J.K. LASSER'S™

Your Income Tax

1998

Prepared by the

J.K. LASSER INSTITUTE™

MACMILLAN • USA

Staff for This Book

J.K. Lasser Editorial

Elliott Eiss, Member of the New York Bar, Editorial Director of the J.K. Lasser Institute™
Bernard Greisman, Member of the New York Bar, Senior Consultant to the J.K. Lasser Institute™
Connor Murphy, Senior Contributing Editor
Regina Fitzpatrick, Contributing Editor
Angelo C. Jack, Editorial/Layout-Production Editor
Francisco Rios, Editorial Assistant
Lloyd Short, Senior Vice President
Maryam Banikarim, Publishing Brand Manager
Gordon Macomber, President, Macmillan General Reference

Outside Contributors

Carolyn Francis, Proofreading and Copyediting
Bill Hamill, Proofreading
Michael Kim, Production Assistant
Joan Griffitts, Indexing

Special Thanks

Kevin Umeh, Mary Grace Whalen, Nick Petro, Sharon Lee, Brian Phair, Andrea Weinreb, Michele Laseau, Michael Freeland, Paul Gillow, Trudy Coler, John Ley, Kathy Nebenhaus, Claire Smith, John Hunt, Julie Hughes, Bud Bressner, Ken Robinson, Jeff Valler, Peter Monte, Stephen Bent

Macmillan General Reference

Macmillan General Reference
A Simon & Schuster Macmillan Company
1633 Broadway
New York, NY 10019-6785

Publisher's Note: *Your Income Tax* is published in recognition of the great need for useful information regarding the income tax laws, for the millions of men and women who must fill out returns. We believe the research and interpretation by the J.K. Lasser Institute™ of the nation's tax laws to be authoritative and of help to taxpayers. Reasonable care has been taken in the preparation of the text. Taxpayers are cautioned, however, that this book is sold with the understanding that the publisher and the contributors to this book are not engaged in rendering legal, accounting, or other professional services herein. Taxpayers with specific tax problems are urged to seek the professional advice of a tax accountant, lawyer, or preparer.

The publisher and contributors to this book specifically disclaim any responsibility for any liability, loss or risk (financial, personal or otherwise) which may be claimed or incurred as a consequence, directly or indirectly, of the use and/or application of any of the contents of this book.

ISBN 0-02-861996-X

How to Use *Your Income Tax 1998*

Tax alert symbols.   Throughout the text of *Your Income Tax*, these special symbols alert you to advisory tips about filing your return and tax planning opportunities:

 Filing Tip or Filing Instruction . . . . . . A **filing tip** or **filing instruction** helps you prepare your 1997 return.

 Planning Reminder . . . . A **planning reminder** highlights year-end tax strategies for 1997 or planning opportunities for 1998 and later years.

 Caution . . . . A **caution** points out potential pitfalls to avoid and areas where IRS opposition may be expected.

 Law Alert . . . . A **law alert** indicates recent changes in the tax law and pending legislation before Congress.

 Court Decision . . . . A **court decision** highlights key rulings from the Tax Court and other federal courts.

The federal income tax law, despite efforts of simplification, remains a maze of statutes, regulations, rulings, and court decisions written in technical language covering thousands and thousands of pages. For over 60 years, J.K. Lasser's™ *Your Income Tax* has aided and guided millions of taxpayers through this complex law. Every effort has been made to provide a direct and easy-to-understand explanation that shows how to comply with the law and at the same time take advantage of tax-saving options and plans.

The 1998 edition of *Your Income Tax*—our 61th edition—continues this tradition. To make maximum use of this tax guide, we suggest that you use these aids:

Contents at a glance. Page v shows the nine major parts of the book and directly leads you to each part.

Contents chapter-by-chapter. The contents, on pages vii-xxii list the chapters in *Your Income Tax*. References direct you to sections within a particular chapter. Thus a reference to *21.1* directs you to Chapter 21 and then to section 1 within that chapter. Section and page references are provided in the index at the back of the book.

New tax law highlights. On pages xxiii-xxv , you will be alerted to key provisions of the Tax Relief Act of 1997 which provides substantial tax benefits, some of which you may be able to claim on your 1997 tax return and others which you may take advantage of in 1998 and later years.

Filing tax basics. Pages 1-6 alert you to filing requirements, filing addresses shown on a map of IRS Service Centers, and a calendar with 1998 filing deadlines.

Glossary of tax terms. The tax law is a technical subject with its own particular terminology. All of the major tax terms are defined in this special glossary starting on **page 725.**

Contents at a Glance

Contents Chapter-by-Chapter

PART 5   PERSONAL TAX SAVINGS PLANS   447

New Tax Law Highlights

Along with new tax benefits, the Taxpayer Relief Act of 1997 brings in its wake tax complexity. There are restrictive phase-out rules, increased holding periods and delayed effective dates. For those who can take advantage of the new benefits, complexity is a small price to pay. For further details on the new law, send for your free copy of the Supplement with the coupon at the front of the book.

Changes Effective In 1997

Holding period rules for capital gains in 1997. For sales occurring after July 28, 1997, there is a new mid-term holding period and a new long-term holding period. A long-term holding period is more than 18 months; a mid-term holding period is more than 12 months but not more than 18 months. For sales made before July 29, 1997, the prior long-term capital gain holding period of more than a year applies. *See 5.2.*

Capital gains rates in 1997. These capital gain rates apply in 1997:

1. The 28% tax ceiling remains in the law and applies to net long-term capital gains on sales before May 7, 1997 and to net mid-term gains occurring after July 28, 1997. *See 5.2.*

2. The new reduced rates of 10% or 20% apply to net gains on sales after May 6 but before July 29, 1997 of capital assets held for more than 12 months and also to net capital gains on sales after July 28, 1997 of capital assets held for more than 18 months. The 10% rate applies to net capital gains falling within the 15% bracket; the 20% rate for net capital gains falling within the 28%, 31%, 36% and 39.6% brackets. *See 5.2.*

3. A 25% tax rate may apply to gain attributed to depreciation on the sale of depreciable real estate on or after May 7, 1997. *See 44.2.*

Principal residence exclusion for sales after May 6, 1997. The promised windfall to homeowners with appreciated principal residences is a reality. Homeowners can now avoid tax on gain of up to $250,000 if single and up to $500,000 if married and filing jointly. The exclusion applies to sales of principal residences made on or after May 7, 1997. You must have owned and used the residence as a principal residence for two out of the last five years before the date of sale. You do not have to buy replacement property, and you can take advantage of the exclusion as many times as you can meet the two-year ownership and residency rule.

Homeowners who realized gains exceeding the exclusion will be taxed on the excess gain. For further details, *see 29.2.*

Short sales against the box after June 8, 1997. Generally, you may no longer defer tax on gain to a later year by transacting a short sale against the box. Under a new law applying to constructive sales after June 8, 1997, gain on a short sale against the box is realized in the year of the short sale, not in the year that the sale is closed. However, there is an exception for certain sales closed within 30 days after the end of the year; *see 30.6.*

Worthless short-sale property after August 5, 1997. If you sell stock short and the stock becomes worthless before you close the short sale, under the new law, you will realize taxable gain when the stock became substantially worthless. The new law applies to property that became substantially worthless after August 5, 1997.

Rollover of gain from small business stock. Gain on the sale after August, 5, 1997 of qualifying small business stock held for more than six months may be rolled over tax free to other small business stock. The rollover must be made within 60 days of the sale. To qualify as a small business, the gross assets of the corporation must be no more than $50 million when the stock is issued. An active business requirement must also be met. If the reinvestment in a qualifying small business is for less than the sale proceeds, your gain is taxed to the extent of the difference. *See 5.6.*

New carry back and carry forward periods for net operating loss in tax years beginning after August 5, 1997. The new carry-back period is two years; the new carry-forward period is 20 years. However, the prior law three-year carryback still applies to disaster losses incurred by farmers and small business persons in presidentially declared disaster areas. *See 40.18.*

Replacement property bought from a related person. For involuntary conversions after June 8, 1997, property acquired from certain close relatives and related parties does not qualify as replacement property if the aggregate gain exceeds $100,000.

State or local officials paid on a fee basis. Such officials may now deduct business expenses as an above-the-line deduction. This break is retroactive to tax years starting after 1986.

Forfeiture of earned income credit for 10 years. Effective January 1, 1997, taxpayers who fraudulently claim the credit may forfeit the right to the credit for a ten-year period; for a two-year period if the credit is claimed recklessly, *see 25.10.*

Preparer penalty for lack of due diligence. Effective January 1, 1997, income tax preparers who do not show due diligence in determining eligibility for the earned income tax credit will be fined a $100 penalty for each failure.

Exchanges of personal property. For transfers after June 8, 1997, you may no longer transact tax-free exchanges of personal property used predominantly in the U.S. for similar property used predominantly outside the U.S.

Repeal of excess distribution and retirement accumulation taxes. The 15% excise tax imposed on excess distributions from qualified retirement plans, tax-sheltered annuities, and IRAs is repealed for excess distributions received after December 31, 1996. The additional 15% estate tax imposed on excess retirement accumulations is repealed for estates of decedents dying after December 31, 1996.

Disaster relief. In the event of a Presidentially declared disaster, the Treasury can postpone tax-related deadlines for up to 90 days for those affected by the disaster. Effective for deadlines expiring after August 5, 1997.

Sales of livestock. Cash-method farmers who are forced to dispose of livestock before the year they ordinarily would have due to flood or other weather related conditions in an area designated for federal assistance may now elect to defer the income to the next tax year.

   A flood or weather related sale of livestock held for breeding, draft or dairy purposes in excess of the number that otherwise would have been sold is treated as an involuntary conversion. Therefore, taxpayers may defer the gain if proceeds from the sale are reinvested. Both provisions are effective for sales or exchanges after 1996.

Changes Effective After 1997

Child tax credit. Starting in 1998, a taxpayer may claim an annual tax credit of $400 per child. As of January 1, 1999, the credit will be $500 per child. An eligible child must be under the age of 17 by the close of the tax year in which the credit is claimed. The child must also be a dependent child, grandchild, stepchild or foster child of the taxpayer.

   The credit is reduced by $50 for each $1,000 (or fraction thereof) that modified adjusted gross income (MAGI) exceeds the phaseout threshold. For single taxpayers, the phaseout starts at MAGI of $75,000, for joint filers at MAGI of $110,000 and for married filing separately at $55,000. See 25.16.

The Hope Scholarship credit is a tax credit for tuition and related expenses incurred in the first two years of post-secondary education. It is effective for expenses paid in 1998 for an academic period starting in 1998. The credit is a maximum of $1,500 per student per year. The credit is structured on 100% of the first $1,000 of tuition costs and 50% of the second $1,000. This credit is allowable only for two taxable years, regardless of how long the student attends school to complete two years of credits. See 38.6.

   The Hope credit and the Lifetime Learning credit (below) both are phased out for taxpayers with MAGI between $40,000 and $50,000 for single persons, and between $80,000 and $100,000 for joint return filers.

The Lifetime Learning credit covers tuition and related expenses paid after June 30, 1998 for an academic period beginning after that date. It applies to costs of undergraduates, graduate students, and those acquiring or improving their job skills through a training program. Students who are learning job skills may claim the credit even for part-time attendance. The credit is based on 20% of up to $5,000 of tuition costs. Starting in 2002, the credit increases to 20% on up to $10,000 of qualified expenses. There is no limit on the number of years the credit can be claimed.

   The Lifetime Learning Credit and the Hope Credit may not be claimed in the same year , or in any year that funds are withdrawn from an Educational IRA. See 38.6.

Student loan interest deduction. Starting in 1998, a student paying interest on a student loan may claim an above-the-line deduction of up to $1,000. This amount will increase to $1,500 in 1999, $2,000 in 2000 and finally caps at $2,500 in 2001. The deduction is subject to an income phaseout. See 38.7.

Educational IRA. You may be able to accumulate a limited amount of tax-free savings for education expenses in an Educational IRA. Starting in 1998, you may make nondeductible annual contributions of up to $500 per child to an Educational IRA if you are not barred by the income phaseout rules at 38.8. The account must be used to pay for post-secondary school tuition, and expenses for room, board, books, and supplies if the individual is a full-time student.

   Contributions must be made in cash, and may not be made after the beneficiary reaches age 18. Contributions to an Educational IRA do not count against contributions to other IRA's. See 38.8.

Penalty-free withdrawals from IRAs. After 1997, the 10% tax penalty for distributions before age 59 1/2 will not apply to withdrawals from an IRA for up to $10,000 of first-time homebuyer expenses and for higher education costs such as tuition, books, room, and board.

   The $10,000 limit for first-time homebuyer expenses is a lifetime cap. A first-time homebuyer may be the IRA owner, the owner's spouse, or the child, grandchild or ancester of the owner or spouse who has not had a property interest in a principal residence for the last two years. First-time home-buyer expenses must be used within 120 days of distribution for such costs as buying or building a principal residence, including settlement, financing or closing costs. See 8.12 and 8.20.

Roth IRA. Starting in 1998, if you have compensation income (salary or self-employed) you may contribute up to $2,000 to a Roth IRA, subject to a phaseout for single taxpayers with MAGI between $95,000 and $110,000, and for joint return filers with MAGI between $150,000 and $160,000. Contributions are not deductible, but earnings accumulate in the Roth IRA tax-free. Taxpayers with MAGI of up to $100,000 can also make a taxable conversion or rollover of a regular IRA to a Roth IRA without paying the 10% penalty tax for early withdrawals. Married people filing separately may not take advantage of rollover provisions. If the assets are rolled over before January 1, 1999, the taxable distribution can be ratably spread over a four-year tax period beginning with the tax year in which the distribution was made. After a five-year holding period, Roth IRA distributions are tax free if you are age $59^{1}/_{2}$ or older, are disabled, or use the distribution to pay qualified first-time homebuyer expenses. See 8.20.

Deduction phase-out for regular IRA's. Starting in 1998 and continuing through 2007, the income phaseout range for making deductible IRA contributions by active participants in employer retirement plans will increase. The phase out range for single persons in 1998 increases to $30,000 - $40,000 of MAGI. For married persons filing jointly in 1998, the phaseout range increases to $50,000 - $60,000 of MAGI. See 8.4.

Also starting in 1998, a spouse who is not an active participant in an employer plan will not be treated as an active participant merely because his or her spouse is a participant. However, under a special rule, the deduction limit for the non-participant spouse filing jointly will be phased out if modified adjusted gross income is between $150,000 and $160,000. *See 8.4.*

Unified Estate and Gift Tax Credit. Under prior law, each individual was entitled to make a combination of lifetime gifts and testamentary transfers of up to $600,000 in value without paying gift or estate tax. For estates of decedents dying and gifts made after 1997, the present $600,000 effective unified estate and gift tax exemption will be increased in small steps until it reaches $1 million in 2006. The phase in will be slow, starting with an increase to a $625,000 exemption in 1998. *See 39.5.*

Exclusion for family owned business. Starting in 1998, if more than 50% of an estate's value consists of a qualifying family-owned business interest, an exclusion may be allowed in calculating the value of the gross estate, but only to the extent that the exclusion and the amount exempted under the unified credit does not exceed $1.3 million. There must be material participation in the business for five of the eight years preceding the decedent's death by the decedent or members of the decedent's family. The business interest must pass to a family member of the decedent or to certain employees of the business. The exclusion is subject to numerous technical requirements; *see* the Supplement for further details.

Gift tax exclusion adjusted for inflation For gifts made after December 31, 1998, the $10,000 gift tax exclusion may be increased by an inflation adjustment.

Estimated income tax threshold increased. For tax years beginning in l998, no estimated tax penalty will be imposed if the tax due, reduced by withholding taxes, is less than $1,000. Further, the safe harbor percentage based on the prior year's tax for high income taxpayers will drop from 110% to 100% for purposes of estimating 1998 taxes. In 1999, it will increase to 105% of tax of the prior year. *See 27.1.*

Dependent standard deduction increased. Starting in 1998, the standard deduction of a dependent may be figured as the dependent's earned income plus $250 if this amount is higher than the annual floor which for 1997 was $650. *See 13.5.*

Mileage rate for charitable deductions. Starting in 1998, the mileage rate for volunteer workers is increased to 14 cents per mile, up from 12 cents per mile allowed in 1997.

Tax payment by credit card. As of May 5, 1998, the IRS is authorized to accept tax payments by any commercially accepted means authorized by the Treasury, including electronic funds transfer, credit cards, and debit cards.

Three-year averaging for farmers. For taxable years beginning after December 31,1997 and before January 1, 2001, farmers may elect to average farm income over the current and prior three years.

Foreign earned income. The 1997 foreign earned income exclusion of $70,000 will increase to $72,000 in 1998, $74,000 in 1999, $76,000 in 2000, $78,000 in 2001, and $80,000 in 2002 and later years.

Parking benefits. Starting in 1998, employer-provided parking qualifying for the monthly exclusion ($170 in 1997) may be offered in lieu of taxable cash compensation. Before 1998, parking benefits had to be provided in addition to, and not in place of, cash compensation.

Liberal home office rule postponed to 1999. If you work outside of your home but use an office in your home for administrative purposes you currently may not claim an office expense deduction, even if you have no other place to do your office work.

For tax years beginning after December 31, 1998, a home office may qualify as a principal place of business as long as it is used to conduct administrative or management activities. You will have to show that there is no other location where you conduct substantial administrative or management activities. *See 40.12.*

Special Tax Situations

Retirees

Self-Employed Persons

Employees

Armed Forces Personnel

Medical Care

Computer Owners

What You May Exclude from Gross Income

Alimony, which does not meet rules of Chapter 37

Annuity payments that repay your cost; *7.22*

Armed Forces benefits and pay; *35.2, 35.4*

Armed Forces disability pensions; *35.2*

Borrowed money returned to you; *2.9*

Casualty insurance and other reimbursement losses not exceeding basis of property; *18.15*

Child support; *37.5*

Clergymen's rental or parsonage allowances; *3.12*

Combat or hazardous duty area pay; *35.4*

Damages for personal injury; *11.7*

Death benefits of up to $5,000 received as beneficiary of employee dying before August 21, 1996; *7.28*

Dependent care assistance from qualified employer plan, within limits; *3.7*

Dividends on life insurance policies until net premiums you paid for the contract are recovered; *4.11*

Education assistance under employer plans; *3.6*

Employer contributions to a qualified pension plan for employee's benefit, within limits; *7.25*

Employer contributions to tax-sheltered annuities for employee's benefit, within limits; *7.25*

Employer furnished meals or lodging for the convenience of the employer; *3.11*

Employer paid business subscriptions or reimbursed membership dues in professional associations; *3.8*

Flexible spending arrangement reimbursements, subject to certain limits; *3.14*

Foreign earned income up to $70,000 ($72,000 in 1998); *36.2*

Forgiven debts that meet tax exclusion rules; *11.8*

Free or low-cost company services or products; *3.15*

Gifts; *11.4*

Government disability pensions; *2.13*

Group-term life insurance premiums paid by employer for coverage up to $50,000; *3.3*

Health and accident coverage under employer plans; *3.1*

Home sale profit of up to $250,000 if single, $500,000 if married on joint return on sales after May 6, 1997; *29.2*

Improvements by lessees; *42.15*

Inherited money or property; *11.4*

Interest credited on frozen deposits; *4.13*

Interest on Series EE bonds issued after 1989 if used for tuition and income tests met; *38.4*

Interest earned on qualified employer retirement plans or IRA's until withdrawal; *7.17, 8.1*

Interest received on tax-exempt government bonds; *4.24*

IRA distributions timely rolled over to another IRA; *8.10*

Job placement assistance, subject to certain limitations; *3.8*

Life insurance received because of the death of the insured; *33.7*

Like-kind exchanges of investment property; *6.1*

Liquidating distributions that are a return of capital; *44.12*

Moving expense reimbursements under accountable plan; *12.8*

Mileage allowance from employer up to IRS limit; *20.33, 43.1*

Overtime meal money and cab fare; *3.9*

Pre-tax salary deferrals to 401(k) or other qualified retirement plans, within limits; *7.18*

Refund of state or local tax for year you claimed standard deduction; *11.5*

Reimbursed business travel and entertainment expenses under accountable plan; *20.30*

Reimbursed medical expenses for permanent physical injury from qualifying employer plan; *3.2*

Rollovers from one qualified employer retirement plan to another, or to an IRA; *7.8, 8.10*

Scholarship awards covering degree candidate's tuition and related fees; *38.1*

Social Security benefits, if under base amount; *34.3*

Stock dividends and stock options; *4.6*

Vanpool, transit pass or employer-provided parking, within limits; *3.5*

Worker's compensation benefits; *2.12*

What You May Deduct

Alimony paid under the rules of Chapter 37

Amortized bond premium; *4.17*

Appraisal costs for donated property; *14.12*

Bad debts subject to limits for nonbusiness loans; *5.9*

Bank deposit loss in insolvent bank; *5.9, 18.4*

Burglary losses; *18.8*

Business expenses; *40.6 – 40.11*

Business gifts up to $25; *20.25*

Business use or rental of a car; *19.12*

Capital loss within limits; *5.17*

Casualty losses within limits; Chapter 18

Charges for services on rental property, e.g., water, sewer, trash; *9.2*

Charitable contributions; Chapter 14

Christmas presents and other holiday gifts to employees, clients, or customers up to $25 a person; *2.4*

Clothing, uniforms, costumes, laundering, and cleaning; *19.6*

Condominium owner's interest and real estate taxes; *15.9*

Convention (business or professional) expenses; *20.12*

Depletion of oil and gas wells, other natural deposits, and timber; *9.14, 9.15*

Depreciation of home computers or cellular telephones, subject to restrictions; *19.9*

Depreciation of leasehold improvements; *42.15*

Depreciation of rental building; *9.2, 42.13*

Depreciation of rental property furniture and appliances; *9.2*

Disaster losses; *18.2*

Education-cost of tuition, books, if required to keep your job or improve job or professional skills; *19.16*

Embezzlement losses; *18.8*

Employment agency fees; *19.7*

Foreign housing costs if self-employed within limits; *36.3*

Foreign income tax and property taxes; *16.12*

Gambling losses to extent of gambling gains; *11.3*

Half of self-employment tax liability; *46.3*

Health care insurance premiums; *17.5*

Home mortgage interest; *15.1*

Impairment-related work expenses; *19.4*

Income tax return preparation fees; *19.25*

Individual retirement account (IRA) contributions, within limits; *8.2 – 8.4*

Investment interest within limits; *15.10*

Job-search expenses; *19.7*

Keogh plan contributions within limits; *41.5*

Legal expenses; *19.26*

Long-term care insurance and services; *17.15*

Losses on small business stock; *5.3*

Magazine subscriptions used for business or professional purposes; *19.5*

Malpractice insurance; *40.6, 40.7*

Medical and dental expenses within limits; *17.1*

Medical savings accounts (MSAs); *17.17*

Moving expenses to new job location; *12.3*

Nurses' wages; *17.12*

Points paid on purchase or improvement of principal residence; *15.8*

Real estate taxes; *16.6*

Rent for business property; *9.1*

Repairs of business or income-producing property; *9.3*

Schooling costs for a mentally or physically handicapped dependent; *17.10*

Simplified Employee Pension (SEP) contributions, within limits; *8.16, 8.17*

Standard deduction; Chapter 13

State and local income taxes; *16.2*

State and local personal property tax; *16.3*

Taxes that are business expenses; *16.11*

Tools used on your job having a life of less than a year; *19.11*

Travel expenses necessary to maintain property; *9.2*

Travel costs to take education courses; *19.22*

Travel costs to get medical care; *17.9*

Work clothes and uniforms; *19.6*

Worthless securities; *5.8*

Frequently Asked Questions

Q. How can I check on the status of my refund?

A. Call the IRS Tele-tax number to get automated refund information. See 46.6 for the number for your area.

Q. I just completed my return and find that I owe the IRS money that I can not pay. What should I do?

A. You should file your return even if you cannot pay all of the amount owed. File by April 15, 1998, and pay as much as possible. By filing on time, you avoid the late filing penalty. By paying as much of the amount as possible, you reduce the amount of interest and late payment penalty you will owe. See 46.3, 47.5

Q. Can I ask to make installment payments on the amount I owe on any 1997 return?

A. Yes. You may request an installment arrangement on Form 9465. However, you will be charged interest and possibly a late payment penalty on the tax not paid by April 15, 1998, even if your request to pay in installments is granted. See 46.3

Q. If I am unable to finish my return by April 15, 1998, how can I get an extension?

A. You can get a four-month extension by filing Form 4868 by April 15, 1998. By filing for the extension, you avoid the late filing penalty. However, Form 4868 does not extend the time to pay your income tax. You will have to pay interest, and possibly late payment penalties. See 46.3.

Q. What can I do to make sure I will not owe the IRS tax on my 1998 return?

A. You can either increase the amount of income tax withheld from your pay or make estimated tax payments to meet your 1998 tax liability. See 27.1.

Q. How can I get forms and publications?

A. Call 1-800-TAX-FORM (1-800-829-3676) or visit your local IRS office. A local library, bank, or post office may have tax forms. Forms may also be obtained by using a computer modem to access Fedworld, an IRS information service. See the IRS site on the world wide web located at http://www.irs.ustreas.gov or direct dial by modem at (703) 321-8020.

Q. If my father has Social Security benefits over $2,650, can I claim him as my dependent?

A. Yes, if the Social Security is not taxable under the rules of 34.3. Dependents other than certain children must have gross income of less than $2,650, but gross income does not include nontaxed items such as gifts, tax-exempt interest, or nontaxable Social Security. See 21.3.

Q. My aunt was solely dependent on me for years. Last spring she died. Can I claim an exemption for her in 1997?

A. Yes. You get the full exemption of $2,650 for the year even though she lived only a few months in 1997. The same rule applies to dependents born during the year. For example, if your child was born in late December you may claim a full $2,650 exemption for the child. See 21.3.

Q. I supported my father for only three months during 1997; my brother took care of him the rest of the time. But I contributed more than 50% of his support. Who may claim the exemption?

A. You do. The test is not the "time" of support but the value of the support. You get the exemption because you furnished more than half of his support during the whole year. See 21.3, 21.7.

Q. My sister and I have been taking care of our parents. We split the support 50-50. Who may claim the exemption?

A. If you and another support the same person, the one furnishing more than half of the support is entitled to the credit. Here you and your sister furnish equal support. You may decide between yourselves who is to claim the exemption. The one who claims the exemption must attach Form 2120, the Multiple Support Agreement, to his or her return. See 21.7, 21.10.

Q. I am paid on a percentage of my sales. But I got an advance on my next year's pay. Is that taxed?

A. Yes, if it is an unrestricted advance, one where you can keep the money. If your employer does not have a policy of demanding repayment for unearned commissions, the advance is taxable. However, if it is really a loan which you must repay if you do not earn the amount, it is not taxed. See 2.1, 2.5.

Q. I bought some stock on the dividend record date. The corporation declared a dividend to holders of record on July 17, 1997, and I bought the stock that same day. Do I pay a tax on this?

A. No. You do not include the dividend on your return. The dividend is paid to the seller of the stock, who must report it as income. See 4.9.

Q. I hear that some stock dividends are not taxed. How can I tell which I can exclude from my tax return?

A. Keep the dividend statements and other literature accompanying your distributions. They usually tell you exactly how to treat dividends on your return. See 4.8.

Q. My father died last year and I received $100,000 as the beneficiary under his insurance policy. Do I report the payment?

A. No. Life insurance payments are not subject to income tax. See 33.7.

Q. I received $10,000 under my uncle's will. Is that taxed?

A. No. Inheritances are exempt from tax. But any income (say, the interest you earn) from this property after you receive it is taxed. See 11.4.

Q. In October 1997, I sold my house at a profit of $100,000. I am age 45 and have owned and lived in the house for 20 years. Can I avoid tax on the profit, even though I do not intend to buy a new house?

A. Yes. Under the new law, you do not pay tax on the profit. If you had sold the house before May 7, 1997, you would have incurred tax under the prior law which allowed tax deferral only on the purchase of a new principal residence. See Chapter 29.

Q. I sold my principal residence at a loss. Can I deduct that loss on my return?

A. No. You cannot. Loss deductions are not allowed for personal-use property. See Chapter 29.

Q. My son worked in my shop during the summer. I paid him $2,100 and withheld taxes from his wages. This was his only income. May I deduct the wages and still claim an exemption for him as my dependent?

A. If you paid your son reasonable wages you may deduct what you paid him as a business expense. Since your son's wages were under $2,650 you may claim him as your dependent, assuming you provided most of his support. If at the end of the year he was under age 19 or a full-time student under age 24, he could be your dependent even if his income were $2,650 or more. He should also file a separate tax return to get a refund of the taxes withheld from his pay. See 1.11, 21.6.

Q. How can I make certain that a scientific organization to which I am planning to donate some money is qualified to receive deductible donations?

A. Ask organization officials for proof of their qualified status, or check IRS Publication 78, which lists most qualified organizations. See 14.1.

Q. May I deduct my unreimbursed costs for gasoline and oil while doing work for a charitable organization?

A. Yes. The expenses are deductible if you claim itemized deductions on your return. In 1997, you may deduct a flat 12-cents-a-mile if that is greater than actual costs. In 1998, 14-cents-a-mile may be claimed. Do not forget to deduct expenses for uniforms required for your charity work. See 14.1, 14.4.

Q. Do I need to get a receipt from a charity for a cash donation?

A. Yes, if you gave $250 or more. If you gave under $250, your cancelled check is acceptable substantiation; a receipt is optional. For donations of $250 or more, get the receipt by the time you file. The charity should include in the receipt an estimate of the value of any benefits you received. See 14.15.

Q. In 1997, I paid state taxes for two taxable years. I prepaid my 1997 state income tax before the end of 1997, and I previously paid my 1996 state tax in 1997. Can I deduct both?

A. Yes. Your payment of the 1997 income tax before it was due does not affect your right to deduct the amount, provided the state accepts it as a tax payment and it is a reasonable approximation of what you owe. See 16.3.

Q. My personal camera and video equipment were stolen from my apartment. I do not know who did it. Can I deduct the loss?

A. A theft loss may be claimed as an itemized deduction, but as a practical matter the deduction may not be allowed because it does not exceed 10% of your adjusted gross income. Even if it exceeded this and the $100 floor, the IRS could disallow the loss if you are audited and argue that there is no proof of a theft. If there were witnesses to a break-in, see if you can get their statements. Report-ing a theft to the police or offering a reward does not prove a theft occurred, but having a police record that there was a robbery would help you support the deduction. See 18.8.

Q. Can I get a bad debt loss for a salary which I earned but was not paid?

A. No. If you are on the cash basis (and most individuals are), you cannot get the deduction for unpaid salary, rent, or fees. On the cash basis you do not include salary as income until you are paid. Merely being entitled to payment but not receiving it does not entitle you to a deduction. See 2.2 , 5.9.

Q. I loaned money to my sister-in-law. She has not paid back the loan. Can I claim a bad debt loss?

A. Yes, if there was an enforceable promise to repay at the time the debt was created and you can show that she became financially unable to pay in 1997. The deduction would be claimed as a short-term capital loss. If the advance you made was really a gift and you did not expect to be repaid, you may not take a deduction. See 5.10.

Q. Can I make a deductible contribution to an IRA if I contribute to a 401 (k) plan at work?

A. It depends on your income. For active plan participants, IRA deductions for 1997 are phased out over a modified adjusted gross income range of $25,000-$35,000 for single persons, or $40,000-$50,000 for married persons filing jointly. See 8.4 for new law rules.

Q. Can I take an IRA deduction for the amount I contributed to a 401(k) plan in 1997?

A. No. A 401(k) plan is not an IRA. However, the amount contributed is not included as income in Box 1 of your W-2 Form, so you don't pay tax on it this year. See 7.17.

Q. What is "itemizing"? How can it help me?

A. You should itemize if you have deductible expenses that exceed your standard deductions. You itemize deductions by filing Schedule A with Form 1040. On Schedule A, you list amounts you paid during the year for items such as medical and dental care, state and local income taxes, real estate taxes, home mortgage interest, casualty losses, gifts to charity and miscellaneous job costs, investment expenses and tax preparation fees. See 13.2.

Q. I refinanced my home in 1997 and paid "points". Can I deduct the entire amount as interest on my 1997 return?

A. No. Points paid solely to refinance your home may not be deducted in the year paid. Instead, they must be deducted over the life of the loan. See 15.7 – 15.8.

Q. What are the deductible mileage rates for 1997?

A. The rate for business travel is 31.5 cents per mile. The rate for travel for medical care and moving expenses is 10 cents per mile. The rate for travel for deductible volunteer work is 12 cents per mile. See 12.3, 14.4, 17.9, 20.33, 43.1.

Q. I withheld Social Security taxes from the wages of a person who cared for my child while I worked in 1997. How do I report the withheld taxes?

A. You report the withholdings, as well as your own employer's share of Social Security and Medicare taxes, on Schedule H. You pay the taxes when you file your personal 1997 return. See 25.8.

30 Checkpoints Before Filing

1. Check that you have filed the correct tax returns. Use Form l040EZ or Form 1040A only if it will save you time and not cause you to give up tax-savings deductions or credits that can only be claimed on Form 1040.

2. Check your arithmetic.

3. Check that you have indicated the correct filing status. If you are married, review whether filing separately would save you more than filing jointly. If you are single and support a dependent, check whether you may claim head of household status.

4. Check that your Social Security number is written correctly, and the number is written on all schedules and statements attached to your return.

5. Check the amount of your itemized deductions against the standard deduction allowed for your filing status. Claim the larger deduction. Check that you have claimed the additional standard deduction allowed if you are age 65 or over, or blind.

6. Check that all tax withholdings are entered on your return so they can be credited against your tax liabilities.

7. Check when using the tax tables that the tax taken is from the line and column applicable to your filing status.

8. Check that a refund amount shown on your return is correct and indicate whether you want the refund in cash or credited to your first estimated tax installment payment for 1998.

9. Check that the amount of tax liability indicated on your return and the amount written on your check or money order is the same. Also, your check or money order should include your Social Security number and note that it is in payment of your 1997 tax liability.

10. Check that all the necessary schedules and statements are attached to your tax return. Make two copies of the return, one for your own records and one for the state income tax authorities.

11. Check that you have signed the return. If you are filing jointly, check that your spouse has also signed.

12. Check that in calculating the amount of taxable Social Security benefits you use the base amounts applicable to your filing status.

13. Check whether you are entitled to a tax credit for excess FICA taxes withheld on your wages if you worked for more than one employer.

14. Check whether you are liable for Alternative Minimum Tax (AMT), especially if you have substantial itemized deductions.

15. Check whether you received a refund of state income taxes and correctly determined how much of the refund is taxable as a recovery of a tax benefit.

16. Check passive loss restrictions if you have income or losses from real estate investments.

17. Check that your withdrawals from IRAs and employer retirement accounts meet the minimum distribution requirements if you are age $70^1/_2$ or over.

18. Check the amount you contributed to your IRA against income limits that may reduce or eliminate your deduction if you are covered by an employer retirement plan.

19. Check if you are self-employed, that you have figured your self-employment tax, claimed a deduction for 50% of the tax, and claimed a deduction for Keogh or SEP plan contributions.

20. Check that you have attached all your withholding tax statements. Also check whether the statements are accurate. If not, ask your employer or other payer for a corrected copy.

21. Check whether you must begin to make estimated tax installments or whether your rate of withholding is in line with your estimated tax for 1998.

22. Check that you have claimed all deductible interest expenses. If you have been claiming amortizable points in prior years, include the amount deductible this year. If the mortgage ended early, deduct the balance of amortizable points this year.

23. Check that you have used the correct cost basis for sales of property bought in prior years.

24. Check that you have not reported tax-exempt interest as taxable interest.

25. Check your deductible auto expenses against the IRS allowance. Claim the larger amount.

26. Check that your Forms 1099 are accurate. If the forms are inaccurate ask the payer to prepare corrected forms.

27. Check if you are entitled to the tax credit for child and dependent care, that you prepare Form 2441 if filing a Form 1040, or Schedule 1, if filing a Form 1040A and attach the additional forms to the return.

28. Check that all documentary evidence including power of attorney or court certificate of legal representative is attached to a return not signed by the taxpayer.

29. Check if deducting alimony that the name and Social Security number of your former spouse is reported on Line 30a, Form 1040.

30. Check if filing for a deceased taxpayer, that the date of death of the deceased is on the return.

Part 1

Filing Basics

In this part, you will learn these income tax basics:

- Whether you must file a return
- When and where to file your return
- Which tax form to file
- What filing status you qualify for
- When filing separately is an advantage for married persons
- How to qualify as head of household
- How filing rules for resident aliens and nonresident aliens differ

Do You Have to File a 1997 Tax Return?

If you are—	You must file if gross income is at least—
Single	
Under age 65	$6,800
Age 65 or older on or before January 1, 1998	7,800
Married, living together at the end of 1997	
Filing a joint return—both spouses under age 65	12,200
Filing a joint return—one spouse age 65 or older	13,000
Filing a joint return—both spouses age 65 or older	13,800
Filing a separate return	2,650
Married, living apart at the end of 1997	
Filing a joint or separate return	2,650
Head of a household maintained for a child or other relative *(see 1.10)*	
Under age 65	8,700
Age 65 or older on or before January 1, 1998	9,700
Widowed in 1996 or 1997 and have a dependent child *(see 1.6)*	
Under age 65	9,550
Age 65 or older on or before January 1, 1998	10,350

Marital status. For 1997 tax purposes, marital status is generally determined as of December 31, 1997. Thus, if you were divorced or legally separated during 1997, you are not considered married for 1997 tax purposes, and you must use the filing threshold for single persons unless you qualify as a head of household *(1.10)*, or you remarried in 1997 and are filing a joint return with your new spouse.

If your spouse died in 1997 and you were living together on the date of death, use the filing threshold shown for married persons living together at the end of 1997. If not living together on the date of death, the $2,650 filing threshold applies, unless you remarried during 1997 and are filing jointly with your new spouse.

Age 65. Whether you are age 65 or older is generally determined as of the end of the year, but if your 65th birthday is on January 1, 1998, you are treated as being age 65 for 1997 tax purposes.

Gross income. Gross income is generally all the income that you received in 1997, except for items specifically exempt from tax.

Include wages, tips, self-employment fees (Chapter 45), taxable scholarships (Chapter 38), taxable interest and dividends (Chapter 4), capital gains (Chapter 5), taxable pensions and annuities (Chapter 7), rents (Chapter 9), and trust distributions (Chapter 11). Home sale proceeds that are tax free (Chapter 29) and tax-free foreign earned income (Chapter 36) are nevertheless considered gross income for purposes of the filing test.

Exclude tax-exempt interest (Chapter 4), Social Security (provided provisional income is below the floor specified in Chapter 34), tax-free fringe benefits (Chapter 3), qualifying scholarships (Chapter 38), and life insurance (Chapter 33).

Other situations when you must file. Even if you are not required to file under the gross income tests, you must file a 1997 return if:

- You are self-employed and your net self-employment earnings for 1997 are $400 or more (Chapter 45), *or*
- You are entitled to a refund of taxes withheld from your wages or a refund based on the earned income credit for working families (Chapter 25), *or*
- You received any earned income credit payments in advance from your employer (Chapter 25), or
- You owe any special tax such as alternative minimum tax (Chapter 23), IRA penalty (Chapter 8), and FICA on tips (Chapter 26), *or*
- You are a nonresident alien with a U.S. business or tax liability not covered by withholding; *see* Form 1040NR.

Filing tests for dependents. If you can be claimed as a dependent by your parent, or by any other taxpayer, see the rules on the next page to determine if you must file a return.

Filing Tests for Dependents

The income threshold for filing a tax return is generally lower for an individual who may be claimed as a dependent than for a nondependent. If your 1997 gross income was $2,650 or more, you may be claimed as a dependent only by your parent, and only if you were either under age 19 or a full-time student under age 24. This income test and the other tests for dependents are explained in *21.1*.

If under the tests at *21.1*, you may be claimed as a dependent by someone else, use the chart on this page to determine if you must file a 1997 return. Include as *unearned* income taxable interest and dividends, capital gains, pensions, annuities and distributions of unearned income from a trust. *Earned* income includes wages, tips, self-employment income, and taxable scholarships or fellowships (Chapter 38). *Gross* income is the total of unearned and earned income.

For married dependents, the filing requirements in the chart assume that the dependent is filing a separate return and not a joint return (Chapter 1). Generally, a married person who files a joint return may not be claimed as a dependent by a third party who provides support; *see 21.13*.

If you are the parent of a dependent child who was under age 14 at the end of 1997 and who had only investment income, you may elect to report the child's income on your own return instead of filing a separate return for the child; *see 24.5* for the election rules.

File a 1997 Return If You Are—

Single dependent under age 65 and not blind and:

- You had at least $1 of unearned income and gross income of at least $650; *or*
- You had no unearned income and earned income exceeding $4,150.

Single dependent and either age 65 or more or blind:

- You had earned income exceeding $5,150 ($6,150 if age 65 or older and also blind); *or*
- You had unearned income exceeding $1,650 ($2,650 if age 65 or older and also blind); *or*
- You had gross income exceeding the larger of $650 or your earned income up to $4,150, *plus* $1,000 ($2,000 if age 65 or older and also blind).

Married dependent under age 65 and not blind:

- You had at least $1 of unearned income and gross income of at least $650; *or*
- You had no unearned income and earned income exceeding $3,450; *or*
- You had gross income of at least $5 and your spouse itemizes deductions on a separate return.

Married dependent and either age 65 or more or blind:

- You had earned income exceeding $4,250 ($5,050 if age 65 or older and also blind; *or*
- You had unearned income exceeding $1,450 ($2,250 if age 65 or older and also blind); *or*
- You had gross income exceeding the larger of $650 or your earned income up to $3,450, *plus* $800 ($1,600 if age 65 or older and also blind); *or*
- Your gross income was at least $5 and your spouse itemizes deductions on a separate return.

Where To File

If you are filing—	File with the Internal Revenue Service Center—
A personal return	For your place of legal residence. If you received an IRS packet of forms with a pre-addressed envelope, use it if the envelope address is the same as the Center shown below for your residence.
A business return	For the location of your principal place of business.
As a U.S. citizen working abroad	At Philadelphia, PA 19255-0002.
As a service member in the Armed Forces	For the place you are stationed. If you have an APO or FPO address, file with the Service Center at Philadelphia, PA 19255-0002.

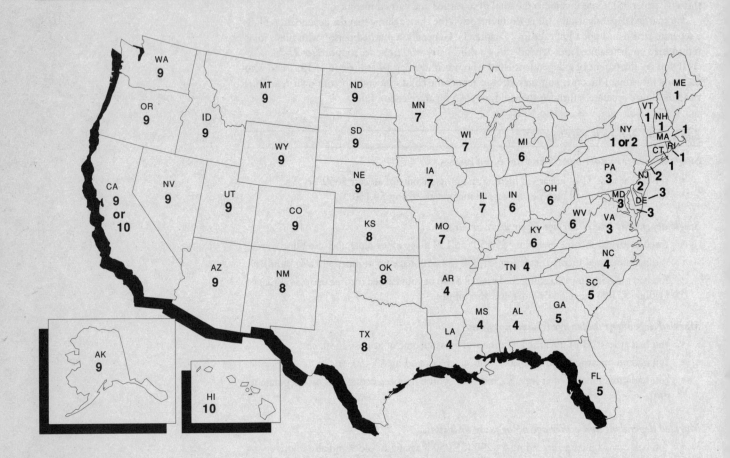

Key To Service Center Map

Key	Mailing Address—
1.	Internal Revenue Service Center, Andover, Massachusetts 05501-0002. *New York residents* file here if they reside outside of New York City or counties of Nassau, Rockland, Suffolk, or Westchester.
2.	Internal Revenue Service Center, Holtsville, New York 00501-0002. *New York residents* in New York City or counties of Nassau, Rockland, Suffolk, or Westchester file here.
3.	Internal Revenue Service Center, Philadelphia, Pennsylvania 19255-0002. *Residents of the District of Columbia* file here.
4.	Internal Revenue Service Center, Memphis, Tennessee 37501-0002.
5.	Internal Revenue Service Center, Atlanta, Georgia 39901-0002.
6.	Internal Revenue Service Center, Cincinnati, Ohio 45999-0002.
7.	Internal Revenue Service Center, Kansas City, Missouri 64999-0002.
8.	Internal Revenue Service Center, Austin, Texas 73301-0002.
9.	Internal Revenue Service Center, Ogden, Utah 84201-0002. *California residents* file here if living in the counties of: Alpine, Amador, Butte, Calaveras, Colusa, Contra Costa, Del Norte, El Dorado, Glenn, Humboldt, Lake, Lassen, Marin, Mendocino, Modoc, Napa, Nevada, Placer, Plumas, Sacramento, San Joaquin, Shasta, Sierra, Siskiyou, Solano, Sonoma, Sutter, Tehama, Trinity, Yolo, and Yuba.
10.	Internal Revenue Service Center, Fresno, California 93888-0002. *California residents* file here if not listed under Key 9 above.

Filing Deadlines (On or Before)

January 15, 1998
Pay the balance of your 1997 estimated tax. If you do not meet this date, you may avoid an estimated tax penalty for the last quarter by filing a final return for 1997 and paying the balance of your 1997 tax by February 2, 1998.

Farmers and fishermen: File your single 1997 estimated tax payment by this date. If you do not, you may still avoid an estimated tax penalty by filing a final tax return and paying the full tax by March 2, 1998.

February 2, 1998.
Make sure you have received a Form W-2 from each employer for whom you worked in 1997.

April 15, 1998
File your 1997 tax return and pay the balance of your tax. If you cannot meet the April 15 deadline, you may file Form 4868 to obtain an automatic four-month filing extension. However, interest will still be charged for taxes not paid by this date, and late payment penalties will be imposed unless at least 90% of your tax liability is paid by this date. If you cannot pay the full amount of tax you owe when you file your return, you can file Form 9465 to request an installment payment arrangement.

If on this date you are a U.S. citizen or resident living and working abroad or in military service outside the U.S. or Puerto Rico, you have an automatic two-month filing extension until June 15, 1998.

Pay the first installment of your 1998 estimated tax by this date.

June 15, 1998
Pay the second installment of your 1998 estimated tax. You may amend your estimate at this time.

If on April 15 you were a U.S. citizen or resident living and working abroad or in military service outside the U.S. or Puerto Rico, file your 1997 return and pay the balance due. You may obtain an additional two-month filing extension until August 17, 1998, by filing Form 4868.

If you are a nonresident alien who did not have tax withheld from your wages, file Form 1040NR by this date and pay the balance due.

August 17, 1998
File your 1997 return if you received an automatic four-month filing extension using Form 4868. Also file your 1997 return and pay the balance due if on April 15 you were a U.S. citizen or resident living and working abroad or in military service outside the U.S. or Puerto Rico, and by June 15 you qualified for an additional two-month extension by filing Form 4868.

September 15, 1998
Pay the third installment of your 1998 estimated tax. You may amend your estimate at this time.

December 31, 1998
If self-employed, this is the last day to set up a Keogh plan for 1998.

January 15, 1999
Pay the balance of your 1998 estimated tax.

April 15, 1999
File your 1998 return and pay the balance of your tax. Pay the first installment of your 1999 estimated tax by this date.

15th day of the 4th month after the fiscal year ends
File your fiscal year return and pay the balance of the tax due. If you cannot meet the filing deadline, apply for an automatic four-month filing extension on Form 4868.

1998

JANUARY
S	M	T	W	T	F	S
				1	2	3
4	5	6	7	8	9	10
11	12	13	14	15	16	17
18	19	20	21	22	23	24
25	26	27	28	29	30	31

FEBRUARY
S	M	T	W	T	F	S
1	2	3	4	5	6	7
8	9	10	11	12	13	14
15	16	17	18	19	20	21
22	23	24	25	26	27	28

MARCH
S	M	T	W	T	F	S
1	2	3	4	5	6	7
8	9	10	11	12	13	14
15	16	17	18	19	20	21
22	23	24	25	26	27	28
29	30	31				

APRIL
S	M	T	W	T	F	S
			1	2	3	4
5	6	7	8	9	10	11
12	13	14	15	16	17	18
19	20	21	22	23	24	25
26	27	28	29	30		

MAY
S	M	T	W	T	F	S
					1	2
3	4	5	6	7	8	9
10	11	12	13	14	15	16
17	18	19	20	21	22	23
24	25	26	27	28	29	30
31						

JUNE
S	M	T	W	T	F	S
	1	2	3	4	5	6
7	8	9	10	11	12	13
14	15	16	17	18	19	20
21	22	23	24	25	26	27
28	29	30				

JULY
S	M	T	W	T	F	S
			1	2	3	4
5	6	7	8	9	10	11
12	13	14	15	16	17	18
19	20	21	22	23	24	25
26	27	28	29	30	31	

AUGUST
S	M	T	W	T	F	S
						1
2	3	4	5	6	7	8
9	10	11	12	13	14	15
16	17	18	19	20	21	22
23	24	25	26	27	28	29
30	31					

SEPTEMBER
S	M	T	W	T	F	S
		1	2	3	4	5
6	7	8	9	10	11	12
13	14	15	16	17	18	19
20	21	22	23	24	25	26
27	28	29	30			

OCTOBER
S	M	T	W	T	F	S
				1	2	3
4	5	6	7	8	9	10
11	12	13	14	15	16	17
18	19	20	21	22	23	24
25	26	27	28	29	30	31

NOVEMBER
S	M	T	W	T	F	S
1	2	3	4	5	6	7
8	9	10	11	12	13	14
15	16	17	18	19	20	21
22	23	24	25	26	27	28
29	30					

DECEMBER
S	M	T	W	T	F	S
		1	2	3	4	5
6	7	8	9	10	11	12
13	14	15	16	17	18	19
20	21	22	23	24	25	26
27	28	29	30	31		

1999

JANUARY
S	M	T	W	T	F	S
					1	2
3	4	5	6	7	8	9
10	11	12	13	14	15	16
17	18	19	20	21	22	23
24	25	26	27	28	29	30
31						

FEBRUARY
S	M	T	W	T	F	S
	1	2	3	4	5	6
7	8	9	10	11	12	13
14	15	16	17	18	19	20
21	22	23	24	25	26	27
28						

MARCH
S	M	T	W	T	F	S
	1	2	3	4	5	6
7	8	9	10	11	12	13
14	15	16	17	18	19	20
21	22	23	24	25	26	27
28	29	30	31			

APRIL
S	M	T	W	T	F	S
				1	2	3
4	5	6	7	8	9	10
11	12	13	14	15	16	17
18	19	20	21	22	23	24
25	26	27	28	29	30	

MAY
S	M	T	W	T	F	S
						1
2	3	4	5	6	7	8
9	10	11	12	13	14	15
16	17	18	19	20	21	22
23	24	25	26	27	28	29
30	31					

JUNE
S	M	T	W	T	F	S
		1	2	3	4	5
6	7	8	9	10	11	12
13	14	15	16	17	18	19
20	21	22	23	24	25	26
27	28	29	30			

JULY
S	M	T	W	T	F	S
				1	2	3
4	5	6	7	8	9	10
11	12	13	14	15	16	17
18	19	20	21	22	23	24
25	26	27	28	29	30	31

AUGUST
S	M	T	W	T	F	S
1	2	3	4	5	6	7
8	9	10	11	12	13	14
15	16	17	18	19	20	21
22	23	24	25	26	27	28
29	30	31				

SEPTEMBER
S	M	T	W	T	F	S
			1	2	3	4
5	6	7	8	9	10	11
12	13	14	15	16	17	18
19	20	21	22	23	24	25
26	27	28	29	30		

OCTOBER
S	M	T	W	T	F	S
					1	2
3	4	5	6	7	8	9
10	11	12	13	14	15	16
17	18	19	20	21	22	23
24	25	26	27	28	29	30
31						

NOVEMBER
S	M	T	W	T	F	S
	1	2	3	4	5	6
7	8	9	10	11	12	13
14	15	16	17	18	19	20
21	22	23	24	25	26	27
28	29	30				

DECEMBER
S	M	T	W	T	F	S
			1	2	3	4
5	6	7	8	9	10	11
12	13	14	15	16	17	18
19	20	21	22	23	24	25
26	27	28	29	30	31	

Choosing Which Tax Form To File

There are three individual tax forms: Form 1040, Form 1040A, and Form 1040EZ. Use the simplified Form 1040EZ or Form 1040A only if you find the return will save you time and not cause you to give up tax-saving deductions or credits that are only available if you file Form 1040. To help you make your selections, fill in the following chart.

By checking the box that indicates your tax status, income, expenses, and credit items, you will be guided in choosing which form to use.

Item—	Form 1040EZ*—	Form 1040A*—	Form 1040—
Single	☐[1]	☐	☐
Head of household		X	X
Married filing jointly	X[1]	X	X
Married filing separately		X	X
Widow and widower		X	X
Exemption for dependents		X	X
Wages, salary	X	X	X
Interest	X[2]	X	X
Dividends		X	X
Unemployment compensation	X	X	X
Self-employment income			X
Pension-annuity		X	X
IRA distributions		X	X
Rents and royalties			X
Gains and loss from property sales			X
Alimony			X
State tax refunds			X
Social Security benefits		X	X
IRA deduction		X	X
Alimony paid			X
Moving expenses			X
Self-employed health insurance			X
$\frac{1}{2}$ of self-employment tax			X
Medical Savings Account deduction			X
Penalty for early withdrawal of savings			X
Deduction for Keogh, SEP, and SIMPLE plans			X
Employee business expenses			X
State and local income taxes			X
Real estate taxes			X
Home mortgage interest, investment and business interest			X
Charitable contributions			X
Medical and dental expenses			X
Casualty and theft losses			X
Miscellaneous deductions (investment expenses, tax preparation)			X
Credit for child and dependent care		X	X
Earned income credit	X[3]	X	X
Credit for elderly and totally disabled		X	X
Foreign tax credit			X
All other credits			X
Estimated tax payments and estimated tax penalty		X	X
Advance earned income credit (EIC) payments		X	X
Self-employment tax			X
Penalty tax on an IRA			X
Alternative minimum tax			X
Social Security tax on tips not reported to your employer			X
Uncollected Social Security tax on tips shown on your Form W-2			X
"Kiddie" tax on child's return		X	X
"Kiddie" tax on parent's return			X
Household employee taxes		X	X
All other taxes or penalties			X

*Taxable income less than $50,000.

[1] Under age 65 and not blind on January 1, 1998.

[2] Up to $400.

[3] If you did not receive any advance earned income credit payments.

Chapter 1

Filing Status

The filing status you use when you file your return determines the tax rates that will apply to your taxable income; *see 1.2.* Filing status also determines the standard deduction you may claim if you do not itemize deductions *(see 13.1)* and your ability to claim certain other deductions, credits, and exclusions.

This chapter explains the five different filing statuses: single, married filing jointly, married filing separately, head of household, and qualifying widow(er). If you are married, filing a joint return is generally advantageous, but there are exceptions discussed in *1.3.* If you are unmarried and are supporting a child who lives with you, you may qualify as a head of household *(see 1.10),* which would enable you to use more favorable tax rates than those allowed for single taxpayers. If you were widowed in either 1996 or 1995 and in 1997 a dependent child lived with you, you may be able to file as a qualifying widow(er) for 1997, which allows you to use joint return rates.

Special filing situations, such as for children, nonresident aliens, and deceased individuals, are also discussed in this chapter.

Importance of Filing Status

1.1 Which Filing Status Should You Use?

Your filing status generally depends on whether you are married at the end of the year, and, if unmarried, whether you maintain a household for a qualifying dependent. The five filing statuses are:
single, married filing jointly, married filing separately, head of household, and qualifying widow or
widower.

If you are *married at the end of the year*, you may file jointly *(1.4)* or separately *(1.3)*. If you lived
apart from your spouse for the last half of 1997 and your child lived with you, you may qualify as
an "unmarried" head of household *(see 1.10)*, which allows you to apply more favorable tax rates
than you could as a married person filing separately.

If you are *unmarried at the end of the year*, your filing status is single unless you meet the tests for
a head of household or qualifying widow(er). Generally, you are a head of household if you pay
more than 50% of the household costs for a relative who lives with you, or a parent, whether or not
he or she lives with you; *see 1.10*. You generally are a qualifying widow(er) if you were widowed in
1996 or 1995 and in 1997 you pay more than 50% of the household costs for you and your dependent child; *see 1.6*. The tax rates for heads of households and for qualifying widow(ers) are more
favorable than those for single taxpayers; *see 1.2*.

The filing status you use determines the tax rates that apply to your taxable income, as shown in
1.2, as well as the standard deduction you may claim *(see 13.1)* if you do not itemize deductions.
Certain other deductions, credits, or exclusions are also affected by filing status. For example, if
you are married, certain tax benefits are only allowed if you file jointly, but more deductions overall
may be allowed in certain cases if you file separately; *see 1.3*. The deduction for personal exemptions is phased out for high income taxpayers at levels based upon filing status; *see 21.15*.

Marital status determined at the end of the year. If on the last day of the year you are
divorced from your spouse under a final decree of divorce or separate maintenance, you are treated
as unmarried for the entire year. However, if at the end of the year you are living apart from your
spouse or are separated under a provisional decree that has not yet been finalized, you are still considered married.

If at the end of the year you live together in a common law marriage that is recognized by the
law of the state in which you live or the state where the marriage began, you are treated as married.

If your spouse dies during the year, you are treated as married for that entire year and may file
a joint return for you and your deceased spouse, assuming you have not remarried before year's
end; *see 1.6*.

1.2 Tax Rates Based on Filing Status

The most favorable tax brackets apply to married persons filing jointly and qualifying widow(ers)
who also use the joint return rates. The least favorable brackets are those for married persons filing
separately, but filing separately may still be advisable for married couples in certain situations, as
discussed in *1.3*. The table on the next page compares 1997 tax rate brackets.

If you are unmarried at the end of the year, do not assume that your filing status is single. If
your child lives with you in a home you maintain, you generally may file as a head of household *(see
1.10)*, which allows you to use more favorable tax rates than a single person. If you were widowed
in either of the two prior years and maintain a household for your dependent child, you generally
may file as a qualified widow(er), which allows you to use favorable joint return rates; *see 1.6*.

If you are married but for the second half of the year you lived with your child apart from your
spouse, and you and your spouse agree not to file jointly, head of household tax rates may be available, which are more favorable than those for married persons filing separately.

Applying the tax table or tax rate schedule. If your taxable income is less than $100,000,
you will look up your tax in the tax tables which are shown in Part VIII of this book. If your taxable
income is $100,000 or more, you figure your tax using the tax rate schedules, also in Part VIII.
Chapter 22 has examples of applying the tax tables or rate schedules to determine your regular income
tax liability. The tables and rate schedules are in Part VIII of this book.

Taxable Income Brackets for 1997

	15% bracket ends at—	*28% bracket ends at—*	*31% bracket ends at—*	*36% bracket ends at—*	*39.6% bracket applies to—*
Married filing separately	$ 20,600	$ 49,800	$ 75,875	$ 135,525	over $ 135,525
Single	24,650	59,750	124,650	271,050	over 271,050
Head of Household	33,050	85,350	138,200	271,050	over 271,050
Married filing jointly or Qualifying widow(er)	41,200	99,600	151,750	271,050	over 271,050

Married Taxpayers

1.3 Filing Separately Instead of Jointly

Filing a joint return will save taxes for a married couple where one spouse earns all, or substantially all, of the taxable income. If both you and your spouse earn taxable income, you should figure your tax on joint and separate returns to determine which method provides the lower tax.

Separate returns may save taxes where filing separately allows you to claim more deductions. On separate returns, larger amounts of medical expenses, casualty losses or miscellaneous deductions may be deductible because lower adjusted gross income floors apply. Unless one spouse earns substantially more than the other, separate and joint tax rates are likely to be the same, regardless of the type of returns filed. The Example on page 11 illustrates how filing separately can save you taxes.

Suspicious of your spouse? If you suspect that your spouse may be evading taxes and may not meet tax liabilities due on a joint return, you may want to file a separate return. By filing separately, you avoid liability for unpaid taxes due on a joint return, plus interest and penalties. Although the *innocent spouse* rules may protect some spouses who file jointly, it is difficult to qualify for this protection; *see 1.4 and 1.5.*

Standard deduction restriction on separate returns. Keep in mind that if you and your spouse file separately, both must either itemize or claim the standard deduction, which is $3,450 in 1997 for married persons filing separately *(13.3)*. Thus, if one spouse itemizes, the other spouse must also itemize even if he or she would get a larger deduction from the $3,450 standard deduction.

Joint return required for certain benefits. Also be aware that certain tax benefits may be claimed by married persons only if they file jointly.

If you want to take advantage of the $25,000 rental loss allowance *(10.2)* or the credit for the elderly (Chapter 34), you must file jointly unless you live apart for the whole year. You must file jointly to claim an IRA deduction for a nonworking spouse *(8.3)*. A joint return is also required to claim the dependent care credit or the earned income credit (Chapter 25), unless you live apart for the last six months of the year. Furthermore, if you receive Social Security benefits, one-half of your benefits are generally subject to tax on a separate return, because on a separate return you are not allowed a base amount exemption; *see* Chapter 34.

Alternative Minimum Tax (AMT). If you are subject to AMT, filing separately may allow a full AMT exemption on one of the separate returns if your spouse's income does not come within the phase-out range for the exemption; *see* Chapter 23.

Filing Status If Married at the End of 1997

Filing Jointly	*Filing Separately*	*Living Apart from Spouse: Filing as Unmarried Head of Household*
Married couples may pay less tax by filing jointly. Filing jointly allows the use of joint return rates.	Filing separately may be advisable where both spouses earn taxable income and have separate deductions, as explained at 1.3. You are required to use tax rates for married persons filing separately in these cases:	If you lived apart from your spouse during the last half of 1997, and your child lived with you for most of the year, you may qualify for tax purposes as "unmarried" and use head of household rates, which are lower than rates for married persons filing separately.

Married couples may pay less tax by filing jointly. Filing jointly allows the use of joint return rates.

You may file a joint return if you are legally married on the last day of 1997.

You need not live together provided you are legally married. A couple legally separated under a final decree of divorce or separate maintenance as of the end of 1997 may *not* file a joint return.

You may file jointly if your spouse died during 1997; *see 1.5.*

If one spouse is a nonresident alien, you may file jointly *only* if you make a special election to be taxed on your worldwide income; *see 1.8.*

You *must* file jointly to make an IRA deduction on behalf of a nonworking spouse *(8.3).* To claim the credit for the elderly (Chapter 34), you must file jointly unless you lived apart for the entire year or qualify as head of household. You must file jointly to claim the dependent care credit or the earned income credit (Chapter 25), unless you live apart and qualify as a head of household.

On a joint return, each spouse is liable for the entire tax. If one spouse does not pay, the other spouse may be liable even though all of the income was earned by the spouse who failed to pay the tax. An "innocent" spouse who files a joint return may be relieved of fraud penalties and tax liability in certain circumstances; *see 1.4.*

For community property rules; *see 1.9.*

Filing separately may be advisable where both spouses earn taxable income and have separate deductions, as explained at 1.3. You are required to use tax rates for married persons filing separately in these cases:

1. Your spouse files a separate return. If you are experiencing marital discord, you may be forced to file separately unless your spouse consents to a joint return.
2. You or your spouse is claimed by someone else as a dependent; see 21.13.
3. You and your spouse have different tax reporting years. If you report on the calendar year but your spouse reports on a fiscal year, you must file separately unless you get permission from the IRS to change your reporting year (Form 1128). This bar to joint filing does not apply when your tax year begins on the same day, but ends because of the death of either or both spouses. A spouse who has never filed a tax return may elect to use the other spouse's tax year as his or her first tax year; then they can file a joint return. That a husband and wife had different tax years before their marriage is no bar to a joint return.
4. You or your spouse is a nonresident alien and you do not make an election to be taxed on your worldwide income; see 1.8.

If you lived apart from your spouse during the last half of 1997, and your child lived with you for most of the year, you may qualify for tax purposes as "unmarried" and use head of household rates, which are lower than rates for married persons filing separately.

The following four tests must be met for you to file separately from your spouse as a head of household:

1. Your spouse was not a member of your household during the last six months of 1997.
2. You maintain your home as a household which was the principal place of abode for your child, adopted child, or stepchild for more than half of 1997. However, a foster child must be a member of your household for the entire year.
3. You are entitled to claim the child as a dependent. Ignore this test if the noncustodial spouse claims the exemption for the child under the rules of 21.11.
4. You provide over half of the cost of supporting the household.

Filing Status If Not Married at the End of 1997

Single	*Head of Household*	*Qualifying Widow(er)*

If you are not married at the end of 1997, use the rate for single individuals, unless you qualify as a surviving spouse or a head of household.

If you are widowed, you are "unmarried" and use rates for single individuals regardless of the number of years you were married. There is an exception for recent widows or widowers supporting children, as explained in the "qualifying widow(er)" column.

If at the end of the year you are not married, you may use special head-of-household rates if you meet these tests:

1. You are not married at the end of the year.
2. You maintain a household for more than half of 1997 for your child or grandchild, or for a dependent relative. The household must be your home and the main residence of your relative except that a dependent parent need not live with you. However, you must maintain a dependent parent's separate household for the entire year to claim head of household status based on that support.
3. You pay more than one-half the cost of the household.
4. You are a U.S. citizen or resident alien during the entire tax year.

These rules are explained in detail in 1.10.

If you are a widow or widower and your spouse died in 1995 or 1996, you may use 1997 joint return tax rates if you meet these four tests:

1. You maintain your home as the main home of your child for the entire year and you furnish over half the cost of maintaining the household.
2. You are entitled to claim the child as a dependent; see 21.1.
3. In the year your spouse died, you could have filed a joint return.
4. You did not remarry before January 1, 1998.

If you meet these tests, your filing status is qualifying widow or widower; see 1.6.

EXAMPLE

Mike Palmer's 1997 adjusted gross income (AGI) is $65,000 and his wife Fran has AGI of $50,000. Mike has deductible medical expenses of $7,000; Fran's are $1,000. Mike has an $8,000 casualty loss *(18.12)* on property owned in his name. He also has unreimbursed miscellaneous expenses of $2,600 and Fran has $500. Mike has deductible mortgage interest expenses of $5,000 and Fran has $2,000. Mike's deductible state and local taxes are $2,000; Fran's are $1,000. Neither of them claims exemptions for dependents.

As the example worksheet below shows, filing separate returns saves Mike and Fran an overall $1,090, because they can deduct more on separate returns. If they filed jointly they would have received no deduction for medical expenses and casualty losses because the deductions would have been eliminated by the higher adjusted gross income floors. If they file separately, the 3% reduction of itemized deductions *(13.8)* applies to Mike but not Fran because only Mike's AGI exceeds the $60,600 threshold. If they file jointly, the 3% reduction does not apply because their AGI is below the $121,200 threshold for joint returns. The phaseout of personal exemptions *(22.15)* does not apply regardless of how they file.

Item	Mike (Separately)	Fran (Separately)	Joint Return
1. **AGI**	**$65,000**	**$50,000**	**$115,000**
Medical expenses	7,000	1,000	8,000
Less 7½% of AGI	4,875	3,750	8,625
2. Allowable medical	2,125	0	0
3. Taxes	2,000	1,000	3,000
4. Mortgage interest	5,000	2,000	7,000
Casualty loss	8,000	0	8,000
Less 10% of AGI	6,500		11,500
5. Allowable casualty	1,500		0
Miscellaneous expenses	2,600	500	3,100
Less 2% of AGI	1,300	1,000	2,300
6. Allowable miscellaneous	1,300	0	800
7. **Total itemized** *(Lines 2–6)*	**11,925**	**3,000**	**10,800**
*Less 3% reduction**	132	0	0
8. **Net itemized**	**11,793**	**3,000**	**10,800**
9. Personal exemptions	2,650	2,650	5,300
10. **Net itemized plus exemptions**	**14,443**	**5,650**	**16,100**
11. Taxable income *(Line 1 minus Line 10)*	50,557	44,350	98,900
12. **Tax liability**	**11,506**	**9,747**	**22,343**
Total tax filing separately			21,253
Savings from filing separately			*1,090*

* $132 reduction = 3% (65,000 AGI – 60,600 floor)

1.4 Both Spouses Liable on Joint Returns

When you sign a joint return, you and your spouse may be held individually liable for the entire tax due, plus interest and any penalties. You may be held liable for the entire tax even if your spouse earned all the income.

If you divorce, you remain jointly liable for the tax due on joint returns filed before the divorce. You remain liable even if your divorce agreement provides that your ex-spouse is responsible for taxes on the prior joint returns; the IRS is not bound by your agreement.

In one case, the Tax Court held that a settlement between the IRS and a bankrupt husband did not extend to the wife. The wife was not involved in the bankruptcy proceeding and the IRS could get a separate assessment against her for the balance of the joint return deficiency.

In limited cases, an innocent spouse may avoid liability, as discussed in *1.5*.

Proposals have been made to change the joint liability standard to one of proportionate liability based on each spouse's share of the joint return income and deductions. However, Congress has not yet acted on such proposals.

Planning Reminder

Switching from Separate to Joint Return

If you and your spouse file separate returns, you have three years from the due date (without extensions) to change to a joint return. If a joint return is filed, you may not change to separate returns once the due date has passed. The filing of separate or joint estimated tax installments (Chapter 27) does not commit you to a similar tax return.

Filing Tip

Can Filing Separately Avoid Exemption Phaseout or Itemized Deduction Reduction?

Filing separately will sometimes allow either you or your spouse to avoid part of the personal exemption phaseout *(21.15)* or the 3% reduction to specified itemized deductions *(13.8)*. If you file jointly and have total 1997 adjusted gross income (AGI) exceeding $181,800, the exemption phaseout applies. If you file separately, the phaseout does not apply to the spouse reporting separate AGI of $90,900 or less. On the other hand, where your joint AGI is $181,800 or less, a spouse reporting AGI over $90,900 on a separate return will be subject to the phaseout although no phaseout would apply on a joint return.

If for 1997 you itemize deductions, the deductions for taxes, mortgage interest, charitable donations, and miscellaneous deductions are reduced by 3% of AGI exceeding $121,200 on a joint return, or exceeding $60,600 on a separate return. If you file separately, the reduction does not apply on a separate return showing AGI of $60,600 or less. Where joint AGI is $121,200 or less, a spouse filing separately with separate AGI over $60,600 is subject to the 3% reduction although no reduction would apply on a joint return.

Court Decision

Innocent Spouse Relief for Overstatement of Cost of Goods Sold

The Tax Court made it easier to qualify as an innocent spouse by holding that an overstatement of the cost of goods sold by the other spouse when computing business income is an omission of income, rather than an excess deduction. Since it is not a deduction, it is not necessary for the "innocent" spouse to show that the cost of the goods claimed by the other spouse had no factual or legal basis. The IRS has agreed to follow the Tax Court position.

Signing the joint return. Both you and your spouse must sign the joint return. Under the following rules, if your spouse is unable to sign, you may sign for him or her.

If, because of illness, your spouse is physically unable to sign the joint return, you may, with the oral consent of your spouse, sign his or her name on the return followed by the words "By _____, Husband (or Wife)." You then sign the return again in your own right and attach a signed and dated statement with the following information: (1) the return being filed, (2) the tax year, (3) the reason for the inability of the sick spouse to sign, and (4) that the sick spouse has consented to your signing.

To sign for your spouse in other situations, you need authorization in the form of a power of attorney, which must be attached to the return. IRS Form 2848 may be used.

If your spouse does not file, you may be able to prove you filed a joint return even if your spouse did not sign and you did not sign as your spouse's agent where:

- You intended it to be a joint return—your spouse's income was included (or the spouse had no income).
- Your spouse agreed to have you handle tax matters and you filed a joint return.
- Your answers to the questions on the tax return indicate you intended to file a joint return.
- Your spouse's failure to sign can be explained.

EXAMPLE

The Hills generally filed joint returns. In one year, Mr. Hill claimed joint return filing status and reported his wife's income as well as his own; in place of her signature on the return, he indicated that she was out of town caring for her sick mother. She did not file a separate return. The IRS refused to treat the return as joint. The Tax Court disagreed. Since Mrs. Hill testified that she would have signed had she been available, her failure to do so does not bar joint return status. The couple intended to make a joint return at the time of filing.

1.5 Innocent Spouse Rules

Generally, you and your spouse are each liable for the entire tax due on a joint return, plus any interest and penalties; *see 1.4*. However, you may be relieved of joint return liability if tax was underpaid because your spouse omitted income or claimed excessive deductions or credits.
To avoid liability as *an innocent spouse*, the following three conditions must be met:

1. There is a tax understatement exceeding $500 due to either (a) the omission of gross income by your spouse, or (b) your spouse's claim of deductions or credits that have no basis in fact or law, and the tax understatement exceeds a specified percentage of your adjusted gross income.

   In determining whether gross income has been omitted, community property rules (1.9) are disregarded, except that rental income or other income derived from property is treated as owned equally by the spouses.

   If the tax understatement is due to your spouse's claim of invalid deductions or credits, the liability must exceed a specific percentage of your adjusted gross income for the taxable year preceding the year in which the IRS mails a deficiency notice. If your adjusted gross income in the year preceding the mailing of a deficiency notice was $20,000 or less, the tax understatement attributable to your spouse's improper deductions must exceed 10% of the preceding year's adjusted gross income. If adjusted gross income in the preceding year was more than $20,000, the tax understatement for which relief is sought must exceed 25% of the preceding year's adjusted gross income. If you had remarried as of the end of the preceding year, your new spouse's income must be included to determine your adjusted gross income for purposes of applying the 10% and 25% tests.

2. In signing the joint return, you did not know and had no reason to know of the understatement. Where relief from tax liability is based on your spouse's omission of income, mere knowledge of the underlying transaction that produced the omitted income (such as a tax-sheltered investment) has been held to be enough to defeat innocent spouse status. According to the Tax Court, knowledge of the underlying transaction can also defeat innocent spouse relief based on the other spouse's claim of deductions or credits with no basis in law or fact. However, in improper deduction cases, several appeals courts have held that knowledge of the underlying transaction will not block relief for a spouse who shows that at the time the joint return was signed, he or she could not be reasonably expected to know that the improper deduction would substantially lower the tax due. The innocent spouse's level of education and involvement in the couple's financial affairs is taken into account.

3. Taking into account all the circumstances, it would be inequitable to hold the innocent spouse liable for the tax. The IRS will consider the extent to which the "innocent" spouse benefitted from the tax underpayment beyond normal support in deciding the "equity" issue.

1.6 Death of Your Spouse

You do not lose the right to file a joint return when your spouse dies during the year. In general, a joint return is filed by you and the executor or administrator. But you alone may file a joint return if you are otherwise entitled to file jointly and:

1. The deceased did not file a separate return, and
2. Someone other than yourself has not been appointed as executor or administrator before the due date for filing the return. An executor or administrator appointed after the joint return is filed may revoke the joint return within the one-year period following the due date.

   If you do file jointly, you include on the return all of your income and deductions for the full year and your deceased spouse's income and deductions *up to the date of death (see 1.12).*

   As a surviving spouse, you may not file a joint return for you and your deceased spouse if:

1. You remarry before the end of the year of your spouse's death. In this case you may file jointly with your new spouse. A final return for the deceased spouse must be filed by the executor or administrator using the filing status of married filing separately.
2. You or your deceased spouse has a short year because of a change in annual accounting period.
3. Either of you was a nonresident alien at any time during the tax year; but *see 1.8.*

Executor or administrator may revoke joint return. If an executor or administrator is later appointed, he or she may revoke a joint return that you alone have filed by filing a separate return for the decedent. Even if you have properly filed a joint return for you and the deceased spouse (as just discussed), the executor or administrator is given the right to revoke the joint return. But a state court held that a co-executrix could not refuse to sign a joint return where it would save the estate money. To revoke the joint return, the executor must file a separate return within one year of the due date (including extensions). The executor's separate return is treated as a late return; interest charges and a late filing penalty apply. The joint return that you filed is deemed to be your separate return. Tax on that return is recalculated by excluding items belonging to your deceased spouse.

Signing the return. A joint return reporting your deceased spouse's income should list both of your names. Where there is an executor or administrator, the return is signed by you as the surviving spouse and the executor or administrator in his or her official capacity. If you are the executor or administrator, sign once as surviving spouse and again as the executor or administrator. Where there is no executor or administrator, you sign the return, followed by the words, "taxpayer and surviving spouse."

Surviving spouse's liability. If a joint return is filed and the estate cannot pay its share of the joint income tax liability, you, as the surviving spouse, may be liable for the full amount. Once the return is filed and the filing date passes, you can no longer change the joint return election and file a separate return unless an administrator or executor is appointed after the due date of the return. In that case, as previously discussed, the executor may disaffirm the joint return.

If you will be appointed executor or administrator and are concerned about estate insolvency, it may be advisable to hedge as follows: (1) File separate returns. If it is later seen that a joint return is preferable, you have three years to change to a joint return. (2) File jointly but postpone being appointed executor or administrator until after the due date of the joint return. In this way, the joint return may be disaffirmed if the estate cannot cover its share of the taxes.

Qualifying Widows or Widowers With Dependent Child.

If your spouse died in either 1995 or 1996 and you meet the following three requirements, your 1997 filing status is *qualifying widow or widower*, which allows you to use joint return rates on an individual return.

1. You did not remarry before 1998 (if you did remarry you may file a joint return with your new spouse).
2. You may claim as your dependent (*see* Chapter 21) in 1997 a child, stepchild, adopted child, or foster child who lived with you during 1997 (except for temporary absences) and you paid over half the cost of maintaining your home.
3. You were able to file jointly in the year of your spouse's death, even if you did not do so.

Caution

Invalidated Prior Divorce
The IRS and Tax Court do not allow a joint return with a new spouse if a prior divorce decree has been declared invalid by a state court. The federal appeals court for the Second Circuit allows the joint return; the Ninth Circuit does not.

If you meet all these tests, use the 1997 tax table or rate schedule for qualifying widows or widowers, the same schedule used by married couples filing jointly; *see 1.2.*

Spouse's death before 1995. If your spouse died before 1995 and you did not remarry before 1998, you may be able to use head of household rates for 1997 if you qualify under the rules of *1.10.*

1.7 Divorce or Separation Decree Bars Joint Return

A final decree of divorce or separate maintenance entered into before the end of 1997 prevents you from filing a joint return. Unless you qualify as head of household *(1.10)*, you must use the rates for single individuals. You may not claim an exemption for a divorced or legally separated spouse, even if you contribute all of his or her support, but *see 21.2* if the divorce or separation is not final.

If you are married but live apart from your spouse and care for a child, you may be able to qualify as a head of household; *see 1.10.*

If, before a final decree of divorce has been made, you are separated under an "interlocutory" decree or temporary order, you are still considered married and may file a joint return. Once the decree is made final, the privilege to file jointly ends. Alimony paid during the period covered by the interlocutory decree is deducted by one spouse and reported by the other spouse as income if separate returns are filed.

If a divorce decree is interlocutory but another state waives the waiting period and permits a spouse to remarry, the IRS will recognize the new marriage and allow the filing of joint returns by the newly married couple. But a court has refused to allow a joint return where a new marriage took place in Mexico during the interlocutory period in violation of California law.

1.8 Nonresident Alien Spouse

Filing Tip

Nonresident Alien Becomes Resident
Where one spouse is a U.S. citizen or resident and the other is a nonresident alien who becomes a resident during the tax year, the couple may make a special election to file a joint return for that year and be taxed on their worldwide income. Thereafter, neither spouse may make the election again even if married to a new spouse. Tests for determining status as a resident or nonresident alien are at *1.16.*

If either you or your spouse was a nonresident alien *(1.14)* during *any part* of the year, a joint return may be filed only if both of you make a special election to be taxed on your worldwide income. Thus, if you are a U.S. citizen and your spouse is a nonresident alien at the beginning of the year who becomes a resident *(1.14)* during the year, the special election to file jointly must be made.

If the election is not made, you may be able to claim your nonresident alien spouse as an exemption on a return filed as married filing separately, but only if the spouse had no income and could not be claimed as a dependent by another taxpayer; *see 21.2.* If the alien spouse becomes a resident before the beginning of the next tax year, you may file jointly for that year.

If one spouse is a nonresident alien and the couple does not make the election to file jointly, certain community property rules do not apply; *see 1.9.*

Election to file a joint return. Where a U.S. citizen or resident is married to a nonresident alien, the couple may file a joint return if both elect to be taxed on their *worldwide income.* The requirement that one spouse be a U.S. citizen or resident need be met only at the close of the year. Joint returns may be filed in the year of the election and all later years until the election is terminated.

A couple that makes the election must keep books and records of their worldwide income and give the IRS access to such books and records. If either spouse does not provide the necessary information to the IRS, the election is terminated. Furthermore, the election is terminated if either spouse revokes it or dies; revocation before the due date of the return is effective for that return. The election automatically terminates for the year of death of either spouse. However, if the survivor is a U.S. citizen or resident, he or she may claim the benefits of being a qualifying widow(er); *see 1.6.* The election to file jointly also terminates if the couple is legally separated under a decree of divorce or separate maintenance. Termination is effective as of the beginning of the taxable year of the legal separation. If neither spouse is a citizen or resident for any part of the taxable year, an election may not be made and an existing election is suspended. If an election is suspended it may again become effective if either spouse becomes a U.S. citizen or resident. Once the election is terminated, neither spouse may ever again make the election to file jointly.

Electing to file a joint return does not terminate the special withholding on the nonresident alien's income.

1.9 Community Property Rules

If you live in Arizona, California, Idaho, Louisiana, Nevada, New Mexico, Texas, Washington, or Wisconsin, the income and property you and your spouse acquire during the marriage is generally regarded as community property. Community property means that each of you owns half of the community income and community property, even if legal title is held by only one spouse. But note that there are some instances in which community property rules are disregarded for tax purposes; these instances are clearly highlighted in the pertinent sections of this book.

Separate property may still be owned. Property owned before marriage generally remains separate property; it does not become community property when you marry. Property received during the marriage by one spouse as a gift or an inheritance from a third party is generally separate property. In some states, if the nature of ownership cannot be fixed, the property is presumed to be community property.

In some states, income from separate property may be treated as community property income. In other states, income from separate property remains the separate property of the individual owner.

Divorce or separation. If you and your spouse divorce, your community property automatically becomes separate property. A separation agreement or a decree of legal separation or of separate maintenance may or may not end the marital community, depending on state law.

Community income rules may not apply to separated couples. If a husband and wife in a community property state file separate returns, each spouse must generally report one-half of the community income. However, a spouse may be able to avoid reporting income earned by his or her spouse if they live apart during the entire calendar year and do not file a joint return.

To qualify, one or both spouses must have earned income for the year and none of that earned income may be transferred, directly or indirectly, between the spouses during the year. One spouse's payment to the other spouse solely to support the couple's dependent children is not a disqualifying transfer. If the separated couple qualifies under these tests, community income is allocated as follows:

- Earned income (excluding business or partnership income) is taxed to the spouse who performed the personal services.
- Business income (other than partnership income) is treated as the income of the spouse carrying on the business.
- Partnership income is taxed to the spouse entitled to a distributive share of partnership profits.

Innocent spouse rules applied to community property. As discussed above, community property rules may not apply to earned income where spouses live apart for the entire year and file separate returns. In addition, a spouse who files a separate return may be relieved of tax liability on community income which is attributable to the other spouse if he or she does not know (or have reason to know) about the income and if it would be inequitable under the circumstances for him or her to be taxed on such income. This rule applies to all tax years not closed by the statute of limitations.

The IRS may disregard community property rules and tax income to a spouse who treats such income as if it were solely his or hers and who fails to notify the other spouse of the income before the due date of the return (including extensions).

Death of spouse. The death of a spouse dissolves the community property relationship, but income earned and accrued from community property before death is community income.

Moving from a community property to a common law (separate property) state. Most common law states (those which do not have community property laws) recognize that both spouses have an interest in property accumulated while residing in a community property state. If the property is not sold or reinvested, it may continue to be treated as community property. If you and your spouse sell community property after moving to a common law state and reinvest the proceeds, the reinvested proceeds are generally separate property, which may be held as joint tenants, or in another form of ownership recognized by common law states.

Moving from a common law to a community property state. Separate property brought into a community property state generally retains its character as separately owned property. However, property acquired by a couple after moving to a community property state is generally owned as community property. In at least one state (California), personal property which qualifies as community property is treated as such, even though it was acquired when the couple lived in a common law state.

Supporting a dependent with separate rather than community income. Filing a Form 2120 multiple support agreement is not necessary where either parent can prove that he or she has income which is considered separate income rather than community income; that parent may be able to satisfy the more-than-50% support test. In certain community property states, the law may provide that income of a husband and wife living apart is considered separate income rather than community income.

 Filing Tip

Claiming Dependents on Separate Returns
Married parents in community property states who plan to file separate returns should be aware that neither parent may be able to claim an exemption for a dependent child. Where all of the couple's income is considered community income, each parent on a separate return is treated as having provided exactly one-half of the child's support, regardless of who actually paid it. Since neither parent has provided more than one-half of the support, neither can claim the child as a dependent.

To avoid this result, parents whose sole income is community income and who want to file separately should consider signing a multiple support agreement, Form 2120, designating which parent may claim the exemption.

Filing as Head of Household

1.10 Qualifying as Head of Household

If you are unmarried at the end of 1997, maintain a household for a child, parent, or other relative, and are a U.S. citizen or resident *(see 1.16)* the entire year, you can file as "head of household." Tax rates are lower for a head of household than for a person filing as single *(see 1.2)* and the standard deduction is higher (Chapter 13). If you are married but for the last half of 1997 you lived apart from your spouse, you may be treated as unmarried and able to qualify for head of household tax rates and standard deduction, which are more favorable than those for a married person filing separately; *see* Test 1.

Test 1. Are you unmarried? You are "unmarried" for 1997 head of household purposes if you are any one of the following:

- *Single as of the end of 1997.*
- *A widow or widower and your spouse died before 1997.* If a dependent child lives with you, *see 1.6* to determine if you may use the even more advantageous filing status of qualifying widow(er). If your spouse died in 1997, you are treated as married and cannot qualify as a 1997 head of household, but a joint return may be filed; *see 1.6.*
- *Legally separated or divorced under a final court decree as of the end of 1997.* A custody and support order does not qualify as a legal separation. A provisional decree (not final), such as a support order *pendente lite* (while action is pending) or a temporary order, has no effect for tax purposes until the decree is made final.
- *Married but living apart from your spouse.* You are considered unmarried for 1997 if your spouse was not a member of your household during the *last six months* of 1997, you file separate returns, and you maintain a household for more than half the year for a dependent child, stepchild, or adopted child. A foster child qualifies if he or she is a member of your household for the whole year. You must be able to claim the child as a dependent unless your spouse (the noncustodial parent) has the right to the exemption under the rules of *21.11.*
- *Your spouse was a nonresident alien during any part of 1997 and you do not elect to file a joint return reporting your joint worldwide income (1.8).*

Test 2: Did you maintain a home for a qualifying relative? You must pay more than half of the costs of maintaining a household for a qualifying relative, and that relative must live with you in that home unless he or she is your parent. Your parent does not have to live with you, but you must pay more than half the costs of your parent's household, whether your parent lives alone, with someone else, or in a senior citizen residence.

Relative generally must be your dependent. The table on the next page shows the relatives who may qualify you to claim head of household status. As the table shows, the relative generally must be your dependent, except for children and grandchildren who are unmarried as of the end of the year. Under another exception, if you are a divorced or separated parent of a *married* child and you meet the other tests, you may claim head of household status even though you waive the exemption for the child in favor of the other parent, or the other parent may claim the exemption under a pre-1985 agreement *(see 21.11).*

If you live apart from your spouse for the last six months of the year and maintain a home for a child, stepchild, adopted child, or foster child, the child, *whether married or unmarried*, must be your dependent unless the dependency exemption is claimed by the other parent because you have waived the exemption or the other parent is entitled to the exemption under a pre-1985 agreement *(21.11).*

You are *not* eligible for head of household status if the qualifying relative is your dependent only because you are allowed to claim the exemption under a multiple support agreement (Form 2210).

Costs of maintaining the household. You must pay for *more than half* of the property taxes, mortgage interest, rent, utility charges, upkeep and repairs, domestic help, property insurance, and food eaten in the household. Do not consider the rental value of the lodgings provided the dependent or clothing, education costs, medical expenses, vacation costs, life insurance premiums, transportation costs, and the value of your work around the house. However, these expenses may be considered in figuring your support contribution in determining whether you may claim the child or other relative as a dependent; *see 21.7.*

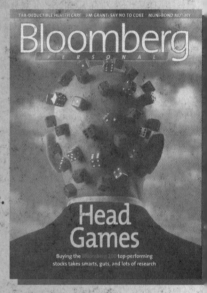

QUALIFYING RELATIVES FOR HEAD OF HOUSEHOLD PURPOSES

Relationship	Does relative have to be your dependent?	Does the relative have to live with you?
Unmarried child, stepchild or adopted child	No*	Yes
Unmarried foster child	Yes	Yes
Unmarried grandchild or great-grand child	No	Yes
Married child, stepchild, adopted child, foster child, grandchild, or great-grandchild	Yes*	Yes
Parent	Yes	No
Stepparent	Yes	Yes
Grandparent	Yes	Yes
Brother, sister, half brother, half sister, stepbrother, stepsister	Yes	Yes
Father-in-law, mother-in-law	Yes	Yes
Son-in-law, daughter-in-law	Yes	Yes
If related by blood: uncle, aunt, niece, nephew	Yes	Yes

*See the text under "Dependent requirement" above for a contrary rule that may apply in the case of divorced or legally separated parents, or parents living apart during the last half of the year.

EXAMPLE

Your mother lived with your sister in your sister's apartment, which cost $5,000 to maintain in 1997. Of this amount, you contributed $3,000, your sister $2,000. Your mother has no income and did not contribute any funds to the household. You qualify as head of household: For 1997, you paid over half the cost of maintaining the home for your mother, who also qualifies as an exemption on your return. A child or dependent relative other than your parent would have to live with you to enable you to file as head of household.

Two-family house.   A mother was allowed head of household status by the Tax Court in the following case. She and her unmarried daughter rented one floor of a multilevel home. A married daughter lived on a different floor with her family. Parts of the home were shared. According to the court, the mother was a head of household, based on support of her unmarried daughter. Although she did not pay more than half of the total household expenses, she paid more than half the expenses attributable to her and her unwed daughter.

Do you have to live in the home you maintain? You generally must pay more than half of the cost of a home that is your qualifying relative's principal residence for more than half the year. If your parent is the qualifying relative and he or she does not live with you, the home must be the parent's principal residence for the *entire* year. If the relative is not your parent, then, according to the IRS, the home you maintain for the relative must also be your principal residence for more than half the year. Some courts have held that the taxpayer must live for a "substantial" period of time in the same house as the dependent. An appeals court in one case allowed a mother to claim head of household status where she maintained a home for a child in one state and had her principal residence in another state. In the Example on the next page, the Tax Court upheld the IRS position.

Household Costs for the Year

1. Property taxes $ _____
2. Mortgage interest   _____
3. Rent paid   _____
4. Insurance   _____
5. Utilities   _____
6. Domestic help   _____
7. Repairs and upkeep   _____
8. Food eaten in the home   _____
9. Total of Lines 1–8   _____
10. 50% of Line 9 $ _____

If you paid more than the amount on Line 10, you "maintain" the household for purposes of Test 2 on page 16.

Filing Tip

Child May Be Head of Household

You may qualify as a head of household for filing purposes although not head of the family. For example, a son who earns more than his father and contributes more than half of the cost of maintaining the family may qualify as a head of household. That the father, not the son, exercises family control does not matter. The important factor is a dollar test: whether the head of household for tax purposes contributed more than half the cost of maintaining the household that is his or her home and the principal home of the qualifying dependents.

EXAMPLE

Doctors advised McDonald that her mentally ill son might become self-sufficient if he lived in a separate residence, but one nearby enough for her to provide supervision. She took the advice and kept up a separate home for her son that was about a mile from her own home. She frequently spent nights at his home and he at hers. The Tax Court agreed with the IRS that McDonald could not file as head of household since her principal residence was not the same as her son's.

Temporary absences disregarded. In determining whether you and a dependent relative lived together for more than half the year, temporary absences are ignored if the absence is due to illness, or being away at school, on a business trip, on vacation, serving in the military, or staying with a parent under a child custody agreement. The IRS requires that it be reasonable to expect your qualifying child or dependent to return to your household after such a temporary absence, and that you continue to maintain the household during the temporary absence. Under this rule, you would lose the right to file as head of household if your dependent moved into his or her own permanent residence before the end of the year.

You may claim head of household status when your qualifying relative is confined to a hospital or a sanitarium and his or her absence is temporary and you continue to maintain a household in expectation of his or her return.

In the year a qualifying relative is born or dies, meeting the residence test for the portion of the year the dependent is alive allows you to claim head of household status.

Tax Returns for Children

 Filing Tip

Kiddie Tax for Children Under Age 14

Children who are under age 14 at the end of 1997 generally must use Form 8615 to figure their 1997 tax if they had more than $1,300 of investment income; *see 24.4.* On Form 8615, the investment earnings over $1,300 are taxed at the parent's top tax rate. However, in certain cases under the rules of *24.5,* parents may elect to report their children's investment income on their own return.

1.11 Filing for Your Child

The income of your minor child is *not* included in your return unless you make a special election to report a child's investment income under the rules of *24.5.* A minor is considered a taxpayer in his or her own right. If the child is required to file a return, but is unable to do so because of age or for any other reason, the parent or guardian is responsible for filing the return.

A tax return must be filed for a dependent child who had more than $650 of gross income, where any of it was from investments. If your child had only earned income (for personal services) and no investment income, a tax return must be filed if the earned income exceeded $4,150.

If the child is unable to sign the return, the parent or guardian should sign the child's name in the proper place, followed by the words, "by (signature), parent (or guardian) for minor child." A parent is liable for tax due on pay earned by the child for services, but not on investment income.

A child who is not required to file a return should still do so for a refund of taxes withheld.

Social Security numbers. A parent or guardian must obtain a Social Security number for a child before filing the child's first income tax return. The child's Social Security number must also be provided to banks, brokers, and other payers of interest and dividends to avoid penalties and backup withholding; *see 26.12.* To obtain a Social Security number, file Form SS-5 with your local Social Security office. If you have applied for a Social Security number but not yet received it by the filing due date, write "applied for" on the tax return in the space provided for the number.

Whether or not you are filing a return for a child, you must obtain and report on your return a Social Security number for a child whom you are claiming as a dependent; *see 21.14.*

Wages you pay your children. You may deduct wages paid to your children in your business. Keep records showing that their activities are of a business rather than personal nature.

Withholding for children. Children with wages are generally subject to withholding and should file Form W-4 with their employer. An exemption from withholding may be claimed only in limited cases. For example, in 1997, a child with any investment income who expected to be claimed as another taxpayer's dependent could claim an exemption from withholding only if the expected amount of investment income plus wages was $650 or less (this amount may change annually). Furthermore, the child must certify on Form W-4 that he or she had no federal tax liability in the prior year and expects no liability in the current year for which the withholding exemption is sought.

Wages you pay to your own children under age 18 for working in your business are not subject to FICA taxes (Social Security and Medicare); *see 26.10.*

Filing for a Deceased or Incompetent Person

1.12 Return for Deceased

When a person dies, another taxpaying entity is created-the decedent's estate. Until the estate is fully distributed, it will generally earn income for which a return must be filed. For example, Carlos Perez dies on June 30, 1997. The wages and bank interest he earned through June 30 is reported on his final income tax return, Form 1040, which is due by April 15, 1998. Income earned on the account from July 1 is reported on Form 1041, the income tax return for the estate. Form 1041 must be filed if the estate has gross income of $600 or more.

What income tax returns must be filed? If the decedent died after the close of the taxable year, but before the income tax return was filed, the following must be filed:

1. Income tax return for prior year;
2. Final income tax return, covering earnings in period from beginning of taxable year to date of death; and
3. Estate income tax return, covering earnings in period after decedent's death.

If the decedent died after filing a return for the prior tax year, then only 2 and 3 are filed.

EXAMPLE

Steven Jones died on March 31, 1998, before he could file his 1997 tax return. The 1997 income tax return must be filed by April 15, 1998. A final income tax return to report earnings from January 1, 1998, through March 31, 1998, will have to be filed on April 15, 1999. Jones's estate will have to file an income tax return on Form 1041 to report earnings and other income that were not paid to Jones before April 1, 1998.

Who is responsible for filing? The executor, administrator, or other legal representative is responsible for filing all returns. For purposes of determining whether a final income tax return for the decedent is due, the annual gross income test at page 2 is considered in full. You do not prorate it to the part of the year decedent lived. A surviving spouse may assume responsibility for filing a joint return for the year of death if no executor or administrator has been appointed and other tests are met (1.6). However, if a legal representative has been appointed, he or she must give the surviving spouse consent to file a joint return for the year of the decedent's death. In one case, a state court held that a co-executrix could not refuse consent and was required to sign a joint return where it would save the estate money.

How do you report the decedent's income and deductions? You follow the method used by the decedent during his or her life to account for the income up to the date of death. The income does not have to be put on an annual basis. Each item is taxed in the same manner as it would have been taxed had the decedent lived for the entire year.

If the deceased owned U.S. Savings Bonds, see 4.29.

When one spouse dies in a community property state (1.9), how should the income from the community property be reported during the administration of the estate? The IRS says that half the income is the estate's and the other half belongs to the surviving spouse.

Medical expenses of the decedent. If the estate pays the decedent's medical expenses within one year of the date of death, the expenses can be deducted on the decedent's last return, subject to the regular 7.5% of adjusted gross income floor (17.4). However, the expenses are not deductible for income tax purposes if they are deducted for estate tax purposes. To deduct such medical expenses on the decedent's last return, a statement must be filed affirming that no estate tax deduction has been taken and that the rights to the deduction have been waived.

Partnership income. The final return includes partnership income or loss only from a partnership year that ends within the decedent's tax year. Thus, if a partner dies in July 1997 and the partnership's taxable year ends December 31, 1997, no partnership income or loss is included on the partner's final 1997 return. It is reported by the partner's executor or other successor in interest on the estate's income tax return.

Exemptions allowed on a final return. These are generally the same exemptions the decedent would have had if he or she had not died. You do not reduce the exemptions because of the shorter taxable year. If the deceased had contributed more than one-half of a dependent's annual support, a dependency exemption is claimed on his or her final return.

Filing Instruction

Decedent's Final Return

Do not report on the decedent's final return income that is received after his or her death, or accrues after or because of death if the decedent used the accrual method. This income is considered "income in respect of a decedent," and is taxed to the estate or beneficiary receiving the income in the year of the receipt. On the decedent's final return, only deductible expenses paid up to and including the date of death may be claimed. If the decedent reported on the accrual basis, those deductions accruable up to and including the date of death are deductible. If a check for payment of a deductible item was delivered or mailed before the date of the decedent's death, a deduction is allowable on the decedent's last return, even though the check was not cashed or deposited until after the decedent's death. If the check was not honored by the bank, the item is not deductible.

Planning Reminder

Promptly Closing the Estate
To expedite the closing of the decedent's estate, an executor or other personal representative of the decedent may file Form 4810 for a prompt assessment. Once filed, the IRS has 18 months to assess additional taxes. Without making the request, the IRS has three years from the due date of the return to make assessments. Form 4810 must be filed separately from the final return, but should be sent to the District Director for the IRS district in which the return is filed.

Estimated taxes. No estimated tax need be paid by the executor after the death of an unmarried individual; the entire tax is paid when filing the final tax return. But where the deceased and a surviving spouse paid estimated tax jointly, the rule is different. The surviving spouse is still liable for the balance of the estimated tax unless an amended estimated tax voucher is filed. Further, if the surviving spouse plans to file a joint return *(1.6)* which includes the decedent's income, estimated tax payments may be required; *see* Chapter 27.

Where the estate has gross income, estimated tax installments are not required on Form 1041-ES for the first two years after the decedent's death.

Signing the return. An executor or administrator of the estate signs the return. If it is a joint return, *see 1.6.*

When a refund is due on a final return. The decedent's final return may also be used as a claim for a refund of an overpayment of withheld or estimated taxes. Form 1310 may be used to get the refund, but the form is not required if you are a surviving spouse filing a joint return for the year your spouse died. If you are an executor or administrator of the estate and you are filing Form 1040, 1040A, or 1040EZ for the decedent, you do not need Form 1310, but you must attach to the return a copy of the court certificate showing your appointment as personal representative.

1.13 Return for an Incompetent Person

A legal guardian of an incompetent person files Form 1040 for an incompetent whose gross income meets the filing tests on page 2. Where a spouse becomes incompetent, the IRS says the other spouse may file a return for the incompetent without a power of attorney, if no legal guardian has been appointed. For example, during the period an individual was in a mental hospital, and before he was adjudged legally incompetent, his wife continued to operate his business. She filed an income tax return for him and signed it for him although she had no power of attorney. The IRS accepted the return as properly filed. Until a legal guardian was appointed, she was charged with the care of her husband and his property.

The IRS had accepted a joint return filed by a wife in her capacity as legal guardian for her missing husband. However, the Tax Court has held that where one spouse is mentally incompetent, a joint return may not be filed because the incompetent spouse was unable to consent to a joint return; an appeals court agreed.

How Resident and Nonresident Aliens File

1.14 How a Nonresident Alien Is Taxed

A nonresident alien is generally taxed only on income from U.S. sources. A nonresident alien's income that is *effectively connected* with a U.S. business or capital gains from the sale of U.S. real estate are subject to tax at regular U.S. rates. Other capital gains are not taxed unless a nonresident alien has a U.S. business or is in the U.S. for 183 days during the year. Generally, investment income of a nonresident alien from U.S. sources that is *not effectively connected* with a U.S. business is subject to a 30% tax rate (or lower rate if provided by treaty).

Nonresident aliens who are required to file must do so on Form 1040NR. If you are a nonresident alien, get a copy of IRS Publication 519, U.S. Tax Guide for Aliens. It explains how nonresident aliens pay U.S. tax.

Dual status. In the year a person arrives in or departs from the U.S., both resident and nonresident status may apply.

EXAMPLE
On May 1, 1997, Leon Marchand arrived on a nonimmigrant visa and was present in the U.S. for the rest of the year. From January 1 to April 31, 1997, he is a nonresident; from May 1 to the end of the year, he is a resident, under the 183-day test *(1.16)*. Despite "dual status," he does not file two returns. Since he is a resident on the last day of the year, he files Form 1040 and reports income on the basis of his status for each part of the year. The income for the nonresident portion of the year should be shown on a separate schedule.

Certain restrictions apply to dual status taxpayers. For example, a joint return may not be filed, unless you and your spouse agree to be taxed as U.S. residents for the entire year.

For details on filing a return for a dual status year, *see* IRS Publication 519 and the instructions to Form 1040NR.

1.15   How a Resident Alien Is Taxed

A resident alien is taxed on worldwide income from all sources, just like a U.S. citizen. The exclusion for foreign earned income may be claimed if the foreign physical presence test is satisfied or if the bona fide residence test is met by an individual residing in a treaty country; *see 36.5*. A resident alien may generally claim a foreign tax credit; *see 36.14*. A resident alien's pension from a foreign government is subject to regular U.S. tax. A resident alien working in the United States for a foreign government is not taxed on the wages if the foreign government allows a similar exemption to U.S. citizens.

1.16   Who Is a Resident Alien?

The following tests determine whether an alien is taxed as a U.S. resident. Intent to remain in the U.S. is not considered.

You are treated as a resident alien and taxed as a U.S. resident if you meet either of the following tests for 1997:

1. You have been issued a "green card," which grants you the status of lawful permanent resident. If you were outside the U.S. for part of 1997 and then became a lawful permanent resident, see the rules for dual tax status on the next page.

2. You meet a 183-day substantial presence test. Under this test, you are treated as a U.S. resident if you were in the U.S. for at least 31 days during the calendar year and have been in the U.S. for 183 days within the last three years (the current year and the two preceding calendar years). The 183-day test is complicated and there are several exceptions.

   To determine if you meet the 183-day test for 1997, the following cumulative times are totaled. Each day in the U.S. during 1997 is counted as a full day. Each day in 1996 counts as $\frac{1}{3}$ of a day; each day in 1995 counts as $\frac{1}{6}$ of a day. Note that you must be physically present in the U.S. for at least 31 days in the current year. If you are not, the 183-day test does not apply.

   Other exceptions to the substantial presence test are: commuting from Canada or Mexico; keeping a tax home and close contacts or connections in a foreign country; having a diplomat, teacher, trainee, or student status; being a professional athlete temporarily in the U.S. to compete in a charitable sports event; or being confined in the U.S. for certain medical reasons. These exceptions are explained in the following paragraphs.

Commute from Mexico or Canada.   If you regularly commute to work in the U.S. from Mexico or Canada, commuting days do not count as days of physical presence for the 183-day test.

Tax home/closer connection exception.   If you are in the United States for less than 183 days during 1997, show that you had a closer connection with a foreign country than with the U.S., and keep a tax home there for the year, you generally will not be subject to tax as a resident under the substantial presence test. Under this exception, it is possible to have a U.S. abode and a tax home in a foreign country. A tax home is usually where a person has his or her principal place of business; if there is no principal place of business, it is the place of regular abode. Proving a tax home alone is not sufficient; the closer connection relationship must also be shown.

To claim the closer connection exception, you must file Form 8840 explaining the basis of your claim. The tax home/closer connection test does not apply to an alien who is present for 183 days or more during a year or who has applied for a "green card." A relative's application is not considered as the alien's application.

Exempt-person exception.   Days of presence in the U.S. are not counted under the 183-day test if you are considered an exempt person such as a teacher, trainee, student, foreign government-related person, or professional athlete temporarily in the U.S. to compete in a charitable sports event.

To exclude days of presence as a teacher, trainee, student, or professional athlete, you must file Form 8843 with the IRS.

A foreign government-related person is any individual temporarily present in the U.S. who (1) has diplomatic status or a visa which the Secretary of the Treasury (after consultation with the Secretary of State) determined represents full-time diplomatic or consular status; or (2) is a full-time employee of an international organization; or (3) is a member of the immediate family of a diplomat or international organization employee.

A teacher or trainee is any individual other than a student who is temporarily present in the U.S. under a "J" or "Q" visa and who substantially complies with the requirements for being so present.

 Caution

Who is a Resident?
An alien's mere presence in the U.S. does not make him or her a "resident." An alien is generally treated as a "resident" only if he or she is a lawful permanent resident who has a "green card" or meets a substantial presence test; *see 1.16*.

A student is any individual who is temporarily present in the U.S. under either an "F," "J," "M," or "Q" visa and who substantially complies with the requirements for being so present.

The exception generally does not apply to a teacher or trainee who has been exempt as a teacher, trainee, or student for any part of two of the six preceding calendar years. However, if during the period you are temporarily present in the U.S. under an "F," "J," "M," or "Q" visa and all of your compensation is received from outside the U.S., you may qualify for the exception if you were exempt as a teacher, trainee, or student for less than four years in the six preceding calendar years. The exception also does not apply to a student who has been exempt as a teacher, trainee, or student for more than five calendar years, unless you show that you do not intend to reside permanently in the U.S. and that you have substantially complied with the requirements of the student visa providing for temporary presence in the U.S.

Medical exception. If you plan to leave but cannot physically leave the U.S. because of a medical condition that arose in the U.S., you may be treated as a nonresident, even if present here for more than 183 days during the year. You must file Form 8843 to claim the medical exception.

Tax treaty exceptions. The lawful permanent residence test and the substantial physical presence test do not override tax treaty definitions of residence. Thus, you may be protected by a tax treaty from being treated as a U.S. resident even if you would be treated as a resident under either test.

Dual tax status in first year of residency. If you first became a lawful permanent resident of the U.S. (received a green card) during 1997 and were not a U.S. resident during 1996, your period of U.S. residency begins with the first day in 1997 that you are present in the U.S. with the status of lawful permanent resident. Before that date, you are a nonresident alien. This means that if you become a lawful permanent resident after January 1, 1997, you have a dual status tax year. On Form 1040, you attach a separate schedule showing the income for the part of the year you are a nonresident.

To figure tax for a dual status year, see IRS Publication 519 and the instructions to Form 1040NR.

You also may have a dual status year if you were not a U.S. resident in 1996, and in 1997 you are a U.S. resident under the 183-day presence test. Your period of U.S. residency starts on the first day in 1997 for which you were physically present; before that date you are treated as a nonresident alien. However, if you meet the 183-day presence test (but not the green card test) and also spent 10 days or less in the U.S. during a period in which you had a closer connection to a foreign country than to the U.S., you may disregard the 10-day period. The purpose of this exception is to allow a brief presence in the U.S. for business trips or house hunting before the U.S. residency period starts.

Planning Reminder

Is 1997 First Year of Residency?
If you were not a resident during 1996 but in 1997 you satisfy both the lawful resident (green card) test and the 183-day presence test, your residence begins on the earlier of the first day you are in the U.S. while a lawful permanent resident and the first day of physical presence.

EXAMPLES

1. Manuel Riveras, who has never before been a U.S. resident, lives in Spain until May 15, 1997. He moves to the U.S. and remains in the U.S. through the end of the year, thereby satisfying the physical presence test. On May 15, he is a U.S. resident. However, for the period before May 15, he is taxed as a nonresident.

2. Same facts as in Example 1, but Riveras attends a meeting in the U.S. on February 2 through 8. On May 15, he moves to the U.S.; May 15, not February 2, is the starting date of the residency. During February, he had closer connection to Spain than to the U.S. Thus, his short stay in February is an exempt period.

First-year choice. If you do not meet either the green card test or the 183-day substantial presence test for the year of your arrival in the U.S. or for the immediately preceding year, but you do meet the substantial presence test for the year immediately following the year of your arrival, you may elect to be treated as a U.S. resident for part of the year of your arrival. To do this, you must (1) be present in the U.S. for at least 31 consecutive days in the year of your arrival; and (2) be present in the U.S. for at least 75% of the number of days beginning with the first day of the 31-consecutive-day period and ending with the last day of the year of arrival. For purposes of this 75% requirement, you may treat up to five days of absence from the U.S. as days of presence within the U.S.

Do not count as days of presence in the U.S. days for which you are an *exempt individual* as discussed earlier.

You make the first-year election to be treated as a U.S. resident by attaching a statement to Form 1040 for the year of your arrival. A first-year election, once made, may not be revoked without the consent of the Internal Revenue Service.

If you make the election, your residence starting date for the year of your arrival is the first day of the earliest 31-consecutive-day period of presence that you use to qualify for the choice. You are treated as a U.S. resident for the remainder of the year.

Last year of residence. You are no longer treated as a U.S. resident as of your *residency termination date*. If you do not have a green card but are a U.S. resident for the year under the 183-day presence test, and you leave the U.S. during that year, your residency termination date is the last day you are present in the U.S., provided that: (1) after leaving the U.S. you had a closer connection to a foreign country than to the U.S. and had your tax home in that foreign country for the rest of the year, and (2) you are not treated as a U.S. resident for any part of the next calendar year.

If during the year you give up your green card (lawful permanent resident status) and meet tests (1) and (2), your residency termination date is the first day that you are no longer a lawful permanent resident. If during the year you meet both the green card test and the 183-day presence test and meet tests (1) and (2), your residency termination date is the *later* of the last day of U.S. presence or the first day you are no longer a lawful permanent resident. If tests (1) and (2) are not met, the residency termination date is the last day of the calendar year. In the year of your residency termination date, the filing rules for dual status taxpayers at *1.14* apply.

1.17 When an Alien Leaves the United States

Current law generally requires an alien who leaves the U.S., regardless of how long the trip is, to obtain a "sailing permit," technically known as a "certificate of compliance." The permit states that you have fulfilled your income tax obligations to the U.S. Without it, unless you are excused from obtaining one, you will be required at your point of departure to file a tax return and pay any tax due. You should apply for a sailing permit from your local District Director of Internal Revenue about two weeks, but no earlier than 30 days, before your departure. See IRS Publication 519 for further details.

1.18 Expatriation Tax

Special tax rules apply to U.S. citizens who renounce their citizenship and long-term residents who end their residency if tax avoidance is one of their principal purposes for leaving. A long-term resident is someone who was a lawful permanent resident (with a green card) in at least eight of the last fifteen years ending with the last year of residency. For a ten-year period, such individuals are subject to regular U.S. tax on income and gains from U.S. sources.

The law presumes a tax avoidance purpose in certain cases. For 1997, tax avoidance is presumed if (1) the departing individual's average net income tax for the last five years before losing citizenship or terminating residency was more than $100,000, or (2) net worth when citizenship or residency ended was $500,000 or more. These dollar amounts are subject to annual adjustments for inflation.

All individuals who lose their citizenship or who end long-term residency must file information statements with the federal government; *see* IRS Publication 519.

 Law Alert

Proposed Changes to "Sailing Permit"

Given widespread noncompliance with the sailing permit requirements, proposals have been made to replace the rules. One proposal would require a resident alien who is permanently leaving the U.S. to file a tax return within 90 days.

Part 2

Reporting Your Income

In this part, you will learn what income is taxable and what income is tax-free and how to report income on your tax return.
Pay special attention to—

- Form W-2, which shows your taxable wages and provides other important information on fringe benefits received (Chapter 2).
- Tax-free fringe benefit plans available from your employer (Chapter 3).
- Reporting rules for interest and dividend income (Chapter 4).
- Reporting gains and losses from sales of property. (Chapter 5).
- Rules for tax-free exchanges of like-kind property (Chapter 6).
- Planning for retirement distributions. Lump-sum distributions from employer plans may qualify for special averaging or tax-free rollover (Chapter 7).
- IRA contributions and distributions. Penalties for distributions before age 59 $\frac{1}{2}$ and after age 70 $\frac{1}{2}$ may be avoided by advance planning (Chapter 8).
- Restrictions on rental losses where a rented residence is used personally by you or by family members during the year (Chapter 9).
- Passive activity restrictions. Losses from rentals or passive business operations are generally not allowed, but certain real estate professionals are exempt from the loss restrictions, and for others, a special rental loss allowance of up to $25,000 may be available (Chapter 10).
- Reporting refunds of state and local taxes. A refund of previously deducted taxes is generally taxable unless you had no benefit from the deduction (Chapter 11).
- Cancellation of debts. When your creditor cancels debts you owe, you generally have taxable income, but there are exceptions for debts discharged while you are bankrupt or insolvent (Chapter 11).
- Damages received in court proceedings. Learn when these are tax free and when taxable (Chapter 11).

Chapter 2

Taxable Wages, Salary, and Other Compensation

Except for tax-free fringe benefits (*see* Chapter 3), practically everything you receive for your work or services is taxed, whether paid in cash, property, or services. Your employer will generally report your taxable compensation on Form W-2 and other information returns, such as Form 1099 for certain retirement payments and compensatory distributions of securities. Do not reduce the amount you report on your return by withholdings for income taxes, Social Security taxes, union dues, or U.S. Savings Bond purchases. Your Form W-2 does not include in taxable pay your qualifying salary-reduction contributions to a retirement plan, although the amount may be shown on the form.

Attach Copy B of Form W-2 to your return; do not attach Form 1099 unless there are withholdings.

Unemployment benefits are fully taxable. The benefits are reported to the IRS on Form 1099-G. You do not have to attach your copy of Form 1099-G to your return.

Key to Your Form W-2	
Amount In—	*What You Should Know—*
Box 1	***Taxable wages and tips.*** Your taxable wages and tips are listed in Box 1. Taxable fringe benefits that are shown in Box 12 will also be included in Box 1 as other compensation. The value of tax-free fringe benefits is not shown on Form W-2.
	Mileage or per diem travel allowances will not be reported in Box 1 as taxable wages unless they exceed the IRS rate. *See* Box 13.
	Do not decrease the amount shown in Box 1 by the amount your employer withholds for income taxes, Social Security taxes, disability insurance payments, hospitalization insurance premiums, U.S. Savings Bonds, union dues, or payments to a creditor who has attached your salary. Box 1 does not include salary reduction contributions to a retirement plan.
	Compensation shown in Box 1 must be reported on Line 7 of Form 1040 or 1040A, or Line 1 of Form 1040EZ.
Box 2	***Federal tax withholdings.*** This is the amount of federal income tax withheld from your pay. Enter the amount on Line 54, Form 1040, Line 29a, Form 1040A, or on Line 7, Form 1040EZ. If the withheld amount plus your estimated tax installments exceed your tax liability, you are entitled to a refund for the excess payments.
Boxes 3, 4, and 7	***Social Security withholdings.*** Withholdings for Social Security coverage are at a rate of 6.20% on up to $65,400 of 1997 wages and tips. If your wages were $65,400 or more, Box 4 should show the maximum tax of $4,054.80. If you worked for more than one employer, and a total of more than $4,054.80 was withheld for Social Security taxes, you claim the excess as a tax payment on your tax return; see 26.10.
	Wages subject to Social Security withholdings are shown in Box 3. Elective salary deferrals to a 401(k) plan or SIMPLE plan are included; Social Security withholding applies, although the deferrals are not subject to income tax and are not included in Box 1. Similarly, employer payments of qualified adoption expenses (Chapter 3) are included in Box 3 although not included in Box 1 taxable wages. Tips you reported to your employer are shown separately in Box 7. The total of Boxes 3 and 7 should not exceed $65,400.
Boxes 5–6	***Medicare tax withholdings.*** Wages, tips, elective salary deferrals, and employer-paid adoption expenses subject to Social Security tax (Boxes 3 and 7) are also subject to a 1.45% Medicare tax, except that there is no wage base limit for Medicare tax. Thus, the Medicare wages shown in Box 5 are not limited to the $65,400 maximum for Box 3. For example, if your wages were $100,000, the amount shown in Box 3 (Social Security wages) would be $65,400, but in Box 5, the full $100,000 would be reported.
	In Box 6, total Medicare withholdings are reported. On wages of $100,000, the Medicare tax would be $1,450 (1.45% × $100,000).
Box 8	***Allocated tips.*** If you worked in a restaurant employing at least 10 people, your employer will report in Box 8 your share of 8% of gross receipts unless you reported tips at least equal to that share *(26.8)*. The amount shown here is not included in Box 1 wages, but you must add it to wages on Line 7 of Form 1040; you cannot file Form 1040A or 1040EZ.
Box 9	***Advance earned income payment.*** If you filed a Form W-5 asking for a part of the credit to be added to your wages, the amount of the advance is shown in Box 9. You report the advance as a tax liability when you file Form 1040 or 1040A. *See* Chapter 25 for details on claiming the earned income credit for 1997, and for advanced earned income payments.
Box 10	***Dependent care benefits.*** Reimbursements from your employer for dependent care expenses and the value of employer-provided care services under a qualifying plan *(3.4)* are included in Box 10. Amounts in excess of $5,000 are also included as taxable wages in Boxes 1, 3, and 5. Generally, amounts up to $5,000 are tax free, but you must determine the amount of the exclusion on Form 2441 if you file Form 1040, or on Schedule 2 if you file Form 1040A. The tax-free amount reduces expenses eligible for the dependent care credit; *see* Chapter 25.
Box 11	***Nonqualified plan distributions.*** Distributions shown in Box 11 are from a nonqualified deferred compensation plan, or a Section 457 plan *(7.21)*. Do not report these distributions separately since they have already been included as taxable wages in Box 1.
Box 12	***Taxable fringe benefits.*** If you received taxable fringe benefits, your employer shows the amount in Box 12 unless it is reportable in Box 10 or Box 13. For example, the taxable value of using a company car for personal trips *(3.7)*, may be included in Box 12. Do not separately report the Box 12 amount as income, since it has already been included in Box 1 as taxable wages.

Amount In—	*What You Should Know—*
Box 13	**Elective deferrals to retirement plans.** If you made elective salary deferrals to an employer retirement plan, Box 15, "deferred compensation," will be checked and your contribution (including any excess over the annual deferral limit) is shown in Box 13. Deferrals to a 401(k) plan *(7.18)* should be labeled with Code D. For example, if you made pre-tax salary deferrals of $4,500 to a 401(k) plan, your employer would enter D 4500 in Box 13. Code E is used for deferrals to a 403(b) tax-sheltered annuity plan *(7.20)*, Code F for deferrals to a simplified employee pension *(8.17)*, Code G for deferrals (including non-elective as well as elective) to a Section 457 plan *(7.21)*, Code H for elective deferrals to a pension plan created before June 25, 1959, and funded only by employee contributions and Code S for salary-reduction deferrals to a SIMPLE IRA.
	Travel allowance reimbursements. If you received a flat mileage allowance from your employer for business trips *(20.33)*; or a per diem travel allowance to cover meals, lodging, and incidentals *(20.32)*; and the allowance exceeded the IRS rate, the amount up to the IRS rate (the nontaxable portion) is shown in Box 13 using Code L. Do not separately report this amount as income since that excess is included as taxable wages in Box 1.
	Group-term life insurance over $50,000. The cost of coverage over $50,000 is taxable. It is shown in Box 13 using Code C. It is also included in Box 1 wages, Box 3 Social Security wages, and Box 5 Medicare wages and tips.
	If you are a retiree or other former employee who received group-term coverage over $50,000, any uncollected Social Security tax is shown using Code M; and uncollected Medicare tax, using Code N. The uncollected amount must be reported on Form 1040 in the section for "Other Taxes"; include it on the line for your "total tax" and write "uncollected tax" next to it.
	Nontaxable sick pay. If you contributed to a sick pay plan, an allocable portion of benefits received is tax free and is shown using Code J.
	Uncollected Social Security and Medicare taxes on tips. If your employer could not withhold sufficient Social Security on tips, the uncollected amount is shown using Code A. For uncollected Medicare tax, Code B is used. This amount must be reported on Form 1040 in the section for "Other Taxes"; include the amount on the line for your "total tax" and write "uncollected tax" next to it.
	Excess golden parachute payments. If you received an "excess parachute payment," Code K identifies the 20% penalty tax on the excess payment. This withheld amount is included in Box 2, but is reported on Form 1040 in the section for "other taxes," on the line for "total tax."
	Moving expense reimbursements. Tax-free employer reimbursments (or payments to movers) for deductible moving expenses (Chapter 12) are shown with Code P.
	Employer contributions to medical savings account. Total employer contributions to a medical savings account are shown with Code R. Contributions exceeding the excludable limit (Chapter 3) are included as taxable wages in Box 1.
	Employer-financed adoption benefits. With Code T, your employer shows qualified adoption expenses paid by the employer *(3.5)* or pre-tax contributions you made to an adoption plan account under a cafeteria plan *(3.13)*.
Box 14	**Miscellaneous payments.** Your employer may use Box 14 to report payments such as union dues, educational assistance, health insurance premiums, or voluntary after-tax contributions to profit-sharing or pension plans.
Box 15	**Statutory employee.** If this box is checked you get a tax break. You report your wage income and deductible job expenses on Schedule C. This treatment allows job expenses to avoid the 2% adjusted gross income (AGI) floor on Schedule A. *See 40.5.* Your earnings are not subject to income tax withholding, but are subject to Social Security and Medicare taxes.
	Pension plan. If the box "pension plan" is checked, this indicates that you were an active participant in an employer plan at some point during the year. As an active participant, you may be unable to make deductible IRA contributions; IRA deductions start to phase out if your AGI exceeds $25,000 (single) or $40,000 (married filing jointly); *see* Chapter 8.
	Household employee. The "Hshld. emp." box will be checked if you worked in the employer's home as a baby-sitter, housekeeper, cook, or butler, or you did similar household work.
	Deferred compensation. The box "deferred compensation" is checked if you made salary deferrals to a 401(k) plan *(7.18)*, tax-sheltered 403(b) annuity *(7.20)*, SIMPLE IRA *(8.18)* or simplified employee pension plan *(8.17)*. In Box 13, the employer lists the total elective deferrals to these plans.
Boxes 18 and 21	**State and local taxes.** If you itemize, deduct on Schedule A state and local tax withholdings shown in Boxes 18 and 21.

Sample Form W-2

You should receive your Form W-2 for 1997 from your employer by February 2, 1998.
Note: Box 3 below includes the wages in Box 1 and a $1,000
401(k) elective deferral shown in Box 13 with Code D; see the
Key to Form W-2 on the preceding pages.

a Control number		OMB No. 1545-0008	
b Employer's identification number 08 - XIXOXIX		**1** Wages, tips, other compensation 35,000	**2** Federal income tax withheld 5,840
c Employer's name, address, and ZIP code ABC Painting Co, Inc 432 Combard Ave City. State XXIII		**3** Social security wages 36,000	**4** Social security tax withheld 2232
		5 Medicare wages and tips	**6** Medicare tax withheld 522
		7 Social security tips	**8** Allocated tips
d Employee's social security number OXI-XX-IX00		**9** Advance EIC payment	**10** Dependent care benefits
e Employee's name, address, and ZIP code Richard Turco 86 Portland Court City. State IXXXI		**11** Nonqualified plans	**12** Benefits included in box 1 1,500
		13 See Instrs. for box 13 D 1000.00	**14** Other

15 Statutory employee ☐	Deceased ☐	Pension plan ☐	Legal rep. ☐	Hshld. emp. ☐	Subtotal ☐	Deferred compensation ☐

16 State	Employer's state I.D. No.	**17** State wages, tips, etc.	**18** State income tax	**19** Locality name	**20** Local wages, tips, etc.	**21** Local income tax
State	11-XIXOXIX	32,000	1,580	City	32,000	765

Department of the Treasury—Internal Revenue Service

Form W-2 **Wage and Tax Statement** **1997**
Copy B To Be Filed With Employee's FEDERAL Tax Return

This information is being furnished
to the Internal Revenue Service.

5 WA

Reporting Compensation

2.1 Salary and Wage Income

The key to reporting your pay is Form W-2, sent to you by your employer. It lists your taxable wages, which may include not only your regular pay, but also other taxable items, such as taxable fringe benefits. A guide to the important information listed on Form W-2 is on pages 28 and 29.

Your employer reports your taxable pay under a simple rule. Unless the item is specifically exempt from tax, you are taxed on practically everything you receive for your work whether paid in cash, property, or services. Taxed pay includes:

Back pay	Honoraria
Bonuses	Jury fees
Commissions	Salaries
Director's fees	Severance pay
Sick pay	Dismissal pay
Employee prizes or awards	Tips
Expense allowances or reimbursements	Vacation pay
under nonaccountable plans	Wages

The items that the law specifically excludes from tax are discussed in Chapter 3. The most common tax-free benefits are employer-paid premiums for health and accident plans and certain group-term life insurance plans for coverage up to $50,000.

Withholdings for retirement plans. Amounts withheld from wages as your contribution to your pension or profit-sharing account are generally taxable unless they are tax-deferred under the limits allowed for Section 401(k) plans *(7.18)*, simplified employee pension plans *(8.17)*, SIMPLE plans *(8.18)*, or tax-sheltered annuity plans *(7.20)*. Tax-deferred amounts are reported in Box 13 of Form W-2.

Wages withheld for compulsory forfeitable contributions to a nonqualified pension plan are not taxable if these conditions exist:

1. The contribution is forfeited if employment is terminated prior to death or retirement.
2. The plan does not provide for a refund of employee contributions and, in the administration of the plan, no refund will be made. Where only part of the contribution is subject to forfeiture, the amount of withheld contribution not subject to forfeiture is taxable income.

You should check with your employer to determine the status of your contributions.

Assigning your pay. You may not avoid tax on income you earned by assigning the right to payment to another person. For example, you must report earnings that you donate to charity, even if they are paid directly by your employer to a charity. If you claim itemized deductions, you may claim a contribution deduction for the donation; *see* Chapter 14.

The IRS allowed an exception for doctors working in a clinic. The doctors were not taxed on fees for treating patients with limited income (teaching cases) where they were required to assign the fees to a foundation.

Salary advances. Salary paid in advance for services to be rendered in the future is generally taxable in the year received if it is subject to your free and unrestricted use.

Child's wages. A parent is not taxed on wages paid for a child's services even if payment is made to the parent. However, a parent is taxed on income from work contracted for by the parent even if the child assists in the labor. For example, a parent whose children helped her with part-time work at home claimed that the children should be taxed on 70% of the income since they did 70% of the work. The IRS claimed that the parent was taxable on all the income because she, not the children, was the true earner, and the Tax Court agreed. Although the company knew that the children were doing part of the work, it had no agreement with them.

Employee leave-sharing plan. Some companies allow employees to contribute their unused leave into a "leave fund" for use by other employees who have suffered medical emergencies. If you use up your regular leave and benefit from additional leave that has been donated to the plan, the benefit is taxable and will be reported as wages on Form W-2.

 Caution

Severance Pay Taxable
You must pay tax on severance pay received upon losing a job. The severance pay is taxable even if you signed a waiver releasing your former employer from potential future damage claims. The waiver does not change the nature of the payments from taxable pay to tax-free personal injury damages; *see 11.7.*

Court Decision

Tax on Assigned Contingent Fee

An attorney who took a medical malpractice case on a contingent fee basis agreed to split the net fee with his ex-wife pursuant to their divorce agreement. After a favorable settlement, the attorney's take was approximately $40,000 after expenses, half of which went to his ex-wife. Each paid tax on his or her share. The attorney argued that his partial assignment of the fee could shift the tax liability because collection was contingent on the outcome of the lawsuit. However, the IRS and the Tax Court held that the attorney was liable for the tax on the entire contingent fee, and an appeals court agreed. The attorney transferred only the right to receive income. Although his fee was contingent upon the successful outcome of the case, once the fee materialized, it was indisputably compensation for his personal services.

"Golden parachute" payments. Golden parachute arrangements are agreements to pay key employees additional compensation upon a change in company control. If you receive such a payment, part of it may be deemed to be an "excess payment" under a complex formula in the law. You must pay a 20% penalty tax on the "excess" amount in addition to regular income tax on the total. The excess amount should be identified on Form W-2 with Code K in Box 13; *see* the Key to Your Form W-2 at the beginning of this chapter.

If the golden parachute payment was reported on Form 1099-MISC, it will be included in Box 7 as non-employee compensation. If you are self-employed, report the total compensation on Schedule C *(40.5)* and compute self-employment tax on Schedule SE *(45.3)*.

Any "excess parachute payment" should be separately labeled in Box 13 of Form 1099-MISC. Multiply the excess payment by 20% and report it in the section of Form 1040 for "other taxes," on the line for "total tax."

2.2 Year-End Paychecks

As an employee, you use the cash basis method of accounting. This means that you report all income items in the year they are actually received and deduct expenses in the year you pay them.

You are also subject to the "constructive receipt rule," which requires you to report income not actually received but which has been credited to your account, subject to your control, or put aside for you. Thus, if you received a paycheck on December 31, 1997, you must report the pay on your 1997 return, even though you do not cash or deposit it to your account until 1998. This is true even if you receive the check after banking hours and cannot cash or deposit it until the next year.

If your employer does not have funds in the bank and asks you to hold the check before depositing it, you do not have taxable income until the check is cashed. If pay for services rendered in 1997 is paid by check dated for 1998, the pay is taxable in 1998.

The IRS has ruled that an employee who is not at home on December 31 to take delivery of a check sent by certified mail must still report the check in that year. However, where an employee was not at home to take certified mail delivery of a year-end check that she did not expect to receive until the next year, the Tax Court held that the funds were taxable when received in the following year.

2.3 Pay Received in Property Is Taxed

Your employer may pay you with property instead of cash. You report the fair market value of the property as wages.

> **EXAMPLE**
>
> For consulting services rendered, Kate Chong receives a check for $10,000 and property having a fair market value of $5,000. She reports $15,000 as wages.

If you receive your company's stock as payment for your services, you include the value of the stock as pay in the year you receive it. However, if the stock is nontransferable or subject to substantial risk of forfeiture, you do not have to include its value as pay until the restrictions no longer apply. You must report dividends on the restricted stock in the year you receive the income.

If you receive your employer's note which has a fair market value, you are taxed on the value of the note less what it would cost you to discount it. If the note bears interest, report the full face value. But do not report income if the note has no fair market value. Report income on the note only when payments are made on it.

A debt cancelled by an employer is taxable income.

Salespeople employed by a dealer have taxable income on receipt of "prize points" redeemable for merchandise from a distributor.

2.4 Gifts From Employers

A payment may be called a gift but still be taxable income. Any payment made in recognition of past services or in anticipation of future services or benefits is taxable even if the employer is not obligated to make the payment. Exceptions for employee achievement awards are discussed at *3.10*.

To prove a gift is tax free, you must show that the employer acted with pure and unselfish motives of affection, admiration, or charity. This is difficult to do, given the employer-employee relationship. A gift of stock by majority stockholders to key employees has been held to be taxable.

2.5 When Commissions Are Taxed

Earned commissions are taxable in the year they are credited to your account and subject to your drawing, whether or not you actually draw them.

On your 1997 tax return, you do not report commissions which were earned in 1997 but which cannot be computed or collected until a later year.

EXAMPLE

Arno Jeffers earns commissions based on a percentage of the profits from realty sales. In 1997 he draws $10,000 from his account. However, at the end of 1997 the full amount of his commissions is unknown because profits for the year have not been figured. In January 1998, his 1997 commissions are computed to be $15,000, and the $5,000 balance is paid to him. The $5,000 is taxable in 1998 even though earned in 1997.

Advances against unearned commissions.   Under standard insurance industry practice, an agent who sells a policy does not earn commissions until premiums are received by the insurance company. However, the company may issue a cash advance on the commissions before the premiums are received. Agents have claimed that they may defer reporting the income until the year the premiums are earned. The IRS, recognizing that in practice companies rarely demand repayment, requires that advances be included in income in the year received if the agent has full control over the advanced funds. A repayment of unearned commissions in a later year is deducted on Schedule A; *see 2.9.*

Salespeople have been taxed on commissions received on property bought for their personal use. In one case, an insurance agent was taxed on commissions paid to him on his purchase of an insurance policy. In another case, a real estate agent was taxed on commissions he received on his purchase of land. A salesman was also taxed for commissions waived on policies he sold to friends, relatives, and employees.

Kickback of commission.   An insurance agent's kickback of his or her commission is taxable where agents may not under local law give rebates or kickbacks of premiums to their clients. The commissions are income and may not be offset with a business expense deduction; illegal kickbacks may not be deducted.

However, in one case, a federal appeals court allowed an insurance broker to avoid tax when he did not charge clients the basic first-year commission. The clients paid the broker the net premium (gross premium less the commission), which he remitted to the insurance company. The IRS and Tax Court held that the commissions were taxable despite the broker's voluntary waiver of his right to them. He could not deduct them because his discount scheme violated state anti-rebate law (Oklahoma). On appeal, the broker won. The Tenth Circuit Court of Appeals held that since the broker never had any right to commissions under the terms of the contracts he structured with his clients, he was not taxed on the commissions. The court cautioned that if the broker had remitted the full premium (including commission) to the insurance company and then reimbursed the client after having received the commission from the company, the commission probably would have been taxable.

Caution

Earned Commissions Credited to Your Account

You may not postpone tax on earned commissions credited to your account in 1997 by not drawing them until 1998 or a later year. However, where a portion of earned commissions is not withdrawn because your employer is holding it to cover future expenses, you are not taxed on the amount withheld.

2.6 Unemployment Benefits Are Taxable

All unemployment benefits you receive in 1997 from a state agency or the federal government are treated as taxable income. You should receive Form 1099-G, showing the amount of the payments. Report the payments separately from wages on Line 19 of Form 1040, Line 12 of Form 1040A or Line 3 of Form 1040EZ.

Supplemental unemployment benefits paid from company- financed funds are taxable as wages and not reported as unemployment compensation. Such benefits are usually paid under guaranteed annual wage plans made between unions and employers.

Unemployment benefits from a private or union fund to which you voluntarily contribute dues are taxable as "other" income on Form 1040, but only to the extent the benefits exceed your contributions to the fund. Your contributions to the fund are not deductible.

Worker's compensation payments are not taxable; *see 2.12.*

Taxable unemployment benefits include federal trade readjustment allowances (1974 Trade Act), airline deregulation benefits (1978 Airline Deregulation Act), and disaster unemployment assistance (1974 Disaster Relief Act).

Repaid Settlement Benefits. If you had to repay supplemental unemployment benefits to receive trade readjustment allowances (1974 Trade Act), taxable unemployment benefits are reduced by repayments made in the same year. If you repay the benefits in a later year, the benefits are taxed in the year of receipt and a deduction may be claimed in the later year. If the repayment is $3,000 or less, the deduction is added to your other adjustments to income on Line 31 of Form 1040. If the repayment exceeds $3,000, a deduction or a credit may be claimed under the rules of *2.9.*

2.7 Strike Pay Benefits and Penalties

Strike and lockout benefits paid out of regular union dues are taxable as wages unless the payment qualifies as a gift, as discussed below. However, if you have made voluntary contributions to a strike fund, benefits you receive from the fund are tax free up to the amount of your contributions and are taxable to the extent they exceed your contributions.

Strike benefits as tax-free gifts. Here are factors indicating that benefits are gifts: Payments are based on individual need; they are paid to both union and nonunion members; and no conditions are imposed on the strikers who receive benefits.

If you receive benefits under conditions by which you are to participate in the strike and the payments are tied to your scale of wages, the benefits are taxable.

EXAMPLE

A striking union pilot claimed that strike benefits were tax-free gifts because they were funded by assessments paid by other union pilots who were not on strike. The IRS and Tax Court held that the benefits were taxable. They were not gifts because they were not motivated by a "detached and disinterested generosity." The union was promoting its own self-interest by giving pilots an incentive to support the strike. The non-striking pilots contributed to the strike fund as an obligation of union membership. The strikers were eligible for benefits only if they agreed to perform any strike activities requested by the union, did not fly for airlines in dispute with the union, and did not take actions that could adversely affect the outcome of the dispute.

Strike pay penalties. Pay penalties charged striking teachers are not deductible. State law may prohibit public school teachers from striking and charge a penalty equal to one day's pay for each day on strike if they do strike. For example, when striking teachers returned to work after a one-week strike, a penalty of one week's salary was deducted from their pay. Although they did not actually receive pay for the week they worked after the strike, they earned taxable wages. Furthermore, the penalty is not deductible. No deduction is allowed for a fine or penalty paid to a government for the violation of a law.

2.8 Deferring Tax on Pay

If you want to avoid current tax on pay, you may contract with your employer to defer pay to future years. To reduce possible IRS opposition, it is advisable to enter into a deferral compensation arrangement before the year in which the services are to be performed; for example, agree in 1998 to defer pay for 1999 services to 2000 or later years. Furthermore, to defer pay to a future period, you must take some risk. You cannot have any control over your deferred pay account. If you are not confident of your employer's ability to pay in the future, you should not enter into a deferred pay plan.

Before agreeing to a deferral arrangement, consider the possibility that if tax rates are raised further, you may be subject to a higher tax on deferred pay than if you had received and paid tax currently on the income.

If IRS tests are met, a trust arrangement, commonly nicknamed a "rabbi trust," can be used by an employer to hold deferred pay contributions; *see 2.14.*

An employee is not taxed on employer contributions to a qualified cash or deferred arrangement (401(k) plan) even though the employee had the option to take the cash; *see 7.17.* Qualified salary reductions under a simplified employee pension plan (SEP) *(8.17),* SIMPLE IRA *(8.18),* or tax-sheltered annuity plan *(7.20)* are also not taxed, even though you could have received cash currently.

2.9 Did You Return Income Received in a Prior Year?

Did you return income in 1997 such as salary or commissions which you reported in a prior taxable year because it appeared you had an unrestricted right to it in the earlier year? If so, you may deduct the repayment as a miscellaneous itemized deduction. If the repayment of wages exceeds $3,000, the deduction is claimed on Line 27 of Schedule A and is not subject to the 2% adjusted gross income (AGI) floor (19.1). However, the law is not clear on the issue of whether a deduction of $3,000 or less is subject to the 2% floor; the IRS takes the position that the 2% floor applies.

Option of tax credit or deduction for repayments over $3,000. If your repayment exceeded $3,000, you may claim the repayment as an itemized deduction, *or* you may claim a tax credit, based upon a recomputation of the prior year's tax; *see* the Filing Instruction on this page.

Repayment of supplemental unemployment benefits. Where repayment is required to qualify for trade readjustment allowances, you may deduct the repayment from gross income. Claim the deduction on Line 31 of Form 1040, and to the left of the line write "subpay TRA." The deduction is allowed even if you do not itemize. If repayment exceeds $3,000, you have the choice of a deduction or claiming a tax credit based on a recomputation of your tax for the year supplemental unemployment benefits were received, as explained in the Filing Instruction on this page.

Repayment of disallowed travel & entertainment expenses. If a "hedge" agreement between you and your company requires you to repay salary or travel and entertainment ("T & E") expenses if they are disallowed to the company by the IRS, you may claim a deduction in the year of repayment. According to the IRS, you may not recalculate your tax for the prior year and claim a tax credit under the rules of Section 1341. However, an appeals court rejected the position taken by the IRS and allowed a tax recomputation under Section 1341 to an executive who returned part of a disallowed salary under the terms of a corporate by-law.

2.10 Waiver of Executor's and Trustee's Commissions

Commissions received by an executor for services performed are taxable as compensation. An executor may waive commissions without income or gift tax consequences by giving a principal legatee or devisee a formal waiver of his or her right to commissions within six months after the initial appointment or by not claiming commissions at the time of filing the usual accountings.

The waiver may not be recognized if he or she takes any action that is inconsistent with the waiver. An example of an inconsistent action would be the claiming of an executor's fee as a deduction on an estate, inheritance, or income tax return.

A *bequest* received by an executor from an estate is tax free if it is not compensation for services.

 Filing Instruction

Repayments Exceeding $3,000
If a repayment in 1997 exceeds $3,000, a special law (Code section 1341) gives this alternative: Instead of claiming an itemized deduction from 1997 income, you may recompute your tax for the prior year as if the income had not been reported. The difference between the actual tax paid in the prior year and the recomputed tax may be claimed as a credit on your 1997 return. The credit is claimed on Line 59 of Form 1040; write next to the line "IRC 1341." If you claim the repayment as a miscellaneous itemized deduction, enter it on Line 27 of Schedule A, where it is not subject to the 2% floor. Choose either the credit or the itemized deduction, whichever gives you the larger tax reduction. The Section 1341 credit does not apply to the refund of income arising from the sale of inventory items.

Disability and Workers' Compensation

2.11 Sick Pay Is Taxable

Sick pay is generally taxable as wages unless it qualifies as workers' compensation under the rules of *2.12*. Payments received under accident or health plans are tax free if you paid the premiums; *see 17.4*. Payments from your employer's plan for certain serious permanent injuries are tax free; *see 3.2*.

Disability pensions are discussed at *2.13*.

Sick pay received from your employer is subject to income tax withholding as if it were wages. Sick pay from a third party such as an insurance company is not subject to withholdings unless you request it on Form W-4S.

2.12 Workers' Compensation Is Tax Free

You do not pay tax on workers' compensation payments for job-related injuries or illness. However, your employer might continue paying your regular salary but require you to turn over your workers' compensation payments. Then you are taxed on the difference between what was paid to you and what you returned.

Caution

Job-Related Injury or Illness

Not all payments for job-related illness or injury qualify as tax-free workers' compensation. Unless the statute or regulation authorizing your disability payment restricts awards to on-the-job injury or illness, your payment is taxable. Even if your payments are in fact based upon job related injury or illness, they are taxed if other individuals can receive payments from the plan for disabilities that are not work related; *see* the Kane Example on this page.

Court Decision

Is Sick Leave Tax-Free Workers' Compensation?

According to the Tax Court, sick leave may qualify as tax-free workers' compensation if it is paid under a specific workers' compensation statute or similar government regulation that authorizes the sick leave payment for job-related injuries or illness; *see* Examples 1, 3, and 4 on this page.

EXAMPLE

John Wright was injured while at work and was out of work for two months. His company continues to pay his weekly salary of $475. He also receives workers' compensation of $100 a week from the state, which is tax free. He gives the $100 back to his employer. The balance of $375 a week is considered taxable wages.

To qualify as tax-free workers' compensation, the payments must be made under the authority of a *law* (or regulation having force of a law) that provides compensation for on-the-job injury or illness. Payments made under a labor agreement do *not* qualify as tax-free workers' compensation; *see* the Examples at the end of this section.

EXAMPLE

Kane, a federal district judge, suffered from sleep apnea, a condition characterized by a cessation of breathing during sleep, which was aggravated by the stress of his judicial work. He received a retirement disability payment of $65,135.

A federal appeals court held that the payment was taxable because it was paid under a statute which did not specifically require that the payments be for work-related injuries. Here, the federal law under which the judge received his payments provided benefits for all permanent disabilities, whether or not job related.

Effect of workers' compensation on Social Security. In figuring whether Social Security benefits are taxable *(34.2)*, workers' compensation that reduces Social Security or equivalent Railroad Retirement benefits is treated as a Social Security (or Railroad Retirement) benefit received during the year. Thus, the workers' compensation may be indirectly subject to tax under *34.3*.

EXAMPLES

1. A teacher, injured while working, received full salary during a two-year sick leave. She argued that the payments, made under board of education regulations, were similar to workers' compensation and thus tax free. The IRS disagreed; the regulations were not the same as a workers' compensation statute. The Tax Court supported the teacher. The payments were made because of job-related injuries and were authorized by regulations having the force of law.

2. A disabled New York City policeman argued that sick leave payments in 1978 under a union labor contract were tax-free workers' compensation because his disability was work related. However, the IRS, Tax Court, and an appeals court disagreed. The payments were made under a labor contract and not a workers' compensation statute or pursuant to government regulations. Furthermore, even if authorized by a statute or regulations, the officer's sick leave would be taxable since under the labor contract, officers received sick pay whether or not their injury or illness was work related.

   A change in New York City law now qualifies sick leave payments to firefighters and police officers for line-of-duty injuries as tax-free workers' compensation.

3. The IRS, relying on the court decision in Example 2, claimed that a police officer in Lynbrook, N.Y., was subject to tax on line-of-duty disability pay because the payment was under a labor agreement with the Police Benevolent Association (PBA). The Tax Court supported the police officer's claim that the payments were authorized by a specific New York State law requiring full salary for job-related police injuries. The PBA agreement did not affect the officer's rights to those state law payments. Lynbrook treated the case as a workers' compensation claim and in fact received reimbursement from the state workers' compensation board for the payments made to the officer.

4. A Los Angeles sheriff injured on the job retired on disability and, under the Los Angeles workers' compensation law, was allowed to elect sick pay in lieu of the regular workers' compensation amount because the sick pay was larger. The IRS argued that the sheriff had merely received taxable sick pay because he would have received the same amount as sick pay if his injuries had been suffered in a personal accident. However, the Tax Court allowed tax-free treatment. The sick leave was paid under a workers' compensation law that applied solely to work-related injuries. The fact that sick leave may also have been available to other employees under other laws does not mean that it may not be included as an option under a workers' compensation statute.

The IRS announced that it does not agree with the Tax Court's decision allowing full tax-free treatment. According to the IRS, benefits up to the regular workers' compensation amount should be tax free but excess amounts should be taxed.

2.13 Employer and Federal Government Disability Pensions

Disability pensions financed by your employer are reported as wage income unless they are for severe permanent physical injuries that qualify for tax-free treatment under the rules of *3.2* or they are tax-free government payments as discussed in this section.

If you receive little or no Social Security and your other income is below a specified threshold, you may be eligible to claim a tax credit for disability payments received while you are under the age of 65 and permanently and totally disabled; *see 34.7.*

Taxable disability pensions are reported as wages until you reach the minimum retirement age under the employer's plan. After reaching minimum retirement age, payments are reported as a pension under the rules of *7.25.*

Federal government services. Certain disability pensions from the military or federal government agencies are tax free. Military disability benefits from the Veterans Administration are tax free, as are payments for combat and terrorist attack-related injuries. Other disability pensions for personal injuries or sickness resulting from active service in the armed forces are taxable if you joined the service after September 24, 1975.

Military disability payments are tax free if before September 25, 1975, you were entitled to military disability benefits or if on that date you were a member of the armed forces (or reserve unit) of the U.S. or any other country or were under a binding written commitment to become a member. A similar tax-free rule applies to disability pensions from the following government agencies if you were entitled to the payments before September 25, 1975, or were a member of the service (or committed to joining) on that date: The Foreign Service, Public Health Service, or National Oceanic and Atmospheric Administration. The exclusion for pre-September 25, 1975, service applies to disability pensions based upon percentage of disability. However, if a disability pension was based upon years of service, you do not pay tax on the amount that would be received based upon percentage of disability.

Veterans Administration benefits. Disability pensions from the Veterans Administration (now called the Department of Veterans Affairs) are tax free. Military retirees who receive disability benefits from other government sources are not taxed on amounts equal to the benefits they would be entitled to receive from the VA. If you retire from the military and are later given a retroactive award of VA disability benefits, retirement pay during the retroactive period is tax free (other than a lump-sum readjustment payment upon retirement) to the extent of the VA benefit.

Pension based on combat-related injuries. Tax-free treatment applies to payments for combat-related injury or sickness which is incurred as a result of any one of the following activities: (1) as a direct result of armed conflict; (2) while engaged in extra-hazardous service, even if not directly engaged in combat; (3) under conditions simulating war, including maneuvers or training; or (4) which is caused by an instrumentality of war, such as weapons.

Terrorist attacks. Tax-free treatment applies to a disability pension paid to a civilian U.S. employee for injuries incurred as a direct result of a violent attack which the Secretary of State determines to be a terrorist attack and which occurred while the employee was working for the United States in the performance of official duties outside the United States.

Pay Plans for Executives

2.14 Deferred Pay Plans

The major objective of a deferred pay plan is to postpone the tax on pay benefits to a year in which you will be in a lower tax bracket than in the year you provide the services. However, a deferred pay plan is generally not advisable where a projection of future income shows that there probably will be no substantial income decline, and/or the tax bracket differentials will not be wide. An after-tax dollar in hand for current use is preferable to an expected tax saving that may not materialize.

As discussed at *2.8,* a deferral arrangement will succeed in postponing tax only if there is an element of risk. An employee with control over the pay account will be treated by the IRS as in "constructive receipt," and thus currently taxable on employer contributions.

Rabbi trusts. If IRS tests are met, employer contributions to a "rabbi trust" are not taxed until distributions from the trust are received or made available. The trust must be irrevocable and the trust assets must be subject to the claims of the employer's creditors in the event of insolvency or bankruptcy. Employees and their beneficiaries have no preferred claim on the trust assets. *See* a model rabbi trust agreement in Revenue Procedure 92-64.

Pension and profit-sharing plans. A company qualified pension or profit-sharing plan offers the following benefits: (1) you do not realize current income on your employer's contributions to the plan on your behalf; (2) funds contributed by both your employer and you compound tax free within the plan; (3) if you receive a lump-sum distribution, tax on employer contributions may in certain cases be reduced by a special averaging rule *(7.4)*; and, (4) if you receive a lump-sum distribution in company securities, unrealized appreciation on those securities is not taxed until you finally sell the stock.

In plan years starting in 1997, the maximum amount of compensation that can be taken into account for purposes of determining qualified employer plan contributions and benefits is $160,000. The $160,000 limit may be adjusted annually for inflation.

Where you are allowed to choose the type of payout from a qualified plan, make sure that you compare the tax on receiving a lump-sum distribution with the projected tax cost of deferring payments over a period of years or rolling over the distribution to an IRA account; *see 7.3* and *7.8.* Distributions before age 59 ½ are generally subject to penalties, but *see* exceptions at *7.14.*

401(k) plan. If your company has a profit-sharing or stock bonus plan, it has the opportunity to give you additional tax-sheltered pay; *see 7.17.* The tax law allows the company to add a cash or deferred pay plan, called a "401(k) plan." If your company permits salary-reduction deferrals to a 401(k) plan, you may be able to make contributions on a pre-tax basis up to the annual limit set by law, which for 1997 was $9,500. However, the limit may be reduced for highly compensated employees in order for the company to satisfy nondiscrimination requirements; *see 7.18.*

2.15 Insurance Plans May Be Tax Free

Company-financed insurance gives employees benefits at low or no tax cost.

Group life insurance. Group insurance plans may furnish not only life insurance protection but also accident and health benefits. Premium costs are low and tax deductible to the company while tax free to you unless you have nonforfeitable rights to permanent life insurance, or, in the case of group-term life insurance, your coverage exceeds $50,000; *see 3.3.* Even where your coverage exceeds $50,000, the tax incurred on your employer's premium payment is generally less than what you would have to pay privately for similar insurance.

It may be possible to avoid estate tax on the group policy proceeds if you assign all of your ownership rights in the policy, including the right to convert the policy, and if the beneficiary is other than your estate. Where the policy allows assignment of the conversion right, in addition to all other rights, and state law does not bar the assignment, you are considered to have made a complete assignment of the group insurance for estate tax purposes.

The IRS has ruled that where an employee assigns a group life policy and the value of the employee's interest in the policy cannot be ascertained, there is no taxable gift. This is so where the employer could simply have stopped making payments. However, there is a gift by the employee to the assignee to the extent of premiums paid by the employer. That gift is a present interest qualifying for the $10,000 annual exclusion.

Split-dollar insurance. Where you want more insurance than is provided by a group plan, your company may be able to help you get additional protection through a split-dollar insurance plan. Under the basic split-dollar plan, your employer purchases permanent life insurance on your life and pays the annual premium to the extent of the yearly increases in the cash surrender value of the policy. You pay only the balance of the premium. At your death, your employer is entitled to part of the proceeds equal to the cash surrender value or any lesser amount equalling the total premiums he or she paid. You have the right to name a beneficiary to receive the remaining proceeds which, under most policies, are substantial compared with the employer's share.

The IRS has ruled that you must report as taxable income an amount equal to the one-year term cost of the declining life insurance protection to which you are entitled, less any portion of the premium provided by you. According to the IRS, there is an additional tax liability to employees under "equity split-dollar plans" that allow the employees to receive the cash surrender value in excess of the premiums paid by the employer. For example, a company paid in a lump sum the premium on a life insurance policy for an executive and it was projected that the cash surrender value would exceed the employer's premium payment in the fourth policy year. The IRS ruled that once the cash surrender value of the policy exceeds the premiums that are returnable to the employer upon the employer's death (or termination of the agreement upon the executive's leaving the company), the employee must report as income the excess cash surrender value. This is in addition to the income realized on the one-year term cost for the declining insurance protection.

2.16 Stock Appreciation Rights (SARs)

SARs are a form of cash bonus tied to an increase in the price of employer stock. Each SAR entitles an employee to receive cash equal to the excess of the fair market value of one share on the date of exercise over the value on the date the SAR was granted.

> **EXAMPLE**
>
> When a stock is worth $30 a share, you get 100 SARs exercisable within five years. Two years later, when the stock price increases to $50 a share, you exercise the SAR and receive $2,000. You are taxed when you receive the cash.

An executive may realize taxable income when he or she becomes entitled to the maximum SAR benefit allowed by the company plan. For example, in 1993, when company stock is worth $30, an executive is granted 100 SARs exercisable within five years. By exercising the SARs, the executive may receive cash equal to the appreciation up to $20 per share. If the stock appreciates to $50 per share in 1998, the executive realizes taxable income of $2,000 ($20 per share × 100) in 1998, even if he or she does not exercise the SARs. The reason is that once the stock value appreciated to $50, the maximum SAR benefit of $20 was realized.

Performance shares. The company promises to make an award of stock in the future, at no cost to you, if the company's earnings reach a set level. You are taxed on the receipt of stock (unless the stock is restricted, as discussed in *2.17*).

2.17 Stock Options and Restricted Stock

Executives receiving qualified statutory stock options generally do not incur tax liability either at the time the option is granted or when the option is exercised, although the option spread may be subject to AMT; *see* Chapter 23. Qualified statutory options include incentive stock options and options under an employee stock purchase plan. Receipt of a nonqualified stock option may result in an immediate tax.

Incentive stock options (ISOs). A corporation may provide its executives with incentive stock options to acquire its stock (or the stock of its parent or subsidiaries). For regular income tax purposes, ISOs meeting tax law tests are not taxed when granted or exercised. Income or loss is not reported until you sell the stock acquired from exercising the ISO. The option must be exercisable within ten years of the date it is granted and the option price must be at least equal to the fair market value of the stock when the option is granted. If the fair market value of stock for which ISOs may first be exercised in a particular year exceeds $100,000 (valued at date of grant), the excess is not considered a qualifying ISO.

For alternative minimum tax (AMT) consequences, *see* Chapter 23.

Gain or loss on sale of option stock. If the stock acquired by the exercise of the ISO is held for more than one year after acquisition and more than two years after the ISO was granted, you have long-term capital gain or loss on the sale, equal to the difference between the selling price of the stock and the option price you paid when you exercised the ISO. If you sell before meeting the one-year and two-year holding period tests, a gain on the sale is treated as ordinary income to the extent of the option spread—the excess of the value of the stock when you exercised the option over the option price. Any gain in excess of the spread is reported as capital gain.

Employee stock purchase plans. These plans allow employees to buy their company's stock, usually at a discount. The plan must be nondiscriminatory and meet tax law tests on option terms. Options granted under qualified plans are not taxed until the shares acquired are sold. If you sell the shares more than two years after the granting of the option, and more than one year after you acquired the stock, gain on the sale is reported as ordinary wage income to the extent the option price was less than the fair market value of the shares when the option was granted. Any excess gain is capital gain; *see 5.2* for the tax rate on net capital gains. For sales before the end of the two-year/one-year holding period, the amount reportable as ordinary wage income is the excess of the value of the shares when the option was exercised over the option price.

 Caution

Watch SAR Expiration Date

If the rights increase in value, keep a close watch on the expiration date. Do not let them expire before exercise. If you do, not only will you lose income but you will be taxed on income you never received. According to the IRS, an employee who does not exercise the SARs is taxed as if they had been exercised immediately before they expire. The IRS claims that an employee has constructive receipt of income immediately before they expire. At that time, the amount of gain realized from the SARs is fixed because the employee can no longer benefit from future appreciation in value.

Nonqualified stock options. Where a nonqualified option has no ascertainable fair market value, as is generally the case for options that are not actively traded on a public exchange, no income is realized on the receipt of the option. When the option is exercised, you are taxed on the difference between the fair market value of the stock when you exercise the option and the option price. If a nonqualified stock option has an ascertainable fair market value, the value of the option less any amount you paid is taxable under the restricted property rules as ordinary wage income in the first year that your right to the option is freely transferable or not subject to a substantial risk of forfeiture. For other details and requirements, *see* IRS regulation Section 1.83-7.

Nonqualified stock options may be granted in addition to or in place of incentive stock options. There are no restrictions on the amount of nonqualified stock options that may be granted.

When sale of stock is treated as grant of option. If company stock is purchased on the basis of the executive's promissory note and he or she is not personally liable, the company can recover only its stock in the event of default on the note. If the stock value drops, he or she may walk away from the deal with no personal risk. According to an IRS regulation, the deal may be viewed as an option arrangement. Application of the IRS regulation would give the executive ordinary taxable income when the stock is purchased if the value of the stock at the time of purchase exceeds the purchase price. For example, on July 1, 1996, a corporation sells 100 shares of its stock to an executive. The stock has a fair market value on that date of $25,000 and the executive executes a nonrecourse note secured by the stock in that amount, plus 8% annual interest. An annual payment of $5,000 of principal, plus interest, is required beginning the following year. In 1997, the executive collects the dividends, votes the stock, and pays the interest on the note but no principal. In 1998, when the stock has appreciated in value to $30,000, the executive pays off the note. Under the IRS regulation, the executive would realize ordinary income upon payment of the nonrecourse note to the extent of the difference between the amount paid ($25,000 in 1998) and the value of the stock ($30,000).

Stock subject to restricted property rules. If in return for performing services you receive company stock or other property subject to restrictions, special tax rules apply. Stock subject to restrictions is taxed as pay in the first year in which it is substantially vested, meaning that it is either transferable or not subject to a substantial risk of forfeiture. A risk of forfeiture exists where your rights are conditioned upon the future performance of substantial services. Generally, taxable income is the difference between the amount, if any, that you pay for the stock and its value at the time the risk of forfeiture is removed. The valuation at the time the forfeiture restrictions lapse is not reduced because of restrictions imposed on the right to sell the property. However, restrictions which will never lapse do affect valuation.

SEC restrictions on insider trading are considered a substantial risk of forfeiture, so that there is no tax on the receipt of stock subject to such restrictions. However, the SEC permits insiders to immediately resell stock acquired through exercise of an option granted at least six months earlier. As the stock acquired through such options is not subject to SEC restrictions, the executive is subject to immediate tax upon exercise of an option held for at least six months.

If the stock is subject to a restriction on transfer to comply with SEC pooling-of-interests accounting rules, the stock is considered to be subject to a substantial restriction.

Note: The tax rules for restricted property are not restricted to employees. They also apply to independent contractors who are compensated for services with restricted stock or other property.

Election to include value of restricted stock in income when received. Although restricted stock is generally not taxable until the year in which it is substantially vested, you may elect to be taxed in the year you receive it on the unrestricted value (as of the date received), less any payment you made. The election must be made by filing a statement with the IRS no later than 30 days after the date the stock is transferred to you. The election may not be revoked without the consent of the IRS.

If you make the election, you are treated as an investor and later appreciation in value is not taxed as pay when your rights to the stock become vested. To figure gain or loss when you sell the stock, your cost basis for the stock is increased by the amount of income you reported as pay under the election. If you forfeit the stock after the election is made, a capital loss is allowed for your cost minus any amount realized on the forfeiture.

Planning Reminder

Electing Immediate Tax on Restricted Stock

If you expect restricted stock to appreciate, consider making an election to be immediately taxed on the value of the restricted stock, minus your cost. If you make the election, any appreciation in value that has accrued since the election was made will not be taxable when the stock becomes substantially vested. Tax on appreciation will not be due until the stock is sold.

2.18 Educational Benefits for Employees' Children

Private foundations. The IRS has published guidelines under which a private foundation established by an employer may make tax-free grants to children of employees. An objective, non-discriminatory program must be adopted. If the guidelines are satisfied, employees are not taxable on the benefits provided their children. Advance approval of the grant program must be obtained from the IRS.

IRS guidelines require:

- Grant recipients must be selected by a scholarship committee which is independent of the employer and the foundation. Former employees of the employer or the foundation are not considered independent.
- Eligibility for the grants may be restricted to children of employees who have been employed for a minimum of up to three years, but eligibility may not be related to the employee's position, services, or duties.
- Once awarded, a grant may not be terminated if the parent leaves his job with the employer, regardless of the reason for the termination of employment. If a one-year grant is awarded or a multi-year grant is awarded subject to renewal, a child who reapplies for a later grant may not be considered ineligible because his parent no longer works for the employer.
- Grant recipients must be based solely upon objective standards unrelated to the employer's business and the parent's employment such as prior academic performance, aptitude tests, recommendations from instructors, financial needs, and conclusions drawn from personal interviews.
- Recipients must be free to use the grants for courses which are not of particular benefit to the employer or the foundation.
- The grant program must not be used by the foundation or employer to recruit employees or induce employees to continue employment.
- There must be no requirement or suggestion that the child or parent is expected to render future employment services.

The grant program must also meet a percentage test. The number of grants awarded in a given year to children of employees must not exceed (1) 25% of the number of employees' children who were eligible, applied for the grants, and were considered by the selection committee in that year; or (2) 10% of the number of employees' children who were eligible during that year, whether or not they applied. Renewals of grants are not considered in determining the number of grants awarded.

Educational benefit trusts and other plans. A medical professional corporation set up an educational benefit plan to provide the payment of college costs to the children of "key" employees. The plan defined a key employee as an employee who was salaried at over $15,000. To receive benefits, the child must have been a candidate for a degree within two years after graduating from high school. If an eligible employee quit for reasons other than death or permanent disability, his or her children could no longer receive benefits except for expenses actually incurred before termination. The company made annual contributions to the trust for which a bank was trustee. According to the IRS, amounts contributed to the trust are a form of pay to qualified employees, as they are contributed on the basis of employment and earnings record, rather than on the basis of competitive standards such as need, merit, or motivation. However, employees are not currently taxable. The right to have their children receive benefits is conditioned upon each employee's future performance of services. Furthermore, there is a substantial risk of forfeiture. Tax is not incurred until a child has a vested right to receive benefits; here, vesting does not occur until a child becomes a candidate for a degree at an educational institution, has actually incurred educational expenses, and his or her parent is employed by the company. Once the right to receive a distribution from the plan becomes vested, the parent of the child who has incurred the expenses is taxable on the amount of the distribution. The company may then claim a deduction for the amount reported as income by the employee.

The Tax Court and appeals court have upheld the IRS position in similar plans.

Caution

Primary Purpose Determination

If all guidelines other than the percentage test are satisfied, the IRS will determine whether the primary purpose of the program is to educate the children. If it is, the grants will be considered tax-free scholarships or fellowships; if it is not, the grants are taxed to the parent-employee as extra compensation.

Chapter 3

Fringe Benefits

Employer-furnished fringe benefits are exempt from tax if the tests discussed in this chapter are met.

The most common tax-free benefits are accident and health plans, group-term life insurance plans, dependent care plans, education assistance plans, tuition reduction plans, cafeteria plans, and plans providing employees with discounts, no-additional-cost services, or employer-subsidized meal facilities.

Highly compensated individuals may be taxed on certain benefits from such plans if nondiscrimination rules are not met.

Starting in 1997, employer-provided adoption benefits for a child under age 18 or a disabled person may be tax-free up to $5,000, $6,000 for a child with special needs; *see 3.5.*

Also starting in 1997, employees of qualifying small employers who have medical coverage through a high-deductible plan may be able to set up a medical savings account (MSA) to pay for medical costs not covered by insurance; *see 3.1.*

Health, Accident, Group Insurance, and Death Benefits

3.1 Tax-Free Health and Accident Coverage Under Employer Plans

You are not taxed on *contributions or insurance premiums* your employer makes to a health, hospitalization, or accident plan to cover you, your spouse, or your dependents. If you are temporarily laid off and continue to receive health coverage, the employer's contributions during this layoff period are tax free. If you are retired, you do not pay tax on insurance paid by your former employer. Medical coverage provided to the family of a deceased employee is tax free since it is treated as a continuation of the employee's fringe-benefit package.

Key to Fringe Benefits	
Fringe Benefit—	*Tax Pointer—*
Athletic facilities	The fair market value of athletic facilities, such as gyms, swimming pools, golf courses, and tennis courts, is tax free if the facilities are on property owned or leased by the employer (not necessarily the main business premises) and substantially all of the use of the facilities is by employees, their spouses, and dependent children. Such facilities must be open to all employees on a nondiscriminatory basis in order for the company to deduct related expenses.
Child or dependent care plans	The value of day care services provided or reimbursed by an employer under a written, nondiscriminatory plan is tax free up to a limit of $5,000, or $2,500 for married persons filing separately. Expenses are excludable if they would qualify for the dependent care credit; *see* Chapter 25. On your tax return, you must report employer-provided benefits to figure the tax-free exclusion. Tax-free employer benefits reduce eligibility for the dependent care tax credit; *see 3.4.*
De minimis (minor) fringe benefits	These are small benefits that are administratively impractical to tax, such as occasional supper money and taxi fares for overtime work, company parties or picnics and occasional theater or sporting event tickets; *see 3.9.*
Discounts on company products and services	Services from your employer that are usually sold to customers are tax free if your employer does not incur additional costs in providing them to you; *see 3.15.* Merchandise discounts and other discounted services are also eligible for a tax-free exclusion; *see 3.16.*
Education plans	A new law has retroactively extended the up-to-$5,250 exclusion to employer-financed undergraduate courses beginning before June 1, 2000; *see 3.6.*
Employee achievement awards	Achievement awards are taxable unless they qualify under special rules for length of service or safety achievement; *see 3.10.*
Group-term life insurance	Premiums paid by employers are not taxed if policy coverage is $50,000 or less; *see 3.3.*
Health and accident plan benefits	Premiums paid by an employer are tax free. Benefits under an employer plan are also generally tax free; *see 3.1* and *3.2.*
Interest-free or low-interest loans	Interest-free loans received from your employer may be taxed; *see 4.30.*
Tuition reductions	Tuition reductions for courses below the graduate level are generally tax free. Graduate students who are teaching or research assistants are not taxed on tuition reduction unless the reduction is compensation for teaching services; *see 3.6.*
Working condition benefits	Benefits provided by your employer that would be deductible if you paid the expenses yourself are a tax-free working condition fringe benefit. Company cars are discussed at *3.7* and other working condition benefits at *3.8.*

If your employer provides health and accident coverage to your live-in companion, the coverage is taxable to you where the companion is not recognized as a "spouse" under state law or "dependent" status is barred (even if support and household membership tests in Chapter 21 are met) because the relationship violates local law. Furthermore, under the 1996 Defense of Marriage Act, a gay or lesbian companion is not treated as a spouse for federal tax purposes.

If you are age 65 or older, Medicare premiums paid by your employer are not taxed. If you retire and have the option of receiving continued coverage under the medical plan or a lump-sum payment covering unused accumulated sick leave instead of coverage, the lump-sum amount is reported as income at the time you have the option to receive it. If you elect continued coverage, the amount reported as income may be deductible as medical insurance if you itemize deductions; *see 17.5.*

Long-term Care Coverage. After 1996, an employee is not taxed on employer-provided long-term care coverage that pays benefits in the event the employee becomes *chronically ill*, as defined at *17.15.* However, the coverage is not tax free if provided through a cafeteria plan *(3.13)* and reimbursements of long-term care expenses may not be made through a flexible spending arrangement *(3.14).*

Medical Savings Account Contributions for Employees of Small Employers Offering High-Deductible Plans

If you work for a small employer (*see* below) that provides health insurance coverage under a high-deductible plan, you may set up a medical savings account (MSA) that can be used to pay unreimbursed medical costs. If you are eligible, your employer may make contributions to your MSA which are tax free to you, subject to the limits discussed below. If the employer does not contribute, you may make deductible contributions up to the same limits; *see* Chapter 12 for claiming the deduction. An MSA may be set up with an insurance company, bank, or any institution qualified to offer IRAs. Distributions from MSAs are discussed in *3.2.*

However, the law authorizing MSAs allows only 750,000 MSAs to be set up between 1997 and 2000, and there are separate annual limits for the years before 2000. MSA benefits are thus generally available only if you or your employer sets up an MSA for you before the IRS announces that the cut-off limit has been reached. Employees who first become eligible to join a high-deductible plan after the cut-off date may qualify in certain cases.

MSA eligibility. To be eligible for an MSA, you must be under age 65 and work for a "small" employer, one that had an average of 50 or fewer employees during either of the two preceding years. You must be covered by a high-deductible health plan, which by law must have a deductible of: (1) at least $1,500 and no more than $2,250 for individual coverage, or (2) at least $3,000 and no more than $4,500 for family coverage.

The IRS has ruled that a high-deductible family plan may not set a lower deductible for individual family members. For example, a plan does not qualify if it sets an overall annual family deductible of $3,000 but allows an individual who incurs expenses exceeding $1,500 to receive benefits.

Out-of-pocket costs must be limited to $3,000 for individual plans and $5,500 for family coverage.

Generally, you are not eligible for an MSA if you have any other health insurance in addition to the high-deductible plan coverage, except for policies covering only disability, vision or dental care, long-term care, accidental injuries, or plans that pay a flat amount during hospitalization. If you are a Medicare beneficiary, you are not eligible for an MSA. However, under a new law, starting in 1999, Medicare beneficiaries may be able to combine a "MedicarePlus MSA" with high-deductible insurance as an alternative to traditional Medicare coverage.

Employer contribution limits. Your employer's contributions to your MSA are tax free up to an annual limit of 65% of the plan deductible if you have individual coverage and 75% of the deductible for family coverage. The limit is reduced on a monthly basis if you are not covered for the entire year. If your employer makes *any* contributions to your account, you may not make any contributions for that year. In addition, if your spouse's employer contributes to his or her MSA, you cannot contribute to your MSA. If your employer (or spouse's employer) does not contribute, you may make deductible contributions up to the above employer contribution limits. Your deduction is claimed on Line 24 of Form 1040. Contributions exceeding the annual limit are subject to a 6% penalty.

Filing Pointer

Deducting Medical Savings Account Contributions

If you work for a qualifying small employer who has a high-deductible health plan, you may make deductible contributions to a medical savings account (MSA) if the employer does not contribute to your account for the year. Contributions are reported on Form 8853, and the deduction is claimed directly from gross income on Line 24 of Form 1040. *See also 17.17.*

Self-employed also eligible. A self-employed person may make deductible contributions to an MSA up to the employer contribution limits discussed above; *see* Chapter 17 for deduction details.

Benefits received from employer plan. *See 3.2* for the types of health and accident plan benefits that qualify for tax-free treatment.

Access and Portability Rules for Group Health Plans

New laws designed to expand access to health care coverage apply in plan years starting after June 30, 1997. Employers are subject to daily penalties if they do not comply with the rules, but small employers with an average of no more than 50 employees in the preceding year are exempt.

Generally, a group health plan may not bar eligibility to an employee and his or her dependents because of health status or medical history. A plan may exclude coverage for specified conditions or procedures, or limit such coverage, but only if there is no discrimination among similarly situated employees based on health-related factors.

Preexisting conditions can bar coverage only in limited circumstances. Coverage may be denied for a condition that was diagnosed or treated within six months before enrollment. However, the exclusion cannot last more than 12 months or 18 months for those who enroll late, and the 12-or-18-month period must be reduced by creditable coverage the employee had before enrollment in the new plan if there was no break in the prior coverage of more than 62 days. Coverage may not be denied to women pregnant on the enrollment date. Newborn children who are enrolled within 30 days of birth must be covered and if the parent changes jobs and enrolls in a new plan without a break in coverage of more than 62 days, the new plan may not exclude the child. A similar protective rule applies to adopted children under age 18 who are enrolled within 30 days of the adoption.

Continuing coverage for group health plans (COBRA coverage). Employers are subject to daily penalties unless they offer continuing group health and accident coverage to employees who leave the company and to spouses and dependent children who would lose coverage in the case of divorce or the death of the employee. The employer may charge the employee or beneficiary a premium of up to 102% of the regular premium imposed under the plan for the applicable (individual or family) coverage. The employer must wait at least 45 days after continuing coverage is elected to require payment of premiums.

Continuing coverage rules do not apply to small employers who in the previous calendar year had fewer than 20 employees on a typical day, or government agencies and churches. For other employers, continuing coverage must be offered in these situations:

1. An employee with coverage who voluntarily or involuntarily leaves the company—unless termination is for gross misconduct. Employees who would lose coverage because of a reduction in hours must also be offered continuing coverage. Continuing coverage must also be offered for the employee's spouse and dependent children who were covered before the employee's termination or reduction in hours. If accepted, the coverage must last for at least 18 months. Within this period, an employee who elects continuing coverage is protected against the possibility of a coverage gap if he or she joins a new company that limits group health coverage for pre-existing conditions; the old employer's continuing coverage must remain available.

    Extended coverage may apply to disabled individuals. The coverage period is extended from 18 months to 29 months for individuals who notify the plan administrator within 60 days of a determination under Title II or XVI of the Social Security Act that they are disabled. Before 1997, the disability had to exist when employment terminated or hours were reduced. After 1996, the coverage extension applies if the disability exists at any time during the first 60 days of continuing coverage. During the extended coverage period, the maximum premium that can be charged is increased from 102% to 150% of the applicable premium.

2. On the death of a covered employee, continuing coverage must be offered to the surviving spouse and dependent children who are beneficiaries under the plan on the day before the death. Coverage must be for at least 36 months.

3. If a covered employee obtains a divorce or legal separation, continuing coverage must be offered to the spouse and dependent children for at least 36 months.

4. If a covered employee becomes eligible for Medicare benefits, continuing coverage under the employer's plan must be offered to the employee's spouse and dependent children for at least 36 months.

 Caution

Cost of Continuing Coverage
If you leave your job and elect continuing health coverage, you may be charged a premium of 102% of the regular cost of similar coverage under the plan. If the COBRA coverage period is extended because you are disabled, you may be charged 150% of the regular premium during the extended period.

5. If a dependent child becomes ineligible under the plan upon reaching a certain age, continuing coverage must be offered for at least 36 months.

6. If an employee with health coverage takes unpaid leave under the Family and Medical Leave Act of 1993 (FMLA) upon the birth or adoption of a child or to deal with a serious family illness, and the employee does not return to work following the leave, continuing coverage must be offered as of the last day of the leave. Continuing coverage must also be offered to the employee's spouse and dependent children if they would otherwise lose coverage.

Employers must provide written notice of the continuing coverage option. If one of the previously discussed qualifying events occurs, the eligible employees, spouses, and/or dependent children generally have 60 days to elect continuing coverage.

3.2 Tax-Free Payments From Employer Health and Accident Plans

There are two general categories of tax-free benefits paid from employer-financed health and accident plans: (1) reimbursements of medical expenses, and (2) payments for permanent physical injuries. In addition, payments from a long-term care insurance contract or medical savings account may be tax free. Details on these categories are below.

Tax-free benefits from qualifying long-term care policy. Payments from a qualifying long-term care policy *(meeting the tests in 17.15)* are tax free if they reimburse long-term care expenses. If payments are received in 1997 under a per diem plan that provides a flat daily amount, the tax-free limit is $175 per day unless you can show that you had actual expenses for long-term services equal to part or all of the excess over the $175 limit. *See 17.15* for further details.

Tax-free benefits from medical savings account. If you work for a small business employer and have a qualifying medical savings account (MSA), earnings accumulate in the account tax free. Withdrawals from an MSA are tax free if used to pay deductible medical costs for you, your spouse, or dependents. Withdrawals used for any other purpose are taxable and a taxable distribution before age 65 or becoming disabled is also subject to a 15% penalty. *See* Chapter 17 for further details.

Taxable payments. Benefits that are not tax free under the above rules are *fully taxable* if: (1) your employer paid all the premiums; and (2) you were not required to report the premiums as taxable income. If you and your employer each paid part of the premiums and you were not taxed on your employer's payment, the portion of the benefits allocable to the employer's contribution is taxed to you. You are not taxed on benefits to the extent that you paid the premiums with after-tax contributions. Examples of figuring the taxable portion of the benefits are at 17.4.

Reimbursed Medical Expenses

Tax-free payments generally include specific reimbursements of medical expenses for yourself, your spouse, or any dependent. Payment does not have to come directly to you to be tax free; it may go directly to your medical care providers.

Caution

Reimbursed Cosmetic Surgery
An employer's reimbursement of expenses for cosmetic surgery is taxable unless you had surgery to correct disfigurement from an accident, disease, or congenital deformity.

Tax-free treatment applies only for reimbursed expenses, not amounts you would have received anyway, such as sick leave that is not dependent on actual medical expenses.

Reimbursements for cosmetic surgery do *not* qualify for tax-free treatment, unless the surgery is for disfigurement related to congenital deformity, disease, or accidental injury.

Reimbursements for your *dependents'* medical expenses are tax free, even if you may not claim them as personal exemptions because they had more than $2,650 of income or filed a joint return. Furthermore, if you are divorced and your children have health coverage under your plan, reimbursements of their expenses are not taxable to you, even if your ex-spouse claims them as dependents; *see 21.11.*

A qualifying dependent does *not* include a live-in mate where the relationship violates local law.

If the reimbursement is for medical expenses you deducted in a previous year, the reimbursement may be taxable. *See 17.4* for the rules on reimbursements of deducted medical expenses.

If you receive payments from more than one policy in excess of your actual medical expenses, the excess is taxable if your employer paid the entire premium; *see* Examples in *17.4.*

Self-employed health plan for spouse. A self-employed person is not considered an "employee" for purposes of the tax-free reimbursement rule for medical expenses. However, the IRS in a ruling allowed a self-employed person who hired his spouse to claim a full business deduction on Schedule C for reimbursements of family medical expenses under a written health plan covering all employees, their spouses, and their dependents. The employee-spouse was reimbursed for medical expenses incurred by her husband (the business owner), herself, and their dependent children. She was not taxed on the reimbursements; *see 40.5.*

Executives taxed in discriminatory self-insured medical reimbursement plans.
Although reimbursements from an employer plan for medical expenses of an employee and his or her spouse and dependents are generally tax free, this exclusion does not apply to certain highly compensated employees and stockholders if the plan is self-insured and it discriminates on their behalf. A plan is self-insured if reimbursement is not provided by an unrelated insurance company. If coverage is provided by an unrelated insurer, these discrimination rules do not apply. If a self-insured plan is deemed discriminatory, rank-and-file employees are not affected; only highly compensated employees are subject to tax.

Highly compensated participants subject to these rules include employees owning more than 10% of the employer's stock, the highest paid 25% of all employees (other than employees who do not have to be covered under the law), and the five highest paid officers.

If highly compensated employees are entitled to reimbursement for expenses not available to other plan participants, any such reimbursements are taxable to them. For example, if only the five highest paid officers are entitled to dental benefits, any dental reimbursements they receive are taxable. However, routine physical exams may be provided to highly compensated employees (but not their dependents) on a discriminatory basis. This exception does not apply to testing for, or treatment of, a specific complaint.

If highly compensated participants are entitled to a higher reimbursement limit than other participants, any excess reimbursement over the lower limit is taxable to the highly compensated participant. For example, if highly compensated employees are entitled to reimbursements up to $5,000, while all others have a $1,000 limit, a highly compensated employee who receives a $4,000 reimbursement must report $3,000 ($4,000 received minus $1,000 lower limit) as income.

A separate nondiscrimination test applies to plan *eligibility*. The eligibility test requires that the plan benefit: (1) 70% or more of all employees, or (2) 80% or more of employees eligible to participate, provided that at least 70% of all employees are eligible. A plan not meeting either test is considered discriminatory unless proven otherwise. In applying these tests, employees may be excluded if they have less than three years of service, are under age 25, do part-time or seasonal work, or are covered by a union collective bargaining agreement. A fraction of the benefits received by a highly compensated individual from a nonqualifying plan is taxable. The fraction equals the total reimbursements to highly compensated participants divided by total plan reimbursements; benefits available only to highly compensated employees are disregarded. For example, assume that a plan failing the eligibility tests pays total reimbursements of $50,000, of which $30,000 is to highly compensated participants. A highly compensated executive who is reimbursed $4,500 for medical expenses must include $2,700 in income:

$$4,500 \times \frac{30,000}{50,000}$$

Taxable reimbursements are reported in the year during which the applicable plan year ends. For example, in early 1998 you are reimbursed for a 1997 expense from a calendar-year plan. If under plan provisions the expenses are allocated to the 1997 plan year, the taxable amount should be reported as 1997 income. If the plan does not specify the plan year to which the reimbursement relates, the reimbursement is attributed to the plan year in which payment is made.

Permanent Physical Injuries

Payments from an employer plan are tax free if they are for the permanent loss of part of the body, permanent loss of use of part of the body, or for permanent disfigurement of yourself, your spouse, or a dependent. To be tax free, the payments must be based on the kind of injury and have no relation to the length of time you are out of work or prior years of service. If the employer's plan does not specifically allocate benefits according to the nature of the injury, the benefits are taxable even if an employee is in fact permanently disabled.

EXAMPLE
After he loses a foot in an accident, Marc Jones receives $5,000 as specified in his employer's plan. The payment is tax free as it does not depend on how long Jones is out from work.

 Filing Tip

Permanent Physical Injuries
An employer's payment for permanent disfigurement or permanent loss of bodily function is tax free if the payment is based solely on the nature of the injury. Whether or not you qualify for this exclusion, you may deduct as an itemized deduction any unreimbursed medical expense you have in connection with these injuries subject to the 7.5% adjusted gross income floor; *see 17.1* for details.

An appeals court held that severe hypertension does not involve loss of a bodily part or function and thus does not qualify for the exclusion.

Disability payments from profit-sharing plan. The Tax Court has held that a profit-sharing plan may provide benefits that qualify for the exclusion for permanent disfigurement or permanent loss of bodily function. The plan must clearly state that its purpose is to provide qualifying tax-free benefits, and a specific payment schedule must be provided for different types of injuries. Without such provisions, payments from the plan are treated as taxable retirement distributions.

3.3 Group-Term Life Insurance Premiums

You are not taxed on your employer's payments of premiums on a policy of up to $50,000 on your life. You are taxed only on the cost of premiums for coverage of over $50,000 as determined by the IRS rates shown in the table on the next page. On Form W-2 your employer should include the taxable amount as wages in Box 1 and separately label the amount in Box 13. You may not avoid tax by assigning the policy to another person.

If two or more employers provide you with group-term insurance coverage, you get only one $50,000 exclusion. You must figure the taxable cost for coverage over $50,000 by using the IRS rates on the next page.

Regardless of the amount of the policy, you are not taxed if, for your entire tax year, the beneficiary of the policy is a tax-exempt charitable organization or your employer.

Your payments reduce taxable amount. If you pay part of the cost of the insurance, your payment reduces dollar-for-dollar the amount includible as pay on Form W-2.

EXAMPLE

Lynda Jackson is a 52-year-old executive provided with $200,000 of group-term coverage. The taxable amount is $864, based on $150,000 of excess coverage. For every $1,000 of coverage over $50,000, the taxable amount is $0.48 (premium) × 12 (months), or $5.76. Thus, for excess coverage of $150,000, the taxable amount is $864 ($5.76 × $150,000/$1,000).

If she paid $120 towards the coverage, the taxable amount would be reduced to $744 ($864 − $120).

Retirees. If you retired before 1984 at normal retirement age or on disability and are still covered by a company group-term life insurance policy, you are not taxed on premium payments made by your employer even if coverage is over $50,000. If you retired after 1983 because of disability and remain covered by your company's plan, you are not taxed even if coverage exceeds $50,000. Furthermore, if you retired after 1983 and are not disabled, you may qualify for tax-free coverage over $50,000 if the following tests are met:

1. The insurance is provided under a plan existing on January 1, 1984, or under a comparable successor plan;
2. You were employed during 1983 by the company having the plan, or a predecessor employer; and
3. You were age 55 or over on January 1, 1984.

However, even if the three tests are met, you may be taxed under the rule below for discriminatory plans if you retired after 1986 and were a key employee.

Key employees taxed under discriminatory plans. The $50,000 exclusion is not available to key employees unless the group plan meets nondiscrimination tests for eligibility and benefits. Key employees include those who during the year or during any of the four preceding years were: (1) more than 5% owners; (2) more than 1% owners earning over $150,000; (3) one of the 10 largest owners with compensation over $30,000; and (4) officers with 1997 pay over $62,500 (this amount may be adjusted annually for inflation). If the plan discriminates, a key employee's taxable benefit is based on the larger of (1) the actual cost of coverage, and (2) the amount for coverage using the IRS rate table.

The nondiscrimination rules also apply to former employees who were "key" employees when they separated from service. The discrimination tests are applied separately with respect to active and former employees.

Group-term life insurance for dependents. Employer-paid coverage for your spouse or dependents is a tax-free *de minimis* fringe benefit *(3.9)* if the policy is $2,000 or less. For coverage over $2,000, you are taxed on the excess of the cost (determined under the IRS table below) over your after-tax payments for the insurance, if any.

Permanent life insurance. If your employer pays premiums on your behalf for permanent non-forfeitable life insurance, you report as taxable wages the cost of the benefit, less any amount you paid. A permanent benefit is an economic value that extends beyond one year and includes paid-up insurance or cash surrender value, but does not include, for example, the right to convert or continue life insurance coverage after group coverage is terminated. Where permanent benefits are combined with term insurance, the permanent benefits are taxed under formulas found in IRS regulations.

Taxable Rates for Insurance Coverage over $50,000

Age—*	Monthly premium per $1,000 of coverage above $50,000—
Under 30	$0.08
30–34	0.09
35–39	0.11
40–44	0.17
45–49	0.29
50–54	0.48
55–59	0.75
60–64	1.17
65–69	2.10
70 and over	3.76

* Age is determined at end of year.

Dependent Care, Adoption Benefits, and Educational Assistance

3.4 Dependent Care Assistance

The value of qualifying day-care services provided by your employer under a written, nondiscriminatory plan is generally not taxable up to a limit of $5,000, or $2,500 if you are filing separately. The same tax-free limits apply if you make pre-tax salary deferrals to a flexible spending account for reimbursing dependent care expenses *(3.14)*. However, you may not exclude from income more than your earned income. If you are married and your spouse earns less than you do, your tax-free benefit is limited to his or her earned income. If your spouse does not work, all of your benefits are taxable unless he or she is a full-time student or is disabled. If a full-time student or disabled, your spouse is treated as earning $200 a month if your dependent care expenses are for one dependent, or $400 a month if the expenses are for two or more dependents.

Expenses are excludable only if they would qualify for the dependent care credit; *see* Chapter 25. If you are being reimbursed by your employer, the exclusion is not allowed if dependent care is provided by a relative who is your dependent (or your spouse's dependent) or by your child under the age of 19. You must give your employer a record of the care provider's name, address, and tax identification number. The identifying information also must be listed on your return.

Reporting employer benefits on your return. Your employer will show the total amount of your dependent care benefits in Box 10 of your Form W-2. Any benefits over $5,000 will also be included as taxable wages in Box 1 of Form W-2 and as Social Security wages (Box 3) and Medicare wages (Box 5).

If you file Form 1040, you must report the benefits on Part III of Form 2441. If you file Form 1040A, you report the employer benefits on Schedule 2. On these forms, you determine both the tax-free and taxable (if any) portions of the employer-provided benefits. If any part is taxable, that amount must be included on Line 7 of your return as wages and labeled "DCB."

Follow IRS instructions for identifying the care provider (employer, baby-sitter, etc.) on Form 2441 or on Schedule 2 of Form 1040A.

The tax-free portion of employer benefits reduces eligibility for the dependent care credit; see Chapter 25.

3.5 Adoption Benefits

If your employer pays or reimburses you for qualifying adoption expenses under a written, nondiscriminatory plan, up to $5,000 may be tax free starting in1997; the excludable limit increases to $6,000 for the adoption of a child with special needs. If you have other qualifying adoption expenses, you may also be able to claim a tax credit up to a separate $5,000 or $6,000 limit; both the

Caution

Figuring Tax-Free Exclusion for Employer-Provided Dependent Care

You cannot assume that your employer-provided dependent care benefit is completely tax free merely because your employer has not included any part of it in Box 1 of Form W-2 as taxable wages. Although up to $5,000 of benefits are generally tax free, the tax-free amount is reduced where you or your spouse earns less than $5,000 or where you file separately from your spouse. You must show the amount of your qualifying dependent care expenses and figure the tax-free exclusion on Form 2441 if you file Form 1040, or on Schedule 2 of Form 1040A.

exclusion and the credit may be claimed for the same adoption if they are not for the same expenses. The exclusion and the credit are subject to similar limitations, including a phaseout based on income. *See* Chapter 25 for a full discussion of the credit.

Employer-provided adoption assistance may be for any child under age 18, or a person physically or mentally incapable of self-care. A "special needs" designation may be made for a child who is a U.S. citizen or resident where special factors (such as physical condition) indicate that adoption assistance is required.

Reporting employer benefits and claiming the exclusion on your return. You must file Form 8839 to report your employer's payments and to claim the tax-free exclusion. If you are married, you generally must file a joint return to exclude the benefits as income. However, if you are legally separated or if you lived apart from your spouse for the last six months of the year, the exclusion may be available on a separate return; *see* Form 8839 for details.

The $5,000 exclusion limit ($6,000 for a special needs child) applies to each effort to adopt an eligible child. The limit applies per child, not per year. The exclusion applies to adoption fees, attorney fees, court costs, travel expenses, and other expenses directly related to a legal adoption. Expenses for adopting your spouse's child and the costs of a surrogate-parenting arrangement do *not* qualify.

The exclusion applies in the year your employer pays the qualifying expenses *unless* you are adopting a foreign child. If the child is not a U.S. citizen or resident when the adoption effort begins, the exclusion is available only in the year the adoption becomes final. For example, if in 1997 your employer pays for expenses of adopting a foreign child but the adoption has not become final by the end of the year, you must report the employer's payment as 1997 income. You will claim the exclusion on Form 8839 in the year the adoption is final.

The allowable exclusion is phased out if your modified adjusted gross income is between $75,000 and $115,000 (including the employer's adoption assistance and adding back certain tax-free income from foreign sources). Figure the tax-free amount on Form 8839. If your modified adjusted income is $115,000 or more, employer-paid adoption expenses are fully taxable.

If you paid adoption expenses in 1997 that were not reimbursed by your employer, and the adoption was final in 1997, you may be able to claim the adoption credit; *see* Chapter 25.

3.6 Education Assistance Plans

If your employer pays for job-related courses, the payment is tax free to you provided that the courses do not satisfy the employer's minimum education standards and do not qualify you for a new profession. If these tests are met, the employer's education assistance is a tax-free working condition fringe benefit *(3.8)*.

Even if not job related, your employer's payment for *undergraduate* courses beginning before June 1, 2000, is tax free up to $5,250, provided the assistance is under a qualifying Section 127 plan meeting nondiscriminatory tests. A new law has extended the exclusion for *undergraduate* courses to courses beginning before June 1, 2000; the prior law exclusion had expired June 30, 1997. This exclusion does not apply to graduate-level courses.

Tuition reductions. Employees and retired employees of educational institutions, their spouses, and their dependent children are not taxed on tuition reductions for *undergraduate* courses provided the reduction is not payment for teaching or other services. Widows or widowers of deceased employees or of former employees also qualify. Officers and highly paid employees may claim the exclusion only if the employer plan does not discriminate on their behalf. The exclusion applies to tuition for undergraduate education at any educational institution, not only the employer's school.

Graduate students who are teaching or research assistants at an educational institution are not taxed on tuition reductions for courses at that school if the tuition reduction is in addition to regular pay for the teaching or research services.

The graduate student exclusion for tuition reductions applies only to teaching and research assistants, and not to faculty or other staff members (or their spouses and dependents) who take graduate courses and also do research for or teach at the school. However, if the graduate courses are work related, a tuition reduction for faculty and staff may qualify as a tax-free working condition fringe benefit *(3.8)*.

 Law Alert

Retroactive Extension of $5,250 Exclusion

A new law retroactively extended the up-to-$5,250 exclusion for education assistance provided by employers under nondiscriminatory plans. Prior law allowed the exclusion for undergraduate courses begun before July 1, 1997. Under the new law, you are not taxed on up to $5,250 of qualifying employer assistance for undergraduate courses beginning after June 30, 1997, and before June 1, 2000.

Company Cars, Working Conditions and *De Minimis* Benefits, and Employee Achievement Awards

3.7 Company Cars, Parking, and Transit Passes

The costs of commuting to a regular job site are not deductible *(20.2)*, but employees who receive transit passes or travel to work on an employer-financed van get a tax break by not having to pay tax on some or all of such benefits. Where a company car is provided, the value of personal use is generally taxable, as discussed below.

Company cars. The use of a company car is tax free under the working condition fringe benefit rule *(3.8)*, provided you use the car for business. If you use the car for personal driving, you may be taxed on the value of such personal use. Your company has the responsibility of calculating taxable income based on IRS tables that specify the value of various priced cars. For certain cars, a flat mileage allowance may be used to measure personal use. You are also required to keep for your employer a mileage log or similar record to substantiate your business use. Your employer should tell you what type of records are required.

Regardless of personal use, you are not subject to tax for a company vehicle that the IRS considers to be of limited personal value. These are ambulances or hearses; flatbed trucks; dump, garbage, or refrigerated trucks; one-passenger delivery trucks (including trucks with folding jump seats); tractors, combines, and other farm equipment; or forklifts. Also not taxable is personal use of school buses, passenger buses (seating at least 20), and moving vans where such personal use is restricted; and police or fire vehicles, or an unmarked law enforcement vehicle, where personal use is authorized by a government agency.

Demonstration cars. The value of a demonstration car used by a full-time auto salesperson is tax free as a working condition fringe benefit if the use of the car facilitates job performance and if there are substantial personal use restrictions, including a prohibition on use by family members and for vacation trips. Furthermore, mileage outside of normal working hours must be limited and personal driving must generally be restricted to a 75-mile radius around the dealer's sales office.

Chauffeur services. If chauffeur services are provided for both business and personal purposes, you must report as income the value of the personal services. For example, if the full value of the chauffeur services is $30,000 and 30% of the chauffeur's workday is spent driving on personal trips, then $9,000 is taxable (30% of $30,000), and $21,000 is tax free.

If an employer provides a bodyguard-chauffeur for business security reasons, the entire value of the chauffeur services is considered a tax-free working condition fringe benefit if: (1) the automobile is specially equipped for security; and (2) the bodyguard is trained in evasive driving techniques and is provided as part of an overall 24-hour-a-day security program. If the value of the bodyguard-chauffeur services is tax free, the employee is still taxable on the value of using the vehicle for commuting or other personal travel.

How your employer reports taxable automobile benefits. Social Security and Medicare tax must be withheld. Income tax withholding is not required, but your employer may choose to withhold income tax. If income tax is *not* withheld, you must be notified of this fact so that you may consider the taxable benefits when determining whether to make estimated tax installments; *see* Chapter 27. Whether or not withholdings are taken, the taxable value of the benefits is entered on your Form W-2 in Box 12, or on a separate Form W-2 for fringe benefits.

A special IRS rule allows your employer to include 100% of the lease value of using the car on Form W-2, even if you used the car primarily for business. Your employer must specifically indicate on Form W-2 or on a separate statement if 100% of the lease value has been included as income on your Form W-2. If it has, you should compute a deduction on Form 2106 for the business use value of the car. However, this deduction, plus any unreimbursed car operating expenses, may be claimed only as a miscellaneous itemized deduction on Schedule A subject to the 2% AGI floor; *see 19.1.*

Your employer may also decide to treat fringe benefits provided during the last two months of the calendar year as if they were paid during the following year. If this election is made for a company car in 1997, only the value of personal use from January through October is taxable in 1997; personal use in November and December is taxable in 1998. If your employer elects this special year-end rule, you should be notified near the end of the year or when you receive Form W-2.

Company planes. Under rules similar to those for company cars, employees who use a company airplane for personal trips are taxable on the value of the flights, as determined by the employer using IRS tables.

Employer-provided transit passes and van pooling. For regular employees, up to $65 a month is tax free in 1997 for the combined value of employer-provided transit passes plus commuting on an employer's van or bus. For example, if in 1997 the monthly value of a transit pass was $70, $5 per month was treated as taxable wages. If the value of benefits was less than $65 in any month, the unused exclusion cannot be carried over to later months. For years after 1997, the $65 monthly exclusion may be adjusted for inflation.

Qualifying transit passes include tokens, fare cards, or vouchers for mass transit or private transportation businesses using highway vehicles seating at least six passengers.

Qualifying van or bus pool vehicles must seat at least six passengers and be used at least 80% of the time for employee commuting; on average, the number of employees must be at least half the seating capacity.

The up-to-$65 monthly exclusion generally applies to cash reimbursements from the employer under a bona fide reimbursement arrangement. However, cash advances are taxable. If an employer has access to vouchers readily exchangeable for transit passes, the vouchers must be used; in that case, cash reimbursements would be taxable.

If your employer gives you a choice between a transit pass worth $50 per month and an extra $50 of pay each month, $50 will be reported as income on your Form W-2 for each month, whether you take the cash or transit pass. Furthermore, if your employer reduces your pay by $50 per month to provide a $50 monthly transit pass, the $50 monthly reduction will be reported as pay on Form W-2 even though you chose otherwise excludable transit pass benefits.

The $65 exclusion applies only to regular employees. For partners, more than 2% S corporation shareholders, and independent contractors who are provided transit passes, the IRS allows up to $21 per month as a tax-free *de minimis* benefit. If the monthly value exceeds $21, the full value is taxable and not just the excess over $21.

Parking provided by employer. For regular employees, the value of employer-provided parking spots or subsidized parking is tax free in 1997 up to a limit of $170 per month. Parking must be on or near the employer's premises, at a mass transit facility such as a train station or car pooling center. The value of parking benefits exceeding $170 per month is taxable in 1997. For years after 1997, the $170 monthly cap may be adjusted for inflation.

The tax will generally apply to employees working in major urban business districts where parking is costly, or in suburban areas where commercial lots are available.

Commuter parking benefits for self-employed partners or more than 2% S corporation shareholders do not qualify for an exclusion and are fully taxable. However, parking benefits provided by the employer while away from the regular office, such as on one-day business trips to other company locations, are generally treated as tax-free working condition fringe benefits *(3.8)* or *de minimis* benefits *(3.9)*. Parking benefits provided to independent contractors are also generally tax free as *de minimis* benefits.

According to the IRS, parking benefits are to be valued according to the regular commercial price for parking at the same or nearby locations. For example, if an employer in a rural or suburban location provides free parking for employees and there are no commercial parking lots in the area, the employee parking is tax free. Where free parking is available to both business customers and employees, the employee parking is considered to have "zero" value unless the employee has a *reserved* parking space that is closer to the business entrance than the spaces allotted to customers.

If the value of the right of access to a parking space exceeds $170 in a month, an employee will be taxed on the excess even if he or she actually uses the space for only a few days during the month.

If the employee pays a reduced monthly price for parking in 1997, there is a taxable benefit for that month only if the price paid plus the $170 exclusion is less than the value of the parking.

3.8 Working Condition Fringe Benefits

An employer-provided benefit that would be deductible by you if you paid for it yourself *(19.3)* is a tax-free working condition fringe benefit. Under IRS regulations, such benefits include:

Company car or plane. The value of a company car or plane is tax free to the extent that you use it for business; *see 3.5* for more on company cars.

Employer-paid business subscriptions or reimbursed membership dues in professional associations.

Law Alert

Parking Benefits After 1997
Starting in 1998, an employer may offer employees the choice of receiving parking benefits instead of cash salary as part of a "cafeteria" plan; *see 3.13*. If you elect the parking, you are not taxed, provided the value does not exceed the monthly tax-free limit. The monthly limit of $170 in 1997 may be increased for 1998 by an inflation factor.

Product testing. This is a limited exclusion for employees who test and evaluate company manufactured goods away from company premises.

Employer-provided education assistance. Employer-paid undergraduate and graduate courses may be a tax-free working condition fringe benefit if the courses maintain or improve job skills but are not needed to meet your employer's minimum educational requirements, and they do not prepare you for a new profession.

Job-placement assistance. According to the IRS, job placement services are tax free so long as they are geared to helping the employees find jobs in the same line of work and the employees do not have an option to take cash instead of the benefits. The employer must also have a business purpose for providing such assistance, such as maintaining employee morale.

For tax-free treatment, there is no nondiscrimination requirement; different types of job placement assistance may be offered, or no assistance at all, in the case of discharged employees with readily transferable skills. Tax-free benefits include the value of counseling on interviewing skills and resume preparation. Executives may be given secretarial support and the use of a private office during the job search.

Job placement benefits received as part of a severance pay arrangement are taxable to the extent that cash could have been elected. An offsetting deduction can be claimed only as a miscellaneous itemized deduction subject to the 2% adjusted gross income-floor *(19.3)*.

3.9 *De Minimis* Fringe Benefits

Small benefits that would be administratively impractical to tax are considered tax-free *de minimis* (minor) fringe benefits. Examples are personal use of company copying machines, company parties, or tickets for the theater or sporting events. Other *de minimis* benefits include:

Occasional overtime meal money or cab fare. If you work overtime and occasionally receive meal money or cab fare home, the amount is tax free. The IRS has not provided a numerical standard for determining when payments are "occasional."

Company eating facility. The operation of a subsidized eating facility for employees is a tax-free *de minimis* fringe benefit if it is located on or near the business premises, and the cost of the meals to employees equals or exceeds the company's operating costs. If meals are not tax-free de minimus benefits under this rule, they may still qualify for tax-free treatment where they are provided for a noncompensatory business purpose as discussed at *3.11*.

Highly compensated employees or owners with special access to executive dining rooms may not exclude the value of their meals as a *de minimis* fringe benefit; however, the meals may be tax free under rules of *3.11* if meals must be taken on company premises.

Commuting under unsafe circumstances. If you are asked to work outside of your normal working hours and due to unsafe conditions your employer provides transportation such as taxi fare, the first $1.50 per one-way commute is taxable but the excess over $1.50 is tax free. This exclusion is not available to certain highly compensated employees and officers, corporate directors, or owners of 1% or more of the company.

Even when working their regular shift, hourly employees who are not considered highly compensated are taxed on only $1.50 per one-way commute if their employer pays for car service or taxi fare because walking or taking public transportation to or from work would be unsafe. The excess value of the transportation over $1.50 is tax free. These rules can apply to day-shift employees who work overtime as well as night-shift employees working regular hours so long as transportation is provided because of unsafe conditions.

3.10 Employee Achievement Awards

Achievement awards are taxable unless they meet special rules for awards of tangible personal property (such as a watch, television, or golf clubs) given to you in recognition of length of service or safety achievement. Cash awards, gift certificates and similar items are taxable.

As a general rule, if your employer is allowed to deduct the cost of a tangible personal property *award*, you are not taxed. The employer's deduction limit, and therefore the excludable limit for you, is $400 for awards from nonqualified plans and $1,600 for awards from qualified plans or from a combination of qualified and nonqualified plans. If your employer's deduction is less than the item's cost, you are taxed on the greater of: (1) the difference between the cost and your employer's deduction, but no more than the award's fair market value; or (2) the excess of the item's fair market value over your employer's deduction. Deduction tests for achievement awards are discussed at *20.25*. Your employer must tell you if the award qualifies for full or partial tax-free treatment.

 Caution

Underpriced Award Items
If the value of an achievement award item is disproportionately high compared to the employer's cost, the IRS may conclude that the award is disguised compensation, in which case the entire value would be taxable to you.

An award will not be treated as a tax-free safety achievement award if employee safety achievement awards (other than those of *de minimis* value) were granted during the year to more than 10% of employees (not counting managers, administrators, clerical employees, or other professional employees). An award made to a manager, administrator, clerical employee, or other professional employee for safety achievement does not qualify for tax-free treatment.

Tax-free treatment also does not apply when you receive an award for length of service during the first five years of employment or when you previously received such awards during the last five years, unless the prior award qualified as a *de minimis* fringe benefit.

Meals and Lodging

Court Decision

House One Block Away

Two federal courts held that a school superintendent received tax-free lodging where the home was one block away from the school and separated by a row of other houses. This met the business premises test. The IRS disagrees with the result and says that it will continue to litigate similar cases arising outside of the Eighth Circuit in which the case arose. The Eighth Circuit includes the states of Arkansas, Iowa, Minnesota, Missouri, Nebraska, and North and South Dakota.

Caution

Partners Are Not Employees

The IRS does not consider partners or self-employed persons as employees and so does not allow them to exclude the value of partnership-provided meals and lodging.

3.11 Employer-Furnished Meals or Lodging

The value of employer-furnished *meals* is not taxable if furnished on your employer's business premises for his or her convenience. The value of *lodging* is not taxable if, as a condition of your employment, you must accept the lodging on the employer's business premises for the employer's convenience.

The key words here are: business premises, convenience of the employer, and condition of employment. For *meals*, you must satisfy the business premises and convenience of employer tests. For *lodging*, you must satisfy these two tests plus the condition of employment test.

Business premises test. The IRS generally defines business premises as the place of employment, such as a company cafeteria in a factory for a cook or an employer's home for a household employee. The Tax Court has a more liberal view, extending the area of business premises beyond the actual place of business in such cases as these:

- A house provided a hotel manager, although located across the street from the hotel. The IRS has agreed to the decision.
- A house provided a motel manager, two blocks from the motel. However, a court of appeals reversed the decision and held in the IRS's favor.
- A rented hotel suite that is used daily by executives for a luncheon conference.

Convenience of employer. This requires proof that an employer provides the free meals or lodging for a business purpose other than providing extra pay. If meals and lodging are described in a contract or state statute as extra pay, this does not bar tax-free treatment provided they are *also* furnished for other substantial, noncompensatory business reasons; for example, you are required to be on call 24 hours a day, or there are inadequate eating facilities near the business premises.

Generally, the value of meals furnished before or after working hours or on nonworking days is taxable, but there are exceptions; *see* the Examples below.

EXAMPLES

1. A waitress who works from 7 a.m. to 4 p.m. is furnished two meals a day without charge. Her employer encourages her to have her breakfast at the restaurant before working, but she is required to have her lunch there. The value of her breakfast and lunch is not income because it is furnished during her work period or immediately before or after the period. But say she is also allowed to have free meals on her days off and a free supper on the days she works. The value of these meals is taxable; they are not furnished during or immediately before or after her work period.

2. A hospital maintains a cafeteria on its premises where all of its employees may eat during their working hours. No charge is made for these meals. The hospital furnishes meals to have the employees available for emergencies. The employees are not required to eat there. Since the hospital furnishes the meals in order to have employees available for emergency call during meal periods, the meals are not income to any of the hospital employees who obtain their meals at the hospital cafeteria.

3. You are required to occupy living quarters on your employer's business premises as a condition of employment. The value of any meal furnished to you without charge on your employer's premises is excluded from taxable income.

4. To assure bank teller service during the busy lunch period, a bank limits tellers to 30 minutes for lunch and provides them with free meals in a cafeteria on the premises so they can eat within this time period. The value of the meals is tax free.

Meal charges. Your company may charge for meals on company premises and give you an option to accept or decline the meals. However, by law, the IRS must disregard the charge and option factors in determining whether the meals are furnished for a noncompensatory business reason, as required by the convenience-of-employer test.

Where your employer provides meals on business premises at a fixed charge which is subtracted from your pay whether you accept the meals or not, the amount of the charge is excluded from your taxable pay. If the meal is provided for the employer's convenience, as in the previous Examples, the value of the meals received is also tax free. If it is not provided for the employer's convenience, the value is taxable whether it exceeds or is less than the amount charged.

Lodging must be condition of employment. This test requires evidence that the lodging is necessary for you to perform your job properly, as where you are required to be available for duty at all times. The IRS may question the claim that you are required to be on 24-hour duty. For example, at one college, rent-free lodgings were provided to teaching and administrative staff members, maintenance workers, dormitory parents who supervised and resided with students, and an evening nurse. The IRS ruled that only the lodgings provided to the dorm parents and the nurse met the tax-free lodging tests because for the convenience of the college, they had to be available after regular school hours to respond to emergencies.

If you are given the choice of free lodging at your place of employment or a cash allowance, the lodging is not considered to be a condition of employment, and its value is taxable.

If the lodging qualifies as tax free, so does the value of employer-paid utilities such as heat, electricity, gas, water, sewerage, and other utilities. Where these services are furnished by the employer and their value is deducted from your salary, the amount deducted is excluded from taxable wages on Form W-2. But if you pay for the utilities yourself, you may not exclude their cost from your income.

 Caution

Housing as Job Requirement
If housing is provided to some employees with a certain job and not others, the IRS may hold that the lodging is not a condition of employment. For example, the IRS taxed medical residents on the value of hospital lodging where other residents lived in their own apartments.

EXAMPLE

Tyrone Jones is employed at a construction project at a remote job site. His pay is $600 a week. Because there are no accessible places near the site for food and lodging, the employer furnishes meals and lodging for which it charges $120 a week, which is taken out of Jones's pay. Jones reports only the net amount he receives—$480. The value of the meals and lodging is a tax-free benefit.

Are Your Board and Lodging Tax Free?

Yes—	No—
Hotel executives, managers, housekeepers, and auditors who are required to live at the hotel. Domestics, farm laborers, fishermen, canners, seamen, servicemen, building superintendents, and hospital and sanitarium employees who are required to have meals and lodging on employer premises. Restaurant and other food service employees who have meals furnished during or immediately before or after working hours. Employees who must be available during meal periods for emergencies. Employees who, because of the nature of the business, must be given short meal periods. Workers who must use company-supplied facilities in remote areas. Park employees who voluntarily live in rent-free apartments provided by a park department in order to protect the park from vandalism.	Your employer gives you a cash allowance for your meals or lodgings. You have a choice of accepting cash or getting the meals or lodging. For example, under a union contract you get meals, but you may refuse to take them and get an automatic pay increase. A state hospital employee is given a choice. He or she may live at the institution rent free or live elsewhere and get extra pay each month. Whether he or she stays at the institution or lives outside, the extra pay is included in his or her income. A waitress, on her days off, is allowed to eat free meals at the restaurant where she works.

Groceries. An employer may furnish unprepared food, such as groceries, rather than prepared meals. Courts are divided on whether the value of the groceries is excludable from income. One court allowed an exclusion for the value of nonfood items, such as napkins and soap—as well as for groceries—furnished to a doctor who ate at his home on the hospital grounds so that he would be available for emergencies.

Cash allowances. A cash allowance for meals and lodging is taxable. Only meals furnished in kind are permitted tax-free treatment.

Faculty lodging. Teachers and other employees (and their spouses and dependents) of an educational institution, including a state university system or academic health center, do not have to pay tax on the value of school-provided lodging if they pay a minimal rent. The lodging must be on or near the campus. The minimal required rent is the smaller of: (1) 5% of the appraised value of the lodging; or (2) the average rental paid for comparable school housing by persons who are neither employees nor students. Appraised value must be determined by an independent appraiser and the appraisal must be reviewed annually.

For purposes of the 5% minimum rent rule, academic health centers include medical teaching hospitals and medical research organizations with regular faculties and curricula in basic and clinical medical science and research.

> **EXAMPLE**
>
> Carol Eng, a professor, pays annual rent of $6,000 for university housing appraised at $100,000. The average rent for comparable university housing paid by non-employees and non-students is $7,000. She does not have to pay any tax on the housing since her rental payments exceed 5% of the appraised housing value (5% of $100,000, or $5,000). If her rent was $4,000, she would have to report income of $1,000 ($5,000 minimum required rent-$4,000).

Peace Corps and VISTA volunteers. Peace Corps volunteers working overseas may exclude subsistence allowances from income under a specific code provision. The law does not provide a similar exclusion for the small living expense allowances received by VISTA volunteers.

3.12 Minister's Rental Allowance

A duly ordained minister pays no tax on the rental value of a home provided as part of his or her pay. If a minister is provided with a rental allowance rather than a home itself, the allowance is tax free if the entire amount is used to pay rent (including the rent of a furnished or unfurnished apartment or house, garage, and utilities).

A housing allowance is also tax free if used as a down payment to buy a house, or used to pay mortgage installments, or for utilities, interest, tax, and repair expenses of the house. Any part of the allowance not used for these housing purposes is taxed. For example, that part of an allowance used to pay rent on business or farm property or for food or the services of a maid is taxed.

A minister who rents his or her home while abroad on church business may exclude his or her rental allowance only up to amounts used for capital improvements. These amounts are treated as expenses of keeping up his or her regular home. The balance of the rental allowance is taxable compensation even though he or she had expenses for maintenance, interest, taxes, repairs, and utilities during the rental period. The expenses may be deducted from rental income.

Who qualifies for tax-free allowance? Tax-free treatment is allowed to ordained ministers, rabbis, and cantors who receive housing allowances as part of their compensation for ministerial duties. Retired ministers qualify if their allowance is furnished in recognition of past services.

The IRS has allowed the tax-free exclusion to ministers working as teachers or administrators for a parochial school, college, or theological seminary which is an integral part of a church organization. A traveling evangelist was allowed to exclude rental allowances from out-of-town churches to maintain his permanent home. Church officers who are not ordained, such as a "minister" of music (music director) or "minister" of education (Sunday School director), do not qualify.

The IRS has generally barred an exclusion to ordained ministers working as executives of nonreligious organizations even where services or religious functions are performed as part of the job. The Tax Court has focused on the duties performed. A minister employed as a chaplain by a municipal police department under church supervision was allowed a housing exclusion, but the exclusion was denied to a minister-administrator of an old-age home that was not under the authority of a church and a rabbi who worked for a religious organization as director of inter-religious affairs.

Planning Reminder

Allowance Must Be Authorized

The church or local congregation must officially designate the part of the minister's compensation that is a rental allowance. To qualify for tax-free treatment, the designation must be made in advance of the payments. Official action may be shown by an employment contract, minutes, a resolution, or a budget allowance.

Allowance subject to self-employment tax. Although parsonage allowances are not taxable income, they are reported as self-employment income for Social Security purposes; *see* Chapter 45. If you do not receive a cash allowance, report the rental value of the parsonage as self-employment income. Rental value is usually equal to what you would pay for similar quarters in your locality. Also include as self-employment income the value of house furnishings, utilities, appurtenances supplied—such as a garage—and the value of meals furnished that meet the rules at *3.11.*

Cafeteria Plans and Flexible Spending Arrangements

3.13 Cafeteria Plans Provide Choice of Benefits

"Cafeteria plans" is a nickname for plans that give an employee a choice of selecting either cash or at least one qualifying nontaxable benefit. You are not taxed when you elect qualifying nontaxable benefits, although cash could have been chosen instead. A cafeteria plan may offer tax-free benefits such as group health insurance or life insurance coverage, long-term disability coverage, dependent care or adoption assistance, or medical expense reimbursements. Starting in 1998, parking benefits *(3.7)* may also be included. Long-term care insurance may *not* be offered through a cafeteria plan.

Employees may be offered a premium-only plan (POP), which allows them to purchase group health insurance coverage or life insurance on a pre-tax basis using salary reduction contributions.

Under a flexible spending arrangement (FSA), employees may be allowed to make tax-free salary-reduction contributions to a medical or dependent care reimbursement plan; *see 3.14.*

A qualified cafeteria plan must be written and not discriminate in favor of highly compensated employees and stockholders. If the plan provides for health benefits, a special rule applies to determine whether the plan is discriminatory. If a plan is held to be discriminatory, the highly compensated participants are taxed to the extent they could have elected cash. Furthermore, if key employees *(3.3)* receive more than 25% of the "tax-free" benefits under the plan, they are taxed on the benefits.

3.14 Flexible Spending Arrangements

A flexible spending arrangement (FSA) allows employees to get reimbursed for medical or dependent care expenses from an account they set up with pre-tax dollars. Under a typical FSA, you agree to a salary reduction which is deducted from each paycheck and deposited in a separate account. As expenses are incurred, you are reimbursed from the account.

Funds from a *health FSA* may be used to reimburse you for the annual deductible under your employer's regular health plan, co-payments you must make to physicians, and any other expenses that your health plan does not cover. These may include eye examinations, eyeglasses, routine physicals, and orthodontia work for you and your dependents. However, a health FSA may *not* be used to pay for health insurance premiums, including premiums for coverage under a plan of your spouse or dependent. Also, expenses for long-term care services *cannot* be reimbursed under a health FSA.

The tax advantage of an FSA is that your salary reduction contributions are not subject to federal income tax or Social Security taxes, allowing your medical or dependent care expenses to be paid with pre-tax rather than after-tax income. The salary deferrals are also exempt from state and local taxes except in New Jersey and Pennsylvania; check with the administrator of your employer's plan.

In the case of a health FSA, paying medical expenses with pre-tax dollars allows you to avoid the 7.5% adjusted gross income (AGI) floor *(17.1)* that limits itemized deductions for medical costs.

However, to get these tax advantages, you must assume some risk. Under a "use it or lose it rule," if your out-of-pocket expenses for the year are less than your contributions, the balance is forfeited, as discussed below.

FSA election to contribute generally irrevocable. The IRS has imposed restrictions on FSAs that make them unattractive for many employees. An election to set up an FSA for a given year must be made before the start of that year. You elect how much you want to contribute during the coming year and that amount will be withheld from your pay in monthly installments. Once the election takes effect, you may not discontinue contributions to your account and elect to receive the amounts as compensation unless there is a change in family status.

Caution

Estimating FSA Contributions
Because of the "use-it-or-lose-it" rule for FSA contributions, make a conservative estimate of your expenses when you make your election. This is particularly true for medical expenses which are generally difficult to project in advance.

Filing Tip

Tax-Free Dependent Care Reimbursements
Whether all or only part of your dependent care FSA reimbursements are tax free is figured on Part III of Form 2441 if you file Form 1040. If you file Form 1040A, the calculation is made on Part III of Schedule 2.

Use-it-or-lose-it rule. Only expenses incurred during the plan year may be reimbursed, and a "use-it-or-lose-it" rule applies: any unused account balance at the end of the plan year is forfeited. Unused amounts may not be refunded to you or carried over to the next year. There is a grace period, generally until April 15 of the following year, to submit reimbursement claims for expenses incurred during the previous year.

Although there are some differences in the reimbursement rules for health care and dependent care FSAs, as discussed below, the "use-it-or-lose-it" feature applies to both.

EXAMPLE

At the end of 1997 you elect to make 1998 salary reduction contributions of $600 to a health care FSA. If you incur only $500 of reimbursable medical expenses during the year, the $100 balance is forfeited; you are not allowed to carry it forward to 1999.

Health care FSA. At all times during the year, you may receive reimbursements up to your designated limit, even if your payments to the FSA are less. For example, if you elect to make salary-reduction contributions of $100 per month to a health care FSA, and you incur $500 of qualifying medical expenses in January, you may get the full $500 reimbursement even though you have paid only $100 into the plan. Your employer may not require you to accelerate contributions to match reimbursement claims.

You may *not* receive tax-free reimbursements for cosmetic surgery expenses unless the surgery is necessary to correct a deformity existing since birth or resulting from a disease or from injury caused by an accident. Nonqualifying reimbursements are taxable.

Employees on medical or family leave. Employees who take unpaid leave under the Family and Medical Leave Act (FMLA) to deal with medical emergencies or care for a newborn child may either continue or revoke their coverage during FMLA leave. If the coverage continues, the maximum reimbursement selected by that employee must be available at all times during the leave period. If the coverage is terminated, the employee must be reinstated under the FSA after returning from the leave, but no reimbursement claims may be made for expenses incurred during the leave.

Dependent care FSA. You may contribute to a dependent care FSA if you expect to have dependent care expenses qualifying for the tax credit discussed in Chapter 25, but if you contribute to a dependent care FSA, *any tax-free reimbursement from the account reduces the expenses eligible for the credit.* If you are married, both you and your spouse must work in order for you to receive tax-free reimbursements from an FSA, unless your spouse is disabled or a full-time student; *see 3.7.*

The maximum tax-free reimbursement under the FSA is $5,000, but if either you or your spouse earns less than $5,000, the tax-free limit is the lesser earnings. If your spouse's employer offers a dependent care FSA, total tax-free reimbursements for both of you are limited to $5,000. Furthermore, if you are considered a highly compensated employee, your employer may have to lower your contribution ceiling below $5,000 to comply with nondiscrimination rules.

Unlike health FSAs, an employer may limit reimbursements from a dependent care FSA to your account balance. For example, if you contribute $400 a month to the FSA, and in January you pay $1,500 to a day care center for your child, your employer may reimburse you $400 a month as contributions are made to your account.

Free or Low-Cost Company Products or Services

3.15 Company Services Provided at No Additional Cost

Employees are not taxed on the receipt of services usually sold by their employer to customers where the employer does not incur additional costs in providing them to the employees. Examples are free or low-cost flights provided by an airline to its employees; free or discount lodging for employees of a hotel; and telephone service provided to employees of telephone companies. These tax-free fringes also may be provided to the employee's spouse and dependent children; retired employees, including employees retired on disability; and widows or widowers of deceased or retired employees. Tax-free treatment also applies to free or discount flights provided to parents of airline employees. Benefits provided by another company under a reciprocal arrangement, such as standby tickets on another airline, may also qualify as tax free.

The employer must have excess service capacity to provide the service and not forego potential revenue from regular customers. For example, airline employees who receive free reserved seating on company planes must pay tax on the benefit because the airline is foregoing potential revenue by reserving seating that could otherwise be sold.

Highly compensated employees.   Highly compensated employees can receive tax-free company services only if the same benefits are available to other employees on a nondiscriminatory basis. Highly compensated employees in 1997 include employees owning more than a 5% interest in 1997 or 1996, and employees who in 1996 had compensation over $80,000. Employers have the option of including only the top-paid 20% in the over $80,000 category.

Line of business limitations.   If a company has two lines of business, such as an airline and a hotel, an employee of the airline may not receive tax-free benefits provided by the hotel. However, there are exceptions. An employee who provides services to both business lines may receive benefits from both business lines. Benefits from more than one line in existence before 1984 may also be available under a special election made by the company for 1985 and later years. Your employer should notify you of this tax benefit.

3.16 Discounts on Company Products or Services

The value of discounts on company products is a tax-free benefit if the discount does not exceed the employer's gross profit percentage. For example, if a company's profit percentage is 40%, the maximum tax-free employee discount for merchandise is 40% of the regular selling price. If you received a 50% discount, then 10% of the price charged customers would be taxable income. The employer has a choice of methods for figuring profit percentage.

Discounts on services that are not tax free under *3.15* for no-additional-cost services qualify for an exclusion, limited to 20% of the selling price charged customers. Discounts above 20% are taxable. An insurance policy is treated as a service. Thus, insurance company employees are not taxed on a discount of up to 20% of the policy's price.

Some company products do not qualify for the exclusion. Discounts on real estate and investment property such as securities, commodities, currency, or bullion are taxable. Interest-free or low-interest loans given by banks or other financial institutions to employees are not excludable. The loan is subject to tax under the rules of *4.31*.

The line of business limitation discussed at *3.15* for no-additional-cost services also applies to qualified employee discounts. Thus, if a company operates an airline and a hotel, employees who work for the airline may generally not receive tax-free hotel room discounts. However, if a special election was made by the company, employees may receive tax-free benefits from any line of business in existence before 1984.

Highly compensated employees are subject to the nondiscrimination rules discussed at *3.15* for no-additional-cost services.

EXAMPLE

The airline that you work for gives you a free round-trip ticket with a confirmed seat to California. The benefit is not tax free under the rule for no-additional-cost services *(3.15)*, but a 20% tax-free discount is allowed. If customers are charged $600 for comparable tickets, $120 is a tax-free benefit (20% of $600) and $480 is taxable.

Chapter 4

Dividend and Interest Income

Dividends and interest paid to you in 1997 are reported to the IRS on Forms 1099.

You will receive copies of:

- Forms 1099-DIV, for dividends
- Forms 1099-INT, for interest
- Forms 1099-OID, for original issue discount

Report the amounts shown on the Forms 1099 on your tax return. The IRS uses the Forms 1099 to check the income you report. If you fail to report income reported on Forms 1099, you will receive a statement asking for an explanation and a bill for the tax deficiency. If you receive a Form 1099 that you believe is incorrect, contact the payer for a corrected form.

Do not attach your copies of Forms 1099 to your return. Keep them with a copy of your tax return.

Schedules A&B (Form 1040) 1997

OMB No. 1545-0074   Page **2**

Name(s) shown on Form 1040. Do not enter name and social security number if shown on other side.

Your social security number

Schedule B—Interest and Dividend Income

Attachment
Sequence No. **08**

**Part I
Interest
Income**

(See pages 13
and B-1.)

Note: If you had over $400 in taxable interest income, you must also complete Part III.

Note: If you received a Form 1099-INT, Form 1099-OID, or substitute statement from a brokerage firm, list the firm's name as the payer and enter the total interest shown on that form.

1 List name of payer. If any interest is from a seller-financed mortgage and the buyer used the property as a personal residence, see page B-1 and list this interest first. Also, show that buyer's social security number and address ▶

	Amount
National Savings Bank	925
Chase Manhattan Bank	515
Municipal Bonds	350
Total	1,790
Less: Tax Exempt Interest	(350)

2 Add the amounts on line 1 . . . . **2** | 1,440
3 Excludable interest on series EE U.S. savings bonds issued after 1989 from Form 8815, line 14. You MUST attach Form 8815 to Form 1040 . . . . . . ▶ **3** | 0
4 Subtract line 3 from line 2. Enter the result here and on Form 1040, line 8a ▶ **4** | 1,440

**Part II
Dividend
Income**

(See pages 13
and B-1.)

Note: If you received a Form 1099-DIV or substitute statement from a brokerage firm, list the firm's name as the payer and enter the total dividends shown on that form.

Note: If you had over $400 in gross dividends and/or other distributions on stock, you must also complete Part III.

5 List name of payer. Include gross dividends and/or other distributions on stock here. Any capital gain distributions and nontaxable distributions will be deducted on lines 7 and 8 ▶

	Amount
Auto Company	126
Bio-Chem Corp	217
Utility Corp	155
Mutual Fund XYZ	810
($500 ordinary; $310 capital gain distribution)	

6 Add the amounts on line 5 . . . . **6** | 1,308
7 Capital gain distributions. Enter here and on Schedule D, line 14* **7** | 310
8 Nontaxable distributions. (See the inst. for Form 1040, line 9.) **8**
9 Add lines 7 and 8 . . . . **9** | 310
10 Subtract line 9 from line 6. Enter the result here and on Form 1040, line 9 . ▶ **10** | 998

*If you don't need Schedule D to report any other gains or losses, see the instructions for Form 1040, line 13, on page 14.

**Part III
Foreign
Accounts
and
Trusts**

(See
page B-2.)

You must complete this part if you **(a)** had over $400 of interest or dividends; **(b)** had a foreign account; or **(c)** received a distribution from, or were a grantor of, or a transferor to, a foreign trust.

	Yes	No
11a At any time during 1997, did you have an interest in or a signature or other authority over a financial account in a foreign country, such as a bank account, securities account, or other financial account? See page B-2 for exceptions and filing requirements for Form TD F 90-22.1		✓
b If "Yes," enter the name of the foreign country ▶		
12 During 1997, did you receive a distribution from, or were you the grantor of, or transferor to, a foreign trust? If "Yes," you may have to file Form 3520 or 926. See page B-2		✓

For Paperwork Reduction Act Notice, see Form 1040 instructions.

Schedule B (Form 1040) 1997

Key to Dividend Reporting

Type of Dividend Payment—	How and Where To Report—
Cash dividends	Dividends paid out of a corporation's earnings and profits are taxable. The corporation will report taxable dividends to you on Form 1099-DIV (or equivalent statement). On Form 1040, report dividends on Line 9; Schedule B must be filed where total dividends exceed $400. If you file Form 1040A, report dividends on Line 9, and if total dividends exceed $400, complete Part II of Schedule 1. Dividends may not be reported on Form 1040EZ.
Dividends on accounts in credit unions, cooperative banks, savings and loan associations, mutual savings banks, and building and loan associations	Distributions from these financial institutions are called "dividends" but are actually interest and are reported to you on Form 1099-INT.
Life insurance policy dividends	Dividends on individual life insurance policies are actually a refund of your premiums and are not taxed unless they exceed the total premiums paid.
Money-market mutual-fund dividends	Cash dividends paid by a money-market mutual fund are reported on Form 1099-DIV. Report them on Line 9 of Form 1040, and include them on Schedule B if your total dividends exceed $400. On Form 1040A, report the dividends on Line 9, and fill out Part II of Schedule 1 if total dividends exceed $400. Do not confuse money-market funds managed by mutual funds with bank money-market accounts. Bank money-market accounts pay interest reported on Form 1099-INT, not dividends.
Mutual-fund distributions	Mutual funds may pay several kinds of dividends. On Form 1099-DIV, the fund will report total distributions in Box 1a. This total includes: (1) fully taxable ordinary dividends that are also reported in Box 1b of Form 1099-DIV; (2) long-term capital gain distributions that are also reported in Box 1c of Form 1099-DIV; and (3) nontaxable distributions that are also listed in Box 1d. Form 1099-DIV for 1997 will include dividends declared before the end of the year, even if not actually paid to you until January 1998. How to report these dividends on your return is detailed in *4.3 and 32.5.*
Nominee distribution—joint accounts	If you receive dividends on stock held as a nominee for someone else, or you receive a Form 1099-DIV that includes dividends belonging to another person, such as a joint owner of the account, you are considered to be a "nominee recipient." If the other owner is someone other than your spouse, you should file a separate Form 1099-DIV showing you as the payer and the other owner as the recipient of the allocable income. Give the owner a copy of Form 1099-DIV by February 2, 1998, so the dividends can be reported on his or her 1997 return. File the Form 1099-DIV, together with a Form 1096 ("Transmittal of Information Return"), with the IRS by March 2, 1998. On your Schedule B, you list on Line 5 the total amount reported to you on Form 1099-DIV. Several lines above Line 6, subtract the nominee distribution (the amount allocable to the other owner) from the total dividends. Thus, the nominee distribution is not included in the taxable dividends shown on Line 6, Schedule B.
Return of capital distributions	A distribution that is not paid out of earnings is a nontaxable return of capital, that is, a partial payback of your investment. The company will report the distribution on Form 1099-DIV as a nontaxable distribution. You must reduce the cost basis of your stock by the nontaxable distribution. If your basis is reduced to zero by a return of capital distributions, any further distributions are taxable as capital gains, which you report on Schedule D. You must use Form 1040 if you received any return of capital distributions; Form 1040A or Form 1040EZ may not be used. If your total dividends, including nontaxable returns of capital, are $400 or less, you do not report the nontaxable distribution on your return unless your basis has been reduced to zero. In that case, further distributions are taxable and are reported on Schedule D. If your total dividends exceed $400, list the nontaxable dividend on Line 5 of Schedule B, along with your other dividends. Then, on Line 8, you subtract the nontaxable distribution from the total.
Stock dividends and stock splits	If you own common stock and receive additional shares of the same company as a dividend, the dividend is generally not taxed. A dividend is taxed where you had the option to receive cash instead of stock, or if the stock is of another corporation. Preferred shareholders are generally taxed on stock dividends. Taxable stock dividends are discussed at *4.7 and 4.8.* Your corporation will determine whether stock dividends are taxable and report the taxable amount on Form 1099-DIV. If you receive additional shares as part of a stock split, the new shares are not taxable; although you own more shares, your ownership percentage has not changed.

Reporting Dividends

4.1 Reporting Corporate Dividends

Dividends paid out of current or accumulated earnings of a corporation are subject to tax. Most dividends fall into this class, except for stock dividends and stock rights on common stock which are generally not taxed; *see 4.6.*

Dividends that are paid to you during 1997 are reported to the IRS by the company on Form 1099-DIV. The IRS uses this information as a check on your reporting of dividends. You receive a copy of Form 1099-DIV. You do not have to attach it to your tax return.

Publicly held corporations generally inform stockholders of the tax consequences of stock dividends and other distributions. Keep such letters with your tax records. You may also want to consult investment publications such as Moody's or Standard & Poor's annual dividend record books for details of dividend distributions and their tax treatment.

4.2 Dividends From a Partnership, S Corporation, Estate, or Trust

You report dividend income you receive as a member of a partnership, stockholder in an S corporation, or as a beneficiary of an estate or trust. The fiduciary of the estate or trust should advise you of the dividend income to be reported on your return.

A distribution from a partnership or S corporation is reported as a dividend only if it is portfolio income derived from nonbusiness activities. Your allowable share of the dividend will be shown on the Schedule K-1 you receive from the partnership or S corporation.

4.3 How Mutual-Fund Distributions Are Taxed

Mutual funds (open-ended, regulated investment companies) pay their shareholders several kinds of dividends and other distributions. Whether the distribution is received by you or reinvested by the fund, you must report it on your return.

The fund will send you Form 1099-DIV (or a similar written form), giving you a breakdown of the type of dividends paid during the taxable year. The Form 1099-DIV from your mutual fund may include several types of dividends or other distributions. The gross amount shown in Box 1a must be reported on your return. The Box 1a total includes ordinary dividends from Box 1b, capital gain distributions from Box 1c, nontaxable return of capital distributions from Box 1d, and in the case of a non-publicly offered fund, your share of fund expenses from Box 1e. *Dividends that you reinvested instead of receiving in cash are included in Box 1a.*

Dividends from a fund's foreign investments are included in the appropriate boxes of Form 1099-DIV, and the fund will indicate in Boxes 3 and 4 any foreign tax paid, which you may claim as a tax credit or deduction; *see 36.14.*

Form 1099-DIV for 1997 will include a dividend received in January 1998 so long as it was declared and was payable in October, November, or December of 1997.

See Chapter 32 for a closer look at the types of dividends reported on Form 1099-DIV, as well as the rules for figuring gain or loss when you sell mutual-fund shares.

4.4 Real Estate Investment Trust (REIT) Dividends

Dividends from a real estate investment trust (REIT) are shown on Form 1099-DIV. Ordinary dividends reported in Box 1b are fully taxable. Dividends designated by the trust as capital gain distributions in Box 1c are reported by you as long-term capital gains regardless of how long you have held your trust shares. A loss on the sale of REIT shares held for six months or less is treated as a long-term capital loss to the extent of any capital gain distribution received before the sale. However, this long-term loss rule does not apply to sales under periodic redemption plans.

4.5 Taxable Dividends of Earnings and Profits

You pay tax on dividends only when the corporation distributing the dividends has earnings and profits. Publicly held corporations will tell you whether their distributions are taxable. If you hold stock in a close corporation, you may have to determine the tax status of its distribution. You need to know earnings and profits at two different periods:

1. Current earnings and profits as of the *end of the current taxable year*. A dividend is considered to have been made from earnings most recently accumulated.
2. Accumulated earnings and profits as of the *beginning of the current year*. However, when current earnings and profits are large enough to meet the dividend, you do not have to make this computation. It is only when the dividends exceed current earnings (or there are no current earnings) that you match accumulated earnings against the dividend.

The tax term "accumulated earnings and profits" is similar in meaning to the accounting term "retained earnings." Both stand for the net profits of the company after deducting distributions to stockholders. However, "tax" earnings may differ from "retained earnings" for the following reason: Surplus accounts, the additions to which are not deductible for income tax purposes, are ordinarily included as tax earnings.

EXAMPLES

1. During 1997, Corporation A paid dividends of $25,000. At the beginning of 1997 it had accumulated earnings of $50,000. It lost $25,000 during 1997. You are fully taxed on your dividend income in 1997 because the corporation's net accumulated surplus exceeds its dividends.
2. At the end of 1996, Corporation B had a deficit of $200,000. Earnings for 1997 were $100,000. In 1997, it paid stockholders $25,000. The dividends are taxed; earnings exceeded the dividends.

4.6 Stock Dividends on Common Stock

If you own common stock in a company and receive additional shares of the same company as a dividend, the dividend is generally not taxable; *see 30.4* and *30.5* for the method of computing cost basis of stock dividends and rights and sales of such stock.

Exceptions to tax-free rule. A stock dividend on common stock is taxable when (1) you may elect to take either stock or cash; (2) there are different classes of common stock, one class receiving cash dividends and another class receiving stock; or (3) the dividend is of convertible preferred stock; *see 4.8* for further details on taxable stock dividends.

Fractional shares. If a stock dividend is declared and you are only entitled to a fractional share, you may be given cash instead. To save the trouble and expense of issuing fractional shares, many companies directly issue cash in lieu of fractional shares or they set up a plan, with shareholder approval, for the fractional shares to be sold and the cash proceeds distributed to the shareholders. Your company should tell you how to report the cash payment. According to the IRS, you are generally treated as receiving a tax-free dividend of fractional shares, followed by a taxable redemption of the shares by the company. You report on Schedule D capital gain or loss equal to the excess of the cash over the basis of the fractional share; long- or short-term treatment depends on the holding period of the original stock. In certain cases, a cash distribution may be taxed as an ordinary dividend and not as a sale reported on Schedule D; your company should tell you if this is the case.

Stock rights. The rules that apply to stock dividends also apply to distributions of stock rights. If you, as a common stockholder, receive rights to subscribe to additional common stock, the receipt of the rights is not taxable provided the terms of the distribution do not fall within the taxable distribution rules of *4.8*.

4.7 Dividends Paid in Property

A dividend may be paid in property such as securities of another corporation or merchandise. You report as income the fair market value of the property. A dividend paid in property is sometimes called a *dividend in kind*.

EXAMPLE

You receive one share of X corporation stock as a dividend from the G company of which you are a stockholder. You received the X stock when it had a market value of $25; you report $25, the value of the property received.

Corporate benefits. On an audit, the IRS may charge that a benefit given to a shareholder-employee is a taxable dividend.

Filing Tip

Stock Splits Are Not Taxed

The receipt of stock under a split-up is not taxable. Stock splits resemble the receipt of stock dividends, but they are not dividends. They do not represent a distribution of surplus as in the case of stock dividends. The purpose of a split-up is generally to reduce the price of individual shares in order to increase their marketability. The basis of the old holding is divided among the new shares in order to find the basis for the new shares; *see 30.4.*

☐ CORRECTED (if checked)

PAYER'S name, street address, city, state, ZIP code, and telephone no.	**1a** Gross dividends and other distributions on stock (Total of 1b, 1c, 1d, and 1e) $ *810*	OMB No. 1545-0110 19**97** Form **1099-DIV**	**Dividends and Distributions**

PAYER'S name: *Mutual Fund XYZ*
1011 Lincoln Drive
City, State 010X0

1b Ordinary dividends $ *500*

PAYER'S Federal identification number *XI-01X0110*	RECIPIENT'S identification number	**1c** Capital gain distributions $ *310*	**2** Federal income tax withheld $	**Copy B For Recipient**

RECIPIENT'S name: *Carl Blake*

1d Nontaxable distributions $ | **3** Foreign tax paid $

Street address (including apt. no.): *46 Washington Street*

1e Investment expenses $ | **4** Foreign country or U.S. possession

City, state, and ZIP code: *City, State 111X0*

Liquidation Distributions

This is important tax information and is being furnished to the Internal Revenue Service. If you are required to file a return, a negligence penalty or other sanction may be imposed on you if this income is taxable and the IRS determines that it has not been reported.

Account number (optional) | **5** Cash $ | **6** Noncash (Fair market value) $

Form **1099-DIV**   (Keep for your records.)   Department of the Treasury - Internal Revenue Service

4.8 Taxable Stock Dividends

The most frequent type of stock dividend is not taxable: the receipt by a common stockholder of a common stock dividend; *see 4.6.*

Taxable stock dividends.   The following stock dividends are taxable:

- Stock dividends paid to holders of preferred stock. However, no taxable income is realized where the conversion ratio of convertible preferred stock is increased only to take account of a stock dividend or split involving the stock into which the convertible stock is convertible.
- Stock dividend elected by a shareholder of common stock who had the choice of taking stock, property, or cash. A distribution of stock that was immediately redeemable for cash at the stockholder's option was treated as a taxable dividend.
- Stock dividend paid in a distribution where some shareholders receive property or cash and other shareholders' proportionate interests in the assets, or earnings and profits of the corporation are increased.
- Distributions of preferred stock to some common shareholders and common stock to other common shareholders.
- Distributions of convertible preferred stock to holders of common stock, unless it can be shown that the distribution will not result in the creation of disproportionate stock interests.

Constructive stock dividends.   You may not actually receive a stock dividend, but under certain circumstances, the IRS may treat you as having received a taxable distribution. This may happen when a company increases the ratio of convertible preferred stock.

4.9 Who Reports the Dividends

Stock held by broker in street name.   If your broker holds stock for you in a street name, dividends earned on this stock are received by the broker and credited to your account. You report all dividends credited to your account in 1997. The broker is required to file an information return on Form 1099 (or similar form) showing all such dividends.

If your statement shows only a gross amount of dividends, check with your broker if any of the dividends represented nontaxable returns of capital.

 Planning Reminder

Dividend Reinvestment in Company Stock
Your company may allow you to take either cash dividends or automatically reinvest the dividends in company stock. If you elect the stock plan, and pay fair market value for the stock, the full cash dividend is taxable.

If the plan lets you buy the stock at a discount price, the amount of the taxable dividend is the fair market value of the stock on the dividend payment date, plus any service fee charged for the acquisition. The basis of the stock is also fair market value at the dividend payment date. The service charge may be claimed as an itemized deduction subject to the 2% adjusted gross income floor; *see 19.24.* If at the same time you also have the option to buy additional stock at a discount and you exercise the option, you have additional dividend income for the difference between the fair market value of the optional shares and the discounted amount you paid for the shares.

Dividends on stock sold or bought between ex-dividend date and record date. Record date is the date set by a company on which you must be listed as a stockholder on its records to receive the dividend. However, in the case of publicly traded stock, an ex-dividend date, which usually precedes the record date by several business days, is fixed by the exchange to determine who is entitled to the dividend.

If you buy stock before the ex-dividend date, the dividend belongs to you and is reported by you. If you buy on or after the ex-dividend date, the dividend belongs to the seller.

If you sell stock before the ex-dividend date, you do not have a right to the dividend. If you sell on or after the ex-dividend date, you receive the dividend and report it as income.

The dividend declaration date and date of payment do not determine who receives the dividend.

Stock sold short. For a discussion of how to treat a payment to a broker for dividends paid on stock sold short, *see* Chapter 30.

Nominees or joint owners. If you receive dividends on stock held as a nominee for another person, other than your spouse, give that owner a Form 1099-DIV and file a copy of that return with the IRS, along with a Form 1096 ("Transmittal of U.S. Information Return"). The actual owner then reports the income. List the nominee dividends on Schedule B of Form 1040 (or Schedule 1, Form 1040A) along with your other dividends, and then subtract the nominee dividends from the total.

Follow the same procedure if you receive a Form 1099-DIV for an account owned *jointly* with someone other than your spouse. Give the other owner a Form 1099-DIV, and file a copy with the IRS, along with a Form 1096. The other owner then reports his or her share of the joint income. On your return, you list the total dividends shown on Forms 1099-DIV and avoid tax by subtracting from the total the nominee dividends reported to the other owner.

EXAMPLE

You receive Form 1099-DIV showing dividends of $960 including a $200 nominee distribution. You prepare a Form 1099-DIV for the actual owner showing the $200 distribution, and file a copy of the form with the IRS, plus Form 1096. On your own Schedule B, report the nominee distribution along with your other dividends and then subtract it from the total.

Dividend Income	Amount
Mutual Fund	$ 310
Computer Inc.	450
Utility Inc.	200
Subtotal	$ 960
Less: Nominee distribution	(200)
Net dividends	$ 760

4.10 Year Dividends Are Reported

Dividends are generally reported on the tax return for the year in which the dividend is unqualifiedly credited to your account or when you receive the dividend check. However, a dividend declared and made payable in October through December by a mutual fund *(4.3)* or by a real estate investment trust (REIT) is taxable in the year it is declared, if it is paid during January of the following year.

Dividends received from a corporation in a year after the one in which they were declared, when you held the stock on the record date, are taxed in the year they are received; *see* Example 4 below.

EXAMPLES

1. A corporation declares a dividend payable on December 29, 1997. It follows a practice of paying dividends by checks that are mailed so that stockholders do not receive them until January 1998. You report this dividend on your 1998 return.

2. On December 31, 1997, a dividend is declared by a mutual fund. You receive it in January 1998. The dividend is taxable in 1997, when declared, and not 1998 when received.

3. On December 31, 1997, a dividend is credited by a corporation to a stockholder's account and made immediately available. The dividend is taxable in 1997, as the crediting is considered constructive receipt in 1997, even though the dividend is not received until 1998 or a later year.

4. You own stock in a corporation. In April 1996, the corporation declared a dividend. But it provided that the dividend will be paid when it gets the cash. It finally pays the dividend in September 1997; the dividend is taxable in 1997.

4.11 Distribution Not Out of Earnings: Return of Capital

A return of capital or "nontaxable distribution" reduces the cost basis of the stock. If your shares were purchased at different times, reduce the basis of the oldest shares first. When the cost basis is reduced to zero, further returns of capital are taxed as capital gains on Schedule D, or on Line 13 of Form 1040 if you do not need Schedule D to report other transactions. Whether the gain is short-term or long term depends on the length of time you have held the stock. The company paying the dividend will usually inform you of the tax treatment of the payment.

Life insurance dividends. Dividends on insurance policies are not true dividends. They are returns of premiums you previously paid. They reduce the cost of the policy and are not subject to tax until they exceed the net premiums paid for the contract. Interest paid or credited on dividends left with the insurance company is taxable. Dividends on VA insurance are tax free, as is interest on dividends left with the VA.

Where insurance premiums were deducted as a business expense in prior years, receipts of insurance dividends are either included in income or taken as a reduction of the insurance expense deduction of the current year. Dividends on capital stock of an insurance company are taxable.

Reporting Interest Income

4.12 Reporting Interest on Your Tax Return

You must report all taxable interest. If you earn over $400 of taxable interest, you list the payers of interest on Schedule B if you file Form 1040, or on Part I of Schedule 1 if you file Form 1040A. Form 1040EZ may not be used if your taxable interest exceeds $400. You must also list tax-exempt interest on your return even though it is not taxable.

You must also list interest that has been shown on Forms 1099 in your name although it may not be taxable to you. For example, you may have received interest as a nominee or as accrued interest on bonds bought between interest dates. In these cases, list the amounts reported on Form 1099 along with your other interest income on Schedule B if you file Form 1040, or Schedule 1 if you file Form 1040A. On a separate line, label the amount as "Nominee distribution," or "Accrued interest," and subtract it from the total interest shown. Accrued interest is discussed at *4.15* and in the "Who Reports Interest Income" chart on page 69. Nominee distributions are discussed further in the chart on page 69.

If you received interest on a frozen account *(4.13)*, include the interest from Form 1099 on Schedule B if you file Form 1040, or on Schedule 1 if you use Form 1040A. On a separate line, write "frozen deposits" and subtract the amount from the total interest reported.

You do not have to list the payers of interest if your interest receipts are $400 or less, unless you have to reduce the interest shown on Form 1099 by nontaxable amounts such as accrued interest, nominee distributions, or frozen deposit interest.

Joint accounts. If you receive a Form 1099-INT for interest on an account you own with someone other than your spouse, you should file a nominee Form 1099-INT with the IRS to indicate that person's share of the interest, together with Form 1096 ("Transmittal of Information Return"). Give a copy of the Form 1099-INT to the other person. When you file your own return, you report the total interest shown on Form 1099-INT and then subtract the other person's share so you are taxed only on your portion of the interest; see the Example below.

Do not follow this procedure if you contributed all of the funds and set up the joint account merely as a "convenience" account to allow the other person to automatically inherit the account when you die. In this case, you report all of the interest income.

EXAMPLE

Your Social Security number is listed on a bank account owned jointly with your sister. You each invested 50% of the account principal and have agreed to share the interest income. You receive a Form 1099-INT for 1997 reporting total interest of $1,500 on the account. By February 2, 1998, prepare and give to your sister another Form 1099-INT which identifies you as the payer and her as the recipient of her share, or $750 interest. Send a copy of the Form 1099-INT and a Form 1096 to the IRS no later than March 2, 1998. Your sister will report the $750 interest on her return. On your Form 1040, report the full $1,500 interest on Line 1 of Schedule B, along with your other interest income. Above Line 2, subtract the $750 belonging to your sister to avoid being taxed on that amount; label the subtraction "Nominee distribution."

4.13 Interest on Frozen Accounts Not Taxed

If you have funds in a bankrupt or insolvent financial institution that "freezes" your account by limiting withdrawals, you do not pay tax on interest allocable to the "frozen" deposits. The interest is taxable when withdrawals are permitted. Officers and owners of at least a 1% interest in the financial institution, or their relatives, may not take advantage of this rule and must still report interest on frozen deposits.

If you report interest on Schedule B of Form 1040 or on Schedule 1 of Form 1040A, report the full amount shown on Form 1099-INT, even if the interest is on a "frozen" deposit. Then, on a separate line, subtract the amount allocable to the frozen deposit from the total interest shown on the Schedule; label the subtraction "frozen deposits." Thus the interest on the frozen deposit is not included on the line of your return showing taxable interest.

Lost deposits. If you lose funds because of a financial institution's bankruptcy or insolvency, and you can reasonably estimate such a loss, you may deduct the loss as a nonbusiness bad debt, as a casualty loss, or as a miscellaneous itemized deduction; *see 18.4*.

Refund opportunity. If you reported interest on a frozen deposit on a tax return for 1994–1996, you may file a refund claim for the tax paid on the interest; *see* Chapter 38.

4.14 Interest Income on Debts Owed You

You report interest earned on money which you loan to another person. If you are on the cash basis, you report interest in the year you actually receive it or when it is considered received under the "constructive receipt rule." If you are on the accrual basis, you report interest when it is earned, whether or not you have received it.

See 4.31 for minimum interest rates required for loans and *4.18* when OID rules apply.

Where partial payment is being made on a debt, or when a debt is being compromised, the parties may agree in advance which part of the payment covers interest and principal. If a payment is not identified as either principal or interest, the payment is first applied against interest due and reported as interest income to the extent of the interest due.

Interest income is not realized when a debtor gives you a new note for an old note where the new note includes the interest due on the old note.

If you give away a debtor's note, you report as income the collectible interest due at the date of the gift. To avoid tax on the interest, the note must be transferred before interest becomes due.

4.15 Reporting Interest on Bonds Bought or Sold

Where you buy or sell bonds between interest dates, interest is included in the price of the bonds. The purchaser does not report as income the interest that accrued before he or she owned the bond. The seller reports the accrued interest. The purchaser reduces the basis of the bond by the accrued interest reported by the seller. The following Examples illustrate these rules.

EXAMPLES
1. *Purchase.* On April 30, you buy for $5,250 a $5,000 corporate bond bearing interest at 8% per year, payable January 1 and July 1. The purchase price of the bond included accrued interest of $133 for the period January 1–April 30.

Interest received on 7/1	$200
Less: Accrued interest	133
Taxable interest	$ 67

Form 1099 sent to you includes the $133 of accrued interest. On Schedule B of Form 1040, you report the total interest of $200 received on July 1 and then on a separate line subtract the accrued interest of $133. Write "Accrued Interest" on the line where you show the subtraction.

Your basis for the bond is $5,117 ($5,250 – $133) for purposes of figuring gain or loss on a later sale of the bond.

Continued on page 71

Who Reports Interest Income

If interest is—	It is reported by—
Joint account interest	The person whose Social Security number is reported to the bank (or other payer) on Form W-9 when the account is opened. If the other owner is not your spouse, and you receive a Form 1099-INT for the interest, you should report all the income on your return and also file a nominee Form 1099-INT with the other owner to indicate the other owner's share of the interest. These rules are discussed in the next item. Do not file a nominee form if you contributed all the funds and named a joint owner so that he or she may automatically inherit the account. You report all the interest.
Nominee distribution	If you receive a Form 1099-INT that includes interest belonging to someone other than you or your spouse, file a nominee Form 1099-INT with the IRS to indicate that person's income, and give a copy to that person. Complete a Form 1099-INT on which you are listed as the payer and the other person is listed as the recipient. Give the Form 1099-INT to the other owner by February 2, 1998. File Form 1099-INT plus Form 1096 ("Transmittal of Information Return") with the IRS by March 2, 1998. On your own Form 1040 or Form 1040A, you list the nominee interest, along with the other interest reported to you on Forms 1099-INT. Then subtract the nominee interest from the total. *See 4.12* for an example of nominee reporting.
Accrued interest on a bond bought between interest payment dates	Interest accrued between interest payment dates is part of the purchase price of the bond. This amount is taxable to the seller as explained at *4.15*. If you received a Form 1099-INT that includes accrued interest on a bond, include the interest on Line 1 of Schedule B, and then on a separate line above Line 2 subtract the accrued interest from the Line 1 total.
Custodian account of a minor (Uniform Gifts to Minors Act)	The interest is taxable to the child. For a child under age 14, net investment income exceeding $1,300 is subject to tax at the parent's top tax rate; *see* Chapter 24.

☐ CORRECTED (if checked)

PAYER'S name, street address, city, state, and ZIP code
National Savings Bank
333 Sunshine Drive
City, State 010XX

Payer's RTN (optional)

OMB No. 1545-0112

1997

Interest Income

Form **1099-INT**

PAYER'S Federal identification number OX-XX100X1
RECIPIENT'S identification number OX1-OO-XX11

1 Interest income not included in box 3 $ 925

Copy B
For Recipient

RECIPIENT'S name
Christine Blake

2 Early withdrawal penalty $
3 Interest on U.S. Savings Bonds and Treas. obligations $

Street address (including apt. no.)
46 Washington Street

4 Federal income tax withheld $

City, state, and ZIP code
City, State 111X0

5 Foreign tax paid

6 Foreign country or U.S. possession

Account number (optional) $

This is important tax information and is being furnished to the Internal Revenue Service. If you are required to file a return, a negligence penalty or other sanction may be imposed on you if this income is taxable and the IRS determines that it has not been reported.

Form **1099-INT**

(Keep for your records.)

Department of the Treasury - Internal Revenue Service

Key to Interest Income Rules

Item—	Pointer—
Forms 1099-INT	Forms 1099-INT, sent by payers of interest income, simplify the reporting of interest income. The forms give you the amount of interest to enter on your tax return. Although they are generally correct, you should check for mistakes and notify payers of any error and request a form marked "corrected." If tax was withheld (26.12), claim this tax as a payment on your tax return. The IRS will check interest reported on your return against the Forms 1099-INT sent by banks and other payers.
Deposits in a savings account	Interest credited to your account in 1997 is taxable for 1997. This is true for a "passbook" savings account even though you do not present your passbook to have the interest entered. Dividends on deposits or accounts in the following institutions are reported as interest income: mutual savings banks; cooperative banks; domestic building and loan associations; and domestic and federal savings and loan associations.
Savings certificates, deferred interest	The interest element on certificates of deposit and similar plans of more than one year is treated as original issue discount (OID) and is taxable on an annual basis. The bank notifies you of the taxable OID amount on Form 1099-OID. If you discontinue a savings plan before maturity, you may have a loss deduction for forfeited interest, which is listed on Form 1099-INT or Form 1099-OID; see 4.16. Tax on interest can be deferred on a savings certificate with a term of one year or less. Interest is taxable in the year it is available for withdrawal without substantial penalty. Where you invest in a six-month certificate before July 1, the entire amount of interest is paid six months later and is taxable in the year of payment. However, when you invest in a six-month certificate after June 30, only interest actually paid or made available for withdrawal without substantial penalty is taxable in the year of issuance. The balance is taxable in the year of maturity. You can defer interest to the following year by investing in a six-month certificate after June 30, provided the payment of interest is specifically deferred to the year of maturity by the terms of the certificate. Similarly, interest may be deferred to the following year by investing in longer term certificates of up to one year, provided that the crediting of interest is specifically deferred until the year of maturity.
U.S. Savings Bonds— Series E, EE	The increase in redemption value of these Savings Bonds is interest income. You do not have to report the annual increase in value until the year in which you cash the bond or the year in which the bond finally matures, whichever is earlier; see 4.28.
U.S. Savings Bonds— Series H, HH	Semiannual interest on these bonds is taxable when received.
U.S. Treasury bills	If your T-bill matured in 1997, report as interest the difference between the amount received at redemption and your cost. If in 1997 you sold a bill before maturity, you may have a capital loss, or a gain that is partly interest income and partly capital gain; see 4.27.
Zero Coupon Bonds	The interest element is treated as original issue discount (OID) and is taxable annually. You receive a Form 1099-OID reporting the taxable amount.
Interest on funds invested abroad	Interest must be reported in U.S. dollars. If foreign tax has been paid, you may be entitled to a deduction or credit; see 36.14. See also 36.12 for blocked currency reporting rules.
Bearer or coupon bonds	Interest coupons due and payable in 1997 are taxable on your 1997 return regardless of when they were presented for collection. For example, a coupon due January 1997 and presented for payment in 1996 is taxable in 1997. Similarly, a December 1997 coupon presented for payment in 1998 is taxable in 1997.
Corporate obligations in registered form	You report interest when received or made available to you. See 4.15 on how to treat interest when you buy or sell bonds between interest dates.
Interest on state and local government obligations	Although you may receive a Form 1099-INT for interest on state or municipal bonds, you do not pay federal tax on the interest. You are required to list the tax-exempt interest on your tax return, although it is not taxable. The interest may be subject to state income tax.
Borrowing to meet minimum deposit requirements for savings certificates	Interest expenses may be deductible as itemized investment interest deductions (15.10). Report the full amount of interest income listed on Form 1099-INT, even if you do not take interest deductions.
Insurance proceeds	You report interest paid on insurance proceeds left with an insurance company or included in installment payments (under optional modes of payment). Exception: A surviving spouse of an insured who died before October 23, 1986, is not taxed on up to $1,000 a year of interest included in installment payments.
Interest on prepaid premium	Taxable interest is reported by insurance company on Form 1099-INT.
Interest on tax refunds	Interest on tax refunds is fully taxable.
Bank gifts	To attract new deposits, banks and thrifts may offer cash, televisions, toasters, and the like as inducements. The gifts are taxable as interest and reported on Form 1099-INT.
Interest on withdrawn life insurance dividends	If you can withdraw the interest annually, you report the interest in the year it is credited to your account. However, if, under the terms of the insurance policy, the interest can be withdrawn only on the anniversary date of the policy (or some other specified date), then you report the interest in the year in which the anniversary date of the policy (or some other specified date) falls. Interest on GI insurance dividends on deposit with the Department of Veterans Affairs (VA) is not taxable.

Continued from page 68

2. *Sale.* On April 30, you sell for $5,250 a $5,000 8% bond with interest payable January 1 and July 1. The sales price included interest of $133 accrued from January 1–April 30. Your cost for the bond was $5,000. On your return, you report interest of $133 and capital gain of $117.

You receive	$ 5,250
Less: Accrued interest	133
Sales proceeds	$ 5,117
Less: Your cost	5,000
Capital gain	$ 117

Redemptions, bankruptcy, reorganizations. On a redemption, interest received in excess of the amount due at that time is not treated as interest income.

EXAMPLE

You hold a $5,000 9% bond with interest payable January 1 and July 1. The company can call the bonds for redemption on any interest date. In May, the company announces it will redeem the bonds on July 1. But you may present the bond for redemption beginning with June 1 and it will be redeemed with interest to July 1. On June 1 you present the bond and receive $ 5,225 – $ 5,000 principal, $187.50 interest to June 1, and $37.50 extra interest to July 1. The $37.50 is treated as a capital gain; the $187.50 is interest.

Taxable interest may continue on bonds after the issuer becomes bankrupt, if a guarantor continues to pay the interest when due. The loss on the bonds will occur only when they mature and are not redeemed or when they are sold below your cost. In the meantime, the interest received from the guarantor is taxed.

Bondholders exchanging their bonds for stock, securities, or other property in a tax-free reorganization, including a reorganization in bankruptcy, have interest income to the extent the property received is attributable to accrued but unpaid interest; *see* Internal Revenue Code Section 354.

Bonds selling at a flat price. When you buy bonds with defaulted interest at a "flat" price, a later payment of the defaulted interest is not taxed. It is a tax-free return of capital that reduces your cost of the bond. This rule applies only to interest in default at the time the bond is purchased. Interest that accrues after the date of your purchase is taxed as ordinary income.

4.16 Forfeiture of Interest on Premature Withdrawals

Banks usually impose an interest penalty if you withdraw funds from a savings certificate before the specified maturity date. You may lose interest if you prematurely withdraw funds in order to switch to higher paying investments, or if you need the funds for personal use. In some cases, the penalty may exceed the interest earned so that principal is also forfeited to make up the difference.

If you are penalized, you must still report the full amount of interest credited to your account. However, on Form 1040, you may deduct the full amount of the penalty-forfeited principal as well as interest. The deductible penalty-forfeited amount is shown in Box 2 of Form 1099-INT sent to you. You may claim the deduction, even if you do not itemize deductions. On Form 1040, enter the deduction on Line 29, marked "Penalty on early withdrawal of savings."

Loss on redemption before maturity of a savings certificate. If you redeem a long-term (more than one year) savings certificate for a price less than the stated redemption price at maturity, you are allowed a loss deduction for the amount of original issue discount (OID) reported as income but not received. The amount of the loss is the excess of: (1) the OID reported as income for the period you held the certificate, over (2) the excess of the amount received upon the redemption over the issue price. Claim the deduction on Line 31 of Form 1040. The basis of the obligation is reduced by the amount of the deductible loss.

Do not include in the computation any amount based on a fixed rate of simple or compound interest that is actually payable or is treated as constructively received at fixed periodic intervals of one year or less.

Premiums and Discounts on Bonds

4.17 Amortization of Bond Premium

Bond premium is the extra amount paid for a bond in excess of its principal or face amount when the value of the bond has increased due to falling interest rates. Investors may elect to amortize the premium on a taxable bond by deducting it over the life of the bond. Amortizing the premium annually is usually advantageous because it gives an annual deduction to offset the interest income from the bond. Basis of the bond is reduced by the amortized premium. If you claim amortization deductions and hold the bond to maturity, basis is reduced by the entire amortized premium and you have neither gain nor loss at redemption.

You may not claim a deduction for a premium paid on a *tax-exempt* bond; however, you must still decrease your basis by the premium.

Dealers in bonds may not deduct amortization but must include the premium as part of cost.

Capital loss alternative to amortizing premium. If you do not elect to amortize the premium on a taxable bond, you will realize a capital loss when the bond is redeemed at par or you sell it for less than you paid for it. For example, you bought a $1,000 corporate bond for $1,300 and did not amortize the $300 premium; you will realize a $300 capital loss when the bond is redeemed at par: $1,000 proceeds less $1,300 cost basis ($1,000 face value plus $300 premium). You could realize a capital gain if you sell the bond for more than the premium price you paid.

Determining the amortizable amount for the year. The annual amortizable premium is based on the yield-to-maturity method (also called constant-yield method) if the bond was issued after September 27, 1985. This method is the same as the optional constant-yield method for reporting market discount discussed at *4.20*. *See* IRS Publication 1212 or consult a tax professional for making the complex computations.

For bonds issued before September 28, 1985, a monthly straight-line method or a constant-yield method based upon IRS Revenue Ruling 82-10 could be used.

For taxable bonds subject to a *call* before maturity, the amortization computation is based on the earlier call date if that results in a smaller amortization deduction.

Taxable bonds acquired before 1988. You also may offset interest income by the amortizable premium for bonds acquired after October 22, 1986, but before 1988; otherwise, the allocated premium must be treated as investment interest subject to the limits at *15.10*.

For bonds acquired before October 23, 1986, the allocable premium is fully deductible on Schedule A as a miscellaneous deduction not subject to the 2% floor *(19.1)*.

Effect of amortization election on other bonds you acquire. The election to amortize does not have to be made in the year you acquire the bond. If you elect to amortize the premium for one bond, you must also amortize the premium on all similar bonds owned by you at the beginning of the tax year, and also to all similar bonds acquired thereafter. An election to amortize may not be revoked without IRS permission. If you file your return without claiming the deduction, you may not change your mind and make the election for that year by filing an amended return or refund claim. If an election is made after the first year, the premium allocable to earlier years is included in your cost basis for the bond and will result in capital loss when the bond is redeemed at par or sold for less than basis.

Callable bonds. On taxable bonds, amortization is based either on the maturity or earlier call date, depending on which date gives a smaller yearly deduction. This rule applies regardless of the issue date of the bond. If the bond is called before maturity, you may deduct as an ordinary loss the unamortized bond premium in the year the bond is redeemed.

Convertible bonds. A premium paid for a convertible bond that is allocated to the conversion feature may not be amortized.

Tax-exempt bonds. You may not take a deduction for the amortization of a premium paid on a tax-exempt bond. When you dispose of the bond, you amortize the premium for the period you held the bond and reduce the basis of the bond by the amortized amount.

If the bond has call dates, the IRS may require the premium to be amortized to the earliest call date.

Filing Tip

How To Deduct Amortized Premium

If you paid a premium on a taxable bond during 1997, you offset interest income on the bond by the amortizable premium. You must file Form 1040 and show the reduction on Schedule B. Report the full interest from the bond on Line 1 of Schedule B, along with the rest of your interest income. On a separate line, subtract the premium from a subtotal of the other interest. Label the subtraction "ABP Adjustment."

This interest offset rule applies to all taxable bonds acquired at a premium after 1987; *see 4.17* for bonds acquired before 1988.

Planning Reminder

Amortized Premium Reduces Basis

You reduce the cost basis of the bond by the amount of the premium taken as a deduction.

If you hold the bond to maturity, the entire premium is amortized and you have neither gain nor loss on redemption of the bond. If before maturity you sell the bond at a gain (selling price exceeds your basis for the bond), you realize long-term capital gain if you held the bond long term. A sale of the bond for less than its adjusted basis gives a capital loss.

Acquisition premium paid on bonds with original issue discount. If you paid more than the original issue price plus accumulated OID from the date of issue, that excess, called *acquisition premium*, reduces the amount of OID that you have to include in income; *see 4.18*.

4.18 Discount on Bonds

There are two types of bond discounts: original issue discount and market discount.

Market discount. Market discount arises when the price of a bond declines because its interest rate is less than the current interest rate. For example, a bond originally issued at its face amount of $1,000 declines in value to $900 because the interest payable on the bond is less than the current interest rate. The difference of $100 is called market discount. The tax treatment of market discount is explained in *4.20*.

Original issue discount (OID). OID arises when a bond is issued for a price less than its face or principal amount. OID is the difference between the principal amount (redemption price at maturity) and the issue price. For publicly offered obligations, the issue price is the initial offering price to the public at which a substantial amount of such obligations were sold. All obligations that pay no interest before maturity, such as zero coupon bonds, are considered to be issued at a discount. For example, a bond with a face amount of $1,000 is issued at an offering price of $900. The $100 difference is OID.

Generally, part of the OID must be reported as interest income each year you hold the bond, whether or not you receive any payment from the bond issuer. This is also true for certificates of deposit (CDs), time deposits, and similar savings arrangements with a term of more than one year, provided payment of interest is deferred until maturity. OID is reported to you by the issuer (or by your broker if you bought the obligation on a secondary market) on Form 1099-OID; *see 4.19* for reporting OID.

Exceptions to OID. OID rules do *not* apply to: (1) obligations with a term of one year or less held by cash-basis taxpayers; *see 4.21;* (2) tax-exempt obligations, except for certain stripped tax-exempts; *see 4.26;* (3) U.S. Savings Bonds; (4) an obligation issued by an individual before March 2, 1984; and (5) loans of $10,000 or less from individuals after March 1, 1984.

You may disregard OID that is less than one-fourth of one percent (.0025) of the principal amount multiplied by the number of full years from the date of original issue to maturity. On most long-term bonds, the OID will exceed this amount and must be reported.

> **EXAMPLES**
> 1. A 10-year bond with a face amount of $1,000 is issued at $980. One-fourth of one percent (.0025) of $1,000 times 10 is $25. As the $20 OID is less than $25, it may be ignored for tax purposes.
> 2. Same facts as in Example 1 except that the bond is issued at $950. As OID of $50 is more than the $25, OID must be reported under the rules explained at *4.19*.

Bond bought at premium or acquisition premium. Generally, if you pay more than the face amount for a bond originally issued at a discount, you do *not* report OID as ordinary income. When you dispose of a bond bought at a premium, the difference between the sale or redemption price and your basis is a capital gain or loss; *see 4.17*.

However, this rule does not apply if you pay more than the original issue price plus accumulated OID from the date of issue. Your excess payment, called the "acquisition premium," reduces the amount of OID you must report as income. The rules for computing the reduction to OID depend on when the bond was purchased. For bonds purchased after July 18, 1984, OID is reduced by a fraction, the numerator of which is the acquisition premium; the denominator is the OID remaining after your purchase date to the maturity date. *See* IRS Publication 1212 for further details on how to make the computation.

4.19 How To Report Original Issue Discount (OID) on Your Return

The issuer of the bond (or your broker) will make the OID computation and report in Box 1 of Form 1099-OID the OID for the actual dates of your ownership during the calendar year. However, the amount shown in Box 1 of Form 1099-OID must be adjusted if you bought the obligation at a premium or acquisition premium, if the obligation is a stripped bond or stripped coupon, or if you received Form 1099-OID as a nominee for someone else.

If you did not receive a Form 1099-OID, contact the issuer or check IRS Publication 1212 for OID amounts.

Premium. If you paid more than the face amount for a bond originally issued at discount, you do not have to report any OID as income. Report the amount shown on Form 1099-OID and then subtract it as discussed in the Filing Tip on this page.

Acquisition premium. The amount that is shown in Box 1 of Form 1099-OID is not correct if you pay an acquisition premium (more than original issue price *plus* accumulated OID) because such premium reduces the amount of OID you must report as income. See IRS Publication 1212 to recompute OID. On your return, report the amount shown on Form 1099-OID and then reduce it, as discussed in the Filing Tip on this page.

Stripped bonds or coupons. The amount that is shown in Box 1 of Form 1099-OID may not be correct for a stripped bond or coupon; *see 4.22*. If it is incorrect, adjust it following the rules in Publication 1212 and report the proper amount, as discussed in the Filing Tip on this page.

Nominee. If you receive a Form 1099-OID for an obligation owned by someone else, other than your spouse, you must file another Form 1099-OID for that owner. The OID computation rules shown in IRS Publication 1212 should be used to compute the other owner's share of OID. You file the other owner's Form 1099-OID and a transmittal Form 1096 with the IRS, and give the other owner a copy of the Form 1099-OID. On your own tax return, report the amount shown on the Form 1099-OID you received and then reduce it, as discussed in the Filing Tip on this page.

Periodic interest reported on Form 1099-OID. If in addition to OID there is regular interest payable on the bond, such interest will be reported in Box 2 of Form 1099-OID. Report the full amount as interest income if you held the bond for the entire year. If you acquired the bond or disposed of it during the year, *see 4.15* for figuring the interest allocable to your ownership period.

REMICS. If you are a regular interest holder in a REMIC (real estate mortgage investment conduit), Box 1 of Form 1099-OID shows the amount of OID you must report on your return and Box 2 includes periodic interest other than OID. If you bought the regular interest at a premium or acquisition, the OID shown on Form 1099-OID must be adjusted as discussed above. If you are a regular interest holder in a single-class REMIC, Box 2 also includes your share of the REMIC's investment expenses. These expenses should be listed in a separate statement and are deductible on Schedule A as a miscellaneous itemized deduction subject to the 2% adjusted gross income floor; *see 19.24*.

Filing Tip

Reporting OID and Recomputed OID

If you are reporting the full amount of OID from Box 1 of Form 1099-OID, as previously explained, include the amount as interest on your Form 1040, 1040A, or 1040EZ. However, if you are reporting less OID than the amount shown in Box 1 of Form 1099-OID, you must file Form 1040 and fill out Schedule B. Include the full amount shown in Box 1 of Form 1099-OID on Line 1 of Schedule B, along with other interest income. Make a subtotal of the Line 1 amounts and subtract from it the OID you are not required to report. Write "OID Adjustment" on the line where you show the subtraction, or "Nominee distribution," if that is the reason for the reduction. If you are reporting more OID than the amount shown in Box 1 of Form 1099-OID, add the additional amount to the subtotal of the interest on Line 1 of Schedule B, and label it "OID Adjustment."

Your basis for the obligation is increased by the taxable OID for purposes of figuring gain on a sale or redemption; *see 4.23*.

4.20 Reporting Income on Market Discount Bonds

Market discount arises where the price of a bond declines below its face amount because it carries an interest rate that is below the current rate of interest.

When you realize a profit on a market discount bond, the portion of the profit equal to the accrued discount must be reported as ordinary interest income rather than as capital gain. Alternatively, an election may be made to report the accrued market discount annually instead of in the year of disposition.

These rules apply to taxable as well as tax-exempt bonds *bought after April 30, 1993*. However, there are these exceptions: (1) bonds with a maturity date of up to one year from date of issuance; (2) installment obligations; and (3) U.S. Savings Bonds. Furthermore, you may treat as zero any market discount that is less than one-fourth of one percent (.0025) of the redemption price multiplied by the number of full years after you acquire the bond to maturity. Such minimal discount will not affect capital gain on a sale.

Bonds bought before May 1, 1993. For bonds bought before May 1, 1993, application of the market discount rules depends on whether the bond is taxable or tax exempt, and in the case of taxable bonds, the issue date.

Tax-exempt bonds bought before May 1, 1993, are *not* subject to the market discount interest income rule; all the gain at disposition is capital gain.

If you bought a *taxable* bond before May 1, 1993, the market discount interest income rule applies if the bond was issued *after* July 18, 1984. If the bond was issued before July 19, 1984, the market discount interest income rule does *not* apply; however, a portion of the gain on disposition can still be treated as interest income if you borrowed money to purchase or carry a market discount bond acquired after July 18, 1984. As discussed in the next paragraph, interest deductions for such loans are restricted and in the year you sell the bond, gain is treated as interest income to the extent of the deferred interest that is deductible in the year of disposition.

Deferral of interest deduction and ordinary income at disposition if you borrow to buy market discount bonds after July 18, 1984. If you took such a loan, your interest expense is deductible only to the extent it exceeds the interest income earned on the bond for the year (including OID income, if any) *plus* any market discount allocated to the days you held the bond during the year. The limitation on the interest deduction applies to bonds you acquire after July 18, 1984, regardless of the issue date of the bond. The allocation of market discount is based on either the ratable-accrual method or constant-interest method; *see* below.

You can avoid this interest deduction limitation if you elect to report the market discount annually as interest income; *see* below for "How to figure accrued market discount."

In the year you dispose of the bond, you may deduct the interest expenses that were disallowed in prior years because of the above limitations. *Gain* on the disposition is interest income to the extent of the deferred interest you may deduct in the year of disposition; the balance is capital gain.

You may choose to deduct disallowed interest in a year before the year of disposition if you have net interest income from the bond. Net interest income is interest income for the year (including OID) less the interest expense incurred during the year to purchase or carry the bond. This election lets you deduct any disallowed interest expense to the extent it does not exceed the net interest income of that year. The balance of the disallowed interest expense is deductible in the year of disposition.

> **EXAMPLE**
>
> In 1997, you borrowed to buy a market discount bond. During 1997, your interest expense is $1,000. Income from the bond is $900 and ratable market discount allocated to the annual holding period is $75. Thus, only $25 is deductible investment interest ($1,000 – $975), subject to the limitations on investment interest; *see 15.10*.
>
> A similar interest deduction limitation will apply every year you hold the bond, assuming you do not elect to report the market discount annually.
>
> In the year you dispose of the bond, interest deferred under the limitation will be deductible, subject to the limits of *15.10*. Gain on the disposition will be treated as interest income to the extent of this deferred interest deduction.

How to figure accrued market discount. Where the market discount rules apply, gain is taxed as ordinary interest income to the extent of the market discount accrued to the date of sale. There are two methods for figuring the accrued market discount. The basic method, called the *ratable accrual method*, is figured by dividing market discount by the number of days in the period from the date you bought the bond until the date of maturity. This daily amount is then multiplied by the number of days you held the bond to determine your accrued market discount; *see* Example 1 below.

Instead of using the ratable accrual method to compute accrual of market discount you may elect to figure the accrued discount for any bond under an optional *constant-yield* (economic-accrual) method. If you make the election, you may not change it. The constant-yield method initially provides a smaller accrual of market discount than the ratable method, but it is more complicated to figure. It is generally the same as the constant-yield method used in IRS Publication 1212 to compute taxable OID *(4.19)*. For accruing market discount, treat your acquisition date as the original issue date and your basis for the market discount bond (immediately after you acquire it) as the issue price when applying the formula in Publication 1212.

Bonds held to maturity. If you do not report the discount annually and hold a bond until maturity, the discount is reported as interest income in the year of redemption; *see* Example 2 below. You have the option of reporting the market discount annually instead of at sale; *see* below for annual reporting.

Reporting discount annually. Rather than report market discount in the year you sell the bond, you may elect, in the year you acquire the bond, to report market discount currently as interest income. You may use either the ratable accrual method, as in Example 3 below, or the elective constant-interest method discussed earlier. Your election to report annually applies to all market discount bonds subject to the interest income rule that you later acquire. You may not revoke the election without IRS consent. If the election is made, the interest deduction deferral rule discussed earlier does not apply. Furthermore, the election could provide a tax advantage if you sell the bond at a profit and you can benefit from lower tax rates applied to net long-term capital gains.

EXAMPLES

1. You buy a taxable bond at a market discount of $200. There are 1,000 days between the date of your purchase and the maturity date. The daily accrual rate is 20 cents. You hold the bond for 600 days before selling it for a price exceeding what you paid for the bond. Under the ratable accrual method, up to $120 of your profit is market discount taxable as interest income (600 × $0.20).

2. You paid $9,100 for a $10,000 bond maturing in 1998. If you hold the bond to maturity, you will receive $10,000, giving you a gain of $900 equal to the market discount. The entire $900 market discount will be taxable as interest income in 1998 when the bond is redeemed.

3. In 1996, you buy at a $200 discount a bond that was issued after July 18, 1984. There are 1,000 days between the date of your purchase and the maturity date, so that daily accrual is 20 cents. You elect to report the market discount currently using the ratable accrual method. If you held the bond for 112 days in 1997, on your 1997 return you report $22 as interest income (112 × $0.20).

Partial principal payments on bonds acquired after October 22, 1986. If the issuer of a bond (acquired by you after October 22, 1986) makes a partial payment of the principal (face amount), you must include the payment as ordinary interest income to the extent it does not exceed the accrued market discount on the bond. *See* IRS Publication 550 for options on determining accrued market discount. A taxable partial principal payment reduces the amount of remaining accrued market discount when figuring your tax on a later sale or receipt of another partial principal payment.

Market discount on a bond originally issued at a discount. A bond issued at original issue discount may later be acquired at a market discount because of an increase in interest rates. If you acquire at market discount an OID bond issued after July 18, 1984, the market discount is the excess of: (1) the issue price of the bond plus the total original issue discount includible in the gross income of all prior holders of the bond over (2) what you paid for the bond.

Exchanging a market discount bond in corporate mergers or reorganizations. If you hold a market discount bond and exchange it for another bond as part of a merger or other reorganization, the new bond is subject to the market discount rules when you sell it. However, under an exception, market discount rules will not apply to the new bond if the old market discount bond was issued before July 19, 1984, and the terms of interest rates of both bonds are identical.

4.21 Discount on Short-Term Obligations

Short-term obligations (maturity of a year or less) may be purchased at a discount from face value. If you are on the cash basis, you report the discount as interest income in the year the obligation is paid. The interest is reported on Form 1099-INT.

EXAMPLE

In May 1996, you paid $920 for a short-term note with a face amount of $1,000. In January 1997, you receive payment of $1,000 on the note. On your 1997 tax return, you report $80 as interest.

Discount must be currently reported by dealers and accrual-basis tax-payers. Discount allocable to the current year must be reported as income by accrual-basis taxpayers, dealers who sell short-term obligations in the course of business, banks, regulated investment companies, common trust funds, certain pass-through entities, and for obligations identified as part of a hedging transaction. Current reporting also applies to persons who separate or strip interest coupons from a bond and then retain the stripped bond or stripped coupon; the accrual rule applies to the retained obligation.

For short-term *governmental* obligations (other than tax-exempts), the acquisition discount is accrued in daily installments under the ratable method, unless an election is made to use the constant-interest method.

For short-term *nongovernmental* obligations, OID is generally taken into account instead of acquisition discount; but an election may be made to report the accrued acquisition discount. *See* IRS Publication 550 for details.

Basis in the obligation is increased by the amount of acquisition discount (or OID for nongovernmental obligations) that is currently reported as income.

Interest deduction limitation for cash-basis investors. A cash-basis investor who borrows funds to buy a short-term discount obligation may not fully deduct interest on the loan unless an election is made to report the accrued acquisition discount as income. If the election is not made, a complicated formula limits deductible interest to the excess of the interest expense for the year over the taxable interest from the bond during the year less (1) the portion of the discount allocated to the days you held the bond during the year, and (2) the portion of interest not taxable for the year under your method of accounting. Any interest expense disallowed under this limitation is deductible in the year in which the obligation is disposed.

The interest deduction limitation does *not* apply if you elect to include in income the accruable discount as explained in *4.20*. The election applies to all short-term obligations acquired during the year and also in all later years.

Gain or loss on disposition of short-term obligations for cash-basis investors. If you have a gain on the sale or exchange of a discounted short-term *governmental* obligation (other than tax-exempt local obligations), the gain is ordinary income to the extent of the ratable share of the acquisition discount received when you bought the obligation. Follow the computation shown in *4.27* for Treasury bills to figure this ordinary income portion. Any gain over this ordinary income portion is short-term capital gain; a loss would be a short-term capital loss.

Gain on short-term *nongovernmental* obligations is treated as ordinary income up to the ratable share of OID. The formula for figuring this ordinary income portion is similar to that shown in *4.27* for short-term governmental obligations, except that the denominator of the fraction is days from original issue to maturity, rather than days from acquisition. A constant yield method may also be elected to figure the ordinary income portion. Gain above the computed ordinary income amount is short-term capital gain (*see* Chapter 5). For more information, *see* IRS Publication 550.

4.22 Stripped Coupon Bonds and Stock

Brokers holding coupon bonds may separate or strip the coupons from the bonds and sell the bonds or coupons to investors. Examples include zero-coupon instruments sold by brokerage houses that are backed by U.S. Treasury bonds (such as CATS and TIGRS).

The U.S. Treasury also offers its version of zero coupon instruments, with the name STRIPS, which are available from brokers and banks.

Brokers holding preferred stock may strip the dividend rights from the stock and sell the stripped stock to investors.

If you buy a stripped bond or coupon, the spread between the cost of the bond or coupon and its higher face amount is treated as original issue discount (OID). This means that you annually report a part of the spread as interest income. For a stripped bond, the amount of the original issue discount is the difference between the stated redemption price of the bond at maturity and the cost of the bond. For a stripped coupon, the amount of the discount is the difference between the amount payable on the due date of the coupon and the cost of the coupon. The rules for figuring the amount of OID to be reported annually are in IRS Publication 1212. *See 4.19* for reporting OID.

If you strip a coupon bond, interest accrual and allocation rules prevent you from creating a tax loss on a sale of the bond or coupons. You are required to report interest accrued up to the date of the sale and also add the amount to the basis of the bond. If you acquired the obligation after October 22, 1986, you must also include in income any market discount that accrued before the date you sold the stripped bond or coupons. The method of accrual depends on the date you bought the obligation; *see* IRS Publication 1212. The accrued market discount is also added to the basis of the bond. You then allocate this basis between the bond and the coupons. The allocation is based on the relative fair market values of the bond and coupons at the date of sale. Gain or loss on the sale is the difference between the sales price of the stripped item (bond or coupons) and its allocated basis. Furthermore, the original issue discount rules apply to the stripped item which you keep (bond or coupon). Original issue discount for this purpose is the difference between the basis allocated to the retained item and the redemption price of the bond (if retained) or the amount payable on the coupons (if retained). You must annually report a ratable portion of the discount.

4.23 Sale or Retirement of Bonds and Notes

Gain or loss on the sale, redemption, or retirement of debt obligations issued by a government or corporation is generally capital gain or loss. If the bond was issued before 1955, there is capital gain or loss only if the obligation was issued with interest coupons or in registered form on or before March 1, 1954.

Caution

Recomputing Form 1099-OID Amount

Do not report the amount shown in Box 1 of Form 1099-OID for a stripped bond or coupon; that amount must be recomputed under complicated rules described in IRS Publication 1212. *See 4.19* for reporting the recomputed OID on your return.

A redemption or retirement of a bond at maturity must be reported as a sale on Schedule D of Form 1040 *(5.6)* although there may be no gain or loss realized.

Corporate bonds with OID issued after 1954 and before May 28, 1969, and government bonds with OID issued before July 2, 1982. If the bonds were originally issued at a discount (OID), you report your ratable monthly share of the OID element as ordinary income when the bonds are sold or redeemed; any gain exceeding OID is reported as capital gain. However, if there was an intention to call before maturity, gain is ordinary income to the full extent of the OID. A loss is a capital loss. IRS Publication 1212 has examples for figuring the amount taxable as ordinary income.

Corporate bonds with OID issued after May 27, 1969, and government bonds with OID issued after July 1, 1982. The accrued amount of OID is reported annually as interest income *(see 4.19)* and added to basis; this includes the accrued OID for the year the bond is sold. If the bonds are sold or redeemed before maturity, you realize capital gain for the proceeds over the adjusted basis (as increased by accrued OID) of the bond, provided there was no intention to call the bond before maturity. If at the time of original issue there was an intention to call the obligation before maturity, the entire OID that has not yet been included in your income is taxable as ordinary income; the balance is capital gain.

Market discount on bonds is taxable under the rules at *4.20.*

Tax-exempts. *See 4.26* for discount on tax-exempt bonds.

Obligations issued by individuals. If you hold an individual's note issued after March 1, 1984, for over $10,000, accrued OID must be reported annually *(4.19)* and added to basis. Gain on your sale of the note is subject to the rules discussed above for corporate and government OID bonds.

If the note is $10,000 or less (when combined with other prior outstanding loans from the same individual), OID is not reported annually provided you are not a professional lender and tax avoidance was not a principal purpose of the loan. On a sale of the note at a gain, your ratable share of the OID is taxed as ordinary income; any balance is capital gain. A loss is a capital loss.

Tax-Free Interest on State and Local Government Obligations

4.24 State and City Interest Generally Tax Exempt

Generally, you pay no tax on interest on bonds or notes of states, cities, counties, the District of Columbia, or a possession of the United States. This includes bonds or notes of port authorities, toll road commissions, utility services activities, community redevelopment agencies, and similar bodies created for public purposes. Bonds issued after June 30, 1983, must be in registered form for the interest to be tax exempt. Interest on federally guaranteed obligations is generally taxable, but *see* exceptions at *4.25.*

Check with the issuer of the bond to verify the tax-exempt status of the interest.

Private activity bonds. Interest on so-called private activity bonds is generally taxable (*see 4.25*), but there are certain exceptions. For example, interest on the following bonds is tax exempt even if the bond may technically be in the category of private activity bonds; qualified student loan bonds; exempt facility bonds; qualified small issue bonds; qualified mortgage bonds and qualified veterans' mortgage bonds; qualified redevelopment bonds; and qualified 501(c)(3) bonds issued by charitable organizations and hospitals.

However, while interest on such bonds is not subject to regular tax, interest that you receive on such bonds issued after August 7, 1986, is considered a tax preference item that may be subject to alternative minimum tax; *see* Chapter 23.

Check with the issuer for the tax status of a private activity bond.

4.25 Taxable State and City Interest

Interest on certain state and city obligations is taxable. These taxable obligations include federally guaranteed obligations, mortgage subsidy bonds, private activity bonds, and arbitrage bonds.

Federally guaranteed obligations. Interest on state and local obligations issued after April 14, 1983, is generally taxable if the obligation is federally guaranteed, but there are exceptions allowing tax exemptions for obligations guaranteed by the Federal Housing Administration, Department of Veterans Affairs, Bonneville Power Authority, Federal Home Loan Mortgage Corporation,

 Filing Tip

Reporting on Schedule B or Schedule 1

On your 1997 return, you must list the amount of tax-exempt interest received during the year although it is not taxable. On Form 1040, you list the tax-exempt interest on Line 8b. On Form 1040A, you list the amount on Line 8b. On Form 1040EZ, you write "TEI" and then the amount of tax-exempt interest to the right of the last word on Line 2, but do not include it in the taxable interest shown on Line 2.

Federal National Mortgage Association, Government National Mortgage Corporation, Resolution Funding Corporation, and Student Loan Marketing Association.

Mortgage subsidy bonds.   Interest on bonds issued by a state or local government after April 24, 1979, may not be tax exempt if funds raised by the bonds are used for home mortgages. There are exceptions for certain qualified mortgage bonds and veterans' bonds. Check on the tax-exempt status of mortgage bonds with the issuing authority.

Private activity bonds.   Generally, a private activity bond is any bond where more than 10% of the issue's proceeds are used by a private business whose property secures the issue, or if at least 5% of the proceeds (or $5 million if less) are used for loans to parties other than governmental units. Interest on such bonds is generally taxable, but there are exceptions as discussed in *4.24*. Check on the tax status of the bonds with the issuing authority.

Arbitrage bonds.   These are state and local bonds issued after October 9, 1969, used to provide funds for reinvestment in higher yielding instruments except where the bond proceeds are part of a required reserve or replacement fund or are being invested temporarily before the purposes of a bond issue can be fulfilled. Interest on arbitrage bonds is taxable.

4.26 Tax-Exempt Bonds Bought at a Discount

Original issue discount (OID) on tax-exempt obligations is not taxable, and on a sale or redemption, gain attributed to OID is tax exempt. Gain attributed to market discount is capital gain or ordinary income depending on whether the bond was purchased before May 1, 1993, or on or after that date; *see 4.20*.

Original issue discount tax-exempt bond.   This arises when a bond is issued for a price less than the face amount of the bond. The discount is considered tax-exempt interest. Thus, if you are the original buyer and hold the bond to maturity, the entire amount of the discount is tax free. If before maturity you sell a bond that was issued before September 4, 1982, and acquired before March 2, 1984, your part of the OID is tax free. On a disposition of a tax-exempt bond issued after September 3, 1982, and acquired after March 1, 1984, you must add to basis accrued OID before determining gain or loss. OID must generally be accrued using a constant- yield method; *see* IRS Publication 1212.

When bonds issued after June 8, 1980, are redeemed before maturity, the portion of the original issue discount earned to the date of redemption is tax-free interest; the balance is capital gain. Bonds issued with an intention to redeem before maturity are not subject to this rule; all interest is tax exempt.

Amortization of premiums is discussed at *4.17*.

Market discount tax-exempts.   A market discount arises when a bond originally issued at not less than par is bought at below par because its market value has declined. If *before* May 1, 1993, you bought at a market discount a tax-exempt bond which you sell for a price exceeding your purchase price, the excess is capital gain. If the bond was held long term, the gain is long term. A redemption of the bond at a price exceeding your purchase price is similarly treated.

However, for market discount tax-exempt bonds purchased *after* April 30, 1993, the ordinary income rules discussed at *4.20* apply.

Stripped tax-exempt obligations.   OID is not currently taxed on a stripped tax-exempt bond or stripped coupon from the bond if you bought it before June 11, 1987. However, for any stripped bond or coupon you bought or sold after October 22, 1986, OID must be accrued and added to basis for purposes of figuring gain or loss on a disposition. Furthermore, if you bought the stripped bond or coupon after June 10, 1987, part of the OID may be taxable; *see* Publication 1212 for figuring the tax-free portion.

Interest on Treasury Securities and U.S. Savings Bonds

4.27 Treasury Bills, Notes, and Bonds

Interest on securities issued by the federal government is fully taxable on your federal return. However, interest on federal obligations is not subject to state or local income taxes. Interest on Treasury bills, notes, and bonds is reported on Form 1099-INT. *See 30.14* and *30.18* for investment information on Treasury securities.

Treasury bonds and notes. Treasury notes have maturities of two to 10 years. Treasury bonds have maturities of over 10 years. You report the fixed or coupon interest as interest income in the year the coupon becomes due and payable. Treasury bonds and notes are capital assets; gain or loss on their sale, exchange, or redemption is reported as capital gain or loss on Schedule D; *see* Chapter 5. If you purchased a federal obligation below par (at a discount) after July 1, 1982, *see 4.18* for the rules on reporting original issue discount. If you purchased a Treasury bond or note above par (at a premium), you may elect to amortize the premium; *see 4.17.* If you do not elect to amortize and you hold the bond or note to maturity, you have a capital loss.

Treasury bills. These are short-term U.S. obligations issued at a discount with maturities of three, six, or 12 months. On a bill held to maturity, you report as interest the difference between the discounted price and the amount you receive on a redemption of the bills at maturity.

Treasury bills are capital assets and a loss on a disposition before maturity is taxed as a capital loss. If you are a cash-basis taxpayer and have a gain on a sale or exchange, ordinary income is realized up to the amount of the ratable share of the discount received when you bought the obligation. This amount is treated as interest income and is figured as follows:

$$\frac{\text{Days T-bill was held}}{\begin{array}{c}\text{Days from acquisition}\\ \text{to maturity}\end{array}} \quad \times \quad \begin{array}{c}\text{T-bill's value at maturity}\\ \textit{minus} \text{ your cost}\end{array}$$

Any gain over this amount is capital gain; *see* the Example below. Instead of using the above fractional computation for figuring the ordinary income portion of the gain, an election may be made to apply the constant interest method. This method follows the OID computation rules shown in IRS Publication 1212 for obligations issued after 1984, except that the acquisition cost of the Treasury bill would be treated as the issue price in applying the Publication 1212 formula.

Accrual-basis taxpayers and dealers who are required to currently report the acquisition discount element of Treasury bills using either the ratable accrual method or the constant yield method *(4.20)* do not apply the above formula on a sale before maturity. In figuring gain or loss, the discount included as income is added to basis.

> **EXAMPLE**
>
> In May 1997, you buy at original issue a six-month $10,000 Treasury bill (180-day maturity) for $9,650. You sell it 90 days later for $9,800. Your entire gain of $150 ($9,800 – $9,650) is taxed as interest income on your 1997 return. Under the ratable daily formula, gain up to $175 would be treated as interest income:
>
> $$\frac{90 \text{ days held}}{\begin{array}{c}180 \text{ days from}\\ \text{acquisition to maturity}\end{array}} \quad \times \quad \$350 \text{ discount} = \$175$$

Interest deduction limitation. Interest incurred on loans used to buy Treasury bills is deductible by a cash-basis investor only to the extent that interest expenses exceed the following: (1) the portion of the acquisition discount allocated to the days you held the bond during the year; and (2) the portion of interest not taxable for the year under your method of accounting. The deferred interest expense is deductible in the year the bill is disposed of. If an election is made to report the acquisition discount as current income under the rules in *4.21* for governmental obligations, the interest expense may also be deducted currently. The election applies to all future acquisitions.

4.28 Interest on U.S. Savings Bonds

Savings Bond Tables: The Supplement will contain redemption tables showing the 1997 year-end values of Series E and EE U.S. Savings Bonds.

Series E and EE Bonds. Series EE bonds have been available since 1980; before 1980, Series E bonds were issued. Both Series E and Series EE bonds may be cashed for what you paid for them plus an increase in their value over stated periods of time. *See 30.22* for investment information on U.S. Savings Bonds.

The increase in redemption value is taxable as interest, but you do not have to report the increase in value each year on your federal return. You may defer *(4.29)* the interest income until the year in which you cash the bond or the year in which the bond finally matures, whichever is earlier.

Planning Reminder

Tax Deferral: T-Bill Maturing Next Year

If you are a cash-basis taxpayer, you may postpone the tax on Treasury bill interest by selecting a Treasury bill maturing next year. Income is not recognized until the date on which the Treasury bill is paid at maturity, unless it has been sold or otherwise disposed of earlier.

But if you want, you may report the annual increase by merely including it on your tax return. If you use the accrual method of reporting, you must include the interest each year as it accrues. Savings bond interest is not subject to state or local taxes.

If you initially choose to defer the reporting of interest and later want to switch to annual reporting, you may do so. You may also change from the annual reporting method to the deferral method. *See 4.29* for rules on changing reporting methods.

Education funding. If you buy EE bonds to pay for educational expenses upon redemption, you may be able to exclude the accumulated interest from income. *See* Chapter 38.

Bonds for child. Interest on savings bonds bought in the name of a child will be taxed to the child, even if the parent paid for the bonds and is named as beneficiary. Unless an election is made to report the increases in redemption value annually, the accumulated interest will be taxable to the child in the year he or she redeems the bond, or if earlier, when the bond finally matures. However, if the interest is reported annually by a child under age 14, or the child is under age 14 in the year bonds are redeemed, the interest may be subject to tax at the parent's top rate under the *kiddie tax; see* Chapter 24. For example, if a child under age 14 has 1997 investment income over $1,300, the excess is taxed at the parent's top tax rate on the child's 1997 return; *see 24.3*. To avoid kiddie tax, savings bond interest may be deferred, as discussed in *4.29*.

Where the kiddie tax for children under age 14 *(24.3)* does not apply, making the election to report the interest annually may be advisable, such as where the child has little or no other income and the bond interest can be offset by personal deductions. For example, a dependent child is not allowed to claim a personal exemption, but he or she may claim a 1997 standard deduction of at least $650; *see 13.5*. If the election to report the savings bond interest currently was made for 1997, up to $650 of the interest would be offset by the standard deduction, assuming the child had no other income.

You may make an election on behalf of your child to report the savings bond interest annually if your child is unable to file his or her own return. To make the election, report the accumulated bond interest and add a statement that the interest will be reported each year. In a later year, the child may change from annual reporting to the deferral method under the rules discussed in *4.29*.

Bonds must be reissued to make gift. Assume you have bought E or EE bonds and had them registered in joint names of yourself and your daughter. The law of your state provides that jointly owned property may be transferred to a co-owner by delivery or possession. You deliver the bonds to your daughter and tell her they now belong to her alone. According to Treasury regulations, this is not a valid gift of the bonds. The bonds must be surrendered and reissued in your daughter's name.

If you do not have the bonds reissued and you die, the bonds are taxable in your estate. Ownership of the bonds is a matter of contract between the United States and the bond purchaser. The bonds are nontransferable. A valid gift cannot be accomplished by manual delivery to a donee unless the bonds also are surrendered and registered in the donee's name in accordance with Treasury regulations.

Series HH. These bonds are issued only in exchange for E or EE bonds, or for Freedom shares. They are issued at face value and pay semiannual interest that is taxable when received.

To be exchanged for HH bonds, the E or EE bonds must have a redemption value of at least $500. If the total value is not a multiple of $500, you will receive cash for the difference. You report the cash received as interest income to the extent of the unreported interest earned on the EE bonds exchanged.

For example, if you trade EE bonds with a redemption value of $3,723.35 for HH bonds, you get $3,500 in HH bonds and cash of $223.35. Report the cash as interest income to the extent it is unreported interest on the EE bonds exchanged.

Series H. These bonds were available before 1980. They were bought at face value and pay semi-annual interest that is taxable when received. If you obtained Series H bonds in an exchange for Series E bonds, and you did not report the E bond interest annually, you do not have to report the interest due on the old E bonds until the H bonds are redeemed or mature, whichever occurs first. H bonds issued after January 1957 cease earning interest when they mature in 30 years. At maturity, or on a disposal before maturity, you must report as interest the accumulated interest from any exchanged E bonds.

Freedom shares. These savings notes were available between 1967 and 1970. They have maturities of 30 years. As with E bonds, owners may defer the reporting of interest until the notes mature.

 Planning Reminder

Changing to Deferral Method for Children

If your children under age 14 have been reporting the annual increases in value on their savings bonds, and they are subject to the "kiddie" tax *(24.3)*, consider making the election on Form 3115 to change to the deferral method. The election would defer tax on the interest that under the kiddie tax is subject to tax at your top marginal tax rate.

4.29 Deferring U.S. Savings Bond Interest

You do not have to make a special election on your tax return in order to defer the interest on Series E or EE savings bonds. You may simply postpone reporting the interest until the year you redeem the bond or the year in which it reaches final maturity, whichever is earlier. If you choose to defer the interest, you may decide in a later year to begin annual reporting of the increase in value. You may also switch from annual reporting to the deferral method. These options are discussed below.

Changing from deferral to annual reporting. If you have deferred reporting of annual increases in value and want to elect to report annual increases on your 1997 return, make sure you report as 1997 interest income the total of all prior and 1997 increases in value. But next year, report only the increases accruing then, plus increases accruing on bonds newly purchased. Suppose you do not include the annual increase on your 1997 return and later change your mind. If the due date of the return has passed, it is too late to make the election. You may not file an amended return reporting the increase in value for 1997. You have to wait until next year's return to make the election.

Changing from annual reporting to deferral. If you have been reporting annual increases in value, you may change your method and elect to defer interest reporting until the bonds mature or are redeemed. You make the election by filing Form 3115 and attaching it to your federal income tax return for the year of the change. At the top of Form 3115, write "Filed Under Rev. Proc. 89-46." You must identify the bonds for which the election is being made. You may make the election on your 1997 tax return; file the return by the due date plus extensions. You must continue to use the deferred method for at least five years following the year of the change.

Extended maturity periods. E bonds may be held for additional periods of maturity after their initial maturity dates. Bonds held for additional periods increase in value and may be cashed in at any time. If you chose to postpone paying tax on accumulated interest, you may continue to postpone the tax during the extended period. You would then report the entire accumulated interest at the final maturity date or in the year you redeem the bond, whichever occurs earlier.

Co-Owners of E and EE Bonds. How to report interest on the bond depends on how it was bought or issued:

1. You paid for the entire bond: Either you or the co-owner may redeem it. You are taxed on all the interest, even though the co-owner cashes the bond and you receive no proceeds. If the other co-owner does cash in the bond, he or she will receive a Form 1099-INT reporting the accumulated interest. However, since that interest is taxable to you, the co-owner should give you a nominee Form 1099-INT, as explained in the rules for nominee distributions on page 69 in the chart "Who Reports Interest Income."
2. You paid for only part of the bond: Either of you may redeem it. You are taxed on that part of the interest which is in proportion to your share of the purchase price. This is so even though you do not receive the proceeds.
3. You paid for part of the bond, and then had it reissued in another's name. You pay tax only on the interest accrued while you held the bond. The new co-owner picks up his or her share of the interest accruing afterwards.
4. You and another person were named co-owners on a bond bought as a gift by a third party. You are taxed on 50% of the interest income; your co-owner is taxed on the remaining half.

Changing the form of registration. Changing the form of registration of an E or EE bond may result in tax. Assume you use your own funds to purchase a bond issued in your name, payable on your death to your son. Later, at your request, a new bond is issued in your son's name only. The increased value of the original bond up to the date it was redeemed and reissued in your son's name is taxed to you as interest income.

The Examples below show changes in registration that do not result in an immediate tax.

EXAMPLES

1. Jones buys an E bond and has it registered in his name and in the name of his son as co-owner. Jones has the bonds reissued solely in his own name; he is not required to report the accumulated interest at that time.
2. You and your spouse each contributed an equal amount toward the purchase of a $1,000 E bond, which was issued to you as co-owners. You later have the bond reissued as two $500 bonds, one in your name and one in your spouse's name. Neither of

Caution

When Accumulated Interest Becomes Taxable

You may not indefinitely defer the tax on E bond interest. E bonds cease earning interest once the bonds reach their final maturity date. For example, bonds issued during 1957 cease earning interest in 1997, 40 years from the date of issuance. On your 1997 return, you must pay tax on all the accumulated interest on 1957 bonds—unless the bonds are traded for new HH bonds in multiples of $500. E bonds issued in 1967 also reach final maturity in 1997, 30 years from the date of issuance. Exchanging E bonds for HH bonds will continue the tax deferral on E bond interest. *See 30.22* for a listing of final maturity dates.

Filing Tip

Form 1099-INT When Bond Is Cashed

When you cash in an E or EE bond, you receive Form 1099-INT that lists as interest the difference between the amount received and the amount paid for the bond. The form may show more taxable interest than you are required to report because you have regularly reported the interest or a prior owner reported the interest. Report the full amount shown on Form 1099-INT on Schedule B if you file Form 1040, or on Part I of Schedule 1 if you file Form 1040A, along with your other interest income. Enter a subtotal of the total interest and then, on a separate line, reduce the subtotal by the savings bond interest that was previously reported and identify the reduction as "Previously Reported U.S. Savings Bond Interest." The interest is exempt from state and local taxes.

you has to report the interest earned to the date of reissue. But if you bought the $1,000 bond entirely with your own funds, you report half the interest earned to the date of reissue.

3. You add another person's name as co-owner to facilitate a transfer of the bond on death. The change in registration does not result in a tax.

Transfer to a spouse. Interest on U.S. Savings Bonds transferred to a spouse in a divorce or settlement may result in tax to the transferor; *see 6.6.*

Transfer to a trust. If you transfer U.S. Savings Bonds to a trust giving up all rights of ownership, you are taxed on the accumulated interest to date of transfer. If, however, you are considered to be the owner of the trust and the interest earned before and after the transfer is taxable to you, you may continue to defer reporting the interest.

Transfer to a charity. Tax on the accumulated E or EE bond interest is not avoided by having the bonds reissued to a philanthropy. Further, tax may not be deferred by first converting E bonds to HH bonds and then reissuing the HH bonds in the philanthropy's name. The IRS held that by having the bonds reissued in the philanthropy's name, the owner realized taxable income on the accumulated bond interest.

Transfer of an E or EE bond at death. If an owner does not report E or EE bond interest annually and dies before redeeming the bond, the income tax liability on the interest accumulated during the deceased's lifetime becomes the liability of the person who acquires the bond, unless an election is made to report the accrued interest in the decedent's final income tax return; *see 1.12.* If the election is not made on the decedent's final return, the new owner may choose to report the accumulated interest annually, or defer reporting it until the bond is redeemed or reaches final maturity, whichever is earlier. If the election is made on the decedent's final return, the new owner is taxable only on interest earned after the date of death.

Estate tax. Where an estate tax has been paid on bond interest accrued during the owner's lifetime, the new bondholder may claim the estate tax as a miscellaneous itemized deduction in the year that he or she pays tax on the accumulated interest. The deduction is not subject to the 2% adjusted gross income floor *(19.1).*

Minimum Interest for Loans and Seller-Financed Debt

4.30 Minimum Interest Rules

The law requires a minimum rate of interest to be charged on loan transactions unless a specific exception covers the transaction. Where minimum interest is not charged, the law imputes interest as if the parties agreed to the charge.

The rules are complicated and have been subject to several revisions. There are different minimum interest rates and reporting rules depending on the nature of the transaction. The following discussion provides the important details for understanding the rules. For specific cases and computations, we suggest that you consult IRS regulations for details not covered in this book.

There are two broad classes of transactions:

Loans. These are generally covered by Internal Revenue Code Section 7872. Below-market or low-rate interest loans are discussed at *4.31.*

Seller-financed sales of property. These are covered by either Internal Revenue Code Section 1274 or Section 483. Seller-financed sales are discussed at *4.32.* If parties fail to charge the minimum required interest rate, the same minimum rate is imputed by law.

4.31 Interest-Free or Below-Market Interest Loans

For many years, the IRS tried to tax interest-free or below-market interest loans. However, court decisions supported taxpayers who argued that such loans did not result in taxable income or gifts. To reverse these decisions, the IRS convinced Congress to pass a law imposing tax on interest-free or low-interest loans made by individuals and businesses. You may not make interest-free or low-interest loans to a relative who uses the loan for personal or investment purposes without adverse income tax consequences, unless the exception discussed in this section for $10,000 or $100,000 loans applies.

Given the complexity of these loan rules, you and your tax advisor should carefully review regulations to the Internal Revenue Code Section 7872 when drafting a loan agreement.

How the imputed interest rules work. If interest at least equal to the applicable federal rate set by the IRS is not charged, the law generally treats a below-market interest loan as two transactions:

1. The law assumes that the lender has transferred to the borrower an amount equal to the "foregone" interest element of the loan. In the case of a loan between individuals, such as a parent and child, the lender is subject to gift tax on this element; in the case of a stockholder borrowing from a company, the element is a taxable dividend; in the case of a loan made to an employee, it is taxable pay.

   Note: For *gift tax* purposes *(33.1)*, a term loan is treated as if the lender gave the borrower the excess of the amount of the loan over the present value of payments due during the loan term. Demand loans are treated as if the lender gave the borrower annually the amount of the foregone interest.

2. The law assumes that imputed interest equal to the applicable federal rate is paid by the borrower to the lender. The borrower may be able to claim a deduction for the interest if the funds are used to buy investment property; *see 15.10.*

A husband and wife are treated as one person for purposes of imputing interest.

No tax withholding is required on interest imputed by the rules of the section.

Charging the applicable federal rate avoids the imputed interest rules. Gift loans qualifying for the $10,000 and $100,000 exceptions are not subject to imputed interest rules. For other loans, the rules imputing income to you as the lender may be avoided by charging interest at least equal to the applicable federal rate. Applicable federal rates are set by the IRS monthly and published in the Internal Revenue Bulletin; you can also get the rates from your local IRS office. For a term loan, the applicable rate is the one in effect as of the day on which the loan is made, computed semiannually. The short-term rate applies to loans of three years or less; the mid-term rate to loans over three and up to nine years; the long-term rate applies to loans over nine years. For a demand loan, the applicable federal rate is the short-term rate in effect at the start of each semi-annual period (January and July).

Different computations for different types of loans. There are two general classes of loans: (1.) Gift loans, whether term or demand, and nongift demand loans, and (2) nongift term loans.

The distinction is important for figuring and reporting imputed interest. For example, in the case of nongift term loans, the imputed interest element is treated as original issue discount; *see 4.19.*

Gift loans and nongift loans payable on demand. As a lender, you are taxable on the "foregone interest," that is, the interest that you would have received had you charged interest at the applicable federal rate over any interest actually charged. The borrower may be able to claim an interest deduction if the funds are used to buy investment property; see 15.10.

Nongift term loans. A term loan is any loan not payable on demand. As a lender of a nongift term loan, you are taxable on any excess of the loan principal over the present value of all payments due under the loan. The excess is treated as original issue (OID) which you report annually as interest income; *see 4.19.*

Gift loans may be exempt from imputed interest rules

In certain cases, gift loans of up to $10,000 may avoid the imputed interest rules. Under another exception, for gift loans of up to $100,000 imputed interest may be completely avoided or limited, depending on the borrower's net investment income.

The $10,000 gift loan exception. In the case of a gift loan to an individual, no interest is imputed to any day on which the aggregate outstanding amount of all loans between the parties is not over $10,000, provided the loan is not attributed to the purchase or carrying of income-producing assets.

The $100,000 gift loan exception. An exception in the law may allow you to give another person an interest-free or low-interest loan of up to $100,000 without having interest income imputed to you; *see* the Planning Reminder on this page.

Planning Reminder

Gift Loans up to $100,000

If you give a child or other relative an interest-free loan to buy a home or start a business, the imputed interest rules will not apply provided (1) the total outstanding loan balance owed to you by the borrower at all times during the year does not exceed $100,000, and (2) the borrower's net investment income *(15.10)* is $1,000 or less.

If the borrower's net investment income for the year exceeds $1,000, the imputed interest rules apply, but the imputed interest is limited to his or her net investment income. If on any day during the year the outstanding loan balance owed to you by the borrower exceeds $100,000, interest will be imputed for that day under the regular rules. If a principal purpose of a loan is the avoidance of federal taxes, imputed interest is not limited to the borrower's net investment income.

EXAMPLES

1. At the beginning of 1997, you make a $45,000 interest-free loan to your son, payable on demand, which he uses for a down payment on a home. This is the only outstanding loan between you and your son. In 1997, your son's net investment income is $650. Since the loan does not exceed $100,000, and your son's net investment income does not exceed $1,000, the imputed interest rules do not apply; you do not have to report the "foregone interest" as interest income.

    For gift tax purposes, the foregone interest is a taxable gift. For example, assume that the applicable federal rate for 1997 is 6%. The taxable gift would be the foregone interest of $2,700 ($45,000 × 6%), but *see 33.1* for the annual gift tax exclusion of $10,000 per donee and other gift tax reporting details.

2. Same facts as in Example 1 above except that your son's net investment income is $1,500. Since net investment income exceeds $1,000, the imputed interest income rules apply, but the imputed interest is limited to the $1,500 of net investment income. Thus, although the foregone interest using the applicable federal rate is $2,700, you report only $1,500 of imputed interest income.

Exceptions for compensation-related loans. A $10,000 exception applies for compensation-related and corporate-shareholder loans, provided the principal purpose of the loan is not tax avoidance. Certain low-interest loans given to employees by employers to buy a new residence in a new job location are exempt from the imputed interest requirements.

Loans to continuing care facilities. Senior citizens moving into a community with a continuing care facility are required to pay a fee to the facility. The fee may be treated as a "loan" subject to the imputed interest rules to the extent the fee is refundable and it exceeds specified limits. These rules are discussed in Chapter 34.

Reporting imputed interest. Imputed interest is generally treated as transferred by the lender to the borrower and retransferred by the borrower to the lender on December 31 in the calendar year of imputation and is reported under the regular accounting method of the borrower and lender.

EXAMPLE

On January 1, 1997, Jones Company makes a $200,000 interest-free demand loan to Frank, an employee. The loan remains outstanding for the entire 1997 calendar year. Jones Company has a taxable year ending September 30. Frank is a calendar year taxpayer. For 1997, the imputed compensation payment and the imputed interest payment are treated as made on December 31, 1997.

With gift loans between individuals, interest computed during the borrower's taxable year is treated for both the lender and the borrower as earned on the last day of the borrower's taxable year. Treasury regulations to Section 7872 provide rules for figuring "foregone" interest. Where a demand loan is in effect for the entire calendar year, an "annual blended rate" issued by the IRS to simplify reporting may be used to compute the imputed interest. The blended rate is not available if the loan was not outstanding for the entire year or if the loan balance fluctuated; computations provided by Treasury regulations must be used.

Tax return statement requirements. A lender reporting imputed interest income or a borrower claiming an interest deduction must attach statements to their income tax returns reporting the interest, how it was calculated, and the names of the parties and their tax identification numbers.

4.32 Minimum Interest on Seller-Financed Sales

The law requires minimum interest charges for seller-financed sales. If the minimum rate is not charged, the IRS imputes interest at the minimum applicable rate requiring both buyer and seller to treat part of the purchase price as interest even though it is not called interest in the sales contract. Generally, interest at the applicable federal rate (AFR) must be charged; *see* the chart at the end of this section for minimum required rates. For example, investment property is sold on the installment basis for $100,000 and the parties fail to charge adequate interest. Assume the IRS imputes interest of $5,000. For tax purposes, $95,000 is allocated to the sale of the property and the principal amount of the debt; the balance is imputed interest of $5,000, taxable to the seller and deductible by the buyer if allowed under the rules of Chapter 15.

However, when the property is *personal-use* property, such as a residence to be used by the buyer, imputed interest rules do not apply to the buyer. Thus, the buyer may not deduct the imputed interest. His or her deduction is limited to the payment of interest stated in the contract if a deduction is allowed under the home mortgage interest rules in Chapter 15.

Two statute classes. The minimum or imputed interest rules are covered by two Internal Revenue Code statutes: Sections 1274 and 483. Under both, the same minimum interest rates apply but the timing of interest reporting is different, as discussed below.

Section 483 applies to any payment due more than six months after the date of sale under a contract which calls for some or all payments more than one year after the date of sale. If the sales price cannot exceed $3,000, Section 483 does not apply. Transactions within Section 483 are sales or exchanges of: (1) principal residences; (2) any property if total payments, including interest and any other consideration to be received by the seller, cannot exceed $250,000; (3) farms if the total price is $1 million or less; and (4) sales of land between family members to the extent the aggregate sales price of all sales between the same parties in the same year is $500,000 or less.

If the selling price exceeds the respective $250,000, $1 million, or $500,000 amount listed in (2) through (4) above, the sale is subject to Section 1274 reporting rules provided some or all payments are due more than six months after the date of sale. Section 1274 also applies to all other transactions where neither the debt instrument nor the property being sold is publicly traded as long as some payments are deferred more than six months.

Timing of interest reporting. One important practical difference between the two statutes covering minimum interest involves the timing of the reporting and deducting of interest.

Under Section 483, a seller and lender use their regular reporting method for imputed interest. For a cash-basis seller, interest is taxed when received; a cash-basis buyer deducts interest when paid if a deduction is allowable. However, if too much interest is allocated to a payment period, the excess interest is treated as prepaid interest, and the deduction is postponed to the year or years interest is earned. Section 483 also describes imputed interest as unstated interest.

Under Section 1274, the interest element is generally reported by both buyer and seller according to the OID accrual rules, even if they otherwise report on the cash basis. Where the seller financing is below an annual threshold ($2,659,900 for 1997 sales), the parties can elect the cash method to report the interest regardless of the OID and accrual rules if: (1) the seller-lender is on a cash-basis method and is not a dealer of the property sold; and (2) the seller and buyer jointly elect to use the cash method. The cash-basis election binds any cash-basis successor of the buyer or seller. If the lender transfers his interest to an accrual-basis taxpayer, the election no longer applies; interest is thereafter taxed under the accrual-method rules. The OID rules also do not apply to a cash-basis buyer of personal-use property; here, the cash-basis debtor deducts only payments of interest required by the contract, assuming a deduction is allowed under the home mortgage rules of Chapter 15.

Figuring Applicable Federal Rate (AFR). There is no imputed interest if the sales contract provides for interest that is at least equal to the AFR. *See* the chart on the next page for determining the AFR.

Assumptions of loans. The imputed interest rules of Sections 1274 and 483 do not generally apply to debt instruments assumed as part of a sale or exchange, or if the property is taken subject to the debt, provided that neither the terms of the debt instrument nor the nature of the transactions are changed.

Important: In planning deferred or installment sales, review Treasury regulations to the Internal Revenue Code Sections 483 and 1274 for further examples and details.

Minimum Interest Rate for Seller Financing

Type	Description
Applicable federal rates	The IRS determines the AFR rates which are published at the beginning of each month in the Internal Revenue Bulletin. There are three AFR rates depending on the length of the contract: *Short-term AFR*—A term of three years or less. *Mid-term AFR*—A term of over three years but not over nine years. *Long-term AFR*—A term of over nine years. The parties may choose the lowest AFR for the three-month period ending with the month in which a binding written sales contract is entered into. Thus, if the AFR for either of the prior two months is lower than the AFR for the month of contract, the lowest of the three AFRs applies. If insufficient interest is charged, the total unstated interest is allocated to payments under an OID computation.
9% safe harbor rate	If seller financing in 1997 is $3,723,800 or less, the minimum required interest is the lower of 9% compounded semiannually and the applicable federal rate (AFR). The amount of seller financing is the stated principal amount under the contract. If the seller-financed amount exceeds $3,723,800, the minimum interest rate is 100% of the AFR. For sales after 1997, the threshold for the 9% safe harbor will be indexed for inflation. The 9% safe harbor provides a benefit only if it is less than the AFR, but in recent years the AFR has been lower than 9%. Thus, until prevailing interest rates increase, charging interest at the AFR will allow a lower rate than the 9% safe harbor. IRS regulations allow the parties to use an interest rate lower than the AFR if it is shown that the borrower could obtain a loan on an arm's-length basis at lower interest.
Seller-financed sale-leaseback transactions	Interest equal to 110% of AFR must be charged.
Sales of land between family members	To the extent that the sales price does not exceed $500,000 during a calendar year, the minimum interest rate is 6%, compounded semiannually. To prevent multiple sales from being used to avoid the $500,000 limit, the $500,000 ceiling applies to all land sales between family members during the same year. To the extent that the $500,000 sales price limit is exceeded, the general 9% or 100% of AFR rules apply.

Chapter 5

Reporting Property Sales

New tax rate and holding period rules apply to sales of capital gain property in 1997. The new rules require that you organize your 1997 sales according to specified sales periods so that you may take advantage of the lower tax rates for long-term capital gains allowed by the new law. The new rules are explained in *5.2*.

Capital losses for 1997 are deductible from capital gains and up to $3,000 of ordinary income, $1,500 if you are married filing separately. Losses exceeding the $3,000 or $1,500 limit may be carried over to 1998; *see 5.3*.

Sales of capital assets are reported on Schedule D. This includes most assets held for investment or personal purposes; *see 5.1*. If in 1997 you sold property and will be receiving payments in a later year, you may report the sale as an installment sale on Form 6252 and spread the tax on your gain over the installment period; *see 5.25*. Sales of business assets are reported on Form 4797. As discussed in *44.8*, most assets used in a business are considered Section 1231 assets, and capital gain or ordinary loss treatment may apply depending upon the result of a netting computation made on Form 4797 for all such assets sold during the year.

Special types of sale situations are detailed in other chapters. *See* Chapter 29 for the home sale exclusion and tax deferral opportunities available on the sale of a principal residence. *See* Chapter 32 for figuring gain or loss on the sale of mutual-fund shares.

Tax-free exchanges of property are discussed in Chapter 6.

Figuring Capital Gains and Losses

5.1 Reporting Sales and Exchanges of Property

The tax treatment of gains and losses is not the same for all types of property sales. Tax reporting generally depends on your purpose in holding the property, as shown in the table below.

When capital gain or loss treatment does not apply. As the table below indicates, certain sales do not qualify for capital gain or loss treatment. Business inventory and property held for sale to customers are not capital assets. Depreciable business and rental property are not capital assets, but you may still have capital gain on the sale, depending on the netting computation for Section 1231 assets discussed at *44.8*.

Although assets held for *personal* use, such as a car or vacation home, are technically capital assets, you may not deduct a capital loss on their sale, even though profits are capital gain.

Certain other assets held for investment or personal use are excluded by law from the capital asset category. These include copyrights, literary or musical compositions, letters, memoranda, or similar property that: (1) you created by your personal efforts, or (2) were acquired as a gift from the person who created the property or for whom the property was prepared or produced. Also excluded are letters, memoranda, or similar property prepared or produced for you by someone else. Finally, U.S. government publications obtained from the government for free or for less than the normal sales price do not qualify as capital assets.

Gains and Losses from Sales and Exchanges of Property

If you sell—	Your gain is—	Your loss is—	Reported on—
Stocks, mutual-fund shares, bonds, and land held for investment.	*Capital gain.* Net short-term capital gains are subject to ordinary income tax rates and lower rates apply to mid-term and long-term capital gains; *see 5.2.*	*Capital loss.* Capital losses are deductible from capital gains with only $3,000 of any excess deductible from ordinary income, $1,500 if married filing separately; *see 5.3.*	Schedule D
Business inventory held for sale to customers. Also, accounts or notes receivable acquired in the ordinary course of business or from the sale of inventory or property held for sale to customers, or acquired for services as an employee.	*Ordinary income.* Such property is excluded by law from the definition of capital assets.	*Ordinary loss.* Ordinary loss is not subject to the $3,000 deduction limit imposed on capital losses. However, passive loss restrictions of Chapter 10 may defer the time when certain ordinary losses are deductible.	Schedule C if self-employed; Schedule F if a farmer; Form 1065 for a business operated as a partnership; Form 1120 or 1120S for an incorporated business.
Depreciable residential rental property or trucks, autos, computers, machinery, fixtures, or equipment used in your business.	*Capital gain or ordinary income.* Section 1231 as explained in *44.8* determines whether gain is taxable as ordinary income or capital gain.	*Ordinary loss if there is a net Section 1231 loss; see 44.8.* However, if you are considered to be an investor in a passive activity, *see 10.12* and *10.13*.	Form 4797
Vacation home, car, jewelry, furniture, art objects, and coin or stamp collection held for personal use.	*Capital gain.* Where an asset is held both for personal and business use, such as an auto, the asset is treated as two separate assets for purposes of figuring gain or loss; *see 44.12.* Tax on all or part of a profit from a sale of a principal residence may be avoided or deferred; *see* Chapter 29.	*Not deductible.* Losses on assets held for personal use are not deductible although profits are taxable. However, a sale of personal assets by an executor of an estate is assumed to be profit-seeking. The estate may claim a loss on the sale of a personal asset. If you sell your principal residence, the sale is reported on Form 2119 whether you have a gain or loss. Taxable gain, if any, is figured on Form 2119 and is also entered on Schedule D.	

Stock is generally treated as a capital asset, but losses on *Section 1244 stock* of qualifying small businesses may be claimed as ordinary losses on Form 4797, rather than on Schedule D as capital losses subject to the $3,000 annual deduction limit ($1,500 if married filing separately) for losses in excess of capital gains. The ordinary loss rules for Section 1244 stock are in Chapter 30 .

Home sale exclusion or deferral. If you qualify under the rules explained in Chapter 29, you may be able to avoid tax on all or part of the gain from the sale of your principal residence.

Small business stock deferral or exclusion. As discussed in 5.6, taxable gains from the sale of publicly traded securities may be postponed if you roll over the proceeds to stock or a partnership interest in an SSBIC (specialized small business investment company). Furthermore, under a new law, gains from the sale after August 5, 1997, of qualifying small business stock may be deferred by making a tax-free rollover to other small business stock.

Gain on the sale of qualifying small business stock issued after August 10, 1993, and held for more than five years, will qualify for a 50% exclusion.

Like-kind exchanges of business or investment property. Exchanges of *like-kind* business or investment property are subject to special rules that allow gain to be deferred, generally until you sell the property received in the exchange; *see 6.1.* When property received in a tax-free exchange is held until death, the unrecognized gain escapes tax forever because the basis of property in the hands of an heir is generally the fair market value of the property at the date of death; *see* 5.21. A loss on a like-kind exchange is not deductible.

5.2 New Capital Gains Rates and Holding Periods

The 1997 Tax Act rewards long-term investors with a lower tax rate on net long-term capital gains while at the same time complicating tax reporting by changing the "long term" holding period and creating a new "mid-term" holding period for sales after July 28, 1997.

The new capital gain rate is 20% for taxpayers whose regular top tax bracket is 28%, 31%, 36%, or 39.6%. The new capital gain rate is 10% for taxpayers in the 15% bracket. These rates apply to (1) sales after May 6, 1997, and before July 29, 1997, if the property was held more than 12 months, and (2) sales after July 28, 1997, if the property was held more than 18 months. The new holding period rules for sales after May 6, 1997, are explained below.

Gains from collectibles such as art, antiques, rugs or coins are not eligible for the new rates and remain subject to the 28% maximum rate that applied under prior law. On the sale of depreciable real estate, the gain allocable to depreciation is taxed at a 25% rate; only gains exceeding depreciation are eligible for the new 20% or 10% rate. On the sale of qualifying small business stock *(see 5.6)* issued after August 10, 1993, and held more than five years, 50% of the capital gain is excludable from income and the taxable 50% is subject to a maximum rate of 28%; the new 20% or 10% rate is not applicable.

The new law does not change the deductibility of capital losses, although the characterization of losses as short term, mid-term, or long term affects the way they are grouped with capital gains on Schedule D. Capital losses remain fully deductible against capital gains, with only $3,000 of any excess ($1,500 if married filing separately) deductible from other types of income.

Key Dates for Reporting 1997 Sales

The date of sale and your holding period will determine the tax treatment of your 1997 sales on Schedule D:

Sales before May 7, 1997. You have short-term gain or loss if you held the property for one year or less and long-term gain or loss if you held it more than one year. The maximum tax rate is 28% on *net capital gains*, the excess of long-term gains over short-term losses realized during this period.

Sales after May 6, 1997, and before July 29, 1997. Gains on assets held for more than one year generally qualify for the new law rate of 20%, 10% for those in the 15% bracket. There are exceptions for gains on collectibles or gains attributable to real estate depreciation, which remain subject to a maximum 28% rate.

Gains on capital assets held for one year or less are short-term gains, fully taxable at your regular top rate.

Sales after July 28, 1997. For sales after July 28, 1997, there are three possible tax results based on the following holding periods: long term, mid-term, and short term.

1. Gains on property held for one year or less are treated as short-term capital gains, fully taxable at your regular top rate.

2. Gains on property held for more than one year but not more than 18 months are treated as *mid-term gains* subject to a maximum 28% tax rate. Thus, when you sell for more than one year but less than 18 months, your gains are treated as they would be if the law had not changed. If your regular top bracket exceeds 28%, you benefit from the 28% maximum rate. The fact that you do not meet the new long-term holding period of more than 18 months will not result in your gains being taxed at your regular 31%, 36%, or 39.6% top rate, as long as the more-than-one-year holding period is met.

If your regular top bracket is 28% or 15%, mid-term gains are taxed at your regular rate, the same way as your short-term capital gains.

3. Gains on assets held over 18 months are subject to the new long-term gain rate of 20% or 10% (if in the 15% bracket), with the exception of collectibles gain or gain from depreciation on real estate.

Revised Schedule D for 1997. When this book went to press, the IRS had not yet released a revised version of Schedule D for 1997 that reflects the new law. If available, Schedule D will be in the Supplement to this book, along with any updates on the reporting rules for 1997 capital gains and losses.

Sales after 1997. The capital gain rules discussed above for sales after July 28, 1997, will apply in 1998 and later years, with one further change scheduled for assets purchased after December 31, 2000. If property purchased after 2000 is held for more than five years, the capital gain tax rate will be further reduced to 18%, 8% for those in the 15% bracket.

EXAMPLE

Jones, who is in the 31% tax bracket, made the following sales of stock in 1997:

- On May 2, he sold 100 shares of Tech. Inc. stock, held for 13 months, at a gain of $2,000.
- On May 9, he sold 200 shares of Best Co. stock, held for 13 months, at a gain of $3,000.
- On July 29, he sold 100 shares of Orange Co. stock, held for 14 months, at a gain of $4,000.
- On August 14, he sold 500 shares of Steel Inc. stock, held for 19 months, at a gain of $5,000.
- On September 10, he sold 100 shares of Amalgamated Inc. stock, held for 11 months, at a gain of $1,500.

Jones's gains are subject to the following tax rates:

Lot sold—	New 20% rate—	28% rate—	31% rate—
May 2		X	
May 9	X		
July 29		X	
August 14	X		
September 10			X

5.3 Capital Losses and Carryovers

Capital losses are fully deductible against capital gains on Schedule D, and if losses exceed gains, you may deduct the excess from up to $3,000 of other income on Form 1040. Net losses over $3,000 are carried over to future years. The $3,000 limit is reduced to $1,500 for married persons filing separately. In preparing your 1997 Schedule D, remember to include any capital loss carryovers from your 1996 return.

Death of taxpayer cuts off carryover. If an individual dies and on his or her final income tax return net capital losses, including prior year carryovers, exceed the $3,000 or $1,500 limit, the excess may not be deducted by the individual's estate. If the deceased individual was married, his or her unused individual losses may not be carried over by the surviving spouse; *see 5.4.*

Carryover if you have "negative" taxable income. A special computation may increase your carryover deduction where you have "negative" taxable income. If without considering personal exemptions you have a "negative taxable income," a net capital loss may not provide a tax benefit because other deductions have reduced taxable income to zero. In this case, you may be allowed a capital loss carryover for all or part of your net capital loss.

To determine the amount of the carryover, follow the steps of the worksheet in the Form 1040 instructions. You first will figure how much of your net loss is treated as "used up" in the current year. The balance of the loss, if any, is carried over to the next year.

5.4 Capital Losses of Married Couples

On a joint return, the capital asset transactions of both spouses are combined and reported on one Schedule D. A carryover loss of one spouse may offset capital gains of the other spouse on a joint return. Where you and your spouse separately incur net capital losses, $3,000 is the maximum capital loss deduction that may be claimed for the combined losses on your joint return. This limitation may not be avoided by filing separate returns. If you file separately, the deduction limit for each return is $1,500. Neither of you may deduct any of the other's losses on a separate return.

> **EXAMPLE**
>
> In 1997, you individually incurred net long-term capital losses of $5,000 and your spouse incurred net long-term losses of $4,000. If you file separate returns, the maximum amount deductible from ordinary income on each return is $1,500. The balance must be carried forward to 1998.
>
> If you had net losses below the $1,500 limit, you could not claim any part of your spouse's losses on your separate return.

Death of a spouse. The IRS holds that if a capital loss is incurred by a spouse on his or her own property and that spouse dies, the surviving spouse may not claim any unused loss carryover on a separate return.

> **EXAMPLE**
>
> In 1994, Alex Smith realized a substantial net long-term capital loss on separately owned property, which was reported on a 1994 joint return filed with his wife, Anne. Part of the excess loss was carried over to the couple's 1995 joint return, and in 1996, before the carryover loss was used up, Alex died. Anne could claim the unused carryover, up to the $3,000 limit, on a joint return filed for 1996, the year of Alex's death. However, any remaining loss carryover to 1997 or later years is lost. Although the loss was originally reported on a joint return, Anne may claim only her allocable share of the loss on her individual returns for years after 1996. However, since the loss property was owned solely by Alex, no part of the loss is allocable to Anne.

5.5 Losses May Be Disallowed on Sales to Related Persons

A loss on a sale to certain related taxpayers may not be deductible, even though you make the sale in good faith, the sale is involuntary (for example, a member of your family forecloses a mortgage on your property), or you sell through a public stock exchange and related persons buy the equivalent property; *see* Examples 1 and 2 below.

Related parties. Losses are not allowed on sales between you and your brothers or sisters (whether by the whole or half blood), parents, grandparents, children, or grandchildren. Furthermore, no loss may be claimed on a sale to your spouse; the tax-free exchange rules of *6.6* apply.

A loss is disallowed where the sale is made to your sister-in-law, as nominee of your brother. This sale is deemed to be between you and your brother. But you may deduct the loss on sales to your spouse's relative (for example, your brother-in-law or spouse's step-parent) even if you and your spouse file a joint return.

The Tax Court has allowed a loss on a direct sale to a son-in-law. In a private ruling, the IRS allowed a loss on a sale of a business to a son-in-law where it was shown that his wife (the seller's daughter) did not own an interest in the company. Losses have been disallowed upon withdrawal from a joint venture and from a partnership conducted by members of a family. Family members have argued that losses should be allowed where the sales were motivated by family hostility. The Tax Court ruled that family hostility may not be considered; losses between proscribed family members are disallowed in all cases.

Losses are barred on sales between an individual and a controlled partnership or controlled corporation (where that individual owns more than 50% in value of the outstanding stock or capital interests).

 Filing Tip

Carryovers From Joint or Separate Returns

If you or your spouse has a capital loss carryover from a year in which separate returns were filed, and you are now filing a joint return, the carryovers from the separate returns may be combined on the joint return. If you previously filed jointly and are now filing separately, any loss carryover from the joint return may be claimed only on the separate return of the spouse who originally incurred the loss.

Losses may also be disallowed in sales between controlled companies, a trust and its creator, a trust and a beneficiary, a partnership and a corporation controlled by the same person (more than 50% ownership), or a tax-exempt organization and its founder. Under the 1997 Tax Act, an estate and a beneficiary of that estate are also treated as related parties, except where a sale is in satisfaction of a pecuniary bequest; this rule applies to taxable years beginning after August 5, 1997. Check with your tax counselor whenever you plan to sell property at a loss to a buyer who may fit one of these descriptions.

Related buyer's resale at profit. Sometimes, the disallowed loss may be saved. When you sell to a related party who resells the property at a profit, he or she gets the benefit of your disallowed loss. Your purchaser's gain up to the amount of your disallowed loss is not taxed; *see* Example 5 below.

EXAMPLES

1. You sell 100 shares of A Co. stock to your brother for $1,000. They cost you $5,000. You may not deduct your $4,000 loss.

2. The stock investments of a mother and son were managed by the same investment counselor. But neither the son nor mother had any right or control over the other's securities. The counselor followed separate and independent policies for each. Without the son's or his mother's prior approval, the counselor carried out the following transactions: (1) on the same day, he sold at a loss the son's stock in four companies and bought the same stock for the mother's account; and (2) he sold at a loss the son's stock in a copper company, and 28 days later bought the same stock for his mother. The losses of the first sale were disallowed, but not the losses of the copper stock sale because of the time break of 28 days. However, the court did not say how much of a minimum time break is needed to remove a sale-purchase transaction from the rule disallowing losses between related parties.

3. In calculating the stock owned, not only must the stock held in your own name be taken into account, but also that owned by your family. You also add (1) the proportionate share of any stock held by a corporation, estate, trust, or partnership in which you have an interest as a shareholder, beneficiary, or partner; and (2) any other stock owned individually by your partner.

4. You own 30% of the stock of a company. A trust in which you have a one-half beneficial interest owns 30%. Your partner owns 10% of the stock of the same company. You are deemed the owner of 55% of the stock of that company (30%, plus one-half of 30%, plus 10%).

5. Smith bought securities in 1990 which cost $10,000. In 1993, he sold them to his sister for $8,000. The $2,000 loss was not deductible by Smith. His sister's basis for the securities is $8,000. In 1997, she sells them for $9,000. The $1,000 gain is not taxed because it is washed out by part of the brother's disallowed loss. If she sold the securities for $11,000, then only $1,000 of the $3,000 gain would be taxed.

5.6 Deferring or Excluding Gain on Small Business Stock Investment

To encourage investments in certain "small" businesses, the tax law provides special gain deferral provisions, discussed below.

Rollover from small business stock to small business stock. Gain on the sale after August 5, 1997, of qualifying small business stock held for more than six months may be rolled over tax free to other small business stock. The rollover must be made within 60 days of the sale. To qualify as a small business, the gross assets of the corporation must be no more than $50 million when the stock is issued. An active business requirement must also be met. If the reinvestment in a qualifying small business is for less than the sale proceeds, your gain is taxed to the extent of the difference. Your basis in the small business stock acquired during the 60-day period is reduced by the amount of the deferred gain.

To elect deferral, follow the the instructions to Schedule D.

Rollover from publicly traded securities to SSBIC. You may be able to defer taxable gain on the sale of publicly traded securities provided the sale proceeds are rolled over within 60 days into common stock or a partnership interest in a "specialized small business investment com-

Planning Reminder

Possible Exclusion In 1998 or Later Years

A 50% exclusion from income will be available for sales of qualifying small business stock issued after August 10, 1993, provided the stock is held for more than five years before the sale. A qualifying small business is one eligible for rollover treatment; *see 5.6.* Under the 1997 Tax Act, 42% of the excluded gain will be treated as a preference item for purposes of the alternative minimum tax (*see* Chapter 23).

pany," or SSBIC. The entire gain is deferrable if the cost of your SSBIC stock or partnership interest is at least equal to the sale proceeds. If the SSBIC investment is less than the sale proceeds, your gain is taxed to the extent of the difference.

To elect deferral, you must report the sale on Schedule D, and attach an explanation of your SSBIC investment; follow the Schedule D instructions. The deferred gain reduces the basis of your SSBIC stock or partnership interest.

An SSBIC is a small business (partnership or corporation) licensed by the Small Business Administration to invest in small businesses which are owned by socially or economically disadvantaged individuals.

Limit on deferrable amount. The amount of gain you may annually elect to roll over to an SSBIC is limited to $50,000, or $25,000 if you are married filing separately. There is a lifetime limit of $500,000, or $250,000 if married filing separately.

5.7 Sample Entries of Capital Asset Sales

You report many different types of transactions on Schedule D: sales of securities; mutual-fund shares; worthless personal loans; sales of stock rights and warrants; sales of land held for investment; and in some cases sales of personal residences.

Different types of Schedule D entries are illustrated in the sample worksheet on the next page. The entries correspond to the following transactions. For each transaction, assume that broker's commissions and state and local transfer taxes, if any, are added to the cost of the stock. The Supplement to this book will include the 1997 Schedule D.

1. *Sale of stock (short-term gain)*—You bought 200 shares of Buma Rubber stock on July 22, 1997, for $400. On October 7, 1997, you sell the 200 shares for $600.

2. *Sale of stock received as a gift (short-term loss)*—Your father gave you a gift of 100 shares of Ajax Auto stock on March 12, 1997, which he had bought on February 15, 1990, for $4,000. The value of the stock at the time of the gift was $3,000. You sell the stock on March 25, 1997, for $2,500. Since the value of the stock at the time of the gift was less than your father's basis, your basis for loss purposes is the date-of-gift value *(5.21)* and the holding period begins on the day after the date of the gift *(5.16)*.

3. *Worthless personal loan (short-term loss)*—You loaned $500 to your friend, Dan Debtor, on May 1, 1990. He was adjudged bankrupt on March 15, 1997. A worthless personal debt is deducted as a short-term capital loss; *see 5.9*. The IRS requires that you explain the deduction in a statement attached to your return. The statement should show: (1) the nature of the debt; (2) the name of the debtor and his or her relationship, if any, to you; (3) when the debt was due; (4) how you tried to collect it; and (5) how you determined it was worthless.

4. *Sale of mutual-fund shares (short-term gain)*—You bought 160 shares of the XYZ Mutual Fund on February 4, 1997, for $4,000. On August 5, you bought another 240 shares for $6,480. You sell 200 of the shares on September 23, 1997, for $6,000. You decide to use the average basis method (single category) to figure the basis of the sold shares. Your average basis is $26.20 per share, the total cost basis of $10,480 divided by 400 shares. Thus, your basis for the 200 sold shares is $5,240 (200 × $26.20). *See* Chapter 32 for further details on basis of mutual-fund shares.

5. *Sale of stock (long-term gain)*—You bought 100 shares of Acme Steel stock on October 1, 1991, for $5,000. On December 12, 1997, you sell the 100 shares for $6,000.

6. *Sale of stock received as a gift (long-term gain)*—Your father gave you a gift of 100 shares of Crown Auto stock on March 18, 1997, which he had bought on May 18, 1983, for $4,000. The fair market value of the stock at the time of the gift was $8,800. On March 24, 1997, you sell the stock for $9,000. Your father paid no gift tax under the annual $10,000 exclusion *(33.1)*. Since the date-of-gift value ($8,800) exceeded your father's basis ($4,000), your basis is your father's basis of $4,000 *(5.21)* and your holding period includes your father's holding period *(5.16)*.

7. *Worthless bond*—On August 10, 1981, you bought a $5,000 bond of Rail Co. at par. The bond became completely worthless during 1997; *see 5.8*.

IRS review. The IRS compares the proceeds that are reported on Schedule D with the selling prices reported on Form 1099-B and Form 1099-S. If you receive an incorrect Form 1099-B or 1099-S, report the proper amount and attach a statement explaining the difference between the amount you entered on Schedule D and the amount shown on the Form 1099.

Worksheet: Sales of Capital Assets

Short-Term Capital Gains and Losses—

(a) Description of property (Example: 100 sh. XYZ Co.)	(b) Date acquired (Mo., day, yr.)	(c) Date sold (Mo., day, yr.)	(d) Sales price (see page D-3)	(e) Cost or other basis (see page D-3)	(f) LOSS If (e) is more than (d), subtract (d) from (e)	(g) GAIN If (d) is more than (e), subtract (e) from (d)
200 sh - Buma Rubber	7-22-97	10-7-97	600	400		200
100 sh - Ajax Auto	3-12-97	3-25-97	2,500	3,000	500	
) Dan Debtor	Worthless Loan —			Statement Attached	500	
) XYZ 200 sh Mutual Fund	"Various"	9-23-97	6,000	5,240		760

Long-Term Capital Gains and Losses—

(a)	(b)	(c)	(d)	(e)	(f)	(g)
(5) 100 sh - Acme Steel	10-1-91	12-12-97	6,000	5,000		1,000
(6) 100 sh - Crown Auto	5-18-83	3-24-97	9,000	4,000		5,000
(7) Worthless Bond Rail Co.	8-10-81	Worthless		5,000	5,000	

Worthless Securities and Bad Debt Deductions

5.8 Worthless Securities

You may deduct as a capital loss on Schedule D the cost basis of securities that have become worthless in 1997. Capital loss treatment applies unless ordinary loss treatment is available for worthless Section 1244 stock; *see* Chapter 30.

A loss of worthless securities is deductible only in the year the securities become completely worthless. The loss may not be deducted in any other year. Because it is sometimes difficult to determine the year in which a security becomes completely worthless, the law allows you to file a refund claim within seven years from the due date of the return for the proper year (the year the security actually became completely worthless).

You may not claim a loss for partially worthless stock. However, if there is a market for it, sell the stock and deduct the loss.

To support a deduction for 1997, you must show:

1. The stock had some value in 1996. That is, you must be ready to show that the stock did not become worthless in a year prior to 1997. If you learn that the stock did become worthless in a prior year, file an amended return for that year; see Filing Pointer on refunds in the next column.
2. The stock became totally worthless in 1997. You must be able to present facts fixing the time of loss during this year. For example, the company went bankrupt, stopped doing business, and is insolvent. Despite evidence of worthlessness, such as insolvency, the stock may be considered to have some value if the company continues to do business, or there are plans to reorganize the company. No deduction may be claimed for a partially worthless corporate bond.

If you are making payments on a negotiable note you used to buy the stock that became worthless and you are on the cash-basis method, your payments are deductible losses in the years the payments are made, rather than in the year the stock became worthless.

If the security is a bond, note, certificate, or other evidence of a debt incurred by a corporation, the loss is deducted as a capital loss, provided the obligation is in registered form or has attached interest coupons. A loss on a worthless corporate obligation is always deemed to have been sustained on the last day of the year, regardless of when the company failed during the year.

If the obligation is not issued with interest coupons or in registered form, or if it is issued by an individual, the loss is treated as a bad debt. If you received the obligation in a business transaction, the loss is fully deductible. You may also make a claim for a partially worthless business bad debt. If it is a nonbusiness debt, the loss is a capital loss and no claim may be made for partial worthlessness; *see* 5.9.

When to deduct worthless stock. If at the end of 1997 a company is in financial trouble but you are not sure whether its condition is hopeless, it is advisable to claim the deduction for 1997 to protect your claim. This advice was given by a court: "The taxpayer is at times in a very difficult position in determining in what year to claim a loss. The only safe practice, we think, is to claim a loss for the earliest year when it may possibly be allowed and to renew the claim in subsequent years if there is a reasonable chance of its being applicable for those years."

If you claim the deduction for 1997 and it turns out that complete worthlessness did not occur until a later year, claim the deduction for the proper year and then file an amended return for 1997 to eliminate the deduction.

Long-term or short-term loss. A sale is presumed to have occurred at the end of the year, regardless of when worthlessness actually occurred during the year.

EXAMPLE

You bought 100 shares of Z Co. stock on July 1, 1980. On March 15, 1997, the stock is considered wholly worthless. The loss is deemed to have been incurred on December 31, 1997. The loss is deducted as a long-term capital loss; the holding period is from July 2, 1980, to December 31, 1997.

Ordinary loss on Small Business Investment Company (SBIC) stock. On Form 4797, investors may take ordinary loss deductions for losses on the worthlessness or sale of SBIC

Filing Tip

Refund Deadline for Worthless Stock

You have seven years from the due date of your return to claim a refund based on a deduction of a bad debt or worthless security.

For example, if you have held securities that you learn became worthless in 1990, you still have until April 15, 1998, to file for a refund of 1990 taxes by claiming a deduction for the worthless securities on an amended return (Form 1040X) for 1990.

Planning Reminder

Selling Before the Security Becomes Worthless

To claim a deduction for worthless stock or bonds, you must be able to prove that the stock became completely worthless in the year for which you are claiming the deduction. Sometimes you can avoid the problem of proving worthlessness by selling while there is still a market for the security. For example, a company is on the verge of bankruptcy, but in 1998 there is some doubt about the complete worthlessness of its securities. You might sell the securities for whatever you can get for them and claim the loss on the sale. However, if the security became worthless in a prior year, say in 1997, a sale for a nominal sum in 1998 will not give you a deduction in 1998.

stock. The loss may also be treated as a business loss for net operating loss purposes. However, a loss realized on a short sale of SBIC stock is deductible as a capital loss. A Small Business Investment Company is a company authorized to provide small businesses with equity capital. Do not confuse investments in these companies with investments in small business stock (Section 1244 stock) discussed at Chapter 30.

S corporation stock. If an S corporation's stock becomes worthless during the taxable year, the basis in the stock is adjusted for the stockholder's share of corporate items of income, loss, and deductions before a deduction for worthlessness is claimed.

Bank deposit loss. If you lose funds in a bank that becomes insolvent, you may claim the loss as a nonbusiness bad debt *(5.9)*, a casualty loss *(18.4)*, or in some cases, an investment expense *(19.24)*.

5.9 Tax Consequences of Bad Debts

When you lend money or sell on credit and your debtor does not repay, you may deduct your loss. The type of deduction depends on whether the debt was incurred in a business or personal transaction. This distinction is important because business bad debts receive favored tax treatment.

Business bad debt. A business bad debt is fully deductible from gross income on Schedule C if you are self-employed, or on Schedule F if your business is farming. In addition, you may deduct partially worthless business debts. You must use the specific charge-off method for deducting business bad debts. If you use the accrual method for reporting income for services, you may be able to account for bad debts by not having to accrue income that you do not expect to collect; see IRS Publication 535 for details.

Examples of business debt transactions:

- You sell merchandise on credit and later the buyer becomes insolvent and does not pay.
- You are in the business of making loans and a loan goes bad.
- You sell your business, but retain some accounts receivable. Later, some of these become worthless.
- You liquidate your business and are unable to collect its outstanding accounts.
- You operate as a promoter of corporations.
- You finance your lessees, customers, or suppliers to help your business.
- You lend money to protect your professional and business reputation.
- You lend money to insure delivery of merchandise from a supplier.
- You make a loan to your employer to keep your job.

Nonbusiness bad debt. A nonbusiness bad debt is deducted as a short-term capital loss on Schedule D. This is a limited deduction. In 1997, you deduct it from capital gains, if any, and $3,000 of other income. Any excess is deductible as a capital loss carryover in 1998 and later years; see *5.3.* You may not deduct partially worthless nonbusiness bad debts. The debt must be totally worthless.

Examples of nonbusiness bad debts:

- You enter into a deal for profit which is not connected with your business; for example, debts arising from investments are nonbusiness bad debts.
- You make a personal loan to a family member or friend with a reasonable hope of recovery and are not in the business of making loans.
- You are assigned a debt that arose in the assignor's business. The fact that he or she could have deducted it as a business bad debt does not make it your business debt. A business debt must arise in your business.
- You pay liens filed against your property by mechanics or suppliers who have not been paid by your builder or contractor. Your payment is considered a deductible bad debt when there is no possibility of recovering reimbursement from the contractor and a judgment obtained against him or her is uncollectible.
- You lose a deposit on a house when the contractor becomes insolvent.
- You loan money to a corporation in which you are a shareholder, and your primary motivation is to protect your investment rather than your job; *see 5.11.*
- You had an uninsured savings account in a savings association which went into default; *see 18.4.*
- You are held secondarily liable on a mortgage debt assumed but not paid by a buyer of your home. Your payment to the bank or other holder of the mortgage is deductible as a bad debt if you cannot collect it from the buyer of the home.

 Caution

Accounts and Notes Receivable
You may claim a bad debt deduction for accounts and notes receivable on unpaid goods or services only if you have included the amount due as gross income. Thus, if a client or customer fails to pay a bill for services rendered, you do not have a deductible bad debt where you have not reported the amount as income.

5.10 Four Rules To Prove a Bad Debt Deduction

To determine whether you have a bad debt deduction in 1997, read the four rules explained below. Pay close attention to the fourth rule, which requires proof that the debt became worthless in the year the deduction is claimed. Your belief that your debt is bad, or the mere refusal of the debtor to pay, is not sufficient evidence. There must be an event, such as the debtor's bankruptcy, to fix the debt as worthless.

Rule 1. You must have a valid debt. You have no loss if your right to repayment is not fixed or depends upon some event which may not happen. Thus, advances to a corporation already insolvent are not valid debts. Nor are advances that are to be repaid only if the corporation has a profit. Voluntary payment of another's debt is also nondeductible. If usurious interest was charged on a worthless debt, and under state law the debt was void or voidable, the debt is not deductible as a bad debt. However, where the lender was in the business of lending money, a court allowed him to deduct the unpaid amounts as business losses.

If advances are made to a company that has lost outside borrowing sources and is thinly capitalized, with heavy debt-to-equity ratio, this indicates that the advances are actually capital contributions and not loans.

Rule 2. A debtor-creditor relationship must exist at the time the debt arose. You have a loss if there was a promise to repay at the time the debt was created and you had the right to enforce it. If the advance was a gift and you did not expect to be repaid, you may not take a deduction. Loans to members of your family, to a controlled corporation, or to a trust may be treated as gifts or contributions to capital.

Rule 3. The funds providing the loan or credit were previously reported as income or part of your capital. If you are on the cash basis, you may not deduct unpaid salary, rent, or fees. On the cash basis, you do not include these items in income until you are paid.

Rule 4. You must show that the debt became worthless during 1997. To prove the debt became worthless in 1997, you must show:

First, that the debt had some value at the end of the previous year (1996), and that there was a reasonable hope and expectation of recovering something on the debt. Your personal belief unsupported by other facts is not enough.

Second, that an identifiable event occurred in 1997—such as a bankruptcy proceeding—that caused you to conclude the debt was worthless. In the case of a business debt which has become partially worthless, you need evidence that the debt has declined in value. Additionally, reasonable collection steps must have been undertaken. That you cancel a debt does not make it worthless. You must still show that the debt was worthless when you cancelled it. You do not have to go to court to try to collect the debt if you can show that a court judgment would be uncollectible.

Third, that there is no reasonable hope the debt may have some value in a later year. You are not required to prove that there is no possibility of ever receiving some payment on your debt. You are not expected to be an extreme optimist.

Effect of statute of limitations. A debt is not deductible merely because a statute of limitations has run against the debt. Although the debtor has a legal defense against your demand for payment, he or she may still recognize the obligation to pay. A debt is deductible only in the year it becomes worthless. This event—for example, the debtor's insolvency—may have occurred even before the statute became effective. What if your debtor recognized his or her moral obligation to pay in spite of the expiration of the statute of limitations, but dies before paying? Your claim would be defeated if the executor raises the statute of limitations. You have a bad debt deduction in the year you made the claim against the estate.

Guarantor or endorsement losses as bad debts. If you guarantee a loan and must pay it off after the principal debtor defaults, your payment is deductible as a business bad debt if you had a business reason for the guarantee. For example, to protect a business relationship with a major client, you guarantee the client's loan. Your payment on the guarantee qualifies as a business bad debt. If as a result of your payment, you have a legal right to recover the amount from the client (right of subrogation or similar right), you may not claim a bad debt deduction unless that right is partially or totally worthless.

A loss on a guarantee may be a nonbusiness bad debt if you made the guarantee to protect an investment, such as where you are a main shareholder of a corporation and guarantee a bank loan to the company. No deduction is allowed if you guaranteed the loan as a favor to a relative or friend. *Bank deposit losses are discussed at 18.4.*

Planning Reminder

Debt Worthless Before Due

You do not have to wait until the debt is due in order to deduct a bad debt. Claim the deduction for the year that you can prove worthlessness occurred.

5.11 Loans by Stockholders

It is a common practice for stockholders to make loans to their corporations or to guarantee loans made by banks or other lenders. If the corporation fails and the stockholder is not repaid or has to make good on the guarantee, he or she is generally left with a nonbusiness bad debt (nonbusiness bad debts are deductible only as a short-term capital loss on Schedule D; *see 5.9*) unless he or she can prove that a business loan was made (business bad debts are fully deductible on Schedule C). To prove a business loan, the stockholder usually has to show one of these facts:

1. He or she is in the business of making loans and the loan was made in that capacity; or he or she is in the business of promoting corporations for a fee or for profits on their sale.
2. He or she made the loan to safeguard the business.
3. He or she wanted to protect his or her job with the company.

Court Decision

Loan to Protect Job

A Supreme Court test requires a shareholder-employee claiming a business bad debt deduction to show that the primary and dominant motive of the loan was to protect his or her job, rather than investment in the company; *see* the Examples at *5.11*.

EXAMPLES

1. To determine an executive's motive for making a loan, the Supreme Court reviewed his salary, outside income, investment in the company, and the size of his loan. His pay was $12,000 ($7,000 after tax); his outside income was $30,000. He had a $38,900 investment in the company and loaned it $165,000. On the basis of these figures, the Court concluded he could not have advanced $165,000 to protect an after-tax salary of $7,000. He was protecting his investment, not his job, and only a nonbusiness bad debt could be claimed.

2. Litwin founded several energy start-up companies after he retired in 1974 from the Litwin Corporation. In 1980, he founded AFS, to which he made loans of $150,000 and guaranteed another $350,000 of loans. AFS went bankrupt in 1984.

   A federal appeals court followed the Supreme Court's approach (Example 1) to determine that Litwin had an employment-related motive for the loans. His primary reason for setting up the company was to stay employed and remain "useful" to society. Given his background and advanced age, his best chance for ongoing employment was to start his own company. The majority of his time and energy was spent on AFS, even after he sold his controlling interest in the corporation and had only limited opportunities to capitalize on his remaining investment. True, Litwin deferred his salary for three years, but evidence showed that he intended to draw a salary in the future. Most importantly, Litwin took a sizeable risk when he personally guaranteed loans that exceeded his investment in AFS. The court noted that a taxpayer is probably not attempting to protect an investment in a company when guaranteed loans far exceed the value of the investment.

Loan to key employees.   A loan by a stockholder to key employees was held to be a business bad debt in the following case.

EXAMPLE

Carter, the president and majority owner of two corporations, loaned money to two key employees to buy stock in the corporations. He wanted to guarantee the employees' future participation in the company. Both corporations went bankrupt, and the employees defaulted on the loans. Carter deducted both loans as business bad debts, contending he was protecting his job.

The IRS argued he had a nonbusiness bad debt; he was merely protecting his investment as a stockholder. The Tax Court disagreed. He made the loans to encourage the future of a business which would provide him salary income rather than dividends or appreciation on his stock.

5.12 Family Bad Debts

The IRS views loans to relatives, especially to children and parents, as gifts, so that it is rather difficult to deduct family bad debts.

To overcome the presumption of a gift when you advance money to a relative, take the same steps you would in making a business loan. Take a note, set a definite payment date, and require interest and collateral. If the relative fails to pay, make an attempt to collect. Failure to enforce collection of a family debt is viewed by the courts as evidence of a gift, despite the taking of notes and the receipt of interest.

Husband's default on child support—a basis for wife's deductible bad debt? A wife who supports her children when her husband defaults on court-ordered support payments may consider claiming her expenses as a nonbusiness bad debt deduction, arguing that her position is similar to a guarantor who pays a creditor when the principal debtor defaults. The IRS does not agree with the grounds of such a claim and will disallow the deduction; its position is supported by the Tax Court.

The federal appeals court for the Ninth Circuit left open the possibility that such a claim may have merit if a wife can show: (1) what she spent on the children; and (2) that her husband's obligation to support was worthless in the year the deduction is claimed.

The Tax Court has subsequently reiterated its position that defaulted child support payments are not a basis for a bad debt deduction. Following these Tax Court decisions, the IRS also announced its continuing opposition to the Ninth Circuit's suggestion that a deduction may be possible. The IRS holds that since the support obligation of the defaulting spouse is imposed directly by the divorce court, the other parent who pays support to make up for the arrearage has no "basis" to support a bad debt deduction.

Holding Period for Capital Assets

5.13 Counting the Months in Your Holding Period

The period of time you own a capital asset before its sale or exchange determines whether capital gain or loss is short term, long term, or mid-term.

Rules for counting the holding period:

1. A holding period is figured in months and fractions of months.
2. The beginning date of a holding month is generally the day after the asset was acquired. The same numerical date of each following month starts a new holding month regardless of the number of days in the preceding month.
3. The last day of the holding period is the day on which the asset is sold.

As a rule of thumb, use the numerical date on which you acquired the asset as the numerical date ending a holding month in each following month. However, if you acquire an asset on the last day of a month, a holding month ends on the last day of a following calendar month, regardless of the number of days in each month.

> **EXAMPLES**
> 1. On September 11, 1997, you buy stock. The holding months begin on September 12, October 12, November 12, December 12, and end on October 11, November 11, December 11, etc. Under the new law for sales after July 28, 1997, long-term capital gain rate apply to property held for more than 18 months; *see 5.2.*
> 2. You buy stock on November 30. A holding month ends on December 31, January 31, February 28 (or 29 in a leap year), etc.

5.14 Holding Period for Securities

Rules for counting your holding period for various securities transactions are as follows:

Stock sold on a public exchange. The holding period starts on the day after your purchase order is executed (trading date). The day your sale order is executed (trading date) is the last day of the holding period, even if delivery and payment are not made until several days after the actual sale (settlement date).

> **EXAMPLES**
> 1. On June 3, you sell a stock at a profit. Your holding period ends on June 3, although proceeds are not received until June 6.
> 2. You sell stock at a gain on a public exchange on December 27, 1997. The gain must be reported in 1997 even though the proceeds are received in 1998. The installment sale rule does not apply; *see 5.25.*

Stock subscriptions. If you are bound by your subscription but the corporation is not, the holding period begins the day after the date on which the stock is issued. If both you and the company are bound, the acceptance of the subscription by the corporation is the date of acquisition, and your holding period begins the day after.

Tax-free stock rights. When you exercise rights to acquire corporate stock from the issuing corporation, your holding period for the stock begins on the day of exercise, not on the day after. You are deemed to exercise stock rights when you assent to the terms of the rights in the manner requested or authorized by the corporation. An option to acquire stock is not a stock right.

Stock sold from different lots. If you purchased shares of the same stock on different dates and cannot determine which shares you are selling, the shares purchased at the earliest time are considered the stock sold first; this is called the FIFO (first-in, first-out) method; *see 30.2*.

> **EXAMPLE**
> You purchased 10 shares of ABC stock on May 3, 1985, 10 shares of ABC stock on May 1, 1987, and 10 shares of ABC stock on September 2, 1988. In 1997, you sell 25 shares of ABC stock, and are unable to determine when those particular shares were bought. Using the "first-in, first-out" method, 10 shares are from May 3, 1985, 10 shares from May 1, 1987, and five shares from September 2, 1988. *See also 30.2*.

Commodities. If you acquired a commodity futures contract, the holding period of a commodity accepted in satisfaction of the contract includes your holding period of the contract, unless you are a dealer in commodities.

Employee stock options. When an employee exercises a stock option, the holding period of the acquired stock begins on the day after the option is exercised. If an employee option plan allows the exercise of an option by giving notes, the terms of the plan should be reviewed to determine when ownership rights to the stock are transferred. The terms may affect the start of the holding period for the stock.

Wash sales. After a wash sale, the holding period of the new stock includes the holding period of the old stock for which a loss has been disallowed; *see 30.6*.

Other references. Stock dividends, *see 30.3*; short sales, *see 30.5*; and convertible securities, *see 30.7*.

5.15 Holding Period for Real Estate

The holding period starts the day after the date of acquisition, which is the earlier of: (1) the date title passes to you; and (2) the date you take possession and you assume the burdens and privileges of ownership. In disputes involving the starting and closing dates of a holding period, you may refer to the state law that applies to your sale or purchase agreement. State law determines when title to property passes.

If you convert a residence to rental property and later sell the house, the holding period includes the time you held the house for personal purposes.

Year-end sale. The date of sale is the last day of your holding period even if you do not receive the sale proceeds until the following year. For example, you sell land at a gain on December 29, 1997, receiving payment in January 1998. The holding period ends on December 29, although the sale is reported in 1998 when the proceeds are received. Note that the December 29th gain transaction can be reported in 1997 by making an election to "elect out" of installment reporting; *see 5.27*. A sale at a loss is reported in 1997.

5.16 Holding Period for Gifts, Inheritances, and Other Property

Gift property. If, in figuring a gain or loss, your basis for the property under *5.21* is the same as the donor's basis, you add the donor's holding period to the period you held the property. If you sell the property at a loss using as your basis the fair market value at the date of the gift *(5.21)*, your holding period begins on the day after the date of the gift.

Inherited property. The law gives an automatic holding period of more than one year for inherited property. Follow the Schedule D instructions for reporting the sale of inherited property.

Where property is purchased by the executor or trustee and distributed to you, your holding period begins the day after the date on which the property was purchased.

Partnership property. When you receive property as a distribution in kind from your partnership, the period your partnership held the property is added to your holding period. But there is no adding on of holding periods if the partnership property distributed was inventory and was sold by you within five years of distribution.

Involuntary conversions. When you have an involuntary conversion and elect to defer tax on gain, the holding period for the qualified replacement property generally includes the period you held the converted property. A new holding period begins for new property if you do not make an election to defer tax.

Figuring Your Profit or Loss

5.17 Calculating Gain or Loss

In most cases, you know if you have realized an *economic* profit or loss on the sale or exchange of property. You know your cost and selling price. The difference between the two is your profit or loss. The computation of gain or loss for tax purposes is similarly figured, except that the basis adjustment rules may require you to increase or decrease your cost or selling price and the amount-realized rules may require you to increase the selling price. As a result, your gain or loss for tax purposes may differ from your initial calculation.

Figuring Gain or Loss on Schedule D

1. Amount realized or total selling price *(5.18)*. $_____
2. Cost or other unadjusted basis *(5.20)*. $_____
3. *Plus:* Improvements; certain legal fees *(5.24)*. $_____
4. *Minus:* depreciation, casualty losses *(5.24)*. $_____
5. Adjusted basis: 2 *plus* 3 *minus* 4. $_____
6. Add selling expenses to 5. This is the total cost shown on Schedule D. $_____ $_____
7. Gain or loss: Subtract 6 from 1. $_____

> **EXAMPLE**
> You sell rental property to a buyer who pays you cash of $50,000 and assumes your $35,000 mortgage. You bought the property for $55,000 and made $12,000 of permanent improvements. You deducted depreciation of $7,250. Selling expenses were $2,000. Your gain on the sale is $23,250, figured as follows:
>
> | | | |
> |---|---|---|
> | 1. Amount realized *(5.18)* | | |
> | Cash | $50,000 | |
> | Assumed mortgage | 35,000 | |
> | | $85,000 | |
> | 2. Original cost | 55,000 | |
> | 3. *Plus* improvements | 12,000 | |
> | | $67,000 | |
> | 4. *Minus* depreciation | 7,250 | |
> | 5. Adjusted basis | 59,750 | |
> | 6. *Plus* selling expenses* | 2,000 | |
> | 7. Total cost: Combined result of Lines 2–6 | 61,750 | |
> | 8. Gain: Subtract Line 7 from Line 1 | $23,250 | |

*Selling expenses on Schedule D. When reporting a sale on Schedule D, IRS instructions require you to include *selling expenses* (Step 6) in the column for *cost,* rather than as a reduction to the sales price. The only exception is where a broker has reported net sale proceeds (gross proceeds *less* selling expenses) on Form 1099-B; you would then report the *net* amount as the sales price. Where a broker has reported the *gross* sales price on Form 1099-B, the IRS wants you to treat sales commissions as an addition to cost (rather than a reduction to selling price) so that it can compare the gross amount shown on Form 1099-B with the sales price reported on your return.

Using the facts in the previous Example, you report the gross selling price of $85,000 in column (d) of Schedule D. In column (e), enter the adjusted basis of $59,750 *plus* the selling expenses of $2,000 for a total of $61,750. The final result, a gain of $23,250 ($85,000 − $61,750), is the same as if the selling price were reduced by the selling expenses.

5.18 Amount Realized Is the Total Selling Price

Amount realized is the tax term for the total selling price. It includes cash, the fair market value of additional property received, and any of your liabilities which the buyer agrees to pay. The buyer's note is included in the selling price at fair market value. This is generally the discounted amount that a bank or other party will pay for the note.

Sale of mortgaged property. The selling price includes the amount of the unpaid mortgage. This is true whether or not you are personally liable on the debt, and whether or not the buyer assumes the mortgage or merely takes the property subject to the mortgage. The full amount of the unpaid mortgage is included, even where the value of the property is less than the unpaid mortgage. *See also 31.10* for computing amount realized on foreclosure sales.

If, at the time of the sale, the buyer pays off the existing mortgage or your other liabilities, you include the payment as part of the sales proceeds.

> **EXAMPLES**
> 1. You sell property subject to a mortgage of $60,000. The seller pays you cash of $30,000 and takes the property subject to the mortgage. The sales price or "amount realized" is $90,000.
> 2. A partnership receives a nonrecourse mortgage of $1,851,500 from a bank to build an apartment project. Several years later, the partnership sells the project for the buyer's agreement to assume the unpaid mortgage. At the time, the value of the project is $1,400,000 and the partnership basis in the project is $1,455,740. The partnership figures a loss of $55,740, the difference between basis and the value of the project. The IRS figures a gain of $395,760, the difference between the unpaid mortgage and basis. The partnership claims the selling price is limited to the lower fair market value and is supported by an appeals court. The Supreme Court reverses, supporting the IRS position. That the value of property is less than the amount of the mortgage has no effect on the rule requiring the unpaid mortgage to be part of the selling price. A mortgagor realizes value to the extent that his or her obligation to repay is relieved by a third party's assumption of the mortgage debt.

5.19 Finding Your Cost

In figuring gain or loss, you need to know the "unadjusted basis" of the property sold. This term refers to the original cost of your property if you purchased it. The general rules for determining your unadjusted basis are in *5.20*. Basis for property received by gift or inheritance is in *5.21;* rules for surviving joint tenants are in *5.22*. Keep in mind that you have to adjust this figure for improvements to the property, depreciation, or losses; *see 5.24*.

5.20 Unadjusted Basis of Your Property

To determine your tax cost for property, first find in the following section the unadjusted basis of the property, and then increase or decrease that basis as explained at *5.24*.

Property you bought. Unadjusted basis is your cash cost plus the value of any property you gave to the seller. If you assumed a mortgage or bought property subject to a mortgage, the amount of the mortgage is part of your unadjusted basis.

Purchase expenses are included in your cost, such as commissions, title insurance, recording fees, survey costs, and transfer taxes.

When you buy real estate, you usually reimburse the seller for property taxes he or she paid that cover the period after you took title. If you bought the property before 1954, you add such payments to basis. If you bought the property after 1953, taxes paid are not added to basis because they are immediately deductible in the year paid; *see 16.6*. However, if at the closing you also paid property taxes attributable to the time the seller held the property, you add such taxes to basis.

> **EXAMPLE**
> You bought a building for $120,000 in cash and a purchase money mortgage of $60,000. The unadjusted basis of the building is $180,000.

Property obtained for services. If you paid for the property by providing services, the value of the property, which is taxable compensation, is also your adjusted basis.

Property received in taxable exchange. Technically, your unadjusted basis for the new property is the fair market value of the surrendered property at the time of exchange. In practice, however, the basis usually is equal to the fair market value of the property received. *See* below for "tax-free" exchanges.

> **EXAMPLE**
>
> You acquire real estate for $35,000. When the property has a fair market value of $40,000, you exchange it for machinery also worth $40,000. You have a gain of $5,000 and the basis of the machinery is $40,000.

Property received in a "tax-free" exchange. The computation of basis is made on Form 8824. If the exchange is completely tax free (6.1), your basis for the new proprty will be your basis for the property you gave up in the exchange, plus any additional cash and exchange expenses you paid. If the exchange is partly nontaxable and partly taxable because you received "boot" (6.3), your basis for the new property will be your basis for the property given up in the exchange, decreased by any cash received and by any liabilities on the property you gave up, and increased by any cash and exchange expenses you paid, liabilities on the property you received, and gain taxed to you on the exchange. Gain is taxed to the extent you receive "boot," in the form of cash or a transfer of liabilities that exceeds the liabilities assumed in the exchange; see 6.3 for a discussion on taxable boot. *The Example at 6.3 illustrates the basis computation.*

> **EXAMPLES**
> 1. You exchange investment real estate, which cost you $20,000, for other investment real estate. Both properties have a fair market value of $35,000 and neither property is mortgaged. You pay no tax on the exchange. The unadjusted basis of the new property received in the exchange is $20,000.
> 2. Same facts as in Example 1 but you receive real estate worth $30,000 and cash of $5,000. On this transaction, you realize gain of $15,000 (amount realized of $35,000 less your basis of $20,000), but only $5,000 of the gain is taxable, equal to the cash "boot" received. Your basis for the new property is $20,000 figured this way:
>
> | | |
> |---|---:|
> | Basis of old property | $20,000 |
> | *Less:* Cash received | 5,000 |
> | | 15,000 |
> | *Plus:* Gain recognized | 5,000 |
> | Basis of new property | $20,000 |

Property received from a spouse or former spouse. As explained at *6.6,* tax-free exchange rules apply to property transfers after July 18, 1984, to a spouse, or to a former spouse where the transfer is incident to a divorce. The spouse receiving the property takes a basis equal to that of the transferor. Certain adjustments may be required where a transfer of mortgaged property is made in trust.

If you received property before July 19, 1984, under a prenuptial agreement in exchange for your release of your dower and marital rights, your basis is the fair market value at the time you received it.

New residence purchased under tax deferral rule. If you sell your old principal residence and buy a qualifying replacement under the rules of Chapter 29, your basis for the new house is what you paid for it, less any gain that was not taxed on the sale of the old residence.

Property received as a trust beneficiary. Generally, you take the same basis the trust had for the property. But if the distribution is made to settle a claim you had against the trust, your basis for the property is the amount of the settled claim.

If you received a distribution in kind for your share of trust income before June 2, 1984, the basis of the distribution is generally the value of the property to the extent allocated to distributable net income. For distributions in kind after June 1, 1984, in taxable years ending after June 1, 1984, your basis is the basis of the property in the hands of the trust. If the trust elects to treat the distribution as a taxable sale, your basis is generally fair market value.

Property acquired with involuntary conversion proceeds. If you acquire replacement property with insurance proceeds from destroyed property, or a government payment for condemned property, basis is the cost of the new property decreased by deferred gain; see *18.23* for figuring the deferred gain. If the replacement property consists of more than one piece of property, basis is allocated to each piece in proportion to its respective cost.

EXAMPLE

A building with an adjusted basis of $100,000 is destroyed by fire. The owner receives an insurance award of $200,000, realizing a gain of $100,000. He buys a building as a replacement for $150,000. Of the $100,000 gain, $50,000 is taxable, while the remaining $50,000 is deferred. Taxable gain is limited to the portion of the insurance award not used to buy replacement property ($200,000 – $150,000). The basis of the new building is $100,000:

Cost of the new building	$150,000
Less: deferred gain	50,000
Basis	$100,000

5.21 Basis of Property You Inherited or Received as a Gift

Special basis rules apply to property you received as a gift or that you inherited. Gifts from a spouse are subject to the rules of *6.6*. If you are a surviving joint tenant who received full title to property upon the death of the other joint tenant, *see 5.22*.

Basis of Property Received as Gift

If the fair market value of the property *equalled or exceeded* the donor's adjusted basis *(5.24)* at the time you received the gift, your basis for figuring gain or loss when you sell it is the donor's adjusted basis plus all or part of any gift tax paid; *see* the gift tax rule below.

If on the date of the gift, the fair market value was less than the donor's adjusted basis, your basis for purposes of figuring gain is the donor's adjusted basis, and your basis for figuring loss is the fair market value on the date of the gift.

EXAMPLES

Assume that in 1986 you received a gift of stock from your father which you sold in 1997. His adjusted basis was $1,000.

The basis you use to determine gain or loss depends on whether the fair market value of the stock on the date of the gift equalled or exceeded your father's $1,000 adjusted basis. If it did, your basis is your father's $1,000 basis and you will realize a gain if your selling price exceeds $1,000, as on Line 1 below, or a loss if the selling price is below $1,000, as on Line 4.

If the value of the stock on the date of the gift was less than $1,000 (father's basis) then you have: a gain if you sell for more than $1,000, as on Line 5; a loss if you sell for less than the $1,000 date-of-gift value, as on Line 2; or neither gain nor loss if you sell for more than the date-of-gift value but no more than $1,000 (father's basis), as on Line 3.

If value of the gift at receipt was—	And you sold it for—	Your basis is—	Your gain is—	Your loss is—
1. $3,000	$2,000	$1,000	$1,000	
2. 700	500	700		$200
3. 300	500	*	none	none
4. 1,500	500	1,000		500
5. 500	1,200	1,000	200	

*On Line 3 of the Example, where you sell for more than the date-of-gift value but for no more than the donor's basis, there is neither gain nor loss. To see if you have a gain, you use the donor's $1,000 basis as your basis, but on a sale for $500, you have a loss ($500) and not a gain. To see if you have a loss, you use the $300 date-of-gift value of the stock as your basis, but on a sale for $500, you have a gain ($200) and not a loss. Thus, you have neither gain nor loss under the basis rules which require you to use the donor's basis for determining if you have a gain, and the date of gift value for determining if you have a loss.

Did the donor pay gift tax?   If the donor paid a gift tax *(33.1)* on the gift to you, your basis for the property is increased under these rules:

1. For property received after December 31, 1976, the basis is increased for the gift tax paid by an amount which bears the same ratio to the amount of tax paid as the net appreciation in the value of the gift bears to the amount of the gift after taking into account the $10,000 annual gift tax exclusion *(33.1)*. The increase may not exceed the tax paid. Net appreciation in the value of any gift is the amount by which the fair market value of the gift exceeds the donor's adjusted basis immediately before the gift. *See* Example 2 below.

2. For property received after September 1, 1958, but before 1977, basis is increased by the gift tax paid on the property but not above the fair market value of the property at the time of the gift.

3. For property received before September 2, 1958, the gift tax paid increases the basis. But this increase may not be more than the excess of the fair market value of the property at the time of the gift over the basis of the property in the donor's hands. Ask the donor or his or her advisor for these amounts.

EXAMPLES

1. In 1975, your father gave you rental property with a fair market value of $78,000. The basis of the property in his hands was $60,000. He paid a gift tax of $15,000 on the gift. The basis of the property in your hands is $75,000 ($60,000 + $15,000).

2. In 1997, your father gave you rental property with a fair market value of $178,000. His basis in the property was $160,000. He paid a gift tax of $44,560 on a taxable gift of $168,000, after claiming the $10,000 annual exclusion. The basis of the property in your hands is your father's basis increased by the gift tax attributable to the appreciation. Gift tax attributable to the appreciation is:

   $$\frac{\text{Appreciation}}{\text{Gift } minus \text{ annual exclusion}} \times \text{Gift tax paid}$$

   $$\frac{\$18,000}{\$168,000} \times \$44,560 = \$4,774$$

   Your basis for figuring gain or loss or depreciation is $164,774 ($4,774 + $160,000 father's basis).

Gift you received before 1921.   Your basis is the fair market value of the property at the time of the gift.

Depreciation on property received as a gift.   If the property is depreciable *(see* Chapter 42), your basis for computing depreciation deductions is the donor's adjusted basis *(5.24)*, plus all or part of the gift tax paid by the donors as previously discussed.

When you sell the property, you must adjust basis *(5.24)* for depreciation claimed. If accelerated depreciation is claimed and you sell at a gain, you are subject to the ordinary income recapture rules discussed at *44.1*.

Basis of Inherited Property

Your basis for inherited property is generally the fair market value of the property on the date of the decedent's death, regardless of when you acquire the property. If the decedent died after October 21, 1942, and the executor elected to use an *alternate valuation date* after the death, your basis is the alternate value at that date.

If you owned the property jointly with the deceased, *see 5.22*.

If you inherit appreciated property that you (or your spouse) gave to the deceased person within one year of his or her death, your basis is the decedent's basis immediately before death, not its fair market value.

If the inherited property is subject to a mortgage, your basis is the value of the property, and not its equity at the date of death. If the property is subject to a lease under which no income is to be received for years, the basis is the value of the property—not the equity.

You might be given the right to buy the deceased person's property under his or her will. This is not the same as inheriting that property. Your basis is what you pay—not what the property is worth on the date of the deceased's death.

If property was inherited from a decedent dying after 1976 and before November 7, 1978, and the executor elected to apply a carryover basis to all estate property, your basis is figured with reference to the decedent's basis. The executor must inform you of the basis of such property.

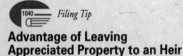

Filing Tip

Advantage of Leaving Appreciated Property to an Heir

Since your basis for inherited property is the value at the decedent's death or alternate valuation date, income tax is completely avoided on the appreciation in value that occurred while the decedent owned the property.

Community property. Upon the death of a spouse in a community property state, one-half of the fair market value of the community property is generally included in the deceased spouse's estate for estate tax purposes. The surviving spouse's basis for his or her half of the property is 50% of the total fair market value. For the other half, the heirs of the deceased spouse also have a basis equal to 50% of the fair market value.

5.22 • Joint Tenancy Basis Rules for Surviving Tenants

The basis of a surviving joint tenant generally depends on whether the joint tenancy was held with a spouse or with someone other than a spouse.

Qualified joint interest rule for survivor of spouse who died after 1981. A "qualified joint interest" rule applies to a joint tenancy with right of survivorship where the spouses are the only joint tenants, and to a tenancy by the entirety between a husband and wife. Where the surviving spouse is a U.S. citizen, the general rule for deaths occurring *after 1981* is as follows: One-half of the fair market value of the property is includable in the decedent's gross estate. This is true regardless of how much each spouse contributed to the purchase price. Fair market value is fixed at the date of death, or six months later if an estate tax return is filed and the optional alternate valuation date is elected.

The surviving spouse's basis equals the one-half estate tax share, plus one-half of the original cost basis for the property; *see* Example 1 below. If no estate tax return was due because the value of the estate was below the filing threshold, the surviving spouse's basis is one-half of the fair market value of the property at the date of death (alternate valuation is not available) plus one-half of the original cost basis. If depreciation deductions for the property were claimed before the date of death, the surviving spouse must reduce basis by his or her share (under local law) of the depreciation; *see* Example 2 below.

If the surviving spouse is *not* a U.S. citizen on the due date of the estate tax return, the basis rule is generally the same as the rule discussed below for unmarried joint tenants.

Spousal joint tenancies created before 1977. The IRS claims that regardless of when the joint tenancy was created, the above 50% estate tax inclusion rule and the 50% stepped-up basis rule apply where the death of the first spouse occurs after 1981. However, two federal appeals courts have held that these rules do not apply to pre-1977 spousal joint tenancies; *see* Example 3 below.

EXAMPLES

1. John and Jennifer Jones jointly own a house that cost them $50,000 in 1979. John paid $45,000 of the purchase price and Jennifer $5,000. In 1997, John dies when the house is worth $200,000. One-half, or $100,000, is included in his estate although he contributed 90% of the purchase price. For income tax purposes, Jennifer's basis for the house is $125,000.

One-half of cost basis	$25,000
Inherited portion	100,000
Jennifer's basis	$125,000

2. Same facts as in Example 1 except that the home was rental property for which $20,000 of depreciation deductions had been allowed before John's death. Under local law, Jennifer had a right to 50% of the income from the property and, thus, a right to 50% of the depreciation. Her basis for the property is $115,000: $125,000 as shown in Example 1, reduced by $10,000, her share of the depreciation.

3. The Gallensteins purchased farm property in 1955 as joint tenants; Mr. Gallenstein provided all the funds. When he died in 1987, Mrs. Gallenstein claimed that 100% of the property was includible in her husband's gross estate and she had a stepped-up basis for that full amount. The IRS argued that under the rules for estates of spouses dying after 1981, her basis was 50% of the date-of-death value. The federal appeals court for the Sixth Circuit (Kentucky, Michigan, Ohio, and Tennessee) agreed with Mrs. Gallenstein. The appeals court held that pre-1977 spousal joint tenancies were not affected when the law was changed to provide a 50% estate tax inclusion and 50% stepped-up basis for spousal deaths after 1981. For pre-1977 spousal joint tenancies, the prior law rule continues to apply: 100% of the date-of-death value of jointly held property is included in the estate of the first spouse to die unless it is shown that the survivor contributed towards the purchase. Thus, in this case, Mrs. Gallenstein's basis was 100% of the value of the property and she realized no taxable gain when she sold the property at a price equal to that stepped-up basis.

The Fourth Circuit Appeals Court (Maryland, North Carolina, South Carolina, Virginia, West Virginia) has agreed with the Sixth Circuit's *Gallenstein* approach of allowing a 100% stepped-up basis for a pre-1977 spousal joint interest.

If the statute of limitations has not expired, a surviving spouse who reported gain on a sale of property using the 50% basis rule should consult with his or her tax adviser about filing a refund claim based upon the 100% basis rule in the Gallenstein case. However, the IRS may reject such refund claims outside the Sixth and Fourth Circuits.

Unmarried joint tenants. If you are a surviving joint tenant who owned property with someone other than your spouse, your basis for the entire property is your basis for your share before the joint owner died plus the fair market value of the decedent's share at death (or on the alternate valuation date if the estate uses the alternate date). Even if the estate is too small to require the filing of an estate tax return, you may still include the decedent's share of the date-of-death value in your basis. However, if no estate tax return is required, you may not use the alternate valuation date basis.

EXAMPLE

You and your sister bought a home in 1950 for $20,000. She paid $12,000, and you paid $8,000. Title to the house was held by both of you as joint tenants. In 1997, when she died, the house was worth $150,000. Since she paid 60% of the cost of the house, 60% of the value at her death, $90,000, is included in her estate tax return (or would be included if an estate tax return was due). Your basis for the house is now $98,000—the $8,000 you originally paid plus the $90,000 fair market value of your sister's share at her death.

Exception for pre-1954 deaths. Where property was held in joint tenancy and one of the tenants died before January 1, 1954, no part of the interest of the surviving tenant is treated, for purposes of determining the basis of the property, as property transmitted at death. The survivor's basis is the original cost of the property.

Survivor of spouse who died before 1982. The basis rule for a surviving spouse who held property jointly (or as tenancy by the entirety) with a spouse who died before 1982 is generally the same as the above rule for unmarried joint tenants. However, special rules applied to qualified joint interests and eligible joint interests are discussed below.

EXAMPLE

A husband and wife owned rental property as tenants by the entirety that they purchased for $30,000. The husband furnished two-thirds of the purchase price ($20,000) and the wife furnished one-third ($10,000). Depreciation deductions taken before the husband's death were $12,000. On the date of his death in 1979, the property had a fair market value of $60,000. Under the law of the state in which the property is located, as tenants by the entirety, each had a half interest in the property. The wife's basis in the property at the date of her husband's death is $44,000, computed as follows:

Interest acquired with her own funds	$10,000
Interest acquired from husband ($\frac{2}{3}$ of $60,000)	40,000
	$50,000
Less: Depreciation of $\frac{1}{2}$ interest not acquired by reason of death ($\frac{1}{2}$ of $12,000)	6,000
Wife's basis at date of husband's death	$44,000

If she had not contributed any part of the purchase price, her basis at the date of her husband's death would be $54,000 ($60,000 fair market value less $6,000 depreciation).

Qualified joint interest and eligible joint interest where spouse died before 1982. Where, after 1976, a spouse dying before 1982 elected to treat realty as a "qualified joint interest" subject to gift tax, such joint property was treated as owned 50–50 by each spouse, and 50% of the value was included in the decedent's estate. Thus, for income tax purposes, the survivor's basis for the inherited 50% half of the property is the estate tax value; the basis for the other half is determined under the gift rules detailed in *5.21*. Personal property is treated as a "qualified joint interest" only if it was created or deemed to have been created after 1976 by a husband and wife and was subject to gift tax.

Where death occurred before 1982 and a surviving spouse materially participated in the operation of a farm or other business, an estate may elect to treat the farm or business property as an "eligible joint interest," which means that part of the investment in the property may be attributed to the surviving spouse's services and that part is not included in the deceased spouse's estate. Where such an election was made, the survivor's basis for income tax purposes includes the estate tax value of property included in the decedent's estate.

5.23 Allocating Cost Among Several Assets

Allocation of basis is generally required in these cases: when the property includes land and building; the land is to be divided into lots; securities or mutual-fund shares are purchased at different times; stock splits; and in the purchase of a business.

Purchase of land and building. To figure depreciation on the building, part of the purchase price must be allocated to the building. The allocation is made according to the fair market values of the building and land. The amount allocated to land is not depreciated.

Purchase of land to be divided into lots. The purchase price of the tract is allocated to each lot, so that the gain or loss from the sale of each lot may be reported in the year of its sale. Allocation is not made ratably, that is, with an equal share to each lot or parcel. It is based on the relative value of each piece of property. Comparable sales, competent appraisals, or assessed values may be used as guides.

Securities. *See 30.3* for details on methods of identifying securities bought at different dates. *See* 30.4 for allocating basis of stock dividends and stock splits and 30.5 for allocating the basis of stock rights.

Mutual-fund shares. *See 32.9* for determining the basis of mutual-fund shares where purchases were made at different times.

Purchase price of a business. *See 44.9* for allocation rule.

5.24 How To Find Adjusted Basis

After determining the *unadjusted* cost basis for property under the rules at *5.20–5.23,* you may have to increase it or decrease it to find your *adjusted basis,* which is the amount used to figure your gain or loss on a sale, as shown at *5.17.*

1. **Additions to basis.** You add to unadjusted basis the cost of these items:
   - *All permanent improvements and additions to the property and other capital costs,* such as the cost of repairing your property after a casualty (for example, repair costs after a fire or storm).
   - *Legal fees,* including fees incurred for defending or perfecting title, or for obtaining a reduction of an assessment levied against property to pay for local benefits.
   - *Sale of unharvested land.* If you sell land with unharvested crops, add the cost of producing the crops to the basis of the property sold.

2. **Deductions from basis.** You reduce cost basis for these items:
   - *Return of capital,* such as dividends on stock paid out of capital or out of a depletion reserve when the company has no available earnings or surplus; *see 4.11.*
   - *Losses from casualties,* including insurance awards and payments in settlement of damages to your property.

EXAMPLE
Your vacation home, which cost $75,000, is damaged by fire. You deducted the uninsured loss of $10,000 and spent $11,000 to repair the property. Several years later, you sell the house for $90,000. To figure your profit, increase the original cost of the house by the $11,000 of repairs and then reduce basis by the $10,000 casualty loss to get an adjusted basis of $76,000 ($75,000 + $11,000 – $10,000). Your gain on the sale is $14,000 ($90,000 – $76,000).

Depletion allowances; *see 9.15.*

Depreciation, first-year expensing deduction, ACRS deductions, amortization, and obsolescence on property used in business or for the production of income. In some years, you may have taken more or less depreciation than was allowable.

If you claim less than what was allowable, you must deduct from basis the allowable amount rather than what was actually claimed. You may file an amended return to claim the full allowable depreciation for a year. If the amended return deadline has passed, you may still get a deduction for the unclaimed depreciation by filing for an accounting method change under IRS Revenue Procedure 96-31; a deduction for the entire amount is allowed for the year of the accounting change.

If you took more depreciation than was allowable, you may have to make the following adjustments: If you have deducted more than what was allowable and you received a tax benefit from the deduction, you deduct from basis the full amount of the depreciation. But if the excess depreciation did not give you a tax benefit, because income was eliminated by other deductions, the excess is not deducted from basis. These rules affect all tax years after 1951.

Amortized bond premium; *see 4.17.*

Cancelled debt excluded from income. If you did not pay tax on certain cancellations of debt because of bankruptcy or insolvency, or on qualifying farm debt or business real property, you reduce basis of your property for the amount forgiven under the rules at *11.7* and *11.8*.

Investment credit. Where the full investment credit was claimed in 1983 or later years, basis was reduced by one-half the credit.

Reporting an Installment Sale

5.25 Tax Advantage of Installment Sales

If you sell property at a *gain* in 1997 and you will receive one or more payments in a later year or years, you may use the installment method to defer tax unless the property is publicly traded securities or you are a dealer of the property sold. If you report the sale as an installment sale on Form 6252, your profit is taxed as installments are received. You may elect not to use the installment method if you want to report the entire profit in the year of sale; *see* Example 1 below and *5.27*.

Losses may not be deferred under the installment method.

How the installment method works. For each year you receive installment payments, report your gain on Form 6252. Installment income from the sale of a capital asset is then transferred to Schedule D. If your gain in the year of sale is long-term capital gain, gain in later years is also long term; short-term treatment in the year of sale applies also to later years. Interest payments you receive on the deferred sale installments are reported with your other interest income on Schedule B of Form 1040, not on Form 6252.

Installment income from the sale of business or rental property is figured on Form 6252 and then entered on Form 4797. If you make an installment sale of depreciable property, any *depreciation recapture* (44.1) is reported as income in the year of disposition. The recaptured amount is first figured on Form 4797 and then entered on Form 6252. On Form 6252, recaptured income is added to basis of the property for purposes of figuring the gross profit ratio for the balance of gain to be reported, if any, over the installment period; *see also 44.7*.

Installment sales of business or rental property for over $150,000 may be subject to a special tax if deferred payments exceed $5 million; *see 5.35*.

EXAMPLES
1. In 1997, you sell real estate for $100,000 that you bought in 1985 for $44,000. Selling expenses were $6,000. You are to receive $20,000 in 1997, 1998, and 1999; and $40,000 in 2000, plus interest of 9% compounded semiannually. Your gross profit is $50,000 ($100,000 contract price less $44,000 cost and $6,000 selling expenses). For installment sale purposes, your gross profit percentage, which is the percentage of each payment that you must report, is 50% ($50,000 profit ÷ $100,000 contract price). When the buyer makes the installment note payments, you report the following:

	You report	
In	*Payment of:*	*Income of:*
1997	$20,000	$10,000
1998	20,000	10,000
1999	20,000	10,000
2000	40,000	20,000
Total	$100,000	$50,000

In 1997, you file Form 6252 to figure your gross profit and gross profit percentage. You report only $10,000 as profit on Schedule D (or Form 4797, if applicable). If you do not want to use the installment method, you make an election by reporting the entire gain of $50,000 on Schedule D or Form 4797.

The buyer's interest payments are separately reported as interest income on Form 1040.

2. On December 21, 1997, you sell a building for $150,000, realizing a profit of $25,000. You take a note payable in January 1998. You report the gain in 1998. Receiving a lump-sum payment in a taxable year after the year of sale is considered an installment sale.

Year-end sales of publicly traded stock or securities. You have no choice about when to report the gain from a sale of publicly traded stock or securities made at the end of 1997. Any gain must be reported in 1997, even if the proceeds are not received until early 1998. The sale is not considered an installment sale.

Farm property. A farmer may use the installment method to report gain from the sale of property that does not have to be inventoried under his method of accounting. This is true even though such property is held for regular sale.

Dealer sales. Generally, dealers must report gain in the year of sale for personal property regularly sold on an installment plan, or real estate held for resale to customers. However, the installment method may be used by dealers of certain time shares (generally time shares of up to six weeks per year) and residential lots, but only if an election is made to pay interest on the tax deferred by using the installment method. For further details, see the instructions to Schedule C of Form 1040.

5.26 Figuring the Taxable Part of Installment Payments

On the installment method, a portion of each payment other than interest represents part of your gain and is taxable. This taxable gain amount is based on the gross profit percentage or ratio, which is figured by dividing gross profit by the selling price or the contract price. The contract price is the same as the selling price unless an adjustment is made for an existing mortgage assumed or "taken subject to" by the buyer. The term *contract price* is used in the computation to describe only payments which the seller receives or is considered to have received. Thus, it does not include the buyer's assumption of an existing mortgage; *see* below for the mortgage adjustment to contract price. By following the line-by-line instructions to Form 6252, you get the gross profit percentage. Selling price, contract price, and gross profit are explained in the following paragraphs.

Interest equal to the *lesser* of 100% of the applicable federal rate and 9% compounded semiannually must generally be charged on a deferred payment sale. Otherwise, the IRS treats part of the sale price as interest; *see 4.32.*

EXAMPLE

On December 7, 1997, you sell real estate for $100,000. The property had an adjusted basis of $56,000. Selling expenses are $4,000. You are to receive installment payments of $25,000 in 1997, 1998, 1999, and 2000, plus interest at 9%, compounded semiannually. The gross profit percentage of 40% is figured as follows:

Selling price (contract price)	$100,000
Less: Adjusted basis and selling expenses	60,000
Gross profit	$ 40,000

$$\frac{\text{Gross profit}}{\text{Contract price}} = \frac{\$40,000}{\$100,000} = 40\% \text{ (gross profit percentage)}$$

In 1997, you report a profit of $10,000 (40% of $25,000) on Form 6252. Interest received is separately reported as income on your Form 1040. Similarly, in each of the following three years, a profit of $10,000 is reported so that by the end of four years, the entire $40,000 profit will have been reported.

Selling price. Include cash, fair market value of property received from the buyer, the buyer's notes (at face value), and any outstanding mortgage on the property that the buyer assumes or takes subject to. If, under the contract of sale, the buyer pays off an existing mortgage or assumes liability for any other liens on the property, such as taxes you owe, or pays the sales commissions, such payments are also included in the selling price.

 Law Alert

Lower Capital Gain Rates

Installment sale proceeds received after May 6, 1997, qualify for the new lower capital gain rates if received on a sale of property held more than 18 months, or more than 12 months if the sale was before July 29, 1997; *see 5.2.*

Interest, including interest imputed under the rules of *4.32*, is not included in the selling price. Notes of a third party given to you by the buyer are valued at fair market value.

Gross profit and gross profit percentage. Gross profit is the selling price *less* what the IRS calls installment sale basis, which is the total of adjusted basis of the property *(5.24)*, selling expenses, such as brokers' commissions and legal fees, and recaptured depreciation income, if any *(44.1)*.

Divide the gross profit by the contract price to get the gross profit percentage. Each year, you multiply this percentage by your payments to determine the taxable amount under the installment method.

Contract price where the buyer takes subject to or assumes an existing mortgage. To figure the gross profit percentage first reduce the selling price by the amount of your existing mortgages that the buyer assumes or takes the property subject to. The reduced amount is the *contract price*. You then divide your gross profit by the contract price to get the gross profit percentage.

If the mortgage exceeds your installment sale basis (total of adjusted basis of the property, selling expenses, and depreciation recapture), you are required to report the excess as a payment received in the year of sale and also increase the *contract price* by that excess amount. Where the mortgage equals or exceeds your installment sale basis, the gross profit percentage will be 100%; *see* Example 3 below.

In a wraparound mortgage transaction, the buyer does not assume the seller's mortgage or take the property subject to it, but instead makes payments that cover the seller's outstanding mortgage liability. At one time, the IRS treated a wraparound mortgage transaction as an assumption of a mortgage by the buyer and required a reduction of the selling price by the mortgage. The Tax Court rejected the IRS position, and the IRS acquiesced in the decision. Currently, the IRS does not require a reduction of selling price for a wraparound mortgage in the Form 6252 instructions or in Publication 537. However, a temporary regulation requiring the reduction has not been withdrawn; *see* Example 4 below.

EXAMPLES

1. You sell a building for $300,000. The building was secured by an existing mortgage of $50,000 which you pay off at the sale closing from the buyer's initial payment. The contract price is $300,000.

2. Same facts as in Example 1, but the buyer assumes the mortgage of $50,000. The contract price is $250,000 ($300,000 – $50,000).

3. You sell a building for $90,000. The buyer will pay you $10,000 annually for three years and assume an existing mortgage of $60,000. The adjusted basis of the property is $45,000. Selling expenses are $5,000. The total installment sale basis is $50,000 ($45,000 plus $5,000). The mortgage exceeds this basis by $10,000 ($60,000 – $50,000). This $10,000 excess is included in the contract price and treated as a payment made in the year of sale. The contract price is $40,000:

Selling price	$90,000
Less: Mortgage	60,000
	$30,000
Add: Excess of mortgage ($60,000) over installment sale basis ($50,000)	10,000
Contract price	$40,000
Selling price	$90,000
Less: Installment sale basis	50,000
Gross Profit	$40,000
Gross profit percentage ($40,000 gross profit ÷ $40,000 contract price)	100%

4. Abel sells real property worth $2 million, encumbered by a mortgage of $900,000. Installment sale basis (adjusted basis plus selling costs) is $700,000. The buyer pays $200,000 cash and gives an interest-bearing wraparound mortgage note for $1.8 million. Abel remains obligated to pay off the $900,000 mortgage. The gross profit ratio is 65% ($1,300,000 gross profit ÷ $2,000,000 contract price). In the year of sale, Abel reports the $200,000 cash of which 65% of $200,000, or $130,000, is taxable income.

Change of selling price. If the selling price is changed during the period payments are outstanding, the gross profit percentage is refigured on the new selling price. The adjusted profit ratio is then applied to payments received after the adjustment.

EXAMPLE

Jones sold real estate in 1994 for $100,000. His basis, including selling expenses, was $40,000, so his gross profit was $60,000. The buyer agreed to pay, starting in 1995, five annual installments of $20,000 plus 10% interest. As the gross profit percentage was 60% ($60,000 ÷ $100,000), Jones reported profit of $12,000 (60% of $20,000) on the installments received in 1995 and 1996.

In 1997, the parties renegotiated the sales price, reducing it from $100,000 to $85,000, and reducing payments for 1997, 1998, and 1999 to $15,000. Jones's original profit of $60,000 is reduced to $45,000 ($85,000 revised sales price *less* $40,000 basis). Of the $45,000 profit, $12,000 was reported in 1995 and an additional $12,000 in 1996. To get the revised profit percentage, Jones must divide the $21,000 of profit not yet received by the remaining sales price of $45,000 ($85,000 less $40,000 installments in 1995 and 1996). The revised profit percentage is 46.67% ($21,000 ÷ $45,000). In 1997, 1998, and 1999, Jones reports profit of $7,000 on each $15,000 installment (46.67% of $15,000).

Paymnts received. Payments include cash, the fair market value of property, and payments on the buyer's notes. Payments do not include receipt of the buyer's notes or other evidence of indebtedness, unless payable on demand or readily tradable. "Readily tradable" means registered bonds, bonds with coupons attached, debentures, and other evidences of indebtedness of the buyer that are readily tradable in an established securities market. This rule is directed mainly at corporate acquisitions. A third-party guarantee (including a standby letter of credit) is not treated as a payment received on an installment obligation.

If the buyer has assumed or taken property subject to a mortgage that exceeds your installment sale basis (adjusted basis plus selling expenses plus depreciation recapture, if any), you include as a payment in the year of the sale the excess of the mortgage over the installment basis; see the Johnson Example below.

EXAMPLE

Johnson sells a building for $160,000, subject to a mortgage of $60,000. Installments plus interest are to be paid over five years. His adjusted basis in the building was $30,000 and his selling expenses were $10,000, so his installment sale basis is $40,000 and his gross profit is $120,000 ($160,000 – $40,000). The contract price is also $120,000, the selling price of $160,000 less $40,000, the part of the mortgage that did not exceed the installment sale basis.

The $20,000 difference between the $60,000 mortgage and the installment sale basis of $40,000 is part of the contract price and is also treated as a payment received in the year of sale. Since the mortgage exceeds Johnson's installment sale basis, he is treated as having recovered his entire basis in the year of sale, and all installment payments will be taxable, as his gross profit ratio is 100%: gross profit of $120,000 ÷ contract price of $120,000. In the year of sale, Johnson must report as taxable gain 100% of the installment payment received, plus the $20,000 difference between the mortgage and his installment sale basis.

Pledging installment obligation as security. If, as security for a loan, you pledge an installment obligation from a sale of property of more than $150,000 (excluding farm or personal-use property), the net loan proceeds must be treated as a payment on the installment obligation. The net loan proceeds are treated as received on the later of the date the loan is secured and the date you receive the loan proceeds. These pledging rules do not apply if the debt refinances a debt that was outstanding on December 17, 1987, and secured by the installment obligation until the refinancing. If the refinancing exceeds the loan principal owed immediately before the refinancing, the excess is treated as a payment on the installment obligation. See the Form 6252 instructions.

Recapture of depreciation or first-year expensing deduction. The entire recaptured amount under *44.1 – 44.3* is reported in the year of sale, even though you report the sale on the installment basis. An installment sale does not defer the reporting of the recaptured deduction. You also add the recaptured amount to the basis of the sold asset to compute the amount of the remaining gain to be reported on each installment. See the instructions to Form 6252.

5.27 Electing Not To Report on the Installment Method

If any sale proceeds are to be received after the year of sale, you must file Form 6252 and use the installment method unless you "elect out" by making a timely election to report the entire gain in the year of sale. If you want to report the entire gain in the year of sale, include it on Schedule D or Form 4797 by the due date for filing your return (plus extensions) for the year of sale. Do not use Form 6252. After the due date (plus extensions), a change from the installment method to full reporting in the year of sale may be made only with IRS consent. The IRS will give consent only in rare cases where it finds "good cause." The IRS may give consent if your tax preparer erroneously reported on the installment method and you promptly ask IRS permission to change to reporting of the entire gain. A change in the tax law is not considered "good cause" by the IRS. For example, sellers who before 1986 reported on the installment basis on the assumption that their payments would be taxed at favorable capital gain rates, wanted to amend their returns and report the entire gain in the year of sale after the 1986 Tax Act repealed the capital gain exclusion. The IRS would not allow the change.

Switching from full reporting to installment method. If you do report the entire gain in the year of sale, you may change to the installment method on an amended return only with the consent of the IRS. In a private ruling, the IRS refused to allow a seller to use the installment method after inadvertently including the entire gain from the sale on his return. Although reporting of the entire gain was a mistake, this was treated as an election not to use the installment method. The IRS refused permission to revoke the election on the grounds that a second chance to apply the installment method would be tax avoidance. However, in other private rulings, permission to revoke was granted where the seller's accountant erroneously reported the entire gain.

In one case, a seller "elected out" in a year in which he planned to deduct a net operating loss carryforward from an installment sale gain. In a later year, the IRS substantially reduced the loss. The seller then asked the IRS to allow him to revoke the "election out" so he could use the installment method. The IRS refused in a private ruling, claiming that the seller asked for the revocation to avoid tax. The installment sale would defer gain to a later year, which is a tax avoidance purpose.

5.28 Restriction on Installment Sales to Relatives

The installment sale method is not allowed where you sell depreciable property to a controlled business, or to a trust in which you or your spouse is a beneficiary.

Further, if you sell property to a relative on the installment basis, and the relative later resells the property, you could lose the benefit of installment reporting. If the family member's resale is within two years of the original sale, the original seller is taxed on that sale under the two-year rule discussed below.

> **EXAMPLE**
>
> In 1997, Jones sells land to his son for $250,000, realizing a profit of $100,000. The son agrees to pay in five annual installments of $50,000 starting in 1998. Later in 1997, the son sells the land to a third party for $260,000. Jones Sr. reports his profit of $100,000 in 1997, even though he received no payment that year. Payments other than interest received by Jones Sr. after 1997 are tax free because he reported the entire profit in 1997.

Two-year rule for property other than marketable securities. If you make an installment sale to a related party of property other than marketable securities, you are taxed on a second sale by the related party only if it occurs within two years of the initial installment sale and before all payments from the first installment sale are made. Related parties include a spouse, child, grandchild, parent, grandparent, brother or sister, controlled corporation (50% or more direct or indirect ownership), any S corporation in which you own stock or partnership in which you are a partner, a trust in which you are a beneficiary, or a grantor trust of which you are treated as the owner. You are treated as owning stock held by your spouse, brothers, sisters, children, grandchildren, parents, and grandparents.

You must report as additional installment sale income: (1) the proceeds from the related party's sale or the contract price from the initial installment sale, whichever is less, minus (2) installment payments received from the related party as of the end of the year. The computation is made in Part III of Form 6252.

The two-year period is extended during any period in which the buyer's risk is lessened by a put on the property, an option by another person to acquire the property, or a short sale or other transaction lessening the risk of loss.

Filing Tip

"Electing Out" of Installment Reporting

When you have losses to offset your gain in the year of sale, installment sale reporting may not be advantageous. In such a case, you may want to report the full gain in the year of sale so the gain may be offset by the losses. However, there is a risk. If the losses are later disallowed by an IRS audit, you may not be given a second chance to use the installment method to spread the gain over the payment period. The IRS *may* not allow you to revoke your "election out" on the grounds that to do so would result in tax avoidance.

The two-year cutoff does not apply to the sale of marketable securities. For such marketable securities, you can be taxed on any related party's sale occurring before you receive all the payments under the initial installment sale.

Marketable securities are:

1. Securities listed on the New York Stock Exchange, the American Stock Exchange, or any city or regional exchange in which quotations appear on a daily basis, including foreign securities listed on a recognized foreign, national, or regional exchange;
2. Securities regularly traded in the national or regional over-the-counter market, for which published quotations are available;
3. Securities locally traded for which quotations can readily be obtained from established brokerage firms;
4. Units in a common trust fund; and
5. Mutual fund shares for which redemption prices are published.

Exceptions to two-year rule. There are exceptions to this related-party rule. Second dispositions resulting from an involuntary conversion of the property will not be subject to the related-party rule so long as the first disposition occurred before the threat or imminence of conversion. Similarly, transfers after the death of the person making the first disposition or the death of the person acquiring the property in the first disposition are not treated as second dispositions. Also, a sale or exchange of stock to the issuing corporation is not treated as a first disposition. Finally, you may avoid tax on a related party's second sale by satisfying the IRS that neither the initial nor the second sale was made for tax avoidance purposes.

Where you transfer property to a related party, the IRS has two years from the date you notify it that there has been a second disposition to assess a deficiency with respect to your transfer.

Sales of depreciable property to related party. Installment reporting is not allowed for sales of depreciable property made to a controlled corporation or partnership (50% control by seller) and between such controlled corporations and partnerships. In figuring control of a corporation, you are considered to own stock held by your spouse, children, grandchildren, brothers or sisters, parents, and grandparents. Installment reporting is also disallowed on a sale to a trust in which you or a spouse is a beneficiary unless your interest is considered a remote contingent interest whose actuarial value is 5% or less of the trust property's value. On these related-party sales, the entire gain is reported in the year of sale, unless the seller convinces the IRS that the transfer was not motivated by tax avoidance purposes.

On a sale of depreciable property to a related party, if the amounts of payments are contingent (for example, payments are tied to profits), the seller must make a special calculation. He or she must treat as received in the year of sale all noncontingent payments plus the fair market value of the contingent payments if such value may be reasonably ascertained. If the fair market value of the contingent payments may not be reasonably calculated, the seller recovers basis ratably. The purchaser's basis for the acquired property includes only amounts that the seller has included in income under the basis recovery rule. Thus, the purchaser's basis is increased annually as the seller recovers basis.

5.29 Contingent Payment Sales

Where the final selling price or payment period of an installment sale is not fixed at the end of the taxable year of sale, you are considered to have transacted a "contingent payment sale." Special rules apply where a maximum selling price may be figured under the terms of the agreement or there is no fixed price but there is a fixed payment period, or there is neither a fixed price nor a fixed payment period.

Stated maximum selling price. Under IRS regulations, a stated maximum selling price may be determined by assuming that all of the contingencies contemplated under the agreement are met. When the maximum amount is later reduced, the gross profit ratio is recomputed.

EXAMPLE

Smith sells stock in Acme Co. for a down payment of $100,000 plus an amount equal to 5% of the net profits of Acme for the next nine years. The contract provides that the maximum amount payable, including the $100,000 down payment but exclusive of interest, is $2,000,000. Smith's basis for the stock is $200,000; $2,000,000 is the selling price and contract price. Gross profit is $1,800,000. The gross profit ratio is 90% ($1,800,000 ÷ $2,000,000). Thus, $90,000 of the first payment is reportable as gain and $10,000 as a recovery of basis.

Fixed period.   When a stated maximum selling price is not determinable but the maximum payment period is fixed, basis—including selling expenses—is allocated equally to the taxable years in which payment may be received under the agreement. If, in any year, no payment is received or the amount of payment received is less than the basis allocated to that taxable year, no loss is allowed unless the taxable year is the final payment year or the agreement has become worthless. When no loss is allowed in a year, the basis allocated to the taxable year is carried forward to the next succeeding taxable year.

> **EXAMPLE**
>
> Brown sells property for 10% of the property's gross rents over a five-year period. Brown's basis is $5,000,000. The sales price is indefinite and the maximum selling price is not fixed under the terms of the contract; basis is recovered ratably over the five-year period.
>
> | Year | Payment | Basis recovered | Gain |
> |------|---------|-----------------|------|
> | First | $1,300,000 | $1,000,000 | $300,000 |
> | Second | 1,500,000 | 1,000,000 | 500,000 |
> | Third | 1,400,000 | 1,000,000 | 400,000 |
> | Fourth | 1,800,000 | 1,000,000 | 800,000 |
> | Fifth | 2,100,000 | 1,000,000 | 1,100,000 |

No stated maximum selling price or fixed period.   If the agreement fails to specify a maximum selling price and payment period, the IRS may view the agreement as a rent or royalty income agreement. However, if the arrangement qualifies as a sale, basis (including selling expenses) is recovered in equal annual increments over a 15-year period commencing with the date of sale. If in any taxable year no payment is received or the amount of payment received (exclusive of interest) is less than basis allocated to the year, no loss is allowed unless the agreement has become worthless. Excess basis not recovered in one year is reallocated in level amounts over the balance of the 15-year term. Any basis not recovered at the end of the 15th year is carried forward to the next succeeding year, and to the extent unrecovered, carried forward from year to year until basis has been recovered or the agreement is determined to be worthless. The rule requiring initial level allocation of basis over 15 years may not apply if you prove to the IRS that a 15-year general rule will substantially and inappropriately defer recovery of basis.

In some cases, basis recovery under an income forecast type of method may also be allowed.

An installment sale with payments to be made in foreign currency or tangible payment units (such as bushels of wheat) is a contingent payment sale, but basis is allocated as if payment were fixed in U.S. dollars.

> **EXAMPLE**
>
> In 1996, Jones sells property for 10,000 English pounds. In 1997, 2,500 pounds are payable. In 1998, the balance of 7,500 pounds is payable. Basis in the property is $2,000. In 1997, 25% of the basis, or $500 (25% of $2,000), is allocated to the first payment. In 1998, $1,500 (75% of $2,000) is allocated to the second payment.

5.30 Using Escrow and Other Security Arrangements

You sell property and the sales proceeds are placed in escrow pending the possible occurrence of an event such as the approval of title or your performance of certain contractual conditions. The IRS may argue that installment reporting is not allowed unless there are escrow restrictions preventing immediate payment.

If the terms of the escrow involve no genuine conditions that prevent you from demanding immediate payment, there will be immediate tax. Substitution of an escrow account for unpaid notes or deeds of trust disqualifies installment reporting.

> **EXAMPLES**
>
> 1. Anderson sold stock and mining property for almost $5 million. He agreed to place $500,000 in escrow to protect the buyer against his possible breaches of warranty and to provide security for certain liabilities. The escrow agreement called for Anderson to direct the investments of the escrow fund and receive income from the fund in excess of $500,000.

The IRS claimed that in the year of sale Anderson was taxable on the $500,000 held in escrow on the ground that Anderson's control of the fund rendered the fund taxable immediately. Anderson argued he was only taxable as the funds were released to him, and the Tax Court agreed. The fund was not under his unqualified control. He might never get the fund if the liabilities materialized. Although Anderson had a free hand with investment of the money, he still lacked ultimate ownership.

2. Rhodes sold a tract to a buyer who was willing to pay at once the entire purchase price of $157,000. But Rhodes wanted to report the sale on the installment basis over a period of years. The buyer refused to execute a purchase money mortgage on the property to allow the installment sale election (required under prior law) because he wanted clear and unencumbered title to the tract. As a solution, Rhodes asked the buyer to turn over the purchase price to a bank, as escrow agent, which would pay the sum over a five-year period.

   The escrow arrangement failed to support an installment sale. Rhodes was fully taxable on the entire price in the year of the sale. The buyer's payment was unconditional and irrevocable. The escrow arrangement involved no genuine conditions that could defeat Rhodes's right to payment, as the buyer could not revoke, alter, or end the arrangement.

3. In January, an investor sold real estate for $100,000. He received $10,000 as a down payment and six notes, each for $15,000, secured by a deed of trust on the property. The notes, together with interest, were due annually over the next six years. In July, the buyer deposited the remainder of the purchase price with an escrow agent and got the seller to cancel the deed of trust.

   The agreement provides that the escrow agent will pay off the buyer's notes as they fall due. The buyer remains liable for the installment payments. The escrow deposit is irrevocable, and the payment schedule may not be accelerated by any party under any circumstances. According to the IRS, the sale, which initially qualified as an installment sale, is disqualified by the escrow account.

5.31 Minimum Interest on Deferred Payment Sales

The tax law requires a minimum amount of interest to be charged on deferred payment sales. The rules for imputing interest are discussed at *4.32*. Imputed interest is included in the taxable income of the seller. Imputed interest is deductible by the buyer if the property is business or investment property, but not if it is used substantially all the time for personal purposes.

5.32 Dispositions of Installment Notes

A sale, a gift, an exchange or other transfer or cancellation of mortgage notes or other obligations received in an installment sale has tax consequences. If you sell or exchange the notes or if you accept less than face value in satisfaction of the obligation, gain or loss results to the extent of the difference between the basis of the notes and the amount realized. For example, if in satisfaction of an installment note, the buyer gives you other property worth less than the face value of the note, you have gain (or loss) to the extent your amount realized exceeds (or is less than) your *basis* in the installment note. The basis of an installment note or obligation is the face value of the note less the income that would be reported if the obligation were paid in full; *see* Example 2 below.

Gain or loss is long term if the original sale was entitled to long-term capital gain treatment. This is true even if the notes were held short term. If the original sale resulted in short-term gain or ordinary income, the sale of the notes gives short-term gain or ordinary income, regardless of the holding period of the notes.

Suppose you make an installment sale of your real estate, taking back a land contract. Later a mortgage is substituted for the unpaid balance of the land contract. The IRS has ruled that the substitution is not the same as a disposition of the unpaid installment obligations. There is no tax on the substitution.

 Filing Tip

Installment Reporting on Escrow Allowable

If an escrow arrangement imposes a substantial restriction, the IRS may allow installment reporting. An example of a substantial restriction: Payment of the escrow is tied to the condition that the seller refrain from entering a competing business for a period of five years. If, at any time during the escrow period, he or she engaged in a competing business, all rights to the amount then held in escrow would be forfeited.

EXAMPLES
1. You sell a lot for $20,000 which cost you $10,000. In the year of the sale, you received $5,000 in cash and the purchaser's notes for the remainder of the selling price, or $15,000. A year later, before the buyer makes a payment on the notes, you sell them for $13,000 cash:

   Selling price of property $20,000

Cost of property	10,000
Total profit	$10,000
Profit percentage, or proportion of each payment returnable as income, is 50% ($10,000 total profit ÷ $20,000 contract price)	
Unpaid balance of notes	$15,000
Amount of income reportable if notes were paid in full (50% of $15,000)	7,500
Adjusted basis of the notes	$7,500

Your profit on the sale is $5,500 ($13,000 – $7,500). It is capital gain if the sale of the lot was taxable as capital gain.

2. You sell a lot on the installment basis for $200,000 which cost you $120,000. In the year of sale, you received $20,000 in cash and the buyer's note for $180,000. Your gross profit percentage is 40% ($80,000 total profit ÷ $200,000 contract price).

Two years later, the buyer is facing financial difficulties and is unable to make payments on the $180,000 note. In satisfaction of the installment note, the buyer agrees to give you two other parcels of real estate, each worth $50,000. By accepting less than the $180,000 face value of the note in satisfaction of the obligation, you realize an $8,000 capital loss; the difference between the amount you realize and your basis in the installment obligation is figured as follows:

Amount realized ($50,000 for each parcel)	$100,000
Face value of note	180,000
Less: Amount of income reportable if note was paid in full given 40% profit percentage (40% of $180,000 = $72,000)	72,000
Basis in installment note	$108,000

The difference between the $100,000 amount realized and $108,000 basis gives you an $8,000 loss. Assuming your profit on the original sale was long-term capital gain, the loss would be deducted as a long-term capital loss.

Gift of installment obligation. If the installment obligations are disposed of other than by sale or exchange, such as when you make a gift of the installment obligations to someone else, gain or loss is the difference between the basis of the obligations and their fair market value at the time of the disposition. If an installment obligation is *cancelled* or otherwise becomes unenforceable, the same rule for determining gain or loss applies.

A gift of installment obligations to a person or charitable organization is treated as a taxable disposition. Gain or loss is the difference between the basis of the obligations and their fair market value at the time of the gift. If the notes are donated to a qualified charity, you may claim a contribution deduction for the fair market value of the obligations at the time of the gift.

Transfer to spouse or former spouse. A transfer of installment obligations to your spouse or a transfer to a former spouse that is incident to a divorce is treated as a tax-free exchange under the rules of 6.6 unless the transfer is in trust.

Transfer at death. A transfer of installment obligations at the death of the holder of the obligation is not taxed as a disposition. As the notes are paid, the estate or beneficiaries report income in the same proportion as the decedent would have, had he or she lived. A transfer of installment obligations to a revocable trust is also not taxed. However, the estate is subject to tax if the obligation is cancelled, becomes unenforceable, or is transferred to the buyer because of the death of the obligation holder.

5.33 Repossession of Personal Property Sold on Installment

When a buyer defaults and you repossess personal property, either by a voluntary surrender or a foreclosure, you may realize gain or loss. The method of calculating gain or loss is similar to the method used for disposition of installment notes; *see 5.32.* Gain or loss is the difference between the fair market value of the repossessed property and your basis for the installment obligations satisfied by the repossession. This rule is followed whether or not title has been kept by you or transferred to the buyer. The amount realized is reduced by costs incurred during the repossession. The basis of the obligation is face value less unreported profit.

If the property repossessed is bid in at a lawful public auction or judicial sale, the fair market value of the property is presumed to be the purchase or bid price, in the absence of proof to the contrary.

Gain or loss in the repossession is reported in the year of the repossession.

EXAMPLE

In December 1996, you sell furniture for $1,500—$300 down and $100 a month plus 9% interest beginning January 1997. You reported the installment sale on your 1996 tax return. The buyer defaulted after making three monthly payments. You foreclosed and repossessed the property; the fair market value was $1,400. The legal costs of foreclosure were $100. The gain on the repossession in 1997 is computed as follows:

Fair market value of property repossessed		$1,400
Basis of the buyer's notes at time of repossession:		
Selling price	$1,500	
Less: Payments made	600	
Face value of notes at repossession	$ 900	
Less: Unrealized profit (assume gross profit percentage of 33 $\frac{1}{3}$ × $900)	$ 300	
	$ 600	600
Gain on repossession		$ 800
Less: Repossession costs		100
Taxable gain on repossession		$ 700

Repossession gain or loss keeps the same character as the gain or loss realized on the original sale. If the sale originally resulted in a capital gain, the repossession gain is also a capital gain.

Your basis in the repossessed property is its fair market value at the time of repossession.

Real property.   Repossessions of real property are at *31.13*.

5.34 Boot in Like-Kind Exchange Payable in Installments

An exchange of like-kind property is tax free unless boot is received. "Boot" may be cash or notes. If you transfer property subject to a mortgage and the amount of the mortgage you give up exceeds the mortgage you assume on the property received, that excess is boot; *see 6.3*. Boot is taxable, and if payable in installments, the following rules apply. Contract price is reduced by the fair market value of like-kind property received. Gross profit is reduced by gain not recognized. "Payment" does not include like-kind property.

The same treatment applies to certain tax-free reorganizations that are not treated as dividends, to exchanges of certain insurance policies, exchanges of the stock of the same corporation, and exchanges of United States obligations.

EXAMPLE

In 1997, property with an installment sale basis (basis plus selling expenses) of $400,000 is exchanged for like-kind property worth $200,000, plus installment obligations of $800,000, of which $100,000 is payable in 1998, plus interest. The balance of $700,000 plus interest will be paid in 1999. The contract price is $800,000 ($1 million selling price less $200,000 like-kind property received). The gross profit is $600,000 ($1 million less $400,000 installment sale basis). The gross profit ratio is 75% (gross profit of $600,000 ÷ contract price of $800,000). Like-kind property is not treated as a payment received in the year of sale, so no gain is reported in 1997. In 1998, gain of $75,000 will have to be reported (75% gross profit ratio × $100,000 payment), and in 1999 there will be a gain of $525,000 (75% of $700,000 payment).

5.35 "Interest" Tax on Sales over $150,000 plus $5 Million Debt

If deferred payments from installment sales of over $150,000 exceed $5 million, an interest charge is imposed on the tax-deferred amount. The special tax applies to sales of business or rental personal property as well as real estate for over $150,000.

Farm property and personal-use property, such as a residence, are exempt from the tax.

How to report interest tax. The interest charge is an additional tax. The method of computing the interest tax is complicated; the rules are in Internal Revenue Code Section 453A. In general, you compute the ratio of the face amount of outstanding installment obligations in excess of $5 million to the face amount of all outstanding installment obligations. This ratio is multiplied by the year-end unrecognized gain on the obligation, the top tax rate (Chapter 22), and also by the IRS interest rate for the last month of the year.

The interest tax is reported on Line 53 of Form 1040, the line for total tax. The tax is considered personal interest, and is not deductible; *see* Chapter 15.

Pledge rule for property sales over $150,000. If as security for a debt you pledge an installment obligation received on a sale of property exceeding $150,000 (other than farm property or personal-use property), the net proceeds of the secured debt are treated as a payment on the installment obligations, as discussed at *5.26.*

Dealer sale of time shares and residential lots. The above interest tax and pledging rules do not apply to installment obligations from the sale of certain time-share rights (generally time shares of up to six weeks per year) or residential lots. However, under a separate rule, the seller must pay interest on tax deferred under the installment method; *see* the instructions to Schedule C of Form 1040 for reporting the interest charge as an additional tax.

Chapter 6

Tax-Free Exchanges of Property

You may exchange property without incurring a tax in the year of exchange if you meet the rules of this chapter. Gain may be taxed upon a later disposition of the property because the basis of the property received in the exchange is usually the same as the basis of the property surrendered in the exchange. Thus, if you exchange property with a tax basis of $10,000 for property worth $50,000, the basis of the property received in exchange is fixed at $10,000, even though its fair market value is $50,000. The gain of $40,000 ($50,000 – $10,000), which is not taxed, is technically called "unrecognized gain." If you later sell the property for $50,000, you will realize a taxable gain of $40,000 ($50,000 – $10,000).

Where property received in a tax-free exchange is held until death, the unrecognized gain escapes tax forever because basis of the property in the hands of an heir is generally the value of the property at the date of death. If the exchange involves the transfer of boot, such as cash or other property, gain on the exchange is taxable to the extent of the value of boot.

You may not exchange tax-free U.S. real estate for foreign real estate.

Tax-free exchanges between related parties may become taxable if either party disposes of the exchanged property within a two-year period.

6.1 Trades of Like-Kind Property

You may not have to pay tax on gain realized on the "like-kind" exchange of business or investment property. By making a qualifying exchange, you can defer the gain. For tax-free treatment, you must trade property held for business use or investment for like-kind business or investment property. If the properties are not simultaneously exchanged, the time limits of *6.4* must be satisfied. Gain is *completely* tax free only if you do not receive any "boot"; as discussed in *6.3*, gain is taxed to the extent of boot received. Where gain on a qualifying exchange is deferred and not immediately taxed, it may be taxable in a later year when you sell the property because your basis for the new property is generally the same as the basis for the property you traded; basis is discussed at *5.20*.

If you make a qualifying like-kind exchange with certain related parties, tax-free treatment may be lost unless both of you keep the exchanged properties for at least two years; *see 6.5*.

The term *like-kind* refers to the nature or character of the property, that is, whether real estate is traded for real estate. It does not refer to grade or quality, that is, whether the properties traded are new or used. In the case of real estate, land may be traded for a building, farm land for city lots, or a leasehold interest of 30 years or more for an outright ownership in realty. Trades of personal property are discussed at *6.2*.

> **EXAMPLES**
> 1. Jones, a real estate investor, purchased a parcel for investment in 1985 for $5,000. In 1996, he exchanged it for another parcel, Parcel B, which had a fair market value of $50,000. The gain of $45,000 was not taxed in 1996.
> 2. Same facts as above, except that in 1997 Jones sells Parcel B for $50,000. His taxable gain is $45,000. The "tax-free" rules have the effect of deferring tax on appreciation. Tax is finally imposed when the exchanged item is sold.
> 3. Same facts as in 1 above, but the value of Parcel B was $3,000. Jones could not deduct the loss in 1996. The basis of the parcel is $5,000. If Jones sells Parcel B in 1997 for $3,000, he may deduct a loss of $2,000.

Losses. If a loss is incurred on a like-kind exchange, the loss is not deductible, whether you receive only like-kind property or "unlike" property together with like-kind property. However, a deductible loss may be incurred if you give up unlike property as part of the exchange; the loss equals any excess of the adjusted basis of the unlike property over its fair market value.

Reporting an exchange. You must file Form 8824 to report an exchange of like-kind property. If you figure a recognized gain or loss on Form 8824, you also must report the exchange on Schedule D (investment property) or Form 4797 (business property).

See 6.5 for reporting an exchange with a related party.

Property not within the tax-free trade rules:

Property used for personal purposes (except for exchanges of personal residences; *see* Chapter 29)
Foreign real estate
Property held for sale
Inventory or stock-in-trade
Securities; *see 6.2* for exception
Notes
Partnership interest; *see* below

See also 31.4 for tax-free exchanges of realty and *6.11* for tax-free exchanges of insurance policies.

Exchange of partnership interests. Exchanges of partnership interests in different partnerships are not within the tax-free exchange rules. Under IRS regulations, tax-free exchange treatment is denied regardless of whether the interests are in the same or different partnerships.

If you made an election to exclude a partnership interest from the application of partnership rules, your interest is treated as interest in each partnership asset, not as an interest in the partnership.

Real estate in foreign countries. You may not make a tax-free exchange of U.S. real estate for foreign real estate. However, in the case of an involuntary conversion *(18.22)*, a tax-free reinvestment may be made in foreign real estate.

 Law Alert

Personal Property Used Predominantly in U.S.

You may no longer make tax-free exchanges of personal property used predominantly in the U.S. for personal property used predominantly outside the U.S. The new law applies to transfers after June 8, 1997, in tax years ending after that date. An exception applies for contracts binding as of June 8, 1997.

6.2 Personal Property Held for Business or Investment

An exchange of depreciable tangible personal property held for productive business or investment use may qualify for tax-free treatment if it meets either the general like-kind test of *6.1* or a more specific "like-class" test created by IRS regulations. The assumption of liabilities is treated as "boot"; *see 6.3.* Where each party assumes a liability of the other party, the respective liabilities are offset against each other to figure boot, if any.

Under the like-class test, there are two types of "like" classes: (1) General Asset Classes; and (2) Product Classes. The like-class test is satisfied if the exchanged properties are both within the same General Asset Class or the same Product Class. A specific asset may be classified within only one class. Thus, if an asset is within an Asset Class, it may not be within a Product Class. The Asset Class or Product Class is determined as of the date of the exchange. This limitation may disqualify an exchange when exchanged assets do not fit within the same Asset Class and are not allowed to qualify within the Product Class; *see* the Brown Example below.

General Asset Classes. There are 13 classes of depreciable tangible business property. Here are some of the asset classifications: office furniture, fixtures, and equipment (class 00.11); information systems: computers and peripheral equipment (class 00.12); data handling equipment, except computers (class 00.13); airplanes and helicopters, except for airplanes used to carry passengers or freight (class 00.21); automobiles and taxis (class 00.22); light trucks (class 00.241); heavy trucks (class 00.242); and over-the-road tractor units (class 00.26). For example, trades of trucks in class 00.241 would be of like class.

Product Classes. Under a coding system of the Standard Industrial Classification Manual (SIC), tangible depreciable assets are assigned a four-digit product-class number. For example, a grader is exchanged for a scraper. Neither item is within a General Asset Class, but both are in the same Product Class as SIC Code 3533. They are, therefore, of a like class.

EXAMPLES
1. Baker exchanges a personal computer used in his business for a printer. Both assets are productively used in business and are in the same General Asset Class of 00.12; the exchange meets the like-class test.

2. Brown exchanges an airplane (asset class 00.21) used in her business for a heavy truck (asset class 00.242). The exchanged properties are not of a like class. Furthermore, since each property is within a specific General Asset Class, the Product Class test may not be applied to qualify the exchange. Brown must report any gain realized on the exchange because the properties also do not meet the general like-kind test.

Intangible personal property and goodwill. Exchanges of intangible personal property (such as a patent or copyright) or nondepreciable personal property must meet the general like-kind test to qualify for tax-free treatment; the like-class tests do not apply. However, regulations close the door for qualifying exchanges of goodwill in an exchange of going businesses. According to the regulations, goodwill or going concern value of one business can never be of a like kind to goodwill or going concern value of another business.

Exchanges of multiple properties. Generally, exchanges of assets are considered on a one-to-one basis. Regulations provide an exception for exchanges of multiple properties, such as on an exchange of businesses. Transferred assets are separated into exchange groups. An exchange group consists of all properties transferred and received in the exchange which are of a like kind or like class. All properties within the same General Asset Class or same Product Class are in the same exchange group. For example, automobiles and computers are exchanged for other automobiles and computers; two exchange groups are set up-one for the automobiles and the other for the computers. If the aggregate fair market values of the properties transferred and received in each exchange group are not equal, the regulations provide calculations for setting up a residual group for purposes of calculating taxable gain, if any.

All liabilities of which a taxpayer is relieved in the exchange are offset against all liabilities assumed by the taxpayer in the exchange, regardless of whether the liabilities are recourse, nonrecourse, or are secured by the specific property transferred or received. If excess liabilities are assumed by the taxpayer as part of the exchange, regulations provide rules for allocating the excess among the properties.

6.3 Receipt of Cash and Other Property—"Boot"

If, in addition to like-kind *(6.1)* property, you receive cash or other property (unlike kind), gain is taxable up to the amount of the cash or other property received. The additional cash or other property is called "boot." If a loss was incurred on the exchange, the receipt of boot does not permit you to deduct the loss unless it is attributable to *unlike*-kind property you gave up in the exchange.

If you transfer mortgaged property, the amount of the mortgage is part of your boot. If both you and the other party transfer and receive mortgaged property, the party giving up the larger debt treats the excess as taxable boot. The party giving up the smaller debt does not have boot; *see also 31.4*. If you pay cash to the other party, add this to the mortgage you receive in figuring which party has given up the larger debt.

Form 8824. The computation of boot, gain (or loss), and basis of the property received is made on Form 8824.

EXAMPLE

Jones owns an apartment house with a fair market value of $220,000, subject to an $80,000 mortgage. His adjusted basis is $100,000. Jones exchanges his building for Smith's apartment building, which has a value of $250,000, subject to a $150,000 mortgage. Jones also receives $40,000 in cash. Smith's adjusted basis for the building he trades is $175,000. Smith and Jones each pay $5,000 in exchange expenses.

The sample Forms 8824 for Jones and Smith on the next page show how they report the exchange. On Line 15, they show the boot received; their taxable gain is limited to this boot. For Jones, boot is the cash boot of $40,000. For Smith, the Line 15 boot is $30,000:

Mortgage transferred to Jones		$150,000
Less: Mortgage assumed by Smith	$80,000	
Plus: Cash paid by Smith	40,000	120,000
		$ 30,000

On Line 18, Jones and Smith increase their basis for the buildings they traded by exchange expenses and the net amounts paid to the other party. For Jones, the Line 18 total of $175,000 includes:

Adjusted basis of building traded		$100,000
Exchange expenses		5,000
Net mortgage assumed:		
Mortgage assumed	$150,000	
Less: Mortgage transferred	80,000	70,000
		$175,000

For Smith the Line 18 total of $180,000 includes:		
Adjusted basis of building traded		$175,000
Exchange expenses		5,000
Net amount paid:		
Mortgage assumed	$80,000	
Cash paid	40,000	
	120,000	
Less: Mortgage transferred	150,000	0
		$180,000

Line 25 shows the basis of the buildings Jones and Smith receive in the exchange.

6.4 Time Limits for Deferred Exchanges

Assume you own property which has appreciated in value. You want to sell it and reinvest the proceeds in other property, but you would like to avoid having to pay tax on the appreciation. You can avoid the tax if you are able to arrange an exchange for similar property.

The problem is that it may be difficult to find a buyer who has property you want in exchange, and the time for closing the exchange is restricted. If IRS tests are met, intermediaries and security arrangements may be used without running afoul of constructive receipt rules that could trigger an immediate tax.

Sample Form 8824 for Jones (see Example on previous page)

Part III	Realized Gain or (Loss), Recognized Gain, and Basis of Like-Kind Property Received		

Caution: *If you transferred **and** received **(a)** more than one group of like-kind properties, or **(b)** cash or other (not like-kind) property, see instructions under **Multi-Asset Exchanges**.*

Note: *Complete lines 12 through 14 ONLY if you gave up property that was not like-kind. Otherwise, go to line 15.*

12	Fair market value (FMV) of other property given up	**12**	
13	Adjusted basis of other property given up	**13**	
14	Gain or (loss) recognized on other property given up. Subtract line 13 from line 12. Report the gain or (loss) in the same manner as if the exchange had been a sale	**14**	
15	Cash received, FMV of other property received, plus net liabilities assumed by other party, reduced (but not below zero) by any exchange expenses you incurred. See instructions	**15**	40,000
16	FMV of like-kind property you received	**16**	250,000
17	Add lines 15 and 16	**17**	290,000
18	Adjusted basis of like-kind property you gave up, net amounts paid to other party, plus any exchange expenses **not** used on line 15. See instructions	**18**	175,000
19	**Realized gain or (loss).** Subtract line 18 from line 17	**19**	115,000
20	Enter the smaller of line 15 or line 19, but not less than zero	**20**	40,000
21	Ordinary income under recapture rules. Enter here and on Form 4797, line 17. See instructions	**21**	- 0 -
22	Subtract line 21 from line 20. If zero or less, enter -0-. If more than zero, enter here and on Schedule D or Form 4797, unless the installment method applies. See instructions	**22**	40,000
23	**Recognized gain.** Add lines 21 and 22	**23**	40,000
24	Deferred gain or (loss). Subtract line 23 from line 19. If a related party exchange, see instructions	**24**	75,000
25	**Basis of like-kind property received.** Subtract line 15 from the sum of lines 18 and 23	**25**	175,000

Sample Form 8824 for Smith (see Example on previous page)

Part III	Realized Gain or (Loss), Recognized Gain, and Basis of Like-Kind Property Received		

Caution: *If you transferred **and** received **(a)** more than one group of like-kind properties, or **(b)** cash or other (not like-kind) property, see instructions under **Multi-Asset Exchanges**.*

Note: *Complete lines 12 through 14 ONLY if you gave up property that was not like-kind. Otherwise, go to line 15.*

12	Fair market value (FMV) of other property given up	**12**	
13	Adjusted basis of other property given up	**13**	
14	Gain or (loss) recognized on other property given up. Subtract line 13 from line 12. Report the gain or (loss) in the same manner as if the exchange had been a sale	**14**	
15	Cash received, FMV of other property received, plus net liabilities assumed by other party, reduced (but not below zero) by any exchange expenses you incurred. See instructions	**15**	30,000
16	FMV of like-kind property you received	**16**	220,000
17	Add lines 15 and 16	**17**	250,000
18	Adjusted basis of like-kind property you gave up, net amounts paid to other party, plus any exchange expenses **not** used on line 15. See instructions	**18**	180,000
19	**Realized gain or (loss).** Subtract line 18 from line 17	**19**	70,000
20	Enter the smaller of line 15 or line 19, but not less than zero	**20**	30,000
21	Ordinary income under recapture rules. Enter here and on Form 4797, line 17. See instructions	**21**	-0-
22	Subtract line 21 from line 20. If zero or less, enter -0-. If more than zero, enter here and on Schedule D or Form 4797, unless the installment method applies. See instructions	**22**	30,000
23	**Recognized gain.** Add lines 21 and 22	**23**	30,000
24	Deferred gain or (loss). Subtract line 23 from line 19. If a related party exchange, see instructions	**24**	40,000
25	**Basis of like-kind property received.** Subtract line 15 from the sum of lines 18 and 23	**25**	180,000

Caution

Strict Time Limits
No extensions of time are allowed if the 45-day or 180-day statutory deadlines cannot be met. If extra time is needed for finding suitable replacement property, it is advisable to delay the date of your property transfer because the transfer date starts the 45-day identification period.

Time limits for completing exchanges. You generally have up to 180 days to complete an exchange, but the deadline may end sooner. Specifically, property will not be treated as like-kind property if received (1) more than 180 days after the date you transferred the property you are relinquishing; or (2) the due date of your return (including extensions) for the year in which you made the transfer, whichever is earlier. Furthermore, the property to be received must be identified within 45 days after the date on which you transferred property.

If the transaction involves more than one property, the 45-day identification period and the 180-day exchange period are determined by the earliest date on which any property is transferred. When the identification or exchange period ends on a Saturday, Sunday, or legal holiday, the deadline is not advanced to the next business day (as it is when the deadline for filing a tax return is on a weekend or holiday).

How to identify property. You must identify replacement property in a written document signed by you and either hand delivered, mailed, telecopied, or otherwise sent before the end of the 45-day identification period to a person involved in the exchange other than yourself or a related party. The identification may also be made in a written agreement. The property must be unambiguously described by a legal description or street address.

You may identify more than one property as replacement property. However, the maximum number of replacement properties that you may identify without regard to the fair market value is three properties. You may identify any number of properties provided the aggregate fair market value at the end of the 45-day identification period does not exceed 200% of the aggregate fair market value of all the relinquished properties as of the date you transferred them. If, as of the end of the identification period, you have identified more than the allowable number of properties, you are generally treated as if no replacement property has been identified.

Receipt of security. In a deferred exchange, you want financial security for the buyer's performance and compensation for delay in receiving property. To avoid immediate tax, you must not make a security arrangement that gives you an unrestricted right to funds before the deal is closed.

> **EXAMPLE**
> You and Jones agree to enter a deferred exchange under the following terms and conditions. On May 17, 1997, you transfer to Jones real estate which has been held for investment; it is unencumbered and has a fair market value of $100,000. On or before July 1, 1997 (the end of the 45-day identification period), you must identify like-kind replacement property. On or before November 13, 1997 (the end of the 180-day exchange period), Jones is required to buy the property and transfer it to you. At any time after May 17, 1997, and before Jones has purchased the replacement property, you have the right, upon notice, to demand that he pay you $100,000 instead of acquiring and transferring the replacement property. However, you identify replacement property, and Jones purchases and transfers it to you. According to the regulations, you have an unrestricted right to demand the payment of $100,000 as of May 17, 1997. You are therefore in constructive receipt of $100,000 on that date. Thus, the transaction is treated as a taxable sale, and the transfer of the real property does not qualify as a tax-free exchange. You are treated as if you received the $100,000 for the sale of your property and then purchased replacement property.

Safe harbor tests for security arrangements. If one of the following safe harbors applies to your security arrangement, you are not taxed as if a sale were made.

The first two "safe harbors" cover transfers dealing directly with the buyer. The third allows the use of professional intermediaries who, for a fee, arrange the details of the exchange. The fourth allows you to earn interest on an escrow account. The safe harbors generally prohibit you from receiving money or other non-like-kind property before replacement property is received. The terms of the agreement govern whether your right to receive the funds is limited as required by the safe harbor rules; possible state law complications are disregarded.

1. The transferee may give you a mortgage, deed of trust, or other security interest in property (other than cash or a cash equivalent), or a third-party guarantee. A standby letter of credit may be given if you are not allowed to draw on such standby letter except upon a default of the transferee's obligation to transfer like-kind replacement property.

2. The transferee may put cash or a cash equivalent in a qualified escrow account or a qualified trust. The escrow holder or trustee must not be related to you. Your rights to receive, pledge, borrow, or otherwise obtain the cash must be limited. For example, you may obtain the cash after all of the

replacement property to which you are entitled is received. After you identify replacement property, you may obtain the cash after the later of (1) the end of the identification period; and (2) the occurrence of a contingency beyond your control that you have specified in writing. You may receive the funds after the end of the identification period if within that period you do not identify replacement property. In other cases, there can be no right to the funds until the exchange period ends.

3. You may use a *qualified intermediary* if your right to receive money or other property is limited (as discussed in safe harbor rule 2, above). A qualified intermediary is an unrelated party who, for a fee, acts to facilitate a deferred exchange by entering into an agreement with you for the exchange of properties pursuant to which the intermediary acquires your property from you, acquires the replacement property, and transfers the replacement property to you. The acquisitions may be on the intermediary's own behalf or as the agent of any party to the transaction.

   The transfer of property that is facilitated by the use of a qualified intermediary may occur through a "direct deed" of legal title by the current owner of the property to you. The transferee of your property does *not* have to receive title to the property you want and then transfer it to you.

   There are restrictions on who may act as an intermediary. You may not employ any person as an intermediary who is your employee or is related to you or has generally acted as your professional adviser such as an attorney, accountant, investment broker, real estate agent, or banker in a two-year period preceding the exchange. Related parties include family members and controlled businesses or trusts *(see 5.5)*, except that for purposes of control, a 10% interest is sufficient under the intermediary rule. The performance of routine financial, escrow, trust, or title insurance services by a financial institution or title company within the two-year period is not taken into account. State laws which may be interpreted as fixing an agency relationship between the transferor and transferee or fixing the transferor's right to security funds are ignored.

   In a simultaneous exchange, the intermediary is not considered the transferor's agent.

4. You are permitted to receive interest or a "growth factor" on escrowed funds if your right to receive the amount is limited as discussed under safe harbor rule 2.

Payment of acquisition and closing costs. The use of funds from a security account to pay specific acquisition and closing costs such as commissions, prorated taxes, and recording and transfer fees will not result in constructive receipt of the remaining funds.

6.5 Exchanges Between Related Parties

Tax-free treatment of like-kind exchanges between related persons may be lost, if either party disposes of property received in the exchange within two years after the date of the last transfer that was part of the exchange. Any gain not recognized on the original exchange is taxable as of the date of the later disposition of the original like-kind property by either party within the two-year period. If a loss was not recognized, the loss becomes deductible if allowed under the rules of *33.10*. This two-year rule does not apply to transfers made under a written binding contract that was in effect on and after July 10, 1989, or to the exceptions listed below.

Indirect dispositions of the property within the two-year period, such as transfer of stock of a corporation or interests in a partnership that owns the property, may also be treated as taxable dispositions.

Related parties. Related persons falling within the two-year rule include your children, grandchildren, parent, brother, or sister, controlled corporations or partnerships (more than 50% ownership), and a trust in which you are a beneficiary. A transfer to a spouse is not subject to the two-year rule unless he or she is a nonresident alien.

Plan to avoid two-year rule. If you set up a prearranged plan under which you first transfer property to an unrelated party who within two years makes an exchange with a party related to you, the related party will not qualify for tax-free treatment on that exchange.

Exceptions. No tax will be incurred on a disposition made because of death; in an involuntary conversion provided the original exchange occurred before the threat of the conversion; or if you can prove that neither the exchange nor the later disposition was for a tax avoidance purpose.

6.6 Property Transfers Between Spouses and Ex-Spouses

All transfers between spouses are tax-free, *other than* transfers to a nonresident alien spouse, certain trust transfers of mortgaged property, and transfers of U.S. Savings Bonds; these exceptions are discussed below. The tax-free exchange rules apply to transfers during marriage as well as to property settlements incident to a divorce. A transfer is "incident to a divorce" if it occurs either within one year after the date the marriage ceases or, if later, is related to the cessation of the marriage,

Filing Tip

Filing Form 8824
The IRS requires related parties who exchange property to file Form 8824 for the year of the exchange and also for the two years following the exchange. If either party disposes of the property received in the original exchange in any of these years, the deferred gain must be reported in the year of disposition as if the property had been sold.

Planning Reminder

Recipient Spouse Bears Tax Consequences

Under the tax-free exchange rules, there is no taxable gain or deductible loss on the transfer of property, even if cash is received for the property or the other spouse (or former spouse) assumes liabilities or gives up marital rights as part of a property settlement. The spouse who receives property may incur tax on a later sale because his or her basis in the property is the same as the transferor-spouse's basis; *see* the Examples on the right. Because the transferee bears the tax consequences of a later sale, he or she should consider the potential tax on the appreciation in negotiating a marital settlement. In a marital settlement, the transferee spouse can lessen the tax burden by negotiating for assets that have little or no unrealized appreciation.

Planning Reminder

Transfers to Third Parties

A transfer to a third party on behalf of a spouse or former spouse qualifies for tax-free exchange treatment where the transfer is required by a divorce or separation instrument, or if you have your spouse's or former spouse's written request or consent for the transfer. The transfer is treated as if made to your spouse or former spouse, who then retransfers the property to the third party. A written request or consent must specifically state that the tax-free exchange rules of Code Section 1041 are intended, and you must receive it before filing the tax return for the year of the transfer; but *see* divorce-related stock redemption on the right.

such as a transfer authorized by a divorce decree. Under temporary regulations, any transfer pursuant to a divorce or separation agreement occurring within six years of the end of the marriage is considered "incident to a divorce." Later transfers qualify only if a transfer within the six-year period was hampered by legal or business disputes such as a fight over the property value.

Nonresident alien. The tax-free exchange rule does not apply to transfers to a nonresident alien spouse or former spouse. A transfer before June 22, 1988, to a former spouse who was a nonresident alien was subject to the tax-free exchange rule if the transfer was "incident to a divorce."

EXAMPLES

1. In a property settlement accompanying a divorce, a husband plans to transfer to his wife stock worth $250,000 that cost him $50,000. In deciding whether to agree to the transfer, the wife should be aware that her basis for the stock will be $50,000; if she sells the stock, she will have to pay tax on the $200,000 gain. This tax cost should be accounted for in arriving at the settlement.

2. Basis of the property in the hands of the transferee-spouse is not increased even if cash is paid as part of the transfer. For example, a husband received a house originally owned by the wife as part of a marital settlement. Her basis for the house was $32,200. He paid her $18,000 cash as part of the settlement and when he later sold the house for $64,000, he argued that his basis for purposes of computing profit was $50,200—the wife's $32,200 basis plus his $18,000 cash payment. The IRS refused to consider the cash payment as part of basis, and the Tax Court agreed that the carryover basis rule applies.

Is a divorce-related redemption of stock in a closely held corporation subject to the tax-free exchange rules? The IRS has consistently disputed tax-free treatment for a spouse whose closely held corporation's stock is redeemed as part of an overall divorce settlement. It argues that a stock redemption between one spouse and a closely held corporation results in a taxable sale and does not fall within the exception for transfers to third parties, discussed above in the Planning Reminder on the left. To hedge against the possibility that a court may rule against its position that the redeeming spouse should be taxed on the proceeds, the IRS will maintain a fallback position: If the redeeming spouse is not taxable, the nonredeeming shareholder should be treated as having received a taxable constructive dividend as a result of the redemption.

EXAMPLES

1. The IRS position that a closely held corporation's redemption of one spouse's stock is taxable was rejected by a federal district court and the Ninth Circuit Court of Appeals, which held that a wife was not taxable on the redemption of her stock by the couple's closely held corporation where the redemption was pursuant to their divorce agreement and incorporated into the divorce decree. The Ninth Circuit viewed the transfer as if the husband had received the stock directly from the wife and then transferred it to the company.

   After the Ninth Circuit held that the redemption was not taxable to the wife, the IRS argued in a separate case against the nonredeeming husband that he received a taxable constructive dividend. However, the Tax Court disagreed, holding that there was no dividend to the husband because under state law he was merely a guarantor; he was not primarily and unconditionally obligated to buy the stock. The IRS did not appeal the Tax Court decision.

   In this unusual case, the IRS is in the position of being unable to collect tax on the redemption proceeds from either the transferor or transferree spouse.

2. The Tax Court refused to follow the Ninth Circuit decision referred to in Example 1 and denied tax-free treatment to a redeeming spouse although the redemption was required by the divorce decree. The Tax Court held that the redemption did not satisfy an obligation of the nonredeeming spouse, and thus it was not paid on his behalf.

Transfers of U.S. Savings Bonds. The IRS has ruled that the tax-free exchange rules do not apply to transfers of U.S. Savings Bonds. For example, if a husband has deferred the reporting of interest on E or EE bonds and transfers the bonds to his ex-wife as part of a divorce settlement, the deferred interest is taxed to him on the transfer. The wife's basis for the bonds is the husband's basis plus the income he realizes on the transfer. When she redeems the bonds, she will be taxed on the interest accrued from the date of the transfer to the redemption date.

Payment for release of community property interest in retirement pay. The Tax Court allowed tax-free treatment for a payment made to a wife for releasing her community property claim to her husband's military retirement pay. The IRS had argued that the tax-free exchange rules discussed in this section did not apply to the release of rights to retirement pay that would otherwise be subject to ordinary income tax. The Tax Court disagreed, holding that the tax-free exchange rule applies whether the transfer is for relinquishment of marital rights, cash, or other property.

Transfers in trust. The tax-free exchange rules generally apply to transfers in trust for the benefit of a spouse or a former spouse if incident to a divorce. However, if the trust property is mortgaged, the transferor spouse must report a taxable gain to the extent that the liabilities assumed by the transferee spouse plus the liabilities to which the property is subject (even if not assumed) exceed the transferor's adjusted basis for the property. If the transferor realizes a taxable gain under this rule, the transferee's basis for the property is increased by the gain.

Sole proprietorship sale to spouse. Tax-free exchange rules may apply to a sale of business property by a sole proprietor to a spouse. The buyer spouse assumes a carryover basis even if fair market value is paid. The transferor is not required to recapture previously claimed depreciation deductions or investment credits. However, the transferee is subject to the recapture rules on premature dispositions or if the property ceases to be used for business purposes.

Agreements existing on July 18, 1984. The tax-free exchange rules generally apply to transfers made after July 18, 1984. Transfers made under agreements in effect before July 19, 1984, are subject to the tax-free rule only if both spouses make an election to have the tax-free rule apply. The election must be made on a signed statement attached to the first tax return filed by the transferor-spouse for the year in which the first transfer occurs. The transferor must also attach the statement to returns for later years in which a transfer is made under the election.

6.7 Tax-Free Exchanges of Stock

Gain on the exchange of common stock for other common stock (or preferred for other preferred of the same company) is not taxable. Similarly, loss realized on such an exchange is not deductible. The exchange may take place between the stockholder and the company or between two stockholders.

An exchange of preferred stock for common, or common for preferred, in the same company, is generally not tax free, unless the exchange is part of a tax-free recapitalization. In such exchanges, the company should inform you of the tax consequences.

Convertible securities. Conversion of securities under a conversion privilege is tax free under the rules discussed at *30.8*.

6.8 Joint Ownership Interests

The change to a tenancy in common from a joint tenancy is tax free. You may convert a joint tenancy in corporate stock to a tenancy in common without income-tax consequences. The transfer is tax free even though survivorship rights are eliminated. Similarly, a partition and issuance of separate certificates in the names of each joint tenant is also tax free.

A joint tenancy and a tenancy in common differ in this respect. On the death of a joint tenant, ownership passes to the surviving joint tenant or tenants. But on the death of a tenant holding property in common, ownership passes to his or her heirs, not to the other tenant or tenants with whom the property was held.

A tenancy by the entirety is a form of joint ownership recognized in some states and can be only between a husband and wife.

Dividing properties held in common. A division of properties held as tenants in common may qualify as tax-free exchanges.

For example, three men owned three pieces of real estate as tenants in common. Each man wanted to be the sole owner of one of the pieces of property. They disentangled themselves by exchanging interests in a three-way exchange. No money or property other than the three pieces of real estate changed hands, and none of the men assumed any liability of the others. The transactions qualified as tax-free exchanges and no gain or loss was recognized.

Receipt of boot. Exchanges of jointly owned property are tax free as long as no "boot," such as cash or other property, passes between the parties; *see 6.3*.

 Caution

Trust Transfer of Leveraged Property
You will not be able to avoid gain on heavily mortgaged property transferred to a trust for your spouse or to a former spouse under a divorce decree. The excess of the liabilities on the property over your adjusted basis is taxable gain.

Caution

Consider Taxable Transfer

Before making a property transfer to a closely held corporation, consult an accountant or an attorney on the tax consequences. It may not be to your advantage to fall within the tax-free exchange rules. This is so when you have property with potential losses or you wish the corporation to take a stepped-up basis for property.

6.9 Setting Up Closely Held Corporations

Tax-free exchange rules facilitate the organization of a corporation. When you transfer property to a corporation that you control solely in exchange for corporate stock, no gain or loss is recognized on the transfer. For control, you alone or together with other transferrers (such as partners, where a partnership is being incorporated) must own at least 80% of the combined voting power of the corporation and 80% of all other classes of stock immediately after the transfer to the corporation. If you receive securities in addition to stock, the securities are treated as taxable "boot." The corporation takes your basis in the property, and your basis in the stock received in the exchange is the same as your basis in the property. Gain not recognized on the organization of the corporation may be taxed when you sell your stock, or the corporation disposes of the property.

EXAMPLE

You transfer a building worth $100,000, which cost you $20,000, to your newly organized corporation in exchange for all of its outstanding stock. You realize an $80,000 gain ($100,000 – $20,000) which is not recognized. Your basis in the stock is $20,000; the corporation's basis in the building is $20,000. The following year, you sell all your stock to a third party for $100,000. The $80,000 gain is now recognized.

Transfer of liabilities. When assets subject to liabilities are transferred to the corporation, the liability assumed by the corporation is not treated as a taxable "boot," but your stock basis is reduced by the amount of liability. The transfer of liabilities may be taxable when the transfer is part of a tax avoidance scheme, or the liabilities exceed the basis of the property transferred to the corporation.

6.10 Exchanges of Coins and Bullion

An exchange of "gold for gold" coins or "silver for silver" coins may qualify as a tax-free exchange of like-kind investment property. An exchange is tax free if both coins represent the same type of underlying investment. An exchange of bullion-type coins for bullion-type coins is a tax-free like-kind exchange. For example, the exchange of Mexican pesos for Austrian coronas has been held to be a tax-free exchange as both are bullion-type coins.

However, an exchange of silver bullion for gold bullion is not tax free. Silver and gold bullion represent different types of property. Silver is an industrial commodity, whereas gold is primarily an investment in itself. Similarly, an exchange of U.S. gold collector's coins for South African Krugerrands is taxable. Krugerrands are bullion-type coins whose value is determined solely by metal content, whereas the U.S. gold coins are numismatic coins whose value depends on age, condition, number minted, and artistic merit, as well as metal content. Although both coins appear to be similar in gold content, each represents a different type of investment.

6.11 Tax-Free Exchanges of Insurance Policies

These exchanges of insurance policies are considered tax free:

Life insurance policy for another life insurance policy, endowment policy, or an annuity contract.
Endowment policy for another endowment policy that provides for regular payments beginning no later than the date payments would have started under the old policy, or in exchange for an annuity contract.
Annuity contract for another annuity contract with identical annuitants.

These exchanges are not tax free:

Endowment policy for a life insurance policy, or for another endowment policy that provides for payments beginning at a date later than payments would have started under the old policy.
Annuity contract for a life insurance or endowment policy.
Transfers of life insurance contracts where the insured is not the same person in both contracts. The IRS held that a company could not make a tax-free exchange of a key executive policy where the company could change insured executives as they leave or join the firm.

Planning Reminder

Financially Troubled Insurer

If your annuity contract or insurance policy is with an insurance company that is in a rehabilitation, conservatorship, insolvency, or a similar state proceeding, you may surrender the policy and make a tax-free reinvestment of the proceeds in a new policy with a different insurance company. The transfer must be completed within 60 days. If a government agency does not allow you to withdraw your entire balance from the troubled insurance company, you must assign all rights to any future distributions to the issuer of the new contract or policy. Full details are in IRS Revenue Procedure 92-44.

Chapter 7

Retirement and Annuity Income

Retirement planning may be the final frontier for achieving substantial tax shelter benefits. For employees, coverage in a qualified employer retirement plan is a valuable fringe benefit, as employer contributions are tax free within specified limits. Certain plans allow you to make tax-free contributions of salary under a salary reduction arrangement. An advantage of all qualified retirement plans is that earnings accumulate tax free until withdrawal.

Along with tax savings opportunities come technical restrictions and pitfalls. For example, retirement plan distributions eligible for rollover are subject to a mandatory 20% withholding tax if you do not instruct your employer to make a direct trustee-to-trustee transfer of the distribution to an IRA or another qualified employer plan.

This chapter discusses tax treatment of annuities and employer plan distributions, including how to avoid tax penalties, such as for distributions before age $59\frac{1}{2}$. IRAs are discussed in Chapter 8. Retirement plans for self-employed individuals are discussed further in Chapter 41.

Under the rubric of "simplification," previously allowed benefits, such as lump-sum averaging and the death benefit exclusion, have been restricted or eliminated by Congress; the new laws are highlighted in the text.

Key to Tax-Favored Retirement Plans

Type—	General Tax Considerations—	Tax Treatment of 1997 Distributions—
Company qualified plan	A company qualified pension or profit-sharing plan offers these benefits: (1) You do not realize current income on your employer's contributions to the plan on your behalf. (2) Income earned on funds contributed to your account compounds tax free. (3) Your employer may allow you to make voluntary contributions. Although these contributions may not be deducted, income earned on the voluntary contributions is not taxed until withdrawn.	If you receive a lump sum after age 59 ½, tax on employer contributions may be reduced by a special averaging rule; *see 7.4*. If you receive a lump-sum distribution in company securities, unrealized appreciation on those securities is not taxed until you finally sell the stock; *see 7.10*. Distributions before age 59 ½ are generally subject to penalties, but there are exceptions; *see 7.14*. Rather than pay an immediate tax, you may elect to roll over a lump-sum payment to an IRA account; *see 7.8*. If you collect your retirement benefits as an annuity over a period of years, *see 7.25*.
Keogh or self-employed plans	You may set up a self-employed retirement plan called a Keogh plan if you earn self-employment income through your performance of personal services. You may deduct contributions up to limits discussed in Chapter 41; income earned on assets held by the plan is not taxed. You must include employees under rules explained in Chapter 41.	As a self-employed person, you generally may not withdraw funds until age 59 ½ unless you are disabled. Premature withdrawals are subject to a 10% penalty. Qualified distributions to self-employed persons or to beneficiaries at death may qualify for favored lump-sum treatment under the rules of *7.2*.
IRA	Anyone who has earned income may contribute to an IRA, but the contribution is deductible only if certain requirements are met. Your status as a participant in an employer retirement plan and your income determine whether you may claim a full $2,000 IRA deduction, a partial deduction, or no deduction at all. *See* Chapter 8 for these deduction limitations. Where deductible contributions are allowed, IRAs offer these benefits: (1) deductions of up to $2,000 for single persons, $4,000 for married couples filing jointly and (2) income earned on IRA accounts is not taxed until the funds are withdrawn. This tax-free build-up of earnings also applies where you make nondeductible IRA contributions under the rules of Chapter 8.	An IRA withdrawal in 1997 before age 59 ½ is subject to a 10% penalty but there are exceptions if you are disabled, have substantial medical expenses, pay medical premiums while unemployed, or receive payments in a series of substantially equal installments: *see 8.12* for exception details. Starting at age 70 ½, you must receive minimum annual distributions to avoid a 50% penalty; *see 8.14*. IRA distributions are fully taxable unless you have previously made nondeductible contributions; *see 8.8*.
SEP	A simplified employee pension plan set up by your employer allows the employer to contribute to an IRA more than you can under regular IRA rules. You do not have to include in 1997 income any employer contributions to your account. If your employer qualifies, you may be allowed to make elective deferrals of salary to the plan, up to $9,500 in 1997; *see also 8.17*.	Withdrawals are taxable under rules explained above for IRAs.
Deferred salary or 401(k) plans	If your company has a profit-sharing or stock bonus plan, the tax law allows the company to add a cash or deferred pay plan which can operate in one of two ways: (1) Your employer contributes an amount for your benefit to your trust account. You are not taxed on your employer's contribution. (2) You agree to take a salary reduction or to forego a salary increase. The reduction is placed in a trust account for your benefit. The reduction is treated as your employer's contribution. In 1997, the maximum salary reduction is $9,500. Income earned on the trust account accumulates tax free until it is withdrawn.	Withdrawals are penalized unless you have reached age 59 ½, become disabled, or meet other exceptions listed at *7.14*. If you receive a qualifying lump sum after age 59 ½, tax on the lump sum may be computed under the rules of *7.2*.

Distributions From Qualified Retirement Plans

7.1 Retirement Distributions on Form 1099-R

On Form 1099-R, payments from pensions, annuities, IRAs, SIMPLE IRAs, insurance contracts, profit-sharing, and other employer plans are reported to you and the IRS. Social security benefits are reported on Form SSA-1099; *see* Chapter 34 for the special rules to apply in determining the taxable portion of Social Security benefits.

Here is a guide to the information reported on Form 1099-R. A sample form is on the next page.

Box 1. The total amount received from the payer is shown here without taking any withholdings into account. If you file Form 1040, report the Box 1 total on Line 15a if the payment is from an IRA, or on Line 16a if from a pension or an annuity. However, if the amount is a qualifying lump-sum distribution for which you are claiming averaging, use Form 4972; *see 7.4.*

If you file Form 1040A, report the Box 1 total on Line 10a if from an IRA, or on Line 11a if from a pension or an annuity.

If you are receiving the distribution as a beneficiary of an employee who died before August 21, 1996, you may be entitled to a $5,000 death benefit exclusion; *see 7.28.*

If an exchange of insurance contracts was made, the value of the contract will be shown in Box 1, but if the exchange qualified as tax free, a zero taxable amount will be shown in Box 2a and Code 6 will be entered in Box 7.

Boxes 2a and 2b. The taxable portion of distributions from employer plans and insurance contracts may be shown in Box 2a. The taxable portion does not include your after-tax contributions to an employer plan, or insurance premium payments.

If the payer cannot figure the taxable portion, the first box in 2b should be checked; Box 2a should be blank. You will then have to figure the taxable amount yourself. A payment from a pension or an annuity is only partially taxed if you contributed to the cost and you did not recover your entire cost investment before 1997. *See 7.22* (commercial annuity) or *7.25* (employee annuity) for details on computing the taxable portion if you have an unrecovered investment.

The payer of an IRA distribution will probably not compute the taxable portion, and in this case, the total distribution from Box 1 will be entered as the taxable portion in Box 2a. This amount is fully taxable unless you have made nondeductible contributions; *see 8.8.*

If the payment is from an employer plan and the "total distribution" box has been checked in 2b, *see 7.2* for possible rollover and special averaging options. The taxable amount in Box 2a should not include net unrealized appreciation in any employer securities included in the lump sum or the value of an annuity contract included in the distribution.

Box 3. If the payment is a lump-sum distribution, and you participated in the plan before 1974, the amount shown here may be treated as capital gain; *see 7.5.*

Box 4. Any federal income tax withheld is shown here. Do not forget to include it on Line 54 of Form 1040 or Line 29a of Form 1040A. If Box 4 shows any withholdings, attach Copy B of Form 1099-R to your return.

Box 5. If you made after-tax contributions to your employer's plan, or paid premiums for a commercial annuity or insurance contract, your contribution is shown here, less any such contributions previously distributed. IRA or SEP contributions (*see* Chapter 8) are not shown here.

Box 6. If you received a qualifying lump-sum distribution that includes securities of your employer's company, the net unrealized appreciation is shown here. Unless you elect to pay tax on it currently *(7.10),* this amount is not taxed until you sell the securities. If you did not receive a qualifying lump sum, the amount shown here is the net unrealized appreciation attributable to your after-tax employee contributions which are also not taxed until you sell the securities; *see 7.10.*

Box 7. In Box 7, the payer will indicate if the distribution is from an IRA or SEP and enter codes that are used by the IRS to check if you have reported the distribution correctly, including the 10% penalty for distributions before age 59 ½.

If you are under age 59 ½ and the employer knows that you qualify for an exception to the 10% early distribution penalty *(7.14),* such as the exception for separation of service after age 55, your employer will enter Code 2 in Box 7. Code 3 will be used if the disability exception applies. Code 4 is the exception for distributions paid to beneficiaries. If Code 1 is entered, this indicates that you were under age 59 ½ at the time of the distribution and as far as the payer knows, no penalty exception applies. However, although Code 1 is entered, you may not be subject to a penalty. For example, you may qualify for the medical expense exception *(7.14)* or you may have made a tax-free rollover instead of having your employer make a direct rollover under the rules of 7.8. If the employer did make a direct rollover, Code G will be entered if the direct rollover was to an IRA, and Code H if to another employer's qualified plan or tax-sheltered annuity.

If you are at least age 59 ½, Code 7 should be entered.

If you are the beneficiary of a deceased employee, Code 4 should be entered. The 10% early distribution penalty does not apply.

If you contribute to a 401(k) plan and are a highly compensated employee, your employer may have to make a corrective distribution to you of contributions (and allocable income) that exceed allowable nondiscrimination ceilings. In this case, the employer will enter Code 8 if the corrective distribution is taxable in 1997, Code P if taxable in 1996, or Code D if taxable in 1995.

If you receive a lump-sum distribution that qualifies for special averaging, Code A will be entered; *see 7.4* for averaging rules.

Box 8. If the value of an annuity contract was included as part of a lump sum you received, the value of the contract is shown here. It is not taxable when you receive it and should not be included in Boxes 1 and 2a. For purposes of computing averaging on Form 4972, this amount is added to the ordinary income portion of the distribution; *see 7.4.*

Box 9. If several beneficiaries are receiving payment from an employer plan total distribution, the amount shown in Box 9a is your share of the distribution.

Boxes 10–15. The payer may make entries in these boxes to show state or local income tax withholdings.

7.2 Lump-Sum Distributions

If you are entitled to a lump-sum distribution from a company retirement plan or self-employed Keogh plan, you may avoid current tax by asking your employer to make a direct rollover of your account to an IRA or another qualified employer plan. If the distribution is made to you, 20% will be withheld, but it is still possible to make a tax-free rollover within 60 days; *see 7.8* for rollover details.

☐ CORRECTED (if checked)

PAYER'S name, street address, city, state, and ZIP code	**1** Gross distribution $ 174,384	OMB No. 1545-0119 **1997** Form **1099-R**	Distributions From Pensions, Annuities, Retirement or Profit-Sharing Plans, IRAs, Insurance Contracts, etc.
Microcom Computers 360 Vista Circle City, State X100X	**2a** Taxable amount $ 174,384		
	2b Taxable amount not determined ☐	Total distribution ☐	**Copy B**
PAYER'S Federal identification number 01-XX10X00	RECIPIENT'S identification number 011-XX-1XX0	**3** Capital gain (included in box 2a) $ 7,241	**4** Federal income tax withheld $ 34,876.80	**Report this income on your Federal tax return. If this form shows Federal income tax withheld in box 4, attach this copy to your return.**
RECIPIENT'S name Mitchell Brewster		**5** Employee contributions or insurance premiums $	**6** Net unrealized appreciation in employer's securities $	
Street address (including apt. no.) 86 Puddle Road		**7** Distribution code 7A	IRA/ SEP/ SIMPLE ☐	**8** Other $ %	This information is being furnished to the Internal Revenue Service.
City, state, and ZIP code City, State X1X1X		**9a** Your percentage of total distribution %	**9b** Total employee contributions $	
Account number (optional)		**10** State tax withheld $ $	**11** State/Payer's state no. State	**12** State distribution $ $
		13 Local tax withheld $ $	**14** Name of locality City	**15** Local distribution $ $

Form **1099-R**   Department of the Treasury - Internal Revenue Service

If you receive a lump-sum and do not make a rollover, the taxable part of the distribution must be reported as ordinary pension income unless you qualify for special averaging as discussed below. A taxable distribution before age 59 ½ is also subject to a 10% penalty unless you qualify for an exception; *see 7.14*.

Special averaging method. If a lump-sum distribution is not rolled over, tax may be computed using special averaging if you have not previously elected averaging after 1996 *(see 7.4)* and all of the following tests are met:

(1) you were at least age 59 ½ when the distribution was made, or you were self-employed and the distribution was made after you became totally disabled before age 59 ½,
(2) you participated in the plan for at least five years before the year of the distribution,
(3) the plan was a "qualified" plan meeting tax law tests,
(4) you received all that is due from the plan within one of your taxable years.

Under test (4), a series of payments may qualify as a lump-sum distribution provided you receive them within the same tax year. Lump-sum treatment is not lost if you receive in one year a qualifying lump-sum distribution after separation from service, and in the next year, you receive a payment that is attributable to your last year of work; the later payment is not part of the "balance" that must be received within one of your tax years. If your employer has more than one plan of the same kind (more than one profit-sharing plan or several stock bonus plans), you must receive your entire balance from all of such plans within the same tax year to use special averaging. For averaging purposes, the account balance does not include deductible voluntary contributions you made after 1981 and before 1987; these are not eligible for averaging.

If you meet these rules and were born before 1936, you may figure tax on the lump sum using either 10-year or five-year averaging; *see 7.4* . If you participated in the plan before 1974, you may elect to apply a 20% rate to the pre-1974 part of the distribution if 20% is lower than the averaging rate.

If you were born after 1935, five-year averaging, but not 10-year, may be elected for a qualifying lump sum. If you anticipate becoming eligible for a lump sum over the next few years, note that this averaging benefit will be available only through 1999. Five-year averaging has been repealed for years after 1999.

See 7.4 for further details on electing averaging.

Important: If you are married, you must generally obtain your spouse's consent to elect a lump-sum distribution; *see 7.11*.

Withholding tax. An employer must withhold a 20% tax from a lump-sum distribution that is paid to you and not rolled over directly by the employer; *see 7.8* for further details.

Beneficiaries. A surviving spouse who receives a lump-sum distribution upon the death of an employee may avoid tax by making a tax-free rollover to an IRA. Beneficiaries other than surviving spouses may not make a tax-free rollover; *see 7.8*.

If the deceased employee was born before 1936 or had reached age 59 ½ , any beneficiary (not just a surviving spouse) may elect special averaging or capital gain treatment for a lump-sum distribution of the account; *see 7.7*.

Court ordered lump-sum distribution to a spouse or former spouse. A distribution received by a spouse or former spouse of an employee under a qualified domestic relations order (QDRO) may be eligible for tax-free rollover, or, in some cases, special averaging treatment; *see 7.12*.

7.3 Should You Average or Make a Rollover?

If you receive a lump-sum distribution but are not eligible for averaging under the tests at *7.2*, you may avoid current tax by rolling over the distribution. To avoid withholding tax on the distribution, you must have your employer directly transfer the distribution to an IRA or qualified plan of another employer. The IRS allows the plan of a new employer to accept a rollover from your old employer even though you are not yet able to contribute to the new plan because of a minimum length of service or age requirement.

If you receive the distribution, a 20% tax will be withheld. If you later decide to make a rollover, you have 60 days from the time of receiving the distribution to do so; *see 7.8*. However, to avoid tax on the entire distribution, you will have to include in the rollover an amount equal to the withheld tax. Withholding is discussed further at *7.8* and *26.11*.

Caution

Prior Rollover Bars Averaging
Even if you receive a distribution that meets the lump-sum tests, you may not claim averaging if you previously received a distribution from the same plan that was rolled over tax free *(7.8)* to an IRA or to another qualified employer plan.

If you *can* average, you should determine whether paying tax currently using the averaging method *(7.4)* will be more favorable to you than making a tax-free rollover. If you receive more than one lump sum during the year, you must make the same choice for all of them; you may not roll over one distribution and claim averaging for another.

If you need the lump-sum payout immediately or may need it within a few years, pay tax now using special averaging.

If you qualify for special averaging but do not plan to use the funds until retirement, estimate whether you will build a larger retirement fund by rolling over the distribution and letting earnings accumulate tax free, or by using special averaging and investing the funds to give you the greatest after-tax return. This is not an easy projection. You must consider the number of years to retirement, your expected tax bracket at retirement, and the estimated yield you can earn on your funds. Generally speaking, a person who is not planning to retire for many years may get a greater after-tax return by making a rollover and then taking withdrawals over his or her life expectancy at retirement.

Finally, your age and the rule that allows you to elect averaging only once are factors in determining how to handle a lump sum. If you were born after 1935, you will have a choice at all only for a lump-sum distribution received before 2000. After 1999, you will be unable to elect averaging and a rollover will be the only alternative to paying regular tax on the full distribution for the year it is made. If you receive a qualifying lump sum before 2000, you may not want to pass up your only opportunity to elect five-year averaging.

On the other hand, if you were born before 1936, 10-year averaging will still be available for a lump-sum distribution received after 1999. You then must consider the one-time-only rule for averaging *(7.4)*. If you receive a qualifying lump sum before 2000 upon separation from service but you plan to continue working for someone else, electing averaging for the current distribution will bar you from applying averaging to any lump-sum distribution you receive from another employer plan. If you would like to preserve the option of electing averaging for a future lump sum, you could ask your former employer to make a direct rollover of the current distribution to the plan of your new employer, or to an IRA that could serve as a "conduit" to another employer's plan. If you later join a plan that accepts rollovers from the "conduit IRA," the transfer could be made and 10-year averaging could apply to a qualifying distribution from the new plan.

An IRA rollover cannot be revoked to claim averaging. If you make a rollover to an IRA, you cannot change your mind and cancel the IRA account in order to apply special averaging. The rollover election is irrevocable, according to an IRS regulation which has been upheld by the Tax Court. If an IRA rollover account is revoked, the entire distribution is taxable as ordinary income, and a 10% penalty may be imposed if the recipient is under age 59 ½ *(7.14)*.

Disqualification of retirement plan. If you receive a lump-sum distribution from a plan which loses its exempt status, the IRS may argue that the distribution does not qualify for lump-sum treatment. Under the IRS position, you may not roll over the distribution to an IRA or elect special averaging. The Tax Court previously took the position that if the plan qualified when contributions were made, an allocable portion of the distribution was a qualified lump sum. However, the majority of appeals courts that reviewed Tax Court decisions on this issue supported the IRS position. In response, the Tax Court reversed its position and adopted the harsher IRS approach: no part of the distribution qualifies for rollover or averaging if the plan loses its exempt status.

7.4 Averaging on Form 4972

If you meet the age test and the other lump-sum qualifying tests discussed at *7.2*, you may elect averaging on Form 4972 for a 1997 lump-sum distribution.

Age test. There are two age tests for averaging and your averaging options depend on which test you meet:

Were you born before 1936? If you were born before 1936, you may elect on Form 4972 either a 10-year averaging method based on 1986 tax rates for single persons, or a five-year averaging method based on single person rates for the year in which the lump sum is received.

Were you born after 1935? If you were born after 1935, you may elect five-year averaging for a qualifying distribution made after you reach age 59 ½. Ten-year averaging is not allowed.

If you were born after June 30, 1938, you will not reach age 59 ½ until 1998 at the earliest and thus a 1997 lump-sum distribution cannot qualify for averaging.

Note: Five-year averaging will not be allowed after 1999.

Planning Reminder

Five-Year Averaging Repealed After 1999

If you were born after 1935, the opportunity to claim five-year averaging for a lump-sum distribution after age 59 ½ ends in 1999. Starting in 2000, five-year averaging is repealed. If you were born before 1936, the right to use 10-year averaging will not be affected after 1999 but the five-year averaging option will not be available.

Form 4972—Worksheet

Part II   **Complete this part to choose the 20% capital gain election** (See instructions.) Do not complete this part unless the participant was born **before** 1936.

6	Capital gain part from box 3 of Form 1099-R	6	7241
7	Multiply line 6 by 20% (.20)	7	1448
	If you also choose to use Part III, go to line 8. Otherwise, include the amount from line 7 in the total on Form 1040, line 38, or Form 1041, Schedule G, line 1b, whichever applies.		

Part III   **Complete this part to choose the 5- or 10-year tax option** (See instructions.)

8	Ordinary income from Form 1099-R, box 2a minus box 3. If you did not complete Part II, enter the taxable amount from box 2a of Form 1099-R	8	167,143
9	Death benefit exclusion for a beneficiary of a plan participant who died before August 21, 1996	9	0
10	Total taxable amount. Subtract line 9 from line 8	10	167,143
11	Current actuarial value of annuity (from Form 1099-R, box 8)	11	0
12	Adjusted total taxable amount. Add lines 10 and 11. If this amount is $70,000 or more, **skip** lines 13 through 16, and enter this amount on line 17	12	167,143
13	Multiply line 12 by 50% (.50), but **do not** enter more than $10,000 13		
14	Subtract $20,000 from line 12. If the result is less than zero, enter -0- 14		
15	Multiply line 14 by 20% (.20) 15		
16	Minimum distribution allowance. Subtract line 15 from line 13	16	
17	Subtract line 16 from line 12	17	167,143
18	Federal estate tax attributable to lump-sum distribution	18	0
19	Subtract line 18 from line 17	19	167,143
	If line 11 is blank, skip lines 20 through 22 and go to line 23.		
20	Divide line 11 by line 12 and enter the result as a decimal	20	.
21	Multiply line 16 by the decimal on line 20	21	
22	Subtract line 21 from line 11	22	

5-year tax option

23	Multiply line 19 by 20% (.20)	23	33,429
24	Tax on amount on line 23. Use the Tax Rate Schedule for the 5-Year Tax Option in the instructions	24	6,156
25	Multiply line 24 by five (5). If line 11 is blank, skip lines 26 through 28, and enter this amount on line 29	25	30,780
26	Multiply line 22 by 20% (.20) 26		
27	Tax on amount on line 26. Use the Tax Rate Schedule for the 5-Year Tax Option in the instructions 27		
28	Multiply line 27 by five (5)	28	
29	Subtract line 28 from line 25. (Multiple recipients, see page 3 of the instructions.) . . .	29	30,780

Note: *Complete lines 30 through 36 ONLY if the participant was born before 1936. Otherwise, enter the amount from line 29 on line 37.*

10-year tax option

30	Multiply line 19 by 10% (.10)	30	16,714
31	Tax on amount on line 30. Use the Tax Rate Schedule for the 10-Year Tax Option in the instructions	31	2,851
32	Multiply line 31 by ten (10). If line 11 is blank, skip lines 33 through 35, and enter this amount on line 36	32	28,510
33	Multiply line 22 by 10% (.10) 33		
34	Tax on amount on line 33. Use the Tax Rate Schedule for the 10-Year Tax Option in the instructions 34		
35	Multiply line 34 by ten (10)	35	
36	Subtract line 35 from line 32. (Multiple recipients, see page 3 of the instructions.) . . .	36	28,510
37	Compare lines 29 and 36. Generally, you should enter the **smaller** amount here (see instructions) . . . . ▶	37	28,510
38	Tax on lump-sum distribution. Add lines 7 and 37. Also, include in the total on Form 1040, line 38, or Form 1041, Schedule G, line 1b, whichever applies . . . . ▶	38	29,958

Averaging on 1997 returns.   If you meet the age test and were a participant in the plan for five or more years before 1997, follow IRS instructions to Form 4972 for applying averaging to a qualifying lump-sum distribution received during 1997. If you received more than one qualified lump sum, you may elect averaging for one of the distributions only if you elect averaging for all.

The amount eligible for averaging is the taxable portion of the distribution shown in Box 2a of Form 1099-R. You may also elect to add to the Box 2a amount any net unrealized appreciation in employer securities (shown in Box 6) included in the lump sum. If you are receiving the distribution as a beneficiary of a plan participant who died before August 21, 1996, follow the instructions to Form 4972 for claiming a death benefit exclusion that reduces the Box 2a taxable portion.

If you were born before 1936 and the distribution includes capital gain (Box 3 of Form 1099-R) and you want to apply the special 20% capital gain rate *(7.5)*, you should subtract the capital gain in Box 3 from the taxable amount in Box 2a and apply averaging to the balance of ordinary income.

Tables for applying the 10-year and 5-year averaging methods are included in the 1997 instructions to Form 4972. In most cases, except where extremely large distributions (over $348,756) are received, 10-year averaging will provide the lower tax.

Whichever averaging method you use, the tax computed on Form 4972 is reported on Form 1040, Line 39, as an additional tax. It is completely separate from the tax computed on your other income reported on Form 1040.

EXAMPLE

Mitchell Brewster retired from Microcom Computers in 1997 at age 65. He received a lump-sum distribution of $174,384 at the end of 1997. The Form 1099-R provided by Microcom shows in Box 3 a capital gain portion of $7,241, attributable to pre-1974 participation.

On Form 4972, Mitchell applies the special 20% rate to the capital gain portion for a tax of $1,448. He then figures the tax on the $167,143 ordinary income part of the distribution under the five-year and ten-year averaging methods. As shown on the Form 4972 worksheet on page 137, the tax using ten-year averaging is lower than the five-year averaging tax. Mitchell's total tax on the distribution is $29,958, the sum of the $28,510 tax under 10-year averaging and the $1,448 tax on the capital gain portion. In Mitchell's case, the special 20% capital gains rate is advantageous because it results in a lower tax than if the capital gain were treated as ordinary income subject to the averaging computation.

Community property.   Only the spouse who has earned the lump sum may use averaging. Community property laws are disregarded for this purpose. If a couple files separate returns and one spouse elects averaging, the other spouse is not taxed on the amount subject to the computation.

EXAMPLE

A husband in a community property state receives a lump-sum distribution of which the ordinary income portion is $10,000. He and his wife file separate returns. If averaging is not elected, $5,000, or one-half, is taxable in the husband's return and the other $5,000 in his wife's return. However, if he elects the averaging method, only he reports the $10,000 on Form 4972.

Pre-1974 capital gain portion of distribution.   If you were born before 1936 and a portion of your 1997 lump-sum distribution is attributable to plan participation before 1974 *(7.5)*, you may treat it as ordinary income eligible for averaging, or you may elect to treat it as capital gain part taxed at a flat 20% rate; *see also 7.5.*

7.5 Capital Gain Treatment for Pre-1974 Participation

The portion of a qualifying lump-sum distribution attributable to pre-1974 participation is eligible for a 20% capital gain rate if you were born before 1936.

On Form 1099-R, the company paying the lump-sum distribution shows the capital gain portion in Box 3. The ordinary income portion is Box 2a (taxable amount) *minus* Box 3.

Born before 1936.   You may elect to treat the pre-1974 portion as capital gain subject to a flat rate of 20% on Form 4972. The tax on the balance of the distribution may be figured under the averaging method. The 20% rate for the capital gain portion is fixed by law, and applies regardless of the tax rate imposed on your other capital gains. Alternatively, you may elect to treat the capital

Planning Reminder

Once in a Lifetime Election
You are allowed to elect averaging only once after 1986. If you elect averaging for a 1997 distribution, you will not be able to claim averaging again if you join another company and receive a lump-sum distribution from the new employer. On the other hand, if you do not claim averaging for a qualifying 1997 lump-sum distribution because you expect to receive another distribution in the future from a new employer, keep in mind the new law that repeals five-year averaging after 1999.

If before 1987 you elected 10-year averaging and were under age 59 1/2, you may elect averaging for a 1997 distribution. However, if you were over age 59 1/2 when you made the pre-1987 election, you are barred from electing averaging again.

gain portion as ordinary income eligible for averaging. You may not elect to report any portion of the pre-1974 portion of a 1997 lump-sum distribution as long-term capital gain on Schedule D.

Under the one-time election rule, if you elect to apply the averaging and/or 20% capital gain rule for a 1997 distribution, you may not elect averaging or capital gain treatment for any later distribution.

Capital gain treatment not allowed for individuals born after 1935. If you were born after 1935, you may *not* treat any portion of it as capital gain. You may not apply the flat 20% rate to the pre-1974 portion of the lump-sum distribution, or include any part of it as capital gain on your 1997 Schedule D. An election to claim capital gain treatment on Schedule D was phased out between 1987 and 1991. If you made such an election, you will not be allowed to claim five-year averaging for a lump-sum distribution received after age 59 ½.

7.6 Lump-Sum Distribution Upon Separation From Service

You may receive a lump-sum distribution from a qualified employer retirement plan when you separate from service, that is, when you resign, retire, or are fired from your job. Your age, not the fact that you have separated from service, determines your right to claim special averaging:

If you are at least age 59 ½ on the date of the distribution, you may elect either special averaging *(see 7.4)* or tax-free rollover treatment *(see 7.8)*.

If you have *not* reached age 59 ½ on the date of the distribution, tax-free rollover is allowed but not special averaging. If a rollover is not made under the rules of 7.8, the distribution is fully taxable and it will also be subject to the 10% penalty for early withdrawals, unless one of the exceptions at 7.14 applies.

Separation-from-service test for pre-1996 distributions of individuals born before 1936. Before 1996, an individual born before 1936 could claim averaging for a lump-sum distribution received *before* age 59 ½, if the distribution was on account of separation from service. This separation-from-service exception is now irrelevant. If you were born before 1936, any lump-sum distribution received in 1997 qualifies for averaging under the regular age 59 ½ rule.

If before 1996 you elected averaging for a lump-sum distribution received following a merger or reorganization but before you were age 59 ½, the IRS may challenge the election if you continued working for the successor firm. The IRS may argue that there was no separation from service. However, if you can show that there was a substantial change in your job responsibilities following the merger or reorganization, this may be evidence of a separation from service.

7.7 Lump-Sum Payments Received by Beneficiary

A beneficiary of a deceased employee may elect special averaging on Form 4972 for a qualifying lump-sum distribution *(7.2)* received because of the employee's death, provided the employee was at least age 59 ½. A beneficiary may elect averaging, even though the deceased employee was in the plan for less than five years. Furthermore, the age of the beneficiary is irrelevant.

Either 10-year or five-year averaging may be claimed if the employee was born before 1936. If the employee was born after 1935 and was at least age 59 ½, five-year averaging may be used. If the employee was born before 1936 and had participated in the plan before 1974, a 20% capital gain election may be elected for that portion of the distribution *(7.5)*, and the averaging method applied to the balance.

Form 4972 is used to compute tax under the averaging method or to make the 20% capital gain election *(7.5)*. Follow the Form 4972 instructions to claim the up-to-$5,000 death benefit exclusion for a 1997 distribution *(7.28)* where the plan participant died before August 21, 1996. Any federal estate tax attributable to the distribution reduces the taxable amount on Form 4972. Any election made as a beneficiary does not affect your right to elect lump-sum treatment for a distribution from your own plan.

A lump sum paid because of an employee's death may qualify for capital gain and averaging treatment, although the employee received annuity payments before death.

An election may be made on Form 4972 only once as the beneficiary of a particular employee. A beneficiary who receives more than one lump-sum distribution for the same beneficiary in the same year must treat them all the same way. Averaging must be elected for all of the distributions on a single Form 4972 or for none of them.

Payment received by a second beneficiary (after the death of the first beneficiary) is not entitled to lump-sum treatment or the death benefit exclusion.

 Filing Tip

Lump Sums to Multiple Beneficiaries

A lump-sum distribution to two or more individuals may qualify for averaging and capital gain treatment. Each beneficiary may separately elect the averaging method for the ordinary income portion, even though other beneficiaries do not so elect. Follow the Form 4972 instructions for multiple recipients.

Beneficiaries of self-employed individuals who receive a qualifying lump-sum distribution from a Keogh plan apply the same rules as beneficiaries of deceased employees, as just discussed.

Distribution to trust or estate. If a qualifying lump sum is paid to a trust or an estate, the employee, or, if deceased, his or her personal representative, may elect averaging.

> **EXAMPLE**
>
> Gunnison's father was covered by a company benefit plan. The father died, as did Gunnison's mother, before benefits were fully paid out. Gunnison received a substantial lump sum. He argued that he collected on account of his father's death. The IRS disagreed.
>
> The Tax Court and an appeals court sided with the IRS. Gunnison was entitled to the payment following his mother's death, not his father's death. For special lump-sum treatment, the payout must arise solely on account of the death of the covered employee.

7.8 Tax-Free Rollovers

Almost all taxable distributions received from a qualified corporate or self-employed pension, profit-sharing, stock bonus, or annuity plan are eligible for tax-free rollover. The major exceptions are your *after-tax* contributions, substantially equal periodic payments over your lifetime or over a period of at least 10 years, and minimum distributions *(7.13)* required after age 70 $\frac{1}{2}$; *see* below for other ineligible distributions.

Caution: If you roll over a partial distribution, a later lump-sum distribution from the plan will not qualify for averaging; see 7.4.

Rollover options. If you want to make a tax-free rollover of an eligible rollover distribution, you should instruct your employer to directly roll over the funds to an IRA you designate or to the plan of your new employer. You could also choose to have the distribution paid to you, and within 60 days you could make a tax-free rollover yourself. *However, to avoid the 20% mandatory withholding tax, you must elect to have the plan make a direct rollover. If an eligible rollover distribution is paid to you, the 20% withholding tax applies. Your employer must provide you with written notice concerning the rollover options and the withholding tax rules.*

Rollover from employer plan to IRA after age 70 $\frac{1}{2}$. Starting with the year you reach age 70 $\frac{1}{2}$, you may no longer make IRA contributions. However, if you are over age 70 $\frac{1}{2}$ and you receive an eligible rollover distribution from your employer's plan, you may instruct your employer to make a direct rollover of the distribution to an IRA as discussed below. If you receive the distribution from the employer, a 20% tax will be withheld; you may make a tax-free rollover within 60 days of the distribution; *see* next column for the discussion of "personal rollovers". In the year of the rollover, you must receive a minimum distribution from the IRA; *see 8.13.*

Beneficiaries. The only beneficiary who may make a tax-free rollover is a surviving spouse as discussed later in this section.

Distributions that may not be rolled over. Any lump-sum or partial distribution from your account is eligible for rollover *except for the following*:

- Payments that are part of a series of substantially equal payments made at least annually over a period of 10 years or more or over your life or life expectancy (or the joint lives or joint life and last survivor expectancies of you and your designated beneficiary).
- Minimum required distributions after attaining age 70 $\frac{1}{2}$ or retiring *(7.13)*.
- Distributions of your voluntary after-tax contributions to the plan. These are nontaxable when distributed to you and thus are not eligible for rollover or subject to withholding.
- Corrective distributions of excess 401(k) plan contributions and deferrals.
- Dividends on employer stock.
- Life insurance coverage costs.
- Loans that are deemed to be taxable distributions because they exceed the limits of *7.16*.

For all of the taxable distributions that are *ineligible* for rollover, you may elect to completely avoid withholding on Form W-4P.

Direct Rollover to IRA or Another Employer Plan

If you choose to have your employer make a direct rollover of an eligible rollover distribution to an IRA or another qualified plan, you avoid tax on the payment and no tax will be withheld. If you are changing jobs and want a direct rollover to the plan of the new employer, make sure that the plan accepts rollovers; if it does not, choose a direct rollover to an IRA.

Planning Reminder

IRA Conduit Between Employer Plans

An IRA may be used as a conduit between two company plans. The funds in the IRA may be transferred to another qualified plan of a company which employs you, provided the plan of your new employer accepts rollovers. A qualifying lump-sum distribution from the new employer plan may be eligible for special averaging; *see 7.4.* The IRA must consist of only the assets (or proceeds from the sale of such assets) distributed from the first qualified plan and income earned on the account. You may not contribute to the account set up as a conduit. You may set up another IRA to which you make annual contributions. In such a case, you will have two accounts, one consisting of the assets (or proceeds from the assets' sale) of the plan of your prior employer and the other of your own contributions.

When you select the direct rollover option, your employer may transfer the funds directly by check or wire to the new plan, or you may be given a check payable to the new plan which you deliver.

In choosing a direct rollover to an IRA, the terms of the payer-employer's plan will determine whether you may divide the distribution among several IRAs or whether you will be restricted to one IRA. For example, you may want to split up your distribution into several IRAs, but the employer may force you to select only one. After the direct rollover is made, you may then diversify your holdings by making tax-free trustee-to-trustee transfers to other IRAs.

You may elect to make a direct rollover of part of your distribution and to receive the balance. The portion paid to you will be subject to 20% withholding and is not eligible for special averaging. The IRS allows plan administrators to bar a partial direct rollover if the rollover amount is less than $500.

A direct rollover will be reported by the payer plan to the IRS and to you on Form 1099-R, although the transfer is not taxable. The direct rollover will be reported in Box 1 of Form 1099-R, but zero will be entered as the taxable amount in Box 2a. In Box 7, Code G should be entered if the direct rollover was to an IRA and Code H if to another qualified employer plan or to a tax-sheltered annuity.

Personal Rollover After Receiving a Distribution

If you do not tell your employer to make a direct rollover of an eligible rollover distribution, and you instead receive the distribution yourself, you will receive only 80%; 20% will be withheld. Withholding does not apply to the portion of the distribution consisting of net unrealized appreciation from employer securities that is tax-free under the rules of 7.10.

Although you receive only 80% of the eligible rollover distribution, the full amount is required as a taxable distribution on Form 1099-R. To avoid tax you must roll it over within 60 days to an IRA or another employer plan.However, to roll over 100% of the distribution you will have to use other funds to replace the 20% withheld. If you roll over only the 80% received, the 20% balance will be taxable; *see* the John Anderson Example below. For the taxable part which is not rolled over, you may not use special averaging or capital gain treatment even if you meet the age test of 7.4. In addition, if the distribution was made to you before you reached age 59 $\frac{1}{2}$, the taxable amount will be subject to a 10% penalty unless you are disabled, separating from service after reaching age 55, or have substantial medical expenses (7.14).

The rollover amount *may not* include your voluntary after-tax contributions to the qualified plan; they are tax free to you when you receive them. The rollover *may* include salary deferral contributions that were excludable from income when made, such as qualifying deferrals to a 401(k) plan. The rollover may also include accumulated deductible employee contributions (and allocable income) made after 1981 and before 1987. Your employer's retirement plan may invest in a limited amount of life insurance which is then distributed to you as part of a lump-sum retirement distribution. You may be able to roll over the life insurance contract to the qualified plan of your new employer but not to an IRA. The law bars investment of IRA funds in life insurance contracts.

You may not claim a deduction for your rollover to an IRA.

EXAMPLE

In January 1998, John Anderson retires. He is due a lump-sum distribution of $100,000 from a qualified plan of his company. If he instructs his employer to make a direct rollover of the amount to an IRA, there is no tax withholding and the $100,000 is transferred to the IRA tax free.

Now assume that John decides not to choose a direct rollover because he is planning to use the funds to invest in a business. The plan will pay him $80,000 and withhold a tax of $20,000 which John will apply to his 1998 tax liability. But, say, a month later John changes his mind about the investment and now wants to roll over his benefits to an IRA. He must make the rollover within 30 days; that is because 30 days of the 60-day rollover period have already passed. Furthermore, to avoid tax on the entire distribution, he must deposit $100,000 in the IRA, even though $20,000 tax has been withheld. If he does not have the $20,000, he must borrow the $20,000 and deposit it in the IRA. If he rolls over only $80,000, he must report $20,000 as a taxable distribution on his 1998 return and if John is under age 59 $\frac{1}{2}$, the 10% penalty for early withdrawals would apply; based on these facts, John does not qualify for a penalty exception (7.14).

Reporting a personal rollover on your return. When you receive a distribution from the old plan, the payer will report as the taxable amount on Form 1099-R the full amount before withholding, although 20% has been withheld. However, if you make a rollover yourself within the 60-day period, the rollover reduces the taxable amount on your tax return. For example, if in 1997 you were entitled to a $100,000 lump-sum distribution and received $80,000 after mandatory 20% withholding and then you rolled over the full $100,000 to an IRA, report $100,000 on Line 16a of Form 1040 or Line 11a of Form 1040A, but enter zero as the taxable amount on Line 16b or Line 11b. If you roll over only part of the distribution, the amount of the lump sum *not* rolled over is entered as the taxable amount. Remember to include the 20% withholding on the line for federal income tax withheld.

Figuring the 60-day period for personal rollovers. A rollover must be completed by the 60th day following the day on which you receive the distribution.

The IRS has strictly applied the 60-day requirement for personal rollovers even where failure to meet the deadline is not the taxpayer's fault. For example, an investor wanted to transfer a lump-sum distribution from a terminated company plan to an IRA. The company plan had been invested in five different funds maintained by a mutual fund "family," and the investor merely wanted to reregister his account as an IRA while keeping the same fund investments. However, his written instructions were followed for only four of the funds because of a clerk's error. The failure to reregister the fifth account was not discovered and corrected until six months later. An unsympathetic IRS held that the amount from the fifth fund, $15,100, was a taxable distribution because it was not rolled over within the 60-day period.

In a similar case, the Tax Court allowed tax-free rollover treatment where Merrill Lynch made a bookkeeping error by failing to properly record a rollover of a lump-sum distribution of cash and stock from a company plan. The cash was deposited into the IRA within the 60-day period but the stock was not. The court held that the date of the rollover was fixed when the taxpayer signed the necessary documentation and transferred the funds to establish the IRA within the 60-day period.

Extension of 60-day rollover period for frozen deposits. If you receive a qualifying distribution from a retirement plan and deposit the funds in a financial institution which becomes bankrupt or insolvent, you may be prevented from withdrawing the funds in time to complete a rollover within 60 days. If this happens, the 60-day period is extended while your account is "frozen." The 60-day rollover period does not include days on which your account is frozen. Further, you have a minimum of 10 days after the release of the funds to complete the rollover.

Multiple rollover accounts allowed. You may wish to diversify a distribution in different investments. There is no limit on the number of rollover accounts you may have. A lump-sum distribution may be rolled over to several IRAs or retirement annuities.

Rollover by Surviving Spouse

A surviving spouse is the only beneficiary who may make a tax-free rollover. If you are your deceased spouse's beneficiary, you may roll over your interest in his or her qualified plan account. You may choose to have the plan make a direct rollover to your IRA; you cannot make the rollover to your employer's qualified plan. The advantage of choosing the direct rollover is to avoid a 20% withholding. If the distribution is paid to you, 20% will be withheld. You may make a rollover within 60 days, but to completely avoid tax, you must include in the rollover the withheld amount, as illustrated in the John Anderson Example on page 141. If you receive the distribution but do not make the rollover, you will be taxed on the distribution, but if your spouse was age 59 ½ or older, you may be able to use special averaging (7.4) to compute the tax. As a surviving spouse, you are not subject to the 10% penalty for premature distributions (7.14) even if you are under age 59 ½.

Rollover of distribution received under a divorce or support proceeding. In a qualified domestic relations order (QDRO) meeting special tax law tests, a state court may give you the right to receive all or part of your spouse's or former spouse's retirement benefits. You can choose to have the payment made to you or you can instruct the plan to make a direct rollover to an IRA or to your employer's qualified plan if it accepts rollovers. Alternatively, if the distribution is paid to you, 20% withholding will apply. You may complete a rollover within 60 days under the rules for personal rollovers discussed earlier. If you do not make the rollover, the payments you receive are taxable, but you may be able to elect special averaging; *see 7.12*. If only part of the distribution is rolled over, the balance is taxed in the year of receipt. In figuring your tax, you are allowed a prorated share of your former spouse's cost investment, if any. You may not elect averaging or capital gain treatment for the portion not rolled over. You are not subject to the 10% penalty for premature distributions even if under age 59 ½.

Nonspouse beneficiaries. If you are a beneficiary other than a spouse, you cannot choose to have the plan make a direct rollover and you cannot make a rollover yourself if payment is made to you. Distributions must begin under the payment rules for beneficiaries discussed at 7.13, unless special averaging is available for a lump-sum distribution of the account; *see 7.4*.

Caution

IRA Rollover Election Is Irrevocable

A rollover from an employer plan to an IRA is irrevocable, according to the IRS. At the time of the rollover, you must elect in writing to irrevocably treat the contribution as a rollover. If a qualifying lump-sum distribution is made to you after you are age 59 ½, and you roll it over, you may not later change your mind in order to to claim averaging. Before making a rollover, figure what the current tax would be on the lump-sum distribution under the special averaging method. Compare it with an estimate of the regular tax that will be payable on a later distribution of the rolled-over account from the IRA.

Other points to consider in deciding whether to roll over a lump sum are discussed at 7.3.

7.9 Rollover of Proceeds From Sale of Property

A lump-sum distribution from a qualified plan may include property, such as non-employer stock; *see 7.10* for employer securities. If you plan to roll over the distribution, you may find that a bank or other plan trustee does not want to take the property. You cannot get tax-free rollover treatment by keeping the property and rolling over cash to the new plan. If you sell the property, you may roll over the sale proceeds to an IRA as long as the sale and rollover occur within 60 days of receipt of the distribution. If you roll over all of the proceeds, you do not recognize a gain or loss from the sale; the proceeds are treated as part of the distribution. If you make a partial rollover of sale proceeds, you must report as capital gain the portion of the gain that is allocable to the retained sale proceeds.

If you receive cash and property, and you sell the property but only make a partial rollover, you must designate how much of the rolled-over cash is from the employer distribution and how much from the sale proceeds. The designation must be made by the time for filing your return (plus any extensions) and is irrevocable. If you do not make a timely designation, the IRS will allocate the rollover between cash and sales proceeds on a ratable basis; the allocation will determine tax on the retained amount.

If you made after-tax contributions to the plan, you may not roll over the portion of the distribution equal to your contributions.

7.10 Distribution of Employer Securities

When a plan distributes securities of your company, the value of the securities may or may not be subject to tax at the time of the distribution. The amount reported as income depends on the value of the securities, the amount contributed by the company toward their purchase, and whether or not the distribution qualifies as a total lump-sum payment.

Lump-sum payments. If you receive appreciated securities as part of a lump-sum distribution, net unrealized appreciation (increase in value since purchase of securities) is not subject to tax at the time of distribution unless you elect to treat it as taxable. This exclusion for net unrealized appreciation applies to distributions meeting the lump-sum tests at *7.2*, except that the five-year participation test does *not* have to be met.

Assuming the election to treat the unrealized appreciation as current income is not made, only the amount of the employer's contribution is subject to tax. Tax on the appreciation is delayed until the shares are later sold by you at a price exceeding cost basis. If, when distributed, the shares are valued at below the cost contribution of the employer, the fair market value of the shares is subject to tax. If you contributed to the purchase of the shares and their value is less than your contribution, you do not realize a loss deduction on the distribution. You realize a loss only when the stock is sold or becomes worthless *(5.7)* at a later date. If a plan distributes worthless stock, you may deduct your contributions to the stock as a miscellaneous itemized deduction subject to the 2% of adjusted gross income floor.

The net unrealized appreciation in employer's securities is shown in Box 6 of the Form 1099-R received from the payer. It is not included in the taxable amount in Box 2a.

Election to waive tax-free treatment. You may elect to include the unrealized appreciation in employer securities as income. You might consider making this election when you want to accelerate income to the current year by taking into account the entire lump-sum distribution. If you are claiming averaging or capital gain treatment on Form 4972 *(7.4)*, follow the form instructions for adding the unrealized appreciation to the taxable distribution. If you are not filing Form 4972, the election to include the unrealized appreciation as income is made by reporting it on Line 16a (pensions and annuities) of Form 1040.

EXAMPLES

1. *Shares valued below your cost contribution.* You contributed $500 and your employer contributed $300 to buy 10 shares of company stock having at the time a fair market value of $80 per share. When you retire, the fair market value of the stock is $40 per share, or a total of $400. You do not realize income on the distribution, and you do not have a deductible loss for the difference between your cost contribution and the lower fair market value. Your contribution to the stock is its basis. This is $50 per share. If you sell the stock for $40 per share, you have a capital loss of $10 per share. However, if you sell the stock for $60 per share, you have gain of $10 per share.

2. *Appreciated shares.* You receive 10 shares of company stock which was purchased entirely with the employer's funds. Your employer's cost was $50 a share. At the time of a lump-sum distribution, the shares are valued at $80 a share. Your employer's contribution of $50 a share, or $500, is included as part of your taxable distribution. The appreciation of $300 is not included, assuming you do not elect to be taxed currently on the appreciation. The cost basis of the shares in your hands is $500 (the amount currently taxable to you). The holding period of the stock starts from the date of distribution. However, if you sell the shares for any amount exceeding $500 and up to $800, your profit is long-term gain regardless of how long you held the shares. If you sell for more than $800, the gain exceeding the original unrealized appreciation of $300 is subject to long-term capital gain treatment only if the sale is long term from the date of distribution. Thus, if within a month of the distribution you sold the shares for $900, $300 would be long-term gain; $100 would be short-term gain.

Other than lump-sum payments. If you receive appreciated securities in a distribution that does not meet the lump-sum tests of *7.2* (disregarding the five-year participation requirement), you report as ordinary income the amount of the employer's contribution to the purchase of the shares and the appreciation allocated to the employer's cost contribution. You do not report the amount of appreciation allocated to your own after-tax contribution to the purchase.

EXAMPLE

A qualified plan distributes 10 shares of company stock with an average cost of $100, of which the employee contributed $60 and the employer, $40. At the date of distribution, the stock had a fair market value of $180. The portion of the unrealized appreciation attributable to the employee's contribution is $48 (60% of $80); the employer's is $32 (40% of $80). The employee reports $72 as income: the employer's cost of $40 and the employer's share of appreciation which is $32. The basis of each share is $132, which includes an employee contribution of $60 and the $72 reported as taxable income. Net unrealized appreciation and cost contributions must be supplied by the company distributing the stock.

7.11 Survivor Annuity for Spouse

If you have been married for at least a year, the law generally requires that payments of vested benefits be in a specific annuity form to protect your surviving spouse. All defined benefit and money purchase plans must provide benefits in the form of a *qualified joint and survivor annuity (QJSA)* unless you, with the written consent of your spouse, elect a different form of benefit. A qualified joint and survivor annuity must also be provided by profit-sharing or stock bonus plans, unless you do not elect a life annuity payment and the plan provides that your nonforfeitable benefit is payable in full upon your death to your surviving spouse, or to another beneficiary if the spouse consents or there is no surviving spouse.

Under a QJSA, you receive an annuity for your life and your surviving spouse receives an annuity for his or her life that is no less than 50% of the amount payable during your joint lives. You may waive the QJSA only with your spouse's consent. Without the consent, you may not take a lump-sum distribution or a single-life annuity ending when you die. A single-life annuity pays higher monthly benefits during your lifetime than the qualified joint and survivor annuity.

The law also requires that a *qualified pre-retirement survivor annuity (QPSA)* be paid to your surviving spouse if you die before the date vested benefits become payable. For example, under a defined contribution plan such as a profit-sharing plan, the QPSA payments must be equal to those under a single-life annuity valued at 50% or more of your account balance. The QPSA is automatic unless you, with your spouse's consent, agree to a different benefit.

Your plan should provide you with a written explanation of these annuity rules within a reasonable period before the annuity starting date, as well as the rules for electing to waive the joint and survivor annuity benefit and the pre-retirement survivor annuity.

Plan may provide exception for marriages of less than one year. The terms of a plan may provide that a QJSA or QPSA will not be provided to a spouse of the plan participant if the couple has been married for less than one year as of the participant's annuity starting date (QJSA) or, if earlier, the date of the participant's death (QPSA).

Planning Reminder

Spouse Must Consent in Writing to Your Waiver

Your spouse must consent in writing to your waiver of a required annuity and the selection of a different type of distribution. A spouse's consent must be witnessed by a plan representative or notary public. An election to waive the qualified joint and survivor annuity may be made during the 90-day period ending on the annuity starting date. An election to waive the qualified pre-retirement survivor annuity may be made any time after the first day of the plan year in which you reach age 35. A waiver is revocable during the time permitted to make the election.

Cash out of annuity. If the present value of the QJSA is $5,000 or less for a plan year beginning after August 5, 1997, your employer may "cash out" your interest without your consent by making a lump-sum distribution of the present value of the annuity before the annuity starting date. For plan years beginning before August 6, 1997, the cash-out limit was $3,500. After the annuity starting date, you and your spouse must consent to a cash-out. Written consent is required for a cash-out it the present value of the annuity exceeds the $5,000 or $3,500 limit. Similar cash-out rules apply to QPSA.

7.12   Court Distributions to Former Spouse

As a part of a divorce-related property settlement, or to cover alimony or support obligations, a state domestic relations court can require that all or part of a plan participant's retirement benefits be paid to a spouse, former spouse, child or other dependent. Administrators of pension, profitsharing, or stock bonus plans are required to honor a qualified domestic relations order (QDRO) that meets specific tax law tests. For example, the QDRO generally may not alter the amount or form of benefits provided by the plan, but it may authorize payments after the participant reaches the earliest retirement age, even if he or she continues working. A QDRO may provide that the recipient spouse is entitled to all, some, or none of the spousal survivor benefits payable under the plan.

QDRO distributions to spouse or former spouse. If you are the spouse or former spouse of an employee and you receive a distribution pursuant to a QDRO, the distribution is generally taxable to you. However, you may make a tax-free rollover to an IRA or to a qualified plan, as discussed at 7.8. Furthermore, if your spouse or former spouse (the plan participant) was born before 1936 or was over age 59 $\frac{1}{2}$, a distribution of your entire share of the benefits is eligible for special averaging, provided the distribution, if received by your spouse (or former spouse), would satisfy the lump-sum distribution tests of 7.2. If your spouse (or former spouse) was born before 1936, you may use Form 4972 to claim either 10-year or five-year averaging, and possibly the 20% capital gain election; see 7.4. If your spouse (or former spouse) was born after 1935 but was at least age 59 $\frac{1}{2}$ when the distribution was made, only five-year averaging is available on Form 4972. Transfers from a governmental or church plan pursuant to a qualifying domestic relations order are also eligible for special averaging or rollover treatment.

For these tax rules to apply, the court order must contain specific language required to create a QDRO. The recipient spouse (or former spouse) must be assigned rights to the plan participant's retirement benefits plan, and must be referred to as an "alternate payee" in the court decree. The decree must identify the retirement plan and indicate the amount and number of payments subject to the QDRO. Both spouses must be identified by name and address.

If the above information is not clearly provided in the decree, QDRO treatment may be denied and the plan participant taxed on the retirement plan distributions, rather than the spouse who actually receives payments.

Distributions to a child or other dependent. Payments from a QDRO are taxed to the plan participant, not to the dependent who actually receives them, where the recipient is not a spouse or former spouse.

7.13   When Retirement Benefits Must Begin

The longer you can defer taking retirement distributions from your company plan or self-employed Keogh plan, the greater will be the tax-free buildup of your retirement fund. To cut off this tax deferral, the law requires minimum distributions to begin by a specified date.

Under prior law, the required beginning date for receiving minimum distributions was no later than April 1 of the calender year following the calender year in which an employee reached age 70 $\frac{1}{2}$.

However, under new law taking effect in 1997, employees who continue to work after the year in which they reach age 70 $\frac{1}{2}$ may delay their first required minimum distribution until April 1 of the year following the year of retirement. For example, if you reach age 70 $\frac{1}{2}$ in 1998 and do not retire until 2001, your first required minimum distribution does not have to be made until April 1, 2002, the year after the year of retirement.

This delayed required beginning date does not apply to those owning a business interest of more than 5%. For such more-than-5% owners, the required beginning date is still April 1 of the year following the year in which age 70 $\frac{1}{2}$ is reached.

Planning Reminder

Drafting a QDRO
Drafting a QDRO involves technical details which legal counsel must carefully review. To ease the drafting burdens and reduce litigation over the effet of QDRO provisions, Congress passed a law requiring the IRS to provide sample language for inclusion in a QDRO that meets tax law requirements. The IRS sample language and a discussion of QDRO requirements is in IRS Notice 97-11.

Planning Reminder

Contact Plan Administrator
The rules for determining minimum required distributions are complicated. Contact your employer's plan administrator well in advance to determine your options in selecting beneficiaries and figuring a payment schedule. Also, consult with your tax adviser about the choice between the term-certain method and the recalculation method if your plan allows you to make an election.

Caution

Effect of Waiting Until April Deadline

You have until April 1 of the year after the year in which you reach age 70 ½ to take your first distribution, or if later, until April 1 of the year following the year of retirement. However, if no distribution is taken during your 70 ½ year, or retirement year (whenever is later), you will have to take two distributions during the following year. For example, if you retire and reach age 70 ½ in 1998, and delay receipt of your first distribution until between January and April 1, 1999, you must also receive a distribution for 1999 by December 31, 1999. This could substantially increase your 1999 taxable income, and possibly subject more of your Social Security benefits to tax; for further details *see* Chapter 34.

Caution

Penalty for Insufficient Distributions

Before you reach your required beginning date, set up a payment schedule with your employer's plan administrator. You will be subject to a 50% penalty if you fail to take a distribution from the plan by the required beginning date or you receive a distribution that is insufficient under the required distribution methods. Unless waived by the IRS, the 50% penalty will apply to the difference between the amount you should have received and the amount you did receive. The IRS may waive the penalty if you show that the shortfall was due to reasonable error and that you are taking steps to correct it. To apply for a waiver, compute the penalty on Form 5329 and attach a letter of explanation. Individuals who made a special election before 1984 to receive distributions under pre-1984 rules will not be subject to the penalty.

How Much Must You Receive After the Required Beginning Date?

The required beginning date rules apply to distributions from all qualified corporate and self-employed Keogh plans, qualified annuity plans, and Section 457 plans of tax-exempt organizations. The rules also apply to distributions from tax-sheltered annuities *(7.20)* but only for benefits accrued after 1986; there is no mandatory beginning date for tax-sheltered annuity benefits accrued before 1987. When you begin distributions under the required beginning date rule, you may spread payments over your life, over the joint lives of yourself and any designated beneficiary, or over a specific period that does not exceed your life expectancy or the joint life expectancies of yourself and any designated beneficiary. To determine your life expectancy, use Table V shown at *7.23.* For joint life expectancies, *see* the sample table at the end of Chapter 8.

Once you choose your beneficiary and a payment period, the plan administrator should figure the minimum required distributions you must receive annually.

Required minimum distributions based on life expectancy. In figuring the payout schedule, the terms of the plan may require that your life expectancy, and the life expectancy of a spousal beneficiary, be recalculated annually. Alternatively, the plan may allow you to choose between the recalculation method and a term-certain method. The initial joint life expectancy under both methods is your single life expectancy or the joint life expectancy of you and your designated beneficiary as of the year in which you reach age 70 ½ or in which you retire, whichever is later. Under the term-certain method, the initial life expectancy is reduced by one in each later year. Under the recalculation method, the initial life expectancy is reduced more slowly because the recalculated life expectancy is based on your age on your birthday in each year. Although the recalculation method generally allows you to spread out distributions over a longer period than the term-certain method, the term-certain method generally has advantages after the death of you or your beneficiary by requiring smaller minimum distributions for the survivor.

Basing payments on the joint life expectancies of yourself and a younger beneficiary will extend the withdrawal period, but the law imposes a limit if the beneficiary is someone other than your spouse. For example, a beneficiary more than 10 years younger than you will be treated as being only 10 years younger, regardless of actual age. This requirement does not affect payments required for spouses under the qualified joint and survivor annuity rule of *7.11.* As discussed at *7.11,* your plan must automatically provide annuity benefits in the form of a qualified joint and survivor annuity if you are married, unless you and your spouse elect otherwise.

Minimum distributions that you are required to take under these rules may not be rolled over tax free.

Payouts to Beneficiaries

The distribution rules for beneficiaries depend on whether the employee or self-employed plan participant had started to receive required minimum distributions under the above rules.

If an employee dies after the start of required minimum distributions. In this case, beneficiaries must continue to take distributions at least as rapidly as under the method being used by the plan participant during his or her lifetime. For example, if an employee had elected under the term-certain method to receive benefits over the 24-year joint life expectancy for himself and his beneficiary, but died after 10 years, the beneficiary would have to receive installments over the remaining 14 years but could elect to accelerate payments over a shorter period. Where the employee's life expectancy had been recalculated annually, the minimum required distributions to the beneficiary are based on his or her remaining single life expectancy; that is, the single life expectancy in the first distribution year reduced by one for each elapsed year.

A beneficiary who chooses a lump-sum distribution instead of installment payments may claim special averaging if the employee met the age test; *see 7.7.* A surviving spouse may also elect a tax-free rollover; *see 7.8.*

A surviving spouse receiving an annuity under the survivor benefit rules of *7.11* receives payments over his or her lifetime, starting at the participant's death.

If an employee dies before required minimum distributions have begun. In this case, distribution rules depend on who the beneficiary is and the terms of the plan. The plan may give the beneficiary the option of (1) taking distributions annually over his or her life expectancy, or (2) completing all distributions by the end of the fifth year following the year of the employee's death. On the other hand, the plan may specify which method must be used or place restrictions on use of the life expectancy method, such as limiting it to a specific term of years. If the plan does not specify the method and the beneficiary does not make an election by December 31 of the year following the year of death, the life expectancy method discussed below must be used by a surviving spouse; a beneficiary other than a surviving spouse must use the five-year method. For a lump-sum distribution, a beneficiary may use special averaging if the employee would have qualified; *see 7.7*. A surviving spouse may make a tax-free rollover of a lump sum; *see 7.8*.

Life expectancy method. If the plan gives the beneficiary the option of taking distributions over his or her life expectancy, the distribution starting date depends on who the beneficiary is:

A *surviving spouse* who is not receiving annuity payments under the rules of *7.11* may delay the start of distributions until the later of: (1) December 31 of the year in which the deceased spouse would have reached age 70 ½, and (2) December 31 of the year after the year of the employee's death. By that later date, the surviving spouse must take the first distribution based upon his or her life expectancy.

A *nonspouse beneficiary* has until December 31 of the year following the year of the employee's death to take the first distribution under his or her life expectancy. If he or she has the option to elect this life expectancy method but fails to do so by December 31 of the year following the year of the employee's death, the five-year method must be used.

Five-year method. Under this method, all distributions must be completed by December 31 of the fifth year following the year of the employee's death. For example, if an employee dies on January 6, 1997, the entire account must be distributed to the beneficiary by December 31, 2002, under the five-year method.

7.14 Penalty for Distributions Before Age 59 ½

A 10% penalty generally applies to taxable distributions received before you reach age 59 ½ from a qualified corporate or Keogh plan, qualified annuity plan, and tax-sheltered annuity plan, but there are several exceptions. For example, the penalty does not apply to distributions made to you after separation from service if the separation occurs during or after the year in which you reach age 55. A full list of exceptions is shown below.

If no exception applies, the penalty is 10% of the taxable distribution. If you make a tax-free rollover *(7.8)*, the distribution is not taxable and not subject to the penalty. If a partial rollover is made, the part not rolled over is taxable and subject to the penalty. The 10% penalty must be figured on Form 5329, which is attached to your Form 1040.

A similar 10% penalty applies to IRA distributions before age 59 ½; *see 8.12* for IRA penalty rules. The penalty for pre-age 59 ½ distributions from deferred annuities is at *7.22*. The penalty does *not* apply to Section 457 plans of tax-exempt employers or state or local governments.

Exceptions to the penalty. The following distributions are exempt from the 10% penalty, even if received before age 59 ½. If your employer "knows" that an exception applies, a code for the exception will be entered in Box 7 of Form 1099-R on which the distribution is reported.

- Distributions that you roll over tax free under the "direct rollover" or "personal rollover" rules of *7.8*.
- Distributions made on account of your total disability.
- Distributions after separation from service if you are age 55 or over in the year you retire or leave the company.
- Distributions used to pay deductible medical expenses exceeding 7.5% of adjusted gross income (whether or not an itemized deduction for medical expenses is claimed).
- Distributions received after separation from service which are part of a series of substantially equal payments (at least annually) over your life expectancy, or over the joint life expectancy of yourself and your designated beneficiary. If you claim the exception and begin to receive such a series of payments but then before age 59 ½ you receive a lump sum or change the distribution method and you are not totally disabled, a recapture penalty tax will apply. The recapture tax applies the 10% penalty to all amounts received before age 59 ½, as if the exception had never been allowed, plus interest for that period. The recapture tax also applies to payments received before age 59 ½ if substantially equal payments are not received for at least five years.
- Distributions paid to an alternate payee pursuant to a qualified domestic relations court order (QDRO).
- Distributions made pursuant to a designation under the 1982 Tax Act (TEFRA).
- Distributions to an employee who separated from service by March 1, 1986, provided that accrued benefits were in pay status as of that date under a written election specifying the payout schedule.

Corrective distributions from 401(k) plans. If you are considered a highly compensated employee and excess elective deferrals or excess contributions are made on your behalf, a distribution of the excess to you is not subject to the penalty.

Beneficiaries exempt from the penalty. If you are the beneficiary of a deceased plan participant, you are not subject to the 10% penalty, regardless of your age or the participant's age.

Filing Form 5329 for exceptions. If your employer correctly entered a penalty exception code in Box 7 of Form 1099-R, you do not have to file Form 5329 to claim the exception. You also do not have to file Form 5329 if you made a tax-free rollover of the entire taxable distribution. You must file Form 5329 if you qualify for an exception, other than the rollover exception, that is not indicated in Box 7 of Form 1099-R.

7.15 Excess Distribution Penalty Repealed

There is no longer a penalty for receiving "too much" in annual retirement distributions. The 1997 Tax Act repealed the 15% excess distribution penalty for distributions received after 1996. Even without the 1997 Act, there would have been no excess distribution penalty for 1997 distributions because a 1996 law had suspended the penalty for three years—1997, 1998, and 1999. A year later, Congress decided to repeal, and not merely suspend, the penalty. For 1996, the 15% penalty generally applied to distributions exceeding $155,000, or $775,000 for lump sums eligible for averaging.

Extra 15% estate tax also repealed. The 1997 Act also repeals the 15% estate tax on excess retirement accumulations. The repeal applies to estates of individuals dying after December 31, 1996. Under prior law, an extra 15% estate tax was imposed on the balance in retirement plans that exceeded the present value of a benefit exempt from the income tax penalty on excess distributions.

7.16 Restrictions on Loans From Company Plans

Within limits, you may receive a loan from a qualified company plan, annuity plan, 403(b) plan, or government plan without triggering tax consequences. The maximum loan you can receive without tax is the lesser of 50% of your vested account balance, and $50,000, but the $50,000 limit is subject to reductions where there are other loans outstanding; *see* below. Loans must be repayable within five years, unless they are used for buying your principal residence. Loans that do not meet these guidelines are treated as taxable distributions from the plan.

These rules generally apply only to employees. For a self-employed person, a retirement plan loan is a prohibited transaction that usually results in penalties; *see 41.9.*

If your vested accrued benefit is $20,000 or less, you are not taxed if the loan, when added to other outstanding loans from all plans of the employer, is $10,000 or less. However, as a practical matter, your maximum loan may not exceed 50% of your vested account balance because of a Labor Department rule that allows only up to 50% of the vested balance to be used as loan security. Loans in excess of the 50% cap are allowed only if additional collateral is provided.

If your vested accrued benefit exceeds $20,000, then the maximum tax-free loan depends on whether you borrowed from any employer plan within the one-year period ending on the day before the date of the new loan. If you did not borrow within the year, you are not taxed on a loan that does not exceed the lesser of $50,000 and 50% of the vested benefit.

If there were loans within the one-year period, the $50,000 limit must be further reduced. The loan, when added to the outstanding loan balance, may not exceed $50,000 less the excess of (1) the highest outstanding loan balance during the one-year period (ending the day before the new loan), over (2) the outstanding balance on the date of the new loan. This reduced $50,000 limit applies where it is less than 50% of the vested benefit; if 50% of the vested benefit was the smaller amount, that would be the maximum tax-free loan.

Planning Reminder

Borrowing From Your Company Retirement Account

You generally may obtain a tax-free loan from your employer's retirement plan up to the lesser of 50% of your vested account balance or $50,000. *See 7.16* for lower tax-free loan limits where you have other outstanding loans, and for repayment requirements.

> **EXAMPLE**
>
> Your vested plan benefit is $200,000. Assume that in December 1997 you borrow $30,000 from the plan. On November 1, 1998, when the outstanding balance on the first loan is $20,000, you want to take another loan without incurring tax.
>
> You may borrow an additional $20,000 without incurring tax: The $50,000 limit is first reduced by the outstanding loan balance of $20,000—leaving $30,000. The reduced $30,000 limit is in turn reduced by $10,000, the excess of $30,000 (the highest loan balance within one year of the new loan) over $20,000 (the loan balance as of November 1).

Repayment period. Generally, loans within the previously discussed limits must be repayable within five years to avoid being treated as a taxable distribution. However, if you use the loan to purchase a principal residence for yourself, the repayment period may be longer than five years; any reasonable period is allowed. This exception does not apply if the plan loan is used to improve your existing principal residence, to buy a second home, or to finance the purchase of a home or home improvements for other family members; such loans are subject to the five-year repayment rule.

Level loan amortization required. To avoid tax consequences on a plan loan, you must be required to repay using a level amortization schedule, with payments at least quarterly. According to Congressional committee reports, you may accelerate repayment, and the employer may use a variable interest rate and require full repayment if you leave the company.

Giving a demand note does not satisfy the repayment requirements. The IRS and Tax Court held the entire amount of an employee's loan to be a taxable distribution since his demand loan did not require level amortization of principal and interest with at least quarterly payments. It did not matter that the employee had paid interest quarterly and actually repaid the loan within five years.

If required installments are not made, the entire loan balance must be treated as a "deemed distribution" from the plan under IRS proposed regulations. However, the IRS allows the plan administrator to permit a grace period of up to one calendar quarter. If the missed installment is not paid by the end of the grace period, there is at that time a deemed distribution in the amount of the outstanding loan balance.

Under IRS proposed regulations, loan repayments may be suspended for up to one year if the borrower takes a leave of absence during which he or she is paid less than the installments due. However, the installments after the leave must at least equal the original required amount and the loan must be repaid by the end of the allowable repayment period (five years if not used to buy a principal residence). For example, when his vested account balance is $80,000, Joe Smith takes out a $40,000 nonprincipal residence loan on July 1, 1997 to be repaid with interest in level monthly installments of $825 over five years. He makes nine payments and then takes a year of unpaid leave. When he returns to work he can either increase his monthly payment to $1,130 or resume paying $825 a month and on June 30, 2002 repay the entire balance owed in a lump sum.

Spousal consent generally required to get a loan. All plans subject to the joint and survivor rules of 7.11 must require spousal consent in order to be able to use your account balance as security for the loan in case you default. Check with your plan administrator for consent requirements.

Interest deduction limitations. If you want to borrow from your account to buy a first or second residence, and you are not a "key" employee (3.3), you can obtain a full interest deduction by using the residence as collateral for the loan. Your account balance may not be used to secure the loan. Key employees are not allowed any interest deduction for plan loans.

If you use a plan loan for investment purposes and are not a key employee, and the loan is not secured by your elective deferrals (or allocable income) to a 401(k) plan or tax-sheltered annuity, the loan account interest is deductible up to investment income; see 15.10. Interest on loans used for personal purposes is not deductible, unless your residence is the security for the loan.

 Caution

Unpaid Loan Taxable If You Leave Job

If you leave your company before your loan is paid off, the company will reduce your vested account balance by the outstanding debt. For example, if your vested account balance is $100,000, and the outstanding loan is $20,000, your account balance is reduced to $80,000, which your company pays you in a lump sum. However, according to the IRS, you are treated as if you received the entire $100,000. If you do not roll over (7.8) the entire $100,000, you will be taxed on the portion not rolled over, and possibly be subject to the 10% penalty for pre-age 59 ½ withdrawals; see 7.14. To avoid tax on the $20,000, you would have to use other resources or borrow funds in order to complete a total rollover within the 60-day period. If making a rollover to a new employer's plan, it might be possible to get an immediate $20,000 loan from the new plan, which could be put right back into the plan to complete the rollover.

401(k), 403(b), and Government Tax-Deferred Savings Plans

7.17 Tax Benefits of 401(k) Plans

If your company has a profit-sharing or stock bonus plan, it has the opportunity of giving you additional tax-sheltered pay. The tax law allows the company to add a cash or deferred pay plan, called a 401(k) plan.

Your company may offer to contribute to a 401(k) plan trust account on your behalf if you forego a salary increase, but in most plans, contributions take the form of salary-reduction deferrals. Under a salary-reduction agreement, you elect to contribute a specified percentage of your wages to the 401(k) plan instead of receiving it as regular salary. In addition, your company may match a portion of your contribution. A salary-reduction deferral is treated as a contribution by your employer that is not taxable to you if the annual contribution limits are not exceeded.

Salary-reduction deferrals. Making elective salary deferrals allows you to defer tax on salary and get a tax-free buildup of earnings within your 401(k) plan account until withdrawals are made.

 Law Alert

SIMPLE 401(k) Plans Starting in 1997

An employer that does not maintain another qualified plan is deemed to satisfy 401(k) plan nondiscrimination requirements if employee elective deferrals are limited to $6,000 and the employer either matches the first 3% of compensation deferred to the plan or contributes 2% of compensation for all eligible employees with at least $5,000 in compensation. All contributions must be 100% vested.

An annual limit applies to salary-reduction deferrals; for 1997, the limit was $9,500. The maximum deferral is lower for employees of "small" employers who adopt a SIMPLE 401(k); for 1997, the maximum SIMPLE elective salary deferral was $6,000. The deferral limits may be increased for 1998 by an inflation factor. *See 7.18* for further details on the deferral limits.

Elective deferrals within the annual limit are *pre-tax* contributions so they are not subject to income tax withholding. However, the contributions are subject to Social Security and Medicare withholdings.

Your employer may not require you to make elective deferrals in order to obtain any other benefits, apart from matching contributions. For example, benefits provided under health plans or other compensation plans may not be conditioned on your making salary deferrals to a 401(k) plan.

Distributions. Withdrawals from a 401(k) plan before age 59 $\frac{1}{2}$ are restricted, as explained at *7.19*. A lump-sum distribution after age 59 $\frac{1}{2}$ may be eligible for averaging under the rules of *7.4*. Mandatory 20% withholding applies to a lump-sum as well as other distributions that are eligible for averaging; exceptions are at *7.8*.

Nondiscrimination rules. The law imposes strict contribution percentage tests to prevent discrimination in favor of employees who are highly compensated. If these tests are violated, the employer is subject to penalties and the plan could be disqualified unless the excess contributions (plus allocable income) are distributed back to the highly compensated employees within specified time limits.

SIMPLE 401(k). Nondiscrimination tests are eased for employers who adopt a 401(k) plan with SIMPLE contribution provisions. A SIMPLE 401(k) may be set up only by employers who in the preceding year had no more than 100 employees with compensation of at least $5,000. An employer who contributes to a SIMPLE 401(k) must report on a calendar-year basis and may not maintain another qualified plan for employees eligible to participate in the SIMPLE plan.

If the SIMPLE contribution requirements are met, the plan is considered to meet 401(k) nondiscrimination requirements. Employee elective deferrals may not exceed $6,000. The employer must either match the employee deferral, up to 3% of compensation, *or* contribute 2% of compensation for all eligible employees, whether or not they make elective deferrals. All contributions are nonforfeitable. No other type of contribution is allowed. In figuring the 3% or 2% employer contributions, compensation is subject to an annual compensation ceiling; for 1997 it was $160,000.

Partnership plans. Partnership plans that allow partners to vary annual contributions are treated as 401(k) plans by the IRS. Thus, elective deferrals are subject to the annual limit *(7.18)* and the special 401(k) plan nondiscrimination rules apply.

7.18 Limit on Salary Reduction Deferrals

The law limits the maximum tax-free salary reduction contribution you can make. For 1997, the limit is $9,500. The $9,500 limit may be increased after 1997 by an inflation factor. Employer plans must limit elective deferrals to the annual tax-free ceiling; otherwise, the plan could be disqualified. Certain highly compensated employees may be unable to take advantage of the maximum tax-free ceiling ($9,500 in 1997) because of restrictions imposed by nondiscrimination tests.

To avoid the strict nondiscrimination tests for employee elective deferrals and employer matching contributions, an employer may make contributions after 1996 to a SIMPLE 401(k); *see 7.17*.

The annual salary-reduction limit ($9,500 for 1997) applies to total salary reduction deferrals made to 401(k) plans as well as to 403(b) tax-sheltered annuity plans *(7.20)* and simplified employee pension plans established before 1997 *(8.16)*. If you participate in more than one such plan, the limit applies to the total salary reductions for all the plans.

An employer may make matching or other contributions, provided the total contribution for the year, including the employee's pre-tax salary deferral and any employee after-tax contributions, does not exceed the *lesser* of 25% of compensation or the annual limit for defined contribution plans, which for 1997 was $30,000.

Correcting excess deferrals. A single plan must apply the annual limit on salary deferrals ($9,500 for 1997) in order to maintain qualified status. However, if you participate in more than one plan, and the total salary deferrals for the year exceed the annual limit, the IRS requires you to report the excess as wages on Line 7 of Form 1040. Furthermore, by April 15 of the year following the year of the excess, you should allocate the excess among the plans and withdraw it, plus income allocable to the excess. If you do, the corrective distribution is not taxable; the distribution of the excess income is taxable in the year it is distributed. If an excess deferral allocated to a 401(k) plan or 403(b) tax-sheltered annuity is *not* withdrawn by the April 15 deadline, it will be taxed again when distributed from the plan. If an excess deferral to a salary-reduction SEP set up before 1997 *(see 8.17)* is not withdrawn by the April 15 deadline, it is treated as a regular IRA contribution that could be subject to the penalty for excess IRA contributions *(see 8.7)*. Excess deferrals (and earnings) distributed by the April 15 deadline are not subject to the 10% penalty for premature distributions *(7.14)* even if you are under age 59 ½.

7.19 Withdrawals From 401(k) Plans Restricted

By law, you may not withdraw funds attributable to elective salary reduction contributions until you reach age 59 ½, are separated from service, become totally disabled, or show financial hardship. Under IRS rules, it is difficult to qualify for hardship withdrawals; *see* below. Lump-sum withdrawals are also allowed if the plan terminates, or the corporation sells its assets or its interest in a subsidiary and you continue to work for the buyer or the subsidiary. However, the hardship provision and age 59 ½ withdrawal allowance do not apply to certain "pre-ERISA" money purchase pension plans (in existence June 27, 1974).

Withdrawals before age 59 ½. Withdrawals for medical disability, financial hardship, or separation from service are subject to the 10% penalty for premature withdrawals unless you meet one of the exceptions listed at *7.14*.

Loans. If you are allowed to borrow from the plan, the loan restrictions at *7.16* apply.

Qualifying for hardship withdrawals. IRS regulations restrict hardship withdrawals of pre-tax salary deferrals. If you qualify under the following restrictive rules you may withdraw your elective deferrals. However, income allocable to elective deferrals may be withdrawn only if it was credited to your account as of the end of the last plan year ending before July 1, 1989; the plan may provide an even earlier cutoff date for income.

The IRS requires you to show an immediate and heavy financial need that cannot be met with other resources.

Financial need includes the following expenses (this list may be expanded by the IRS in rulings):

- Purchase of a principal residence for yourself (but not mortgage payments);
- Tuition, related fees and room and board for the next 12 months of post-secondary education for yourself, your spouse, children, or other dependents;
- Medical expenses previously incurred for yourself, your spouse or dependents, or expenses incurred to obtain medical care for such persons;
- Preventing your eviction or mortgage foreclosure; and
- Paying funeral expenses for a family member.

Even if you can show financial need, you may not make a hardship withdrawal if you have other resources to pay the expenses. You do not have to provide your employer with a detailed financial statement, but you must state to your employer that you cannot pay the expenses with: compensation, insurance, or reimbursements; liquidation of your assets without causing yourself hardship by virtue of the liquidation; stopping your contributions, including salary deferrals, to the plan; other distributions or nontaxable loans from plans of any employer; or borrowing from a commercial lender. Your spouse's assets, as well as those of your minor children, are considered to be yours unless you show that they are not available to you. For example, property held in trust for a child or under the Uniform Gifts to Minors Act is not treated as your property.

Under a special rule, you are considered to lack other resources if you have taken all available distributions from all plans of the employer, including nontaxable loans, and you suspend making any contributions to any of the employer's qualified and nonqualified deferred compensation plans for at least 12 months after receipt of the hardship distribution. Furthermore, all of the employer's plans must provide that for the year after the year of the hardship distribution, elective contributions must be limited to the excess of the annual salary deferral limitation over the elective contributions made for the year of the hardship distribution.

7.20 Annuities for Employees of Tax-Exempts and Schools (403(b) Plans)

If you are employed by a state or local government public school, or by a tax-exempt religious, charitable, scientific, or educational organization, or are on the civilian staff or faculty of the Uniformed Services University of the Health Sciences (Department of Defense), you may be able to arrange for the purchase of a nonforfeitable tax-sheltered annuity. Another name for such a tax-sheltered annuity is a 403(b) plan. A 403(b) plan may invest funds for employees in mutual-fund shares as well as in annuity contracts.

 Caution

Reduced Deferral Limit for Highly Compensated Employees

To avoid discrimination problems an employer may set a lower limit for elective salary deferrals by highly compensated employees than the ceiling generally allowed ($9,500 for 1997).

If, after contributions are made, the plan fails to meet the nondiscrimination tests, the excess contributions will either be returned to the highly compensated employees or kept in the plan but recharacterized as after-tax contributions. In either case, the excess contribution is taxable. Form 1099-R will indicate the excess contribution.

For years after 1997, employers may avoid the nondiscrimination tests by meeting the SIMPLE plan contribution rules; *see 7.17*.

The purchase of the annuity is generally made through a reduction of salary which is used to pay for the contract. The amount of the salary reduction used to buy the contract is not taxable if it comes within specified limits. The tax rules for computing the exclusion are complicated, as there are several limitations and exceptions.

Note: As the following contribution rules for tax-sheltered annuities have been stated in general terms and are subject to Treasury regulations, we suggest that you also consult your employer or the issuer of the contract. IRS Publication 571 has detailed examples.

Tax-free exclusion allowance.   The tax-sheltered salary-reduction contribution, called the exclusion allowance, is generally 20% of your pay multiplied by the number of years of service with your employer less tax-free contributions made in prior years by your employer to a tax-sheltered annuity or to any qualified plan. Salary reductions count as tax-free employer contributions. Under this formula, you may not be allowed to exclude any part of the current year's salary reduction because of employer contributions in prior years. Further, even though allowed by the 20% of *pay/ years* of service formula, the maximum tax-free salary reduction may not exceed the lower of 25% of your pay and the annual ceiling on elective deferrals, which for 1997 is $9,500. However, employees with at least 15 years of service may be able to defer an additional $3,000 each year. *See* below for details of the $9,500 limit and the exceptions.

EXAMPLE

Carol Grossinger, a public school teacher earning $30,000, agreed to a $2,400 salary reduction for 1997 to be used to purchase an annuity contract. The employer also contributed $1,800 to a pension trust for the teacher's account. For 1997, the entire salary reduction contribution is tax free as it is within the $5,520 exclusion allowance (20% of the reduced salary of $27,600 × one year service). Starting in 1998, pay is not reduced by elective salary-reduction contributions when figuring the 20% exclusion allowance. In later years, part or all of the reduction may be taxed because the exclusion allowance is reduced by prior tax-free employer contributions including salary-reduction contributions you made in the prior years.

Alternative contribution ceilings.   Subject to the maximum salary reduction limit ($9,500 for 1997), employees of schools, hospitals, churches, health and welfare service agencies, and home health service agencies may be able to elect tax-free contributions that exceed 25% of pay, or that exceed the exclusion allowance. There are three alternative methods, but only one may be elected and an election is irrevocable.

One alternative allows such employees to irrevocably elect a limitation equal to the *lower* of (1) the general 20% of pay exclusion allowance, (2) 25% of pay plus $4,000, and (3) $15,000. Another alternative election allows such employees to make an irrevocable election to disregard the general 20% exclusion allowance. If the election is made, the tax-free contribution equals the contribution limit for defined contribution plans, the *lesser* of 25% of pay and $30,000.

The third alternative allows such employees in the year of separation from service to elect a tax-free contribution limit equal to the *lower* of (1) $30,000, (2) the exclusion allowance, taking into account no more than 10 years of service, and (3) the annual limit on salary-reduction deferrals, which is $9,500 for 1997. This limit may be used only once.

Church employees.   A church employee whose adjusted gross income is $17,000 or less is allowed a minimum exclusion allowance equal to the *lesser* of $3,000 and his or her includable compensation. In addition, an election may be made permitting contributions exceeding the 25% of pay test, up to $10,000 per year; however, there is a lifetime contribution limit of $40,000.

$9,500 salary deferral limit for 1997.   Even if allowed by the general exclusion allowance rule, the maximum tax-free salary reduction from a tax-sheltered annuity plan cannot exceed the *lower* of 25% of pay and an annual limit, which for 1997 was $9,500. If you work for more than one employer, the $9,500 limit applies to all tax-sheltered annuity arrangements in which you participate. An increased limit for certain employees with 15 years of service is discussed below.

The $9,500 salary-reduction limit may be increased after 1997 by an inflation factor.

If, in addition to a tax-sheltered annuity, you make salary deferrals to a 401(k) plan or simplified employee pension plan, the annual salary reduction limit applies to the total deferrals; *see 7.18.* If you defer more than the annual limit, the excess is taxable. Further, if a salary reduction deferral in excess of the annual limit is made and the excess is not distributed to you by April 15 of the following year, the excess will be taxed twice—not only in the year of deferral but again in the year it is actually distributed. To avoid the double tax, any excess deferral plus the income attributable to such excess should be distributed no later than April 15 of the year following the year in which the excess deferral is made; *see 7.18*.

If your employer makes separate contributions in addition to your salary-reduction deferrals, the total of elective salary reductions (not to exceed the annual limit) plus the employer contributions may be up to the contribution limit for defined contribution plans, which is generally the lower of 25% of pay and $30,000; the $30,000 ceiling may be increased after 1997.

Special catch-up election for certain employees with 15 years of service. If allowed under the general 20% of *pay/years* of service exclusion formula, and by the 25% of pay limit, the annual salary reduction ceiling ($9,500 for 1997) is increased by $3,000 for employees of educational organizations, hospitals, churches, home health service agencies, and health and welfare service agencies who have completed 15 years of service. However, the extra $3,000 annual deferral may not be claimed indefinitely. There is a lifetime limit of $15,000 on the amount of extra deferrals allowed. Furthermore, the extra deferrals may not be claimed after lifetime elective deferrals to the plan exceed $5,000 multiplied by your years of service.

Distributions from tax-sheltered annuities. Distributions attributable to salary-reduction contributions to a 403(b) tax-sheltered annuity are allowed only when an employee reaches age 59 ½, separates from service, becomes disabled, suffers financial hardship, or dies. Annuity payments are taxed under the general rules for employees, discussed at *7.25*. Payments are fully taxable if the only contributions to the plan were salary-reduction contributions excluded from income (pre-tax contributions) under the annual limits discussed earlier in this section.

Non-annuity distributions from a tax-sheltered annuity do not qualify for special averaging *(7.4)*, but a tax-free rollover of a distribution may be made to another tax-sheltered annuity or IRA unless the distribution is not eligible for rollover under the rules at *7.8*. If you do not choose to have the payer of the distribution make a direct rollover, mandatory 20% withholding will be applied. You may then personally make a rollover within 60 days, but you would have to include the withheld amount in the rolled-over amount to avoid tax on the entire distribution. See *7.8* for further rollover and withholding details.

Benefits accruing after 1986 are subject to the required beginning date rules of *7.13* and a penalty may be imposed for failure to take minimum required distributions. Benefits accrued before 1987 are not subject to the required minimum distribution rules until the year you reach age 75.

To change tax-sheltered annuity investments, you may direct the issuer of your current annuity contract to make a direct transfer of your account to a different issuer. The transfer is tax free, provided that distributions with respect to salary reduction contributions are allowed under both contracts only when the employee reaches age 59 ½, separates from service, becomes disabled, suffers financial hardship, or dies.

7.21 Deferred Pay Plans for Government Employees

Federal government employees may make tax-free salary-reduction contributions to the Federal Thrift Savings Fund. Employees of state and local governments and of tax-exempt organizations may be able to make tax-free salary-reduction contributions to a Section 457 deferred compensation plan.

Federal employees. Federal employees may elect to defer up to 10% of their basic pay to the Federal Thrift Savings Fund, but no more than the limit on elective deferrals. The deferral limit for 1997 is $9,500, the same as for 401(k) plans; *see 7.18*. The limit is subject to increases for inflation. Deferrals are not taxed until distributed from the plan. The deferred amount is counted as wages for purposes of computing Social Security taxes and benefits.

Distributions from the Thrift Savings Fund are generally fully taxable. However, lump-sum distributions are eligible for special averaging under the rules of *7.4*, or tax-free rollover treatment; *see 7.8*. If you separate from service before the year in which you reach age 55, you are subject to the 10% penalty for premature distributions unless you are disabled or qualify for the medical exception discussed at *7.14*.

Section 457 state and local government plans. State and local governments may set up deferred compensation plans which allow employees to defer annually up to the *lesser* of 33 ⅓% of includible compensation (not including the deferrals), or an annual limit which for 1997 was $7,500. The $7,500 limit may be increased for 1998 by an inflation adjustment.

A limited "catch-up" provision allows employees in the last three years before reaching normal retirement age to defer larger amounts, provided that the full $7,500 or 33 ⅓% limit has not been used in prior years. The catch-up deferral, figured under IRS regulations, may not exceed $15,000. Deferred pay and income allocable to the deferrals is not taxed until the year it is distributed or made available to the employee. Distributions are fully taxable; averaging and rollover treatment may not be claimed.

The annual deferral limit does not apply to vacation leave, sick leave, disability pay, compensatory time, severance pay, or death benefits plans.

If an employee participates in more than one Section 457 plan, the annual limit applies to total deferrals under all the plans. Furthermore, if an employee also participates in a tax-sheltered annuity plan, simplified employee pension (SEP), 401(k) plan, or Section 501(c)(18) plan (created before June 25, 1959, and funded solely by employee contributions), the annual Section 457 plan limit is reduced by tax-free deferrals to the other plan.

Distributions to employees or beneficiaries generally may not be made before the year the employee turns age 70 ½, the employee separates from service, or faces an "unforeseeable" emergency, assuming the plan allows payment in cases of emergency. Under IRS regulations, an unforeseeable emergency generally means severe financial hardship resulting from a sudden illness or accident of the employee or a dependent, or loss of property due to a casualty. If the employee can obtain funds by ceasing deferrals to the plan or by liquidating assets without causing himself or herself severe financial hardship, payment from the plan is not allowed. The regulations specifically prohibit payments from the plan to purchase a home or pay for a child's college tuition.

In plan years beginning after August 5, 1997, a one-time in-service distribution may be made if the account balance is $5,000 or less and there have been no plan deferrals in the prior two-year period. The limit was $3,500 for plan years beginning before August 6, 1997.

See 7.13 for required distribution starting dates after age 70 ½ and minimum pay-out rules. Where an employee dies before receiving distributions, the account balance must be paid to nonspouse beneficiaries over a period of 15 years or less. Payments to a surviving spouse may be made over the spouse's life expectancy.

Note: Check with your employer for other details on Section 457 contributions and distribution rules.

Tax-exempt organizations eligible.   Section 457 plans may also be set up by nongovernmental tax-exempt organizations other than churches.

Reporting Commercial Annuities

7.22 Figuring the Taxable Part of Your Annuity

Tax treatment of a distribution depends on whether you receive it before or after the annuity starting date, and on the amount of your investment. A cash withdrawal before age 59 ½ from an annuity contract is generally subject to a 10% penalty but there are exceptions; the penalty is discussed at the end of this section. If your annuity is from an employer plan and it started after July 1, 1986, *see 7.25.*

The *annuity starting date* is either the first day of the first period for which you receive a payment or the date on which the obligation under the contract becomes fixed, whichever is later. If your monthly payments start on August 1 for the period starting July 1, July 1 is your annuity starting date.

Payments before the annuity starting date.   If your commercial annuity contract was purchased *after* August 13, 1982, withdrawals before the annuity starting date are taxable to the extent that the cash value of the contract, immediately before the distribution, exceeds your investment in the contract. This rule also applies to withdrawals that are attributed to investments made after August 13, 1982, where the contract was purchased before August 14, 1982. Loans under the contract or pledges are treated as cash withdrawals. Withdrawals from contracts bought by a qualified retirement plan are discussed at *7.25.*

If the contract was purchased before August 14, 1982, withdrawals *before* the annuity starting date are taxable only if they exceed your investment. Loans are tax free and are not treated as withdrawals subject to this rule. Where additional investments were made after August 13, 1982, cash withdrawals are first considered to be tax-free distributions of the investment before August 14, 1982. If the withdrawal exceeds this investment, the balance is fully taxable to the extent of earnings on the contract, with any excess withdrawals treated as a tax-free recovery of the investment made after August 14, 1982.

Payments on or after the annuity starting date.   If the withdrawal is a regular annuity payment, that part of the annuity payment allocated to your cost investment is treated as a nontaxable return of the cost; the balance is taxable income earned on the investment. You may find the taxable part of your annuity payment by following the six steps listed below under "Taxable Portion of Annuity Payments." If you have a variable annuity, the computation of the tax-free portion is discussed following Step 6.

Payments on or after the annuity starting date that are not part of the annuity, such as dividends, are generally taxable, but there are exceptions. If the contract is a life insurance or endowment contract, withdrawals of earnings are tax free to the extent of your investment, unless the contract is a modified endowment contract.

Payments on a complete surrender of the contract or at maturity are taxable only to the extent they exceed your investment.

Taxable Portion of Annuity Payments

If the payer of the contract does not provide the taxable amount in Box 2a of Form 1099-R, you can compute the taxable amount of your commercial annuity using the following steps.

If you have an employee annuity *(7.25)* that started before July 2, 1986, you also can use the following six steps to figure your taxable payment. If your employee annuity started after July 1, 1986, you may use a simplified method discussed at *7.26*.

Step 1: Figure your investment in the annuity contract. If you have no investment in the contract, annuity income is fully taxable; therefore, ignore Steps 2 through 6.

If your annuity is—	Your cost is—
Single premium annuity contract	The single premium paid.
Deferred annuity contract	The total premiums paid.
A gift	Your donor's cost.
An employee annuity	The total of your after-tax contributions to the plan *plus* your employer's contributions which you were required to report as income; *see 7.25*.
With a refund feature	The value of the refund feature.

From cost, you subtract the following items:

- Any premiums refunded, and rebates or dividends received on or before the annuity starting date.
- Additional premiums for double indemnity or disability benefits.
- Amounts received under the contract before the annuity starting date to the extent these amounts were not taxed; *see* above.
- Value of a refund feature; *see* below.

Value of refund feature. Your investment in the contract is reduced by the value, if any, of the refund feature.

Your annuity has a refund feature when these three requirements are present: (1) The refund under the contract depends, even in part, on the life expectancy of at least one person; (2) the contract provides for payments to a beneficiary or the annuitant's estate after the annuitant's death; and (3) the payments to the estate or beneficiary are a refund of the amount paid for the annuity.

The value of the refund feature is figured by using a life expectancy multiple which may be found in Treasury Table III or Table VII depending on the date of your investment; the tables are in IRS Publication 939.

Where an employer paid part of the cost, the refund is figured on only the part paid by the employee.

The refund feature is considered to be *zero* if (1) for a joint and survivor annuity, both annuitants are age 74 or younger, the payments are guaranteed for less than 2 ½ years, and the survivor's annuity is at least 50% of the first annuitant's (retiree's) annuity; or (2) for a single-life annuity without survivor benefits, the payments are guaranteed for less than 2 ½ years and you are age 57 or younger if using the new (unisex) annuity tables, age 42 or younger if male and using the old annuity tables, or age 47 or younger if female and using the old annuity tables.

Also subtract from cost any tax-free recovery of your investment received *before* the annuity starting date, as previously discussed.

Step 2: Find your expected return. This is the total of all the payments you are to receive. If the payments are to be made to you for life, your expected return is figured by multiplying the amount of the annual payment by your life expectancy as of the nearest birthday to the annuity starting date. The annuity starting date is the first day of the first period for which an annuity payment is received. For example, on January 1 you complete payment under an annuity contract providing for monthly payments starting on July 1 for the period beginning June 1. The annuity starting date is June 1. Use that date in computing your investment in the contract under Step 1 and your expected return.

If payments are for life, you find your life expectancy in IRS tables included in IRS Publication 939. The table for single life annuities is in *7.23*. When using the table, your age is the age at the birthday nearest the annuity starting date. If you have a joint and survivor annuity and after your death the same payments are to be made to a second annuitant, the expected return is based on your joint life expectancy. Use Treasury Table II in IRS Publication 939 to get joint life expectancy if the entire investment was before July 1, 1986. Use Treasury Table VI if any investment was made after June 30, 1986. If your joint and survivor annuity provides for a different payment amount to the survivor, you must separately compute the expected return for each annuitant; this method is explained in Publication 939. Adjustments to the life expectancy multiple are required when your annuity is payable quarterly, semiannually, or annually. The required adjustment is discussed in *7.23*.

If the payments are for a fixed number of years or for life, whichever is shorter, find your expected return by multiplying your annual payments by a life expectancy multiple found in Treasury Table IV if your entire investment was before July 1, 1986, or Table VIII if any investment was made after June 30, 1986.

If payments are for a fixed number of years (as in an endowment contract) without regard to your life expectancy, find your expected return by multiplying your annual payment by the number of years.

Note: See 7.23 for more information on the life expectancy tables.

Step 3: Divide the investment in the contract (Step 1) by the expected return (Step 2). This will give you the tax-free percentage of your yearly annuity payments. The tax-free percentage remains the same for the remaining years of the annuity, even if payments increase due to a cost-of-living adjustment. A different computation of the tax-free percentage applies to variable annuities; *see* below.

If your annuity started before 1987, and you live longer than your projected life expectancy (shown in the IRS table), you may continue to apply the same tax-free percentage to each payment you receive. Thus, you may exclude from income more than you paid. However, if your annuity starting date is after 1986, your lifetime exclusion may not exceed your cost investment, less the value of any refund feature. Once you have recovered your cost, further payments are fully taxable.

If your annuity starting date is after July 1, 1986, and you die before recovering your investment, a deduction is allowed on your final tax return for the unrecovered cost. If a refund of the investment is made under the contract to a beneficiary, the beneficiary is allowed the deduction. The deduction is claimed as a miscellaneous itemized deduction that is not subject to the 2% adjusted gross income floor; *see* Chapter 19.

Step 4: Find your total annuity payments for the year. For example, you received 10 monthly payments of $100 as your annuity began in March. Your total payments are $1,000, the monthly payment multiplied by 10.

Step 5: Multiply the percentage in Step 3 by the total in Step 4. The result is the nontaxable portion (or excludable amount) of your annuity payments.

Step 6. Subtract the amount in Step 5 from the amount in Step 4. This is the part of your annuity for the year which is subject to tax.

Note: An example of figuring the taxable and nontaxable portions for a single life annuity is in *7.23*.

Variable annuities. If you have a variable annuity that pays different benefits depending on cost-of-living indexes, profits earned by the annuity fund, or similar fluctuating standards, the tax-free portion of each payment is computed by dividing your investment in the contract (Step 1) by the total number of payments you expect to receive. If the annuity is for a definite period, the total number of payments equals the number of payments to be made each year multiplied by the number of years you will receive payments. If the annuity is for life, you divide the amount you invested in the contract by a multiple obtained from the appropriate life expectancy table; *see* Step 2. The result is the tax-free amount of annual annuity income.

If you receive a payment that is *less* than the nontaxable amount, you may elect when you receive the next payment to recalculate the nontaxable portion. The amount by which the prior nontaxable portion exceeded the payment you received is divided by the number of payments you expect as of the time of the next payment. The result is added to the previously calculated nontaxable portion, and the sum is the amount of each future payment to be excluded from tax. A statement must be attached to your return explaining the recomputation.

EXAMPLES

1. Andrew Taylor's total investment of $12,000 for a variable annuity was made after June 30, 1986. The annuity starting date is January 1, 1997. The annuity will be paid starting July 1, 1997, in varying annual installments for life. Andrew's age (nearest birthday) at the January 1 starting date is 65. He uses a life expectancy multiple of 20.0, the amount shown in Table V on page 159 for a person age 65. The amount of each payment excluded from tax is:

Investment in the contract	$12,000
Multiple (from Table V)	20.0
Amount of each payment excluded from tax ($12,000 ÷ 20)	$600

   If the first payment is $920, then 320 ($920 – $600) will be included in Andrew's 1997 income.

2. Assume that, after receiving the 1997 payment of $920 in Example 1, Andrew receives $500 in 1998 and $1,200 in 1999. None of the 1998 payment is taxed, as $600 is excludable from each annual payment. Andrew may also elect to recompute his annual exclusion starting with the 1999 payment. The exclusion is recomputed as follows:

Amount excludable in 1998	$600
Amount received in 1998	500
Difference	$100
Multiple as of 1/1/99 (*see* Table V on page 159 for age 67)	18.4
Amount added to previously determined annual exclusion ($100 ÷ 18.4)	$5.43
Revised annual exclusion for 1999 and later years ($600 + $5.43)	$605.43
Amount taxable in 1999 ($1,200 – $605.43)	$594.57

Penalty on Premature Withdrawals From Deferred Annuities

As discussed above, withdrawals before the annuity starting date may be taxable or tax free, depending on whether investments were made after August 13, 1982.

Withdrawals before age 59 $\frac{1}{2}$ are also generally subject to a penalty of 10% of the amount includable in income. A withdrawal in 1997 from an annuity contract is penalized unless:

1. You have reached age 59 $\frac{1}{2}$ or have become totally disabled.
2. The distribution is part of a series of substantially equal payments, made at least annually over your life expectancy or over the joint life expectancies of you and a beneficiary. If you can avoid the penalty under this exception and you change to a nonqualifying distribution method within five years or before age 59 $\frac{1}{2}$, such as where you receive a lump sum, a recapture tax will apply to the payments received before age 59 $\frac{1}{2}$.
3. The payment is received by a beneficiary or estate after the policyholder's death.
4. Payment is from a qualified retirement plan, tax-sheltered annuity, or IRA; in this case the penalty rules of *7.14* (qualified plans) or *8.8* (IRAs) apply.
5. Payment is allocable to investments made before August 14, 1982.
6. Payment is from an annuity contract under a qualified personal injury settlement.
7. Payment is from a single-premium annuity where the starting date is no more than one year from the date of purchase.
8. Payment is from an annuity purchased by an employer upon the termination of a qualified retirement plan and held until you separated from service.

If no exception applies, you compute the 10% penalty on Form 5329. The penalty is 5% instead of 10% if as of March 1, 1986, you were receiving payments under a specific schedule pursuant to your written election. Attach an explanation to Form 5329 if you are applying the 5% rate.

7.23 Life Expectancy Tables

IRS unisex actuarial tables must be used if you made any investment in the annuity contract after June 30, 1986. Generally, life expectancies are longer under the unisex tables than under the prior male-female tables. The unisex life expectancy table for single life annuities is IRS Table V, shown on page 159. A sample of the unisex table for ordinary joint life and last survivor annuities is at the end of Chapter 8. The full table is Table VI, in IRS Publication 939.

If your entire investment was before July 1, 1986, you use the older male/female tables. The tables, IRS Tables I through IV, are in Publication 939. Table I, shown on page 159, is for single life expectancies. Table II, for ordinary joint life and last survivor annuities, is in Publication 939.

You may make an irrevocable election to use the unisex tables for all payments received under the contract, even if you did not make an investment after June 30, 1986.

If you invested in the contract both before July 1, 1986, and after June 30, 1986, and you are the first person to receive annuity payments under the contract, you may make a special election to use the prior tables for the pre-July 1986 investment and the unisex tables for the post-June 1986 investment. *See* IRS Publication 939 for further information. Treasury Regulation 1.72-6(d) has examples showing how to figure the post-June 1986 and pre-July 1986 investments.

Birthday nearest annuity starting date.   In looking up single life or joint life expectancy in the applicable table, use your age (and the age of a joint annuitant) at the birthday nearest to the annuity starting date. The number in the table next to this age is the life expectancy multiple used to figure the tax-free and taxable portions of a monthly annuity; *see* the following Examples.

Adjustments for nonmonthly payments.   An adjustment is required when your annuity payments are received quarterly, semi-annually, or annually; *see* Example 3 below.

EXAMPLES

1. Bill Jones was 66 years old on March 14, 1997. On April 1, he received his first monthly annuity check of $1,000. This covered his annuity payment for March. Bill's annuity starting date was March 1, 1997, and his entire investment was before July 1, 1986.

    Looking at Table I on page 159 under "Male" at age 66 (age on birthday nearest January 1 starting date), Bill finds the multiple 14.4. (He does not have to adjust that multiple because the payments are monthly.) Bill multiplies the 14.4 by $12,000 ($1,000 a month for a year) to find his expected return of $172,800. Say the annuity cost Bill $129,600. He divides his expected return into the investment in the contract (the cost) and gets his exclusion percentage of 75%. In every year for the rest of his life, Bill receives tax free 75% of his annuity payments and is taxable on 25%. In 1997, Bill receives $9,000 ($1,000 in April through December) and reports $2,250 as the taxable amount:

Amount received	$9,000
Amount excludable (75%)	6,750
Taxable portion	$2,250

    For 1998 and later years, Bill will receive annuity payments for the full year. The amount received will be $12,000; amount excludable, $9,000; and taxable portion, $3,000.

2. Same facts as in Example 1 except there was an investment after June 30, 1986, and Table V is used. Looking at Table V under age 66, Bill finds the multiple 19.2. The same multiple applies to males and females. Multiplying the19.2 by $12,000 gives an expected return of $230,400. Using a cost of $129,600, the exclusion percentage is 56.25% ($129,600 ÷ $230,400). For 1997, Bill reports annuity income as follows:

Amount received	$9,000.00
Amount excludable (56.25%)	5,062.50
Taxable portion	$3937.50

    For 1998 and later years in which annual payments of $12,000 are received, the amount excludable will be $6,750, and the taxable portion, $5,250.

3. You receive quarterly annuity payments. Your first payment comes on January 15, covering the first quarter of the year. Since the period between the starting date of January 1 and the payment date of January 15 is less than one month, you adjust the life expectancy multiple according to the table at the bottom of page 159, by adding 0.1. If the life expectancy multiple from the IRS table was 14.4, the adjusted multiple is 14.5.

TABLE I: Investments Before July 1, 1986

Ages			Ages			Ages		
Male	Female	Multiples	Male	Female	Multiples	Male	Female	Multiples
6	11	65.0	41	46	33.0	76	81	9.1
7	12	64.1	42	47	32.1	77	82	8.7
8	13	63.2	43	48	31.2	78	83	8.3
9	14	62.3	44	49	30.4	79	84	7.8
10	15	61.4	45	50	29.6	80	85	7.5
11	16	60.4	46	51	28.7	81	86	7.1
12	17	59.5	47	52	27.9	82	87	6.7
13	18	58.6	48	53	27.1	83	88	6.3
14	19	57.7	49	54	26.3	84	89	6.0
15	20	56.7	50	55	25.5	85	90	5.7
16	21	55.8	51	56	24.7	86	91	5.4
17	22	54.9	52	57	24.0	87	92	5.1
18	23	53.9	53	58	23.2	88	93	4.8
19	24	53.0	54	59	22.4	89	94	4.5
20	25	52.1	55	60	21.7	90	95	4.2
21	26	51.1	56	61	21.0	91	96	4.0
22	27	50.2	57	62	20.3	92	97	3.7
23	28	49.3	58	63	19.6	93	98	3.5
24	29	48.3	59	64	18.9	94	99	3.3
25	30	47.4	60	65	18.2	95	100	3.1
26	31	46.5	61	66	17.5	96	101	2.9
27	32	45.6	62	67	16.9	97	102	2.7
28	33	44.6	63	68	16.2	98	103	2.5
29	34	43.7	64	69	15.6	99	104	2.3
30	35	42.8	65	70	15.0	100	105	2.1
31	36	41.9	66	71	14.4	101	106	1.9
32	37	41.0	67	72	13.8	102	107	1.7
33	38	40.0	68	73	13.2	103	108	1.5
34	39	39.1	69	74	12.6	104	109	1.3
35	40	38.2	70	75	12.1	105	110	1.2
36	41	37.3	71	76	11.6	106	111	1.0
37	42	36.5	72	77	11.0	107	112	0.8
38	43	35.6	73	78	10.5	108	113	0.7
39	44	34.7	74	79	10.1	109	114	0.6
40	45	33.8	75	80	9.6	110	115	0.5
						111	116	0.0

TABLE V: Investments After June 30, 1986

Age	Multiple	Age	Multiple	Age	Multiple
5	76.6	42	40.6	79	10.0
6	75.6	43	39.6	80	9.5
7	74.7	44	38.7	81	8.9
8	73.7	45	37.7	82	8.4
9	72.7	46	36.8	83	7.9
10	71.7	47	35.9	84	7.4
11	70.7	48	34.9	85	6.9
12	69.7	49	34.0	86	6.5
13	68.8	50	33.1	87	6.1
14	67.8	51	32.2	88	5.7
15	66.8	52	31.3	89	5.3
16	65.8	53	30.4	90	5.0
17	64.8	54	29.5	91	4.7
18	63.9	55	28.6	92	4.4
19	62.9	56	27.7	93	4.1
20	61.9	57	26.8	94	3.9
21	60.9	58	25.9	95	3.7
22	59.9	59	25.0	96	3.4
23	59.0	60	24.2	97	3.2
24	58.0	61	23.3	98	3.0
25	57.0	62	22.5	99	2.8
26	56.0	63	21.6	100	2.7
27	55.1	64	20.8	101	2.5
28	54.1	65	20.0	102	2.3
29	53.1	66	19.2	103	2.1
30	52.2	67	18.4	104	1.9
31	51.2	68	17.6	105	1.8
32	50.2	69	16.8	106	1.6
33	49.3	70	16.0	107	1.4
34	48.3	71	15.3	108	1.3
35	47.3	72	14.6	109	1.1
36	46.4	73	13.9	110	1.0
37	45.4	74	13.2	111	0.9
38	44.4	75	12.5	112	0.8
39	43.5	76	11.9	113	0.7
40	42.5	77	11.2	114	0.6
41	41.5	78	10.6	115	0.5

Multiple Adjustment Table

If the number of whole months from the annuity starting date to the first payment date is—	0–1	2	3	4	5	6	7	8	9	10	11	12
And payments under the contract are to be made:												
Annually	+0.5	+0.4	+0.3	+0.2	+0.1	0.0	0.0	–0.1	–0.2	–0.3	–0.4	–0.5
Semiannually	+0.2	+0.1	0.0	0.0	–0.1	–0.2						
Quarterly	+0.1	0.0	–0.1									

7.24 When You Convert Your Endowment Policy

When an endowment policy matures, you may elect to receive a lump sum, an annuity, an interest option, or a paid-up life insurance policy. If you elect—

A lump sum. You report the difference between your cost (premium payments less dividends) and what you receive.

An annuity before the policy matures or within 60 days after maturity. You report income in the years you receive your annuity. *See 7.22* for how to report annuity income. Use as your investment in the annuity contract the cost of the endowment policy less premiums paid for other benefits such as double indemnity or disability income. If you elect the annuity option more than 60 days after maturity, you report income on the matured policy as if you received the lump sum; *see* above rule. The lump sum is treated as the cost investment in the annuity contract.

An interest option before the policy matures. You report only the interest as it is received, provided you do not have the right to withdraw the policy proceeds. If you have the right to withdraw the proceeds, you are treated as in constructive receipt; the difference between your cost and what you receive would be taxed as if you had received a lump sum.

Paid-up insurance. You report the difference between the present value of the paid-up life insurance policy and the premium paid for the endowment policy. In figuring the value of the insurance policy, you do not use its cash surrender value, but the amount you would have to pay for a similar policy with the company at the date of exchange. Your insurance company can give you this figure. The difference is taxed at ordinary income tax rates.

Tax-free exchange rules apply to the policy exchanges listed at *6.11*.

Sales of endowment, annuity, or life insurance policies are taxable as ordinary income, not as capital gains.

The proceeds of a veteran's endowment policy paid before the veteran's death are not taxable.

Employee Annuities

7.25 Reporting Employee Annuities

Tax treatment of your employee annuity payments depends on the amount of your contributions and your annuity starting date.

Fully taxable payments. If you did not contribute to the cost of a pension or employee annuity, and you did not report as income your employer's contributions, you are fully taxed on payments after the annuity starting date. On your 1997 return, you report fully taxable payments on Line 16b of Form 1040 or Line 11b of Form 1040A.

An employee is taxed on the full value of a nonforfeitable annuity contract which the employer buys him or her if the employer does not have a qualified pension plan. Tax is imposed in the year the policy is purchased. A qualified plan is one approved by the IRS for special tax benefits.

If your annuity started before July 2, 1986, and payments within the first three years under the contract exceeded your cost investment, payments were not taxable until they exceeded your cost investment. On your 1997 return, your payments are fully taxable.

Disability pension before minimum retirement age. Disability payments received before you reach the minimum retirement age (at which you would be entitled to a regular retirement annuity) are fully taxable as wages. After minimum retirement age, payments are treated as an annuity subject to the cost recovery rules of *7.22* or the simplified rules of *7.26*.

Partially taxable payments. If you and your employer both contributed to the cost of your annuity, the part of each payment allocable to your investment is tax free and the balance is taxable.

On Form 1099-R, the payer of a pension or annuity may tell you how much is taxable. If not, you may make the tax-free calculation under either (1) the "simplified" method explained at *7.26;* or (2) for a $50 fee, ask the IRS to calculate the taxable amount.

Cost and cost adjustments are explained in *7.27* and *7.28*.

Changing cost-recovery methods. If your annuity starting date was before November 19, 1996, you can switch from the regular six-step method of *7.22* to the simplified method *(7.26)* or from the simplified to the regular method within the period for filing an amended return *(49.1)* for the first year. For example, if your annuity started in April 1996 and on your 1996 return you used the six-step method, and later realize within the amendment period that you could get a larger tax-free return with the simplified method, you may file amended returns for 1996 and later years using the simplified method to recompute your tax-free exclusion for all the years. After recomputing the tax-free percentage of each payment under the new method, use that same percentage every year until your investment has been completely recovered.

7.26 Simplified Rule for Calculating Taxable Employee Annuity

If your annuity starting date is *after November 18, 1996*, you must use the simplified method explained below to figure the tax-free portion of your annuity payments from a qualified employer plan, qualified employee annuity, or 403(b) tax-sheltered annuity. The only exception is for annuitants who are age 75 or older at the time payments begin and who have payments guaranteed for at least five years; they must use the six-step method discussed at *7.22* for commercial annuities.

A beneficiary receiving a survivor annuity may use the simplified method if the employee used it.

Figuring taxable and tax-free payments under the simplified method. Under the simplified method, a level tax-free portion is determined for each monthly payment with the following steps.

Step 1. Figure your investment in the contract as of the annuity starting date. Include premiums you paid and any after-tax contributions you made to the employer's pension plan; *see 7.27*. Beneficiaries may increase the investment by any allowable death benefit exclusion, up to $5,000, but only if the employee died before August 21, 1996; *see 7.28*.

Step 2. Divide the investment from Step 1 by the number of monthly payments shown in Table I or Table II below, using your age at the birthday preceding the annuity starting date. The result is the tax-free recovery portion of each monthly payment. The tax-free portion remains the same if a spouse or other beneficiary receives payments under a joint and survivor annuity after the employee's death.

Use either Table I or Table II, described below. Table II reflects a new law for annuities based on more than one life if the annuity starting date is after December 31, 1997.

Table I: Use this table if the annuity starting date is after November 18, 1996, and before January 1, 1998, whether the annuity is based on a single life or the life of more than one annuitant. Also use it if the annuity starting date is after December 31, 1997, and the annuity is based on one life only.

Table II: Use this table if the annuity starting date is after December 31, 1997, and benefits are based on the life of *more than* one annuitant. For example, this table applies to a 50% joint and survivor annuity, if the annuity starting date is after 1997.

Table I

Age of primary annuitant at starting date	Number of monthly payments
55 and under	360
56–60	310
61–65	260
66–70	210
71 and over	160

Table II

Combined ages of annuitants	Number of payments
Not more than 110	410
More than 110 but not more than 120	360
More than 120 but not more than 130	310
More than 130 but not more than 140	260
More than 140	210

Step 3. Multiply the Step 2 result by the number of monthly payments received during the year; this is the total tax-free payment for the current year. However, if any part of your cost was previously recovered tax free in years after 1986, the tax-free amount is limited to the excess of your investment from Step 1 over the prior year recoveries.

Step 4. Subtract the Step 3 tax-free payment from the total pension received this year; this is the taxable pension you must report on Form 1040 or Form 1040A. If the payer of the annuity shows a higher taxable amount on Form 1099-R, use the amount figured here.

EXAMPLE

Fred Smith, age 65, retires, and beginning January 1, 1997, he receives an annuity of $1,000 per month for the joint lives of him and his wife Betty. His investment in the plan was $30,000. To figure the tax-free portion of each payment, he divides his $30,000 investment by 260; *see* Table I on page 161. The result, $115.38, is the tax-free portion of each monthly payment ($30,000 ÷ 260 = $115.38) and $884.62 ($1,000 − $115.38) is taxable. For 1997, he reports $10,615 of his pension as taxable income (12 × $884.62); $1,385 is tax free (12 × $115.38).

If Fred dies before the receipt of 260 payments, Betty will also exclude $115.38 from each payment she receives until a total of 260 payments (hers and Fred's) have been recovered. If she dies before the 260th payment, a deduction for the unrecovered investment is allowed on her final income tax return; the deduction is a miscellaneous itemized deduction not subject to the 2% AGI floor.

If the annuity starting date was after 1997, Fred and Betty would use Table II to figure the tax-free portions of the joint-life annuity payments.

Annuity starting date before November 19, 1996. The IRS allowed an optional version of the simplified method where the annuity starting date was after July 1, 1986, and before November 19, 1996.

The number of payments used to figure the tax-free portion of each payment was smaller than that shown in Table I on page 161. For those 55 and under, the number of payments is 300; if age 56–60, 260; if age 61–65, 240; if age 66–70, 170; and if 71 or over, 120.

Since the IRS method is optional for annuities starting before November 19, 1996, an individual who started to use the six-step commercial annuity method at *7.22* may be able to switch to the IRS method by timely filing amended returns for the first year of the annuity and the later years.

7.27 Cost of Employee Annuity

For purposes of figuring the tax-free recovery of your investment under the general rules of *7.22* or the simplified rule of *7.26,* include the following items paid as of the annuity starting date as your cost in an employee annuity:

- Premiums paid by you or by after-tax withholdings from your pay.
- Payments made by your employer and reported as additional pay.
- Premiums paid by an employer in a nonapproved plan for your benefit give you immediate income if you have nonforfeitable rights to the policy.
- Premiums paid by your employer, which, if the amounts had been paid to you directly, would have been tax free to you because you were working abroad; *see* Chapter 36.
- Pre-1939 contributions by a city or state to its employees' pension fund. (Before 1939, salaries to state and city employees were tax free for federal income tax purposes.)

If you are a beneficiary of a deceased employee, *see 7.28.*

7.28 Death Benefit Exclusion Repealed

If you are the beneficiary of an employee who died after August 20, 1996, you are not eligible for any death benefit exclusion. However, if you are the beneficiary of an employee (or self-employed plan participant) who died before August 21, 1996, you may be able to claim a death benefit exclusion of up to $5,000 to reduce the tax on 1997 payments received on behalf of the employee.

Death benefit exclusion under prior law rules. The repeal of the death benefit exclusion does not apply to beneficiaries of employees dying before August 21, 1996. As beneficiary, you may be entitled to all or part of the up-to-$5,000 exclusion. If the employee had more than one beneficiary, the total exclusion for that employee is $5,000, and it must be divided among you and the other beneficiaries in proportion to the benefits received.

If you are receiving a survivor annuity, the allowable exclusion is added to the cost of the annuity *(7.27)* to figure the tax-free and taxable portion of the payments under the simplified method *(7.26)* or general method *(7.22)*. If you are the survivor under a joint and survivor annuity, you may *not* claim the death benefit exclusion if the deceased had received any payment under the joint and survivor contract after reaching minimum retirement age.

If as a beneficiary you receive a one-time death benefit payment that is *not* made from an employer retirement plan, report as "Other income" on Form 1040 the excess of the payment over the allowable death benefit exclusion.

7.29 Withdrawals Before Annuity Starting Date

You generally may not make tax-free withdrawals from your employer's plan before the annuity starting date, even if your withdrawals are less than your investment. On a withdrawal before the annuity starting date, you must pay tax on a portion of the withdrawal unless the exceptions below apply. The portion of the withdrawal allocable to your investment is recovered tax free; the portion allocable to employer contributions and income earned on the contract is taxed. To compute the tax-free recovery, multiply the withdrawal by this fraction:

$$\frac{\text{Your total investment}}{\text{Your vested account balance or accrued benefit}}$$

Your investment and vested benefit are determined as of the date of distribution.

Exceptions. More favorable investment recovery rules are allowed in the following cases:

1. *Employer plans in effect on May 5, 1986.* If on May 5, 1986, your employer's plan allowed distributions of employee contributions before separation from service, the above pro-rata recovery rule applies only to the extent that the withdrawal exceeds the total investment in the contract on December 31, 1986.

   For example, assume that as of December 31, 1986, you had an account balance of $9,750, which included $4,000 of your own contributions. If the plan on May 5, 1986, allowed pre-retirement distributions of employee contributions, you may receive withdrawals up to your $4,000 investment without incurring tax. Thus, if you have not made previous withdrawals and receive a $3,000 distribution in 1994, it is not subject to tax.

2. *Separate accounts for employee contributions.* A defined contribution plan (such as a profit-sharing plan) is allowed to account for employee contributions (and earnings on the contributions) separately from employer contributions. If separate accounting is maintained, withdrawals of employee contributions from the separate account may be made tax free. A defined benefit pension plan may also maintain employee contributions (and earnings) in a separate account to which actual earnings and losses are allocated.

Note: Both of the exceptions just discussed are complicated and you should consult your plan administrator to determine if the exceptions apply and how to make the required calculations.

7.30 Civil Service Retirement

As discussed at *7.26*, the simplified method must be used to compute the tax-free and taxable portions of each withdrawal if your annuity starting date is after November 18, 1996.

If you leave federal government service before retirement or transfer to a job not under the federal retirement system and you are not entitled to an immediate annuity, you may receive a refund of your contributions (plus any interest). If the refund exceeds your contributions, the excess is taxable.

Retirees with a life-threatening illness may be able to elect a reduced annuity in order to receive a lump-sum credit for their total contributions to the plan; *see* IRS Publication 721 for figuring the taxable portion of the lump sum if the election was made.

Cost of civil service annuity. For purposes of figuring the tax-free portion of each annuity payment your *cost* equals the withholdings from your federal government pay that were contributed to the Civil Service retirement fund. Also, if you repaid to the retirement fund amounts that you previously had withdrawn, or paid into the fund to receive full credit for certain uncovered service, the entire amount you paid, including that designated as interest, is part of your cost. You may not claim an interest deduction for any amount designated as interest.

The annuity statement you received when your annuity was approved shows your "total contributions" to the retirement fund (your cost) and the "monthly rate" of your annuity benefit. The monthly rate is the rate before adjustment for health benefits coverage and life insurance, if any.

A future increase in your civil service pension or your survivor's benefit is not treated as annuity income but is reported in full as miscellaneous income and is not reduced by the exclusion ratio. However, an increase effective on or before a survivor's civil service annuity commences must be taken into account in computing the expected return or in determining the aggregate amount receivable under the annuity.

A lump-sum payment for accrued annual leave received upon retirement is not part of your annuity. It is treated as a salary payment and is taxable as ordinary income.

If you made voluntary contributions to the retirement fund that you use to fund an additional monthly benefit, you report the portion of your annuity attributable to the voluntary contributions as a separate annuity, taxable under the rules at 7.26. If you made voluntary contributions, an information return which you receive each year will state the portion of your monthly payments attributable to your voluntary contributions. If instead of increasing your monthly benefit you receive a refund of your voluntary contributions plus accrued interest, the interest is taxable in the year you receive it.

7.31 Retired Military Personnel Allowed Annuity Election

If, when you retire from the military, your pay is reduced to provide an annuity for your spouse or certain child beneficiaries, you do not report that part of your retirement pay used to fund the annuity.

For example, you are eligible to receive retirement pay of $500 a month. You elect to receive $400 a month to obtain an annuity of $200 a month for your spouse on your death. You report $400 a month for tax purposes during your lifetime, rather than the $500. On your death, your spouse generally will report the full $200 a month received as income.

Veteran's benefit deposits.   If you elected to receive veteran's benefits instead of some or all of your retirement pay, you may have been required to deposit with the U.S. Treasury an amount equal to the reduction for the annuity. If so, you do not report retirement pay until it equals the amount deposited.

Beneficiaries.   If all of the retired person's consideration for the contract (previously taxed reductions) has not been offset against retirement income at the time of death, the beneficiary excludes all payments under the contract until the exclusions equal the remaining consideration for the contract not previously excluded by the deceased. As soon as this amount is excluded, the beneficiary reports all later payments as income.

Contributions to a regular IRA of up to $2,000 a year are deductible for 1997 if you and your spouse do not have retirement plan coverage where you work. If you have coverage, you may claim a deduction if your adjusted gross income is below a specified phase-out range; *see 8.4.*

If you work for a qualifying small employer that sets up a SIMPLE IRA, you may elect to defer up to $6,000 of your pay to the plan; *see 8.18.* Under a special type of IRA, a simplified employee pension (SEP) set up by your employer, you may make larger tax-sheltered contributions than you may make to a regular IRA; *see 8.16.*

IRA distributions that you received in 1997 are fully taxable, except to the extent you have made nondeductible contributions. You must file Form 8606 to figure the tax-free portion of distributions allocable to nondeductible contributions; *see 8.9.*

IRA distributions received before age 59 $\frac{1}{2}$ are generally subject to a penalty (*see 8.12* for exceptions). Minimum distributions from an IRA must begin after you reach age 70 $\frac{1}{2}$; *see 8.14.*

New law opportunities in 1998. Starting in 1998, new IRA benefits will be available. If you have retirement plan coverage where you work, the income range for making deductible IRA contributions is increased; *see 8.4.* An individual who is not covered by an employer plan, but whose spouse is, will be able to claim a $2,000 IRA deduction if modified adjusted gross income is less than $150,000; *see 8.4.*

For long-term planning, an important change is the introduction of the Roth IRA, a new type of nondeductible IRA which offers a tax-free buildup of earnings and allows tax-free withdrawals after a five-year period if you are over age 59 $\frac{1}{2}$; *see 8.20.*

Starting and Contributing to an IRA

8.1 Starting an IRA

There are two ways in which you may set up an IRA: (1) by making annual contributions which may be deductible *(see 8.4* for deduction rules) or nondeductible *(see 8.5* and *8.20)* and (2) by rolling over a distribution received from a qualified employer plan or from another IRA. Both types of IRA accounts provide tax-free accumulation of earnings until withdrawals are made. The rollover option also allows you to avoid immediate tax when you receive a lump-sum payment upon retirement, changing jobs, or disability; *see 7.8.* Tax-free interest compounding can produce the following funds for retirement:

Invest $2,000 on January 1, every year for—	With interest compounded daily		
	6%	8%	10%
		gives you—	
5 years	$12,015	$12,794	$13,633
10 years	28,233	31,879	36,109
15 years	50,125	60,349	73,164
20 years	79,676	102,820	134,252
25 years	119,563	166,176	234,962
30 years	173,405	260,688	400,993

IRA restrictions. Weigh the benefits from tax deductions for IRA contributions *(8.3)* and from tax-free compounding against these restrictions: Generally, you may not freely withdraw IRA funds until the year you reach age 59 $\frac{1}{2}$ or become disabled. If you take money out before that time, you are subject to a penalty; *see 8.8.* Pledging the account as collateral is treated as a taxable distribution from the account; *see 8.8.* In the year you reach age 70 $\frac{1}{2}$, you may no longer make IRA contributions, and you must start to withdraw *(8.14)* from the account. All IRA withdrawals are fully taxable except for amounts allocable to nondeductible contributions; *see 8.8* and *8.9.* Special averaging for lump-sum distributions does not apply. Excess contributions *(8.7)* are penalized.

If your IRA loses value because of poor investments, you may not deduct the loss. A loss is allowed only if you make nondeductible contributions which you have not recovered when the account is depleted; *see 8.9.*

Types of IRAs. You may set up an IRA as:

1. *An individual retirement account* with a bank, savings and loan association, federally insured credit union, or other qualified person as trustee or custodian. An individual retirement account is technically a trust or custodial account. Your contribution may be invested in vehicles such as certificates of deposit, mutual funds, and certain limited partnerships.
2. *An individual retirement annuity* by purchasing an annuity contract (including a joint and survivor contract for the benefit of you and your spouse) issued by an insurance company; no trustee or custodian is required. The contract, endorsed to meet the terms of an IRA, is all that is required. Contracts issued after November 6, 1978, must provide for flexible premiums up to $2,000 a year, so that if your compensation changes, your payment may also change. As borrowing or pledging of the contract is not allowed under an IRA, the contracts will not contain loan provisions. Endowment contracts issued after November 6, 1978, that provide life insurance protection may not be used as individual retirement annuities.

You may set up one type of IRA one year and choose another form the next year. You also may split your contribution between two or more investment vehicles. For example, you are eligible to contribute $2,000. You may choose to put $1,000 into an investment retirement annuity and $1,000 into an individual retirement account with your local bank.

You do not have to file any forms with your tax return when you set up or make contributions to a deductible IRA. Form 8606 must be attached to Form 1040 or Form 1040A if you make nondeductible IRA contributions; *see 8.6.* The bank or company where you set up your IRA will report your contribution to the IRS on Form 5498, and you should receive a copy.

Self-Directed IRA. If you wish to take a more active role in managing your IRA investments, you may set up a "self-directed" IRA using an IRS model form. The model trust (Form 5305) and the model custodial account agreement (Form 5305-A) meet the requirements of an exempt indi-

Caution

Investment Restrictions for Self-Directed IRA

If you have a self-directed IRA, you may not invest in collectibles, such as art works, gems, stamps, antiques, rugs, metals, or guns. Coins are not allowed except for state-issued coins or certain U.S. minted gold and silver coins. Starting in 1998, investments are allowed in certain platinum coins, as well as certain gold, silver, platinum, or palladium bullion held by the trustee. Assets used to acquire a prohibited collectible are treated as distributions and are taxed.

vidual retirement account and so do not require a ruling or determination letter approving the exemption of the account and the deductibility of contributions made to the account. If you use this method, you still have to find a bank or other institution or trustee to handle your account or investment. Investments in a self-directed IRA are subject to restrictions; *see* the Caution this page.

SIMPLE IRA. If you work for a company with 100 or less workers, your employer may set up a SIMPLE IRA to which you may make salary-reduction contributions; *see 8.18.*

Trustee's fees and brokerage commissions. Trustee's fees paid to set up or manage an IRA are not considered IRA contributions provided they are separately billed. They are investment expenses which may be deducted as a miscellaneous itemized deduction subject to the 2% adjusted gross income floor; *see 19.1.* However, broker's commissions that are paid when you make investments for your IRA are not separately deductible, according to the IRS. They are considered IRA contributions subject to the $2,000 contribution limit.

Contributions after the end of the taxable year. You have until April 15, 1998 (the regular filing due date for your 1997 return), to make deductible or nondeductible IRA contributions for 1997. You must make your contribution by April 15, 1998, even if you get an extension to file your return. If you are short of cash, you may borrow the funds to make the contribution without jeopardizing the deduction. If an IRA deduction entitles you to a refund, you can file your return early, claim the IRA deduction, and if you receive the refund in time, apply it towards an IRA contribution before the due date.

8.2 Contributions Must Be Based on Earnings

You may make IRA contributions for 1997 of up to $2,000, provided you have wage, salary, or net self-employment earnings and that you have not reached age $70 \frac{1}{2}$ by the end of the year. If your earned income is less than $2,000, the contribution limit is 100% of your pay or net earned income if self-employed. Contributions for 1997 may be made up to the filing deadline of April 15, 1998; this is the deadline even if you obtain a filing extension.

If you are married, you may each contribute up to $2,000 to an IRA, as long as your combined compensation covers the contributions; *see 8.3.*

Contributions up to these limits are *fully deductible* on your 1997 return if *neither you nor your spouse* is an active participant in an employer or self-employed retirement plan. Deductions for active plan participants are phased out for single persons with adjusted gross income over $25,000, and married persons filing jointly with adjusted gross income over $40,000. The phase-out rules are discussed at *8.4.* Whether you should make nondeductible IRA contributions is discussed at *8.6.*

IRA contributions must be based on payments received for rendering personal services, such as salary, wages, commissions, tips, fees, bonuses, jury fees, or net earnings from self-employment (less Keogh plan contributions on behalf of the self-employed). Compensation does *not* include:

1. Investment income such as interest, dividends, or profits from sales of property;
2. Deferred compensation, pensions, or annuities; or
3. Income earned abroad for which the foreign earned income exclusion is claimed.

> **EXAMPLE**
>
> A trader whose sole income was derived from stock dividends and gains in buying and selling stocks contributed to an IRA. The IRS disallowed the deduction on the grounds that his income was not earned income.

If you live in a community property state, the fact that one-half of your spouse's income is considered your income does not entitle you to make contributions to an IRA. The contributions must be based on pay earned through your services.

Only cash contributions are deductible; contributions paid by check are considered cash for this purpose.

Working for spouse. If you work for your spouse, you may make an IRA contribution provided you actually perform services and receive an actual payment of wages. A wife who worked as a receptionist and assistant to her husband, a veterinarian, failed to meet the second test. Her husband did not pay her a salary. Instead, he deposited all income from his business into a joint bank account held with his wife. In addition, no federal income tax was withheld from her wages. In a ruling, the IRS held that the wife could not set up her own IRA, even though she performed services; she failed to receive actual payment. Depositing business income into a joint account is

Caution

Broker's Restriction on IRA Transfers

Before you invest in an IRA, carefully review the terms of the agreement for restrictions. One investor, who put his IRA in a brokerage account, was not allowed by the trustee to transfer from one account to another. Furthermore, the trustee reserved some of the IRA funds to cover broker fees and other transfer costs. The investor asked the IRS if these restrictions violated the tax law. The IRS, in a private letter ruling, said there was no violation. An IRA is a contractual agreement between the IRA trustee and the participant. Although the tax laws do not place limitations on direct IRA-to-IRA transfers, the trustees of a particular account may restrict such transfers.

neither actual nor constructive payment of the wife's salary. Furthermore, any deduction claimed for the wife's wages was disallowed.

Self-employed may make IRA contributions. IRA contributions may be based on net self-employment earnings (*45.1*), after taking into account deductible Keogh or SEP retirement plan contributions (*41.5*) and the deduction for one-half of self-employment tax liability (*45.3*). If you have a net loss for the year, you may not make an IRA contribution unless you also have wages.

If you have more than one self-employed activity, you must aggregate profits and losses from all of your self-employed businesses to determine if you have net income on which to base an IRA contribution. For example, if one self-employed business produces a net profit of $15,000 but another a net loss of $20,000, you may not make an IRA contribution based on the net profit of $15,000 since you have an overall loss. This netting rule does not apply to salary or wage income. If you are an employee who also has an unprofitable business, you may make an IRA contribution based on your salary.

If you have a self-employed retirement plan from your business, you are considered an active participant in a retirement plan for purposes of the adjusted gross income phase-out rules discussed at *8.4*.

Taxable alimony treated as compensation. A divorced spouse with little or no earnings in 1997 may treat taxable alimony as compensation, giving a basis for deductible IRA contributions. If you are divorced, you make an IRA contribution equal to 100% of taxable alimony up to $2,000. However, the deduction may be reduced or eliminated if you are an active participant in an employer plan and your adjusted gross income exceeds the $25,000 threshold for unmarried individuals; *see 8.4*. Taxable alimony is alimony paid under a decree of divorce or legal separation, or a written agreement incident to such a decree; *see* Chapter 37. It does not include alimony payments made under a written agreement that is not incident to such a decree.

No deductible contributions allowed for those age 70 $\frac{1}{2}$. Even if you still have earnings, you may not make deductible contributions to your IRA for the year in which you reach age 70 $\frac{1}{2}$, or any later year. For example, if you were born in the last six months of 1926 or the first six months of 1927, you will reach age 70 $\frac{1}{2}$ in 1997 and may not make any deductible IRA contributions for 1997 or later years.

If you have a nonworking spouse under age 70 $\frac{1}{2}$, you may contribute up to $2,000 to his or her IRA, even though no contribution may be made to your own deductible IRA because you have reached age 70 $\frac{1}{2}$; *see 8.3*.

Under a new law, contributions to a nondeductible Roth IRA may be made after 1997 even if you are over age 70 $\frac{1}{2}$, provided you have compensation (*8.2*) to support the contribution and your income is within the limit allowed under the Roth IRA contribution rules; *see 8.20*.

8.3 IRA Contributions for Married Couples

If both you and your spouse earned compensation in 1997 of at least $2,000, and you are each under 70 $\frac{1}{2}$ at the end of the year, each of you may make an IRA contribution for 1997 of up to $2,000 by April 15, 1998. Under the liberalized spousal IRA rule that takes effect in 1997, the $2,000 per spouse limit applies even if only one of you works, provided you file jointly and your combined compensation is at least $4,000. *See* below for details on the 1997 spousal IRA rule.

Contributions up to the $2,000 limit are fully deductible if *neither* you nor your spouse is covered by an employer retirement plan. If either spouse is an active plan participant, your deduction may be reduced or eliminated by a phase-out rule which is based on your modified adjusted gross income (MAGI) and whether you file jointly or separately.

Deduction phase-out rule for spouses filing jointly for 1997. If you and your spouse file a joint return for 1997 and either of you is an active participant in an employer retirement plan, the phase-out rule applies only if your modified adjusted gross income (MAGI) on the joint return exceeds $40,000. Contributions are fully deductible if modified adjusted gross income (MAGI) on the joint return is $40,000 or less. Limited deductions are allowed if joint MAGI is between $40,000 and $50,000 under the phase-out rules explained at *8.4*. No deduction is allowed for either spouse if joint return MAGI is $50,000 or more.

EXAMPLE

In 1997, Ray earns a salary of $20,000, his wife Ann earns $15,000, and neither is covered by an employer retirement plan. On a 1997 joint return, each of them may claim an IRA deduction of up to $2,000, for a maximum of $4,000. Even if only one of them worked, the maximum deduction would be $2,000 for each of them under the spousal IRA rules discussed below.

If either Ray or Ann is an active participant in an employer plan, they are still allowed the maximum $4,000 deduction provided their combined MAGI on a 1997 joint return is $40,000 or less. If joint return MAGI is over $40,000 but less than $50,000, each may claim a limited deduction; *8.4*.

Deduction phase-out rule for married persons filing separately for 1997. If you are married, live together at any time during 1997, file separately, and either of you is an active participant in an employer plan, the other spouse is also considered an active participant. Both of you are subject to the $0 to $10,000 AGI deduction phaseout; *see 8.4*.

If you live apart for all of 1997, you each figure IRA deductions as if single. Thus, the more favorable deduction phase-out range of $25,000 to $35,000 applies if you are covered by an employer retirement plan; *see 8.4*. If you are *not* covered, you may claim a full deduction on your separate return.

Spousal IRA deduction on 1997 joint return for nonworking or low earning spouse. Before 1997, the maximum total IRA deduction for a married couple on a joint return was $2,250 where one spouse did not work or had earnings of under $250. For 1997, the deductible limit on a joint return is generally $2,000 for each spouse, the same as for two-earner couples, as long as their combined compensation is at least $4,000. The $2,000 deduction limit for each spouse is subject to the 1997 phase-out rules for active plan participants discussed at *8.4*. Thus, if modified adjusted gross income (MAGI) on a 1997 joint return is between $40,000 and $50,000, the $2,000 limit per spouse is phased out, with no deduction allowed at MAGI of $50,000 or more.

The spousal IRA rule in effect allows the lower earning spouse to "borrow" his or her spouse's compensation in order to reach the maximum $2,000 deductible limit. Thus, if one spouse does not work and the other spouse has compensation of $4,000 or more, the $2,000 limit for each spouse applies, unless it is reduced under the phase-out rule *(8.4)* for active plan participants.

Specifically, the lower earning spouse has a deductible limit equal to the *lesser* of:

(1) $2,000, and

(2) the lower earning spouse's compensation, plus the excess of the higher earning spouse's compensation over the deductible contribution for the higher earning spouse.

If either spouse is an active participant in an employer retirement plan and the couple's joint MAGI for 1997 exceeds $40,000, the deduction phase-out rules of *8.4* will reduce or eliminate the $2,000 limit in the above computation for the lower-earning spouse; see Example 3 below.

 Law Alert

Higher Spousal IRA Contributions in 1997

A new law effective in 1997 increases the maximum IRA deduction for a married couple filing jointly from $2,250 to $4,000, up to $2,000 each, as long as their combined compensation is at least that much.

EXAMPLES

1. Ted and Lynn Baker file a joint return for 1997. Lynn has 1997 compensation of $42,000 and Ted, a full-time student, does not work. Their modified adjusted gross income *(8.4)* is $43,000. Lynn is not an active plan participant *(see 8.4)* so the IRA deduction phase-out rules do not apply. Lynn's deductible IRA limit under the regular rule is $2,000 (lesser of $2,000 limit and compensation of $42,000). Ted's deductible limit under the spousal IRA rule is also $2,000: the lesser of (1) $2,000 and (2) $40,000, the excess of Lynn's $42,000 compensation over her deductible $2,000 limit.

2. If Lynn's compensation in Example 1 was $2,500, her deductible IRA limit would still be $2,000. Ted's limit would be $500: the lesser of (1) $2,000 and (2) $500, the excess of Lynn's compensation of $2,500 over her $2,000 deduction limit. Their combined deduction limit is their compensation of $2,500.

   If Ted had compensation of $1,000, his deductible IRA limit would increase by $1,000, to $1,500. In that case, Lynn and Ted's combined deductible IRA limit would equal their combined compensation of $3,500.

3. Assume the facts of Example 1 except that Lynn is an active participant in a retirement plan where she works. Since she is an active plan participant and the joint return MAGI exceeds $40,000, the deduction phase-out rule at *8.4* applies. Under the phase-out rule, the $2,000 deduction limit is reduced to $1,400; *see* the Table on page 171 *(8.4)* which shows a $1,400 limit where excess MAGI is $3,000 ($43,000 MAGI over $40,000 phase-out threshold). The $1,400 phase-out limit applies to both Lynn and Ted. It applies to Lynn because it is less than her compensation. It applies to Ted because it is less than $40,600, the excess of Lynn's $42,000 compensation over her $1,400 phase-out limit.

If you are divorced, you may not maintain a spousal account for your former spouse. If you contributed to an account on behalf of your nonworking spouse and then divorce later in the year, the contribution is an excess contribution. IRAs based on alimony are discussed at 8.2.

An amount distributed to one spouse may not be rolled over to an IRA account of the other spouse, except in the case of divorce or death; see 8.11.

If you already have an IRA for yourself and you want to make contributions on behalf of your nonworking spouse, you may do so by merely opening a new IRA for your spouse and continuing your present IRA for yourself. However, if you have an annuity or endowment contract, check with your insurance agent about any contract restrictions on reducing your premium payments. Before setting up a single IRA with subaccounts for you and your spouse, check IRS regulations covering their use.

Contributions for spouses under age 70 ½. If you are over age 70 ½ and still working, you may contribute to a spousal IRA if your spouse is nonworking and is under age 70 ½ at the end of the year. The entire contribution of up to $2,000 must be allocated to the nonworking spouse. No contribution may be made to your own account for the year in which you reach age 70 ½, or any later year. However, after 1997, you may contribute to a Roth IRA even if you are over age 70 ½, provided your compensation is within the Roth IRA limits; see 8.20.

8.4 Deduction Restrictions for Active Participants in Employer Plan

If you are covered by an employer retirement plan, including a self-employed plan, you may be unable to make deductible IRA contributions. When you have coverage, your right to claim a full $2,000 deduction, a limited deduction, or no deduction at all depends on your modified adjusted gross income (MAGI). If you are married, and one spouse has employer plan coverage for 1997, you are both considered to have coverage in most cases; see below.

If you do *not* have employer plan coverage, or if you are married and neither of you has coverage (see rule for spouses below), an IRA deduction of up to $2,000 is allowed as long as you have compensation of $2,000 or more. The deduction phase-out rules do not apply, regardless of your income.

Generally, you are considered to be "covered" by a retirement plan if you are an *active participant* in the plan for any part of the plan year ending within your taxable year; see the Sara Wartes Example below. If you are an employee, your 1997 Form W-2 should indicate whether you are covered for the year; if you are, the "pension plan" box within Box 15 of Form W-2 should be checked. Active participation in a self-employed Keogh plan or SEP (Chapter 41) is treated as employer plan coverage for purposes of the IRA deduction phase-out rules. Active participation is explained further at 8.5.

Law Alert

New Spousal Participation Rule After 1997

Starting in 1998, a spouse who is not an active participant in an employer plan will not be treated as an active participant merely because his or her spouse is a participant. However, under a special phase-out rule, the deduction limit for a *nonparticipant* spouse filing jointly will be phased out if modified adjusted gross income (MAGI) is between $150,000 and $160,000.

EXAMPLE

Sara Wartes, a college teacher, quit her job in 1988 and withdrew all of the contributions she had made to her employee pension plan. The Tax Court held that Sara could not claim an IRA deduction in that year. Sara was an active participant in the college plan during 1988 and under the phase-out rules based upon adjusted gross income, no IRA deduction was allowed. The court noted that the active participation test is not made at the end of the year. Participation in a company plan at any time during the year triggers the deduction phase-out rules. This is true even where a person has forfeitable benefits.

Spouse is an active plan participant. If you are married filing jointly for 1997, and either of you is considered an active plan participant for the year, you are both considered to be active plan participants for purposes of figuring your 1997 IRA deductions. The same rule applies if you are married filing separately for 1997 and you lived together at any time during the year.

If you are married filing separately and you lived apart for all of 1997, your spouse's plan participation does not affect your IRA deduction. Take into account only your own participation, if any, and if you are an active participant, your IRA deduction under the phase-out rules is figured as if you were single. If you are not an active participant, you may claim the full $2,000 deduction.

Modified adjusted gross income (MAGI) determines your deduction limit if you or your spouse is an active plan participant. If either you or your spouse is an active plan participant, you still may be allowed a full or limited deduction, but this will depend on whether your 1997 modified adjusted gross income (MAGI) is within the phase-out range shown below for your filing status.

MAGI is generally equal to the total income shown on your return *minus* adjustments to income other than for IRA deductions. However, if you are claiming an exclusion for employer-provided adoption assistance or interest on U.S. EE Savings Bonds used for tuition, you must *add back* that interest to adjusted gross income to get MAGI. If you worked abroad and are claiming the foreign earned income exclusion *(36.1)*, or a foreign housing exclusion or deduction *(36.3)*, these amounts also must be added back to adjusted gross income to get MAGI.

The deduction phase-out rules apply for 1997 only if your MAGI exceeds $25,000 if you are single or head of household, or $40,000 if married filing jointly or a qualifying widow or widower. If married filing separately and you lived with your spouse at any time during the year, the phase-out applies to the first $10,000 of MAGI on each separate return. If you file separately and did not live together at all during the year, you are treated as if you were single.

Higher phase-out threshold for 1998. For 1998, a new law increases the phase-out threshold for single persons to $30,000, and for married persons filing jointly to $50,000.

FIGURING YOUR 1997 IRA DEDUCTION UNDER THE PHASE-OUT RULES

If you are an active plan participant for 1997, or you are considered to be a participant because of your spouse's participation (as discussed earlier), the $2,000 IRA deduction limit is phased out where your 1997 modified adjusted gross income (MAGI) exceeds a phase-out threshold.

Phase-out threshold for 1997 returns. The phase-out threshold for 1997 returns is:

- $25,000 if you are single, head of household, or married filing separately and treated as single because you lived apart from your spouse for all of 1997;
- $40,000 if you are married filing jointly or a qualifying widow or widower; *and*
- $0 if you are married filing separately and lived with your spouse at any time in 1997.

The phase-out applies to the first $9,999 of MAGI exceeding the $25,000, $40,000, or zero phase-out threshold. If your MAGI exceeds the threshold by $10,000 or more, you are not allowed any IRA deduction.

Phase-out Range for $2,000 Deduction Limit on 1997 Returns

If your phase-out threshold (see above) is—	Deduction limit is phased out if MAGI is—	No deduction if MAGI is—
$25,000	$25,001–$34,999	$35,000 or more
$40,000	$40,001–$49,999	$50,000 or more
$0	$0–9,999	$10,000 or more

Using the Deduction Limit Table. If your MAGI is within the $9,999 phase-out range, you can refer to the Deduction Limit Table on page 172 to look up your maximum IRA deduction limit for 1997. To use the Table, figure your *excess MAGI* by subtracting the phase-out threshold from your MAGI. If the excess MAGI is less than $10,000, refer to the Table. Keep in mind that you may make deductible contributions up to the phase-out limit from the Table only if your compensation is at least that much. If the excess MAGI is $10,000 or more, you are not allowed any IRA deduction.

Using the Table saves you the trouble of figuring the deduction limit yourself. The Table reflects the following phase-out formula in the law: Deduction limit equals $2,000 minus 20% of the MAGI exceeding the phase-out threshold. A result that is not a multiple of $10 is rounded up to the next highest multiple of $10. If the rounded up amount is less than $200, it is increased to $200. The law allows the $200 deduction to taxpayers with MAGI in the final $1,000 of the phase-out range, such as single persons with MAGI over $34,000 but less than $35,000, whose deduction limit would otherwise be below $200.

Spouses filing jointly. If you are filing jointly with your spouse and both of you work, the phase-out limit is the deductible limit for each of you as long as your individual compensation equals or exceeds that limit; *see* Example 2 below. If you are filing jointly and one of you does not work or has compensation of under $2,000, the phase-out limit from the Table (or formula) applies to each

Law Alert

Income Phase-out Limits Increased Starting in 1998

Starting in 1998, taxpayers who are covered by employer retirement plans will have a greater opportunity to claim IRA deductions. For single individuals, the phase-out range in 1998 will be $30,000–$40,000. For married couples filing jointly, the phase-out range in 1998 will be $50,000–$60,000. From 1999 through 2002, these ranges will expand each year by an additional $1,000 at each end. Starting in 2003, bigger jumps will apply, until the phase-out range reaches $50,000–$60,000 in 2005 for single persons and $80,000–$100,000 in 2007 for married persons filing jointly.

IRA Deduction Limit Table for 1997—*See* page 171 for figuring excess MAGI.

If Excess MAGI Is			If Excess MAGI Is			If Excess MAGI Is		
From—	*Up to—*	*Your Maximum Deduction Is—*	*From—*	*Up to—*	*Your Maximum Deduction Is—*	*From—*	*Up to—*	*Your Maximum Deduction Is—*
$0.00	$49.00	$2,000.00	$3,050.00	$3,099.00	$1,390.00	$6,100.00	$6,149.00	$780.00
$50.00	$99.00	$1,990.00	$3,100.00	$3,149.00	$1,380.00	$6,150.00	$6,199.00	$770.00
$100.00	$149.00	$1,980.00	$3,150.00	$3,199.00	$1,370.00	$6,200.00	$6,249.00	$760.00
$150.00	$199.00	$1,970.00	$3,200.00	$3,249.00	$1,360.00	$6,250.00	$6,299.00	$750.00
$200.00	$249.00	$1,960.00	$3,250.00	$3,299.00	$1,350.00	$6,300.00	$6,349.00	$740.00
$250.00	$299.00	$1,950.00	$3,300.00	$3,349.00	$1,340.00	$6,350.00	$6,399.00	$730.00
$300.00	$349.00	$1,940.00	$3,350.00	$3,399.00	$1,330.00	$6,400.00	$6,449.00	$720.00
$350.00	$399.00	$1,930.00	$3,400.00	$3,449.00	$1,320.00	$6,450.00	$6,499.00	$710.00
$400.00	$449.00	$1,920.00	$3,450.00	$3,499.00	$1,310.00	$6,500.00	$6,549.00	$700.00
$450.00	$499.00	$1,910.00	$3,500.00	$3,549.00	$1,300.00	$6,550.00	$6,599.00	$690.00
$500.00	$549.00	$1,900.00	$3,550.00	$3,599.00	$1,290.00	$6,600.00	$6,649.00	$680.00
$550.00	$599.00	$1,890.00	$3,600.00	$3,649.00	$1,280.00	$6,650.00	$6,699.00	$670.00
$600.00	$649.00	$1,880.00	$3,650.00	$3,699.00	$1,270.00	$6,700.00	$6,749.00	$660.00
$650.00	$699.00	$1,870.00	$3,700.00	$3,749.00	$1,260.00	$6,750.00	$6,799.00	$650.00
$700.00	$749.00	$1,860.00	$3,750.00	$3,799.00	$1,250.00	$6,800.00	$6,849.00	$640.00
$750.00	$799.00	$1,850.00	$3,800.00	$3,849.00	$1,240.00	$6,850.00	$6,899.00	$630.00
$800.00	$849.00	$1,840.00	$3,850.00	$3,899.00	$1,230.00	$6,900.00	$6,949.00	$620.00
$850.00	$899.00	$1,830.00	$3,900.00	$3,949.00	$1,220.00	$6,950.00	$6,999.00	$610.00
$900.00	$949.00	$1,820.00	$3,950.00	$3,999.00	$1,210.00	$7,000.00	$7,049.00	$600.00
$950.00	$999.00	$1,810.00	$4,000.00	$4,049.00	$1,200.00	$7,050.00	$7,099.00	$590.00
$1,000.00	$1,049.00	$1,800.00	$4,050.00	$4,099.00	$1,190.00	$7,100.00	$7,149.00	$580.00
$1,050.00	$1,099.00	$1,790.00	$4,100.00	$4,149.00	$1,180.00	$7,150.00	$7,199.00	$570.00
$1,100.00	$1,149.00	$1,780.00	$4,150.00	$4,199.00	$1,170.00	$7,200.00	$7,249.00	$560.00
$1,150.00	$1,199.00	$1,770.00	$4,200.00	$4,249.00	$1,160.00	$7,250.00	$7,299.00	$550.00
$1,200.00	$1,249.00	$1,760.00	$4,250.00	$4,299.00	$1,150.00	$7,300.00	$7,349.00	$540.00
$1,250.00	$1,299.00	$1,750.00	$4,300.00	$4,349.00	$1,140.00	$7,350.00	$7,399.00	$530.00
$1,300.00	$1,349.00	$1,740.00	$4,350.00	$4,399.00	$1,130.00	$7,400.00	$7,449.00	$520.00
$1,350.00	$1,399.00	$1,730.00	$4,400.00	$4,449.00	$1,120.00	$7,450.00	$7,499.00	$510.00
$1,400.00	$1,449.00	$1,720.00	$4,450.00	$4,499.00	$1,110.00	$7,500.00	$7,549.00	$500.00
$1,450.00	$1,499.00	$1,710.00	$4,500.00	$4,549.00	$1,100.00	$7,550.00	$7,599.00	$490.00
$1,500.00	$1,549.00	$1,700.00	$4,550.00	$4,599.00	$1,090.00	$7,600.00	$7,649.00	$480.00
$1,550.00	$1,599.00	$1,690.00	$4,600.00	$4,649.00	$1,080.00	$7,650.00	$7,699.00	$470.00
$1,600.00	$1,649.00	$1,680.00	$4,650.00	$4,699.00	$1,070.00	$7,700.00	$7,749.00	$460.00
$1,650.00	$1,699.00	$1,670.00	$4,700.00	$4,749.00	$1,060.00	$7,750.00	$7,799.00	$450.00
$1,700.00	$1,749.00	$1,660.00	$4,750.00	$4,799.00	$1,050.00	$7,800.00	$7,849.00	$440.00
$1,750.00	$1,799.00	$1,650.00	$4,800.00	$4,849.00	$1,040.00	$7,850.00	$7,899.00	$430.00
$1,800.00	$1,849.00	$1,640.00	$4,850.00	$4,899.00	$1,030.00	$7,900.00	$7,949.00	$420.00
$1,850.00	$1,899.00	$1,630.00	$4,900.00	$4,949.00	$1,020.00	$7,950.00	$7,999.00	$410.00
$1,900.00	$1,949.00	$1,620.00	$4,950.00	$4,999.00	$1,010.00	$8,000.00	$8,049.00	$400.00
$1,950.00	$1,999.00	$1,610.00	$5,000.00	$5,049.00	$1,000.00	$8,050.00	$8,099.00	$390.00
$2,000.00	$2,049.00	$1,600.00	$5,050.00	$5,099.00	$990.00	$8,100.00	$8,149.00	$380.00
$2,050.00	$2,099.00	$1,590.00	$5,100.00	$5,149.00	$980.00	$8,150.00	$8,199.00	$370.00
$2,100.00	$2,149.00	$1,580.00	$5,150.00	$5,199.00	$970.00	$8,200.00	$8,249.00	$360.00
$2,150.00	$2,199.00	$1,570.00	$5,200.00	$5,249.00	$960.00	$8,250.00	$8,299.00	$350.00
$2,200.00	$2,249.00	$1,560.00	$5,250.00	$5,299.00	$950.00	$8,300.00	$8,349.00	$340.00
$2,250.00	$2,299.00	$1,550.00	$5,300.00	$5,349.00	$940.00	$8,350.00	$8,399.00	$330.00
$2,300.00	$2,349.00	$1,540.00	$5,350.00	$5,399.00	$930.00	$8,400.00	$8,449.00	$320.00
$2,350.00	$2,399.00	$1,530.00	$5,400.00	$5,449.00	$920.00	$8,450.00	$8,499.00	$310.00
$2,400.00	$2,449.00	$1,520.00	$5,450.00	$5,499.00	$910.00	$8,500.00	$8,549.00	$300.00
$2,450.00	$2,499.00	$1,510.00	$5,500.00	$5,549.00	$900.00	$8,550.00	$8,599.00	$290.00
$2,500.00	$2,549.00	$1,500.00	$5,550.00	$5,599.00	$890.00	$8,600.00	$8,649.00	$280.00
$2,550.00	$2,599.00	$1,490.00	$5,600.00	$5,649.00	$880.00	$8,650.00	$8,699.00	$270.00
$2,600.00	$2,649.00	$1,480.00	$5,650.00	$5,699.00	$870.00	$8,700.00	$8,749.00	$260.00
$2,650.00	$2,699.00	$1,470.00	$5,700.00	$5,749.00	$860.00	$8,750.00	$8,799.00	$250.00
$2,700.00	$2,749.00	$1,460.00	$5,750.00	$5,799.00	$850.00	$8,800.00	$8,849.00	$240.00
$2,750.00	$2,799.00	$1,450.00	$5,800.00	$5,849.00	$840.00	$8,850.00	$8,899.00	$230.00
$2,800.00	$2,849.00	$1,440.00	$5,850.00	$5,899.00	$830.00	$8,900.00	$8,949.00	$220.00
$2,850.00	$2,899.00	$1,430.00	$5,900.00	$5,949.00	$820.00	$8,950.00	$8,999.00	$210.00
$2,900.00	$2,949.00	$1,420.00	$5,950.00	$5,999.00	$810.00	$9,000.00	$9,999.00	$200.00
$2,950.00	$2,999.00	$1,410.00	$6,000.00	$6,049.00	$800.00	$10,000.00	or more	$0.00
$3,000.00	$3,049.00	$1,400.00	$6,050.00	$6,099.00	$790.00			

of you under the special spousal IRA rules, provided your combined compensation is at least double the phase-out limit; *see* Example 3 at *8.3*.

Nondeductible contributions. Any contributions exceeding the amount allowed under the above rules are treated as nondeductible IRA contributions. *See 8.6* for further details.

Figuring your IRA deduction if you receive Social Security benefits. If you or your spouse *(8.3)* is an active participant in an employer plan and either of you receives Social Security benefits, you need to make an extra computation before you can figure whether an IRA deduction is allowed. Follow the rules of *34.3* to determine if part of your Social Security benefits would be subject to tax, assuming no IRA deduction were claimed. If none of your benefits would be taxable, you follow the regular rules above for determining IRA deductions. If part of your Social Security benefits would be taxable, MAGI for IRA purposes is increased by the taxable benefits. The allowable IRA deduction is then taken into account to determine the actual amount of taxable Social Security.

EXAMPLES

(Examples assume coverage under a company retirement plan. MAGI is defined on page 171.)

1. **Single or head of household.** Rob Porter is single and for 1997 has MAGI of $26,343. His MAGI exceeds the $25,000 phase-out floor for single persons by $1,343. As the table on the preceding page shows, the maximum IRA deduction limit is $1,740 for someone with excess MAGI of $1,343. Using the table saves Rob the trouble of computing the $1,740 deduction limit under the phase-out formula:

   1. Excess of MAGI over phase-out threshold
      for single persons ($26,343 – $25,000) $1,343.00
   2. 20% of step 1   268.60
   3. $2,000 minus step 2 $1,731.40
   4. Round step 3 to the next highest multiple of $10.
      This is the deductive limit.   1,740.00

   If Rob contributed $2,000 to the IRA, $260 will be treated as a nondeductible contribution unless it is withdrawn by the filing due date *(see 8.6)*.

2. **Married filing jointly.** Ted Baker and his wife, Lynn, have a joint modified adjusted gross income in 1997 of $43,000. They file a joint return. Each of them works but only Lynn is an active participant in an employer plan. Ted is also considered an active participant under the 1997 IRA rules for married couples filing jointly. The maximum 1997 IRA deduction for *each of them* is $1,400. Their excess MAGI is $3,000 ($43,000 MAGI – $40,000 phase-out threshold on a joint return). As the table on the preceding page shows, the deduction limit is $1,400 where excess MAGI is $3,000.

8.5 Active Participation in Employer Plan

Active participants in an employer retirement plan are subject to the adjusted gross income tests for deducting contributions as discussed at *8.4*. Married individuals are generally treated as active participants if either spouse has plan coverage; *see 8.3*. An employer retirement plan means:

1. A qualified pension, profit-sharing, or stock bonus plan, including a qualified self-employed Keogh plan, SIMPLE IRA, or simplified employee pension (SEP) plan;
2. A qualified annuity plan;
3. A tax-sheltered annuity; and
4. A plan established for its employees by the United States, by a state or political subdivision, or by any agency or instrumentality of the United States or a state or political subdivision, but *not* eligible state Section 457 plans.

Form W-2. If your employer checks the "Pension plan" box within Box 15 of your 1997 Form W-2, this indicates that you were an active participant in your employer's retirement plan during the year. If you want to make a contribution before you receive your Form W-2, check the following guidelines and consult your plan administrator for your status.

Type of plan. Under any type of plan, if you are considered an active participant for any part of the plan year ending with or within your taxable year, you are treated as an active participant for the entire taxable year. Because of this plan year rule, you may be treated as an active participant even if you worked for the employer only part of the year. Under IRS guidelines, it is possible to be treated as an active participant in the year of retirement and even in the year after retirement if your employer maintains a fiscal year plan.

The plan year rule works differently for defined benefit pension plans than for defined contribution plans such as profit-sharing plans, 401(k) plans, money purchase pension plans, and stock bonus plans. These rules are discussed below.

If you are married, and either of you is treated as an active participant for 1997, so is the other. The only exception is if you file separately and live apart for the whole year; *see 8.4.*

Defined benefit pension plans. You are treated as an active participant in a defined benefit pension plan if, for the plan year ending with or within your taxable year, you are eligible to participate in the plan. Under this rule, as long as you are eligible, you are treated as an active participant, even if you decline participation in the plan or you fail to make a mandatory contribution specified in the plan. Furthermore, you are treated as an active participant even if your rights to benefits are not vested.

Defined contribution plan. For a defined contribution plan, you are generally considered an active participant if "with respect to" the plan year ending with or within your taxable year (1) you make elective deferrals to the plan; (2) your employer contributes to your account; or (3) forfeitures are allocated to your account. If any of these events occur, you are treated as an active participant for that taxable year, even if you do not have a vested right to receive benefits from your account.

EXAMPLES
1. Pat O'Neil joins a company that has a 401(k) plan (a type of defined contribution plan) with a plan year starting July 1 and ending the following June 30. He is not eligible to participate in the plan year ending June 30, 1997. He elects to defer 6% of his 1997 salary to the 401(k) plan for the plan year ending June 30, 1998. Although he makes elective deferrals to the plan during 1997, he is *not* considered an active participant for 1997 because his contributions were made for the plan year ending in 1998. He *will* be considered an active participant in 1998, even if he decides not to defer any part of his 1998 salary for the plan year ending June 30, 1999.
2. Clarise Jones's employer has a defined benefit pension plan with a plan year starting July 1 and ending the following June 30. She is not excluded from participating. If she retired during September 1997, she is considered an active participant for 1997 because she was eligible to participate during the plan year ending during 1997. She will also be considered an active participant for 1998. Although she will retire before the end of the plan year starting July 1, 1997, and ending June 30, 1998, she will still be eligible to participate during part of that plan year (July 1, 1997, until retirement in September 1997), and since the 1997–1998 plan year ends within her 1998 tax year, she will be considered an active participant for 1998.

8.6 Nondeductible IRA Contributions

If you are not allowed to deduct any IRA contributions for 1997 because of the phase-out rule *(8.4)*, you may make *nondeductible* contributions of up to $2,000, or $4,000 if married filing jointly, where you have compensation of at least that much. If a deduction of less than $2,000 is allowed under the phase-out rules, you may make a nondeductible contribution to the extent the maximum contribution limit of $2,000 exceeds the deductible limit figured under *8.4.* Thus, if you are limited to a $1,800 deduction because your adjusted gross income is within the deduction phase-out range *(8.4)*, you may make a $200 nondeductible contribution. As with deductible contributions, nondeductible contributions for 1997 may be made up to the April 15, 1998 filing due date (without extensions). The advantage of making nondeductible contributions is that earnings on the account accumulate tax free until withdrawn.

If you are considering making a nondeductible IRA contribution, *see 8.20* for the rules on the new Roth IRA, which becomes available January 1, 1998. If you are not barred from making Roth IRA contributions because of your income level, the Roth IRA has advantages over the pre-Roth type of nondeductible IRA. For example, after a five-year period, completely tax-free withdrawals may be made from a Roth IRA if you are age 59 ½ or older, you are disabled, or you withdraw no more than $10,000 for first-time home-buyer expenses. With a pre-Roth nondeductible IRA, withdrawals are partially taxed if any deductible contributions were previously made. Furthermore, contributions after age 70 ½ may be made only to a Roth IRA, and mandatory required minimum distributions are not required from a Roth IRA, as they are for other IRAs.

Law Alert

New Nondeductible Roth IRA Available in 1998

A Roth IRA is a new type of nondeductible IRA which offers significant tax and retirement planning advantages. Nondeductible contributions of up to $2,000 may be made if modified adjusted gross income is below $95,000 if you are single, $150,000 if married filing jointly. In general, after the five-year period beginning with the first taxable year for which a Roth IRA contribution was made, tax-free withdrawals may be made if you are age 59 ½ or older, you are disabled or you have qualifying first-time home-buyer expenses. Existing IRAs may be rolled over to Roth IRAs if your modified adjusted gross income is $100,000 or less. *See 8.20* for further details.

Form 8606. You must file Form 8606 to report nondeductible IRA contributions unless you withdraw the contribution as discussed below. You also must list on Form 8606 the value of all of your IRAs as of the end of the year, including amounts based on deductible contributions. If you are married and you and your spouse both make nondeductible contributions, you must each file a separate Form 8606. A $50 penalty may be imposed for not filing Form 8606 unless there is reasonable cause. Furthermore, if you overstate the amount of designated nondeductible contributions made for any taxable year, you are subject to a $100 penalty for each such overstatement unless you can demonstrate that the overstatement was due to reasonable cause. You may file an amended return for a taxable year and change the designation of IRA contributions from deductible to nondeductible or nondeductible to deductible.

If you make contributions during the year, you may not know whether you will be allowed to claim a deduction under the phase-out rules of *8.4*. For example, you may have employer plan coverage but might not know whether your 1997 MAGI will exceed the $35,000 limit (single) or $50,000 limit (married filing jointly). You can make your contribution without knowing whether it is deductible or not and figure your deduction when you file your return. Any nondeductible amount would be reported on Form 8606. However, if you do not want to make nondeductible contributions, you may wait until after the end of the year when you can determine your MAGI and active participant status; you have until the April filing due date (without extensions) to make your contribution; for 1997 returns, the filing due date is April 15, 1998.

Withdrawing nondeductible contributions. If you make an IRA contribution for 1997 and later realize it is not deductible, you may make a tax-free withdrawal of the contribution by the filing due date (plus extensions), instead of designating the contribution as nondeductible on Form 8606. To do this, you must also withdraw the earnings allocable to the withdrawn contribution and include the earnings as income on your 1997 return. You might want to make the withdrawal if you incorrectly determined that a contribution would be deductible and you do not want to leave nondeductible contributions in your account. However, making the withdrawal could subject you to bank penalties for premature withdrawals, or other withdrawal penalties imposed by the IRA trustee. Furthermore, if you are under age 59 $\frac{1}{2}$, the 10% premature withdrawal penalty applies to the withdrawn earnings unless one of the exceptions at *8.12* is available.

8.7 Penalty for Excess IRA Contributions

If you contribute more than the allowable amount, whether deductible or nondeductible, the excess contribution may be subject to a penalty tax of 6%. The penalty tax is cumulative. That is, unless you correct the excess, you will be subject to another penalty on the excess contribution in the following year. The penalty tax is not deductible. The penalty is figured in Part II of Form 5329, which must be attached to Form 1040.

The 6% penalty may be avoided by withdrawing the excess contribution by the due date for your return, including extensions, plus any income earned on it. The withdrawn excess is not taxable provided no deduction was allowed for it. The withdrawn income must be reported as income on your return for the year in which the excess contribution was made. If you are under age 59 $\frac{1}{2}$ (and not disabled) when you receive the income, the 10% premature withdrawal penalty applies to the income. Similar rules apply to withdrawals of excess employer contributions to a simplified employee pension plan *(8.16)* made by the due date for your return.

If an excess contribution for 1997 is not withdrawn by the due date for your 1997 return, the 6% penalty will apply to your 1997 return but it may be avoided for 1998 by withdrawing the excess by the end of 1998. You may also avoid a penalty for 1998 by reducing your allowable 1998 IRA contribution by the 1997 excess and then including that amount in your 1998 IRA deduction. *See* IRS Publication 590 and Form 5329 for details.

If you deducted an excess contribution in an earlier year for which total contributions were $2,000 or less, you may make a tax-free withdrawal of the excess by filing an amended return to correct the excess deduction. However, the 6% penalty tax applies for each year that the excess was still in the account at the end of the year.

After the due date of your return, you may make a tax-free withdrawal of excess employer contributions to a simplified employee pension plan *(8.16)* if they are $30,000 or less. However, the 6% penalty tax applies for each year that the excess was still in the account at the end of the year.

See IRS Publication 590 for further information on correcting excess contributions made in a prior year.

Planning Reminder

Form 8606 for IRA Distributions
Keep a copy of each Form 8606 filed showing nondeductible contributions and keep a separate record of deductible contributions. When you make IRA withdrawals, the portion of each withdrawal allocable to nondeductible contributions is not taxed. You may not completely avoid tax even if you withdraw an amount equal to your nondeductible contributions. The tax-free portion of the withdrawal is figured on Form 8606. The rules for figuring tax on withdrawals and a sample Form 8606 are at *8.9*.

Taking Money Out of an IRA

8.8 Taxable IRA Distributions

If all of your IRA contributions were deductible, any IRA distribution you receive that you do not roll over or redeposit within 60 days *(8.10)* will be taxable. Not only are distributions taxable, but the timing and amount of IRA payments is subject to these restrictions:

- Distributions in 1997 before age 59 $\frac{1}{2}$ are subject to a 10% tax penalty, unless you are totally disabled, meet exceptions for paying medical costs, or you receive annual payments under an annuity-type schedule. The penalty and the exceptions are discussed at *8.12.*
- After you reach age 70 $\frac{1}{2}$, you must start to receive annual distributions under a life-expectancy calculation. The required starting date is the April 1 of the year after the year in which you reach age 70 $\frac{1}{2}$. For example, if you reach age 70 $\frac{1}{2}$ during 1997 you must start taking IRA distributions by April 1, 1998. Failure to take the minimum required annual distribution can result in penalties. These rules are discussed in *8.14.*

How to report IRA distributions on your 1997 return. All IRA distributions are reported to you and to the IRS on Form 1099-R; *see* the guide to Form 1099-R on page 133. Form 1099-R must be attached to your return only if federal tax has been withheld. You can avoid withholding by instructing the payer not to withhold on Form W-4P (or a substitute form); *see 26.11.*

If you have never made nondeductible contributions, your IRA withdrawals are fully taxable and should be reported on Line 15b of Form 1040 or Line 10b of Form 1040A. If you have made deductible and nondeductible contributions, complete Form 8606 to figure the nontaxable and taxable portions as discussed in *8.9.* Then you report the total IRA withdrawal on Line 15a of Form 1040 or Line 10a of Form 1040A and enter only the taxable portion on Line 15b or Line 10b, respectively.

If you have an individual retirement annuity, your investment in the contract is treated as zero so all payments are fully taxable. Distributions from an endowment policy due to death are taxed as ordinary income to the extent allocable to retirement savings; to the extent allocable to life insurance, they are considered insurance proceeds.

Proceeds from U.S. retirement bonds (which were issued by the Treasury before May 1982) are taxable in the year the bonds are redeemed. However, you must report the full proceeds in the year you reach age 70 $\frac{1}{2}$ even if you do not redeem the bonds.

Loan treated as distribution. If you borrow from your IRA account or use it as security for a loan, you generally are considered to have received your entire interest. Borrowing will subject the account or the fair market value of the contract to tax at ordinary income rates as of the first day of the taxable year of the borrowing. Your IRA account loses its tax-exempt status. If you use the account or part of it as security for a loan, the portion that is pledged is treated as a distribution. However, under the rollover rules, a short-term loan may be made by withdrawing IRA funds and redepositing them in an IRA within 60 days, subject to the once-a-year rollover rule at *8.10.*

IRS seizure of IRA treated as distribution. The Tax Court has held that an IRS levy of an IRA to cover back taxes is a taxable distribution to the account owner, even though the funds are transferred directly from the account to the IRS and not actually received by the owner. Where the owner is under age 59 $\frac{1}{2}$, the Tax Court has held that the 10% penalty for early withdrawals does not apply to involuntary distributions attributable to an IRS levy.

8.9 Partially Tax-Free Distributions Allocable to Nondeductible Contributions

If you ever made a nondeductible IRA contribution, you must file Form 8606 to report a 1997 distribution from any of your IRAs, even if the distribution is from an IRA to which only deductible contributions were made. All of your IRAs are treated as one contract. If you receive distributions from more than one IRA in the same year, they are combined for reporting purposes on Form 8606. When you withdraw an amount from any IRA during a taxable year and you previously made both deductible and nondeductible IRA contributions, the part of your withdrawal that is allocable to your nondeductible contributions is tax-free; any balance is taxable. You may not claim that you are withdrawing only your tax-free contributions, even if your withdrawal is less than your non-deductible contributions. If you withdraw amounts from your nondeductible account, you will incur tax. You make the computations on Form 8606. The six steps below reflect the IRS method used on Form 8606 to figure the nontaxable and taxable portions of the IRA distributions.

Court Decision

Penalty on Garnished IRA

The Tax Court held that an IRA owner received a taxable distribution when a bank enforced a court's garnishment award for past-due child support by transferring his IRA to his ex-wife. The Tax Court found that the distribution to the owner's former wife was a discharge of indebtedness to her and was constructively received by him. Whether the transfer of funds was voluntary or in settlement of a legal obligation was held to be of no consequence. The 10% tax penalty for distributions before age 59 $\frac{1}{2}$ also applied.

Form 8606—Worksheet

Contributions, Nontaxable Distributions, and Basis

1	Enter your IRA contributions for 1997 that you choose to be nondeductible. Include those made during 1/1/98–4/15/98 that were for 1997. See instructions	**1** *0*
2	Enter your total IRA basis for 1996 and earlier years. See instructions	**2** *6,000*
3	Add lines 1 and 2	**3** *6,000*

Did you receive any IRA distributions (withdrawals) in 1997? — **No** → Enter the amount from line 3 on line 12. Then, **stop** and read **When and Where To File** on page 2.

— **Yes** → Go to line 4.

4	Enter only those contributions included on line 1 that were made during 1/1/98–4/15/98. This amount will be the same as line 1 if all of your nondeductible contributions for 1997 were made in 1998 by 4/15/98. See instructions	**4** *0*
5	Subtract line 4 from line 3	**5** *6,000*
6	Enter the total value of **ALL** your IRAs as of 12/31/97 plus any outstanding rollovers. See instructions	**6** *17,500*
7	Enter the total IRA distributions received during 1997. Do not include amounts rolled over before 1/1/98. See instructions	**7** *5,000*
8	Add lines 6 and 7	**8** *22,500*
9	Divide line 5 by line 8 and enter the result as a decimal (to at least two places). Do not enter more than "1.00"	**9** × *.27*
10	Multiply line 7 by line 9. This is the amount of your **nontaxable distributions for 1997**	**10** *1,350*
11	Subtract line 10 from line 5. This is the **basis in your IRA(s) as of 12/31/97**	**11** *4,650*
12	Add lines 4 and 11. This is your **total IRA basis for 1997 and earlier years**	**12** *4,650*

Taxable Distributions for 1997

13	Subtract line 10 from line 7. Enter the result here and on Form 1040, line 15b; Form 1040A, line 10b; or Form 1040NR, line 16b, whichever applies	**13** *3,650*

The rule requiring you to combine nondeductible and deductible IRAs when making IRA withdrawals will not apply to withdrawals from a Roth IRA set up after 1997. A Roth IRA will be treated separately. After a five-year period, withdrawals after age 59½ are completely tax-free; *see 8.20*.

The payer of an IRA account, such as a bank, will report withdrawals from an IRA account to the IRS on Form 1099-R as if they are taxable. It is up to you to keep records that show the nondeductible contributions you have made. IRS instructions require you to keep copies of all Forms 8606 on which nondeductible contributions have been designated, as well as copies of (1) your tax returns for years you made nondeductible contributions; (2) Forms 5498 showing all IRA contributions and showing the value of your IRAs for each year you received a distribution; and (3) Form 1099-R and Form W-2P showing IRA distributions. According to the IRS, you should keep such records until you have withdrawn all IRA funds.

Follow these steps in determining the tax-free and taxable portion of IRA distributions received during 1997:

Step 1. Total IRA withdrawals during 1997.

Step 2. Total nondeductible contributions to all IRAs made by the end of 1997. Tax-free withdrawals of nondeductible contributions in prior years reduce the total. If you made an IRA contribution for 1997 (including a contribution made between January 1 and April 15, 1998) that may be partly nondeductible because your modified adjusted gross income is within the deduction phase-out range shown in *8.4* for active plan participants, you should include that entire contribution in the Step 2 total.

Step 3. Add Step 1 to the balance of all your IRAs at the end of 1997. If you received an IRA distribution within the last 60 days of 1997 which was rolled over to another IRA within the 60-day rollover period *(8.10) but* not until 1998, add the 1998 rollover to the year-end balance.

Step 4. Divide Step 2 by Step 3. This is the tax-free percentage of your IRA withdrawal.

Step 5. Multiply the Step 4 percentage by Step 1. This amount is tax free.

Step 6. Subtract Step 5 from Step 1. This amount is fully taxable.

EXAMPLE

In 1997, Nick James withdraws $5,000 from his IRA, having made deductible IRA contributions of $8,000 and nondeductible contributions of $6,000 as follows:

Year	Deductible	Nondeductible
1990	$2,000	0
1991	2,000	0
1992	2,000	0
1993	1,000	$1,000
1994	1,000	1,000
1995	0	2,000
1996	0	2,000
	$8,000	$6,000

Assume that at the end of 1997, Nick's total IRA account balance, including earnings, is $17,500, and that this is his first IRA withdrawal. On his 1997 return, $1,350 of the $5,000 IRA withdrawal will be tax free and $3,650 will be taxable.

Step 1.	IRA withdrawal	$5,000
Step 2.	Nondeductible contributions	6,000
Step 3.	IRA balance at end of the year ($17,500) *plus* Step 1	22,500
Step 4.	Tax-free percentage: $6,000 ÷ $22,500	27%
Step 5.	Tax-free withdrawal: 27% × $5,000	1,350
Step 6.	Taxable withdrawal: $5,000 – $1,350	$3,650

The total $5,000 withdrawal should be reported on Line 15a of Form 1040 or on Line 10a of Form 1040A, and the taxable $3,650 portion should be entered on Line 15b (Form 1040) or on Line 10b (Form 1040A).

On the sample Form 8606 worksheet, the $6,000 of nondeductible contributions are shown on Line 2 and the $5,000 withdrawal on Line 7. The tax-free percentage of 27% is shown on Line 9 and the $1,350 tax-free withdrawal on Line 10. The remaining IRA basis of $4,650 ($6,000 – $1,350) is shown on Line 12.

Deductible IRA loss based on unrecovered nondeductible contributions. According to the IRS, a loss may be allowed if all IRA funds have been distributed and you have not recovered your basis in nondeductible contributions.

EXAMPLE

Paula Brown makes nondeductible IRA contributions of $10,000 from 1992–1996. At the end of 1997, she withdraws $6,000. The year-end balance is $8,000. The tax-free portion of the withdrawal is $4,286 ($10,000 nondeductible contributions ÷ $14,000 total of withdrawal plus year-end balance × $6,000 withdrawal).

After the withdrawal, her account balance is $8,000; her basis is $5,714 ($10,000 - $4,286). If because of poor investments the value of the IRA fell to $3,000 by the end of 1998 and she withdrew the entire $3,000 balance, she could claim a $2,714 loss ($5,714 basis – $3,000 distribution).

Planning Reminder

60-Day Loan from IRA

You can take advantage of the rollover rule to borrow funds from your IRA if you need a short-term loan to pay your taxes or other expenses. As long as you redeposit the amount in an IRA within 60 days you are not taxed on the withdrawal; the redeposit is considered a tax-free rollover. You may roll over the funds to a different IRA from the one from which the withdrawal was made. A second withdrawal from the same IRA within one year would be taxable as previously discussed.

8.10 Tax-Free Rollovers and Direct Transfers to IRAs

There are two types of tax-free rollovers that you can make to an IRA. You may roll over funds to an IRA from a qualified company or self-employed retirement plan, as discussed at 7.8. You may also use a rollover to switch funds from one IRA to another, although another option, a direct transfer, may be a more advantageous way of changing IRA investments.

Direct transfer. A *direct transfer* is made by instructing the trustee of an IRA to transfer all or part of your account to another IRA trustee. Direct transfers are tax free because you do not receive the funds. The tax law does not require a waiting period between direct transfers, whereas rollovers are subject to a once-a-year limitation, as discussed below.

For example, assume you have an IRA at Bank "A" and decide to switch your account to Mutual Fund "ABC." The mutual fund will provide you with transfer request forms which you complete and return to the fund, which will then forward the forms to the bank to complete the direct transfer. The transfer from the bank to the mutual fund is tax free. Because the IRA funds were not paid to you, the transfer is not considered a rollover subject to the once-a-year rollover limitation. This means that if within one year you become unhappy with the performance of Mutual Fund "ABC," you may make another tax-free direct transfer of your IRA to Fund "XYZ" or to Bank "B."

Rollover. With a *rollover* you withdraw funds from an IRA and have 60 days to invest in another IRA. To avoid tax on a rollover from one IRA to another, these tests must be met: (1) The amount you receive from your old IRA must be transferred to the new plan within 60 days of your receiving it; and (2) a tax-free rollover may occur only once in a one-year period starting on the date you receive the first distribution. If within that one-year period you receive a distribution from the previously rolled over IRA, the distribution is taxable and if you are under age 59 ½, could be subject to the 10% penalty for premature distributions; *see 8.12*. A *direct transfer* may be used as discussed above if you want to invest in another IRA within the one-year period.

The once-a-year rollover rule applies separately to each of your IRAs. For example, you have one IRA invested in a bank and another IRA invested in a mutual fund. Within the same one-year period, you may roll over the bank IRA to a different IRA and you may also roll over the mutual-fund IRA to a different IRA. However, neither of the new IRAs may be rolled over again within the one-year period starting on the date that you received the distribution from the original IRA plan.

There is an exception to the one-year waiting period between rollovers if the second distribution is made from an insolvent financial institution by the FDIC (Federal Deposit Insurance Corporation) acting as receiver. The exception applies only if the receiver makes the distribution to you because it is unable to find a buyer for the insolvent institution.

Deposits in insolvent financial institutions. The 60-day limit for completing a rollover is extended if the funds are "frozen" and may not be withdrawn from a bankrupt or insolvent financial institution. The 60-day period is extended while the account is frozen and you have a minimum of 10 days after the release of the funds to complete the rollover.

If a government agency takes control of an insolvent bank, you might receive an "involuntary" distribution of your IRA account from the agency. According to the IRS and Tax Court, such a payment is subject to the regular IRA distribution rules. For example, a couple received payment for their $11,000 IRA balance from the Maryland Deposit Insurance Fund after the bank in which the funds were invested became insolvent. The Tax Court held that the payment was taxable, even though the distribution was from a state insurance fund and not from the bank itself. Furthermore, since they were under age 59 ½, the 10% penalty for early distributions *(8.12)* was imposed, even though the distribution was involuntary. The tax and penalty could have been avoided by making a rollover of the distribution within 60 days, but this was not done.

8.11 Transfer of IRA to Spouse at Divorce or Death

If you receive your former spouse's IRA pursuant to a divorce decree or written instrument incident to the decree, the transfer is not taxable to either of you. From the date of transfer the account is treated as your IRA. If you are legally separated, a transfer of your spouse's IRA to you is tax free if made under a decree of separate maintenance or written instrument incident to the decree. The transferred account is then treated as your IRA.

QDRO transfer to IRA. If you receive your share of your spouse's or former spouse's benefits from an employer plan under a qualified domestic relations order (QDRO), the distribution is taxable to you unless you roll it over to an IRA. Special averaging may be available; *see 7.12*. If you roll over only part of a qualifying QDRO distribution, you figure the tax on the retained portion by taking into account a pro-rated share of your former spouse's cost investment.

Surviving spouse. If you inherit your spouse's IRA when he or she dies, you may elect to treat the IRA as your own, or you may receive distributions from the account as a beneficiary. *See 8.15* for a discussion of these options.

8.12 Penalty for IRA Withdrawals Before Age 59 ½

You have to pay a 10% penalty if you receive an IRA distribution before you are age 59 ½, *unless* (1) you make a qualifying rollover to another IRA *(8.10)*, (2) you are totally disabled, (3) you pay medical expenses exceeding 7.5% of adjusted gross income, (4) you receive unemployment compensation for at least 12 consecutive weeks and pay medical insurance premiums, (5) the distribution is one of a series of payments being made under one of several annuity-type methods, or (6) you are a beneficiary receiving IRA distributions following the death of the owner.

Filing Tip

Reporting a Rollover on Your 1997 Return

If you rolled over a qualifying distribution from an employer plan to an IRA *(7.8)*, report the total distribution on Line 16a of Form 1040 or Line 11a of Form 1040A. Enter zero as the taxable amount on Line 16b or Line 11b if the entire amount was rolled over. If only part of the distribution was rolled over, enter the portion not rolled over on Line 16b or Line 11b.

If you rolled over funds from one IRA to another, the total distribution should be reported on Line 15a of Form 1040 or Line 10a of Form 1040A. If the entire distribution was rolled over, enter zero as the taxable amount on Line 15b or Line 10b. Otherwise, enter the amount not rolled over on Line 15b or Line 10b.

If you made a tax-free direct transfer from one IRA to another, you do not have to report it on your return.

Law Alert

Medical Expense Penalty Exceptions

Starting in 1997 there are two new medical-related exceptions to the pre–age 59 ½ penalty. If in the year of the IRA distribution you pay deductible medical expenses that exceed 7.5% of your adjusted gross income, the penalty does not apply to distributions that exceed the 7.5% threshold.

The other new exception applies to IRA owners who receive unemployment benefits for at least 12 consecutive weeks. If medical insurance premiums are paid in the year of the IRA distribution, the penalty does not apply to the extent of the premiums.

The penalty is 10% of the taxable IRA distribution. For example, if before age 59 ½, you withdraw $3,000 from your IRA, you must include the $3,000 as part of your taxable income and, in addition, pay a $300 penalty tax. If part of a premature distribution is tax free because it is allocable to nondeductible contributions (see 8.9) or rolled over to another IRA (8.10), the 10% penalty applies only to the taxable portion of the distribution.

If you are subject to the 10% early distribution penalty but not to the penalties discussed at 8.7, 8.13, or 8.14, the penalty is entered directly on Form 1040, Line 50.

If you do not owe the penalty because you qualify for an exception, you may have to file Form 5329 with Form 1040, depending on whether the payer of the distribution correctly marked the exception in Box 7 of Form 1099-R. If you qualify for the annuity-method exception and the payer correctly indicated that exception by marking Code 2 in Box 7, you do not have to file Form 5329. Similarly, if you are the beneficiary of a deceased IRA owner and the payer has correctly noted that with Code 4 in Box 7, you do not have to file Form 5329 to claim the exception.

If you qualify for the disability exception (see below), it is unlikely that the payer will know of that fact and thus Code 3 (for the disability exception) will probably not be marked in Box 7 of Form 1099-R. In that case, you must file Form 5329 to claim the exception. You also must file Form 5329 if the annuity method or beneficiary exception applies but it is not coded in Box 7 of Form 1099-R.

If you rolled over your entire distribution within 60 days to another IRA (8.10), the penalty does not apply and Form 5329 does not have to be filed.

Spousal beneficiaries. Beneficiaries are exempt from the pre-59 ½ penalty. If you inherit an IRA from your deceased spouse and elect to treat it as your *own* IRA as discussed at 8.15, you are not eligible for the beneficiary exception; distributions from the account before you reach age 59 ½ will be subject to the penalty. The beneficiary exception applies if the account is maintained in the name of your deceased spouse and you are receiving the distribution as a spousal beneficiary under the rules at 8.15.

Disability exception. To qualify for the disability exception, you must be able to show that you have a physical or mental condition that can be expected to last indefinitely or result in death and that prevents you from engaging in "substantial gainful activity" similar to the type of work you were doing before the condition arose.

In one case, a 53-year old stockbroker claimed that his IRA withdrawal of over $200,000 should be exempt from the 10% penalty because he suffered from mental depression. However, the Tax Court upheld the IRS imposition of the penalty because he continued to work as a stockbroker.

Medical expense exception. If you withdraw IRA funds in a year in which you pay substantial medical costs, part of the distribution may avoid the pre-age 59 ½ penalty. If your unreimbursed medical expenses in the year of the distribution exceed 7.5% of your adjusted gross income, the distribution, to the extent of the excess, is not subject to the penalty. The medical costs must be eligible for the itemized medical deduction (see Chapter 17), but the IRA penalty exception applies whether you itemize or claim the standard deduction.

Unemployed person's medical insurance exceptions. If you are unemployed and received unemployment benefits under Federal or state law for at least 12 consecutive weeks, you may make penalty-free IRA withdrawals to the extent of medical insurance premiums paid during the year for you, your spouse, and your dependents. The withdrawals may be made in the year the 12-week unemployment test is met, or in the following year. However, the penalty exception does not apply to distributions made more than 60 days after you return to the work force.

Self-employed persons who are ineligible by law for unemployment benefits may be treated as meeting the 12-week test, and thus eligible for the exception, under regulations to be issued by the IRS.

Annuity-Schedule Payments Avoid 10% Penalty

You may avoid the penalty if you are willing to receive annual distributions under one of the annuity-type methods discussed in this section. Before arranging an annuity-type schedule, consider these points: all of the payments will be taxable (unless allocable to non-deductible contributions under 8.8), and if you do not continue the payments for a minimum number of years, the IRS will impose the 10% penalty for all taxable payments received before age 59 ½, plus interest charges.

The payments must continue for five years, or until you reach age 59 ½, whichever period is *longer*. Thus, if you are in your 40s, you would have to continue the scheduled payments until you

 Law Alert

New IRA Penalty Exceptions Available in 1998

Starting in 1998, the pre–age 59 ½ penalty will not apply to IRA distributions used for qualifying higher education and home-buying expenses. Note that the distributions remain taxable; only the penalty for early withdrawals is avoided if the distributions qualify.

A penalty exception is allowed for IRA distributions after 1997 used to pay higher education expenses, including graduate school costs, for you, your spouse, your children, or your grandchildren. Eligible expenses include tuition, room and board, fees, books, supplies, and equipment that you pay after 1997 for courses starting after 1997.

Another penalty exception is allowed for up to $10,000 of qualifying "first-time" home-buyer expenses. The penalty does not apply to IRA distributions after 1997 that are used within 120 days to buy, construct, or reconstruct a principal residence for you, your spouse, child, grandchild, or ancestor of you or your spouse. A qualifying first-time home-buyer is someone who did not have a present ownership interest in a principal residence in the two-year period before the acquisition of the new house. The exception applies only for $10,000 of home-buyer expenses. This is a lifetime cap per IRA owner and not an annual limit.

are age 59 $\frac{1}{2}$. If you are in your mid-50s, the minimum payout period is not as serious a burden, as you only need to continue the scheduled payments for a five-year period, starting with the date of the first distribution, provided that the period ends after you reach age 59 $\frac{1}{2}$. During this minimum period, the arranged annuity-type schedule may not be changed. For example, taking a lump-sum distribution of your account balance before reaching age 59 $\frac{1}{2}$ would trigger the retroactive penalty, plus interest charges. After the minimum payout period, you can discontinue the payments or change the method without penalty.

The minimum payout period rules do not apply to totally disabled individuals or to beneficiaries of deceased IRA owners.

If you would like to take advantage of this penalty exception, you may apply one of the following three payout methods that have been approved by the IRS in private rulings:

1. *Life expectancy method.* This is the easiest method to figure but provides smaller annual payments than the other methods. Figure the annual withdrawal by dividing your account balance by your life expectancy or by the joint life and last survivor expectancy of you and your beneficiary. This is the same method discussed at *8.13* for figuring minimum required distributions after age 70 $\frac{1}{2}$.

For example, you are age 50 in 1998 and have an IRA of $100,000 at the beginning of the year. You may take a penalty-free payment of $3,021 in 1998 ($100,000 account balance ÷ 33.1 life expectancy). Individual life expectancies are shown in Table V at *7.23*. The annual penalty-free amount will generally increase in later years, with the exact amount depending on your account balance and whether you recalculate your life expectancy under the table each year (based on your age) or you simply reduce your life expectancy by one for each year that has elapsed since the year that you received the first payment.

If instead of using your single life expectancy you used the joint life and last survivor expectancy of you and your beneficiary (*see* sample table on page 192) the annual penalty-free amount would be smaller given the longer joint life expectancy. For example, if your beneficiary was age 45, your joint life and last survivor life expectancy would be 42 years (using ages 50 and 45), and the penalty-free withdrawal $2,381 ($100,000 account balance ÷ 42). *See* page 192 for the sample section of the IRS joint life and last survivor life expectancy table. The full IRS Table VI showing joint life and last survivor life expectancy is in IRS Publication 939 and can also be obtained from your IRA trustee.

2. *Amortization method.* Under this method, you amortize your IRA account balance like a mortgage, using the same life expectancy as under Method 1 (your single life expectancy or the joint life and last survivor expectancy of you and your beneficiary) and a long-term interest rate that is reasonable when the payments commence. In private rulings, the IRS approved the use of interest rates based on federal rates, such as the applicable federal rate used for figuring minimum interest on seller-financed sales *(4.32)*, or the rate of interest under Pension Benefit Guaranty Corporation regulations.

Under the amortization method, the annual penalty-free withdrawal will be larger than under Method 1. For example, using an interest rate of 8% (assuming that is a reasonable rate), a 50-year-old with a $100,000 account balance may withdraw $8,679 without penalty in the first year, as opposed to $3,021 under Method 1. The payment in future years will depend on how life expectancy is adjusted.

3. *Annuity factor method.* This method is similar to the amortization method but it allows you to use insurance mortality tables (such as the UP-1984 Mortality Table) that project shorter life expectancy tables than the IRS life expectancy tables used under Methods 1 and 2. If an interest rate of 8% and the UP-1984 mortality table were used for a 50-year-old with a $100,000 account balance, the penalty-free withdrawal in the first year would be $9,002, as opposed to $3,021 under Method 1 or $8,679 under Method 2.

Note: For Methods 2 and 3, you should get the assistance of a tax professional and an actuary to help plan a series of payments that will qualify for the penalty exception.

8.13 Excess Distribution Penalty Repealed

Before 1997, IRA distributions exceeding an annual floor were subject to a 15% penalty. For example, in 1996, IRA distributions over $155,000 were generally subject to the penalty. However, the 1997 Tax Act has repealed the penalty for distributions received after 1996. In a prior law, Congress had suspended the penalty for 1997–1999, but the new law replaces the suspension with outright repeal.

Extra estate tax also repealed. The new law also repeals the additional 15% estate tax that was imposed on excess retirement accumulations. The repeal applies to estates of individuals dying after December 31, 1996.

8.14 Mandatory Distributions After Age 70 ½

By April 1 of the year following the year in which you reach age 70 ½ , you have to start receiving annual IRA distributions under a schedule that meets tax law tests. If you do not receive the minimum amount required by the tax law, a penalty tax of 50% applies to the difference between the minimum amount you should have received and the amount you did receive. The penalty is reported on Form 5329, which must be attached to Form 1040.

> ### EXAMPLE
> During 1997, Chris Calano reaches age 70 ½ and receives $500 from his IRA plan. The minimum amount required to be paid to him was $700. He must pay a penalty tax of $100 (50% of $200), unless it is waived by the IRS.

When must your first required minimum distribution be received? Your required beginning date is April 1 of the year following the year in which you reach age 70 ½ . For example, if you reached age 70 ½ during 1997, you must receive a minimum distribution for 1997 no later than April 1, 1998. You will also have to receive a minimum distribution for 1998 by December 31, 1998. Thus, if you do not take your first distribution during 1997, and wait until between January 1 and April 1, 1998, you will have to make two distributions in 1998, one by April 1 and another by December 31. This could increase your 1998 taxable income substantially. Distributions for later years must be made by December 31 of each year.

If you reach age 70 ½ during 1998, your first distribution must be no later than April 1, 1999. If you have an individual retirement annuity, your insurance company should gear your payments to meet minimum distribution requirements.

Key decisions to make by your required beginning date. By your required beginning date (April 1 of the year after the year you reach age 70 ½), you should designate a beneficiary and elect either the term-certain or recalculation method of adjusting life expectancy. As discussed below, your choices will determine the minimum amount you must receive from your IRA each year, and, in some cases, also determine the payout options for your beneficiaries after your death.

For example, the age of your designated beneficiary affects the calculation of the minimum distributions you must receive, as discussed below under Step 2. If you select a charitable organization as your beneficiary, or your estate as the beneficiary, you will have to use your single life expectancy in figuring your required minimum distributions.

Penalty Waiver for Reasonable Mistakes. The IRS may waive the penalty for insufficient withdrawals if they are due to reasonable error and if steps have been taken in order to remedy the situation. You must submit evidence to account for shortfalls in withdrawals and how you are rectifying the situation. The IRS has indicated that examples of acceptable reasons for insufficient withdrawals include erroneous advice from the sponsoring organization or other pension advisors or that your own good faith efforts to apply the required withdrawal formula produced a miscalculation or misunderstanding of the formula. You should attach your letter of explanation to Form 5329. You must pay the penalty; if the IRS grants a waiver, it will refund the penalty.

Figuring Minimum IRA Distributions

Your IRA trustee should help you figure how much you must withdraw to avoid an IRS penalty. If that does not happen and you must figure the required minimum distribution yourself, follow the five steps below. In general, the required minimum distribution for each year equals the applicable life expectancy divided into the account balance at the end of the prior year. If you have more than one IRA, you must figure the required annual minimum distribution for each IRA separately, although once you have done so, the total required minimum distribution for the year may be withdrawn from any of the accounts in any combination you choose. Figure the required minimum distribution for *each* of your IRAs by following these steps:

Step 1: Find the account balance of your IRA as of the previous December 31. If you reach age 70 ½ during 1997, the account balance to be used for figuring your first required minimum distribution is the account balance for December 31, 1996, even if the actual distribu-

Planning Reminder

Choose Life Expectancy Method

If you have not chosen a life expectancy method by your required beginning date, the terms of the plan may apply the recalculation method as the default method, which could be disadvantageous following your death or the death of your spouse if he or she is your designated beneficiary; see the discussion of life expectancy methods under Step 3 on page 183.

Filing Tip

Penalty Waiver for Reasonable Mistakes

The IRS may waive the penalty for insufficient withdrawals if they are due to reasonable error and if steps have been taken in order to remedy the situation. You must submit evidence to account for shortfalls in withdrawals and how you are rectifying the situation. The IRS has indicated that examples of acceptable reasons for insufficient withdrawals include erroneous advice from the sponsoring organization or other pension advisors or that your own good faith efforts to apply the required withdrawal formula produced a miscalculation or misunderstanding of the formula. You should attach your letter of explanation to Form 5329. You must pay the penalty; if the IRS grants a waiver, it will refund the penalty.

tion for 1997 is not made until the first quarter of 1998 (January 1–April 1). For purposes of figuring your required minimum distribution for 1998, use the 1997 year-end balance, reduced by the first-year distribution if you took it in the first quarter of 1998.

Step 2: Find your life expectancy. For the year you reach age 70 ½ , use the joint life and last survivor life expectancy of you and the beneficiary that was designated by the required beginning date (April 1 of the year after the year you reach age 70 ½). If you name more than one beneficiary, the age of the oldest beneficiary (the shortest life expectancy) is taken into account. Joint life and last survivor life expectancy is found in IRS unisex Table VI, a sample section of which is shown on page 192. The rest of the table is in IRS Publication 939 and can also be obtained from your IRA trustee.

Use only your single life expectancy from Table V at *7.23* if your beneficiary as of the required beginning date is your estate or a charitable organization; the charity or estate has no life expectancy. Your single life expectancy is also used if no beneficiary has been designated by the required beginning date.

The initial joint life and last survivor life expectancy of you and your beneficiary is determined by your ages on your respective birthdays in the year in which you reach age 70 ½ . For example, if you were born in October 1926, you reached age 70 ½ in April 1997 and age 71 on your birthday in October 1997. Assume your beneficiary is age 67 on his or her birthday in 1997. For purposes of figuring your first required IRA distribution for the year 1997 (due by April 1, 1998), your joint life and last survivor expectancy from the table on page 192 is 21.7 years (using ages 71 and 67). For 1998 and later years, the required minimum distributions will depend on whether you choose to recalculate your life expectancies annually or to use the term-certain method; *see* Step 3 below.

Is your nonspouse beneficiary more than 10 years younger than you are? You are not allowed to use the actual joint life expectancy of you and a beneficiary who is more than 10 years younger than you are, unless the beneficiary is your spouse. If your beneficiary is not your spouse, you must treat the beneficiary as being only 10 years younger than yourself, although he or she may be much younger. This 10-year age rule is called the MDIB (minimum distribution incidental benefit) requirement.

For example, if you are age 71 on your birthday in the year you reach age 70 ½ , and your beneficiary is your 20-year-old grandchild, the grandchild is considered to be age 61 for purposes of figuring your initial joint life and last survivor expectancy. In subsequent years, you are each considered to be one year older, so your joint life and last survivor expectancy for the second distribution year is based on ages 72 and 62, for the third year it is based on ages 73 and 63, and so on.

The MDIB requirement applies each year while you are alive, regardless of whether you filed an election with the IRA plan to use the term-certain method or recalculation method of adjusting life expectancy as discussed under Step 3 below. However, the MDIB requirement no longer applies in years after your death. The payout rules to your beneficiary *will* depend on whether you elected the term-certain or recalculation method; *see* Step 3 and the rules for non-spouse beneficiaries at *8.15*.

Step 3: How to adjust life expectancy each year. The initial joint life and last survivor life expectancy for you and your beneficiary has to be adjusted every year to figure the minimum required IRA withdrawal. There are four methods for adjusting life expectancy—the *recalculation* method, the *term-certain* method, the *MDIB* method and the *hybrid* method.

You must use the MDIB rule to figure each of your annual required minimum distributions if your designated beneficiary as of the required beginning date is more than 10 years younger than you are and is not your spouse. This is true regardless of whether you have elected in the IRA plan to use the term-certain or the recalculation method; *see* Step 2 above.

If you do not have to use the MDIB rule for a nonspouse designated beneficiary, a *hybrid* method (*see* below) applies where you do not elect the term-certain method.

If your spouse is your designated beneficiary as of the required beginning date, the recalculation method may apply automatically under the terms of your IRA plan unless an election to use the term-certain method is specifically made by the required beginning date (April 1 of the year after the year you reach age 70 ½). Check your plan to determine whether a specific election is necessary to apply the method you want. The method that takes effect as of the required beginning date cannot be changed.

Recalculation method. Under the recalculation method, your life expectancy may be recalculated annually and so may the life expectancy of a spouse who was designated as your beneficiary as of the required beginning date. If your beneficiary is not your spouse, you may recalculate your own life expectancy under the hybrid method discussed below.

If your spouse is your beneficiary and you both recalculate life expectancy, this means that each year your joint life expectancy from the IRS table is based on your ages at your birthdays in that year. For example, assume that your spouse is your beneficiary and that in 1997, the year you reached age 70 ½ , you were age 71 on your birthday and your spouse was age 67 on his or her birthday. Based on ages 71 and 67, your initial joint life and last survivor life expectancy from the IRS table (page 192) is 21.7 years, for purposes of figuring your required distribution for 1997. If you and your spouse recalculate life expectancies, your adjusted joint life expectancy for 1998, based on ages 72 and 68 (your ages on your birthdays in 1998), would be 20.8 years from the IRS table. For 1999, based on ages 73 and 69, the adjusted joint life expectancy from the IRS table would be 20.0 years, and for 2000 it would be 19.1 years (ages 74 and 70). As you can see, the joint life expectancy is reduced by *less than one* with each annual recalculation; as you grow older, the annual reduction in joint life expectancy becomes even smaller.

Term-certain method.   Under the *term-certain* method, you do not have to use IRS life expectancy tables once you determine your initial joint life and last survivor expectancy for you and your beneficiary. You simply reduce that initial life expectancy by one in each later year. This method may be used with a spouse or non-spouse beneficiary unless you must use the MDIB rule for a non-spouse beneficiary as discussed in Step 2. Thus, if your initial joint life and last survivor expectancy for 1997 based on ages 71 and 67 is 21.7 years, it would be reduced to 20.7 years for 1998, 19.7 years for 1999, 18.7 years for 2000, and so on under the term-certain method.

Should you use the recalculation or term-certain method?   Each method has advantages and disadvantages. The recalculation method generally allows you to conserve principal longer than the term-certain method by requiring you to take slightly smaller annual distributions; life expectancy is reduced each year by less than one under the recalculation method, while under the term-certain method life expectancy is reduced by a full year.

However, there is a disadvantage to the recalculation method if your spouse is your beneficiary and your spouse dies first. After the death of a recalculating owner or recalculating spousal beneficiary, that person's life expectancy is reduced to zero starting in the year after the year of death. Thus, if your recalculating spouse is your designated beneficiary and he or she dies first, you must use your single life expectancy to figure your minimum required distributions starting in the year after the year of your spouse's death; the joint life expectancy rules may no longer be used. Then, when you die, your secondary beneficiary will have to receive the entire account by the end of the year following the year of your death and pay tax on the entire amount. Similar rules would apply to your surviving spouse and your secondary beneficiary if you die before your spouse and your spouse receives distributions from your account as a *beneficiary.* The payout period can be extended where a surviving spouse elects to be treated as the *owner* of the IRA instead of receiving distributions as a beneficiary. The options for surviving spouses are detailed in *8.15.*

If your estate is the beneficiary, these recalculation rules may be particularly costly. Since your life expectancy is reduced to zero as of the year following the year of your death, and the estate has no life expectancy on which distributions may be based, the entire account must be distributed to the estate by the end of the year after the year of your death.

On the other hand, when you elect the term-certain method to figure your minimum required distributions, the balance of the initial joint life expectancy period remains available following the death of you or your beneficiary. This allows the survivor to spread out the distributions, and the tax on the distributions, over the rest of the term-certain period.

Step 4: Divide the account balance from Step 1 by the Step 2 life expectancy.
This is the minimum amount you must receive. If you have more than one IRA, divide Step 1 by Step 2 for each account and *see* Step 5.

Step 5: If you have more than one IRA, total the Step 4 amounts for all the accounts.   This is the minimum you must receive for the year; you are of course free to withdraw more than that. Although you must calculate the minimum required distribution separately for each account, you do not have to make withdrawals from each of them. The total minimum required distribution from all accounts may be taken from any one account, or more than one account if you prefer. For example, if you have five bank IRAs you may take the entire required distribution from the bank where you have the largest balance, or from any other combination of banks. *See* Example 2 below. The entire distribution is taxable unless part is allocable to nondeductible IRA contributions, as explained in *8.8.*

Note: For further information on calculating minimum required distributions, *see* IRS proposed regulations Sections 1.408-8 and 1.401(a)(9)-1. Also *see* the instructions to Form 5329.

Planning Reminder

Hybrid Method May Be Required If Your Beneficiary Is Not Your Spouse

If you do not elect the term-certain method, you must use a *hybrid* method of determining your joint life and last survivor expectancy if your nonspouse designated beneficiary is not more than 10 years younger than you are (so the MDIB rule is inapplicable). Under the hybrid method, you use your age as of your birthday in each year and must adjust the beneficiary's age following the steps in Example 3 at the end of this section.

EXAMPLES

1. Joe Blake reached age 70 ½ in March 1997. A minimum distribution for 1997 must be received by April 1, 1998. As of December 31, 1996, Joe's IRA balance was $26,300. The 1996 year-end balance is used in the computation even if the distribution for 1997 is made in the first quarter of 1998 (by the April 1 deadline). Joe's beneficiary is his wife, who is age 63 on her birthday in 1997. On his 1997 birthday, Joe is age 71.

    Step 1. Account balance of $26,300.

    Step 2. Joint life and last survivor expectancy from the table on page 192 is 24 years, using ages 71 and 63.

    Step 3. Divide Step 1 by Step 2.
    $26,300 ÷ 24 = $1,096. Joe must receive the $1,096 by April 1, 1998.

    The second minimum distribution, due by December 31, 1998, is based upon the 1997 year-end account balance, but if the 1997 distribution was not made until early 1998 (by April 1), the account balance is reduced by that distribution. Thus, assume that Joe took the $1,096 distribution for 1997 in March 1998 and that the 1997 year-end balance is $27,500. For purposes of figuring the required distribution for 1998, an account balance of $26,404 ($27,500 − $1,096) is used.

    Assuming Joe and his wife recalculate their life expectancies, their joint expectancy would be 23.1 (using ages 72 and 64). Thus, the minimum required distribution for 1998, due by December 31, 1998, would be $1,143 ($26,404 ÷ 23.1).

    However, if Joe had elected not to recalculate life expectancy but to use the term-certain method, the first-year joint life expectancy of 24 years would be reduced to 23 years. The minimum 1998 distribution would be $1,148 ($26,404 ÷ 23).

2. Cynthia Lowell has two IRAs. She reached age 70 ½ on January 15, 1997, and thus must receive her first distribution by April 1, 1998. The beneficiary of IRA-1 is her brother, who is age 61 on his birthday in 1997; the account balance of IRA-1 as of December 31, 1996, was $100,000. The beneficiary of IRA-2 is her husband, who was age 74 on his 1996 birthday; the account balance at the end of 1996 was $10,000.

    IRA-1: The first minimum required distribution is $3,952.57. This is the account balance of $100,000 divided by 25.3, the joint life and last survivor expectancy using ages 71 and 61 from the table.

    IRA-2: The first minimum required distribution is $537.63, the account balance of $10,000 divided by 18.6, the joint life and last survivor expectancy using ages 71 and 74.

    The total required distribution of $4,490.20 from both IRAs must be received by April 1, 1998. Cynthia may withdraw the money from either one or both of the IRAs.

    If the withdrawal is delayed until the first quarter of 1998, the 1997 year-end balance is reduced by the withdrawal when she figures her minimum required distribution for 1998. The distribution for 1998 must be received by December 31, 1998.

3. Assume that in Example 1, Joe Blake's beneficiary was not his wife but his brother Frank, who was 63 on his birthday in 1997. Also assume that Joe did not elect to use the term-certain method. For 1997, the first distribution year, the required distribution is $1,096 (the same as under Step 3 of Example 1). Assume Joe received the $1,096 distribution in March 1998. To figure the required minimum distribution for 1998, the second distribution year, Joe's recalculated age is 72 (his age on his birthday in 1998). To determine Frank's revised age, and then their joint life and last survivor life expectancy, the following hybrid method computation is made:

    Step 1. Frank's life expectancy in first distribution year of 1997, using age 63. Life expectancy is shown in Table V at *7.23*. 21.6

    Step 2. Number of years that have passed since the first distribution year of 1997 (nearest whole number). 1.0

    Step 3. Remaining life expectancy (Step 1 *minus* Step 2) 20.6

    Step 4. Find the age corresponding to the life expectancy in Table V *(7.23)*, that is closest to, but less than, the Step 3 life expectancy of 20.6. In Table V, 20.6 falls between an expectancy of 20.8 years for age 64 and 20.0 years for age 65; thus, the higher age of 65 is used. 65

    Step 5. Joe's revised age for 1998. 72

Step 6. Joint life and last survivor expectancy using ages 72 and 65
(Steps 4 and 5) from table. 22.5

For 1998, Joe's minimum required distribution using the revised joint life expectancy of 22.5 years is $1,174 ($26,404 account balance ÷ 22.5).

For 1999, Joe's age in Step 5 will be 73, and the computation for Frank will be similar, except that Step 3 remaining life expectancy will be 19.6.

8.15 Inherited IRAs

When an IRA owner dies, the rules for handling the account depend on who the beneficiary is. A surviving spouse beneficiary has certain advantages not available to other beneficiaries.

Surviving Spouse Is Beneficiary of IRA

Treating inherited IRA as your own. If you are the beneficiary of your deceased spouse's IRA, you may elect to treat it as your own IRA by rolling it over to an IRA in your name, by making IRA contributions to the account, or by making rollover contributions into the account from other IRAs or from a qualifying employer-plan distribution; *see 8.10*.

An advantage of treating the amount *as your own* is that if you are under age 70 $\frac{1}{2}$, you may delay the start of your distributions until your required beginning date (April 1 of the year after the year in which you reach 70 $\frac{1}{2}$), at which time your minimum required distributions may be based on the joint life and last survivor life expectancy of yourself and the beneficiary you have designated; *see 8.14*. Even if you are over age 70 $\frac{1}{2}$ when your spouse dies, treating the IRA as your own and naming your own beneficiary generally allows you to take smaller distributions from the account than if you did not treat the IRA as your own but instead took distributions from the account as a beneficiary; *see* below. Distributions from the account are taxable and, if received before age 59 $\frac{1}{2}$, may be subject to the 10% penalty for early withdrawals; *see 8.12*.

Receiving distributions as a beneficiary. If you do not want to treat the account as your own IRA, you may receive payments from the account as a beneficiary; the account stays in the name of your deceased spouse. As a beneficiary, distributions you receive before you are age 59 $\frac{1}{2}$ are not subject to the 10% penalty for early withdrawals *(8.12)*. The payout period for withdrawing funds from the account as a beneficiary depends on when your spouse died:

• If your spouse died *after* starting to receive required minimum distributions under the rules at *8.14* for individuals age 70 $\frac{1}{2}$ and older, and you do not elect to treat the IRA as your own, you generally must receive distributions from the IRA at least as rapidly as your spouse was receiving them.

This means that if your spouse had elected the *term-certain* method *(8.14)* for figuring distributions, you must receive minimum distributions over the balance of the term-certain period. That is, for each year, you divide the account balance at the end of the prior year (see Step 1 at *8.14*) by the joint life and last survivor expectancy for both of you in the year your spouse reached age 70 $\frac{1}{2}$ *minus* one year for each year that has passed. For example, if in the year your spouse reached age 70 $\frac{1}{2}$ your joint life and last survivor life expectancy (Step 2 at *8.14*) was 21.7 years and your spouse died after receiving three annual required minimum distributions under the term-certain method, you use the balance of the term-certain period, or 18.7 years, to figure your first required minimum distribution.

However, if your spouse was *recalculating* life expectancy annually *(8.14)*, his or her life expectancy is treated as zero starting in the year following the year of death. For the years after the year of death, your minimum distributions are based on your single life expectancy, which is either your recalculated expectancy, or, if you were not recalculating, your life expectancy in the first distribution year (shown in Table V at *7.23*), reduced by one for each elapsed year.

• If your spouse died *before* starting to receive required minimum distributions under the rules at *8.14* for individuals age 70 $\frac{1}{2}$ and older, the IRA plan will probably allow you to either (1) withdraw funds from the IRA over your life expectancy, or (2) withdraw the entire account balance by the end of the fifth year following the year of your spouse's death. Some plans allow the account owner to elect the method to be used by the beneficiary, and some plans do not allow a choice but specify the method.

If the life expectancy method is elected or specified for you, you do not have to begin the distributions until the later of (1) December 31 of the year in which your spouse would have reached age 70 $\frac{1}{2}$, or (2) December 31 of the year following the year of your spouse's death.

IRA Beneficiaries Other Than Surviving Spouses

If you inherit an IRA from someone who was not your spouse, you may not treat it as your own IRA account. Thus, you may not make contributions to the account or roll it over to another IRA. You must begin receiving withdrawals from the plan. Distributions you receive as a beneficiary before age 59 ½ are *not* subject to the 10% early withdrawal penalty *(8.12)*. The payout period for withdrawing funds from the account as a beneficiary depends on when the account owner died:

- If the owner died *after* starting to receive required minimum distributions under the rules at *8.14* for individuals age 70 ½ and older, you generally must receive distributions at least as rapidly as the owner was receiving them. If the owner was using the *term-certain method (8.14)*, you must receive minimum distributions over the balance of the term-certain period.

    A similar rule applies if the owner had filed a term-certain election with the IRA plan but was nevertheless required to use the MDIB method because you were more than 10 years younger than the owner (*see* Step 2 at *8.14*). The life expectancy you use to figure your minimum required distributions is the balance of the initial term-certain period-your joint life and last survivor expectancy for the year in which the owner reached age 70 ½ , minus one year for each year that has passed.

    However, if the owner used the hybrid method (*see* Step 3 at *8.14)*, your minimum distributions starting in the year after the year of death are based on your single life expectancy as of the first distribution year (Table V at *7.23*), reduced by one for each elapsed year.

- If the owner died *before* starting to receive required minimum distributions under the rules at *8.14* for individuals age 70 ½ and older, the inherited plan may give you the option of receiving funds from the account over your life expectancy or over the five-year period following the owner's death. Some plans specify which method must be used or permit the owner to designate the method.

    If the IRA plan gives you the choice of taking withdrawals from the account over your life expectancy, you may choose this option by beginning distributions no later than December 31 of the year following the year of the IRA owner's death. If the plan does not allow the life expectancy option, or if you choose the five-year method, you must withdraw the entire account by December 31 of the fifth year following the year of the owner's death.

Planning Reminder

Beneficiary Options

If you inherit an IRA, check the terms of the plan. The plan may give you flexibility in choosing the period over which you may receive distributions from the IRA.

Simplified Employee Pension Plans (SEPs)

8.16 SEP Basics

A simplified employee pension plan (SEP) set up by an employer allows the employer to contribute to an employee's IRA account more money than is allowed under regular IRA rules. For 1997, your employer may contribute and deduct up to 15% of your compensation or $30,000, whichever is less. Your employer's SEP contributions are excluded from your pay and are not included on Form W-2 unless they exceed the limit. If contributions exceed the limit, the excess is included in your gross income and a 6% penalty tax may be imposed unless the excess (plus allowable income) is withdrawn by the due date of the return, plus extensions; *see 8.7.*

Self-employed plans. Self-employed individuals may set up a SEP as an alternative to a Keogh plan; *see* Chapter 41.

Eligibility. A SEP must cover all employees who are at least age 21, earn over $400 in 1997 (this amount is adjusted annually for inflation), and who have worked for the employer at any time during at least three of the past five years. Union employees covered by union agreements may generally be excluded.

SEP salary reduction arrangements. If a qualifying small employer set up a salary reduction SEP before 1997, employees may contribute a portion of their pay to the plan instead of receiving it in cash; *see 8.17.*

SEP distributions. Distributions from a SEP are subject to the regular IRA distribution rules at *8.8.*

Caution

Employees over Age 70 ½

An employee over age 70 ½ may still participate in an employer SEP plan but may not make personal IRA contributions. Minimum distributions from the plan must begin as discussed in *7.13.*

8.17 Salary Reduction SEP Set Up Before 1997

Qualifying small employers may offer employees the option of deferring a portion of their salary to an IRA. There are two types of salary reduction IRAs, with different eligibility and contribution rules: (1) Salary reduction SEPs established before 1997, and (2) "SIMPLE" IRA accounts established after 1996.

After 1996, an employer may establish a SIMPLE plan but not a salary reduction SEP. Rules for SIMPLE IRAs established after 1996 are at *8.18*. A salary reduction SEP that was established before 1997 may continue to receive contributions under the prior law rules discussed below, and employees hired after 1996 may participate in the plan, subject to those rules.

Salary reduction SEPs established before 1997. Salary reductions are allowed for a year only if the employer had no more than 25 employees eligible to participate in the SEP at any time during the prior taxable year. Furthermore, at least 50% of the eligible employees must elect the salary reduction option, and the deferral percentage for highly compensated employees may not exceed 125% of the average contribution of regular employees. State or local government agencies and tax-exempt organizations may not set up salary reduction SEPs.

If salary reductions are allowed, the maximum salary reduction contribution for 1997 is $9,500; the limit is subject to future inflation adjustments. Deferrals over $9,500 are taxable, and if not timely distributed to the employee, can be taxed again when distributed from the plan.

If an employee contributes to both a SEP and a 401(k) plan, the annual limit ($9,500 for 1997) applies to the total salary reductions from both plans. If an employee makes salary reduction contributions to a SEP and also to a tax-sheltered annuity plan *(7.20)*, the annual limit generally applies to the total salary reductions to both plans. In some cases, employees with at least 15 years of service may be able to defer an additional $3,000 to the tax-sheltered annuity plan as discussed at *7.20*.

Salary reduction deferrals are treated as employer contributions. For 1997, total employer contributions including salary reductions may not exceed the lesser of 15% of pay or $24,000. $24,000 is 15% of $160,000, the maximum amount of compensation that the plan may take into account for 1997; this amount may be increased for 1998 by an inflation adjustment.

SIMPLE IRAs

8.18 Who Is Eligible for a SIMPLE IRA?

SIMPLE IRAs are a new type of salary-reduction retirement plan that qualifying small employers may offer their employees. Salary-reduction contributions of up to $6,000 per year may be made by eligible employees, and employers are required to make matching contributions or a flat contribution, as discussed in *8.19*. The SIMPLE IRA replaces the salary-reduction SEP, which after 1996 may be used only by an employer that had established the plan before 1997; *see 8.17*.

Qualifying employers. A SIMPLE IRA may be maintained only by an employer that (1) in the previous calendar year had no more than 100 employees who earned compensation of $5,000 or more and (2) does not maintain any other retirement plan. A self-employed individual who meets these tests may set up a SIMPLE IRA, as discussed in Chapter 41.

In determining whether the 100-employee test is met for the prior year, all employees under the common control of the employer must be counted. For example, Joe Smith owned two businesses in 1997—a computer rental company with 80 employees and a computer repair company with 60 employees. If they all earned at least $5,000, they all count towards the 100 limit, so if Joe decides in 1998 to set up a retirement plan for his businesses, a different type of plan must be used. He may not establish a SIMPLE IRA for either business under the 100-employee limit.

If a SIMPLE IRA is established but the employer in a later year grows beyond the 100-employee limit, the employer generally has a two-year "grace period" during which contributions may continue to be made.

Eligible employees. In general, an employee must be allowed to contribute to a SIMPLE IRA for a year in which he or she is reasonably expected to earn $5,000 or more, provided at least $5,000 of compensation was received in *any two* prior years, whether or not consecutive. If the employer owns more than one business (under common control rules) and sets up a SIMPLE IRA for one of them, employees of the other business must also be allowed to participate if they meet the $5,000 compensation tests. Employees who are covered by a collective bargaining agreement may be excluded if retirement benefits were the subject of good-faith negotiations.

The employer may lower or eliminate the $5,000 compensation requirement in order to broaden participation in the plan. No other conditions on eligibility, such as age or hours of work, are permitted.

SIMPLE IRA contributions and distributions. Contribution and distribution rules for SIMPLE IRAs are discussed in *8.19*.

401(k) SIMPLE plans. An employer with a 401(k) plan that reports on the calendar year may avoid the regular 401(k) nondiscrimination tests by following the contribution rules for SIMPLE IRAs; *see 7.17.*

8.19 SIMPLE IRA Contributions and Distributions

The only contributions that may be made to a SIMPLE IRA are elective salary-reduction contributions by employees and matching or non-elective contributions by employers. All contributions are fully vested and nonforfeitable when made.

Eligible employees *(see 8.18)* may elect each year to make salary-reduction contributions to the plan of up to $6,000 per year. The $6,000 limit may be increased for future years by an inflation adjustment. Salary-reduction contributions are excluded from the employee's taxable pay on Form W-2 and not subject to federal tax withholding. They are subject to FICA withholding for Social Security and Medicare tax.

Eligible employees must be given notice by the employer of their right to elect salary reduction contributions and at least 60 days to make the election. After the first year of eligibility, the election to defer for the upcoming year is made during the last 60 days (at minimum) of the prior calendar year. The employer may provide notice in the form of a model SIMPLE IRA approved by the IRS. Form 5304-SIMPLE allows employees to select a financial insitution to which the contributions will be made. With Form 5305-SIMPLE, the employer selects the financial institution to which contributions are initially deposited, but employees have the right to subsequently transfer their account balances without cost or penalty to another SIMPLE-IRA at a financial institution of their own choosing.

If an employee contributes to a SIMPLE-IRA and also to a 401(k) plan of another employer for the same year, the annual limit on tax-free salary reduction deferrals ($9,500 for 1997) applies. Deferrals over the annual limit are taxable and must be removed to avoid being taxed again when distributed from the plan; *see 7.18.*

Employer contributions. Each year, the employer must make either a matching contribution or a fixed "non-elective" contribution. If the employer chooses matching contributions, the employee's elective salary-reduction contribution generally must be matched, up to a limit of 3% of the employee's compensation. For up to two years in any five-year period, the 3% matching limit may be reduced to as low as 1% for each eligible employee.

Instead of making either the 3% or reduced limit matching contribution, the employer may make a "non-elective" contribution equal to 2% of each eligible employee's compensation. If this option is chosen, the 2% contribution must be made for eligible employees whether or not they elect to make salary reduction contributions for the year. The 2% contribution is subject to an annual compensation limit, which for 1997 was $160,000. Thus, for 1997, the maximum 2% nonelective contribution was $3,200 (2% of $160,000) even if an employee earned more than $160,000. The 3% matching contribution is *not* subject to the annual compensation limit, but only to the $6,000 salary reduction limit.

The employer must notify eligible employees of the type of contribution it will be making for the upcoming year prior to the employees' 60-day election period for making elective salary-reduction contributions.

Planning Reminder

Employer's Intended Contributions
The IRS model notification included with Form 5304-SIMPLE or 5305-SIMPLE requires the employer to tell employees how much the employer will be contributing for the upcoming year; required employer contributions are discussed in the left column.

EXAMPLE

Martin's 1998 salary is $60,000. He elects to make the maximum $6,000 salary-reduction contribution to his employer's SIMPLE IRA plan. If his employer elects the 3% matching rule, the matching contribution is limited to $1,800, 3% of Martin's compensation.

If Martin's salary was $260,000, he could make the $6,000 salary-reduction contribution and the employer's matching contribution would also be $6,000; the 3% match (3% of $260,000 is $7,800) cannot exceed the $6,000 contribution made by Martin.

Distributions from a SIMPLE IRA. A distribution from a SIMPLE IRA is generally subject to the regular IRA distribution rules; *see 8.8.* However, for the first two years, a higher penalty for distributions before age 59 $\frac{1}{2}$ *(see 8.12)* applies. The pre-59 $\frac{1}{2}$ penalty is increased to 25% from 10%, assuming no penalty exception applies, if the distribution is received during the two-year period starting with the employee's initial participation in the plan. After the first two years, the regular 10% penalty applies.

In the initial two-year period, a tax-free rollover or direct trustee-to-trustee transfer *(see 8.10)* of a SIMPLE IRA may be made to another SIMPLE IRA. After the first two years, a tax-free rollover or direct transfer may be made to a regular IRA as well as to a SIMPLE IRA.

Caution

Increased Pre-59 $\frac{1}{2}$ Penalty
In the first two years of SIMPLE IRA participation, the penalty for distributions before age 59 $\frac{1}{2}$ is increased from 10% to 25%.

The mandatory distribution rules that apply to regular IRAs after age 70 $\frac{1}{2}$ also apply to SIMPLE IRAs.

8.20   Roth IRA Available Starting in 1998

The Roth IRA is a new type of nondeductible IRA available after 1997. As with other IRAs, earnings accumulate within a Roth IRA tax free until distributions are made. The key benefit of the Roth IRA is that tax-free distributions of earnings may be received after a five-year period by an individual who is age 59 $\frac{1}{2}$ or older, is disabled, or who pays qualifying first-time home-buyer expenses. However, certain high-income taxpayers are not eligible to make Roth IRA contributions.

The opportunity to receive tax-free distributions is expected to make the Roth IRA an attractive retirement planning alternative. Individuals with modified adjusted gross income up to $100,000 may roll over or convert an existing IRA to a Roth IRA by paying a current tax, as discussed below, in order to gain the future benefit of tax-free distributions. Similarly, individuals who qualify for deductible IRA contributions as well as the Roth IRA should consider whether the tax value of deductible contributions outweighs the advantage of future tax-free distributions from the Roth IRA; distributions from deductible IRAs are taxable.

Contributing to a Roth IRA. Contributions up to $2,000 may be made annually to a Roth IRA if you have compensation of at least that much, provided that your modified adjusted gross income is less than $95,000 if you are single, or less than $150,000 if married filing jointly. A married person filing separately may contribute only if income is less than $15,000. The right to make contributions is phased out for single taxpayers with incomes between $95,000 and $110,000, and for joint filers with incomes between $150,000 and $160,000. The income restrictions for Roth IRA contributions apply regardless of whether you are covered by an employer retirement plan, unlike the deductible IRA phase-out rules *(8.4)*, which apply only to active plan participants.

For purposes of the income restrictions, modified adjusted gross income is figured in the same way as under the regular IRA deduction phase-out rules *(8.4)*, except that a taxable rollover or conversion from a non-Roth IRA to a Roth IRA is disregarded and any deductible IRA contribution is taken into account.

Contributions to a Roth IRA for a year may be made by the April 15 filing due date (without extensions), the same deadline as for other IRAs. Excess contributions are subject to a 6% penalty, unless the excess is withdrawn by the filing due date.

The annual $2,000 contribution limit for a Roth IRA is reduced by contributions to any non-Roth IRA for the year. If deductible contributions *(8.4)* or nondeductible contributions to a non-Roth IRA *(8.6)* are made, the total contribution for the year, including Roth IRA contributions, is limited to $2,000. The Roth IRA does not replace the regular nondeductible contribution rules *(8.6)*. For an individual who is unable to contribute to a Roth IRA because of the income limits, and is unable to make deductible IRA contributions because of the phase-out rules for active plan participants, nondeductible contributions may still be made to a regular IRA under the rules at 8.6. Qualifying rollovers from a non-Roth IRA to a Roth IRA are in addition to the $2,000 limit.

Contributions after age 70 $\frac{1}{2}$ may be made to a Roth IRA, but not to any other type of IRA. In addition, the minimum required distribution rules that apply to other IRAs after age 70 $\frac{1}{2}$ *(8.14)* do not apply to Roth IRAs.

Rollover or Conversion of Regular IRA to Roth IRA. To obtain the benefit of the tax-free withdrawal feature of Roth IRAs (see below), you may make a *taxable* conversion of a regular IRA to a Roth IRA or *taxable* rollover of a distribution from a regular IRA to a Roth IRA. However, the transfer is allowed only if your modified adjusted gross income for the year of the rollover or conversion is $100,000 or less. A married person filing separately may *not* roll over or convert a non-Roth IRA to a Roth IRA, regardless of income.

A conversion could be made by requesting a direct transfer of a regular IRA to a new Roth IRA trustee, or by instructing the trustee of the regular IRA to change the registration of the account to a Roth IRA. A rollover to a Roth IRA must be completed within the usual 60-day rollover period.

The rollover or conversion of a regular IRA to a Roth IRA is treated as a taxable distribution, unless part of the account was allocable to nondeductible contributions (made under the rules at 8.6). If the rollover or conversion is made during 1998, there is this tax break: the tax that would otherwise be due is spread ratably over four years starting with 1998. After 1998, a rollover or conversion is taxable in the year it is made. A rollover or conversion from a regular IRA to a Roth IRA is exempt from the 10% penalty on taxable distributions received before age 59 $\frac{1}{2}$.

Law Alert

Rollover or Conversion to Roth IRA in 1998

If your modified adjusted gross income is $100,000 or less, you may roll over or convert an existing IRA to a Roth IRA. If you do so, the rollover or conversion is generally taxable, unless the transferred amount is allocable to nondeductible contributions. If you are considering making the change, doing so in 1998 will allow you to spread the tax otherwise due ratably over four years. After 1998, a rollover or conversion will be fully taxable (unless allocable to nondeductible contributions) in the year it is made.

Distributions from a Roth IRA. A distribution from a Roth IRA will be *tax free* if:

(1)   It is made *after* the five-year period beginning with the first taxable year for which a Roth contribution was made, *and*

(2)   It is made for any of these reasons:

- the taxpayer is age 59 $\frac{1}{2}$ or older,
- the taxpayer is disabled,
- the taxpayer uses the distribution to pay up to $10,000 of qualifying first-time home-buyer expenses as discussed below,
- the distribution is to a beneficiary following the death of the account owner.

Distributions that do not qualify for tax-free treatment under the above tests are taxable to the extent of earnings and are subject to the 10% penalty for taxable distributions before age 59 $\frac{1}{2}$, unless a penalty exception *(see 8.12)* applies. In determining the taxable amount, distributions are treated as being made first from contributions and then from earnings. Under this rule, if a distribution is less than total contributions to the Roth IRA, it is not taxable or subject to the pre-age 59 $\frac{1}{2}$ penalty even if it is made within the first five years. However, there are indications that Congress may revise the law to prevent this favorable treatment when a taxpayer under age 59 $\frac{1}{2}$ rolls over or converts a regular IRA to a Roth IRA and shortly thereafter makes withdrawals from the Roth IRA; *see* the Supplement for future developments.

Distribution used for up to $10,000 of first-time home-buyer expenses.

Tax-free treatment will apply to a Roth IRA distribution received after the first five-year period and used for up to $10,000 of qualifying "first-time" home-buyer expenses. The $10,000 limit is a lifetime cap per IRA owner, not an annual limitation. Expenses qualify if they are used within 120 days of the distribution to pay the acquisition costs of a principal residence for you, your spouse, your child, or your grandchild, or an ancestor of you or your spouse. The residence does not have to be the homeowner's "first" home. A qualifying first-time home-buyer is considered to be someone who did not have a present ownership interest in a principal residence in the two-year period before the acquisition of the new home. If the home-buyer is married, both spouses must satisfy the two-year test. Eligible acquisition costs include buying, constructing, or reconstructing the principal residence, including reasonable settlement, financing, and closing costs.

Joint Life and Last Survivor Life Expectancy *(See 8.12)*

Ages	45	46	47	48	49	50	51	52	53	54	55	56	57	58	59
40	46.9	46.5	46.2	45.9	45.6	45.3	45.1	44.8	44.6	44.4	44.2	44.1	43.9	43.8	43.7
41	46.3	45.9	45.5	45.2	44.9	44.6	44.3	44.1	43.9	43.6	43.4	43.3	43.1	43.0	42.8
42	45.7	45.3	44.9	44.5	44.2	43.9	43.6	43.3	43.1	42.9	42.7	42.5	42.3	42.1	42.0
43	45.1	44.7	44.3	43.9	43.6	43.2	42.9	42.6	42.4	42.1	41.9	41.7	41.5	41.3	41.2
44	44.6	44.1	43.7	43.3	42.9	42.6	42.2	41.9	41.7	41.4	41.2	40.9	40.7	40.5	40.4
45	44.1	43.6	43.2	42.7	42.3	42.0	41.6	41.3	41.0	40.7	40.4	40.2	40.0	39.7	39.6
46	43.6	43.1	42.6	42.2	41.8	41.4	41.0	40.6	40.3	40.0	39.7	39.5	39.2	39.0	38.8
47	43.2	42.6	42.1	41.7	41.2	40.8	40.4	40.0	39.7	39.3	39.0	38.7	38.5	38.2	38.0
48	42.7	42.2	41.7	41.2	40.7	40.2	39.8	39.4	39.0	38.7	38.4	38.1	37.8	37.5	37.3
49	42.3	41.8	41.2	40.7	40.2	39.7	39.3	38.8	38.4	38.1	37.7	37.4	37.1	36.8	36.6
50	42.0	41.4	40.8	40.2	39.7	39.2	38.7	38.3	37.9	37.5	37.1	36.8	36.4	36.1	35.9
51	41.6	41.0	40.4	39.8	39.3	38.7	38.2	37.8	37.3	36.9	36.5	36.1	35.8	35.5	35.2
52	41.3	40.6	40.0	39.4	38.8	38.3	37.8	37.3	36.8	36.4	35.9	35.6	35.2	34.8	34.5
53	41.0	40.3	39.7	39.0	38.4	37.9	37.3	36.8	36.3	35.8	35.4	35.0	34.6	34.2	33.9
54	40.7	40.0	39.3	38.7	38.1	37.5	36.9	36.4	35.8	35.3	34.9	34.4	34.0	33.6	33.3
55	40.4	39.7	39.0	38.4	37.7	37.1	36.5	35.9	35.4	34.9	34.4	33.9	33.5	33.1	32.7
56	40.2	39.5	38.7	38.1	37.4	36.8	36.1	35.6	35.0	34.4	33.9	33.4	33.0	32.5	32.1
57	40.0	39.2	38.5	37.8	37.1	36.4	35.8	35.2	34.6	34.0	33.5	33.0	32.5	32.0	31.6
58	39.7	39.0	38.2	37.5	36.8	36.1	35.5	34.8	34.2	33.6	33.1	32.5	32.0	31.5	31.1
59	39.6	38.8	38.0	37.3	36.6	35.9	35.2	34.5	33.9	33.3	32.7	32.1	31.6	31.1	30.6

Joint Life and Last Survivor Life Expectancy *(See 8.14)*

Ages	60	61	62	63	64	65	66	67	68	69	70	71	72	73	74	75	76	77	78	79	80
70	26.2	25.6	24.9	24.3	23.7	23.1	22.5	22.0	21.5	21.1	20.6	20.2	19.8	19.4	19.1	18.8	18.5	18.3	18.0	17.8	17.6
71	26.0	25.3	24.7	24.0	23.4	22.8	22.2	21.7	21.2	20.7	20.2	19.8	19.4	19.0	18.6	18.3	18.0	17.7	17.5	17.2	17.0
72	25.8	25.1	24.4	23.8	23.1	22.5	21.9	21.3	20.8	20.3	19.8	19.4	18.9	18.5	18.2	17.8	17.5	17.2	16.9	16.7	16.4
73	25.6	24.9	24.2	23.5	22.9	22.2	21.6	21.0	20.5	20.0	19.4	19.0	18.5	18.1	17.7	17.3	17.0	16.7	16.4	16.1	15.9
74	25.5	24.7	24.0	23.3	22.7	22.0	21.4	20.8	20.2	19.6	19.1	18.6	18.2	17.7	17.3	16.9	16.5	16.2	15.9	15.6	15.4
75	25.3	24.6	23.8	23.1	22.4	21.8	21.1	20.5	19.9	19.3	18.8	18.3	17.8	17.3	16.9	16.5	16.1	15.8	15.4	15.1	14.9
76	25.2	24.4	23.7	23.0	22.3	21.6	20.9	20.3	19.7	19.1	18.5	18.0	17.5	17.0	16.5	16.1	15.7	15.4	15.0	14.7	14.4
77	25.1	24.3	23.6	22.8	22.1	21.4	20.7	20.1	19.4	18.8	18.3	17.7	17.2	16.7	16.2	15.8	15.4	15.0	14.6	14.3	14.0
78	25.0	24.2	23.4	22.7	21.9	21.2	20.5	19.9	19.2	18.6	18.0	17.5	16.9	16.4	15.9	15.4	15.0	14.6	14.2	13.9	13.5
79	24.9	24.1	23.3	22.6	21.8	21.1	20.4	19.7	19.0	18.4	17.8	17.2	16.7	16.1	15.6	15.1	14.7	14.3	13.9	13.5	13.2
80	24.8	24.0	23.2	22.4	21.7	21.0	20.2	19.5	18.9	18.2	17.6	17.0	16.4	15.9	15.4	14.9	14.4	14.0	13.5	13.2	12.8
81	24.7	23.9	23.1	22.3	21.6	20.8	20.1	19.4	18.7	18.1	17.4	16.8	16.2	15.7	15.1	14.6	14.1	13.7	13.2	12.8	12.5
82	24.6	23.8	23.0	22.3	21.5	20.7	20.0	19.3	18.6	17.9	17.3	16.6	16.0	15.5	14.9	14.4	13.9	13.4	13.0	12.5	12.2
83	24.6	23.8	23.0	22.2	21.4	20.6	19.9	19.2	18.5	17.8	17.1	16.5	15.9	15.3	14.7	14.2	13.7	13.2	12.7	12.3	11.9
84	24.5	23.7	22.9	22.1	21.3	20.5	19.8	19.1	18.4	17.7	17.0	16.3	15.7	15.1	14.5	14.0	13.5	13.0	12.5	12.0	11.6
85	24.5	23.7	22.8	22.0	21.3	20.5	19.7	19.0	18.3	17.6	16.9	16.2	15.6	15.0	14.4	13.8	13.3	12.8	12.3	11.8	11.4

Chapter 9

Income From Rents and Royalities

Use Schedule E of Form 1040 to report real estate rental income and expenses. You must also file Form 4562 to claim depreciation deductions for buildings you acquired in 1997.

Use Schedule C instead of Schedule E if you provide additional services for the convenience of the tenants, such as maid service. That is, Schedule C is used to report payments received for the use and occupancy of rooms or other areas in a hotel, motel, boarding house, apartment, tourist home, or trailer court where services are provided primarily for the occupant.

If you rent an apartment or room in the same building in which you live, you report the rent income less expenses allocated to the rental property; *see 9.4.*

The law prevents most homeowners from deducting losses (expenses in excess of income) on the rental of a personal vacation home or personal residence if the owner or close relatives personally use the premises during the year. Tests based on days of personal and rental use determine whether you may deduct losses as explained in *9.7.*

Rental losses may also be limited by the passive activity rules of Chapter 10. Real estate professionals may avoid passive restrictions on rental income, and an investor who actively manages property may deduct rental losses of up to $25,000.

Use Schedule E to report royalties, but if you are a self-employed author, artist, or inventor, report royalty income and expenses on Schedule C.

Business rentals of equipment, vehicles, or similar personal property are reported on Schedule C, not Schedule E.

Rental Income and Deductions

9.1 Reporting Rental Income and Expenses

On the cash basis, you report rent income on your tax return for the year in which you receive payment or in which you "constructively" receive it, such as where payment is credited to your bank account.

On the accrual basis, you report income on your tax return for the year in which you are entitled to receive payment, even if it is not actually paid. However, you do not report accrued income if the financial condition of the tenant makes collection doubtful. If you sue for payment, you do not report income until you win a collectible judgment.

Advance rentals. Advance rentals or bonuses are reported in the year received, whether you are on the cash or accrual basis.

Tenant's payment of landlord's expenses. The tenant's payment of your taxes, interest, insurance, mortgage amortization (even if you are not personally liable on the mortgage), repairs, or other expenses is considered additional rental income to you. If your tenant pays your utility bills or your emergency repairs and deducts the amount from the rent payment, you must include as rental income the full rental amount, not the actual net payment. However, you can claim an offsetting deduction for expenses, such as repairs, that would have been deductible had you paid them.

Tenant's payment to cancel lease. A tenant's payment for cancelling a lease or modifying its terms is considered rental income in the year you receive it regardless of your method of accounting. You may deduct expenses incurred because of the cancellation or modification and any unamortized balance of expenses paid in negotiating the lease.

Insurance. Insurance proceeds for loss of rental income because of fire or other casualty are rental income.

Improvements by tenants. You do not realize taxable income when your tenant improves the leased premises, provided the improvements are not substitute rent payments. Furthermore, when you take possession of the improvements at the time the lease ends, you do not realize income. However, you may not depreciate the value of the improvements as the basis to you is considered zero.

Property or services. If you receive property or services instead of money, include the fair market value of such property or services as rental income.

If you agree upon a specified price for services rendered, that price is generally treated as the fair market value.

Rental losses. Rental income may be offset by deductions claimed for depreciation, mortgage interest, and repair and maintenance costs. However, if these expenses exceed rental income, the resulting loss is subject to deduction limitations. If you do not qualify as a real estate professional *(10.3)*, you generally may not deduct rental losses from other income (such as salary, interest, and dividends). Rental losses may offset only other rental and passive activity income. However, if you perform some management role, you may deduct from other income *real estate* rental losses of up to $25,000, provided your adjusted gross income does not exceed $100,000. The passive activity restrictions have the positive effect of making rental income attractive. Consider purchasing rental property if you have passive tax losses which may be used to offset the rental income.

Passive loss restrictions, which also affect tax credits, are discussed in Chapter 10.

9.2 Checklist of Rental Deductions

The expenses in this section are deductible from rental income on Schedule E of Form 1040 in determining your profit.

Real estate taxes. However, special assessments for paving, sewer systems, or other local improvements are not deductible; they are added to the cost of the land. *See 16.6* through *16.9* for real estate tax deductions.

Construction period interest and taxes. These expenses generally have to be capitalized and depreciated; *see 16.5*.

Caution

Security Deposits

Distinguish advance rentals, which are income, from security deposits, which are not. Security deposits are amounts deposited with you solely as security for the tenant's performance of the terms of the lease, and as such are usually not taxed, particularly where local law treats security deposits as trust funds. If the tenant breaches the lease, you are entitled to apply the sum as rent, at which time you report it as income. If both you and your tenant agree that a security deposit is to be used as a final rent payment, it is advance rent. Include it in your income when you receive it.

Depreciation of a rental building. You may start claiming depreciation in the month the building is ready for tenants. For example, you bought a house in May 1997 and spent June and July making repairs. The house is ready to rent in August and you advertise for tenants. You begin depreciation as of August, even if a tenant does not move in until September or some later month. The month the building is ready for tenants is the month that determines the first-year depreciation write-off under the mid-month convention. *See 9.5* for the monthly-based depreciation rates.

Depreciation for furniture and appliances. Furniture used in your rental property, carpeting, and appliances such as stoves and refrigerators are considered seven-year property under MACRS; *see 42.4.* The seven-year recovery period also applies to office furniture and equipment such as desks and files.

Management expenses.

Maintenance expenses, such as heating, repairs, lighting, water, electricity, gas, telephone, coal, and other service costs; *see 9.3.*

Salaries and wages paid to superintendents, janitors, elevator operators, and service and maintenance personnel.

Traveling expenses to look after the properties. If you travel "away from home" to inspect or repair rental property, be prepared to show that this was the primary purpose of your trip, rather than vacationing or other personal purposes. Otherwise, the IRS may disallow deductions for round-trip travel costs.

Legal expenses for dispossessing tenants. But expenses of long-term leases are capital expenditures deductible over the term of the lease.

Interest on mortgages and other indebtedness. But expenses and fees for securing loans are nondeductible capital expenditures.

Commissions paid to collect rentals. But commissions paid to secure long-term rentals must be deducted over the life of the lease. Commissions paid to acquire the property are capitalized.

Premiums for fire, liability, and plate glass insurance. If payment is made in one year for insurance covering a period longer than one year, you amortize and deduct the premium over the life of the policy, even though you are on a cash basis.

Also deductible is a premium paid to secure a release from a mortgage in order to get a new loan.

Tax return preparation. You may deduct as a rental expense the part of a tax preparation fee allocable to Part 1 of Schedule E (income or loss from rentals or royalties). You may also deduct, as a rental expense, a fee paid to a tax consultant to resolve a tax underpayment related to your rental activities.

Charging below fair market rent. If you rent your property to a friend or relative for less than the fair rental value, you may deduct expenses and depreciation only to the extent of the rental income; *see 9.8.*

Co-tenants. One of two tenants in common may deduct only half of the maintenance expenses although he or she pays the entire bill. A tenant in common who pays all of the expenses of the common property is entitled to reimbursement from the other co-tenant. So one-half of the bill is not his or her ordinary and necessary expense. Each co-tenant owns a separate property interest in the common property which produces separate income for each. Each tenant's deductible expense is that portion of the entire expense which each separate interest bears to the whole, and no more.

Costs of cancelling lease. A landlord may pay the tenant to cancel an unfavorable lease. The way the payment is treated by the landlord depends on the reason for the cancellation. If the purpose of the cancellation is to enable the landlord to construct a new building in place of the old, the cancellation payment is added to the basis of the new building. If the purpose is to sell the property, the payment is added to the cost of the property. If the landlord wants the premises for his or her own use, the payment is deducted over the remaining term of the old lease. If the landlord gets a new tenant to replace the old one, the cancellation payment is also generally deductible over the remaining term of the old lease.

Court Decision

Co-Tenant's Deduction for Real Estate Taxes

The Tax Court allowed a co-tenant to deduct more than her proportionate share of real estate taxes. According to the court, the deduction test for real estate taxes is whether the payment satisfied a personal liability or protects a beneficial interest in the property. In the case of co-tenants, nonpayment of taxes by the other co-tenants could result in the property being lost or foreclosed. To prevent this, a co-tenant who pays the tax is protecting his or her beneficial interest and, therefore, is entitled to deduct the payment of the full tax.

EXAMPLE

Handlery Hotels, Inc., had to pay its lessee $85,000 to terminate a lease on a building three years before the lease term expired. Handlery entered into a new 20-year lease at more favorable terms with another lessee. Handlery amortized the $85,000 cancellation payment over the three-year unexpired term of the old lease. The IRS claimed that the payment had to be amortized over the 20-year term of the new lease because it was part of the cost of obtaining the new lease. A federal district court agreed with the IRS, but an appeals court sided with Handlery. Since the unexpired lease term is the major factor in determining the amount of the cancellation payment, the cost of cancellation should be amortized over that unexpired term.

9.3 Distinguishing Between a Repair and an Improvement

Maintenance and repair expenses are not treated in the same way as expenses for improvements and replacements. Only maintenance and incidental repair costs are deductible against rental income. Repairs that add to the value or prolong the life of the property or adapt the property to new uses are capital improvements. Capital improvements may not be deducted currently but may be depreciated under the rules at *42.13.* If you make improvements to property before renting it out, add the cost of the improvements to your basis in the property.

A repair keeps your property in good operating condition. For example, repairs include painting, fixing gutters or floors, fixing leaks, plastering, and replacing broken windows. However, putting a recreation room in an unfinished basement, paneling a den, putting up a fence, putting in new plumbing or wiring, putting on a new roof, and paving a driveway are all examples of capital improvements depreciable under *42.13.*

Repairs may not be separated from capital expenditures when part of an improvement program; *see* Example 2 below.

EXAMPLES

1. The costs of painting the outside of a building used for business purposes and the costs of papering and painting the inside are repair costs and may be deducted. The replacement of a roof or a change in the plumbing system is a capital expenditure which may be depreciated under MACRS; *see 42.13.*

2. Amanda Jones buys a dilapidated business building and has the building renovated and repaired. The total cost comes to about $130,000, of which $17,800 is deducted as repairs. But the repair deduction is disallowed because it is a capital expenditure. When a general improvement program is undertaken, you may not separate repairs from improvements. They become an integral part of the overall betterment and a capital investment, although they could be characterized as repairs when viewed independently.

Normal maintenance or major improvement?   Normal maintenance expenses were distinguished from major improvement costs in a case involving a major hotel where improvements and maintenance were generally done at the same time. The operators of the hotel capitalized the cost of the improvements but claimed expense deductions for the cost of painting and repapering rooms. The IRS disallowed the deductions, claiming they were part of the improvement program. The operators claimed that the papering and painting were normal and usual maintenance work required to keep the hotel in first-class condition. The Tax Court disagreed and sided with the IRS. However, on appeal, the appeals court allowed the deduction. The "rehabilitation doctrine" does not apply where it can be shown that repairs are part of a normal range of ongoing maintenance. Here, the painting and papering only served to maintain the first-class status of the hotel. The fact that the work was done under a general improvement plan does not defeat the deduction. Any commercial enterprise, such as a hotel, that annually spends large sums of money on replacements and repairs must do so under a detailed plan and budget.

 Planning Reminder

Repairs and Improvments
What if repairs and improvements are unconnected and not part of an overall improvement program? Assume you repair the floors of one story and improve another story by cutting new windows. You may probably deduct the cost of repairing the floors provided you have separate bills for the jobs. To safeguard the deduction, schedule the work at separate times so that the two jobs are not lumped together as an overall improvement program.

How To Report Rentals of Residential and Vacation Homes

Court Decision

Rented Room That Are Not Separate Dwelling Units

A rental loss was denied to an owner of a two-story, four-bedroom house when he rented out two bedrooms to separate tenants after he lost his job. Although individual locks were placed on the doors of the rented bedrooms, the tenants and the owner shared access to the kitchen, bathroom, and other parts of the house. The Tax Court held that the rented rooms were not separate and distinct from the rest of the house which the owner used. The house was a single dwelling unit shared by the owner and tenants and under the personal-use rules of *8.7*, the owner could not claim a rental loss.

9.4 Reporting Rents From a Multi-Unit Residence

If you rent out an apartment or room in a multi-unit residence in which you also live, you report rent receipts and deduct expenses allocated to the rented part of the property on Schedule E of Form 1040. Expenses allocated to rental are deductible, whether or not you itemize deductions. You deduct interest and taxes on your personal share of the property as itemized deductions on Schedule A of Form 1040 if you itemize deductions.

If expenses exceed rental income on Schedule E, your loss deduction is subject to the passive loss rules of Chapter 10. The loss, if it comes within the $25,000 allowance *(10.2)* or the exception for real estate professionals *(10.3)*, may be deducted from any type of income. If you cannot claim the allowance, the loss may be deducted only from passive activity income.

If your only passive activity losses are rental losses of $25,000 or less from actively managed rental real estate and your modified adjusted gross income is $100,000 or less, you do not have to use Form 8582 to deduct losses under the $25,000 allowance; *see 10.12.*

EXAMPLE

You bought a three-family house in 1974. You occupy one apartment as a personal residence. The house cost you $30,000 ($27,000 for the building and $3,000 for the land). It had a useful life of 30 years. Two-thirds of the basis of the building has been subject to depreciation, or $18,000 (²/₃ of $27,000). Assuming straight-line depreciation of $600 ($18,000 cost ÷ 30 years), this is how you deduct expenses in a taxable year:

	Total	Deduct itemized deductions	Deduct on Schedule E	Not deductible
Taxes	$600	$200	$400	
Interest	390	130	260	
Repairs	300		200	$100
Depreciation	600		600	
	$1,890	$330	$1,460	$100

The taxes and interest allocated to personal use are deductible on Schedule A if you itemize deductions. Repairs allocated to your apartment are nondeductible personal expenses.

If you or close relatives personally use the rented portion during the year and expenses exceed income, loss deductions may be barred under the rules of *9.7.*

9.5 Depreciation on Converting a Home to Rental Property

When you convert your residence to rental property, you may depreciate the building. You figure depreciation on the *lower* of:

• Fair market value of the building at the time you convert it to rental property; *and*
• Adjusted basis. This is your original cost for the building, exclusive of land, plus permanent improvements minus casualty or theft loss deductions claimed on prior tax returns.

You claim MACRS depreciation based on a 27 ½ -year recovery period. The specific rate for the year of conversion is the rate for the month in which the property is ready for tenants. For example, you move out of your home in May and make some minor repairs. You advertise the house for rent in June. Depreciation starts in June because that is when the home is ready for rental, even if you do not actually obtain a tenant until a later month. Under a mid-month convention, the house is treated as placed in service during the middle of the month. This means that one-half of a full month's depreciation is allowed for that month. In the table on the next page, the monthly depreciation rates for the year the property is placed in service and the next 11 years are shown. The table incorporates the mid-month convention.

EXAMPLE

In 1987, you bought a house for $125,000, of which $100,000 is allocated to the house; the $25,000 balance is allocated to the land. In June 1997 you move out of the house and rent it. At that time, the fair market value of the house exclusive of the land is $150,000. The depreciable basis of the house is the lower adjusted basis of $100,000. The depreciation rate for placing the house in service in June is 1.970%, as shown in the table below. Thus, your 1997 depreciation deduction is $1,970 ($100,000 × 1.970%).

Depreciating a rented cooperative apartment. If you rent out a co-op apartment, you may deduct your share of the total depreciation claimed by the cooperative corporation. The method for computing your share depends on whether you bought your co-op shares as part of the first offering. If you did, follow these steps: (1) Ask the co-op corporation officials for the total real estate depreciation deduction of the corporation, not counting depreciation for office space that cannot be lived in by tenant-shareholders. (2) Multiply Step 1 by the following fraction: number of your co-op shares divided by total shares outstanding. The result is your share of the co-op's depreciation, but you may not deduct more than your adjusted basis.

The computation is more complicated if you bought your co-op shares after the first offering. You must compute your depreciable basis as follows. Increase your cost for the co-op shares by your share of the co-op's total mortgage. Reduce this amount by your share of the value of the co-op's land and your share of the commercial space not available for occupancy by tenant-stockholders. Your "share" of the co-op's mortgage, land value, or commercial space is the co-op's total amount for such items multiplied by the fraction in Step 2, that is, the number of your shares divided by the total shares outstanding. After computing your depreciable basis, multiply that basis by the depreciation percentage for the month your apartment is ready for rental.

Basis to use when you sell a rented residence. For purposes of figuring gain, you use adjusted basis at the time of the conversion, plus subsequent capital improvements, and minus depreciation and casualty loss deductions. For purposes of figuring loss, you use the *lower* of adjusted basis or fair market value at the time of the conversion, plus subsequent improvements and minus depreciation and casualty losses. You may have neither gain nor loss to report; this would happen if you figure a loss when using the above basis rule for gains, and you figure a gain when using the basis rule for losses.

Have an appraiser estimate the fair market value of the house when it is rented. The appraisal will help support your basis for depreciation or a loss deduction on a sale if your return is examined.

Depreciation on a vacant residence. If you move from your house before it is sold, you generally may not deduct depreciation on the vacant residence while it is held for sale. The IRS will not allow the deduction, and, according to a Tax Court case, a deduction is possible only if you can show that you held the house, expecting to make a profit on an increase in value over and above the value of the house when you moved from it. That is, you held the house for sale on the expectation of profiting on a future increase in value after abandoning the house as a residence.

Depreciation: Use the Row for the Month the Residence Is Ready for Rental in the First Rental Year

Month—	1	2	3	4	5	6	7	8	9	10	11	12
Year												
1	3.485%	3.182%	2.879%	2.576%	2.273%	1.970%	1.667%	1.364%	1.061%	0.758%	0.455%	0.152%
2–9	3.636	3.636	3.636	3.636	3.636	3.636	3.636	3.636	3.636	3.636	3.636	3.636
10	3.637	3.637	3.637	3.637	3.637	3.637	3.636	3.636	3.636	3.636	3.636	3.636
11	3.636	3.636	3.636	3.636	3.636	3.636	3.637	3.637	3.637	3.637	3.637	3.637
12	3.637	3.637	3.637	3.637	3.637	3.637	3.636	3.636	3.636	3.636	3.636	3.636

9.6 Renting to a Relative

The tax law distinguishes between a rental of a unit used by a close relative as a principal residence, and a rental of a unit that is not the relative's principal residence, such as a second home or vacation home. It is easier to deduct a rental loss on the principal residence rental.

On a fair market rental of a unit used by the close relative as a principal residence, your relative's use is *not* considered personal use by you that could bar a loss under the personal-use test of *9.7*. A relative's use of the unit as a second or vacation home *is* attributed to you in applying the personal-use test at *9.7*, even if you receive a fair market value rent.

Close relatives who come within these rules are: brothers and sisters, half-brothers and half-sisters, spouses, parents, grandparents, children, and grandchildren.

Fair market rental is the amount a person who is not related to you would be willing to pay. The most direct way to determine fair market rental is to ask a real estate agent in your neighborhood for comparative rentals.

9.7 Personal Use and Rental of a Residential Unit During the Year

The number of days of personal and rental use determines how you must report income and expenses of a residential unit in which you live part of a taxable year and rent or offer for rent for the days you do not live there.

Before reading the daily-use tests, list your days of use in 1997:
Fair market rental days:_____
Personal-use days:_____

Personal-use days may also include rental days to family members listed at *9.6* and use days under co-ownership agreements. *See 9.8* for details on personal-use days.

Rental of less than 15 days during the taxable year.   If rent days are less than 15 days in the taxable year, you do not report the rental income and the only deductions allowed are those you would be allowed anyway as a homeowner. That is, if you itemize deductions on Schedule A, you deduct mortgage interest, real estate taxes, and casualty losses, if any. No other rental expenses such as depreciation and maintenance expenses are deductible. Interest is generally fully deductible if the home qualifies as a first or second home under the mortgage interest rules of Chapter 15.

Rental of 15 days or more in the taxable year.   A daily-use test determines whether your use of the unit during the taxable year is treated as residential use which requires you to figure your deductions under the allocation rules of *9.9* that limit your deductions to the rental income. You are considered to have used the unit as a residence if personal-use days exceed the *larger* of 14 days and 10% of fair market rental days. When the unit is treated as a residence, rental expenses are deductible on Schedule E only to the extent of rental income, following the rules of *9.9*. Expenses not deductible in the current year under this limitation may be carried forward and will be deductible up to rental income in the following year. The deduction limit is irrelevant if your rental income exceeds expenses. You report the rental income and claim the deductible expenses on Schedule E.

If your personal-use days do not exceed the larger of 14 days and 10% of the fair market rental days, your rental deductions are not limited by the personal-use test. However, a loss deduction is subject to the passive activity loss restrictions discussed at *10.1*.

Caution

Restrictions Apply to Any Dwelling Unit

The daily-use tests of *9.7* apply to any "dwelling unit" you rent out which is also used as a residence during the year by yourself or other family members. A dwelling unit may be a house, apartment, condominium, cooperative, house trailer, mini motor home, boat, or similar property with basic living accommodations, including any appurtenant structure such as a garage. A dwelling unit does not include property used exclusively as a hotel, motel, inn, or similar establishment.

> **EXAMPLES**
> 1. In 1997, you rented out a condominium unit in Florida at a fair market rental for 260 days. If you used the unit personally for 27 or more days, the condominium is considered a residence subject to the allocation rules of *9.9* because your personal use exceeds 26 days, 10% of the fair market rental days. If you used the unit for 26 days or less, you may treat the unit for the taxable year as rental property and you may deduct a loss, if any, subject to the passive activity rules of *10.1*.
>
>   Where rental days exceed 140 days, as a rule of thumb, you can figure that for every 10 days of fair-rent use, you may use the unit personally for one day.   Thus, if you rented a vacation unit for 11 months, you could personally use it for a month or so without jeopardizing a deduction of a rental loss (rental of 330 days would permit 33 days of personal use).

2. Assume the same unit as in Example 1 but you rented the unit for 130 days. If you used the unit personally for 14 days or less, you may treat the unit as a rental property. To be treated as a residence, your personal use would have to exceed 14 days, since 14 days is greater than 10% of the rental days.

9.8 Counting Personal-Use and Rental Days

In applying the personal-use test of *9.7*, personal-use days are:

- Days you used the residence for personal purposes other than days primarily spent making repairs or getting the property ready for tenants.
- Days on which the residence is used by your spouse, children, grandchildren, parents, brothers, sisters, or grandparents. However, if such a relative pays you a fair rental value to use the home as a principal residence, the relative's use is not considered personal use by you. If you rent a vacation home to such relatives, their use is considered personal use by you even if they pay a fair rental value amount.

  The same rules apply to days of use by a relative of a co-owner of the property.
- Days on which the residence is used by any person under a reciprocal arrangement that allows you to use some other dwelling during the year.
- Days on which you rent the residence to any person for less than fair market value.
- Days that a co-owner of the property uses the residence, unless the co-owner's use is under a shared-equity financing agreement discussed later in this section.

An owner is not considered to have personally used a home that is used by an employee if the value of such use is tax-free lodging required as a condition of employment; *see 3.11*.

Shared-equity financing agreements for co-owners. Use by a co-owner is not considered personal use by you if you have a shared-equity financing agreement under which: (1) the co-owner pays you a fair rent for using the home as his or her principal residence; and (2) you and your co-owner each have undivided interests for more than 50 years in the entire home and in any appurtenant land acquired with the residence.

Any use by a co-owner which does not meet these two tests is considered personal use by you if, for any part of the day, the home is used by a co-owner or a holder of any interest in the home (other than a security interest or an interest under a lease for fair rental) for personal purposes. For this purpose, any other ownership interest existing at the time you have an interest in the home is counted, even if there are no immediate rights to possession and enjoyment of the home under such other interest. For example, you have a life estate in the home and your friend owns the remainder interest. Use by either of you is personal use.

 Planning Reminder

Shared-Equity Financing Agreements

As an investor, you can help finance the purchase of a principal residence for a family member or other individual. The rental income you receive for your ownership share in the property may be offset by deductions for your share of the mortgage interest, taxes, and operating expenses you pay under the terms of the agreement, as well as depreciation deductions for your percentage share. Rental losses are subject to the passive loss restrictions of Chapter 10.

The other co-owner living in the house may claim itemized deductions for payment of his or her share of the mortgage interest and taxes.

EXAMPLES

1. A son rented a condominium in Florida to his parents, who split their time between the Florida apartment and the home they owned in Illinois. Although the parents paid a fair amount for the Florida condo, the son's rental deductions were limited by the IRS and the Tax Court to interest and real estate taxes that did not exceed the rental income. The parents' rental days were attributed to the son under the 14 day/10% rental day limit since the home in Illinois, and not the Florida apartment, was their principal residence.

2. You and your neighbor Joe are co-owners of a vacation condominium. You rent the unit out whenever possible; Joe uses the unit for two weeks every year. As Joe owns an interest in the unit, both of you are considered to have used the unit for personal purposes during those weeks.

3. You and your neighbor Tom are co-owners of a house under a shared-equity financing agreement. Tom lives in the house and pays you a fair rental price. Even though Tom has an interest in the house, the days he lives there are not counted as days of personal-use by you because Tom rents the house as a main home under a shared-equity financing agreement.

4. You rent a beach house to Jane. Jane rents her house in the mountains to you. You each pay a fair rental price. You are using your house for personal purposes on the days that Jane uses it because your house is used by Jane under an arrangement that allows you to use her house.

Rental of principal residence prior to sale. You are not considered to have made any personal use of a principal residence which you rent or try to rent at a fair rental for (1) a consecutive period of 12 months or more, *or* (2) for a period of less than 12 months that ends with the sale or exchange of the residence. For example, you move out of your principal residence on May 31, 1998, offering it for rental as of June 1. You rent it from June 15 until mid-November, when you sell the house. Under the special rental period rule, your use of the house from January 1 until May 31, 1998, is *not* counted as personal use. This means that deductions for the rental period are not subject to the allocation rules and restrictions of *9.9.*

Rental pool arrangements. Pool arrangements have been devised to avoid the loss restriction by attempting to increase the days the home is held for a fair rental value. They have not been successful. Courts have ruled that only days on which a home is actually rented count as fair rental days, not days of availability through the rental pool.

In proposed regulations, the IRS also holds that a rental pool is not a basis for counting fair rental days. However, the proposed regulations permit rental pool participants to elect to average the actual rental of their units. Unanimous consent is required to elect the averaging rule. If the election is made, the number of rental days for a unit is determined by multiplying the aggregate number of days that all units in the rental pool were rented at fair rental during the pool season by a fraction. The numerator of the fraction is the number of participation days of a particular unit; the denominator is the aggregate number of participation days of all the units.

The IRS may apply the rental pool rule to a rental guarantee option. The Tax Court supported the IRS position, but an appeals court did not, in the following Example.

EXAMPLE

Razavi owned a condo in Florida and elected to take a rental guarantee option from the resort operator over a three-year period. The annual guaranteed rent was $21,000 plus 40% of rentals over $52,500. In 1987, the resort actually received gross rentals of $48,300 for the unit, but Razavi received $21,000 under the guarantee and claimed a rental loss deduction. The IRS disallowed the loss because it claimed that Razavi personally used the unit for 27 days, exceeding 10% of the 200 days the unit had actually been rented.

Razavi claimed that the 27 days were less than 10% of the 338 days covered by a rental guarantee. That is, the guarantee covered 365 days less 27 days of personal use. The Tax Court disagreed on the grounds that the guarantee was based on a rental period of between 142 days and 179 days and this was far below the 270 rental days needed to support his 27 personal-use days.

The Sixth Circuit allowed the loss. The $21,000 guarantee was a fair rental for the entire year based on rentals of comparable units. Although Razavi probably could have earned more than $21,000 with daily or weekly rentals, such short-term rentals also would have carried added risks and responsibilities that he was able to avoid by choosing the rent guarantee.

9.9 Allocating Expenses to Rental Days

When you rent out your home for part of the year at fair market value and also use it personally on some days during the taxable year, expenses are allocated between personal and rental use. By law, deductible expenses of renting are limited by this fraction:

$$\frac{\text{Days of fair market rental}}{\text{Total days of rental and personal use}}$$

The number of days a vacation home is held out for rent but not actually rented is not counted as rental days.

There is a conflict of opinion between the IRS and the courts over the issue of whether this formula applies also to interest and taxes. According to the courts, interest and taxes are allocated on a daily basis. Thus, if a house is rented for 61 days in the year, one-sixth of the deductible interest and taxes (61/365) is deducted first from the rental income. This rule allows a larger amount of other expenses to be deducted from rental income than is allowed under the IRS application of the formula; *see* Example 2 on the next page.

Claiming expenses if personal use bars a loss deduction. If your personal use of a residence exceeds the 14-day /10% test of *9.7*, the residence was rented for at least 15 days during the year, and the expenses allocated to rental use exceed rental income, the allocable rental expenses are deducted from rental income in a specific order:

1. The rental portion of the following expenses is fully deductible on Schedule E of Form 1040, even if the total exceeds rental income: deductible home mortgage interest *(15.1)*, real estate taxes, deductible casualty and theft losses (Chapter 18), and directly related rental expenses. Directly related rental expenses are rental expenses not related to the use or maintenance of the residence itself, such as office supplies, rental agency fees, advertising, and depreciation on office equipment used in the rental activity .
2. If there is any rental income remaining after the income is reduced by the expenses in Step 1, the balance is next offset by the rental portion of operating expenses for the residence itself, such as utilities, repairs, and insurance. Do not include depreciation on the rental part of the home in this group.
3. If any rental income remains after Step 2, depreciation on the rental portion of the residence may be deducted from the balance.

Step 1expenses, as well as the expenses from Steps 2 and 3 that offset rental income, are deducted on the applicable lines of Schedule E. Operating expenses from Step 2 and depreciation from Step 3 that exceed the balance of rental income are carried forward to the next year as rental expenses for the same property. In the next year, the carried-over expenses are deductible only to the extent of rental income from the property for that year, even if your personal use of the residence does *not* exceed the 14-day/10% test of *9.7* for that year.

If you itemize deductions, you claim the *personal-use* portion of deductible mortgage interest, real estate taxes, and casualty and theft losses on Schedule A of Form 1040.

Interest expenses. If you personally use a rental vacation home for more than the greater of 14 days and 10% of the fair market rental days *(9.7)*, the residence may be treated as a qualifying second residence under the mortgage interest rules; *see 15.1*. The interest on a qualifying second home is generally fully deductible and is not subject to disallowance under the passive activity restrictions of Chapter 10. As shown above, the portion of the deductible mortgage interest allocable to the rental portion is deducted from rental income (along with taxes) before other expenses.

EXAMPLES

1. You rent out your vacation home for 61 days in 1997, receiving rent of $2,000. You use it yourself for 61 days. You may deduct expenses only up to the amount of this income because your personal use exceeds the 14-day/10% rental test. Your

   expenses are mortgage interest of $1,600, real estate taxes of $800, and maintenance and utility costs of $1,200. Depreciation (based on 100% rental use) is $1,500. Assume the vacation home is a qualifying second home (*15.1*), so that all the interest is deductible under the mortgage interest rules. Under the IRS method, one-half of all the expenses (61 rental days divided by 122 total days of use), including the interest and taxes, are deducted in this order:

Rent income		$2,000
Less: Interest	$800	
Taxes	400	1,200
		$ 800
Less: Maintenance		600
		$ 200
Less: Depreciation		$ 200

   Under the Tax Court's method of allocating interest and taxes, one-sixth of the interest and taxes (61/365) would be deducted from rental income, rather than one-half as under the IRS method.

   The balance of the depreciation is not deductible. It may be carried forward to the following year.

   The balance of interest and taxes is deductible as itemized deductions provided you claim itemized deductions on Schedule A of Form 1040.

   If the vacation home were not a qualifying second residence under *15.1*, the interest would not be deducted with taxes from the $2,000 of rental income, but would be treated as an operating expense and deducted along with the maintenance expenses.

2. The Boltons paid interest and property taxes totaling $3,475 on their vacation home. Maintenance expenses (not including depreciation) totaled $2,693. The Boltons stayed at the home 30 days and rented it for 91 days, receiving rents of $2,700. Because the personal use for 30 days exceeded the 14-day limit, the Boltons could deduct rental expenses only up to the gross rental income of $2,700, reduced by interest and taxes allocable to rental. In figuring the amount of interest and taxes deductible from rents, they divided the number of rental days, or 91, by 365, the number of days in the year. This gave them an allocation of 25%. After subtracting $868 for interest and taxes (25% of $3,475) from rental income, they deducted $1,832 ($2,700 – $868) of maintenance expenses from rental income.

The IRS argued that 75% of the Boltons' interest and tax payments had to be allocated to the rental income. The IRS used an allocation base of 121 days of personal and rental use. Thus, the IRS allocated 75% (91/121) of the interest and taxes, or $2,606, to gross rental income of $2,700. This allocation allowed only $94 maintenance expenses to be deducted ($2,700 – $2,606).

The Tax Court sided with the Boltons and an appeals court (the Ninth Circuit) agreed. The IRS method of allocating interest and taxes to rental use is bizarre. Interest and taxes are expenses that accrue ratably over the year and are deductible even if a vacation home is not rented for a single day. Thus, the allocation to rental use should be based on a ratable portion of the annual expense by dividing the number of rental days by the number of days in a year.

The Tenth Circuit appeals court also supports the Tax Court allocation method.

9.10 Rentals Lacking Profit Motive

If you rent a residential unit for 15 days or more and a loss is not barred under the personal-use limitation of 9.7, the IRS may attempt to disallow a loss by claiming that you had no profit motive in placing the unit up for rent. If the IRS makes such an argument, you must try to prove a profit motive under 40.9. Any loss disallowed under these grounds may not be carried over to a later year.

EXAMPLES

1. *(Loss allowed.)* In 1973, Clancy purchased a house and land in a coastal resort area of California. Prior to the purchase, Clancy was told by a renting agent that he could expect reasonable income and considerable appreciation from the property. Previously, he had sold similar property in the same development at a profit. After the purchase, Clancy spent $5,000 to prepare the house for rental, and gave a rental agency the exclusive right to offer the property for rent. The house was available for rent 95% of the time in 1973, and 100% of the time in 1974. However, rentals proved disappointing, totaling only $280 in 1973 and $1,244 in 1974, despite the active efforts of the agency to rent the property. However, the house did appreciate in value and was eventually sold at a profit of $14,000. In 1973 and 1974, Clancy deducted rental expenses of approximately $21,000 which the IRS disallowed. The IRS claimed that the house was not rental property used in a business. Furthermore, as Clancy knew that he could not make a profit from the rentals, he could not be considered to hold the property for the production of income.

   The Tax Court agrees that the expenses are not deductible business expenses. But this does not mean that they are not deductible as expenses of income production. Although the rental income from the property was minimal, Clancy acquired and held the property expecting to make a profit on a sale. He had previously sold similar property at a profit and was told to expect considerable rental income as well as appreciation from the new house. Where an owner holds property, as Clancy did here, because he believed that it may appreciate in value, such property is held for the production of income. Further evidence that Clancy held the property to make a profit: He rarely used it for personal purposes and an agent actively sought to rent it.

2. *(Loss allowed.)* Nelson bought a condominium, hired a rental agent, and even advertised in the *Wall Street Journal* and *Indianapolis Star*. He also listed the unit for sale. During 1974, he was unable to rent the apartment but deducted expenses and depreciation of over $6,100, which the IRS disallowed. The IRS argued that he did not buy the unit to make a profit but to shelter substantial income from tax. The Tax Court disagreed. Although his efforts to rent were not successful in 1974, he was successful

in later years in renting the unit. He rarely visited the apartment other than to initially furnish it. When he went on vacation, he went abroad or to other vacation spots.

3. *(Loss disallowed.)* The Lindows purchased a condominium which they rented out during the prime winter rental season. However, over an eight-year period their expenses consistently exceeded rental income. The Tax Court agreed with the IRS that expenses in excess of rental income were not deductible. Substantial, repeated losses, even after the initial years of operation, indicate that the operation was not primarily profit-oriented. The rental return during the prime rental season could not return a profit. Even if the condominium were fully rented for the entire prime rental season, annual claimed expenses would exceed rent income. The couple also used the unit for several months and intended to live there on retirement. They did not consider putting the unit up for sale with an agent. Finally, that they had detailed records of income and expenses did not prove a business venture. Records, regardless of how detailed, are insufficient to permit the deduction of what are essentially personal expenses.

IRS may challenge losses claimed on temporary rental before sale. If you are unable to sell your home and must move, it may be advisable to put it up for rent. This way you may be able to deduct maintenance expenses and depreciation on the unit even if it remains vacant. However, the IRS has disallowed loss deductions for rentals preceding a sale on the ground that there was no "profit motive" for the rental under the rules of *40.9.* Courts have allowed loss deductions in certain cases.

EXAMPLES

1. The IRS and Tax Court disallowed a loss deduction for rental expenses under the "profit-motive rules" *(40.9)* where a principal residence was rented for 10 months until it could be sold. According to the Tax Court, the temporary rental did not convert the residence to rental property. Since the sales effort was primary, there was no profit motive for the rental. Thus, no loss could be claimed; rental expenses were deductible only to the extent of rental income. The favorable side of the Tax

   Court position: Since the residence was not converted to rental property, the owners could defer tax on the gain from the sale by buying a new home. An appeals court reversed the Tax Court and allowed both tax deferral and a loss deduction. The rental loss was allowed since the old home was actually rented for a fair rental price. Furthermore, the owners had moved and could not return to the old home, which was rented almost continuously until sold.

2. In 1976, a couple bought a condo apartment in Pompano Beach, Florida. In 1983, they decided to move and listed the unit for either sale or rent with a local real estate broker. Sale of the unit was difficult because of the saturation of the Florida real estate market. Rental of the unit was also difficult because the condominium association's rules barred the rental of condominium units on a seasonal basis. The unit remained unrented until it was sold in 1986 for a substantial gain. In 1984, the couple deducted a $9,576 rental loss ($7,596 for maintenance expenses and $1,980 for depreciation). The IRS disallowed the deduction as not incurred in a bona fide rental activity. The Tax Court allowed the deduction. The couple made an honest and reasonable effort to rent the condominium. Lack of rental income was caused by a slack rental market and the condominium association rules prohibiting short-term rentals.

 Planning Reminder

Passive Income Exception
Certain working oil and gas interests are exempt from the passive activity loss restrictions; *see 10.10.*

Royalty Income and Deductions

9.11 Reporting Royalty Income

Royalties are payment for use of patents or copyrights or for the use and exhaustion of mineral properties. Royalties are taxable as ordinary income and are reported on Schedule E (Form 1040). Depletion deductions relating to the royalties are also reported on Schedule E. If you own an operating oil, gas, or mineral interest, or are a self-employed writer, investor, or artist, you report royalty income, expenses, and depletion on Schedule C.

Examples of Royalty Income

License fees received for use, manufacture, or sale of a patented article.

Renting fees received from patents, copyrights, and depletable assets (such as oil wells).

Authors' royalties including advance royalties if not a loan.

Royalties for musical compositions, works of art, etc.

Proceeds of sale of part of your rights in an artistic composition or book—for example, sale of motion picture or television rights.

Royalties from oil, gas, or other similar interests; *see 9.16.* To have a royalty, you must retain an economic interest in the minerals deposited in the land which you have leased to the producer. You usually have a royalty when payments are based on the amount of minerals produced. However, if you are paid regardless of the minerals produced, you have a sale which is taxed as capital gain if the proceeds exceed the basis of the transferred property interest. Bonuses and advance royalties which are paid to you before the production of minerals are taxable as royalty income and are entitled to an allowance for depletion. However, bonuses and advanced royalties for gas and oil wells and geothermal deposits are not treated as gross income for purposes of calculating percentage depletion. If the lease is terminated without production and you received a bonus or advanced royalty, you report as income previously claimed depletion deductions. You increase the basis of your property by the restored depletion deductions.

9.12 Production Costs of Books and Creative Properties

Freelance authors, artists, and photographers may deduct their costs of producing original works in the years that the expenses are paid or incurred. The uniform capitalization rules that generally apply to property that you produce *(see 40.2)* do not apply.

You qualify for current expense deductions if you are self-employed and you *personally create* literary manuscripts, musical or dance scores, paintings, pictures, sculptures, drawings, cartoons, graphic designs, original print editions, photographs, or photographic negatives or transparencies. However, the exception to the uniform capitalization rules does not apply, and thus current deductions are not allowed for expenses relating to motion picture films, videotapes, printing, photographic plates, or similar items.

If you conduct business as an owner-employee of a personal service corporation, and you are a qualifying author, artist, or photographer, the corporation may claim current deductions related to your expenses in producing books or other eligible creative works. Substantially all of the corporation's stock must be owned by you and your relatives.

Hobby loss restrictions. Authors and artists with expenses exceeding income may be barred by the IRS from claiming loss deductions; *see 40.9.*

9.13 Deducting the Cost of Patents or Copyrights

If you create an artistic work or invention for which you get a government patent or copyright, you may depreciate your costs over the life of the patent or copyright. Basis for depreciation includes all expenses which you are required to capitalize in connection with creating the work such as the cost of drawings, experimental models, stationery, and supplies; travel expenses to obtain material for a book; fees to counsel; government charges for patent or copyright; and litigation costs in protecting or perfecting title.

If you purchased the patent or artistic creation, depreciate your cost over the remaining life of the patent or copyright. If your cost for a patent is payable annually as a fixed percentage of the revenue derived from use of the patent, the depreciation deduction equals the royalty paid or incurred for that year. However, if a copyright or patent is acquired in connection with the acquisition of a business, the cost is amortizable over a 15-year period as a Section 197 intangible; *see 42.13.*

If you inherited the patent or rights to an artistic creation, your cost is the fair market value either at the time of death of the person from whom you inherited it *(5.21)* or the alternate valuation date if elected by the executor *(39.4).* You get this cost basis even if the decedent paid nothing for it. Figure your depreciation by dividing the fair market value by the number of years of remaining life.

If your patent or copyright becomes valueless, you may deduct your unrecovered cost or other basis in the year it became worthless.

9.14 Intangible Drilling Costs

Intangible drilling and development costs include wages, fuel, repairs, hauling, and supplies incident to and necessary for the preparation and drilling of wells for the production of oil or gas, and geothermal wells. For wells you are developing in the United States, you can elect to deduct the costs currently as business expenses or treat them as capital expenses subject to depreciation or depletion.

Electing current deductions. The election applies only to costs of drilling and developing items that do not have a salvage value. You must make this election by deducting the expenses on your income tax return for the first tax year in which you pay or incur the costs.

Tax-shelter investors may deduct prepayments of drilling expenses only if the well is "spudded" within 90 days after the close of the taxable year in which the prepayment is made. The prepayment must also have a business purpose, not be a deposit, and not materially distort income. The investor's deduction is limited to his or her cash investment in the tax shelter. For purposes of this limitation, an investor's cash investment includes loans that are not secured by his or her shelter interest or the shelter's assets and loans that are not arranged by the organizer or promoter. If the above tests are not met, a deduction may be claimed only as actual drilling services are provided.

Recapture of intangible drilling costs for oil, gas, geothermal, or mineral property. Upon the disposition of oil, gas, geothermal, or other mineral property placed in service after 1986, ordinary income treatment applies to previously claimed deductions for intangible drilling and development costs for oil, gas, and geothermal wells, and to mineral development and exploration costs. Depletion deductions under *9.15* are also generally subject to this ordinary income treatment upon disposition of the property.

For oil, gas, or geothermal property placed in service before 1987, ordinary income treatment applies on the disposition of a working or operating interest to the extent that intangible drilling and development cost deductions exceeded what would have been allowed if the costs had been deducted through cost depletion. Recapture for geothermal property applies only to wells commenced after September 30, 1978.

AMT and intangible drilling costs. If you are an independent oil or gas producer or royalty owner, intangible drilling costs for oil and gas production are not treated as tax preference items for purposes of alternative minimum tax (AMT). However, the reduction in your AMT income from not treating intangible drilling costs as a tax preference is limited. The reduction may not exceed 40% of your AMT income, figured as if excess intangible drilling costs were still a tax preference item and without regard to any AMT net operating loss deduction; *see* the instructions to Form 6251.

9.15 Depletion Deduction

Properties subject to depletion deductions are mines, oil and gas wells, timber, and exhaustible natural deposits.

Two methods of computing depletion are: (1) cost depletion; and (2) percentage depletion. If you are allowed to compute under either method, you must use the one that produces the *larger* deduction. In most cases, this will be percentage depletion. For timber, you must use cost depletion.

Cost depletion. The cost depletion of minerals is computed as follows: (1) divide the total number of units (tons, barrels) remaining in the deposit to be mined into the adjusted basis of the property; (2) multiply the unit rate found in Step 1 by the number of units for which payment is received during the taxable year if you are on the cash basis, or the units sold if you are on the accrual basis.

Adjusted basis is the original cost of the property, less depletion allowed, whether computed on the percentage or cost depletion method. It does not include nonmineral property such as mining equipment. Adjusted basis may not be less than zero.

Timber depletion is based on the cost of timber (or other basis in the owner's hands) and does not include any part of the cost of land. Depletion takes place when standing timber is cut. Depletion must be computed by the cost method, not by the percentage method. However, instead of claiming the cost depletion method, you may elect to treat the cutting of timber as a sale subject to capital gain or loss treatment. For further details, *see* IRS Publication 535.

Percentage depletion. Percentage depletion is based on a certain percentage rate applied to annual gross income derived from the resource. In determining gross income for percentage depletion, do not include any lease bonuses, advance royalties, or any other amount payable without regard to production. A deduction for percentage depletion is allowed even if the basis of the property is already fully recovered by prior depletion deductions. The percentage to be applied depends upon the mineral involved; the range is from 5% up to 22%. For example, the maximum 22% depletion deduction applies to sulphur, uranium, and U.S. deposits of lead, zinc, nickel, mica, and asbestos. A 15% depletion percentage applies to U.S. deposits of gold, silver, copper, iron ore, and shale. For timber, cost depletion must be used.

Taxable income limit. For properties other than oil and gas, the percentage depletion deduction *may not exceed* 50% of taxable income from the property computed without the depletion deduction. In computing the 50% limitation, a net operating loss deduction is not deducted from gross income. A 100% taxable income limit applies to oil and gas properties; *see 9.16.*

Note: As an independent oil or gas producer, or royalty owner, you do not have to treat a portion of your depletion deduction as a preference item for AMT purposes; *see* Chapter 23.

Oil and gas property. Percentage depletion for oil and gas wells was repealed as of January 1, 1975, except for the following exemptions: (1) small independent producers and royalty owners; and (2) for gas well production. *See 9.16* for these oil and gas percentage depletion exemptions.

9.16 Oil and Gas Percentage Depletion

Small independent producers and royalty owners generally are allowed to deduct percentage depletion at a 15% rate for domestic oil and gas production. However, a higher rate may be allowed for qualifying "marginal" production, as discussed on the next page. The deduction is subject to a taxable income limit.

The 15% rate applies to a small producer exemption which equals the gross income from a maximum daily average of 1,000 barrels of oil or 6 million cubic feet of natural gas, or a combination of both. Gross income from the property does not include advanced royalties or lease bonuses that are payable without regard to the actual production.

The depletable natural gas quantity depends on an election made annually by independent producers or royalty owners to apply part of their 1,000-barrel-per-day oil limitation to natural gas. The depletable quantity of natural gas is 6,000 cubic feet times the barrels of depletable oil for which an election has been made. The election is made on an original or amended return or on a claim for credit or refund. For example, if your average daily production is 1,200 barrels of oil and 6.2 million cubic feet of natural gas, your maximum depletable limit is 1,000 barrels of oil, which you may split between the oil and gas. You could claim depletion for 500 barrels of oil per day and for 3 million cubic feet of gas per day: 3 million cubic feet of gas is the equivalent of the remaining 500 barrels of oil limit (500 barrels × 6,000 cubic feet depletable gas quantity equals 3 million cubic feet of gas).

Transferees who received their interest in a "proven" oil or gas property after October 11, 1990 are allowed percentage depletion under the regular rules.

Transferees receiving "proven" properties after 1974 and before October 12, 1990, are not allowed percentage depletion *unless* the transfer was made because of the death of the prior owner, a tax-free transfer to a controlled corporation, a transfer between commonly-controlled corporations, or changes in beneficiaries of a trust where the changes are due to births, adoptions, or deaths within a single family.

Ineligible retailers and refiners. The small producer exemption is not allowed to any producer who owns or controls a retail outlet for the sale of oil, natural gas, or petroleum products. It is also not allowed to a refiner who refines more than 50,000 barrels of oil on any one day of the taxable year; the limit is based on inputs of crude oil into the refinery process, rather than outputs. A taxpayer is not treated as a retailer where gross sales of oil and gas products are less than $5 million in any one year or if all sales of oil or natural gas products occur outside the United States, and none of the taxpayer's domestic production is exported. Bulk sales of oil or natural gas to industrial or utility customers are not to be treated as retail sales.

Figuring average daily domestic production. Average daily production is figured by dividing your aggregate production during the taxable year by the number of days in the taxable year. If you hold a partial interest in the production (including a partnership interest), production rate is found by multiplying total production of such property by your income percentage participation in such property.

The production over the entire year is averaged regardless of when production actually occurred. If average daily production for the year exceeds the 1,000-barrel or 6-million-cubic-feet limit, the exemption must be allocated among all the properties in which you have an interest.

Taxable income limits on percentage depletion. The percentage depletion deduction for a small producer or royalty owner may not exceed the *lesser* of (1) 100% of the taxable income from the property before the depletion allowance and (2) 65% of your taxable income from all sources computed without regard to the depletion deduction allowed under the small producer's exemption, any net operating loss carry-back, and any capital loss carry-back.

Under the 1997 Tax Act, The above 100% limit is suspended for production from marginal production properties during taxable years starting after 1997 and before 2000.

Limitations where family members or related businesses own interests. The daily exemption rate is allocated among members of the same family in proportion to their respective production of oil. Similar allocation is required where business entities are under common control. This affects interests owned by you, your spouse, and minor children; by corporations, estates, and trusts in which 50% of the beneficial interest is owned by the same or related persons; and by a corporation which is a member of the same controlled group.

Higher depletion for marginal production. Independent producers and royalty owners are allowed a higher depletion rate for *marginal production,* defined as oil or natural gas from "stripper well property" or property producing substantially all "heavy" oil. A stripper well property is one from which average daily production, divided by the number of all producing wells on the property, is 15 or less "barrel equivalents." A barrel equivalent is a barrel of oil or 6,000 cubic feet of natural gas.

The 15% rate is increased by 1% for each whole dollar that the "reference price" (the average annual wellhead price as estimated by the IRS) of domestic crude oil for the previous year was below $20 per barrel. For example, the IRS determined that the reference price for 1996 was $18.46, so the allowable depletion rate for qualifying production in 1997 is 16% ($20.00 – $18.46 = $1.54, rounded down to 1.00, is the 1% increase to the 15% floor).

The higher rate applies only up to the maximum depletable limit, which is the average daily production of up to 1,000 barrels a day of oil, or 6 million cubic feet of gas. If the taxpayer has production from "marginal properties" eligible for the higher depletion rate, as well as production from other properties subject to the 15% rate, the marginal production is taken into account first in applying the 1,000-barrel or 6-million-cubic-feet overall limit. However, a special election may be made to prorate the overall limit among all production, whether marginal or non-marginal.

Chapter 10

Loss Restrictions: Passive Activities and At-Risk Limits

The passive activity law was legislated to discourage tax-shelter investments, but its reach went beyond tax shelters to cover all real estate investors and persons who invest in businesses as "silent partners" or who are not involved full time in the business. The passive activity law prevents an investor from deducting what the law defines as a passive loss from salary, self-employment income, interest, dividends, or retirement income. Such losses are deductible only from income from other passive activities. Losses disallowed by the passive activity rules are suspended and carried forward to later taxable years and become deductible only when passive income is realized or substantially all of the activity is sold.

Casualty and theft losses are not passive losses unless they are of the type usually occurring in a business, such as shoplifting theft losses.

On your tax return, passive income items and allowable deductible items are reported as regular income and deductions. For example, rental income and allowable deductions are reported on Schedule E. However, before you make these entries, you may have to prepare Form 8582, which identifies your passive income and losses and helps you to determine whether passive loss items are deductible.

10.1 Rental Activities

Rental income and losses are automatically treated as passive unless they are earned or incurred by a professional real estate person *(10.3)* or the rentals are considered by law to be business activity as discussed below. Even where rental income or loss is earned by a professional or is considered to be business income, the passive loss restrictions may still apply if the material participation activity rules of *10.6* are not met.

If you are not a real estate professional and have real estate rental losses, you may be able to deduct without restriction a loss of up to $25,000 under the rules of *10.2*.

The passive activity rules apply to rental income and losses from rentals of apartments and commercial office space (whether long- or short-term); long-term rentals of office equipment, automobiles, and/or a vessel under a bareboat charter or a plane under a dry lease (no pilot or captain and no fuel); and net-leased property. A property is under a net lease if the deductions (other than rents and reimbursed amounts) are less than 15% of rental income or where the lessor is guaranteed a specific return or is guaranteed against loss of income.

Rentals treated as business activity. Although rental activities are generally treated as "passive," the following six activities are excluded from the category of rental activity. However, income or loss from these activities may still be treated as passive income or loss if you fail to meet one of the business material participation tests of *10.6*.

1. **Incidental rental of investment property, property used in a business, or property rented to an employee for the convenience of an employer.** The rental of investment property is treated as a business activity if the principal purpose for holding the property during the tax year is to realize gain from its appreciation, and the gross rental income from the property for the tax year is less than 2% of the lower of the unadjusted basis of the property and fair market value of the property. The rental of business property is treated as incidental if the property was (1) predominantly used in a business during the tax year or during at least two of the five tax years that immediately precede the tax year and (2) gross rental income from the property for the tax year is less than 2% of the lesser of the unadjusted basis of the property and the fair market value of the property.

EXAMPLE

Kyle Gail owns unimproved land with a fair market value of $400,000 and an unadjusted basis of $300,000. He holds it for the principal purpose of realizing gain from its appreciation. To help reduce the cost of holding the land, he leases it to a rancher for grazing purposes at an annual rental of $3,500. The gross rental income of $3,500 is less than 2% of the lower of the fair market value and the unadjusted basis of the land. The rental of the land is not a rental activity.

2. **The average period of customer use of the property is seven days or less.** You figure the average for the year by dividing the aggregate number of days in all rental periods that end during the tax year by the number of rentals. Each period during which a customer has a continuous or recurring right to use the property is treated as a separate rental.

   This exception covers short-term rentals of vacation units, autos, video cassettes, tuxedos, and hotel and motel rooms.

EXAMPLE

The Toups purchased a cottage in Callaway Gardens, a vacation resort south of Atlanta, Georgia. The unit was rented for short-term periods of seven days or less during the year to resort guests. The resort's operator was the sole managing and rental agent. Over a three-year period, they deducted net losses of $46,848. The IRS disallowed the losses as passive activity losses. The Toups argued that they were not passive investors but material participants in the operation. They claimed they spent more than 300 hours each year preparing an annual budget and cash flow analysis and meeting with other owners to set rentals and inspect the grounds.

The Tax Court sided with the IRS. The losses were passive because the Toups did not materially participate in the resort operation. They had nothing to do with running the resort on a day-to-day basis. Their activity was merely that of investors.

Planning Reminder

Vacation Home Rentals

If you rent out a vacation unit for an average rental period of seven days or less at a loss, the loss is treated as a business loss deductible from nonpassive income if you meet the material participation tests of *10.6*. If you do not materially participate, the loss is not deductible. The loss does not qualify for the up-to-$25,000 rental loss allowance discussed in *10.2* because the property is not treated as rental property.

3. **The average period of customer use of the property is more than seven days but is 30 days or less, and you provide significant personal services.** Personal services include only services performed by individuals and do not include (a) services necessary to permit the lawful use of the property; (b) construction or repair services that extend the useful life of the property for a period substantially longer than the average period of customer use; and (c) services that are provided with long-term rentals of high-grade commercial or residential real property such as cleaning and maintenance of common areas, routine repairs, trash collection, elevator service, and security guards.

   Note: For purposes of Exceptions 2 and 3, if more than one class of property is rented as part of the same activity, average period of customer use is figured separately for each class. The average period of customer use (as explained in Exception 2) is multiplied by the ratio of gross rental income from that class to the total rental income from the activity; *see* the Form 8582 instructions.

4. **Regardless of the average period of customer use, extraordinary personal services are provided so that rental is incidental.** This applies to institutions providing hospital patients room and board.

5. **Providing property to a partnership or S corporation which is not engaged in rentals.** If you own an interest in a partnership or S corporation and you contributed property to it as an owner, the contributed property is not considered a rental activity. For example, if as a partner you contribute property to a partnership, your distributive share of partnership income will not be considered as income from a rental activity. However, this exception will not apply if the partnership is engaged in a rental activity.

6. **The property is generally allowed for the nonexclusive use of customers during fixed business hours** such as operating a golf course. The customers are treated as licensees, not lessees.

Grouping rental and nonrental business activities. Where you conduct rental as well as nonrental business activities, you may not group a rental activity with a nonrental activity, unless one of the activities is considered insubstantial in relation to the other. No guidelines are provided for determining what is "substantial" or "insubstantial."

Under an exception, a rental of property to a business may be grouped together with the business, although one activity is insubstantial to the other, provided each business owner has the same proportionate ownership in the rental activity.

Real property rentals and personal property rentals. An activity involving the rental of realty and one involving the rental of personal property may not be treated as a single activity, unless the personal property is provided in connection with the real property or the realty is provided in connection with the personal property.

10.2 Rental Real Estate Loss Allowance of up to $25,000

If you are not a real estate professional *(10.3)* but perform some management role in a real estate rental venture, you may deduct up to $25,000 of a real estate rental loss against your regular, nonpassive income such as wages. The loss allowance is claimed on Form 8582. The allowance is phased out if your modified adjusted gross income is between $100,000 and $150,000.

The allowance applies only to real estate rentals not excluded from the rental category by the rules of *10.1*. For example, short-term vacation home rentals averaging seven days or less do *not* qualify for the allowance. The allowance also does not apply to any rentals of equipment or other personal property.

A trust may not qualify for the $25,000 allowance. Thus, you may not circumvent the $25,000 ceiling or multiply the number of $25,000 allowances by transferring rental real properties to one or more trusts. However, an estate may qualify for the allowance if the decedent actively participated in the operation. The estate is treated as an active participant for two years following the death of the owner.

Married filing separately. If you file separately and at any time during the taxable year live with your spouse, you may not claim the allowance. If you are married but live apart from your spouse for the entire year and file a separate return, the $25,000 allowance and the adjusted gross income phase-out range are reduced by 50%. Thus, the maximum allowance on your separate return is $12,500 and this amount is phased out by 50% of AGI over $50,000. Therefore, if your AGI exceeds $75,000, no allowance is allowed.

Active participation test must be met. To qualify for the allowance, you must meet an *active participation test.* Having an agent manage your property does not prevent you from meeting the test, but you must show that you or your spouse participates in management decisions, such as selecting tenants, setting rental terms, and reviewing expenses. The IRS may not recognize your

Planning Reminder

Rental of Personal Residence

Renting a personal residence is not treated as a passive rental activity if you personally use the home for more than the greater of (1) 14 days and (2) 10% of the days the home is rented for a fair rental amount. On Schedule E, you may claim a full deduction for the rental portion of real estate taxes and mortgage interest, assuming the home is a principal residence or qualifying second home under the mortgage interest rules *(15.1)*.

See 9.9 for limitations on deductions of other rental expenses.

activity as meeting the test if you merely ratify your manager's decisions. You (together with your spouse) must also have at least a 10% interest in the property. Limited partners are not considered active participants and do not qualify for the allowance.

If a decedent actively participated in property held by an estate, the estate is deemed to actively participate for the two years following the death of the taxpayer.

EXAMPLES
1. You live in New York and own a condominium in Florida that you rent through an agent. You set the rental terms and give final approval to any rental arrangement. You also have final approval over any repairs ordered by the agent. You are an active participant and may claim the $25,000 rental allowance.
2. A married couple who owned a time-share interest in an ocean-front condominium rented the condo during their allotted period to vacationers. They claimed a rental loss which the IRS held did not qualify for the up-to-$25,000 allowance. Since the average rental period for their unit was seven days or less, the rentals were excluded from the category of rental activity; see 10.1.

Figuring the $25,000 allowance. First match income and loss from all of your rental real estate activities in which you actively participate. A net loss from these activities is then applied to net passive income (if any) from other activities to determine the $25,000 allowance. Gains from pre-1987 installment sales are passive income if the sold property was from an activity that would have been considered passive had the passive activity rules been in effect before 1987. If you rent out a personal residence, rental income or loss may be exempt from the passive activity rules; see the Planning Reminder on page 212. The allowance may not be used against carryover losses from prior taxable years when you were not an active participant.

EXAMPLE
David Chung has a $90,000 salary, $15,000 income from a limited partnership, and a $26,000 loss from rental real estate in which he actively participated. The $26,000 loss is first reduced by the $15,000 of passive income. The remaining balance of the $11,000 rental loss is deducted from the salary income.

Phaseout of the $25,000 allowance. For purposes of the allowance phaseout, *modified adjusted gross income* (MAGI) is adjusted gross income shown on your return, but you should disregard:

Any passive activity income or loss.
Any loss allowed under *10.3* for real estate professionals.
Taxable Social Security and railroad retirement payments (Chapter 34). For example, if your adjusted gross income on Form 1040 is $90,000, and that includes $5,000 of taxable Social Security benefits, your modified adjusted gross income is $85,000.
Deductible IRA contributions (Chapter 8).
The deduction on Form 1040 for one-half of self-employment tax liability (Chapter 46).
Excluded interest on U.S. Savings Bonds used for paying tuition in the year the bonds are redeemed. If you are allowed to exclude the interest from income for regular tax purposes (Chapter 33) the interest must still be included for purposes of the allowance phaseout.
Employer-provided adoption assistance that is a tax-free fringe benefit (Chapter 3). The assistance must be included in MAGI for purposes of applying the allowance phase-out rule.

A rental loss which is carried over because it exceeds the allowance may be deductible in a later year if you continue to meet the active participant rule.

EXAMPLES
1. In 1997, Liz Blake had $120,000 in salary, $5,000 of partnership income from a limited partnership and a $31,000 loss from a rental building in which she actively participates. She may deduct only $15,000 of the rental loss. The remaining $11,000 must be carried over to 1998. Her deduction and carryover are computed as follows:

Modified adjusted gross income	$120,000
Less: amount not subject to phaseout	100,000
Amount subject to phaseout	$ 20,000
Phase-out percentage	50%

 Filing Tip

Rental Allowance Based on Income
The rental loss allowance is phased out when your modified adjusted gross income is over $100,000. For every dollar of income over $100,000, the loss allowance is reduced by 50 cents. When your modified adjusted gross income reaches $150,000, the allowance is completely phased out. An explanation of modified adjusted gross income and an example of how the phaseout works is under the heading "Phaseout of the $25,000 allowance" on this page.

IF MODIFIED AGI IS	LOSS ALLOWANCE IS
Up to $100,000	$25,000
110,000	20,000
120,000	15,000
130,000	10,000
140,000	5,000
150,000 or more	0

 Planning Reminder

Proving Management Activites
To take advantage of the $25,000 loan allowance, make sure you have proof of active management, such as approving leases and repairs.

Portion of allowance phased out	$ 10,000
Maximum rental allowance offset	$ 25,000
Less: Amount phased out	10,000
Deductible rental loss allowance offset in 1997	$ 15,000
Passive loss from rental real estate	$ 31,000
Less: Passive income from partnership	5,000
Passive activity loss	$ 26,000
Less: Deductible rental loss allowance in 1997	15,000
Carryover loss to 1998	$ 11,000

2. In 1998, Liz's modified adjusted gross income is below the phase-out range and she continues to actively participate in the rental building, which incurred a loss of $5,000. Under the allowance, she may deduct a rental loss of $16,000 (the current loss plus the carryover loss).

Real estate allowance for tax credits.   On Form 8582-CR, a deduction equivalent of up to $25,000 may allow a credit that otherwise would be disallowed. You must meet the active participation test in the year the credit arose. The $25,000 allowance is generally subject to the regular MAGI phase-out rule.

To claim low-income housing and rehabilitation credits *(9.8)*, you need not meet the active participant test. Furthermore, for rehabilitation credits, and credits for low-income housing property placed in service before 1990, the phaseout for the $25,000 allowance starts at MAGI of $200,000 ($100,000 if married filing separately and living apart the entire year); thus, the deduction equivalent is completely disallowed when MAGI reaches $250,000. The phaseout is figured on Form 8582-CR. There is no MAGI phaseout for low-income housing property placed in service after 1989, unless you have a pass-through interest in a partnership or S corporation that you acquired before 1990. No low-income housing credit may be claimed for an investment exempted from the passive activity rules under *10.14*.

The *deduction equivalent* of a credit is the amount which, if allowed as a deduction, would reduce your tax by an amount equal to the credit. For example, a tax credit of $1,000 for a taxpayer in the 28% bracket equals a deduction of $3,571 and would come within the $25,000 allowance provided you actively participated. In the 28% bracket, the equivalent of a $25,000 deduction is a tax credit of $7,000 ($25,000 × 28%). Thus, if you have a rehabilitation credit of $8,000 and you are in the 28% bracket, the $25,000 allowance may allow you to claim $7,000 of the credit, while $1,000 of the credit would be carried forward to the following year.

If in one year you have both losses and tax credits, the $25,000 allowance applies first to the losses, then to tax credits from rental real estate with active participation, then to tax credits for rehabilitation or low-income housing placed in service before 1990, and finally to tax credits for low-income housing placed in service after 1989.

The allowance and net operating losses.   If losses are allowed by the $25,000 allowance but your nonpassive income and other income are less than the loss, the balance of the loss may be treated as a net operating loss and may be carried back and forward; *see 40.17* for further details.

10.3   Real Estate Professionals

You may be able to treat rental real estate income and loss as nonpassive income and loss by meeting the following two tests:

Test 1. Your personal services in real estate businesses meet the 50% and 750 hours tests explained below.

Test 2. You materially participate in the rental real estate activity. Here, you consider only services in the rental activity. You may not combine hours of participation in nonrental activities with rental real estate activities to meet this test. To meet the material participation requirement, you may make an election to aggregate all of your rental real estate activities.

The material participation tests applied to real estate businesses and real estate rental activities are the same as applied to non-real estate businesses as explained at *10.6*.

Qualifying as a real estate professional (Test 1).   You must meet the following two activity tests:

1. More than 50% of your personal services in all of your businesses must be performed in real property businesses in which you materially participate *(10.6)*. For this purpose, a real prop-

erty business means any real property development, redevelopment, construction, reconstruction, acquisition, conversion, rental operation, management, leasing, or brokerage trade or business. Real estate financing is not included; and

2. More than 750 hours of your services are in real property businesses in which you materially participate *(10.6)*.

For a married couple filing jointly, both the "50% of services test" and the "750 hours test" must be met by one of the spouses individually, without regard to the other spouse's services, although the other spouse's participation counts in determining whether you materially participate in the real property businesses under Test 2.

Personal services performed as an employee are not treated as performed in a real estate business unless you are considered a "more than 5% owner" in the employer. That is, you must own more than 5% of the outstanding stock or more than 5% of total combined voting powers of all stock issued by the corporation. In a noncorporate employer such as a partnership, you must own more than a 5% capital or profit interest.

A closely held C corporation qualifies under the real estate professional rules if in a taxable year more than 50% of the gross receipts of the corporation are from a real property business in which the corporation materially participates under the rules at *10.15*.

Rental real estate activity material participation (Test 2).   Generally, each interest in rental real estate property is treated as a separate activity. However, you may elect to treat all of your interests as one rental activity as discussed below. If, under the rules of *10.1*, you group a rental real estate activity with a business activity, that rental activity is not treated as rental real estate for purposes of the real estate professional rules.

Attorneys who specialize in real estate practice while participating in a rental business may not treat the legal practice as material participation for purposes of qualifying as real estate professionals.

Election to aggregate rental real estate activities.   If in a prior year rental real estate activities were treated separately, you may elect to aggregate activities for any year you qualify as a real estate professional by attaching a statement to your original tax return for that year. The statement must contain a declaration that you are a qualifying real estate professional and are treating all of your rental real estate activities as a single activity under Internal Revenue Code Section 469(c)(7)(A). The election is binding for all future years in which you qualify as a real estate professional, even if there are intervening years in which you do not qualify. In the nonqualifying years, the election has no effect. You may not revoke the election in a later year unless there has been a material change in circumstances that you explain in a statement attached to your original return for the year of revocation. That the election no longer gives you a tax advantage is not a basis for a revocation.

If the election to aggregate is made, prior-year suspended losses from any of the aggregated rental real estate activities may be used to offset net income in the current year from the aggregated activity, regardless of which of the rental activities produced the income.

Rental loss allowance may apply to nonqualifying rental activity.   A real estate professional may also claim the $25,000 rental loss allowance. For example, you are a real estate professional and meet the material participation test for one rental real estate activity but not for another and do not elect to aggregate. Losses from the nonqualifying activity qualify for the rental allowance. Furthermore, suspended prior year losses from the qualifying activity may also be deductible under the rental loss allowance, as illustrated in the following Example.

 Planning Reminder

Tax Break for Real Estate Professionals

Proving professional status allows you to avoid passive loss limitations. You improve your ability to meet the material participation tests of *10.6* by aggregating your rental real estate activities. However, you may not want to aggregate activities if you have passive losses from non–real estate activities and have rental income from an operation which if treated as passive income could be offset by the losses.

Also be aware that if you elect to group all of your rental real estate activities as one activity and later sell one of the rental properties, you will probably be unable to deduct suspended losses from that property because of the rule that requires "substantially all" of your interest in an activity (here, the combined activity) to be disposed of in order to deduct suspended losses; *see 10.13*.

EXAMPLE

Jane Morton owns a rental building in Manhattan and a rental building in Newark. In 1997, she qualifies as a real estate professional. She does not elect to treat the two buildings as one activity. She materially participates in the operations of the Manhattan building, which has $100,000 of disallowed passive losses from prior years and a $20,000 passive loss for 1997. She does not materially participate in the operation of the Newark building, which has $40,000 of rental income for 1997. Jane also has $50,000 of income from other nonpassive sources.

The $20,000 loss from the Manhattan building is treated as nonpassive and offsets $20,000 of the $50,000 nonpassive income from other sources.

Jane can also use $40,000 of the $100,000 prior year suspended losses from the Manhattan building to offset the $40,000 of passive income from the Newark building in 1997. Of the $60,000 remaining suspended loss, $25,000 may be deducted under the rental loss allowance.

The rental loss allowance is deducted from the $30,000 of remaining nonpassive income, leaving Jane with $5,000 of nonpassive income for 1997. The balance of suspended losses of $35,000 ($60,000 – $25,000 rental allowance) may be used in 1998 to offset income from the Newark building or passive income from other sources.

Interests in S corporations and partnerships. Your interest in rental real estate held by a partnership or an S corporation is treated as a single interest in rental real estate if the entity grouped its rental real estate as one rental activity. If not, each rental real estate activity of the entity is treated as a separate interest in rental real estate. However, you may elect to treat all interests in rental real estate, including the rental real estate interests held by an S corporation or partnership, as a single rental real estate activity.

If you hold a fifty-percent or greater interest in the capital, income, gain, loss, deduction, or credit in a partnership or S corporation for the taxable year, each interest in rental real estate held by the entity is treated as a separate interest in rental real estate, regardless of the entity's grouping of activities. However, you may elect to treat all interests in rental real estate, including your share of the rental real estate interests held by the entities, as a single rental real estate activity.

Limited partners. Generally, a person who has a limited partnership interest in rental real estate must establish material participation by participating for more than 500 hours during the year or meeting Test 5 or Test 6 at *10.6*. This material participation rule also generally applies if an election is made to aggregate limited partnership interests in rental real estate with other rental real estate interests. However, these more stringent rules may be avoided if less than 10% of the gross rental income for the taxable year from all rental real estate activities is attributed to limited partnership interests. In such a case, you may make the election to aggregate all rental real estate activities and determine material participation under any of the seven tests of *10.6*.

10.4 Participation May Avoid Passive Loss Restrictions

To avoid passive activity treatment of income and loss from a business investment, you must show material participation in that activity. The word "activity" does not necessarily relate to one specific business. If you invest in several businesses, you may be able to treat all or some of those activities as one activity or treat each separately.

Determining aggregate or separate treatment for your activities is discussed at *10.5* and material participation tests are discussed at *10.6*.

For a rental activity, material participation tests apply only if you are trying to qualify for the passive activity exception for real estate professionals at *10.3*. For other rental real estate operators or investors, an "active" participation test which requires only certain management duties may allow you to deduct rental losses of up to $25,000; *see 10.2*.

10.5 Classifying Business Activities as One or Several

If you are in more than one activity, determining aggregate or separate treatment is important for:

Deducting suspended losses when you dispose of an activity. If the activity is considered separate from the others, you may deduct a suspended loss incurred from that activity when you dispose of it. If it is not separate from the others, the suspended loss is deductible only if you dispose of substantially all of your investment; *see 10.13*.

Applying the material participation rules of *10.6*. If activities are separate and apart from each other, the material participation tests are applied to each activity separately. If the activities are aggregated as one activity, material participation in one activity applies to all.

Earmarking a business activity. You may use any reasonable method under the facts and circumstances of your situation to determine if several business activities should be grouped together or treated separately. To be grouped together, the IRS says that the activities should be "an appropriate economic unit" for measuring gain or loss. For making this determination, the IRS sets these general guidelines: (1) similarities and differences in types of business; (2) the extent of common control; (3) geographic location; (4) the extent of common ownership; and (5) interdependencies between the activities. Interdependency is measured by the extent to which several business activities buy or sell among themselves, use the same products or services, have the same customers and employees, or use a single set of books and records.

Caution

Consistent treatment required

Once you treat activities separately or group them together as a single activity, the IRS generally requires you to continue the same treatment in later taxable years. You can regroup activities only if the original treatment was "clearly inappropriate" or has become clearly inappropriate because of a material change in circumstances.

The IRS will not require that all five factors be present for grouping for multiple activities.

Rental activities. Rental activities may not be grouped with business activities unless one of the exceptions discussed at *10.1* applies.

> **EXAMPLE**
>
> Lance Jones has a significant interest in a bakery and a movie theater at a shopping mall in Baltimore and in a bakery and a movie theater in Philadelphia. The IRS does not explain what constitutes a significant interest. In grouping his activities into appropriate economic units based on the relevant facts and circumstances, Jones could: (1) group the theaters and bakeries into a single activity; (2) place the two theaters into one group and the bakeries into a second group; (3) put his Baltimore businesses into one group and his Philadelphia businesses in another group; or (4) treat the two bakeries and two movie theaters as four separate activities.
>
> Once he chooses a grouping, he must consistently use that grouping for all future years unless a material change makes the grouping inappropriate. His decision is also subject to IRS review and, if questioned, he must show the factual basis for his grouping.

IRS may regroup activities. The IRS may regroup your activities if your grouping does not reflect one or more appropriate economic units and a primary purpose of the grouping is to circumvent the passive loss rules.

> **EXAMPLE**
>
> Five doctors operate separate medical practices and also invest in tax shelters that generate passive losses. They form a partnership to operate X-ray equipment. In exchange for the equipment contributed to the partnership, each doctor receives limited partnership interests. The partnership is managed by a general partner selected by the doctors. Partnership services are provided to the doctors in proportion to their interests in the partnership and service fees are set at a level to offset the income generated by the partnership against individual passive losses. Under these facts, the IRS will not allow the medical practices and the partnership to be treated as separate activities as this would circumvent the passive loss limitations by generating passive income from the partnership to offset the tax-shelter losses. The IRS will require each doctor to treat his or her medical practice and interests in the partnership as a single activity.

Partnerships and S corporations. A partnership or S corporation must group its activities under the facts and circumstances test. Once a partnership or S corporation determines its activities, the partners or shareholders are bound by that decision and may not regroup them. The partners and shareholders then apply the facts and circumstances test to combine the partnership or S corporation activities with, or separate them from, their other activities.

Special rule for certain limited partners and limited entrepreneurs. A limited entrepreneur is a person with an ownership interest who does not actively participate in management. A limited entrepreneur or limited partner in films, videotapes, farming, oil and gas, or the renting of depreciable property generally may combine each such activity only with another of such activities in the same type of business, and only if he or she is a limited entrepreneur or partner in both. Grouping of such activities with other activities in the same type of business in which he or she is *not* a limited partner or entrepreneur is allowed if the grouping is appropriate under the general facts and circumstances test.

10.6 Material Participation Tests for Business

The IRS has seven tests for determining material participation in a business. Some tests require only a minimum amount of work, such as 500 hours a year and others only 100 hours. You need to meet only one of the seven tests to qualify as a material participant. If you do, then the income and loss from that business is treated as *nonpassive*.

The tests apply whether you do business as a sole proprietor, in an S corporation, or partnership. Losses and credits passed through S corporations and partnerships are subject to passive activity rules.

If you are a limited partner, you are not by law a material participant unless you satisfy certain conditions discussed at *10.11*.

 Planning Reminder

Proof of Material Participation
Material participation must be determined on an annual basis. Show proof of your participation by keeping an appointment book, calendar, or log of the days and time spent in the operation. If you want to treat contacts by phone as material activity, keep a log of phone calls showing the time and purpose of the calls.

Your tax position towards the IRS participation rules will depend on whether the particular activity produces income or loss. If you have passive activity losses from other activities, you may prefer to have a profitable business activity treated as a passive activity in order to offset the income by the losses from passive activities. On the other hand, if the business activity operates at a loss and you do not have passive income from other sources, you may want to meet the material participation test for that business activity in order to claim current loss deductions. IRS strategy in reviewing your activities would be the opposite. If your return was under audit, an agent would attempt to prevent you from treating income from a business activity as passive. For example, the IRS, by applying Tests 5 and 6, can prevent a retired person from treating post-retirement income from a prior business or profession as passive income to offset passive losses from another activity. If you realize a loss in one passive activity, Test 4 may prevent you from generating passive income by merely reducing your participation in another activity.

Material participation results in nonpassive treatment. There are two key terms: material participation and significant participation. If you materially participate by meeting one of the seven IRS tests, your activity is not a passive activity. For example, under Test 1, work for more than 500 hours in an activity is considered material participation. Under Test 4, significant participation is work for more than 100 hours but less than 500 hours at an activity in which you do not otherwise materially participate. The IRS applies a significant participation rule to convert passive activity income into nonpassive income and to convert several significant participation activities into material participation if the total participation in those activities exceeds 500 hours; *see* Test 4.

Work by you or your spouse that counts as participation. Any work you do in a business in which you have an ownership interest is treated as "participation." If you are married, work by your spouse in the activity during the tax year is treated, for purposes of the following tests, as participation by you. This is true even if your spouse does not own an interest in the business or if you file separately. However, the following type of work is *not* treated as participation:

1. Work that is not of a type customarily done by an owner of an activity, if one of the principal reasons for the performance of the work is to avoid the passive loss rules (*see* the Example below).

2. An investor's review of financial statements or analysis which is unrelated to day-to-day management or operation of the activity.

EXAMPLE

An attorney owns an interest in a professional football team for which he performs no services. He anticipates a net loss from the football activity and to qualify as a material participant, he hires his wife to work 15 hours a week as an office receptionist for the team. Although a spouse's participation in an activity generally qualifies as participation by both spouses, the receptionist work here does not qualify as participation because (1) it is not the type of work customarily done by an owner of a football team and (2) the attorney hired his spouse to avoid disallowance of a passive loss.

IRS Tests for Material Participation

If you meet one of the following tests for the year in question, you are considered to have materially participated in that activity, and therefore the activity is considered *nonpassive* for that year. Tests 5 and 6 prevent retired individuals from treating post-retirement income as passive income.

Test 1. You participate in the activity for more than 500 hours during the tax year.
Test 2. Your participation in the activity for the tax year constitutes substantially all of the participation in the activity of all individuals including non-owners for the year.
Test 3. You participate in the activity for more than 100 hours during the tax year, and your participation is at least as great as that of any other person including non-owners for that year.

EXAMPLE

Joan Brown and Pat Collins are partners in a moving van business which they conduct entirely on weekends. They both work for eight hours each weekend. Although neither partner participates for more than 500 hours (Test 1), they are each treated as material participants under Test 3 because they participate for more than 100 hours and no one else participates more.

Caution

Overcoming Investor Status

The IRS will not recognize time spent as an investor as "participation" unless you can show you are involved in daily operations or management of the activity. According to the IRS, this requires you to be at the business site on a regular basis. Even if you do appear daily, the IRS may ignore such evidence if there is an on-site manager or you have full-time business obligations at another site. Activity of an investor includes the studying and reviewing of financial reports for your own use which are considered unrelated to management decisions. If you invest in a business that is out of state or a distance from your home, you may also find it difficult to prove material participation.

Test 4. You are active in several enterprises but each activity does not in itself qualify as material participation. However, if you spend more than 100 hours in each activity and the total hours of these more-than-100-hours activities exceeds 500, you are treated as a material participant in each of these activities. This test is described as the significant participation test.

EXAMPLES

1. Mike Smith is a full-time accountant with ownership interests in a restaurant and shoe store. He works 150 hours in the shoe store and 360 hours in the restaurant. Under the significant participation test (Test 4), Smith is considered a material participant in both activities, as the total hours of both exceed 500.
2. Carl Young invests in five businesses. In activity (a) he works 110 hours; in activity (b), 100 hours; in activity (c), 125 hours; in activity (d), 120 hours; and in activity (e), 140 hours. He does not qualify under the significant participation test (Test 4). Although his total hours in the five activities exceed 500, activity (b) is ignored in the total count because the hours did not exceed 100. The total of the four other activities is 495.
3. Assume that Young worked one hour more for activity (b). It and all of the other activities would be considered as meeting the significant material participation test. The total hours are 596. Assuming that activity (a) totaled 125 hours and activity (b) remained at 100 hours or less, he would meet the test for all of the activities except for activity (b), which did not exceed 100 hours. The total of the four qualified activities is 510 hours.

Test 5. You materially participated in the activity for any five tax years during the 10 tax years preceding the tax year in question. The five tax years do not have to be consecutive. Use only Test 1 for determining material participation in years before 1987. Thus, if you are retired but meet the five-out-of-10-year participation test, you are currently considered a material participant, with the result that net income is treated as nonpassive, rather than passive. If you retired from a personal service profession, an even stricter rule applies; *see* Test 6.

Test 6. In a personal service activity, you materially participated for any three tax years preceding the tax year in question. The three years do not have to be consecutive. Use only Test 1 for determining material participation in years before 1987. Examples of personal services within this test are the professions of health, law, engineering, architecture, accounting, actuarial science, the performing arts, consulting, or any other trade or business in which capital is not a material income-producing factor.

Test 7. Under the facts and circumstances test, you participate in the activity on a regular, continuous, and substantial basis. *According to the IRS, you do not come within this test if you participate less than 100 hours in the activity.*

Retired farmers. Retired or disabled farmers are treated as materially participating in a farming activity if they materially participated for five of the eight years preceding their retirement or disability. A surviving spouse is also treated as materially participating in a farming activity if the real property used in the activity meets the estate tax rules for special valuation of farm property passed from a qualified decedent and the surviving spouse actively manages the farm.

Limited partners; *see 10.11.*

Participant rules for personal service and closely held corporations; *see 10.15.*

10.7 Tax Credits of Passive Activities Limited

You may generally not claim a tax credit from a passive activity unless you report and pay taxes on income from a passive activity. Furthermore, the tax allocated to that income must be at least as much as the credit. If the tax credit exceeds your tax liability on income allocable to passive activities, the excess credit is not allowed. Use Form 8582-CR to figure the allowable credit. Suspended credits are not allowed when property is disposed of. The credits may be used only when passive income is earned.

EXAMPLE

Ben Wall has a $1,000 credit from a passive activity. He does not report income from any passive activity. He may not claim the credit because no part of his tax is attributed to passive activity income. The credit is suspended until he has income from a passive activity and he incurs tax on that income. All or part of the credit may then be claimed to offset the tax. If he disposed of his interest before using a suspended credit, the credit may no longer be claimed but the election to reduce basis, discussed below, could be made.

Credits for real estate activities.   As discussed at *10.2*, more favorable tax credit rules apply to real estate activities.

Basis adjustment for suspended credits.   If the basis of property was reduced by tax credits, you may elect on Form 8582-CR to add back a suspended credit to the basis when your entire interest in an activity is disposed of. If the property is disposed of in a transaction that is not treated as a fully taxable disposition under *10.13*, then no basis adjustment is allowed.

EXAMPLE

Mark places in service rehabilitation credit property and claims an allowable credit of $50, which also reduces basis by $50. However, under the passive loss rule, he is prevented from claiming the credit. In a later year, he disposes of his entire interest in the activity, including the property whose basis was reduced. He may elect to increase basis of the property by the amount of the original basis adjustment.

10.8 Nonpassive Income and Losses

The purpose of the passive loss rules is to prevent you from deducting passive losses from nonpassive income. Passive losses are generally losses from business activities in which you do not materially participate or from rental activities which generate losses which are not deductible under the $25,000 allowance or do not qualify you as a real estate professional. In some cases, as explained in *10.9*, passive income may be treated as nonpassive income.

Where you do not materially participate in a business activity, passive income or loss is determined by matching income and expenses of that activity. Portfolio income earned by the activity or any pay that you earn is not included to determine passive income or loss.

Portfolio income is nonpassive income and broadly defined as income that is not derived in the ordinary course of business of the activity. Portfolio income includes interest, dividends, annuities, and royalties from property held for investment. However, interest income on loans and investments made in the business of lending money or received on business accounts receivable is generally not treated as portfolio income; *see 10.9* for special recharacterization rules. Similarly, royalties derived from a business of licensing property is not portfolio income to the person who created the property or performed substantial services or incurred substantial costs.

Portfolio income also includes gains from the sale of properties that produce portfolio income or are held for investment.

Expenses allocable to portfolio income, including interest expenses, do not enter into the computation of passive income or loss.

Sale of property used in activity.   Gain realized on the sale of property used in the activity is treated as passive activity income if at the time of disposition the activity was passive; *see* the exception at *10.16*. Under this rule, if you transact an installment sale, the treatment of installment payments depends on your status at the time of the initial sale. If you were not a material participant, installment payments in a later year are treated as passive income, even if you become a material participant in the later years.

Installment payments from a pre-1987 installment sale are treated as passive income if the activity would have been considered passive had the passive activity rules been in effect before 1987.

Although gain on the sale of property is generally passive income if the activity is passive at the time of sale, there is an exception that could recharacterize the gain as nonpassive income if the property was formerly used in a nonpassive activity; *see 10.16* for details.

Compensation for personal services is not passive activity income.   The term "compensation for personal services" includes only (1) earned income, including certain payments made by a partnership to a partner and representing compensation for the services of the partner; (2) amounts included in gross income involving the transfer of property in exchange for the performance of services; (3) amounts distributed under qualified plans; (4) amounts distributed under retirement, pension, and other arrangements for deferred compensation of services; and (5) Social Security benefits includible in gross income.

Passive activity gross income also does not include (1) income from patent, copyright, or literary, musical, or artistic compositions, if your personal efforts significantly contributed to the creation of the property; (2) income from a qualified low-income housing project; (3) income tax refunds; and (4) payments on a covenant not to compete.

Passive activity deductions. Deductible expenses that offset passive income of an activity must be related to the passive activity, such as real property taxes. The following are *not* considered passive activity deductions:

Casualty and theft losses if similar losses do not recur regularly in the activity.

Charitable deductions.

Miscellaneous itemized deductions subject to the 2% AGI floor.

State, local, and foreign income taxes.

Carryovers of net operating losses or capital losses.

Expenses clearly and directly allocable to portfolio income.

Loss on the sale of property producing portfolio income.

Loss on the sale of your entire interest in a passive activity to an unrelated party. The loss is allowed in full; *see 10.13.*

Interest deductions. Interest expenses attributable to passive activities are treated as passive activity deductions and are not subject to the investment interest limitations. For example, in 1997, if you have net passive loss of $100, $40 of which is of interest expense, the entire $100 is a passive loss. $40 of the loss is not subject to the investment interest limitation of *15.10.* Similarly, income and loss from passive activities generally are not treated as investment income or loss in figuring the investment interest limitation.

If you rent out a vacation home that you personally use for more than the greater of 14 days and 10% of the fair market rental days *(9.7)*, you may treat the residence as a qualified second residence under the mortgage interest rules; *see 15.1.* Interest on such a qualifying second home is generally fully deductible, and the deductible interest *(15.1)* is *not* treated as a passive activity deduction. The rental portion of the interest is deducted on Schedule E of Form 1040 and the personal-use portion on Schedule A if itemized deductions are claimed; *see 9.9.*

10.9 Passive Income Converted Into Nonpassive Income

There is an advantage in treating income as passive income when you have passive losses that may offset the income. However, the law may prevent you from treating certain income as passive income. The conversion of passive income to nonpassive income is technically called "recharacterization." This may occur when you do not materially participate in the business activity, but are sufficiently active for the IRS to consider your participation as significant. Recharacterization may also occur when you rent nondepreciable property or sell development rental property. As discussed at *10.16,* gain on the sale of property used in a passive activity may be recharacterized as nonpassive income if the property was formerly used in a nonpassive activity.

Significant participation. The IRS compares income and losses from all of your activities in which you work more than 100 hours but less than 500 and which are not considered material participation under the law. If you show a net aggregate gain, part of your gain is treated as nonpassive income according to the computation illustrated in the following Example.

EXAMPLE

Carol Warren invests in three business activities—A, B, and C. She does not materially participate in any of the activities during 1997 but participates in Activity A for 105 hours, in Activity B for 160 hours, and in Activity C for 125 hours. Her net passive income or loss from the three activities is:

	A	B	C	Total
PA gross income	$600	$700	$900	$2,200
PA deductions	(200)	(1,000)	(300)	(1,500)
Net passive income	$400	($ 300)	$600	$700

Carol's passive activity gross income from significant participation passive activities of $2,200 exceeds passive activity deductions of $1,500. A ratable portion of her gross income from significant participation activities with net passive income for the tax year (Activities A and C) is treated as gross income that is not from a passive activity. The ratable portion is figured by dividing:

1. The excess of her passive activity gross income from significant participation over passive activity deductions from such activities (here $700) by

2. The net passive income of only the significant participation passive activities having net passive income (here $1,000). The ratable portion is 70%.

Thus, $280 of gross income from Activity A ($400 × 70%) and $420 of gross income from Activity C ($600 × 70%) is treated as nonpassive gross income. This adjustment prevents $700 from being offset by passive losses from another activity.

Net interest income from passive equity-financed lending.   Gross income from "equity-financed lending activity" is treated as nonpassive income to the extent of the lesser of the equity-financed interest income or net passive income. An activity is an "equity-financed lending activity" for a tax year if (1) the activity involves a trade or business of lending money; and (2) the average outstanding balance of the liabilities incurred in the activity for the tax year does not exceed 80% of the average outstanding balance of the interest-bearing assets held in the activity.

Incidental rental of property by development activity.   Where gains on the sale of rental property are attributable to recent development, passive income treatment may be lost if the sale comes within the following tests: (1) the rental started less than 12 months before the date of disposition; and (2) you materially participated or significantly participated in the performance of services enhancing the value of the property. The 12-month period starts at the completion of the development services that increased the property's value.

Rental of property with an insubstantial depreciable basis.   This rule prevents you from generating passive rental income with vacant land or land on which a unit is constructed that has a value substantially less than the land. If less than 30% of the basis of rental property is depreciable, and you have net passive income from rentals (taking into account carried-over passive losses from prior years), the net passive income is treated as nonpassive income. Basis here is generally adjusted basis without any adjustments.

> **EXAMPLES**
> 1. A limited partnership buys vacant land for $300,000, constructs improvements on the land at a cost of $100,000, and leases the entire property. After the rental period, the partnership sells the property for $600,000, realizing a gain. The unadjusted basis of the depreciable improvements of $100,000 is only 25% of the basis of the property of $400,000. The rent and the gain allocated to the improvements are treated as nonpassive income.
> 2. In 1989, Shirley offset a passive rental loss from an investment in a limited partnership, LP, which was a substantial owner of a general partnership, GP, against rental income from an investment in a joint venture, JV. JV had leased to GP land on which GP constructed a shopping center. The IRS held that the rental income from JV was nonpassive rental income within the 30% test and could not be offset by the passive rental loss. The Tax Court agreed and also rejected Shirley's attempt to aggregate her investment activities in JV and LP as one activity. The operations of each group, JV, LP, and GP, were separate and not owned by the same person. She was not the direct owner of any of the units. Further, the aggregation rule does not apply to property falling within the 30% test.

Property rented to nonpassive activity (self-rental property).   You may not generate passive income by renting property to a business in which you materially participate.

Licensing of intangible property.   Your share of royalty income in a partnership, S corporation, estate, or trust is treated as nonpassive income if you invested after the organization created the intangible property, performed substantial services, or incurred substantial costs in the development or marketing of it. See Publication 925 for further details.

Planning Reminder

Limited Liability for Oil or Gas Well

A working interest in an oil or gas well is exempt from the passive activity restrictions if your liability is not limited. The following forms of loss protection are disregarded and, thus, are not treated as limiting your liability: protection against loss by an indemnification agreement; a stop-loss agreement; insurance; or any similar arrangement or combination of agreements.

10.10   Working Interests in Oil and Gas Wells

Working interests are generally not treated as passive activities. This is true whether you hold your interest directly or through an entity, provided your liability is not limited. As long as you have unlimited liability, you need not materially participate in the activity. A working interest is one burdened with the financial risk of developing and operating the property, such as a share in tort liability (for example, uninsured losses from a fire); some responsibility to share in additional costs; responsibility for authorizing expenses; receiving periodic reports about drilling, completion, and expected production; and the possession of voting rights and rights to continue operations if the present operator steps out.

Limited liability.   If you hold a working interest through any of the following entities, the entity is considered to limit your liability and you are subject to the passive loss rules: (1) a limited partnership interest in a partnership in which you are not a general partner; (2) stock in a corporation; or (3) an interest in any entity other than a limited partnership or corporation that, under applicable state law, limits the liability of a holder of such interest for all obligations of the entity to a determinable fixed amount.

Working interests are considered on a well-by-well basis. Rights to overriding royalties or production payments, and contract rights to extract or share in oil and gas profits without liability for a share of production costs, are not working interests.

10.11   Partnership Rules

If you are a partner, your level of personal participation in partnership activity during the partnership year determines whether your share of income or loss is passive or nonpassive. Generally, limited partners are subject to passive activity treatment, but there are some exceptions. On Schedule K-1 of Form 1065, the partnership will identify each activity it conducts and specify the income, loss, deductions, and credits from each activity.

> **EXAMPLE**
> Don Bailey is a general partner of a fiscal year partnership that ends on March 31, 1997. During that fiscal year he was inactive. Since he did not materially participate, his share of partnership income or loss reported in 1997 is passive activity income or loss, even if he becomes active from April 1, 1997, to the end of 1997.

Not treated as passive income are payments for services and certain guaranteed payments made in liquidation of a retiring or deceased partner's interest unless attributed to unrealized receivables and goodwill at a time the partner was passive.

Gain or loss on the disposition of a partnership interest may be attributed to different trade, investment, or rental activities of the partnership. The allocation is made according to a complicated formula included in IRS regulations.

Payments to a retired partner.   Gain or loss is treated as passive only to the extent that it would be treated as such at the start of the liquidation of the partner's interest.

Limited partners.   A limited partner is generally not considered to be a material participant in a partnership activity, and, thus, treats income or loss as passive, except in these cases:

1. The limited partner participates for more than 500 hours during the tax year; *see* Test 1 in *10.6*.
2. The limited partner materially participated in the partnership during prior years under either Test 5 or Test 6 at *10.6*.
3. The limited partner is also a general partner at all times during the partnership tax year that ends with or within the partner's taxable year.

To determine material participation in rental real estate activities under the special rules for real estate professionals, Test 1 or Test 5 of *10.6* must generally be met, but *see* the exception at *10.3*.

A limited partner is not considered to be an "active participant" and thus does not qualify for the $25,000 rental loss allowance under *10.2*.

10.12   Form 8582

The purpose of Form 8582 is to assemble in one place items of income and expenses from passive activities in order to determine the effect of the passive loss rules on these items. After this determination, income and allowable deductions are reported as regular income and deductions in appropriate schedules attached to your tax return. For example, net profits of a self-employed person who is not active in the business are reported on Schedule C, sales of capital assets of a passive activity are reported on Schedule D, your share of partnership income and allowable deductions is reported on Schedule E, rental income and allowable deductions are reported on Schedule E.

Schedule D or Form 4797.   Gains or losses from the sale of assets from a passive activity or from the sale of a partial interest which is less than "substantially all" of your entire interest in a passive activity are reported on Schedule D or on Form 4797 (sale of business property, *see* Chapter 44). The gain is also entered on Form 8582. Losses must first be entered on Form 8582 to *see* how much, if any, is allowable under the passive loss restrictions before an amount can be entered as a loss on Schedule D or Form 4797.

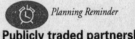

Planning Reminder

Publicly traded partnerships (PTPs).
A PTP is a partnership whose interests are traded on established securities exchanges or are readily tradable in secondary markets. PTPs that are not treated as corporations for tax purposes are subject to special rules that allow losses to be used only to offset income from the same PTP. See the instructions to Form 8582.

A disposition of an insubstantial part of your interest in the activity does not allow a deduction of suspended passive losses from prior years. When you dispose of your *entire* interest in a passive activity to a nonrelated party in a fully taxable transaction, your losses for the year plus prior year suspended losses from the activity are fully deductible. The same rule applies to a partial disposition only if you are disposing of *substantially all* of the activity and you have proof of the current year and prior year suspended losses allocable to the disposed-of portion. You net the gain or loss from the disposition with the net income or loss from current year operations and any prior year suspended passive losses. If the netting gives you an overall gain, you need to file Form 8582 only if you have other passive activities. If you have an overall loss after the netting, you do not file Form 8582.

Schedule E. If you have a net profit from rental property or other passive activity reported on Schedule E and you also have losses from other passive activities, the income reported on Schedule E is also entered on Form 8582. A net loss from rental activities generally must be entered on Form 8582 but Form 8582 is not needed if you qualify for the full $25,000 allowance *(10.2)* for rental real estate losses and meet these tests:

Your only passive activities are rental real estate activities and you have no suspended prior year passive losses from such activities;

You have no credits related to passive activities;

You actively participated in the rental real estate operations;

Your total losses from the rental real estate activities are $25,000 or less ($12,500 or less if married filing separately and you lived apart from your spouse all year);

Your modified adjusted gross income is $100,000 or less ($50,000 or less if married filing separately and you lived apart from your spouse all year); and

You do not own any interest in a rental real estate activity as a limited partner or beneficiary of a trust or estate.

If you have a loss from a passive interest in a partnership, trust, estate, or S corporation, you first determine on Form 8582 whether the loss is deductible on Schedule E.

Schedule F. A passive activity farm loss is entered on Form 8582 to determine the deductible loss. If only part of the loss is allowed, only that portion is claimed on Schedule F. A net profit from passive farm activities is also entered on Form 8582 to offset losses from other passive activities.

Other tax forms. Other forms tied to Form 8582 are Form 4797 (sale of business assets or equipment), Form 4835 (farm rental income), and Form 4952 (investment interest deductions). For further details *see* Form 8582; also *see* IRS Publication 925 for filled-in sample forms.

10.13 Suspended Losses Allowed on Disposition of Your Interest

Losses and credits that may not be claimed in 1997 because of the passive activity limitations are suspended and carried forward to 1998 and later years. The carryover lasts indefinitely, until you have passive income against which to claim the losses and credits. No carryback is allowed. What if you have suspended losses and later materially participate in the business in which the loss was realized? The losses remain as passive losses but may offset nonpassive income of that activity.

Caution

Partial Disposition
To deduct suspended passive losses on a disposition of part of an activity, the part disposed of must constitute substantially all of the activity; *see 10.13.*

> **EXAMPLE**
>
> In 1997, Nick Milo was not a material participant in a business activity and his share of losses was $10,000, which was suspended because he had no passive income. In 1998, he becomes a material participant in the business and his share of income is $1,000. The $1,000 is treated as nonpassive income, and he may apply $1,000 of the suspended loss to offset that income.

Allocation of suspended loss. If your suspended loss is incurred from several activities, you allocate the loss among the activities using the worksheets accompanying Form 8582. The loss is allocated among the activities in proportion to the total loss. If you have net income from significant participation activities (Test 4 of *10.6*), such activities may be treated as one single activity in making the allocation; see instructions to Form 8582.

Disposition of a passive interest. A fully taxable sale of your interest to a nonrelated person will allow you to claim suspended deductions from the activity. Worthlessness of a security in a passive activity is treated as a disposition. An abandonment also releases suspended losses.

On a disposition, the suspended losses plus any current year income or loss from the activity are combined with the gain or loss from the disposition; *see* the Examples below and follow the instructions to Form 8582 for reporting the net gain or loss.

Partial disposition. You may for the taxable year in which there is a disposition of *substantially all* of an activity treat the part disposed of as a separate activity. You must show: (1) the amount of prior year suspended deductions and credits allocable to that part of the activity for the taxable year, and (2) the amount of gross income and any other deductions and credits allocable to that part of the activity for the taxable year.

$3,000 capital loss limit. Capital losses incurred on a disposition of a passive interest are also subject to the general $3,000 loss limitation of *5.3*.

EXAMPLES

1. Jill Stein has a 5% interest in a limited partnership with an adjusted basis of $42,000. In 1997, she sells her interest in the partnership to an unrelated person for $50,000. For 1997, she has a current year loss from the partnership (shown on Schedule K-1) of $3,000. She also has $2,000 of suspended passive losses from prior years that have been carried forward to 1997. Jill's $8,000 gain from the sale of her interest is combined on Form 8582 with the current year loss and suspended losses giving her an overall gain of $3,000, figured as follows:

Sales price		$50,000
Less: Adjusted basis		$42,000
Gain		$8,000
Less: Current year loss	$3,000	
Suspended losses	$2,000	$5,000
Overall gain		$3,000

   If Jill has *other* passive activities, the $8,000 gain would be reported as current year income on Form 8582. The $3,000 current year loss and $2,000 suspended losses would also be entered on Form 8582.

   If this was Jill's *only* passive activity, she does not have to file Form 8582. The gain from the sale is reported on Schedule D and the current year and suspended losses are reported as nonpassive losses on Schedule E.

2. Assume that Jill's suspended losses from prior years were $10,000 instead of $2,000. She has an overall loss of $5,000 after combining the gain from the sale of $8,000, the current year loss of $3,000, and the suspended losses of $10,000.

   Since there is an overall loss after combining the gain and losses, Jill does not file Form 8582. The current year loss plus the suspended losses are reported as nonpassive losses on Schedule E and the gain from the disposition on Schedule D.

3. Assume in Example 1 that Jill sold her interest for $30,000 instead of $50,000. She would have a $12,000 loss on the sale ($42,000 adjusted basis *less* $30,000 sales price). Combining the loss with the current year loss of $3,000 and the $2,000 of suspended losses, she has an overall loss of $17,000.

   Since there is an overall loss, Jill does not file Form 8582. The current year loss plus the suspended losses are reported as nonpassive losses on Schedule E. The $12,000 loss on the sale is reported on Schedule D as a capital loss. Under the regular rules for capital losses, the loss will offset capital gains for 1997 and any excess will be deductible only up to $3,000 *(5.3)*. Assuming the $3,000 limit applies, Jill has a $9,000 capital loss carryover to 1998.

Gifts. When a passive activity interest is given away, you may not deduct suspended passive losses. The donee's basis in the property is increased by the suspended loss if he or she sells the property at a gain. If a loss is realized by the donee on a sale of the interest, the donee's basis may not exceed fair market value of the gift at the time of the donation.

Death. On the death of an investor in a passive interest, suspended losses are deductible on the decedent's final tax return, to the extent the suspended loss exceeds the amount by which the basis of the interest in the hands of the heir is increased.

EXAMPLE

An owner dies holding an interest in a passive activity with a suspended loss of $8,000. After the owner's death, the heir's stepped-up basis for the property (equal to fair market value) is $6,000 greater than the decedent's basis. On the decedent's final return, $2,000 of the loss is deductible ($8,000 – $6,000).

Installment sales.   If the passive activity interest is sold at a profit on the installment basis, suspended losses are deducted over the installment period in the same ratio as the gain recognized each year bears to the gain remaining to be recognized as of the start of the year. For example, if in the year of sale you report 20% of your total gain under the installment method, 20% of your suspended losses are also allowed.

10.14 Suspended Tax Credits

If you have tax credits that were barred under the passive activity rules, they may be claimed only in future years when you have tax liability attributable to passive income. However, in the year you dispose of your interest, a special election may be available to decrease your gain by the amount of your suspended credit; *see* below.

Basis election for suspended credits.   If you qualify for an investment credit (under transition rules) or a rehabilitation credit, you are required to reduce the basis of the property even if you are unable to claim the credit because of the passive activity rules. If this occurs and you later dispose of your entire interest in the passive activity, including the property whose basis was reduced, your gain will be increased by virtue of the basis reduction although you never benefited from the credit. To prevent this, you may reduce the taxable gain by electing to increase the pretransfer basis of the property by the amount of the unused credit.

EXAMPLE

Dan Brown places in service rehabilitated credit property qualifying for a $50 credit, but the credit is not allowed under the passive loss rules. However, his basis is still reduced by $50. In a later year, Brown makes a taxable disposition of his entire interest in the activity and in the rehabilitation property. Assuming that no part of the suspended $50 credit has been used, Brown may elect to increase his basis in the property by the unused $50 credit.

10.15 Personal Service and Closely Held Corporations

To prevent avoidance of the passive activity rules through use of corporations, the law imposes restrictions on income and loss offsets in closely held C corporations and personal service corporations.

Unless the material participation tests discussed in this section are met, the activities of a personal service corporation or a closely held corporation are considered passive activities, subject to the restrictions on loss deductions and tax credits. For purposes of these passive activity rules, a closely held C corporation is a corporation in which more than 50% in value of the stock is owned by five or fewer persons during the last half of the tax year.

A personal service corporation is a C corporation the principal activity of which is the performance of personal services by the employee-owners. Personal services are services in the fields of health, law, engineering, architecture, accounting, actuarial sciences, performing arts, or consulting. An employee-owner is any employee who on any day in the tax year owns any stock in the corporation. If an individual owns any stock in a corporation which in turn owns stock in another corporation, the individual is deemed to own a proportionate part of the stock in the other corporation. Further, more than 10% of the corporation's stock by value must be owned by owner-employees for the corporation to be a personal service corporation.

Material participation.   A personal service corporation or closely held corporation is treated as materially participating in an activity during a tax year *only if* either:

1. One or more stockholders are treated as materially participating in the activity and they directly or indirectly hold in the aggregate more than 50% of the value of the corporation's outstanding shares; *or*
2. The corporation is a closely held corporation and in the 12-month period ending on the last day of the tax year, the corporation had at least one full-time manager, three full-time employees, none of whom own more than 5% of the stock, and business deductions exceeded 15% of gross income from the activity.

A stockholder is treated as materially participating or significantly participating in the activity of a corporation if he or she satisfies one of the seven tests in *10.6* for material participation. For purposes of applying the significant participation test (Test 4 at *10.6*), an activity of a personal service or closely held corporation will be treated as a significant participation activity for a tax year *only if:*

1. The corporation is not treated as materially participating in the activity for the tax year; and
2. One or more individuals, each of whom is treated as significantly participating in the activity directly or indirectly, hold in the aggregate more than 50% of the value of the outstanding stock of the corporation. Furthermore, in applying the seven participation tests, all activities of the corporation are treated as activities in which the individual holds an interest in determining whether the individual participates in an activity of the corporation; and the individual's participation in all activities other than activities of the corporation is disregarded in determining whether his or her participation in an activity of the corporation is treated as material participation under the significant participation test (Test 4 at *10.6*).

Closely held corporation's computation of passive loss.   Even if a closely held corporation does not meet the material participation tests above, it still qualifies for a slight break from the passive loss restrictions. A closely held corporation may use passive activity deductions to offset not only passive activity gross income but also *net active income.* Generally, net active income is taxable income from business operations, disregarding passive activity income and expenses, and also disregarding portfolio income and expenses; *see 10.8.* Passive activity losses cannot offset portfolio income.

If a corporation stops being closely held, its passive losses and credits from prior years are not allowable against portfolio income but continue to be allowable only against passive income and net active income.

Tax liability on net active income may be offset by passive activity credits.

10.16 Sales of Property and of Passive Activity Interests

Generally, gain on the sale or disposition of property is passive or nonpassive, depending on whether your activity is passive or nonpassive in the year of sale or disposition. Thus, gain on the sale of property used in a rental activity is treated as passive income, and gain on property used in a nonrental business is passive if you did not materially participate in the business in the year of sale. However, exceptions may prevent you from generating passive income by arranging certain sales described in this section. For example, gain on the sale of substantially appreciated property formerly used in a nonpassive activity may be treated as nonpassive income, even if sold by a passive activity.

Where you transact an installment sale, treatment of gain in later years depends on your status in the year of sale. For example, if you were considered a material participant in a business, all gain is treated as nonpassive income, including gain for later installments. If you were in a rental activity or were not a material participant in a nonrental business, the gain is treated as passive income, unless the exceptions in this section apply.

Current gain from a pre-1987 installment sale is passive income if the activity would have been passive, assuming the passive activity rules were in effect at the time of the sale.

Gain on appreciated property formerly used in nonpassive activity.   Gain from a disposition of substantially appreciated property is treated as passive activity income if the property was used in a passive activity for either 20% of its holding period or the entire 24-month period ending on the date of the disposition. Property is substantially appreciated if fair market value exceeds 120% of its adjusted basis.

EXAMPLE

In 1989, Andy Jones buys a building for use in a business in which he materially participates until March 31, 1999. On April 1, 2000, he rents the building. On December 31, 2001, he sells the building. Gain from the sale is treated as not from a passive activity. The building was used in a passive rental activity for 21 months before disposition (April 1, 2000, through December 31, 2001). Thus, it was not used in a passive activity for the entire 24-month period ending on the date of the sale. Further, the 21-month period during which the building was used in a passive activity is less than 20% of Jones's holding period of 12 years.

Property used in more than one activity in a 12-month period preceding disposition. You are required to allocate the amount realized on the disposition and the adjusted basis of the property among the activities in which the property was used during a 12-month period preceding the disposition. For purposes of this rule, the term "activity" includes personal use and holding for investment. The allocation may be based on the period for which the property is used in each activity during the 12-month period. However, if during the 12-month period the value of the property does not exceed the lesser of $10,000 and 10% of the value of all property used in the activity at the time of disposition, gain may be allocated to the predominant use.

> **EXAMPLE**
>
> Joe Smith sells a personal computer for $8,000. During the 12-month period that ended on the date of the sale, 70% of Smith's use of the computer was in a passive activity. Immediately before the sale, the fair market value of all property used in the passive activity, including the personal computer, was $200,000. The computer was predominantly used in the passive activity during the 12-month period ending on the date of the sale. The value of the computer, $8,000, did not exceed the lesser of $10,000 and 10% of the $200,000 value of all property used in the activity immediately before the sale. Thus, the amount realized and the adjusted basis are allocated to the passive activity.

Disposition of partnership and S corporation interests. Gain or loss from the disposition of an interest in a partnership and S corporation is generally allocated among the entity's activities in proportion to the amount that the entity would have allocated to the partner or shareholder for each of its activities if the entity had sold its interest in the activities on an "applicable valuation date."

Gain is allocated only to appreciated activities. Loss is allocated only to depreciated activities. The entity may select either the beginning of its tax year in which the holder's disposition occurs or the date of the disposition as the applicable valuation date.

Claiming suspended loss on disposition of interest in passive activity. A fully taxable sale of your entire interest or of substantially all of your interest to a nonrelated person will allow you to claim suspended loss deductions from the activity. These rules are fully discussed in 10.13.

Dealer's sale of property similar to property sold in the ordinary course of business. IRS regulations set down complex tests which determine whether the result of the sale is treated as passive or nonpassive income or loss.

At-Risk Rules

 Filing Tip

Form 6198

If you have invested an amount for which you are not at risk, such as a nonrecourse loan, you generally must file Form 6198 to figure a deductible loss. However, nonrecourse financing for real estate that secures the loan is treated as an at-risk investment in most cases; *see 10.18.*

10.17 At-Risk Limits

The at-risk rules prevent investors from claiming losses in excess of their actual tax investment by barring them from including nonrecourse liabilities as part of the tax basis for their interest. Almost all ventures are subject to the at-risk limits. Real estate placed in service after 1986 is subject to the at-risk rules as well, but most real estate nonrecourse financing can qualify for an exception; *see 10.18.*

> **EXAMPLE**
>
> Crystal Parker invests cash of $1,000 in a venture and signs a nonrecourse note for $8,000. In 1997, her share of the venture's loss is $1,200. The at-risk rules limit her deduction to $1,000, the amount of her cash investment; as she is not personally liable on the note, the amount of the liability is not included as part of her basis for loss purposes.

Losses disallowed under the at-risk rules are carried over to the following year; *see 10.21.*

Form 6198. If you have amounts that are not at risk, you must file Form 6198 to figure your deductible loss. A separate form must be filed for each activity. However, if you have an interest in a partnership or S corporation that has more than one investment in any of the following four categories, the IRS currently allows you to aggregate all of the partnership or S corporation activities within each category. For example, all partnership or S corporation films and videotapes may be treated as one activity in determining amounts at risk. The aggregation rules may be changed by the IRS; *see* the instructions to Form 6198.

1. Holding, producing, or distributing motion picture films or videotapes;
2. Exploring for or exploiting oil or gas properties;
3. Exploring for, or exploiting, geothermal deposits (for wells commenced on or after October 1, 1978); *and*
4. Farming. For this purpose, farming is defined as the cultivation of land and the raising or harvesting of any agricultural or horticultural commodity—including raising, shearing, breeding, caring for, or management of animals. Forestry and timber activities are not included, but orchards bearing fruits and nuts are within the definition of farming. Certain activities carried on within the physical boundaries of the farm may not necessarily be treated as farming.

In addition to the previous categories, the law treats as a single activity all leased depreciable business equipment (Section 1245 property) that is placed in service during any year by a partnership or S corporation.

Exempt from the at-risk rules are C corporations which meet active business tests and are not in the equipment leasing business or any business involving master sound recording, films, videotapes, or other artistic, literary, or musical property. For details on the active business tests, as well as a special at-risk exception for equipment leasing activities of closely held corporations, *see* IRS Publication 925.

The at-risk limitation applies only to tax losses produced by expense deductions which are not disallowed by reason of another provision of the law. For example, if a prepaid interest expense is deferred under the prepaid interest limitation *(15.14)*, the interest will not be included in the loss subject to the risk limitation. When the interest accrues and becomes deductible, the expense may be considered within the at-risk provision. Similarly, if a deduction is deferred because of farming syndicate rules, that deduction will enter into the computation of the tax loss subject to the risk limitation only when it becomes deductible under the farming syndicate rules.

Effect of passive loss rules.   Where a loss is also subject to the at-risk rules, you apply the at-risk rules first. If the loss is deductible under the at-risk rules, the passive activity rules then apply. On Form 6198 (at risk), you figure the deductible loss allowed as at risk and then carry the loss over to Form 8582 to determine the passive activity loss.

10.18   What Is At Risk?

The following amounts are considered at risk in determining your tax position in a business or investment:

Cash;
Adjusted basis of property that you contribute; and
Borrowed funds for which you are personally liable to pay.

At-risk basis is figured as of the end of the year. Any loss allowed for a year reduces the at-risk amount as of the start of the next year. Therefore, if a loss exceeds your at-risk investment, the excess loss will not be deductible in later years unless you increase your at-risk investment; *see* the Examples below and *10.21*.

Personal liability alone does not assure that the borrowed funds are considered at risk. The lender must have no interest in the venture other than as creditor.

> **EXAMPLE**
> Julie Kahn, an investor, pays a promoter of a book purchase plan $45,000 for a limited partnership interest. The promoter is the general partner. Kahn pays $30,000 cash and gives a note for $15,000 on which she is personally liable. Her amount at risk is $30,000; the $15,000 personal liability note is not counted because it is owed to the general partner.

Special at-risk rule for real estate financing.   For real property placed in service after 1986, you may treat nonrecourse financing from unrelated commercial lenders or from government agencies as amounts at risk if the financing is secured by the real estate. Loans from the seller or promoter do not qualify. Third-party nonrecourse debt from a related lender, other than the seller or a promoter, may also be treated as at risk, providing the terms of the loan are commercially reasonable and on substantially the same terms as loans involving unrelated persons.

If you acquired an interest after 1986 in a partnership or S corporation, the above at-risk rules apply to your share of real estate losses, regardless of when the partnership or S corporation placed the property in service.

Pledges of other property.   If you pledge personally owned real estate used outside the activity to secure a nonrecourse debt and invest the proceeds in an at-risk activity, the proceeds may be considered part of your at-risk investment. The proceeds included in basis are limited by the fair market value of the property used as collateral (determined as of the date the property is pledged as security) less any prior (or superior) claims to which the collateral is subject.

Partners.   A partner is treated as at risk to the extent that basis in the partnership is increased by the share of partnership income. That partnership income is then used to reduce the partnership's nonrecourse indebtedness will have no effect on a partner's amount at risk. If the partnership makes actual distributions of the income in the taxable year, the amount distributed reduces the partner's amount at risk. A buy-sell agreement, effective at a partner's death or retirement, is not considered for at-risk purposes.

EXAMPLES

1. On January 2, 1995, Paul Reed, an investor, contributes $5,000 cash to a farming venture. He also borrows $3,000 from a bank for which he is personally liable and contributes it. By the end of 1995, he pays off $750 of the loan. The venture has no income or losses in 1995. His at-risk basis as of December 31, 1995, is $7,250, determined as follows:

Contributions	$ 5,000
Recourse financing	3,000
	$ 8,000
Less: Partial loan repayment	750
Amount at risk as of 12/31/95	$ 7,250

2. Same as Example 1, but on February 1, 1996, he borrows $10,000 on a nonrecourse basis. He pays off $1,000 on the personal liability loan and $500 on the nonrecourse loan. The venture earns $3,000 and distributes $2,000 to him. The at-risk basis as of December 31, 1996, is $7,250, determined as follows:

Amount at risk as of 1/1/96		$ 7,250
Plus: Income		3,000
		$10,250
Less: Repayment of personal liability loan	$1,000	
Distribution	2,000	3,000
Amount at risk as of 12/31/96		$ 7,250

Payment on the nonrecourse loan with funds or other nonrecourse loans from only the activity does not affect the amount at risk.

3. Same as Example 2, but on March 1, 1997, the investor contributes $2,500 and pays off the personal liability loan. The venture has losses of $10,500 for 1997. As of December 31, 1997, the investor's amount at risk is $8,500, determined as follows:

Amount at risk as of 1/1/97	$7,250
Plus: Contribution	2,500
	$9,750
Less: Payment of personal liability loan	1,250
Amount at risk as of 12/31/97	$8,500

The investor's loss deduction is limited to the amount at risk of $8,500. The $2,000 disallowed loss is carried over to 1998.

Note: The above adjustments to basis are only for at-risk purposes. Basis for depreciation and computing gain or loss on a sale is controlled by the adjusted basis rules at 5.20.

Activities begun before 1976.   A special rule determines the amount at risk as of the first day of the first tax year after 1975. Again, you start with the amounts considered at risk. Losses incurred and deducted in taxable years before 1976 first reduce the basis allocated to amounts considered not at risk, such as nonrecourse loans. If the losses exceed the amount not at risk, the excess reduces the at-risk investment. Distributions reduce at-risk amounts. *See* the instructions to Form 6198.

10.19 Amounts Not At Risk

The following may not be treated as part of basis for at-risk purposes in determining your tax position in a business or investment:

Liabilities for which you have no personal liability, except in the case of certain real estate financing; *see 10.18.*

Liabilities for which you have personal liability, but the lender also has a capital or profit-sharing interest in the venture.

Recourse liabilities convertible to a nonrecourse basis.

EXAMPLE

David Krepp, an investor, purchases cattle from a rancher for $10,000 cash and a $30,000 note payable to the rancher. Krepp is personally liable on the note. In a separate agreement, the rancher agrees to care for the cattle for 6% of Krepp's net profits from the cattle activity. Krepp is considered at risk for $10,000; he may not increase the amount at risk by the $30,000 borrowed from the rancher.

Money borrowed from a relative listed at 5.5 who has an interest in the venture, other than as a creditor, or from a partnership in which you own more than a 10% interest.

Funds borrowed from a person whose recourse is solely your interest in the activity or property used in the activity.

Amounts for which your economic loss is limited by a nonrecourse financing guarantee, stop-loss agreement, or other similar arrangement.

Investments protected by insurance or loss reimbursement agreement between you and another person. If you are personally liable on a mortgage but you separately obtain insurance to compensate you for any mortgage payments, you are at risk only to the extent of the uninsured portion of the personal liability. You may, however, include as at risk any amount of premium paid from your personal assets. Taking out casualty insurance or insurance protecting you against tort liability is not considered within the at-risk provisions, and such insurance does not affect your investment basis.

EXAMPLES

1. Some commercial feedlots in livestock feeding operations may reimburse investors against any loss sustained on sales of the livestock above a stated dollar amount per head. Under such "stop-loss" orders, an investor is at risk only to the extent of the portion of his or her capital against which he or she is not entitled to reimbursement. Where a limited partnership makes an agreement with a limited partner that, at the partner's election, his or her partnership interest will be bought at a stated minimum dollar amount (usually less than the investor's original capital contribution), the partner is considered at risk only to the extent of his or her investment exceeding the guaranteed repurchase price.

2. A TV film promoter sold half-hour TV series programs to individual investors. Each investor gave a cash down payment and a note for which he or she was personally liable for the balance. Each investor's note, which was identical in face amount, terms, and maturity date, was payable out of the distribution proceeds from the film. Each investor also bought from the promoter the right to the unpaid balance on another investor's note. The promoter arranged the distribution of the films as a unit and was to apportion the sales proceeds equally among the investors.

   The IRS held that each investor is not at risk on the investment evidenced by the note. Upon maturity, each may receive a payment from another investor equal to the one that he or she owes.

3. A gold mine investment offered tax write-offs of four times the cash invested. For $10,000 cash, an investor buys from a foreign mining company a seven-year mineral claim lease to a gold reserve. Under the lease, he or she can develop and extract all of the gold in the reserve. At the same time, he or she agrees to spend $40,000 to develop the lease before the end of the year. To fund this commitment, the investor authorizes the promoter to sell an option for $30,000 to a third party who is to buy all the gold to

be extracted. The $30,000 along with the $10,000 down payment is to be used to develop the reserve. The promoter advises the investor that he or she may claim a $40,000 deduction for certain development costs.

The IRS ruled that $30,000 is not deductible because the amount is not "risk capital." The investor gets $30,000 by selling an option that can be exercised only if gold is found. If no gold is found, he or she is under no obligation to the option holder. His or her risk position for the $30,000 is substantially the same as if he or she had borrowed from the option holder on a nonrecourse basis repayable only from his or her interest in the activity.

The Tax Court struck down a similar plan on different grounds. Without deciding the question of what was at risk, the court held that the option was only a right of first refusal. Thus, $30,000 was taxable income to the investor in the year of the arranged sale.

Limited partner's potential cash call.   Under the terms of a partnership agreement, limited partners may be required to make additional capital contributions under specified circumstances. Whether such a potential cash call increases the limited partner's at-risk amount has been a matter of dispute.

In one case, the IRS and Tax Court held that a limited partner was not at risk with respect to a partnership note where, under the terms of the partnership agreement, he could be required to make additional capital contributions if the general partners did not pay off the note at maturity. The possibility of such a potential cash call was too uncertain; the partnership might earn profits to pay off the note and even if there were losses, the general partners might not demand additional contributions from the limited partners.

However, a federal appeals court reversed, holding that the limited partner was at risk because his obligation was mandatory and "economic reality" insured that the general partners would insure their rights by requiring the additional capital contribution.

In another case, limited partners relied upon the earlier favorable federal appeals court decision to argue that they were at risk where they could be required by the general partners to make additional cash contributions, but only in order to cover liabilities or expenses that could not be paid out of partnership assets. So long as the partnership was solvent, the limited partners could "elect out" of the call provision. Because of this election, the Tax Court held that the limited partners' obligation was contingent, rather than unavoidable as in the earlier federal appeals court case. Thus, the cash call provision did not increase their at-risk amount.

10.20 At-Risk Investment in Several Activities

If you invest in several activities, each is generally treated separately when applying the at-risk limitation on Form 6198. You generally may not aggregate basis, gains, and losses from the activities for purposes of at-risk limitations. Thus, income from one activity may not be offset by losses from another; the income from one must be reported while the losses from the other may be nondeductible because of at-risk limitations.

However, you may aggregate activities that are part of a business you actively manage. Activities of a business carried on by a partnership or S corporation qualify if 65% or more of losses for the year are allocable to persons who actively participate in management.

The law allows partnerships and S corporations to treat as a single activity all depreciable equipment (Section 1245 property) which is leased or held for lease and placed in service in any tax year. Furthermore, you may aggregate all partnership or S corporation activities within the four categories of films and videotapes, oil and gas properties, geothermal properties, and farms; *see 10.17.*

10.21 Carryover of Disallowed Losses

A loss disallowed in a current year by the at-risk limitation may be carried over and deducted in the next taxable year, provided it does not fall within the at-risk limits or the passive loss limits in that year. The loss is subject to an unlimited carryover period until there is an at-risk basis to support the deduction. This may occur when additional contributions are made to the business or when the activity has income which has not been distributed.

Gain from the disposition of property used in an at-risk activity is treated as income from the activity. In general, the reporting of gain will allow a deduction for losses disallowed in previous years to be claimed in the year of disposition.

10.22 Recapture of Losses Where At Risk Is Less Than Zero

To prevent manipulation of at-risk basis after a loss is claimed, there is a special recapture rule. If the amount at risk in an activity is reduced to below zero because of a distribution or a change in the status of an indebtedness from recourse to nonrecourse, income may be realized to the extent of the negative at-risk amount. The taxable amount may not exceed the amount of losses previously deducted.

The recaptured amount is not treated as income from the activity for purposes of determining whether current or suspended losses are allowable.

The recaptured amount is treated as a deduction allowable to that activity in the following year.

Income From: Prizes, Gambling, Gifts, State Tax Refunds, Damages, Debt Cancellations, Partnerships, S Corporations, Trusts And Estates

Income items discussed in this chapter are reported on Line 10 or 21 of Form 1040 or on a Schedule E and then transferred to Line 17 of Form 1040.

- Taxable state tax refunds are reported on Line 10 of Form1040.

- Prizes, gambling winnings, and awards are reported on Line 21 of Form 1040.

- Your share of partnership, S Corporation, trust or estate income or loss is reported in Schedule E according to Schedule K-1 statements provided you by the entity.

Further reporting details are discussed in this chapter.

11.1 Prizes and Awards

Prizes; Lottery and Gambling Winnings

Prizes and awards are taxable income except for an award or prize that meets *all* these four tests:

1. It is for outstanding educational activities, literary, or civic achievement.
2. You were selected without any action on your part.
3. You do not have to perform services.
4. You assign the prize or award to a government unit or tax-exempt charitable organization. You must make the assignment before you use or benefit from the award. You may not claim a charitable deduction for the assignment.

Prize taxed at fair market value. A prize of merchandise is taxable at fair market value. For example, where a prize of first-class steamship tickets was exchanged for tourist-class tickets for a winner's family, the taxable value of the prize was the price of the tourist tickets. What is the taxable fair market value of an automobile won as a prize? In one case, the Tax Court held that the taxable value was what the recipient could realize on an immediate resale of the car.

Employee achievement awards. The above restrictions on tax-free treatment do not apply to awards from employers for length of service or safety achievement. The rules for such employee awards are at *3.10* and *20.25*.

11.2 Lottery and Sweepstake Winnings

Sweepstake, lottery, and raffle winnings are taxable as "other income" on Line 21 of Form 1040. The cost of tickets is deductible only to the extent you report winnings, and only if you itemize deductions. The deduction is claimed on Schedule A as a miscellaneous deduction that is *not* subject to the 2% adjusted gross income (AGI) floor (Chapter 19). For example, if you buy state lottery tickets and win a 1997 drawing, you may deduct the cost of your losing tickets in 1997 up to the amount of your winnings.

When a minor wins a state lottery and the prize is held by his or her parents as custodians under the Uniform Gifts to Minors Act, the prize is taxed to the minor in the year the prize is won.

Installment payments. If winnings are payable in installments, you pay tax only as installments are received. This is true even if the payer is required by state law to buy a surety bond as security for future installments. That the payments are secured does not make them immediately taxable where you have no choice in the way payments are made. If you have the chance to elect a lump-sum payment but instead choose installments, you are in "constructive receipt," and thus are taxable on the entire amount in the year the prize is awarded.

11.3 Gambling Winnings and Losses

Gambling winnings are taxable. Losses from gambling are deductible only up to the gains from gambling. You may not deduct a net gambling loss even though a particular state says gambling is legal. Nor does it matter that your business is gambling. You may not deduct the loss even if you are a professional gambler.

If you are not a professional gambler, gambling income is included on Form 1040 as "other income" on Line 21. Gambling losses (not exceeding the amount of the gains) are deductible as "miscellaneous deductions" on Schedule A. The losses are *not* subject to the 2% AGI floor (Chapter 19). According to the IRS, professional gamblers who bet only for their own account are not in a business and must deduct losses (up to gains) as itemized deductions. However, the Supreme Court has held that full-time gamblers may deduct losses as business expenses even if they place wagers only for themselves. According to the Supreme Court, in order to be considered engaged in a business, a gambler must prove that he or she bets full time to earn a livelihood and not merely as a hobby.

Caution

Splitting Lottery Winnings
To split income, potential lottery winnings may be divided among family members or others before the prize is won. You might buy the lottery ticket in your name and the names of others. The prize is shared and each portion separately taxed. However, the IRS has not allowed income splitting after the prize is won. In one case, a couple who bought a winning lottery ticket that under state law was payable to only one person proved they shared the ticket before the drawing by having their attorneys draw up a joint ownership agreement.

To prove your losses in the event your return is questioned, you must retain evidence of losses.

Court Decision

Gambler Not Taxed on Cancelled Gambling Debt

The federal appeals court for the Third Circuit (New Jersey, Pennsylvania, and Delaware) held that the settlement by an Atlantic City casino of a gambler's $3.4 million debt for $500,000 was not taxable. The debt was not enforceable under New Jersey law because the casino did not comply with state regulations on issuance of credit. Furthermore, the gambling chips were not "property" securing the debt; they had no economic value outside the casino.

EXAMPLES
1. To appear on the Wheel of Fortune, Whitten traveled from Chicago to Los Angeles, spending $1,820 for transportation, meals, and lodging. When he won cash prizes of $14,850 plus an automobile, he tried to offset his winnings by the travel costs, claiming they were gambling losses on Schedule A not subject to the 2% AGI floor. The IRS and Tax Court disagreed; travel costs are not like wager or bet losses.

2. Trump Casino in Atlantic City gave Libutti, a high roller at its gaming tables, over $2.5 million in "comps" during a three-year period in which he lost over $8 million. The comps included 10 expensive automobiles, jewelry, European vacations, and tickets to sporting events. Libutti reported the comps as income and then claimed a matching miscellaneous deduction for gambling losses not subject to the 2% floor. The IRS disallowed the deduction, claiming that the comps were not gambling income because they were perks given to stimulate his desire to gamble at Trump's, and not winnings from the success of his wagers.
   The Tax Court disagrees. Libutti would not have received the comps unless he gambled at high stakes in Trump's casino. Although the comps did not directly hinge on the success or failure of his wagers, the comps were sufficiently related to his gambling losses to allow the deduction.

11.4   Gifts and Inheritances

Gifts and inheritances you *receive* are not taxable. Income earned from gift or inherited property after you receive it is taxable.

Describing a payment as a gift or inheritance will not necessarily shield it from tax if it is, in fact, a payment for your services. Treatment of gifts to employees is covered at *2.4*.

A sale of an expected inheritance from a living person is taxable as ordinary income.

Planning Reminder

Gifts You Make

You may have to file a gift tax return if your gifts to an individual within the year exceed $10,000; *see 33.1*.

EXAMPLES
1. An employee is promised by his employer that he will be remembered in his will if he continues to work for him. The employer dies but fails to mention the employee in his will. The employee sues the estate, which settles his claim. The settlement is taxable.

2. A nephew left his uncle a bequest of $200,000. In another clause of the will, the uncle was appointed executor, and the bequest of the $200,000 was described as being made in lieu of all commissions to which he would otherwise be entitled as executor. The bequest is considered tax-free income. It was not conditioned upon the uncle performing as executor. If the will had made the bequest contingent upon the uncle's acting as executor, the $200,000 would have been taxed.

3. An attorney performed services for a friend without expectation of pay. The friend died and in his will left the attorney a bequest in appreciation for his services. The payment was considered a tax-free bequest. The amount was not bargained for.

4. A lawyer agreed to handle a client's legal affairs without charge; she promised to leave him securities. Twenty years later, under her will, he inherited the securities. The IRS taxed the bequest as pay. Both he and the client expected that he would be paid for legal services. If she meant to make a bequest from their agreement, she should have said so in her will.

Planning Reminder

Campaign Contributions

Campaign contributions are not taxable income to a political candidate if the funds are used for political campaign expenses or some similar purposes. Detailed records of receipts and disbursements are advisable to avoid tax on the political funds. Also nontaxable are contributions that are intended for the candidate's unrestricted personal use and qualify as gifts.

State Tax Refunds and Other Recovered Deductions

11.5 Refunds of State and Local Income Tax Deductions

A refund of state or local income tax is not taxable if you did not previously claim the tax as an itemized deduction in a prior year. For example, if you claimed the standard deduction on your 1996 return and in 1997 you received a refund for state tax withheld from your 1996 wages, the refund is not taxable on your 1997 return.

If you did claim the refunded tax as an itemized deduction, the refund is taxable only to the extent that your itemized deductions exceeded the standard deduction you could have claimed in the prior year. If, in addition to the tax refund, you received recoveries of other itemized deductions, the same computation applies to determine the taxable portion of the total recovery; *see 11.6.*

To help you figure the taxable portion of 1996 itemized deductions recovered in 1997, 1996 standard deduction amounts are shown in the table at the end of this section.

The computation of the taxable refund is different if, in the year the refunded item was claimed, you were subject to the 3% reduction of itemized deductions. In this case, the IRS provides a special method explained in Publication 525.

EXAMPLE

On your 1996 return, you filed as a single taxpayer. You claimed itemized deductions of $4,300, of which $2,300 was for state and local taxes, $1,500 was for mortgage interest and $500 was for charitable contributions. Your deductions exceeded by $300 the $4,000 standard deduction you could have claimed. The deductions were not subject to the 3% reduction discussed at *13.8*.

In 1997, you received from the state a $750 refund for 1996 state taxes. You must report $300 of the refund as income on your 1997 Form 1040. The taxable recovery is limited to the $300 difference between the itemized deductions claimed and the $4,000 standard deduction for 1996.

If you had a *negative* taxable income in 1996, the taxable recovery figured under the above rule is reduced by the negative amount. If you had a negative taxable income of $100 in 1996, only $200 of the refund would be taxable instead of $400.

Allocating a refund recovery. If in 1997 you received a refund of state or local taxes and also a recovery of other deductions, and only part of the total recovery is taxable, you allocate the taxable amount of the recovery according to the ratio between the state tax refund and the other recovery. You do this by first dividing the state refund by the total of all itemized deductions recovered. The resulting percentage is then applied to the taxable recovery to find the amount to report as the tax refund on Line 10 of Form 1040; other taxable recoveries are reported on Line 21.

EXAMPLE

In 1997, you received a refund of state income taxes of $500 and a recovery of other itemized expenses of $2,000 deducted in 1996. You figure that only $1,500 of the recovery is taxable because your total 1996 itemized deductions were $1,500 more than the standard deduction you could have claimed. As a state tax refund is reported separately from other recoveries, you must find how much of the taxable recovery is attributed to the refund. By dividing the state tax refund by the amount of the total recovery, you find that 20% is attributed to the refund ($500/$2,500). Thus, 20% of the taxable recovery, or $300 (20% of $1,500), is reported as a state refund on Line 10, Form 1040, and the balance of $1,200 on Line 21, Form 1040. Also attach a statement showing that the allocation of recoveries required the reporting on Line 10, Form 1040, of an amount less than the actual state refund shown on Form 1099-G.

Refund of state tax paid in installments over two tax years. If you pay estimated state or local income taxes, your last tax installment may be in the year you receive a refund. In this case, you allocate the refund between the two years; see the following Example.

EXAMPLE

Your estimated state income tax for 1996 was $4,000, which you paid in four equal installments. You made your fourth payment in January 1997. No state income tax was withheld during 1996. In 1997, you received a tax refund of $400. You claimed itemized deductions each year on your federal return. You allocate the $400 refund between 1996 and 1997. As you paid 75% ($3,000 ÷ $4,000) of the estimated tax in 1996, 75% of the $400 refund, or $300, is allocated to 1996. On your 1997 return, you include $300 as income on Line 10, Form 1040. You also attach a statement explaining that the amount on Line 10 is less than the $400 refund shown on the Form 1099-G received from the state because of the allocation required by the estimated tax payment in 1997.

When you figure your 1997 deduction for state income taxes, you reduce the $1,000 paid in January by $100. Your 1997 deduction for state income taxes will include the January net amount of $900 plus any estimated taxes paid in 1997 for 1997, any state income tax withheld during 1997, and any 1996 tax paid with your state income tax return filed in 1997.

Note: If the $300 refund allocated to 1996 in the previous Example was more than the excess of your 1996 itemized deductions over the 1996 standard deduction you could have claimed, you report only that excess as 1997 income. If in 1996 you were subject to the 3% reduction to itemized deductions, see IRS Publication 525 for figuring the taxable portion of the refund. Also *see 11.6* for reducing the taxable amount if you had a negative taxable income, or if you recovered a bad debt or other non-itemized deduction

1996 Standard Deduction for Figuring Recoveries of 1996 Itemized Deductions

If you were—	*1996 standard deduction was—*
Married filing jointly	$6,700
Single	4,000
Head of household	5,900
Married filing separately	3,350
Qualifying widow or widower	6,700
Single age 65 or over	5,000
Single and blind	5,000
Single age 65 or over and also blind	6,000
Married filing jointly with:	
One spouse age 65 or over	7,500
Both spouses age 65 or over	8,300
One spouse blind under age 65	7,500
Both spouses blind under age 65	8,300
One spouse age 65 or over and also blind	8,300
One spouse age 65 or over and other spouse blind and under age 65	8,300
One spouse age 65 or over and also blind; other spouse blind and under age 65	9,100
Both spouses age 65 or over and also blind	9,900
Qualifying widow or widower age 65 or over	7,500
Qualifying widow or widower and blind	7,500
Qualifying widow or widower age 65 or over and also blind	8,300
Head of household age 65 or over	6,900
Head of household and blind	6,900
Head of household age 65 or over and also blind	7,900
Married filing separately age 65 or over[*]	4,150
Married filing separately and blind[*]	4,150
Married filing separately age 65 or over and also blind[*]	4,950

[*] *If you are claiming your spouse as an exemption (21.2), add $800 if he or she was either blind or age 65 or older; add $1,600 if he or she was both blind and age 65 or older.*

11.6 Other Recovered Deductions

The income rule applied to refunds of state income tax in *11.5* applies also to the recovery of other items for which you claimed a tax deduction, such as a refund of adjustable rate mortgage interest *(15.1)*, reimbursement of a deducted medical expense *(17.4)*, a reimbursed casualty loss *(18.1)*, a return of donated property which was claimed as a charitable deduction *(14.1)*, and a payment of debt previously claimed as a bad debt *(5.9)*.

EXAMPLE

In 1996, you filed a joint return and claimed itemized deductions of $8,000, which exceeded your standard deduction of $6,700. You were not subject to the 3% reduction to itemized deductions. In 1997, you received the following recoveries for amounts deducted in 1996:

Medical expenses	$ 200
State income tax refund	400
Interest expense	325
Total	$ 925

The total recovery of $925 is taxable. It is less than $1,300, the excess of your itemized deductions over the allowable standard deduction ($8,000 – 6,700). You report the state and local income tax refund of $400 on Line 10, Form 1040, and the balance of $525 on Line 21, Form 1040.

If the total recovery had been $2,500 instead of $925, $1,300 would be taxable (the excess of $8,000 over $6,700). The $1,200 balance would be tax free.

Tax credit in prior year. If you recover an item deducted in a prior year in which tax credits exceeded your tax, you refigure the prior year tax to determine if the recovery is taxable. Add the amount of the recovery to taxable income of the prior year and figure the tax on the increased taxable income. If your tax credit exceeds the recomputed tax, do not include the recovery in income. If the tax credit is less than the recomputed tax, include the recovery in income to the extent the recovery reduced your tax in the prior year.

Alternative minimum tax in the prior year. If you were subject to the alternative minimum tax (AMT) in the year the recovered deduction was claimed, recompute your regular and AMT tax for the prior year based on the taxable income you reported plus the recovered amount. If inclusion of the recovery does not change your total tax, you do not include the recovery in income. If your total tax increases by any amount, you include the recovery in income to the extent the deduction reduced your tax in the prior year.

Recovery of previously deducted items used to figure carryover. A deductible expense may not reduce your tax because you have an overall loss. If in a later year the expense is repaid or the obligation giving rise to the expense is cancelled, the deduction of that expense will be treated as having produced a tax reduction if it increased a carryover that has not expired by the beginning of the taxable year in which the forgiveness occurs. For example, you are on the accrual basis and deducted, but did not pay, rent in 1996. The rent obligation is forgiven in 1997. The 1996 rent deduction is treated as having produced a reduction in tax, even if it resulted in no tax savings in 1996 if it figured in the calculation of a net operating loss that has not expired or been used by the beginning of 1997, the year of forgiveness. The same rule applies to other carryovers such as the investment credit carryover.

 Filing Pointer

Negative Taxable Income

If your taxable income was a negative amount in the year in which the recovered item was deducted, you reduce the recovery includible in income by the negative amount. For example, if the taxable recovery would be $1,700 but you had a negative taxable income of $500 for the year the deduction was claimed, only $1,200 is taxable.

Damages and Debt Cancellation

11.7 How Legal Damages Are Taxed

Awards recovered through legal action, whether fixed by a court or a settlement between the parties, are generally taxable, unless they qualify as compensation for a personal injury, such as damages awarded for a physical injury in an auto accident. Interest paid on a tax-free damage award is taxable.

When damages compensate for the loss of property, you have taxable gain if the damages exceed adjusted basis of the property. A deductible loss will generally be allowed when the recovery is less than adjusted basis. The nature of the gain or loss takes on the same character (that is, capital gain or loss or ordinary income gain or loss) as the property lost.

Discrimination and other nonphysical injury awards. Damages received after August 20, 1996, are tax free only if on account of a physical injury or physical sickness, including awards for emotional distress attributable to a physical injury or physical sickness.

Damages received in discrimination or other nonphysical injury cases are taxable with one exception: Damages up to the amount of actual medical care expenses attributable to emotional distress are tax free. Apart from the medical care exception, emotional distress, including physical symptoms such as insomnia, headaches and stomach disorders, is not by itself considered a physical injury or sickness.

Punitive damages. Punitive damages are taxable, even if they relate to a physical injury or sickness. This law specifically applies to damages received after August 20, 1996, but a 1996 Supreme Court decision held that punitive damages were taxable even under the prior law because punitive

 Planning Reminder

Legal Fees

If the damages are tax free, you may not deduct your litigation costs. If your damages are fully taxed, you deduct all of your litigation costs. If your damages are only partially taxed, then you deduct only that portion of your litigation costs attributed to the taxed damages.

When your attorney receives payment of taxable damages and then turns over the money after deducting his or her fee, you are taxed in the year you receive your share.

Legal fees that are deductible as miscellaneous expenses are subject to the 2% adjusted gross income floor; *see* Chapter 19.

damages do not provide compensation for injuries, but are intended to punish wrongdoing by the defendant who was sued.

11.8 Cancellation of Debts You Owe

If your creditor cancels or reduces a debt you owe, you realize taxable income unless you can prove the creditor intended a gift or the cancellation qualifies for an exclusion. Exclusions are allowed for discharges of farm or business real estate debt and debts of insolvent and bankrupt persons, as explained below.

Form 1099-C. You should receive Form 1099-C from a federal government agency, credit union or bank that cancels or forgives a debt you owe of $600 or more. The IRS receives a copy of the form. Generally, the amount of canceled debt shown in Box 2 of Form 1099-C must be reported as "other income" on Line 21 of Form 1040, unless one of the exclusions discussed below applies.

Discounted mortgage repayment. A prepayment of a home mortgage at a discount is taxable. The income is reported on Line 21, Form 1040. The tax treatment of a foreclosure sale or voluntary conveyance to a creditor is discussed at *31.10*.

> **EXAMPLE**
> A bank allows a homeowner to prepay a low-interest mortgage of $20,000 for $18,000. The discount of $2,000 is taxable as ordinary income.

Law Alert

Loans Cancelled by Foundations
A new law also allows tax-free treatment for student loans cancelled by educational organizations after August 5, 1997. The loan must be made under a program that encourages students to provide public service by working in occupations or areas with unmet needs and the services must be under the direction of a governmental unit or tax-exempt charity. Services to the lender organization do not qualify.

Cancellation of student loans. A cancelled student loan is taxable income with this exception: If a loan by a government agency, by a government-funded loan program of an education organization, or by a qualified hospital organization is cancelled because you worked for a period of time in certain geographical areas for certain types of employers, such as practicing medicine in rural areas or teaching in inner-city schools, then the cancelled amount is not taxable. The Tax Court held that a student loan cancelled by the State of Alaska was taxable. The Alaska law conditioned forgiveness only on working in Alaska and there was no requirement that work be in a special area for specified employers.

Debts discharged in bankruptcy. A discharge of a debt in a Title 11 bankruptcy case is not taxable, but is used to reduce specified "tax attributes" on Form 982 in this order:

1. Net operating losses and carryovers—dollar for dollar of debt discharge;
2. Carryovers of the general business credit—$33^1/_3$ cents for each dollar of debt discharge;
3. AMT minimum tax credit as of the beginning of the year immediately after the taxable year of the discharge—$33^1/_3$ cents for each dollar of debt discharge;
4. Net capital losses and carryovers-dollar for dollar of debt discharge;
5. Basis of depreciable and nondepreciable assets—dollar for dollar of debt discharge (but not below the amount of your total undischarged liabilities);
6. Passive activity loss and credit carryovers—dollar for dollar of debt discharge for passive losses; $33^1/_3$ cents for each dollar of debt discharge in the case of passive credits; and
7. Foreign tax credit carryovers—$33^1/_3$ cents for each dollar of debt discharge.

After these reductions, any remaining balance of the debt discharge is disregarded. On Form 982, you may make a special election to first reduce the basis of any depreciable assets before reducing other tax attributes in the order above. Realty held for sale to customers may be treated as depreciable assets for purposes of the election. The election allows you to preserve your current deductions, such as a net operating loss carryover or capital loss carryover, for use in the following year. The election also will have the effect of reducing your depreciation deductions for years following the year of debt cancellation. If you later sell the depreciable property at a gain, the gain attributable to the basis reduction will be taxable as ordinary income under the depreciation recapture rules of *44.1*.

Separate bankruptcy estate. If you are an individual debtor who files for bankruptcy under Chapter 7 or 11 of the Bankruptcy Code, a separate "estate" is created consisting of property that belonged to you before the filing date. This bankruptcy estate is a new taxable entity, completely separate from you as a taxpayer. The estate is represented by a trustee who manages the estate for the benefit of any creditors. The estate earns its own income and incurs expenses. The trustee reports the estate's income or loss on a separate return (Form 1041). The creation of a separate bankruptcy estate also gives you a "fresh start"; with certain exceptions, wages you earn and property you acquire after the bankruptcy case has begun belong to you and do not become part of the bankruptcy estate.

A separate estate is not created for an individual who files for bankruptcy under Chapter 12.

In a Title 11 case, the tax attribute reductions are made to the attributes in the bankruptcy estate. Reductions are not made to attributes of an individual debtor that come into existence after the bankruptcy case begins or that are treated as exempt property under bankruptcy rules. Basis reduction does apply to property transferred by the bankruptcy estate to the individual.

Debts discharged while you are insolvent. If your debt is cancelled outside of bankruptcy while you are insolvent, the cancellation does not result in taxable income to the extent of the insolvency. Insolvency means that liabilities exceed the fair market value of your assets immediately before the discharge of the debt. The discharged debt is not taxed to the extent of your insolvency and is applied to the reduction of tax attributes on Form 982 in the same manner as to a bankrupt individual. If the cancelled debt exceeds the insolvency, any remaining balance is treated as if it were a debt cancellation of a solvent person and, thus, it is taxable unless it is a qualifying farming debt or business real estate debt as discussed later in this section.

See the Example below for the IRS approach to figuring insolvency upon a debt cancellation.

EXAMPLE

In 1992, Jones borrowed $1,000,000 from Chester and signed a note payable for that amount. Jones was not personally liable on the note, which was secured by an office building valued at $1,000,000 that he bought from Baker with the proceeds of Chester's loan. In 1997, when the value of the building declined to $800,000, Chester agreed to reduce the principal of the loan to $825,000. At the time, Jones held other assets valued at $100,000 and owed another person $50,000.

To determine the extent of Jones's insolvency, the IRS compares the value of Jones's assets and liabilities immediately before the discharge. According to the IRS, his assets total $900,000: the building valued at $800,000 plus other assets of $100,000. His liabilities total $1,025,000: the other debt of $50,000 plus the liability on the note, which the IRS considered to be $975,000, equal to the $800,000 value of the building and the discharged debt of $175,000. Jones is insolvent by $125,000 ($1,025,000 in liabilities *less* $900,000 in assets). As $175,000 was the amount of the discharged debt and Jones was insolvent to the extent of $125,000, only $50,000 is treated as taxable income.

Partnership debts. When a partnership's debt is discharged because of bankruptcy, insolvency, or if it is qualified farm debt or business real estate debt that is cancelled, the discharged amount is allocated among the partners. Bankruptcy or insolvency is tested not at the partnership level, but separately for each partner. Thus, a bankrupt or insolvent partner applies the allocated amount to reduce the specified tax attributes as previously discussed. A solvent partner may not take advantage of the rules applied to insolvent or bankrupt partners, even if the partnership is insolvent or bankrupt.

Purchase price adjustment for solvent debtors. If you buy property on credit and the seller reduces or cancels the debt arising out of the purchase, the reduction is generally treated as a purchase price adjustment (reducing your basis in the property). Since the reduction is not treated as a debt cancellation, you do not realize taxable income on the price adjustment. This favorable price adjustment rule applies only if you are solvent and not in bankruptcy, you have not transferred the property to a third party, and the seller has not transferred the debt to a third party, such as with the sale of your installment contract to a collection company.

Qualified farm debt. A solvent farmer may avoid tax from a discharge of indebtedness by an unrelated lender, including any federal, state, or local government agency, if the debt was incurred in farming or is a farm business debt secured by farmland or farm equipment used in the farming business. You are eligible for this relief only if 50% or more of your total gross receipts for the preceding three taxable years was derived from farming. The excluded amount first reduces tax attributes such as net operating loss carryovers and business tax credits. The excluded amount then reduces the farmer's basis in all property other than farmland, and then the basis in land used in the farming business.

Filing Pointer

Price Adjustments Not Taxed

If you bought property on credit and the seller cancels or reduces your purchase-related debt, this is a price adjustment, not a taxable cancellation of debt; *see 11.8* for details.

Business real estate debt. A solvent taxpayer may elect to avoid tax on a discharge of qualifying real property business debt. Such a discharge may occur where the fair market value of the property securing the debt has fallen in value. This relief applies to debt discharges after 1992. The debt must have been incurred or assumed in connection with business real property and must be secured by such property. A debt incurred or assumed after 1992 must be incurred or assumed to buy, construct, or substantially improve real property used in a business, or to refinance such acquisition debt (up to the refinanced amount). Debt incurred after 1992 to refinance a pre-1993 business real property debt (up to the refinanced amount) also qualifies. The debt must be secured by the property. Discharges of farm indebtedness do not qualify but may be tax free under the separate rules discussed earlier.

The maximum amount that can be excluded from income is the excess of the outstanding loan principal (immediately before the discharge) over the fair market value (immediately before the discharge) of the real property securing the debt, less any other outstanding qualifying real property business debts secured by the property. The excludable amount also may not exceed the taxpayer's adjusted basis for all depreciable real property held before the discharge. The excluded amount reduces basis in all depreciable real property.

Effect of basis reduction on later disposition of property. A reduction of basis is treated as a depreciation deduction so that a profitable sale of the property at a later date may be subject to the rules of recapture of depreciation; *see 44.1.*

Partners, S Corporation Shareholders, and Trust and Estate Beneficiaries

11.9 Schedule K-1

Although partnerships, S corporations, trusts, and estates are different types of tax entities, they share a common tax-reporting characteristic. The entity itself generally does not pay income taxes. As a partner, shareholder, or beneficiary, you report your share of the entity's income or loss. The entity files a Schedule K-1 with the IRS which indicates your share of the income, deductions, and credits passed through from the entity. You will receive a copy of the Schedule K-1, which you should keep for your records; it does not have to be attached to your tax return.

11.10 How Partners Report Partnership Profit and Loss

A partnership files Form 1065, which informs the IRS of partnership profit or loss and each partner's share on Schedule K-1. The partnership pays no tax on partnership income; each partner reports his or her share of partnership net profit or loss and special deductions and credits, whether or not distributions are received from the partnership, as shown on Schedule K-1. Income that is not distributed or withdrawn increases the basis of a partner's partnership interest.

Your share reported to you on Schedule K-1 (Form 1065) is generally based on your proportionate capital interest in the partnership, unless the partnership agreement provides for another allocation.

Your partnership must give you a copy of Schedule K-1 (Form 1065), which lists your share of income, loss, deduction, and credit items, and where to report them on your return. For example, your share of income or loss from a business or real estate activity is reported on Schedule E and is subject to passive activity adjustments, if any. Interest and dividends are reported on Schedule B, royalties on Schedule E, and capital gains and losses on Schedule D. Your share of charitable donations is claimed on Schedule A if you itemize deductions. Tax preference items for alternative minimum tax purposes are also listed.

Health insurance premiums. A partnership that pays 1997 premiums for health insurance for partners has a choice. It may treat the premium as a reduction in distributions to the partners. Alternatively, it may deduct the premium as an expense and charge each partner's share as a guaranteed salary payment taxable to the partner. The partner reports the guaranteed payment shown on Schedule K-1 as nonpassive income on Schedule E and may deduct 40% of the premium on Line 27, Form 1040.

Guaranteed salary and interest. A guaranteed salary which is fixed without regard to partnership income is reported as ordinary income. If you receive a percentage of the partnership income with a stipulated minimum payment, the guaranteed payment is the amount by which the minimum guarantee exceeds your share of the partnership income before taking into account the minimum guarantee.

Interest on capital is reported as interest income.

Self-employment tax. As a partner, you pay 1997 self-employment tax on your partnership profits, including a guaranteed salary and other guaranteed payments. The self-employment tax is explained in Chapter 45. Limited partners do not pay self-employment tax, unless guaranteed payments are received; *see 45.2.*

Special allocations. Partners may agree to special allocations of gain, income, loss, deductions, or credits disproportionate to their capital contributions. The allocation should have a substantial economic effect to avoid an IRS disallowance. The IRS will not issue an advance ruling on whether an allocation has a substantial economic effect. If the allocation is rejected, a partner's share is determined by his or her partnership interest.

To have substantial economic effect, a special allocation must be reflected by adjustments to the partners' capital accounts; liquidation proceeds must be distributed in accordance with the partners' capital accounts, and following a liquidating distribution, the partners must be liable to the partnership to restore any deficit in their capital.

If there is a change of partnership interests during the year, items are allocated to a partner for that part of the year he or she is a member of the partnership. Thus, a partner who acquires an interest late in the year is barred from deducting partnership expenses incurred prior to his entry into the partnership. If the partners agree to give an incoming partner a disproportionate share of partnership losses for the period after he or she becomes a member, the allocation must meet the substantial economic effect test to avoid IRS disallowance.

See IRS regulations to Code Section 704, IRS Publication 541, and Form 1065 instructions for further details.

Reporting transfers of interest to IRS. If you transfer a partnership interest that includes an interest in partnership receivables and appreciated inventory, you must report the disposition to the partnership within 30 days, or, if earlier, by January 15 of the calendar year after the year of the transfer. The partnership in turn files a report with the IRS on Form 8308. You must also attach a statement to your income tax return describing the transaction and allocating basis to the receivables and inventory items. The IRS wants to keep track of such dispositions because partners have to pay ordinary income tax on the portion of profit attributable to the receivables and inventory.

For transfers before August 6, 1997, the ordinary income rule for appreciated inventory applies to inventory with a fair market value exceeding 120% of adjusted basis. Under a new law for transfers after August 5, 1997, the profit attributable to *all* inventory is ordinary income unless the transfer is pursuant to a contract binding on and after June 8, 1997.

Within 30 days of your transfer, provide the partnership with a statement that includes the date of the exchange and identifies the transferee (include Social Security number if known). You can be penalized for failure to notify the partnership. You and your transferee should receive a copy of the Form 8308 which the partnership will send to the IRS along with its Form 1065.

Generally, the partnership must file a separate Form 8308 for each transfer but the IRS may allow a composite Form 8308 for the calendar year if there were at least 25 reportable transfers.

Recognition of gain by partner on distribution of contributed property. Under a restrictive law (Code Section 737), a partner who contributes appreciated property to a partnership may incur tax on the pre-contribution gain if within five years *other* property is received from the partnership that is valued at more than the partner's basis in the partnership. Under another law (Code Section 704(c)(1)(B)), if appreciated property contributed by a partner is distributed to a *different* partner within five years of the contribution, the contributing partner is taxed on the pre-contribution gain as if the property had been sold at fair market value on the date of distribution. The five-year period under both of these statutes is extended to seven years by a new law, effective for contributions to partnerships after June 8, 1997. The five-year rule will continue to apply if there was a binding contract to contribute a fixed amount of property in effect on and after June 8, 1997.

 Filing Instruction

Partnership Elections
The partnership, not the individual partners, makes elections affecting the computation of partnership income such as the election to defer involuntary conversion gains, to amortize organization and start-up costs, and to choose depreciation methods, including first-year expensing. An election to claim a foreign tax credit is made by the partners.

Caution

Partner May Be Taxed on Pre-Contribution Gain

The rules subjecting partners to tax on pre-contribution gain when they contribute property and the partnership makes a later distribution are complicated and hedged with restrictions. Consult a tax advisor before making transfers of appreciated property to, or taking distributions from, a partnership.

11.11 When a Partner Reports Income or Loss

You report your share of the partnership gain or loss for the partnership year which ends in your tax reporting year. If you and the partnership are on a calendar-year basis, you report your share of the 1997 partnership income on your 1997 income tax return. If the partnership is on a fiscal year ending March 31, for example, and you report on a calendar year, you report on your 1997 return your share of the partnership income for the whole fiscal year ending March 31, 1997—that is, partnership income for the fiscal year April 1, 1996, through March 31, 1997.

If a Section 444 election of a fiscal year is made on Form 8716, a special tax payment must be computed for each fiscal year and if the computed payment exceeds $500, it must be paid to the IRS. The tax payment is figured and reported on Form 8752. The tax does not apply to the first tax year of a partnership's existence but Form 8752 must still be filed. In later years, a refund of prior payments is available to the extent the prior payments exceed the payment required for the current fiscal year. For example, if the required payment was $12,000 for the fiscal year July 1, 1997–June 30, 1998, and the required payment for the fiscal year starting July 1, 1998, is $10,000, a $2,000 refund may be claimed on Form 8752. Refunds of prior-year payments also are available if the fiscal-year election is terminated and a calendar year adopted or if the partnership liquidates.

See *IRS Publication 541 for further information on partnership reporting.*

11.12 Partnership Loss Limitations

Your share of partnership losses may not exceed the adjusted basis of your partnership interest. If the loss exceeds basis, the excess loss may not be deducted until you have partnership earnings to cover the loss or contribute capital to cover the loss. The basis of your partnership interest is generally the amount paid for the interest (either through contribution or purchase) *less* withdrawals plus accumulated taxed earnings that have not been withdrawn.

A partner's basis is not increased by accrued but unpaid expenses such as interest costs and accounts payable unless the partnership uses the accrual accounting method. However, basis is increased by capitalized items allocable to future periods such as organization and construction period expenses.

Partners are subject to the "at-risk" loss limitation rules. These rules limit the amount of loss that may be deducted to the amount each partner personally has at stake in the partnership such as contributions of property and loans for which the partner is personally liable. *See 10.17* for a discussion of the "at-risk" rules.

Furthermore, if the IRS determines that a tax-shelter partnership is not operated to make a profit, deductions may be disallowed even where there is an "at-risk" investment.

Finally, any loss not barred by these limitations may be disallowed under the passive activity rules discussed in Chapter 10.

11.13 Unified Tax Audits of Partnerships

Tax audits of both a partnership of more than 10 partners and its partners must be at the partnership level. To challenge the partnership treatment of an item, the IRS must generally audit the partnership, not the individual partner. To avoid a personal audit of a partnership item, a partner should report partnership items as shown on the partnership return or identify any inconsistent treatment on his or her return. Otherwise, the IRS may assess a deficiency without auditing the partnership.

For a partnership-level audit, the partnership names a "tax matters partner" (TMP) to receive notice of the audit. If one is not named, the IRS will treat as a TMP the general partner having the largest interest in partnership profits at the end of the taxable year involved in the audit. Notice of the audit must also be given to the other partners. All partners may participate in the partnership audit. If the IRS settles with some partners, similar settlement terms must be offered to the others.

Within 90 days after the IRS mails its final determination, the TMP may appeal to the Tax Court; individual partners have an additional 60 days to file a court petition if the TMP does not do so. An appeal may also be filed in a federal district court or the claims court if the petitioning partner first deposits with the IRS an amount equal to the tax that would be owed if the IRS determination were sustained. A Tax Court petition takes precedence over petitions filed in other courts. The first Tax Court petition filed is heard; if other partners have also filed petitions, their cases will be dismissed. If no Tax Court petitions are filed, the first petition filed in federal district court or the claims court takes precedence. Regardless of which petition takes precedence, all partners who hold an interest during the taxable year involved will be bound by the decision (unless the statute of limitations with respect to that partner has run out).

Exception for 10 or fewer partners. The unified audit rules do not apply if there are 10 or fewer partners. The exception applies if all the partners are individuals (but not nonresidents), estates of deceased partners, or C corporations. C corporations are allowed under this exception under a new law effective for taxable years ending after August 5, 1997. A husband and wife (and their estates) are treated as one partner.

11.14 Stockholder Reporting of S Corporation Income and Loss

S corporations are subject to tax reporting rules similar to those applied to partnerships. However, shareholders who work for the corporation are treated as employees for FICA purposes. They do not pay self-employment tax on their salary income or other receipts from the corporation.

Your company must give you a copy of Schedule K-1 (Form 1120S), which lists your share of income or loss, deductions, and credits that must be reported on your return. For example, your share of business income or loss is reported on Schedule E and is subject to passive activity adjustments, if any. Interest and dividends from other corporations are reported on Schedule B, capital gains and losses on Schedule D, Section 1231 gains or losses on Form 4797, and charitable donations on Schedule A. Tax preference items for alternative minimum tax purposes are also listed.

Health insurance premimums paid by an S corporation for more than 2% stockholders are treated as wages, deductible on Form 1120-S by the corporation and reported to the stockholder on Form W-2.

A more-than-2% shareholder who reports premiums as wages for 1997 may deduct 40% of the premium on Line 27 of Form 1040 as an adjustment to income.

Allocation to shareholders. The following items are allocated to and pass through to the shareholders based on the proportion of stock held in the corporation:

- Gains and losses from the sale and exchange of capital assets and Section 1231 property, as well as interest and dividends on corporate investments and losses. Investment interest expenses subject to the rules of *15.10* also pass through.
- Tax-exempt interest. Tax-exempt interest remains tax free in the hands of the stockholders but increases the basis of their stock. Dividends from other companies may qualify for the exclusion.
- First-year expense deduction.
- Charitable contributions made by the corporation.
- Foreign income or loss.
- Foreign taxes paid by the corporation. Each stockholder elects whether to claim these as a credit or deduction.
- Tax preference items.
- Recovery of bad debts and prior taxes.

If your interest changed during the year, your pro rata share must reflect the time you held the stock.

The Tax Court and several federal appeals courts have held that an S corporation shareholder's basis is not increased by guaranteeing a loan to the corporation where there is no actual economic outlay. The Tax Court disagrees with the approach of another federal appeals court that allowed an increased basis where the lender looked to the guarantor-shareholder as the primary obligor on the guaranteed loan.

Passive activity rules limit loss deductions. Losses allocated to you may be disallowed under the passive activity rules discussed at Chapter 10.

Basis adjustments. Because of the nature of S corporation reporting, the basis of each shareholder's stock is subject to change. Basis is increased by the pass-through of income items and reduced by the pass-through of loss items and the receipt of distribution. Because income and loss items pass through to stockholders, an S corporation has no current earnings and profits. An income item will not increase basis, unless you actually report the amount on your tax return. The specific details and order of basis adjustments are listed in IRS Publication 589.

Planning Reminder

Basis Limits Loss Deductions.
Deductible losses may not exceed your basis in S corporation stock and loans to the corporation. If losses exceed basis, the excess loss is carried over and becomes deductible when you invest or lend an equivalent amount of money to the corporation. This rule may allow for timing a loss deduction. In a year in which you want to deduct the loss, you may contribute capital to the corporation. If a carryover loss exists when an S election terminates, a limited loss deduction may be allowed.

Family S Corporations

The IRS has the authority to change the amounts of items passed through to stockholders to properly reflect the value of services rendered or capital contributed by family members of one or more S corporation shareholders. If you are the member of a family of an S corporation shareholder and perform services or furnish capital to the corporation without receiving reasonable compensation, the IRS may reallocate salary or interest income to you from the other shareholders to reflect the value of your services or capital. The term "family" includes only a spouse, parents, ancestors, children, and any trusts for the benefit of such relatives.

Consistent Reporting by Beneficiaries

On tax returns filed after August 5, 1997, beneficiaries of trusts and estates must report items consistently with the Schedule K-1 provided by the trust or estate. If an item is treated inconsistently and a statement identifying the inconsistency is not attached to the return, the IRS may make a summary assessment for additional tax without issuing a deficiency notice.

Trust Sale of Capital Gain Property Within Two Years of Transfer

Under prior laws, if a trust sold appreciated property within two years of receiving it by gift or bargain sale, gain was taxed to the trust at the same rate that the transferor would have paid if the transferor sold the property. This rule for taxing gain did not apply if the transferor died and then the trust sold the property within the two-year period.

The rule taxing gain to the trust at the transferor's rate has been repealed, effective for sales after August 5, 1997.

EXAMPLES
1. A calendar-year corporation incurs a loss of $10,000. Smith and Jones each own 50% of the stock. On May 1, Smith sells all of his stock to Harris. For the year, Smith was a shareholder for 120 days, Jones for 365 days, and Harris for 245 days. The loss is allocated on a daily basis; the daily basis of the loss is $27.3973 ($10,000 divided by 365 days). The allocation is as follows:

   Smith: $1,644 ($27.3973 × 120 days × 50% interest)
   Jones: $5,000 ($27.3973 × 365 days × 50% interest)
   Harris: $3,356 ($27.3973 × 245 days × 50% interest)

2. Same facts as in Example 1, except that on May 1, Smith sells only 50% of his stock to Harris. The allocation for Smith accounts for his 50% interest for 120 days and his 25% interest for the remainder of the year.

   Smith: $3,322 ($27.3973 × 120 days × 50% plus $27.3973 × 245 days × 25%)
   Jones: $5,000 (as above)
   Harris: $1,678 ($27.3973 × 245 days × 25%)

11.15 How Beneficiaries Report Estate or Trust Income

Trust or estate income is treated as if you had received the income directly from the original source instead of from the estate or trust. This means capital gain remains capital gain, ordinary income is fully taxed, and tax-exempt income remains tax free. Tax preference items of a trust or estate are apportioned between the estate or trust and beneficiaries, according to allocation of income.

You report your share of trust or estate income on Schedule B as shown on the Schedule K-1 (Form 1041) sent to you by the trustee. Dividends and interest from the trust are reported on Schedule B of Form 1040 and capital gains on Schedule D. Income or loss from real estate or business activities shown on Schedule K-1 is reported by you on Schedule E, subject to the passive activity restrictions discussed in Chapter 10.

Reporting rule for revocable grantor trusts. A grantor who sets up a revocable trust or keeps certain powers over trust income or corpus must report all of the trust income, deductions, and credits. This rule applies if a grantor retains a reversionary interest in the trust that is valued at more than 5% of the trust (valued at the time the trust is set up); *see* Chapter 33. If a grantor is also a trustee of a revocable trust and all the trust assets are in the United States, filing Form 1041 is not necessary. The grantor simply reports the trust income, deductions, and credits on Form 1040. This reporting rule is optional for revocable trusts created before 1981. Grantors of such trusts who want to report trust income on their own returns without having to file Form 1041 must first file a final Form 1041 for the current tax year with a notation on the form alerting the IRS that in later years they will report trust income on their own returns; *see* the instructions to Form 1041.

11.16 Repeal of Throwback Rule for Distributions of Accumulated Trust Income

Where you are the beneficiary of an accumulation trust, the trust accumulates income on which it pays tax. When the trust distributes income to you, the trustee tells you what part of the distribution is attributable to current income reported under the general rules of *11.15* and how much is attributable to accumulations of prior income. If you receive a distribution of accumulated income from a trust, contact the trustee or an experienced tax practitioner for advice in computing your tax on the accumulation.

For distributions made in trust taxable years beginning before August 6, 1997, tax on the accumulation distribution is figured on Form 4970, subject to a throwback rule. Under a new law, however, the throwback rule has been repealed for distributions made by most domestic trusts in trust taxable years beginning after August 5, 1997. The throwback rule continues to apply to distributions from domestic trusts that were formerly foreign trusts, or which were created before March 1, 1984, and subject to the rules for multiple trusts with a tax avoidance purpose. The throwback rules continue to apply to foreign trusts.

Throwback rule for distributions not affected by new law repeal. Distributions of accumulated income are subject to tax, provided the accumulation exceeds the distributable net income of the trust for the year. However, under the throwback rule, only that portion of the accumulation distribution that would have been included in the beneficiary's income had it been distributed when earned is currently taxed. Thus, tax-exempt interest is never taxed. Income accumulated prior to the beneficiary's reaching the age of 21 and the years before a beneficiary was born is not subject to the throwback rule unless distributions are made under a multiple trust rule explained in the instructions to Form 4970.

Although a beneficiary pays a tax in the year of receiving the accumulation distribution, tax is computed as if the accumulated income were actually distributed in the years in which it was earned. For the year of the accumulation distribution, the beneficiary pays tax on the sum of: (1) a tax on taxable income exclusive of the accumulation distribution; (2) a tax on the accumulation distribution computed using a short-cut method that takes into account taxable income in three of the five years preceding the year of distribution; and (3) an interest charge in the case of a foreign trust.

In preparing your return, the tax on your regular taxable income is computed on Form 1040; the tax on the distribution is computed on Form 4970 and added to the tax on Form 1040.

Where a trust has already been subject to estate tax or the generation-skipping transfer tax, the partial tax on a distribution is reduced by the estate or generation-skipping tax attributable to the accumulated income. The reduction is limited by a special statutory formula for determining the pre-death portions.

Where the beneficiary receives an accumulation distribution from more than two trusts for the same year, tax for the distributions from the third trust is computed under the method described above, except that no credit is given for any taxes previously paid by the trust with respect to the accumulation distribution. A *de minimis* rule provides that accumulation distributions are not subject to the multiple trust rule unless the distribution equals or exceeds $1,000.

Trust for the benefit of a spouse. Where a spouse creates a trust for the benefit of the other spouse, income of the trust is taxed to the spouse who created the trust as income is earned. Trust transfers before October 10, 1969, are not subject to this rule.

11.17 Deductions for Income Subject to Estate Tax

If you receive income which was earned by, but not paid to, a decedent before death, you are said to have "income in respect of a decedent." You report the income, and if an estate has paid a federal estate tax on the income, you may deduct part of the estate tax allocated to the income. No deduction is allowed for state death taxes. Ask the executor of the estate for data in computing the deduction.

> **EXAMPLE**
>
> When Jim Bennett's uncle died, he was owed a fee of $1,000. He also had not collected accrued bond interest of $500. Bennett, as the sole heir, will collect both items and pay income tax on them. These items are called income in respect of a decedent. Assume that an estate tax of $390 was paid on the $1,500. Bennett collects the $1,000, which he reports on his income tax return. He may deduct $260, computed as follows:
>
> $$\frac{\$1,000}{\$1,500} \times \$390, \text{ or } \$260$$
>
> When he collects the $500, he will deduct the balance, or $130 ($390 – $260).

Schedule A deduction. The deduction is generally claimed on Line 27 of Schedule A as a miscellaneous itemized deduction that is *not* subject to the 2% AGI floor. However, if you receive long-term capital gain income, such as an installment payment on a sale transacted before a decedent's death, the estate tax attributed to the capital gain item is not claimed as a miscellaneous deduction. The deduction is treated as if it were an expense of sale and, thus, reduces the amount of gain.

 Filing Instruction

Lump-sum Distributions From Qualified Retirement Plans

When a beneficiary receiving a lump-sum distribution because of an employee's death reports the distribution using the special averaging method (Chapter 7), the taxable amount of the distribution must be reduced by the estate taxes attributable to the distribution. See the Form 4972 instructions when calculating the tax under averaging.

Claiming Deductions

In this part, you will learn how to reduce your tax liability by claiming deductions from gross income, and either the standard deduction or itemized deductions. Pay special attention to—

- Deductions you may claim directly from gross income in arriving at adjusted gross income. These are allowed even if you claim the standard deduction. *See* Chapter 12.

- The standard deduction. Although the standard deduction (*See* Chapter 13) may provide an automatic tax reduction, read the chapters on itemized deductions to see that you have not overlooked itemized deductions for charitable donations, interest expenses, state and local taxes, medical expenses, casualty and theft losses, miscellaneous expenses for job costs and investment expenses.

- The 3% reduction of certain itemized deductions discussed in Chapter 13 if your 1997 adjusted gross income, or AGI (Line 32 of Form 1040), exceeds $121,200 (or $60,600 if you are married and file separate returns).

- Personal exemptions. Each personal exemption claimed on your 1997 return—for yourself, your spouse, your children, and other dependents, is the equivalent of a $2,650 deduction. *See* Chapter 21 for exemptions rules, including the phaseout of exemptions for certain high-income taxpayers.

- Other deductions which are discussed in the following chapters:

<table>
<tr><td>Chapter 40</td><td>Business expenses</td></tr>
<tr><td>Chapter 9</td><td>Rental expenses</td></tr>
<tr><td>Chapter 43</td><td>Automobile expenses</td></tr>
</table>

Chapter 12

Deductions Allowed in Figuring Adjusted Gross Income

Adjusted gross income (AGI) is the amount used in figuring the 7.5% floor for the medical expense deductions *(17.1)*, the 10% floor for personal casualty and theft losses *(18.11)*, the 2% floor for miscellaneous itemized deductions *(19.1)*, the charitable contribution percentage limitations *(14.17)*, and the 3% reduction of itemized deductions *(13.7)*.

If you follow the instructions and order of the tax return, you will arrive at adjusted gross income automatically. But if you are planning the tax consequences of a transaction in advance of preparing your return, *12.1* will explain how to figure adjusted gross income (AGI).

There is an advantage in being able to claim deductions directly from gross income in arriving at adjusted gross income, since the deduction is allowed even if you claim the standard deduction and do not itemize deductions on Schedule A of Form 1040. This chapter will explain the deductions that qualify for the direct deduction from gross income.

Expenses Deductible Directly From Gross Income

12.1 Figuring Adjusted Gross Income (AGI)

Adjusted gross income is the difference between gross income in Step 1 and the deductions listed in Step 2.

Step 1. Figure gross income.   This is all income received by you from any source, such as wages, salary, tips, gross business income, income from sales and exchanges of property, interest and dividends, rents, royalties, annuities, pensions, etc. But gross income does not include such items as tax-free interest from state or local bonds *(4.24)*, tax-free parsonage allowance *(3.12)*, tax-free insurance proceeds (Chapter 33), gifts and inheritances *(11.1)*, Social Security benefits which are not subject to tax under the rules of *34.3,* tax-free scholarship grants (Chapter 33), tax-free board and lodging *(3.11)*, and other tax-free fringe benefits (Chapter 3).

Step 2. Deduct from gross income only the following items:

Repayment of supplemental unemployment benefits required because of receipt of trade readjust ment allowances *(2.9)*

Forfeiture of interest penalties because of premature withdrawals *(4.16)*

Capital loss deduction up to $3,000 *(5.3)*

IRA contributions *(8.4)*

Rent and royalty expenses (Chapter 9)

50% of self-employed tax liability *(12.2)*

Health insurance deduction if self-employed *(12.2)*

Jury duty pay turned over to your employer *(12.2)*

Performing artists qualifying expenses *(12.2)*

Reforestation expenses *(12.2)*

Moving expenses *(12.3)*

Alimony payments *(37.1)*

Business expenses (Chapter 40)

Net operating losses *(40.17)*

Keogh or SEP retirement plan contributions for yourself (Chapter 41)

Step 3. The difference between Steps 1 and 2 is adjusted gross income.

12.2 Claiming Deductions From Gross Income

Many deductions that are deductible directly from gross income in arriving at adjusted gross income are deducted on Form 1040 schedules devoted to a specific activity, such as business deductions claimed on Schedule C (Chapter 40), capital losses claimed on Schedule D (Chapter 5), and real estate rental expenses on Schedule E (Chapter 9). Where an expense is not claimed on a specific schedule, it is deducted on Lines 23–31 of Form 1040. IRA deductions on Form 1040A are claimed on Line 15.

Here is a list of the deductions claimed on Lines 23–31 of Form 1040. Many of them are discussed in detail elsewhere in this book. Moving expenses are discussed at *12.3–12.8.* The others are discussed below.

IRA deduction—Line 23 of Form 1040; Line 15 of Form 1040A.   Enter your deductible IRA contribution here, including a contribution for your spouse if you file jointly. The deductible limits, including the phaseout rules for individuals covered by employer retirement plans, are explained in Chapter 8.

Medical savings account (MSA) deduction—Line 24 of Form 1040.   If you are self employed or employed by a qualifying small business and have high-deductible health coverage, a deduction for contributions to a MSA may be allowed. *See 17.17* for the MSA rules.

Moving expenses—Line 25 of Form 1040.   Deductible moving expenses are discussed in this chapter at *12.3–12.8.*

50% of self-employment tax—Line 26 of Form 1040.   After you figure your self-employment tax liability on Schedule SE, you deduct 50% of it here as an income tax deduction. *See* Chapter 45 for the calculation of self-employment tax.

Self-employed health insurance deduction—Line 27.   If you were self-employed in 1997, you may claim a special deduction on Form 1040, Line 27, for 40% of health insurance premiums paid in 1997 for yourself, your spouse, and your dependents. The deduction is also al-

Law Alert

Self-Employed Health Insurance

Under the new law, the deductible percentage of health insurance that may be deducted from gross income by a self-employed person will increase starting in 2000. There is no change to the prior law percentages of 40% for 1997, and 45% for 1998 and 1999. In 2000 and 2001, the percentage increases to 50%, to 60% in 2002, to 80% for 2003 through 2005, to 90% in 2006 and finally to 100% in 2007 and later years.

lowed if you received wages from an S corporation in which you were more than a 2% shareholder.

If you have a qualified long-term care policy, the deductible portion of the premiums under the rules at *17.15* is included in the 40% deduction.

The 40% deduction may not exceed your net profit from the business under which the health premiums are paid, less deductions claimed on Line 26 (50% of self-employment tax) and Line 28 (Keogh, SEP or SIMPLE retirement plan contributions).

The 40% deduction may not be claimed for any month during 1997 that you were eligible to participate in an employer's subsidized health plan, including a plan of your spouse's employer. If the deduction would be barred for any month because of such eligibility, and you have long-term care coverage that is not employer subsidized, you may claim the 40% deduction for the allowable portion of the long-term care premiums *(17.15)*.

Any balance of premiums not deductible under the special 40% rule may be claimed as an itemized medical expense subject to the 7.5% income floor *(17.4)*.

In 1998, the deduction percentage will be 45%.

Keogh plan contributions and self-employed SEP or SIMPLE deductions—Line 28. *See* Chapter 41 for further details.

Penalty on early savings withdrawals—Line 29, *see 4.16.*

Alimony paid—Line 30a, *see* Chapter 37.

Jury duty pay turned over to employer—Line 31. If you receive your regular pay while on jury duty and turn over your jury duty fees to your employer, report the fees as other income on Line 21, Form 1040, claim an offsetting deduction on Line 31. Write "Jury pay" next to Line 31.

Expenses of performing artists—Line 31. As a performing artist, you may deduct job expenses from gross income, whether or not itemized deductions are claimed, if you have:

1. Two or more employers in the performing arts during 1997 with at least $200 of earnings from at least two of them.
2. Expenses from acting or other services in the performing arts that exceed 10% of gross income from such work; and
3. Adjusted gross income (before deducting these expenses) that does not exceed $16,000.

If you are married, a joint return must be filed to claim the deduction, unless you lived apart from your spouse during the whole year. The $16,000 adjusted gross income limitation applies to your combined incomes. If both spouses are performing artists, the $16,000 adjusted income limit applies to the combined incomes, but each spouse must separately meet the two-employer test and 10% expense test for his or her job expenses to be deductible on the joint return.

You report the performing artist expenses on Form 2106 (or Form 2106-EZ where eligible) and enter the total as a "write-in amount" on Line 31 of Form 1040, instead of on Schedule A. Write "QPA" next to Line 31. If you do not meet the tests, the expenses are deducted on Schedule A subject to the 2% AGI floor.

State and local officials—Line 31. A new law allows state and local officials paid on a fee basis to deduct from gross income unreimbursed business expenses. Follow IRS instructions to Line 31 for identifying the expenses.

Repayment of supplemental unemployment benefits—Line 31. As explained at *2.9,* you may claim a deduction from gross income for the repayment or in some cases a tax credit. If the deduction is claimed, label it "subpay TRA" on Line 31.

Reforestation amortization—Line 31. If you do not have to file Schedule C or F to report income from a timber activity, an amortization deduction for qualifying reforestation expenses may be claimed on Line 31. Amortization is allowed over an 84-month period; *see* Code Section 194 for details. On Line 31, the amortization deduction should be labeled "RFST".

 Law Alert

State and Local Officials

If you are a state or local government employee paid on a fee basis, business expenses related to your duties are now deductible from gross income on Line 31 of Form 1040. If you were unable to claim a deduction for such expenses in a year prior to 1997 because of the 2% floor on miscellaneous expenses *(19.3)*, you may be able to claim it on a timely-filed amended return; *see 49.1.*

Moving Costs to New Job Location

12.3 What Moving Costs Are Deductible

You may deduct unreimbursed expenses of moving your household goods and traveling to a new job location, provided you meet
- A 50-mile distance test, and
- A time test for remaining in the new location.

You claim the moving expense deduction as an adjustment to gross income on Form 1040, Line 25, whether you claim the standard deduction or itemized deductions.

If your expenses are reimbursed, you do not have to report the reimbursement, provided your employer reimburses you under an accountable plan; *see 20.3*1 and *21.8*.

If the distance test *(21.4)* and time test *(12.5–12.6)* are met, you may deduct on your 1997 return the following unreimbursed moving expenses incurred during 1997:

1. *Traveling costs of yourself and members of your household en route from your old to the new locality.* Here, you include the costs of transportation and lodging for yourself and household members while traveling to your new residence. Lodging before departure for one day after the old residence is unusable and lodging for the day of arrival at the new locality are included. If you use your own car, you may either deduct your actual costs of gas, oil, and repairs (but not depreciation) during the trip or take a deduction based on the rate of 10¢ a mile. Also add parking fees and tolls. Meal expenses are not a deductible moving expense.
2. *The actual cost of moving your personal effects and household goods.* This includes the cost of packing, crating, and transporting furniture and household belongings, in-transit storage up to 30 consecutive days, insurance costs for the goods, and the cost of moving a pet or shipping an automobile to your new residence. You may also deduct expenses of moving your effects from a place other than your former home, but only up to the estimated cost of such a move from your former home. Also deduct the cost of connecting or disconnecting utilities when moving household appliances. The cost of connecting a telephone in your new home is not deductible.

In one case, a moving expense deduction was allowed for the cost of shipping a sailboat. The IRS had disallowed the deduction, claiming the sailboat was not a "personal effect." The Tax Court, however, allowed the deduction based on these facts: the couple were active sailors and frequently used the boat; they lived on the sailboat for two weeks immediately before they moved and also for nine weeks after they arrived in the new location; and they kept on board personal effects such as a refrigerator, kitchen utensils, and chairs. According to the court, the boat was so "intimately related" to their lifestyle that it should be considered a deductible personal effect.

It is not necessary for you and members of your household to travel together or at the same time to claim the deduction or the expenses incurred by each member.

Delay in moving to new job location. You may delay moving to the area of a new job location. A delay of less than one year does not jeopardize a deduction for moving expenses. Furthermore, if you move to the new job area within one year, your family may stay in the old residence for a longer period. Their later moving expenses will generally be deductible, even though incurred after one year. For example, the IRS allowed a moving expense deduction to a husband who immediately moved to a new job location, although his wife and children did not join him until 30 months after he began the new job. They delayed so that the children could complete their education. The IRS held that since part of the moving expenses were incurred within one year, the moving expenses incurred later were also deductible.

Nondeductible expenses. You may not deduct the cost of travel incurred for a maid, nurse, chauffeur, or similar domestic help (unless the person is also your dependent), expenses of refitting rugs and drapes, forfeited tuition, car tags or driver's license for the state you move to, losses on disposing of memberships in clubs, mortgage penalties, expenses for trips to sell your old house, or loss on the sale of the house. Furthermore, when your employer reimburses you for such costs, you realize taxable income equal to the amount of the reimbursement.

You may not deduct the cost of transporting furniture which you purchased en route from your old home.

You may not deduct the cost of pre-move house-hunting trips, temporary living expenses, or expenses of selling, purchasing, or leasing the old or new residence, such as attorneys' fees, real estate fees, or costs of settling an unexpired lease. Meal expenses while traveling to your new residence are not deductible.

12.4 The Distance Test

The distance between your new job location and your former home must be at least 50 miles more than the distance between your old job location and your former home. For this purpose, your home may be a house, apartment, trailer, or even a houseboat, but not a seasonal residence such as a summer cottage. If you had no previous job or you return to full-time work after a long period of unemployment or part-time work, the new job location must be at least 50 miles from your former home. Self-employed individuals are also subject to the mileage test.

Filing Tip

Meeting the Mileage Test

Use the following worksheet to see if your move satisfies the 50-mile test. Find the shortest of the most commonly traveled routes in measuring the distances.

Distance between	In miles
1. Old residence and new job location	_____
2. Old residence and old job location	_____
3. Difference (must be at least 50 miles)	_____

The location of your new residence is not considered in applying the mileage test. However, if the distance between your new residence and the new job location is more than the distance between your old residence and new job location, your moving expenses may be disallowed unless you can show (1) you are required to live there as a condition of employment; or (2) an actual decrease in commuting time or expense results.

If you worked for more than one employer, you find the shortest of the most commonly traveled routes from your old residence to your former principal place of employment.

Your job location is where you spend most of your working time. If you work at various locations, the job location is where you report to work. If you work for several employers on a short-term basis and get jobs through a union hall system, the union hall is considered your job location.

Moving overseas. A member of the Armed Services may deduct the cost of moving his or her family to an overseas post.

If you take a new job overseas, and qualify for the foreign earned income exclusion, moving expenses allocable to the excluded income are not deductible; see 36.7.

Alien moving to the U.S. The deduction is not limited to U.S. citizens and residents. An alien may deduct the cost of travel here to work at a full-time position.

EXAMPLES

1. Your company's office is in the center of a metropolitan area. You live 18 miles from your office. You are transferred to a new office and buy a new house. To deduct moving costs, you must show that the location of the new office is at least 50 miles from your previous residence.
2. Your old job was four miles from your former residence and your new job is 55 miles from your former residence. You move to a house that is less than 50 miles from your old house. Nevertheless, you have met the 50-mile test since your new job is 51 miles further from your former home than your old job was.

12.5 The 39-Week Test for Employees

In addition to meeting the distance test (12.4), you must work in the locality of the new job as a full-time employee for at least 39 weeks during the 12-month period immediately following your arrival at the new job location. You do not need to have a job prior to your arrival at the new location. Your family does not have to arrive with you. The 39 weeks of work need not be consecutive or with the same employer. You may change jobs provided you remain in the same general commuting area for 39 weeks. The 39-week test does not apply to employees who become disabled and lose their jobs, or who die.

If you are temporarily absent from work through no fault of your own, due to illness, strikes, shutouts, layoffs, or natural disasters, your temporary absence is counted in the 39 weeks.

EXAMPLE

You accept a position with a company 600 miles from your former position. You move to the new location. After you have worked in the new position 14 weeks, you resign and take another job with a nearby company. You may add the 14 weeks of work with the first company to 25 weeks with the second company to meet the 39-week requirement.

Job transfers. The 39-week period is also waived if you are transferred from your new job for your employer's benefit. However, it must be shown that you could have satisfied the 39-week test except for the transfer.

What if *you* initiate the transfer? The IRS held in a ruling that the 39-week test is not waived if an employee initiates the transfer, even if the employer approves. An individual was not allowed to deduct the costs of moving across the country to take a government position when, within 39 weeks of taking the position, he applied for and took another government job in another area. The IRS disallowed the deduction, although the government reimbursed part of the employee's moving expenses to the new job post, thereby indicating that it considered the transfer to be in the government's interest. According to the IRS, the waiver of the 39-week test applies to transfers initiated by employers, not by employees.

 Planning Reminder

Loss of Job

If you lose your job for reasons other than your willful misconduct, the 39-week requirement is waived. Should you resign or lose your job for willful misconduct, a part-time job will not satisfy the 39-week test. The time test is not waived because you reach mandatory retirement age first, where this retirement was anticipated.

Full-time status. This is determined by the customary practices of your occupation in the area. If work is seasonal, off-season weeks count as work weeks if the off-season period is less than six months and you have an employment agreement covering the off-season.

Joint returns. On a joint return, either spouse may meet the time test. But the work time of one spouse may not be added to the time of the other spouse.

EXAMPLE

Smith moves from New York to a new job in Denver. After working full time for 30 weeks, he resigns from his job and cannot find another position during the rest of the 12-month period. He may not deduct his moving expenses. But assume that Mrs. Smith also finds a job in Denver at the same time as her husband and continues to work for at least 39 weeks. Since she has met the 39-week test, the moving expenses from New York to Denver paid by her husband are deductible, provided they file a joint return. However, if Mrs. Smith had worked for only nine weeks, her work period could not be added to her husband's to meet the 39-week test.

12.6 The 78-Week Test for the Self-Employed and Partners

In addition to meeting the distance test *(12.4)*, you must work full time in the area of the new business for at least 78 weeks during the 24 months immediately following your arrival, of which at least 39 weeks occur in the first 12 months. The full-time work requirement may prevent semi-retired hobbyists, students, or others who work only a few hours a week in self-employed trades or occupations from claiming the deduction.

You are considered to have obtained employment at a new principal place of work when you have made substantial arrangements to begin such work.

The time test is waived if disability or death prevents compliance.

Change of employee or self-employed status. If you start work at a new location as an employee and then become self-employed before meeting the 39-week employee time test, you must meet the 78-week test. Time spent as an employee is counted along with the time spent self-employed in meeting the test.

If, during the first 12 months, you change from working as a self-employed person to working as an employee, you may qualify under the 39-week employee time test, provided you have 39 weeks of work as an *employee.* If you do not have 39 weeks as an employee in the first 12 months, you must meet the 78-week test.

Joint returns. Where you file a joint return, you deduct moving expenses if either you or your spouse can satisfy the time test based on individual work records.

12.7 Claiming Deductible Moving Expenses

Qualifying unreimbursed moving expenses *(21.1)* incurred during 1997 are deductible on your 1997 return whether you claim the standard deduction or itemize deductions. Report your expenses and nontaxable employer reimbursements on Form 3903. Qualifying unreimbursed moving expenses from Form 3903 are then deducted on Form 1040, Line 25, as an adjustment to gross income.

Claiming the deduction before meeting the time test. If the due date for filing your tax return arrives before you can satisfy the applicable time test, you may, nevertheless, deduct unreimbursed moving expenses. If you file your return without taking the deduction, you may file an amended return after meeting the time test to claim the deduction.

EXAMPLE

You move to a new location on November 1, 1997. At the end of the year, you have worked in your new position only nine weeks. You deduct your moving expenses on your 1997 tax return even though you did not complete the 39- or 78-week period of work. But if, after you file the 1997 return, you move from the location before completing the applicable 39-week or 78-week work period, you must report as income the amount of moving expenses deducted in 1997 on the return for the year you move from the location. Alternatively, you may file an amended 1997 return on which you eliminate the deduction.

12.8 Reimbursements of Moving Expenses

If your employer reimburses you for deductible moving expenses *(12.3)* under an accountable plan, the reimbursement should not be reported as salary or wage income on Form W-2. The requirements for an accountable plan are similar to those discussed for business travel expenses at *20.31*.

A reimbursement for expenses that do *not* qualify for a deduction, such as pre-move house-hunting costs, temporary living expenses, meal costs or real estate expenses is reported as compensation on your Form W-2.

On Form 3903, you report your deductible expenses in excess of nontaxable reimbursements, and enter the deductible amount on Form 1040, Line 25, as an adjustment to gross income.

If in 1997 you had deductible moving expenses which you claim on your 1997 return, and you receive a reimbursement for the expenses in 1998, you report your employer's reimbursement as compensation in 1998.

Reimbursements on the sale of a home. To encourage or facilitate an employee's move, an employer may reimburse the employee for a loss incurred on the sale of his or her home. The IRS taxes such reimbursements as pay.

Chapter 13

Claiming the Standard Deduction or Itemized Deductions

Claim the standard deduction only if it exceeds your allowable itemized deductions for mortgage interest, property taxes, medical costs, charitable donations, casualty losses, and miscellaneous deductions for job costs and investment expenses. Generally, a single person may claim a 1997 standard deduction of $4,150; a head of household, $6,050; a married couple filing jointly, or a qualifying widow(er), $6,900; and a married person filing separately, $3,450. Larger standard deductions are allowed to those who are age 65 or over or blind, and lower standard deductions are allowed to dependents with only investment income.

Before deciding whether to itemize or claim the standard deduction, read Chapters 14 through 20 to see that you have not overlooked any itemized deductions. To itemize, you must file Form 1040 and report your deductions on Schedule A.

Key to Itemized Deductions and the Standard Deduction for 1997

Item—	Explanation—	Limitations and Examples—
Standard deduction	The standard deduction is fixed by law according to your filing status and age. The standard deduction in 1997 is: $6,900 if you are married filing jointly or a qualifying widow or widower. $4,150 if you are single. $6,050 if you are a head of household. $3,450 if you are married filing separately. If you are age 65 or over or blind, your standard deduction is substantially larger; see 13.4.	Married persons filing separately may not use the standard deduction if their spouses itemize deductions. The standard deduction may not be claimed by a nonresident or dual-status alien or on a return filed for a short taxable year caused by a change in accounting period. A lower standard deduction of $650 is allowed to dependents with only unearned income; see 13.5.
Itemized deductions	You should itemize deductions on Schedule A if your deductions exceed the standard deduction for your filing status. Itemized deductions include charitable contributions, interest expenses, local and state taxes, medical and dental costs, casualty and theft losses, job and investment expenses, and educational costs.	There is no dollar limit on the amount of itemized deductions. But individual itemized deductions are subject to limitations and some taxpayers are subject to a 3% reduction as explained below. **EXAMPLE** You are single and may claim the standard deduction of $4,150 for 1997. However, your itemized deductions are $5,000. You claim $5,000 on Schedule A of Form 1040.
3% reduction	If your 1997 adjusted gross income (AGI) exceeds $121,200, itemized deductions other than medical expenses, casualty and theft losses, gambling losses, and investment interest expenses are reduced by 3% of the excess AGI over $121,200. If you are married filing separately, the reduction applies if your AGI exceeds $60,600; see 13.7.	The total reduction may not exceed 80% of your deductions. **EXAMPLE** Your joint return adjusted gross income (AGI) for 1997 is $156,600. Your itemized deductions for mortgage interest, state income taxes, and charitable donations are $20,000. The AGI excess over $121,200 is $35,400. Therefore, itemized deductions are reduced by $1,062 (3% of $35,400). On Schedule A you may deduct $18,938 ($20,000 – $1,062).
Charitable contributions	You may deduct donations to religious, charitable, educational, and other philanthropic organizations that have been approved to receive deductible contributions; see 14.1.	The contribution deduction is generally limited to 50% of adjusted gross income. Lower ceilings apply to property donations and contributions to foundations. The deductible amount is included in the 3% reduction explained above.
Interest expenses	You may deduct interest on qualified home mortgages, points, home equity loans, and interest on loans to carry investments.	Interest on investment loans is deductible only up to extent of net investment income. Interest on personal and consumer loans is not deductible. Interest on home mortgages that do not meet tests of 15.1 is not deductible. Interest on home mortgages and points are included in the 3% reduction explained above.
Taxes	You may deduct payments of state, local, and foreign real property and income taxes, as well as state and local personal property taxes. You claim your deduction on the tax return of the year in which you paid the taxes, unless you report on the accrual basis; see 16.6.	No dollar limitation. The deductible amount is included in the 3% reduction explained above.

Item—	Explanation—	Limitations and Examples—
Medical expenses	You may deduct payments of medical expenses for yourself and dependents. A checklist of over 100 deductible medical items is at *17.2.* Deductible drug costs are limited to drugs prescribed by a physician.	Only expenses in excess of 7.5% of adjusted gross income are deductible.
Casualty and theft losses	You may deduct personal property losses caused by storms, fires, and other natural events and as the result of theft.	Each individual casualty loss must exceed $100 and the total of all losses during the year must exceed 10% of adjusted gross income; *see 18.11.*
Job expenses	You may deduct unreimbursed costs of union dues, job educational courses, work clothes, entertainment, travel, and looking for a new job.	Included as miscellaneous expenses of which only the excess over 2% of adjusted gross income is deductible; *see 19.1.* The 2% floor does not apply to performing artists *(12.2)*, handicapped employees, or job-related moving expenses *(12.3)*. The deductible amount is included in the 3% reduction explained above.
Investment expenses and tax preparation costs	You may deduct investment expenses and other expenses of producing and collecting income, expenses of maintaining income-producing property, expenses of tax return preparation, refunds, and audits.	Included as miscellaneous expenses of which only the excess over 2% of adjusted gross income is deductible; *see 19.1.*

13.1 Claiming the Standard Deduction

On your 1997 return, you are allowed a standard deduction, which may be claimed regardless of your actual expenses. The standard deduction is not integrated into the tax rate schedules or tax tables. On your return, you deduct the standard deduction from adjusted gross income (AGI), assuming you do not claim itemized deductions on Schedule A of Form 1040; *see* the Example below.

The *basic standard deduction* is allowed if you are under age 65 and not blind. The amount is adjusted each year to reflect inflation. For 1997, the basic standard deduction is:

$6,900 if married filing jointly or a qualifying widow(er);
$6,050 if filing as a head of household;
$4,150 if single; and
$3,450 if married filing separately.

A married person filing separately must itemize deductions and may not claim any standard deduction if the other spouse itemizes on a separate return; *see 13.3.*

Age 65 or older or blind.   For taxpayers age 65 or over, or taxpayers of any age who are blind, the basic standard deduction is increased by an additional amount; *see 13.4.*

Dependents.   Individuals who may be claimed as dependents by other taxpayers are generally limited to a $650 standard deduction, unless they have earned income; *see 13.5.*

Dual-status alien.   You are generally not entitled to any standard deduction if for part of the year you are a nonresident and part of the year a resident alien. However, a standard deduction may be claimed on a joint return if your spouse is a U.S. citizen or resident and you elect to be taxed on your worldwide income; *see 1.8.*

EXAMPLE

Ben Green is age 25 and single. In 1997, he has salary income of $35,000 and interest income of $2,000. He is not covered by a company retirement plan and contributed $2,000 to an IRA. Green claims the standard deduction because his itemized deductions are less than $4,150.

Gross income:		
Salary	$35,000	
Interest income	2,000	$37,000
Deduction from gross income:		
IRA (8.3)		2,000
Adjusted gross income		$35,000
Less: Standard deduction		4,150
		$30,850
Less: Exemption (21.1)		2,650
Taxable income		$28,200

13.2 When To Itemize

Claim the standard deduction only if it exceeds your allowable itemized deductions for charitable donations, certain local taxes, interest, allowable casualty loss, miscellaneous expenses, and medical expenses. If your deductions exceed your standard deduction, you elect to itemize by claiming the deductions on Schedule A of Form 1040. However, if you are married filing separately and your spouse itemizes deductions, you also must itemize, even if the standard deduction exceeds your itemized deductions; *see 13.3.*

EXAMPLE

Ellen Bates is single and her 1997 adjusted gross income is $35,000. Her itemized deductions total $5,200. As the $4,150 standard deduction is less than her itemized deductions, she claims itemized deductions of $5,200 on Schedule A.

13.3 Husbands and Wives Filing Separate Returns

If you file separate returns for 1997, you and your spouse must first decide whether you will claim itemized deductions or limit yourselves to a standard deduction of $3,450 each. You must make the same election. That is, if one spouse has itemized deductions exceeding $3,450 and elects to itemize, the other spouse must also itemize, even if his or her itemized deductions are less than $3,450.

On a separate return, each spouse may deduct only those itemized expenses for which he or she is liable. This is true even if one spouse pays expenses for the other. For example, if a wife owns property, then the interest and taxes imposed on the property are her deductions, not her husband's. If he pays them, neither one may deduct them on separate returns. The husband may not because they were not his liability. The wife may not because she did not pay them. This is true also of casualty or theft losses.

Claiming itemized deductions when you are living apart from your spouse. When a husband and wife are divorced or legally separated under a decree of divorce or separate maintenance, they are free to compute their tax as they see fit, without reference to the return of the other spouse. They are treated as single. If one spouse has itemized deductions, that spouse may elect to claim them, and the other spouse is not required to itemize. The standard deduction is not limited to $3,450. Head of household tax rates may be available under the rules of *1.10.*

If a husband and wife are separated but do not have a decree of divorce or separate maintenance, both must either itemize or claim the 1997 standard deduction of $3,450. There is an exception if you are married and live apart from your spouse and meet the following conditions:

- Your spouse was not a member of your household during the last six months of 1997.
- You maintained as your home a household which was, for more than half of 1997, the principal place of abode for your child, adopted child, foster child, or stepchild.
- You are entitled to claim the child as a dependent (21.1) or the child's other parent has the right to the exemption under the rules of *21.11.*
- You provide over half the cost of supporting the household.

If you satisfy these conditions and file a separate return, you generally may file your return as a head of household; however, a foster child must live with you for the entire year (except for temporary absences) to qualify you for head of household status. You may elect to itemize without regard

Filing Instruction

Changing an Election
If you filed your return using the standard deduction and want to change to itemized deductions, or you itemized and want to change to the standard deduction, you may do so within the three-year period allowed for amending your return. If you are married and filing separately, each of you must consent to and make the same change; you both must either itemize or claim the standard deduction.

to whether your spouse itemizes or not. If you elect not to itemize, your 1997 standard deduction as a head of household is $6,050 if you are under age 65 and not blind. If you are age 65 or over or blind, your standard deduction is substantially larger; *see 13.4.*

13.4 Standard Deduction If 65 or Older or Blind

A larger standard deduction is provided for persons who are age 65 or over or who are blind. The larger deduction for blindness is allowed regardless of age.

Age and blindness are determined as of December 31, 1997. However, if your 65th birthday is January 1, 1998, you may claim the standard deduction for those age 65 or over on your 1997 return.

Your total standard deduction consists of two parts: (1) The basic standard deduction shown in *13.1* for your filing status; plus (2) an extra standard deduction for being age 65 or older, or blind. The amount of the extra deduction is $1,000 if you are filing as single or head of household; $800 if you are married, whether filing jointly or separately, or your filing status is qualifying widow(er). The chart below lists the total standard deduction, including the extra amount.

If you are married filing separately, you may claim the standard deduction only if your spouse also claims the standard deduction on his or her return.

Check applicable boxes

	65 or older	Blind
Yourself	☐	☐
Your spouse if claiming spouse as exemption *(21.2)*	☐	☐
Total checks____		

If you are—	Number of checks are—	Standard deduction is—
Single	1	$5,150
	2	6,150
Married filing jointly or qualified widow or widower *(1.6)*	1	7,700
	2	8,500
	3	9,300
	4	10,100
Married filing separately	1	4,250
	2	5,050
	3	5,850
	4	6,650
Head of household *(1.10)*	1	7,050
	2	8,050

13.5 Standard Deduction for Dependents

The following restrictive rules apply to you only if you may be claimed as a dependent. If you earn gross income of $2,650 or more in 1997, you may *not* be claimed as a dependent by anyone other than your parent, and you may be claimed by your parent only if you are under age 19 or a full-time student under age 24; *see 21.6.* If you are *not* a dependent because of the $2,650 income test, your standard deduction is shown in *13.1* or in *13.4.* If you *may* be claimed as a dependent, your standard deduction is figured under the rules below. You *may* elect to itemize deductions if these exceed the allowable standard deduction. If you are married and your spouse itemizes on a separate return, you *must* itemize; *see 13.3.*

Dependent under age 65 and not blind. If you can be claimed as another taxpayer's dependent for 1997, your standard deduction is the greater of $650 or *earned income,* but no more than the basic standard deduction shown in *13.1* for your filing status. If you have wages over $650, your deduction equals the wages, up to the regular standard deduction for nondependents. For example, if you had interest income of $400 and wages from a short-term job of $500, your standard deduction is $650 (the greater of $650 and earned income of $500). If you are your parent's dependent *(21.6)* and earn wages exceeding $2,650, your standard deduction equals the wages up to $4,150, the maximum amount for a single dependent who is under age 65 and not blind.

Dependents age 65 or older or blind.   Your standard deduction is figured in two steps:

Step 1. The greater of $650 and earned income up to the basic standard deduction amount shown in *13.1; plus*

Step 2. $800 if you are married or a qualifying widow or widower, or $1,000 if single or head of household. If you are age 65 or older and you are also blind, add $1,600 if married or a qualifying widow or widower, or $2,000 if single or head of household.

The worksheets below incorporate these steps for computing your 1997 standard deduction.

Standard Deduction for Dependents in 1997 With Earned Income of $650 or Less

If your filing status is—	*Standard deduction is—*
Single or head of household	
Under age 65 and not blind	$ 650
Age 65 or older or blind	1,650
Age 65 or older and blind	2,650
Married, or qualifying widow(er)	
Under age 65 and not blind	$ 650
Age 65 or older or blind	1,450
Age 65 or older and blind	2,250

Standard Deduction for Dependents in 1997 Who Are Under Age 65 and Not Blind with Earned Income Exceeding $650

1. Enter your earned income.[*] $_____
2. Enter:

   $4,150 if you are single,
   $6,050 if head of household,
   $6,900 if qualifying widow(er) or married filing jointly, or
   $3,450 if married filing separately.   _____

3. Enter the smaller of Lines 1 and 2. This is your standard deduction.   _____

Standard Deduction for Dependents in 1997 Who Are Age 65 or Older or Blind With Earned Income Exceeding $650

1. Enter your earned income.[*] $_____
2. Enter:

   $4,150 if you are single,
   $6,050 if head of household,
   $6,900 if qualifying widow(er) or married filing jointly, or
   $3,450 if married filing separately.   _____

3. Enter the smaller of Lines 1 and 2.   _____
4. Enter:

   $1,000 if you are single or head of household and
   are either age 65 or older or blind.
   $800 if you are married filing jointly or separately,
   or a qualifying widow(er) and are either age 65 or older or blind.
   If both age 65 or older and blind, the $1,000 or $800 amounts are
   doubled to $2,000 and $1,600.   _____

5. Add Lines 3 and 4. This is your standard deduction.   _____

 Law Alert

Higher Standard Deduction for Certain Dependents in 1998
For certain dependents with earned income, a higher standard deduction will be allowed after 1997; the new rule is discussed in *13.5.*

[*]*Include pay for services and taxable scholarships (38.1). However, if your gross income (earned and unearned) is $2,650 or more, you may be claimed as a dependent only by your parent, and only if you are under age 19 or a full-time student under age 24; see 21.6.*

EXAMPLES

1. Jane Dell claims her widowed mother, Beth, who is age 67, as her dependent for 1997. Beth has interest income of $500, wages of $2,000, and Social Security benefits of $10,000 that are exempt from tax under the rules of *34.3*. Beth's standard deduction is $3,000: $2,000 (the greater of $650 and her earned income of $2,000) plus $1,000, the additional deduction for a single person over age 65. Beth's taxable income is zero. Although her gross income of $2,500 is below the filing threshold (*see* filing tests for dependents on page 3), she should file a tax return to obtain a refund of income tax withheld from her wages.

2. Same as Example 1 except Beth's wages are $500 and interest income is $2,000. Her standard deduction is $1,650: $650 (the greater of $650 and $500 of earned income) plus the additional standard deduction of $1,000. Beth must file a tax return since her investment income exceeds $1,650 (*see* filing tests for dependents on page 3). Her taxable income is $850 ($2,500 – $1,650 standard deduction). She cannot claim a personal exemption for herself since she is Jane's dependent *(21.1)*.

Dependents' standard deduction in 1998. In 1998, an individual who may be claimed as a dependent may add $250 to earned income in figuring the allowable standard deduction. The deduction will be the larger of:

1. The annual floor, which was $650 for 1997 but may be increased for 1998, *and*
2. Earned income plus $250, but no more than the basic standard deduction for a nondependent.

For example, assume that for 1998, the annual floor increases to $700 from $650. If a dependent has $450 or less of earned income for 1998, the standard deduction will be $700. The $250 addition to earned income does not provide a benefit in this case because it does not raise the standard deduction over the $700 floor. However, if earnings exceed $450, the deduction would exceed the $700 floor. For example, if earnings were $600, the standard deduction would be $850 ($600 + $250), as that exceeds the $700 floor.

After 1998, the $250 additional amount may be increased by an inflation adjustment.

13.6 Prepaying or Postponing Itemized Expenses

Before the end of the year, check your records for payments of deductible itemized expenses. If you find that your payments up to that time are slightly less than the allowable standard deduction for that year, accelerating payment of an expense that you would otherwise pay in the following year could allow you to itemize. For example, at the end of 1997, you may make an additional charitable contribution, or pay a state or local tax bill not due until 1998, or extend by one year professional association dues or job-related subscriptions. You cannot deduct prepayments of interest, insurance premiums, or rent on investment property.

On the other hand, making the year-end payment might still not increase your deductions enough to itemize. In that case, you would get no tax benefit from the payment. By postponing the payment until the next year, you may make it easier to itemize on that year's return.

If your year-to-year payments of itemized expenses have consistently been below the standard deduction, a prepayment or postponement strategy may allow you to itemize in at least one of two consecutive years, enabling you to reduce your taxes over the two-year period without increasing your overall expenditures; *see* the following Example.

EXAMPLE

With only a few days remaining in 1997, you determine that your itemized deductions will be $4,000. You are single and expect to have the same amount of expenses in 1998. Instead of taking the $4,150 standard deduction, you could prepay a state income tax of $1,000 to raise your itemized deductions to $5,000. You would then itemize your deductions for 1997 and this would result in an $850 increase in deductions ($5,000 – $4,150). If you cannot itemize in 1998, you will claim a standard deduction that as a result of an inflation adjustment exceeds the $4,150 amount allowed for 1997; the projected amount for 1998 is $4,250. *See* the Supplement for the official figure.

13.7 3% Itemized Deduction Reduction

If your 1997 adjusted gross income (AGI) exceeds $121,200 ($60,600 if married filing separately) some of your itemized deductions are disallowed. First figure your itemized deductions under the regular rules; *see* Chapters 14 through 20 for details and limitations on specific types of expenses. Then reduce the total of otherwise allowable itemized deductions by the following, which are *not* subject to the 3% reduction:

- Medical and dental expenses
- Investment interest
- Casualty losses
- Theft losses
- Gambling losses

The balance of your itemized deductions are generally reduced by 3% of the excess of your AGI over the $121,200 (or $60,600) threshold. Use the worksheet below to figure the reduction. The 3% reduction creates an added tax cost to earning additional income; *see* 28.2.

Worksheet for 3% Reduction

1. Enter your 1997 adjusted gross income. $_____
2. Enter $121,200 ($60,600 if married filing separately). _____
3. Subtract Line 2 from Line 1. _____
4. Multiply the amount on Line 3 by 3% (.03). _____
5. Enter total allowable itemized deductions from Schedule A before the 3% reduction. _____
6. Enter the amount included on Line 5 for allowable medical and dental expenses, investment interest, casualty or theft losses, and gambling losses. These deductions are *not* subject to the reduction. _____
7. Subtract Line 6 from Line 5.* _____
8. Multiply the amount on Line 7 by 80% (.80). _____
9. Enter the smaller of Line 4 and Line 8. This is the disallowed amount. _____
10. Subtract Line 9 from Line 5. This is the net amount of itemized deductions you may claim on your 1997 return. $_____

*If the amount on Line 7 is zero, the reduction does not apply.

EXAMPLE

Dan Sommer is single and his 1997 adjusted gross income on Form 1040 is $193,600. On Schedule A, Dan reports $31,000 of itemized expenses, after applying the 7.5% floor for itemized medical costs and the 2% floor for miscellaneous itemized deductions. Since his AGI exceeds $121,200, part of his itemized deduction will be disallowed.

Medical expense deduction (after 7.5% floor)	$ 1,000
State and local income taxes	16,000
Real estate taxes	2,000
Home mortgage interest	5,000
Charitable donation	6,000
Miscellaneous expenses (after 2% floor)	1,000
Total	$31,000

All of the deductions except medical expenses are subject to the 3% reduction.

Following the steps of the worksheet shown above, Dan figures that $2,172 of his deductions are disallowed, leaving a net deduction of $28,828:

1.	Adjusted gross income	$193,600
2.	*Less:* threshold	121,200
3.	Excess	72,400
4.	3% of Line 3	2,172
5.	Itemized deductions	31,000
6.	*Less:* medical deductions (not subject to the 3% reduction)	1,000
7.	Itemized deductions subject to the 3% reduction	30,000
8.	80% of Line 7	24,000
9.	Smaller of (4) and (8) is disallowed	2,172
10.	Net itemized deductions allowable on Schedule A (Line 5 *less* Line 9)	$28,828

The Sample Schedule A on the next page shows the reduced deduction on Line 28 ($31,000 – $2,172 disallowed = $28,828).

Name(s) shown on Form 1040: **Don Sommer**

Your social security number: XXO OX XIIX

Section	No.	Description		Amount
Medical and Dental Expenses		Caution: *Do not include expenses reimbursed or paid by others.*		
	1	Medical and dental expenses (see page A-1)	1	15,520
	2	Enter amount from Form 1040, line 33. **2** 193,600		
	3	Multiply line 2 above by 7.5% (.075)	3	14,520
	4	Subtract line 3 from line 1. If line 3 is more than line 1, enter -0-	4	1,000
Taxes You Paid (See page A-1.)	5	State and local income taxes	5	16,000
	6	Real estate taxes (see page A-2)	6	2,000
	7	Personal property taxes	7	0
	8	Other taxes. List type and amount ▶	8	
	9	Add lines 5 through 8	9	18,000
Interest You Paid (See page A-2.)	10	Home mortgage interest and points reported to you on Form 1098	10	5,000
	11	Home mortgage interest not reported to you on Form 1098. If paid to the person from whom you bought the home, see page A-3 and show that person's name, identifying no., and address ▶	11	
Note: Personal interest is not deductible.	12	Points not reported to you on Form 1098. See page A-3 for special rules	12	
	13	Investment interest. Attach Form 4952, if required. (See page A-3.)	13	
	14	Add lines 10 through 13	14	5,000
Gifts to Charity	15	Gifts by cash or check. If you made any gift of $250 or more, see page A-3	15	6,000
If you made a gift and got a benefit for it, see page A-3.	16	Other than by cash or check. If any gift of $250 or more, see page A-3. You **MUST** attach Form 8283 if over $500	16	
	17	Carryover from prior year	17	
	18	Add lines 15 through 17	18	6,000
Casualty and Theft Losses	19	Casualty or theft loss(es). Attach Form 4684. (See page A-4.)	19	
Job Expenses and Most Other Miscellaneous Deductions	20	Unreimbursed employee expenses—job travel, union dues, job education, etc. You **MUST** attach Form 2106 or 2106-EZ if required. (See page A-4.) ▶	20	
	21	Tax preparation fees	21	300
(See page A-5 for expenses to deduct here.)	22	Other expenses—investment, safe deposit box, etc. List type and amount ▶ Tax Court Legal Fees $ 4,572	22	4,572
	23	Add lines 20 through 22	23	4,872
	24	Enter amount from Form 1040, line 33. **24**		
	25	Multiply line 24 above by 2% (.02)	25	3,872
	26	Subtract line 25 from line 23. If line 25 is more than line 23, enter -0-	26	1,000
Other Miscellaneous Deductions	27	Other—from list on page A-5. List type and amount ▶	27	
Total Itemized Deductions	28	Is Form 1040, line 33, over $121,200 (over $60,600 if married filing separately)? **NO.** Your deduction is not limited. Add the amounts in the far right column for lines 4 through 27. Also, enter on Form 1040, line 35, the **larger** of this amount or your standard deduction. **YES.** Your deduction may be limited. See page A-5 for the amount to enter. ▶	28	28,828

For Paperwork Reduction Act Notice, see Form 1040 instructions. Cat. No. 11330X Schedule A (Form 1040) 1997

266

Chapter 14

Charitable Contribution Deductions

By making deductible donations, you help your favorite philanthropy and at the same time receive a tax benefit. Donations to organizations qualified to receive deductible contributions give you a tax reduction if you itemize deductions. For example, if you are in the 28% tax bracket, a donation of $1,000 reduces your taxes by $280. By donating appreciated securities and real estate held long term, you can increase the amount of your tax savings by avoiding the tax that would have been owed if you had sold the property and donated the proceeds. If you do volunteer work for a qualified charity, you may deduct your unreimbursed expenses.

If you contributed at least $250 to a charity in 1997, you must get a written receipt from the organization to substantiate the donation. A cancelled check is not sufficient evidence for a cash donation of $250 or more; *see 14.15.*

Also be aware that if you claim deductions for property valued at more than $500, you must attach Form 8283 to Form 1040. If the value you claimed exceeds $5,000, you also may have to obtain a written appraisal.

There are deduction ceilings depending on the type of donation and the nature of the charity. The ceiling for cash donations made to public philanthropies is 50% of adjusted gross income, and for gifts of capital gain property, 30% of adjusted gross income. For other ceilings, *see 14.17.*

If your adjusted gross income exceeds $121,200 ($60,600 if married filing separately), your charitable contribution deduction is subject to the 3% reduction of itemized deductions explained in *13.7.*

Qualifying Charitable Donations

14.1 Deductible Contributions

Charitable contributions are deductible only as itemized deductions on Schedule A of Form 1040. The deduction is subject to the 3% reduction of total itemized deductions explained at *13.7* if your adjusted gross income exceeds $121,200 ($60,600 if married filing separately).

You may deduct donations to religious, charitable, educational, and other philanthropic organizations approved by the IRS to receive deductible contributions; *see* the listing later in this section. If you are unsure of the tax status of a philanthropy, ask the organization about its status, or check the IRS list of tax-exempt organizations (IRS Publication 78). Donations to the federal, state, and local government are also deductible.

Substantiating your donations.   Keep a cancelled check or receipt from the charity as proof of donations under $250. For donations of $250 or more, you need to obtain a written acknowledgment that notes any benefits or goods that you received in exchange. *See 14.15* for details on the substantiation requirements.

Year-end donations.   You deduct donations on the tax return filed for the year in which you paid them in cash or property. A contribution by check is deductible in the year you give the check, even if it is cashed in the following year. A check mailed and dated on the last day of 1997 is deductible in 1997. A postdated check with a 1998 date is not deductible until 1998. For checks of $250 or more, get a written receipt by the filing due date of your return. A pledge or a note is not deductible until paid. Donations made through a credit card are deductible in the year the charge is made. Donations made through a pay-by-phone bank account are not deductible until the payment date shown on the bank statement.

Delivering securities.   If you are planning to donate appreciated securities near the end of the year, make sure that you consider these delivery rules in timing the donation. If you unconditionally deliver or mail a properly endorsed stock certificate to the donee or its agent, the gift is considered completed on the date of delivery or mailing, provided it is received in the ordinary course of the mails. If you deliver the certificate to your bank or broker as your agent, or to the issuing corporation or its agent, your gift is not complete until the stock is transferred to the donee's name on the corporation's books. This transfer may take several weeks, so, if possible, make the delivery at least three weeks before the end of the year to assure a current deduction.

Debts.   You may assign to a charity a debt payable to you. A deductible contribution may be claimed in the year your debtor pays the charity.

Limits on deduction.   Depending on the nature of the organization and the donated property, a deduction ceiling of 50%, 30%, or 20% of adjusted gross income applies. In general, the deduction ceiling is 50% for cash contributions and 30% for contributions of appreciated property held long term. *See 14.17* for details on the deduction ceilings. Where donations in one year exceed the percentage limits, a five-year carryover of the excess may be allowed; *see 14.18*.

A deduction may also be limited under the 3% reduction rule discussed at *13.7*.

Organizations Qualifying for Deductible Donations

The following types of organizations may qualify to receive deductible contributions:

The United States, a U.S. possession, a state, city, or town or Indian tribal government.   The gift must be for public purposes. The gift may be directed to a government unit, or it may be to a government agency such as a state university, a fire department, a civil defense group, or a committee to raise funds to develop land into a public park. Donations may be made to the Social Security system (Federal Old Age and Survivors Insurance Trust Fund). Donations may be made to the federal government to help reduce the national debt; checks should be made payable to "Bureau of the Public Debt."

A domestic nonprofit organization, trust, community chest, fund, or foundation that is operated exclusively for one of the following purposes:

Religious. Payments for pew rents, assessments, and dues to churches and synagogues are deductible.
Charitable. In this class are organizations such as Boy Scouts, Girl Scouts, American Red Cross, Community Funds, Cancer Societies, CARE, Salvation Army, Y.M.C.A., and Y.W.C.A.
Scientific, literary, and educational. Included in this group are hospitals, research organizations, colleges, universities, and other schools that do not maintain racially discriminatory policies; and leagues or associations set up for education or to combat crime, improve public morals, and aid public welfare.

Prevention of cruelty to children or animals.

Fostering amateur sports competition. However, the organization's activities may not provide athletic facilities or equipment.

Domestic nonprofit veterans' organizations or auxiliary units.

A domestic fraternal group operating under the lodge system. The contributions must be used exclusively for religious, charitable, scientific, literary, or educational purposes; or for the prevention of cruelty to children or animals.

Nonprofit cemetery and burial companies, where the voluntary contribution benefits the whole cemetery, not only your plot.

Legal services corporations established under the Legal Services Corporation Act. Such corporations provide legal assistance to financially needy people in noncriminal proceedings.

14.2 Nondeductible Contributions

The following types of contributions are not deductible:

1. Payments to political campaign committees or political action committees.
2. Payments to an organization that devotes a substantial part of its activities to lobbying, trying to influence legislation, or carrying on propaganda or whose lobbying activities exceed certain limits set by the law, causing the organization to lose its tax-exempt status. The IRS has disallowed contributions to a civic group opposing saloons, nightclubs, and gambling places, although the group also aided libraries, churches, and other public programs.
3. Donations to or on behalf of specific individuals, even if needy or worthy. Generally, scholarships for specific students, or gifts to organizations to benefit only certain groups. However, the IRS in private rulings has allowed deductions for scholarship funds which are limited to members of a particular religion, so long as that religion is open to all on a racially nondiscriminatory basis, and to scholarship funds open only to male students.
4. Gifts to organizations such as:
   Fraternal groups—except when they set up special organizations exclusively devoted to charitable, educational, or other approved purposes.
   Professional groups such as those organized by accountants, lawyers, and physicians—except when they are specially created for exclusive charitable, educational, or other philanthropic purposes. The IRS will disallow unrestricted gifts made to state bar associations, although such organizations may have some public purposes. Some courts have allowed deductions for donations to bar associations on the ground that their activities benefit the general public. However, an appeals court disallowed deductible donations to a bar association that rates candidates for judicial office.
   Clubs for social purposes—fraternities and sororities are generally in this class. Unless an organization is exclusively operated for a charitable, religious, or other approved purpose, you may not deduct your contribution, even though your funds are used for a charitable or religious purpose.
5. Donations to civic leagues, communist or communist-front organizations, chambers of commerce, business leagues, or labor unions.
6. Contributions to a hospital or school operated for profit.
7. Purchase price of church building bond. To claim a deduction, you must donate the bond to the church. The amount of the deduction is the fair market value of the bond when you make the donation. Interest on the bond is income each year, under the original issue discount rules of *4.19,* where no interest will be paid until the bond matures.
8. Donations of blood to the Red Cross or other blood banks.
9. Contributions to foreign charitable organizations or directly to foreign governments. Thus, a contribution to the State of Israel was disallowed. Similarly, contributions to international charitable organizations are nondeductible; but *see 14.1.*

Donation of services. You may not deduct the value of volunteer work you perform for charities. But you can deduct unreimbursed expenses incurred during such work; *see 14.4.*

Free use of property. You may not deduct the rental value of property you allow a charity to use without charge. That is, if you allow a charity rent-free use of an office in your building, you may not deduct the fair rental value. You also have no deduction when you lend money to a charity without charging interest.

To raise money for a charity, supporters of the organization may donate rental time for their vacation home, to be auctioned off to the public. No deduction is allowed for donating the rental time; *see 14.10.*

 Caution

Foreign Charities

You may deduct donations to domestic organizations that distribute funds to charities in foreign countries, as long as the U.S. organization controls the distribution of the funds overseas. An outright contribution to a foreign charitable organization is not deductible. Some exceptions to this ban are provided by international treaties. A limited exception applies to contributions to certain Canadian or Mexican organizations if you have income from Canadian or Mexican sources. For details, write IRS, Assistant Commissioner International, 950 L'Enfant Plaza, S.W., Washington, D.C. 20024.

 Caution

Donations Which Provide You with Goods or Services

Except for certain token benefits and memberships which are disregarded for tax purposes, you may not deduct a contribution to a qualified charity to the extent that you receive goods, services, or financial benefits in exchange; *see 14.3.*

You may not deduct tuition payments to a parochial or other church-sponsored school for the education of your children if secular courses that lead to a recognized degree are provided. Payments exceeding the usual tuition charge are deductible. Similarly, fees paid to a tax-exempt rest home in which you live, or to a hospital for the care of a particular patient, are not deductible if any benefit is received from the contribution. A gift to a retirement home, over and above monthly fees, is not deductible if the size or type of your quarters depends on the gift.

Parents' support payments of children serving as Mormon missionaries. According to the Supreme Court, support payments made by parents directly to their children who serve as missionaries are not deductible because the church does not control the funds.

14.3 Contributions That Provide You With Benefits

A contribution to a qualifying organization *(14.1)* is generally deductible only to the extent that you intend to give more than the value of benefits you receive and actually do so. You may rely on a written estimate from the organization of the value of any benefits given to you unless it appears to be unreasonable. However, as discussed later in this section, certain token items and membership benefits do not reduce the amount of your deduction.

If you contribute $75 or less and receive benefits, the organization may tell you the value of the benefits. If your contribution *exceeds* $75, the organization by law *must* give you a written statement that estimates the value of the benefits provided to you and instructs you to deduct only the portion of your contribution that exceeds the benefits. However, the disclosure statement does not have to be provided to you if you receive only token benefits, or if you receive from a religious organization only "intangible religious benefits."

EXAMPLES

1. You contribute $200 to a philanthropy and receive a book which you have seen on sale for prices ranging between $18 and $25. The charity estimates the value at $20. As the estimate is between the typical retail prices, it is acceptable to the IRS. Although the book sold at a price as high as $25, you may treat the $20 estimate as fair market value and claim a deduction of $180.

2. A charitable organization sponsors an art auction and provides a catalogue which lists the items being auctioned and estimates of fair market value. The catalogue lists the value of a vase at $100. At the auction, you bid and pay $500 for the vase. As you were aware of the estimate before the auction and paid more for the vase, you may deduct $400 as a contribution.

Dues. Dues paid to a qualified tax-exempt organization are deductible to the extent they exceed the value of benefits or privileges from the organization for the dues, such as monthly bulletins or journals, use of a library, or the right to attend luncheons and lectures. As discussed above, you generally must be provided with an estimate of any benefits you received if your donation exceeds $75; *see 14.3*.

If dues are paid to a social club with the understanding that a specified part goes to a qualifying charity *(14.1)*, you may claim a charitable deduction for dues earmarked for the charity. If the treasurer of your club is actually the agent of the charity, you take the deduction in the year you give him or her the money. If the treasurer is merely your agent, you may take the deduction only in the year the money is turned over to the charity.

Benefit tickets. Tickets to theater events, tours, concerts, and other entertainments are often sold by charitable organizations at prices higher than the regular admission charge. The difference between the regular admission and the higher amount you pay is deductible as a charitable contribution. If you decline to accept the ticket or return it to the charity for resale, your deduction is the price you paid.

The charity should explain to you how much is deductible. The charity must provide an explanation where you paid more than $75; *see* above.

If the benefit ticket price is the same or less than the regular admission price, you have no deduction unless you refuse to accept the ticket or you return the ticket to the charity for resale.

If you purchase season tickets to a charity-sponsored series of programs and your average cost per program equals or is less than the cost for individual performances, your deduction for a returned ticket depends upon how long you held the tickets. Generally, you may deduct only your cost. However, if you have held the ticket for more than a year, you may deduct the fair market value, the price the charity will charge on resale of the ticket.

You may not deduct the cost of raffle tickets, bingo games, or other types of lotteries organized by charities.

EXAMPLE

A couple claimed a full deduction for regular-price tickets to a high-school fund-raising event that they did not attend. They argued that they were entitled to the deduction because they received no benefit from their ticket purchase. The IRS disallowed the deduction and the Tax Court agreed, holding that a donor receives a benefit by merely having the right to attend the event. To claim a deduction for the price of the tickets the couple should have returned them to the charity.

Donation for the right to buy athletic stadium tickets.   If you contribute to a public or nonprofit college or university scholarship program and receive the right to buy preferential seating at the school's football stadium or other sports arena, you may deduct 80% of the contribution to the scholarship program. The cost of any tickets you buy is not deductible. The deduction is allowed only if you receive the right to buy tickets rather than tickets themselves. For example, if in exchange for a substantial donation you receive a lifetime season ticket, no deduction is allowed.

Token Items and Membership Benefits That Do Not Reduce Your Deduction

Token items.   Popular fund-raising campaigns, such as those for museums, zoos, and public TV, offer token items such as calendars, tote bags, tee shirts, and other items carrying the organization's logo. You are allowed a full deduction for your contribution if the item is considered to be of insubstantial value under IRS guidelines.

The charity must tell you how much of your contribution is deductible in the solicitation that offers the token item. If the items are insubstantial in value, the charity should tell you that your payment is fully deductible. For example, if in 1997 you contributed at least $34.50, and the offered items cost the charity no more than $6.90, the value of the benefits is ignored and a full 1997 deduction is allowed. A full deduction for 1997 is also allowed if the items were worth no more than 2% of the contribution, or $69, whichever was less. The $34.50, $6.90, and $69 amounts change annually for inflation.

Newsletters or program guides that are not of commercial quality are treated as token items having no fair market value or cost if their primary purpose is to inform members about the organization's activities, and they are not available to nonmembers by paid subscription or through newsstand sales.

Publications with articles written for compensation and advertising are treated as commercial-quality publications for which the organization must figure value to determine if a full deduction is allowed under the "insubstantial value" test. Professional journals, whether or not they have such articles and advertising, will generally be treated as commercial-quality publications that must be valued.

Membership benefits.   If you contribute $75 or less for an annual membership in a qualified charity *(see 14.1)* you may deduct your entire payment under IRS guidelines provided either of the following is true:

1. You receive membership privileges that can be exercised frequently, such as free or discounted parking or admission, or discounts on gift shop or mail order merchandise, *or*
2. Your membership entitles you to admission to events that are open only to members and the organization's reasonably projected cost per person for each event excluding overhead (as of the time the membership package is offered) is no more than the annual limit for "low cost articles." For 1997, the "low cost article" limit is $6.90.

If you pay more than $75 for a membership package, the IRS allows you and the organization to disregard the benefits available under a $75-or-less package.

14.4 Unreimbursed Expenses of Volunteer Workers

If you work without pay for an organization listed at *14.1,* you may deduct as charitable contributions your unreimbursed expenses in providing the services. This includes commuting expenses to and from its place of operations, and meals and lodging on a trip away from home for the organization.

To qualify for the deduction, the expenses must be incurred for a domestic organization which authorizes you to travel. You may not deduct the value of your donated services.

Keep records, such as cancelled checks, to substantiate the amount of your out-of-pocket expenses. To deduct an unreimbursed expense of $250 or more, such as for a plane ticket or a luncheon you hosted on behalf of the organization, IRS regulations require that for each such expense, a statement be obtained from the charitable organization that acknowledges the services you provide. The acknowledgment must describe the services, and state whether you were provided any goods or services by the charity. If so, an estimate of their value must be given unless the benefits

 Law Alert

Volunteer's Auto Allowance After 1997

Starting in 1998, the flat mileage allowance for volunteer workers as a charitable contribution increases to 14¢ a mile from 12¢ a mile.

are "intangible religious benefits." The acknowledgment must be obtained by the date you file your return, but if you file after the April 15 due date (or extended due date if you get an extension), the acknowledgment must be obtained by the due date of your return including extensions.

Deductible expenses. If in 1997 you used your car in providing volunteer services for a charity, you may deduct either the actual operating costs of your car or a flat mileage rate of 12¢ a mile allowed by the IRS. Parking fees and tolls are deductible under both methods.

The 12¢-a-mile deduction rate is not mandatory. If your out-of-pocket expenses are greater, you may deduct your actual costs of operating the automobile exclusively for charitable work, such as the cost of gas and oil, in addition to tolls and parking fees. You may not deduct repairs, depreciation, or insurance costs.

Starting in 1998, the automobile allowance increases to 14¢ a mile.

> **EXAMPLE**
>
> Jill Patton is a volunteer worker for a philanthropy. In the course of her volunteer work during 1997, she drove her car 1,000 miles. She may claim a contribution deduction of $120, plus tolls and parking.

Also deductible as charitable contributions are:

Uniform costs required in serving the organization

Cost of telephone calls, and cost of materials and supplies you furnished such as stamps or stationery

Travel expenses, including meals and lodging on overnight trips away from home as an official delegate to a convention of a church, charitable, veteran, or other similar organization. If you are a member but not a delegate, you may not deduct travel costs, but you may deduct expenses paid for the benefit of your organization at the convention.

The IRS does not allow a deduction for "babysitting" expenses of charity volunteer workers. Although incurred to make the volunteer work possible, babysitting costs are a nondeductible personal expense. Furthermore, the expense is not a dependent care cost; it is not related to a paying job.

Recreational purposes may bar travel expense deduction. To claim a charitable deduction for travel expenses of a research project for a charitable organization, you must show the trip had no significant element of personal pleasure, recreation, or vacation.

> **EXAMPLES**
> 1. Al Jones sails from one Caribbean island to another and spends eight hours a day counting whales and other forms of marine life as part of a project sponsored by a charitable organization. According to the IRS, he may not claim a charitable deduction for the cost of the trip.
> 2. Sara Smith works on an archaeological excavation sponsored by a charitable organization for several hours each morning, with the rest of the day free for recreation and sightseeing. According to the IRS, she may not deduct the cost of the trip.
> 3. Myra Scott, a member of a chapter of a local charitable organization, travels to New York City and spends the entire day at the required regional meeting. According to the IRS, she may deduct her travel expenses as a charitable donation, even if she attends a theater in the evening.

14.5 Support of a Student in Your Home

A limited charitable deduction is allowed for support of an elementary or high school student in your home under an educational program arranged by a charitable organization. If the student is not a relative or your dependent, you may deduct as a charitable contribution your support payments up to $50 for each month the student stays in your home. For this purpose, 15 days or more of a calendar month is considered a full month. You may not deduct any payments received from the charitable organization if any reimbursements are received for the student's maintenance. The only exception is that if you prepay a "one-time" expense such as a hospital bill or vacation for the child at the request of the child's parents or the sponsoring charity, and you are later reimbursed, you may deduct your unreimbursed expenses.

To support the deduction, be prepared to show a written agreement between you and the organization relating to the support arrangement. Keep records of amounts spent for such items as food, clothing, medical and dental care, tuition, books, and recreation in order to substantiate your deduction. No deduction is allowed for depreciation on your house.

Planning Reminder

Foster Parent Expenses

If you receive payments from a state agency to reimburse you for the costs of caring for a foster child in your home, and you can show that your support costs exceed the reimbursements, the excess is deductible as a charitable contribution. Keep detailed records to substantiate your support payments.

14.6 What Kind of Property Are You Donating?

The tax law does not treat all donations of appreciated property in the same way. Whether the full amount of the fair market value of the property is deductible depends on the type of property donated, your holding period, the nature of the philanthropy, and the use to which the property is put by the philanthropy.

Save records to support the market value and cost of donated property. Get a receipt or letter from the charitable organization acknowledging and describing the gift. You *must* get a receipt for donations of property valued at $250 or more; *see 14.15*. Lack of substantiation may disqualify an otherwise valid deduction. Furthermore, if the total claimed value of your 1997 property donations exceeds $500, you must report the donation on Form 8283, which you attach to Schedule A, Form 1040. *See also 14.12* for when you need an appraisal of the value of the property.

Figuring value. When donating securities listed on a public exchange, fair market value is readily ascertainable from newspaper listings of stock prices. It is the average of the high and low sales price on the date of the donation.

To value other property, such as real estate or works of art, you will need the services of an experienced appraiser. Fees paid to an appraiser are not deductible as a charitable contribution, but rather as a miscellaneous itemized deduction *(19.25)* subject to the 2% adjusted gross income floor.

Fair market value deductible for intangible personal property (such as securities) and real estate held long term. Fair market value is deductible where you have held such property long term (longer than one year) and you give it to a publicly supported charity or to a private foundation that qualifies as a 50% limit organization, but you may not deduct more than 30% of adjusted gross income as discussed at *14.17*. A five-year carryover for the excess is allowed; *see 14.18*. If the donation exceeds the 30% ceiling, you may consider a special election which allows you to apply the 50% ceiling; *see 14.19*.

A contribution of appreciated securities or real estate held long term has two tax advantages that reduce the real cost of making the contribution:

1. Your taxes are reduced by the deduction of the fair market value of the property. For example, you donate appreciated stock which is selling at $1,000. You are in the 28% tax bracket. The deduction for the donation reduces your taxes by $280.
2. You avoid the tax you would have paid on a sale of the stock. Assume that your cost for the stock was $400. On a sale at $1,000, you would pay tax of $168 (28% of $600 profit). By donating the stock, you save that $168 plus $280 from the $1,000 deduction, for a total tax savings of $448. Your "cost" for donating the $1,000 asset is $552 ($1,000 – $448).

The IRS ruled that you may not claim a deduction on donated stock if you retain the voting rights, even though the charity has the right to receive dividends and sell the stock. The right to vote is considered a substantial interest and is crucial in protecting a stockholder's investment.

If planning a year-end donation of securities, keep in mind that the gift is generally not considered complete until the properly endorsed securities are mailed or delivered to the charity or its agent; *see 14.1*.

Deduction limited to cost for property not held long term and ordinary income property. This is property which, if sold by you at its fair market value, would not result in long-term capital gain. The deduction for donations of this kind is restricted to your cost for the property. Examples include: stock and other capital assets held by you for one year or less, inventory items donated by business, farm crops, Section 306 stock (preferred stock received as a tax-free stock dividend, usually in a closely held corporation), and works of art, books, letters, and memoranda donated by the person who prepared or created them. *See 14.9* for art objects. For example, a former Congressman claimed a charitable deduction for the donation of his papers. His deduction was disallowed. His papers were ordinary income property, and since his cost basis in the papers was zero, he could claim no deduction.

 Law Alert

Long-Term Holding Period
In this chapter, references to property held long term are to property held more than one year by the donor.
The 1997 Tax Act did not change this rule.

EXAMPLE

Bob James holds short-term stock which cost him $1,000. It is now worth $1,500. If he donates it to a philanthropy, his deduction would be limited to $1,000. He would get no tax benefit for the appreciation of $500. On the other hand, if the stock were held long-term, he could claim a deduction for the full market value of the stock on its donation.

Tangible personal property held long term. Items such as furniture, books, equipment, fixtures (severed from realty), jewelry, and art objects are tangible personal property. When held long term, deductions for donations of this type of asset may be subject to restrictions which will limit your deduction to cost basis. If the philanthropy to which you donate the property does not put it to a use that is related to its tax-exempt charitable function, the deduction must be reduced by the amount of long-term capital gain that would have been realized if the property had been sold at fair market value. If the charity must sell your gift to obtain cash for its exempt purposes, your donation is treated as being put to a nonrelated use by the charity, and your deduction must be reduced by the long-term gain element.

If the donation of tangible personal property is to a 50% deduction limit organization such as a church or college, and you must reduce the deduction as a *nonrelated* gift, the reduced gift is then subject to the 50% annual deduction ceiling of *14.17*. If the organization's use of the property is *related* to its tax-exempt charitable purposes, and it is a 50% limit organization, you may deduct the property's fair market value subject to the 30% of adjusted gross income deduction ceiling; *see 14.17*. Alternatively, you may elect to deduct up to 50% of adjusted gross income by reducing the deduction by the long-term gain; *see 14.19*.

EXAMPLE

You contribute a painting held long term to a college that displays it in a library where art students may study it. The college's use of the painting is related to its tax-exempt educational purposes and you may deduct fair market value. However, if the college sold the painting and used the proceeds for educational purposes, its use would be treated as nonrelated, and you would have to reduce your deduction by the long-term capital gain element. However, if on the date of the donation you could reasonably anticipate that the painting would not be sold (or put to another nonrelated use), you may deduct fair market value, even if it is in fact sold at a later date.

Donating mortgaged property. A donation of mortgaged property may be taxable. Before you give mortgaged property to a charity, have an attorney review the transaction. You may deduct the excess of fair market value over the amount of the outstanding mortgage. However, you may realize a taxable gain. The IRS and Tax Court treat the transferred mortgage debt as cash received in a part-gift, part-sale subject to the bargain-sale rules discussed at *14.8*. You will realize a taxable gain if the transferred mortgage exceeds the portion of basis allocated to the sale part of the transaction. This is true even if the charity does not assume the mortgage.

EXAMPLE

Bob Hill donates to a college land held long-term which is worth $250,000 and subject to a $100,000 mortgage. His basis is $150,000. Hill's charitable contribution deduction is $150,000 ($250,000 – $100,000). He also is considered to have made a bargain sale for $100,000 (transferred mortgage debt) on which he realized $40,000 long-term capital gain. 40% of the transaction is treated as a bargain sale:

$$\frac{\$100,000 \text{ (amount of mortgage)}}{\$250,000 \text{ (fair market value)}} = 40\%$$

Basis allocated to sale: 40% of $150,000, or $60,000

Amount realized	$100,000
Allocated basis	60,000
Gain	$ 40,000

Donating capital gain property to private non-operating foundations. You generally may not deduct the full fair market value of gifts of capital gain property to private non-operating foundations that are subject to the 20% deduction ceiling for non-50% limit organizations discussed at *14.17*. (Capital gain property is property which, if sold by you at fair market value, would result in long-term capital gain.) The deduction must be reduced by the long-term gain that would have been realized if the property had been sold at fair market value. In other words, your deduction is limited to your cost basis.

An exception is available for certain contributions of stock to a private non-operating foundation; *see* the Law Alert on this page.

Law Alert

Stock Donation to Private Foundation

A deduction for fair market value is allowed on a donation made before July 1, 1998, to a non-operating private foundation of appreciated publicly traded stock held long term. If you or family members donate more than 10% of any corporation's stock, the fair market value deduction is allowed only for the first 10%.

The deduction for fair market value had expired May 31, 1997, but the 1997 Tax Act extended it from June 1, 1997, through June 30, 1998.

U.S. Saving Bonds.   You may not donate U.S. Saving Bonds, such as EE bonds, because you may not transfer them. They are non-negotiable. You must first cash the bonds and then give the proceeds to the charity, or surrender the bonds and have new ones registered in the donee's name. When you do this, you have to report the accrued interest on your tax return. Of course, you will get a charitable deduction for the cash gift.

Gift of installment obligations.   You may deduct your donation of installment notes to a qualified philanthropy. However, if you received them on your sale of property which you reported on the installment basis, you may realize gain or loss on the gift of the notes; see *5.32*. The amount of the contribution is the fair market value of the obligation, not the face amount of the notes.

14.7   Property That Has Declined Below Cost

Unless the charity needs the property for its own use, you should not donate business or investment property whose value has declined below your cost. You may not claim a deductible loss when you make a gift. When the property is held for investment or business purposes, you may get the loss deduction by first selling the property and then a charitable deduction by donating the cash proceeds of the sale.

> **EXAMPLE**
>
> Betty Dunn owns securities which cost $20,000 several years ago but which have declined in value to $5,000. A donation of these securities gives a charitable contribution of $5,000. But selling the securities for $5,000 to make a cash donation provides a long-term capital loss of $15,000.

If the property is a personal asset such as clothing or an automobile, you may not deduct a loss on the sale. It makes no difference whether you sell the property and donate the sales proceeds or donate the property.

14.8   Bargain Sales of Appreciated Property

A sale of appreciated property to a philanthropy for less than fair market value allows you to claim a charitable deduction while receiving proceeds from the sale. However, you must pay a tax on part of the gain attributed to the sale. That is, the transaction is broken down into two parts: the sale and the gift.

To compute gain on the sale, you allocate the adjusted basis of the property between the sale and the gift following these steps:

Step 1.   Divide the sales proceeds by the fair market value of the property. If the property is mortgaged, include the outstanding debt as sale proceeds.

Step 2.   Apply the Step 1 percentage to the adjusted basis of the property. This is the portion of basis allocated to the sale.

Step 3.   Deduct the resulting basis of Step 2 from the sales proceeds to find the gain.

You may deduct the donated appreciation if full market value would be deductible on a straight donation (no sale) under the rules of *14.6*. Thus, the donated appreciation is deductible if the property is securities or real estate held long term (*see* Law Alert on page 273), or long-term tangible personal property related to the charity's exempt function; *see* Example 1 below. However, if a deduction for the property (assuming no sale) would be reduced to cost basis under *14.6*, your charitable deduction on the sale is also reduced; *see* Example 2 below. This reduction affects sales of capital gain property held short term; ordinary income property; tangible personal property not related to the charity's exempt function; depreciable personal property subject to recapture; and sales of capital gain property to private non-operating foundations.

> **EXAMPLES**
>
> 1. Lana Briggs sells to a university for $12,000 stock held long term. The adjusted basis of the stock is $12,000, and the fair market value is $20,000. On the sale, she recouped her investment and donated the appreciation of $8,000, but, at the same time, she realized taxable gain of $4,800 computed as follows: The percentage of basis applied to the sale is 60% ($12,000 sale proceeds ÷ $20,000 fair market value). Thus, 60% of the $12,000 basis, or $7,200, is allocated to the sale. Gain on the sale equals the $12,000 sale proceeds less the $7,200 allocated basis, or $4,800.

Filing Instruction

Donating Used Clothing or Furniture

If you donate used clothing, furniture, or household appliances, deduct their fair market value, which is usually much less than your original cost. For your records, get a statement from the donee organization acknowledging the gift and describing the property. Also keep a record of your original cost. If the claimed value of your 1997 donation exceeds $500, you must complete Form 8283; *see 14.12*. For each individual contribution with a claimed value of $250 or more, you must get a receipt as explained in *14.15*.

2. Joel Marx sells to his church stock held short term for his basis of $4,000. The stock is worth $10,000. Using the allocation method in Example 1, 40% ($4,000 sale proceeds ÷ $10,000 fair market value) of his $4,000 basis, or $1,600, is allocated to the sale. Thus, he has a short-term capital gain of $2,400 ($4,000 sale proceeds – $1,600 allocated basis). Furthermore, his deductible charitable contribution is also $2,400, equal to the 60% of basis allocated to the gift (60% of $4,000 = $2,400).

Basis allocation applies even if a deduction is barred by the annual ceiling. The basis allocation rules for determining gain on a bargain sale apply even if the annual deduction ceilings *(14.17)* bar a deduction in the year of the donation and in the five-year carryover period.

EXAMPLE

The Hodgdons contributed real estate valued at $3.9 million but subject to mortgage debt of $2.6 million. The IRS treated the mortgage debt as sales proceeds and figured gain based on the difference between the debt and the portion of basis allocated to the sale element. The Hodgdons claimed that the basis allocation rule, which increased the amount of their gain, should not apply. Earlier in the year, they had made another donation that used up their charitable deduction ceiling for that year as well as for the following five-year carryover period. The Tax Court held that the basis allocation rule applied because a charitable deduction was "allowable," even if the contribution did not actually result in a deduction in the carryover period.

14.9 Art Objects

You may claim a charitable deduction for a painting or other art object donated to a charity. The amount of the deduction depends on (1) whether you are the artist; (2) if you are not the artist, how long you owned it; and (3) the type of organization receiving the gift.

If you are the artist, your deduction is limited to cost regardless of how long you held the art work or to what use the charity puts it. In the case of a painting, the deduction would be the lower of either the cost for canvas and paints, or the fair market value.

If you owned the art work short term, your deduction is limited to cost, under the rules applying to donations of ordinary income property at *14.6.*

If you owned the art work long term (see 14.6), your deduction depends on how the charity uses the property. If the charity uses it for its exempt purposes, you may deduct the fair market value. However, if the charity uses it for unrelated purposes, your deduction is reduced by 100% of the appreciation. A donation of art work to a general fund-raising agency would be reduced because the agency would have no direct use for it. It would have to sell the art work and use the cash for its exempt purposes.

Appraisals. Be prepared to support your deduction with detailed proof of cost, the date of acquisition, and how value was appraised. The appraisal fee is treated as a "miscellaneous" itemized deduction subject to the 2% adjusted gross income floor; *see 19.25.* See also *14.12* for appraisal requirements.

The IRS has its own art advisory panel to assess whether the fair market value claimed for donated art works is reasonable.

Requesting advance valuation of art from IRS. To avoid a later dispute, you may ask the IRS for an advance valuation of art that you have had appraised at $50,000 or more. A request for an IRS Statement of Value (SOV) may be submitted for income tax, gift tax or estate tax purposes. The IRS has the discretion to value items appraised at less than $50,000 if the SOV request includes at least one item appraised at $50,000 or more, and the IRS determines that the valuation is in the best interest of efficient tax administration.

A request for an SOV must be submitted to the IRS before filing the tax return reporting the donation. The request must include a copy of an appraisal for the item of art and a $2,500 fee, which pays for an SOV for up to three items of art. There is an additional charge of $250 for each item of art over three. It takes the IRS between six and 12 months to issue an SOV.

If the IRS agrees with the value reported on the appraisal, the IRS will issue an SOV approving the appraisal. If not, the IRS will issue a different SOV listing the reason it disagrees with the appraised amount. Regardless of whether you agree with the IRS appraisal, the SOV must be attached

Filing Instruction

Appraisal Required

If you claim a deduction for art of $20,000 or more, you must attach a signed copy of a qualifying appraisal to Form 8283 and file it with your return; *see 14.12* for further details.

to and filed with the return reporting the donation. If you file the return before the SOV is issued, a copy of the SOV must be attached to your return and on receipt of the SOV, an amended return must be filed with the SOV attached. For further SOV details, *see* IRS Revenue Procedure 96-15.

EXAMPLES

1. You give your college a painting which you have owned for many years. Its cost was $100 but it is now worth $1,000. The school displays the painting in its library for study by students. This use is related to the school's educational purposes. Your donation is deductible at fair market value. If, however, the school proposed to sell the painting and use the proceeds for general education purposes, its use would not be considered related. Your deduction would be reduced by the $900 appreciation to $100. That the school sells the painting does not necessarily reduce the donation if you show that, when you made the gift, it was reasonable to anticipate that your gift would not be put to such unrelated use.

2. You donate to the Community Fund a collection of first edition books held for many years and worth $5,000. Your cost is $1,000. Since the charity is a general fund-raising organization, its use of your gift is not related. Your deduction would be $1,000 ($5,000 *less* $4,000).

3. You contribute to a charity antique furnishings you owned for years. The antiques cost you $500 and are now worth $5,000. The charity uses the furnishings in its office in the course of carrying on its functions. This is a related use. Your contribution deduction is $5,000.

Donating a partial interest in an art collection. You may deduct the value of a donated partial interest in an art collection, such as where you give a museum the right to exhibit the works for a specific period during the year. The deduction is allowed even if the museum does not take possession of the art works, provided it has the right to take possession.

Keeping a reversionary interest. The IRS may question a charitable deduction where you do not completely relinquish control over the donated property. However, if the possibility of the property reverting back to you is considered to be remote, a deduction may be allowed. For example, a taxpayer who donated her art collection to a museum was allowed to claim a charitable deduction even though she retained the right to decide where and how the art would be displayed. Disputes concerning art displays would be settled by a mutually acceptable museum curator. If the museum breached a condition, it had a period of time to cure the violation. If the violation was not cured, the ownership would revert back to the donor. The IRS allowed the deduction; the retained rights were fiduciary in nature and the possibility of the art reverting to the donor was so remote as to be negligible.

14.10 Interests in Real Estate

No deduction is allowable for the fair rental value of property you allow a charity to use without charge even in direct furtherance of its charitable functions as, for example, a thrift shop.

If you donate an undivided fractional part of your entire interest, a deduction will be allowed for the fair market value of the proportionate interest donated.

A donation of an option is not deductible until the year the option to buy the property is exercised.

Remainder interest in a home or farm. You may claim a charitable deduction for a gift of the remainder value of a residence or farm donated to a charity, even though you reserve the use of the property for yourself and your spouse for a term of years or life. Remainder gifts generally must be made in trust. However, where a residence or farm is donated, the remainder interest must be conveyed outright, not in trust. A remainder interest in a vacation home or in a "hobby" farm is also deductible. There is no requirement that the home be your principal residence or that the farm be profit-making.

Contribution of real property for conservation purposes. A deduction may be claimed for the contribution of certain partial interests in real property to government agencies or publicly supported charities for exclusively conservational purposes. Deductible contributions include: (1) your entire interest in real property other than retained rights to subsurface oil, gas, or other minerals; (2) a remainder interest; or (3) an easement, restrictive covenant, or similar property restriction granted in perpetuity. The contribution must be in perpetuity and further at least one of the

Caution

Donating Vacation Home Use Not Advisable

To raise funds, a charitable organization may ask contributors who own vacation homes to donate use of the property which the charity then auctions off to the public. Be warned that if you offer your home in this way you will not only be denied a charitable deduction for your generosity, but you may jeopardize your deduction for rental expenses. A deduction is not allowed for giving a charity the free use of your property. *See* the Example on the right.

following "conservation purposes"—preservation of land areas for outdoor recreation, education, or scenic enjoyment; preservation of historically important land areas or structures; or the protection of plant, fish, and wildlife habitats or similar natural ecosystems.

To obtain the deduction, there must be legally enforceable restrictions that prevent you from using your retained interest in the property in a way contrary to the intended conservation purpose. The donee organization must be prohibited from transferring the contributed interest except to other organizations that will hold the property for exclusively conservational purposes. If you retain an interest in subsurface oil, gas, or minerals, surface mining must generally be specifically prohibited. However, there is a limited exception where the mineral rights and surface interests have been separately owned since June 12, 1976. A deduction will be allowed if the probability of surface mining is so remote as to be considered negligible. The exception does not apply if you are related to the owner of the surface interest or if you received the mineral interest (directly or indirectly) from the surface owner.

EXAMPLE

To help a charity raise money, one owner allowed the charity to auction off a week's stay in his vacation home, and the highest bidder paid the charity a fair rental. The IRS ruled that not only was the owner's donation not deductible, but the one week stay by the bidder was considered personal use by the owner for purposes of figuring deductions for rental expenses. True, if the owner had directly rented the property to the bidder, the bidder's payment of a fair rental value would have been counted as a rental day and not a personal use day. However, the donation for charitable use is not a business rental, and the bidder's rental payment to the charity is not considered a payment to the owner.

Furthermore, the bidder's use of the home pushed the owner over the personal use ceiling, which in turn prevented him from deducting a rental loss. A rental loss may not be claimed if personal use of a home exceeds the greater of 14 days and 10% of the number of days the home is rented at fair rental value *(9.7)*. Here, the owner personally used the home for 14 days and rented the home for 80 days. The rental expenses exceeded rental income. If the bidder's use of the home was not considered his personal use, the owner could have deducted the loss because his personal use did not exceed the 14-day limit (which was more than 10% of the 80 rental days). However, by adding the bidder's seven days of use to the owner's 14 days, the resulting 21 days of personal use exceeded the 14-day ceiling.

14.11 Life Insurance

You may deduct the value of a life insurance policy if the charity is irrevocably named as beneficiary and you make both a legal assignment and a complete delivery of the policy. A deduction may be disallowed where you reserve the right to change the beneficiary.

The amount of your deduction generally depends on the type of policy donated. Your insurance company can furnish you with the information necessary to calculate your deduction. In addition, you may deduct premiums you pay after you assign the policy.

Deducting premium payments on donated policy. If you assign a life insurance policy to a charity and continue to pay the premiums, you generally may deduct the premiums. However, in states where charities do not have an "insurable interest" in the donor's life, the IRS may challenge income tax and gift tax deductions for the premium payments. The IRS took this position in a private ruling interpreting New York law. In response, New York amended its insurance code to allow individuals to buy a life insurance policy and immediately transfer it to a charity. The IRS then revoked the earlier ruling but it did not announce a change in its position. Thus, the IRS may challenge premium deductions of donors in other states where a charity's insurable interest is not clearly provided by state law.

14.12 Form 8283 and Written Appraisal Requirements

Attach Form 8283 to your Form 1040 if the total deduction claimed for all of your donations of property in 1997 exceeds $500. The IRS may disallow your deduction if you fail to attach Form 8283.

If you are claiming a deduction exceeding $5,000 for an item, or for a group of similar items (such as coins, stamps, books, paintings, or buildings), you need a written appraisal, which must be summarized in Part I, Section B of Form 8283. The appraiser must complete Part III in Section

Form 8283—Worksheet

Noncash Charitable Contributions

Form **8283**
(Rev. October 1995)

Department of the Treasury
Internal Revenue Service

▶ **Attach to your tax return if you claimed a total deduction of over $500 for all contributed property.**
▶ **See separate instructions.**

OMB No. 1545-0908

Attachment
Sequence No. **55**

Name(s) shown on your income tax return

Identifying number

Note: *Figure the amount of your contribution deduction before completing this form. See your tax return instructions.*

Section A—List in this section **only** items (or groups of similar items) for which you claimed a deduction of $5,000 or less. Also, list certain publicly traded securities even if the deduction is over $5,000 (see instructions).

Part I — Information on Donated Property—If you need more space, attach a statement.

1	(a) Name and address of the donee organization	(b) Description of donated property
A	Red Cross City, State 11XXX	Blankets and used clothing
B	Community Food Center City, State 11XXX	Station Wagon - 1988 (8 cylinders, 100,000 miles)
C		
D		
E		

Note: *If the amount you claimed as a deduction for an item is $500 or less, you do not have to complete columns (d), (e), and (f).*

	(c) Date of the contribution	(d) Date acquired by donor (mo., yr.)	(e) How acquired by donor	(f) Donor's cost or adjusted basis	(g) Fair market value	(h) Method used to determine the fair market value
A	7-24-97				$50 00	thrift shop value
B	11-18-97	4-6-88	Purchase	$15,000	$2,500 00	Blue Book Value
C						
D						
E						

B of Form 8283. However, you do not need a written appraisal for publicly traded securities and nonpublicly traded stock of $10,000 or less. Keep the appraisal for your records unless you donate art valued at $20,000 or more. In that case, you must attach a complete copy of the appraisal to Form 8283. Furthermore, you may be asked by the IRS to submit a color photograph (8" × 10") or a slide of the art (4" × 5").

If you need an appraisal, get one from an unrelated professional no earlier than 60 days before your gift, and you must receive it by the due date (including extensions) of your return on which you claim the deduction.

For property donations exceeding $5,000, the donee organization must acknowledge the receipt of the property on Part IV, Section B of Form 8283.

Penalty for overvaluation. You may be penalized for a substantial overvaluation of donated property; *see 14.16.*

Appraisal fees. A fee paid to an appraiser is not considered a charitable deduction but is deductible as a "miscellaneous" expense subject to the 2% adjusted gross income floor; *see 19.25.*

14.13 Business Inventory

Self-employed business owners generally may not deduct more than cost for donations of inventory. If a charitable deduction is claimed, costs incurred in a year prior to the year of donation must be removed from opening inventory and excluded from the cost of goods sold when figuring business gross profit for the year of the contribution.

No contribution deduction is allowed for a gift of merchandise which was produced or acquired in the year donated. Instead, the cost is added to the cost of goods sold to figure gross profit for the year of the contribution. Business deductions are not subject to the percentage limitation applied to donations.

14.14 Donations Through Trusts

Outright gifts are not the only way to make deductible gifts to charities. You may transfer property to a charitable income trust or a charitable remainder trust to provide funds for charity.

 Caution

Charity Reports Transfer Within Two Years

If the charity sells or otherwise disposes of appraised property within two years after your gift, it must notify the IRS on Form 8282 and send you a copy. The IRS could compare the selling price received by the charity with the value you claimed on Form 8283. Reporting on Form 8282 is not required by the charity if in Part II, Section B of Form 8283 you indicated that the appraised value of the item was not more than $500. Similar items such as a collection of books by the same author, stereo components, or place settings of silverware may be treated as one item. Reporting is also not required for donated property that the organization uses or distributes without consideration, if this use furthers the organization's exempt function or purpose.

A charitable income trust involves your transfer of property to a trust directed to pay income to a charity you name, for the term of the trust, and then to return the property to you or to someone else. A charitable remainder trust is one which provides income for you or another beneficiary for life, after which the property passes to a charity.

Trust arrangements require the services of an experienced attorney who will draft the trust in appropriate form and advise you of the tax consequences.

Deductions for gifts of income interests in trust. Current law is designed to prevent a donor from claiming an immediate deduction for the present value of trust income payable to a charity for a term of years. In limited situations, you may claim a deduction if either: (1) You give away all of your interests in the property to qualifying *(14.1)* organizations. For example, you put your property in trust, giving an income interest for 20 years to a church and the remainder to a college. A deduction is allowed for the value of the property. Or (2) you create a unitrust or annuity trust, and are taxed on the income. A unitrust for this purpose provides that a fixed percentage of trust assets is payable to the charitable income beneficiary each year. An annuity trust provides for payment of a guaranteed dollar amount to the charitable income beneficiary each year. A deduction is allowed for the present value of the unitrust or annuity trust interest.

Because income remains taxable to the grantor, alternative (2) will probably not be chosen, unless the income of the trust is from tax-exempt securities. If such a trust is created, a tax may be due if the donor dies before the trust ends or is no longer the taxable owner of trust income. The law provides for recapture of part of the tax deduction, even where the income was tax exempt.

Charitable remainder trusts. A charitable deduction is allowable for transfers of property to charitable remainder trusts only if the trust meets these requirements: The income payable for a noncharitable income beneficiary's life or a term of up to 20 years must be guaranteed under a unitrust or annuity trust. If a donor gives all of his or her interests in the property to the charities, the annuity or unitrust requirements need not be satisfied. The value of the charitable deduction allowable for a gift in trust is determined by IRS tables.

Planning Reminder

Life Income Plans

A philanthropy may offer a life income plan (pooled income fund) to which you transfer property or money in return for a guaranteed income for life. After your death, the philanthropy has full control over the property. If you enter such a plan, ask the philanthropy for the amount of the deduction that you may claim for the value of your gift.

Reporting Charitable Contributions

14.15 Records Needed To Substantiate Your Contributions

The type of records you must keep to substantiate your donations generally depends on their amount and whether you are contributing cash or property. The requirements are stricter for contributions of $250 or more than for smaller contributions.

Contributions under $250. A cancelled check or a dated receipt is proof of a donation under $250. For a property donation, your receipt should contain a description of the property. You should keep records showing the fair market value of the property and your cost basis.

You need a receipt and explanation from the charity for contributions of $250 or more. A written receipt or acknowledgment is necessary to prove charitable contributions of $250 or more. You may not rely on a cancelled check to document a cash contribution of $250 or more. The receipt requirement does not apply if the donation is less than $250, but if the contribution exceeds $75, you must be given a disclosure statement from the charity estimating the value of any benefits you received in return for the donation.

The IRS exempts from the receipt requirement grantors of a charitable lead trust, charitable remainder annuity trust, or charitable remainder unitrust. Since a specific charity does not have to be designated as beneficiary at the time the trust transfer is made, there may be no organization available to provide a receipt.

Content of receipt. A receipt for a donation of $250 or more may be a letter, form, or postcard. If you gave cash, the amount of the donation must be shown. If you gave property, the property must be described in the receipt or acknowledgment, but the charity does not have to value it.

The receipt must state whether or not you have received any goods or services from the charity in exchange for the contribution. If you have, the receipt must include a statement describing such benefits and estimating their value. However, "token" items and certain membership benefits, as described in *14.3,* do not have to be described or valued. There is also an exception if the only benefits received are "intangible" religious benefits, such as admission to religious ceremonies; these do not have to be described or valued, but the statement must indicate that they are the sole benefits provided.

Filing Tip

Right To Buy Athletic Stadium Tickets

The IRS considers 20% of the amount paid for the right to buy college or university athletic seating to be the fair market value of the right. You may deduct 80% *(see 14.3)*. When your payment is $312.50 or more, you are considered to have made a contribution of at least $250 ($250 = 80% of $312.50), requiring a written acknowledgment from the charity.

Payments throughout the year.   For purposes of the $250 receipt threshold, each payment is generally considered separate. Thus, for small donations made during the year, you do not have to obtain a receipt even if they total $250 or more.

If contributions are made by payroll deductions from your wages, the amount withheld from each paycheck is treated separately. A receipt is not required unless withholding on a single paycheck is at least $250. A pay stub or Form W-2 from the employer indicating the amount of a single withholding over $249 is considered a valid "receipt"; a pledge card or other document from the charity must state that you have not received benefits in exchange for the payroll deduction contribution.

Deadline for 1997 donation receipts.   For a 1997 contribution, the deadline for obtaining a receipt is the date you file your 1997 return. If you file after the filing due date or extended due date, get the receipt by the due date or extended due date.

A charity must provide a disclosure statement if you contribute more than $75 and receive benefits.   If you contribute more than $75 but less than $250 to a charity, you do not have to get a written receipt but the charity is required to give you a "disclosure" statement that estimates the value of any benefits you received, such as concert tickets or books. The statement will tell you to deduct only the excess of your contribution over the value of the benefits. If a required disclosure statement is not provided when contributions are solicited, it must be provided when you make a contribution exceeding $75.

Proving Your Donations

If you contribute—	You need—
$75 or less	A cancelled check or receipt from the charity
More than $75 but less than $250	A cancelled check or receipt from the charity. If you received benefits, the charity is required to give you a "disclosure" statement that estimates the value of any benefits you received, such as concert tickets or books. The statement will tell you to deduct only the excess of your contribution over the value of the benefits. If a required disclosure statement is not provided when contributions are solicited, it must be provided when you make a contribution exceeding $75. The disclosure statement is not required if the only benefits you receive are "token items" as discussed in *14.3*. Nor is it required where you contribute to a religious organization and the only benefits you receive are "intangible religious benefits". An example of an intangible religious benefit would be admission to religious ceremonies. A Congressional committee report also suggests that tuition for wholly religious education that does not lead to a recognized degree would qualify.
$250 or more	A receipt or acknowledgment from the charity. You may not rely on a cancelled check to document a cash contribution of $250 or more. A receipt is also required for a donation of property if you are claiming a deduction of $250 or more. If you received any goods or services from the charity in exchange for the contribution, the receipt generally must estimate their value. The deadline for obtaining receipts is the date you file your return. If you file after the filing due date or extended due date, get the receipt by the due date or extended due date. Where the contribution is $250 or more, and both the receipt requirement and the disclosure requirement apply, the charity may satisfy both requirements with the same document. If your total deduction for all property donations exceeds $500, you must report the contributions on Form 8283. If you are not allowed to deduct fair market value for a property donation under the rules of *14.6*, you must attach a statement to Form 8283 explaining the reduction for the appreciation. For property deductions exceeding $5,000, you need a written appraisal as discussed in *14.12*.

14.16 Penalty for Substantial Overvaluation of Property

If the IRS disallows a portion of your claimed deduction for appreciated property on the grounds that you have overvalued it, you may be subject to a penalty as well as additional tax. The penalty applies only for substantial overvaluations that result in a tax underpayment exceeding $5,000. There are two levels of penalty, depending on the extent of overvaluation:

20% penalty. If the value claimed is 200% or more of the correct amount and results in a tax underpayment exceeding $5,000, the penalty is 20% of the resulting tax underpayment.

40% penalty. If the value claimed is 400% or more of the correct amount and results in a tax underpayment exceeding $5,000, the penalty is 40% of the resulting underpayment.

In determining whether the 200% or 400% overvaluation threshold is met, each property claimed on your return is considered separately. Thus, if on the same return you overvalue Property A by 180% and Property B by 250%, the penalty may be imposed only against Property B, even though on an aggregate basis the overvaluation for both properties is at least 200%.

If there is an overvaluation of at least 200% for more than one property, the resulting tax underpayments are combined to determine if the $5,000 underpayment threshold has been met. For example, Property C is overvalued by 300%, resulting in a $1,000 tax underpayment, and Property D is overvalued by 400%, for a tax underpayment of $4,500. As the total underpayment exceeds $5,000, both overvaluations are subject to the penalty.

Reliance on appraisal may avoid penalty. Even though you have an overvaluation subject to the penalty, you may avoid it under a reasonable cause exception if you relied on an appraisal, but only if the appraisal and the appraiser who prepared it were qualified under IRS regulations and, in addition, you made a good faith, independent investigation of the value of the property.

A professional appraiser who knowingly overvalues charitable deduction property is subject to a $1,000 penalty.

14.17 Ceiling on Charitable Contributions

Unless you make donations that are very substantial in relation to your adjusted gross income (Line 32, Form 1040), you do not have to be concerned with the deduction ceilings discussed in this section. For cash contributions, the deduction ceiling is generally 50% of adjusted gross income, but in some cases a 30% limit applies. For property donations, the deduction limit is generally 30% of adjusted gross income although it sometimes is 50% or even 20%. As detailed below, the specific limit for each donation depends on whether it is made to a "50% limit organization" and whether it is capital gain property. Where you have made contributions subject to different ceilings, the ceilings are applied in a specific order and are subject to an overall ceiling of 50% of adjusted gross income. If your deduction is limited by any of the ceilings, a five-year carryover is allowed for the excess; see 14.18.

Even if none of your charitable contributions are subject to the ceilings, your overall charitable deduction is subject to the 3% reduction to itemized deductions if your 1997 adjusted gross income exceeds $121,200 ($60,600 if married filing separately); see 13.7.

Volunteer expenses. The deduction ceiling for unreimbursed expenses you incur doing volunteer work for a charity (14.4) is 50% of adjusted gross income if your services were for a 50% limit organization such as a church or college (see the list below), or 30% of adjusted gross income if the services were on behalf of an organization other than a 50% limit organization.

30% limit for contributions for the use of an organization. If a donation is treated as for the use of, rather than directly to, any organization, it is deductible under the 30% ceiling described below for contributions to organizations that are not 50% limit organizations.

This 30% ceiling applies to a charitable unitrust or annuity trust income interest that is deductible under the rules of 14.14. A charitable remainder trust transfer is also subject to the 30% limit if the trust provides that after the death of the income beneficiary, the property is to be held in the trust for the benefit of the charity, rather than distributed to the charity.

Deductible expenses for supporting a student in your home (see 14.5) are considered to be for the use of a charitable organization and thus subject to the 30% ceiling for contributions to organizations that are not 50% limit organizations.

Planning Reminder

Advance Valuation of Art from IRS

To protect against the possibility of a valuation dispute that could lead to a penalty where you are claiming a deduction of at least $50,000 for a work of art, you may request a valuation from the IRS prior to the time you file. *See 14.9* for obtaining the IRS valuation.

Contributions to 50% Limit Organizations

Organizations in the 50% limit category include churches, schools, publicly supported charities, and private foundations in the list below. Cash contributions to such organizations are deductible up to 50% of adjusted gross income and contributions of capital gain property held long term generally are deductible up to 30% of adjusted gross income.

The 50% deduction ceiling also applies to donations to the United States, Puerto Rico, a U.S. possession, a state, a political subdivision of a state or U.S. possession, or an Indian tribal government.

50% ceiling.   Contributions of cash, ordinary income property, and capital gain property held short term are deductible up to 50% of adjusted gross income if made to the following types of charitable organizations:

Churches, synagogues, mosques, and other religious organizations.

Schools, colleges, and other educational organizations that normally have regular faculties and student bodies in attendance on site.

Hospitals and medical research organizations associated with hospitals.

Government-supported or publicly supported foundations for state and municipal universities colleges.

Religious, charitable, educational, scientific or literary organizations that receive a substantial part of their financial support from the general public or a government unit. Libraries, museums, drama, opera, ballet and orchestral societies, community funds, the American Red Cross, Heart Fund, and the United Way are in this category. Also included are organizations to prevent cruelty to children or animals, or to foster amateur sports (provided they do not provide athletic facilities or equipment).

Private operating foundations.

Private non-operating foundations that distribute their contributions annually to qualified charities within 2 ½ months after the end of their taxable year.

Private non-operating foundations that pool donations and allow donors to designate the charities to receive their gifts, if the foundation pays out all income within 2 ½ months after the end of the tax year.

Organizations that normally receive more than one-third of their support from the general public or governmental units.

30% ceiling for capital gain property held long term.   The deduction ceiling is generally 30% (not 50%) of adjusted gross income where you donate to a 50% limit organization property that would have resulted in long-term capital gain had you sold it at fair market value.

The 30% ceiling applies where the fair market value of the property is deductible under the rules of *14.6.* This includes donations of appreciated securities and real estate held long term. It also includes donations of appreciated tangible personal property (such as furniture or art) held long term where the organization's use of your gift is directly related to its tax-exempt charitable purposes.

However, you may elect to apply the 50% ceiling instead of the 30% ceiling to such property donations if you reduce the fair market value of the property by the appreciation; *see 14.19.*

If you donate tangible personal property held long term that is *not* used by the organization for its tax-exempt charitable purposes, so that your deduction must be reduced for the appreciation *(14.6),* the reduced amount is deductible under the 50% ceiling.

Contributions to Non–50% Limit Organizations

If a contribution is made to a qualifying organization that is *not* in the above list of 50% limit organizations, a 30% or 20% deduction ceiling applies. Organizations in this category include veterans' organizations, fraternal societies, nonprofit cemeteries and private non-operating foundations that do not meet the payout requirements for 50% limit status.

The 30% limit applies to contributions of cash, ordinary income property, and capital gain property held short term. The 20% limit applies to contributions of capital gain property held long term (more than one year). However, the actual ceiling may be less than 30% or 20% of adjusted gross income where in the same year you have made contributions to 50% limit organizations. In that case, follow Steps 2 and 4 of the following section on applying the deduction ceilings.

 Filing Tip

Cash Gifts

A donation of cash to a church, college, or publicly supported charity is deductible up to 50% of your adjusted gross income; *see* the list on this page of organizations to which contributions eligible for the 50% limit may be made.

 Law Alert

Long-Term Holding Period

In this chapter, references to property held long term are to property held more than one year by the donor.

The 1997 Tax Act did not change this rule.

Applying the Deduction Ceilings

The various deduction ceilings are applied in a specific order, with the total deduction for the year limited to 50% of adjusted gross income. Check above for the ceilings that apply to your donations and then apply the ceilings in the following order. *See 14.19* for carryover rules if a portion of your deduction is barred by the deduction ceilings.

1. 50% deduction ceiling for contributions to 50% limit organizations.
2. 30% of adjusted gross income ceiling for contributions to organizations that are *not* 50% limit organizations, except for contributions of capital gain property subject to the 20% ceiling under Step 4 below.

   If any contributions to 50% limit organizations were made, including donations of capital gain property that are subject to the 30% ceiling under Step 3 below, this Step 2 ceiling is the lesser of (1) 30% of adjusted gross income and (2) 50% of adjusted gross income minus the contributions to the 50% limit organizations.
3. 30% of adjusted gross income ceiling for contributions of capital gain property to 50% limit organizations.

   If contributions qualifying for the 50% ceiling (Step 1) were made, your deduction for these 30% limit contributions is the lesser of (1) 30% of adjusted gross income and (2) 50% of adjusted gross income minus the contributions qualifying for the 50% ceiling.
4. 20% of adjusted gross income ceiling for contributions of capital gain property to organizations that are not 50% limit organizations.

   If contributions are deductible under any of the other ceilings (Steps 1–3), you may deduct contributions subject to the 20% ceiling only to the extent that there is any adjusted gross income remaining under the overall 50% adjusted gross limit.

EXAMPLES

1. Linda Jones in 1997 contributes to a church $22,000 in cash and land held long term valued at $35,000. Her adjusted gross income is $100,000, so the total deduction for the year may not exceed $50,000 under the 50% overall limit. Since the $22,000 cash contribution subject to the 50% ceiling is considered first, the deduction for the land (subject to the 30% ceiling under Step 3 above) is limited to $28,000, the difference between the $50,000 overall limit and the $22,000 cash gift. Jones may carry over the unused $7,000 donation attributable to the land.
2. Earl Smith in 1997 has an adjusted gross income of $100,000. He contributes land worth $40,000 to a college, deductible under the 30% ceiling of Step 3 above. He also contributes $30,000 in cash to a non-operating private foundation subject to the 30% ceiling of Step 2 above. The 30% limitation for cash gifts to non-operating private foundations is applied before the 30% limitation applicable to gifts of capital gain property to public charities. The deduction for the cash gift is reduced to $10,000 (50% of $100,000 adjusted gross income, or $50,000, minus $40,000 gift to college). The deduction for the land is limited to $30,000 (30% of $100,000). Accordingly, Smith's charitable contribution deduction for 1997 is $40,000 ($10,000 + $30,000).

   Smith is allowed to carry over *(14.18)* the amounts disallowed by the ceilings: $20,000 ($30,000 – $10,000) for the cash gift and $10,000 ($40,000 – $30,000) for the land.

14.18 Five-Year Carryover for Excess Donations

If you make donations that are not deductible because they exceed the 50%, 30%, or 20% of adjusted gross income ceilings discussed in *14.17,* you may carry over the excess over the next five years. In each carryover year, the original percentage ceiling applies. For example, where contributions of appreciated long-term intangible personal property or real estate (or tangible personal property put to a related use by the charity) exceed the 30% ceiling for capital gain property *(14.17)*, the excess remains subject to the 30% ceiling in the carryover years.

In any carryover year, you must first figure your deduction for contributions in the current year under the applicable 50%, 30%, or 20% ceilings. For each category of property carried over, the carryover contributions are deductible only after the deduction for current year donations is figured. The total deduction in the carryover year, for both current year and carryover contributions, cannot exceed 50% of adjusted gross income for the carryover year.

Filing Instruction

Carryover for Excess Contributions

If you contribute cash and property in the same year, your deductions may be subject to different limits, such as 50% of adjusted gross income for the cash and 30% for the property. Follow the steps and examples on this page for applying the ceilings.

If your donation exceeds the limits, you may carryover the excess for five years.

Planning Reminder

Project Your Income

When planning substantial donations that may exceed the annual ceiling, make a projection of your income for at least five years. Although the carryover period of five years will probably absorb most excess donations, it is possible that the excess may be so large that it will not be completely absorbed during the year of the contribution and the five-year carryover period. It is also possible that your income may drop in the future so that you cannot adequately take advantage of the excess.

EXAMPLE

In 1997, you contribute to a university stock held long term with a fair market value of $19,000. The contribution is subject to the 30% ceiling for capital gain property *(14.17)*. You also have a $2,000 carryover from 1996 for a cash gift to your church which in 1997 remains subject to the 50% ceiling. Your 1997 adjusted gross income is $40,000. Under the 30% ceiling, the deduction for the contribution of stock is limited to $12,000 (30% of $40,000 adjusted gross income). Since the overall deduction limit is $20,000 (50% of $40,000 adjusted gross income), the $2,000 carryover from 1996 is fully deductible. The total deduction on your 1997 return is $14,000 ($12,000 plus $2,000 carryover). You carry over to 1998 the $7,000 balance from the gift of stock that could not be deducted in 1997 because of the 30% ceiling.

14.19 Election To Reduce Property Gift Appreciation

Although the 30% ceiling generally applies to long-term intangible property (such as securities) and real estate contributed to 50% limit organizations *(see 14.17)*, you may elect the 50% ceiling, provided you reduce the fair market value of the property by 100% of the appreciation on all such donations during the year. The reduction also applies to donations of tangible personal property related in use to the organization's charitable function. In most cases, this election should be made only where the amount of appreciation is negligible. Where there is substantial appreciation, the increase in the deduction may not make up or exceed the required 100% reduction, which allows you to claim a deduction only for your cost basis in the property. If the election is made in a year in which there are carryovers of capital gain property subject to the 30% ceiling, the carryovers are subject to reduction; *see* IRS Publication 526.

The election of the 50% ceiling is made by attaching a statement to your original return or amended return filed by the original due date. Even where no formal electing statement is made, claiming a deduction without the appreciation in order to come within the 50% ceiling is treated as an election. A formal or "informal" election is not revocable unless a material mistake is shown. A revocation based on a reconsideration of tax consequences is not considered sufficient grounds.

Chapter 15

Itemized Deduction for Interest Expenses

On Schedule A of Form 1040, you may deduct three types of interest charges:

- Home mortgage interest
- Points
- Investment interest

These deductions are also subject to limitations:

- Home mortgage interest and points are subject to the 3% reduction of itemized deductions if your adjusted gross income (AGI) exceeds $121,200 ($60,600 for married persons filing separate returns).
- Investment interest is deductible only up to the amount of net investment income but is not included in the 3% reduction computation. The 3% reduction rule is discussed at *13.7*.

Interest on personal loans (such as loans to buy autos and other personal items and credit card finance charges) is not deductible.

Interest on loans for business purposes is fully deductible on Schedule C. Interest on loans related to rental property is fully deductible from rental income on Schedule E.

Whether interest is a business, investment, or a personal expense generally depends upon the use made of the money borrowed, not on the kind of property used to secure the loan. However, interest on a loan secured by a first or second home may be deductible as home equity mortgage interest regardless of how you use the loan.

Passive activity interest. Interest on loans used to finance an investment in a passive activity is subject to the limitations of Chapter 10. However, if you rent out a second home that qualifies as a second residence, the portion of mortgage interest allocable to rental use is deductible as qualified mortgage interest and is not treated as a passive activity expense.

Home Mortgage Loans

15.1 Home Mortgage Interest

You generally may deduct on Schedule A (Form 1040) qualifying mortgage interest on up to two residences (*see* two-residence limit below). However, if your 1997 adjusted gross income exceeds $121,200 ($60,600 if married filing separately), your mortgage interest deduction is subject to the 3% reduction of itemized deductions; *see 13.7.*

Mortgage loan obtained after October 13, 1987. Whether you can take a full mortgage interest deduction for a loan taken out after October 13, 1987, depends on the amount of the mortgage debt and how you use the proceeds. Loans used to buy, construct, or improve a first or second home are called *home acquisition loans,* and up to $1 million of such debt qualifies for a mortgage interest deduction, $500,000 if married filing separately. Loans used for any other purpose are called *home equity loans* by the tax law, and up to $100,000 of such debt qualifies for an interest deduction; the home equity limit is $50,000 for married persons filing separately.

To deduct interest on a home acquisition or home equity loan, the loan must be *secured* by your main home or a second home. For the loan to be "secured," it must be recorded or satisfy similar requirements under state law. For example, if a relative gives you a loan to help you purchase a home, the relative must take the legal steps required to record the loan with local authorities; otherwise, you may not deduct interest on the loan.

Home acquisition loans are further discussed at *15.2. Home equity loans* are discussed at *15.3.* If you *refinance* your mortgage, *see 15.7.*

Mortgage loan obtained before October 14, 1987. You may deduct all of the interest on a loan secured by a first or second home if the loan was obtained before October 14, 1987. Technically, such loans are considered home acquisition debt, but they are treated as "grandfathered debt" exempt from the $1 million loan limit ($500,000 for married persons filing separately).

However, the amount of your pre-October 14, 1987, loan reduces the $1 million limit (or $500,000) on home acquisition debt after October 13, 1987; *see 15.2.* It also reduces the fair market value limit for home equity debt; *see 15.3.* If you *refinance* your loan, *see 15.7.*

Two-residence limit for qualifying mortgage debt. The rules for deducting qualifying acquisition debt or home equity debt apply to loans secured by your principal residence and one other residence. A residence may be a condominium or cooperative unit, houseboat, mobile home, or house trailer that has sleeping, cooking, and toilet facilities. If you own more than two houses, you decide which residence shall be considered your second residence. Interest debt secured by the second residence is deductible under the rules for acquisition debt *(15.2)* or home equity debt *(15.3).*

A residence that you rent out for any part of the year may be treated as a second residence only if you use it for personal nonrental purposes for more than the greater of 14 days or 10% of the rental days. In counting rental days, include days that the home is held out for rental or listed for resale. In counting days of personal use, use by close relatives generally qualifies as your personal use; *see 9.6.*

Interest on debt secured by a residence other than your principal or second home may still be deductible, if you use the proceeds for investment or business purposes; *see 15.12.*

Interest on mortgage credit certificates. Under special state and local programs, you may obtain a "mortgage credit certificate" to finance the purchase of a principal residence or to borrow funds for certain home improvements. Generally, a qualifying principal residence may not cost more than 90% of the average area purchase price, 110% in certain targeted areas. A tax credit for interest paid on the mortgage may be claimed. The credit is computed on Form 8396 and claimed on Line 44 of Form 1040. The credit equals the interest paid multiplied by the certificate rate set by the governmental authority but the maximum annual credit is $2,000. Interest not qualifying for the credit is deductible as home mortgage interest.

EXAMPLE

You pay $5,000 interest for a mortgage issued under a qualifying mortgage credit certificate. Under its terms, you are allowed a tax credit of $750. You may claim the balance of your mortgage interest, or $4,250 ($5,000 – $750), as an itemized deduction. If the allowable credit exceeds tax liability, a three-year carryover is allowed.

If you buy a home using a qualifying mortgage credit certificate and sell that home within nine years, you must recapture part of the tax credit on Form 8828.

 Planning Reminder

Mortgage Interest on a Third Home

Interest on debt secured by a residence *other than* your principal or second home may still be deductible, if you use the proceeds for investment or business purposes; *see 15.12.*

15.2 Home Acquisition Loans

Under the mortgage interest rules, a qualifying "home acquisition loan" is a loan used to buy, build, or substantially improve your principal residence or second home, provided the debt is secured by that same residence.

Interest paid on such home acquisition loans is fully deductible if the total debt does not exceed $1,000,000, or $500,000 if you are married filing separately. The $1,000,000 (or $500,000) limit applies to acquisition loans taken out after October 13, 1987.

If your mortgages, taken after October 13, 1987, exceed the $1,000,000 (or $500,000) limit, you must use IRS worksheets included in Publication 936 to figure the amount of your deductible interest. Furthermore, if you incurred substantial loans before October 14, 1987, and later purchase a new home, your deduction for the mortgage for the new home may be limited. The $1 million limit for acquisition debt after October 13, 1987, is reduced by the amount of outstanding pre-October 14, 1987, debt.

Although interest on a pre-October 14, 1987, debt is generally fully deductible regardless of the size of the loan, refinancing a pre-October 14, 1987, debt for more than the existing balance subjects the excess to the $1 million ceiling; see 15.7.

Generally, a debt qualifies as being incurred in buying, constructing, or improving a residence if you satisfy IRS tracing rules (15.12) that prove the use of the loan proceeds for such residential purposes. Even if you cannot prove under the tracing rules that a loan was used to buy a residence, a loan will be treated by the IRS as incurred for buying a house to the extent you can show acquisition expenses within 90 days before, or 90 days after, incurring the loan. Special construction loan and improvement loan rules are discussed in 15.4 and 15.5.

Interest on a mortgage to buy or build a home other than your principal residence or qualifying second home is treated as nondeductible personal interest. If a nonqualifying home is rented out, the part of the mortgage interest that is allocable to the rental activity is treated as passive activity interest subject to the limitations of Chapter 10; the interest allocable to your personal use is nondeductible personal interest.

A married couple filing jointly may designate as a second residence a home owned or used by either spouse.

If a married couple files separately, each spouse may generally deduct interest on debt secured by one residence. However, both spouses may agree in writing to allow one of them to deduct the interest on a principal residence plus a designated second residence.

Cooperatives. In the case of housing cooperatives, debt secured by stock as a tenant-stockholder is treated as secured by a residence. The cooperative should provide you with the proper amount of your deductible interest. If the stock cannot be used to secure the debt because of restrictions under local law or the cooperative agreement, the debt is still considered to be secured by the stock if the loan was used to buy the stock. For further details on allocation rules, see IRS Publication 936.

Line-of-credit mortgages. If you had a line-of-credit mortgage on your home on October 13, 1987, and you borrowed additional amounts on this line of credit after that date, the additional borrowed amounts are treated as a mortgage taken out after October 13, 1987. If the newly borrowed amounts are used to buy, build, or improve your first or second home, they are treated as home acquisition debt subject to the $1 million or $500,000 limit. If used for any other purpose, the amounts are subject to the home equity debt rules at 15.3.

Mortgage interest paid after house destroyed. If your principal residence or second home (15.1) is destroyed and the land is sold within a reasonable period of time following the destruction, the IRS treats the property as a residence for purposes of deducting interest payments on the mortgage during the period between the destruction of the residence and the sale of the land. In one case, the IRS allowed the interest deduction where a sale of land took place 26 months after the destruction of a home by a tornado.

If the destroyed residence is reconstructed and reoccupied within a reasonable period of time following the destruction, the property will continue to be treated as a residence during that period, and the interest payments on the mortgage on the property will be deductible. The IRS allowed an interest deduction where reconstruction began 18 months after, and was completed 34 months after, destruction of the home.

15.3 Home Equity Loans

For interest deduction purposes, qualifying home equity debt is the *lesser* of:

1. $100,000, or $50,000 if married filing separately, *and*
2. The fair market value of your principal residence and second home, *reduced* by the amount of acquisition debt *(15.2)* and by any "grandfathered" pre-October 14, 1987, mortgages *(15.1)*. According to the IRS, fair market value, acquisition debt, and grandfathered debt are determined on the date that the last debt was secured by the home.

The debt must be secured by your first or second home to qualify. If you have a second home as well as a principal residence, the above limitation under (1) and (2) applies to the total debt for both houses. Interest on a qualifying home equity loan is deductible regardless of the way you spend the proceeds, unless it is used to buy tax-exempts *(15.11)*.

On loans exceeding the home equity debt limit, interest may be deductible if the proceeds are used for investment or business purposes. Otherwise, interest on the excess is nondeductible personal interest.

> **EXAMPLES**
> 1. You bought your house in 1986 for $200,000 subject to a mortgage of $150,000. When the mortgage principal is $120,000 and the fair market value of the house is $210,000, you take out a home equity loan. Interest on a home equity loan of up to $90,000 is fully deductible. Qualifying home equity debt may not exceed the difference between the fair market value of the house ($210,000) and the current acquisition debt ($120,000). If the value of the house exceeded $220,000, you could have borrowed up to the $100,000 limit as a qualifying home equity loan.
> 2. The fair market value of your house is $200,000 and the current mortgage is $160,000. You may deduct interest on a home equity loan of up to $40,000 ($200,000 – $160,000).

A loan may qualify partially as acquisition debt and partially as home equity debt where part of it is used to refinance an existing acquisition debt. The refinanced amount is still considered acquisition debt. Debt in excess of the refinanced amount is either home equity debt subject to the $100,000 ceiling or home acquisition debt subject to the $1 million ceiling, depending on how the proceeds are used; *see 15.7.*

15.4 Home Construction Loans

Interest on a home construction loan may be fully deductible from the time construction begins for a period of up to 24 months while construction takes place. Within the 24-month period, the loan is considered acquisition debt subject to the $1 million ceiling *(15.2)*, provided that the home is a principal residence or second home when it is actually ready for occupancy. Furthermore, the loan proceeds must be directly traceable to home construction expenses, including the purchase of a lot, and the loan must be secured by the lot to be treated as acquisition debt. According to the IRS, if construction begins before a loan is incurred, the loan is treated as acquisition debt to the extent of construction expenses within the 24-month period *before* the loan. In determining when a loan is "incurred" for purposes of this 24-month rule, you can treat the date of a written loan application as the date the loan was "incurred," provided you receive the loan within 30 days after loan approval.

Interest incurred on the loan before construction begins is treated as nondeductible personal interest (*see* Example 1 on the next page). If construction lasts more than 24 months, interest after the 24-month period also is treated as nondeductible personal interest.

Interest on loans taken out within 90 days *after* construction is completed may qualify for a full deduction. The loan is treated as acquisition debt to the extent of construction expenses within the last 24 months before the residence was completed, plus expenses through the date of the loan (*see* Example 2 on the next page). For purposes of the 90-day rule, the loan proceeds generally are treated as received on the loan closing date. However, a debt may be considered "incurred" on the date a written loan application is made, provided the loan proceeds are actually received within 30 days after loan approval. If a loan application is made within the 90-day period and it is rejected, and a new application with another lender is made within a reasonable time after the rejection, a loan from the second lender will be considered timely even if more than 90 days have passed since the end of construction.

 Filing Tip

Mortgage Fees Not Deductible
You may not deduct expenses incurred in obtaining a mortgage loan, such as loan assumption fees or costs of an appraisal or credit report.

 Planning Reminder

Home Equity Loan To Pay Consumer Debts
Interest on consumer loans is not deductible, but you can use a home equity line-of-credit mortgage to pay off existing consumer debts and finance future consumer expenses. However, although interest on a home equity loan is fully deductible for regular tax purposes if within the $100,000 limit, the interest is not allowed for purposes of alternative minimum tax, unless used to improve your first or second home; *see 23.2.*

EXAMPLES

1. On January 12, 1997, you borrow $100,000 to buy a residential lot. The loan is secured by the lot. You begin construction of a principal residence on January 1, 1998, and use $250,000 of your own funds for construction expenses. The residence is completed December 31, 1999.

   The interest paid in 1997 is nondeductible personal interest. It was paid before the 24-month qualifying construction period which started January 1, 1998, and ended December 31, 1999.

   Interest paid in 1998 and 1999 is fully deductible as the $100,000 loan is treated as acquisition debt for the 24-month construction period.

2. Same facts as Example 1, but on March 17, 2000, you take out a $300,000 mortgage on the completed house to raise funds. You use $100,000 of the loan proceeds to pay off the $100,000 loan on the lot and keep the balance.

   All of the interest on the $300,000 loan is fully deductible because the loan qualifies as acquisition debt; $100,000 of the debt is treated as acquisition debt used for construction, since it was used to refinance the original 1997 debt to purchase the lot. The $200,000 balance is also treated as a construction loan under the 90-day rule. It was borrowed within 90 days after the residence was completed, and it reimbursed construction expenses of at least $200,000 incurred within 24 months before the completion date.

3. On January 12, 1997, you purchased a residential lot and began building a home on the lot using $45,000 of your personal funds. The home was completed on October 31, 1997. On November 29, 1997, you received a loan of $36,000 that was secured by the home. The debt may be treated as taken out to build the home as it was taken out no later than 90 days after the home was completed, and expenditures of at least $36,000 were made within the period of 24 months before the home was completed.

15.5 Home Improvement Loans

Loans used for substantial home improvements are treated as acquisition debt subject to the $1 million ceiling for loans after October 13, 1987; *see 15.2.* Include only the cost of home improvements that must be added to the basis of the property because they add to the value of the home or prolong useful life. Repair costs are not considered.

EXAMPLE

Your current acquisition mortgage is $100,000. You borrow $20,000 to build a new room. Your qualifying acquisition debt is now $120,000.

If substantial improvements to a home are begun but not completed before a loan is incurred, the loan will be treated as acquisition debt (assuming the debt is secured by the home) to the extent of improvement expenses made within 24 months before the loan. If the loan is incurred within 90 days after an improvement is completed, the loan is treated as acquisition debt (assuming the debt is secured by the home) to the extent of improvement expenses made within the period starting 24 months before completion of the improvement, and ending on the date of the loan.

15.6 Mortgage Payment Rules

Payments to the bank or lending institution holding your mortgage may include interest, principal payments, taxes, and fire insurance premiums. Deduct only interest and tax payments. You may not deduct the payments of mortgage principal and insurance premiums.

In the year you sell your home, check your settlement papers for interest charged up to the date of sale; this amount is deductible.

Mortgage credit. If you qualify for the special tax credit for interest on qualified home mortgage certificates, you only deduct interest in excess of the allowable credit; *see 15.1.*

Jointly owned property. When mortgaged property is jointly owned, a joint owner who pays the entire interest charge may deduct the amount of the entire payment.

Prepayment penalty. A penalty for prepayment of a mortgage is deductible as interest.

Mortgage assistance payments. You may not deduct interest paid on your behalf under Section 235 of the National Housing Act.

Caution

Mortgage Interest Reported on Form 1098

Banks and other lending institutions report mortgage interest payments of $600 or more to the IRS on Form 1098. You should receive a copy of Form 1098 or a similar statement by February 2, 1998, showing your mortgage payments in 1997. Deductible points *(15.8)* paid on the purchase of a principal home are included on Form 1098.

Delinquency charges for late payment. According to the IRS, a late payment charge is deductible as mortgage interest if it was *not* for a specific service provided by the mortgage holder. In one case, the Tax Court agreed with the IRS that delinquency charges imposed by a bank were not interest where they were a flat percentage of the installment due, regardless of how late payment was. The late charges were primarily imposed by the bank to recoup costs related to collection efforts, such as telephone calls, letters, and supervisory reviews. They were also intended to discourage untimely payments by imposing a penalty.

Graduated payment mortgages. Monthly payments are initially smaller than under the standard mortgage on the same amount of principal, but payments increase each year over the first five- or 10-year period and continue at the increased monthly amount for the balance of the mortgage term. As a cash-basis taxpayer, you deduct the amount of interest actually paid even though, during the early years of the mortgage, payments are less than the interest owed on the loan. The unpaid interest is added to the loan principal, and future interest is figured on the increased unpaid mortgage loan balance. The bank, in a year-end statement, will identify the amount of interest actually paid. (An accrual-basis taxpayer may deduct the accrued interest each year.)

Reverse mortgage loan. Homeowners who own their homes outright may in certain states cash in on their equity by taking a "reverse mortgage loan." Typically, 80% of the value of the house is paid by a bank to a homeowner in a lump sum or in installments. Principal is due when the home is sold or when the homeowner dies; interest is added to the loan and is payable when the principal is paid. The IRS has ruled that an interest deduction may be claimed by a cash-basis homeowner only when the interest is paid, not when the interest is added to the outstanding loan balance.

Shared appreciation mortgage. Under a shared appreciation mortgage (SAM) for a personal residence, the lender agrees to charge a fixed rate of interest that is lower than the prevailing market rate. In return, the homeowner promises to pay a percentage of the appreciation on the property at a later date to make up the difference. The fixed-rate interest is deductible when paid and the percentage of appreciation is also treated as interest which you can deduct in the year of payment, subject to the limits of *15.2*. For example, you agree to pay interest of 9% plus 40% of the appreciation in the value of the property within 10 years or earlier if you sell the house or pay off the mortgage. If, at the end of 10 years, the residence is not sold or the loan repaid, you may refinance at the prevailing rate the outstanding balance plus the interest based on the appreciation. If you refinance with the same lender, you may not claim an immediate deduction for the extra interest. The execution of a note is not considered payment. The amount covering the extra interest is deducted ratably over the period of the new loan. If you refinance with another lender and use the funds to pay off the old loan plus the extra interest, the extra interest is deductible in the year of payment, subject to the limits of *15.2*.

Redeemable ground rents. These are deductible as mortgage interest if: (1) the land you lease is for a term exceeding 15 years (including renewal periods) and is freely assignable; (2) you have a present or future right to end the lease and buy the entire interest; and (3) the lessor's interest in the land is primarily a security interest. Payments to end the lease and buy the lessor's interest are not deductible ground rents.

Filing Tip

Joint Liability on Mortgage

If you do not personally receive a Form 1098 but a person (other than your spouse with whom you file a joint return) who is also liable for and paid interest on the mortgage received a Form 1098, you deduct your share of the interest and attach a statement to your Schedule A showing the name and address of the person who received the form. If you are the payer of record on a mortgage on which there are other borrowers entitled to a deduction for the interest shown on the Form 1098 you received, provide them with information on their share of the deductible amount.

15.7 Interest on Refinanced Loans

When you refinance a mortgage on a first or second home *(15.1)* for the same amount as the remaining principal balance on the old loan, there is no change in the tax treatment of interest. In other words, if interest was fully deductible on the old loan, then it is fully deductible on the new loan.

If you refinance a home mortgage for more than the existing balance, the deductibility of interest on the excess amount depends upon how you use the funds and the amount of refinancing. If the excess amount is used to buy, build, or substantially improve your first or second home, then it is considered home acquisition debt; *see 15.2*. If the excess plus all other home acquisition loans does not exceed $1 million ($500,000 if married filing separately), the interest is fully deductible. If the excess is used for any other purpose, such as to pay off credit card debt or to finance a child's education, the excess is considered home equity debt; *see 15.3*. If the excess plus all other home equity loans does not exceed $100,000 ($50,000 if married filing separately), the interest is fully deductible. If the refinanced loan is partly home acquisition debt and partly home equity debt, the overall limit of $1.1 million applies ($1 million home acquisition debt and $100,000 home equity debt), or, if married filing separately, $550,000 ($500,000 home acquisition debt and $50,000 home equity debt).

Interest paid on loans in excess of home acquisition and home equity debt ceilings is generally treated as nondeductible personal interest unless the proceeds are used for business or investment purposes; *see 15.12.*

EXAMPLE

In 1992, Robert and Michelle Stein purchased a home for $250,000. They put $50,000 down and obtained a $200,000, 30-year mortgage secured by the home. In 1997, when their house is worth $300,000 and there is a $175,000 principal balance on the mortgage, they refinance to take advantage of lower interest rates. The refinanced mortgage is for $225,000, payable over 20 years. The Steins use $175,000 to pay off the old mortgage, $30,000 to purchase a car and to pay off credit card debt, and the remaining $20,000 to build a new deck on their home.

The interest on up to $175,000 of the debt incurred to pay off the old mortgage is fully deductible; the amount equals the outstanding balance before refinancing and also falls within the $1 million home acquisition debt ceiling. The $20,000 used to remodel the house is also treated as home acquisition debt. Interest on this amount is fully deductible; the amount falls within the $1 million ceiling when added to the $175,000.

The $30,000 used to buy a car and pay off credit cards is treated as home equity debt. Interest on this amount is fully deductible; the amount falls within the $100,000 ceiling.

Court Decision

Current Deduction for Points on Refinancing

Huntsman replaced a three-year loan used to purchase his principal residence with a 30-year mortgage. He deducted $4,400 of points paid on the new mortgage. The IRS and the Tax Court held that the points had to be deducted over the 30-year loan term.

The Federal Appeals Court for the Eighth Circuit disagreed and allowed a full deduction in the year the points were paid. The first loan was temporary and merely a step in obtaining permanent financing for the purchase of the principal residence.

The IRS has announced that in areas outside of the Eighth Circuit, it will continue to disallow full deductions in the year of payment for points paid on refinancings. The Eighth Circuit includes only these states: Minnesota, Iowa, North and South Dakota, Nebraska, Missouri, and Arkansas. In these states, the IRS will not challenge deductions for points on refinancing agreements similar to Huntsman's which replace short-term financing with long-term permanent financing.

In a later case, the Tax Court held that the *Huntsman* exception does not apply where a borrower refinances a long-term mortgage to take advantage of lower interest rates; the points must be deducted over the term of the new mortgage.

Pre-October 14, 1987, loans. Refinanced pre-October 14, 1987, loans are not subject to the $1 million home acquisition and $100,000 home equity debt ceilings during the period of the original loan term. However, after the end of the original loan term, the ceilings apply to the refinanced amount as explained above. Furthermore, where a refinanced pre-October 14, 1987, debt exceeds the remaining principal balance, the excess is also subject to the $1 million home acquisition and $100,000 home equity debt ceilings.

EXAMPLE

In 1981, Anton and Julia Johnson purchase a home for $400,000. They put $80,000 down and obtain a $320,000, 30-year mortgage secured by their home. In 1997, the house is worth $500,000 and $250,000 is the principal balance remaining on the loan. In 1997, to take advantage of lower interest rates the Johnsons refinance and obtain a $360,000, 20-year mortgage. They use $250,000 to pay off the old mortgage, $90,000 as a down payment on a summer home, and the remaining $20,000 to pay for their daughter's college tuition. They file a joint return.

The interest on up to $250,000 of the debt incurred to pay off the old mortgage is fully deductible; the amount equals the outstanding balance immediately before refinancing. The $90,000 used as a down payment on a summer home is treated as home acquisition debt. Interest paid on this amount is fully deductible; the amount was used to buy a second home and it does not exceed the $1 million ceiling when added to the $250,000 mortgage on the first home. The $20,000 used towards their daughter's college tuition is treated as home equity debt. The interest on this amount is fully deductible; the amount is less than the $100,000 home equity debt ceiling.

Had the Johnsons used $110,000 for college tuition, to buy a new car, and pay off credit card debt, only the interest paid on up to $100,000 of debt would be deductible; interest on the $10,000 excess debt would have been treated as nondeductible personal interest.

Points Paid on Refinancing

The IRS does not allow a current deduction for points on a refinanced mortgage. According to the IRS, the points must be deducted ratably over the loan period, unless part of the new loan is used for home improvements. Thus, if you pay points of $2,400 when refinancing a 20-year loan on your principal residence, the IRS allows you to deduct only $10 a month, or $120 each full year.

A federal appeals court has rejected the IRS allocation rule where points are paid on a long-term mortgage which replaces a short-term loan; *see* the Court Decision alert.

If part of a refinancing is used for home improvements to a principal residence, the IRS allows a deduction for a portion of the points allocable to the home improvements.

EXAMPLE

In June 1997, Craig Smith refinances his home mortgage, which has a principal of $80,000 outstanding. The new loan is for $100,000, payable over 15 years starting in July 1997. Craig uses $80,000 to pay off the old $80,000 balance and the remaining $20,000 is used for home improvements. Assume that at the closing of the new loan, Smith pays points of $2,000 from his separate funds. In the year of payment he may deduct $400 allocable to the 20% of the loan used for home improvements. He may also deduct the ratable portion of the $1,600 balance of the points, which must be deducted over the period of the new loan. The ratable portion is $53 ($1,600 ÷ 180-month loan term × 6 months in 1997). Thus, Craig's total deduction for points in 1997 is $453 ($400 + $53).

Mortgage ends early.   If you are ratably deducting points on a refinanced loan and you refinance again, or the mortgage ends early because you prepay it or the lender forecloses, you can deduct the remaining points in the year the mortgage ends.

15.8 "Points"

Lenders sometimes charge "points" in addition to the stated interest rate. The points increase the lender's up-front fees, but in return borrowers generally are charged a lower interest rate over the loan term. Points are either treated as a type of prepaid interest *(15.14)* or as a nondeductible service fee, depending on what the charge covers. If the points qualify as interest, they are deductible over the term of the loan unless they are paid on the purchase or improvement of your principal residence as discussed in this section.

Points are treated as interest if your payment is solely for your use of the money and is not for specific services performed by the lender which are separately charged. Whether a payment is called "points" or a "loan origination fee" does not affect its deductibility if it is actually a charge for the use of money. The purpose of the charge—that is, for the use of the money or the services rendered—will be controlling. For example, you may not deduct points that are fees for services, such as appraisal fees, preparation of a mortgage note or deed of trust, settlement fees, notary fees, abstract fees, commissions, and recording fees.

If you are *selling* property and you assume the buyer's liability for points, do not deduct the payment as interest but include it as a selling expense that reduces the amount realized on the sale.

Deduction for Points on Purchase or Improvement of Principal Residence

Points are generally treated as prepaid interest *(15.14)* that must be deducted over the period of the loan. However, there is an exception for points you pay on a loan to buy or improve your principal residence. The points on such loans are deductible in the year paid if these tests are met: (1) the loan is secured by your principal residence; (2) the charging of points is an established business practice in the geographic area in which the loan is made; (3) the points charged do not exceed the points generally charged in the area; (4) the amount of points is computed as a percentage of the loan and specifically earmarked on the loan closing statement either as "points," "loan origination fees," or "loan discount"; and (5) you pay the points directly to the lender; *see* "Points withheld from the principal," below.

Points paid by seller are deductible by buyer.   The seller's payment is treated as an adjustment to the purchase price which the seller gives to you as the buyer and which you then turn over to the lender to pay off the points. You must reduce your cost basis for the home by the seller-paid points.

Points withheld from the principal.   Points withheld from the principal of a loan used to buy your principal residence are treated as if you paid them directly to the lender, if, at or before closing, you have made a down payment, escrow deposit, or earnest money payment that is at least equal to the amount of points withheld. These payments must have been from your own funds and not from funds that have been borrowed from the lender as part of the overall transaction.

Caution

Points Reported to the IRS

Points you paid in 1997 on the purchase of your principal residence will be reported to the IRS by the lender on Form 1098 if they meet the five tests explained earlier. Seller-paid points are also included on Form 1098. Form 1098 is used by the IRS to check on the deduction you claim for points on Line 10 of Schedule A. Points paid on an improvement loan for your principal residence are deductible on Line 12 of Schedule A if they meet the tests; they are not shown on Form 1098.

If the loan is used to *improve* your principal residence, the points are not immediately deductible if withheld from the loan principal. You must pay the points with funds that have not been obtained from the lender to claim the full deduction in the year of payment. Otherwise, the deduction must be spread over the loan term.

Points on second home.   If you pay points on a mortgage secured by a second home or a vacation home, the points are not fully deductible in the year of payment; you must claim the deduction ratably over the loan term.

Points paid on refinancing.   The IRS does not allow a current deduction for points on a refinanced mortgage (*see 15.7* for further information).

Deduct balance of points if mortgage ends early.   If you are deducting points over the term of the loan because a full first-year deduction is not allowed, you are allowed to deduct the balance in the year the mortgage ends, such as when you refinance or prepay the loan, or the lender forecloses. For example, if you refinanced your mortgage in 1993 and paid points, those points had to be amortized over the loan term (*15.7*). If in 1997 you refinance again and pay points again, the balance of the points from the 1993 loan are deductible on your 1997 return, and the points on the new loan must be amortized over the loan term.

15.9   Cooperative and Condominium Apartments

Cooperative apartments.   If you are a tenant-stockholder of a cooperative apartment, you may deduct your portion of:

> Interest paid by the cooperative on its debts, provided you do not pay interest on more than two residences; *see 15.1*. This includes your pro rata share of the permanent financing expenses (points) of the cooperative on its mortgage covering the housing project.
> Taxes paid by the cooperative (*16.6*). However, if the cooperative does not own the land and building but merely leases them and is required to pay real estate taxes under the terms of the lease, you may not deduct your share of the tax payment.

In some localities, such as New York City, rent control rules allow tenants of a building converted to a cooperative to remain in their apartments even if they do not buy into the co-op. A holdover tenant may prevent some co-op purchasers from occupying an apartment. The IRS ruled that the fact that a holdover tenant stays in the apartment will not bar the owner from deducting his or her share of the co-op's interest and taxes.

Condominiums.   If you own an apartment in a condominium, you have a direct ownership interest in the property and are treated, for tax purposes, just as any other property owner. You may deduct your payments of real estate taxes and mortgage interest. You may also deduct taxes and interest paid on the mortgage debt of the project allocable to your share of the property. The deduction of interest from condominium ownership is also subject to the two-residence limit of *15.1*. If your condominium is used part of the time for rental purposes, you may deduct expenses of maintenance and repairs and claim depreciation deductions subject to the rules of *9.7*.

Investment Loans

15.10   Investment Interest Limitations

Interest paid on margin accounts and debts to buy or carry other investments is deductible up to the amount of net investment income on Schedule A. If you do not have investment income such as interest, you may not deduct investment interest. Investment interest in excess of net investment income may be carried forward and deducted from next year's net investment income.

You compute the deduction for investment interest on Form 4952, which must be attached to Form 1040. The deduction is *not* subject to the 3% reduction of itemized deductions if your adjusted gross income exceeds $121,200 ($60,600 if married filing separately); *see 13.7*.

What is investment interest?   It is all interest paid or accrued on debts incurred or continued to buy or carry investment property such as interest on securities in a margin account. However, interest on loans to buy tax-exempt securities is not deductible; *see 15.11*.

Investment interest does not include any qualified residence interest (*15.1*), production period interest that is capitalized (*16.4*), or interest related to a passive activity.

Investment property includes property producing portfolio income (interest, dividends, or royalties not realized in the ordinary course of business) under the passive activity rules of Chapter 10, and property in activities that are not treated as passive activities, even if you do not materially participate, such as working interests in oil and gas wells.

Passive activity interest is not investment interest.   Interest expenses incurred in a passive activity such as rental real estate *(10.1)*, or a limited partnership or S corporation in which you do not materially participate *(10.6)*, are taken into account on Form 8582 when figuring net passive income or loss. This includes interest incurred on loans used to finance your investment in a passive activity. Do not treat passive activity interest as investment interest on Form 4952.

However, interest expenses allocable to *portfolio* income (non–business activity interest, dividends, or royalties) from a limited partnership or S corporation are investment interest and not passive interest. The investment interest will be listed separately on Schedule K-1 received from the partnership or corporation.

Computing the Deduction

Deductible investment interest is limited to net investment income. Net investment income is the excess of investment income over investment expenses. The key terms *investment income* and *investment expenses* are defined below.

Investment income.   Investment income is generally gross income from property held for investment, such as interest, dividends, annuities, and royalties. Income or expenses considered in figuring profit or loss of a passive activity (Chapter 10) is not considered investment income or expenses. Property subject to a net lease is not treated as investment property, as it is within the passive activity rules.

If you have net capital gains *(5.2)* from the sale of investment property (such as stocks or mutual-fund shares), you must specifically elect to include such net capital gains as investment income on Form 4952. If you make this election, you may not apply preferential capital gain rates to the amount of the net capital gains treated as investment interest on Form 4952. *See* the IRS instructions to Form 4952 and to the IRS capital gain worksheet in the Form 1040 instructions.

Investment expenses.   There are expenses, other than interest, directly connected with the production of investment income. However, for purposes of determining net investment income, only those investment expenses (other than interest) allowable after figuring the 2% floor for miscellaneous itemized deductions *(19.24)* are taken into account. The 2% floor will bar a deduction for some of the miscellaneous itemized deductions. For purposes of this net investment income computation, assume that miscellaneous itemized deductions other than investment expenses are disallowed first.

Net investment income.   Reducing investment income by investment expenses gives you net investment income. Your deduction for investment interest expenses is limited to this amount; any excess interest expense for 1997 may be carried over to 1998, as discussed below.

Where to enter the deduction on your return.   The deduction figured on Form 4952 is generally entered on Line 13 of Schedule A as investment interest. However, if the interest is attributable to royalties, you may have to enter the interest on Schedule E; follow the Form 4952 instructions. Furthermore, there is an additional complication if you have investment interest for an activity for which you are not "at risk" (Chapter 10). After figuring the investment interest deduction on Form 4952, you must enter the portion of the interest that is attributable to the at-risk activity on Form 6198. The amount carried over to Form 6198 is subtracted from the investment interest deduction claimed on Form 4952.

Carryover to 1998.   Investment interest in excess of net investment income for 1997 may be carried forward to 1998 and is deductible in 1998 to the extent that when added to 1998 investment interest expenses it does not exceed net investment income.

Caution

Interest on Loans To Buy Market Discount Bonds and Treasury Bills
Limits apply to the deduction for interest on loans used to buy or carry market discount bonds *(4.20)* and Treasury bills *(4.27)* acquired after July 18, 1984.

EXAMPLE

For 1997, Larry Jones has $10,000 of investment income from interest and dividends. He has investment expenses, other than interest, of $3,200, after taking into account the 2% floor on miscellaneous itemized deductions. His investment interest expense from securities margin account loans is $8,000. Jones also has income of $2,000 from a passive partnership investment.

Jones's net investment income is $6,800: $10,000 of investment income *less* $3,200 of non-interest investment expenses. The passive activity income from the partnership is not included in investment income.

Jones's investment interest deduction for 1997 is limited to the $6,800 of net investment income. The $1,200 of investment interest in excess of net investment income ($8,000 – $6,800) is carried forward to 1998.

15.11 Debts To Carry Tax-Exempt Obligations

When you borrow money in order to buy or carry tax-exempt bonds, you may not deduct any interest paid on your loan. Application of this disallowance rule is clear where there is actual evidence that loan proceeds were used to buy tax-exempts or that tax-exempts were used as collateral. But sometimes the relationship between a loan and the purchase of tax-exempts is less obvious, as where you hold tax-exempts and borrow to carry other securities or investments. IRS guidelines explain when a direct relationship between the debt and an investment in tax-exempts will be inferred so that no interest deduction is allowed. The IRS will *not* infer a direct relationship between a debt and an investment in tax-exempts in these cases:

1. The investment in tax-exempts is not substantial. That is, it is not more than 2% of the adjusted basis of the investment portfolio and any assets held in an actively conducted business.

2. The debt is incurred for a personal purpose. For example, an investor may take out a home mortgage instead of selling his tax-exempts and using the proceeds to finance the home purchase. Interest on the mortgage is deductible under the rules of *15.1.*

3. The debt is incurred in connection with the active conduct of a business and does not exceed business needs. But if a person reasonably could have foreseen when the tax-exempts were purchased that he or she would have to borrow funds to meet ordinary and recurrent business needs, the interest expenses are not deductible.

The guidelines infer a direct relationship between the debt and an investment in tax-exempts in this type of case: An investor in tax-exempts has outstanding debts not directly related to personal expenses or to his or her business. The interest will be disallowed even if the debt appears to have been incurred to purchase other portfolio investments. Portfolio investments include transactions entered into for profit, including investments in real estate, which are not connected with the active conduct of a business; *see* the Example below.

Mutual funds. If you receive tax-exempt interest dividends from a mutual fund during the year, you may deduct interest on a loan used to buy or carry the mutual fund shares only to the extent it can be allocated to taxable dividends you also receive.

> **EXAMPLE**
>
> An investor owning $360,000 in tax-exempt bonds purchased real estate in a joint venture, giving a purchase money mortgage and cash for the price. He deducted interest on the mortgage. The IRS disallowed the deduction, claiming the debt was incurred to carry tax-exempts. A court allowed the deduction. A mortgage is the customary manner of financing such a purchase. Furthermore, since the purchase was part of a joint venture, the other parties' desires in the manner of financing had to be considered.

Planning Reminder

Keep Loans Separate

To safeguard your investment and business interest deductions, you must earmark and keep a record of your loans. You should avoid using loan proceeds to fund different types of expenditures.

15.12 Earmarking Use of Loan Proceeds

The IRS has set down complex record keeping and allocation rules for claiming interest deductions on loans used for business or investment purposes, or for passive activities. The rules deal primarily with the use of loan proceeds for more than one purpose and the commingling of loan proceeds in an account with unborrowed funds. The thrust of the rules is to base deductibility of interest on the *use* of the borrowed funds. The allocation rules do not affect mortgage interest deductions on loans secured by a qualifying first or second home; *see 15.1.*

Keep separate accounts for business, personal, and investment borrowing. For example, if you borrow for investment purposes, keep the proceeds of the loan in a separate account and use the proceeds only for investment purposes. Do not use the funds to pay for personal expenses. Furthermore, do not deposit loan proceeds in an account funded with unborrowed money, unless you intend to use the proceeds within 30 days of the deposit. By following these directions, you can pinpoint your use of the proceeds to a specific expenditure, such as for investment, personal, or business purposes, and the interest on the loan may be treated as incurred for that purpose. The 30-day rule is discussed below.

The IRS treats undisbursed loan proceeds deposited in an account as investment property, even though the account does not bear interest. When proceeds are disbursed from the account, the use of the proceeds determines how interest is treated; see Examples 1 and 2 later in this section.

30-day disbursement rule. If you deposit borrowed funds in an account with unborrowed funds, a special 30-day rule allows you to treat payments from the account as made from the loan proceeds. Where you make more than one disbursement from such an account, you may treat any expenses paid within 30 days before or after deposit of the loan proceeds as if made from the loan proceeds. Thus, you may allocate interest on the loan to that disbursement, even if earlier payments from the account have been made; *see* Example 3 below. If you make the disbursement after 30 days, the IRS requires you to allocate interest on the loan to the first disbursement; *see* Example 4 below. Furthermore, if an account includes only loan proceeds and interest earned on the proceeds, disbursements may be allocated first to the interest income and then to the loan proceeds.

Allocation period. Interest is allocated to an expenditure for the period *beginning* on the date the loan proceeds are used or treated as used, and *ending* on the earlier of either the date the debt is repaid or the date it is reallocated.

Accrued interest is treated as a debt until it is paid, and any interest accruing on unpaid interest is allocated in the same manner as the unpaid interest is allocated. Compound interest accruing on such debt, other than compound interest accruing on interest that accrued before the beginning of the year, may be allocated between the original expenditure and any new expenditure from the same account on a straight-line basis. That is done by allocating an equal amount of such interest expense to each day during the taxable year. In addition, you may treat a year as *twelve 30-day months* for purposes of allocating interest on a straight-line basis.

Payments from checking account. A disbursement from a checking account is treated as made at the time the check is written on the account, provided the check is delivered or mailed to the payee within a reasonable period after the writing of the check. You may treat checks written on the same day as written in any order. A check is presumed to be written on the date appearing on the check and to be delivered or mailed to the payee within a reasonable period thereafter. However, the presumption may not apply if the check does not clear within a reasonable period after the date appearing on the check.

Change in use of property. You must reallocate interest if you convert debt-financed property to a different use; for example, when you buy a business auto with an installment loan, interest paid on the auto is business interest, but if during the year you convert the auto to personal use, interest paid after the conversion is personal interest.

Order of repayment. If you used loan proceeds to repay several different kinds of debt, the debts being repaid are assumed to be repaid in the following order: (1) personal debt; (2) investment debt and passive activity debt other than active real estate debt; (3) debt from a real estate activity in which you actively participate; (4) former passive activity debt; and (5) business debt. *See* Example 5 below. Payments made on the same day may be treated as made in any order.

EXAMPLES

1. On January 1, you borrow $10,000 and deposit the proceeds in a non-interest-bearing checking account. No other amounts are deposited in the account during the year and no part of the loan is repaid during the year. On April 1, you invest $2,000 of the proceeds in a real estate venture. On September 1, you use $4,000 to buy furniture.

   From January 1 through March 31, interest on the entire undisbursed $10,000 is treated as investment interest. From April 1 through August 31, interest on $2,000 of the debt is treated as passive activity interest, and interest on $8,000 of the debt is treated as investment interest. From September 1 through December 31, interest on $4,000 of the debt is treated as personal interest; interest on $2,000 is treated as passive activity interest; and interest on $4,000 is treated as investment interest.

2. On September 1, you borrow money for business purposes and deposit it in a checking account. On October 15, you disburse the proceeds for business purposes. Interest incurred on the loan before the disbursement of the funds is treated as investment interest expense. Interest starting on October 15 is treated as business interest. However, you may elect to treat the starting date for business interest as of the first of the month in which the disbursement was made—that is, October 1—provided all other disbursements from the account during the same month are similarly treated.

3. On September 1, you borrow $5,000 to invest in stock and deposit the proceeds in your regular checking account. On September 10, you buy a TV and stereo for $2,500 and on September 11 invest $5,000 in stock, using funds from the account. As the stock

investment was made within 30 days of depositing the loan proceeds in the account, interest on the entire loan is treated as incurred for investment purposes.

4. Same facts as in Example 1, but the TV and stereo were bought on October 1 and the stock on October 31. As the stock investment was not made within 30 days, the IRS requires you to treat the purchase of the TV and the stereo for $2,500 as the first purchase made with the loan proceeds of $5,000. Thus, the 50% of loan interest that is allocated to the stereo purchase is nondeductible.

5. On July 12, Smith borrows $100,000 and immediately deposits the proceeds in an account. He uses the proceeds as follows:

August 31	$40,000 for passive activity
October 5	$20,000 for rental activity
December 24	$40,000 for personal use

On January 19 of the following year, Smith repays $90,000. Of the repayment, $40,000 is allocated as a repayment of the personal expenditure, $40,000 of the passive activity, and $10,000 of the rental activity. The outstanding $10,000 is treated as debt incurred in a rental activity.

Timing of Interest Deductions

15.13 Year To Claim an Interest Deduction

As a cash-basis taxpayer, you deduct interest in the year of payment except for prepayments of interest; *see 15.14*. Giving a promissory note is not considered payment. Increasing the amount of a loan by interest owed, as with insurance loans, is also not considered payment and will not support a deduction. If a person pays your interest obligation with the understanding you will repay him or her, you take the deduction in the year the interest is paid, not when you repay him or her. However, an accrual-basis taxpayer generally deducts interest in the year the interest accrues; *see 40.2*.

Here is how a cash-basis taxpayer treats interest in the following situations:

On a life insurance loan, where proceeds are used for a deductible (nonpersonal) purpose, you claim a deduction in the year in which the interest is paid. You may not claim a deduction when the insurance company adds the interest to your debt. You may not deduct your payment of interest on an insurance loan after you assign the policy.

On a margin account with a broker, interest is deductible in the year in which it is paid or your account is credited after the interest has been charged. But an interest charge to your account is not payment if you do not pay it in cash or the broker has not collected dividends, interest, or security sales proceeds which may be applied against the interest due. Note that the interest deduction on margin accounts is subject to investment interest limitations; *see 15.10*.

For partial payment of a loan used for a deductible (nonpersonal) purpose, interest is deductible in the year the payment is credited against interest due. When a loan has no provision for allocating payments between principal and income, the law presumes that a partial payment is applied first to interest and then to principal, unless you agree otherwise. Where the payment is in full settlement of the debt, the payment is applied first to principal, unless you agree otherwise. Where there is an involuntary payment, such as that following a foreclosure sale of collateral, sales proceeds are applied first to principal, unless you agree to the contrary. *See also 15.12* for the effect of payments on the allocation of debt proceeds.

Note renewed. You may not deduct interest by merely giving a new note. You claim a deduction in the year the renewed note is paid. The giving of a new note or increasing the amount due is not payment. The same is true when past due interest is deducted from the proceeds of a new loan; this is not a payment of the interest.

15.14 Prepaid Interest

If you prepay interest on a loan used for *investment* or *business* purposes you may not deduct interest allocable to any period falling in a later taxable year. The prepaid interest must be deducted over the period of the loan, whether you are a cash basis or accrual basis taxpayer.

Planning Reminder

Using Borrowed Funds To Pay Interest

To get an interest deduction you must pay the interest; you may not claim a deduction by having the creditor add the interest to the debt. If you do not have funds to pay the interest, you may borrow money to pay the interest. The borrowed funds must be from a different creditor. The IRS disallows deductions where a debtor borrows from the same creditor to make interest payments on an earlier loan. The second loan is considered a device for getting an interest expense deduction without actually making payments. Courts tend to side with the IRS.

Points paid on the purchase of a *principal residence* are generally fully deductible in the year paid; *see 15.8*. Points paid on refinancing generally are not deductible; *see 15.7*.

Treatment of interest included in a level payment schedule. Where payments of principal and interest are equal, a large amount of interest allocated to the payments made in early years of a loan will generally not be considered prepaid interest. However, if the loan calls for a variable interest rate, the IRS may treat interest payments as consisting partly of interest, computed under an average level effective rate, and partly of prepaid interest allocable to later years of the loan. An interest rate which varies with the "prime rate" does not necessarily indicate a prepaid interest element.

When you borrow money for a deductible purpose and give a note to the lender, the amount of your loan proceeds may be less than the face value of the note. The difference between the proceeds and the face amount is interest discount. For loans that do not fall within the OID rules of *4.18*, such as loans of a year or less, interest is deductible in the year of payment if you are on the cash basis. If you use the accrual basis, the interest is deductible as it accrues.

EXAMPLE

In February 1996, you borrow $1,000 for an investment and receive $900 in return for your $1,000 note. You repay the full loan in January 1997. You are on the cash basis. You do not deduct the interest of $100 when the note is given. The $100 interest is deductible when the loan is paid in 1997. If the loan proceeds were used for personal purposes, none of the interest is deductible in 1997.

For loans that fall within OID rules, your lender should provide a statement showing the interest element and the tax treatment of the interest.

Chapter 16

Deductions for Taxes

If you itemize deductions on Schedule A, you may deduct your 1997 payments of state, local, and foreign income taxes and real property taxes, as well as state and local personal property taxes. State and local sales taxes are not deductible.

To increase your deduction for state and local taxes, consider making a year-end prepayment of estimated tax liability. You also may be able to increase withholdings from your pay to increase your deduction.

If you pay transfer taxes on the sale of securities or investment real estate, the taxes are not deductible. However, they increase your cost basis when figuring your profit or loss.

Taxes paid in operating a business are generally deductible, except for sales taxes, which are added to the cost of the property.

Taxes claimed as itemized deductions are subject to the 3% reduction of itemized deductions if your adjusted gross income exceeds $121,200, or $60,600 if married filing separately; *see 13.7.*

16.1 Deductible Taxes

You may deduct as itemized deductions on Schedule A your 1997 payments of:

- State, local, and foreign income taxes
- State, local, and foreign real property taxes
- State and local personal property taxes

In figuring deductible state or local income taxes, include the amount of state or local income tax withheld from your 1997 pay and any estimated tax you paid in 1997 to state or local authorities. Also, do not forget to include tax that you paid in 1997 when you filed your 1996 state and local tax returns.

Taxes incurred in your business are generally deductible on Schedule C; *see 16.11.*

If your 1997 adjusted gross income exceeds $121,200, or $60,600 if married filing separately, your deduction for taxes is subject to the 3% reduction computation explained at *13.7.*

Claim the deduction for deductible taxes on the tax return for the year in which you paid the taxes, unless you report on the accrual basis; *see 16.8.*

Checklist of Taxes

Type of tax—	Deductible as itemized deduction—
Admission	No
Alcoholic beverage	No
Assessments for local benefits	No
Automobile license fees not qualifying as personal property tax	No
Cigarette	No
Customs duties	No
Driver's license	No
Estate—federal or state	No
Excise—federal or state, for example, on telephone service	No
Gasoline—federal	No
Gasoline and other motor fuel—state and local	No
Gift taxes—federal and state	No
Income—federal (including alternative minimum tax)	No
Income—state, local, or foreign	Yes
Inheritance tax	No
Mortgage tax	No
Personal property—state or local	Yes
Poll	No
Real estate (state, local, or foreign)	Yes
Regulatory license fees (dog licenses, parking meter fees, hunting and fishing licenses)	No
Sales and use tax on personal property	No
Social Security	No
Tolls	No
Transfer taxes on securities and real estate	No

16.2 Nondeductible Taxes

Sales taxes on personal property are not deductible as itemized deductions. Transfer taxes paid on the sale of securities or investment real estate are not separately deductible, but you may increase your cost basis by the transfer tax in figuring profit or loss on Schedule D.

Gasoline taxes.   State and local taxes on gasoline used for personal purposes are not deductible. If you travel for business, the taxes are deductible as part of your gasoline expenses.

Filing Tip

Refund Credited to State Estimated Tax

If you were entitled to a refund on your 1996 state tax return and you credited the overpayment towards your 1997 estimated state tax, do not forget to include the credited amount with other 1997 payments of state and local income tax on your 1997 Schedule A.

16.3 Deducting State Income Taxes

You may deduct on your 1997 return state and local income taxes withheld from your pay and estimated state and local taxes paid in 1997. Also deduct the balance of your 1996 state and local taxes you paid during 1997. If in 1998 you pay additional state income tax on your 1997 income, you deduct the payment on your 1998 tax return.

State income taxes may be claimed only as itemized deductions, even if attributed solely to business income. That is, state income taxes may not be deducted as business expenses from gross income.

To increase your itemized deductions on your 1997 return, consider prepaying state income taxes before the end of 1997. The prepayment is deductible provided the state tax authority accepts prepayments and state law recognizes them as tax payments. The IRS has ruled, however, that prepayments are not deductible if you do not reasonably believe that you owe additional state tax. Do not make prepayments if you may be subject to alternative minimum tax; *see* Chapter 23.

If you report on the accrual basis and you contest a tax liability, claim the deduction in the year of payment.

You may deduct on your federal return state and local income taxes allocable to interest income that is exempt from federal tax but not state and local income tax. However, state and local taxes that are allocated to other federal exempt income are not deductible. For example, state income tax allocated to a cost-of-living allowance exempt from federal income tax is not deductible as a state tax.

Mandatory employee contributions to the following state disability or unemployment insurance funds are deductible as state income taxes: California Unemployment Insurance Code; New Jersey Non-occupational Disability Benefit Fund; New York Nonoccupational Disability Benefit Fund; Rhode Island Temporary Disability Benefit Fund; West Virginia Unemployment Compensation Trust Fund; and the Alabama State Unemployment Fund.

However, employee contributions to a private or voluntary disability plan in California, New Jersey, or New York have been held by the IRS to be nondeductible.

Mandatory employee contributions to a state unemployment fund are deductible.

Note: A refund of state income taxes claimed as an itemized deduction may have to be reported as income; *see 11.5.*

16.4 When Taxes and Interest Are Capitalized

Uniform capitalization rules (Code Section 263A) may prevent you from deducting taxes and interest incurred on business and investment real estate during a construction or development period; *see 40.2.* According to a Tax Court decision, the development period for land started when a development plan was submitted to zoning authorities. The developer was required to capitalize real estate taxes on the raw land, even though no actual development had occurred.

Where property such as nonproductive and undeveloped land is *not* subject to the uniform capitalization rules of Code Section 263A, you may elect to capitalize taxes and interest instead of deducting them. You capitalize the expenses by adding these amounts to the basis of the property. Capitalization may be to your advantage if you do not need the immediate deduction because you have little or no income to offset, or because you do not have itemized deductions or expect a greater tax benefit by adding the taxes to the basis.

Making the election. Attach to your return a statement of expenses you elect to capitalize; IRS permission is not required. The election must apply to all similar expenses for the same project. An election for unimproved and unproductive real property applies only for the year for which it is made.

16.5 Assessments

Assessments by homeowner's association not deductible as taxes. Assessments paid to a local homeowner's association for the purpose of maintaining the common areas of the residential project and for promoting the recreation, health, and safety of the residents are not deductible as real property taxes.

Assessments for government services. If property is used solely as your residence, you may not deduct charges for municipal water bills (even if described as a "tax"), sewer assessments, assessments for sanitation service, or title registration fees. A permit fee to build or improve a personal residence is added to the cost basis of the house.

Assessments for local benefits are deductible if they cover maintenance or repairs of streets, sidewalks, or water or sewer systems, or interest costs on such maintenance. However, assessments for construction of streets, sidewalks, or other local improvements that tend to increase the value of your property are not deductible as real estate taxes. You add such assessments to your cost basis for the property.

If you are billed a single amount, you may deduct the portion allocable to assessments for maintenance or repairs. The burden is on you to support the allocation.

16.6 Deducting Real Estate Taxes

You may deduct payments of real estate tax on your property if you claim itemized deductions on Schedule A. The monthly mortgage payment to a bank or other mortgage holder generally includes amounts allocated to real estate taxes, which are paid to the taxing authority on their due date. Mortgage payments allocated to real estate taxes are deductible in the year you make the payments only if the mortgage holder actually pays the taxes to the tax authority by the end of that year. Typically, banks will furnish you with a year-end statement of disbursements to taxing authorities, indicating dates of payment.

16.7 Tenants' Payment of Taxes

You generally may not deduct a portion of your rent as property taxes. This is so even where state or local law identifies a portion of the rent as being tied to tax increases.

Tenants have been allowed a deduction for property taxes in the following areas: In Hawaii tenants with leases of 15 years or more may deduct the portion of the rent representing taxes. In California, tenants who have their names placed on the tax rolls and who pay the taxes directly to the taxing authority may claim a deduction.

In New York, liability for tax is placed directly on the tenant and the landlord is a collecting agent for paying over the tax to the taxing authorities; the landlord also remains liable for the tax. The IRS ruled that it will not permit tenants to deduct a portion of rent as a payment of taxes.

> **EXAMPLE**
>
> A municipal rent control ordinance allowed landlords to charge real property tax increases to the tenants as a monthly "tax surcharge." The ordinance stated that the surcharge was not to be considered rent for purposes of computing cost-of-living rental increases. The IRS ruled that the tenant may not deduct the "tax surcharge" as a property tax. The tax is imposed on the landlord, not on the tenant. The city ordinance, which permitted the landlord to pass on the tax increases to a tenant, did not shift liability for the property taxes from the landlord to the tenant. For federal tax purposes, the surcharge is merely an additional rental payment by the tenant. Similarly, "rates tax" or "renters' tax" imposed on tenants was ruled to be nondeductible because the tax is imposed on the person using the property rather than the property itself.

16.8 Allocating Taxes When You Sell or Buy Realty

When property is sold, the buyer and seller apportion the real estate taxes imposed on the property during the "real property year." A "real property year" is the period which a real estate tax covers. This allocation is provided for you in a settlement statement at the time of closing. If you want to figure your own allocations, your local tax authority can give you the "real property year" of the taxes you plan to apportion. With this information, you then make the following allocation. If *you* are the:

Seller, you deduct that portion of the tax covering the beginning of the real property year through the day before the sale.

Buyer, you deduct the part of the tax covering the date of the sale through the end of the real property year.

> **EXAMPLE**
>
> The real property year in East County starts April 1 and ends March 31. On July 2, 1997, you sell realty located in East County to Jones. Assume the real estate tax for the real property year ending March 31, 1998, is $1,000. You deduct $252 ($\frac{92}{365}$ of $1,000, since there are 92 days in the period beginning April 1 and ending July 1, 1997). Jones deducts $748 ($\frac{273}{365}$ of $1,000, since there are 273 days in the period beginning July 2, 1997, and ending March 31, 1998).

Filing Tip

Cooperative Apartments

Tenant-stockholders of a cooperative housing corporation may deduct their share of the real estate taxes paid by the corporation. However, no deduction is allowed if the corporation does not own the land and building but merely leases them and pays taxes under the lease agreement. *See also 15.9.*

Information returns. The IRS requires real estate agents to report in Box 5 of Form 1099-S the buyer's share of real estate taxes on a residence. For example, Smith sells her house in Green County, where the real estate tax is paid annually in advance. In the year of sale she paid $1,200 in real estate taxes. Assuming that the home is sold at the end of the ninth month of the real property tax year, the amount of the real estate tax allocable to the buyer is $300 ($100 per month × 3 months). This amount, which is shown as paid by the seller in advance on an HUD-1 (Uniform Settlement Statement) form provided at the closing, must be reported by the real estate agent as the buyer's share of the real estate tax in Box 5 of Form 1099-S.

The allocation just discussed is mandatory whether or not your contract provides for an allocation. However, you do not allocate taxes of a real property year when:

Property is sold before the real property year. This rule prevents the seller from deducting any part of the tax for that year, even though it became a personal liability or lien while he or she owned the property. The buyer gets the deduction because he or she owns the property for the entire real property year.

Property is sold after the real property year. This rule prevents the buyer from deducting the tax even though it becomes a personal liability or lien after he or she takes possession of the property. The seller gets the deduction because the tax covers the property year in which the seller owns the property. The allocation is limited to a tax covering a property year during which both the seller and the buyer own the property.

When to deduct allocated taxes. After you have made the allocation based on the "real property year," you then must fix the year in which you deduct your share of the allocated tax. Here you consider your method of reporting your income—cash or accrual basis—and the date on which either you or the other party became liable for the tax or paid the tax. If neither you nor the other party is liable for the tax under local law, then the party who holds the property at the time the tax became a lien on the property is considered liable. Check the following rules to determine when you deduct the apportioned tax:

Seller on the cash basis—If the buyer is liable for the tax under local law, the seller may deduct his or her share of the allocated tax either in the year of the sale or a later year when the tax is actually paid. If the seller is liable for the tax under local law, and the tax is not payable until after the sale date, the seller may deduct the tax either in the year of sale or in the year he or she pays the tax.

Buyer on the cash basis—If the seller is liable for the tax under local law, the buyer may deduct the tax either in the year of sale or when the tax is actually paid. If the buyer is liable for the tax, he or she deducts the tax in the year the tax is paid.

Seller on the accrual basis—The seller accrues his or her share of the tax on the date of the sale, unless taxes have been accrued ratably over the years. If this is so, the last accrual is the sale date.

Buyer on the accrual basis—If the seller is liable for the tax, the buyer accrues his or her share of the tax on the date of the sale, unless taxes are accrued ratably. If taxes are accrued ratably, the accrual begins with the date of sale. If the buyer is liable for the tax, he or she deducts the tax in the return for the year the tax accrues unless an election is made to accrue ratably from the date of sale.

Seller's deduction in excess of the allocated amount is taxed. If, in the year before the sale, the seller deducts an amount for taxes in excess of the allocated amount, the excess must be reported as income in the year of the sale. This may happen when the seller is on the cash basis and pays the tax in the year before the sale.

Law Alert

Form 1099-S

A residence sale after May 6, 1997, generally does not have to be reported on Form 1099-S if the seller gives the real estate agent responsible for the closing written assurance that the home was the seller's principal residence and that the full gain on the sale is excludable from income (*see* Chapter 29).

EXAMPLE

A real property tax of $1,000 is due and payable on November 30 for the following calendar year. On November 30, 1996, Keith Jones, who uses the cash basis and reports on a calendar year, pays the 1997 tax. On June 30, 1997, he sells the real property. Under the apportionment rule, Jones is allowed to deduct only $493 ($180/365 of $1,000, since there are 180 days in the period from January 1 to June 29, 1997) of the tax for the 1997 real property tax year. But Jones has already deducted the full amount in the 1996 return. Therefore, he reports as income that part of the tax deduction which he was not entitled to under the apportionment.

Buyer may not deduct payment of seller's back taxes.   The back taxes paid are added to the cost of the newly purchased property. The amount realized by the seller is increased by the buyer's payment of back taxes.

Seller's payment upon buyer's failure to pay.   If a buyer is obligated to pay taxes under a land contract but fails to pay, the owner who pays the tax may deduct the payment if the tax is assessed to him or her.

Buyer of foreclosed property.   If you buy realty at a tax sale and you do not receive immediate title to the property under state law until after a redemption period, you may not be able to deduct payment of realty taxes for several years.

16.9 Who May Deduct Real Property Taxes

A person who pays a property tax must have an ownership interest in the property to deduct the payment. The following table summarizes who may deduct payments of real property taxes.

If the tax is paid by—	Then it is deductible by—
You, for your spouse	Neither, if your spouse has title to the property, and you each file a separate return. This is true even if the mortgage requires you to pay the taxes. The tax is deductible on a joint return.
You, as owner of a condominium	You deduct real estate tax paid on your separate unit. You also deduct your share of the tax paid on the common property.
Your cooperative apartment or corporation	You deduct your share of real estate tax paid on the property; see 15.9. But if the organization leases the land and building and pays the tax under the terms of the lease, you may not deduct your share.
A life tenant	A court allowed the deduction to a widow required to pay the taxes under a will for the privilege of occupying the house during her life.
A tenant	The tenant of a business lease may deduct the payment of tax as additional rent, not tax. The tenant of a personal residence may not deduct the payment as either a tax or rent expense, unless placed on the real estate assessment rolls, so the tax is assessed directly against him or her; see 16.7.
You, as a local benefit tax to maintain, repair, or meet interest costs arising from local benefits	You deduct only that part of the tax which you can show is for maintenance, repair, or interest. If you cannot make the allocation, no deduction is allowed. If the benefit increases the value of the property, you add the nondeductible assessment to the basis of the property.
One whose property was foreclosed for failure to pay taxes	You may not deduct the taxes paid out of the proceeds of the foreclosure sale if your interest in the property ended with the foreclosure.
Tenant by the entirety or joint tenant	The tenant who is jointly and severally liable and who pays the tax. If real property is owned by husband and wife as tenants by the entirety or joint tenants, either spouse may deduct the taxes paid on a separate return or a joint return.

If the tax is paid by—	Then it is deductible by—
Tenant in common	When property is owned as a tenancy in common, under an IRS rule, a tenant may deduct only his or her share of the tax, even if the entire tax was paid. However, in one case the Tax Court allowed a deduction for the full amount where a co-tenant's payment protected her against the possibility of foreclosure in the event the other co-tenants failed to pay their share of the taxes; *see 9.2.*
A mortgagee	No deduction. If tax is paid before the foreclosure, it is added to the loan. If paid after the foreclosure, it is added to the cost of property.

Filing Tip

Value Portion of License Fee

If an automobile license fee is based partly on value and partly on weight or other tests, the tax attributed to the value is deductible. For example, assume a registration fee based on 1% of value, plus 40¢ per hundred-weight. The part of the tax equal to 1% of value qualifies as an *ad valorem* tax and is deductible as a personal property tax on Schedule A.

16.10 Automobile License Fees

You may not deduct an auto license fee based on weight, model, year, or horsepower. But you may deduct a fee based on the value of the car as a state personal property tax if these three tests are met: (1) the fee is an *ad valorem* tax, based on a percentage of value of the property; (2) it is imposed on an annual basis, even though it is collected more or less frequently; and (3) it is imposed on personal property. This third test is met even though the tax is imposed on the exercise of a privilege of registering a car or for using a car on the road.

The majority of state motor vehicle registration fees are not *ad valorem* taxes and do not qualify for the deduction. Various states and localities impose *ad valorem* or personal property taxes on motor vehicles that may qualify for the deduction. If you pay fees or taxes on your auto in these states, we suggest you contact a state or local authority to verify the amount of tax qualifying: Arizona, California, Colorado, Connecticut, Georgia, Indiana, Iowa, Maine, Massachusetts, Minnesota, Mississippi, Montana, Nebraska, Nevada, New Hampshire, Oklahoma, Washington, and Wyoming.

16.11 Taxes Deductible as Business Expenses

That a tax is not deductible as an itemized deduction does not mean you may not deduct it elsewhere on your return. For example, you may generally deduct property taxes incurred as a cost of doing business on Schedule C. Here are some other examples:

If you pay excise taxes on merchandise you sell in your business, you deduct the tax as a business expense.

If you pay Social Security taxes (FICA) on your employees' wages, you deduct the tax as a business expense on Schedule C.

If you pay sales tax on business property, you add the tax to the cost of the property for depreciation purposes. If the tax is paid on nondepreciable property, the tax is included in the currently deductible cost.

If you pay sales tax on a deductible business meal, the tax is deductible as part of the meal costs, subject to the cost limit discussed at *20.26.*

50% self-employment tax deduction. One-half of the self-employment tax figured on Schedule SE is deductible from gross income on Line 26 of Form 1040, rather than on Schedule C; *see 45.3.*

Note: If you are not a material participant in the business, your Schedule C expenses are subject to passive activity limitations; *see* Chapter 10.

16.12 Foreign Taxes

You may deduct your payment of foreign real property taxes and income and excess profits taxes as itemized deductions. Where you pay foreign income or excess profits tax, you have an election of either claiming the tax as a deduction or a credit. Claiming the credit may provide a larger tax savings; *see 36.14.*

Chapter 17

Medical and Dental Expense Deductions

Tax relief for the high cost of medical care is limited. Medical expenses are deductible only if you itemize and only if you have expenses exceeding 7.5% of your adjusted gross income. Expenses up to 7.5% of AGI are not deductible.

Carefully review the list of deductible expenses in this chapter so that you do not overlook any deductible expenses. Include payments of doctors' fees, health care premiums, prescription medicines, travel costs for obtaining medical care, and eligible home improvements.

If you are married, both you and your spouse work, and one of you has substantial medical expenses, filing separate returns may result in a lower overall tax.

Deductible medical expenses are *not* subject to the 3% reduction of itemized deductions that applies on 1997 returns if adjusted gross income exceeds $121,200 ($60,600 if married filing separately).

Starting in 1997, qualifying long-term care expenses may be treated as medical expenses subject to the 7.5% of AGI floor, including a specified deductible amount of premiums paid for a qualifying long-term care contract; *see 17.15.*

Medical savings accounts (MSAs) are now available to self-employed individuals and employees of certain small businesses; *see 17.17.*

17.1 Medical Expenses Must Exceed 7.5 % of AGI

The tax law provides only a limited opportunity to deduct medical costs for you, your spouse, and your dependents. A wide range of expenses, such as those listed on page 310, qualify as deductible medical expenses. However, you may not be able to claim the deduction because of a percentage floor. You may deduct only expenses exceeding 7.5% of your adjusted gross income (AGI). Adjusted gross income is explained at *12.1*. For 1997, adjusted gross income is shown on Line 32 of Form 1040.

Married persons filing joint returns figure the 7.5% limit on combined adjusted gross income.

On your 1997 return, you may deduct expenses paid in 1997 by cash or check (unless the check is postdated to 1998) for yourself, your spouse *(17.6)*, or dependents *(17.7)*. If you borrow to pay medical or dental expenses, you claim the deduction in the year you use the loan proceeds to pay the bill, not in the later year when you repay the loan. If you paid medical or dental expenses by credit card in 1997, the deduction is allowed in 1997, although you do not pay the charge bill until 1998.

You may not deduct medical expenses for which you have been reimbursed by insurance or other awards *(17.4)*. Furthermore, reimbursement of medical expenses deducted in prior tax years may be taxable income *(11.6)*.

EXAMPLES

1. Frank Ryan's adjusted gross income (AGI; *see 12.1*) is $20,000 for 1997. His unreimbursed medical expenses were $1,000 for doctor and dentist visits, $210 for prescribed drugs and medicines, and $625 for medical insurance premiums. If he itemizes deductions on Schedule A, he may deduct medical expenses of $335, figured this way:

Unreimbursed expenses	$1,000
Premiums	625
Drugs	210
Total	$1,835
Less: 7.5% of adjusted gross income (7.5% of $20,000)	1,500
Medical expense deduction	$335

2. Same as Example 1 except that Frank's AGI is $30,000, not $20,000. Here, Frank may not claim any medical deduction because his expenses of $1,835 do not exceed $2,250, 7.5% of his AGI.

17.2 Allowable Medical Care Costs

In determining whether you have paid deductible medical expenses exceeding the 7.5% AGI floor *(17.1)*, include the cost of diagnosis, cure, mitigation, treatment, or prevention of disease or any treatment that affects a part or function of your body. Also include qualifying costs you paid for your spouse *(17.6)* and your dependents *(17.7)*. *See* the checklist on the next page.

Expenses that are *solely* for cosmetic reasons are not deductible. Also, expenses incurred to benefit your general health are not deductible even if recommended by a physician; *see 17.3*.

Medicine and drugs. To be deductible, medicines and drugs other than insulin must be obtainable solely through a prescription by a doctor. Insulin is deductible even though a prescription may not be required. Marijuana is not deductible even if prescribed by a doctor in a state allowing the prescription. You may not deduct the cost of over-the-counter medicines and drugs, such as aspirin and other cold remedies, even if you have a doctor's prescription.

Special foods. The cost of special foods or beverages is not a deductible medical expense if the food or beverages substitute for those normally consumed.

EXAMPLE

To alleviate an ulcer, your doctor puts you on a special diet. According to the IRS, the cost of your food and beverages is not deductible. The special diet replaces the food you normally eat.

The Tax Court has set its own standard for deducting the extra cost of special foods as medical costs. The test is to show a medical need for taking the special food and the extra cost of the health food over ordinary food. Only the extra cost is deductible.

Deductible Medical Expenses

Professional Services

Chiropodist
Chiropractor
Christian Science practitioner
Dermatologist
Dentist
Gynecologist
Neurologist
Obstetrician
Ophthalmologist
Optician
Optometrist
Orthopedist
Osteopath
Pediatrician
Physician
Physiotherapist
Plastic surgeon; but see 17.3.
Podiatrist
Practical or other nonprofessional nurse for medical services only; not for care of a healthy person or a small child who is not ill. Costs for medical care of elderly person unable to get about or person subject to spells are deductible; see 17.12.
Psychiatrist
Psychoanalyst
Psychologist
Registered nurse
Surgeon
Unlicensed practitioner services are deductible if the type and quality of the services are not illegal.

Dental Services

Artificial teeth
Cleaning teeth
Dental X-rays
Extracting teeth
Filling teeth
Gum treatment
Oral surgery
Straightening teeth

Equipment and Supplies

Abdominal supports
Air conditioner where necessary for relief from an allergy or for relieving difficulty in breathing; see 17.13.
Ambulance hire
Arches

Artificial eyes, limbs
Autoette (auto device for handicapped person)
Back supports
Braces
Contact lenses
Cost of installing stair-seat elevator for person with heart condition; see 17.13.
Crutches
Elastic hosiery
Eyeglasses
Fluoridation unit in home
Hearing aids
Heating devices
Invalid chair
Iron lung
Orthopedic shoes—excess cost over cost of regular shoes
Oxygen or oxygen equipment to relieve breathing problems caused by a medical condition
Reclining chair if prescribed by doctor
Repair of special telephone equipment for the deaf
Sacroiliac belt
Special mattress and plywood bed boards for relief of arthritis or spine
Splints
Truss
Wheelchair
Wig advised by doctor as essential to mental health of person who lost all hair from disease

Medical Treatments

Abortion
Acupuncture
Blood transfusion
Childbirth delivery
Diathermy
Electric shock treatments
Hearing services
Hydrotherapy (water treatments)
Injections
Insulin treatments
Navajo healing ceremonies ("sings")
Nursing
Organ transplant
Prenatal and postnatal treatments
Psychotherapy

Sterilization
Radial keratotomy
Radium therapy
Ultraviolet ray treatments
Vasectomy
Whirlpool baths
X-ray treatments

Medicines and Drugs

Cost of prescriptions only; over-the-counter medicine is not deductible.

Laboratory Examinations and Tests

Blood tests
Cardiographs
Metabolism tests
Spinal fluid tests
Sputum tests
Stool examinations
Urine analyses
X-ray examinations

Hospital Services

Anesthetist
Hospital bills
Oxygen mask, tent
Use of operating room
Vaccines
X-ray technician

Premiums for Medical Care Policies

See 17.5 for how to deduct:
Blue Cross and Blue Shield
Contact lens replacements
Federal Voluntary Medicare (Part B) and Federal Medicare (Part A) by persons not covered by Social Security
Health insurance covering hospital, surgical, and other medical expenses
Membership in medical service cooperative

Miscellaneous

Alcoholic inpatient care costs
Asylum; see 17.11.
Birth control pills or other birth control items prescribed by your doctor
Braille books—excess cost of Braille works over cost of regular editions

Childbirth classes for expectant mother
Clarinet lessons advised by dentist for treatment of tooth defects
Convalescent home—for medical treatment only; see 7.11.
Drug treatment center—inpatient care costs
Fees paid to health institute where the exercises, rubdowns, etc., taken there are prescribed by a physician as treatments necessary to alleviate a physical or mental defect or illness
Kidney donor's or possible kidney donor's expenses
Lead-based paint removal to prevent a child who has had lead poisoning from eating the paint. The cost of repainting the scraped area is not deductible.
Legal fees for guardianship of mentally ill spouse where commitment was necessary for medical treatment
Lifetime care—advance payments made either monthly or as a lump sum under an agreement with a retirement home; see 17.11.
Long-term care costs for chronically ill; see 17.15.
Nurse's board and wages, including Social Security taxes paid on wages
Remedial reading for child suffering from dyslexia
Sanitarium and similar institutions; see 17.11.
School—payments to a special school for a mentally or physically impaired person if the main reason for using the school is its resources for relieving the disability; see 17.10.
"Seeing-eye" dog and its maintenance
Special school costs for physically and mentally handicapped children; see 17.10.
Telephone-teletype costs and television adapter for closed caption service for deaf person
Wages of guide for a blind person

Nondeductible Medical Expenses

Antiseptic diaper service

Athletic club expenses

Babysitting fees to enable you to make doctor's visits

Boarding school fees paid for healthy child while parent is recuperating from illness

Bottled water bought to avoid drinking fluoridated city water

Cost of divorce recommended by a psychiatrist

Cost of hotel room suggested for sex therapy

Cost of moving away from airport noise by person suffering a nervous breakdown

Cost of trips prescribed by a doctor for a "change of environment" to boost an ailing person's morale

Dance lessons advised by a doctor as physical and mental therapy or for the alleviation of varicose veins or arthritis

Divorced spouse's medical bills; but see 17.7 to deduct them as alimony

Domestic help; but see 17.12 if nursing duties are performed

Ear piercing

Funeral, cremation, burial, cemetery plot, monument, or mausoleum

Health programs offered by resort hotels, health clubs, and gyms

Illegal operations and drugs

Marijuana, even if prescribed by a physician in a state permitting the prescription

Marriage counseling fees

Massages recommended by physician for general stress reduction

Maternity clothes

Premiums on policies guaranteeing you a specified amount of money each week in the event of hospitalization

Scientology fees

Smoking program to improve your general health is not deductible even if suggested by a doctor.

Special food or beverage substitutes; but see 17.2

Tattooing

Toothpaste

Transportation costs of a disabled person to and from work

Travel costs to favorable climate when you can live there permanently

Travel costs to look for a new place to live—on a doctor's advice

Tuition and travel expenses to send a problem child to a particular school for a beneficial change in environment; see 17.10

Weight-loss program to improve general health

How Your Medical Expense Deduction Is Reduced by the 7.5% Limit

If your adjusted gross income is	\$200	\$300	\$400	\$500	\$600	\$700	\$800	\$900	\$1,000	\$1,500	\$2,000
\$2,000	50	150	250	350	450	550	650	750	850	1,350	1,850
3,000	0	75	175	275	375	475	575	675	775	1,275	1,775
4,000	0	0	100	200	300	400	500	600	700	1,200	1,700
5,000	0	0	25	125	225	325	425	525	625	1,125	1,625
6,000	0	0	0	50	150	250	350	450	550	1,050	1,550
7,000	0	0	0	0	75	175	275	375	475	975	1,475
8,000	0	0	0	0	0	100	200	300	400	900	1,400
9,000	0	0	0	0	0	25	125	225	325	825	1,325
10,000	0	0	0	0	0	0	50	150	250	750	1,250
11,000	0	0	0	0	0	0	0	75	175	675	1,175
12,000	0	0	0	0	0	0	0	0	100	600	1,100
13,000	0	0	0	0	0	0	0	0	25	525	1,025
14,000	0	0	0	0	0	0	0	0	0	450	950
15,000	0	0	0	0	0	0	0	0	0	375	875
18,000	0	0	0	0	0	0	0	0	0	150	650
20,000	0	0	0	0	0	0	0	0	0	0	500
25,000	0	0	0	0	0	0	0	0	0	0	125
30,000	0	0	0	0	0	0	0	0	0	0	0
40,000	0	0	0	0	0	0	0	0	0	0	0
50,000	0	0	0	0	0	0	0	0	0	0	0

Your medical expenses are / *You may deduct*

EXAMPLES

1. Anna Von Kalb suffered from hypoglycemia and her physician prescribed a special high protein diet, which required her to consume twice as much protein as an average person and exclude all processed foods and carbohydrates. She spent $3,483 for food, and deducted 30%, or $1,045, as the extra cost of her high protein diet. The IRS disallowed the deduction, claiming that the protein supplements were a substitute for foods normally consumed. The Tax Court disagreed. The high protein food did not substitute for her usual diet but helped alleviate her hypoglycemia. Thus, she may deduct its additional expense.

2. The Bechers suffered from allergies and were advised by a physician to eat organically grown food to avoid the chemicals in commercial food. The Bechers claimed a medical expense deduction of $2,255, the extra cost of buying organic food.
   The IRS disallowed the deduction and the Tax Court agreed. They did not present evidence that their allergies could be cured by limiting their diet to organic food. That the food was beneficial to their general health and was prescribed by a doctor is not sufficient for a deduction.

Childbirth classes. A mother-to-be may deduct the cost of classes instructing her in Lamaze breathing and relaxation techniques, stages of labor, and delivery procedures. If her husband or other childbirth "coach" also attends the classes, the portion of the fee allocable to the coach is not deductible, nor are costs of classes on early pregnancy, fetal development, or caring for newborns.

17.3 Nondeductible Medical Expenses

The most common nondeductible medical expense is the cost of over-the-counter medicines and drugs, such as aspirin and other cold remedies. A deduction for over-the-counter medicines is disallowed even if you have a doctor's prescription. Also *see* the checklist on page 311.

Cosmetic surgery. A medical expense deduction is allowed for cosmetic surgery if it is necessary to improve a disfigurement related to a congenital abnormality, disfiguring disease or an accidental injury.

You may not deduct the cost of cosmetic surgery or other procedures that do not have a medical purpose. Thus, face lifts, hair transplants, electrolysis, and liposuction intended to improve appearance are generally not deductible. In one case, the Tax Court allowed an exotic dancer to claim a depreciation deduction for breast implants essential for her business; *see 19.8.*

Exercise, stop-smoking, and weight-reduction programs. If you incur costs for such programs to improve your *general* health, the costs are not deductible even if your doctor has recommended them. However, if your doctor has recommended a program as treatment for a *specific* condition, the IRS has indicated that the cost would be deductible.

17.4 Reimbursements Reduce Deductible Expenses

Insurance or other reimbursements of your medical costs reduce your potential medical deduction. Reimbursements for loss of earnings or damages for personal injuries and mental suffering do not have to be taken into account. A reimbursement first reduces the medical expense for which it is paid. The excess is then applied to your other deductible medical costs.

EXAMPLE

Gail Hurz paid $800 in medical insurance premiums. She paid doctor and hospital bills totaling $700 and purchased prescription drugs costing $150. Group hospitalization insurance reimbursed $300 for doctors and hospital bills and $25 for medicines and drugs. Her adjusted gross income is $15,000. Her deduction is computed as follows:

Prescription drugs	$150
Medical care expenses	700
Premiums	800
Total	$1,650
Less reimbursement	325
	$1,325
Less: 7.5% of $15,000	1,125
Medical expense deduction	$200

Personal injury settlements or awards. Generally, a cash settlement recovered in a personal injury suit does not reduce your medical expense deduction. The settlement is not treated as reimbursement of your medical bills. But when part of the settlement is specifically earmarked by a court or by law for payment of hospital bills, the medical expense deduction is reduced.

If you receive a settlement for a personal injury that is partly allocable to future medical expenses, you reduce medical expenses for these injuries by the allocated amount until it is used up.

Fake claims. Medical reimbursements for fake injury claims are treated as taxable income; *see* the following Example.

> **EXAMPLE**
>
> Dodge, with the aid of a "friendly" doctor, arranged to be hospitalized for alleged back injuries and realized over $200,000 from HIP policies. The IRS charged that the insurance proceeds were taxable income. Dodge argued they were tax-free reimbursements of medical costs.
>
> The Tax Court sided with the IRS. The tax-free rules cover the payment of legitimate medical costs. Here there were no legitimate medical costs of actual injuries. Dodge took out the policies in a scam arrangement with the doctor.

Reimbursements in excess of your medical expenses. If you paid the entire premium of the policy, the excess payment is not taxed. If you and your employer each contributed to the policy, you generally have to include in income that part of the excess reimbursement which is attributable to employer premium contributions not included in your gross income.

However, you do not have to report any excess reimbursements that are tax-free payments for permanent disfigurement or loss of bodily functions, as discussed in *3.1*.

If your employer paid the total cost of the policy and the contributions were not taxed to you, you report as income all of your excess reimbursement, unless it covers payment for permanent injury or disfigurement.

For the treatment of insurance reimbursements of long-term care costs, see *17.15*.

> **EXAMPLES**
>
> 1. Henry Knight pays premiums of $240 and $120 for two personal health insurance policies. His total medical expenses are $900. He receives $700 from one insurance company and $500 from the other. The excess reimbursement of $300 ($1,200 – $900) is not taxable because he paid the entire premium on the policy.
> 2. Lionel Guest's employer paid premiums of $1,800 for two employee health insurance policies covering medical expenses. Guest's medical expenses in one year are $900. He receives $1,200 from the two companies. The entire $300 excess is taxable because Guest's employer paid the total cost of the policy and the contributions were not taxed to him.
> 3. Kay Brown's employer paid a premium of $1,000 for a group health policy covering Brown, and Brown herself paid $300 for a personal health policy. Her medical expenses are $900. She receives reimbursements of $1,200, $700 under her employer's policy and $500 under her own policy. Brown's reimbursements exceed expenses by $300, but the taxable portion attributed to her employer's premium contribution is $175, computed this way:
>
> | | |
> |---|---|
> | Reimbursement allocated to Brown's policy ($500 ÷ $1,200) × $900 | $375 |
> | Reimbursement allocated to employer's policy ($700 ÷ $1,200) × $900 | $525 |
> | Taxable excess allocated to employer's policy ($700 – $525) | $175 |
>
> 4. Mike Green's employer paid $1,200 for a health insurance policy but contributed only $450 and deducted $750 from Green's wages. Green also paid $300 for a personal health insurance policy. His medical expenses are $900. He recovered $700 from the employer's policy and $500 from his personal policy. The excess attributable to the employer's policy is $175 (computed as in Example 3 above). However, the taxable portion is only $65.63. Both Green and his employer contributed to the cost of the

employer's policy and a further allocation is necessary:	
Green's contribution	$750
Employer's contribution	450
Total cost of policy	$1,200
Ratio of employer's contribution to annual cost of policy (450 ÷ 1,200, or 37.50%)	
Taxable portion: 37.50% of excess reimbursement of $175	$65.63

Reimbursement in a later year may be taxed.   If you took a medical expense deduction in one year and are reimbursed for all or part of the expense in a later year, the reimbursement may be taxed in the year received. The reimbursement is generally taxable income to the extent the deduction reduced your tax in the prior year. For further details for figuring taxable income on a recovery of a prior deduction, *see 11.6.*

EXAMPLES

1. In 1996, Anna Gurchani had adjusted gross income of $12,000. She claimed itemized deductions which exceeded her allowable standard deduction by $1,000; on her Schedule A, Gurchani listed medical expenses of $1,300. She deducted $700, computed as follows:

Medical expenses	$1,300
Less: 7.5% of $12,000	900
Allowable deduction	$400

   In 1997 she collects $300 from insurance, reimbursing part of her 1996 medical expenses. If she had collected that amount in 1996, her medical expense deduction would have been $100. The entire reimbursement of $300 is subject to tax in 1997. It is the amount by which the 1996 deduction of $400 exceeds the deduction of $100 that would have been allowed if the reimbursement had been received in 1996.

2. Same facts as in Example 1 above, but Anna did not deduct medical expenses in 1996 because she did not itemize deductions. The reimbursement in 1997 is not taxable.

17.5   Premiums of Medical Care Policies

You may deduct as medical expenses premiums paid for medical care policies covering yourself, your spouse *(17.6),* or dependents *(17.7).* There is no separate deduction for health insurance premiums. All qualifying premiums are treated as medical expenses subject to the overall 7.5% limit. Include premium for Medicare Part B supplemental insurance. Payment for coverage under Medicare (Part A) is deductible by those over age 65 who are not covered by Social Security. Deductions may be claimed for membership payments in associations furnishing cooperative or free-choice medical services, group hospitalization, or clinical care policies, including HMOs (health maintenance organizations) and medical care premiums paid to colleges as part of a tuition bill, if the amount is separately stated in the bill.

Deduct premiums for health insurance providing reimbursements for hospital, surgical, drug costs, and other medical expenses. Also deductible are premiums paid for contact lens replacement and premiums on policies providing solely for indemnity for hospital and surgical expenses.

Premiums paid before you reach age 65 for medical care insurance for protection after you reach age 65 are deductible in the year paid if they are payable on a level payment basis under the contract (1) for a period of 10 years or more; or (2) until the year you reach age 65 (but in no case for a period of less than five years).

Premiums for qualifying long-term care policies are deductible subject to the limits explained in *17.15.*

Nondeductible premiums.   You may *not* deduct premiums for a policy guaranteeing you a specified amount each week (not to exceed a specified number of weeks) in the event you are hospitalized. Also, no deduction may be claimed for premiums paid for a policy which compensates you for loss of earnings while ill or injured, or for loss of life, limb, or sight. If your policy covers both medical care and loss of income or loss of life, limb, or sight, no part of the premium is deductible unless (1) the contract or separate statement from the insurance company states what part of the premium is allocated to medical care; and (2) the premium allocated to medical care is reasonable.

You may not deduct part of the car insurance premiums for medical insurance coverage for persons injured by or in your car where the premium covering you, your spouse (17.6), or your dependents (17.7) is not stated separately from the premium covering medical care for others.

Self-employed deduction of 40%.   If you were self-employed in 1997, you may claim a special deduction on Form 1040, Line 27, for 40% of health insurance premiums paid in 1997 for yourself, your spouse, and your dependents. The deduction is also allowed if you received wages from an S corporation in which you were more than a 2% shareholder.

The 40% deduction may not be claimed for any month during 1997 that you were eligible for coverage under an employer's subsidized health plan, including a plan of your spouse's employer. Also, the deduction may not exceed your net earnings from the business under which the health premiums are paid. *See 12.2* for further details on the 40% deduction.

Any balance of premiums not deductible under the special 40% rule may be claimed as an itemized medical expense subject to the 7.5% income floor (17.1).

17.6   Expenses of Your Spouse

You may deduct as medical expenses your payments of medical bills for your spouse if you were married *either* at the time the expenses were incurred or at the time the bills were paid. That is, you may deduct your payment of your spouse's medical bills even though you are divorced or widowed, if, at the time the expenses were incurred, you were married. Furthermore, if your spouse incurred medical expenses before you married and you pay the bills after you marry, you may deduct the expense.

> **EXAMPLES**
> 1. Your spouse has doctor bills covering an operation performed in 1996, before you were married. You married in 1997. You pay those bills in 1997. You may claim a 1997 medical expense deduction for your payment.
>
> 2. In October 1996, your spouse had dental work done. In February 1997, you are divorced; in April 1997, you pay your former spouse's dental bills. You may deduct the payment on your 1997 tax return.
>
> 3. In 1997, you pay medical expenses for your spouse who died in 1996. You remarry in 1997. On a 1997 joint return filed with your new spouse, you may deduct your payment of your deceased spouse's medical expenses.

Filing separately in community property states.   If you and your spouse file separately and live in a community property state, any medical expenses paid out of community funds are treated as paid 50% by each of you. Medical expenses paid out of separate funds of one spouse can be deducted only by that spouse.

17.7   Expenses of Your Dependents

You may deduct your payment of medical bills for your children or other dependents, subject to the 7.5% floor at *17.1*. You may deduct the expenses of a person who was your dependent either at the time the medical services were provided or at the time you paid the expenses. In determining dependent status for medical expense purposes, you may disregard two of the regular tests listed at *21.1* for claiming an exemption for a dependent. You may deduct the medical costs of a person who qualifies as your dependent under the relationship test, the support test, and the citizen or resident test. The gross income test and the joint return test do not have to be met. *See* Examples 1–3 on the next page.

A child may not deduct medical expenses paid with his or her parent's welfare payments; *see* Example 4 on the next page.

Divorced and separated parents.   You may be able to deduct your payment of your child's medical costs, even though your ex-spouse is entitled to claim the child as a dependent. For purposes of the medical deduction, the child is considered to be the dependent of *both* parents if (1) they are divorced or legally separated under a court agreement, separated under a written agreement, or married but living apart during the last six months of 1997; (2) the child was in the custody of one or both parents for more than half of 1997; and (3) more than half of the child's 1997 support was provided by both parents.

Filing Tip

Should spouses file separately?
If you are married and both you and your spouse have separate incomes, and one of you has substantial medical expenses, consider filing separate returns. This way the 7.5% floor will apply separately to your individual incomes, not to the higher joint income. To make sure which option to take—filing jointly or separately— you compute your tax on both types of returns and choose the one giving the lower overall tax; *see 1.2.*

EXAMPLES

1. You contribute more than half of your married son's support, including a payment of a medical expense of $800. Because he filed a joint return with his wife, you may not claim him as a dependent *(21.13)*. But you still may include your payment of the $800 medical expense with your other qualifying medical expenses since you contributed more than half of his support.

2. Your mother, a U.S. citizen, underwent an operation in November 1996. You paid for the operation in February 1997. You may deduct the cost of the operation in 1997 if you furnished more than one-half of your mother's support in either 1996 or 1997.

3. Same facts as Example 5, except your mother is a citizen and resident of Italy. You may not deduct the cost of the operation. She is not a U.S. citizen or a resident of the United States, Canada, or Mexico and thus does not qualify as a dependent for exemption purposes *(21.12)* or for medical deduction purposes.

4. A son is the legal guardian of his mother who is mentally incompetent. As guardian, he received his mother's state welfare and Social Security benefits, which he deposited in his personal bank account and used to pay part of his mother's medical expenses. On his tax return, he claimed a deduction for the total medical expenses paid on behalf of his mother. The court held that he could deduct only medical expenses in excess of the amounts received as welfare and Social Security payments. The benefits, to the extent used to pay medical expenses, represented the mother's payments in her own behalf.

Adopted children. You may deduct medical expenses of an adopted child if you may claim the child as a dependent either when the medical services are rendered or when you pay the expenses. An adopted child may be claimed as a dependent when a court has approved the adoption. In the absence of a court decree, the child is your dependent if he or she was placed in your home by an authorized agency and was a member of your household the rest of the year; *see 21.3*. If he or she has not been placed in your custody by an authorized agency, you have to show that the child lived in your home for the entire year.

If you reimburse an adoption agency for medical expenses it paid under an agreement with you, you are considered to have paid the expenses. But reimbursement of expenses incurred and paid before adoption negotiations does not qualify them as your medical expenses and you may not deduct them.

You may not deduct medical expenses for services rendered to the natural mother of the child you adopt.

Multiple support agreements. You may be able to deduct your payment of a relative's medical expenses although you do not contribute more than one-half of his or her support. You must meet the tests for a multiple support agreement; *see 21.10*. If your relative has a gross income of $2,650 or more, you may still deduct your payment of medical expenses provided the other tests for multiple support are met.

You may deduct only the amount you actually pay for the relative's medical expenses. If you are reimbursed by others who signed the multiple support agreement, you must reduce your deduction by the amount of reimbursement.

EXAMPLE

Ingrid Fromm and her brother and sister share equally in the support of their mother. Part of their mother's support includes medical expenses. Should the three of them share in the payment of the bills or should only one of them pay the bills? The answer: Payment should be made by the person who may claim the mother as a dependent under a multiple support agreement. Only that person may deduct the payment. If Ingrid is going to claim her as an exemption, she should pay the bill. She may deduct the payment although she did not contribute more than half of her mother's support. If her brother and sister reimburse her for part of the bill, she must reduce her medical deduction by the amount of the reimbursement. Neither Ingrid's brother nor her sister may deduct this share. Thus, a deduction is lost for these amounts.

17.8 Decedent's Medical Expenses

If you pay the medical expenses of your deceased spouse or dependent *(17.7)*, you may claim the payment as a medical expense in the year you pay the expenses, whether that is before or after the person's death.

If the executor or administrator of the estate pays the decedent's medical expenses within one year after the date of death, an election may be made to treat the expenses as if the deceased had paid them in the year the medical services were provided. The executor or administrator may file an amended return for the year the services were provided and claim them as a medical deduction for that year, assuming the period for filing the amended return *(49.1)* has not passed.

If the election is made by the executor to claim the expenses as an income tax deduction, they may not be claimed as a deduction on the estate tax return. The executor must file a statement with the decedent's income tax return that the expenses have not been deducted on the estate tax return and the estate waives its right to deduct them for estate tax purposes.

If medical expenses are claimed as an income tax deduction, the portion of the expenses that are below the 7.5% floor, and, therefore, not deductible, may not be deducted on the estate tax return. Although the expenses were not actually deducted, the IRS considers them to be part of the overall income tax deduction.

EXAMPLE

Oscar Reyes incurred medical expenses of $500 in 1996 and $300 in 1997. He died June 1, 1997, without having paid these expenses. He had already filed his 1996 return before the due date. In August 1997, his executor pays the $800 in medical expenses. The executor may file an amended return for 1996, claim a medical expense deduction for the $500, and get a refund for the increased deductions. The executor may claim the remaining $300 as a medical expense deduction on Reyes' final return for 1997.

17.9 Travel Costs May Be Medical Deductions

You may deduct the cost of travel to a place where you receive medical treatment or which is prescribed as a place that will help relieve a specific chronic ailment. Trips to and from a doctor's office are the most common type of deductible travel expense.

The amount of the deduction is limited to the cost of transportation, such as the cost of operating a car or fares for public transportation. If you use your automobile, you may deduct a flat rate of 10¢ a mile and, in addition, you may deduct parking fees and tolls. If, however, auto expenses exceed this standard mileage rate, you may deduct your actual out-of-pocket costs for gas, oil, repairs, tolls, and parking fees. Do not include depreciation, general maintenance, or car insurance.

EXAMPLE

You drive your car to a doctor's office for treatment. You made 40 such round trips of 25 miles each. As the total mileage is 1,000, you claim $100 (1,000 × 10¢) as medical expenses. If you incurred tolls or parking fees during the trips, you add these expenses to the deduction.

Lodging expenses. Your lodging expenses while away from home are not deductible as medical expenses unless the trip is primarily to receive treatment from a doctor in a licensed hospital, hospital-related out-patient facility, or a facility equivalent to a hospital. Food expenses are not deductible.

EXAMPLE

Polyak spent the winter in Florida on the advice of her doctor to alleviate a chronic heart and lung condition. While in Florida, she stayed in a rented trailer that cost $1,426. She saw a physician for treatment of an infection and to renew medications. She deducted the trailer costs as a medical deduction, which the IRS and Tax Court disallowed. Although her Florida trip was primarily for mitigating her condition, she did not travel to receive medical care from a physician in a licensed hospital or related out-patient facility. The medical care was routine and incidental to her travel to Florida. Her deduction for transportation costs to Florida was not contested by the IRS, which conceded that the trip was primarily for and essential to her health.

The deduction for lodging while receiving treatment at a licensed hospital, outpatient clinic, or hospital-equivalent facility is limited to $50 per night per person. For example, the limit is $100 if a parent travels with a sick child. The IRS ruled that the $50 allowance could be claimed by a parent for a six-week hotel stay while her eight-year-old daughter was treated in a nearby hospital for serious injuries received in an automobile accident. The mother's presence was necessary so that she could sign release forms.

Deductible Transportation Costs

Examples of travel costs which have been allowed as medical deductions by rulings or court decisions are:

- Nurse's fare if nurse is required on trip
- Parent's fare if parent is needed to accompany child who requires medical care
- Parent's fare to visit his child at an institution where the visits are prescribed by a doctor
- Trip to visit specialist in another city
- Airplane fare to a distant city in which a patient used to live to have a checkup by a family doctor living there. That he could have received the same examination in the city in which he presently lived did not bar his deduction.
- Trip to escape a climate that is bad for a specific condition. For example, the cost of a trip from a northern state to Florida during the winter on the advice of a doctor to relieve a chronic heart condition is deductible. The cost of a trip made solely to improve post-operative condition by a person recovering from a throat operation was ruled deductible.
- Travel to an Alcoholics Anonymous club meeting if membership in the group has been advised by a doctor
- Disabled veteran's commuting expenses where a doctor prescribed work and driving as therapy
- Wife's trip to provide nursing care for an ailing husband in a distant city. The trip was ordered by her husband's doctor as a necessity.
- Driving prescribed as therapy
- Travel costs of kidney transplant donor or prospective donor

Nondeductible Transportation Costs

- Trip for the general improvement of your health
- Traveling to areas of favorable climates during the year for general health reasons, rather than living permanently in a locality suitable for your health
- Meals while on a trip for medical treatment—even if cost of transportation is a valid medical cost. However, a court has allowed the deduction of the extra cost of specially prepared food.
- Trip to get "spiritual" rather than medical aid. For example, cost of a trip to the Shrine of Our Lady of Lourdes is not deductible.
- Moving a family to a climate more suitable to an ill mother's condition. Only the mother's travel costs are deductible.
- Moving household furnishings to area advised by physician
- Operating an auto or special vehicle to go to work because of disabled condition. The cost of wheelchair, autoette, or special auto devices for handicapped persons is deductible.
- Convalescence cruise advised by a doctor for a patient recovering from pneumonia
- Loss on sale of car bought for medical travel
- Medical seminar cruise taken by patient whose condition was reviewed by physicians taking the cruise

17.10 Schooling for the Mentally or Physically Handicapped

You may deduct as medical expenses the costs of sending a mentally or physically handicapped person to a special school or institution to overcome or alleviate his or her handicap. Such costs may cover:

- Teaching of Braille or lip reading
- Training, caring for, supervising, and treating a mentally retarded person
- Cost of meals and lodgings, if boarding is required at the school
- Costs of regular education courses also taught at the school, provided they are incidental to the special courses and services furnished by the school

The parent of a child with psychological problems may deduct only that part of a private school fee directly related to psychological aid given to the child.

The fact that a particular school or camp is recommended for an emotionally disturbed child by a psychiatrist will not qualify the tuition as a deduction if the school or camp has no special program geared to the child's specific personal problem. However, you may deduct the costs of maintaining a mentally retarded person in a home specially selected to meet the standards set by a psychiatrist to aid in an adjustment from life in a mental hospital to community living.

Payment for future medical care expenses is deductible if immediate payment is required by contract.

EXAMPLES

1. An emotionally disturbed child was sent to a private school maintaining a staff of three psychologists. His father deducted the school fee of $6,270 as a medical expense. The IRS disallowed the amount, claiming that the child, who was neither mentally retarded nor handicapped, was sent to school primarily for an education. The Tax Court allowed the father to deduct $3,000 covering the psychological treatment.

2. A retarded boy had been excluded from several schools for the mentally handicapped because he needed close attention. The director of a military academy had extensive experience in training young boys. Although it was not the usual practice of the academy to enroll mentally handicapped children, the director accepted the boy on a day-to-day basis as a personal challenge. The Tax Court held that the cost of both tuition and transportation to bring the boy to and from the school were deductible medical expenses. The primary purpose of the training given the boy was not ordinary education but remedial training designed to overcome his handicap. But note that, in other cases, a deduction for tuition of a military school to which a child was sent in order to remove him from a tense family environment, and the cost of a blind boy's attendance at a regular private school which made a special effort to accommodate his Braille equipment, were disallowed.

17.11 Senior Citizen Care Facilities

A payment for meals and lodging to a nursing home, convalescent home, home for the aged, or sanitarium is a deductible medical expense if the patient is confined for medical treatment.

If you cannot prove that the patient entered the home for medical care (which would permit a deduction for meals and lodging in addition to medical costs), you may nevertheless deduct that part of the cost covering actual medical and nursing care.

In an unusual case, a court allowed a medical expense deduction for apartment rent of an aged parent.

EXAMPLE

A doctor recommended to Ungar that his 90-year-old mother, convalescing from a brain hemorrhage, could receive better care at less expense in accommodations away from a hospital. A two-room apartment was rented, hospital equipment installed, and nurses engaged for seven months. The rent totaled $1,400. Ungar's sister, who worked in her husband's shoe store, nursed her mother for six weeks. Ungar paid the wages of a clerk who was hired to substitute for his sister in the store. Ungar deducted both the rent and wages as medical expenses. The IRS disallowed them; a Tax Court reversed the IRS's decision. The apartment rent was no less a medical expense than the cost of a hospital room. As for the clerk's wages, they too were deductible medical costs. The clerk was hired specifically to allow the daughter to nurse her mother, thereby avoiding the larger, though more direct, medical expense of hiring a nurse.

Establishing medical purpose.   The following facts are helpful in establishing the full deductibility of payments to a nursing home, convalescent home, home for the aged, or sanitarium:

- The patient entered the institution on the direction or suggestion of a doctor.
- Attendance or treatment at the institution had a direct therapeutic effect on the condition suffered by the patient.
- The attendance at the institution was for a specific ailment rather than for a "general" health condition. Simply showing that the patient suffers from an ailment is not sufficient proof that he or she is in the home for treatment.

Payment for future lifetime care.   Generally, no deduction is allowed for prepayment of medical expenses for services to be performed in a later taxable year. However, in the Examples below, the IRS allowed a deduction where there was a current obligation to pay.

1. A 78-year-old man entered into an agreement with a retirement home. For a lump-sum payment, the home agreed to provide lifetime care, including medical care, medicine, and hospitalization. The lifetime care fee was calculated without regard to fees received from other patients and was not insurance. The home allocated 30% of the lump-sum payment to medical expenses based on its prior experience. The IRS holds that this part of the payment is deductible in the year paid. It holds that the legal obligation to pay the medical expenses was incurred at the time the lump-sum payment was made, even though medical services would not be performed until a future time, if at all. Should any portion of the lump-sum payment be refunded, that part attributable to the deducted amount must be reported as income; *see 12.8*.

2. Parents contracted with an institution to care for their handicapped child after their death. The contract provided for payments as follows: 20% on signing, 10% within 12 months, 10% within 24 months, and the balance when the child enters. Payment of specified amounts at specified intervals was a condition imposed by the institution for its agreement to accept the child for lifetime care. Since the obligation to pay was incurred at the time payments were made, they are deductible as medical expenses, although the medical services were not to be performed until a future time, if at all.

3. A couple entered a retirement home which would provide them with accommodations, meals, and medical care for life. They paid a founder's fee of $40,000 and a monthly fee of $800. If they leave the home, they may get a refund of a portion of the founder's fee. Fifteen percent of the monthly fee and 10% of the founder's fee will be used for medical care and 5% of the founder's fee will be used for construction of a health facility. On the basis of these figures, the couple may deduct as medical costs 10% of the founder's fee and 15% of the monthly fee. However, the portion of the founder's fee for the possible health facility does not qualify as a medical expense. Finally, any refund of the founder's fee received in a later year may be income to the extent medical deductions were previously claimed for the fees.

17.12 Nurses' Wages

The costs of a nurse attending an ill person are deductible. Costs include any Social Security or Medicare (FICA) tax paid by you. You may deduct the expenses of a nurse who is not registered or licensed so long as he or she provides you with medical services. Medical services include giving medications, changing dressings, and bathing and grooming the patient. If the nurse also performs domestic services, deduct only that part of the pay attributable to medical services for the patient.

The cost of an attendant's meals is included in your medical expenses. Divide total food costs among the household members to determine the attendant's share.

Costs eligible for tax credit.   If, in order to work, you pay a nurse to look after a physically or mentally disabled dependent, you may be able to claim a credit for all or part of the nurse's wages as a dependent care expense. You may not, however, claim both a credit and a medical expense deduction. First, you claim the nurse's wages as a dependent care cost. If not all of the wages are allowed as care costs because of the expense limits (Chapter 25), the remaining balance is deductible as a medical expense.

The salary of a clerk hired specifically to relieve a wife from her husband's store in order to care for her ill mother was allowed as a medical expense; *see* the Ungar Example in *17.11*.

1. Dodge's wife was arthritic. He was advised by her doctor to have someone take care of her to prevent her from falling. He moved her to his daughter's home and paid the daughter to care for her mother. He deducted the payments to his daughter. The IRS disallowed the deduction, claiming that the daughter was not a trained nurse. The Tax Court allowed that part of the deduction specifically attributed to nursing aid. Whether a medical service has been rendered depends on the nature of the services rendered, not on the qualifications or title of the person who renders them. Here, the daughter's services, following the doctor's advice, qualify as medical care.

2. An attendant hired by a quadriplegic performs household duties, in addition to caring for his medical and personal needs. The quadriplegic pays him wages and also provides food and lodging. According to the IRS, a medical expense deduction is allowable only for that portion of the wages attributable to medical and personal care. The

wages are apportioned on the basis of time spent performing nursing-type services and time spent performing household duties. The same allocation is used to determine the portion of the cost of the attendant's meals which are deductible as a medical expense. However, the attendant's lodging is not deductible as a medical expense, unless the quadriplegic shows additional expenditures directly attributable to lodging the attendant, such as paying increased rent for an apartment with another bedroom for the attendant.

17.13 Home Improvements as Medical Expenses

A disease or ailment may require the construction of special equipment or facilities in a home: A heart patient may need an elevator to carry him or her upstairs; a polio patient, a pool; and an asthmatic patient, an air cleaning system.

You may deduct the full cost of minor equipment installed for a medical reason if it does not increase the value of your property, as, for example, the cost of a detachable window air conditioner. Where equipment increases the value of your property, you may generally take a medical deduction only to the extent that the cost of the equipment exceeds the increase in the value of the property. This increased-value test does *not* apply to certain structural changes to a residence made by a handicapped person, as discussed at the end of this section. If the equipment does not increase the value of the property, its entire cost is deductible, even though it is permanently fixed to the property.

EXAMPLE

Mike Gerard's daughter suffered from cystic fibrosis. While there is no known cure for the disease, doctors attempt to prolong life by preventing pulmonary infection. One approach is to maintain a constant temperature and high humidity. A doctor recommended that Gerard install a central air-conditioning unit in his home for his daughter. It cost $1,300 and increased the value of his home by $800. The $500 balance was a deductible medical expense.

Deducting cost of swimming pool. If swimming is prescribed as physical therapy, the cost of constructing a home swimming pool may be partly deductible as a medical expense but only to the extent the cost exceeds the increase in value to the house. However, the IRS is likely to question any deduction because of the possibility that the pool may be used for recreation. If you can show that the pool is specially equipped to alleviate your condition and is not generally suited for recreation, the IRS will allow the deduction unless the expense is considered to be "lavish or extravagant." For example, the IRS allowed a deduction for a pool constructed by an osteoarthritis patient. His physician prescribed swimming several times a day as treatment. He built an indoor lap pool with specially designed stairs and a hydrotherapy device. Given these features, the IRS concluded that the pool was specially designed to provide medical treatment.

In one case the IRS tried to limit the cost of a luxury indoor pool built for therapeutic reasons to the least expensive construction. The Tax Court rejected the IRS position, holding that a medical expense is not to be limited to the cheapest form of treatment; on appeal, the IRS position was adopted.

If, instead of building a pool, you buy a home with a pool, can you deduct the part of the purchase price allocated to the pool? The Tax Court said no. The purchase price of the house includes the fair market value of the pool. Therefore, there is no extra cost above the increase in the home's value that would support a medical expense deduction.

The operating costs of an indoor pool were allowed by the Tax Court as a deduction to an emphysema sufferer.

A deduction is barred where the primary purpose of the improvement is for personal convenience rather than medical necessity.

EXAMPLES

1. Ken Cherry was advised by his doctor to swim to relieve his severe emphysema and bronchitis. He could not swim at local health spas; they did not open early enough or stay open late enough to allow him to swim before or after work. His home was too small for a pool. He bought a lot and built a new house with an indoor pool. He used the pool several times a day, and swimming improved his condition; if he did not swim, his symptoms returned. Cherry deducted pool operating costs of $4,000 for

fuel, electricity, insurance, and repairs. The IRS disallowed the deductions, claiming that the pool was used for personal recreation. Besides, it did not have special medical equipment. The Tax Court allowed the deduction. Cherry built the pool to swim in order to exercise his lungs. That there was no special equipment is irrelevant; Cherry did not need special ramps, railings, a shallow floor, or whirlpool. Finally, his family rarely used the pool.

2. Doug Haines broke his leg in a skiing accident and underwent various forms of physical therapy, including swimming. To aid his recovery, his physician recommended that he install a swimming pool at his home. The Tax Court agreed with the IRS that the cost of the pool was not deductible. Although swimming was beneficial to his condition, he needed special therapy only for a limited period of time, and he could have gotten it at less cost at a nearby public pool. Finally, because of weather conditions, the pool could not be used for about half of the year.

Cost of maintaining and operating improvement. The expense of maintaining and operating equipment installed for medical reasons may be claimed as a medical expense, even if the cost of the equipment and its installation is not deductible under the rules in this section.

Handicapped persons. The increased-value test does not apply to a handicapped person who makes structural changes to a residence such as adding ramps, modifying doorways and stairways, installing railings and support bars, and altering cabinets, outlets, fixtures, and warning systems. Such improvements are treated for medical deduction purposes as not increasing the value of the house. Lifts, but not elevators, also are in this category. The full cost of such improvements is added to other deductible expenses and the total is deductible to the extent that it exceeds the 7.5% AGI floor.

17.14 Costs Deductible as Business Expenses

The following Examples illustrate cases in which expenses are deductible as business expenses rather than as medical expenses. Claiming a business deduction is preferable because the deduction is not subject to the 7.5% adjusted gross income floor.

Costs of a checkup required by your employer are business expenses and are not subject to the 7.5% AGI floor.

EXAMPLE

An airline pilot is required by his company to take a semi-annual physical exam at his own expense. If he fails to produce a resultant certificate of good health, he is subject to discharge. The cost of such checkups certifying physical fitness for a job is an ordinary and necessary business expense. If the doctor prescribes a treatment or further examinations to maintain the pilot's physical condition, the cost of these subsequent treatments or examinations may be deducted only as medical expenses, even though they are needed to maintain the physical standards required by the job. Thus, a professional singer who consults a throat specialist may not deduct the fee as a business expense. The fee is a medical expense subject to the 7.5% AGI floor.

The Tax Court allowed a licensed social worker working as a therapist to deduct psychoanalysis costs as an education expense.

Handicapped persons. Some expenses incurred by a physically handicapped person due to his or her handicap may be deductible as business expenses rather than as medical expenses. A business expense deduction may be allowed if the expense is necessary for you to satisfactorily perform your job and is not required or used, except incidentally, for personal purposes.

If you are self-employed, claim the deduction on Schedule C.

If you are an employee, the expenses are listed on Form 2106 and if not reimbursed, entered on Schedule A. The expenses are a fully deductible miscellaneous itemized deduction; the 2% AGI floor does *not* apply.

EXAMPLES

1. A professor is paralyzed from the waist down and confined to a wheelchair. When he attends out-of-town business meetings, he has his wife, a friend, or a colleague accompany him to help him with baggage, stairs, narrow doors, and to sit with him on airplanes when airlines will not allow wheelchair passengers without an attendant. While he does not pay them a salary, he does pay their travel costs. He may deduct these costs as business expenses. They are incurred solely because of his occupation.

2. An attorney uses prostheses due to bilateral amputation of his legs and takes medication several times a day for other ailments. On both personal and business trips, his wife or a neighbor accompanies him to help him travel and receive medication. He may deduct the out-of-town expenses paid for his neighbor only as a medical expense. The neighbor's services are not business expenses because assistance in personal activities is regularly provided. When his wife accompanies him, he may deduct her transportation costs as a medical expense; her food and lodging are nondeductible ordinary living expenses.

17.15 Long-Term Care Costs of Chronically ill

You may deduct as medical expenses (subject to the 7.5% income floor) your unreimbursed expenses for qualifying long-term care services that you require because you are "chronically ill" or because your spouse or dependent is chronically ill.

Chronically ill. A chronically ill person is someone who has been certified by a licensed health care practitioner within the preceding 12 months as being unable to perform for a period of at least 90 days at least two of the following activities without substantial assistance: eating, toileting, dressing, bathing, continence, or transferring. Also qualifying as chronically ill is someone who requires substantial supervision because of severe cognitive impairment, such as from Alzheimer's disease.

Qualifying long-term care services for a chronically ill individual are broadly defined as necessary diagnostic, preventive, therapeutic, curing, treating, mitigation, and rehabilitative services, and also maintenance or personal care services. The services must be provided under a plan of care prescribed by a licensed health care practitioner, who may be a physician, a registered nurse, a licensed social worker, or other individual meeting Treasury requirements. Services provided by a spouse or relative are deductible only if that person is a licensed professional; services provided by a related corporation or partnership do not qualify.

Deductible premium costs of long-term care policies. Depending on your age, all or part of your premium payments for a qualified long-term care policy may be included as deductible medical expenses, subject to the 7.5% adjusted gross income floor. To qualify, the policy must provide for long-term care services for the chronically ill (*see* above). The amount of the deductible premium depends on your age at the end of the year. For 1997, the maximum deductible premium amounts are: $200 if you are age 40 or younger at the end of 1997; $375 for those age 41 through 50; $750 for those age 51 through 60; $2,000 for those age 61 through 70; and $2,500 for those over age 70. These limits may be increased after 1997 by an inflation factor.

If you are considering purchase of a long-term care insurance policy, make sure that it qualifies for the tax treatment explained in this section. A qualified contract must provide only for coverage of qualified long-term care services and be guaranteed renewable; it may not provide for a cash surrender value or money that can be assigned, pledged, or borrowed; it may not reimburse expenses covered by Medicare except where Medicare is a secondary payer or the contract makes *per diem* payments.

Benefits paid by long-term care policies. Benefits for an indemnity-type contract are tax free to the extent they pay or reimburse long-term care expenses. Benefits paid from a *per diem* type contract are tax free up to $175 a day in 1997. (The $175 limit may be adjusted in 1998 for inflation.) If *per diem* payments are received for the full year, the 1997 exclusion is $63,875. If *per diem* payments exceed $175, the excess over $175 is tax free to the extent of unreimbursed long-term care costs. Any balance of the excess is taxable.

EXAMPLE

In 1997, you receive *per diem* long-term care benefits of $225 under a qualifying long-term care policy. Your actual daily costs are above $225. No part of the benefit payments is taxable provided you have proof of actual costs.

17.16 Life Insurance Used To Pay Medical Costs of Terminally ill

A person who is terminally ill may be forced to cash in a life insurance policy to pay medical bills and other living expenses. With the increase of terminally ill patients, especially those suffering from AIDS, and the high cost of medical care, insurance companies have developed life insurance policies with accelerated death benefit clauses. Where a policy lacks an accelerated payment clause, it is also possible to sell a life insurance policy to a viatical settlement company that specializes in buying policies from ill persons who require funds to pay expenses.

Accelerated death benefits and viatical settlements proceeds received by terminally individuals are *not taxed*.

Life Insurance used by chronically ill. A chronically ill individual may sell a life insurance policy to a viatical settlement company to pay for long-term care costs. However, tax-free treatment is determined under the tax rules applied to long-term care policies in *17.15*. Thus, if the proceeds exceed the $175 *per diem* limit and also exceed actual long-term care costs, the excess is taxable. Accelerated life insurance proceeds paid under a long-term care rider are also subject to the rules of *17.15*.

17.17 Medical Savings Accounts (MSAs)

Medical Savings Accounts (MSAs) are designed to lower the costs of providing medical expense reimbursement plans for employees of certain small businesses and self-employed persons. To do this, a medical plan combines a high-deductible insurance policy with a special funded account to cover the payment of ordinary medical expenses below the insurance deductible. More specifically, an MSA plan combines:

1. A high-deductible health insurance policy with premiums fixed by law. For single persons, the deductible must be between $1,500 and $2,250. For family coverage, the deductible must be between $3,000 and $4,500. Annual out-of-pocket costs excluding premiums must be limited to $3,000 for single coverage and $5,500 for family coverage.

2. A medical savings account, or MSA, to which annual contributions may be made based on the amount of the deductible set by the health insurance policy. For single persons, the maximum contribution is 65% of the deductible charged for single person coverage. For family coverage, the maximum contribution is 75% of the deductible for family coverage.

Self-employed. Here are the tax consequences of an MSA plan if you are self employed:

1. You may deduct the health insurance premium element. For 1997, you may deduct 40% of the health insurance premium payments made in 1997 directly from gross income on Line 27 of Form 1040; *see 12.2* for restrictions. The balance of premiums not deductible on Line 27 may be treated as a medical expense deductible on Schedule A if your total medical expenses exceed 7.5% of your adjusted gross income.

2. You report your contribution to the MSA on Form 8853 and deduct the contribution directly from gross income on Line 24 of Form 1040.

Income earned on the MSA will accumulate tax free and withdrawals used to pay medical expenses will not be taxed. By paying medical expenses from the MSA, you are in effect using funds that you had fully deducted when the contributions were made. If you did not have the MSA and used your regular funds to pay unreimbursed expenses, you would be unable to deduct the payments unless the total medical expenses paid in the year exceeded 7.5% of adjusted gross income.

Withdrawals from an MSA that are not used to pay medical expenses are taxable and also subject to a 15% penalty tax, but the penalty does not apply if you are age 65 or older, or disabled.

Other contribution and distribution details on MSAs may be found in IRS Notice 96-53.

EXAMPLE

Jones, who is self-employed, buys an MSA contract in 1997 which has a monthly charge of $452.50 a month. Of this amount, $265 is for family health coverage with a $3,000 deductible for health insurance. The balance of $187.50 is deposited monthly in an MSA. The $187.50 monthly MSA contribution is $1/_{12}$ of $2,250, the maximum annual MSA contribution based on 75% of the $3,000 deductible. Jones makes 10 monthly payments during the year. On Line 27 of Form 1040, Jones can deduct $1,060 (40% of $2,650 in premiums) and he can include the balance of the premiums as part of medical expenses subject to the 7.5% adjusted gross income floor on Schedule A. He also reports on Form 8853 and deducts on Line 24 of Form 1040 the MSA contribution of $1,875. Without counting any deduction of premiums on Schedule A, Jones is able to deduct at least $2,935 of the payments of $4,525 made in 1997.

Employees of qualifying small businesses. Small business employers having an average of 50 or less employees in either of the two prior calendar years may provide MSA plans for their employees. The employer may fully finance the contracts or pay for the insurance element while allowing the employee to contribute to the MSA account. If the employer finances the full costs of the plan, the payments are not taxed under the rules at *3.1.* If the employer contributes less than the maximum allowed to an employee's MSA, the employee is not allowed to make any MSA contribution for that year; *see 3.1.* If the employee contributes to the MSA, the employee reports the contribution on Form 8853 and may deduct the contribution from gross income on Line 24 of Form 1040. Any health insurance premiums paid by the employee are combined with other medical expenses paid during the year with the total being deductible only to the extent it exceeds 7.5% of adjusted gross income.

Withdrawals by the employee from the MSA are subject to the rules discussed above for self-employed individuals.

Chapter 18

Casualty and Theft Losses and Involuntary Conversions

The tax treatment of an unreimbursed casualty or theft loss depends on the purpose for which you held the damaged, destroyed, or stolen property. A loss of property held for:

• *Personal purposes* is deducted as an itemized deduction on Schedule A (Line 19). Each loss to personal-use property must be reduced by $100; *see 18.11.* The loss also is subject to the 10% adjusted gross income floor *(18.11)* and the sudden events tests of *18.5.*

The itemized deduction claimed for personal use property is not subject to the 3% reduction computation; *see 13.7.*

• *Income-producing purposes,* such as negotiable securities, is deducted on Schedule A (Line 22). The loss deduction is subject to the 2% AGI floor. It is not subject to the $100 and 10% adjusted gross income floors, or the sudden event test. The 3% reduction *(13.7)* does apply to a loss deduction for income-producing property claimed on Line 22 of Schedule A.

• *Business or rental purposes* is claimed as a loss on Form 4797. It is not subject to any floor or the sudden event test.

Use Form 4684 to determine the tax treatment of a casualty or theft. It has been designed to direct you to the proper method of treating the casualty or theft, and to the schedule for reporting your loss, or gain if compensation for your loss exceeded the basis of the property. If you suffer more than one casualty or theft in 1997, use separate Forms 4684 to figure the loss for each event.

If you have realized a gain, you may defer tax by replacing or repairing the property; *see 18.18.*

Appraisal fees and other incidental costs, such as taking photos to establish the amount of the loss, are claimed as a miscellaneous itemized deduction on Line 22 of Schedule A.

18.1 When To Deduct a Casualty or Theft Loss

Generally, you deduct a casualty loss in the year the casualty occurs, regardless of when you repair or replace damaged or destroyed property. But say a casualty occurs in one year and you do not discover the damage until a later year, or you know damage has been inflicted, but you do not know the full extent of the loss because you expect reimbursement in a later year. Here is what to do:

If you reasonably expect reimbursement in a later year. You should deduct in the year the casualty occurred only that part of your loss (after applying the personal property floors of *18.11*) for which you do not expect reimbursement. For example, if you expect a full insurance recovery in 1998 for a 1997 loss, you would take no deduction on your 1997 return.

If you do not expect any reimbursement and deduct a loss in 1997, but you receive insurance or other reimbursement in 1998, the reimbursement is taxable in 1998 to the extent that the 1997 deduction gave you a tax benefit by reducing your 1997 taxable income; *see 11.6.* You may not amend your 1997 tax return.

EXAMPLE

In 1969, Hurricane Camille destroyed oceanfront real estate owned jointly by two brothers. The buildings were insured under two policies which included wind damage but not losses resulting from floods, tidal waves, or water. The insurers, claiming the tidal wave had caused the destruction, denied their claim. The brothers consulted an attorney about the possibility of suit against the insurance companies, but there seemed little likelihood of recovery, so they deducted their shares of the casualty loss in 1969. However, in January 1970, the adjusters of both companies changed their decisions, reimbursing the brothers for more than two-thirds of their loss. One of the brothers filed an amended 1969 tax return, reducing the previously reported casualty loss.

The IRS claimed that the insurance recovery is taxable in the year of receipt, 1970, to the extent that the prior deduction reduced 1969 income. The brother claimed that he made an error in claiming the deduction in 1969 because he had a reasonable prospect of reimbursement. Thus it was proper to reduce the deduction by the reimbursement on an amended return.

The Tax Court disagreed. Tax liability is based on facts as they exist at the end of each year. A recovery in a later tax year does not prove that a reasonable prospect of recovery existed in the earlier year. Amendments to previously filed tax returns may be made only to correct mathematical errors or miscalculations, not to rearrange facts and readjust income for two years.

If your reimbursement is less than you expected. Assume you took no loss deduction in 1997 because you expected to recover your entire loss in 1998—but the insurance company refuses to pay your claim. When do you deduct your loss? You deduct your loss in the year you find that you have no reasonable prospect of recovery. For example, you sue the company in 1998, with a reasonable prospect of winning your claim. However, in 1999, a court rules against you. You deduct your loss in 1999, subject to the personal property floors of *18.11.*

If you, as lessee, are liable to the lessor for damage to property, you may deduct the loss in the year you pay the lessor.

If you do not discover the loss until a later year. In this case, IRS regulations do not specifically allow a deduction for the loss in the year it is discovered, but court decisions have. In one case, an unseasonable blizzard damaged a windbreak planted to protect a house, buildings, and livestock. The damage to the evergreens did not become apparent until the next year, when about half of the trees died and the others were of little value. The court held that the loss occurred in the later year. In another case, hurricane damage did not become apparent for two years. The Tax Court allowed the deduction in the later year. Where drought damage occurs, *see 18.5.*

If your loss is in a federal disaster area. If your property is damaged in an area eligible for federal disaster assistance, you have a choice of years for which the loss may be claimed; *see 18.2.*

If reimbursements exceed your adjusted basis for the property. Receiving reimbursements in excess of adjusted basis results in a gain that you must report on your return unless you acquire qualifying replacement property and elect to defer the gain; *see 18.18.*

If a loss deduction was claimed in a prior year, you must report the reimbursement as income to the extent the prior deduction reduced your taxable income in the year claimed; *see 11.6.*

18.2 Disaster Losses

If you suffer a loss from a disaster in an area declared by the President as warranting federal assistance, you may deduct the loss either on the return for the year of the loss or on the return of the prior tax year. *See 18.12* for figuring the deductible loss.

Filing Tip

Claiming Disaster Loss for Prior Year

You make an election for the prior year in a signed statement attached to your return (original or amended) or refund claim. List the date of the disaster and where the property was located (city, town, county, and state). To amend a filed return for the prior year, use Form 1040X. Consider making the election if the deduction on the return of the prior year gives a greater tax reduction than if claimed on the return for the year in which the loss occurred or you want a refund of all or part of the tax paid for the prior year.

You may elect to claim the deduction on a tax return for the previous year any time on or before the *later* of (1) the due date (without extensions) of the return for the year of the disaster; or (2) the due date considering any extension for filing the return for the prior tax year. In the case of a 1997 disaster loss claimed on a 1996 return, you generally have until April 15, 1998, to amend a 1996 tax return to claim a disaster loss occurring during 1997. In the case of a 1998 disaster loss claimed on a 1997 return, you generally have until April 15, 1999, to amend a 1997 tax return to claim a disaster loss occurring during 1998.

Revoking your decision.   After making your election of which year to claim the disaster loss, you have 90 days in which to revoke it. After the 90-day period, the election becomes irrevocable. However, where an early election is made, you have until the due date for filing your return for the year of the disaster to change your election. Your revocation of an election is not effective unless you repay any credit or refund resulting from the election within the revocation period. A revocation made before you receive a refund will not be effective unless you repay the refund within 30 days after you receive it.

Homeowners forced to relocate.   If you were forced to relocate or demolish your home in a disaster area, you may be able to claim a loss even though the damage, such as from erosion, does not meet the sudden event test of *18.5*. For example, after a severe storm, there is danger to a group of homes from nearby mudslides. State officials order homeowners to evacuate and relocate their homes. Disaster loss treatment is allowed provided: (1) the President has determined that the area warrants federal disaster relief; (2) within 120 days of the President's order, you are ordered by the state or local government to demolish or relocate your residence; and (3) the home was rendered unsafe by the erosion or other disaster. The law applies to vacation homes and rental properties, as well as to principal residences.

If these tests are met, the loss in value to your home is treated as a disaster loss so that you may elect to deduct the loss either in the year the demolition or relocation order is made or in the prior taxable year.

Fiscal year.   If you are on a fiscal year, an election may be made for disaster losses occurring after the close of a fiscal year on the return for that year. For example, if your fiscal year ends June 30, and you suffer a disaster loss anytime between July 1, 1997, and June 30, 1998, you may elect to deduct it on your return for the fiscal year ending June 30, 1997.

Law Alert

IRS Interest Abatement

If the IRS extends the due date to file tax returns and pay taxes for a person in an area declared after 1996 to be a disaster area, the IRS must also abate interest on past-due taxes for the period covered by the extension.

Disaster relief grants and loans.   Cancellation of part of a disaster loan under the Disaster Relief Act is treated as a reimbursement that reduces your loss; *see 18.12*. Grants to disaster victims under the Disaster Relief Act are not taxable, but the grant is considered a reimbursement reducing your deductible loss.

IRS interest abatement.   For declared disasters occurring in 1997, the IRS will abate interest for the period covered by an extension to file tax returns and pay taxes.

Insurance Proceeds for Damaged Principal Residence

Generally, you have a taxable gain if you receive insurance proceeds in excess of your adjusted basis for your home or its contents. However, under a special rule, if your principal residence (whether owned or rented) is damaged by a Presidentially declared disaster, you pay no tax on gain from insurance proceeds received for *unscheduled* personal property damaged or destroyed in the home. Personal property is *unscheduled* if it is not separately listed on a schedule or rider to the basic policy.

In addition, insurance proceeds received for the home itself or for *scheduled* property are treated as received for a single item of property. Gain on this combined insurance pool may be deferred by reinvesting in replacement property that is similar or related in service or use to either the damaged residence or its contents. If the cost of a new principal residence and/or contents equals or exceeds the combined insurance pool, you may elect to defer any gain attributable to the insurance recovery; *see 18.20* for making the election. The deferred gain reduces your basis in the replacement property. The period for purchasing replacement property ends four years after the end of the first tax year in which any part of your gain is realized. If the cost of the replacement property is less than the combined insurance pool, your gain is taxed to the extent of the unspent reimbursement.

EXAMPLES

1. Your home was destroyed by a flood in 1997. The county in which your home was located was declared a disaster area. You received insurance proceeds in 1997 as follows: $200,000 for the home; $25,000 for unscheduled personal property in the home; $10,000 for a stamp collection and $5,000 for jewelry which were kept in your home and were scheduled property on your insurance policy.

   The $25,000 received for the unscheduled personal property is not taxed.

   You can choose to postpone reporting any gain on the remaining proceeds of $215,000 if you acquire property similar or related in service or use to your home, jewelry, or stamp collection. If you use all of the proceeds to purchase a new principal residence, you may postpone all of your gain even if you do not purchase any jewelry or stamps. As long as the total cost of replacement property is at least $215,000, you may defer all of the gain, regardless of how the reinvestment is divided between the residence and household contents. New household contents may be either scheduled or unscheduled property.

   If you invest less than $215,000, you must include the gain in income to the extent the proceeds exceed the amount used for property similar to your home, jewelry, or stamp collection.

   To postpone gain, you must purchase the replacement property before 2000. The replacement period ends December 31, 2001, four years after the close of the first year (1997) in which any gain was realized. Your basis in the replacement property is cost minus the amount of any postponed gain.

2. You rent an apartment as your principal residence. Your apartment and its contents were completely destroyed by a hurricane in 1997; the county in which your apartment was located was declared a disaster area. You received insurance proceeds of $17,000 for unscheduled personal property in your apartment. The proceeds are not taxable.

Sale of land following disaster. If your principal residence is destroyed in a Presidentially declared disaster, and you decide to relocate elsewhere and sell the underlying land, the IRS treats the sale and the destruction as a single involuntary conversion. The land sale proceeds are combined with your insurance recovery for purposes of figuring deferrable gain when a replacement residence is purchased. All of the gain resulting from the insurance recovery may be deferred if a new principal residence is purchased within the four-year replacement period and it costs at least as much as the combined insurance and sales proceeds.

The same gain deferral rule applies if a Presidentially declared disaster destroys a second residence such as a vacation home that qualifies for a mortgage interest deduction (15.1), but in that case the replacement period is two years (18.21) instead of four years.

The two-year replacement period also applies where the damage is to a principal residence but a Presidential disaster declaration is not made.

EXAMPLE

Your principal residence is destroyed in 1997 by a tornado that is declared a disaster by the President. You receive in 1997 insurance proceeds of $120,000. You decide not to rebuild and in 1998, you sell the underlying land for $10,000.

If your basis for the property (land and house) was $100,000, your gain from the insurance recovery is $20,000 ($120,000 insurance – $100,000 basis). The $100,000 tax-free insurance recovery reduces your basis in the property to zero, so on the later sale of the land there is a $10,000 gain that could not be deferred if the land sale was treated separately. However, since the sale of the land is treated by the IRS as part of the original involuntary conversion occurring when the home was destroyed, the overall gain of $30,000 ($20,000 from insurance and $10,000 from land sale) is eligible for deferral if you buy a qualifying replacement residence.

All of the gain may be deferred if you buy a new principal residence at a cost of at least $130,000, equal to the total insurance and land sale proceeds. The residence must be purchased before 2001. The replacement period ends December 31, 2001, four years after the close of the first year (1997) in which any gain was realized.

If the destroyed home had been a second home rather than your principal residence, the same gain deferral rules would apply except that the replacement period would end December 31, 1999.

18.3 Who May Claim the Loss Deduction

The casualty and theft loss deduction may be claimed only by the owner of the property. For example, a husband filing a separate return may not deduct the loss of jewelry belonging to his wife; only she may deduct it on her separate return.

On jointly owned property, the loss is divided among the owners. If you and your spouse own the property jointly, you deduct the entire loss on a joint return. If you file separately, each owner deducts his or her share of the loss on each separate return.

If you have a legal life estate in the property, the loss is apportioned between yourself and those who will get the property after your death. The apportionment may be based on actuarial tables that consider your life expectancy.

You may claim a casualty loss for property lost or destroyed by your dependent if you own the property. You may not claim a loss deduction for destroyed property that belongs to your child who has reached majority, even though he or she is still your dependent.

Lessee. A person leasing property may be allowed to deduct payments to a lessor that compensate for a casualty loss. A tenant was allowed to deduct as a casualty loss payment of a judgment obtained by the landlord for fire damage to the rented premises which had to be returned in the same condition as at the start of the lease. However, the Tax Court does not allow a deduction for the cost of repairing a rented car, as the lessee has no basis in the car.

Damage to nearby property. The casualty must have caused damage to your property. Damage to a nearby area which lowered the value of your property does not give you a loss deduction.

EXAMPLE

You buy or lease a lot on which to build a cottage. Along with your purchase or lease, you have the privilege of using a nearby lake. The lake is later destroyed by a storm and the value of your property drops. You may not deduct the loss. The lake is not your property. You had only a privilege to use it, and this is not an ownership right which supports a casualty loss deduction.

18.4 Bank Deposit Losses

If a bank in which you deposit funds fails and your loss is not covered by insurance, generally you may claim your loss either as a bad debt deduction or casualty loss. Furthermore, if none of the deposits were federally insured, an investment loss may be claimed.

Bad debt. You may claim a bad debt deduction for a loss of a bank deposit in the year there is no reasonable prospect of recovery from the insolvent or bankrupt bank. You claim the loss as a short-term capital loss on Schedule D unless the deposit was made in your business. A nonbusiness bad debt deduction is deductible from capital gains. If you do not have capital gains or the bad debt loss exceeds capital gains, only $3,000 of the loss may offset other income. The remaining loss is carried over. A lost deposit of business funds is claimed as a business bad debt; *see 5.9.*

Casualty loss. You may elect to take a casualty loss deduction for the year in which the loss can be reasonably estimated. The loss is subject to the 10% AGI floor for casualty losses. Once the casualty loss election is made, it is irrevocable and will apply to all other losses on deposits in the same financial institution.

The casualty loss election may allow you to claim the loss in an earlier year because you do not have to wait until the year there is no prospect of recovery as required in the case of bad debts. The casualty loss election may also be advisable if other casualty losses may absorb all or part of the 10% AGI floor. The casualty loss election is not allowed to stockholders of the bank with more than a 1% interest, officers of the bank, or their relatives.

Investment loss. If *none* of your deposits were federally insured and you reasonably estimate that you will not recover the funds, up to $20,000 ($10,000 if married filing separately) may be claimed on Schedule A as an investment loss subject to the 2% adjusted gross income floor for miscellaneous itemized deductions. The $20,000 limit (or $10,000) applies to total losses from any one financial institution, regardless of how many accounts you have. A separate $20,000 deduction limit applies to each financial institution. The $20,000 (or $10,000) limit is reduced by any insurance proceeds authorized by *state* law that you reasonably expect to receive. If your other miscellaneous deductions exceed 2% of adjusted gross income, claiming investment loss treatment may be preferable to treating the loss as a casualty subject to the 10% floor or a bad debt subject to the $3,000 limit. If you claimed a bad debt deduction for a lost deposit in a prior year and you qualify for the investment loss, you may file an amended return to claim the investment loss if the statute of limitations has not passed.

Reasonable estimate of casualty or investment loss. Generally, the trustees of the troubled bank will provide depositors with an estimate of the expected recovery and loss. In the year of that determination, you may claim the estimated loss deduction. If you deduct an estimated loss that is less than you are entitled to, you may claim the additional loss in the year of the final determination as a bad debt. If you deduct more than the actual loss, the excess loss must be reported as income in the year of the final determination. Failure to claim the loss in the year in which the loss can first be reasonably estimated does not bar a deduction in a later year.

For any particular year, only one election may be made for losses in the same bank. If you elect the up-to-$20,000 investment loss for losses in one bank and your loss exceeds the limit, the balance may not be claimed as a casualty deduction. Similarly, if you elect casualty loss treatment, the amount that is not deductible because of the $100 and 10% of the adjusted gross income floors is not deductible under the $20,000 investment loss rule.

18.5 Sudden Event Test for Personal Property Losses

A loss of personal-use property must result from a sudden and destructive force. Chance or a natural phenomenon must be present. Examples include earthquakes, hurricanes, tornadoes, floods, severe storms, landslides, and fires. Loss due to vandalism during riots or civil disorders also is treated as a casualty loss. Damage to your car from an accident is generally deductible; *see 18.7*. Courts have allowed deductions for other types of accidents; *see* Example 2 below. The requirement of suddenness is designed to bar deductions for damage caused by a natural action such as erosion, corrosion, and termite infestation occurring over a period of time.

Foreseeable events and preventable accidents. The IRS may try to disallow a deduction by claiming that the loss was foreseeable and therefore not a deductible casualty loss; *see* the Examples at the end of this section.

EXAMPLES

1. A homeowner claimed a loss for water damage to wallpaper and plaster. The water entered through the window frame. The loss was disallowed. He gave no evidence that the damage came from a sudden or destructive force, such as a storm. The damage may have been caused by progressive deterioration.

2. Mr. White accidentally slammed the car door on his wife's hand. In pain, she shook her hand vigorously. A diamond flew out of her ring's setting, which was loosened by the impact. It was never found. The IRS disallowed the deduction, contending that a casualty loss requires a cataclysmic event. The Tax Court disagreed. A deductible casualty loss occurs whenever an accidental force is exerted against property, and its owner is powerless to prevent the damage because of the suddenness. The IRS has accepted the decision.

3. A boat, which was in a poor state of repair, was equipped with a pump that automatically began operating when the water in the hull rose above a certain level. One day, the dockside power source failed, and the boat sank at its mooring within four hours. The IRS claimed that no deductible type of casualty occurred because the leakage was a chronic problem. The Tax Court allowed the deduction. The sinking was not a direct result of the boat's leaking hull, but of the failure of the on-board water pump.

4. Floods damaged 12 homes which were razed by local authorities for safety reasons. Although Finkbohner's home suffered only minor damage, he claimed that the removal of the neighboring homes decreased the attractiveness of the neighborhood and made it more susceptible to crime. He estimated that the value of his home fell from $120,000 to $95,000 and claimed a casualty loss for the $25,000 difference.

   The IRS disallowed the loss on the grounds that it was not based on actual physical damage. It allowed a deduction only for the cost of repairs, about $1,200. A federal district court jury allowed a $12,500 casualty loss after being instructed by the trial judge that permanent buyer resistance after the flood damage to the neighborhood is basis for a loss deduction.

   An appeals court upheld the loss because permanent buyer resistance affected the value of the home. The court distinguished Finkbohner's case from that of a homeowner who, after a flood and mudslide, was barred from deducting a loss based on fears of future floods. In that situation, the owner was trying to claim a loss that could only be deducted, if and when a future disaster occurred, by the future owner. Here, the buyer resistance confronting Finkbohner was not based on expected future casualties, but on changes to their neighborhood that already occurred.

Is drought damage deductible?   The IRS does not generally allow deductions for drought damage. An agent may argue that the loss resulted from progressive deterioration which does not fit the legal definition of a personal casualty loss. Courts have allowed deductions for severe drought where the damages occur in the same year as the drought.

If the damage becomes noticeable a year later, a court will view this as evidence of progressive deterioration which does not qualify as a deductible casualty. Where there are drought conditions, inspect your property for damage before the end of the year and claim a deduction for the damage in that year to negate an IRS argument that damage was caused by progressive deterioration.

Damage to surrounding property.   Loss due to buyer resistance because of damage to surrounding property is generally not deductible. However, a deduction was allowed by a federal district court and an appeals court.

Termites.   Termite damage is generally nondeductible since it often results from long periods of termite infestation. Proving a sudden action in the sense of fixing the approximate moment of the termite invasion is difficult. Some courts have allowed a deduction, but the IRS will bar deductions for termite damage under any conditions based on a study that found that serious termite damage results only after an infestation of three to eight years. Examples of other nondeductible casualty losses are at *18.9*.

Damage to trees.   The destruction of trees by southern pine beetles over a period of 5–10 days was held by the IRS to be a casualty. One court decided similarly where the destruction occurred over a 30-day period. For figuring the casualty deduction for tree and shrub damage, *see 18.6.*

Deduction despite faulty construction.   A plumber stepped on a pipe which was improperly installed. Resulting underground flooding caused damage of over $20,000. The IRS argued that this was caused by a construction fault and is not a casualty loss. The Tax Court disagreed. The plumber caused the damage. Improper construction was only an element in the causative chain.

Caution

Loss Prevention Measures

The cost of preventive measures, such as burglar alarms or smoke detectors, or the cost of boarding up property against a storm, is not deductible.

EXAMPLES

1. Heyn owned a hillside lot on which he contracted for the building of a home. A soil test showed a high proportion of fine-grain dense sandstone, which is unstable. His construction contract called for appropriate shoring up and support. But, because of the contractor's negligence, a landslide occurred. The IRS disallowed the loss on the ground that it was not a "casualty" because the danger was known before Heyn undertook the project and because of the negligence involved. The court disagreed. The contractor's negligence is not a factor in determining whether there was a casualty. For example, an automobile collision is considered a casualty, even if caused by negligent driving. Foreseeability is not a factor. A weather report may warn property owners to take protective steps against an approaching hurricane, but losses caused by the hurricane are deductible. The IRS has agreed to accept the decision.

2. Mrs. Kane placed her dirty ring in a glass of ammonia. Not knowing the contents of the glass, her husband emptied it into the sink and started the automatic garbage disposal, crushing the ring. The court allowed a full deduction for the loss which it said resulted from a destructive force. That Mr. Kane was negligent has no bearing on whether the event was a casualty.

3. At Christmas time in 1982, Hananel left his 1974 Plymouth Valiant in Chicago in an area in which the city was towing away cars to make room for construction work. When he returned a week later, he found that his car was missing and reported it stolen. A month later, he learned that the city pound had towed the car away and then crushed it because its ownership could not be determined. He claimed a casualty loss for the car. The IRS disallowed the deduction, claiming that the towing and crushing was not an unforeseeable event, and thus did not qualify as a casualty.

    The Tax Court agreed that Hananel could have foreseen that leaving the car on the street subjected it to being towed. He was negligent. However, the penalty for this is a towing charge. He could not have foreseen its destruction. Therefore, the destruction occurred from an unusual and unexpected event, and he was allowed to claim a casualty loss deduction.

4. Destruction of a lawn through the careless use of weed killer has been held to be a casualty.

18.6 Damage to Trees and Shrubs

Not all damage to trees and shrubs qualifies as a casualty loss. The damage must be occasioned by a sudden event; *see 18.5*. Destruction of trees over a period of 5–10 days by southern pine beetles is deductible. One court allowed a deduction for similar destruction over a 30-day period. However, damage by Dutch Elm disease or lethal yellowing disease has been held to be gradual destruction not qualifying as a casualty loss. The Tax Court has allowed a deduction for the cost of removing infested trees.

If shrubbery and trees on *personal-use property* are damaged by a sudden casualty, you figure the loss on the value of the entire property before and after the casualty. You treat the buildings, land, and shrubs as one complete unit; *see* Example 2 below.

In fixing the loss on *business or income-producing property*, however, shrubs and trees are valued separately from the building; *see* Example 1 below.

EXAMPLES

1. Wayne Smith bought an office building for $90,000. The purchase price was allocated between the land ($18,000) and the building ($72,000). Smith planted trees and ornamental shrubs on the grounds surrounding the building at a cost of $1,200. When the basis of the building had been depreciated to $66,000, a hurricane caused extensive property damage. The fair market value of the land and building immediately before the hurricane was $18,000 and $80,000; immediately afterwards it was $18,000 and $52,000. The fair market value of the trees and shrubs immediately before the casualty was $2,000 and immediately afterwards, $400. Insurance of $15,000 is received to cover damage to the building. Deductible losses are figured separately for the building and the trees and shrubs. The deduction for the building is $13,000, computed as follows:

Value of building immediately before casualty	$80,000
Less: Value immediately after casualty	52,000
Loss in value	$28,000
Less: Insurance received	15,000
Deduction allowed	$13,000

The deduction for the trees and shrubs is $1,200:

Value immediately before casualty	$2,000
Less: Value of trees immediately after casualty	400
Loss in value	$1,600*

*However, the deductible loss cannot exceed the adjusted basis of the property, $1,200.

2. Same facts as in Example 1, except that Smith purchases a personal residence instead of an office building. Smith's adjusted gross income is $25,000, and this is his only loss. No allocation of the purchase price is necessary for the land and house because the property is not depreciable. Likewise, no individual evaluation of the fair market values of the land, house, trees, and shrubs is necessary. The amount of the deduction for the land, house, trees, and shrubs is $12,000, computed as follows:

Value of property immediately before casualty		$100,000
Less: Value of property immediately after casualty		70,400
Loss in value		$29,600
Less: Insurance received	$15,000	
10% floor ($2,500) and $100 floors	2,600	17,600
Deduction allowed		$12,000

18.7 Deducting Damage to Your Car

Damage to your car in an accident may be a deductible casualty loss unless caused by your willful conduct, such as drunken driving.

You may not deduct legal fees and costs of a court action for damages or money paid for damages to another's property because of your negligence while driving for commuting or other personal purposes. But if at the time of the accident you were using your car on business, you may deduct as a business loss a payment of damages to the other party's car. For purposes of a business

Court Decision

Failure To Winterize Car

The Tax Court held that the loss of an engine because of a failure to use anti-freeze is not deductible as a casualty loss since the damage is not the result of a destructive force or accident but of personal neglect.

loss deduction, driving between two locations of the same business is considered business driving but driving between locations of two separate businesses is considered personal driving. Therefore, the payment of damages arising from an accident while driving between two separate businesses is not deductible.

A court has allowed deductions for damage resulting from a child pressing the starter button of a car and from flying stones while driving over a temporary road. In a private letter ruling, the IRS disallowed a loss for damage to a race car by an amateur racer on the ground that in races, crashes are not an unusual event and so do not constitute a casualty.

If the deduction is questioned, be prepared to show the amount, if any, of your insurance recovery. A deduction is allowed only for uninsured losses. Not only must the loss be proved, but also that it was not compensated by insurance.

Towing costs are not included as part of the casualty loss.

A parent may not claim a casualty loss deduction for damage to a car registered in a child's name, although the parent provided funds for the purchase of the car.

Expenses of personal injuries arising from a car accident are not a deductible casualty loss.

Automobile used partly for business.   When you use an automobile partly for personal use and partly for business, your loss is computed as though two separate pieces of property were damaged—one business and the other personal. The $100 and 10% floors reduce only the loss on the part used for personal purposes.

18.8   Theft Losses

The taking of property must be illegal under state law to support a theft loss deduction. That property is missing is not sufficient evidence to sustain a theft deduction. It may have been lost or misplaced. So if all you can prove is that an article is missing or lost, your deduction may be disallowed. Sometimes, of course, the facts surrounding the disappearance of an article indicate that it is reasonable to assume that a theft took place. A deduction has been allowed for the theft of trees.

You deduct a theft loss in the year you discover the property was stolen. If you have a reasonable chance of being reimbursed for your loss, you may not take a deduction until the year in which you learn there is no reasonable prospect of recovery.

A legal fee paid to recover stolen property has been held to be deductible as part of the theft loss. To figure the amount of a theft loss deduction, *see 18.12.*

Fraud by building contractors.   A deduction was allowed when a building contractor ran away with a payment he received to build a residence. The would-be homeowner was allowed a theft loss deduction for the difference between the money he advanced to the contractor and the value of the partially completed house. In another case, a theft deduction was allowed for payments to subcontractors. The main contractor had fraudulently claimed that he had paid them before he went bankrupt.

Embezzlement losses are deductible as theft losses in the year the theft is discovered. However, if you report on a cash basis, you may not take a deduction for the embezzlement of income you have not reported. For example, an agent embezzled royalties of $46,000 due an author. The author's theft deduction was disallowed. The author had not previously reported the royalties as income; therefore, she could not get the deduction.

Fraudulent sales offers.   Worthless stock purchases made on the representation of false and fraudulent sales offers are deductible as theft losses in the year there is no reasonable prospect of recovery. However, the illegal sale of unregistered stock does not support a theft loss deduction.

Kidnapping ransom.   Payment of ransom to a kidnapper is generally a deductible theft loss. However, the expense of trying to find an abducted child is not a theft loss.

Fortune tellers.   The Tax Court allowed a theft loss deduction in New York, where fortune telling is by law a theft-related offense. The law assumes that telling fortunes or promising to control occult forces is a form of fraud. An exception is made for fortune telling at shows for the purpose of entertaining or amusement. That a person voluntarily asks for advice does not bar the deduction. According to the court, a gullible person who gives money to fortune tellers in the belief that he or she will be helped is still defrauded or swindled. Theft is a broad term and includes theft by swindling, false pretenses, and any other form of guile. In this case, the taxpayer, who was suffering from mental depression, had become attached to two fortune tellers whom he claimed took him for over $19,000.

Planning Reminder

Proving a Theft

Get statements from witnesses who saw the theft or police records documenting a break-in to your house or car. A newspaper account of the crime might also help.

When you suspect a theft, make a report to the police. Even though your reporting does not prove that a theft was committed, it may be inferred from your failure to report that you were not sure that your property was stolen. But a theft loss was allowed where the loss of a ring was not reported to the police or an attempt made to demand its return from the suspect, a domestic employee. The owner feared being charged with false arrest.

Riot losses.   Losses caused by fire, theft, and vandalism occurring during riots and civil disorders are deductible. When a reception is canceled because of a curfew, no loss deduction is allowed for perishable food that is discarded.

To support your claim of a riot loss, keep evidence of the damage suffered and the cost of repairs. Photographs taken prior to repairs or replacement, lists of damaged or missing property, and police reports would help to establish and uphold your loss deduction.

Foreign government confiscations.   The IRS and courts have disallowed deductions for confiscations of personal property by foreign governments.

Swindled by friend.   A theft loss deduction was allowed to a widow who gave her old beau over $2 million to acquire stock for her in his bank. He used the money to pay his personal debts. The IRS barred the theft loss, arguing that the widow failed to prove fraud. A district court disagreed and allowed the deduction. Under Oklahoma state law, a person who makes a promise in return for cash has committed larceny by fraud if he never intended to return the funds or make good on the promise. Here, that the widow gave him the money voluntarily does not bar a theft loss deduction. She parted with the funds based upon his false claim that he would invest the money for her when he had no intention of doing so, but planned all along to pay off his debts with the funds.

18.9   Nondeductible Losses

Certain losses, though "casualties" for you, may not be deducted if they are not due to theft, fire, or from some other sudden natural phenomenon. The following have been held to be nondeductible losses:

- Termite damage; *see 18.5*
- Carpet beetle damage
- Dry rot damage
- Damages for personal injuries or property damage to others caused by your negligence
- Legal expenses in defending a suit for your negligent operation of your personal automobile
- Legal expenses to recover personal property wrongfully seized by the police
- Expenses of moving to and rental of temporary quarters
- Loss of personal property while in storage or in transit
- Loss of passenger's luggage put aboard a ship. The passenger missed the boat and the luggage could not be traced.
- Accidental loss of a ring from your finger
- Injuries resulting from tripping over a wire
- Loss by husband of joint property taken by his wife when she left him
- Loss of a valuable dog which strayed and was not found
- Damage to a crop caused by plant diseases, insects, or fungi
- Damage to property from drought in an area where a dry spell is normal and usual
- Damage to property caused by excavations on adjoining property
- Damage from rust or corroding of understructure of house
- Moth damage
- Dry well
- Losses occasioned by water pockets, erosion, inundation at still water levels, and other natural phenomena (There was no sudden destruction.)
- Amount paid to a public library for damages to a book you borrowed
- Death of a saddle horse after eating a silk hat
- A watch or spectacles dropped on the ground
- Sudden drop in the value of securities
- Loss in earnings of a lawyer resulting from his illness
- Loss of contingent interest in property due to the unexpected death of a child
- Improper police seizure of private liquor stock
- Chinaware broken by a family pet
- Temporary fluctuation in value
- Loss of tree from Dutch Elm disease and lethal yellowing disease
- Loss of trees after horse ate bark
- Damage to property from local government construction project
- Fire purposely set by owner
- Engine damage due to failure to use anti-freeze

Note: Some of the above items may be allowed as business expenses.

Filing Instruction

If Stolen Property Is Recovered
If you claim a theft loss and in a later year the property is returned to you, you must refigure your loss deduction. If the refigured deduction is lower than the amount you claimed, the difference must be reported as income in the year of the recovery. To recalculate the loss, follow the steps in *18.12* for figuring deductible losses, but in Step 1, compute the loss in fair market value from the time the property was stolen until you recovered it. The lower of this loss in value, if any, and your adjusted basis for the property is then reduced by insurance reimbursements and the personal floors *(18.11)* to get the recalculated loss.

Key To Proving a Casualty Loss

To prove—	You need this information—
That a casualty actually occurred	With a well-known casualty, like regional floods, you will have no difficulty proving the casualty occurred, but you must prove it affected your property. Photographs of the area, before and after, and newspaper stories placing the damage in your neighborhood are helpful. If only your property is damaged, there may be a newspaper item on it. Some papers list all the fire alarms answered the previous day. Police, fire, and other municipal departments may have reports on the casualty.
The cost of repairing the property	Cost of repairs is allowed as a measure of loss of repairing the value if it is not excessive and the repair merely restored your property to its condition immediately before the casualty. Save cancelled checks, bills, receipts, and vouchers for expenses of clearing debris and restoring the property to its condition before the casualty.
The value immediately before and after the casualty	Appraisals by a competent expert are important. Get them in writing—in the form of an affidavit, deposition, estimate, appraisal, etc. The expert—an appraiser, engineer, or architect—should be qualified to judge local values. Any records of offers to buy your property, either before or after the casualty, are helpful. Automobile "blue books" may be used as guides in fixing the value of a car. But an amount offered for your car as a trade-in on a new car is not usually an acceptable measure of value.
Cost of your property—the deductible cannot be more than that	A deed, contract, bill of sale, or other document probably shows your original cost. **loss** Bills, receipts, and canceled checks show the cost loss cannot be more than that of improvements. One court refused to allow a deduction because an owner failed to prove the original cost of a destroyed house and its value before the fire. In another case, estimates were allowed where a fire destroyed records of cost. A court held that the homeowner could not be expected to prove cost by documents lost in the fire that destroyed her property. She made inventories after the fire and again at a later date. Her reliance on memory to establish cost, even though inflated, was no bar to the deduction. The court estimated the market value based on her inventories. If you acquired the property by gift or inheritance, you must establish an adjusted basis in the property from records of the donor or the executor of the estate; *see 5.21* and *5.22*.

18.10 Proving a Casualty Loss

If your return is audited, you will have to prove that the casualty occurred and the amount of the loss. The time to collect your evidence is as soon after the casualty as possible. The Key To Proving a Casualty Loss above, indicates the information that you will need when computing your loss under the steps explained in *18.12*.

18.11 Floors for Personal-Use Property Losses

Casualty and theft losses to personal-use property are subject to "floors" that will reduce, and in some cases eliminate, your deduction. For each casualty or theft, a $100 reduction applies after the loss is computed under the steps of *18.12*. In addition, personal casualty and theft losses (after the $100 reduction) are deductible only to the extent they exceed 10% of your adjusted gross income.

The $100 floor. The $100 floor reduces casualty and theft losses of property used for personal purposes; *see* Step 4 of *18.12*. The $100 floor does not apply to losses of business property or property held for the production of income such as securities. If property used both in business and personal activities is damaged, the $100 offset applies only to the loss allocated to personal use.

For each casualty or theft during the year, a separate $100 reduction applies. For example, you are involved in five different casualties during the year. There will be a $100 offset applied to each of the five losses. But when two or more items of property are destroyed in one event, only one $100 offset is applied to the total loss. For example, a storm damages your residence and also your car parked in the driveway. You figure the loss on the residence and car separately, but only one $100 offset applies to the total loss.

Form 4684—Worksheet

Form **4684**	**Casualties and Thefts**	OMB No. 1545-0177

► See separate instructions.
► Attach to your tax return.

Department of the Treasury
Internal Revenue Service

► **Use a separate Form 4684 for each different casualty or theft.**

19 96

Attachment
Sequence No. **26**

Name(s) shown on tax return | Identifying number

SECTION A—Personal Use Property (Use this section to report casualties and thefts of property **not** used in a trade or business or for income-producing purposes.)

1 Description of properties (show type, location, and date acquired for each):

Property **A** *Residence* 2-8-87
Property **B** *Furniture* 3-15-88
Property **C**
Property **D**

Properties (Use a separate column for each property lost or damaged from one casualty or theft.)

		A	B	C	D
2	Cost or other basis of each property	76,000	5,000		
3	Insurance or other reimbursement (whether or not you filed a claim). See instructions	2,000	500		
	Note: *If line 2 is **more than** line 3, skip line 4.*				
4	Gain from casualty or theft. If line 3 is **more than** line 2, enter the difference here and skip lines 5 through 9 for that column. See instructions if line 3 includes insurance or other reimbursement you did not claim, or you received payment for your loss in a later tax year				
5	Fair market value **before** casualty or theft	167,500	2,000		
6	Fair market value **after** casualty or theft	162,500	0		
7	Subtract line 6 from line 5	5,000	2,000		
8	Enter the **smaller** of line 2 or line 7	5,000	2,000		
9	Subtract line 3 from line 8. If zero or less, enter -0-	3,000	1,500		

10	Casualty or theft loss. Add the amounts on line 9. Enter the total	**10**	4,500
11	Enter the amount from line 10 or $100, whichever is **smaller**	**11**	100
12	Subtract line 11 from line 10	**12**	4,400
	Caution: *Use only one Form 4684 for lines 13 through 18.*		
13	Add the amounts on line 12 of all Forms 4684	**13**	4,400
14	Combine the amounts from line 4 of all Forms 4684	**14**	-0-
15	• If line 14 is **more than** line 13, enter the difference here and on Schedule D. Do not complete the rest of this section (see instructions). • If line 14 is **less than** line 13, enter -0- here and continue with the form. • If line 14 is **equal to** line 13, enter -0- here. Do not complete the rest of this section.	**15**	-0-
16	If line 14 is **less than** line 13, enter the difference	**16**	4,400
17	Enter 10% of your adjusted gross income (Form 1040, line 32). Estates and trusts, see instructions	**17**	2,800
18	Subtract line 17 from line 16. If zero or less, enter -0-. Also enter result on Schedule A (Form 1040), line 19. Estates and trusts, enter on the "Other deductions" line of your tax return	**18**	1,600

For Paperwork Reduction Act Notice, see page 1 of separate instructions.   Cat. No. 12997O   Form **4684** (1996)

Filing Tip

$100 Floor for Married Couples
Where a husband and wife file a joint return, only one $100 floor applies to a casualty loss suffered by either spouse, whether the property is owned jointly or separately. If separate returns are filed, each spouse must reduce his or her half of the loss on jointly owned property by $100. If the property is owned by one spouse, only that spouse can claim a casualty loss on a separate return.

The $100 floor is applied after taking into account insurance proceeds received and insurance you expect to receive in a later year.

The $100 floor applies separately to the loss of each individual whose property has been damaged by a single casualty, even where the damaged property is owned by two or more individuals. The only exception is for a married couple filing jointly who apply only one $100 floor to their losses from a single casualty.

EXAMPLES

1. Two sisters own and occupy a house which is damaged in a storm. Each sister applies the $100 floor to figure her separate deduction.

2. Your house is partially damaged by a fire which also damages the personal property of a houseguest. You are subject to one $100 floor and the houseguest is subject to a separate $100 floor.

10% AGI floor. The 10% adjusted gross income (AGI) floor applies to the total of all losses occurring during the taxable year to personal-use property. The Example below illustrates the application of the $100 floor to each separate casualty event and the 10% AGI floor to the total losses.

EXAMPLE

In January 1997, you have an uninsured jewelry theft loss of $1,000, and in July 1997 uninsured damage of $3,000 to your personal car. Your adjusted gross income is $25,000. Your deduction is $1,300 figured as follows:

Theft loss	$1,000	
Less	100	$ 900
Car damage	3,000	
Less	100	2,900
Total loss		3,800
Less 10% of $25,000		2,500
Deductible loss		$1,300

18.12 Figuring Your Loss on Form 4684

The deductible loss is usually the difference between the fair market value of the property before and after the casualty or theft *less* (1) reimbursements received for the loss; and (2) $100 if the property was used for personal purposes. However, the loss may not exceed your adjusted basis *(5.24)* for the property, which for many items will be your cost. If your adjusted basis is less than the loss in value, your deduction is limited to basis, less reimbursements and the $100 floor for personal-use assets. After figuring all allowable casualty and theft losses for personal-use property, the total is deductible only to the extent it exceeds the 10% adjusted gross income floor *(18.11)*. Use the following five-step method for figuring the deductible amount.

Steps for calculating your deductible loss. The following five steps reflect the procedure on Form 4684 for computing a casualty or theft loss. Form 4684 is used to report casualties or thefts of personal-use property, business property, or income-producing property. However, if your loss is to business inventory, you do not have to use Form 4684, but may take the loss into account when figuring the cost of goods sold; *see* Inventory losses later in this section.

To figure your deductible loss, follow these five steps:

Step 1. Compute the loss in fair market value of the property. This is the difference between the fair market value immediately before and immediately after the casualty. You will need written appraisals to support your claim for loss of value. You may not claim sentimental or aesthetic values or a fluctuation in property values caused by a casualty; you must deal with cost or market values of what has been lost. If the value of your property has been lowered because of damage to a nearby area, you do not have a deductible loss since your own property has not been damaged. No deduction may be claimed for estimated decline in value based on buyer resistance in an area subject to landslides.

For household items, the Tax Court has allowed losses based on cost less depreciation, rather than on the decrease in fair market value; *see* the first Example on page 340.

Step 2. Compute your adjusted basis for the property. This is usually the cost of the property plus the cost of improvements, less previous casualty loss deductions and depreciation if the property is used in business or for income-producing purposes. Unadjusted basis of property acquired other than by purchase is explained at *5.20*. Adjusted basis is explained at *5.24*.

Step 3. Take the lower of Step 1 and 2. The lower amount, reduced by the adjustments in Step 4, is your casualty loss, with one exception: Where property used for business or income-producing purposes is totally destroyed, and before the casualty its market value is less than its adjusted basis, the measure of the loss is the adjusted basis, *less* any salvage value.

Step 4. Reduce the loss in Step 3 by the insurance proceeds or other compensation for the loss; *see 18.15*. If the property was used for personal purposes, also reduce the loss by $100; *see 18.11*.

Step 5. If the property was used for personal purposes, the loss is allowed only if it exceeds 10% of your adjusted gross income. If you have more than one personal casualty or theft, reduce the total combined loss by 10% of adjusted gross income; only the excess is deductible; *see 18.11*.

Caution

Incidental Expenses

Expenses that are incidental to a casualty or theft, such as medical treatment for personal injury, temporary housing, fuel, moving, or rentals for temporary living quarters, are not deductible as casualty losses.

Law Alert

Appraisals for Disaster Relief

A new law allows the IRS to accept an appraisal that is used to obtain federal loans or loan guarantees following a Presidentially declared disaster as proof of the amount of a casualty loss. However, IRS guidelines are needed to implement the rule; *see* the Supplement for any developments.

EXAMPLES

1. Your home, which cost $76,000 in 1987, was damaged by a fire. The value of the house before the disaster was $167,500, but afterwards $162,500. The furniture cost $5,000 in 1988. Its value before the fire was set at $2,000. It was totally destroyed. The insurance company reimbursed you $2,000 for your house damage and $500 for your furnishings. This was the only casualty for the year. Your adjusted gross income is $28,000. You figure your loss for the furniture separately from the loss on the house but apply only one $100 reduction *(18.11)* because the damage was from a single casualty.

    1. Decrease in home's fair market value:

Value of house before fire	$167,500
Value of house after fire	162,500
Decrease in value	$ 5,000
2. Adjusted basis:	$ 76,000
3. Loss sustained (lower of 1 and 2)	$5,000
Less: Insurance	2,000
Loss on house	$3,000
4. Loss on furnishings (decreased value)*	$2,000
Less: Insurance	500
Loss on furnishings	$1,500
5. Total loss ($3,000 and $1,500)	$4,500
Less: $100 floor	100
Casualty loss (subject to 10% floor)	$4,400

    After applying the 10% adjusted gross income floor, you may deduct $1,600 on Schedule A ($4,400 – $2,800 or 10% of $28,000).

    See the sample Form 4684 on page 337 for how this loss is reported.

    *The loss for the furnishings on Line 4 is $2,000, the decrease in fair market value, as this is lower than the $5,000 basis.

2. Depreciable business property with a fair market value of $1,500 and an adjusted basis of $2,000 is totally destroyed. Because property used in your business was totally destroyed (*see* Step 3 above), your loss is measured by your adjusted basis of $2,000, which is larger than the $1,500 loss in fair market value. Salvage value, if any, reduces your deduction, but you disregard the $100 floor applied to casualty losses on personal property. If the property was used for personal purposes, the loss would have been limited to the $1,500 loss in market value less $100, leaving a loss of $1,400 subject to the 10% adjusted gross income floor.

Inventory losses. A casualty or theft loss of inventory is automatically reflected on Schedule C in the cost of goods sold, which includes the lost items as part of your opening inventory. Any insurance or other reimbursement received for the loss must be included as sales income.

You may separately claim the inventory loss as a casualty or theft loss on Form 4684 instead of automatically claiming it as part of the cost of goods sold. If you do this, you must eliminate the items from inventory by lowering either opening inventory or purchases when figuring the cost of goods sold.

Cost less depreciation method for household items. The Tax Court has allowed casualty loss deductions based on cost less depreciation, rather than on the difference in fair market value immediately before and after the casualty. *See* the following Example.

Filing Instruction

Reporting on Form 4684

If you are claiming a loss for personal-use property, use Section A on page one of Form 4684. If you suffered more than one casualty or theft during the year, use a separate Form 4684 for each one. The total deductible casualty or theft loss from Section A of Form 4684 is then entered on Schedule A of Form 1040.

If you are claiming a loss for property used in your business or income-producing activity, use Section B on page 2 of Form 4684. Losses from income-producing property are generally entered on Schedule A as a miscellaneous itemized deduction subject to the 2% adjusted gross income floor. Losses from business property are generally netted against gains and the result entered on Form 4797; follow the instructions to Form 4684.

Planning Reminder

Keep Records of Deductible Losses

If your property is damaged, you must reduce the basis of the damaged property by the casualty loss deduction and compensation received for the loss; *see 5.24*. When you later sell the property, gain or loss is the difference between the selling price and the reduced basis.

EXAMPLE

Basing a deduction on the difference between the value of furnishings immediately before and immediately after a casualty may limit your deduction to the going price for second-hand furnishings. A homeowner whose furniture was destroyed by fire claimed that the fair market value immediately before the fire should be original cost less depreciation. He based his figures on an inventory prepared by certified public adjusters describing each item, its cost and age. The deduction figured this way came to approximately $27,500 ($55,000 cost, less $13,000 depreciation, a $14,400 insurance recovery, and the $100 floor).

The IRS estimated that the furniture was worth $15,304 before the fire and limited the deduction to $804 after setting off the insurance and the $100 floor. The Tax Court disagreed. The householder's method of valuing his furniture is consistent with methods used by insurance adjusters who have an interest in keeping values low. He is not limited to the amount his property would bring if "hawked off by a secondhand dealer or at a forced sale." However, in another case, the court refused to allow the cost less depreciation formula where the homeowner's inventory list was based on memory.

18.13 Personal and Business Use of Property

For property held partly for personal use and partly for business or income-producing purposes, a casualty or theft loss deduction is computed as if two separate pieces of property were damaged, destroyed, or stolen. Follow the steps of *18.12* for figuring the allowable loss, but apply the $100 and 10% of adjusted gross income floors only to the personal part of the loss.

EXAMPLE

A building with two apartments, one used by the owner as his home and the other rented to a tenant, is damaged by a fire. The fair market value of the building before the fire was $169,000 and after the fire, $136,000. Its cost basis was $120,000. Depreciation taken before the fire was $14,000. The insurance company paid $20,000. The owner has adjusted gross income of $40,000. This is his only loss this year. He has a business casualty loss of $6,500 and a deductible personal casualty loss of $2,400 figured as follows:

	Business	Personal
1. Decrease in value of building:		
Value before fire ($169,000)	$84,500	$84,500
Value after fire ($136,000)	(68,000)	(68,000)
Decrease in value	$16,500	$16,500
2. Adjusted basis of building:	$60,000	$60,000
Less: Depreciation	(14,000)	
Adjusted basis	$46,000	$60,000
3. Loss sustained (lower of 1 and 2)	$16,500	$16,500
Less: Insurance (total $20,000)	($10,000)	($10,000)
4. Loss	$6,500	$6,500
Less: $100 floor and 10% of adjusted gross income	—	(4,100)
Deductible casualty loss	$6,500	$2,400

18.14 Repairs May Be a "Measure of Loss"

The cost of repairs may be treated as evidence of the loss of value (Step 1 of *18.12*), if the amount is not excessive and the repairs do nothing more than restore the property to its condition before the casualty. An estimate for repairs will not suffice; only actual repairs may be used as a measure of loss. However, where you measure your loss by comparing appraisals of value for before and after the casualty, repairs may be considered in arriving at a post-casualty value even though no actual repairs are made.

Deduction not limited to repairs. A casualty loss deduction is not limited to repair expenses where the decline in market value is greater, according to a federal appeals court; *see* the next Example.

EXAMPLE

Connor claimed that the market value of his house dropped $93,000 after it was damaged by fire. His $52,000 cash outlay in repairing the house was reimbursed by insurance. He claimed a casualty loss of approximately $40,000, the uncompensated drop in market value. The IRS barred the deduction. The house was restored to pre-casualty condition. The cost of the repairs is a realistic measure of the loss, and, as the expense was fully compensated by insurance, Connor suffered no loss. A federal appeals court disagreed. The house dropped $70,000 in market value, of which $20,000 was uncompensated by insurance. The deduction is measured by the uncompensated difference in value before and after the casualty. It is not limited to the cost of repairs, even where the repair expense is less than the difference in fair market values. Had the repairs cost more than this difference, the IRS would not have allowed a larger deduction.

18.15 Insurance Reimbursements

You reduce the amount of your loss *(18.12)* by insurance proceeds, voluntary payments received from your employer for damage to your property, and cash or property received from the Red Cross. Also reduce your loss by reimbursements you expect to receive in a later year; *see 18.1*. However, cash gifts from friends and relatives to help defray the cost of repairs do not reduce the loss where there are no conditions on the use of the gift. Also, gifts of food, clothing, medical supplies, and other forms of subsistence do not reduce the loss deduction nor are they taxable income.

Cancellation of part of a disaster loan under the Disaster Relief Act is treated as a partial reimbursement of the loss and reduces the amount of the loss. Payments from an urban renewal agency to acquire your damaged property under the Federal Relocation Act of 1970 are considered reimbursements reducing the loss.

Insurance payments for the cost of added living expenses because of damage to a home do not reduce a casualty loss. The payments are treated separate and apart from payments for property damage. Payments for excess living costs are generally not taxable; *see 18.16*.

Passive activity property loss reimbursements. A reimbursement of a casualty or theft loss deduction is not considered passive activity income if the original loss was not treated as a passive deduction; *see 10.1*. The reimbursement may be taxed under the rule of *11.6*.

Realizing a gain from insurance. If you receive insurance proceeds in excess of your adjusted basis for the property, you generally realize a gain, which you may be able to defer by buying replacement property; *see 18.18*.

18.16 Excess Living Costs Paid by Insurance Are Not Taxable

Your insurance contract may reimburse you for excess living costs when a casualty or a threat of casualty forces you to vacate your house. The payment is tax free if these tests are met:

1. Your principal residence is damaged or destroyed by fire, storm, or other casualty or you are denied use of it by a governmental order because of the occurrence or threat of the casualty.

2. You are paid under an insurance contract for living expenses resulting from the loss of occupancy or use of the residence.

Whether you have a taxable or tax-free reimbursement is figured at the end of the period you were unable to use your residence. Thus, if the dislocation covers more than one taxable year, the taxable income, if any, will be reported in the taxable year in which the dislocation ended.

The tax-free amount includes only excess living costs paid by the insurance company. The excess is the difference between (1) the actual living expenses incurred during the time you could not use or occupy your house, and (2) the normal living expenses which you would have incurred for yourself and members of your household during the period. Living expenses during the period may include the cost of renting suitable housing and extraordinary expenses for transportation, food, utilities, and miscellaneous services. The expenses must be incurred for items and services (such as laundry) needed to maintain you in the same standard of living that you enjoyed before the loss and must be covered by the policy.

Where a lump-sum settlement does not identify the amount covering living expenses, an allocation is required to determine the tax-free portion. In the case of uncontested claims, the tax-free portion is that part of the settlement which bears the same ratio to total recovery as increased living expense bears to total loss and expense. If your claim is contested, you must show the amount reasonably allocable to increased living expenses consistent with the terms of the insurance contract, but not in excess of coverage limitations specified in the contract.

 Caution

Failure To Make an Insurance Claim

If you are insured for your full loss and do not file a claim because you do not want to risk cancellation of liability coverage, you may not claim a deduction. If you do not file an insurance claim but your loss exceeds the coverage, the noncovered loss is deductible. For example, if you have a $500 deductible on your automobile insurance policy, a loss of up to $500 for car damage would be allowed, subject to the $100 and 10% of adjusted gross income floors.

The exclusion from income does not cover insurance reimbursements for loss of rental income or for loss of or damage to real or personal property; such reimbursements for property damage reduce your casualty loss; *see 18.15.*

If your home is used for both residential and business purposes, the exclusion does not apply to insurance proceeds and expenses attributable to the nonresidential portion of the house. There is no exclusion for insurance recovered for expenses resulting from governmental condemnation or order unrelated to a casualty or threat of casualty.

The insurance reimbursement may cover part of your normal living expenses as well as the excess expenses due to the casualty. The part covering normal expenses is income; it does not reduce your casualty loss.

EXAMPLES

1. On March 1, your home was damaged by fire. While it was being repaired, you and your spouse lived at a motel and ate meals at restaurants. Costs are $1,200 at the motel, $1,000 for meals, and $75 for laundry services. You make the required March payment of $790 on your home mortgage. Your customary $40 commuting expense is $20 less for the month because the motel is closer to your work. Your usual commuting expense is therefore treated as not being incurred to the extent of the $20 decrease. Furthermore, you do not incur your customary $700 food expense for meals at home, $75 for utilities, and $60 for laundry at home. Your insurance company pays you $1,700 for expenses. The tax-free exclusion for insurance payments is limited to $1,420, computed in the third column. You must report as income $280 ($1,700 – $1,420).

	Expenses from casualty	Expenses not incurred	Increase (Decrease)
Housing	$1,200		$1,200
Utilities		$75	(75)
Meals	1,000	700	300
Transportation		20	(20)
Laundry	75	60	15
Total	$2,275	$855	$1,420

2. Same facts as Example 1 except that you rented the residence for $400 per month and the risk of loss was to the landlord. You did not pay the March rent. The excludable amount is $1,020 ($1,420 less $400 normal rent not incurred). You would have to report as income the excess of the insurance received over the $1,020 exclusion.

18.17 Do Your Casualty Losses Exceed Your Income?

If your casualty or theft losses exceed your income, you pay no tax in 1997. You may also carry the excess loss back to 1994 and file a refund claim for that year. Any remaining loss may be carried back to 1995 and 1996 and carried forward to 1998 through 2012, or you may just carry your loss forward 15 years until it is used up. The excess casualty loss is carried back or forward as a net operating loss. *See 40.17* for net operating loss rules.

Note: The $100 and 10% of adjusted gross income floors for personal casualty losses apply only in the year of loss; you do not again reduce your loss in the carry-back or carryover years.

Taxable Gain From Involuntary Conversions

18.18 Defer Gain by Replacing Property

If your property is destroyed, damaged, stolen, or taken by a government authority, this is considered to be an *involuntary conversion* for tax purposes. If upon an involuntary conversion you receive insurance or other compensation that exceeds the adjusted basis of the property, you realize a taxable gain; but *see* "Principal residence" below.

You may elect to postpone tax on the full gain provided you invest the proceeds in replacement property the cost of which is equal to or exceeds the net proceeds from the conversion. Reinvestment requirements are discussed at *18.21–18.23.* The replacement period for personal-use property is two years; for business and investment property it is two or three years depending on the type of involuntary conversion; for a residence and its contents involuntarily converted due to a Presidentially declared disaster *(see 18.2)* it is four years; *see 18.21* for replacement periods.

Your basis in the replacement property is its replacement cost, minus any postponed gain. If you find that you cannot buy a replacement by the end of the period, ask the IRS for an extension of time *(see 18.21)*.

18.19 Involuntary Conversions Qualifying for Tax Deferral

For purposes of an election to defer tax on gains, "involuntary conversion" is more broadly defined than "casualty loss." You have an involuntary conversion when your property is:

Damaged or destroyed by some outside force.

Stolen.

Seized, requisitioned, or condemned by a governmental authority. If you voluntarily sell land made useless to you by the condemnation of your adjacent land, the sale may also qualify as a conversion. Condemnation of property as unfit for human habitation does not qualify. Condemnation, as used by the tax law, refers to the taking of private property for public use, not to the condemnation of property for noncompliance with housing and health regulations. Similarly, a tax sale to pay delinquent taxes is not an involuntary conversion.

Sold under a threat of seizure, condemnation, or requisition. The threat must be made by an authority qualified to take property for public use. A sale following a threat of condemnation made by a government employee is a conversion if you reasonably believe he or she speaks with authority and could and would carry out the threat to have your property condemned. If you learn of the plan of an imminent condemnation from a newspaper or other news media, the IRS requires you to confirm the report from a government official before you act on the news.

Farmers. Farmers also have involuntary conversions when:

Land is sold within an irrigation project to meet the acreage limitations of the federal reclamation laws;

Cattle are destroyed by disease or sold because of disease; *or*

Draft, breeding, or dairy livestock is sold because of drought. The election to treat the sale as a conversion is limited to livestock sold over the number which would have been sold but for the drought. In some cases, livestock may be replaced with other farm property where there has been soil or other environmental contamination.

Should you elect to postpone gain? An election gives an immediate advantage: tax on gain is postponed and the funds that would have been spent to pay the tax may be used for other investments.

However, as a condition of deferring tax, the basis of the replacement property is generally fixed at the same adjusted basis as the converted property. If your reinvestment exceeds the insurance proceeds, the excess increases the basis of the replacement property. As long as the value of the replacement property does not decline, tax on the original gain is finally incurred when the property is sold.

Consider whether postponement of gain at the expense of a reduced basis for property is advisable, compared to the tax consequences of reporting the gain in the year it is realized.

Special rules for federally declared disaster areas are discussed at *18.2*.

> **EXAMPLE**
>
> Assume a rental building is destroyed by fire and a proper replacement is made. Assume that gain on the receipt of the insurance proceeds is taxable as capital gain. An election is generally not advisable if you have capital losses to offset the gain. However, even if you have no capital losses, you may still decide not to make the election and pay tax in order to fix, for purposes of depreciation, the basis of the new property at its purchase price, if the future depreciation deductions will offset income taxable at a higher rate than the current tax. If there is little or no difference between the two rates so that a net after-tax benefit from the depreciation would not arise, an election might be made solely to postpone the payment of tax.

18.20 How To Elect To Defer Tax

To defer tax on your gain, do not report the gain as income for the year it is realized. Attach to your return a statement giving details of the transaction, including computation of the gain and your intention to buy a replacement if you have not yet done so. *See 18.21* for replacement periods and IRS notification requirements.

If your property is condemned and you are given similar property, no election is necessary. Postponement of tax on the gain is required. For example, the city condemns a store building and gives you another store building the value of which exceeds the cost basis of the old one; gain is not taxed.

Partnerships. The election to defer gain must be made at the partnership level. Individual partners may not make separate elections unless the partnership has terminated, with all partnership affairs wound up. Dissolution under state law is not a termination for tax purposes.

18.21 Time Period for Buying Replacement Property

To defer tax, you generally must buy property similar or related in use *(18.22)* to the converted property within a fixed time period. The replacement period is either two, three, or four years:

1. A two-year replacement period applies for destroyed, damaged, or stolen property, whether used for business, investment, or personal purposes, but *see 18.2* for the four-year period for principal residences in Presidentially declared disaster areas.

   A two-year period also applies to condemned property other than business or investment real estate eligible for the three-year replacement period.

2. A three-year replacement period applies for condemned business or investment real estate, excluding inventory. However, the two-year and not the three-year period applies if the condemned business or investment real estate is replaced by your acquiring control of a corporation that owns the replacement property.

3. A four-year replacement period applies for a principal residence damaged in a Presidentially declared disaster; *see 18.2.*

The two-year period for damaged, destroyed, and stolen property *starts* on the date the property was destroyed, damaged, or stolen, and *ends* two years after the end of the year in which you realize a gain.

For condemnations, the two-year or three-year (investment or non-inventory business real estate) replacement period *starts* on the earlier of (1) the date you receive notification of the condemnation threat, and (2) the date you dispose of the condemned property. The period *ends* two or three years after the end of the year in which gain on the condemnation is realized.

The four-year replacement period *starts* on the date the residence is involuntarily converted and *ends* four years after the end of the first taxable year in which any part of the gain is realized. *See 18.2* for an example of the four-year replacement rule.

Caution

Nullifying Deferral Election on Amended Return

If you elect to defer tax on a gain, intending to buy replacement property, but you fail to make a replacement within the time limit, you must file an amended return for the year of the gain and pay the tax that you had elected to defer. You also must file an amended return and report the gain not eligible for deferral if you invest in property that does not qualify as a replacement, or which costs less than the amount realized from the involuntary conversion.

However, if you elect to defer and make a timely qualifying replacement, you may not change your mind and pay tax on the gain in order to obtain a higher basis *(18.19)* for the replacement property. The Tax Court has agreed with the IRS that the election to defer is irrevocable once a qualified replacement is made within the time limits. Similarly, once you report to the IRS *(18.21)* that a qualified replacement has been made, you may not substitute other replacement property, even if the replacement period has not yet expired.

EXAMPLES

1. On January 10, 1996, a parcel of investment real estate is condemned; the parcel cost $15,000. On February 27, 1996, you received a check for $23,500 from the state. You may defer the tax on the gain of $8,500 if you invest at least $23,500 in other real estate not later than December 31, 1999, the end of the three-year replacement period.

2. Business property was contaminated by dangerous chemicals, and after the Environmental Protection Agency ordered businesses and residents to relocate, the property was sold to the local government under a threat of condemnation. The owner was paid the full pre-contamination fair market value for the property. The owner wanted to defer gain under the three-year replacement rule for condemnations. However, the IRS said that part of the gain was deferrable under the two-year rule and part under the three-year rule. There were two conversions: (1) the contamination, subject to the two-year replacement rule; and (2) the later condemnation, subject to the three-year rule.

   To determine the amount eligible for deferral for each period, an allocation must be made between the proceeds allocable to the destruction of the property and the proceeds allocable to the condemnation.

   According to the IRS, the burden for making the allocation between the two conversions rests with the owner. The government's payments are allocable to the condemnation and, therefore, eligible for the three-year replacement rule, only to the extent of the post-contamination value. Practically speaking, it may be advisable to make the replacement within the two-year period, as it may be difficult to show the contaminated land had any value after the contamination.

Advance payment of award. Gain is realized in the year compensation for the converted property exceeds the basis of the converted property. An advance payment of an award which exceeds the adjusted basis of the property starts the running of the replacement period.

An award is treated as received in the year that it is made available to you without restrictions, even if you contest the amount.

Replacement before actual condemnation.   You may make a replacement after a threat of condemnation. If you buy property before the actual threat, it will not qualify as a replacement even though you still own it at the time of the actual condemnation.

Replacement by an estate.   A person whose property was involuntarily converted may die before he or she makes a replacement. According to the IRS, his or her estate may not reinvest the proceeds within the allowed time and postpone tax on the gain. The Tax Court rejects the IRS position and has allowed tax deferral where the replacement was made by the deceased owner's estate. However, the Tax Court agreed with the IRS that a surviving spouse's investment in land did not defer tax on gain realized by her deceased husband on an involuntary conversion of his land. She had received his property as survivor of joint tenancy and could not, in making the investment, be considered as acting for his estate.

Giving IRS notice of replacement.   If you have not bought replacement property by the time you file your return for the year of the involuntary conversion but you intend to do so, attach a statement to your return describing the conversion and the computation of gain, and state that you intend to make a timely replacement. Then, on the return for the year of replacement, attach a statement giving the details of your replacement property. This notice starts the running of the period of limitations for any tax on the gain. Failure to give notice keeps the period open. Similarly, a failure to give notice of an intention not to replace also keeps the period open. When you do not buy replacement property after making an election to postpone tax on the gain, file an amended return for the year in which gain was realized and pay the tax (if any) on the gain.

Assume you have a gain from an involuntary conversion and do not expect to reinvest the proceeds. You report the gain and pay the tax. In a later year, but within the prescribed time limits, you buy similar property. You may make an election to defer tax on the gain and file a claim for tax refund.

18.22 Types of Qualifying Replacement Property

Although exact duplication is not required, the replacement generally must be *similar or related in use* to the property that was involuntarily converted in order to defer tax. Where *real property* held for productive use in a business or for investment is converted through a *condemnation* or threat of condemnation, the replacement test is more liberal. A replacement merely has to be of a *like kind* to the converted property. Under the *like-kind* test, the replacement of improved property by unimproved property qualifies; *see 6.1.*

Under the *related-use* test, the replacement of unimproved land for improved land does not qualify. Under the *related-use* test, a replacement generally must be closely related in function to the destroyed property. For example, a condemned personal residence must be replaced with another personal residence. The replacement of a house rented to a tenant with a house used as a personal residence does not qualify for tax deferral; the new house is not being used for the same purpose as the condemned one. This functional test, however, is not strictly applied to conversions of rental property. Here, the role of the owner toward the properties, rather than the functional use of the buildings, is reviewed. If an owner held both properties as investments and offered similar services and took similar business risks in both, the replacement may qualify.

You may own several parcels of property, one of which is condemned. You may want to use the condemnation award to make improvements on the other land such as drainage and grading. The IRS generally will not accept the improvements as a qualified replacement. However, an appeals court has rejected the IRS approach in one case.

If it is not feasible to reinvest the proceeds from the conversion of livestock because of soil contamination or other environmental contamination, then other property (including real property) used for farming purposes is treated as similar or related and qualifies as replacement property.

Buying controlling interest in a corporation.   The replacement test may be satisfied by purchasing a controlling interest (80%) in a corporation owning property that is similar or related in service to the converted property.

Business and investment property in a disaster area.   The similar or related-use tests do not have to be met when replacing business or investment property damaged or destroyed in a Presidentially declared disaster area. You may make a qualified replacement by buying any tangible property held for business use. This rule applies retroactively for disaster declarations made after December 31, 1994, in taxable years ending after that date.

Planning Reminder

Extension of Time To Replace

A contract to buy replacement property within the time limits is not considered to qualified replacement. If you cannot replace property within the time required, ask your local District Director for additional time. Apply for an extension before the end of the period. If you apply for an extension within a reasonable time after the statutory period has run out, you must have a reasonable cause for the delay in asking for the extension.

Law Alert

Buying a Replacement From a Relative

Under a new law, buying a replacement from a close relative or a related business organization may not qualify unless the gain on the conversion is $100,000 or less. This rule applies to involuntary conversions occurring after June 8, 1997. Affected related parties are the same as defined for loss transactions discussed at 5.6.

18.23 Cost of Replacement Property Determines Postponed Gain

To fully defer tax, the cost of the replacement property must be equal to or exceed the *net proceeds* from the conversion. If replacement cost is less than the adjusted basis of the converted property, you report the entire gain. If replacement cost is less than the amount realized on the conversion but more than the basis of the converted property, the difference between the amount realized and the cost of the replacement is reported as gain; you may elect to postpone tax on the balance of the gain. *See* Examples 1–3 below.

Condemnation award. The award received from a state authority may be reduced by expenses of getting the award such as legal, engineering, and appraisal fees. The treatment of special assessments and severance damages received when part of your property is condemned is explained at 18.24. Payments made directly by the authority to your mortgagee may not be deducted from the gross award.

Do not include as part of the award interest paid on the award for delay in its payment; you report the interest as interest income. The IRS may treat as interest part of an award paid late, even though the award does not make any allocation for interest.

Relocation payments are not considered part of the condemnation award and are not treated as taxable income to the extent that they are spent for purposes of relocation; they increase basis of the newly acquired property.

Distinguish between insurance proceeds compensating you for loss of profits because of business interruption and those compensating you for the loss of property. Business interruption proceeds are fully taxed as ordinary income and may not be treated as proceeds of an involuntary conversion.

A single standard fire insurance policy may cover several assets. Assume a fire occurs, and in a settlement the proceeds are allocated to each destroyed item according to its fair market value before the fire. In comparing the allocated proceeds to the tax basis of each item, you find that on some items, you have realized a gain; that is, the proceeds exceed basis. On the other items, you have a loss; the proceeds are less than basis. According to the IRS, you may elect to defer tax on the gain items by buying replacement property. You do not treat the proceeds paid under the single policy as a unit, but as separate payments made for each covered item.

EXAMPLES

1. The cost basis of your four-family apartment house is $175,000. It is condemned to make way for a thruway. The net award from the state is $200,000. Your gain is $25,000. If you buy a similar apartment house for $175,000 or less, you report the entire $25,000 gain.

2. Using the same figures as in Example 1, except that you buy an apartment house for $185,000. Of the gain of $25,000, you report $15,000 as taxable gain ($200,000 – $185,000). You may elect to postpone the tax on the balance of the gain, or $10,000.

3. Using the same figures as in Example 1, but you buy an apartment house for $200,000. You may elect to postpone tax on the entire gain because you have invested all of the award in replacement property.

18.24 Special Assessments and Severance Damages

When only part of a property parcel is *condemned* for a public improvement, the condemning authority may:

1. Levy a special assessment against the remaining property, claiming that it is benefited by the improvement. The authority usually deducts the assessment from the condemnation award.
2. Grant an award for severance damages if the condemnation of part of your property causes a loss in value or damage to the remaining property which you keep.

Special assessments reduce the amount of the gross condemnation award. If they exceed the award, the excess is added to the basis of the property. An assessment levied after the award is made may not be deducted from the award.

EXAMPLE

Two acres of a 10-acre tract are condemned for a new highway. The adjusted basis of the land is $30,000, or $3,000 per acre. The condemnation award is $10,000; the special assessment against the remaining eight acres is $2,500. The net gain on the condemnation is $1,500:

Condemnation award		$10,000
Less:		
Basis of two condemned acres	$6,000	
Special assessment	2,500	8,500
Net gain		$1,500

When both the condemnation award and severance damages are received, the condemnation is treated as two separate involuntary conversions: (1) A conversion of the condemned land. Here, the condemnation award is applied against the basis of the condemned land to determine gain or loss on its conversion. And (2) a conversion of part of the remaining land in the sense that its utility has been reduced by condemnation, for which severance damages are paid.

Net severance damages reduce the basis of the retained property. Net severance damages are the total severance damages, reduced by expenses in obtaining the damages and by any special assessment withheld from the condemnation award. If the damages exceed basis, gain is realized. Tax may be deferred on the gain through the purchase of replacement property under the "similar or related in use test" at *18.22,* such as adjacent land or restoration of the property to its original condition.

Allocating the proceeds between the condemnation award and severance damages will either reduce the gain or increase the loss realized on the condemned land. The IRS will allow such a division only when the condemnation authority specifically identifies part of the award as severance damage in the contract or in an itemized statement or closing sheet. The Tax Court, however, has allowed an allocation in the absence of earmarking where the state considered severance damages, and the value of the condemned land was small in comparison to the damages suffered by the remaining property. To avoid a dispute with the IRS, make sure the authority makes this breakdown. Without such identification, the IRS will treat the entire proceeds as consideration for the condemned property.

18.25 Reporting Gains From Casualties

If an involuntary conversion was the result of a *theft* or *casualty,* you have to prepare Form 4684. To report net gains, Form 4684 will direct you to Form 1040, Schedule D, or Form 4797, depending on the type of property involved. Generally, use of Form 4797 reflects the netting requirements for involuntary conversions of business, rental, or royalty property under Section 1231; *see 44.8.*

If the conversion occurred because of a *condemnation,* you use Form 4797 for business or investment property and Schedule D for personal-use property.

Chapter 19

Deducting Job Costs and Other Miscellaneous Expenses

Deductible miscellaneous expenses cover a wide and varied range of items, such as employee travel and entertainment expenses, work clothes expenses, union and employee professional dues, investment expenses, legal expenses, tax preparation expenses, and educational expenses. They also share a common limitation: the 2% adjusted gross income (AGI) floor. If your expenses do not exceed this floor, you may not deduct them. If the expenses exceed the floor, only the excess is deductible on Schedule A, as explained in *19.1*. Some job-related deductions, such as moving expenses and impairment-related work expenses, are not subject to the 2% AGI floor.

In addition to the 2% AGI floor, employees who incur unreimbursed meal and entertainment costs face this further restriction: Only 50% of meal and entertainment costs are deductible.

Miscellaneous deductions, except for gambling losses, are subject to the 3% reduction to itemized deductions *(13.7)* if your adjusted gross income exceeds $121,200 ($60,600 if you are married and file separate returns).

Miscellaneous Expenses on Schedule A

19.1 2% AGI Floor Reduces Miscellaneous Deductions

A floor of 2% of adjusted gross income (AGI) applies to the total of most miscellaneous deductions that are claimed on Schedule A of Form 1040. AGI is the amount on Line 32 of Form 1040. The purpose of the floor is to reduce or eliminate such deductions. Only expenses above the floor are deductible.

If your 1997 AGI exceeds $121,200, or $60,600 if married filing separately, deductible miscellaneous expenses (after applying the 2% AGI floor) are then subject to a further reduction under the 3% reduction computation discussed at *13.7*.

Miscellaneous expenses subject to the 2% AGI floor:

- Unreimbursed travel, meals, and entertainment expenses of employees, *20.1* and *20.31*
- Reimbursed job expenses or expense allowances under nonaccountable plans, *20.32*
- Union dues, *19.5*
- Professional and business association dues, *19.5*
- Work clothes expenses, *19.6*
- Cost of looking for a new job, *19.7*
- Job agency fees, *19.7*
- Tax advice and preparation fees, *19.25*
- Appraisal fees related to casualty losses and charitable property contributions, *19.25*
- Investment expenses, such as IRA custodial fees, safe deposit rentals, and fees to investment counselors, *19.24*
- Employee home office expenses, *19.13*
- Legal fees, *19.26*
- Education costs, *19.15*

Miscellaneous expenses not subject to the 2% AGI floor:

- Moving expenses to a new job location, Chapter 12
- Impairment-related work expenses for handicapped employees, *19.4*
- Gambling losses up to gambling income, *11.3*
- Estate tax attributable to income in respect of a decedent, *11.17*
- The deduction for repayment of amounts held under a claim of right, *2.9*
- Amortizable bond premium on bonds purchased before October 23, 1986, *4.17*
- Unrecovered investments in pension on deceased retiree's final return, *7.22*
- Jury duty fees turned over to employer, *12.2*

EXAMPLES

1. You pay union dues of $280, work clothes costs of $300, and $150 for the preparation of your tax return. Your adjusted gross income (AGI) is $25,000. Your miscellaneous deduction on Schedule A after applying the 2% floor is $230:

Union dues	$280
Work clothes	300
Tax preparation	150
	$730
Less: 2% of $25,000	500
Deductible amount	$230

2. Your adjusted gross income (AGI) is $90,000. You pay the following deductible miscellaneous expenses:

Professional dues	$100
Investment counsel fee	300
Safe deposit box	50
Tax preparation fee	500
Unreimbursed travel expenses	800
	$1,750

   Since the 2% floor of $1,800 (2% × $90,000) exceeds your miscellaneous expenses, none of the expenses are deductible.

19.2 Effect of 2% AGI Floor on Deductions

The table below shows the effect of the 2% AGI floor on miscellaneous deductible expenses. A higher bracket taxpayer may also be subject to the 3% reduction to itemized deductions discussed at 13.7.

If your adjusted gross income (AGI) is—	Miscellaneous expenses must exceed this amount for a deduction—
$10,000	$200
20,000	400
30,000	600
40,000	800
50,000	1,000
60,000	1,200
70,000	1,400
80,000	1,600
90,000	1,800
100,000	2,000
200,000	4,000

19.3 Checklist of Job Expenses Subject to the 2% AGI Floor

The following expenses that are job related—ranging from professional dues and subscriptions to employment agency fees—are subject to the 2% AGI floor and so you may be unable to deduct them; *see 19.2*. Generally, you must file Form 2106 to claim job-related expenses that were not reimbursed by your employer. You enter your expenses and any reimbursements on Form 2106, and the allowable amount is then transferred to Line 20 of Schedule A (unreimbursed employee expenses), where it is subject to the 2% AGI floor along with other miscellaneous deductions; *see 19.1*. If you are using the standard mileage rate of 31.5 cents per mile *(43.1)* for 1997 vehicle expenses, and you were not reimbursed by your employer for any job expenses, you may file Form 2106-EZ.

You may enter your unreimbursed expenses directly on Line 20 of Schedule A without having to complete Form 2106 or Form 2106-EZ if you are not claiming any job-related travel, local transportation, meal, or entertainment expenses and you received no employer reimbursement at all for any of your other job costs (such as education expenses, union dues, or uniforms).

 Filing Tip

Life Insurance Agents and Food Deliverers

Statutory employees, such as full-time life insurance salespersons, may deduct expenses on Schedule C and so avoid the 2% AGI floor; *see 40.5* for further details.

Agency fees for job, *19.7*
Airfares, *20.5*
Auto club membership, *43.2*
Auto expenses, *43.1*
Books used on the job, *19.5*
Bond costs, *19.24*
Car insurance premiums, *43.2*
Cleaning costs, *19.6*
Commerce association dues, *19.5*
Commuting costs, *20.2*
Computers, *19.9*
Convention trips, *20.12, 20.14*
Correspondence course, *19.16*
Depreciation, *42.1*
Dues, *19.5*
Educational expenses, *19.15–19.23*
Employment agency fees, *19.7*
Entertainment expenses, *20.15–20.27*
Equipment, *19.9–19.11*
Foreign travel costs, *20.11, 20.14*
Furniture, *19.13, 12.7*
Garage rent, *43.2*
Gasoline, *43.2*
Gasoline taxes, *43.2*

Gifts, *20.25*
Home office expenses, *19.13*
Hotel costs, *20.5*
House-hunting costs, *12.7*
Instruments, *19.11*
Labor union dues, *19.5*
Laundry, *19.6*
Legal expenses, *19.26*
Local transportation, *20.1*
Lodging, *20.5*
Magazines, *19.5*
Malpractice liability premiums, *40.5*
Meals, *20.3, 20.4*
Medical examinations, *17.2*
Membership dues and fees, *19.5*
Motel charges, *20.5*
Moving expenses, *12.7*
Parking fees, *43.2*
Passport fees for business travel, *20.11*
Pay turned over to employer, *2.9*
Periodicals, *19.5*
Protective clothing, *19.6*
Rail fares, *20.5*
Reimbursed expenses, *20.30–20.34*

Safety helmets, *19.6*
Safety shoes, *19.6*
Secretarial convention, *20.12*
Subscriptions, *19.5*
Taxi fares, *20.5*
Telegrams, *19.14*
Telephone calls, *19.14*
Toll charges, *43.2*
Tools, *19.11*
Trade association dues, *19.5*
Transportation and travel expenses, *20.1*
Tuition, *19.15–19.23*
Typewriter, *19.10*
Uniforms, *19.6*
Union dues, *19.5*
Work clothes, *19.6*

19.4 Job Expenses Not Subject to the 2% AGI Floor

Impairment-related work expenses. Unreimbursed impairment-related work expenses are reported on Form 2106 (or Form 2106-EZ where eligible) and then the unreimbursed portion is entered on Line 27 of Schedule A as a miscellaneous itemized deduction that is *not* subject to the 2% AGI floor. You have to show:

1. You are handicapped. A handicapped person must have a physical or mental disability which results in a functional limitation to employment or which substantially limits one or more major life activities. Generally, showing blindness or deafness will meet this test, but other disabilities that impair your ability to walk, speak, breathe, or perform manual tasks also may qualify if they limit the ability to work.
2. You incur the expenses in order to work. The expenses must be ordinary and necessary to allow you to work. Attendant care services at a place of employment which are necessary for you to work are also deductible.

Expenses of performing artists. As a performing artist, you may deduct job expenses from gross income, whether or not itemized deductions are claimed, *see 12.2*.

You report the performing artist expenses on Form 2106 (or Form 2106-EZ where eligible) and enter the total as a "write-in amount" on Line 31 of Form 1040, instead of on Schedule A. Write "QPA" next to Line 31. If you do not meet the tests, the expenses are deducted on Schedule A subject to the 2% AGI floor.

Moving expenses. Moving expenses to a new job location are not subject to the 2% AGI floor; *see 12.3*.

19.5 Dues and Subscriptions

You may deduct as miscellaneous itemized deductions, subject to the 2% AGI floor on Schedule A, dues paid to a:

- Professional society if you are a salaried lawyer, accountant, teacher, physician, or other professional
- Trade association if it is conducted for the purpose of furthering the business interests of its members
- Stock exchange if you are a securities dealer
- Community "booster" club conducted to attract tourists and settlers to the locality where the members do business
- Chamber of Commerce if it is conducted to advance the business interests of its members

Union costs. Union members may deduct as "miscellaneous" itemized deductions, union dues, and initiation fees. Similarly, non-union employees may deduct monthly service charges to a union. An assessment paid for unemployment benefits is deductible if payment is required as a condition of remaining in the union and holding a union job. Voluntary payments to a union unemployment benefit or strike fund are not deductible.

No deduction is allowed for mandatory contributions to a union pension fund applied toward the purchase of a retirement annuity; the contributions are treated as the cost of the annuity. Furthermore, to the extent that an assessment covers sick, accident, or death benefits payable to you or your family, it is not deductible. Similarly, an assessment for a construction fund to build union recreation centers was disallowed by the Tax Court, even though the payment was required for keeping the job.

Campaign costs for running for union office are not deductible.

Subscriptions. Subject to the 2% AGI floor, you may claim as miscellaneous itemized deductions unreimbursed payments for job-related subscriptions to professional journals and trade magazines.

19.6 Uniforms and Work Clothes

The cost of uniforms and other apparel, including their cleaning, laundering, and repair, is deductible *only* if the clothes are:

1. Required to keep your job; *and*
2. Not suitable for wear when not working.

The deduction is subject to the 2% AGI floor.

Special work clothes. Courts have held that the cost of special work clothes that protect you from injury is deductible even if you are not required to wear them to keep your job. However, you may not deduct the cost of special clothing, such as aprons and overalls, which protect your regular street clothing. Nor may you deduct the cost of ordinary clothes used as work clothes on the grounds that: (1) they get harder use than customary garments receive; (2) they are soiled after a day's work and cannot be worn socially; or (3) they were purchased for your convenience to save wear and tear on your better clothes. For example, a sanitation inspector, a machinist's helper, a carpenter, and a telephone repairman were not allowed to deduct the cost of their work clothes.

Employer allowance. An allowance paid by your employer for work clothes or a uniform is not reported as income, unless you do not substantiate the expenses to your employer. If you do substantiate the expenses, those exceeding the reimbursement are reported on Form 2106, and the deduction is subject to the 2% AGI floor; *see 20.30.*

High-fashion work clothes. That your job requires you to wear expensive clothing is not a basis for deducting the cost of the clothes if the clothing is suitable for wear off the job.

Deductions allowed. Deductions for costs of uniforms and work clothes have been allowed to:

Airline pilot
Bakery salesperson—for a uniform
   with a company label
Baseball player
Bus driver
Cement finisher for gloves, over-
   shoes, and rubber boots
Civilian faculty members of a military school
Commercial fisherman for protec-
   tive clothing, such as oil cloths,
   gloves, and boots
Dairy worker for rubber boots,
   white shirts, trousers, and cap
   worn only while inside the dairy
Entertainer for theatrical clothing
   used solely for performances
Exotic dancer for breast implants
   used as a "stage prop" essential
   to her business; *see* Example 8 in *19.8*
Factory foreman for white coat
   bearing the word "foreman" and
   the name of the company

Factory worker for safety shoes
Firefighter
Hospital attendant for work
   clothes; he came in con-
   tact with patients having
   contagious diseases
Jockey
Letter carrier
Meat cutter for special
   white shoes
Musician for formal wear
Paint machine operator for
   high top shoes and long
   leather gloves
Plumber for special shoes
   and gloves
Police officer
Railroad conductor
Railroad firefighter for
   boots, leather gloves,
   raincoat, caps, and work
   gloves

Filing Tip

Cleaning and Laundering

If you are allowed to deduct the cost of work clothes and uniforms, you also may deduct the cost of cleaning and laundering them. Also, courts have allowed the cost of cleaning and laundering in situations where:

- The clothes could only be worn one day at a time because they became too dirty.
- Dirty clothes were a hazard; they became baggy and might have gotten caught in machinery.
- Clothes were worn only at work and a place for changing clothes was provided by the employer.
- A meat cutter had to wear clean work clothes at all times.

EXAMPLES

1. A painter may not deduct the cost of work clothing consisting of a white cap, a white shirt, white bib overalls, and standard work shoes. The clothing is not distinctive in character as a uniform would be. That his union requires him to wear such clothing does not make it a deductible expense.

2. A tennis pro who taught at private clubs was not allowed to deduct the cost of tennis outfits or shoes required for his job. He did not wear them outside of work and argued that he replaced the shoes every few weeks to reduce the chances of injury. However, the Tax Court upheld the IRS's disallowance of his deductions because the clothes and shoes are suitable for everyday wear; warm-up suits and tennis clothes are fashionable and frequently worn as casual wear. Furthermore, there was no evidence that his tennis shoes reduced chances of injury.

Your claim of a work clothes deduction is helped if your employer requires you to wear a uniform. Uniform costs of reservists and service persons are discussed at 35.8.

19.7 Expenses of Looking for a New Job

You may deduct expenses of looking for a new job in the *same line of work,* whether or not a new job is found. The deduction is subject to the 2% AGI floor. If you are unemployed when seeking a new job, and the period of unemployment has been substantial, the IRS may disallow the deduction.

EXAMPLE

The IRS disallowed the driving expenses of an unemployed secretary on the ground that she was not currently employed. The Tax Court disagreed and held that for purposes of deducting job-hunting expenses, she could still be considered in the business of being a secretary. She had worked as an administrative secretary with Toyota in San Francisco. The firm relocated, resulting in a 100- mile-per-day commute. She quit her job at the end of January 1984. From February to November 1984, she drove her Cadillac El Dorado over 4,600 miles looking for a new job. The Tax Court allowed her a depreciation deduction of $2,880 and $981 for car operating costs.

Expenses of seeking your *first job* are not deductible, even if a job is obtained. Also, expenses of looking for a job in a different line of work are not deductible, even if you get the job.

The IRS may also dispute the deduction of search expenses of a previously employed professional who forms a partnership.

EXAMPLE

A CPA working for a firm decided to go out on his own. After a period of investigation, he formed a partnership with another CPA. The IRS disallowed his deduction of search expenses, claiming his expenses were incurred in a new business. As an employee he was in a different business than that of a self-employed practitioner. Thus, the expenses should be capitalized as a cost of setting up or organizing the partnership. The Tax Court disagreed, allowing the deduction. The travel expenses were incurred to seek work as a CPA, whether as a self-employed or employed CPA.

Travel expenses. If you travel to find a new job in the same line of work, such as an interview in a distant city, you may deduct travel expenses, including living costs. If, during the trip, you also do personal visiting, you may deduct the transportation expenses if the trip was primarily related to your job search. Time spent on personal activity is compared with time spent looking for a job to determine the primary purpose of the trip. If the transportation expenses to and from the destination are not deductible, you may still deduct the expenses of seeking a new job while you are away.

Are you between jobs? If you are between jobs and you continue to see and entertain your former customers, the IRS holds that you may not deduct the cost of entertainment and other business expenses during this period on the ground that you are not in business and earning income. However, the Tax Court in the following case allowed the deduction.

EXAMPLE

Haft was a successful jewelry salesman earning as much as $60,000 a year. In the fall of one year, he left his employer and started to look for a new connection. During the following year, he continued to maintain contacts with his former customers by entertaining buyers and their representatives. He deducted the expenses of entertaining and other business costs. The IRS disallowed the deduction, claiming he was not in business. The court disagreed. His lack of business income was temporary and resulted from a period of transition which lasted a reasonable time.

 Filing Tip

Employment Agency Fee

If your new employer pays the fee under an agreement with an agency, you may disregard the payment for tax purposes. However, if you pay the fee and deduct it as a job search expense and in a later year you are reimbursed by your employer, you must report the reimbursement as taxable income to the extent you received a tax benefit from the earlier deduction; see 11.6.

A company interested in your services may invite you to a job interview and agree to pay all of the trip expenses to its office, even if you are not hired. The company payment is tax free up to your actual expenses.

19.8 Unusual Job Expenses

The following are not typical deductible expenses. However, deductions in the following cases have been allowed.

EXAMPLES

1. *Shoeshine expense of a pilot.* Company rules required a commercial airline pilot to look neat, keep his hair cut, and wear conservative black shoes, properly shined. The pilot deducted as a business expense $100 for his haircuts and $25 for his shoe shines. The IRS disallowed the deductions, but the Tax Court allowed the cost of the shoe shines. The shoes were of a military type which he wore only with his pilot's uniform. The cost of keeping up a uniform is deductible. The haircuts were merely nondeductible personal expenses.

2. *Depreciation on furnishings bought by executive for his company office.* Following a quarrel with an interior decorator, a sales manager bought his own office furniture when his firm moved to new quarters. Rather than complain or ask for reimbursement, he footed the bill and deducted depreciation. The IRS disallowed the deduction, claiming the expense was that of his company. The Tax Court allowed the deduction. The manager's action was unusual, but prudent. He did not want to cause difficulties, and at the same time had to maintain his image as a successful manager. His expenses for furniture were appropriate and helpful.

3. *Salesman's cost of operating a private plane.* Sherman flew his own plane to visit clients in six southern states and deducted $18,000 as operating costs of the plane. The IRS disallowed the deduction, claiming there was no business reason for the plane. He could have taken commercial flights or used a company car to reach his clients. Furthermore, his company did not reimburse him for the private airplane costs, although it would cover costs of his car and commercial air travel. Finally, the amount of airplane expenses was unreasonable compared to his salary of $25,000. Sherman convinced the Tax Court that use of a private airplane was the only reasonable way he could cover his six-state sales area. He showed that most of his clients were not near commercial airports. Although the airplane costs were large in relation to his salary, they were still reasonable and, therefore, deductible.

4. *Executive's purchase of blazers for sales force.* Jetty, the president of an oil equipment manufacturing firm, thought that he could generate goodwill for the company if employees who attended industrial trade shows wore a blazer and vest set in the company colors. He personally paid and deducted $6,725 for 27 blazers and vests. The IRS disallowed the deduction on the grounds that it was a company expense and that Jetty should have sought reimbursement from the company.

   The Tax Court allowed the deduction. Paying for the clothes was a legitimate business expense for Jetty since he depended on bonuses for a large portion of his pay, and, as company president, he had responsibility for seeing to it that there were profits to share in. Furthermore, the outlay was not the type of expense covered by the company's manual on expense reimbursements.

5. *Repayment of layoff benefits to restore pension credit.* When he was laid off, an employee received a lump-sum payment from his company based on his salary and years of service. When he was rehired a year later, he repaid the lump sum in order to restore his pension credits and other benefit rights. The IRS ruled that he may deduct the repayment as a condition of being rehired; the repayment was required to restore employee benefits.

6. *Teaching supplies.* The IRS does not allow teachers a deduction for school supplies. Some courts have been lenient and have allowed teachers to deduct out-of-pocket expenses. In one case, however, a teacher could not convince a court that his deduction for the cost of paper, pens, glue, and other supplies was a business expense. He could not support his claim that the school did not supply enough equipment.

7. *Politician's expenses.* Elected officials may incur out-of-pocket expenses in excess of the allowances received from the government. They may deduct as miscellaneous deductions their payment of office expenses such as salaries, office rent, and supplies. Part-time officials may claim the deduction. The expenses are deductible even if they exceed the official's income.

8. *Depreciation for exotic dancer's breast implants.* Hess, an exotic dancer, enlarged her breasts to the abnormal size of 56N and claimed a $2,088 depreciation deduction for their cost. The IRS disallowed the deduction claiming that cosmetic surgery is a personal expense. The Tax Court disagreed. Hess's expenses were incurred solely in furtherance of her business and not for her own personal benefit. The breast implants were not of the kind that women usually get to enhance their appearance. Rather, Hess enlarged her breasts to a "freakish" size to substantially increase her annual income, which she did. The court also compared the implants to special work clothes *(19.6)*, required for a job and not for personal wear. As an exotic dancer, Hess's large breasts are like a "costume" needed to keep her job. Although she could not remove them daily, she would have, if possible, because they caused her serious medical problems.

Computers, Phones, and Home Office Costs of Employees

19.9 Computers and Cellular Phones

Computers (and peripherals) and cellular phones are treated as "listed property" subject to deduction restrictions: To get a first-year expensing deduction *(42.3)* or to claim any type of depreciation, the computer or cellular phone must be used for the convenience of your employer and also be required as a condition of your job. The IRS strictly interprets these requirements.

Computer. A letter from your employer stating that a computer is needed for your position does not by itself satisfy the deduction tests. Even where your employer encourages use of a personal computer that is used for basic job requirements, the IRS requires proof that you need your own computer to do your job because your employer does not provide one, or because the computer supplied by your employer is not adequate for your job. In the following Examples, the IRS disallowed depreciation writeoffs.

EXAMPLES
1. An electric company offers to help pay for its engineers' personal computers where they will improve productivity. Qualifying engineers receive extra pay and must buy a computer meeting company specifications, take approved computer courses, and agree to restrictions on resale of the computer. An engineer buys a computer and uses it 95% of the time for writing business memos and reports, and studying business flow charts. He does not use the computer for entertainment.

    The IRS held that although the engineer's computer was work related and benefited his employer, buying a computer was not required for his job; it was not "inextricably related" to proper job performance. Further, his participation in the employer's computer program was optional, not mandatory.

2. A professor of nursing, trying to keep her temporary position, bought a personal computer, needing a word processor for independent research papers and to document her qualifications for research grants. The research and external grant support were implied university requirements for faculty appointments. She did not have access to university word-processing equipment during regular work hours; and because of her classroom responsibilities, her research and grant development work had to be done on her own time. To help her pursue outside grants, the university bought her a "modem" that allowed a phone hook-up with its computer at night. Her computer was used 100% for research and grant work.

    As in Example 1, the IRS held that use of the computer was not "inextricably related" to proper job performance and did not qualify for a depreciation writeoff. Furthermore, there was no evidence that employees who did not use computers were professionally disadvantaged.

3. The IRS held that an insurance agent could not deduct depreciation for a laptop computer he used to help develop insurance plans for clients. The insurance company encouraged its agents to buy the computer because office computers were not generally accessible. According to the IRS, it is not enough that the agent's productivity increased or that he used the computer solely for business. Purchasing the computer was optional, not a mandatory job requirement. Employees who did not purchase computers were not professionally disadvantaged.

Court Decision

Tax Court Allows Computer Deduction

The Tax Court allowed a first-year expensing deduction to a working couple who used the same home computer given these facts: The husband, a professor, used it to store historical data; the wife, a state transportation planner, used it to do extensive number crunching. What apparently won the decision for the couple was evidence that (1) the husband did not have access to a computer at the university, and (2) the state office in which the wife worked did not have funds to buy a computer. The court held that the use of the computer was necessary for them to properly do their jobs, and as the purchase of a computer spared their employers from having to provide them with computers, the purchase was for the employers' convenience.

In a later case, a telemarketing sales manager was allowed a first-year expensing deduction for a home computer and printer used to prepare reports. The key to winning the deduction was her supervisor's testimony that as a mid-level manager, she could not enter the office after regular hours to use a company computer, and that she was able to keep up with the volume of sales reports she was required to submit by using her home computer and accessing information via modem.

> 4. The IRS barred a third-grade teacher from deducting the cost of a Macintosh computer because it was not *required* for her job. She bought the computer using an interest-free loan from the school after the school decided that report cards and student evaluations would have to be prepared on a Macintosh instead of being written. The Tax Court and an appeals court sided with the IRS. It may have been convenient for the teacher to use a home computer but it was not required. Other teachers were able to timely complete their duties using school computers.

Cellular phones. The IRS has not released specific guidelines or rulings covering deduction requirements for cellular phones. In general, the "convenience of the employer" and "job condition" tests apply.

Claiming a deduction. If you can meet the "convenience of the employer" and "job condition" tests for a computer or cellular phone purchased in 1997, and you have records to prove that the unit is used more than 50% of the time for your job, you may write off up to $18,000 of the cost under the first-year expensing rules; *see 42.3* or regular five-year MACRS depreciation rates may be used; *see 42.10.* If business use of the unit is 50% or less, you may not use first-year expensing or regular MACRS but you may claim straight-line depreciation.

First-year expensing or depreciation is claimed on Form 4562 and then entered on Form 2106 or Form 2106-EZ along with other job-related costs. The deduction from Form 2106 or Form 2106-EZ is subject to the 2% AGI floor for miscellaneous deductions on Schedule A; *see 19.1.* If business use in a later year is 50% or less, *see 42.10* for recapture rules.

You need to keep records documenting your percentage of business use for a computer or cellular phone.

19.10 Calculators, Copiers, Fax Machines, and Typewriters

The listed property requirements applied to computers and cellular phones *(19.9)* do not apply to calculators, copiers, fax machines, adding machines, and typewriters. This means that the restrictive convenience of the employer and job condition rules do not apply. However, to depreciate the cost of such equipment, you should be ready to prove that you need the equipment for your job, and keep a record of the time it is used for business. To claim first-year expensing *(42.3)*, rather than regular depreciation, you must use the equipment *more* than 50% of the time for business.

19.11 Small Tools

If you furnished your own small tools used on your job, you may deduct their cost if they are not expected to last beyond a year. The deduction is subject to the 2% AGI floor. The cost of tools with a useful life of more than a year must be recovered through depreciation or first-year expensing; *see 42.3.* Be prepared to substantiate your deduction with receipts showing the cost and type of tools purchased, and the business necessity for them.

19.12 Automobile Used for Work

If you buy a car that you use for work, you generally may claim the IRS mileage allowance or deduct actual unreimbursed expenses on Form 2106. If you claim actual expenses, you are allowed to deduct depreciation only if use of the car is required for the job and for the convenience of the employer. For a car bought in 1997, the maximum depreciation deduction is $3,160, reduced by the percentage of personal use.

The IRS standard mileage allowance is discussed at *43.1.*

Depreciation rules, including annual deduction limits, are at *43.3.*

19.13 Employee Home Office Deductions

The law severely limits employees from claiming deductions for home office expenses by setting conditions most employees cannot meet. To deduct office expenses, the office must be *exclusively used* on a *regular* basis as either a—

1. Principal place of business, or
2. Place of business to meet customers, clients, or patients for the convenience of the employer.

Under these tests, the IRS has consistently barred employees from claiming home office deductions.

Exclusive business use means that the space used as an office must not be used for personal purposes such as a family den. Even if you meet this exclusive-use test, a deduction is barred unless the office is used regularly as your principal place of business or to see customers, clients, or patients.

EXAMPLE

A husband and wife both teach in an elementary school. Neither can use the school facilities after 5 p.m. and so they are required to work at home, preparing lessons, constructing charts and learning materials, and reading educational literature. They do this in a room exclusively used for this purpose. Despite exclusive business use of the room, no home office deduction is available; the room is not their principal place of business; *see* Example 1 below.

Principal place of business test. The *Soliman* decision of the Supreme Court provides the following two tests to determine whether a home office is a principal place of business: (1) the relative importance of the work done at each business location; and (2) the amount of time spent at each location. In determining the principal place of business, the IRS first applies Test (1) from *Soliman*, comparing the characteristics of the work done at each business location. Weight is given to the place where patients, clients, or customers are met, where goods are delivered or services are performed; *see* Examples 1 and 2 below. If Test (1) is inconclusive, the IRS applies Test (2) above. The fact that the office serves some business function, such as a place to do administrative paperwork, does not suffice to claim a deduction under current law, as illustrated by the *Soliman* decision in Example 3 below. *See* the Law Alert on this page for a more favorable administrative office rule that will take effect in 1999.

EXAMPLES

1. *Teacher.* Charlie, a teacher, spends 25 hours a week at school and 35 hours a week at home grading papers and tests, and preparing lectures. According to the IRS, the most important part of a teacher's business is to teach and meet with students at the school. The work done at the home office, although essential and more time consuming, is less important than school instruction. Therefore, applying Test (1), the teacher's principal place of business is the school and not the home office.

2. *Plumber.* Joe, a plumber, spends 40 hours a week at customers' homes and 10 hours a week in his home office talking with customers, ordering supplies, and scheduling appointments. Applying Test (1), the IRS holds that a plumber's business is installing and repairing plumbing at customers' homes. The work done from the home office, although essential, is less important and takes less time than Joe's service calls to customers.

3. *Anesthesiologist.* Soliman, an anesthesiologist, deducted expenses of his home office, where he spent 10–15 hours per week doing all of his administrative work and pre-treatment planning. He had no office space at the three hospitals where he administered anesthesia and cared for patients for 30–35 hours per week. The Tax Court allowed the deduction, holding that the home office was essential to his work. The Supreme Court disagreed. That the home office was essential to his practice was irrelevant; his principal place of business was at the hospitals where he practiced.

   According to the Supreme Court, whether a home office is the principal place of business depends on two considerations: (1) The functions at each business location and the relative importance of each. The place where a person is required to meet with clients or patients, deliver goods or perform services is generally the principal place of business, especially if that place has unique or special characteristics, as a hospital does. (2) The time spent at each location if it is difficult to make a determination under (1).

4. Fred Jones, a salesperson, makes most of his sales to customers by telephone or mail from his home office. He spends an average of 30 hours a week there and 12 hours a week visiting prospective customers to deliver products and occasionally take orders. According to the IRS, the essence of Fred's business as a salesperson requires him to make telephone or mail contact with customers primarily from the office in his home. Visiting customers is less important to his business than the activities performed from his home office. Further, a comparison of the 30 hours per week spent in the home office with the 12 hours per week spent visiting customers also supports the conclusion that Fred's home office is his principal place of business. Therefore, he may deduct his home office expenses.

Rentals to employer. Home office deductions may not be claimed by employees who rent home office space to their employer.

 Law Alert

Administrative Office Deductions Allowed Starting in 1999

For tax years beginning after December 31, 1998, a home office will meet the principal place of business test if it is used to conduct administrative or management activities and you can show that there is no other fixed location where you conduct substantial administrative or managerial activities for your business. When the new law takes effect, it will overrule the result in the *Soliman* decision (discussed on this page), which denied a deduction for home offices used largely for administrative purposes. However, for 1997 and 1998, the strict *Soliman* principal place of business test remains a difficult hurdle to overcome.

 Filing Instruction

Office For Sideline Business

If you are an employee and also have a sideline business for which you use a home office, the office expenses are deductible if the office is used regularly and exclusively as your principal place of business or a meeting place with clients, customers, or patients. If the tests are met, you claim you home office expenses as a self-employed person on Form 8829, which you attach to Schedule C. The deduction may not exceed your income from the sideline business. *See 40.11–40.15* for a sample Form 8829 and other deduction details.

Investors. Home office deductions may not be claimed by investors who use a home office to review investments and make investment decisions unless the activity constitutes a business; *see 19.24.*

Deductible expenses. If you satisfy the covenience of the employer test and othe deduction tests discussed earlier, you may deduct, subject to the 2% AGI floor, the allocable business part of the cost of home insurance, maintenance, utilities, rent, and depreciation (if you own your home or apartment). Real estate taxes and mortgage interest are fully deductible on Schedule A, regardless of your use of the home. Expenses, such as maintenance, depreciation, or rent, allocated to your home office use are claimed as miscellaneous expenses on Line 20 of Schedule A, subject to the 2% AGI floor. You must first enter the expenses on Form 2106 if you were partially reimbursed by your employer. Form 2106 (or Form 2106-EZ if you qualify) must also be used if you are claiming automobile or job travel costs. Allocated home office expenses may not exceed income from your job.

You may allocate expenses to the home office by dividing the number of square feet of space used as an office into the total number of square feet in the home. Apply the resulting percentage to the total expenses. If the rooms in your home are approximately the same size, you can divide total rooms in the house by the room used as an office. For example, if one room out of a five-room apartment is used for an office, $\frac{1}{5}$, or 20%, of deductible home expenses are allocated to the use of the office.

To support your deduction, keep records to show how you allocated the expenses, in addition to cancelled checks, receipts, and other evidence of the expenses paid.

You need physical evidence of an office. A bare minimum is a desk, chair, and filing cabinet. Retain business mail directed to your home.

Keep a record of business phone calls you make, particularly charges for long-distance telephone calls, and a diary of business visitors, including those who come to your home for entertainment.

19.14 Telephone Costs

For business calls made outside of your employer's office or at home, keep a record or diary of business calls to support your deduction. To avoid the problem of allocating the costs of a single home phone for both business and personal use, consider installing a separate home phone for business use only. For long-distance business calls, you might ask the phone company to transfer the charges to your office phone.

Deduction barred for basic charge of first phone line. You may not claim as a deductible home office expense any part of the standard monthly charge for the first telephone line into your home. This disallowance rule only applies to the first telephone line. If you have more than one telephone line and use additional lines in a home office, costs for these lines remain deductible, subject to the restrictions at *19.13.* The restriction does not affect deductibility of long-distance calls, phone rentals, or optional services such as call waiting, call forwarding, three-way calling, or extra directory listings.

Deductible Education Costs

19.15 Types of Deductible Education Costs

If you improve your job or professional skills by attending continuing education or refresher classes, advanced academic courses, or vocational training, you may be able to deduct your expenses. As a self-employed business owner or professional, allowable expenses are deductible on Schedule C. However, as an employee, the tax benefit of an educational expense deduction is limited because the expenses are miscellaneous itemized deductions, which, together with any other miscellaneous expenses, are deductible on Schedule A only to the extent that the total exceeds 2% of your adjusted gross income; *see 19.1.*

To deduct education costs, you must show that the following conditions are met:

1. You are employed or self-employed;
2. You already meet the minimum requirements of your job, business, or profession;
3. The course maintains or improves your job or professional skills, or you are required by your employer or by law to take the course to keep your present salary or position; *and*
4. The course does *not* lead to qualification for a new profession or business. The cost of courses preparing you for a new profession is not deductible, even if you take them to improve your skills or to meet your employer's requirements. This rule prevents the deduction of law school

costs; *see 19.17.* Furthermore, the cost of a bar review course or CPA review course is not deductible because it leads to a new profession as an attorney or CPA. If courses lead to qualification for a new business or profession, no deduction is allowed even if you keep your current position.

If your courses meet the above requirements you may deduct the following education costs on Schedule C if self-employed or on Schedule A subject to the 2% AGI floor if the courses are related to your job:

1. Tuition, textbooks, fees, equipment, and other aids required by the courses.

2. Local transportation costs as discussed at *19.22*.

3. Travel to and from a school away from home, and lodging and 50% of meals while at school away from home; *see 19.22.* The IRS will not disallow traveling expenses to attend a school away from home or in a foreign country merely because you could have taken the course in a local school. But it may disallow your board and lodging and expenses at the school if your stay lasts longer than a year.

Further details of the deduction requirements are explained at 19.16.

Nondeductible courses. The cost of courses preparing you for a new profession or for meeting the minimum requirements for your job is not deductible, even if you take them to improve your skills or to meet your employer's requirements *(see 19.16)*.

19.16 Work-Related Tests for Education Costs

You must meet an employment test to deduct educational expenses. Educational costs are not deductible if you are unemployed or inactive in a business or profession. The cost of "brush-up" courses taken in anticipation of resuming work is also not deductible. However, in one case, a court allowed an unemployed teacher to deduct the cost of tuition, fees, and books where the IRS conceded that the teacher, although unemployed, remained in the teaching profession while attending college classes.

You are not considered unemployed when you take courses during a vacation or temporary leave of absence; *see 19.21*.

Course does not meet minimum standards. You may not deduct the cost of courses taken to meet the minimum requirements of your job. The minimum requirements of a position are based on a review of your employer's standards, the laws and regulations of the state you live in, and the standards of your profession or business. That you are presently employed does not in itself prove that you have met the minimum standards for your job.

If minimum standards change after you enter a job or profession, courses you take to meet the new standards are deductible.

The minimum standards for teachers are discussed at *19.19*.

Course must maintain or improve job skills. To be deductible, the education must maintain or improve your current job skills. That you are established in your position and that persons in similar positions usually pursue such education indicates that the courses are taken to maintain and improve job skills. However, the IRS may not allow a deduction for a general education course that is a prerequisite for a job-related course.

If the courses lead to a change of position or promotion within the same occupation, a deduction for their cost will usually be allowed if your new duties involve the same general type of work. If, as a consequence of taking a job-related course, you receive a substantial advancement and the IRS questions the deduction of the course costs, be prepared to prove that you took the course primarily to maintain or improve skills of your existing job. However, if the course leads to qualification for a new profession, the IRS will disallow a deduction even if the course also improves current job skills.

Courses must not lead to qualification for a new profession. If a course improves your current job skills but leads to qualification for a new profession, the course is not deductible. For example, a deduction is not allowed for the cost of law school or medical school courses since they prepare you for a new profession. This is true even if you do not intend to practice medicine or law; *see 19.17* and *19.18*. The IRS with Tax Court approval has also held that a deduction is not allowed for the cost of college courses that are part of a degree program, such as a bachelor of arts or science degree.

If you are practicing your profession, the cost of courses leading to a specialty within that profession is deductible.

 Filing Tip

Are MBA Courses Deductible?
The cost of MBA courses is deductible if the courses enhance the skills required in your current position, are not a minimum job requirement, and do not qualify you for a new business. The IRS may question in a particular case whether there has been a change of business, particularly where taking the courses leads to a promotion. For a deduction, the courses must be related to your existing job responsibilities. The Tax Court has allowed deductions for MBA expenses where individuals with some managerial or administrative experience took the courses to improve job skills.

If your employer requires a master's degree as a minimum entrance requirement for your position, the cost of the courses is not deductible.

In one case, a college graduate who took a summer job before starting MBA courses was not allowed a deduction because he had not yet established himself in a business or employment; the summer position was just a temporary stage between schooling.

If your employer reimburses you for MBA courses that qualify for a deduction, the reimbursement is a tax-free working condition fringe benefit; *see 3.6*.

EXAMPLE

A practicing dentist returned to school full time to study orthodontics while continuing his practice on a part-time basis. When he finished his training, he limited his work to orthodontics. The IRS ruled he may deduct the cost of his studies. His post-graduate schooling improved his professional skills as a dentist. It did not qualify him for a new profession.

Further education required by employer or law. If, to retain your present job or rate of pay, your employer requires you to obtain further education, you may deduct the cost of the courses. The fact that you also qualified for a raise in pay or a substantial advancement in your position after completing the courses should not bar the deduction.

The employer's requirement must be for a bona fide business reason, not merely to benefit you. Only the minimum courses necessary for the retention of your job or rate of pay are considered by the IRS as taken to meet your employer's requirement. You must show any courses beyond your employer's minimum requirements were taken to maintain or improve your job skills.

19.17 Law School Costs

The IRS does not allow deductions for law school courses, because they qualify you for a new profession. Courts support the IRS position. A deduction is not allowed even if you do not intend to practice law. For example, teachers who took law school courses have been disallowed deductions although they intended to continue teaching.

Bar review courses. The costs of bar review courses and the bar exam are not deductible, even where you are seeking admission to the bar of a second state. However, fees paid to state bar admission authorities have been held to be amortizable over an attorney's life expectancy.

Additional legal education. An attorney may deduct the cost of a master's degree program (LL.M.). You must practice as an attorney before the expenses of further legal education are deductible.

EXAMPLE

The Tax Court allowed a lawyer to deduct educational expenses to obtain an LL.M. degree where he worked for a law firm as a beginning lawyer during the summer between graduating from law school and starting work on the LL.M. degree. He was admitted to the state bar before he graduated from law school, and the work he did during the summer was normally assigned to beginning lawyers rather than to law students.

In another case, the IRS and Tax Court did not allow a deduction to a law school graduate who took LL.M. courses before passing the state bar or working as an attorney.

19.18 Courses Taken by Doctors and Nurses

The IRS allows general practitioners to deduct the cost of short refresher courses, even though the courses relate to specialized fields. These courses maintain or improve skills and do not qualify the doctor for a new profession.

A practicing psychiatrist may deduct the cost of attending an accredited psychoanalytic institute to qualify to practice psychoanalysis. A social worker has also been allowed a deduction for the cost of psychoanalysis. In one case, a psychiatrist was allowed by the Tax Court to deduct the cost of personal therapy sessions conducted through telephone conversations and tape cassettes. The court was convinced that the therapy improved his job skills by eliminating psychological blind spots that prevented him from understanding his patient's problems.

A licensed practical nurse may not deduct the costs of a college program which qualifies him or her as a "physician's assistant," which is a new business. Physicians' assistants and practical nurses are subject to different registration and certification requirements under state law, and, more importantly, the physician's assistant may perform duties, such as physical examinations and minor surgery, which go beyond practical nursing duties.

19.19 Courses Taken by Teachers

You must meet the minimum level of education for your present position as set down by law or regulations before you may deduct the cost of courses. The educational requirements are those that existed when you were hired. If your employer set no tests fixing a minimum educational level, you meet the minimum requirements when you become a member of the faculty. Whether you are a faculty member depends on the custom of your employer. You are ordinarily considered a faculty member if: (1) you have tenure, or your service is counted toward tenure; (2) the institution is contributing toward a retirement plan based on your employment (other than Social Security or a similar program); or (3) you have a vote in faculty affairs.

Employed teacher taking courses for teaching certificate. That you are already employed as a teacher, with all the responsibilities of a teacher, may not establish that you have met the minimum educational requirements. A school system which requires a bachelor's degree before granting a permanent teaching certificate may grant temporary or provisional certificates after a person has completed a number of college credits. Renewal of the provisional certificate may be conditioned on the teacher's continuing education for a bachelor's degree. In this case, the IRS will disallow a deduction for the educational costs. The minimum requirements are not met until the teacher has the degree. Current Tax Court decisions follow the IRS position, although in the past the court took a contrary view.

19.20 Professor's Research Expenses

Research costs incurred by a college professor are deductible under this condition: He or she is appointed to lecture and teach with the understanding that research in the field will be carried on with the goal of incorporating the findings in teaching and writing. If this test is met, the IRS is satisfied that the research is an express requirement of the teaching position and that research expenses are deductible job expenses.

Deductible research costs include traveling expenses and stenographic and other costs of preparing a manuscript. If income is later realized from the research in the form of lecture or royalty fees, the previously deducted research costs may not again be deducted in determining the income realized from the research.

Expenses of a research project undertaken for a scholarly publication are not deductible if the research is not linked to an income-producing activity or job requirement.

19.21 Leave of Absence To Take Courses

If you are a teacher, the IRS will allow a deduction for full-time graduate courses you take during a leave of absence if these conditions are met: (1) the absence must not be for more than one year; and (2) upon completion of the education courses, the same type of employment must be resumed, although you may take a job with a new employer. You may also have to show that you had more than a vague intention to go back to your employment—for example, that you were actually negotiating for a new teaching position and that, in fact, you did obtain a position soon after finishing the graduate courses.

19.22 Local Transportation and Travel Away From Home To Take Courses

If your courses meet the requirements at *19.15* and *19.16*, costs of local transportation and travel away from home are deductible.

Local transportation expenses. If your courses qualify for a deduction under *19.16,* you may deduct transportation costs of going from your job directly to school. According to the IRS, the return trip from school is also deductible if you are going to school on a *temporary* basis. If you take a one-time course or a course that lasts a few days or weeks, the IRS considers this temporary and you are allowed a deduction for your transportation to and from school. The IRS position is illustrated in the following Examples.

EXAMPLES

1. You regularly work in Camden, New Jersey, and every night for three weeks you drive from home to attend a refresher course. The course is considered temporary. You may deduct the round-trip transportation costs between home and school. The deduction is allowed regardless of how far you travel.

   If you went directly from your job to the school, you may deduct transportation from work to school, and from school to home.

2. On six consecutive Saturdays, which are nonworkdays for you, you drive from home to attend a qualifying course. This is considered a temporary course. You are allowed a deduction for round-trip transportation between home and school, even though you are traveling on a nonworkday.

Planning Reminder

Teacher's Job Change

Elementary and secondary school teachers may deduct the cost of courses taken to make any of the following job changes: (1) elementary to secondary school classroom teacher; (2) classroom teacher in one subject (such as mathematics) to classroom teacher in another subject (such as English or history); (3) classroom teacher to guidance counselor; or (4) classroom teacher to principal.

The IRS held that a "discussion leader" in a college adult education program could not deduct the costs of a master's degree program that led to certification as a high school guidance counselor because this was a new business. The Tax Court disagreed, holding that the responsibilities of discussion leader are similar to the responsibilities of a school counselor. The court distinguished an earlier decision in which a classroom paraprofessional assistant was not allowed to deduct education costs that qualified her as a classroom teacher. The court considered this as a change in professions. A paraprofessional does not have the same control and responsibilities for classroom work as a classroom teacher.

3. After work, you attend classes twice a week for one year. The IRS does not consider the course to be temporary. You may deduct the cost of going directly from work to school, but the costs of going between home and school are nondeductible.

Travel and living expenses away from home. "Away from home" as explained at *20.6* has a special tax meaning. You are not away from home unless you are away overnight. If you are away from home to attend a qualifying course, you may deduct the cost of travel to and from the site of the course, plus lodging and 50% of meals while you are there.

Expenses of sightseeing, social visiting, and entertaining while taking the courses are not deductible. If personal reasons are your main purpose in going to the vicinity of the school, such as to take a vacation, you may deduct only the cost of the courses and your living expenses while attending school. You may not deduct the rest of your travel costs.

To determine the purpose of your trip, an IRS agent will pay close attention to the amount of time devoted to personal activities relative to the time devoted to the courses.

Is travel itself a form of education? The law says no. No deduction is allowed for costs of travel claimed as a form of education. For example, no deduction will be allowed to a French teacher traveling to France to maintain general familiarity with the French language and culture, or to a social studies teacher traveling to learn about or photograph people and customs.

A deduction may still be allowed for travel that qualifies as a business expense, as, for example, if a teacher must travel abroad to do research that cannot be done elsewhere.

19.23 How To Deduct Education Costs on Your Return

The way you deduct educational expenses on your return depends on your occupational status. If you are:

An employee. If you have education costs that are deductible under *19.16* but which have not been reimbursed by your employer, you generally deduct the expenses on Form 2106 or Form 2106-EZ. However, you do not need Form 2106 or Form 2106-EZ and may report your educational expenses directly on Schedule A as unreimbursed employee expenses if: (1) you are not claiming job expenses for travel, transportation, meals, or entertainment; and (2) you received no reimbursements for education expenses or any other job-related costs. If your expenses were partially reimbursed, you must use Form 2106; Form 2106-EZ may not be used.

Employer reimbursements, including advances of deductible expenses, are not reported as income on your Form W-2 if you substantiate the expenses to your employer and return amounts in excess of the substantiated expenses. If these substantiation tests are not met or if the education costs are not deductible under *19.16,* the expenses are reported as income on your Form W-2, and you must claim them on Form 2106 (or Schedule A if Form 2106 is not needed) as if they were unreimbursed. If your employer pays the tuition directly to the educational institution, you are not required to report the payment in any way on your return.

Unreimbursed costs, such as travel, tuition, books, fees, and meals from Form 2106 or Form 2106-EZ, are deductible only if you claim itemized deductions. They are claimed as miscellaneous itemized deductions and are subject to the 2% AGI floor when included with other miscellaneous deductions on Schedule A.

Teacher on sabbatical. Where a school system has a policy of paying teachers full salary during sabbatical leaves, a teacher on sabbatical may be required to pay a fixed percentage of salary into a fund to pay substitute teachers. A teacher reports the full amount of the salary paid during the sabbatical but may claim payments to the fund as miscellaneous itemized deductions subject a teacher on sabbatical may be required to pay a fixed percentage of salary into a fund to pay substitute teachers. A teacher reports the full amount of the salary paid during the sabbatical but may claim payments to the fund as miscellaneous itemized deductions subject to the 2% AGI floor.

A self-employed business owner or professional. If your education costs qualify under *19.16,* you deduct all of your education costs on Schedule C. You also attach a statement to your return explaining your deduction and the relationship of the education to your position.

A veteran receiving educational benefits from the VA. Educational assistance from the Department of Veterans Affairs (VA) is tax free, whether it covers educational or living expenses. The portion of the payment covering educational costs reduces your deductible educational expenses. If you use only part of the VA payment for qualifying courses, reduce your deduction by the part of the VA reimbursement covering the qualifying courses. The portion of the reimbursement, if any, that covers living expenses does not affect your deduction.

Investment, Legal, and Tax Advice Expenses

19.24 Checklist of Deductible Investment Expenses

The following investment expenses are deductible as miscellaneous expenses on Schedule A subject to the 2% adjusted gross income (AGI) floor. In addition, the 3% reduction for total itemized deductions applies if your adjusted gross income exceeds $121,200, or $60,600 if married filing separately; *see 13.7*.

- Accounting fees for keeping records of investment income.
- Bank deposit loss if not federally insured; *see 18.4*.
- Casualty or theft losses of income-producing property such as stock certificates, but not rental or royalty property; the deduction is figured on Form 4684 and entered on Schedule A.
- Fees for collecting interest and dividends. Also deductible are fees paid to a bank that acts as dividend agent in an automatic dividend reinvestment plan of a publicly owned corporation. Costs of collecting tax-exempt interest are not deductible; expenses deducted on an estate tax return are also not deductible. Fees paid to a broker to acquire securities are not deductible but are added to the cost of the securities. Commissions and fees paid by an investor on the sale of securities reduce the selling price; a dealer, however, may deduct selling commissions as business expenses.
- Fees to set up or administer an IRA. The fees must be billed and paid separately from the regular IRA contribution.
- Guardian fees or fees of committee for a ward or minor incurred in producing or collecting income belonging to the ward or minor or in managing income-producing property of the ward or minor.
- Investment management or investment planner's fees. However, fees allocated to advice dealing with tax-exempt obligations are not deductible.
- Investment fees from non–publicly offered mutual fund, shown in Box 1e of Form 1099-DIV.
- Legal costs; *see 19.26*.
- Premiums and expenses on indemnity bonds for the replacement of missing securities. If part of the expenses are refunded in the year the expenses are paid, only the excess expense is deductible. A refund in a later year is taxable income to the extent the expenses were deducted and reduced your tax; *see 11.6*.
- Proxy fight expenses where the dispute involves legitimate corporate policy issues, not a frivolous desire to gain membership on the board.
- Safe deposit box rental fee or home safe to hold your securities, unless used to hold personal effects or tax-exempt securities.
- Salary of a secretary, bookkeeper, or other employee hired to keep track of your investment income.
- Subscriptions to investment services.
- Travel costs of trip away from home *(20.6)* to look after investments, or to confer with your attorney, accountant, trustee, or investment counsel about the production of income. If you have investment property in a resort area, keep proof that the trip was taken primarily to check your investment property, not to vacation. Nondeductible travel is discussed below.

Computer used to manage investments. Subject to the 2% floor, depreciation may be claimed; *see 42.10*.

Managing investment property. Expenses incurred in managing property held for income are deductible, even if the property does not currently produce income. Similarly, expenses incurred to avoid further losses or to reduce anticipated losses on such property are deductible.

Rental or royalty expenses. Expenses of earning royalty or rental income are deducted directly from the income, rather than as itemized deductions subject to the 2% AGI floor.

EXAMPLE

You pay deductible investment management fees of $1,500; a tax preparation fee of $500; and a safe deposit box fee of $40. Your other miscellaneous expense deductions subject to the 2% floor are $500 for unreimbursed job expenses. Your adjusted gross income is $80,000. Your deduction after applying the 2% AGI floor is $940, figured as follows:

Investment management fees	$1,500
Tax preparation fee	500
Safe deposit box fee	40
Other miscellaneous expenses	500
	$2,540
Less: 2% of $80,000	1,600
Total deductible	$ 940

Caution

Investment Seminars

You may not deduct the cost of an investment or financial planning seminar or similar meeting.

Nondeductible travel costs.   Investors may not deduct the costs of these types of trips:

- Trips to investigate prospective rental property.
- Trips to attend a convention, seminar, or similar meeting that deals with investment, financial planning, or the production or collection of income. Convention costs are deductible only in the case of a business activity; *see 20.12.*
- Trips to attend stockholder meetings. However, in a private letter ruling, one stockholder was allowed a deduction. He owned substantial stockholdings which had lost value because his corporation had been issuing stock to the public at prices below book value. He went to the annual shareholders' meeting to present a resolution requesting management to stop the practice; the resolution passed. Under such circumstances, the IRS held that the trip was directly related to his stockholdings and allowed him the deduction. The IRS distinguished his case from a ruling which bars most stockholders from deducting the cost of travel to an annual meeting. Here the stockholder's purpose in getting the resolution passed was more closely related to his investment activities than if he had attended the meeting, as most stockholders do, to pick up data for future investment moves.

Hobby expenses.   For the limitations on deducting hobby expenses, *see 40.9.*

Home office of an investor.   An investor may not deduct the costs of an office at home unless investing constitutes a business. For example, you get no deduction for use of a home office in your residence where you read financial periodicals and reports, and clip bond coupons. These activities are not considered a business.

> **EXAMPLE**
>
> In his home office, Moller spent 40 hours a week managing four stock portfolios worth over $13 million. However, an appeals court held he could not deduct home office expenses despite the time spent there managing his investment. To deduct home office expenses, Moller had to show he was a trader. A trader is in a business; an investor is not. A trader buys and sells frequently to catch daily market swings. An investor buys securities for capital appreciation and income without regard to daily market developments. Here, Moller was an investor. He was primarily interested in the long-term growth potential of stock. He did not earn his income from the short-term stock turnovers. He had no significant trading profits.

19.25 Costs of Tax Return Preparation and Audits

You may deduct your payment of fees charged for the services listed below, subject to the 2% AGI floor and the 3% reduction if AGI exceeds $121,200 ($60,600 if married filing separately); *see 13.7.*

- Preparing your tax return or refund claim involving any tax;
- Preparing and obtaining a private IRS ruling, including IRS filing fees; and
- Representing you before any examination, trial, or other type of hearing involving any tax.

The term "any tax" covers not only income taxes but also gift, property, estate, or any other tax, whether the taxing authority be federal, state, or municipal.

Tax practitioner's fees.   Deductible fees for services of tax practitioners are claimed on Schedule A as miscellaneous itemized deductions on the tax return for the year in which the fee was paid. For example, if in March 1997 you pay an accountant to prepare your 1996 return, the fee is deductible on your 1997 return.

You deduct fees related to preparing Schedule C or F (and related business Schedules) on the Schedule C or F, thereby avoiding the 2% AGI floor on Schedule A. In one case, the Tax Court allowed a Schedule C deduction for a $55 tax preparation fee claimed by a self-employed lumberjack, although nonbusiness income was also reported on his return. Any allocation to the nonbusiness income would have been minimal. The Court noted that the IRS's position in disallowing the deduction reflected misguided zeal and was not only petty but impractical.

If you report rental or royalty income or loss on Schedule E, you deduct the allocated tax preparation fee on Schedule E.

An accountant's fee for arranging the purchase of real estate was deductible where the purchase was part of a plan to cut taxes; *see* the Collins Example at the end of this section.

Personal checking account fees.   These are nondeductible, even though the checks are used for tax records. Similarly, the per-check fee on an interest-bearing NOW account is nondeductible. However, fees charged on a bank money-market account may be deductible if check writing is severely limited and writing excess checks forfeits the status of the account as a money-market account.

Planning Reminder

Allocate Fees for Tax Advice

There have been disputes over the deductibility of fees charged for general tax advice unconnected to the preparation of a return or a tax controversy. A deduction for fees charged for general tax advice not within these areas may be disallowed, unless the fee can be related to the production of business or investment income or the management of income-producing property. *See* the Examples at the end of *19.25.*

Appraisal fees. Appraisals for determining a casualty loss or charitable donation are miscellaneous expenses.

EXAMPLES

1. Stockholders of a closely held corporation negotiated with a publicly held company for a tax-free exchange of their stock. An accounting firm asked the IRS for a ruling to determine whether the exchange would be taxable or tax free. The accounting fee was $8,602. Of this, $7,602 was for the ruling and $1,000 was for fixing the basis of the new stock. The stockholders deducted the full fee, which the IRS disallowed because the fee was not charged for the preparation of a tax return nor for representation at a contest of a tax liability.

   The Tax Court disagreed in part. The fee paid for the ruling is deductible; it was connected with determining the extent of the stockholders' liability, if any, in the proposed exchange. But a deduction cannot be allowed for the $1,000 charged to determine the basis of the new stock. This was computed for the stockholders' information, not for determining tax liability. The disallowed fee could be added to the cost basis of the stock.

2. Collins paid an accountant $4,511 for tax advice to reduce his tax on a sweepstakes winning. He was advised to buy an apartment house under a contract obligation to make a large prepayment of interest (which was deductible under prior law). The accountant helped prepare contracts, escrow agreements, and other documents to implement the plan. Collins' deduction of his accountant's fee was disallowed. The IRS held that the fee was a capital expense in acquiring the property. The Tax Court disagreed. The accountant was hired to minimize Collins' income tax through the purchase of the building and the terms of the purchase. Therefore, his fee was deductible.

 Filing Tip

Deducting the Cost of This Book
The purchase of *Your Income Tax* in 1997 may be claimed as a miscellaneous expense deduction on your 1997 return. The cost, when included with other miscellaneous expenses, is subject to the 2% AGI floor. If you purchased the book in 1998, include the cost with your other miscellaneous expenses on your 1998 return.

19.26 Deducting Legal Costs

A legal expense is generally deductible if the dispute or issue arose in the course of your business or employment or involves income-producing property. Legal expenses for personal matters are generally not deductible. If you are self-employed, your deduction for legal fees arising from a business-related dispute is claimed on Schedule C.

Legal expenses related to your job as an employee or to investment activities are claimed as miscellaneous itemized deductions subject to the 2% AGI floor. The IRS may disallow the deduction on the ground that the legal dispute does not directly arise from the business or income activity. Thus, for example, the cost of contesting the suspension of a driver's license for drunken driving is not deductible despite a business need for the license; the suspension arose out of a personal rather than a business-related activity. A deduction may also be disallowed where the dispute involves title to property. Legal fees incurred in obtaining an award of tax-free damages are not deductible.

The legal costs of defending against disbarment are deductible.

For the deductibility of legal fees in organizing a new business, *see 40.10.*

Employment suits. The following Examples illustrate when legal costs for job-related matters may be deductible.

EXAMPLES

1. Waldheim, a corporate officer, director, and stockholder, incurred legal fees in a suit to prevent his discharge. His legal costs were deductible.

2. An Army officer was allowed to deduct the cost of successfully contesting a court martial based on charges of misrepresentations in official statements and reports. He would have lost his position had he been convicted.

3. Tellier, a securities dealer, was convicted of mail fraud and securities fraud. He was allowed to deduct legal fees as business expenses related to his securities business. That he was found guilty of the criminal charge does not affect the deductibility of the expense. The deduction of legal expenses is not disallowed on public policy grounds since a defendant has a constitutional right to an attorney.

4. In an alimony action, Gilmore was successful in preventing his wife from securing stock and taking control of corporations from which he earned practically all his income. He was not allowed to deduct his legal costs. The dispute did not arise from an income-producing activity; the fact that an adverse determination of the dispute might affect his income did not make the legal expenses deductible.

Planning Reminder

Lawyer's Bill Should Be Itemized

Your lawyer should bill you separately or itemize fees for services connected with deductible items (collection of taxable alimony or separate maintenance payments; or preparation of tax returns, tax audits, and tax litigation) and nondeductible capital items (expenses incurred in purchase of property or dispute over title).

Filing Tip

Tax Advice and Tax Return Preparation

You may deduct legal fees paid in 1997 for preparing your tax return or refund claim, or for representing you in a trial, examination, or hearing involving any tax; *see 19.25*. Legal fees incurred in defending against a tax imposed by a foreign country are also deductible. However, legal fees incurred in reducing an assessment on property to pay for local benefits are not deductible; the fees are capital expenses which are added to basis.

5. A doctor who attempted to bribe a judge to suspend his sentence for tax evasion was convicted of the bribe attempt and lost his license to practice medicine. He could not deduct his defense costs. His practice of medicine did not give rise to his need for an attorney. The fact that the conviction affected his ability to earn income was merely a consequence of personal litigation.

6. Siket, a police officer, was not allowed to deduct expenses of successfully defending a criminal charge of assault while off duty. The origin of the claim was personal, even though a conviction might have been detrimental to his position as a police officer. The arrest did not occur within the performance of his duties; he was off duty and in a different municipality at the time of the arrest.

Will contests and wrongful death actions.   Legal costs of a will contest are generally not deductible because an inheritance is not taxable income. Similarly, legal fees incurred to collect a wrongful death award (which is tax-free income) are not deductible.

EXAMPLE

Parker, an heir who was left out of his grandmother's estate, sued to recover his inheritance. In a settlement, he received his share of his grandmother's property plus income earned on that property. The allocable portion of legal fees attributed to the income, which was taxable, was deductible; the balance of the fees was not deductible.

Title issues or disputes.   Legal costs related to the acquisition of property or to the determination of title to property, whether such property is business or personal, are nondeductible capital expenditures. They are added to the basis of the property. For example, litigation costs to fix the value of shares of dissident shareholders are not deductible because they are related to the purchase of the stock and are part of the cost of acquisition.

Legal fees incurred to acquire title to stock were also held to be nondeductible.

Where a dispute over property does not involve title, such as in a recovery of income-producing securities loaned as collateral, the Tax Court holds that legal fees are deductible.

Personal injury or marital actions.   Where you recover taxable damages, you may deduct the legal fees. If the damages are not taxable, legal fees are not deductible; *see 11.7*. For legal expenses incurred in marital actions, *see 37.8*.

Collecting Social Security.   If you hire an attorney to press a claim for disputed benefits, such as disability benefits, you may deduct the legal fees only to the extent that your benefits are taxable under the rules of *34.3*. For example, if 50% of your Social Security benefits are taxable, 50% of your legal fees are treated as miscellaneous expenses subject to the 2% AGI floor.

Estate tax planning fee.   All or part of an attorney's fee for estate tax planning services may be deductible. Estate tax planning usually involves tax and non-tax matters. To the extent that the services do not cover tax advice or income-producing property, the fee is not deductible. A bill allocating a fee between deductible and nondeductible services may help support a deduction claimed for the deductible portion of the fee.

Recovery of attorneys' fees from government.   *See* Chapter 47.

Chapter 20

Travel and Entertainment Expense Deductions

Unreimbursed employee travel expenses are deductible but are subject to the 2% adjusted gross income (AGI) floor. If you are self-employed, the 2% floor does not apply. The types of deductible travel expenses are highlighted in the key to deductible travel and entertainment expenses at the beginning of this chapter. Generally, you must be away from home to deduct travel expenses on business trips. On one-day business trips within the general area of your employment, only transportation costs may be deducted; meals may not.

To support your travel expense deductions, keep records that comply with IRS rules as explained at *20.26*. To avoid the 2% AGI floor, consider an "accountable" reimbursement arrangement of your travel expenses with your employer; *see 20.31*.

You report unreimbursed employee transportation and travel expenses on Form 2106 or on new short form 2106-EZ if you are not reimbursed by your company and you do not claim depreciation on a car used for business.

Unreimbursed expenses from Form 2106 or 2106-EZ are entered on Schedule A where they are subject to the 2% AGI floor.

An expense allowance for travel costs is not reported as income on Form W-2 if you substantiated the expenses to your employer and returned any unsubstantiated portion of the allowance; *see 20.31* for details.

If you are self-employed, you deduct travel costs on Schedule C. The 2% AGI floor does not apply, but meal and entertainment expenses are subject to the 50% limitation.

Commuting and Meal Expenses

20.1 Deduction Guide for Travel and Transportation Expenses

The following chart summarizes the rules for deducting travel expenses while "away from home" on business trips, and other deductible travel and transportation expenses; *see 20.6* for when you are away from home. Generally, commuting expenses from your home to your place of business are not deductible; *see 20.2*. However, you may be able to claim a deduction for daily transportation expenses incurred in commuting to a temporary job location; *see* chart below and *20.2*.

Key to Deductible Travel and Transportation Expenses

Your Travel Status—	Tax Rule—
Trips to see customers and clients	You may deduct your transportation expenses but not the cost of personal meals on one-day business trips within the general area of your tax home.
Two job locations for one employer in the same area **EXAMPLE:** Your employer has two business locations in the city in which you live. You work about half of the time in each place—at one location in the morning and at the other in the afternoon.	You deduct transportation expenses from one location to the other. However, if, for personal reasons, such as the choice of a place for eating lunch, you do not go directly from one location to the other, you may deduct your transportation expenses only to the extent that they do not exceed the cost of going directly from the first location to the second. But say your employer has several locations in the same city, but you do not move from one location to another in the same day. You spend the entire day at one place. You may not deduct transportation expenses between your home and the various locations, even if you report to a different location each day.
Two different jobs in the same area **EXAMPLE:** You work for two different employers in the city in which you live. Most of the time you work a full work shift at your principal place of employment. Then you work a part-time shift for your second employer some distance away.	You may deduct the transportation expenses from one job to another within the same working day. But you may not claim the deduction if you return home after the first job and then, after supper, go to your second job.
Permanent job in an area other than where you have your residence **EXAMPLE:** You live with your family in Chicago, but work in Milwaukee. During the week, you stay in a hotel in Milwaukee and eat meals in a restaurant. You return to your family in Chicago every weekend.	Milwaukee is your "home" for tax purposes; *see 20.6*. Thus, your expenses for traveling to Milwaukee and your meals and lodging there are personal, nondeductible expenses.
Temporary assignment in an area other than where you have your residence **EXAMPLE:** You live in Kansas City where you work. You have been assigned to duty in Omaha for 60 days. Occasionally, you return to Kansas City on your days off, but most of the time you stay in Omaha.	You may deduct the necessary expenses for traveling from Kansas City to Omaha and returning to Kansas City after your temporary assignment is completed. You may also deduct expenses for meals and lodging (even for your days off) while you are in Omaha. As discussed at *20.9*, deductions are not allowed on temporary assignments that are *expected* to last more than one year.
Weekend trip home from temporary assignment **EXAMPLE:** Same facts as Example above except that you return home to Kansas City during the weekend.	You are not "away from home" while you are in Kansas City on your days off and your meals and lodging while you are there are not deductible. However, you may deduct your traveling expenses (including meals and lodging, if any) from Omaha to Kansas City and back if they are no more than the amount it would have cost you for your meals and lodging if you had stayed in Omaha. If they are more, your deduction is limited to the amount you would have spent in Omaha. If you retain your room in Omaha while in Kansas City, your expenses of returning to Kansas City on days off are deductible only to the extent of the amount you would have spent for your meals had you stayed in Omaha.

Key to Deductible Travel and Transportation Expenses

Your Travel Status—	Tax Rule—
Temporary job location away from home where there are no living accommodations **EXAMPLE:** You live and work in Chicago. You have been assigned for three months to a construction job located 20 miles outside Nashville. There are no living facilities near the job site and you have to stay at a hotel in Nashville.	Under these circumstances, your necessary expenses in getting to and from your temporary job are business expenses and not commuting expenses. If you were employed at the site for an indefinite period (*20.9*), then the costs of commuting would be nondeductible, regardless of the distance; *see 20.2.*
Taxi trips between customers' locations	The cab fares are deductible; *see 20.2.*
Seasonal jobs in different areas **EXAMPLE:** You live in Cincinnati where you work for eight months each year. You earn the greater share of your annual income from that job. For the remaining four months of the year, you work in Miami. When in Miami, you eat and sleep in a hotel. You have been working on both of these jobs for several years and expect to continue to do so.	You have two recurring seasonal places of employment. Cincinnati is your principal place of employment. You may deduct the costs of your traveling expenses while away from Cincinnati working at your minor place of employment in Miami, including meals and lodging in Miami.
Trailer home moved to different job sites **EXAMPLE:** You are a construction welder. You live in a trailer which you move from city to city where you work on construction projects. You have no other established home.	You may not deduct your expenses for meals and lodging. Each place where you locate becomes your principal place of business and, therefore, you are not "away from home."
Travel to school after work to take job-related courses	You may deduct travel costs if you meet the rules at *19.23.*
Finding a new job in the same line of work **EXAMPLE:** You live in New York. You travel to Chicago for an interview for a new position.	You may deduct the cost of the trip and living expenses in Chicago; *see 19.7.*
Convention trip	You may deduct costs of travel to a business convention under the rules of *20.12*. If you are a delegate to a charitable or veterans' convention, you may claim a charitable deduction for the travel costs; *see 14.4.*
Trip to out-of-town college for educational courses	You deduct the cost of the trip if you meet the rules at *19.23.*
Trip for health reasons	You may deduct the cost of the trip as a medical expense if you meet the rules at *17.9.*

20.2 Commuting Expenses

The cost of travel between your home and place of work is generally not deductible, even if the work location is in a remote area not serviced by public transportation. Nor can you justify the deduction by showing you need a car for faster trips to work or for emergency trips. Travel from a union hall to an assigned job is also considered commuting. If you join a car pool, you may not deduct expenses of gasoline, repairs, or other costs of driving you and your passengers to work.

According to the IRS, if you install a telephone in your car and make calls to clients or business associates while driving to your office, you are still commuting and your expenses are not deductible. Similarly, the deduction is not allowed if you drive passengers to work and discuss business.

Deductible commuting expenses.   The IRS allows these exceptions to its blanket ban on commuting expense deductions.

If you are on a business trip out of town, you may deduct taxi fares or other transportation costs from your hotel to the first business call of the day and all other transportation costs between business calls.

If you use your car to carry tools to work, you may deduct transportation costs where you can prove that they were incurred in addition to the ordinary, nondeductible commuting expenses. The deduction will be allowed even if you would use a car in any event to commute; *see* the Examples below.

EXAMPLES

1. Jones commuted to and from work by public transportation before he had to carry tools. Public transportation cost $2 per day to commute to and from work. When he had to use the car to carry the tools, the cost of driving was $3 a day and $5 a day to rent a trailer to carry the tools. Jones may deduct only the cost of renting the trailer. The IRS does not allow a deduction for the additional $1 a day cost of operating the car. It is not considered related to the carrying of the tools. It is treated as part of the cost of commuting which is not deductible.
2. Same facts as above, but Jones does not rent a trailer. He uses the car trunk to store his tools. He may not claim a deduction because he incurs no additional cost for carrying the tools.
3. Smith uses his car regardless of the need to transport tools. He rents a trailer for $5 a day to carry tools. He may deduct $5 a day under the "additional-cost" rule.

Commuting to a temporary place of work.   Whether you can deduct commuting expenses to a temporary place of work may depend on the location of the temporary assignment and whether you have a regular place of business or a home office which is your principal place of business. According to the IRS, if the temporary location is within the metropolitan area where you live and usually work, you must show either that you have a regular place of business outside your home, or that your principal place of business is your office in your home. If the temporary location is outside the metropolitan area, you may deduct commuting expenses to the temporary location without having to meet either the regular place of business or home office test.

Given the difficulty of proving that a home office is the principal place of business (*19.13*), self-employed persons such as plumbers, electricians, and salespersons who do not have a regular place of business outside the home are prevented from deducting commuting costs *within* the metropolitan area of the home. For example, the IRS barred a self-employed lumberjack who did not have an office outside his home from deducting the cost of driving from home to the first logging site of the day and returning home from the last site.

What is a temporary place of work?   A temporary place of work is any location where you perform services on an irregular basis or for a short-term period, generally a few days or weeks. If you are on a temporary job that lasts longer, it is important to show that the job started out as a temporary assignment and that factors beyond your control extended the time and that you looked for work closer to home.

20.3 Overnight-Sleep Test Limits Deduction of Meal Costs

The overnight-sleep rule prevents the deduction of meal costs on one-day business trips. To be deductible, meal costs must be incurred on a business trip that lasts longer than a regular working day (but not necessarily 24 hours) and requires time off to sleep (not just to eat or rest) before returning home. Taking a nap in a parked car off the road does not meet the overnight-sleep test.

EXAMPLES

1. A New Yorker flies to Washington, D.C., which is about 250 miles away, to see a client. He arrives at noon, eats lunch, and then visits the client. He flies back to New York. He may deduct the cost of the plane fare, but not the cost of the lunch. He was not away overnight nor was he required to take time out to sleep before returning home.

Court Decision

Police Car

An IRS and Tax Court decision that barred police captains' costs of driving their specially equipped cars to and from the stationhouse was reversed by an appeals court.

Court Decision

Self-Employed Person's Office at Home

If you are self-employed and your regular office is outside your home, you may not deduct the cost of commuting to the office or from that office to your home even if you work at home at a second job. However, in several cases, the Tax Court allowed self-employed persons whose home office was their principal place of business (*40.11*) to deduct travel costs beginning with the first business call of the day. The IRS agrees with this approach.

2. Same facts as above except he sleeps overnight in a Washington hotel. He eats breakfast there, and then sees another client and returns home to New York in the afternoon. He may deduct not only the cost of the plane fare but also the cost of the meals while on the trip and the cost of the hotel, since he was away overnight.

3. A trucker's run is from Seattle to Portland and back. He leaves at about 2:00 A.M. and returns to Seattle the same day, getting in at about 6:00 P.M. While in Portland, he is released from duty for about four hours layover time to get necessary sleep before returning to Seattle. He may deduct the cost of meals because he is released at a layover location to obtain necessary sleep. Official release from duty, however, is not a prerequisite for satisfying the sleep or rest test.

Several courts held that the IRS rule was unreasonable and outdated in the world of supersonic travel, and they would have allowed the New Yorker on the one-day trip to Washington, D.C., to deduct the cost of his lunch. The Supreme Court disagreed and upheld the IRS rule as a fair administrative approach.

Meal costs during overtime. Such costs are not deductible if you are not away from your place of business. Thus, for example, a resident physician could not deduct the cost of meals and sleeping quarters at the hospital during overnight or weekend duty.

20.4 IRS Meal Allowance

If you find it difficult to keep records of meal costs while away from home on business trips, you may prefer to claim an IRS meal allowance. The allowance covers, in addition to meals, incidental expenses, such as laundry and tips for services. Self-employed individuals may claim the allowance as well as employees who are not reimbursed for meals under an "accountable" plan; *see 20.31.*

1997 meal allowance. For travel within the continental U.S., the daily allowance for 1997 is usually $30 per day except that in certain high-cost areas designated by the government, the allowance may be $34, $38, or $42 per day. The high-cost areas are generally major metropolitan cities or resort areas. *See* the table on pages 372 and 373 for a list of cities within the continental U.S. that qualify for meal allowance rates over $30 per day for 1997. Also *see* IRS Publication 463 for allowance rate tables.

For travel in Alaska, Hawaii, or other areas outside the continental U.S., an allowance for each location is shown in government tables.

You must keep a record of the time, place, and business purpose of the trips. As long as you have this proof, you may claim the allowance even if your actual costs are less than the allowance.

Transportation industry workers. Employees or self-employed persons in the *transportation industry* may elect to claim a meal allowance of $36 per day for all 1997 travel within the continental U.S. instead of applying the $30, $34, $38, or $42 rate on a trip-by-trip basis. Also, an allowance of $40 per day may be elected for all travel outside the continental U.S.

Claiming the allowance. The allowance is allocated for the first and last day of a trip. The day is divided into four six-hour periods, starting at midnight. For each six-hour period that you are away, you are entitled to 25% of the allowance. If you start your business trip between midnight and 6 A.M., you are considered to be away for the entire day and may claim the full day allowance for the first day. If you start between 6 A.M. and noon, you claim 75% of the allowance for the first day; if you start between noon and 6 P.M., you claim 50% of the allowance for the first day, and 25% if you leave between 6 P.M. and midnight.

If you are an employee and claim a deduction based on the allowance, you must reduce the deduction by 50% on Form 2106 or Form 2106-EZ. Furthermore, if you are an employee, the balance, when added to your other miscellaneous deductions, is subject to the 2% AGI floor on Schedule A. If you are self-employed, the deduction for meals is claimed on Schedule C, where it is subject only to the 50% reduction; *see 40.5.*

Reimbursement plans. If your employer has an "accountable" reimbursement plan (*20.31*), and you are reimbursed for meals up to the allowable rate, the reimbursement will not be reported as income on your Form W-2.

Locations Eligible for $34, $38, or $42 a Day Meal Allowance for Travel on or After January 1, 1997

The allowance applies to the county, parish, borough, and military installation surrounding the city shown. See IRS Publication 463 for a full list of counties. Any changes to the list will be in the Supplement.

STATE	$34	$38	$42
ALABAMA	Gulf Shores and Huntsville	Birmingham and Mobile	
ARIZONA	Flagstaff, Prescott, and Tucson	Grand Canyon Nat'l Park and Kaibab Nat'l Forest if within Coconino County, and Pheonix/Scottsdale	
CALIFORNIA	Clearlake, Eureka, Fresno, Merced, Modesto, Oakland, Redding, Santa Barbara, and Stockton	Monterey, Ontario/Victorville/Barstow, Palm Springs, Sacramento, San Diego, San Luis Obispo, San Mateo/Redwood City, Santa Cruz, Santa Rosa, South Lake Tahoe, Tahoe City, and Visalia	Bridgeport/Mammoth Lakes, Death Valley, Gualala/Point Arena, Los Angeles, Napa, Palo Alto/ San Jose, San Francisco, and Yosemite Nat'l Park Aspen, Keystone/Silverthorne, and Vail
COLORADO	Denver, Durango, Glenwood Springs, and Steamboat Springs	Boulder and Telluride	
CONNECTICUT	New London/Groton and Salisbury/ Lakeville	Bridgeport/Danbury	
DELAWARE	Dover	Lewes and Wilmington	
DISTRICT OF COLUMBIA			Washington, D.C.
FLORIDA	Altamonte Springs, Cocoa Beach, Daytona Beach, Fort Lauderdale, Fort Myers, Gainesville, Gulf Breeze, Orlando, Pensacola, Punta Gorda, St. Augustine, Sarasota, Stuart, and Tallahassee	Naples, Tampa/St. Petersburg, and West Palm Beach	Key West and Miami
GEORGIA	Athens and Savannah	Atlanta	
IDAHO	Boise, Coeur d'Alene, Idaho Falls, McCall, and Stanley	Ketchum/Sun Valley	
ILLINOIS	Champaign/Urbana and Peoria	Rockford	Chicago
INDIANA	Bloomington/Crane, Evansville, and Lafayette	Carmel and Indianapolis	
IOWA	Cedar Rapids		
KANSAS	Wichita		Kansas City
KENTUCKY	Covington and Lexington	Louisville	
LOUISIANA	Baton Rouge and Shreveport		New Orleans
MAINE	Bar Harbor, Kennebunk/Sanford, Kittery, and Rockport	Portland	
MARYLAND	Grasonville, Lexington Park/St. Inigoes/ Leonardtown, Lusby, and Salisbury	Annapolis, Baltimore, Frederick, Saint Michaels	Columbia and Ocean City
MASSACHUSETTS	Cambridge/Lowell, Pittsfield, and Quincy	Andover and Hyannis	Boston and Martha's Vineyard/Nantucket
MICHIGAN	Gaylord, Grand Rapids, Petosky, Sault Ste. Marie, St. Joseph/Benton Harbor/ Niles, and Traverse City	Detroit, Mackinac Island, Pontiac/Troy, and Port Huron	
MINNESOTA		Duluth and Minneapolis/St. Paul	
MISSISSIPPI	Biloxi/Gulfport/Pascagoula/Bay St. Louis, Jackson, and Ridgeland		
MISSOURI	Lake Ozark, Osage Beach, and Springfield		Kansas City and St. Louis
NEBRASKA	Omaha		

Locations Eligible for $34, $38, or $42 a Day Meal Allowance for Travel on or After January 1, 1997

The allowance applies to the county, parish, borough, and military installation surrounding the city shown. See IRS Publication 463 for a full list of counties. Any changes to the list will be in the Supplement.

STATE	$34	$38	$42
NEVADA	Reno	Incline Village, Las Vegas, and Stateline	
NEW HAMPSHIRE	Conway and Portsmouth/Newington	Hanover	
NEW JERSEY	Belle Mead, Flemington, Freehold/Eatontown, Millville, and Tom's River	Atlantic City, Camden/Moorestown, Edison, Parsippany/Dover, and Princeton/Trenton	Newark
NEW MEXICO	Albuquerque, Farmington, Los Alamos, and Taos		Santa Fe
NEW YORK	Batavia, Binghamton, Corning, Kingston, Lake Placid, Monticello, Niagara Falls, Palisades/Nyack, Plattsburgh, Schenectady, Syracuse, and Utica	Albany, Buffalo, Glens Falls, and Saratoga Springs	New York City, Long Island, Rochester, and White Plains
NORTH CAROLINA	Asheville, Duck/Outer Banks, Greensboro/High Point, and Winston-Salem	Charlotte, and Research Park/Raleigh/Durham/Chapel Hill	
OHIO	Akron, Cincinnati/Evendale, Columbus, Springfield, and Toledo	Cleveland	
OREGON	Eugene/Florence	Ashland/Medford, Beaverton, Crater Lake/Klamath Falls, Lincoln City/Newport, and Portland	
PENNSYLVANIA	Allentown, Gettysburg, Harrisburg, Lancaster, Scranton, State College, Warminster, and York	King of Prussia/Ft. Washington, Philadelphia, Pittsburgh, and Valley Forge/Malvern	Chester/Radnor
RHODE ISLAND	East Greenwich		Newport/Block Island and Providence
SOUTH CAROLINA	Charleston, Hilton Head, and Myrtle Beach	Greenville	
TENNESSEE	Gatlinburg and Knoxville	Nashville	
TEXAS	Austin, El Paso, Lubbock, Plano, and San Antonio	Houston	Dallas/Fort Worth and Galveston
UTAH	Bullfrog, Provo, and St. George	Salt Lake City/Ogden	Park City
VERMONT	Burlington, Manchester, and Middlebury		
VIRGINIA	Lynchburg, Roanoke, and Williamsburg	Richmond and Virginia Beach	Alexandria, Charlottesville, Fairfax, Falls Church, and Wintergreen
WASHINGTON	Anacortes/Mt. Vernon/Whidbey Island, Bellingham, Kelso/Longview, Lynnwood/Everett, Ocean Shores, Port Angeles, and Vancouver	Friday Harbor, Seattle, and Spokane	
WEST VIRGINIA	Wheeling		
WISCONSIN	Eau Claire, La Crosse, Lake Geneva, Madison, Milwaukee, Oshkosh, and Racine/Kenosha	Brookfield and Wisconsin Dells	
WYOMING			Jackson

Deducting Travel Expenses Away From Home

20.5 Business Trip Deductions

The following expenses of a business trip *away from home* (20.6) are deductible if not reimbursed by your employer:

- Plane, railroad, taxi, and other transportation fares
- Hotel and lodging expenses
- Meal costs. Only 50% of the cost of the meal is deductible. The business discussion test of *20.16* does not apply to meal costs on business trips provided you eat alone or with your family or personal acquaintances.

- Tips, telephone, and telegraph costs
- Laundry and cleaning expenses
- Baggage charges (including insurance)
- Cab fares or other costs of transportation to and from the airport or station and your hotel. Also deductible are cab fares or other transportation costs, beginning with your first business call of the day, of getting from one customer to another, or from one place of business to another.
- Travel costs to find a new job are deductible; *see 19.7.*
- Entertainment expenses incurred while traveling away from home are deductible under the rules at *20.6.*

Cruise ship. If you travel by cruise ship on a business trip, your deductible cruise costs are limited to twice the highest federal *per diem* rate for travel in the United States on that date multiplied by the number of days in transit.

> **EXAMPLE**
>
> You sail to Europe on business. While you are away, the highest *per diem* federal rate is $223 and the trip lasts five days. The maximum deduction for the cost of the trip is $2,230 (2 × $223 × 5). The double *per diem* rule applies without regard to the 50% limit on meal costs if meals are not separately stated in your bill. If a separate amount for meals or entertainment is included, such amount must be reduced by 50%.
>
> The *per diem* limitation does not apply to cruise ship convention costs that are deductible up to $2,000 a year, if all the ports of call are in the U.S. or U.S. possessions and if the ship is registered in the United States; *see 20.14.* The *per diem* rate also does not apply if the expense comes within an exception to the 50% cost limit rule explained at *20.24.*

Important: Record-keeping requirements. *See* the section beginning at *20.26* for record-keeping rules to support a deduction for unreimbursed travel expenses or to avoid being taxed on employer reimbursements.

20.6 When Are You Away From Home?

You have to meet the "away from home" test to deduct the cost of meals (only 50% deductible) and lodging while traveling.

> **EXAMPLES**
>
> 1. Your residence is in a suburb within commuting distance of New York City where you work full time. Your personal home and tax home are the same, that is, within the metropolitan area of New York City. You are away from home when you leave this area, say for Philadelphia. Meals and lodging are deductible only if you meet the overnight-sleep test; *see 20.3.*
>
> 2. Your residence is in New York City, but you work in Baltimore. Your tax home is Baltimore; you may not deduct living expenses there. But you may deduct travel expenses on a temporary assignment to New York City even while living at your home there.
>
> 3. A construction worker works for a utility company on construction sites in a 12-state area. Assignments are sent from his employer's regional office; he is not required to report to the office. The IRS ruled that his residence, which is in a city in the 12-state area, is his tax home.

Are you constantly on the road? If you move from job to job and do not work within any particular locality, an IRS agent may disallow your travel deductions on the grounds that your tax home is wherever you work; thus, you are never "away from home." You are considered a transient worker.

If your deduction is questioned because you have no regular or main place of business, you may be able to show that your tax home is the area of your residence. If you meet the following three tests, the IRS will treat your residence as your tax home: (1) you do some work in the vicinity of your residence, house, apartment, or room and live there while performing services in the area; (2) you have mortgage expenses or pay rent for the residence while away on the road; (3) the residence is in an area where you were raised or lived for a long time, or a member of your immediate family such as your parent or child lives in the residence, or you frequently return there.

Law Alert

Tax Home Defined

For travel expense purposes, your home is your place of business, employment, or post of duty, regardless of where you maintain your family residence. This tax home includes the entire city or general area of your business premises or place of employment. The area of your residence may be your tax home if your job requires you to work at widely scattered locations, you have no fixed place of work, and your residence is in a location economically suited to your work.

According to the IRS, if you meet only two of these three tests, it will decide on a case-by-case basis if your residence is your tax home. If you meet less than two of the tests, the IRS will not allow a deduction; each of your work locations is treated as your tax home.

If you live in a trailer at each job assignment and have no other home, each job location is your principal place of business and you are "not away from home."

Permanent duty station of service members.   The Supreme Court held that a member of the Armed Forces is not away from home when he or she is at a permanent duty station. This is true even if the service member has to maintain a separate home for family members who are not permitted to live at the duty station.

20.7 Fixing a Tax Home If You Work in Different Locations

If you regularly work in two or more separate areas, your tax home is the area of your principal place of business or employment. You are away from home when you are away from the area of your principal place of business or employment. Therefore, you may deduct your transportation costs to and from your minor place of business and your living costs there.

Professional sports players, coaches, and managers.   When the only business of such persons is the professional sport, their home is the "club town." But if they are in another business in addition to their professional playing, how much time is spent and how much is earned at each place determines whether their club's hometown or the place of their off-season business is their tax home. If it is the club's hometown, they deduct travel and living expenses while away from that town—including the time they are where the second business is. (If the second place is where their families also live, they may not deduct the families' expenses there.) If the town where the other business is located is the tax home, then expenses in the club's hometown may be deducted.

Airline pilots.   It is important for airline pilots who fly in and out of various locations to determine a tax home for income and deduction purposes. Generally, the IRS considers an airline pilot's tax home to be the airport at which the pilot is regularly based. For example, in one case the IRS barred a pilot from claiming the foreign earned income exclusion *(36.1)* because his tax home was deemed to be his base in New York, rather than in London where he and his wife actually lived.

> **EXAMPLES**
> 1. Sherman lived in Worcester, Mass., where he managed a factory. He opened his own sales agency in New York. He continued to manage the factory and spent considerable time in Worcester. The larger part of his income came from the New York business. However, he was allowed to treat New York as his minor place of business and to deduct his travel expenses to New York and his living expenses there because he spent most of his time in Worcester and his income there was substantial.
> 2. Benson, a consulting engineer, maintained a combination residence-business office in a home he owned in New York. He also taught four days a week at a Technological Institute in West Virginia under a temporary nine-month appointment. He spent three-day weekends, holidays, and part of the summer at his New York address. At the Institute, he rented a room in the student union building. The IRS disallowed transportation expenses between New York and West Virginia and meals and lodging there as not incurred while away from home. The Tax Court disagreed. A taxpayer may have more than one occupation in more than one city. When his occupations require him to spend a substantial amount of time in each place, he may deduct his travel expenses, including meals and lodging, at the place away from his permanent residence. That Benson's teaching salary happened to exceed his income from his private practice does not change the result.

20.8 Tax Home of Married Couple Working in Different Cities

When a husband and wife work and live in different cities during the week, one of them may seek to deduct travel expenses away from home. Such deductions have generally been disallowed, but courts have allowed some exceptions. Although for common law purposes the domicile of the husband may be the domicile of the wife, for tax purposes when each spouse works in a different city, each may have a separate tax home.

 Planning Reminder

Determining Your Principal Place of Business

If you have more than one regular place of business, your tax home is your principal place of business. Your principal place of business or employment is determined by comparing: (1) the time ordinarily spent working in each area; (2) the degree of your business activity in each area; and (3) the amount of your income from each area.

No single factor is determinative. The relative importance of each fact will vary depending on the facts of a particular case. For example, where there are no substantial differences between incomes earned in two places of employment, your tax home is probably the area in which you spend more of your time. Where there are substantial income differences, your tax home is probably the area in which you earn more of your income.

EXAMPLES

1. Robert worked in Wilmington, Delaware; his wife, Margaret, worked in New York City. During the weekend, she traveled to Wilmington and deducted, as travel expenses away from home, her living costs in New York and weekend travel expenses to Wilmington. She argued that because she and her husband filed a joint return, they were a single taxable unit, and the tax home of this unit was Wilmington where her husband lived. The deduction was disallowed. That a couple can file a joint return does not give them deductions that are not otherwise available to them as individuals. Margaret's tax home was New York where she worked. Therefore, her expenses there are not deductible. And, as the weekend trips to Wilmington had no relationship to her job, they, too, are not deductible.

2. Hundt and his wife lived in Arlington, Va., but he wrote and directed films in various parts of the country. He wrote screenplays either at his Arlington home or on location, but most of his business came from New York City, where he lived in hotels. One year, he spent 175 days in New York City on business and rented an apartment for $1,200 because it was cheaper than a hotel. He deducted half the annual rent for the New York apartment, the costs of traveling between Arlington and New York, and the cost

   of meals in New York. The IRS disallowed the expenses, finding New York to be his tax home. The court disagreed. Arlington was Hundt's tax home because (1) part of his income came from his creative writing in Arlington; and (2) his travel to other parts of the country was temporary. The fact that most of his income came from New York did not make New York his tax home.

20.9 Deducting Living Costs on Temporary Assignment

A business trip or job assignment away from home *(20.6)* at a single location may last a few days, weeks, or months. If your assignment is considered *temporary*, you may deduct travel costs *(see below)* while there because your tax home has not changed. An assignment is considered temporary by the IRS if you realistically expect it to last less than one year and it actually does last less than one year. If an assignment is realistically expected to last more than a year it is considered *indefinite*, and you cannot deduct your living costs at the area of the assignment because that location becomes your tax home. You can be away for less than a year and still be barred from claiming a deduction if at the time you started the assignment you realistically expected it to last for more than a year. Likewise, employment that is initially temporary may become indefinite due to changed circumstances; *see* the Examples below.

EXAMPLES

1. You are on a job assignment away from home in a single location that is expected to last (and it does in fact last) for one year or less. The IRS will treat the employment as temporary, unless facts and circumstances indicate otherwise. Expenses are deductible.

2. You are sent on a job assignment away from home at a *single* location. You expected that the job would last 18 months. However, due to financial difficulties you were transferred home after 11 months. Even though your assignment actually lasted for less than one year the IRS treats the employment as indefinite because you realistically expected it to last more than one year. Thus, your travel and living expenses while away from home are not deductible.

3. You are sent on a job assignment away from home at a *single* location. You expected that the job would last only nine months. However, due to changed circumstances occurring after eight months, you were asked to remain on the assignment for six more months. The IRS treats the assignment as temporary for eight months, and indefinite for the remaining time you are away from home. Thus, travel and living expenses you paid or incurred during the first eight months are deductible; expenses paid or incurred thereafter are not.

Deductible travel costs on temporary trip. While on a temporary job assignment *expected* to last a year or less, you may deduct the cost of meals and lodging there, even for your days off. If you return home, say for weekends, your living expenses at home are not deductible. You may deduct travel expenses, meals, and lodging en route between your home and your job assignment provided they do not exceed your living expenses had you stayed at the temporary job location. If you keep a hotel room at the temporary location while you return home, you may deduct your round-trip expenses for the trip home only up to the amount you would have spent for meals had you stayed at the temporary workplace.

EXAMPLE

Michaels, a cost analyst for Boeing, lived in Seattle. He traveled for Boeing, but was generally not away from home for more than five weeks. Michaels agreed to go to Los Angeles for a year to service Boeing's suppliers in that area. He rented his Seattle house and brought his family with him to Los Angeles. Ten months later, Boeing opened a permanent office in Los Angeles and asked Michaels to remain there permanently. Michaels argued that his expenses for food and lodging during the 10-month period were deductible as "away from home" expenses. The IRS contended that the Los Angeles assignment was for an indefinite period.

The Tax Court sided with Michaels. He was told that the stay was for a year only. He leased his Seattle house to a tenant for one year, planning to return to it. He regarded his work in Los Angeles as temporary until Boeing changed its plans. The one-year period justified his taking the family but did not alter the temporary nature of the assignment.

No regular job where you live. That you do not have regular employment where you live may prevent a deduction of living costs at a temporary job in another city. The IRS may disallow the deduction on the grounds that the expenses are not incurred while away from home; the temporary job site is the tax home.

Caution

Taking Your Family with You

If you take your family with you to a temporary job site, an IRS agent may argue that this is evidence that you considered the assignment to be indefinite. In the Michaels Example on this page, however, such a move was not considered detrimental to a deduction of living expenses at the job location.

Deducting Expenses of a Business-Vacation Trip

20.10 Business-Vacation Trips Within the United States

On a business trip to a resort area, you may also spend time vacationing. If the *primary purpose* of the trip is to transact business and the area is within the United States (50 states and District of Columbia) you may deduct all of the costs of your transportation to and from the area, lodging, and 50% of meal expenses, even if you do spend time vacationing. If the main purpose of the trip was personal, you may not deduct any part of your travel costs to and from the area. The amount of time spent on business as opposed to sightseeing or personal visits is the most important issue in determining your primary purpose. Regardless of the primary purpose of your trip, you are allowed to deduct expenses related to the business you transacted while in the area.

No deductions will be allowed if you attend a convention or seminar where you are given videotapes to view at your own convenience and no other business-related activities or lectures occur during the convention. The trip is considered a vacation.

If your trip is primarily for business, and while at the business destination you extend your stay for a few days for nonbusiness reasons, such as to visit relatives, you deduct travel expenses to and from the business destination.

EXAMPLE

You work in Atlanta and make a business trip to New Orleans. You stay in New Orleans for six days and your total costs, including round-trip transportation to and from New Orleans, meals, and lodging, is $600, which you may deduct subject to the 50% limit for meals. If, on your way home, you spend three days in Mobile visiting relatives and incur an additional $200 in travel costs, your deduction is limited to the $600 (less 50% of meals) you would have spent had you gone home directly from New Orleans.

Reimbursement for weekend travel. If your employer extends your business trip over a weekend to take advantage of discount airfares which require a Saturday night stayover, you may deduct the cost of meals, lodging, and other incidental expenses incurred for the additional night. The reason for the stayover has a business purpose: to cut travel costs. If your employer pays for the expenses directly or if you are reimbursed under an accountable plan (*20.31*), the payment is not taxable to you.

Caution

Primary Business Purpose

If your return is examined, proving the business purpose of your trip depends on presenting evidence to convince an examining agent that the trip, despite your vacationing, was planned primarily to transact business. Keep a log or diary to substantiate business activities.

20.11 Business-Vacation Trips Outside the United States

On a business trip abroad, you may deduct your travel expenses (50% of meals), even though you take time out to vacation, provided you can prove: (1) the primary purpose of the trip was business; and (2) you did not have control over the assignment of the trip.

If the IRS determines that you were primarily on vacation, it will disallow all travel costs except for costs directly related to your business in the area such as registration fees at a foreign business convention; *see 20.14.*

Fixing the date of the trip does not mean that you had control over the assignment. IRS regulations assume that when you travel for your company under a reimbursement or allowance arrangement, you do not control the trip arrangements, provided also that you are not: (1) a managing executive of the company; (2) related to your employer; or (3) have more than a 10% stock interest in the company. You are considered a managing executive if you are authorized without effective veto procedures to decide on the necessity of the trip. You are related to your employer if the employer is your spouse, parent, child, brother, sister, grandparent, or grandchild.

Rule for managing executives and self-employed persons. If you are a managing executive, self-employed, related to your employer, or have a more-than-10% stock interest, you may deduct all transportation costs if:

1. The trip outside the United States took a week or less, not counting the day you leave the U.S. but counting the day you return,

2. If the trip abroad lasted more than a week, you spent less than 25% of your time, counting the days your trip began and ended, on vacation or other personal activities, *or*

3. In planning the trip you did not place a major emphasis on taking a vacation.

If the vacationing and other personal activities took up 25% or more of your time on a trip lasting more than one week, and you cannot prove that the vacation was a minor consideration in planning the trip, you must *allocate* travel expenses between the time spent on business and on personal affairs. The part allocated to business is deductible; the balance is not. To allocate, count the number of days spent on the trip outside the United States, including the day you leave the U.S. and the day you return. Then divide this total into the number of days on which you had business activities; include days of travel to and from a business destination.

If you vacation at, near or beyond the city in which you do business, the expense subject to allocation is the cost of travel from the place of departure to the business destination and back. For example, you travel from New York to London on business and then vacation in Paris before returning to New York. The expense subject to allocation is the cost of traveling from New York to London and back; *see* Example 2. However, if from London you vacationed in Dublin before returning to New York, you would allocate the round-trip fare between New York and Dublin and also deduct the difference between that round-trip fare and the fare between New York and London; *see* Example 3 on the next page.

EXAMPLES

1. You fly from New York to Paris to attend a business meeting for one day. You spend the next two days sightseeing and then fly back to New York. The entire trip, including two days for travel en route, took five days. The plane fare is deductible. The trip did not exceed one week.

2. You fly from Chicago to New York where you spend six days on business. You then fly to London where you conduct business for two days. You then fly to Paris for a five-day vacation after which you fly back to Chicago. You would not have made the trip except for the business that you had to transact in London. The nine days of travel outside the United States away from home, including two days for travel en route, exceeded a week, and the five days devoted to vacationing were not less than 25% of the total travel time outside the U.S. The two days spent traveling between Chicago and New York, and the six days spent in New York, are not counted in determining whether the travel outside the United States exceeded a week and whether the time devoted to personal activities was less than 25%.

   Assume you are unable to prove either that you did not have substantial control over the arrangements of the trip or that an opportunity for taking a personal vacation was not a major consideration in your decision to take the trip. Thus, $\frac{5}{9}$ (five nonbusiness days out of nine days outside the U.S.) of the plane fare from New York to London and from London to New York is not deductible. You may deduct $\frac{4}{9}$ of the New York-to-London round-trip fare, plus lodging, 50% of meals, and other allowable travel costs while in London. No deduction is allowed for any part of the costs of the trip from London to Paris.

3. Same facts as Example 2 except that the vacation is in Dublin, which is closer to the U.S. than London. The allocation is based on the round-trip fare between New York and Dublin. Thus, $\frac{4}{9}$ of the New York to Dublin fare is deductible and $\frac{5}{9}$ is not deductible. Further, the IRS allows a deduction for the excess of the New York-to-London fare over the New York-to-Dublin fare.

Weekends, holidays, and business standby days. If you have business meetings scheduled before and after a weekend or holiday, the days in between the meetings are treated as days spent on business for purposes of the 25% business test just discussed. This is true although you spend the days for sightseeing or other personal travel. A similar rule applies if you have business meetings on Friday and the next scheduled meeting is the following Tuesday; Saturday through Monday are treated as business days. If your trip is extended over a weekend to take advantage of reduced airfares, the additional expense of meals, lodging, and other incidental expenses is deductible; *see 20.10*.

20.12 Deducting Expenses of Business Conventions

Conventions and seminars at resort areas usually combine business with pleasure. Therefore, the IRS scrutinizes deductions claimed for attending a business convention where opportunities exist for vacationing. Especially questioned are trips where you are accompanied by your spouse and other members of your family. Foreign conventions are discussed at *20.14*.

Generally, you may not deduct expenses of attending investment conventions and seminars; *see 19.24*. You also may not deduct the costs of business conventions or seminars where you merely receive a videotape of business lectures to be viewed at your convenience and no other business-related activities occur during the event.

In claiming a deduction for convention expenses, be prepared to show that the convention was connected with your business. Cases and IRS rulings have upheld deductions for doctors, lawyers, and dentists attending professional conventions. One case allowed a deduction to a legal secretary for her costs at a secretaries' convention. If you are a delegate to a business convention, make sure you prove you attended to serve primarily your own business interests, not those of the association. However, it is not necessary for you to show that the convention dealt specifically with your job. It is sufficient that attendance at the convention may advance or benefit your position. If you fail to prove business purpose, the IRS will allocate your expenses between the time spent on your business and the time spent as a delegate. You then deduct only the expenses attributed to your business activities.

EXAMPLES

1. An attorney with a general law practice was interested in international law and relations. He was appointed a delegate to represent the American branch of the International Law Association at a convention in Paris. The attorney deducted the cost of the trip and convention as business expenses which the IRS and a court disallowed. He failed to prove that attending the conference on international law helped his general practice. He did not get any business referrals as a result of his attendance at the convention. Nor did he prove the chance of getting potential business from the conference.

2. An insurance agent doing business in Texas attended his company's convention in New York. One morning of the six-day convention was devoted to a business meeting and luncheon; the rest of the time was spent in sightseeing and entertainment. The company paid for the cost of the trip. The IRS added the reimbursement to the agent's pay and would not let him deduct the amount. The convention in New York served no business purpose. It was merely a method of entertaining company personnel. If there was any valid business to be transacted, the company could have called a meeting in Texas, the area of his home office.

3. A plywood company could not deduct the costs of entertaining 116 customers and employees at a New Orleans hotel during a Superbowl weekend. The company did not reserve conference rooms or make any other arrangements for organized business meetings. The IRS and two federal courts held that although business discussions may have occurred on a random basis, these were secondary to entertainment.

What expenses are deductible?   If the convention trip is primarily for business, you may deduct travel costs both to and from the convention, food costs, tips, display expenses (such as sample room costs), and hotel bills. If you entertain business clients or customers, you may deduct these amounts too.

Food and beverage costs are subject to the 50% cost limitation rule as explained in *20.24*.

EXAMPLE

You attend a business convention held in a coastal resort city primarily for business reasons. During the convention period, you do some local sightseeing, social entertaining, and visiting-all unrelated to your business. You may deduct your traveling expenses to and from the resort, your living expenses at the resort, and other expenses such as business entertaining, sample displays, etc. But you may not deduct the cost of sightseeing, personal entertaining, and social visiting.

Keep records of your payments identifying expenses directly connected with your business dealings at the convention and those which are part of your personal activity, such as sightseeing, social visiting, and entertaining. Recreation costs are not deductible even though a part of your overall convention costs.

Fraternal organizations.   You may not deduct expenses at conventions held by fraternal organizations, such as the American Legion, Shriners, etc., even though incidental business was carried on. However, delegates to fraternal conventions may in some instances deduct expenses as charitable contributions; *see 14.4.*

20.13 Travel Expenses of a Spouse or Dependents

Travel costs of a spouse, dependent, or any other individual who is not a business associate and who accompanies you on a business trip are not deductible unless that person is also your employee and has a bona fide business reason for taking the trip that would justify claiming a deduction if the person took the trip on his or her own.

Even though the travel costs of a non-employee spouse or other person are not deductible, you may deduct the cost of such person's participation in the entertainment of business clients at conventions or business trips if the trip or entertainment meets the tests at *20.21*. Generally, you may deduct the cost of goodwill entertaining of associates immediately before or after convention business meetings. A convention meeting qualifies as a bona fide business meeting.

EXAMPLE

You and your spouse travel by car to a convention. You pay $120 a day for a double room. A single room would have cost $100 a day. Your spouse's presence at the convention was for social reasons. You may deduct the total cost of operating your car to and from the convention city. You may deduct $100 a day for your room. If you traveled by plane or railroad, you would deduct only your own fare.

20.14 Restrictions on Foreign Conventions and Cruises

You may not deduct expenses at a foreign convention outside the North American area unless you satisfy the rules at *20.11* and also can show the convention is directly related to your business and it was as reasonable for the meeting to be held outside the North American area as within it.

Apart from the United States, the North American area includes Mexico, Canada, Puerto Rico, U.S. Virgin Islands, American Samoa, Northern Mariana Islands, Guam, Marshall Islands, Micronesia, Palau and U.S. island possessions.

Conventions may also be held in eligible Caribbean countries that agree to exchange certain data with the U.S. and do not discriminate against conventions held in the United States. Barbados, Bermuda, Costa Rica, Dominica, Dominican Republic, Grenada, Guyana, Honduras, Jamaica, Saint Lucia, and Trinidad and Tobago have qualified and are considered to be within the North American area.

Check with the convention operator about whether the country in which your convention is being held has qualified.

Limited cruise ship deduction.   Up to $2,000 a year is allowed for attending cruise ship conventions if all the ports of call are in the U.S. or U.S. possessions and if the ship is registered in the United States. A deduction is allowed only if you attach to your return statements signed by you and by an officer of the convention sponsor that detail the daily schedule of business activities, the number of hours you attended these activities, and the total days of the trip. Do not confuse the $2,000 limitation with the *per diem* limitation for cruise ship costs discussed at *20.5*. The *per diem* limitation does not apply to cruises that meet the tests for the up-to-$2,000 deduction.

Meals and Entertainment Expenses

20.15 50% Deduction Limit

You may not deduct the full cost of entertainment for customers or clients at restaurants, country clubs, at home, theaters, and sporting events, even if the expenses qualify under the restrictive tests of *20.16*. Only 50% of unreimbursed expenses is deductible and this 50% balance is reduced by the 2% AGI floor if you are an employee. Furthermore, all entertainment costs, including meals, must be backed up with records. If you do not keep adequate records, your deductions will be disallowed. The 50% deduction limit for meals and entertainment is discussed at *20.24*.

20.16 The Restrictive Tests for Meals and Entertainment

You must be prepared to show that meal and entertainment costs are ordinary and necessary to your business, and also:

1. Directly related to the active conduct of your business *(20.17)*, *or*
2. Directly preceding or following a substantial and bona fide business discussion on a subject associated with the active conduct of your business. This test applies to dining and entertainment in which you seek new business or to goodwill entertainment to encourage the continuation of an existing business relationship. Under this test, you may entertain business associates in nonbusiness settings such as restaurants, theaters, sports arenas, and nightclubs, provided the entertainment directly precedes or follows the business discussion. Business associates are: established or prospective customers, clients, suppliers, employees, agents, partners, or professional advisers, whether established or prospective; *see 20.18*.

20.17 Directly Related Dining and Entertainment

The directly related test limits the deduction of dining and entertainment costs at restaurants, nightclubs, on yachts, at sporting events, on hunting trips, and during social events. If such dining or entertainment fails to meet the directly related tests, it may qualify under the rules discussed in *20.18*, which require the holding of a business discussion before or after the entertainment.

The directly related test may be met in one of three ways: (1) under the generally related test; (2) as expenses incurred in a clear business setting; or (3) as expenses incurred for services performed.

Generally related test.   Under this test, you must show a business motive for the dining or entertainment and business activity during the entertainment. You must show that you had more than a general expectation of getting future income or other specific business benefit (other than goodwill). Although you do not have to prove that income or other business benefit actually resulted from the expense, such evidence will help support your claim. What type of business activity will an IRS agent look for? The agent will seek proof that a business meeting, negotiation, or discussion took place during the period of dining or entertainment. It is not necessary that more time be devoted to business than to entertainment. What if you did not talk business? You must prove that you would have done so except for reasons beyond your control.

Clear business setting test.   Expenses incurred in a clear business setting meet the directly related test provided also that you had no significant motive for incurring the expenses other than to further your business. Entertainment of people with whom you have no personal or social relationship is usually considered to have occurred in a clear business setting. For example, entertainment of business representatives and civic leaders at the opening of a new hotel or theatrical production to obtain business publicity rather than goodwill is considered to be entertainment in a clear business setting. Also, entertainment which involves a price rebate is considered to have occurred in a clear business setting, as, for example, when a hotel owner provides occasional free dinners at the hotel for a customer who patronizes the hotel.

Costs of a hospitality room displaying company products at a convention are also a directly related expense.

Caution

Hunting or Fishing Trips
The IRS presumes entertainment during a hunting or fishing trip or on a yacht is not conducive to business discussion or activity. You must prove otherwise.

Entertainment occurring under the following circumstances or in the following places is generally not considered as directly related:

- You are not present during the entertainment.
- The distractions are substantial, as at nightclubs, sporting events, or during a social gathering such as a cocktail party.
- You meet with a group which includes persons other than business associates at cocktail lounges, country clubs, golf and athletic clubs, or at vacation resorts.

Services performed test. An expense is directly related if it was directly or indirectly made for the benefit of an individual (other than an employee) either as taxable compensation for services he or she rendered or as a taxable prize or award. The amount of the expense must be reported on an information Form 1099 (unless the amount is less than $600).

EXAMPLE

A manufacturer provides a vacation trip for retailers whose sales of his products exceed quotas. The value of the vacation is a taxable prize to the retailers. The vacation cost is a directly related entertainment expense for the manufacturer.

20.18 Goodwill Entertainment

Goodwill entertaining may qualify as deductible entertainment. Dining and entertainment costs may be deductible if a substantial and *bona fide* business discussion directly preceded or followed the dining or entertainment.

An officially scheduled meeting at a convention is generally considered a bona fide business discussion.

EXAMPLES

1. During the day, you negotiate with a group of business associates. In the evening, you entertain the group and their spouses at a theater and nightclub. The cost of the entertainment is deductible, even though arranged to promote goodwill.
2. In the evening after a business meeting at a convention, you entertain associates or prospective customers and their spouses. You may deduct the entertainment costs.

20.19 Home Entertaining

The cost of entertaining business customers or clients at home is deductible provided a business discussion occurs before, during, or after the meal. When you claim such a deduction, be ready to prove that your motive for dining with them was business rather than social. Have a record of the entertainment costs, names of the guests, and their business affiliations.

20.20 Your Personal Share

If the entertaining occurred while on a business trip away from home, you deduct your own meal cost as travel expenses away from home. If the entertaining occurred within the locality of your regular place of business, whether you will be allowed a deduction for your share will depend on the agent examining your return. The IRS said in a ruling that an agent will not disallow your deduction of your own part of the meal cost unless he or she finds that you are claiming a substantial amount that includes personal living expenses. In such a case, which generally is limited to situations where personal meals are regularly claimed as part of an "abusive" pattern, the agent will follow the stricter Tax Court rule (sometimes referred to as the "Sutter" rule) and allow only that part of the meal cost that exceeds what you would usually spend on yourself when alone.

20.21 Entertainment Costs of Spouses

A deduction is allowed for the spouses' share of the entertainment costs if they were present during entertainment that qualified as directly related entertainment under the general rule discussed in *20.17*. For goodwill entertainment, the cost of entertainment of the spouses is deductible if your share and the business associate's share of the entertainment is deductible. The IRS recognizes that when an out-of-town customer is accompanied by his or her spouse, it may be impracticable to entertain the customer without the spouse. Under such circumstances, the cost of the spouse's entertainment is deductible if the customer's entertainment costs are also deductible. Furthermore, if your spouse joined the party because the customer's spouse was present, the expenses of your spouse are also deductible.

Planning Reminder

Scheduling Entertainment and Business Discussions

A business discussion generally must take place the same day as the dining or entertainment. If not, and your deduction is questioned, you must give an acceptable reason for the interval between the discussion and the dining or entertainment. IRS regulations recognize that a day may separate a business meeting and the entertainment of an out-of-town customer. He or she may come to your office to discuss business one day and you provide entertainment the next day, or you provide the entertainment on the first day and discuss business the day after.

The IRS does not estimate how long a business discussion should last. But it does warn that a meeting must involve a discussion or negotiation to obtain income or business benefits. It does not require that more time be devoted to the meeting than to the entertainment.

20.22 Entertainment Facilities and Club Dues

You may not deduct the expenses of maintaining and operating facilities used to entertain. By law, entertainment facilities are not considered business assets. Examples of entertainment facilities are yachts, hunting lodges, fishing camps, swimming pools, tennis courts, automobiles, airplanes, apartments, hotel suites, or homes in a vacation area. A season box seat or pass at a sporting event or theater is not considered an entertainment facility.

The disallowance rule applies to operating expenses such as rent, utilities and security, and also to depreciation, but not to such expenses as interest, taxes, and casualty losses which are deductible without having to show business purpose.

A deduction may be allowed for expenses such as the cost of food and drinks incurred at an entertainment facility, if they meet the rules of *20.16* through *20.21*.

Club dues. You may not deduct dues for country clubs, golf and athletic clubs, airline clubs, hotel clubs, business luncheon clubs, and other clubs organized for business, pleasure, recreation, or other social purposes. However, IRS regulations generally allow a deduction for dues paid to (1) civic or public service organizations such as Kiwanis, Lions and Rotary clubs; (2) professional organizations such as medical or bar associations; and (3) chambers of commerce, trade associations, business leagues, real estate boards and boards of trade. The deduction for dues is allowed provided that the organization in (1)–(3) does not have a principal purpose of providing entertainment for members or their guests.

20.23 Restrictive Test Exception for Reimbursements

As an employer, you can deduct expense allowances or other reimbursements of employee expenses that you treat as compensation and from which you withhold federal tax. You are not subject to the 50% deduction limit for meals and entertainment; the employee is.

A similar rule applies to meal allowances or reimbursements that you give to an independent contractor and which you report as compensation on Form 1099-MISC where the contractor does not adequately account for the expenses.

The restrictive tests of *20.16* do not apply to such reimbursements. They are deductible if they are "ordinary and necessary" business expenses, and you have records to back up the deduction.

20.24 50% Cost Limitation on Meals and Entertainment

You may not deduct the full amount of your deductible expenses for business meals and entertainment expenses, such as tickets to sports events. Only 50% of the otherwise allowable amount for food, beverages, and entertainment is deductible.

Taxes and tips are considered part of the cost subject to the 50% limit. If your employer reimburses your expenses, the 50% limit applies to the employer.

The 50% limit applies to both employees and the self-employed. It applies to the $30, $34, $38, or $42 IRS meal allowance deduction; see *20.4*. For employee expenses the limit is taken into account on Form 2106 or 2106-EZ (if you are not reimbursed by your employer and do not claim depreciation for a business car), and on Schedule C for self-employment expenses.

 Law Alert

Transportation Industry Workers

Starting in 1998, individuals subject to Department of Transportation limitations on hours of service, such as interstate truck drivers, may claim a higher deductible percentage of food and beverages when working away from home. The deductible amount is 55% for 1998 and 1999. The deductible percentage will increase further after 1999 until it reaches 80% for 2008 and later years.

EXAMPLES
1. You pay meal and entertainment costs of $5,000. Only $2,500 ($5,000 × 50%) is considered deductible.
2. Same facts as above, but your employer reimburses your costs after you account for the expenses. The employer's deduction is limited to $2,500. You have no deduction.

The deductible amount for a ticket treated as an entertainment expense is restricted to the face value of the ticket. Amounts in excess of face value paid to ticket agencies or scalpers are not deductible. The deductible cost of tickets is also subject to the 50% limitation.

EXAMPLE
You buy from a ticket broker five tickets to entertain clients. The face value of the tickets is $250. You paid $300 for them. The deductible amount is $125 (50% × $250).

Exceptions to 50% cost limitation. In the following cases, you may claim a full deduction for meals and entertainment; the 50% limitation does not apply:

1. As an employer, you pay for an employee's meals and entertainment that is treated as taxable compensation to the employee and as wages for purposes of withholding of income tax.

2. You reimburse an independent contractor for meal and entertainment expenses he or she incurs on your behalf and the contractor does not adequately account for the expenses. You deduct the reimbursements as compensation if they are ordinary and necessary business expenses.

3. As an employer, you incur expenses for recreational, social, or similar activities (including facilities) primarily for the benefit of employees who are not highly compensated employees. For example, the expenses of food, beverages, and entertainment for a company-wide summer party are not subject to the 50% limit.

4. Expenses for meals and entertainment, including the use of facilities made available to the general public, such as a free concert, for advertising or goodwill purposes. For example, the IRS allowed a real-estate broker to fully deduct the cost of free dinners it provided to potential investors who attended its sales presentations. The 50% deduction limitation for meals does not apply to promotional activities that are made available to the general public. The IRS relied on the following example in a 1986 Congressional committee report for purposes of allowing a 100% deduction: A wine merchant provides customers with wine and food to demonstrate the suitability of the wine with certain types of meals. The committee report indicated that the cost of the wine, food, and other costs associated with the wine-tasting function would be fully deductible.

5. Expenses for meals and entertainment sold to the public in your business, such as meal expenses if you run a restaurant, or the cost of providing entertainment if you run a nightclub. These expenses are fully deductible.

6. Food or beverage provided to your employees as a tax-free *de minimis* fringe benefit *(3.8)*. This would include expenses of a cafeteria on your premises for employees where meal charges cover the direct operating cost of the cafeteria.

7. The price of tickets to charitable sports events (including amounts in excess of face value) provided the ticket package includes admission to the event. To qualify, a charitable sports event must: (1) be organized for the primary purpose of benefiting a tax-exempt organization; (2) contribute 100% of its net proceeds to such organization; and (3) use volunteers for substantially all work performed in carrying out the event. According to Congressional committee reports, a golf tournament that donates all its proceeds to charity is eligible to qualify under this exception, even if it offers prize money to the golfers who participate or uses paid concessionaires or security personnel. However, tickets to a college football game or similar scholastic events generally do not qualify because they do not satisfy the requirement that substantially all work be performed by volunteers.

The cost of a charitable sports ticket may include seating, parking, and refreshments.

Skybox rental costs. A skybox is a private luxury seating area at a sports arena. Skybox seats are generally rented for the season or for a series of games such as the World Series. The deductible amount for a rental covering more than one game or performance may not exceed the sum of the face values of non-luxury box seat tickets for the number of seats in the box. The allowable amount is also subject to the 50% cost limitation. Separately stated charges for food or beverage charges at the box are deductible as entertainment expenses and are subject to the 50% cost rule. For example, assume that for two games, you paid $1,480 for a skybox containing 10 seats—$740 per game. The cost of 10 non-luxury box seat tickets for each game was $200, or $400 total. You may deduct 50% of $400 non-luxury face value, or $200. If you had rented the skybox for one game, you could deduct $370 (50% of $740) for that skybox because the special limitation applies only where the rental is for more than one game or other performance.

20.25 Business Gift Deductions Are Limited

Deductions for gifts to business customers and clients are restricted. Your deduction for gifts is limited to $25 a person. You and your spouse are treated as one person in figuring this limitation even if you do not file a joint return and even if you have separate business connections with the recipient. The $25 limitation also applies to partnerships; thus a gift by the partnership to one person may not exceed $25, regardless of the number of partners.

Filing Tip

Allocating Payment Covering Lodging and Meals

A hotel may include meals in a room charge. In such cases, the room charge must be allocated between the meals, and entertainment and lodging. The amount allocated to meals and entertainment is subject to the 50% cost limitation. If you receive a per diem allowance from your employer covering both lodging and meals under an accountable reimbursement plan, you may have to allocate part of the reimbursement to meals in order to deduct expenses in excess of the reimbursement; *see 20.31.*

In figuring the $25 limitation to each business associate, do not include the following items:

1. A gift of a specialty advertising item which costs $4 or less on which your name is clearly and permanently imprinted. This exception saves you the trouble of having to keep records of such items as pens, desk sets, plastic bags, and cases on which you have your name imprinted for business promotion.
2. Signs, displays, racks, or other promotional material which is used on business premises by the person to whom you gave the material.
3. Incidental costs of wrapping, insuring, mailing, or delivering the gift. However, the cost of an ornamental basket or container must be included if it has a substantial value in relation to the goods it contains.

If you made a gift to the spouse of a business associate, it is considered as made to the associate. If the spouse has an independent bona fide business connection with you, the gift is not considered as made to the associate unless it is intended for the associate's eventual use.

If you made a gift to a corporation or other business group intended for the personal use of an employee, stockholder, or other owner of the corporation, the gift generally is considered as made to that individual.

Theater or sporting event tickets given to business associates are entertainment, not gift, expenses if you accompany them. If you do not accompany them, you may elect to treat the tickets either as gifts, which are subject to the $25 limitation, or as entertainment expenses subject to the entertainment expense rules, such as the requirement to show a business conference before or after the entertainment and the 50% cost limitation.

Packaged food or drink given to a business associate is a gift if it is to be consumed at a later time.

Gifts not coming within the $25 limit are: (1) scholarships that are tax free under the rules in Chapter 38; (2) prizes and awards that are tax free under the rule of *11.1*; and (3) awards to employees, discussed below.

Awards to employees. There is an exception to the $25 gift deduction limitation for achievement awards of tangible personal property given to your employees in recognition of length of service or safety achievement. Special deduction limits apply to such achievement awards provided they are given as part of a presentation under circumstances indicating that they are not a form of disguised compensation. For example, awards will not qualify if given at the time of annual salary adjustments, or as a substitute for a prior program of cash bonuses, or if awards discriminate on behalf of highly compensated employees.

The amount of your deduction depends on whether the achievement award is considered a qualified plan award. You may deduct up to $1,600 for all qualified plan awards (safety and length of service) given to the same employee during the taxable year. If the award is not a qualified plan award, the annual deduction ceiling for each employee is $400. The $1,600 overall limit applies if the same employee receives some qualified plan awards and some non-qualified awards during the same year.

To be a qualified plan award, the award for length of service or safety achievement must be given under an established written plan or program that does not discriminate in favor of highly compensated employees. The average cost of all awards under the plan for the year (to all employees) must not exceed $400. In determining this $400 average cost, awards of nominal value are not to be taken into account. In case of a partnership, the deduction limitation applies to the partnership as well as to each partner.

Safety and length of service. A length of service award does not qualify as an employee achievement award if it is given during the employee's first five years. Furthermore, only one length of service award every five years is considered an employee achievement award.

Safety awards granted to managers, administrators, clerical employees, or professional employees are not considered employee achievement awards. Furthermore, if during the year more than 10% of other employees (not counting managers, administrators, clerical employees, or professional employees) previously received safety awards, none of the later awards are subject to the employee achievement award rules.

Employee's tax. The employer's deductible amount for an employee achievement award is tax free to the employee; *see 3.10*. For example, you give a qualified plan award costing $1,800 to an employee. You may deduct only $1,600. The employee is not taxed on the award up to $1,600; the $200 balance is taxable.

Caution

Employee Bonuses

Employee bonuses should not be labeled as gifts. An IRS agent examining your records may, with this description, limit the deduction to $25 unless you can prove the excess over $25 was pay. By describing the payment as a gift, you are inviting an IRS disallowance of the excess over $25. This was the experience of an attorney who gave his secretary $200 at Christmas. The IRS disallowed $175 of his deduction. The Tax Court refused to reverse the IRS. The attorney could not prove that the payment was for services.

Travel and Entertainment Records

20.26 Record-keeping Requirements

Your testimony—even if accepted by an IRS agent or a judge as truthful—is not sufficient to support a deduction of travel and entertainment expenses. By law, your personal claim must be supported by other evidence such as records or witnesses. The most direct and acceptable way is to have records that meet IRS rules discussed in the following pages. Failure to have adequate records will generally result in an examination of your return and in a disallowance of your travel and entertainment expense deductions. Only in unusual circumstances will evidence other than records provide all of the required details of proof.

If your expenses are reimbursed by your company, you must keep records to support the reimbursement arrangement with your company; *see 20.30.*

20.27 Substantiating Deductions for Travel and Entertainment

To satisfy the IRS requirements and to substantiate your expense deductions in the event of an audit, you need two types of records:

1. A diary, account book, or similar record to list the time, place, and business purpose of your travel and entertainment expenses; and
2. Receipts, itemized paid bills, or similar statements for lodging regardless of the amount, and for other expenses of $75 or more. But note these exceptions:

- A receipt for transportation expenses of $75 or more is required only when it is readily obtainable. For example, for air travel receipts are usually provided.
- A cancelled check by itself is not an acceptable voucher. If you cannot produce a bill or voucher, you may have to present other evidence such as a statement in writing from witnesses to prove business purpose of the expense.

Record-keeping rules for attorneys and other independent contractors who are reimbursed are discussed at *20.23.*

A receipted bill or voucher must show (1) the amount of the expense; (2) the date the expense was incurred; (3) where the expense was incurred; and (4) the nature of the expense.

A hotel bill must show the name, location, date, and separate amounts for charges such as lodgings, meals, and telephone calls. A receipt for lodging is not needed if its cost is covered by a *per diem* allowance; *see 20.32.*

A restaurant bill must show the restaurant's name and location, the date and amount of the expense, and, when a charge is made for items other than meals or beverages, a description of the charge.

Diary entries. Your diary does not have to duplicate data recorded on a receipt, provided that a notation in the diary is connected to the receipt. You are also not required to record amounts your company pays directly for any ticket or fare. Credit card charges should be recorded.

Your records for entertainment costs must also show (1) the names of those you entertained; (2) the business purpose served by the entertainment; (3) the business relationship between you and your guests; and (4) the place of entertainment. Inattention to these details of substantiation can cost you the deduction. For example, an executive's company treasurer verified that the executive was required to incur entertainment expenses beyond reimbursed amounts. He also kept a cash diary in which he made contemporaneous notes of the amounts he spent. But he failed to note place, purpose, and business relationship. Consequently, there was no record that tied the expenses to his employment and the deduction was disallowed.

You should keep your diary and supporting records for at least three years after the due date for the return which the records support. However, you may not have to keep these records if the information from them is submitted to your company under the rules applied to reimbursed expenses and allowances described at *20.30.*

Excuses for Inadequate Records

Substantial compliance. If you have made a "good faith" effort to comply with the IRS rules, you will not be penalized if your records do not satisfy every requirement. For example, you would not automatically be denied a deduction merely because you did not keep a receipt.

Planning Reminder

Credit cards

Credit card charge statements for traveling and entertainment expenses meet the IRS tests, provided the business purpose of the expense is also shown. Credit card statements provide space for inserting the names of people entertained, their business relationship, the business purpose of the expense, and the portion of the expense to be allocated to business and personal purposes. These statements generally meet the IRS requirements of accounting to your employer for reimbursed expenses *(20.31)*, provided a responsible company official reviews them.

Accidental destruction of records.   If receipts or records are lost through circumstances beyond your control, you may substantiate deductions by reasonable reconstruction of your expenditures.

Exceptional circumstances.   If, by reason of the "inherent nature of the situation," you are unable to keep adequate records, you may substantially comply by presenting the next best evidence. A supporting memorandum from your files and a statement from the persons entertained may be an adequate substitute. IRS regulations do not explain the meaning of "inherent nature of the situation."

EXAMPLES
1. Bryan's 1966 records were lost by a moving company. He claimed a T&E deduction of $15,301.87. The IRS estimated his T&E and other business expenses as $8,669 on the basis of his 1971 expense records. The Tax Court affirmed the IRS's approach. True, Bryan's loss of records made his burden of proof difficult, but he had to provide a reasonable reconstruction of his records to support his claimed deduction. His testimony of what he incurred in 1966 was not sufficient. A more accurate method was the IRS's use of his 1971 records and receipts.
2. Jackson claimed the IRS lost his records. He left his records with the IRS when he was audited, and the records were never returned. The Tax Court held that to be a good excuse for not producing his records and allowed a deduction on the basis of reconstructed records. Evidence that the IRS lost them: The IRS turned up Jackson's worksheet a year after the audit interview.
3. Murray claimed he lost his records when he was evicted from his apartment for failure to pay rent for a month. The Tax Court accepted his excuse on proof that he had kept records before they were lost. The eviction was beyond his control. However, if the records had been lost during a voluntary move, the loss would not have been excused, as in Example 1.

20.28   Reporting T&E Expenses as Self-Employed Person

You must keep travel and entertainment (T&E) records following the rules of *20.27*. You may claim the meal allowance at *20.4* on overnight business trips. The reimbursement rules of *20.30* do not apply to you.

In preparing your tax return, you report your expenses on the appropriate lines of Schedule C or Schedule C-EZ (if you qualify). You do not use Form 2106. An advantage of reporting on Schedule C (or C-EZ) is that your travel and entertainment expenses (T&E) are not subject to the 2% adjusted gross income (AGI) floor. Only 50% of meals and entertainment costs are deductible.

20.29   Reporting T&E Expenses Where You Are Not Reimbursed

If you are paid a salary with the understanding that you will pay your own expenses and you pay all of your travel an entertainment (T&E) expenses *without* reimbursement, you report all of your salary or commission income as shown on Form W-2. You report your expenses on Form 2106 or Form 2106-EZ (if other tests are met). Meals and entertainment are only 50% deductible. You must also keep records as required by *20.27* to support your deduction. The deductible amount from Form 2106 or Form 2106-EZ is entered on Schedule A as a miscellaneous expense subject to the 2% AGI floor. Therefore, if your total miscellaneous expenses, including the unreimbursed T&E costs, do not exceed 2% of adjusted gross income, none of the miscellaneous expenses will be deductible.

Employer Reimbursement Plans

20.30   Tax Treatment of Reimbursements

Compliance rules are imposed on employees and employers for reporting reimbursed travel and entertainment expenses in order to prevent reimbursement arrangements from being used to avoid the 2% of adjusted gross income (AGI) floor for employee miscellaneous expenses. Plans that allow reimbursements that *do not* comply with the IRS rules are called *nonaccountable plans*. All reimbursements under a nonaccountable plan are reported as salary or wage income on Form W-2. You then deduct your expenses as miscellaneous deductions subject to the 2% AGI floor; *see 20.34*.

If a plan meets the IRS rules, the plan is called an *accountable plan* and reimbursements made by the plan are *not* reported on Form W-2 as taxable wages. You also do not have to deduct expenses, assuming the reimbursement equals your expenses. In other words, there is a bookkeeping "wash" in which the full amount of expenses offsets the reimbursement without being reduced by the 2% AGI floor and in the case of meal and entertainment costs, by the 50% reduction. Even though the employer may only deduct 50% of qualifying meal and entertainment expenses, you are not taxed on any part of a reimbursement of such costs if the accountable plan rules are met.

To qualify a plan as accountable, your employer must see to it that you submit adequate proof of your expenditures, and that you return any excess advances; *see 20.31*. To reduce record-keeping for actual costs, the company may reimburse you according to certain fixed *per diem* allowance rates; *see 20.32*. Your company must also determine how much of the advance or reimbursement, if any, is to be reported on your Form W-2.

EXAMPLE

Your adjusted gross income is $85,000, and you incur T&E expenses of $1,600 which are reimbursed by your company. If the reimbursement arrangement does not meet the IRS rules, the $1,600 reimbursement is reported as wage income on your Form W-2. You may report the expenses on Form 2106 and claim a deduction on Schedule A as a miscellaneous expense subject to the 2% AGI floor. However, if these are your only miscellaneous expenses, you will not get the benefit of a deduction because they do not exceed 2% of $85,000, or $1,700. The $1,600 is fully taxable although spent for T&E.

If your reimbursement arrangement qualified as an accountable plan, and you made an adequate reporting to your employer, the $1,600 would not be reported as income on your Form W-2, and you would not have to be concerned with the 2% floor for miscellaneous itemized deductions. There is a bookkeeping "wash." In other words, you receive a full deduction by substantiating the expenses to your employer.

Reimbursements of club dues or spousal travel costs. If you are reimbursed for nondeductible club dues *(20.22)* or nondeductible travel costs of a spouse or other person *(20.13)*, the reimbursement may be treated by your employer as taxable wages. If it is, you are not allowed an offsetting deduction. If the reimbursement is not treated as taxable wages by your employer, and you substantiate a business purpose for the club dues or for a travel companion's presence, the reimbursement is considered to be a tax-free working condition fringe benefit *(3.8)*.

EXAMPLE

A company pays for the country club dues of an executive. In 1997, it reimbursed dues of $20,000, and the executive used the club for business purposes 40% of the time. If the company does not treat the reimbursement as taxable wages but as a fringe benefit, $8,000 of the reimbursement is not taxable to the executive; $12,000 allocated to personal use is taxable.

20.31 What Is an Accountable Plan?

A reimbursement or allowance arrangement is an accountable plan if it requires you to:

- Adequately account to your employer for your expenses; *and*
- Return to your employer any excess reimbursement or allowance which you do not show was spent for ordinary and necessary business expenses.

If these terms are met and your expenses are fully reimbursed, you do not report the expenses or the reimbursement on your return. If the reimbursement is less than your payment of expenses, you use Form 2106 and Schedule A to claim a deduction for the unreimbursed expenses. The unreimbursed expenses are subject to the 2% AGI floor on Schedule A.

What is an adequate accounting? You adequately account to your employer by submitting bills and an account book, diary, or similar record in which you entered each expense at or near the time you had it. You must account to your employer for all amounts received as advances, reimbursements, or allowances, including amounts charged on a company credit card. Your records and supporting information must meet the rules of *20.27*. You must also pay back any reimbursements or allowances for which you do not adequately account or the nonreturned accounts will be taxable under the rules at *20.34* for nonaccountable plans.

Court Decision

Ask for Reimbursement

If you are entitled to reimbursement from your employer, make sure you ask for reimbursement. Failure to be reimbursed may prevent you from deducting your out-of-pocket expenses. A supervisor whose responsibility was to maintain good relations with his district and store managers entertained them and their families and also distributed gifts among them. His cost was $2,500 for which he could have been reimbursed by his company, but he made no claim. Consequently, the Tax Court disallowed it as a deduction on his return. The expense was the company's; any goodwill he created benefitted it. But because he failed to seek reimbursement, he was not allowed to convert company expenses into his own.

The accounting requirements are eased if you are reimbursed under a *per diem* arrangement covering meals, lodging, and incidental expenses *(20.32)* or you receive a flat mileage allowance *(20.33)*.

Time limits for receiving advances, substantiating expenses, and returning excess payments. The general rule is that these events must occur within a reasonable time. Under an IRS "safe harbor," the following payments are considered to be within a reasonable time:

- Advance payments—if given to you within 30 days before you reasonably anticipate to pay or incur expenses;
- Substantiation of expenses—if provided to your employer within 60 days after the expense is paid or incurred; and
- Return of excess—if done within 120 days after you pay or incur expense.

An employer may set up a "periodic statement method" to meet IRS rules. Here, an employer gives each employee periodic statements (at least quarterly) that list the amounts paid in excess of expenses substantiated by the employee and request substantiation of the additional amounts paid, or a return of the excess, within 120 days of the date of the statement. Substantiation or return within the 120-day period satisfies the reasonable time test.

Allocating reimbursements to meals and entertainment. Only 50% of meals and entertainment expenses are deductible. Therefore, if you adequately account for your expenses, and receive a flat reimbursement that is partly for meals and entertainment, and partly for other expenses, you must allocate part of the reimbursement to meals and entertainment if the employer has not provided an item-by-item breakdown. You must make this allocation if you want to deduct expenses exceeding reimbursements because on Form 2106, you must separately list meals and entertainment costs and reimbursements for meals and entertainment. The allocation is based on the percentage which your meal costs bear to the total T&E expenses.

 Filing Tip

Failure To Timely Return Excess
If you fail to return excess payments within a reasonable time but you meet all of the other tests applied to an accountable plan, such as providing proof of the expenses, only the retained excess is taxed to you as if paid outside of an accountable plan.

> **EXAMPLE**
> You receive an allowance of $1,000 for travel expenses and have total expenses of $1,500, including $300 for meals. The percentage of your meals to total expenses is 20% (300 ÷ 1,500). On Form 2106, you show 20% of the allowance or $200 as the allocable reimbursement for meals. The unreimbursed $100 balance for meals ($300 – $200) must be reduced to $50 by the 50% reduction for meals. You may deduct $400 of the $1,200 in expenses that were not for meals; 80% of the $1,000 travel allowance is allocated to such costs. The total deductible amount of $450 ($50 for meals and $400 for other expenses) is transferred from Form 2106 to Schedule A, where it is deductible as a miscellaneous itemized expense subject to the 2% AGI floor.

20.32 *Per Diem* Travel Allowance Under Accountable Plans

Instead of providing a straight reimbursement for substantiated out-of-pocket travel expenses, an employer may use a *per diem* allowance to cover meals, lodging, and incidental expenses on business trips away from home. Incidental expenses covered by a *per diem* arrangement may include tips, laundry, and cleaning fees, or similar expenses, but, under IRS rules, may not include cab fares, telephone, or telegram costs.

If the *accountable plan* rules *(20.31)* are met and you are not related to the employer, you do not have to give your employer proof of your actual expenses if you receive a *per diem* allowance or reimbursement that is equal to or less than the federal travel rate for the particular area.

For allowances in 1997 covering lodging plus meals and incidental expenses for travel *within* the continental U.S., an employer may use an IRS high-low rate of $109 for most areas or $166 per day for "high-cost" areas, instead of the federal travel rate.

Tables published by the government show the federal travel rate for areas within the continental U.S. (called CONUS locations) and for areas outside the continental U.S., including Hawaii and Alaska (called OCONUS locations). The CONUS federal travel rates and IRS high-low rates are in IRS Publication 1542.

If your employer's method of fixing and reviewing *per diem* arrangements qualifies, you do not have to keep hotel receipts. You do have to account for the time, place, and business purpose of your travel. If you do *not* provide such an accounting for some travel days, you must be required to return the *per diem* allowance received for such days in order for the employer's plan to qualify.

Employees related to the employer. The IRS *per diem* rules that allow you to avoid accounting for actual expenses do not apply if you work for a brother, sister, spouse, parent, child, grandparent, or grandchild. They also do not apply if you are an employee-stockholder who owns more than 10% of the company's stock.

Reporting a *per diem* allowance. If the allowance does not exceed the federal travel rate or IRS high-low rate, the reimbursement is not reported on Form W-2. If your expenses do not exceed the reimbursement, you do not have to report the expenses or the reimbursement on your tax return; *see* Example 1 below. If your expenses exceed the allowance, you may deduct the excess by reporting the expenses and reimbursement on Form 2106. The net amount from Form 2106, after applying the 50% reduction for meals, is claimed on Schedule A as a miscellaneous expense subject to the 2% AGI floor; *see* Example 2 below.

Meal allowance only. If your employer gives you a *per diem* allowance covering only meals and incidental expenses, it is not taxable to you if you are not related to the employer and the allowance does not exceed the IRS meal allowance rates under *20.4.*

For meals *outside* the continental U.S., the meal allowance rates of *20.4* do not apply. The allowable meal allowance rates are listed in the government's OCONUS tables.

Caution

Excess *Per Diem* Allowances
If a *per diem* allowance exceeds the federal travel rate or the IRS high-low rate, the excess will be reported as income on your Form W-2, unless you return the excess; *see* Example 3 on the right. The excess reportable on Form W-2 is also subject to income tax and FICA tax withholding.

EXAMPLES
1. You take a three-day business trip to a locality at a time when the federal travel rate for the area is $106 per day. You account for the date, place, and business purpose of the trip. Your employer reimburses you $106 a day for lodging, meals, and incidental expenses, for a total of $318. Your actual expenses do not exceed this amount. Your employer does not report the reimbursement on your Form W-2. You do not have to report the reimbursement or deduct any expenses on your return.
2. Same facts as Example 1, except that the reimbursement is less than your actual expenses of $330 for which you have records. On Form 2106, you report the $318 reimbursement and your $330 of expenses. You also must allocate part of the allowance to meals to apply the 50% limit. The net amount from Form 2106 is deductible on Schedule A as a miscellaneous expense subject to the 2% AGI limit.
3. Same facts as Example 1, except that you receive a per diem allowance of $114 per day—$8 per day more than the federal travel rate. If you do not return the excess of $24 ($8 × 3 days) within a reasonable time *(20.31)*, your employer must report the $24 as income in Box 1 of your Form W-2. The amount up to the federal travel rate, or $318, will be reported in Box 13 of Form W-2, but not included as income.

20.33 Automobile Mileage Allowance

If your employer pays you a fixed mileage allowance of up to 31.5 cents per mile for 1997, the amount of your automobile expenses is treated as substantiated, provided you show the time, place, and business purpose of your travel. If the allowance is in the form of an advance, it must be given within a reasonable period before the anticipated travel and you must also be required to return within a reasonable period *(20.31)* any portion of the allowance that covers mileage that you have not substantiated.

If these tests are met, the allowance will not be reported as income on Form W-2, and you will not have to report the allowance or expenses on your return; *see* Example 1 in this section. If you do not prove to your employer the time, place, and purpose of your travel the entire reimbursement is treated as paid from a nonaccountable plan and will be reported as income on Form W-2.

If you were given a 1997 mileage allowance in excess of 31.5 cents per mile, the excess will be included as wages on your Form W-2; *see* Example 2. If your allowance was less than 31.5 cents per mile, you may deduct the difference as a miscellaneous itemized deduction subject to the 2% AGI floor; *see* Example 3.

Your employer may reimburse you for parking fees and tolls in addition to the mileage allowance.

EXAMPLES
1. You drive 12,000 miles for business and account to your employer for the time, place, and business purpose of each trip. Your employer reimburses you at the IRS rate of 31.5 cents per mile. None of the reimbursements will be reported as income on your Form W-2, and you do not have to report the reimbursements or any expenses on your return if your expenses do not exceed 31.5 cents per mile.

2. Same as Example 1 except that you were reimbursed at 32 cents per mile. The amount using the IRS rate, or $3,780 (31.5¢ × 12,000 miles), is $60 less than the reimbursement of $3,840 (32¢ × 12,000). The $60 excess over the IRS rate will be reported as wages on your Form W-2.

   If you had records substantiating expenses over 31.5 cents per mile, you could claim them on Form 2106. The excess of your expenses over the IRS rate is shown on Form 2106, and that excess is claimed on Schedule A as a miscellaneous itemized deduction subject to the 2% AGI floor.

3. Same as Example 1 except that you were reimbursed only 20 cents per mile. The reimbursements will not be reported as income on your Form W-2. You may deduct expenses up to the 31.5-cent IRS rate by reporting the expenses and reimbursements on Form 2106. The amount using the IRS rate, or $3,780 (31.5¢ × 12,000 miles), is $1,380 more than the reimbursement of $2,400 (20¢ × 12,000 miles). The $1,380 may be claimed as a miscellaneous itemized deduction on Schedule A subject to the 2% AGI floor.

   If you had records showing actual expenses of more than $3,780, you would claim those expenses on Form 2106 and not use the IRS fixed mileage allowance rate to figure your deduction.

Fixed and variable rate allowance (FAVR).   In lieu of setting the allowance at the IRS standard mileage rate (31.5 cents per mile in 1997), an employer may use a fixed or variable rate allowance, called a FAVR, that gives employees a cents-per-mile rate to cover gas and other operating costs, plus a flat amount to cover fixed costs such as depreciation, insurance and registration. A FAVR allowance must reflect local driving costs and allows employers to set reimbursements at a rate that more closely approximates employee expenses. If your employer sets up a qualifying FAVR under IRS guidelines, you will be required to provide records substantiating your mileage and certain car ownership information. Expenses up to the FAVR limits are deemed substantiated and will not be reported as wages on your Form W-2.

20.34 Reimbursements Under Non-Accountable Plans

A non-accountable plan is one that either does not require you to adequately account for your expenses, or allows you to keep any excess reimbursement or allowances over the expenses for which you did adequately account.

Your employer reports allowances or reimbursements for a nonaccountable plan as part of your salary income in Box 1 of your Form W-2. The allowance is also subject to income tax and FICA tax (Social Security) withholding. To claim deductions, you must use Form 2106 and itemize your deductions on Schedule A. Your expenses are subject to the 2% AGI floor.

Planning Reminder

Importance of Adequate Accounting
If you adequately report expenses to your employer and return excess reimbursements, you are treated as being reimbursed under an accountable plan and generally do not have to report any reimbursement on your return; *see* *20.31.*

Chapter 21

Personal Exemptions

Each personal exemption you claim on your 1997 return is the equivalent of a $2,650 deduction. Exemptions for children, parents, and other dependents are allowed if the tests of this chapter are met.

If you have a high adjusted gross income, you may lose the benefit of your deduction under the phase-out rule discussed in *21.15*.

Number of Exemptions	Deduction Allowed
1	$ 2,650
2	5,300
3	7,950
4	10,600
5	13,250
6	15,900
7	18,550
8	21,200
9	23,850
10	26,500

21.1 How Many Exemptions May You Claim?

On your 1997 return, you may claim a $2,650 exemption for each of the following, provided you are not subject to the phaseout of exemptions for high income taxpayers (*see 21.15*):

- *Yourself.* You claim an exemption for yourself unless you are the dependent of another taxpayer. If someone else can claim you as a dependent for 1997, you may not claim a personal exemption for yourself on your own return; this is true even if the other person does not actually claim you as a dependent. This rule prevents your child or other dependent from claiming an exemption on his or her return if you may claim an exemption for the child or other dependent.
- *Your spouse.* You claim your spouse as an exemption when you file a joint return. If you file a separate return, you claim your spouse as an exemption if he or she has no income and is not a dependent of another person; *see 21.2.*
- *Children, parents, and other dependents.* An individual qualifies as your dependent if the following tests are met for each person claimed:

  1. The relationship test discussed at *21.3* or the member of household test at *21.4*.
  2. The gross income test for dependents, which does not apply to your children who are under age 19 or full-time students under age 24 as of the end of the year; *see 21.5–21.6*.
  3. The 50% support test at *21.7*, or the 10% multiple support test at *21.10*.
  4. The citizenship or residence test for dependents; *see 21.12*.
  5. For dependents who are married, the joint return test; *see 21.13*.

21.2 Your Spouse as an Exemption

Your spouse is not your dependent for tax purposes. An exemption for a spouse is based on the marital relationship, not support. On a joint return, each spouse receives an exemption as a taxpayer.

On a separate return, you may claim your spouse as an exemption if he or she has no gross income and is not the dependent of another taxpayer. You may not claim an exemption for your spouse who has income, *unless you file a joint return which includes that income.* For example, if a wife files a separate return, her husband may not claim her as an exemption, even if she filed the return merely for a refund of taxes withheld on her wages.

If your spouse is a nonresident alien, has no income from U.S. sources, and is not a dependent of another person, you may claim an exemption for your spouse on a separate return.

If divorced or legally separated during the year. You may not claim your former spouse as an exemption if you are divorced or legally separated under a *final* decree of divorce or separate maintenance, even if you provided his or her entire support. However, an interlocutory (not final) decree does not bar you from claiming your spouse as an exemption.

> **EXAMPLE**
>
> An interlocutory (not final) decree of divorce is entered in 1997, and a final decree in 1998. For 1997, the couple may file a joint return on which exemptions for both are claimed. A marriage is not dissolved until a final decree is entered, which in this case is in 1998.

Your spouse died during the year. If you did not remarry and your deceased spouse had gross income, you may claim an exemption for your spouse only if you file a joint return that includes his or her income. You may claim the exemption on a separate return only if your spouse had no gross income and was not a dependent of another taxpayer.

> **EXAMPLE**
>
> Sylvia Smith dies on June 27. Her husband Steve Smith may file a joint return and claim Sylvia as an exemption. They were married as of the date of Sylvia's death. The joint return includes all of Steve's income for the year, but only that part of Sylvia's income earned up to June 27; *see 1.5*.

If you remarry before the end of the year in which your spouse died, you may not claim an exemption for your deceased spouse. If you file a joint return with your new spouse, you may be claimed as an exemption on that return. If you had *no* income for the year, you may be claimed as an exemption on both your deceased spouse's separate return and on a separate return filed by your new spouse, provided no one else may claim you as a dependent.

Planning Reminder

You Must Report I.D. Numbers for Dependents

You must obtain and report on your return the Social Security number of each dependent claimed. Nonresident and resident aliens not eligible for Social Security numbers must have an individual taxpayer identification number; *see 21.14*.

Caution

Phaseout of Exemptions

Your 1997 deduction for exemptions is phased out if your adjusted gross income exceeds these thresholds: $181,800 if married filing jointly; $151,500 if filing as head of household; looses $121,200 if filing as single; and $90,900 if married and filing separately. *See 21.15* for full details.

Tests for Claiming Dependents

TEST 1. RELATIONSHIP OR MEMBER OF HOUSE-HOLD TEST

The person must be either:

Your relative—child, stepchild, adopted child, grandchild, great-grandchild, son- or daughter-in-law, father- or mother-in-law, brother- or sister-in-law, parent, brother, sister, grandparent, step-parent, stepbrother or sister, half-brother or sister, and, if related by blood, an uncle, aunt, niece, or nephew. These relatives do not have to live with you. However, a foster child qualifies only if he or she is a member of your household for the entire year, apart from temporary absences; see 21.3.

Or—any person, whether related or not, who is a member of your household for the entire year, except for temporary absences. The exemption is not allowed if the person was your spouse at any time during the year, or if your relationship with such person is in violation of state law; see 21.4.

TEST 2. GROSS INCOME TEST

Your child—If at the end of 1997 your child was under age 19, or was a full-time student under age 24 (21.6), his or her income does not matter. You can claim the child as your dependent if Tests 3, 4, and 5 are met. However, a child who was age 19–23 and not a full-time student at the end of the year, or who was age 24 or older, may be claimed as your dependent only if his or her gross income was less than $2,650 in 1997.

Other relatives or household members—must have gross income of less than $2,650 in 1997.

For 1998, the $2,650 income limit will be adjusted for inflation.

TEST 3. SUPPORT TEST

You either contribute more than half the dependent's support, or contribute more than 10% and together with others contribute more than half; see 21.7 and 21.10.

Total the dollar amount of support spent on a dependent by you, by others, and by the dependent. If your contribution is:

- *More than 50% of the total spent*—you claim the exemption.
- *More than 10% of the total spent and together with what you and the other contributors gave is more than 50% of the total spent*—you or one of the others who also contributed more than 10% may claim the exemption. You and the others must decide who is to claim the exemption. If you take it, you must attach to your return a Form 2120, "Multiple Support Declaration," signed by each person who contributed more than 10%.
- *Less than 50%, either alone or with the contribution of others*—neither you nor the other contributors may claim the exemption for the dependent.

Special support rules apply to divorced or separated parents; see 21.11.

TEST 4. CITIZENSHIP OR RESIDENT TEST

Your dependent is a United States citizen or national, or a resident of the United States, Canada, or Mexico; see 21.12.

TEST 5. JOINT RETURN TEST

Your married dependent does not file a joint return with his or her spouse; see 21.13 for an exception.

21.3 Test 1. Relationship Test

If the other tests are met (Tests 2–5 in 21.1), you may claim an exemption for a dependent relative listed in this section, even if he or she is an adult, healthy, and capable of self-support. An unrelated person or distantly related person not listed may still qualify as an exemption under the tests at 21.4.

Your children. If your child was born at the end of 1997, you may claim a full $2,650 exemption for that child.

A stillborn child may not be claimed as an exemption. The exemption is allowed for a child who was born alive even if the infant lived for only a moment.

Stepchildren. Your stepchild is considered your child.

Adopted children. A *legally adopted* child is treated as your child. A child is considered legally adopted when a court decree is entered. In states allowing interlocutory (not final) adoption decrees, you may claim the exemption in the year the interlocutory decree is entered.

If a court decree has not been entered, a child may be your dependent provided he or she was placed with you for adoption by an authorized adoption agency and was a member of your household for the rest of the year. If the child has not been placed with you for adoption by an agency, you may claim the child as a dependent *only if* he or she was a member of your household for the entire tax year; see 21.4.

Foster child. A foster child is considered to be your child if he or she is a member of your household for the entire year except for temporary absences.

Other qualifying relatives. The following individuals also meet the relationship test: your parent, grandparent, great-grandparent, step-parent, grandchild, great-grandchild, brother, sister, half-brother, half-sister, stepbrother, stepsister, son- or daughter-in-law, father- or mother-in-law, and brother- or sister-in-law. If related by blood, aunts, uncles, nieces, and nephews also qualify.

Stepchild's husband or wife or child. Your stepchild's spouse does not meet the relationship test. Nor may you claim an exemption for a step-grandchild if you file a separate return. They are not on the list of relatives qualifying. But you may claim them as exemptions on a joint return. On a joint return, it is not necessary that the close relationship exist between the dependent and the spouse who furnishes the chief support. It is sufficient that the relationship exists with either spouse.

> **EXAMPLE**
>
> You contribute more than half of the support of the sister of your wife's mother (your wife's aunt). If you and your wife file a joint return, her aunt is allowed as an exemption on your joint return. But your wife's aunt's husband is not related by blood to you or your wife. You cannot claim an exemption for him, even on a joint return, unless he is a member of your household under the rules of *21.4*.

In-laws. Brother-in-law, sister-in-law, father-in-law, mother-in-law, son-in-law, and daughter-in-law are relatives by marriage. You may claim them as exemptions if you meet the other tests in this chapter.

You may claim an exemption for an in-law who was related to you by marriage and whom you continue to support after divorce or the death of your spouse.

> **EXAMPLE**
>
> Allen has contributed all the support of his father-in-law since he was married. Allen's wife died in 1996. He continued sole support of his wife's father in 1997. Allen may claim him as an exemption in 1997.

Death during the year. If a relative died during 1997 but was supported by you while alive, and you meet the other tests listed in this chapter, you may claim an exemption.

> **EXAMPLE**
>
> On January 21, 1997, your father died. Until that date, you contributed all of his support. You may claim him as an exemption for 1997. The full deduction is taken. Exemptions are not prorated.

 Filing Tip

Nephew, Niece, Uncle, and Aunt

Nephews, nieces, uncles, and aunts must be your blood relatives to qualify under the relationship test. For example, the brother or sister of your father or mother qualifies as your relative; their spouses do not. You may not claim your spouse's nephews, nieces, uncles, or aunts unless you file a joint return.

21.4 Unrelated or Distantly Related Dependents Living With You

A friend or a relative not listed in *21.3*—such as a cousin who lives with you—can be your dependent. You may claim an unrelated or distantly related person as a dependent if the other dependent tests are met *and:*

1. The person is a member of your household; and
2. Your home is his or her principal home for the entire year, except for absences when attending school, vacationing, or being confined to a hospital. You may not claim a friend as an exemption when you live in his or her house even though you provide support. You are living in his or her household—not your own. Also, you cannot claim an exemption for a friend who lives in your house and renders you services in return for your care.

> **EXAMPLES**
>
> 1. Carol Barnes supports her niece Phyllis, who lives in Carol's house all year. Carol can claim Phyllis as a dependent member of her household if Phyllis meets the citizenship test *(21.12)* and has gross income under $2,650 in 1997 *(21.5)*.
> 2. Roger Johnson provides a home for an orphan for seven months. He cannot claim the child as a dependent; the child did not live in his home for the entire year. However, if the child had been placed in his home for adoption by an authorized adoption agency, he or she may be claimed as Johnson's dependent although not a member of his household for the entire year; *see* the adopted children rule at *21.3*.
> 3. Mike Pilla supports a cousin, Janet, who lives in a house owned by him. Mike lives elsewhere and may not claim his cousin as a dependent because they do not live in the same house.

Your spouse or former spouse. Under the tax law, one spouse is not considered a dependent of the other; *see 21.2*. If you are divorced or legally separated during the year, your former spouse cannot qualify as your dependent even if he or she is a member of your household for the whole year.

Caution

Exemption for Unmarried Mate
An exemption for an unmarried mate depends on local law. Where the relationship violates local law, no exemption may be claimed.

EXAMPLE

Ensminger lived in North Carolina with a woman whom he supported. When he claimed an exemption for her, the IRS disallowed the exemption, claiming that under North Carolina law it is a misdemeanor for an unmarried man and woman to live together. When the Tax Court supported the IRS position, Ensminger appealed, arguing that the North Carolina law was an unconstitutional invasion of his right to privacy. The appeals court held that constitutionality was not an issue for the IRS and Tax Court to decide. The states are responsible for regulating domestic affairs. Federal tax law merely follows the direction of state law. If Ensminger lived in a state that did not hold his relationship illegal, he could claim the exemption.

In a similar case, a dependency exemption was allowed where the court ruled cohabitation did not violate Missouri law.

21.5 Test 2. Gross Income Limit for Dependents

A gross income limit applies to—

• Dependents who are not your children—such as parents, in-laws, sisters, brothers, uncles, aunts, and members of your household; *and*
• Your children who at the end of the year are age 19 or over and not full-time students, *or* children who are full-time students age 24 or older at the end of the year; *see 21.6*.

For 1997, the gross income test requires your dependent to have a gross income of less than $2,650. If a dependent has gross income in 1997 of $2,650 or more, he or she may not be claimed as an exemption, even if all of the support is provided by you. The only exception is for your children who are under age 19 or who are full-time students under age 24; *see 21.6*.

Gross income here means taxable income items includible in the dependent's tax return. It does not include nontaxable items such as gifts and tax-exempt bond interest. Gross income for a service-type business is gross receipts without deductions of expenses and for a manufacturing or merchandising business is total sales less cost of goods sold. A partner's share of partnership gross income, not the share of net income, is treated as gross income.

Gross income does not include income earned by a totally and permanently disabled individual at a school operated by a government agency or tax-exempt organization, if the school provides special instruction for alleviating the disability and the income is incidental to medical care received.

Social Security benefits are treated as gross income only to the extent they are taxable under the rules of *34.3*.

EXAMPLES

1. Larry Jones gives $4,000 a year for his father's support. The father owns a two-family house. He lives in one apartment and rents the other for $250 a month, giving him a gross annual income of $3,000. After deducting interest and taxes, his net income is $1,800. Larry may not claim his father as a dependent as his 1997 gross income is not under $2,650.

2. Lisa Burr's son, age 21 and *not* a full-time student *(21.6)* in 1997, received $10,000 in damages for personal injuries suffered in an accident. His only other income was bank interest of $450. Since the damages are excluded from gross income *(11.7)*, the gross income test is satisfied. However, if Lisa's son used part of the damages to support himself, she may claim him as a dependent for 1997 only if her support contributions were larger; *see* the checklist of support items in *21.7*.

3. Kent Dolin's widowed father received $5,000 in Social Security benefits which he used to support himself *(21.7)*. He also received $1,200 in bank interest. Under *34.3*, the benefits are not subject to tax and therefore not treated as gross income. His gross income of $1,200 is below the $2,650 limit. If Kent contributed more than $5,000 to his support, he meets the support test *(21.7)* and may claim his father as a dependent.

21.6 Children Under Age 19 or Full-Time Students Under Age 24

The tax law provides you with a break for dependent children. There is no gross income limit *(21.5)* for—

1. Your children who are under age 24 as of the end of the year if they are full-time students; *and*
2. Your children under age 19 as of the end of the year, whether or not they are students.

Such children may earn *any* amount and still be claimed as your dependents, provided you meet the support test *(21.7)* and the other exemption tests discussed in this chapter.

This rule applies to your child, stepchild, and adopted child. It also applies to a foster child who, for the entire year, is a member of your household. It does not apply to a grandchild, a son- or daughter-in-law, or a brother or sister who is a full-time student; they must have gross income of less than $2,650 in 1997 to qualify as your dependents.

Qualifying as a full-time student. A full-time student is one who attends school full time during at least five calendar months in the tax year. For example: attendance from February through some part of June—or from February through May and then at least one month from September through December—qualifies. The five months do not have to run consecutively. Attendance at a vocational, trade, or technical school for the five-month period qualifies, but not correspondence schools or on-the-job training courses.

> **EXAMPLES**
> 1. Benita Rosa's unmarried daughter, who is age 22, attended college full time until she graduated in June 1997. The gross income test does not apply to her earnings in 1997 because she was a full-time student for at least five months during the year. However, Benita must meet the support test *(21.7)* to claim her daughter as her dependent.
> 2. Peter Block's son John, who is age 19, worked during the first half of the year and then started college in September. Peter may not claim John as an exemption if John earned $2,650 or more. Although John is a full-time student as of the end of the year, he did not attend school for at least five months during the year.

Night school. Your child who attends night school is considered a full-time student *only if* he or she is enrolled for the number of hours or classes that is considered full-time attendance at a similar daytime school.

21.7 Test 3. 50% Support Test

If your dependent has no financial means and you are the only person contributing to his or her support during the year, you can skip the following discussion on support. You meet the support test. You contribute 100% of the dependent's support. If, however, the dependent or other persons or organizations contribute to his or her support, you have to determine whether your contribution exceeds 50% of the dependent's total support.

Meeting the support test. Follow these steps to figure support: (1) Total the value of the support contributed by you, by the dependent, and by others for the dependent. Use the checklists later in this section for determining what to include in total support and what to exclude. (2) Determine your share of the total. If your share is more than 50% of the dependent's total support, you meet the support test. It does not matter how many months or days you provided the support; only the total cost of the support is considered. If the dependent or some other person or organization contributed 50% or more of the dependent's support, you may not take the exemption. If the dependent or someone else did not contribute 50% or more of the support, and you contributed more than 10% of the total support, you may be able to claim the exemption under a multiple support agreement; *see 21.10.*

Divorced or separated parents contributing to support of their children should follow the special support rules at *21.11.*

Students Age 24 or Older
The favorable rule that disregards income of full-time students applies only to students who are under age 24 as of the end of the year. If your child was age 24 or older at the end of 1997 and had gross income of $2,650 or more, you may not claim him or her as a dependent.

Support of Children Earning Income
Although there is no gross income test for your children who are under age 19 or who are full-time students under age 24, you must still meet the support test of *21.7* to claim them as your dependents. If your child has income, be prepared to show either that the income was not used for his or her support, or that your support contributions were larger. Use the checklists at *21.7* for determining what must be treated as "support."

Checklist of Support Items

- Food and lodging; *see 21.8*
- Clothing
- Medical and dental expenses, including premiums paid for health insurance policies and supplementary Medicare
- Education expenses such as tuition, books, and supplies. If your child receives a student loan and is the primary obligor, the loan proceeds are considered his or her own support contribution. This is true even if you are a guarantor of the loan. Scholarships received by full-time students are *not* treated as support; *see* the following checklist of nonsupport items.
- Cars and transportation expenses. Include the cost of a car bought for a dependent as support. If you buy a car but register it in your own name, the cost of the car is *not* support provided by you, but any out-of-pocket expenses you have for operating the car are part of your support contribution.
- Recreation and entertainment. A computer or TV set bought for your child or other dependent is support. Also include costs of summer camp, singing and dancing lessons, and musical instruments, as well as wedding expenses.

Personal savings, Social Security, and tax-free income may be support. In figuring a person's total support, include his or her tax-exempt income, personal savings, and Social Security benefits if actually used for support items such as food, lodging, or clothing. Also include support items that are financed by loans. Income that is invested and not actually spent for support is not included in the earner's total support.

Where husband and wife are paid Social Security benefits in one check made out in their joint names, 50% is considered to be used by each spouse unless shown otherwise.

Government benefits. In figuring whether you have provided more than 50% of the dependent's support, you have to consider certain government benefits as support provided by a third party. For example, welfare, including AFDC (Aid to Families with Dependent Children), food stamps, or housing payments based on need, are state support payments if they are used for support items. G.I. Bill education assistance is support provided by the government.

Foster care payments by a child placement agency to parents are support provided by the agency and not by the parents. The value of board, lodging, and education provided to a child in a state juvenile home is treated as support provided by the state.

When a person joins the Armed Forces, the value of board, lodging, and clothing he or she receives is treated as the government's support contribution. However, if *you* are in the Armed Forces, dependency allotments withheld from your pay and used to support your dependents are included in *your* support contributions for them. Also included in your support contribution is a military quarters allowance covering a dependent.

Checklist of Items Not Counted as Support

- Federal, state, and local income taxes and Social Security taxes paid by the dependent from his or her own income
- Funeral expenses
- Life insurance premiums
- Medicare Part A (basic Medicare) and Part B (Supplementary Medicare benefits). In one case the IRS argued that Medicaid benefits were includible in total support but the Tax Court disagreed, holding that Medicaid is similar to excludable Medicare benefits.
- Medical insurance benefits received by the dependent
- Scholarships received by your child, stepchild, or legally adopted child who is a full-time student for at least five calendar months during the year. Scholarship aid is counted as support contributed by the child if he or she is not a full-time student for at least five months. Naval R.O.T.C. payments and payments made under the War Orphans Educational Assistance Act are scholarships that are not counted as support. State aid to a handicapped child for education or training, including room and board, is a scholarship.

EXAMPLES

1. Anna Chung's son invests half of his earnings from a part-time job and spends the other half on recreation. The invested earnings are not treated as support. If Anna's support payments exceed the amount her son spent for recreation, and no one else contributes to his support, Anna meets the support test.

2. Eric Hill receives Social Security benefits of $6,000 and also $300 in bank interest. He spends $4,400 on food, clothes, transportation, and recreation. The $4,400 spent is his contribution to his own support. Eric's rent, utilities, medical expenses, and other necessities are paid by his son, Mike. If Mike's payments exceed $4,400, and no one else contributes to Eric's support, Mike may claim Eric as a dependent.

3. Social Security benefits paid to children of deceased workers *which are used for their support* are treated as the children's contribution to their own support. Follow this rule even though benefits are paid to you as the child's parent or custodian. If the Social Security benefits used for a child's support are more than half of the child's total support, no one may claim the child as a dependent.

21.8 Lodging and Food as Support

You count as support the *fair rental value* of a room, apartment, or house in which the dependent lives. In your estimate, you include a reasonable allowance for the rental value of furnishings and appliances, and for heat and other utilities. You do *not* add payments of rent, taxes, interest, depreciation, paint, insurance, and utilities. These are presumed to be accounted for in the fair rental estimate. The fair rental value of lodging you furnish a dependent is the amount you could reasonably expect to receive from a stranger for the lodging.

Does dependent live in own home?   If the dependent lives in his or her own home, treat the total fair rental value as his or her own contribution to support. However, if you help maintain his or her home by giving cash, or you directly pay such expenses as the mortgage, real estate taxes, fire insurance premiums, and repairs, you reduce the total fair rental value of the home by the amount you contributed; *see* Example 1 below.

If you lived with your dependent rent-free in his or her home, the fair rental value of lodging furnished to you must be offset against the amounts you spent for your dependent in determining the net amount of your contribution to his or her support.

Food and other similar household expenses.   If the dependent lives with you, you divide your total food expenses equally among all the members of your household, unless you have records showing the exact amount spent on the dependent; *see* the Examples in *21.9*. If he or she does not live with you, you count the actual amount of food expenses spent by or for that dependent.

Do you pay for a relative's care in a health facility?   If you pay part of a relative's expenses for care in a state-supported hospital or nursing home, your payment is a support contribution. If you make a lump-sum contribution covering a relative's stay in an old-age home or other care facility, you prorate your payment over the relative's life expectancy to determine the current support contribution; *see* Examples 2 and 3 below.

EXAMPLES

1. You contribute $7,000 as support to your father who lives in his own home, which has a fair rental value of $8,000 a year. He uses $4,600 of the money you give him to pay real estate taxes. He spends $3,000 of his Social Security for recreation and invests the rest. He has no gross income *(21.5)* and receives no other support. Your father's total support is computed as follows:

Cash contributed by you	$7,000
Fair rental value of house ($8,000 *less* $4,600 for taxes)	3,400
Social Security spent	3,000
Father's total support	$13,400

You may claim your father as a dependent because your contribution of $7,000 exceeds half of his total support.

2. A son secures his father's placement in a religious home for a lump-sum payment of $89,600. The payment was determined on the basis of $11,200 a year over the father's life expectancy of eight years. If the father dies within eight years no refund is due. The son counts $11,200 as an annual contribution to his father's support. If this is more than half of his father's yearly support costs, the son may claim the exemption. If the father fails to reach his life expectancy, the son may *not* deduct any unused part of the $89,600 as a charitable deduction.

3. In 1997, your father was a patient in a state hospital. The state required you to pay part of his expenses and you paid the state $15,000. In the state budget report for 1997, the

average cost of maintaining an individual in the hospital was listed as $25,000. As you contributed over half of your father's support, you may claim him as a dependent. If he required special care, such as private nursing or a major operation, the actual cost to the state agency for maintaining him during the year, rather than the average cost, would be used to measure your father's total support.

21.9 Examples of Allocating Support

The Examples in this section illustrate how you should allocate various support items when your contributions benefit more than one person or when your dependent provides part of his or her own support.

Earmarking support to one dependent. If you are contributing funds to a household consisting of several persons and the amount you contribute does not exceed 50% of the total household support, you may be able to claim an exemption for at least one dependent by earmarking your support to his or her use. Your earmarked contributions must exceed 50% of this dependent's support costs. Mark your checks for the benefit of the dependent, or provide the dependents with a written statement of your support arrangement at the time you start your payments. The IRS says its agents will generally accept such evidence of your arrangement. If you do not designate for whom you are providing support, your contribution is allocated equally among all members of a household (*see* Example 3 on the next page).

EXAMPLES

1. Your father lives in your home with you, your spouse, and your three children. He receives Social Security benefits of $9,800, which are not subject to tax *(34.3)* and half of which ($4,900) he spends for his own clothing, travel, and recreation. You spend $6,600 for food during the year. You also paid his dental bill of $500. You estimate the annual fair rental value of the room furnished him is $3,600. Your father's total support is:

Social Security used for support	$4,900
Share of food costs ($\frac{1}{6}$ of $6,600)	1,100
Dental bill paid by you	500
Rental value of room	3,600
	$10,100

You can claim him as a dependent. You contributed more than half his total support, or $5,200 ($3,600 for lodging, $500 for dental, and $1,100 for food).

2. Your parents live with you, your spouse, and your two children in a house you rent. The fair rental value of their room is $3,000. Your father receives a tax-free government pension of $5,200, all of which he spent equally for your mother and himself for clothing and recreation. Your parents' only other income was $3,000 of tax-exempt interest. They did not make any other contributions towards their own support. Your total expense in providing food for the household is $6,000. You pay heat and utility bills of $1,200. You paid your mother's medical expenses of $600. Your father's total support from all sources is $5,100; your mother's is $5,700, figured as follows:

	Father	Mother
Fair rental value of room	$1,500	$1,500
Pension used for their support	2,600	2,600
Share of food costs ($\frac{1}{6}$ of $6,000)	1,000	1000
Medical expenses for mother		600
	$5,100	$5,700

In figuring your parents' total support, you do not include the cost of heat and utilities, because these are presumed to be included in the fair rental value of the room ($3,000).

The support you furnish your father, $2,500 (lodging, $1,500; food, $1,000), is *not* over half of his total support of $5,100. The support you furnish your mother, $3,100 (lodging, $1,500; food, $1,000; medical, $600), *is* over half of her total support of $5,700. You can claim your mother as a dependent but not your father. Since she did not have taxable income, the gross income test *(21.5)* is satisfied.

3. A husband who lives apart from his family without a divorce or legal separation sends his wife $3,240 to meet household expenses. A son and daughter live with her. The wife contributes from her own funds $6,480; an uncle sends her $1,080. The total amount going to meet household expenses from all sources is $10,800. On a separate return, the husband may not claim any exemptions for his children; his contributions are less than 50% of their total support. As he has not earmarked who is to get his contributions, his payments are allocated equally among the three members of the household. Each is considered to have received $1,080 from him. His contribution of $1,080 is less than half of the total support of $3,600 allocated to each child.

Contributed by:		Allocated to:		
	Wife	Son	Daughter	Total
Wife	$2,160	$2,160	$2,160	$6,480
Husband	1,080	1,080	1,080	3,240
Uncle	360	360	360	1,080
Total	$3,600	$3,600	$3,600	$10,800

4. Same facts as in Example 3 except that the husband notes on his monthly checks of $270 that $180 is for his son and $90 for his daughter. He may claim his son as an exemption on a separate return; he has contributed more than half of the son's support. As total household costs of $10,800 are allocated equally among the three household members, the wife's contribution is reallocated to make up for the difference created by the husband's increased support to the son. Here, the wife is considered to have contributed $3,240 to her own support.

Contributed by:		Allocated to:		
	Wife	Son	Daughter	Total
Wife	$3,240	$1,080	$2,160	$6,480
Husband		2,160	1,080	3,240
Uncle	360	360	360	1,080
Total	$3,600	$3,600	$3,600	$10,800

5. Assume that in Example 4 the mother contributed only $6,240 and her son contributed $240. There would be no change in tax consequences; however, the allocation of support contributions would differ. The son's contribution is added to the total household costs, which are allocated equally among the family members to find how much applies to each person's support. However, in determining support contributions, the son is treated as contributing $240 to his own support.

Contributed by:		Allocated to:		
	Wife	Son	Daughter	Total
Wife	$3,240	$ 840	$2,160	$6,240
Son		240		240
Husband		2,160	1,080	3,240
Uncle	360	360	360	1,080
Total	$3,600	$3,600	$3,600	$10,800

21.10 Multiple Support Agreements

Are you and others sharing the support of one person, but with no one individual providing more than half of his or her total support? You may claim the dependent as an exemption if:

1. You gave more than 10% of the support;
2. The amount contributed by you and others to the dependent's support equals more than half the support;
3. Each contributor could have claimed the exemption—except that he or she gave less than half the support; *and*
4. Each contributor who gave more than 10% agrees to let you take the exemption. Each signs a Form 2120, "Multiple Support Agreement." You then attach the forms to your return.

EXAMPLES

1. You and your two brothers contribute $2,000 each toward the support of your mother. She contributes $1,000 of her own to support herself. Your two sisters contribute $500 each. Thus, the total support comes to $8,000. Of this, each brother gave 25% ($2,000

÷ $8,000), for a total of 75%. Each sister gave 6 $\frac{1}{4}$ % ($500 ÷ $8,000). You or one of your brothers may claim the exemption. The total of your contributions is more than half of your mother's support. Each of you contributed more than 10%. Among yourselves, you must decide which brother is to claim the exemption. If you claim the exemption, your brothers must sign Forms 2120, which you attach to your return. If one of your brothers claims the exemption, you sign a Form 2120, which is attached to the return of the brother who claims the exemption. Since neither of your sisters furnished more than 10%, neither can claim the exemption; they need not sign Forms 2120.

2. Your mother's support totals $6,000; you contribute $1,800; your brother, $1,200; your father, $600; and your mother from her savings contributes $2,400. Assume your father does not file a tax return claiming your mother as an exemption. You and your brother cannot use your father's contribution to meet the more than 50% test required by Rule 2 above. Your father may not join in a multiple support agreement because your mother is not his dependent for tax purposes, although an exemption may be claimed for a wife on the basis of the marital relationship; *see 21.2.*

21.11 Divorced or Separated Parents

A special rule favoring the "custodial parent" applies where divorced or separated parents together provide more than half of their child's total support and one or both of them have custody of the child for more than half the year. The "custodial parent" is the parent who had custody of the child for the greater portion of the year; *see* the custody rules below. Under the special rule, the custodial parent is treated as meeting the support test *(21.7)* for the child even if the noncustodial parent actually paid most of the child's support. Although the custodial parent is considered to have met the support test, and, thus, is generally able to claim an exemption for the child, the parents may arrange for the noncustodial parent to claim an exemption for a child in a divorce decree or separation agreement, or the custodial parent may waive his or her right to the exemption in favor of the noncustodial parent.

You must answer yes to the following three tests for the special parental-support rule to apply; otherwise, the general support rules of 21.7 must be used.

Are you divorced or separated?　For the special rules of this section to apply for 1997, you must be divorced or legally separated under a decree of divorce or separate maintenance, or separated under a written agreement, or live apart at all times during the last six months of 1997.

Did you and the other parent provide over 50% of the child's support?　Neither parent may claim the exemption unless the parents together gave more than 50% of the child's support for 1997. If you remarried, support contributions made during 1997 by your new spouse for the child are treated as your own contributions.

These special rules for parents do *not* apply if several people contributing more than 10% of the support enter into a multiple support agreement *(21.10)* authorizing one of them to claim the exemption.

Was the child in your custody or the custody of both you and the other parent for more than half the year?　If the child was not in the custody of either or both parents for more than half of 1997, the exemption is claimed by the person who contributed more than 50% of the child's support *(see 21.7)*, or, if there is no such person, by the person designated in a multiple support agreement under the rules at *21.10.*

Custodial parent.　If the previously discussed three tests are met and you had custody (defined below) for a greater portion of the year than the other parent, you are treated as meeting the support test regardless of your actual support contribution. Thus, you may claim the exemption unless barred under the other exemption tests. However, you may allow the noncustodial parent to claim the exemption by waiving your right to it. The noncustodial parent may also be able to claim it under the terms of a divorce decree or separation agreement.

Note: If a high-income noncustodial parent would be subject to the exemption phaseout *(21.15)*, it would be advisable for the lower-earning custodial spouse to claim the exemption.

Custody is determined by the terms of a decree of divorce or separate maintenance or a written separation agreement. If a decree or agreement does not determine custody, the parent with physical custody for most of the year is the custodial parent. This physical custody rule also applies if parents have joint custody under a decree or agreement, or if the issue of custody is the subject of legal proceedings as of the end of the year.

If you were divorced or separated during 1997, and before that time you had joint custody of the child, the parent who has custody for the greater period of time after the separation is considered the custodial parent.

Custodial parent's waiver on Form 8332 allows noncustodial parent to claim exemption for child.   As the custodial parent, you may waive the exemption by signing a written declaration on Form 8332. When you use the form for the first time, you indicate whether you are waiving the exemption for that year only or for future years as well. The noncustodial parent attaches Form 8332 to his or her return and claims the exemption for the child. If the exemption has been waived for future years as well, a copy of Form 8332 must be attached to the noncustodial parent's returns for the later years.

Noncustodial parent granted exemption under divorce agreement after 1984.   If you are the noncustodial parent and have been given the unconditional right to the exemption by a divorce decree or separation agreement that went into effect after 1984, you may attach to your return instead of Form 8332 copies of: the page of the agreement allowing you the exemption; the cover page, on which you should write the custodial parent's Social Security number; and the signature page showing the date of the agreement.

Noncustodial parent's exemption under pre-1985 agreement.   If a pre-1985 agreement gives you, as noncustodial parent, the exemption, you must provide at least $600 for the support of the child in 1997. The exemption must be specifically allocated to you in a decree of divorce or separate maintenance or a written agreement executed before January 1, 1985.

21.12   Test 4. The Dependent Must Meet a Citizen or Resident Test

To claim a 1997 exemption for a dependent, the dependent must have at some time during 1997 qualified as a:

- Citizen or resident of the United States;
- United States national (one who owes permanent allegiance to the U.S.; principally, a person born in American Samoa who has not become a naturalized American citizen); *or*
- Resident of Canada or Mexico; *see 1.14.*

Child born abroad.   A child born in a foreign country, one of whose parents is a nonresident alien and whose other parent is a U.S. citizen, qualifies as a U.S. citizen and thus as a dependent if the other tests are met.

If you are a U.S. citizen living abroad, you may claim as a dependent a legally adopted child who is not a U.S. citizen or resident if for the entire year your home was the child's principal residence and he or she is a member of your household.

21.13   Test 5. The Dependent Does Not File a Joint Return

You may not claim an exemption for a dependent who files a joint return with another. For example, if you meet the other four tests entitling you to an exemption for your married daughter as your dependent, but she files a joint return with her husband, you may not claim her as your dependent on your tax return.

Exception.   Even if your dependent files a joint return, you may claim the exemption where the income of each spouse is under the income limit required for filing a return and the couple files a joint return merely to obtain a refund of withheld taxes. Under these circumstances, their return is considered a refund claim, and a dependency exemption may be claimed.

Should dependents file separately?   When a married dependent files a joint return, the parent cannot claim an exemption. The loss of the exemption may cost a parent more than the joint return saves the couple. In such a case, it may be advisable for the couple to file separate returns so that the parent may benefit from the larger tax saving.

If the couple decides to revoke their election to file jointly and then file separately in order to preserve the exemption for a parent, they must do so before the filing date for the return. Once a joint return is filed, the couple may not, after the filing deadline, file separate returns for the same year.

21.14 Reporting Social Security Numbers of Dependents

On your 1997 return, you must list the Social Security number (SSN) of each dependent you claim. Include the SSNs of parents or other adults you claim as dependents, as well as those of children.

An SSN may be obtained from the Social Security Administration for U.S. citizens and aliens who have been lawfully admitted for permanent residence or employment. If a dependent is a resident or nonresident alien ineligible to obtain an SSN, an individual taxpayer identification number (ITIN) must be obtained from the IRS by filing Form W-7.

If you fail to include a correct SSN or ITIN for a dependent claimed on your return, the IRS may disallow the exemption, although it may first contact you and give you an opportunity to provide the number. If an exemption is disallowed, the IRS may assess the extra tax using a summary assessment procedure if you fail to request abatement of the assessment within 60 days of receiving notice; this procedure does not require issuance of a deficiency notice, so there is no appeal to the Tax Court.

If the dependent is a resident of Mexico or Canada, write "MX" or "CN" in the space on your return where the IRS asks for the SSN or ITIN.

To obtain a Social Security number for a dependent child, file Form SS-5 with your local Social Security Administration office. Parents of newborn children may request a number when filing out hospital birth-registration records.

21.15 Phaseout of Personal Exemptions for Higher Income Taxpayers

You will lose part or all of the $2,650 deduction for each 1997 personal exemption if your adjusted gross income (AGI) exceeds the threshold amount for your filing status. *Adjusted gross income* is explained at *12.1*. On your 1997 Form 1040, adjusted gross income is the amount shown on Line 32.

If your 1997 filing status is—	Phaseout applies if AGI exceeds* —	Exemptions completely phased out if AGI exceeds—
Married filing jointly or qualified widow(er)	$181,800	$304,300
Head of household	151,500	274,000
Single	121,200	243,700
Married filing separately	90,900	152,150

These thresholds are adjusted annually for inflation.

How the phaseout increases your marginal tax rate. The phaseout *increases* 1997 marginal rates according to the number of exemptions claimed. For earnings within the $122,500 phase-out range ($61,250 for married filing separately), the effective marginal tax rate increases for each exemption. Thus, taxpayers who support many dependents are hurt more by the phaseout than taxpayers who support few dependents.

Exemption Reduction Worksheet

1. Multiply $2,650 by the number of exemptions claimed on Form 1040, Line 6d.   1_____
2. Enter adjusted gross income (Line 32, Form 1040).   2_____
3. Enter base amount for your filing status:
   Joint return: $181,800
   Single: $121,200
   Head of household: $151,500
   Married filing separately: $90,900   3_____
4. Subtract Line 3 from Line 2.*   4_____
5. Divide Line 4 by $2,500 ($1,250 if married filing separately). Round up to next higher whole number if result is not a whole number (for example, round .005 to 1).   5_____
6. Multiply Line 5 by 2% and enter the number as a decimal.   6_____

7. Multiply Line 1 by Line 6.   7_____

8. Subtract Line 7 from Line 1. **This is the amount that
you deduct for exemptions on Line 37, Form 1040.**   8_____

*If Line 4 is zero or less, your exemptions are not reduced. Enter the amount from Line 1 on Form 1040, Line 37.
If Line 4 is over $122,500 ($61,250 if married filing separately), you may not claim any deductions for exemptions. If Line 4 is more than zero but no more than $122,500 ($61,250 if married filing separately), proceed to Line 5.*

EXAMPLE

Howard and Jessica are married. For 1997, they filed a joint return and claimed four exemptions. They reported adjusted gross income of $188,750 on Line 32 of Form 1040. Their exemptions are reduced by $636 to $9,964, figured as follows:

1. $2,650 × 4		$10,600
2. Adjusted gross income	$188,750	
3. Base for joint return	181,800	
4. Difference	6,950	
5. $6,950 (Line 4) ÷ 2,500 (2.78 rounded up to 3)	3	
6. 3 (Line 5) × 2%	.06(6%)	
7. $10,600 (Line 1) × 6% (Line 6)		636
8. Exemption deduction allowed (Line 1 *less* Line 7)		$9,964

Part 4

Personal Tax Computations

In this part, you will learn how to:

- **Figure your regular tax.** After claiming the standard deduction or itemized deductions *(13.1)* and deducting your allowable personal exemptions *(21.1)*, you figure your regular tax either by looking up the tax in the tax tables or by figuring the tax using the tax rate schedules; *see* Chapter 22.

- **Apply the alternative minimum tax.** If you have reduced your taxable income by certain deductions and tax benefits, you may be subject to the alternative minimum tax (AMT); for further details, *see* Chapter 23.

- **Figure estimated tax payments.** If you have investment and self-employment income, you generally have to pay quarterly estimated tax; *see 27.1.*

- **Compute the "Kiddie Tax."** If your child under age 14 has investment income exceeding $1,300, you must compute tax on that income as if it were your own. "Kiddie Tax" rules are discussed in Chapter 24.

Chapter 22

Figuring Your Regular Income Tax Liability

There are two types of income tax rates: (1) regular rates, which apply to all taxpayers, and (2) alternative minimum tax (AMT) rates, which apply only if certain tax benefits, when added back to your income, result in an AMT tax that exceeds your regular tax.

Most taxpayers do not have to compute the regular tax. They find the tax for their income and filing status in IRS tax tables if their taxable income is less than $100,000. Tax rate schedules must be used to figure your regular income tax if taxable income is $100,000 or more. The tables and rate schedules are printed in Part 8 of this book.

Computation of the alternative minimum tax is more complicated and requires the preparation of Form 6251. AMT is discussed in Chapter 23.

22.1 Taxable Income

Your income tax liability is based on your taxable income. If your taxable income is less than $100,000, you must use the IRS tables to look up your tax; *see 22.2.* If your taxable income is $100,000 or more, you use the tax rate schedules to compute the tax; *see 22.3.*

Taxable income is your adjusted gross income *(12.2)* minus the following: (1) your standard deduction or itemized deductions, whichever you claim (*see* Chapter 13) and (2) deductions for personal exemptions allowed under the rules of Chapter 21. On Form 1040 for 1997, taxable income is entered on Line 38.

On Form 1040A and Form 1040EZ, the computation of taxable income generally takes fewer steps because only limited types of income and deductions may be reported. Itemized deductions may not be claimed. Personal exemptions for dependents may be claimed on Form 1040A but not on Form 1040EZ. *See* the table on page 6 for the types of income and deductions that may not be reported on these forms.

On Form 1040A for 1997, taxable income is entered on Line 22; on Form 1040EZ, it is on Line 6.

22.2 Using the Tax Tables

If you file Form 1040EZ or Form 1040A, you use the tax tables in Part 8 of this book to look up your tax liability. If you file Form 1040, you also use the tax tables if your taxable income is *less* than $100,000; if taxable income is $100,000 or more, you use the tax rate schedules shown in Part 8.

If you use the tax tables, you do not have to compute your tax mathematically. To use the tables you first figure your taxable income *(see 22.1)*, then turn to your income bracket and look for the tax liability listed in the column for your filing status. Filing status (single, married filing jointly, head of household, married filing separately, and qualifying widow(er)) is discussed in Chapter 1.

You may *not* use the tax tables and *must* use the schedules if you file for a short period (less than 12 months) due to a change of accounting period.

Estates and trusts may not use the tax tables.

Tax credits.   After applying the tax tables or rate schedules to get your regular tax liability, you may be able to reduce that liability by claiming tax credits such as the dependent care or earned income credits discussed in Chapter 25, or the business tax credits discussed in Chapter 40.

EXAMPLES

1. You are single and have an adjusted gross income of $25,945 for 1997. You claim one personal exemption and the standard deduction.

Adjusted gross income		$25,945
Less: Standard deduction	$4,150	
Exemption	2,650	6,800
Taxable income		$19,145

Your tax liability from the tax table is $2,869. The tax is shown in the column for single persons with taxable income of at least $19,100 but less than $19,150.

2. You are married filing jointly and have 1997 adjusted gross income of $35,000, itemized deductions of $7,000, and three exemptions.

Adjusted gross income		$35,000
Less: Itemized deductions	$7,000	
Exemptions (3 × $2,650)	7,950	14,950
Taxable income		$20,050

Your tax liability from the tax table is $3,011.

22.3 **Tax Rate Schedules**

There are five tax brackets: 15%, 28%, 31%, 36%, and 39.6%. *See* the tax rate schedules in Part 8 of this book. You compute your 1997 tax using the tax rate schedules if either of the following is true:

- Your taxable income is $100,000 or more; *or*
- You file for a short period due to a change of accounting period.

EXAMPLES

1. You file as a head of household with taxable income of $103,000 for 1997. You use Schedule Z to figure your tax.

Tax on first $85,350	$19,601.50
Tax on excess $17,650 at 31%	5,471.50
Total tax	$25,073.00

2. You are married and file a joint return with taxable income of $130,000 for 1997. You use Schedule Y-1 to figure your tax.

Tax on first $99,600	$22,532
Tax on excess $30,400 at 31%	9,424
Total tax	$31,956

Alternative Minimum Tax (AMT)

The purpose of AMT is to increase your tax if the following benefits result in a regular income tax that is lower than the tax that would apply if the benefits were added back to taxable income. You may owe AMT if you claimed:

- **Itemized deductions,** such as taxes, interest on home equity loans used for nonresidential purposes, medical expenses, and miscellaneous job and investment expenses.
- **Tax benefits,** such as certain tax-exempt interest, accelerated depreciation, and incentive option benefits.

There are no specific tests to determine whether or not you are liable for AMT. You must first figure your regular income tax and then see whether tax benefit items must be added back to taxable income to figure alternative minimum taxable income, on which the AMT is figured. If after claiming the AMT exemption and applying the AMT rates of 26% and 28% the tentative minimum tax exceeds your regular income tax, the excess is your AMT liability, which is added to the regular tax on your return.

AMT liability is figured on Form 6251 and is attached to Form 1040. If you file Form 1040A and report tax-exempt interest from private activity bonds subject to AMT, AMT liability, if any, is figured on a worksheet and the AMT is entered on the line for total tax on Form 1040A.

23.1 Form 6251

You use Form 6251 to compute AMT liability, if any. The following checklist will help you determine if you have to use Form 6251. The checklist items are discussed at *23.2* and *23.3*.

If you check any of the items on the list, you should complete Form 6251 to determine if you are liable for AMT. These items are AMT adjustments and preferences and generally are added back to regular taxable income to calculate alternative minimum taxable income (AMT income). After reducing AMT income by the allowable exemption, the AMT rates are applied. The AMT exemption based on filing status and the phase-out rule for the exemption are discussed in the "Key to AMT Rules" on the next page.

After reducing AMT income by the allowable exemption, a 26% AMT rate generally applies to the first $175,000 of AMT income ($ 87,500 if married filing separately), and a 28% rate applies to any balance of the AMT income. However, a special calculation is made on Form 6251 if you had net capital gains realized after May 6, 1997, that qualify for the new 10% or 20% capital gains rate; *see 5.2*. The effect of the calculation is to apply the same capital gains rate for AMT purposes as for regular income tax purposes.

You report the AMT liability, less any AMT foreign credit, as an additional tax on Form 1040 only to the extent it exceeds your regular income tax (without taking into account the special averaging tax on a lump-sum distribution) *minus* any regular foreign tax credit.

Follow the line-by-line instructions to Form 6251 to figure your AMT liability, if any.

Items subject to AMT: Check: ✓

1. Itemized deductions for taxes, miscellaneous expenses, and medical expenses   ❑
2. Interest on home equity debt used for nonresidential purposes   ❑
3. Accelerated depreciation in excess of straight line   ❑
4. Income from the exercise of incentive stock options   ❑
5. Tax-exempt interest from private activity bonds   ❑
6. Intangible drilling costs   ❑
7. Depletion   ❑
8. Circulation expenses   ❑
9. Mining exploration and development costs   ❑
10. Research and experimental costs   ❑
11. Pollution control facility amortization   ❑
12. Tax-shelter farm income or loss   ❑
13. Passive income or loss   ❑
14. Certain installment sale income   ❑
15. Income from long-term contracts computed under percentage-of-income method   ❑
16. Net operating loss deduction   ❑
17. Foreign tax credit   ❑
18. Investment expenses   ❑

23.2 Adjustments for AMT

The amount of your regular taxable income from Form 1040 (before personal exemptions) will generally be increased by adjustments on Form 6251.

Itemized deductions. If you have claimed itemized deductions for state and local taxes or miscellaneous deductions subject to the 2% AGI floor, you must add back all of such deductions to your regular taxable income (prior to personal exemptions) in order to figure alternative minimum taxable income. If medical expenses are deducted for regular tax purposes, you must add back to income on Form 6251 the *smaller* of the allowable medical deduction from Schedule A and 2.5% of adjusted gross income.

Taxes directly deductible from gross income for business or rental purposes remain deductible for AMT purposes. For AMT purposes *only* the following itemized deductions are *allowed*:

• Charitable contributions. However, if you have carryover deductions from contributions of certain appreciated property made before 1993 or tangible personal property before 1991, you must refigure the AMT carryover using cost basis instead of fair market value of the property. The difference between the regular tax carryover deduction and the refigured AMT carryover deduction is entered as a preference item on Form 6251.

• Medical expenses exceeding 10% of AGI. Do not confuse this limit with the 7.5% limit for regular tax purposes.

• Casualty and theft losses exceeding 10% of AGI

Continued on page 414

Key to AMT Rules

Item—	AMT Rule—
Tax rate	A 26% rate applies to AMT taxable income of $175,000 or less (after the AMT exemption); $87,500 or less for married filing separately. A 28% rate applies to AMT income exceeding the $175,000 or $87,500 threshold.
AMT taxable income	Regular taxable income without personal exemptions, increased or decreased by adjustments and increased by preferences.
AMT exemption	$45,000 if married filing a joint return (or a qualifying widow(er)); $33,750 if single or head of household; *or* $22,500 if married filing a separate return. Under a phase-out rule, these exemption amounts are reduced by 25¢ for each $1 that AMT taxable income exceeds $150,000 for joint filers or a qualifying widow(er), $112,500 if you file as a single person or head of household, and $75,000 for a married person filing separately. The exemption is completely phased out at $330,000 on a joint return and $247,500 on a single or head of household return. On a married person's separate return, the exemption is eliminated if AMT taxable income is $165,000 or more. There is also a penalty if, as a married person, you file a separate return and have AMT taxable income exceeding $165,000. You must increase AMT taxable income by 25% of the excess over $165,000, but the maximum increase is $22,500.
AMT adjustments	Itemized deductions for taxes, certain interest, and most miscellaneous deductions are not allowed. Personal exemptions and the standard deduction are not allowed. MACRS depreciation is figured under the alternative MACRS system for real estate using 40-year straight-line recovery, and, for personal property, the 150% declining balance method. Incentive stock options; *see 23.2.* Mining exploration and development costs are allowable costs amortized over 10 years. For long-term contracts entered into after February 28, 1986, income is figured under the percentage-of-completion method. Pollution control facilities amortization is figured under alternate MACRS. Alternative tax net operating loss is allowed with adjustments. Circulation expenditures must be amortized ratably over three years. Research and experimental expenditures must be amortized ratably over 10 years. Passive activity losses are recomputed; certain tax-shelter farm losses may not be allowed.
AMT preference items	Tax-exempt interest from private activity bonds issued after August 7,1986, *except* for qualifying 501(c) (3) bonds. Accelerated depreciation on real property and leased personal property placed in service before 1987—excess depreciation or amortization taken over straight-line deduction.
Adjusted gross income	In making AMT computations involving adjusted gross income limitations, use adjusted gross income as computed for regular tax purposes.
Partnership AMT	If you are a partner, include for AMT your distributive share of the partnership's adjustments and tax preference items. These are reported on Schedule K-1 (Form 1065). The partnership itself does not pay alternative minimum tax.
Trust or estate AMT	If you are a beneficiary of an estate or trust, consider for AMT your share of distributable net alternative minimum taxable income shown on Schedule K-1 (Form 1041). The estate or trust must pay tax on any remaining alternative minimum taxable income.
S corporation stockholder	If you are a shareholder, consider for AMT your share of the adjustments and tax preference items reported on Schedule K-1 (Form 1120S).
Children subject to "kiddie tax"	Children under age 14 who are subject to the "kiddie tax" *(24.3)* may have to compute AMT liability on Form 6251. The child's AMT exemption for 1997 is generally limited to $1,300 plus his or her earned income. Where the child's parent is not subject to AMT because his or her AMT exemption exceeds AMT income, and the child's share of the parent's unused AMT exemption exceeds $1,300, the child's AMT exemption equals that share plus earned income. A child's AMT for 1997 may be reduced or eliminated if the child's parent or sibling under age 14 had regular tax liability exceeding tentative minimum tax, if any, from Form 6251. By completing a worksheet in the Form 6251 instructions, the child's AMT is limited to the extra tax that the parent would pay if the child's tentative minimum tax liability, plus regular tax, were added to the parents'. In 1998, the AMT exemption for a child subject to the "Kiddie tax" will equal the child's earned income plus $5,000, but no more than the regular AMT $33,750 exemption for single persons.
Nonrefundable credits, such as the child and dependent care credit	The amount of these credits may be reduced because of AMT rules explained at *23.5.*

Continued from page 412
- Unreimbursed moving expenses to a new job location
- Wagering losses
- Claim of right deduction; *see 2.9.*
- Estate-tax deductions for income in respect of a decedent
- Impairment-related work expenses
- Home mortgage interest, *except* for interest on home equity debt, taken out after June 30, 1982, where the loan was not used to buy, build, or substantially improve your first or second home
- Investment interest to the extent of net investment income

The 3% reduction for itemized deductions at *13.7* does not apply for AMT purposes.

Mortgage interest. Less interest may be deductible for AMT purposes than for regular tax purposes. No AMT adjustment is required for home mortgage interest paid on a debt incurred to buy, construct, or substantially rehabilitate your principal residence or qualifying second residence. The residence may be a house, apartment, cooperative apartment, condominium, or mobile home not used on a transient basis.

Interest on a mortgage taken out after June 30, 1982, is not deductible for AMT purposes if the proceeds are used for any purpose other than to buy, build, or substantially improve your principal or second residence. Furthermore, in the case of a mortgage refinanced after June 30, 1982, interest is deductible for AMT purposes only to the extent the new debt does not exceed the amount of the old debt immediately before the refinancing. Interest on the excess is not deductible for AMT purposes.

Interest on a mortgage debt incurred before July 1, 1982, for any purpose qualifies for an AMT deduction if the mortgage was secured by your principal residence or any other home used by you or a family member at the time the mortgage was taken out.

If an interest deduction is claimed on Schedule A for debt that does not qualify under these AMT rules, that interest is added back as an adjustment on Form 6251.

State and local taxes. State and local taxes deducted on Schedule A must be added back to taxable income in figuring AMT. If you received in 1997 a refund of state taxes deducted in a prior year, you enter the refund on Form 6251 as a negative adjustment which reduces taxable income in arriving at AMT taxable income.

MACRS depreciation. Depreciation allowed for AMT may differ from that allowed for regular tax purposes. For property acquired after 1986 other than real estate, the AMT depreciation rate is the 150% declining balance method, switching to the straight-line method when a larger depreciation allowance results. Real property acquired after 1986 is depreciated for AMT over a 40-year period using the straight-line method. Depreciation deductions for films, videotapes, and sound recordings under the unit-of-production method or other method not based on a term of years are not adjusted under AMT.

If, for regular tax purposes, you use the regular 200% declining balance method to depreciate business equipment, the difference between the higher regular depreciation and the lower rate for AMT is an adjustment. You may avoid this adjustment by using the 150% rate for regular tax purposes. For real estate, the adjustment is the difference between the straight-line depreciation claimed for regular tax purposes using the recovery period discussed at *42.13* and the straight-line recovery over the AMT 40-year recovery period.

The adjustment for MACRS may result in providing more depreciation for AMT purposes where the AMT depreciation computation towards the latter part of the useful life of the property provides larger deductions than the regular MACRS deduction.

Filing Instruction

Standard Deduction and Exemptions

If you claimed the standard deduction instead of itemizing deductions on Form 1040, you may not claim the standard deduction as an AMT deduction. Exemptions for yourself and your dependents are also not allowed for AMT purposes. The standard deduction is added back to taxable income as an AMT adjustment. Personal exemptions are disallowed by using as the starting point for figuring AMT the taxable income from Form 1040 before personal exemptions are claimed.

EXAMPLE

In one taxable year when AMT applies, Jones has two assets acquired after 1986. The regular MACRS depreciation for Asset A is $500 and for Asset B, $400. When applying the AMT rules, the depreciation for Asset A is $400 and for Asset B is $450. AMT taxable income is increased by $50. The adjustment accounts for post-1987 MACRS property held in the current year.

Asset A		
Regular depreciation	$500	
AMT depreciation	400	$100
Asset B		
Regular depreciation	$400	
AMT depreciation	450	(50)
Net adjustment to AMT		
Taxable income		$50

Property placed in service before 1987, unless it qualifies under the MACRS transitional rules, is subject to prior law tax preference rules. Prior law creates tax preference items when the ACRS deduction exceeds regular straight line; *see 23.3.* A tax preference item always increases AMT taxable income.

Basis adjustment affects AMT gain or loss.   When post-1986 depreciable assets are sold, gain for AMT purposes is figured on the basis of the property as adjusted by depreciation claimed for AMT purposes. This gain or loss will be different from the gain or loss figured for regular tax purposes where regular MACRS depreciation was used. (This AMT basis rule does not apply to property placed in service before 1987 except for transitional property within the post-1986 rules).

Similarly, recalculations of basis and gain are made for prior AMT adjustments taken for circulation expenditures, research and experimental expenditures, pollution control facilities, and mining exploration and development costs.

Incentive stock option (ISO).   If you exercise ISO options in 1997 and the shares are freely transferable, the excess of the fair market value of the shares at the time of exercise over the option price is treated as an adjustment increasing AMT taxable income. When you sell the stock in a later year, and you are subject to AMT in that year, you may increase the basis of the stock for AMT purposes by the amount of the AMT adjustment reported in 1997.

If you exercise an incentive stock option and you sell the acquired stock in the same year, no AMT adjustment is necessary.

Mining exploration and development costs.   The deduction allowed for regular tax purposes for mining exploration and development costs is amortized ratably over a 10-year period for AMT purposes.

If a mine is abandoned as worthless, all mining exploration and development costs that have not been written off are deductible in the year of abandonment.

Long-term contracts.   The use of the completed contract method of accounting or certain other methods of accounting for long-term contracts is generally not allowable. For AMT, the percentage of completion method must be used. However, there is an exception for home construction contracts.

Amortization of certified pollution control facilities.   For purposes of the alternative minimum tax, the amortization deduction for a certified pollution control facility placed in service after 1986 is determined under alternative MACRS; *see 42.9.*

Research and experimental expenditures.   Costs are amortized over 10 years if incurred in a business in which you are not a material participant.

Passive losses.   The law for AMT distinguishes between farm and nonfarm activities. Generally, no loss is deductible for any tax-shelter farm activity. A tax-shelter farm activity is any farming syndicate or any farming activity in which you do not materially participate. You may be treated as a material participant if a member of your family materially participates or you meet certain retirement or disability tests discussed at *10.7.*

Gains and losses reported for regular tax purposes from tax-shelter farm activities must be refigured by taking into account any AMT adjustments and preferences. However, a refigured loss is not allowed for AMT purposes except to the extent that you are insolvent at the end of the year. The amount of the disallowed loss for AMT purposes may be reduced by the amount of insolvency at the end of the taxable year. This means that you can deduct the loss to the extent of your insolvency. Insolvency is the excess of liabilities over fair market value of assets. Any AMT-disallowed loss is carried forward to later years in which there is gain from that same activity, or until you dispose of the activity.

Passive losses from nonfarming activities are adjusted for preference or adjustment items not allowed for AMT purposes. For example, an adjustment for MACRS depreciation is made directly against the passive loss and is not treated as a separate AMT adjustment item. The loss allowed for AMT purposes is increased by the amount by which you are insolvent at the end of the year. *See* the instructions to Form 6251, which suggest that the AMT adjustment of passive losses be figured on a separate Form 8582 which you do not file.

23.3 Tax Preference Items

The following are tax preference items that increase the amount of 1997 AMT taxable income.

Tax-exempt interest on nonessential private activity bonds.   For AMT purposes, you must include as a tax preference item the tax-exempt interest on qualified private activity bonds

Law Alert

Farmers May Use Installment Method for AMT
Congress has resolved a political controversy by retroactively allowing farmers who make deferred crop sales to use the installment sales method for AMT purposes. The IRS had required farmers who used the installment sales method for regular tax purposes to make an adjustment on Form 6251 to compute AMT liability.

The new law retroactively allows the installment method for 1988 and later years.

issued after August 7, 1986, except for qualified 501(c)(3) bonds used to benefit tax-exempt groups. Generally, private activity bonds issued after August 7, 1986, are subject to AMT, but for certain bonds meeting specific tests, the AMT rule applies to bonds issued on or after September 1, 1986. Interest paid on buying or carrying such bonds is deductible for AMT purposes.

> **EXAMPLE**
> You received $5,000 interest income from a private activity bond issued in 1992. You also had $100 of investment expense related to this bond. You enter $4,900 on Form 6251.

Accelerated depreciation of property acquired before 1987. For real property placed in service before 1987, the difference between the depreciation that would have been allowable if the straight-line method had been used and accelerated depreciation claimed on real property during the taxable year is a tax preference item. The excess is computed separately for each asset depreciated through an accelerated method. For example, if you use ACRS 15-year, 18-year, or 19-year accelerated rates for regular tax purposes, figure the deduction for each such property under the straight-line method and report the excess of your regular tax deduction over the straight-line amount as a preference item.

For personal property leased to others before 1987, the preference item is the excess of the regular tax deduction over the depreciation that would have been allowed under the straight-line method, without regard to salvage value. The excess is computed separately for each asset. For 10-year property, a 15-year recovery period is used.

Note: See 23.2 for the MACRS adjustment rules for post-1986 assets.

Oil and gas preference items generally repealed. Independent oil and gas producers and royalty owners do not have to compute preference items for excess percentage depletion deductions, or for excess intangible drilling costs (only integrated oil companies remain subject to tax preference treatment). *However,* the repeal of the intangible drilling cost preference may result in no more than a 40% reduction in the 1997 AMT taxable income figured as if the drilling cost preference were still in effect and without regard to any AMT net operating loss deduction. *See* the instructions to Form 6251 for making this computation.

23.4 Net Operating Losses

A net operating loss (NOL) claimed for regular tax purposes must be recomputed for AMT after all other AMT adjustments and preference items are taken into account. An NOL deductible for AMT purposes is generally the amount of the regular net operating loss except that in figuring the nonbusiness deduction adjustment *(40.19)* only AMT itemized deductions are taken into account. Thus, for AMT purposes, state and local taxes and certain interest that are not allowable AMT deductions do not reduce nonbusiness income in figuring the NOL adjustment.

In some cases, a net operating loss will eliminate your regular tax but not the AMT. The amount of the NOL deduction that may be deducted from AMT taxable income may not exceed 90% of AMT taxable income before the NOL deduction and the new energy preference adjustment. Net operating losses that are disallowed because of the 90% AMT limit may be carried back under regular NOL rules *(40.17)* but the deduction in the carryback or carryover year is subject to the 90% limit. Carryovers from years beginning after 1982 and before 1987 are figured under prior law rules, subject to the 90% AMT limit.

Deferred minimum tax before 1983 because of NOL. If you had minimum tax liability in a pre-1983 year that was deferred because of a net operating loss, you must pay a minimum tax if, in 1997, you claim the net operating loss carryover deduction from that period. The tax is 15% of the net operating loss carryover deduction. You report the tax on Line 48 of Form 1040 and write in "Deferred Minimum Tax."

23.5 AMT Foreign Tax Credit and Other Tax Credits

The foreign tax credit is the only credit that may be deducted from tentative AMT tax liability. It is figured in the same way as the regular foreign tax credit *(36.15)* after substituting AMT taxable income for regular taxable income.

The AMT foreign tax credit may not offset more than 90% of AMT tax determined without regard to the foreign tax credit and net operating loss deduction. Any foreign tax credit not allowed by the limit may be carried back and forward; *see 36.16* and instructions to Form 6251 for further details.

Other credits limited.   If you have AMT adjustments or preference items, the interplay of technical rules and definitions may reduce nonrefundable credits, such as the dependent care credit and the elderly and disabled credit, even when you are *not* liable for AMT after application of the AMT exemption. The amount of such nonrefundable credits is limited to the regular tax liability less the AMT tax liability. The credit limitation is figured on Form 2441 for the dependent care credit, and on Schedule R for the credit for the elderly and disabled.

Certain nonrefundable business credits may also be limited; follow the instructions to Form 3800.

23.6 AMT Tax Credit From Regular Tax

You may be able to reduce your regular 1997 tax by a tax credit based on prior-year AMT taxes. The credit, which is computed on Form 8801, may be applied against your 1997 regular tax after deducting any credits for dependent care, the elderly or disabled, mortgage interest, foreign taxes, and general business credits. However, the tax credit is allowed only if your regular 1997 tax liability exceeds 1997 tentative alternative minimum tax liability computed on Form 6251. Follow the instructions to Form 8801.

23.7   Avoiding AMT Tax

If you are within the range of the AMT tax, review periodically your income and expenses to determine whether to make certain tax elections, accelerate income, and/or defer the payment of expenses.

There are elections, such as the election of alternative straight-line MACRS depreciation, that may avoid AMT adjustments. However, such elections will increase your regular tax. Similarly, adjustment treatment for mining exploration and development costs, circulation expenses, and research expenses can be avoided by elections to amortize; *see 23.2.*

The following steps may also avoid or soften the impact of the AMT tax:

- Defer deductible expense items to a later year in which your income will be subject to regular tax rates exceeding your AMT tax rate (either 26% or 28% depending on your AMT income). Consider deferring payment of home mortgage interest and medical expenses. You will get a larger tax benefit from the deductions in the later year. In the case of unimproved real estate, consider an election to capitalize taxes and carry charges. Also, do not elect first-year expensing of business equipment.
- Defer if possible the exercise of an incentive stock option to a later year when you are not subject to AMT. The bargain element of an incentive stock option is an adjustment item subject to AMT. This is the difference between the option price and the fair market price of the stock on the date of exercise. If you exercise the option and it is subject to AMT, you may find yourself with an unexpected liability and short of liquid funds to meet your tax liability.

Accelerating income.   If you find that you will be subject to AMT in a current year, you may want to subject additional income in that year to the 26% or 28% AMT tax rate. In such a case, consider accelerating the receipt of income to that year. If you are in business, you might ask for earlier payments from customers or clients. If you control a small corporation, you might prepay salary or pay larger bonuses. But here be careful not to run afoul of reasonable compensation rules. You might also consider paying dividends.

If you hold savings certificates with a six-month maturity in a later year, you might consider an early redemption to the current year. But here weigh the penalty cost of an early forfeiture. Similarly, you might make an early sale of U.S. Treasury bills to the current year.

Chapter 24

Computing the "Kiddie Tax" for Children Under Age 14

Investment income over $1,300 earned by a child under age 14 is taxed at the child's parent's top tax rate. The child's parent or legal representative generally makes this tax computation, which is nicknamed the "kiddie tax."

The kiddie tax applies only to investment income, such as interest, dividends, rents, royalties and profits on the sale of property. Income from wages and self-employment is not subject to the kiddie tax.

As the child's parent, you generally must use Form 8615 to report the child's income and compute the tax which is reported on the child's personal income tax return; see 24.4. The Form 8615 computation has no effect on the treatment of items on your own return or on your tax computation. You may instead elect on Form 8814 to report the child's investment income on your own return, provided the child received only interest and dividend income. This election is generally not advisable. If you elect on Form 8814 to report the child's investment income on your own return, your adjusted gross income will increase and this could adversely affect your right to claim various deductions; see 24.5.

If you are married but file separately, the parent with the larger amount of taxable income is responsible for the kiddie tax computation. If parents are divorced, separated, unmarried, or living apart for the last six months of the year, the parent who has custody of the child for the greater part of 1997 computes the tax. If a child cannot get tax information directly from a parent, the legal representative of the child may ask the IRS for permission on Form 8615.

24.1 Filing Your Child's Return

To discourage substantial income splitting of investment income between parents and minor children, the tax law has complicated income reporting for parents and children by—

1. Imposing a "kiddie tax" that taxes a child's investment income over $1,300 at the parent's top bracket if the child is under 14 years of age at the end of the taxable year; *see 24.3.*
2. Barring a dependent child from claiming a personal exemption on his or her own tax return.
3. Limiting the standard deduction to $650 for a dependent child who has only investment income; *see 13.5.*

Does your child have to file?   For a child who can be claimed as a dependent, the income filing threshold is generally $650. If your dependent child has gross income (earned and investment income) of $650 or less for 1997, he or she is not subject to tax and does not have to file a tax return.

A 1997 return must be filed for a dependent child with gross income of more than $650, but there is this exception: If a dependent child has salary or other earned income but no investment income, a return does not have to be filed unless such earned income exceeds $4,150 in 1997. If your child's only income is from interest and dividends, you may be able to make an election to report the income on your own return; *see 24.5.*

Although a dependent child may not claim a personal exemption on his or her 1997 tax return, the child is allowed to claim a $650 standard deduction. A dependent child with earned income over $650 may claim a standard deduction up to those earnings, but no more than the basic standard deduction, which is generally $4,150; *see 13.1.*

How to file for your child.   If your child was under age 14 as of January 1, 1998, and had investment income of $1,300 or less, follow the regular filing rules and use either Form 1040EZ, 1040A, or Form 1040 to report the child's income and deductions. The "kiddie tax" computation does not apply, so all of the child's income will be taxed at his or her own tax rate. If your child is unable to sign his or her tax return, you must do so; *see 1.11.*

If your child's investment income exceeded $1,300, the kiddie tax computation applies; *see 24.3.* Form 8615 must be filed to compute the kiddie tax unless your child's only income is interest and dividends and you elect to report your child's investment earnings on your own return as discussed at *24.5.* On Form 8615 you must provide your tax identification number and taxable income. Form 8615 is attached to the child's tax return; *see 24.4.*

If your child was age 14 or older as of January 1, 1998, your child should file Form 1040EZ, 1040A, or 1040, depending on the type of income and deductions he or she has. The special kiddie tax rules do not apply.

Child's AMT liability.   A child who has substantial tax-exempt interest, tax preferences, or tax adjustments subject to the alternative minimum tax must compute tentative AMT liability on Form 6251; *see Chapter 23.*

24.2 Children Not Subject to the "Kiddie Tax"

For 1997 returns, the "kiddie tax" computation does *not* apply to—

- A child who was 14 years old or over on January 1, 1998.
- A child under age 14 who had no investment income or whose 1997 gross investment income was $1,300 or less. The kiddie tax computation applies only to investment income exceeding $1,300. Furthermore, children who itemize deductions may in some cases exempt more than $1,300 from the computation; *see 24.3.*
- A child under age 14 if neither parent was alive at the end of 1997.

EXAMPLES

1. At the end of 1997, your son is age 14. He has interest income of $1,400 and salary income of $950 from his part-time job. His standard deduction is $950, the greater of earned income and $650. No personal exemption may be claimed. Assuming he has no itemized deductions, taxable income is $1,400 ($2,350 gross income – $950 standard deduction). The kiddie tax computation based on your top rate does not apply because your son is at least age 14 at the end of the year.

2. In 1997, your five-year-old daughter has interest income of $800. Taxable income of $150 is subject to tax at her own tax rate.

Interest income	$800
Less: standard deduction	650
Taxable income	$150

The kiddie tax computation does not apply because investment income does not exceed $1,300.

24.3 Children Under Age 14 Subject to the "Kiddie Tax"

The "kiddie tax" is a tax on a child's investment income at the parent's top marginal tax rate. It applies for 1997 returns to a child who—

- Was under age 14 on January 1, 1998;
- Had either parent alive at the end of 1997; *and*
- Had investment income for 1997 exceeding $1,300. For a child who has itemized deductions of more than $650 that are directly connected to the production of investment income, the $1,300 exemption is increased, as explained below.

Figuring kiddie tax on child's or parent's return.   The kiddie tax computation is generally made on Form 8615, which must be attached to your child's return. A sample Form 8615 is at the end of this chapter. However, if the only income of your child who is under age 14 is interest and dividends and other tests are met, you may elect on Form 8814 to include your child's investment income on his or her own tax return, instead of computing the kiddie tax on Form 8615; *see* 24.5.

Kiddie tax on Form 8615 applies to investment income exceeding $1,300 floor.   If your child files his or her own return and the "kiddie tax" is computed on Form 8615, your top rate applies to *net investment income*. For purposes of this rule, *net investment income* equals gross investment income minus $1,300 if your child does not itemize deductions on Schedule A. Thus, if your child does not itemize, the first $1,300 of investment income is exempt from the special computation. Investment income exceeding $1,300 is considered net investment income subject to the special computation; *see* Example 3 below.

Include as gross investment income all taxable income that is not compensation for personal services. Include interest income, unless it is tax-exempt interest, dividends, royalties, rents, and profits on the sale of property. Payments from a trust are also included to the extent of distributable net income. Income in custodial accounts is treated as the child's income and is subject to the kiddie tax computation.

Investment earnings on all of your child's property must be considered, even if the property was a gift from you or someone else, or if the property was produced from your child's wages, such as a bank account into which the wages were deposited. The wages themselves, or self-employment earnings, are not considered.

If your child does itemize deductions, and has more than $650 of deductions that are directly connected to the production of investment income, the $1,300 floor is increased. The floor is $650 plus the directly connected deductions. If the directly connected deductions are $650 or less, the regular $1,300 kiddie tax exemption applies, as in Example 4 below. Directly connected itemized deductions are expenses paid to produce or collect income or to manage, conserve, or maintain income-producing property. Only the part of the total expenses exceeding the 2% AGI floor may be deducted. These expenses include custodian fees and service charges, service fees to collect interest and dividends, and investment counsel fees. If, after you subtract the itemized deductions, your child's net investment income exceeds his or her taxable income, you apply the tax to the lower taxable income, rather than to the net investment income.

EXAMPLES

(In all the following Examples, assume the child is your dependent for 1997 and under age 14 on January 1, 1998.)

1. Child has interest income of $480 and no other income for 1997. The child has no income tax liability and does not have to file a return.

Interest income	$480
Less: standard deduction	480
	0

2. Child has interest and dividend income of $900 and no other income for 1997. A standard deduction of $650 may be claimed. The balance of $250 is taxed at the child's regular tax bracket. Form 8615 does not have to be filed and the kiddie tax computation does not apply since investment income does not exceed $1,300.

3. For 1997, child has dividend income of $1,800 and taxable income of $1,150, of which $500 is subject to the kiddie tax computation based on the parent's top tax bracket on Form 8615.

   Figuring taxable income:

Dividend income	$1,800
Less: standard deduction	650
	$1,150

   Income subject to tax at parent's rate:

Investment income	$1,800
Less: $1,300	1,300
	$500

   An example of the actual Form 8615 computation is at *24.4*. As an alternative to computing kiddie tax on $500 on Form 8615, the parent may elect to report the child's dividend income on his or her own return; *see 24.5.*

4. Child has $300 of wages and $1,750 of dividends and interest income for 1997. On Schedule A, the child claims itemized deductions of $400 related to investment income after the 2% AGI floor. The child also has $400 of other itemized deductions. Itemized deductions of $800 are claimed; they exceed the $650 standard deduction.

   Figuring taxable income:

Total income	$2,050
Less: itemized deductions	800
Taxable income	$1,250
Income subject to tax at parent's rate:	
Investment income	$1,750
Less: greater of (1) $1,300 and (2) the sum of $650 and directly related expenses of $400	1,300
Net investment income subject to tax at parent's rate on Form 8615 *(24.4)*; *see 24.5* for parent's alternative election	$450

 Law Alert

Dependent's Standard Deduction in 1998

For children who have earned income, an increased standard deduction limit may provide a tax benefit starting in 1998; *see 13.5.*

24.4 Computing "Kiddie Tax" on Child's Return

If your child is subject to the "kiddie tax" under *24.3*, the tax is computed on Form 8615, which is attached to his or her return, unless you make the parent's election at *24.5*. Before your child's Form 8615 can be completed, your own taxable income must be determined. The amount to be entered on Form 8615 as the parent's taxable income depends on the parent's marital and filing status.

If the parents file a *joint return,* their joint taxable income is entered on Form 8615, along with the net investment income *(24.3)* of all their children under age 14. If the parents file *separate returns,* the larger of the parents' separate taxable incomes is used on the child's Form 8615.

Where parents are legally separated or divorced and custody of the child is shared, Form 8615 should be completed using the taxable income of the parent who has custody for the greater part of the year. If parents are married but living apart, and the custodial parent qualifies as unmarried under Test 1 at *1.10,* that parent's taxable income is used on Form 8615. If the custodial parent is not considered unmarried, the income of the parent with the larger taxable income is used. If the custodial parent has remarried and files a joint return with a new spouse, their joint return taxable income is used on the child's Form 8615. If the parents were never married but they live together with the child, the income of the parent with the larger taxable income is used; if the parents live apart, the income of the parent with custody for most of the year is used on Form 8615.

More than one child subject to kiddie tax.   You file a separate Form 8615 for each child and on each form net investment income of all the children subject to the tax is included. The computed tax is allocated to each of your children, according to his or her share of their combined net investment income. This computation is incorporated in the steps of Form 8615 and by following the order of the form, you will make the proper allocation.

As parents, the kiddie tax computation on Form 8615 does not affect your tax liability or how you compute any limitation on deductions or credits. For example, the addition of the child's net investment income to your taxable income on Form 8615 does *not* affect the adjusted gross income floors for purposes of figuring your deduction for IRA contributions, medical expenses, or miscellaneous expenses.

> **EXAMPLE**
>
> For 1997, Bill and Betty Brown each file Form 1040A. Bill, age 12, has dividend income of $2,100; Betty, age 10, has $1,500. They each claim a standard deduction of $650. Neither may claim a personal exemption because they are claimed as dependents by their parents, Tom and Lilli Brown. Bill's taxable income after claiming the standard deduction is $1,450. Betty's is $850.
>
> Tom and Lilli Brown do not make the election (24.5) to report Bill's and Betty's dividends on their joint return. Forms 8615 are prepared and attached to the children's Forms 1040A, because each child is under age 14 and has more than $1,300 of investment income.
>
> Tom and Lilli report taxable income of $52,000 on their 1997 joint return. They use the IRS tax tables to look up their tax (the tables are in Part 8 at the back of this book). The tax on $52,000 is $9,211. The special computation on Form 8615 does not increase their joint return tax; it determines only the amount of Bill's and Betty's tax.
>
> As shown at the end of this chapter on sample worksheets based on Form 8615, Bill's 1997 tax is $323 and Betty's 1997 tax is $155. If the special computation did not apply, Bill's 1997 tax would be $219 and Betty's tax would be $129. Thus, as a result of the special computation, the total tax bill for the children is increased by $130 ($478 – $348).

Estimating the kiddie tax in case of filing delay.   If you are unable to file your return by April 15, 1998, the child's tax on Form 8615 may be based on an estimate. You may make a reasonable estimate of your taxable income on Form 8615 or may estimate the net investment income of children under age 14 if that information is not yet available. When you have the complete income details, file an amended return.

A reasonable estimate may be based on your 1996 taxable income and the 1996 investment income of the child. If a refund is due, the IRS will pay interest from April 15, 1998, or, if the return was filed late, from the filing date. If additional tax is due on the amended return, interest will be charged from April 15, but no penalty will be imposed.

24.5 Parent's Election To Report Child's Dividends and Interest

Instead of filing a separate return for your child *(24.4)* whose income is subject to the "kiddie tax," you may elect on Form 8814 to compute the kiddie tax on your return if all of the following tests are met:

- The child's income is only from interest and dividends (Alaska Permanent Fund dividends may be included);
- The total interest and dividends are over $650 but less than $6,500;
- Estimated tax payments were not made in the child's name and Social Security number for 1997, and there was no overpayment from the child's 1996 return applied to his or her 1997 estimated tax; *and*
- The child was not subject to 1997 backup withholding.

By making this election, and following the steps of Form 8814, you include in your income the child's interest and dividends to the extent they exceed $1,300. You also figure an additional tax equal to the smaller of $97.50 and 15% of your child's income over $650.

If parents are divorced, separated, unmarried, or living apart for the last six months of the year, the parent whose taxable income would be taken into account on Form 8615 *(24.4)* is the parent who may elect to report the income on his or her own return.

In figuring whether you owe alternative minimum tax (AMT), you must include as a tax preference item interest income your child receives from specified private activity bonds; *see 23.3* and Form 6251 instructions.

Should you make the election?   There is no advantage in making the election, except to skip the paperwork involved in preparing a return in the child's name or returns in your children's names. If you consider this an advantage, you may want to make the election. It may be preferable to take the time to prepare the child's return to keep the child's tax accounting separate from yours.

Including the child's income as your own increases your AGI, which may create these disadvantages:

- Subject you to the exemption phaseout *(21.15)* and 3% reduction computation *(13.7)* for itemized deductions.
- Make it more difficult to deduct job expenses and other miscellaneous itemized deductions, which are subject to a 2% AGI floor *(19.1)*, and medical deductions, subject to a 7.5% AGI floor *(17.1)*.
- Limit a deduction for IRA contributions under the phase-out rules *(8.4)*.
- Limit your ability to claim the special $25,000 rental loss allowance under the passive activity rules *(10.2)*.
- Increase local and state tax liability.

Finally, if you elect to report the child's income on your own return, you may not claim any deductions that your child would have been able to claim on his or her return such as investment expenses or a penalty on premature withdrawals from a savings account. On the other hand, reporting your child's interest or dividends increases your net investment income, which may allow you to claim a larger deduction for investment interest; *see 15.10*. Also, your ceiling for charitable donations may be increased. If you plan to report your child's income on your 1998 return, provide for the tax in your estimated tax payments or withholdings during 1998.

EXAMPLE

Woodrow, age 10, received $2,000 of interest income in 1997. He has no other income and is not subject to backup withholding. No estimated tax payments were made in his name. His parents elect on Form 8814 to include his interest income on their 1997 tax return instead of filing a return for him. They include $700 of the interest ($2,000 – $1,300 floor) on Line 21 (other income) of Form 1040. They also add $97.50 to their tax on Line 39 of Form 1040 and indicate that the amount is from Form 8814.

Form 8615—Worksheet

Child's name shown on return Betty Brown

Child's social security number X10 00 1111

A Parent's name (first, initial, and last). **Caution:** *See instructions on back before completing.* Tom Brown

B Parent's social security number XXX 11 1X11

C Parent's filing status (check one):
☐ Single ☑ Married filing jointly ☐ Married filing separately ☐ Head of household ☐ Qualifying widow(er)

Step 1 Figure child's net investment income

1	Enter child's investment income, such as taxable interest and dividend income. See instructions. If this amount is $1,300 or less, **stop;** do not file this form	1	1,500
2	If the child DID NOT itemize deductions on Schedule A (Form 1040 or Form 1040NR), enter $1,300. If the child ITEMIZED deductions, see instructions	2	1,300
3	Subtract line 2 from line 1. If the result is zero or less, **stop;** do not complete the rest of this form but ATTACH it to the child's return	3	200
4	Enter child's **taxable** income from Form 1040, line 38; Form 1040A, line 22; or Form 1040NR, line 36	4	850
5	Enter the **smaller** of line 3 or line 4	5	200

Step 2 Figure tentative tax based on the tax rate of the parent listed on line A

6	Enter parent's **taxable** income from Form 1040, line 38; Form 1040A, line 22; Form 1040EZ, line 6; TeleFile Tax Record, line J; Form 1040NR, line 36; or Form 1040NR-EZ, line 13. If the parent transferred property to a trust, see instructions	6	52,000
7	Enter the total net investment income, if any, from Forms 8615, line 5, of ALL OTHER children of the parent identified above. **Do not** include the amount from line 5 above	7	800
8	Add lines 5, 6, and 7	8	53,000
9	Tax on line 8 based on the **parent's** filing status. See instructions. If from Capital Gain Tax Worksheet, enter amount from line 4 of that worksheet here ▶	9	9,491
10	Enter parent's tax from Form 1040, line 39; Form 1040A, line 23; Form 1040EZ, line 10; TeleFile Tax Record, line J; Form 1040NR, line 37; or Form 1040NR-EZ, line 14. If from **Capital Gain Tax Worksheet,** enter amount from line 4 of that worksheet here ▶	10	9,211
11	Subtract line 10 from line 9. If line 7 is blank, enter on line 13 the amount from line 11; skip lines 12a and 12b	11	280
12a	Add lines 5 and 7 12a 1,000		
b	Divide line 5 by line 12a. Enter the result as a decimal (rounded to two places)	12b	× .20
13	Multiply line 11 by line 12b	13	56

Step 3 Figure child's tax—If lines 4 and 5 above are the same, enter -0- on line 15 and go to line 16.

14	Subtract line 5 from line 4 14 650		
15	Tax on line 14 based on the **child's** filing status. See instructions. If from Capital Gain Tax Worksheet, enter amount from line 4 of that worksheet here ▶	15	99
16	Add lines 13 and 15	16	155
17	Tax on line 4 based on the **child's** filing status. See instructions. If from Capital Gain Tax Worksheet, check here ▶ ☐	17	129
18	Enter the **larger** of line 16 or line 17 here and on Form 1040, line 38; Form 1040A, line 23; or Form 1040NR, line 37.	18	155

Child's name shown on return Bill Brown

Child's social security number 0XX 11 1111

A Parent's name (first, initial, and last). **Caution:** *See instructions on back before completing.* Tom Brown

B Parent's social security number XXX 11 1X11

C Parent's filing status (check one):
☐ Single ☑ Married filing jointly ☐ Married filing separately ☐ Head of household ☐ Qualifying widow(er)

Step 1 Figure child's net investment income

1	Enter child's investment income, such as taxable interest and dividend income. See instructions. If this amount is $1,300 or less, **stop;** do not file this form	1	2,100
2	If the child DID NOT itemize deductions on Schedule A (Form 1040 or Form 1040NR), enter $1,300. If the child ITEMIZED deductions, see instructions	2	1,300
3	Subtract line 2 from line 1. If the result is zero or less, **stop;** do not complete the rest of this form but ATTACH it to the child's return	3	800
4	Enter child's **taxable** income from Form 1040, line 38; Form 1040A, line 22; or Form 1040NR, line 36	4	1,450
5	Enter the **smaller** of line 3 or line 4	5	800

Step 2 Figure tentative tax based on the tax rate of the parent listed on line A

6	Enter parent's **taxable** income from Form 1040, line 38; Form 1040A, line 22; Form 1040EZ, line 6; TeleFile Tax Record, line J; Form 1040NR, line 36; or Form 1040NR-EZ, line 13. If the parent transferred property to a trust, see instructions	6	52,000
7	Enter the total net investment income, if any, from Forms 8615, line 5, of ALL OTHER children of the parent identified above. **Do not** include the amount from line 5 above	7	200
8	Add lines 5, 6, and 7	8	53,000
9	Tax on line 8 based on the **parent's** filing status. See instructions. If from Capital Gain Tax Worksheet, enter amount from line 4 of that worksheet here ▶	9	9,491
10	Enter parent's tax from Form 1040, line 39; Form 1040A, line 23; Form 1040EZ, line 10; TeleFile Tax Record, line J; Form 1040NR, line 37; or Form 1040NR-EZ, line 14. If from **Capital Gain Tax Worksheet,** enter amount from line 4 of that worksheet here ▶	10	9,211
11	Subtract line 10 from line 9. If line 7 is blank, enter on line 13 the amount from line 11; skip lines 12a and 12b	11	280
12a	Add lines 5 and 7 12a 1,000		
b	Divide line 5 by line 12a. Enter the result as a decimal (rounded to two places)	12b	× .80
13	Multiply line 11 by line 12b	13	224

Step 3 Figure child's tax—If lines 4 and 5 above are the same, enter -0- on line 15 and go to line 16.

14	Subtract line 5 from line 4 14 650		
15	Tax on line 14 based on the **child's** filing status. See instructions. If from Capital Gain Tax Worksheet, enter amount from line 4 of that worksheet here ▶	15	99
16	Add lines 13 and 15	16	323
17	Tax on line 4 based on the **child's** filing status. See instructions. If from Capital Gain Tax Worksheet, check here ▶ ☐	17	219
18	Enter the **larger** of line 16 or line 17 here and on Form 1040, line 38; Form 1040A, line 23; or Form 1040NR, line 37.	18	323

Chapter 25

Family Tax Credits: Dependent Care and Earned Income (EIC) Credits

The dependent care and earned income credits help ease the burden of caring for dependents.

The dependent care credit is for working people who pay care costs which allow them the freedom to work. Depending on your income, the credit is 20% to 30% of up to $2,400 of care expenses for one dependent and up to $4,800 of expenses for two or more dependents. If your adjusted gross income exceeds $28,000, the maximum credit is $480 for one dependent and $960 for two or more dependents.

The earned income credit (EIC) is provided to low-income workers who support children, and a limited credit is allowed to certain workers without qualifying children; *see 25.8*. For 1997, the EIC can be as much as $2,210 if you have one qualifying child *(25.8)*, $3,656 if you have more than one qualifying child, and $332 if you do not have a qualifying child.

If you have one or more qualifying children, the maximum EIC begins to phase out when either earned income or AGI is at least $11,950. If you do not have any qualifying children, the maximum EIC begins to phase out when either earned income or AGI is at least $5,450. You look up the credit amount in IRS tables included in the tax form instructions. The EIC is "refundable"; you will receive a refund from the IRS if the credit exceeds your tax liability.

Dependent Care Credit

25.1 Qualifying for Child or Dependent Care Credit

Did you hire someone to care for your children or other dependents while you work? If so, you may qualify for a tax credit for the expenses. You may claim the credit even if you work part time. The credit is generally available to the extent you have earnings from employment. Your employer may have a plan qualifying for tax-free child care, and, if you are covered, you may be unable to claim a tax credit; *see 25.5*.

Where to claim the credit. The credit is claimed on Form 2441 if you file Form 1040, or on Form 1040A, Schedule 2. The size of the credit depends on the amount of care expenses and income. Depending on your income, the credit is 20% to 30% of up to $2,400 of care expenses for one dependent and up to $4,800 of expenses for two or more dependents. If your adjusted gross income exceeds $28,000, the maximum credit is $480 for one dependent and $960 for two or more dependents. *See* the chart in *25.2*.

Credit requirements. To qualify for the credit, you must:

1. Incur the care expenses in order to earn income. In the case of a married couple, this requires both spouses to work either at full- or part-time positions. An exception to the earned income rule is made for a spouse who is a full-time student or incapacitated (*25.3*). Qualifying care expenses are discussed at *25.5*. Limits on the amount of qualifying costs are discussed at *25.2*.
2. Pay over 50% of the household maintenance costs for a qualifying dependent; *see 25.4*. You must report the dependent's name and Social Security number on Form 2441 or Schedule 2 of Form 1040A.
3. File jointly if you are married, unless you are separated under the rules of *25.6*.
4. Hire someone *other than* your child who is under age 19 at the end of the year, your spouse, or a person you can claim as a dependent; *see 25.5*.
5. Have qualifying expenses in excess of tax-free reimbursements received from your employer; *see 25.5*.
6. Report on your tax return the name, address, and taxpayer identification number (Social Security number for individuals) of the child-care provider; *see* below.

Identifying care provider on your return. You must list the name, address, and taxpayer identification number of the person you paid to care for your dependent on Form 2441 if you file Form 1040, or on Form 1040A, Schedule 2. You do not need the taxpayer identification number if a tax-exempt charity provides the dependent care services. Failure to list the correct name, address, and number may result in a disallowance of the credit. To avoid this possibility, ask the provider to fill out Form W-10 or get the identifying information from a Social Security card, driver's license, or business letterhead or invoice. If a household employee has filled out Form W-4 for you, this may act as a backup record.

Withholding tax for housekeeper. Where you employ help to care for your dependent in your home, you may be liable for FICA (Social Security) and FUTA (unemployment) taxes; *see 25.7*.

25.2 Limits on the Dependent Care Credit

The credit is a percentage of expenses paid for the care of a dependent to allow you to work and earn income. Qualifying expenses are discussed at *25.5*. The credit percentage depends on your income.

Limit on expenses. In figuring the credit, you may only take into account qualifying expenses (*25.5*) up to a limit of $2,400 for one dependent, or $4,800 for two or more dependents. The $2,400 or $4,800 limit applies even if your actual expenses are much greater. Further, the $2,400 or $4,800 limit must be reduced by tax-free benefits received from an employer's dependent care plan. Finally, if your earned income is less than the $2,400 or $4,800 limit, your credit is figured on the lower income amount.

Take into account only 1997 payments for 1997 services. Your credit for 1997 must be based on payments made in 1997 for care services provided in 1997. If you paid for 1996 services in 1997, you may be able to claim an additional credit on your 1997 return, but only in limited circumstances, as discussed at the end of this section. If in 1997 you prepay for 1998 services, you must allocate your payment. Only payments for 1997 services should be counted towards the $2,400 or $4,800 limit when figuring your 1997 credit.

Filing Tip

Employer Reimbursements Reduce Credit

Expenses qualifying for the dependent care credit are reduced by any tax-free reimbursements under a qualified employer dependent care program. That is, the reimbursements reduce the $2,400 expense limit for one dependent, or the $4,800 expense limit for two or more qualifying dependents; *see 25.5*. Your employer will report reimbursements in Box 10 of your Form W-2. You figure the tax-free portion of the reimbursement, and any reduction to the credit expense base, on Form 2441 if you file Form 1040 or on Schedule 2 if you file Form 1040A.

Credit percentage. Depending on your income, a credit percentage of 20% to 30% applies to your expenses up to the $2,400 (one dependent) or $4,800 (two or more dependents) limit. The maximum credit is 30% for families with adjusted gross income of $10,000 or less. For adjusted gross income over $10,000, the 30% credit is reduced by 1% for each $2,000 of adjusted gross income or fraction of $2,000 over $10,000, but not below 20%. The 20% credit applies to adjusted gross incomes exceeding $28,000.

The dependent care credit is nonrefundable; it is limited to your tax liability. Furthermore, if you have tax preference items or adjustments subject to alternative minimum tax (23.1), the dependent care credit may be limited; follow the IRS instructions.

Allowable Credit

Adjusted gross income	Credit percentage	Your maximum credit	
		One dependent	Two or more dependents
$10,000 or less	30%	$720	$1,440
10,001–12,000	29	696	1,392
12,001–14,000	28	672	1,344
14,001–16,000	27	648	1,296
16,001–18,000	26	624	1,248
18,001–20,000	25	600	1,200
20,001–22,000	24	576	1,152
22,001–24,000	23	552	1,104
24,001–26,000	22	528	1,056
26,001–28,000	21	504	1,008
28,001–and over	20	480	960

EXAMPLES

1. You pay $6,000 to a neighbor to care for your two children while you work. Your adjusted gross income is $31,000. The credit percentage of 20% is applied to the maximum expense limit of $4,800, giving you a credit of $960.
2. Same as above except you receive a tax-free reimbursement of $2,500 from your employer's plan. The reimbursement reduces the $4,800 expense limit to $2,300 ($4,800 – $2,500); see 25.5. Your credit is $460 (20% of $2,300). If the tax-free reimbursement were $4,800 or more (it cannot exceed $5,000), no credit would be allowed.

Additional credit for 1997 payment of 1996 dependent care expenses. Payments made in 1997 for 1996 services may be eligible for an additional credit but only if you did not use up the $2,400 or $4,800 expense limit when claiming your 1996 credit.

For example, the cost of day-care services for your child in 1996 was $3,000, half of which you paid in 1996 and half in early 1997. On your 1996 return, a credit was based on the $1,500 of expenses paid in 1996. Since you used only $1,500 of the $2,400 expense limit in 1996, the $900 of "unused" expenses is carried over to 1997. On your 1997 Form 2441 or Schedule 2 of Form 1040A, you multiply $900 by a credit percentage based on your 1996 adjusted gross income. If your 1996 adjusted gross income was $30,000, the credit percentage is 20%. Thus, your additional 1997 credit is $180 (20% of $900). The $180 credit is claimed on Line 9 of Form 2441 or Schedule 2 (Form 1040A), and is in addition to the regular credit for 1997 care services. You must attach a statement explaining the carryover to 1997 and the computation of the additional credit.

25.3 Earned Income Test for Dependent Care Credit

To claim the credit, you must earn wage, salary, or self-employment income figured without regard to community property laws. Expenses for dependent care incurred while looking for a job may be included. However, you must have earnings during the year to claim the credit.

Earned income rule for married couples. Generally, both spouses must work at least part time, unless one is incapable of self-care or is a full-time student. If either you or your spouse earns less than the $2,400 or $4,800 credit base (25.2), the base is limited to the smaller income.

Filing Tip

No Credit if Neither Spouse Works

If both husband and wife are full-time students and neither works, they may not claim the credit for dependent care costs. While one spouse may be considered to have earned income of $200 (or $400) each month, the other spouse's earned income is zero. Care costs eligible for the credit are limited to the lesser amount of earned income, which in this case is zero.

> **EXAMPLE**
>
> John and Mary are married. John earns $4,000. Mary earns $23,500. They incur care costs of $5,000 for their two children, ages 5 and 7. Their adjusted gross income including interest earnings is $27,742; their credit percentage is 21%. The regular $4,800 credit base is limited to John's lower income of $4,000. They may claim a credit of $840 ($4,000 × 21%).

Spouses who are students or disabled. An incapacitated spouse or a spouse who is a full-time student is considered to have earned income of $200 a month if expenses are incurred for one dependent, or $400 a month for two or more such dependents.

A full-time student is one who attends school full time during each of five calendar months during the year.

> **EXAMPLE**
>
> Same facts as in the Example above except John was a full-time student for nine months and earned no income for the year. The credit base is limited to $3,600 ($400 × 9).

25.4 Household and Dependent Tests for Dependent Care Credit

To claim the credit you must maintain as your principal home a household for at least one of the following qualifying persons who lives with you:

1. A child *under the age of 13* whom you may claim as your dependent. If you are divorced or separated, and you had custody of the child for a longer time during the year than the other parent, you may be able to claim the credit even if the other parent is entitled to claim the child as a dependent; *see 25.6.*
2. Your spouse, if physically or mentally incapable of caring for himself or herself.
3. A person, regardless of age, who is physically or mentally incapable of caring for himself or herself. For example, he or she needs help to dress or to take care of personal hygiene or nutritional needs, or requires constant attention to avoid hurting himself or herself or others. Relatives who qualify, if disabled, are listed at *21.3.* A nonrelative may also qualify if he or she is a member of your household for the entire year, except for temporary absences. Generally, the qualifying person must be your dependent, but if he or she has gross income of $2,650 or more, so that you may not claim an exemption *(21.5)* for that person, you may still claim a credit for his or her care costs.

> **EXAMPLE**
>
> You live with your mother, who is physically incapable of caring for herself. You hire a practical nurse to care for her in the home while you are at work. Payments to the nurse qualify as care costs. However, if you placed her in a nursing home, the cost of the nursing home would not qualify as dependent care costs; but *see 17.11* for possible medical expense deduction.

If your child becomes age 13 during the year. Take into account expenses incurred for his or her care prior to the 13th birthday. However, you do not prorate the $2,400 limitation. For example, if your child becomes age 13 on May 1 and you incurred $2,400 in care expenses between January 1 and April 30, the entire $2,400 qualifies for the credit.

You must pay more than half of household costs. You are considered to have maintained a household if you (or you and your spouse) provided more than half the maintenance costs in 1997. You also qualify if you paid more than half the costs during a lesser period in which you had care cost expenses. Rent, mortgage interest, property tax and insurance, utility bills, upkeep, repairs, and groceries are considered maintenance costs. Do not count costs of clothing, education, medical expenses, vacations, life insurance, mortgage principal, and capital improvements, such as replacing a boiler.

In determining costs of maintaining a household for a care period of less than a year, the annual household costs are prorated over the number of calendar months within the period care costs were incurred. A period of less than a calendar month is treated as a calendar month.

Household of two or more families. If two or more families share living quarters, each family is treated as a separate household.

Expenses Qualifying for the Dependent Care Credit • 25.5

EXAMPLES

1. The annual cost of maintaining a household is $6,600, and the period during which child care costs qualified for the deduction is from June 20 to December 31. To meet the household test, you must furnish more than $1,925 in maintaining the household from June 1 to December 31. The allocation covers seven months (June 1 to December 31).

$$^7\!/_{12} \text{ of } \$6,600 = \$3,850$$
$$50\% \text{ of } \$3,850 = \$1,925$$

2. Two women, each with children, share a house. If each pays more than one-half of the household costs for her own family, each is treated as maintaining her separate household for purposes of the credit.

25.5 Expenses Qualifying for the Dependent Care Credit

If you do not receive tax-free dependent care benefits from an employer's plan, you may take into account up to $2,400 of the following types of expenses when figuring the credit for one dependent, or up to $4,800 for two or more dependents. If you receive employer-financed dependent care, tax-free reimbursements reduce the $2,400 or $4,800 base.

1. Costs of caring for your child under age 13, incapacitated spouse, or incapacitated dependent in your home. If you pay FICA or FUTA taxes on your housekeeper's wages *(25.7)*, you may include your share of the tax (employer) as part of the wages when entering your qualifying expenses. Also include your housekeeper's share of FICA tax if you pay it. Note that these taxes may more than offset your allowable credit.

    The manner of care need not be the least expensive alternative. For example, where a grandparent resides with you and may provide adequate care for your child to enable you to work, the cost of hiring someone to care for the child is still eligible for the credit.

2. Ordinary domestic services in your home, such as laundry, cleaning, and cooking (but not payments to a gardener or chauffeur) that are partly for the care of the qualifying person. Expenses for the dependent's food, clothing, or entertainment do not qualify. Food costs for a housekeeper who eats in your home may be added to qualifying expenses.

3. Outside-the-home care costs for a child under age 13, as in a day-care center, day camp, nursery school, or in the home of a babysitter. Outside-the-home care costs also qualify if incurred for a handicapped dependent, regardless of age, provided he or she regularly spends at least eight hours per day in your home. However, the cost of schooling in the first grade or higher does not qualify for the credit. Costs for sleep-away camp also do not qualify for the credit.

    The cost of driving a dependent to or from a day-care center or similar transportation does not qualify for a child-care credit. However, the Tax Court allowed a child-care credit for supervised bus transportation; the transportation was part of the actual child care.

Payments to relatives. No credit may be claimed for payments made to relatives for whom a dependency exemption is allowable *(21.3)*. Thus, if you pay your mother to care for your child and you cannot claim your mother as a dependent, such payments qualify for the credit. The same rule applies for payments to unrelated persons who live with you and qualify as your dependents; *see 21.4*.

No credit may be claimed for payments to your child who is under 19 years of age at the close of the tax year, whether or not you may claim the child as a dependent.

Allocating expenses when employed less than entire year. When an expense covers a period, part of which you were gainfully employed or in active search of gainful employment and part of which you were not employed or seeking employment, you must allocate expenses on a daily basis.

EXAMPLE

You are employed for only two months and 10 days. Monthly care expenses are $300. Eligible care expenses amount to $700 ($300 × 2 months, plus $^1\!/_3$ of $300).

Employer-financed dependent care reduces credit base. Tax-free reimbursements under an employer's dependent care program reduce the $2,400 or $4,800 credit base. For example, if you have one child and you receive a $1,500 reimbursement of child-care costs from your company's plan, the amount eligible for the tax credit is reduced to $900 ($2,400 – $1,500). A reimbursement of $2,400 or more would bar any credit. The $4,800 credit expense limit for two or more dependents is similarly reduced. On your Form W-2, your employer will report the amount of tax-free reimbursement; *see 3.4*.

 Filing Tip

Day-Care Center or Nursery School

The amount you pay to a day-care center or nursery school for a dependent child under age 13 is eligible for the credit, even if it covers such incidental benefits as lunch. However, tuition for a child in first grade or higher is not taken into account. If the dependent is not your child, costs for care outside the home qualify only if the dependent regularly spends at least eight hours per day in your home. Up to $2,400 a year of outside-the-home care expenses may be taken into account in figuring the credit for one dependent, and up to $4,800 for two or more.

If your employer's plan allows you to fund a reimbursement account with salary reduction contributions that are excluded from taxable pay *(3.14)*, reimbursements from the account are considered employer-financed payments that reduce the $2,400 or $4,800 credit base. In deciding whether to make salary reduction contributions, you should determine whether the tax-free reduction will provide a larger tax savings than that provided by the credit. If your tax bracket is higher than 15%, taking the salary reduction is advantageous. Even if you expect to be in the 15% bracket, you should compare the estimated tax savings from the credit with the estimated savings from a salary reduction. You may find that the salary reduction provides the larger tax savings, taking into consideration not only the decrease in federal income tax, but also the Social Security tax and state and local taxes avoided by using the salary reduction. Further, by lowering your adjusted gross income, a salary reduction may enable you to claim a larger IRA deduction if you are subject to the deduction phase-out rule *(8.4)*, or a larger deduction for miscellaneous itemized deductions subject to the 2% floor *(19.1)*.

Allocation if expenses cover noncare services.   If a portion of expenses is for other than dependent care or household services, only the portion allocable to dependent care or household services qualifies. No allocation is required if the nondependent care services are minimal.

> ### EXAMPLES
> 1. A person accepts a full-time position and sends his 12-year-old child to boarding school. The expenses paid to the school must be allocated. The part representing care of the child qualifies; the part representing tuition does not.
> 2. A full-time housekeeper is hired to care for two children, ages 9 and 12. The housekeeper also drives the mother to and from work each day. The driving takes no longer than 30 minutes. No allocation is required because the nondependent care services of chauffeuring are minimal.
> 3. You pay $6,000 for care of your child in your home. The expenses also qualify as medical expenses. Assume your adjusted gross income is $17,000. Your dependent care costs are limited to $2,400 and you may claim a credit of $624 ($2,400 ¥ 26%). The balance of $3,600 is deductible as medical expenses if you itemize deductions on Schedule A. If you had no other medical costs, your medical deduction would be $2,325 after deducting the 7.5% limitation on medical costs ($3,600 − $1,275, or 7.5% of $17,000).

25.6 Dependent Care Credit Rules for Separated Couples

A married person generally must file a joint return to claim the dependent care credit *(25.1)*, but if you are living apart from your spouse you may claim the credit on a separate return if you meet the following tests:

1. You maintain as your home a household which is the principal place of abode of a qualifying person *(25.4)* for more than half the year;
2. You furnish over half the cost of maintaining the household for the entire year; *and*
3. Your spouse was not a member of the household during the *last six months* of the year.

If you satisfy these tests, you are treated as unmarried and may claim the credit on a separate return. You do not have to take your spouse's income into account or show that he or she is employed in order to claim a credit.

Your child may be a qualifying person for purposes of the credit even if you cannot claim the child as your dependent. This favorable rule applies if: you are legally divorced or separated, separated under a written agreement, or you lived apart from your spouse during the last six months of 1997; you or you and the other parent had custody of the child for more than half the year and provided more than half of the child's support; and you are the *custodial parent* (have custody longer than the other parent). If these tests are met, you may claim the credit for care of a dependent child who is under age 13 or physically or mentally incapable of caring for himself or herself even though you waive the dependency exemption on Form 8332 or are unable to claim the exemption under a pre-1985 divorce or separation agreement. The noncustodial parent may not claim the credit even if he or she is allowed the exemption.

Filing Tip

Care Costs Qualifying as Medical Expenses

Care costs, such as a nurse's wages, may also qualify as medical expenses, but you may not claim both the dependent care credit and the medical expenses deduction. If your care costs exceed the amount allowed as dependent care costs, the excess, to the extent it qualifies as a medical expense, may be added to other deductible medical costs.

Employment Taxes for Household Employees

25.7 Paying and Withholding Taxes for Household Employees

If you employ someone to care for your children or disabled dependents in your home, clean your residence, cook, or provide other personal services in or around your home, you may be obligated to pay and withhold Social Security and Medicare taxes (FICA) and also pay federal unemployment taxes (FUTA). FICA or FUTA taxes do not apply if the household worker is the employee of an agency that assigns the position, sets the fee, and requires reports from the worker.

The reporting requirements for FICA are at *25.8,* and the FUTA requirements at *25.9.*

Income taxes. Income tax withholding is not required for a household employee, but if the employee requests it and you agree, you pay the withheld tax under one of the reporting options discussed in *25.8.* Withholdings are based on a Form W-4 (Withholding Allowance Certificate) filed by the employee.

An employee who qualifies for the earned income credit may receive advance payments by giving you Form W-5; *see 25.13.*

25.8 Social Security and Medicare Taxes (FICA) for Household Employees

You generally must pay and withhold Social Security and Medicare taxes (FICA) if you pay cash wages of $1,000 or more to a household employee in 1997. Wages paid to your spouse, child, or parent for household services are generally exempt from this tax, as discussed at the end of this section. Also exempt are wages of any amount paid to a household employee who is under the age of 18 at any time during the year, so long as he or she does not work full time as a household worker. For example, if you hire a student under age 18 as a baby-sitter, Social Security and Medicare taxes do not apply regardless of the amount of wages you pay. However, if wages of $1,000 or more are paid to a person under 18 years of age who works full time as a household employee, Social Security and Medicare taxes apply.

Once payments to non-exempt employees equal or exceed $1,000, the entire amount, including the first $1,000, is subject to FICA taxes.

The $1,000 threshold may be increased for 1998 by an inflation adjustment.

Tax rates. As an employer, you pay FICA at the rate of 7.65% of wages: 6.2% for Social Security and 1.45% for Medicare. For example, you pay a housekeeper $125 a week ($6,500 for the year). You must pay $497.25 in FICA and either withhold the same amount from the housekeeper's wages or pay the housekeeper's share yourself. In the unlikely case that wages exceed the wage limit for Social Security taxes (for example, $65,400 in 1997), there is an extra Medicare tax of 2.9%: 1.45% tax owed by you as the employer and 1.45% owed by the housekeeper. There is no wage limit on the additional 2.9% Medicare tax. You and the employee are each liable for the combined FICA rate of 7.65% (6.20% Social Security plus 1.45% Medicare) where 1997 wages are $65,400 or less. If wages exceed $65,400, the 7.65% rate applies to the first $65,400, and the 1.45% rate applies to the excess.

If you do not withhold the employee's share of FICA taxes, you are liable for the full amount. If you pay the employee's share of FICA taxes instead of deducting it from wages, you must treat your payment as additional wages when you report the employee's wages on Form W-2, but the payment is not considered wages for Social Security and Medicare tax purposes.

How to report and pay federal employment taxes. You compute 1997 FICA tax (Social Security and Medicare) on wages paid to household employees on Schedule H, which you attach to your 1997 Form 1040 or 1040A.

You must include your employer identification number (EIN) on Schedule H. An EIN is a nine-digit number, separate from your Social Security number, that is obtained from the IRS by filing Form SS-4. If you previously obtained an EIN when paying taxes for other employees, use that number on Schedule H.

Form W-2. File a 1997 Form W-2 for each household employee to whom you paid Social Security and Medicare wages, or wages from which you withheld federal income tax. Give copies B, C, and 2 of Form W-2 to your household employee by February 2, 1998, and give copy A to the Social Security Administration by March 2, 1998.

 Caution

Illegal Aliens
Household employees who work for you on a regular basis must verify their U.S. citizenship or their eligibility to work in the U.S. on Form I-9 from the Immigration and Naturalization Service. It is unlawful to knowingly hire an alien who is not legally entitled to work in the U.S.

Estimated Tax. In planning whether to make estimated tax installments during 1998 *(27.1)*, you should include an estimate of employment taxes for household employees as part of your estimate of 1998 income tax liability. Failure to consider the employment taxes could trigger an estimated tax penalty for 1998. For years before 1998, the estimated tax penalty did not apply to household employee taxes.

 Caution

Estimated Tax Penalty for 1998

If you do not have enough income tax withheld or pay enough in estimated tax installments, you may be liable for an estimated tax penalty; *see 27.1*. Beginning in 1998, the penalty can apply to employment taxes for household employees. In planning whether to make estimated tax installments for 1998, take the employment taxes into account.

Reporting rules for self-employed persons who have regular business employees. Self-employed persons who have employees other than household employees may follow one of these two options:

1. Report FICA and FUTA taxes and any income tax withholding for household employees annually on Schedule H, and report FICA taxes and any income tax withholding for other employees quarterly on Form 941 and FUTA taxes annually on Form 940 (or 940-EZ); *or*
2. Report FICA taxes and any income tax withholding for *all* employees (household employees and other employees) quarterly on Form 941 and report FUTA taxes annually for all employees on Form 940 or Form 940-EZ.

Employers of household employees must also give copies of Form W-2 (Wage and Tax Statement) to each employee and to the Social Security Administration, as discussed above.

Reporting rules for an estate. If a person who hired household help dies during the year and the estate continues to employ the employee for domestic work, the estate includes both the wages paid by the decedent and the estate to determine whether taxes are due under the $1,000 test. Thus, if in 1997 a person before dying paid $500 to a domestic and her estate continued to employ the domestic and paid wages of $800, the estate is required to pay FICA taxes on wages of $1,300.

Payments to your parent, child, or spouse. FICA tax does not apply to wages paid to your spouse for domestic services in your home. A similar exception applies to wages paid to your son or daughter under age 21, but note the rule that bars you from basing a dependent care credit on payments made to a child under age 19 *(25.5)*. Further, FICA generally does not apply to wages paid to your father or mother for domestic work in your home unless (1) you are divorced or widowed, or your spouse is disabled; and (2) you have a child living at home who is under age 18 or is disabled.

25.9 Federal Unemployment Taxes (FUTA) for Household Employees

As an employer, you are also liable for FUTA (federal unemployment taxes) if you pay cash wages of $1,000 or more for household services during any calendar quarter, or if you did so in any quarter in the preceding year. You do not pay FUTA on wages paid to your spouse, your parents, or your children under age 21. Your employee is not liable for FUTA.

The FUTA rate for 1997 is 6.2% on the first $7,000 of cash wages. However, there is a credit for payments to a state unemployment fund which reduces FUTA liability.

For wages paid to a household employee in 1997, you will generally report FUTA on Schedule H, which you attach to your Form 1040. If you have regular business employees, *see 25.8* for reporting options.

Earned Income Credit (EIC)

25.10 Qualifying Tests for EIC

For 1997, the earned income credit (EIC) may be claimed not only by workers with qualifying children who meet the tests below, but also, in limited cases, by childless workers.

Claiming the EIC with Qualifying Children

You may claim the EIC on a 1997 return if you:

- Have earned income, such as wages and self-employment earnings, and also modified adjusted gross income of under $25,760 if you have one qualifying child or under $29,290 if you have two or more qualifying children. *See 25.11* for the credit phase-out rules.
- Have a qualifying child who lived with you in your main home in the U.S. for more than six months in 1997; *see* below.
- File a joint return if married.

- File Schedule EIC with your Form 1040 or Form 1040A. On Schedule EIC, you identify and provide information about a qualifying child.
- Are not a qualifying child of another person.
- Include on your return your Social Security number and, if married, that of your spouse.

A qualifying child. A qualifying child is your son, daughter, adopted child, grandchild, stepchild, or foster child who at the end of 1997 was under age 19, or under age 24 and a full-time student, or any age if permanently and totally disabled. To be a full-time student, a child must be enrolled during any five months for classes treated as full time by the school.

Household requirement. The qualifying child must have lived with you in your main home in the U.S. for more than six months. A foster child must have lived with you for all of 1997. Temporary absences for school or vacation count as time lived in your home.

A person in the U.S. armed forces who is stationed outside the U.S. on extended active duty is treated as maintaining a main residence within the U.S.

If you are married, you must file a joint return with your spouse to claim the credit. However, if your spouse did not live in your household for the last six months of the year, and you maintained a home for a child who lived with you for more than half of the year, you may claim the credit as a head of household; *see 1.10.*

Permanently and totally disabled. A person is permanently and totally disabled if: (1) he or she cannot engage in any substantial gainful activity because of a physical or mental condition; and (2) a physician determines that the condition has lasted or is expected to last for at least a year or lead to death.

Married child or qualifying child of another person. You may not take the earned income credit if your child is also a qualifying child of another person who has a higher adjusted gross income in 1997 than you do.

If your child was married at the end of 1997, he or she may be a qualifying child only if the child was claimed as a dependent on Form 1040 or Form 1040A, Line 6, or you waive the exemption in favor of the child's other parent, or the other parent may claim the exemption under a pre-1985 agreement.

If *you* are a qualifying child of another person, you may not claim the EIC even if you have a qualifying child and would otherwise qualify for the credit.

Nonresident aliens. An individual who is a nonresident alien for any part of the year is not eligible for the credit unless he or she is married and an election is made by the couple to have all of their worldwide income subject to U.S. tax.

Claiming the Credit without Qualifying Children

If you do not have a qualifying child, you may claim the EIC on a 1997 return if you:

- Have earned income, such as wages and self-employment earnings, of under $9,770, and also modified adjusted gross income under $9,770. *See 25.11* for the credit phase-out rule.
- Have your main home in the U.S. for more than six months in 1997.
- Are at least 25 but under age 65 at the end of 1997. If filing a joint return, either you or your spouse must satisfy this age test.
- File a joint return if married.
- Are not a dependent of another taxpayer.
- Are not a qualifying child of another taxpayer.
- Include your Social Security number on your return, and, if married, that of your spouse.

The rules discussed earlier for armed forces personnel and nonresident aliens with qualifying children also apply to individuals without children.

25.11 Income Tests for EIC

For purposes of the credit, earned income includes wages, salary, tips, commissions, jury duty pay, union strike benefits, certain disability pensions, tax-free meals and lodging from your employer, the rental value of a parsonage, U.S. military basic quarters and subsistence allowances, combat pay, voluntary salary deferrals, and self-employment earnings.

Disqualifying income. For 1997, an individual is not eligible for the earned income credit if he or she has "disqualified income" exceeding $2,250. Disqualified income includes interest (taxable and tax-exempt), dividends, net rent and royalty income, net capital gain income, and net passive income that is not self-employment income.

Law Alert

Denial of future credits for recklessness or fraud

A new law prohibits a taxpayer who negligently or fraudulently claims the EIC from claiming future credits over a period of several years. The credit is disallowed for two years from the tax year for which it is determined that the EIC claim was claimed recklessly or in disregard of the rules. The period increases to 10 years from the most recent tax year for which it is found that the EIC was claimed fraudulently. The law applies to 1997 and later years.

Law Alert

Recertification required if EIC denied

If the IRS denies an EIC by issuing a deficiency notice, the credit may not be claimed in a future tax year unless the IRS is presented evidence of eligibility to take the credit. Once the IRS certifies eligibility, proof of eligibility is not required again in subsequent tax years unless the IRS again denies the EIC in a deficiency proceeding. This new rule applies in 1997 and later tax years.

Credit phases out with income. If you have one qualifying child *(25.10)*, the 1997 credit begins to phase out in the IRS table *(25.12)* if either earned income or modified adjusted gross income (MAGI) is at least $11,950, and no credit is allowed if either earned income or MAGI is $25,760 or more.

If you have two or more qualifying children, the phaseout of the 1997 credit also begins when either earned income or MAGI is at least $11,950 and the credit is completely phased out if either earned income or MAGI is $29,290 or more.

If you do not have any qualifying children, the phaseout of the credit begins when either earned income or MAGI is at least $5,450, and the credit is completely phased out if either amount is $9,770 or more.

Modified adjusted gross income. For purposes of the EIC phase-out rules, modified adjusted gross income (MAGI) is generally equal to your adjusted gross income but certain losses are disregarded for EIC purposes. These include: net capital losses; net losses from trusts and estates; net losses relating to nonbusiness rents and royalties; and 50 percent of the net losses from businesses, computed separately with respect to sole proprietorships (other than in farming), sole proprietorships in farming, and other businesses.

Starting in 1998, the percentage of disregarded business losses increases from 50% to 75%. Furthermore, the following items must be added back to MAGI: tax-exempt interest, nontaxable pension annuity payments, and nontaxable IRA distributions that are not rolled over to another IRA.

Self-employed. If you were self-employed in 1997, your earned income for credit purposes is the net earnings shown on Schedule SE, *less* the income tax deduction for 50% of self-employment tax claimed on Line 26 of Form 1040. If your net earnings were less than $400, the net amount is your earned income for purposes of the credit. If you had a net loss, the loss is subtracted from any wages or other employee earned income. If you are a statutory employee, the income reported on Schedule C qualifies for the credit.

Foreign earned income. If you work abroad and claim the foreign income exclusion, you may *not* take the credit.

25.12 Look Up EIC in Government Tables

After completing a worksheet in the IRS instructions which determines whether your earned income credit is based on your earned income or modified adjusted gross income *(25.11)*, you then look up the amount of your credit in an IRS table.

If you have children, the table provides a phaseout of the credit once 1997 earnings are at least $11,950. If you have only one qualifying child *(25.8)*, your credit is completely phased out if either earned income or modified adjusted gross income is $25,760 or more. If you have more than one qualifying child, the 1997 credit is completely phased out if either earned income or modified adjusted gross income is $29,290 or more. *See 25.11* for modified adjusted gross income rules.

If you do not have a qualifying child, the phaseout of the credit starts when earned income or modified adjusted gross income is $5,450 or more and no credit is allowed if either amount is $9,770 or more.

> **EXAMPLE**
>
> Jane is divorced. Her only income in 1997 is wages of $10,500. She supports her eight-year-old daughter, who lives with her for the entire year.
> To find her credit, Jane turns to the IRS Table in the instruction book accompanying her return. In the table, the credit shown for her income bracket is $2,210.

25.13 Advance Payment of Earned Income Credit

If you believe you are entitled to an earned income credit, you may file a certificate, Form W-5, with your employer to have a portion of the credit added to your paycheck throughout the year. To get advanced earned income payments you must have a qualifying child *(25.10)*.

If you receive any advance payments, you must report them on Form 1040 or Form 1040A; your employer will include the amount in Box 9 of your Form W-2. If you receive advance payments in excess of the credit you are entitled to, the excess is treated as a tax you owe when you file your return. If the credit you are entitled to exceeds the advance payments, the excess credit reduces any other tax you owe. If the credit exceeds your liability, the difference is refunded to you.

 Law Alert

Workfare payments
After 1997, certain workfare payments under state-subsidized programs are not included in earned income for EIC purposes.

25.14 Qualifying for the Adoption Credit

Starting in 1997, a tax credit of up to $5,000 may be available for the qualifying costs of adopting a child under age 18, or a person who is physically and mentally incapable of self-care. If a state determination has been made that a child is a "special needs" child, the maximum credit is $6,000. The credit is phased out ratably for those with adjusted gross income (after certain adjustments) between $75,000 and $115,000.

The credit is claimed on Form 8839. If you paid qualifying adoption costs in 1997 but the adoption was not final at the end of the year, the credit may *not* be claimed on your 1997 return; *see* *25.15* for the credit timing rules.

Employer plans. As discussed at *3.5*, an exclusion from income is also available to employees if adoption expenses are paid through a qualifying employer program, subject to rules similar to that of the credit. If you receive employer adoption benefits that are less than your adoption expenses, you may be able to claim the credit.

25.15 Claiming the Adoption Credit on Form 8839

The adoption credit is claimed on Form 8839, which you attach to your Form 1040 or 1040A. On Form 8839, you provide the child's name, age, and taxpayer identification number (generally a Social Security number). On Form 8839, you take into account the $5,000 (or $6,000) per child limitation, and reduce the maximum allowable credit if your modified adjusted gross income is over $75,000 and under $115,000. No credit is allowed if modified adjusted gross income is $115,000 or more.

If you are married, you generally must file a joint return to take the adoption credit or exclusion. You may take the credit or exclusion on a separate return if you are legally separated under a decree of divorce or separate maintenance, or if you lived apart from your spouse for the last six months of the tax year and (1) your home is the eligible child's home for more than half the year, and (2) you pay more than half the cost of keeping up your home for the year.

Qualifying Expenses. Qualifying adoption expenses are reasonable and necessary adoption fees, court costs, attorney fees, and other expenses directly related to, and whose principal purpose is for, the legal adoption of an eligible child *(25.14)*. Qualifying expenses do not include expenses paid before January 1, 1997. You may not claim a credit for the costs of a surrogate parenting arrangement or for adopting your spouse's child.

When to claim the adoption credit for a child who is a U.S. citizen or resident. If you pay qualifying expenses in any year before the year the adoption becomes final, the credit may be claimed in the year after the year of the payment, whether or not the adoption is final in that year. If you pay qualifying expenses in the year the adoption becomes final, the credit for those expenses is claimed in that year. If qualifying expenses are paid in any year after the year in which the adoption becomes final, the credit is claimed in the year of payment.

Foreign child. If you adopt a child who is not a U.S. citizen or resident, a credit may not be claimed until the year the adoption becomes final. If adoption expenses are paid after the tax year in which the adoption became finalized, a credit for such expenses is allowed for the tax year of payment.

Unused credit carryforward. The amount of your allowable adoption credit for a year cannot be more than your tax liability for that year, minus the following:

1. Any credit for child and dependent care expenses,
2. Any credit for the elderly or disabled, *and*
3. Your tentative alternative minimum tax.

If your credit is more than this limit, you can carry forward any unused credit for the next five years, or until used, whichever comes first.

> **EXAMPLE**
>
> Virginia and Chuck Murphy begin adoption proceedings in 1997. During 1997, they incur qualifying adoption expenses of $4,000. During 1998, the year in which the adoption is finalized, they incur additional expenses of $2,000. The Murphys may not claim any credit for 1997. A credit may be claimed for 1998, taking into account the expenses of both years, subject to the $5,000 limit ($6,000 if the child is a special needs child) and the income phase-out for 1998.

Law Alert

Eligible Child After 2001
After 2001, the adoption credit applies only to qualified expenses for adopting an eligible child with special needs.

Adoption Credit

435

25.16 Child Tax Credit in 1998

Starting in 1998, taxpayers who have qualifying children under age 17 may be entitled to the new child tax credit. The amount of the credit will be $400 per child in 1998 and increases to $500 per child in 1999 and thereafter.

The credit is phased out if modified adjusted gross income (MAGI) exceeds $110,000 for married couples filing joint returns, $75,000 for single filers, and $55,000 for married persons filing separately. For each $1,000 (or fraction thereof) of AGI in excess of the threshold amount, the credit is reduced by $50. Thus, for a married couple filing a joint return with one child, the $400 per child credit is completely phased out if their MAGI exceeds $119,000 in 1998. The phase-out ranges are not indexed for inflation.

Qualifying child. A "qualifying child" is a child, grandchild, stepchild, or eligible foster child for whom the taxpayer can claim a dependency exemption and who is less than 17 years old as of the close of the tax year. The child must also be a U.S. citizen, resident, or national.

Supplemental credit. Certain parents eligible for the earned income credit may be entitled to a supplemental credit under a complicated formula that will require IRS guidelines for implementation.

The Supplement will have further details, if available, concerning the child tax credit calculations.

Chapter 26

Tax Withholdings

Withholding taxes give the Government part of your income before you have a chance to use it. Withholding tax is imposed on salary and wage income, tip income, certain gambling winnings, pensions, and retirement distributions, but you may avoid withholding on retirement payments; *see 26.11*. Withholding is also imposed on interest and dividends if you do not give your taxpayer identification number to a payer of interest or dividend income.

You may increase or decrease withholdings on your wages by submitting a new Form W-4 to your employer. Withholdings may be reduced by claiming allowances based on tax deductions and credits.

Make sure that tax withholdings meet or help you meet the estimated tax rules that require withholdings plus estimated tax payments to equal 90% of your current year liability or the required percentage of the prior year's liability; *see* Chapter 27.

A 20% withholding rate applies to nonperiodic distributions from an employer retirement plan. You may avoid the withholding by instructing your employer to directly transfer the funds to an IRA or the plan of your new employer; *see 26.11*.

26.1 Withholdings Should Cover Estimated Tax

In fixing the rate of withholding on your wages, pay attention to the tests for determining whether sufficient taxes have been withheld from your pay. A penalty will apply if your wage withholdings plus estimated tax payments do not equal the lesser of 90% of your current tax liability and the required percentage of the prior year's tax; *see 27.1.*

Taxes are withheld from payments made to you for services that you perform as an employee; *see 26.2* for exceptions. By filing Form W-4, you claim exemptions for yourself, your spouse, and dependents. The number of exemptions claimed will either decrease or increase the amount of withholding. You also may claim withholding allowances for itemized deductions and credits such as the credit for the elderly and totally disabled, the foreign tax credit, credit for home mortgages, the general business credit, and earned income credit (if you have not filed for an advance payment of the credit on Form W-5).

26.2 When Income Taxes Are Withheld on Wages

The amount of income tax withheld for your wage bracket depends on your marital status and the number of exemptions you claim. Exemptions for withholding correspond to the exemptions allowed on your tax return; *see 21.1.* You file a withholding certificate, Form W-4, with your employer, indicating your status and exemptions. Without the certificate, your employer must withhold tax as if you are a single person with no exemptions.

Cash payments or the cash value of benefits paid to an employee by an employer are subject to withholding, unless the payments are specifically excluded.

Income Taxes Are Withheld On:

- Payments to employees as salaries, wages, fees, commissions, pensions, retirement pay, vacation allowances, dismissal pay, etc. (whether paid in cash or goods). The withholding rate on separately paid bonuses is 28%. *See 26.11* for withholding on pensions and annuities.
- Sick pay paid by your employer. If a third party pays you sick pay on a plan funded by your employer, you may request withholding by filing Form W-4S.
- Taxable group insurance coverage for amount over $50,000.
- Reimbursements of expenses that do not meet qualifying rules of accountable plans discussed at *20.31.* Also, reimbursements from accountable plans that exceed federal rates if the employee does not return the reimbursement or show that it is substantiated by proof of expenses.
- Pay to members of the U.S. Armed Forces.
- Prize awarded to a salesman in a contest run by his employer.
- Retroactive pay and overtime under Fair Labor Standards Act.
- Taxable supplemental unemployment compensation benefits.

Income Taxes Are Not Withheld On:

- Payments to household workers. However, although income tax withholding is not required, the worker and the employer may make a voluntary withholding agreement; *see 25.7.*
- Payments to agricultural workers, college domestics, ministers of the gospel (except chaplains in the Armed Forces), casual workers, nonresident aliens, public officials who receive fees directly from the public, notaries, jurors, witnesses, precinct workers, etc.; but *see* voluntary withholding agreements, *26.3.*
- Pay for newspaper home delivery by children under age 18.
- Advances for traveling expenses if the employee substantiates expenses to the employer and if the employee returns any unsubstantiated amount; *see 20.31.*
- Value of tax-free board and lodging furnished by an employer.
- Fringe benefits not subject to tax.
- Substantiated reimbursements for deductible moving expenses or medical care benefits under a self-insured medical reimbursement plan.
- Death benefit payments to beneficiary of employee; wages due but unpaid at employee's death and paid to estate or beneficiary.
- Pay for U.S. citizen working abroad or in U.S. possessions to the extent that the pay is tax free; *see* Chapter 36 for rules.
- Employer contributions to SEPs; *see 8.16.*
- Earnings of self-employed persons, as they pay their income taxes currently through estimated tax.

Filing Instruction

Adjust Withholdings
If you do not expect withholdings to meet your final tax liability, ask your employer to withhold a greater amount of tax; *see 26.3.* On the other hand, if the withholding rate applied to your wages results in overwithholding, you may claim extra withholding allowances to reduce withholding during the year; *see 26.5* and *26.6.*

Form W-2. By the end of January, your employer must give you duplicate copies of Form W-2, which is a record of your pay and the withheld income and Social Security taxes. If you leave your job during the year, you may ask your employer for a Form W-2 by making a written request within 30 days of leaving the job.

26.3 Increasing Withholding

For withholding tax purposes, you do not have to claim all your exemptions. This will increase the amount withheld and help reduce the final tax payment on filing your tax return. It may also relieve you of having to make quarterly estimated tax payments, provided the withholdings are sufficient to meet your estimated tax liability; *see 27.1.* A waiver of exemptions for withholding taxes does not prevent you from claiming the "waived" exemptions on your final tax return. The waiver is merely a bookkeeping aid to your company's payroll department. If you find that even a waiver of exemptions does not cover all of the tax you want withheld, you may ask your employer on Form W-4 to withhold additional amounts from each paycheck.

26.4 Avoiding Withholding

If you had no income tax liability in 1997 and expect none for 1998, you may be exempt from income tax withholdings on your 1998 wages. If eligible, students working for the summer, retired persons, and other part-time workers do not have to wait for a refund of withheld taxes they do not owe. The exemption applies only to income tax withholding, not to withholdings for Social Security and Medicare *(26.10).*

However, if you can be claimed as a dependent on another person's tax return, and you have any investment income, you may claim this special exemption only if you expect total income (wages plus investments) to be no more than the minimum standard deduction for dependents, which in 1997 was $650 *(13.5).* If the $650 amount is increased due to an inflation factor, the higher amount will be on the 1998 version of Form W-4.

If you cannot be claimed as a dependent by another person, you can claim the exemption from withholding if your total income is no more than the sum of your personal exemption and the standard deduction for your filing status.

To claim an exemption for 1998, you must file a withholding exemption certificate, Form W-4, with your employer. The form may be obtained from an IRS district office or from your employer. If you will file a joint return for 1998, do not claim an exemption on Form W-4 if the joint return will show a tax. An exemption claimed during 1998 will expire February 16, 1999.

26.5 Withholding Allowances

Too much may be withheld from your pay if you have tax reduction items. The overpayment will be refunded when you file your return, but you lose the use of your money during the year. By filing Form W-4 with your employer, you may avoid this and reduce withholding taxes by claiming additional withholding allowances based on the following: (1) estimated itemized deductions; (2) IRA contribution deductions; (3) alimony deductions; (4) net losses from Schedule C, D, E, or F of Form 1040; and (5) tax credits such as the dependent care credit, credit for the elderly, earned-income credit (if you did not request advance payment on Form W-5), and general business credit.

Working couples filing jointly figure withholding allowances on their combined wage income, deductions, adjustments, and credits, but can divide the total number of allowances between them in any way they wish. On separate returns, the allowances must be figured separately.

If you work for two or more employers at the same time, you figure your allowances based on the total income, and then split the allowances between the two jobs in any way you wish. Do not claim the same allowances with more than one employer at the same time.

File a new Form W-4 each year for withholding allowances based on itemized deductions and credits. Furthermore, you may have to file a new form to increase your withholding if withholding allowances you had been claiming are no longer allowed; *see 26.7.*

A civil penalty of $500 may be imposed if, for purposes of claiming tax withholding allowances, you overstate your itemized deductions and credits or understate your wages without a reasonable basis. There is also a criminal penalty of up to $1,000 plus a jail sentence for willfully supplying false information.

26.6 Special Withholding Allowance

A special withholding allowance designed to eliminate overwithholding may be claimed on Form W-4 by certain employees. The withholding allowance, like an exemption, frees wage income from withholding. An unmarried person may claim this special withholding allowance, provided he or she is not working for more than one employer. If you are married, you may claim the allowance if you work for only one employer and your spouse does not work, or your wages from a second job or your spouse's wages are $1,000 or less. This special allowance is only for withholding purposes. You may not claim it on your tax return.

26.7 When To File New Form W-4

You should file a new Form W-4 any time the number of your exemptions or withholding allowances increases or decreases, such as when a child is born or adopted, you marry, you get a divorce, or your deductible expenses change.

Your employer may make the new Form W-4 effective with the next payment of wages. However, an employer may postpone the new withholding rate until the start of the first payroll period ending on or after the 30th day from the day you submit the revised form.

You must file a new Form W-4 within 10 days if the number of allowances previously claimed by you decreases because: you divorce or legally separate; you stop supporting a dependent; or a dependent for whom you claimed a withholding allowance will receive more than the exemption amount for the year ($2,650 in 1997), but this income restriction does not apply to your child who is under 19 years of age or a student under age 24 as of the end of the year.

The death of a spouse or a dependent in a current year does not affect your withholding until the next year but requires the filing of a new certificate, if possible, by the first business day in December, or within 10 days if the death is in December. However, a widow or widower entitled to joint return rates in the next two years as a qualifying widow or widower with a dependent child (1.6) need not file a new withholding certificate.

When you file on or before December 1, your employer must reduce your withholding as of January 1 of the next year.

26.8 When Tips Are Subject to Withholding

Tips are subject to income tax and FICA (Social Security and Medicare) withholdings. If you receive cash tips amounting to $20 or more in a month, you must report the total amount of tips received during the month to your employer on Form 4070 (or a similar written report). You make the report on or before the 10th day after the end of the month in which the tips are received. (If the 10th day is a Saturday, Sunday, or legal holiday, you must submit the report by the next business day.) For example, tips amounting to $20 or more that are received during January 1998 are reported by February 10, 1998. Your employer may require more frequent reporting.

You include cash tips paid to you in your own behalf. If you "split" or share tips with others, you include in your report only your share. You do not include tips received in the form of merchandise or your share of service charges turned over to you by your employer.

You are considered to have income from tips when you make your report to your employer. However, if you do not report your tips to your employer, you are considered to have tip income when you receive the tips. For example, if you received tips of $200 during December 1997 and reported the tips to your employer on January 8, 1998, the tips are considered paid to you in January 1998, and the $200 is included on your 1998 income tax return. On the other hand, if your tips during December 1997 totaled only $18, you are not required to report the amount to your employer. The tips are considered paid to you in 1997 and must be included in your 1997 income tax return.

Your employer withholds the Social Security, Medicare, and income tax due on the tips from your wages or from funds you give him or her for withholding purposes. If the taxes due cannot be collected on the tips, either from your wages or from voluntary contributions, by the 10th day after the end of the month in which tips are reported, you have to pay the tax when you file your income tax return.

Where wages are insufficient to meet all of the withholding liability, the wages are applied first to Social Security and Medicare tax.

If you have not reported tips of $20 or more in any month, or tips are allocated to you under the special tip allocation rules discussed below, you must compute Social Security and Medicare tax on that amount on Form 4137 and enter it as a tax due on Line 49 of Form 1040; attach Form 4137 to Form 1040. The unreported tips must be included as wages on Line 7 of Form 1040.

 Filing Instruction

Uncollected Social Security and Medicare Taxes

If your employer is unable to collect enough money from your wages during the year to cover the Social Security or Medicare tax on the tips you reported, the uncollected amount is shown on your Form W-2 in Box 13 with Code A next to it for Social Security or Code B for Medicare. You must report the uncollected amount on Line 53 of Form 1040 (Total Tax) as an additional tax due; write "Uncollected Tax on Tips" and show the amount next to Line 53.

Penalty for failure to report tips. Failure to report tip income of $20 or more received during the month to your employer may subject you to a penalty of 50% of the Social Security and Medicare tax due on the unreported tips, unless your failure was due to reasonable cause rather than to willful neglect.

Tips of less than $20 per month are taxable but not subject to withholding.

Tip allocation reporting by large restaurants. To help the IRS audit the reporting of tip income, restaurants employing at least 10 people must make a special report of income and allocate tips based on gross receipts. For purposes of the allocation, the law assumes tip income of at least 8%. If you voluntarily report tips equal to your allocable share of 8% of the restaurant's gross receipts, no allocation will be made to you. However, if the total tips reported by all employees is less than 8% of gross receipts and you do not report your share of the 8%, your employer must make an allocation based on the difference between the amount you reported and your share of the 8% amount. The allocated amount is shown on Form W-2. However, taxes are not withheld on the allocated amount. Taxes are withheld only on amounts actually reported by employees. An employer or majority of employees may ask the IRS to apply a tip percentage of less than 8%, but no lower than 2%.

Reporting allocated tips. Your employer will show allocated tips in Box 8 of your Form W-2. However, this amount will not be included in Box 1 wages and you must add it to income yourself by reporting it on Line 7 of Form 1040. You also must compute Social Security and Medicare tax on the allocated tips on Form 4137 and enter the tax from Form 4137 on Line 49 of Form 1040. You may not use Form 1040A or Form 1040EZ.

26.9 Withholding on Gambling Winnings

Gambling winnings are generally reported on Form W-2G if the amount paid is $600 or more and at least 300 times the amount of the wager; the payer has the option of taking into account the wager in applying the $600 test. Different reporting rules apply to winnings from keno, bingo, and slot machines. Keno winnings are reported on Form W-2G if they are $1,500 or more, *reduced* by the wager. Winnings from bingo or slot machines of $1,200 or more, *not* reduced by the wager, are reported on Form W-2G.

Your winnings from gambling may be subject to 28% withholding. Withholding applies if your winnings exceed:

1. $5,000 from lotteries, sweepstakes, and wagering pools (whether or not state-conducted) including church raffles, *pari-mutuel* betting pools and on- and off-track racing pools; or
2. $5,000 from other wagering transactions, if the proceeds are at least 300 times as large as the amount wagered, such as from wagers on horse races, dog races, or jai alai.

If your winnings exceed the $5,000 threshold the withholding rate applies to your gross winnings less your wagers, and not just the amounts over $5,000. Any withholdings will be shown on Form W-2G.

The IRS requires you to tell the payers of gambling winnings if you are also receiving winnings from identical wagers; winnings from identical wagers must be added together to determine if withholding is required.

If you have agreed to share your winnings with another person, give the payer a Form 5754. The payer will then prepare separate Forms W-2G for each of you.

26.10 FICA Withholdings

FICA withholdings are employee contributions for Social Security and Medicare coverage. Your employer is liable for the tax if he or she fails to make proper withholdings. The amount withheld is figured on your wages and is not affected by your marital status, number of exemptions, or the fact that you may be over age 65 and are collecting Social Security. On Form W-2, Social Security withholdings are shown in Box 4 and Medicare withholdings in Box 6.

Subject to FICA tax are your regular salary, commissions, bonuses, vacation pay, cash tips, group-term insurance coverage over $50,000, the first six months of sick pay, and contributions to cash or deferred (401(k)) pay plans or salary-reduction contributions to a simplified employee pension (SEP) or tax-sheltered annuity. Not subject to tax are the value of tax-free meals and lodgings under *3.11* and reimbursements for substantiated travel or entertainment expenses or for moving expenses.

Excess Social Security and Railroad Retirement withholding. If you have worked for more than one employer during 1997, attach all Copies B of Form W-2 to your return. Check to see that the total withheld in 1997 by your employers does not exceed your liability for Social

Caution

Backup Withholding
Winnings from bingo, keno, and slot machines are not subject to 28% income tax withholding. However, if you do not provide a taxpayer identification number, the payer will withhold tax at the 31% backup withholding rate *(26.12)*.

Security taxes. The maximum 1997 liability for Social Security is $4,054.80, 6.2% on the first $65,400 of salary income. If too much was withheld, claim the excess as a payment on Line 58 of your 1997 Form 1040. On Form 1040A, the excess is added to your total tax payments; you cannot claim the excess on Form 1040-EZ.

Medicare tax is withheld at a rate of 1.45% on *all* salary and wage income.

Employees covered by the Railroad Retirement Tax Act (RRTA) receive Form W-2, which lists total wages paid and withholdings of income and Railroad Retirement taxes. Follow tax form instructions for claiming a credit for excess Railroad Retirement withholding.

If any one employer withheld too much Social Security or Railroad Retirement tax, you cannot claim the excess on your income tax return. You must ask that employer for a refund of the excess.

Wages you pay to your spouse or child.   Wages you pay to your spouse for working in your business are subject to FICA tax and income tax withholding. Wages you pay to your child for working in your business are subject to income tax withholding but exempt from FICA if the child is under age 18. Wages you pay to your child under age 21 or to your spouse for domestic work or child care in your own home are exempt from FICA.

Wages paid to household employees.   *See 25.8* for FICA withholding on wages paid to household employees.

26.11 Withholding on Retirement Distributions

Retirement distributions are subject to withholding taxes, but you may avoid withholdings. The method of avoiding withholding varies with the type of payment.

Periodic payments.   If you receive periodic payments, such as an annuity, withholding is required unless you elect to avoid withholding on Form W-4P, or on a substitute form furnished by the payer. If you are a U.S. citizen or resident alien, withholding may not be avoided on pensions or other distributions paid outside the U.S. or U.S. possessions. Payment must be to your home address within the U.S. (or in a U.S. possession) to avoid withholding.

Unless you tell the payer otherwise, wage withholding tables are used to figure withholdings on periodic payments as if you were married and claiming three withholding exemptions. Withholding allowances may be claimed on Form W-4P for estimated itemized deductions, alimony payments, and deductible IRA contributions.

You may also request that the payer withhold a specific amount of additional tax for each payment.

Nonperiodic payments from IRAs and commercial annuities.   Nonperiodic payments are subject to withholding at a flat 10% rate unless you elect to avoid withholding on Form W-4P (or substitute form). IRA distributions that are payable upon demand are considered nonperiodic and, thus, subject to the 10% withholding rule.

Nonperiodic payments from qualified employer plans.   Employers must withhold 20% from nonperiodic payments, such as lump-sum distributions that are eligible for tax-free rollover but which are paid directly to you. To avoid withholding you must tell your employer to make a direct rollover *(7.8)* of the funds to an IRA or to a defined contribution plan *(8.4)* of your new employer. If you do not instruct your employer to make the direct transfer and elect to personally receive the distribution, 20% will be withheld before payment is made to you.

See 7.8 for a further explanation and an Example showing the effects of the withholding rule where you receive the distribution and then decide to make a rollover yourself.

26.12 Backup Withholding

Backup withholding is designed to pressure taxpayers to report interest and dividend income. You may be subject to backup withholding if you do not give your taxpayer identification number to parties paying you interest or dividend income, you give an incorrect number, or you ignore IRS notices stating that you have underreported interest or dividends. Your taxpayer identification number is your Social Security number or your employer identification number. The backup withholding rate is 31%.

Similarly, backup withholding of 31% can apply to fees of $600 or more (Form 1099-MISC) for work you do as an independent contractor, payments from brokers (Form 1099-B), royalty payments (Form 1099-MISC) and certain gambling winnings *(see 26.9)* if you do not give the payer your taxpayer identification number.

Civil and criminal penalties can be imposed if you provide false information to avoid backup withholding.

 Caution

Employer Plan Distributions
Your employer must withhold 20% from a distribution paid to you if it could have been rolled over tax-free; *see 7.8.*

Chapter 27

Estimated Tax Payments

Income taxes are collected on a pay-as-you-go basis through withholding on wages and pensions, as well as quarterly estimated tax payments on other income. Where all or most of your income is from wages, pensions, and annuities, you will generally not have to pay estimated tax, because your estimated tax liability has been satisfied by withholding. But do not assume you are not required to pay simply because taxes have been withheld from your wages. Always check your estimated tax liability. Withholding may not cover your tax; the withholding tax rate may be below your actual tax rate when considering other income such as interest, dividends, business income, and capital gains.

Your estimated tax must also include liability for self-employment tax and alternative minimum tax (AMT).

You have to make quarterly estimated tax payments during 1998 if your estimated tax liability, after accounting for withholding taxes, is $1,000 or more and the withholding taxes will not be at least 90% of your 1998 tax liability, or 100% of your 1997 tax liability.

Failure to pay a required estimated tax installment is subject to a penalty based on the prevailing IRS interest rate applied to tax deficiences.

Estimated tax payments are made with vouchers included with Form 1040-ES. Residents of Puerto Rico during the entire taxable year also use Form 1040-ES. Nonresident aliens should use Form 1040-ES (NR).

27.1 Estimating Your Tax

There are three stages of reviewing your estimated tax liability:

1. **When you have computed the exact amount of your 1997 tax liability on your 1997 return.** If you owe less than $500 on your 1997 return after taking into account withheld taxes, you are not subject to a penalty. If the tax owed after withholdings is $500 or more, you can now determine whether your 1997 withholdings plus estimated tax installments were at least 90% of your final 1997 tax, shown on Line 53 of Form 1040 or Line 28 of Form 1040A. If they were, you are not subject to a 1997 penalty. If they were not, you are subject to a penalty unless your estimated tax payments were at least 100% or 110% of the final 1996 tax on a return covering a full 12 months. The 100% test applies if your 1996 adjusted gross income was $150,000 or less ($75,000 or less if married filing separately for 1997). If your 1996 adjusted gross income was more than $150,000 (or more than $75,000 if married filing separately for 1997), the 110% test applies.

   If you underestimated your 1997 liability because of an unexpected increase in income during 1997, or if you did not earn income evenly throughout 1997, such as where you operated a seasonal business, you may be able to lower or eliminate the penalty by using the *annualized income installment method.* Under this exception, you may avoid a penalty for an estimated tax installment by figuring the installment that would be due if the income (and deductions) earned before the date for the installment were *annualized.* Form 2210 and IRS Publication 505 have worksheets for applying the annualized income exception. The computation is complicated and its use may be discouraged by the complexity, despite the potential benefits.

2. **When you make an estimate for 1998.** You will generally do this after completing your 1997 return. In planning your 1998 payments, you do not want to pay more than necessary to avoid a penalty. If you expect your 1998 income and deductions to be about the same as in 1997, apply 1998 tax rates (which will be in the Supplement) to your 1997 taxable income, and base your 1998 withholdings and quarterly estimated tax installments on 90% of that tax. If you were subject to self-employment tax or alternative minimum tax in 1997, add 90% of such taxes to your 1998 estimate.

   Safe harbor based on prior year's tax. If you are uncertain of the amount of your 1998 income and deductions, you can play it safe and avoid a possible penalty in 1998 by having withholdings and quarterly estimated tax installments equal 100% of your 1997 tax liability, provided you filed a 1997 return covering a full 12 months.

   If an accurate estimate for 1998 is possible, it is generally advantageous to base your estimated payments on the 90% test rather than the 100% prior year test, as the 100% test will probably result in an overestimation of your liability unless the 1998 liability turns out to be substantially larger than the 1997 liability.

   You may use the worksheet and the tax rate schedule included in the 1998 Form 1040-ES to figure your estimated tax liability and the required annual payment to avoid a penalty under either the 90% current year or 100% prior year liability tests just discussed.

   Reduce your 1998 estimated tax liability by projected 1998 withholdings from wages, pensions, and annuities. If after withholdings your estimated tax is $1,000 or more, you must make estimated tax payments using Form 1040-ES vouchers unless the withholdings will cover at least 90% of your estimated 1998 liability or 100% of your 1997 liability. If withholdings will not cover the amount required under the 90% or 100% tests, you may pay the balance of the estimated tax with the first Form 1040-ES voucher or in four equal installments. The first installment is due April 15, 1998.

   If you are due a refund when you file your 1997 return, it may be credited to your 1998 estimated tax by making an election on your 1997 return. The IRS will credit the refund to the April installment of 1998 estimated tax unless you attach a statement to your return instructing the IRS to apply the refund to later installments.

   Members of a partnership declare their estimated taxes in their individual capacities. Each partner's estimate must include his or her share of the partnership income, whether actually paid or not.

   Farmers or fishermen. In figuring the required annual payment to avoid a penalty for 1998, a farmer or fisherman has to pay only 66 $\frac{2}{3}$ % of the 1998 estimated liability, rather than 90%. A penalty may also be avoided by paying 100% of the 1997 tax, provided a tax return covering a 12-month period was filed for 1997; the 110% test does not apply to a farmer or fisherman. To qualify as a farmer or fisherman under these rules, at least two-thirds of gross income must be from farming or fishing.

3. **When preparing your second, third, or fourth estimated tax installment.** If, during the year, your income, expenses, or exemptions change, refigure your estimated tax liability and adjust your payment schedule as shown in the Examples starting below. Increasing an install-

Law Alert

Estimated Tax Safe Harbor Modified

In planning withholdings and estimated tax installments for 1998, you can avoid a 1998 estimated tax penalty if your payments are at least the lesser of 90% of your 1998 tax liability or 100% of your total 1997 tax liability. The 100% of 1997 liability safe harbor applies regardless of your 1997 income.

If 1998 adjusted gross income exceeds $150,000, 1999 estimated tax payments may be based on 105% of the 1998 tax. For a married person filing separately in 1999, the 105% of 1998 liability rule applies if 1998 adjusted gross income exceeds $75,000 (rather than $150,000). If the $150,000 or $75,000 income threshold for 1998 is not exceeded, the 100% safe harbor rule applies when making your estimate for 1999.

ment payment cannot make up for an underpayment in a prior quarter; *see* Example 2. However, withholding from pay can be allocated equally over all four quarters and, thus, increased withholding may be applied to earlier quarters.

If taxes paid in the previous installments total more than your revised estimate, you cannot obtain a refund at that time. You must wait until you file your final return showing that a refund is due.

EXAMPLES

1. Smith estimates a 1998 tax of $6,000. In April 1998, he pays an installment of $1,500. In June, he amends his estimate, showing a tax of $3,000 instead of $6,000. He refigures the installment schedule by dividing $3,000 by 4, which gives a quarterly payment rate of $750. As he paid $1,500 in April, the $750 overpayment covers his June obligation. By September 15, he pays $750; by January 15, 1999, he pays $750.

2. In September 1998, Jones finds that his estimated 1998 tax liability should be $25,000 rather than his original estimate of $20,000. He paid $5,000 as his April and June installments ($10,000 total). Under the amended schedule, he should have paid $6,250 per quarter ($25,000 ÷ 4), or $12,500 by June 16. Thus, there is a $2,500 underpayment ($12,500 – 10,000).

    To cover the underpayment of $2,500, which carries over to the third quarter, Jones's September installment must be at least $8,750 ($6,250 + $2,500). If less than $8,750 is paid, there will be an underpayment for the third quarter, as third-quarter payments are applied first to the carried-over underpayment of $2,500. The fourth-quarter installment, due by January 15, 1999, will be $6,250. The underpayments for the first two quarters may be subject to a penalty unless covered by one of the exceptions previously discussed.

27.2 Dates for Paying Estimated Taxes

The four installment dates for 1998 estimated tax are: April 15, 1998; June 15, 1998; September 15, 1998; and January 15, 1999. Later installments may be used to amend earlier ones; *see* the Examples at the end of *27.1*. You do not have to file the January 15, 1999, voucher if you file your 1998 tax return and pay the balance of tax due by February 1, 1999.

If you use a fiscal year. A fiscal year is any year other than the calendar year. If you file using a fiscal year, your first estimated installment is due on or before the 15th day of the fourth month of your fiscal year. Amendments may be made on the 15th day of the sixth and ninth months of your fiscal year with the final amendment on the 15th day of the first month of your next fiscal year. Your installments are also due then.

27.3 Estimates by Husband and Wife

A married couple may pay joint or separate estimated taxes. The nature of the estimated tax does not control the kind of final return you file.

Where a joint estimated tax is paid but separate tax returns are filed, you and your spouse can decide on how to divide the estimated payments between you. Either one of you can claim the whole amount, or you can agree to divide it in any proportion. If you cannot agree, the IRS will allocate the estimated taxes proportionally according to the percentage of total tax each spouse owes.

If separate estimated taxes are paid, overpayment by one spouse is not applied against an underpayment by the other when separate final returns are filed.

A joint estimated tax may be made by a husband and wife only if they are both citizens or residents of the United States. Both must have the same taxable year. A joint estimate may not be made by a couple who are divorced or legally separated under a decree. If a joint estimate is made and the spouses are divorced or legally separated later in that year, they may divide the joint payments between them under the above rule for spouses who file separately.

Responsibility for paying estimated tax rests upon each spouse individually. Each must pay if individually required by the rules.

If a joint estimated tax is made and one spouse dies, the estate does not continue to make installment payments. The surviving spouse is required to pay the remaining installments unless he or she amends. Amounts paid on the joint estimate may be divided as agreed upon by the spouse and the estate of the deceased. If they do not agree, the IRS will apportion the payments according to the percentage of the total tax owed by each spouse.

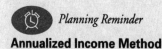

Planning Reminder

Annualized Income Method

If your income typically fluctuates throughout the year, or if your income unexpectedly changes during the year, you may base installment payments on the annualized income method. This method allows you to avoid a penalty for installment periods during which less income is earned by reducing the required estimated tax payment for such periods. To figure your installment payments, use the Annualized Estimated Tax Worksheet in IRS Publication 505. If you base installment payments on the annualized method, you must file Form 2210 with your return to determine if you are subject to an estimated tax penalty.

Planning Reminder

Farmers and Fishermen

Farmers only have to make one installment payment, generally by January 15 of the following year. The payment for 1997 must be made by January 15, 1998, or farmers may file their 1997 returns by March 2, 1998, instead of making an estimated tax payment. To qualify under these rules, a farmer must receive two-thirds of his or her 1996 or 1997 gross income from farming.

Fishermen who expect to receive at least two-thirds of their gross income from fishing pay estimated taxes as farmers do.

27.4 Final Payment for 1997

That you paid an estimated tax for 1997 does not excuse you from filing a tax return on or before April 15, 1998. You must file a final return and pay the difference between the total of your withholding plus your estimated tax payments and your final tax. If your 1997 tax is less than your withholdings and payments, you get a refund from the IRS *or* you can apply the overpayment towards your 1998 estimated tax. You may also split up the amount due you. You may take part of the overpayment as a refund. The other part may be credited to your estimate of 1998 taxes.

Check your mathematics before you apply an overpayment as a credit on your next year's estimate. If you apply too much, the amount credited may not be used to offset any additional tax due that the IRS determines you owe. For example, your 1997 return shows a $500 refund due, and you apply it towards your 1998 estimated tax. However, the IRS determines that you overpaid $200, not $500. You will be billed for the additional $300 tax, plus interest due; you may not offset the extra tax with the credited amount.

27.5 Penalty for Underestimating Your 1997 Tax

Penalties are figured separately for each installment date *(27.2)*. This means that if, after taking into account withholdings from your pay, you underpay an installment, you may owe a penalty for that period even though you overpay later installments to make up the difference. The penalty for each period runs from the installment due date until the amount is paid or until the regular filing date for the final tax return, whichever is earlier.

Withholding payments are treated as if they were payments of estimated tax. In applying them, the total withholdings of the year are divided equally between each installment period unless you want to show the actual payment dates; then they are applied in the period they are actually withheld.

Figure the 1997 penalty for yourself on Form 2210 or let the IRS do it.   You can use Form 2210 to determine any 1997 penalty, but the IRS encourages taxpayers to let the IRS compute any penalty. The IRS will figure the amount of any penalty and bill you for the amount if you do not complete Form 2210.

There is no penalty and you do not have to file Form 2210 if the tax liability shown on your 1997 return is less than $500, after taking into account withholdings. There also is no penalty if you had no tax liability for 1996, you were a U.S. citizen or resident for all of 1996, and your 1996 taxable year included 12 full months.

You *must* attach Form 2210 to your return if: (1) you use the annualized income exception; (2) you do not allocate wage withholdings in four equal amounts; (3) your required estimated tax payment for 1997 is based on 100% or 110% of the prior year's tax and a joint return is filed for either the prior year or the current year but not both, or (4) you claim a penalty waiver; *see* below for waiver rules.

If you *underpaid* for any quarter, the amount of the underpayment reduces the payment made in the following quarter. That is, an underpayment of one quarter is carried over to succeeding quarters on Form 2210. If you underpay for a quarter, any payment you make after that installment date will be applied first to the earlier underpayment. Thus, even if you make the required payment for a quarter, you could still be subject to a penalty for that quarter because your payment is applied to a prior underpayment.

If you *overpaid* in any quarter, the excess carries over to the next quarter. The excess cannot be used to make up an underpayment of the prior quarter. However, these rules apply only to installment payments made with Form 1040-ES vouchers. They do not apply to withholdings, which are allocated equally over the year so that withholdings late in the year can reduce an underpayment for an earlier calendar quarter.

Waiver of penalty for hardship, retirement, or disability.   The IRS may waive the penalty if you can show you failed to pay the estimated tax because of casualty, disaster, or other unusual circumstances.

The IRS may also waive a penalty for a 1997 underpayment if in 1997 or 1996 you retired after reaching age 62 or became disabled, and you failed to make a payment due to reasonable cause and not due to willful neglect. This rule would apply to a 1998 underpayment if you became disabled or retired (after age 62) in 1997 or 1998. To apply for the waiver, attach an explanation on Form 2210 with applicable documentation.

Law Alert

Penalty Threshold Increases for 1998

If your total tax liability for 1997 after withholdings is less than $500, you are not subject to an estimated tax penalty for 1997. For 1998, no estimated tax penalty will apply if the total tax shown on your 1998 return, after withholdings, is less than $1,000.

Planning Reminder

Withholdings Cover Prior Underpayment

You have a choice in allocating withholdings from pay or other income that is subject to withholding: (1) You may treat your entire year's withholdings as having been withheld in equal amounts for each quarter; or (2) you may allocate to each quarter the actual withholdings paid for that quarter. Also, if toward the end of the year, you find that you have underestimated for an earlier quarter, ask your employer to withhold an extra amount which may be allocated equally over the four quarters. This way, you may eliminate the underestimate for the earlier quarters.

Part 5

Personal Tax Savings Plans

The chapters in this part will alert you to special tax saving opportunities and tell you how to take advantage of tax-saving ideas and planning strategies.

Chapter 28

Tax-Saving Ideas and Planning

Tax planning is a year-round activity. By planning income and deduction strategies, you may be able to reduce your tax. You may realize capital gain income subject to lower capital gain rates, defer certain income to a later year in which you expect to pay a lower tax, and accelerate deductions to a higher tax year. Tax-free investments are available and, within limits, income splitting with family members may be possible.

This chapter illustrates basic tax-planning strategies. In subsequent chapters, tax-savings plans for homeowners, families, investors, and executives are discussed.

28.1 When To Defer Income and Accelerate Deductions

When you expect to pay less tax in a future year than in a current year, consider deferring income and accelerating deductions. There are two strategies: (1) to postpone receipt of income to a year of lower tax rates, and/or (2) to claim deductions for losses and expenses in the year you are subject to the higher tax rates. In planning to defer income and accelerate deductions, however, watch these tax-rule limitations.

Postponing income.   You may not defer salary income by not cashing a paycheck or not taking salary that you have earned and that you can receive without restrictions. Under certain conditions, you may contract with your employer to defer the taxable receipt of current compensation to future years. To defer pay to a future period you must take some risk. You cannot have any control over your deferred pay account. If you are not confident of your employer's ability to pay in the future, you should not defer pay.

If you are self-employed and are on the cash basis, you can defer income by delaying your billing at the end of the year or extending the time of collection. If you own a closely held corporation, you can time the payment of dividends and bonuses.

Accelerating deductions.   In accelerating deductions, there are these limitations: You may not deduct prepaid interest and rent. Prepaid interest must be deducted over the period of the loan. Rentals must also be deducted over the rental period. However, you can generally deduct prepayments of state income tax and accelerate your payments of charitable contributions. Annual subscriptions to professional journals and business magazines can be renewed before the end of the year. If the subscription is for more than a year, you may deduct only the first-year prepayment. The cost of the later subscription must be deducted in the later year. Contributions, purchases, and business expenses charged to credit card accounts are deductible in the year of charge, even though you do not pay your charge account bill until the next year. You can also realize losses by selling business or investment property which has lost value in the year you want to incur the loss.

Making an extra donation at the end of the year also may provide an added deduction which may lower your tax. You may deduct a charitable gift made by check on the last day of the year, even if the check is not cashed until the new year begins. Charitable donations may be timed to give you the largest possible tax savings. If, toward the end of the year, you find that you need an extra deduction, you may make a deductible donation in late December. Doing so would be especially beneficial if you know that your tax bracket will be lower the following year; *see* Chapter 14 for further planning details.

Also *see* Chapter 13 for claiming the standard deduction and itemizing deductions in alternate years, and Chapter 23 for planning steps when you may be subject to alternative minimum tax.

Deferring interest income to next year.   Buying six-month certificates after June 30 can defer interest reporting to the next year. As a general rule, you have to report interest credited to your savings account for 1997, even if the account is a passbook account and you did not present the passbook to have the amount entered. Similarly, interest coupons due and payable in 1997 are taxable on your 1997 return, regardless of when they were presented for collection. For example, a coupon due in December 1997, but presented for payment in 1998, is taxable in 1997. However, there are opportunities to defer interest in the following ways:

1. Buy a savings certificate after June 30 with a maturity of six months or more. Interest is taxable in the next year when the certificate matures, provided that interest is specifically deferred until the following year by the terms of the certificate.
2. Buy Treasury bills which come due next year. Six-month bills bought after June 30 will mature in the next year. You can make these purchases through your bank or broker.
3. Buy Series EE bonds. These bonds may be cashed for their purchase price, plus an increase in their value over stated periods of time. The increase in redemption value is taxed as interest. You may defer the interest income until the year you cash the bond or the year the bond finally matures, whichever is earlier.

Timing sales of property.   A sale is generally taxable in the year title to the property passes to the buyer. Since you can control the year title passes, you can usually defer income realized on the sale to the year in which you will pay less tax. Year-end sales of securities are discussed at *30.1.*

28.2 Tax Cost of Earning Over the Thresholds for the Exemption Phaseout and Itemized Deduction Reduction

In figuring the tax cost of earning additional income, consider the phaseout of personal exemptions *(21.15)* or the 3% reduction to itemized deductions *(13.7)*. When extra income, such as from a bonus, a freelance assignment, or a year-end sale of stock, pushes you over the *threshold* for the exemption phaseout or the 3% reduction, or if you already are over the threshold, the marginal tax rate on the extra income will be higher than the stated maximum rate for ordinary income (31%, 36%, or 39.6%), or the 10%, 20%, or 28% rate applied to capital gains. By earning over a threshold amount, your taxable income is increased not only by the earnings over the threshold but also by the amounts disallowed by the phaseout or the 3% reduction.

For the 3% itemized deduction reduction on 1997 returns, the adjusted gross income (AGI) threshold is $121,200, except for married persons filing separately, who are subject to a $60,600 threshold.

For the exemption phaseout, the AGI threshold is $121,200 for single persons, $151,500 for heads of household, $181,800 for married persons filing jointly and qualifying widow(er)s, and $90,900 for married persons filing separately.

Effective rate increase. The amount of the increase in the effective rate due to the exemption phaseout or 3% itemized deduction reduction can be estimated by this equation:

$$\text{Increase in effective rate} = \frac{\text{Top bracket}^* \times \text{disallowed amount}}{\text{Excess income over threshold}}$$

Your top bracket. For example, if you are in the 36% bracket (see the tax rate schedules in Part 8 of this book), take 36% of the disallowed amount.

Key to Tax Planning

Objective—	Explanation—
Earning tax-free income	You can earn tax-free income by— 1. Investing in tax-exempt securities. However, before you invest, determine whether the tax-free return will exceed the after-tax return of taxed income; *see 30.13*. 2. Taking a position in a company that pays tax-free fringe benefits, such as health and life insurance protection. For a complete discussion of tax-free fringe benefits, *see* Chapter 3. 3. Seeking tax-free benefits with scholarship arrangements and educational IRAs; *see* Chapter 38. 4. Taking a position overseas to earn up to $72,000 tax free in 1998; $74,000 in 1999; 76,000 in 2000; *see* Chapter 36. 5. Investing in Roth IRAs; *see 8.20*.
Deferring income	You can defer income to years when you will pay less tax through— 1. Deferred pay plans, which are discussed in Chapter 32. 2. Qualified retirement plans such as through Keogh plans and regular IRA investments; *see* Chapter 41 and Chapter 8. 3. The year-end planning techniques explained in *28.1*. 4. Transacting installment sales when you sell property; *see 5.25*. 5. Investing in U.S. Savings EE bonds; *see 4.28* and *30.21*.
Income splitting	Through income splitting you divide your income among several persons or taxpaying entities that will pay an aggregate tax lower than the tax that you would pay if you reported all of the income. Although the tax law limits income-splitting opportunities, certain business and family income planning can provide tax savings. Family income planning is discussed in Chapter 33.
Tax-free exchanges	You can defer tax on appreciated property by transacting tax-free exchanges as discussed at *6.1* and *31.4*.
Buying a personal residence rather than renting	Homeowners are favored by the tax law. 1. Rather than paying rent, buy a home, condominium, or cooperative apartment. You may deduct interest and taxes. When you sell your house, you may avoid tax on gains of up to $250,000 if single and up to $500,000 if married; *see* Chapter 29. 2. Homeowners can borrow on their home equity and deduct interest expenses; *see 15.3*.

Tax Savings for Residence Sales

A new law may allow you to avoid tax on gain on the sale of a principal residence. If you are single, you may be able to avoid tax on up to $250,000 of gain, $500,000 if you are married and file jointly. This exclusion applies to sales after May 6, 1997, and is explained in *29.1–29.4*.

If you sold your principal residence before May 7, 1997, and you were age 55 or over at the date of sale, you may elect to avoid tax on gain of up to $125,000; *see 29.15*. If you were under age 55 or age 55 or over and do not want to elect to avoid tax, you may defer tax by buying or building another residence; *see 29.5*.

You may not deduct the loss on the sale of a personal residence. Losses on the sale of property devoted to personal use are nondeductible. However, *see 29.13 and 29.14*, which explain under what conditions you may claim a loss deduction on the sale of a residence which you rent out or inherit.

If you rent out a residential property and you or family members also use the residence during the year, rental expenses are subject to the special restrictions discussed at *9.7*.

Form 1099-S. Sales and exchanges of residences before May 7, 1997, are reported to the IRS on Form 1099-S by the attorney or other party responsible for closing the transaction. The IRS may check your return to verify that you have reported proceeds shown on Form 1099-S. A sale or exchange after May 6, 1997, of a principal residence is not reported on Form 1099-S if the seller gives a written assurance that the full amount of the gain is tax free and there is no taxable income because of mortgage subject to subsidized financing assistance; *see 29.10*.

29.1 Sales Date Determines Home Sale Benefits in 1997

The date that you sold your principal residence determines whether you may avoid tax under the new tax law or defer tax or avoid tax if you are 55 or over under the prior tax rules. The date of sale is the date you passed title to the buyer. If the date of sale is:

Before May 7, 1997, you may defer tax on the gain if you buy a new principal residence under the prior law rules explained in *29.5*. If you are 55 or over, you may avoid tax on up to $125,000 of gain under the prior law explained in *29.15*.

After May 6, 1997, you may avoid tax on gain of up to $250,000 if single and 500,000 if married and filing jointly; *see 29.3*. You do not have to buy a replacement residence to get this break. You can take advantage of the tax exclusion every two years; *see 29.2*. If your gain exceeds the exclusion, the excess gain is subject to tax.

EXAMPLE

In October 1997, you sell a principal residence in which you and your wife lived for over 20 years. You realize a gain of $600,000. The excess gain of $100,000 over the $500,000 exclusion is taxed as a long-term capital gain. The gain of $100,000 is taxable, even though you intend to buy a new residence at a price exceeding the sale proceeds of the old residence.

For electing the prior rollover rules for sales occurring before August 6, 1997, and for certain sales occurring after August 5, 1997, *see 29.4*.

Multiple use of a residence.   If you used part of a sold residence for business or rental to tenants, you may have to apportion the sales price and basis of the house between the rental portion and the residential portion. Follow the IRS instructions to Form 2119.

$250,000 or $500,000 Exclusion on Sales After May 6, 1997

29.2 Ownership and Use Tests

You may exclude from income up to $250,000 of gain, $500,000 if married filing jointly, realized on a sale or exchange of a residence after May 6, 1997, if you owned and occupied it as a principal residence for an aggregate of at least two years out of five years before the sale or exchange. Periods of use do not have to be consecutive as long as the periods of use during the five-year period total two years. In counting the period of ownership and use, you may include periods for all residences bought under the prior law rollover rules.

Note: The exclusion is not a one-time benefit. As often as you meet the applicable ownership and use tests, you may claim the exclusion on sales of principal residences.

Less-than-two-year exceptions.   If you are forced to sell before two years of ownership and use because of a change in a place of employment or health or unforeseen circumstances, the gain is prorated. The IRS will define *unforeseen circumstances* in regulations. The excludable gain is generally prorated for the time spent in the residence over the two-year period. For example, you move to a new job location after owning and occupying your house for one year. You are entitled to exclude 50% of the gain.

Sales within two years of August 5, 1997.   Even though you do not satisfy the two-year ownership and use tests and the sale was not due to a change in employment or unforeseen circumstances, you may claim a prorated gain if the following two tests are met:

1. You owned the residence on August 5, 1997, and
2. The sale or exchange occurred during the two-year period beginning August 5, 1997.

Incapacitated homeowner.   A homeowner who becomes physically or mentally incapable of self-care is deemed to use a residence as a principal residence during the time in which the individual owns the residence and resides in a licensed care facility. For this rule to apply, the homeowner must have owned and used the residence as a principal residence for an aggregate period of at least one year during the five years preceding the sale.

Principal residence.   A principal residence is not restricted to one-family houses but includes a mobile home, trailer, houseboat, and condominium apartment used as a principal residence. An investment in a retirement community does not qualify as a principal residence unless you receive equity in the property. In case of a tenant-stockholder of a cooperative housing corporation, the residence ownership requirement applies to the ownership of the stock and the use requirement applies to the house or apartment which the stockholder occupies.

The exclusion may not be claimed by a nonresident alien subject to Code Sec. 877(a)(1) because of giving up U.S. citizenship for tax avoidance purposes.

The exclusion may be claimed by an unrelated person holding a remainder interest.

The exclusion does not apply to the extent of depreciation with respect to business or rental use of the home after May 6, 1997. That portion of the gain is taxable.

29.3 $500,000 Exclusion for Married Couples Filing Jointly

On a 1997 joint return, a married couple may claim a $500,000 exclusion for a sale after May 6, 1997, provided: (1) either spouse owned the residence for at least two years, and (2) both used the residence for at least two years. If only one spouse meets the two-year use and ownership test, the exclusion is limited to $250,000.

> **EXAMPLE**
> 1. You and your wife owned and occupied your principal residence for 10 years. In December 1997, you sell the house for a gain of $450,000. The gain is not taxable if you file jointly.
> 2. As a widower, you used and owned your principal residence for three years. In January 1997, you remarried and you and your wife lived in the house for nine months. In October 1997, you sold the house and realized a gain of $350,000. You may claim an exclusion of $250,000 on your joint return; the balance of $100,000 is taxable. You meet the exclusion tests, not your wife. Thus, the exclusion is limited to $250,000.

A widow or widower may count the period during which a deceased spouse owned the residence.

If a residence is transferred to a taxpayer incident to divorce, the time during which the taxpayer's spouse or former spouse owned the residence is added to the taxpayer's period of ownership. A taxpayer who owns a residence is deemed to use the residence while the taxpayer's spouse or former spouse uses the residence under the terms of a divorce or separation.

29.4 Electing Not To Claim the Exclusion

You may elect not to claim the $250,000/$500,000 exclusion on a particular sale. This election may be helpful where you use two principal residences during a five-year period and plan to sell both within two years of each other. If the first sale will give a lower gain and the second a larger gain, you may elect not to apply the exclusion to the first sale and take advantage of the exclusion for the second sale.

Prior law rollover election for sales after May 6, 1997, and before August 6, 1997. If you do not want not claim the new exclusion or you cannot claim the exclusion because you do not meet the use and ownership tests of *29.2*, you may claim the tax deferment rules of the prior law starting at *29.5* on a sale of a principal residence before August 6, 1997.

Prior law rollover election for certain sales after August 5, 1997. You may take advantage of the prior rollover rules at *29.5* for sale of a principal residence made after August 5, 1997, under a contract binding on August 5, 1997. A similar rule applies to a sale transacted under binding contract as of August 5, 1997, where a replacement residence was acquired before August 6, 1997.

Deferring Tax on Gain on Sales Before May 7, 1997

29.5 Three Tests for Deferring Tax on a Profitable Sale

If you meet the following three tests, you must defer tax (deferral is mandatory) on gain from the sale of your principal residence before May 7, 1997:

Principal residence test (29.6)—requires that you have used your old residence as your principal residence and now use or intend to use your new residence as a principal residence.

Time test (29.7)—requires you to buy or build a new residence and use it within two years before or after you sell your old one.

Investment test (29.8)—requires you to buy or build a residence at a cost at least equal to the amount you received from the sale of the old residence. If the replacement property costs less, part or all of the gain is taxed.

You may not defer tax if, within two years before the sale, you previously deferred tax on a profitable sale of another principal residence. This rule does not apply to a move to a new job location.

If you later sell the new residence after May 6, 1997, you may avoid tax on the gain under the rules of *29.2*.

29.6 Principal Residence Test for Deferring Tax

Deferring tax is allowed only on a sale of your principal residence before May 7, 1997, that meets the time test of *29.7* and the investment test of *29.8*. You may not defer tax on the profitable sale of a second house such as a summer cottage. Nor may you defer tax on the sale of a principal residence by buying a summer home; the new home must also be a principal residence.

An apartment in a multifamily building may be a principal residence. Similarly, where you actively use part of your house for business purposes, such as in operating a farm or a store while living in an apartment in the same building, an allocation is required.

The location of the old and new residences is not relevant. If you buy or build a new home outside the U.S. and begin to use it within the two-year replacement period *(29.7)*, the tax deferral rules apply to the gain realized on a sale of a U.S. residence.

Title to both the old and new home must be in your name. If you place title to the new home in someone else's name, the new home does not qualify. An exception exists for a married couple who file a consent form; *see 29.11*.

29.7 Time Test for Deferring Tax

If you buy or build a new home, you must do so and *begin to use it* within two years before or after you sold your old one. This time test is strictly applied; failure to comply will not be excused for any reason. However, the two-year period is suspended for workers abroad and members of the armed services, as discussed at the end of this section.

Under the rules for involuntary conversions, a four-year replacement period applies to houses destroyed in federal disaster areas; *see 18.2*.

A contract to purchase a new home is *not* sufficient to satisfy the time test. A sale is considered to occur at the earlier of the passage of title or the assumption of the benefits and burdens of ownership.

When you build, you must complete construction and occupy the house within the two-year period.

 Planning Reminder

Types of Qualifying Homes

A qualified residence is not restricted to one-family houses but includes a mobile home, trailer, houseboat, cooperative apartment (tied to stock ownership), and condominium apartment, which you use as a principal residence. An investment in a retirement home community does not qualify if you do not receive equity in the property.

EXAMPLES

1. Bayley sold his house at a profit, started construction on a new house, and elected to defer tax. The new house was not completed before the end of the required time period. A day before the end of the period, Bayley moved some of his furniture into the house but could not live there. The house had no water or sewage connections. He finally moved in two months later. The IRS taxed the gain because the house had not been timely occupied. The Tax Court agreed. Bayley had made the necessary investment but failed to meet the requirement of occupying the house.

2. The Lokans bought land to farm and build a new home. Several months later, they sold their old house at a profit. During construction, they set up a trailer on the property. When one bedroom and a bath in the new house were completed, three children slept in the house; they, plus one other child, slept in the trailer. The house was not fully completed until three years after the sale. The IRS and the Tax Court held that the Lokans did not reside in the new house; the trailer was their principal residence.

Surviving spouse. If a married couple report a sale on a joint return and one spouse dies before a new residence is purchased during the two-year period, the surviving spouse may defer tax on the original sale by making the purchase within the period.

Deferment on entering the Armed Forces. If you go on active duty for more than 90 days, the two-year replacement period is suspended while you are in the service. The suspension applies only if your service began before the end of the two-year replacement period. The suspension generally lasts until your discharge, when the balance of the two-year replacement period starts to run again. However, regardless of the length of service, the replacement period ends *four years* after the date of sale. Thus, even if you remain in the service, you must buy and live in your new home no more than four years after you sell your old home.

Planning Reminder

Deferment for Workers Abroad

If your tax home *(20.6)* is outside the United States, the replacement period is suspended while you are abroad. The suspension applies only if your stay abroad began before the end of the two-year replacement period and lasts until you return from abroad or until four years after the sale, whichever occurs first. Your spouse is also protected by the suspension provided that you both used the old home and new home as your principal residence.

There is a further extension of the replacement period if you are stationed outside the U.S. on extended duty or have to live in government quarters at a remote site after returning from a tour of duty outside the U.S. The replacement period is suspended while you are at the foreign or remote site plus one year after the last day you were so stationed. However, the replacement period ends on the date which is *eight years* after the sale. If your spouse is in the armed forces and you are not, you are also protected by the suspension if you jointly owned the old home and both you and your spouse used the old home and new home as principal residences. If you divorce or separate during the suspension period, your replacement period starts to run again the day after the divorce or separation is final.

A special rule applies if you served in a combat zone *(35.4)*. The replacement period for members of the Armed Forces or nonmilitary support personnel is suspended while in the combat zone or while hospitalized for combat zone injuries (limited to five years of hospitalization in the U.S.) plus an additional 180 days; *see 35.5.*

29.8 Investment Test for Deferring Tax

To defer tax on the full amount of gain from the sale of your principal residence before May 7, 1997, you must buy another principal residence within the replacement period *(29.7)*, and your investment must equal or exceed the adjusted sales price of your old home.

You first have to figure your *actual gain* on Form 2119 by subtracting *adjusted basis* for the sold house from the *amount realized* on the sale. Then, to determine how much of the actual gain may be deferred, you have to figure the *adjusted sales price* and also the *cost of the new home*. If the cost of the new home equals or exceeds the adjusted sales price, no part of the gain is taxable in the year of sale; that is, 100% of your gain is deferred. If the cost of the new house is less than the adjusted sales price, the difference is generally taxable; *see* the Example on the next page. The key terms *adjusted basis, amount realized, adjusted sales price,* and *cost of the new home* are explained in this section.

Amount realized.   This is the selling price of your old house less selling expenses for commissions, advertising, preparing the deed, and other legal and title services. "Points" paid by you as the seller also reduce the selling price. Transfer taxes, stamp taxes, or similar taxes are selling expenses that reduce the amount realized; do not deduct them as taxes on Schedule A.

The selling price includes the amount of the mortgages on the old house, whether the buyer has assumed or bought the property subject to them. If immediately after the sale you discount notes received on a deferred payment contract, include the discounted value of the notes, not the face amounts.

Do not include amounts received for furnishings, such as rugs and furniture, sold with the house. Profit on a sale of furnishings is reported separately; a loss is not deductible.

Adjusted basis.   The adjusted basis of the old house is the original cost, including legal and recording fees, transfer taxes, and other settlement costs paid when you bought the house, plus the cost of home improvements. You must reduce this amount by any depreciation or casualty loss deductions, or energy credits claimed in prior years, and also by any deferred gains from prior home sales. If, when you bought the house, the seller paid any of the points on your mortgage, the seller-paid points reduce basis.

Adjusted sales price.   This is the amount realized on the sale of the old house *less* fix-up costs spent to make your old house saleable, such as papering, painting, and similar repairs. To qualify as fix-up costs, the work must be done within the 90-day period ending on the day on which the contract to sell is entered into and paid for within 30 days after the sale.

Fix-up costs do not include costs of permanent improvements spent to clinch a sale, such as, for example, installing a new roof or furnace. Such improvements are capital expenditures added to the cost basis of the old house.

Qualifying fix-up costs are taken into account only for purposes of figuring the adjusted sales price. They are not deductible in figuring your actual gain and are not separately deductible on your tax return.

Cost of the new house.   You are not required to reinvest the actual cash proceeds of the sale of your old house. You may buy the new house with a small cash payment plus a large mortgage loan. The cost of the new house includes not only cash payments but also any mortgages you assume or take subject to. Also include purchase expenses such as broker's commissions, title search, transfer taxes, and lawyer's fees. Points that you pay on the purchase of a principal residence are generally immediately deductible and not added to basis; *see 15.8.*

If the seller paid points, that amount *reduces* the cost basis of the new home.

If you reinvest proceeds in two homes, you may not figure the investment in both houses. You consider only the investment in your new principal residence.

The present value of future land lease payments may not be added to the cost of your new house.

Construction costs.   When you build a house, include all costs paid for the land and construction of the house during the two years prior to the sale and two years after the sale. Costs paid after the two-year period are not included even if you have incurred liability for them before the end of the two-year period. However, these costs do become a part of the cost of the new house to figure gain or loss if you later sell it. If you inherit or receive as a gift all or part of a new home, do not count the value of that part in figuring whether you have reinvested your gain on the sale of your old residence. However, you may include costs of reconstructing an inherited house to make it habitable.

Remodeling a vacation home as a permanent residence.   A couple, planning to sell their principal home and remodel their vacation home into a permanent residence, asked the IRS if the remodeling costs could be considered as a purchase of a new residence. They planned to add 35% more living space by converting storage space to living areas, putting in a new roof, installing heating and air conditioning systems, and expanding the basement. The IRS answered that the remodeling qualified because of the substantial structural alterations. Furthermore, the remodeling costs were to be paid within the qualifying replacement period discussed at *29.7*.

The IRS warned that merely adding a tennis court, pool, or new roof would not have qualified for tax deferral. However, once major alterations are made, all improvements, such as the construction of a pool, could be considered part of the total renovation cost.

 Filing Tip

How Much Gain Can You Defer?
Compare the adjusted sales price with the cost of the new house. If the cost of the new house is the same or greater than the adjusted sales price of the old house, then none of the actual gain is taxed. But if the cost of the new house is less than the adjusted sales price, you are taxed on the difference—but not on more than your actual gain; *see* the Example on the left.

EXAMPLE

In April 1997, you sold your house for $175,000; its adjusted basis is $124,500. You are under age 55. In February 1997, you painted the exterior at a cost of $800 to make it more attractive to buyers. Brokers' commissions and other selling expenses are $11,500. In October 1997, you buy a new house for $161,000. This is how you compute the amount realized, the adjusted sales price, gain taxable on your 1997 return, and your adjusted basis in the replacement property:

Selling price	$175,000
Less: Selling expenses	11,500
Amount realized	$163,500
Less: Adjusted basis of old house	124,500
Actual gain	$ 39,000
Amount realized	$163,500
Less: Fix-up costs	800
Adjusted sales price	$162,700
Less: Cost of new house	161,000
Taxable gain	$ 1,700

Of the $39,000 gain, $1,700 is taxable in 1997; the balance, $37,300, is not taxable. The cost basis of the new house is reduced by the deferred gain, giving you an adjusted basis of $123,700 ($161,000 – $337,300).

Cost basis of a cooperative apartment.   In addition to the cash paid for the stock in the cooperative, include your share of the cooperative's outstanding mortgage, determined as of the date you purchased the stock if these three tests are met:

1. The mortgage is properly allocated to your apartment. The IRS will accept a mortgage allocation based on the same ratio as your stock interest bears to the total value of all the corporate stock.

2. The corporation retains your stock as a pledge for payment of your annual charges such as interest and principal payments on the mortgage.

3. Your share of corporate assets will be reduced by the unpaid balance of your proportionate share of the mortgage if the corporation is liquidated.

29.9 Reviewing Purchase and Sales Records

Arrange your records into three groups: (1) records of the purchase costs of the old house and improvements; (2) records of the sale of your old house; and (3) records of the new purchase. These are essential for determining the taxable gain on the sale of the old house and the cost basis for the new house.

Sale of the old house. You should have: (1) the sales contract showing the sales price of the old house; (2) a statement showing settlement costs at the closing and allocating taxes and fire insurance; (3) the bill and record of payment of legal fees; (4) records of payment of brokers' fees, if any; (5) a closing statement from the bank holding the mortgage on your old house showing final interest charges up to the date of transfer of title and prepayment penalties, if any; (6) if you incurred fix-up costs, records of when the work was done and when payment was made; and (7) a record of payments for advertising the sale of the house, if any.

You reduce the selling price of the house by payments for brokers' commissions, legal fees, and advertising expenses. The allocated property taxes are deducted according to the rules at *16.8*. Mortgage interest and any prepayment penalty are deductible as interest if you itemize deductions. You may not deduct fire insurance premium payments. The treatment of fix-up costs is explained at *29.8*. The paying off of the principal balance of the mortgage to the bank does not enter into the tax computation.

Keep records for costs of old house. Your records here should show the purchase price of the old house plus title insurance fees, recording fees, transfer taxes, and attorneys' fees. You should have bills or records of capital improvements made to the house for additional rooms, equipment, landscaping, and similar capital items. The cost of such improvements increases your cost basis for the house and thus reduces taxable gain. If you deducted a casualty loss for damage to the house, the deduction reduces the basis of the house.

Purchase of the new residence. Here you should have (1) your contract showing the cost of the new house plus any additional improvements; and (2) the closing statement showing title insurance fees, adjustment of taxes, mortgage fees, and recording fees.

The cost basis of your new house includes the purchase price (even though all or part is covered by a mortgage), attorneys' fees, mortgage fees, title insurance fees, and recording fees less the gain not taxed on the sale of your old home. Deduct taxes according to the allocation rules at *16.8*. The payment of fire insurance premiums on the house is not deductible. *See 15.8* for points.

29.10 Reporting Residence Sales Made Before May 7, 1997

Report the details of the sale of a principal residence on Form 2119, which must be attached to Form 1040. On Form 2119, you compute gain or loss on the sale. If you bought another principal residence, you figure whether all of the gain is deferred and also the basis of the new residence on Form 2119. The exclusion for sellers age 55 or over *(29.15)* is also claimed on Form 2119. If your entire gain does not qualify for tax deferral or the exclusion, enter the taxable gain from Form 2119 on Schedule D, or on Form 6252 if you are receiving installment payments over more than one year *(5.25)*.

If by the time you file your return you have already purchased a new home, details of the purchase are shown on Form 2119. You qualify for deferral if the cost of the new home equals or exceeds the adjusted sale price of the old home.

If you plan to buy a new home within the two-year replacement period but have not yet done so when you file your 1997 return, you indicate your intention on Form 2119; you may postpone the gain from the sale on your 1997 return. If you later make a timely replacement that qualifies for full deferral (purchase price exceeds adjusted sales price of old home), you should notify the IRS by filing a new Form 2119 for 1997. If the purchase price of a replacement home does not at least equal the adjusted sales price of the old home, or if you do not make a timely replacement, you must file an amended return on Form 1040X to report taxable gain for 1997 and attach a new Form 2119 and Schedule D; you will also owe interest on the tax due. You may also file an amended return to claim a refund if you paid tax on a 1997 gain and later buy a new home within the two-year replacement period.

The IRS may tax you on the unreported gain from the sale of your residence during a three-year period that starts when you notify the IRS on Form 2119 of the cost of your new residence, your intention not to buy one, or your failure to acquire one before the required time limit. In the absence of notice, the IRS may assess the tax on unreported taxable gain at any time.

Federal subsidy recapture. If after 1990 your home was financed with the proceeds of a tax-exempt bond or a qualified mortgage credit certificate *(15.1)* and you sell or dispose of the home within nine years of the financing, you may have to recapture the federal subsidy received. Use Form 8828 to figure the amount of the recapture tax, which is reported on Form 1040 as a separate tax.

29.11 Deferral for Married and Divorced Couples

If you are married and title to your new house differs from title to your old house, you and your spouse must file a consent statement to defer tax on a sale before May 7, 1997. This situation arises when you or your spouse individually held title to the old house and now you both hold title jointly to the new house, *or* title to the old house was in your joint names and now only one of you holds title to the new house. The consent, signed by both spouses, may be written on Form 2119 or an attached statement. By consenting, you both agree to divide the gain from the old house and to reduce the basis of the new home by the deferred gain. Consents are ineffective to defer tax unless the old and new houses were principal residences of both spouses.

EXAMPLES
1. John Smith holds title to his condominium apartment. Its cost basis is $70,000. On March 1, 1997, he sells the apartment for an adjusted sales price of $80,000 and realizes $10,000 gain. However, within the year, he and his wife, Alice, contribute $40,000 each to buy a new house for $80,000 in their joint names. John pays no tax on the gain if he and Alice file consent statements in which they agree to allocate the basis of the new house between them. They file the consent on Form 2119 in 1997. John and Alice each have a $35,000 basis in the new house—$80,000 cost, minus $10,000 deferred gain, divided by two.
    If the consent was not filed, John's entire gain of $10,000 would be taxable, since the adjusted sales price of $80,000 exceeded by more than $10,000 his $40,000 share of the cost of the new home; *see 29.8.*
2. Same facts as in Example 1 above, except John and Alice jointly owned the condominium, and the new house is bought by Alice alone and placed in her name. Tax on the gain is deferred if both sign a consent statement. The basis of the new house to Alice is $70,000 ($80,000 cost minus $10,000 deferred gain). Without the consent, only Alice would qualify for deferral, since she reinvested in a new home. John, who did not reinvest, would be taxed on his half of the gain from the old house.

Surviving spouses. Consent requirements are deemed satisfied if one spouse dies after the sale of the old home and before a new home is purchased, and if the surviving spouse purchases and occupies a new principal residence within the replacement period.

Couple replacing premarital homes with single home. If you and your spouse sold separate homes owned before marriage, tax on the gain from both sales is postponed if the combined adjusted sales prices of the two sales is reinvested in a new home within the time limit, you each contribute one-half the purchase price, and you take joint title to the new home. No consent statement is required. Report each sale on a separate Form 2119, attached to your joint return.

Separated couples. If you and your spouse sold your jointly owned home, which was used by both of you as your principal residence *(29.6)*, and buy and live in separate new homes, you may each be able to defer tax. You each report the sale on Form 2119 as if two separate homes were sold. For example, assume that under state law each of you is entitled to half the proceeds. On Form 2119, you each report half of the sales price. If the cost of your new home exceeds your respective half of the old home's adjusted sales price, you defer tax on your half of the gain. The same deferral test applies to your spouse.

If as a result of a divorce or separation you first move out of your jointly owned home which you later sell, the IRS may bar you from deferring tax on the sale on the ground that it was no longer your principal residence.

Divorce after reporting sale on joint return. If a married couple elect to defer tax on a joint return by indicating on Form 2119 that they plan to buy a replacement residence, and then they are divorced, the home sale deferral rules apply separately to each ex-spouse. If within two years of the sale the wife buys a new home and spends at least her share of the adjusted sales price of the old home (sales price less selling expenses less fix-up costs), she can defer her share of the tax. The same is true for her ex-husband. Each spouse who reinvests should follow the reporting rules in *29.10.*

However, if one spouse reinvests in a new home within two years and the other does not, the IRS could assess the tax due on the non-deferred portion of the sale proceeds against either spouse. The spouse who does reinvest could still be held liable because both spouses are liable for any tax owed on a sale that was originally reported on a joint return. To avoid this possibility, a couple that is contemplating divorce when they sell their home might consider filing separate tax returns in the year of sale. If they file jointly, one option may be to place the sales proceeds in escrow until the replacement period ends, with each spouse's share of any tax due to come from the escrow fund before division of sale proceeds. If the proceeds are divided before a divorce agreement is finalized and one spouse will be paying alimony, a provision in the agreement could note the prospective tax liabilities on the home sale and allow the spouse paying alimony to reduce future alimony payments by any tax liability on the sale that is owed but not paid by the other spouse.

EXAMPLE

A couple reported on their 1983 joint return a $150,000 profit on the sale of their jointly owned home. They did not pay an immediate tax because they indicated on Form 2119 that they anticipated buying a new home within two years. The adjusted sales price of the house was $300,000. They divorced in 1984, and in 1985, the husband bought a new home for $120,000; the wife did not buy a new home within two years. Their divorce agreement provided that each spouse would be responsible for half of any tax due in the event that the taxable gain was not completely deferred. The husband wanted to amend the 1983 joint return in order to report as income the $30,000 difference between the cost of his new home ($120,000) and his half of the adjusted sales price of the old home ($150,000, half of $300,000). The IRS said that he also had to include his wife's $75,000 share of the original gain since he was jointly and severally liable with her for any tax due. He also had to pay interest on the total tax due. To recover the tax payment attributable to his wife's failure to buy a new home within two years he would have to sue her under the divorce agreement. If the wife cannot be located, or refuses to sign the amended joint return, the husband must explain this on the amended joint return.

Selling Your House at a Loss

29.12 No Loss Allowed on Personal Residence

A loss on the sale of your principal residence is not deductible. However, you must still report the sale on Form 2119 and attach it to Form 1040. Do not report the loss transaction on Schedule D. If part of your principal residence was used for business in the year of sale, treat the sale as if two pieces of property were sold. Report the personal part on Form 2119 and the business part on Form 4797. A loss is deductible only on the business part.

Second home or vacation home. If you sell at a loss a second home or vacation home (not your principal residence) that was used entirely for personal purposes, you report the loss transaction on Schedule D, even though the loss is not deductible. Instead of entering the loss amount in column (f) of Schedule D, write "Personal Loss." If in the year of sale part of the home was rented out or used for business, allocate the sale between the personal part and the rental or business part; report the personal part on Schedule D and the rental or business part on Form 4797.

Losses allowed. A loss may be claimed if you sell a house that has been converted from personal to rental use; see 29.13. A loss may also be claimed on the sale of a house received as an inheritance or gift if you immediately put it up for sale or rental; see 29.14.

29.13 Loss on Residence Converted to Rental Property

You are not allowed to deduct a loss on the sale of your personal residence. If you convert the house from personal use to rental use you may claim a loss on a sale if the value has declined below the basis fixed for the residence as rental property.

To figure basis for loss purposes, you first need to know the *lower* of (1) your adjusted basis for the house at the time of conversion, and (2) the fair market value at the time of conversion. *Add* to the lower amount the cost of capital improvements made after the conversion, and *subtract* depreciation and casualty loss deductions claimed after the conversion. To deduct a loss, you have to be able to show that this basis exceeds the sales price. For example, if you paid $200,000 for your home and convert it to rental property when the value has declined to $150,000, your conversion date basis for the rental property is $150,000. If the property continues to decline in value, and you sell for $125,000 after having deducted $10,000 for depreciation, you may claim a loss of $15,000 ($140,000 – $125,000). Your loss deduction will not reflect the $50,000 loss occurring before the conversion.

EXAMPLE

In 1987, Adams bought a house in Fort Worth, Texas. He paid $124,000, put in capital improvements and lived there until he was forced to put it on the market when he lost his job. In 1988, he listed the house with a broker for $145,000. After receiving no offers, he decided to lease the house through 1990. By October of 1989 Adams owed $4,551 in property taxes and was three months behind on his mortgage payments. Fearing foreclosure, he sold the house for $130,000.

For purposes of figuring a loss, Adams assumed that the fair market value at the time of conversion was equal to the $145,000 list price. The adjusted basis of the house was $141,026. As this was less than the estimated fair market value of $145,000, he used the $141,026 adjusted basis to figure a loss of $11,026 ($130,000 – $141,026). The IRS claimed the fair market value at the time of conversion was equal to the actual sale price of $130,000. Since basis for the converted property is the lesser of fair market value ($130,000) and adjusted basis ($141,026), Adams had no loss on the sale.

However, the Tax Court allowed a $5,000 loss by fixing the fair market value at the time of conversion at $135,000. It held that Adams sold at a lower price because of his weak financial position of which the buyer took advantage. The court figured the $135,000 as follows: $129,000 fair market value in 1987 (based on an appraisal report, which both parties agree was correct), plus $6,000 of appreciation attributable to the capital improvements made to the property after it was converted.

Profit-making purposes. Renting a residence is a changeover from personal to profit-making purposes. If the house is merely put up for rent or is rented for several months, the IRS may not recognize the house as rental property and disallow the loss deduction. However, the Tax Court has approved a loss deduction where a house was rented on a 90-day lease with an option to buy. The court set down the following two tests for determining when a house is converted to rental property: (1) the rental charge returns a profit; and (2) the lease prevents you from using or reoccupying the house during the lease period. Under the Tax Court approach, you have a conversion to rental property if you have a lease that gives possession of the house to the tenant during the lease period, and if the rent, after deducting taxes, interest, insurance, repairs, depreciation, and other charges, returns you a profit.

Loss allowed on house bought for resale. A loss deduction is also allowed where you acquired the house as an investment with the intention of selling it at a profit, even though you occupied it incidentally as a residence prior to sale. For example, an owner bought a house with the intention of selling it. He lived in it for six years, but during that period it was for sale. He was allowed to deduct the loss on its sale by proving he lived in it to protect it from vandalism and to keep it in good condition so that it would attract possible buyers.

In another case, an architect and builder built a house and offered it for sale through an agent and advertisements. He had a home and no intention to occupy the new house. On a realtor's advice, he moved into the house to make it more saleable. Ten months later, he sold the house at a loss of $4,065 and promptly moved out. The loss was allowed on proof that his main purpose in building and occupying the house was to realize a profit by a sale; the residential use was incidental.

Gain on rented residence. You have a gain on the sale of rental property if you sell for more than your adjusted basis at the time of conversion, plus subsequent capital improvements, and minus depreciation and casualty loss deductions. The sale is subject to the rules of Chapter 44 for depreciable property.

Stock in cooperative apartment. Normally, you get no deduction for a loss on the sale of your stock in a cooperative housing corporation. It makes no difference that you occasionally sublet your apartment. It is still not considered property used in a business. But you may get a loss deduction when there were non-stockholder tenants in the cooperative housing corporation when you bought your stock. Then, you get a partial capital loss deduction if you sell your stock or if it becomes worthless. To figure capital loss:

1. First find the difference between your cost and your selling price. This would ordinarily be your capital loss.
2. Then find the percentage of non-stockholding tenants (based on rental values) in the housing corporation when you bought your stock.
3. Apply this percentage to the loss you figured above. This is the capital loss you are allowed.

See 9.5 for when depreciation may be taken on the basis of the cooperative stock ownership.

 Caution

Temporary Rental Before Sale

A rental loss may be barred on a temporary rental before sale. The IRS and Tax Court held that where a principal residence was rented for several months while being offered for sale, the rental did not convert the home to rental property. Deductions for rental expenses were limited to rental income; no loss could be claimed. A federal appeals court disagreed and allowed a rental loss deduction; also *see 9.7.*

Partially rented home. You may deduct a loss on a home sale if you rented part and occupied part for your own purposes. A loss on a sale is allowable on the rented portion. You report the sale as if two properties were sold. The residential part is reported on Form 2119 and the rental part on Form 4797.

29.14 Loss on Residence Acquired by Gift or Inheritance

You may deduct a loss on the sale of a house received as an inheritance or gift if you personally did not use it and offered it for sale or rental immediately or within a few weeks after acquisition.

If you inherit a residence in which you do not intend to live, it may be advisable to put it up for rent for an ordinary loss deduction. If you merely try to sell, and you finally do so at a loss, you are limited to a capital loss.

EXAMPLES
1. A couple owned a winter vacation home in Florida. When the husband died, his wife immediately put the house up for sale and never lived in it. It was sold at a loss. The IRS disallowed the capital loss deduction, claiming it was personal and nondeductible. The wife argued that her case was no different from the case of an heir inheriting and selling a home, since at the death of her husband her interest in the property was increased. The court agreed with her reasoning and allowed the capital loss deduction.
2. A widow inherited a house owned by her late husband and rented out by his estate. Shortly after getting title to the house, she sold it at a loss which she deducted as an ordinary loss. The IRS limited her to a capital loss deduction. The Tax Court agreed. She could not show any business activity. She did not negotiate the lease with the tenant who was in the house when she received title. She never arranged any maintenance or repairs for the building. Moreover, she sold the property shortly after receiving title, which indicates she viewed the house as investment, not rental, property.

$125,000 Exclusion for Homesellers Age 55 or Over for Sales Before May 7, 1997

29.15 Qualifying for the Exclusion

If you were 55 years of age or older when you sold your principal residence at a profit before May 7, 1997, you may avoid tax on profits up to $125,000 ($62,500 for married persons filing separately). To claim this exclusion, you must (1) elect to avoid tax on Form 2119; (2) be age 55 or over on the date of sale; and (3) have owned and occupied the house as your principal residence for at least three of the five years ending on the day of sale. The age, ownership, and use tests are discussed below. If you excluded gain under prior-law rules for sales before July 27, 1978, you may make an election under these rules.

The election applies to cooperative apartment ownership tied to stock ownership and to condominiums. It also applies to gain realized from an involuntary conversion of your home through fire, storm, or other casualty, or condemnation. Although you avoid tax on gain, you consider the gain as gross income in determining whether you are required to file a return.

The election to exclude gain does not apply where only a partial interest in the home is sold. In a private letter ruling, the IRS refused to permit an exclusion to a homeowner who sold the remainder interest in her home while retaining the right to live in it for life. However, the exclusion is allowed if a homeowner gives away a remainder interest in the house and then sells the retained life interest. The exclusion may be claimed because the life interest is the owner's entire interest in the residence.

The age test. You must be age 55 or over by the date of sale. It is not sufficient that you will be age 55 sometime during the year in which the sale occurs. A sale on the date of your 55th birthday qualifies.

The use and ownership test. You must have owned *and* occupied your home as your principal residence for at least three out of the five years ending on the date of sale. Ownership and use for 36 full months or for 1,095 days (365 × 3) during the five-year period qualifies. The three years need not be consecutive, and the periods of use and ownership may be different. Short, temporary absences for vacations are counted as periods of use, even if the house is rented while you are away.

However, if you are away from the house for a more substantial period, such as a job transfer or sabbatical lasting a year or more, the IRS will not treat that period as your use of the home.

Disabled owners. If an illness required an owner to move to a licensed nursing home or similar state- or city-licensed facility because of mental or physical disability, the period in the facility may be counted as "use" of the residence as long as the person owned and used the residence for at least one year during the five-year period preceding the sale.

Jointly owned residences. If you were married on the date of sale and the home was owned jointly with your spouse, only one of you must meet the age, use, and ownership tests to claim the exclusion on a joint return for the year of sale.

If the home was not jointly owned, the spouse owning the home must meet the age, ownership, and use tests. If you held title but were under age 55, filing a joint return with a spouse over age 55 who did not have title will not qualify you for the exclusion because neither spouse meets all three tests.

If you were married at the time of sale, both spouses must consent to an election of the exclusion, and an election bars either of you from claiming the exclusion again. *See 29.16* for these and other election rules for married couples.

Joint ownership with someone other than spouse. A husband and wife selling a jointly owned residence are considered as one taxpayer for purposes of the exclusion limitation. But if joint owners are not married, each owner who meets the tests for age (55), use (principal residence), and holding period (three of five years) may exclude gain up to $125,000 on his or her interest in the residence. The fact that one owner meets the requirements does not qualify the other for the exclusion.

29.16 The Exclusion and Married Couples

If you were married at the time of a sale before May 7, 1997, and the home is jointly owned, one of you must meet all three tests for the exclusion—age, use, and ownership. If only one of you holds title, that person must meet all the tests. Regardless of who owned the home, both of you must agree to elect the exclusion.

A married person who files a separate return may exclude up to $62,500 of profit, provided the other spouse consents to the election on Form 2119 or in an attached statement. By so consenting, the other spouse is barred from electing the exclusion for a future sale.

If you later decide to revoke the election, you also must have your spouse's consent. If you are divorced after the election but then want to revoke, you must get your former spouse's consent to the revocation. A revocation is made in a signed statement showing (1) your name and Social Security number; (2) the year in which the election was made and filed; and (3) the Internal Revenue office where you filed the election. Attach the revocation to an amended return (Form 1040X) and amended Form 2119.

Only one lifetime election was allowed a married couple. If either you or your spouse previously elected the exclusion, neither of you may make another election.

Death of spouse. A surviving spouse who inherited a residence upon the death of his or her spouse may qualify for the exclusion even before three-out-of-five-year ownership and use tests are satisfied. The surviving spouse is treated as meeting the ownership and use tests and may elect the exclusion on a sale after reaching age 55, provided (1) he or she has not remarried as of the date of the sale; and (2) the deceased spouse met the ownership and use tests and had not previously elected the exclusion or consented to a former spouse's exclusion on a sale after July 26, 1978.

If you were married on the date of sale and your spouse dies after the sale but before you could make an election, your deceased spouse's personal representative (administrator or executor) must join with you in making an election. Similarly, the personal representative must join in a revocation of any election previously made by you and your deceased spouse. Joint elections and revocations are required, even though the residence was separately owned, separate tax returns are filed, or the non-owning spouse does not meet the three-year residence requirement.

In one case, the IRS permitted an election by an executor where a sale was completed after the death of the owner under an executory contract made by the owner prior to his death.

Sale by irrevocable trust. Where a residence is transferred to an irrevocable trust by a married couple, whether they can claim the exclusion on a sale by the trust depends on whether they are treated as the owners of the trust for tax purposes. The IRS in a private ruling held that if they are treated as owners under the grantor trust rules because of retained powers over the property, they may claim the exclusion if they meet the age, ownership, and use tests.

Caution

Part of Home Used for Business

Partial business use of your residence during the five-year period preceding the sale may affect the amount of the exclusion. If you used *part* of your residence for business purposes, for example as a home office, for more than two years during the five-year period preceding the sale, the exclusion does not apply to the gain allocated to that business part of the home. If business use was two years or less, business use is ignored in figuring the exclusion.

Sale by marital trust for surviving spouse.   Property may be left to a marital trust for the benefit of a surviving spouse if there is concern that the survivor may be unable to manage the property. A personal residence may be put into the trust. If the surviving spouse is entitled to all the trust income and has an unlimited power to receive trust corpus upon request or appoint the property to any other person, the surviving spouse is considered the owner of the trust for tax purposes. If the trust sold the personal residence before May 7, 1997, the surviving spouse can elect to claim the $125,000 home sale exclusion, provided he or she was over age 55 on the date of sale and has (1) owned (through the trust) and used the residence as a principal residence for three of the last five years preceding the date of sale; and (2) the $125,000 exclusion was not previously elected by the surviving spouse or the deceased spouse with respect to a prior sale.

29.17   How To Claim the Exclusion

You elect the exclusion on Form 2119 or in a signed statement which you attach to your income tax return for the year of sale. If you do not have Form 2119, write on a separate statement that you elect to exclude from income the gain realized on the sale. In addition, give the following data: (1) your name, age, Social Security number, and marital status as of the date of sale; (2) the dates you bought and sold your residence; (3) the adjusted sale price and the adjusted basis of the property on the date of sale; and (4) the length of any absences during the five years preceding the sale, apart from vacations and other seasonal absences.

Chapter 30

Tax Savings for Investors in Securities

You have the opportunity to control the taxable year in which to realize gains and losses. Gains and losses are realized when you sell, and if there are no market pressures, you can time sales to your advantage. To profit from the low 10% or 20% tax rate on long-term capital gains, pay attention to the more-than-18-month holding period for realizing long-term capital gains on the sale of securities. Realizing long-term capital gains will give you tax savings. However, do not overlook the fact that realizing substantial capital gains may subject you to the exemption phaseout and/or 3% reduction of itemized deductions. The 3% reduction increases the effective capital gain rate and, depending on the number of exemptions phased out, the effective rate will be still higher. Thus, it may be advisable to avoid realizing too much capital gain income in a year you are subject to the exemption phaseout if that income can be deferred to a year in which you will have lower income and not be subject to the phaseout.

The $3,000 limitation ($1,500 for married filing separately) on deducting capital losses from other types of income is a substantial restriction. If you have capital losses exceeding the $3,000 (or $1,500) limit, it is advisable to realize capital gains income that can be offset by the losses.

Security Transactions

30.1 Planning Year-End Securities Transactions

First establish your current gain and loss position for the year. List gains and losses already realized from completed transactions. Then review the records of earlier years to find any carryover capital losses. Include nonbusiness bad debts as short-term capital losses. Then review your paper gains and losses and determine what losses might now be realized to offset actual gains or what gains might be realized to absorb your losses.

If you have already realized net capital losses exceeding $3,000 ($1,500 if married filing separately), you may want to realize capital gains that will be absorbed by the excess loss. Remember, only up to $3,000 (or $1,500) of capital losses exceeding net capital gain may be deducted from other income such as salary, interest, and dividends. Also, project your tax-bracket ranges in the current and next tax year. For example, assume that you are close to the threshold for the phaseout of exemptions and that realizing substantial gains will place you in the exemption phase-out range *(21.15)*. You may want to defer gain transactions to a year in which you will be in a lower bracket or not subject to the phaseout.

December 31 deadline for 1997 gains and losses.   If you want to realize gains on publicly traded securities, you have until December 31, 1997, to transact the sale. Gain is reported in 1997, although cash is not received until the settlement date in 1998. If you do not want to realize the gain in 1997, delay the trade date until 1998.

Losses are also realized as of the trade date; a loss on a sale made by December 31, 1997, is reported on your 1997 return.

Planning for losses.   Realizing losses may pose a problem if you believe the security is due to increase in value sometime in the near future. Although the wash-sale rule *(30.6)* prevents you from taking the loss if you buy 30 days before or after the sale, the following possibilities are open to you.

- If you believe the security will go up, but not immediately, you can sell now, realize your loss, wait 31 days, and then recover your position by repurchasing before the expected rise.
- You can hedge by repurchasing similar securities immediately after the sale provided they are not substantially identical. They can be in the same industry and of the same quality without being considered substantially identical. Check with your broker to see if you can use a loss and still maintain your position. Some brokerage firms maintain recommended "switch" lists and suggest a practice of "doubling up"—that is, buying the stock of the same company and then 31 days later selling the original shares. Doubling up has disadvantages: It requires additional funds for the purchase of the second lot, exposes you to additional risks should the stock price fall, and the new shares take a new holding period.

EXAMPLE

You own 100 shares of Steel Co. stock which cost you $10,000. In November 1997, the stock is selling at $6,000 ($60 a share × 100 shares). You would like to realize the $4,000 loss, but, at the same time, you want to hold on to the investment. You buy 100 shares at a market price of $60 a share (total investment $6,000) and 31 days later sell your original 100 shares, realizing the loss of $4,000. You retain your investment in the new lot. In 1997, November 28 is the last day to buy new shares to allow a loss sale on December 31.

30.2 Earmarking Stock Lots

Keep a record of all your stock transactions, especially when you buy the stock of one company at varying prices. By keeping a record of each stock lot, you may control the amount of gain or loss on a sale of a part of your holdings.

If your stock is held by your broker, the IRS considers that an adequate identification is made if you give instructions to your broker about which particular shares are to be sold, and you receive a written confirmation from the broker or transfer agent within a reasonable time.

How To Identify Securities

If your securities are—	Identify them by—
Registered in your own name	The number, your name, and any other identification which they bear.
In a margin account registered in a "street" name	A specified block or security bought on a designated day at a particular price. A mere intention to sell a particular share without informing the broker is without significance.
New certificates received for old in a recapitalization	Record the new certificate with the lowest number as being in exchange for the old certificate with the lowest number. Do this until all the new certificates are matched with all the old.
Shares exchanged for shares in a reorganization	Allocate each of the new certificates to each of the old in your records. Where the exchange involves several blocks of stock and there is no specific identification, the IRS says you must average your costs.
Shares received in a stock split	Match the new certificates with the old ones surrendered. Identification of your selling securities as the "highest cost" or "lowest cost" stock is insufficient. You have to match at the time of the split-up.
Stock dividends	The lot of stock on which you received the dividend. The new stock is part of the old lot. But, if you receive one certificate for more than one lot, you may have to apply the first-in, first-out rule when you sell.
Acquired by exercise of nontaxed stock rights	The number, or other identification, of the lot you receive by exercising the rights. Each lot you so acquire is considered a separate lot received on the date of subscription.

EXAMPLE

Over a three-year period, you bought the following shares of Acme Steel stock: In 1995, 100 shares at $77 per share; in 1996, 200 shares at $84 per share; and in 1997, 100 shares at $105 per share. When the stock is selling at $90, you plan to sell 100 shares. You may use the cost of your 1997 lot and get a $1,500 loss if, for example, you want to offset some gains or other income you have already earned this year. Or you may get capital gains of varying amounts by either selling the 1995 lot or part of the 1996 lot.

You must clearly identify the lot you want to sell. Say you want a loss and sell the 1997 lot. Unless you identify it as the lot sold, the IRS will hold that you sold the 1995 lot under the "first-in, first-out" rule. This rule assumes that, when you have a number of identical items that you bought at different times, your sale of any of them is automatically the sale of the first you bought. So the cost of your first purchase is what you match against your selling price to find your gain or loss. Here is what to do to counteract the first-in, first-out rule: If you have stock certificates registered in your name, show that you delivered the 1997 stock certificates. If the broker is holding the stock, specifically identify the 1997 lot in your selling instructions and get a written confirmation. *See* the chart in *32.10* for averaging cost on the sale of mutual-fund shares.

30.3 Sale of Stock Dividends

A sale of stock originally received as a dividend is treated as any other sale of stock. The holding period of a *taxable* stock dividend *(4.8)* begins on the day after the date of distribution. The holding period of a *tax-free* stock dividend or stock received in a split *(4.6)* starts from the time you acquired the original stock.

You bought 100 shares of X Co. stock on December 3, 1995. On August 12, 1997, you receive 10 shares of X Co. stock as a tax-free stock dividend. On December 9, 1997, you sell the 10 shares at a profit. You report the sale as long-term capital gain because the holding period of the 10 shares goes back to your original purchase date of December 3, 1995, not August 12, 1997.

Basis of tax-free dividend in the same class of stock. Assume you receive a common stock dividend on common stock. You divide the original cost by the total number of old shares and new shares to find the new basis per share.

You bought 100 shares of common stock for $1,000, so that each share has a basis of $10. You receive 100 shares of common as a tax-free stock dividend. The basis of your 200 shares remains $1,000. The new cost basis of each share is now $5 ($1,000 ÷ 200 shares). You sell 50 shares for $560. Your profit is $310 ($560 – $250).

Basis of tax-free dividend in a different class of stock. Assume you receive preferred stock dividends on common stock. You divide the basis of the old shares over the two classes in the ratio of their values at the time the stock dividend was distributed.

You bought 100 shares of common stock for $1,000. You receive a tax-free dividend of 10 shares of preferred stock. On the date of distribution, the market value of the common stock is $9 a share and that of the preferred stock is $30. That makes the market value of your common stock $900 and your preferred stock $300. So you allocate 75% ($900 ÷ $1,200) of your $1,000 original cost, or $750, to your common stock and 25% ($300 ÷ $1,200) of your cost to the preferred stock.

Basis of taxable stock dividend. The basis of a taxable stock dividend is its fair market value at the time of the distribution. Its holding period begins on the date of distribution. The basis of the old stock remains unchanged.

You bought 1,000 shares of stock for $10,000. The company gives you a choice of a cash dividend or stock (one share for every hundred held). You elect the stock. On the date of the distribution, its market value was $15 a share. The basis of the new stock is $150 (10 × $15). The basis of the old stock remains $10,000.

The tax treatment of the receipt of stock as a dividend and in a split is discussed at *4.6.*

Basis of public utility stock received under dividend reinvestment plan. For several years before 1986, an exclusion was allowed for stock dividends received from public utility companies if the dividends were reinvested in stock. If you claimed the exclusion, the stock takes a zero basis. If you sell the stock, the entire sales proceeds of the stock are reported as long-term capital gain.

30.4 Stock Rights

The tax consequences of the receipt of stock rights are discussed at *4.6.* The following is an explanation of how to treat the sale, exercise, or expiration of nontaxable stock rights. The basis of taxable rights is their fair market value at the time of distribution.

Expiration of nontaxable distributed stock rights. When you allow nontaxable rights to expire, you do not have a deductible loss; you have no basis in the rights.

Sale of nontaxable distributed stock rights. If you sell stock rights distributed on your stock, you treat the sale as the sale of a capital asset. The holding period begins from the date you acquired the original stock on which the rights were distributed.

Purchased rights.   If you buy stock rights, your holding period starts the day after the date of the purchase. Your basis for the rights is the price paid; this basis is used in computing your capital gain or loss on the sale.

If you allow purchased rights to expire without sale or exercise, you realize a capital loss. The rights are treated as having been sold on the day of expiration. When purchased rights become worthless during the year prior to the year they lapse, you have a capital loss which is treated as having occurred on the last day of the year in which they became worthless.

Exercise of stock rights.   You realize no taxable income on the exercise of stock rights. Capital gain or loss on the new stock is recognized when you later sell the stock. The holding period of the new stock begins on the date you exercised the rights. Your basis for the new stock is the subscription price you paid plus your basis for the rights exercised.

Figuring the basis of nontaxable stock rights.   Whether rights received by you as a stockholder have a basis depends on their fair market value when distributed. If the market value of rights is less than 15% of the market value of your old stock, the basis of your rights is zero, unless you elect to allocate the basis between the rights and your original stock. You make the election on your tax return for the year the rights are received by attaching to your return a statement that you are electing to divide basis. Keep a copy of the election and the return.

If the market value of the rights is 15% or more of the market value of your old stock, you must divide the basis of the stock between the old stock and the rights, according to their respective values on the date of distribution.

No basis adjustment is required for stock rights that become worthless during the year of issue.

EXAMPLE

You own 100 shares of M Co. that cost $10 a share. On September 15, there is a distribution of stock rights allowing for the purchase of one additional share of common for each 10 rights held at a price of $13 a share. The common stock is now worth $15 (ex-rights). The rights have a market value of 20¢ each. This is less than 15% of the market value of the stock. You can either: (1) choose not to spread the tax cost of the stock between the old stock and the rights, or (2) elect to spread the tax cost as follows:

Cost of your old stock, 100 shares at $10, or $1,000.

Fair market value of old stock, 100 shares at $15, or $1,500.

Market value of 100 rights at 20¢, or $20.

Market value of both old stock and rights, $1,520.

Apportionment of old stock:

$$\frac{\$1,500}{\$1,520} \times 1,000 = 986.84$$

Your new basis of old stock is $986.84 for 100 shares, or $9.87 a share. The tax cost of the rights is then calculated:

$$\frac{\$20}{\$1,520} \times 1,000 = \$13.16$$

Basis of the rights is $13.16 for 100 rights.

When you exercise your rights and 10 shares are bought, your basis for the new stock is $130 plus the cost of the rights of $13.16, or $143.16.

If the option of allocation is not exercised, the rights have a basis of zero and the basis of the new stock is $130. The basis of the old stock remains $1,000.

30.5 Short Sales

You sell short when you sell borrowed securities, usually borrowed from a broker. You close the short sale when you deliver identical shares to the broker. The short sale is generally considered closed on the date you deliver the replacement shares. This is true whether or not you sold against the box. You sell against the box if at the time of the short sale you held shares identical to the shares sold short. Under a new law, this date of closing rule may not apply to gains on short sales against the box made after June 7, 1997. Under the new law effective for short sales made after June 7, 1997, when you hold an appreciated financial position in the shares, gain on the sale is considered to have been realized at the time of the short sale, not when you close the sale. There is an exception: You close the short sale of an appreciated position before the end of the 30th day after the close of the taxable year and hold an appreciated position 60 days from the date of the closing of the short sale.

EXAMPLE

You sell short 100 shares of Steel Co. for $5,000. You borrowed the stock from your broker. The market declines. Thirteen months later, you buy 100 shares of Steel Co. stock for $3,000, which you deliver to your broker to close the short sale. Your profit of $2,000 is taxed as short-term capital gain. Your profit is short term regardless of how long you kept the sale open.

The acquisition of a *put* (an option to sell) is treated as a short sale if you hold substantially identical securities short term at the time you buy the put. However, the short-sale rules do not apply if on the same day you buy a put and stock which is identified as covered by the put. If you do not exercise the put which is identified with the stock, add its cost to the basis of the stock.

Expenses of short sales.   Before you buy stock to close out a short sale, you pay the broker for dividends paid on stock you have sold short. If you itemize deductions, you may treat your payment as investment interest *(15.10)*, provided the short sale is held open at least 46 days, or more than a year in the case of extraordinary dividends. If the 46-day (or one-year) test is not met, the payment is generally not deductible and is added to basis; in counting the short-sale period, do not count any period during which you have an option to buy or are obligated to buy substantially identical securities, or are protected from the risk of loss from the short sale by a substantially similar position.

Under an exception to the 46-day test, if you receive compensation from the lender of the stock for the use of collateral and you report the compensation as ordinary income, your payment for dividends is deductible to the extent of the compensation; only the excess of your payment over the compensation is disallowed. This exception does not apply to payments with respect to extraordinary dividends.

An extraordinary dividend is generally a dividend that equals or exceeds the amount realized on the short sale by 10% for any common stock or by 5% for any preferred stock dividends. For purposes of this test, dividends on stock received within an 85-day period are aggregated; a one-year aggregation period applies if dividends exceed 20% of the adjusted basis in the stock.

Arbitrage transactions.   Special holding-period rules apply to short sales involved in identified arbitrage transactions in convertible securities and stock into which the securities are convertible. These rules can be found in Treasury regulations to Internal Revenue Code Section 1233.

30.6 Wash Sales

The objective of the wash-sale rule is to disallow a loss deduction where you recover your market position in a security within a short period of time after the sale. Under the wash-sale rule, your loss deduction is barred if within 30 days of the sale you buy *substantially identical* stock or securities, or a "put" or "call" option on such securities. The wash-sale period is 61 days—running from 30 days before to 30 days after the date of sale. The end of a taxable year during this 61-day period does not affect the wash-sale rule. The loss is still denied. If you sell at a loss and your spouse buys substantially identical stock within this period, the loss is also barred.

The wash-sale rule does not apply to gains. It also does not apply to acquisitions by gift, inheritance, or tax-free exchange.

The wash-sale rule applies to investors and traders. It does not apply to dealers.

Loss on sale of part of a stock lot bought less than 30 days ago.   If you buy stock and then, within 30 days, sell some of those shares, a loss on the sale is deductible; the wash-sale disallowance rule does not apply.

EXAMPLE

You buy 200 shares of stock. Within 30 days, you sell 100 shares at a loss. The loss is not disallowed by the wash-sale rule. The wash-sale rule does not apply to a loss sustained in a bona fide sale made to reduce your market position. It does apply when you sustain a loss for tax purposes with the intent of recovering your position in the security within a few days. Thus if, after selling the 100 shares, you repurchase 100 shares of the same stock within 30 days after the sale, the loss is disallowed.

 Filing Tip

Losses on Short Sales

A loss on a short sale is not deductible until shares closing the short sale are delivered to the broker. You may not realize a short-term loss on the closing of a short sale if you held substantially identical securities long term on the date of the short sale. The loss is long term. This rule prevents you from creating short-term losses when you held the covering stock long term. Loss deductions on short sales may be disallowed under the wash-sale rules of *30.6*.

Oral sale-repurchase agreement. The wash-sale rule applies to an oral sale-repurchase agreement between business associates.

Defining "substantially identical." What is substantially identical stock or securities? Buying and selling General Motors stock is dealing in an identical security. Selling General Motors and buying Chrysler stock is not dealing in substantially identical securities.

Bonds of the same obligor are substantially identical if they carry the same rate of interest; that they have different issue dates and interest payment dates will not remove them from the wash-sale provisions. Different maturity dates will have no effect, unless the difference is economically significant. Where there is a long time span between the purchase date and the maturity date, a difference of several years between maturity dates may be considered insignificant. A difference of three years between maturity dates was held to be insignificant where the maturity dates of the bonds, measured from the time of purchase, were 45 and 48 years away. There was no significant difference where the maturity dates differed by less than one year, and the remaining life, measured from the time of purchase, was more than 15 years.

The wash-sale rules do not apply if you buy bonds of the same company with substantially different interest rates; buy bonds of a different company; or buy substantially identical bonds outside of the wash-sale period.

Warrants. A warrant falls within the wash-sale rule if it is an option to buy substantially identical stock. Consequently, a loss on the sale of common stocks of a corporation is disallowed when warrants for the common stock of the same corporation are bought within the period 30 days before or after the sale. But if the timing is reversed—that is, you sell warrants at a loss and simultaneously buy common stock of the same corporation—the wash-sale rules may or may not apply depending on whether the warrants are substantially identical to the purchase stock. This is determined by comparing the relative values of the stock and warrants. The wash-sale rule will apply only if the relative values and price changes are so similar that the warrants become fully convertible securities.

 Planning Reminder

Basis Adjusted for New Stock
Although the loss deduction is barred if the wash-sale rule applies, the economic loss is not forfeited for tax purposes. The loss might be realized at a later date when the repurchased stock is sold, because after the disallowance of the loss, the cost basis of the new lot is fixed as the basis of the old lot and adjusted (up or down) for the difference between the selling price of the old stock and purchase price of the new stock; *see* the Examples on the left.

EXAMPLES
1. You bought common stock of Appliance Co. for $10,000 in 1981. On June 27, 1997, you sold the stock for $8,000, incurring a $2,000 loss. A week later, you repurchased the same number of shares of Appliance stock for $9,000. Your loss of $2,000 on the sale is disallowed because of the wash-sale rule. The basis of the new lot becomes $11,000. The basis of the old shares ($10,000) is increased by $1,000, which is the excess of the purchase price of the new shares ($9,000) over the selling price of the old shares ($8,000).

2. Assume the same facts as in Example 1 except that you repurchase the stock for $7,000. The basis of the new lot is $9,000. The basis of the old shares ($10,000) is decreased by $1,000, which is the excess of the selling price of the old shares ($8,000) over the purchase price of the new shares ($7,000).

3. Assume that in February 1998 you sell the new lot of stock acquired in Example 1 above for $9,000 and do not run afoul of the wash-sale rule. On the sale, you realize a loss of $2,000 ($11,000 − $9,000).

Repurchasing fewer shares. If the number of shares of stock reacquired in a wash sale is less than the amount sold, only a proportionate part of the loss is disallowed.

EXAMPLE
You bought 100 shares of Stock A for $10,000. On December 12, 1997, you sell the lot for $8,000, incurring a loss of $2,000. On January 2, 1998, you repurchase 75 shares of Stock A for $6,000. Three-quarters ($\frac{75}{100}$) of your loss is disallowed, or $1,500 ($\frac{3}{4}$ of $2,000). You deduct the remaining loss of $500 on your return for 1997. The basis of the new shares is $7,500 ($6,000 cost *plus* $1,500 disallowed loss).

Holding period of new stock. After a wash sale, the holding period of the new stock includes the holding period of the old lots. If you sold more than one old lot in wash sales, you add the holding periods of all the old lots to the holding period of the new lot. You do this even if your holding periods overlapped as you purchased another lot before you sold the first. You do not count the periods between the sale and purchase when you have no stock.

 Planning Reminder

Tax Advantage of Wash-Sale Rule
Sometimes the wash-sale rule can work to your advantage. Assume that during December you are negotiating a sale of real estate that will bring you a large capital gain. You want to offset a part of that gain by selling certain securities at a loss. You are unsure just when the gain transaction will go through. It may be on the last day of the year, at which point it may be too late to sell the loss securities before the end of the same year.

You can do this: Sell the loss securities during the last week of December. If the profitable deal goes through before the end of the year, you need not do anything further. If it does not, buy back the loss securities early in January. The December sale will be a wash sale and the loss disallowed. When the profitable real estate sale occurs next year, you can sell the loss securities again. This time the loss will be allowed and will offset the gain.

Losses on short sales.   Losses incurred on short sales are subject to the wash-sale rules. A loss on the closing of a short sale is denied if you sell the stock or enter into a second short sale within the period beginning 30 days before and ending 30 days after the closing of the short sale.

30.7 Convertible Stocks and Bonds

You realize no gain or loss when you convert a bond into stock, or preferred stock into common stock of the same corporation, provided the conversion privilege was allowed by the bond or preferred stock certificate.

Holding period.   Stock acquired through the conversion of bonds or preferred stock takes the same holding period as the securities exchanged. However, where the new stock is acquired partly for cash and partly by tax-free exchange, each new share of stock has a split holding period. The portion of each new share allocable to the ownership of the converted bonds (or preferred stock) includes the holding period of the bonds (or preferred stock). The portion of the new stock allocable to the cash purchase takes a holding period beginning with the day after acquisition of the stock.

Basis.   Securities acquired through the conversion of bonds or preferred stock into common take the same basis as the securities exchanged. Where there is a partial cash payment, the basis of the portion of the stock attributable to the cash is the amount of cash paid; *see* Examples 1 and 2 below.

If you paid a premium for a convertible bond, you may not amortize the amount of the premium that is attributable to the conversion feature.

EXAMPLES

1. On January 2, 1997, you paid $100 for a debenture of A Co. Your holding period for the debenture begins on January 3; *see 5.13*. The debenture provides that the holder may receive one share of A Co. common stock upon surrender of one debenture and the payment of $50. On October 18, you convert the debenture to stock on payment of $50. For tax purposes, you realize no gain or loss upon the conversion regardless of whether the fair market value of the stock is more or less than $150 on the date of the conversion. The basis and holding period for the stock is as follows: $100 basis for the portion attributed to the ownership of the debenture with the holding period beginning January 3; and $50 basis attributed to the cash payment with the holding period for this portion beginning October 20.

2. Same facts as in the above Example, but you acquired the debenture on January 2 through the exercise of rights on that date. Since the holding period for the debenture includes the date of exercise of the rights, *see 30.4*, the portion of the stock allocable to the debenture takes a holding period beginning on January 3.

Investment Opportunities

30.8 Reducing the Tax on Dividend Income

The tax on dividend income may be reduced by the following types of transactions:

- *Selling stock on which a dividend has been declared but not yet paid.* During the period a dividend is declared but not paid, the price of the stock includes the value of the dividend. If you plan to sell stock in this position and figure that the tax on the dividend reflected in the selling price will be less than the tax on the dividend received, transact the sale before the stock goes ex-dividend; *see 4.9.*
- *Investing in companies paying tax-free dividends.* Some companies pay tax-free dividends. A list of companies that do may be provided by your broker. When you receive a tax-free dividend, you do not report the dividend as income as long as the dividend does not exceed your stock basis. A tax-free dividend reduces the tax cost of your stock. Dividends in excess of basis produce capital gain; *see 4.11.*
- *Investing in companies paying stock dividends.* On receipt of a stock dividend, you generally do not have taxable income.

30.9 Treasury Bills and CDs

Short-term paper (maturity of one year or less) provides an opportunity for earning income on funds during periods of uncertainty in the stock and other investment markets. Funds which you do not wish to tie up long term and do not want to remain unproductive may be invested in Treasury bills, notes, or certificates of deposit. These investments offer safety and negotiability, earning current interest rates from the day of purchase to the day of redemption, either on maturity or sale.

Treasury bills.   These are direct obligations of the U.S. Treasury issued to finance budgetary needs. Bills are offered for three-month, six-month, and 12-month maturities in minimum amounts of $10,000 and multiples of $1,000 above the minimum. Bills are sold at a discount at Treasury auctions held at the Federal Reserve Banks, which serve as agents for the Treasury. They are redeemed at face value. Your return on a Treasury bill is the difference between the discount price you pay for the bill and its face value, if you hold it to maturity, or the amount you receive for it on a sale before maturity. The selling price of a Treasury bill before maturity will vary with changes of current interest rates.

You may buy Treasury bills directly without charge from any Federal Reserve Bank, which gives you a receipt indicating that a book entry of your purchase has been recorded. You also may buy or sell Treasury bills through your bank or stockbroker, who will charge you for handling the transaction.

Most investors submit *noncompetitive tenders* (bids) for the Treasury bills they wish to buy. To submit a *competitive* tender, you must specify the price you are willing to pay for your bill, and you run the risk of bidding too low and not getting the bills you want. Noncompetitive tenders do not have to specify a price. They are filled at a price which is the average of the accepted competitive tenders for that specific auction. Check the Federal Reserve Bank or branch in your area for auction dates on Treasury bills. You may also buy or sell Treasury bills through your bank or your stockbroker, who will charge you for handling the transaction.

Figuring the yield on your Treasury bill.   On the day of the auction, the Treasury will figure the average price bid by those who submitted acceptable competitive tenders. The difference between this average price and the full value of the Treasury bill is the *discount* at which the bill is sold. All noncompetitive tenders are filled at this price. The Treasury pays you the difference between the purchase price and the face value.

EXAMPLE

Assume the accepted average bid on three-month bills is $9,850. You gave the government $10,000. To reflect the actual purchase price of $9,850, a "discount" of $150 is paid to you.

Figuring Treasury bill yield.   The equivalent annual yield on your Treasury bill is figured this way:

1. Find the yield on your investment by dividing discount by purchase price.

2. Convert this yield to the annual rate by multiplying the yield by 4.0110 (365 ÷ 91 days to maturity) if the bill is for three months and by 2.0055 (365 ÷ 182 days to maturity) if the bill is for six months.

   On a three-month bill your discount is $100 (cost $9,900); the equivalent annual yield is 0.04051:

$$\frac{\$100}{\$9,900} = 0.0101 \quad 0.0101 \times 4.0110 = 0.04051, \text{ or } 4.051\% \text{ per year}$$

Financial pages of the newspapers report the previous day's auction, including the discount rate and what this amounts to as an annual percentage yield.

Cashing bills before maturity.   If you decide you need funds before the maturity date of your bill, you can sell it through a commercial bank or a securities broker. The Federal Reserve Bank and the Treasury do not handle bills which have not matured.

For bills sold before maturity, current interest rates will determine the amount you receive. The market value of Treasury bills is listed daily in the financial section of newspapers.

At maturity.   Redemption is automatic at maturity, unless you notify the Federal Reserve Bank that you wish to roll over matured bills into new bills. The Treasury will electronically deposit the face amount of the bill into a savings or checking account you have previously designated. If you bought your bill through a bank, the bank will credit your account on the date the bill matures. To roll over your maturing bill, you follow the same procedures as in buying a new bill and use your matured bill as payment. If you purchase bills directly from the Treasury, a payment for the difference between the price of the new bills and the face value of your matured bills will be transferred electronically to your designated account.

Certificates of deposit.   Certificates of deposit (CDs) are another form of short-term investment which offers a high return with safety and negotiability.

Certificates of deposit represent money lent by investors to a bank for a specified short period of time, generally 30, 60, or 90 days, although certificates of deposit for six months to several years are also available.

Purchasing CDs.   Certificates of deposit are generally purchased through your bank or broker. The rate of interest that banks will pay depends on supply and demand in the money market. The interest rate may vary with the size of your investment. For deposits of $100,000 or more, you may be able to get a "heavy duty" CD at a higher rate than offered on smaller deposits.

Before investing, check with the bank for minimum investment requirements, charges, and restrictions on withdrawals, including penalties for withdrawals before maturity. Also *see 30.10* for more on CDs.

If you have an account with a broker, you may prefer to invest in CDs through your broker. The CDs bought through a broker are federally insured up to $100,000. Brokers offer CDs from various banks throughout the U.S. and can provide at times a higher current rate offered by a bank in an area that is not directly accessible to you.

Repurchase agreements (repos).   This investment offered by banks and thrifts allows you to earn high interest rates by sharing in a portion of the bank's portfolio of government securities. The bank is required to repurchase your investment from you at your request. The minimum investment is $1,000; maturities vary, on average, three months. Repos are not FDIC or FSLIC insured, and there is no interest penalty for early repurchase, as long as you hold them for a minimum of a week or more. There may be a small service charge for early repurchase.

Commercial paper.   Periodically during the year, many corporations requiring large sums of money to finance short-term customer receivables offer short-term promissory notes at high rates of interest. These notes are generally referred to as commercial paper. Although much of this paper is sold in units of $100,000 or more, commercial paper in denominations of $25,000 and even less is sometimes available.

Finance companies, automobile manufacturers, and large retail stores are types of businesses which typically issue commercial paper for periods ranging from one week to 270 days.

Investments in commercial paper may not be as liquid as other short-term paper and are subject to greater risks.

Tax-exempt notes are discussed at *30.13.*

30.10   Investing in Savings Institutions

Bank money-market accounts compete with money-market mutual funds. Bank money-market funds generally guarantee for one-week or one-month periods interest rates tied to the Treasury bill rate or the average money-market rate. Bank funds also offer this added attraction: They are federally insured. Bank money-market accounts require certain average monthly balances and if the account falls below the minimum, the interest rate is reduced.

Investments in money-market funds allow you to take advantage of rising interest rates, but if market rates decline, so will your return. Investments in CDs allow you to lock into the highest available interest rate for a fixed period of time if you are concerned with a decline of rates during that period.

Withdrawals generally may be made from money-market accounts without penalty, subject to minimum account requirements. Premature withdrawals from CDs are penalized.

CD investments in savings institutions allow you to lock into high interest rates only for the short term, generally up to five years. If you are concerned that rates will substantially decline in the future, you may want to invest in a currently available investment that fixes a high rate over longer periods, such as bonds with long-term maturities. Bond investments are discussed in *30.11.*

As indicated in *30.9,* stockbrokers may offer to their customers issues of CDs from various banks and may allow you to invest at a slightly higher rate than that offered by a local bank.

Savings certificates versus Treasury bills.   Treasury bills require a minimum $10,000 investment, while certificates keyed to the Treasury bill rate usually require much lower minimums. Treasury bill investments over the minimum must be made in multiples of $1,000; for certificates, additional investments may be made in smaller increments. There is no fee charged for the purchase of certificates, while a fee may be charged to purchase Treasury bills unless purchased directly from the Treasury or a Federal Reserve Bank. Where you do not have the minimum to invest, some institutions may lend the difference at a lower interest rate, typically 1% to 2% over the rate earned on the certificate. Treasury bills have a tax advantage over certificates: interest on savings certificates is subject to state and local taxes; interest on Treasury bills is exempt from state and local taxes. Furthermore, there are penalties for redeeming certificates before maturity. *See 4.16* for taxation of interest and for forfeiture of interest on premature withdrawals.

Investment options vary from bank to bank. Not all banks offer the maximum rates or compound interest in the same manner. Whether interest is compounded daily or annually will affect your rate of return. Each bank also has its own policy on procedures concerning maturity of certificates. Some banks automatically renew the CD for another term at the current rate unless notified to the contrary; some banks will not renew a matured CD without express authority from you. If you fail to act, you may find your funds switched to a day-of-deposit account on maturity. Banking institutions can also change their rules after you have opened an account.

30.11 Investing in Corporate Bonds

When you buy a corporate bond, you are lending money to the issuer of the bonds. You become a creditor of the issuing company. The corporation pledges to pay you interest on specified dates, generally twice a year, and to repay the principal on the date of maturity stated on the bond.

For investment purposes, a bond may be described according to the length of the period of maturity. Short-term bonds usually mature within one to five years, medium-term bonds in five to 20 years, and long-term bonds in 20 or more years.

Where the interest is paid out on a regular schedule, the bond is called a "current income" bond. An accrual or discount bond is a bond on which interest is accumulated and paid as part of the specified maturity value (the bond having been issued at a price lower than the specified maturity value).

Figuring the yield of a bond. The investment value of bonds is generally expressed in rates of yield. There are four types of yield: the nominal or coupon yield; the actual yield; the current market yield; and the net yield to maturity.

The nominal or coupon yield is the fixed or contractual rate of interest stated on the bond. A bond paying 6% has a 6% nominal yield.

The actual yield is the rate of return based on the price at which the bond was purchased. If bought below par, the actual yield will exceed the nominal or coupon yield. If bought at a premium (above par), the actual yield will be less than the coupon or nominal yield. For example, if you paid $850 for a $1,000 bond paying 5% interest, the actual yield is 5.88% ($50 ÷ $850).

The current market yield is the rate of return on the bond if bought at the prevailing market price. It is figured in the same manner as actual yield.

Net yield to maturity represents the rate of return on the bond if it is held to maturity, plus appreciation allocated to a discount purchase or less reductions for any premium paid on a bond selling above par. If you buy a bond below par at a market discount, your annual return is proportionately increased by a part of the discount allocated to the number of years before maturity. If the discount was $50 on a bond with a five-year maturity, then your annual income return on the bond is increased by $10 ($50 ÷ 5). On the other hand, if you bought at a premium, the extra cost is a reduction against your income because you paid more than can be recovered at maturity. This cost is allocated over the remaining life of the bond. Thus, if you bought a five-year bond at $50 over par, your average annual return is reduced by $10 ($50 ÷ 5).

Call privileges may reduce the investment value of the bond. A call privilege gives the issuer a chance to redeem the obligation before maturity if interest rates have declined below the rate fixed by the obligation. A call privilege is a disadvantage to an investor; a favorable investment may be lost at a time the investor may not be able to replace it with another. To take some of the "sting" out of a call provision, the issuer may provide for the payment of a "premium" on the exercise of the call and a minimum period during which the bonds will not be called. The call premium is usually expressed as a percentage of the maturity value, for example, 105%. The amount of the premium varies with the length of the period in which the bond may be called. As the maturity date approaches, the call premium will decrease. Some bonds now carry a guarantee that they will not be called for a specified number of years, such as five or 10 years.

A call privilege generally will not be exercised if the going interest rate remains about the same as, or is higher than, the interest rate of the bond. If interest rates decline below the interest rate of the bond, the bond will probably be called because the issuer can obtain the borrowed money at lower cost elsewhere.

Planning Reminder

Deferring Interest Income

Defer interest income by buying a six-month tax-deferred certificate after June 30. Interest is taxable in the next year when the certificate matures if the terms of the certificate specifically defer the interest to maturity. If your bank offers you the choice of when to receive the interest, deferral is not allowed. You may also defer interest by buying Treasury bills which come due next year.

Interest on bearer bonds issued with coupons attached is paid when a bondholder clips the coupon and deposits it for payment. A registered bond carries the name of the owner, who receives his or her interest by mail from the issuing corporation.

Whether a bond is registered or in bearer form has no effect on its investment quality or yield. A coupon-type or bearer bond may be preferred by institutional investors because it can be transferred by hand without registration. However, this advantage must be weighed against the risks of loss through fire, theft, or casualty.

Issuing and trading bonds. New bond issues are generally placed through investment bankers who usually assist in the preparation of the issue. Often an issue may be sold directly by the issuing organization to an institutional investor. Many newly issued bonds are purchased directly from issuers or from their investment bankers by institutional investors before the bonds are offered to individual investors. Issuers prefer this type of placement as it involves less expense than a public offering. Normally, only the new issues (or part of new issues) which cannot be marketed this way are offered to private investors.

Bonds are also traded on the open market where individuals, as well as institutional buyers, may buy or sell them at competitive, market determined prices, through dealers or brokers.

Bond prices fluctuate in response to changes in interest rates and business conditions. In setting the daily price of a bond, the market weighs the current status, performance, and future prospects of the issuing corporation, as well as the interest rate and maturity period of the bond.

Quotations are based on 100 as equal to par, even though the basic unit for an actual bond may be in denominations of $1,000. A quote of 90 $\frac{1}{2}$ simply means a bond with a face value of $1,000 will cost $905 at market.

Calls under sinking fund redemption. A bond may be called in at par under the terms of a sinking fund arrangement. Not all bonds are called and those that are selected are picked by lot. Redemptions for sinking fund purposes account for only a small percentage of a single bond issue. But some issues may retain the right to use a blanket sinking fund under which they may redeem bonds paying interest at their highest rate.

Put privileges. A put privilege is the flipside of a call privilege. It permits the buyer to sell the bonds at par to the issuer after a stated number of years. This feature is valuable to investors for long-term bonds. If interest rates rise, investors are not locked into low yields.

Current interest rates affect the selling price of bonds so that you may gain or lose on your investment:

1. *If current interest rates increase over the interest rate of your bond, the market value of your bond will decline.* The decline in value has nothing to do with the credit rating of the issue. It simply means that other investors will buy only at terms that will give them the current higher return. If you bought a $1,000 bond paying a rate of 6% at par, and a few months later interest rates go to 8%, another investor will not pay $1,000 for the bond for a 6% return. To match the 8% return on a dollar, the market value of the bond will drop to a level which will return 8% on the money invested, based on its actual 6% return and the period remaining before maturity. Thus, during periods of rising interest rates, the price of bonds issued at lower rates in prior years declines. This can lead to substantial losses, as bond investors learned in 1993–94. Top-quality bonds are not immune from price declines; the highest credit rating will not protect the market value of a low-interest-paying bond. When this happens there also may be bond bargains, as prices on outstanding bonds decrease.

2. *If interest rates decline below the interest rate of your bond, the value of your bond will increase;* but at the same time, the company, if it has an exercisable call option, may redeem the bond to rid itself of the high interest cost and attempt to raise funds at current lower rates. Thus, an early redemption of the bond could upset your long-range investment plans in that particular issue.

With these points in mind, you can understand why investors have shied away from long-term bonds as interest rates rise. Investors prefer shorter-term bonds, which pay lower interest but have more stable value.

Corporate zero coupon bond. A zero coupon bond is a deep discount obligation issued at considerably less than face value and redeemed at face at a set date. No annual interest is paid. A zero coupon bond allows an investor to lock in a return. He or she knows how much will be received at maturity and so avoids the problem of turning over investments at fluctuating short-term rates. However, zero coupon bonds may be subject to "call" provisions, as previously discussed; an early call would upset your projected return. Brokers have lists of zero coupon bonds; the prices

 Caution

Reporting Zero Coupon Bond Discount

Zero coupon bond discount is reported annually as interest over the life of the bond, even though interest is not received. This tax cost tends to make zero coupon bonds unattractive to investors, unless the bonds can be bought for IRA and other retirement plans which defer tax on income until distributions are made.

Zero coupon bonds also may be a means of financing a child's education. A parent buys the bond for the child. The child must report the income, and if the income is not subject to the parent's marginal tax bracket under the "kiddie tax" (Chapter 24), the income subject to tax may be minimal.

The value of zero coupon bonds fluctuates sharply with interest rate changes. This fact should be considered before investing in long-term zero coupon bonds. If you sell zero coupon bonds before the maturity term, at a time when interest rates rise, you may lose part of your investment.

vary with the credit rating of the companies, current market rates, maturity dates, and whether the bond is callable.

Floating rate or variable interest bonds.   For investors unwilling to gamble on the future of interest rates, some bonds have been offered with floating interest rates. The rate is updated periodically, but there may be a floor and ceiling limiting the changes. The market price of the bond should remain near par since its interest rate moves with the market. Although this feature is a form of insurance for the investor, it may not be worth its added cost.

30.12   Treasury Bonds, Notes, and U.S. Agency Obligations

The federal government offers the following obligations for investment opportunities. They are guaranteed by the federal government and are exempt from state and local taxes.

Treasury bonds and notes.   Treasury bonds have maturity dates in excess of 10 years. The minimum denomination is $1,000. Interest is paid semiannually at a rate which varies with each issue. These bonds may be purchased through a commercial bank or directly from the Federal Reserve Bank.

Treasury notes are similar to Treasury bonds but have shorter maturity dates of from two to 10 years. Minimum investments range from $1,000 to $5,000, depending on the issue. Interest is paid semiannually and interest varies with each issue. Notes are purchased from commercial banks or directly from the Federal Reserve Bank.

Treasury notes and bonds are issued in book-entry form only; you do not receive a certificate. Under a direct deposit system, semiannual interest and principal at maturity is electronically deposited in a bank account which you designate.

Zero coupon Treasury bonds.   Certain major brokerage houses have created zero coupon Treasury bonds by stripping the coupons from Treasury bonds and selling the bonds at deep discounts. They have been promoted under such names as TIGRS, LIONS, COUGARS, and CATS as investments suitable for IRAs, retirement plan trusts, and custodian accounts for minors. The U.S. Treasury itself offers its own version of the zero coupon bond under the name STRIPS. The government does not offer STRIPS directly to individual investors, but sells them to banks and brokers who then sell them to the public. Because STRIPS have the direct backing of the U.S. government, they are considered to be the safest zeros and generally yield up to one-tenth of one percent less than brokerage firm or bank created zero coupon bonds, such as TIGRS or CATS. With all zero coupon Treasury obligations, an investor can select a particular maturity date suited to his or her needs, such as the year the investor will start taking IRA distributions or the year a child will start college. For tax reporting rules, *see 30.11* on corporate zero coupon bonds.

Other U.S. obligations, such as savings bonds, are discussed at *30.16* and Treasury bills at *30.9*.

Certain federal agencies, like the Tennessee Valley Authority, offer their own securities. The types of securities offered vary. Such securities must be purchased through brokers or commercial banks.

Federally chartered companies, such as the Government National Mortgage Association ("Ginnie Mae") and the Federal National Mortgage Association ("Fannie Mae"), authorize certain firms and institutions to issue securities based on insured mortgages. While interest on these securities is generally not exempt from state and local taxes, they offer the investor a higher yield than Treasury securities. Some of these obligations carry a U.S. government full faith and credit guarantee; some have only an implied guarantee; and some no backing from the federal government, but risk is generally considered to be negligible.

Ginnie Maes are offered in minimum denominations of $25,000. Monthly payments to security holders include not only interest, but also a return of principal. Rather than buying Ginnie Maes in the open market, you may consider investing in a mutual fund or trust which has a portfolio of such securities. Minimum investment units typically begin at $1,000.

30.13   Investing in Tax-Exempts

Interest on state and local obligations is not subject to federal income tax. It is also exempt from the tax of the state in which the obligations are issued. In comparing the interest return of a tax-exempt with that of a taxable bond, you figure the taxable return that is equivalent to the tax-free yield of the tax-exempt. This amount depends on your tax bracket. For example, a municipal bond of $5,000 yielding 7% is the equivalent of a taxable yield of 9.7% subject to the tax rate of 28%.

 Planning Reminder

Treasury Inflation-Indexed Bonds
The U.S. Treasury now offers bonds indexed to inflation. The bonds pay currently taxable interest at a fixed rate. The principal of the bonds is increased to reflect inflation. Bondholders are also taxed on the inflation adjustment to the principal as if it were interest income received in the year the adjustment is made.

You can compare the value of tax-exempt interest to taxable interest for your tax bracket by using this formula:

$$\frac{\text{Tax-exempt return}}{\text{1 minus your tax bracket}}$$

The denominator of the above fraction is:

0.85 if your tax bracket is 15%
0.72 if your tax bracket is 28%
0.69 if your tax bracket is 31%
0.64 if your tax bracket is 36%
0.604 if your tax bracket is 39.6%

EXAMPLE

You are deciding between a tax-exempt bond and a taxable bond. You want to find which will give you more income after taxes. You have a choice between a tax-exempt bond paying 6% and a taxable bond paying 8%. Your tax bracket is 28%.

You find that the tax-exempt bond is a better buy in your tax bracket as it is the equivalent of a taxable bond paying 8.3%.

$$T = \frac{0.06}{0.72\ (1-0.28)}$$

$$T = .083 \text{ or } 8.3\%$$

The following table shows the amount a taxable bond would have to earn to equal the tax-exempt bond, according to the investor's income tax bracket.

| If top income tax rate is— | A tax-exempt yield of—* | | | | | |
| | 3% | 4% | 5% | 6% | 7% | 8% |
	Is the equivalent of these taxable yields:					
28%	4.2	5.5	6.9	8.3	9.7	11.1
31%	4.3	5.8	7.2	8.7	10.1	11.6
36%	4.7	6.3	7.8	9.4	10.9	12.5
39.6%	5.0	6.6	8.3	9.9	11.6	13.2

*Exemption from the tax of the state issuing the bond will increase the yield.

To lock in high rates, you may have to invest in a long-term bond. However, consider these drawbacks: You may not want to tie up your capital long term. There is the possibility that a future increase in interest rates may reduce the value of your investment if you should need the principal before maturity.

Ratings of tax-exempt bonds. As in the case of commercial bonds, tax-exempt issues are rated by services such as Standard & Poor's and Moody's. In rating a bond, the services will consider the size of the issuer, the amount of its outstanding debt, its past record in paying off prior debts, whether it has competent officials and a balanced budget, its tax assessment and collection record, and whether the community is dominated by a single industry which might be subject to economic change. Generally, an issuer with a good credit rating will offer lower interest rates than one plagued with revenue deficits or similar problems. A basic test is the sufficiency of tax yields or revenues even in times of economic stress.

General obligation bonds will normally be rated higher than revenue bonds because they have the support of the taxing power of the community. Revenue bonds (backed by the revenue of the issuer) may receive high ratings once a capacity to produce earnings is shown.

Purchase and trading of tax-exempts. Tax-exempt municipals are traded over the counter and are generally handled through a firm specializing in this field or having a department for municipals. Prices quoted represent a percentage of par. For example, a par value $5,000 bond quoted at 90 is selling for $4,500 (90% of $5,000); a par value $1,000 bond quoted at 90 is selling for $900 (90% of $1,000). It may not pay to buy tax-exempts unless you intend to hold them to maturity because the additional cost of selling a small order might be as much as a year's interest.

The bid and asked prices of tax-exempt bonds are generally not quoted in the daily newspapers, although some brokerage houses which specialize in them do print such prices. As in the general bond market, an offer of unusually high interest compared with the average bond rates may be an indication that the bonds are riskier than others.

The market for tax-exempts is not as large as the market for stock. This poses a risk if you ever need ready cash and are forced to sell a tax-exempt bond at a discount. If you are concerned with liquidity, restrict your investments to major general obligation bonds of state governments and revenue bonds of major authorities.

Mutual funds.   Instead of purchasing tax-exempts directly, you may consider investing in municipal bond funds. The funds invest in various municipal bonds and, thus, offer the safety of diversity. The value of fund shares will fluctuate with the bond markets. Also, an investment in the fund may be as small as $1,000 compared with the typical $5,000 municipal bond. Check on fees and other restrictions in municipal bond funds.

You may also invest in tax-free money-market mutual funds. These provide ready liquidity and protect the value of your principal by maintaining a $1 value per share. The tax-exempt yield is generally lower than from a municipal bond fund.

Tax-exempt notes.   Although generally bought by banks and large corporations, short-term tax-exempt notes may be available to individuals. The majority of the notes are offered in face amounts of $25,000 and up, but sometimes in denominations of $5,000 and $10,000. They are issued by states and municipalities to tide them over until expected revenues are received or until longer-term money can be raised through an issue of long term bonds. Where rising interest rates have made the cost of long term issues high, a government authority may postpone a long-term offering and try to fill the gap with short-term notes. The interest rates on tax-exempt notes may be higher than on tax-exempt bonds if the authority is willing to pay the extra interest for the short term in the expectation that a future long-term offering may be placed at lower rates.

Interest on these short-term notes is exempt from federal tax. Many of the notes are from housing authorities and issued to pay construction costs on projects for which bonds will eventually be issued. Housing notes are guaranteed by the FHA and, because of their safety, yields are lower than more speculative paper.

Tax law restrictions.   Most municipal bonds that are issued before July 1, 1983, except for housing issues, are in the form of bearer bonds; the owners are not identified, and interest coupons are cashed as they come due. However, state and municipal bonds issued after June 30, 1983, with a maturity of more than one year, as well as obligations of the federal government and its agencies, are in registered form. Principal and interest are transferable only through an entry on the books of the issuer.

In buying state or local bonds, check the prospectus for the issue date and tax status of the bond. The tax law treats bonds issued after August 7, 1986, as follows:

1. "Public-purpose" bonds. These include bonds issued directly by state or local governments or their agencies to meet essential government functions, such as highway construction and school financing. These bonds are generally tax exempt.

2. "Qualified private activity" bonds. These include bonds issued to finance housing and student loans. There are limits on the amount of qualifying private activity bonds an authority may issue. Interest on qualifying bonds issued after August 7, 1986 (or after August 31, 1986, for certain bonds), is tax free for regular income tax purposes, but is a preference item to be added to taxable income if you are subject to alternative minimum tax. Because of the AMT, a nongovernment-purpose bond may pay slightly more interest than public-purpose bonds. These may be a good investment if you are not subject to AMT tax or if your AMT liability is not substantial. Your broker can help you identify such bonds.

3. "Taxable" municipals. These are bonds issued for nonqualifying private purposes. They are subject to federal income tax, but may be exempt from state and local taxes in the states in which they are issued. Generally, bonds issued after August 15, 1986, are subject to this rule.

30.14 Investing in Unit Investment Trusts

A unit investment trust is a closed-end unmanaged portfolio of bonds marketed by investment houses. Yield is fixed for the life of the trust with interest payable semiannually or more frequently. As bonds in the portfolio mature, a unit holder receives a repayment of principal. Unit trusts provide investors with the possibility of locking into high yields for the long term. However, a trust has this disadvantage: If principal is needed before the end of the trust term, an investor may sacrifice substantial amounts of principal if interest rates rise or if the general investment market is shying away from long-term investments; even where the trust may offer a current return equal to market value, its price may be depressed because there may be few investors willing to take the risk of tying up their funds in long-term investments. Despite these drawbacks, the performance of unit trusts has been rated higher than that of similar mutual funds.

Unit trusts hold varying types of debt instruments. Tax-exempt municipal bond trusts, made up of tax-exempt obligations, are generally favored by investors in the top tax brackets. Taxable unit trusts hold investments such as corporate bonds, bank certificates of deposit, and Treasury obligations. Usually, units are offered in denominations of $1,000. An investor pays a front-end sales charge, but no management fee as there is no need for management once a unit trust is closed.

Maturities of the various trusts range as follows: The short-term, tax-exempt average is three years; intermediate, six to 12 years; and long-term, 18 to 30 years. An average for corporate intermediate is six years, with 25 years for long-term.

30.15 Ordinary Loss for Small Business Stock (Section 1244)

Shareholders of qualifying "small" corporations may claim within limits an ordinary loss, rather than a capital loss, on the sale or worthlessness of Section 1244 stock. An ordinary loss up to $50,000, or $100,000 on a joint return, may be claimed on Form 4797. On a joint return, the $100,000 limit applies even if only one spouse has a Section 1244 loss. Losses in excess of these limits are deductible as capital losses. Any gains on Section 1244 stock are reported as capital gain on Schedule D.

An ordinary loss may be claimed only by the original owner of the stock. If a partnership sells Section 1244 stock at a loss, an ordinary loss deduction may be claimed by individuals who were partners when the stock was issued. If a partnership distributes the Section 1244 stock to the partners, the partners may not claim an ordinary loss on their disposition of the stock.

If an S corporation sells Section 1244 stock at a loss, S corporation shareholders may not claim an ordinary loss deduction. The IRS with Tax Court approval limits shareholders' deductions to capital losses (which are deductible only against capital gains plus $3,000 ($1,500 if married filing separately); *see 5.3*).

To qualify as Section 1244 stock:

1. The corporation's equity may not exceed $1,000,000 at the time the stock is issued, including amounts received for the stock to be issued. Thus, if the corporation already has $600,000 equity from stock previously issued, it may not issue more than $400,000 worth of additional stock.

    If the $1,000,000 equity limit is exceeded, the corporation follows an IRS procedure for designating which shares qualify as Section 1244 stock.

    Preferred stock issued after July 18, 1984, may qualify for Section 1244 loss treatment, as well as common stock.
2. The stock must be issued for money or property (other than stock and securities).
3. The corporation for the five years preceding your loss must generally have derived more than half of its gross receipts from business operations and not from passive income such as rents, royalties, dividends, interest, annuities, or gains from the sales or exchanges of stock or securities. The five-year requirement is waived if the corporation's deductions (other than for dividends received or net operating losses) exceed gross income. If the corporation has not been in existence for the five years before your loss, then generally the period for which the corporation has been in existence is examined for the gross receipts test.

Recordkeeping requirements. You must keep records that distinguish between Section 1244 stock and other stock interests. Your records must show that the corporation qualified as a small business corporation when the stock was issued, you are the original holder of the Section 1244 stock, and it was issued for money or property. Stock issued for services does not qualify. In addition, the records should also show the amount paid for the stock, information relating to any property transferred for the stock, any tax-free stock dividends issued on the stock, and the corporation's gross receipts data for the most recent five-year period.

Failure to keep these records will be grounds for disallowing a loss that is claimed on Section 1244 stock.

30.16 Savings Bond Plans

Savings bond purchases give you an opportunity to defer tax; *see 4.28*. EE bonds can be purchased for one-half the face value (ranging from $50 to a maximum of $10,000).

EE bonds issued on or after May 1, 1997, earn interest at rates tied to Treasury securities immediately from the date of purchase through the next 30 years until the bond matures. Interest earned is 90% of the average market yield on five-year Treasury securities for the preceding six months. Interest is earned monthly, and compounded semiannually. Because the interest rates are dependent upon a variable market rate that changes every six months, there is no way to predict when the bond will reach its face value. While a bond earning an average of 5% would reach face value in $14^1/_2$ years and a bond earning 6% would reach face value in 12 years, in the unlikely event that a bonds does not reach face value by the time it is 17 years old, the Treasury will make a one-time adjustment to increase the bond's value to face value at that time.

EE bonds issued on or after May 1, 1997, can be redeemed any time after six months from the date of issue, but bonds cashed in any time before five years are subject to a three-month interest penalty; *see* the Example below.

EXAMPLE

You purchase series EE bonds on May 1, 1997. If you cash them 24 months later, in May 1999, you get your original investment back plus 21 months of interest (instead of 24 months of interest) because of the three-month penalty for redemptions within the first five years of ownership.

EE bonds issued after April 30, 1995, but before May 1, 1997, earn interest at rates tied to Treasury Securities from the date of purchase through original maturity in 17 years. For the first five years they earn a rate (set each May 1 and November 1) that is equal to 85% of the average six-month Treasury bill rate for the preceding three-month period. From five years through 17 years, the rate is 85% of the average yield on five-year Treasury securities during the preceding six-month period.

EE bonds issued before May 1, 1995, earn a guaranteed minimum rate, and if held at least five years, a rate tied to Treasury securities if that is greater than the minimum rate.

Deferring tax on savings bond interest. Unless you report the interest annually, Series E and EE bond interest is deferred *(4.29)* until the year you redeem the bond or it reaches final maturity. When you redeem the bond, the accumulated interest is taxable on your federal return but *not* taxable on your state and local income tax return. If in the year of redemption you use the proceeds to pay for higher education or vocational school costs, the accumulated interest may be tax free for federal tax purposes; *see* Chapter 38.

Interest accrual dates for Series E and Series EE savings bonds. Interest on Series E bonds accrues twice a year. The months of accrual depend on the issue date of the bond, as shown in the chart on page 482. When you cash a bond, you receive the value of the bond as of the last date that interest was added. If you cash a bond in between accrual months, you will not receive interest for the partial period. For example, if interest accrues in February and August, and you cash a bond in during July, you would earn interest only through February.

A similar twice-a-year accrual rule applies to Series EE bonds, except for those issued from March 1993 through April 1995 and those issued on or after May 1, 1997, which accrue interest monthly. *See* the chart on the next page.

Final maturity for savings bonds. Do not neglect the final maturity date for older bonds. After the final maturity date, no further interest will accrue. For example, Series E savings bonds issued in 1957 mature in 1997 and will not earn further interest. E bonds issued in 1967 also reached final maturity in 1997. E bonds issued in 1958 and in 1968 will reach final maturity in 1998. If you have bonds that are maturing, and have deferred the reporting of interest, you may continue the deferral by exchanging the matured bonds for HH bonds. HH bonds are available in multiples of $500, and pay taxable interest semiannually. If the exchange is made, and you choose to continue the deferral, the interest on the E bonds will not be taxed until the HH bonds are cashed or reach maturity. HH bonds mature in 20 years. The exchange may be made within one year after the E bond reaches final maturity.

 Caution

Timing Bond Redemptions
In the year you cash in a savings bond you could lose interest by cashing it in too soon. Interest accrues only twice a year on E bonds and on EE bonds issued prior to March 1, 1993, or between May 1995 and April 1997. Bonds issued at different times have different accrual dates. If you cash your bonds before the accrual date that applies to your bond, you will lose interest. For a list of interest accrual dates, *see* the chart on the next page.

For EE bonds issued after February 1993 and before May 1995, or after April 1997, interest is credited on the first day of each month.

Accrual Dates for Series E and EE Bonds

Issue Date—	Accrual Months—	Example—
February 1957– May 1959 E Bonds	Fifth month after issue month *and* eleventh month after issue month. Bonds reach final maturity 40 years after issue.*	If you have a bond issued in June 1958, interest accrues every November (five months after the June issue month) and every May (11 months after the June issue month).
June 1959– November 1965 E Bonds	Third month after issue month *and* ninth month after issue month. Bonds reach final maturity 40 years after issue.*	If you have a bond issued in September 1964, interest accrues every December (three months after the September issue month) and every June (nine months after the September issue month).
December 1965– May 1969 E Bonds	Sixth month after issue month *and* original issue month. Bonds reach final maturity 30 years after issue.*	If you have a bond issued in October 1968, interest accrues every April (six months after the October issue month) and every October (month of original issue).
June 1969– November 1973 E Bonds	Fourth month after issue month *and* tenth month after issue month. Bonds reach final maturity 30 years after issue.*	If you have a bond issued in July 1971, interest accrues every November (four months after the July issue month) and every May (10 months after the July issue month).
December 1973– June 1980 E Bonds	Sixth month after issue month *and* original issue month. Bonds reach final maturity 30 years after issue.*	If you have a bond issued in May 1979, interest accrues every November (six months after the May issue month) and every May (month of original issue).
January 1980– February 1993 EE Bonds	Sixth month after issue month *and* original issue month. Bonds reach final maturity 30 years after issue.*	If you have a bond issued in June 1990, interest accrues every December (six months after the June issue month) and every June (month of original issue).
March 1993– April 1995 EE Bonds	Interest is credited on the first day of every month for the first five years, then semiannually. Bonds reach final maturity 30 years after issue.*	
May 1995– April 1997 EE Bonds	Sixth month after issue month *and* original issue month. Bonds reach final maturity 30 years after issue.*	If you have a bond issued in August 1995, interest accrues every February (six months after the August issue month) and every August (month of original issue).
On or after May 1, 1997 EE Bonds	Interest is credited on the first day of the month. A three-month interest penalty is imposed if the bond is redeemed before five years. Bonds reach final maturity 30 years after issue.	

*Last interest accrual on final maturity date.

Chapter 31

Tax Savings for Investors in Real Estate

Real estate investors may take advantage of the following tax benefits:

- Sale of investment property may be taxed at capital gain rates and gain attributed to depreciation at recapture rates.
- Depreciation can provide a source of temporary tax-free income; *see 31.1*.
- Rental income can be used to offset passive losses; *see* Chapter 10.
- Tax-free exchanges make it possible to defer tax on exchanges of real estate held for investment; *see 31.4*.

Losses on real estate transactions may be subject to the following disadvantages:

- Rental losses may not be deductible from other income such as salary interest and dividends unless you qualify as a real estate professional or for the special $25,000 rental loss allowance; *see* Chapter 10.
- Compromises of mortgage liability may subject you to tax; *see 31.11*.

Real Estate Investments

31.1 Investing in Real Estate Ventures

A real estate investment should provide a current income return and an appreciation in the value of the original investment. As an additional incentive, a real estate investment may in the early years of the investment return income subject to little or no tax. That may happen when depreciation and other expense deductions reduce taxable income without reducing the amount of cash available for distribution. This tax savings is temporary and limited by the terms and the amount of the mortgage debt on the property. Payments allocated to amortization of mortgage principal reduce the amount of cash available to investors without an offsetting tax deduction. Thus, the amount of tax-free return depends on the extent to which depreciation deductions exceed the amortization payments.

To provide a higher return of tax-free income, at least during the early years of its operations, a venture must obtain a constant payment mortgage that provides for the payment of fixed annual amounts which are allocated to continually decreasing amounts of interest and increasing amounts of amortization payments. Consequently, in the early years, a tax-free return of income is high while the amortization payments are low, but as the amortization payments increase, nontaxable income decreases. When this tax-free return has been substantially reduced, a partnership must refinance the mortgage to reduce the amortization payments and once again increase the tax-free return; *see* Examples 1 and 2 below.

The tax-free return is based on the assumption that the building does not actually depreciate at as fast a rate as the tax depreciation rate. If the building is depreciating physically at a faster rate, the so-called tax-free return on investment does not exist. Distributions to investors (over and above current income return) that are labeled tax-free distributions are, in fact, a return of the investor's own capital.

EXAMPLES

1. A limited partnership of 100 investors owns a building that returns an annual income of $100,000 after a deduction of operating expenses, but before a depreciation deduction of $80,000. Thus, taxable income is $20,000 ($100,000 – $80,000). Assuming that there is no mortgage on the building, all of the $100,000 is available for distribution. (Since the depreciation requires no cash outlay, it does not reduce the cash available for distribution.) Each investor receives $1,000. Taxable income being $20,000, only 20% ($20,000 ÷ $100,000) of the distribution is taxable. Thus, each investor reports as income only $200 of his or her $1,000 distribution; $800 is tax free.

2. Same facts as in Example 1, except that the building is mortgaged, and an annual amortization payment of $40,000 is being made. Consequently, only $60,000 is available for distribution, of which $20,000 is taxable. Each investor receives $600, of which $\frac{1}{3}$ ($20,000 ÷ $60,000), or $200, is taxed, and $400 is tax free. In other words, the $60,000 distribution is tax free to the extent that the depreciation deduction of $80,000 exceeds the amortization of $40,000—namely $40,000. If the amortization payment were increased to $50,000, only $30,000 of the distribution would be tax free ($80,000 – $50,000).

The advantages just discussed are available for investments made by you individually or in partnership with other associates. They are also available to investors in limited partnerships. However, before investing in a limited partnership, consider these disadvantages of limited partnerships:

1. Investors in limited partnerships are by law generally treated as receiving passive activity income or loss. Furthermore, as a limited partner, you may not take advantage of the $25,000 rental loss allowance, as you are not considered an "active participant"; *see 10.2.* In view of the passive activity rules, if you and others join together to buy rental property, you should not organize as a limited partnership if any losses are anticipated. Limited partnerships are advisable only if income is expected or where two or more investment activities will produce income and loss, which will offset each other.

2. Although limited partnerships are organized to prevent double taxation, which occurs in doing business as a corporation, there may be a danger that the partnership could be taxed as a corporation if its operations resemble those of a corporation.

3. Partnership operations do not provide for the diversification of investments or for the free transfer of individual interests. Investors may find it difficult to sell their interests because of

transferability restrictions and a lack of an open market for the sale of their interests. This liquidity problem may be overcome by buying interests sold through public exchanges. However, interests in a publicly traded master limited partnership (MLP) are subject to the passive activity restrictions and in some cases are taxed as corporations; *see 10.11*.

Real estate investment trusts (REITs). The tax treatment of real estate investment trusts resembles that of open-end mutual funds. Distributions generally are taxed to the investors in the trust as dividend income. Distributed long-term capital gains are reported by the investors as long-term gains; *see also 4.4*. If the trust operates at a loss, the loss may not be passed on to the investors.

REMICs. A real estate mortgage investment company (REMIC) holds a fixed pool of mortgages. Investors are treated as holding a regular or residual interest. A REMIC is not a taxable entity for federal income tax purposes. It is generally treated as a partnership, with the residual interest holders as partners.

Investors with regular REMIC interests are treated as holding debt obligations. Interest income is reported on Form 1099-INT and original issue discount (OID) on Form 1099-OID.

The net income of the REMIC, after payments to regular interest holders, is passed through to the holders of residual interests. On Schedule E, residual holders report the income or loss reported to them by the REMIC on Schedule Q of Form 1066.

Reviewing an investment offer. Consider the following pointers in reviewing an offering:

1. If the venture is constructing a development, discount projected income which may be eroded by increasing construction costs caused by inflation, material shortages, and labor disputes. Escalating costs not accounted for in long-term construction can jeopardize the project or income prospects. Adequate cash reserves should be available for emergencies.

2. Check the market conditions. Has there been overconstruction in the area? Is the area changing socially and economically?

3. Check the fees of managers. See that they are reasonable for your area. A promoter may conceal the amount of money he or she is drawing from the project. The promoter may be taking a real estate commission by having a commission paid to a company which he or she controls. A reliable promoter should disclose this fact and be willing to collect the commission only after the investors have recovered their capital. Also check the reasonableness of prepaid management fees and loan fees and whether or not the sale of property to the syndicate is from a corporation in which the syndicator has an interest. If there is such a sale, check its terms, price, interest rates, and whether there is any prepaid interest which may conceal a cash profit payout to the syndicator.

4. Check the experience and reliability of the manager.

31.2 When a Tenancy in Common Is a Partnership

In a tenancy in common, each tenant owns an undivided share in the property. Upon the death of a co-tenant, his or her interest passes to the heirs, not to the other co-tenants as in a joint tenancy.

Tenants in common may or may not be considered as holding the property in a partnership. The determination of whether they are partners affects whether a partnership return must be filed, whether the involuntary conversion election *(18.20)* and first-year expensing election *(42.3)* must be made by the partnership or the co-tenants, and the deductibility of property taxes beyond a co-tenant's percentage of ownership; *see 16.9*.

IRS regulations defining partnerships note that the co-ownership of property which is merely maintained, kept in repair, and rented or leased is not a partnership. This does not create a separate entity for federal tax purposes. *See* IRS Regulation Section 301.7701–1(a)(2).

31.3 Sales of Subdivided Land—Dealer or Investor?

An investor faces a degree of uncertainty in determining the tax treatment of sales of subdivided realty. In some situations, investor status may be preferred, and in others, dealer status.

Capital gain on sale. Investor status allows capital gain treatment. Capital losses may offset the gains. For capital gain, an investor generally has to show that his or her activities were not those of a dealer but were steps taken in a liquidation of the investment. To convince an IRS agent or a court of investment activity, this type of evidence may present a favorable argument for capital gain treatment:

• The property was bought as an investment, to build a residence, or received as a gift or inheritance.
• No substantial improvements were added to the tract.
• The property was subdivided to liquidate the investment.

- Sales came through unsolicited offers. There was no advertising or agents.
- Sales were infrequent.
- There were no previous activities as a real estate dealer.
- The seller was in a business unrelated to real estate.
- The property was held for a long period of time.
- Sales proceeds were invested in other investment property.

Section 1237 capital gain opportunity. Section 1237 is a limited tax provision that provides a capital gain opportunity for subdivided lots only if arbitrary holding period rules and restrictions on substantial improvements are complied with. For example, the lots must generally be held at least five years before sale unless they were inherited. If the lots were previously held for sale to customers, or if other lots are so held in the year of sale, Section 1237 does not apply. Furthermore, substantial improvements must not have been made to the lots. According to the IRS, a disqualifying substantial improvement is one that increases the value of the property by more than 10%. The IRS considers buildings, hard surface roads, or utilities, such as sewers, water, gas, or electric lines, as substantial improvements.

Installment sales. The distinction between an investor and dealer is significant if land is sold on the installment basis. Investor status is preferable if you want to elect the installment method. Dealers may not elect installment sale treatment; *see 5.25.*

Interest expense deductions. The distinction between an investor in land and a dealer is also important in the case of interest expenses. Dealer status is preferable here. Interest expenses incurred by an investor are subject to investment interest deduction limitations; *see* Chapter 15. On the other hand, interest expenses of a dealer in the course of business activities are fully deductible; *see* the Morley Example below.

EXAMPLE

Morley was interested in buying farm acreage to resell at a profit. Two and a half million dollars was set as the purchase price. To swing the deal, Morley borrowed $600,000. A short time later, his attempts to resell the property failed, and he allowed the property to be foreclosed. While he held the property he incurred interest costs of over $400,000, which he deducted. The IRS held the interest was not fully deductible. It claimed the interest was investment interest subject to investment interest restrictions. That is, the debt was incurred to purchase and carry investment property. The IRS position was based on the so-called "one-bite" rule, which holds that a taxpayer who engages in only one venture may not under any circumstances be held to be in a business as to that venture. Morley argued that he bought the property not as an investment property but as business property for immediate resale.

The Tax Court sided with Morley, holding that he held the acreage as ordinary business property. The court rejected the "one-bite" rule. The fact that he had not previously sold business property did not mean that he could not prove that he held acreage for resale. Here, he intended promptly to resell it, and the facts supported his intention.

Passive activity. Income from sales of lots is not considered passive activity income. Thus, losses from sales of land may offset salary and other investment income. If you hold rental property and also sell land, make sure that your accounts distinguish between and separate each type of income. This way income and losses from land sales will not be commingled with rent income subject to the passive activity restrictions of Chapter 10. Your activity in real property development counts towards qualifying you as a real estate professional who may deduct rental losses from nonpassive income if material participation tests are met; *see 10.3.*

31.4 Exchanging Real Estate Without Tax

You may trade real estate held for investment for other investment real estate and incur no immediate tax. The potential tax on the gain is postponed to the time you sell the new property for more than your basis. A tax-free exchange may also defer a potential tax due on gain from depreciation recapture and might be considered where the depreciable basis of a building has been substantially written off. Here, the building may be exchanged for other property which will give off larger tax deductions.

Fully tax-free exchanges. To transact a fully tax-free exchange, you must satisfy these conditions:

- The property traded must be solely for property of a "like kind." The words *like kind* are liberally interpreted. They refer to the nature or character of the property, not its grade, quality, or use. Some examples of like-kind exchanges are: farm or ranch for city property; unimproved land for improved real estate; rental house for a store building; and fee in business property for 30-year or more leasehold in the same type of property; *see 6.1.* You may not make a tax-free exchange of U.S. real estate for real estate in foreign countries.
- The property exchanged must have been held for productive use in your business or for investment and traded for property to be held for productive use in business or investment. Therefore, trades of property used, or to be used, for personal purposes, such as exchanging a residence for rental property, cannot receive tax-free treatment. Special rules, however, apply when you trade your residence for another home; *see* Chapter 29.
- The trade must generally occur within a 180-day period, and property identification must occur within 45 days of the first transfer; *see 6.4* for further details of this test.

A real estate dealer cannot transact a tax-free exchange of property held for sale to customers. Also, an exchange is not tax free if the property received is held for immediate resale.

Tax-free exchanges between related parties are subject to tax if either party disposes of the exchanged property within a two-year period; *see 6.5.*

Disadvantage of tax-free exchange. Although the postponement of tax from a tax-free exchange is equivalent to an interest-free loan from the government equal to the amount you would have owed in taxes had you sold the property, this tax advantage is offset by a disadvantage in the case of an exchange of depreciable real estate. You must carry over the basis of the old property to the new property; *see* the following Example.

> **EXAMPLE**
>
> You have property with a basis of $25,000, now valued at $50,000, that you exchange for another property worth $50,000. Your basis for depreciation for the new property is $25,000.
>
> If—instead of making an exchange—you sell the old property and use the proceeds to buy similarly valued property, the tax basis for depreciation is $50,000, giving you larger deductions than you are getting in the exchange transaction. If increased depreciation deductions are desirable, then it may pay to sell the property and purchase new property. Tax may be spread by transacting an installment sale. Project the tax consequences of a sale and an exchange and choose the one giving the greater overall tax benefits. You may find it preferable to sell the property and purchase new property on which MACRS may be claimed.

A tax-free exchange may be advantageous in the case of land. Land is not depreciable, but it may be exchanged for a depreciable rental building. The exchange is tax free and depreciation may be claimed on the building.

A tax-free exchange is not desirable if the transaction will result in a loss, since you may not deduct a loss in a tax-free exchange. To ensure the loss deduction, first sell the property, then buy new property with the proceeds.

Partially tax-free exchanges. Not all property exchanges are tax free. To be completely tax-free, the exchange must be solely an exchange of like-kind properties. If you receive "boot," such as cash or property that is not of like-kind, gain is taxed up to the amount of the boot.

If you trade mortgaged property, the mortgage released is treated as boot; *see 6.3.* When there are mortgages on both properties, the mortgages are netted. The party giving up the larger mortgage and getting the smaller mortgage treats the excess as boot. *See* the Example below and also the Example in *6.3,* which illustrates how to report an exchange on Form 8824.

If the amount of boot exceeds your actual gain, the entire gain is taxed; taxable boot cannot exceed the amount of your gain.

> **EXAMPLE**
>
> You own a small office building with a fair market value of $170,000, and an adjusted basis of $150,000. There is a $130,000 mortgage on the building. You exchange it for Low's building valued at $155,000, having a $120,000 mortgage, and for $5,000 in cash. You compute your gain in this way:

What you received		
Present value of Low's property		$155,000
Cash		5,000
Mortgage on building traded		130,000
Total received		$290,000
Less:		
Adjusted basis of building traded	$150,000	
Mortgage assumed by you	120,000	270,000
Actual gain on the exchange		$20,000

However, your actual gain of $20,000 is taxed only up to the amount of boot, $15,000.

Figuring boot		
Cash received		$5,000
Mortgage on building traded	$130,000	
Less: Mortgage assumed on Low's property	120,000	10,000
Gain taxed to the extent of boot		$15,000

31.5 Timing Your Real Property Sales

Generally, a taxable transaction occurs in the year in which title or possession to property passes to the buyer. By controlling the year title and possession pass, you may select the year in which to report profit or loss. For example, you intend to sell property this year, but you estimate that reporting the sale next year will incur less in taxes. You can postpone the transfer of title and possession to next year. Alternatively, you can transact an installment sale, giving title and possession this year but delaying the receipt of all or most of the sale proceeds until next year; *see 5.25.*

31.6 Cancellation of a Lease

Payments received by the tenant on the cancellation of a business lease held long term are treated as proceeds received in a Section 1231 transaction; *see 44.8.* Payments received by the tenant on cancellation of a lease on a personal residence or apartment are treated as proceeds of a capital asset transaction. Gain is long-term capital gain if the lease was held long term; losses are not deductible.

Payments received by a landlord from a tenant for cancelling a lease or modifying lease terms are reported as rental income when received; *see 9.1.*

Cancellation of a distributor's agreement is treated as a sale, if you made a substantial capital investment in the distributorship. For example, you own facilities for storage, transporting, processing, or dealing with the physical product covered by the franchise. If you have an office mainly for clerical work, or where you handle just a small part of the goods covered by the franchise, the cancellation is not treated as a sale. Your gain or loss is ordinary income or loss. If the cancellation is treated as a sale, the sale is subject to Section 1231 treatment; *see 44.8.*

31.7 Sale of an Option

The tax treatment of the sale of an option depends on the tax classification of the property to which the option relates.

If the option is for the purchase of property that would be a capital asset in your hands, profit on the sale of the option is treated as capital gain. A loss is treated as a capital loss if the property subject to the option was investment property; if the property was personal property, the loss is not deductible. Whether the gain or loss is long term or short term depends on your holding period.

EXAMPLES

1. You pay $500 for an option to purchase a house. After holding the option for five months, you sell the option for $750. Your profit of $250 is short-term capital gain.
2. The same facts as in Example 1 above, except that you sell the option for $300. The loss is not deductible because the option is related to a sale of a personal residence.

If the option is for a "Section 1231 asset" *(44.8),* gain or loss on the sale of the option is combined with other Section 1231 asset transactions to determine if there is capital gain or ordinary loss.

If the option relates to an ordinary income asset in your hands, then gain or loss would be ordinary income or loss.

If you fail to exercise an option and allow it to lapse, the option is considered to have been sold on the expiration date. Gain or loss is computed according to the rules just discussed.

The party granting the option realizes ordinary income on its expiration, regardless of the nature of the underlying property. If the option is exercised, the option payment is added to the selling price of the property when figuring gain or loss.

31.8 Granting of an Easement

Granting an easement presents a practical problem of determining whether all or part of the basis of the property is allocable to the easement proceeds. This requires an opinion as to whether the easement affects the entire property or just a part of the property. There is no hard and fast rule to determine whether an easement affects all or part of the property. The issue is factual. For example, an easement for electric lines will generally affect only the area over which the lines are suspended and for which the right of way is granted. In such a case, an allocation may be required; *see* Example 1 below. If the entire property is affected, no allocation is required and the proceeds reduce the basis of the property. If only part of the property is affected, then the proceeds are applied to the cost allocated to the area affected by the easement. If the proceeds exceed the amount allocated to basis, a gain is realized. Capital gain treatment generally applies to grants of easements. The granting of a perpetual easement which requires you to give up all or substantially all of a beneficial use of the area affected by the easement is treated as a sale. The contribution to a government body of a scenic easement in perpetuity is a charitable contribution, not a sale.

In reviewing an easement, the IRS will generally try to find grounds for making an allocation, especially where the allocation will result in a taxable gain. In opposition, a property owner will generally argue that the easement affects the entire property or that it is impossible to make an allocation because of the nature of the easement or the particular nature of the property. If he or she can sustain an argument, the proceeds for granting the easement reduce the basis of the entire property; *see* Examples 1–3 below.

Condemnation. If you realize a gain on a grant of an easement under a condemnation or threat of condemnation, you may defer tax by investing in replacement property; *see* 18.18.

EXAMPLES

1. The owner of a 600-acre farm was paid $5,000 by a power company for the right to put up poles and power lines. The right of way covered 20 acres along one boundary which the owner continued to farm. The cost basis of the farm was $60,000, or $100 an acre. The IRS ruled that he had to allocate the basis. At $100 an acre, the allocated basis for the 20 acres was $2,000. Thus, a gain of $3,000 was realized ($5,000 – $2,000).

2. The owner of a tract of unimproved land gave a state highway department a perpetual easement affecting only part of the land. He wanted to treat the payment as a reduction of the basis of the entire tract and so report no gain. The IRS ruled that he had to allocate basis to the portion affected by the road.

3. The owner of farmland gave a transmission company a 50-foot right of way for an underground pipeline that did not interfere with farming. During construction, the right of way was 150 feet. The owner received payments for damages covering loss of rental income during construction and for the 50-foot permanent right of way. The IRS ruled that the damage payment was taxable as ordinary income; the payment for the right of way was a taxable gain to the extent that it exceeded the basis allocated to the acreage within the 50-foot strip.

Release of a restrictive covenant. A payment received for a release of a restrictive covenant is treated as a capital gain if the release involves property held for investment.

EXAMPLE

You sell several acres of land held for investment to a construction company subject to a covenant that restricts construction to residential dwellings. Later, the company wants to erect structures other than individual homes and pays you for the release of the restrictive covenant in the deed. You realize capital gain on receipt of the payment. The restrictive covenant is a property interest and a capital asset in your hands.

31.9 Special Tax Credits for Real Estate Investments

To encourage certain real estate investments, the tax law offers the following tax credits:

Low-income housing credit for buildings placed in service after 1986. Qualifying investors are allowed to claim a tax credit in annual installments over 10 years for qualifying newly constructed low-income housing and also to certain existing structures that are substantially rehabilitated. The amount of the credit depends on whether the building is new and whether federal subsidies are received. To claim the credit, you, as the building owner, must receive a certification from an authorized housing credit agency. The agency allocates a credit to you on Form 8609, which you use to claim the credit on Form 8586. You must attach to your return Form 8586, and, in some cases, also Form 8609 and Schedule A, Form 8609.

Rehabilitation credit for pre-1936 buildings or certified historic structures. On Form 3468, you may claim a 10% tax credit for rehabilitating pre-1936 buildings or a 20% credit for rehabilitating certified historic structures. For both types of rehabilitation credits, you must generally incur rehabilitation expenses of $5,000 or your adjusted basis in the building, whichever is greater.

Certified historic structure. A certified historic structure may be used for residential or non-residential purposes. The National Park Service must certify that a planned rehabilitation is in keeping with the building's historic status designation for the credit to be available.

In one case, a developer who rehabilitated a certified historic structure and donated a conservation easement to a historic society in the same year was required to base the credit computation on the rehabilitation expenses minus the charitable deduction claimed. If the donation had been made in a later year, a portion of the original credit claimed would be subject to recapture.

Pre-1936 buildings. The 10% credit for pre-1936 buildings applies only to nonresidential property. A substantial portion of the building's original structure must be retained after the rehabilitation. At least 75% of the external walls must be intact, with at least 50% kept as external walls. At least 75% of the existing internal structural framework must be kept in place. In one case, the IRS and Tax Court interpreted the 75% external wall test as requiring that at least 75% of the existing external walls be retained in the same place, thereby denying the credit for a pre-1936 building that was relocated and then renovated. However, a federal appeals court disagreed, holding that there is no relocation restriction; the credit is allowed provided at least 75% of the external walls are retained as such after the renovation.

For further details and credit conditions concerning the two types of rehabilitation credits, *see* Form 3468.

Tax credit limitations. Tax credits for low-income housing and rehabilitating historic or pre-1936 buildings may be limited by passive activity restrictions on Form 8582-CR (Chapter 10) and by tax liability limits for the general business credit (Chapter 40).

Foreclosures and Abandonments of Mortgaged Property

31.10 Foreclosures and Voluntary Conveyances to Creditors

If you are unable to meet payments on a debt secured by property, the creditor may foreclose on the property. A foreclosure sale or a voluntary conveyance of the property to the creditor is treated as a sale of the property. If you are personally liable on the debt, and if the value of the property is less than the cancelled debt, you also generally realize ordinary income on the debt cancellation.

Figuring gain or loss. Gain or loss is the difference between your adjusted basis in the property and the amount realized. Determining the amount realized depends on your liability for the debt:

If you are *not* personally liable on the debt, the amount realized includes the full amount of the cancelled debt, regardless of the value of the property.

If you are personally liable, the amount realized includes the portion of the cancelled debt that equals the fair market value of the property. If the fair market value of the property is less than the debt, the foreclosure or voluntary conveyance back to the creditor is treated as two separate transactions:

1. A sale of property. Gain or loss is the difference between adjusted basis and the amount realized, including the cancelled debt up to the fair market value of the property.

2. The receipt of ordinary income upon the cancellation of the debt for less than the face amount of the debt. You generally have cancellation of debt income equal to the excess of the cancelled debt over the fair market value of the property. However, this income may not be taxable, if you come within the exclusion rules of *11.8,* such as being insolvent at the time of the foreclosure. *See also 31.11* for the exclusion on restructurings of business real property debt.

EXAMPLES

1. Jones could not meet the mortgage payments on a condominium which cost him $85,000. He had paid cash of $20,000 and taken a mortgage loan of $65,000 on which he was personally liable. When the remaining balance of the loan was $62,000, he defaulted, and the bank accepted his voluntary conveyance of the unit, canceling the loan. Similar units at the time were selling for $60,000. On the transaction, Jones incurred a loss of $25,000: the difference between his adjusted basis of $85,000 and the fair market value of the unit of $60,000. The loss is not deductible because the unit was held for personal purposes. Jones also recognizes income on the cancellation of the loan because the amount of the debt exceeded the fair market value of the unit by $2,000. This amount is taxable, unless Jones can show he was insolvent at the time of the transfer to the bank; *see 11.8.*

2. Brown invested in a vacant lot. He put down cash of $10,000 and assumed a mortgage of $20,000. When he could not make payments on the mortgage, the bank foreclosed. The net proceeds from the foreclosure sale were $32,000. Brown received $12,000 and realized a capital gain of $2,000 (the difference between his adjusted basis of $30,000 and the amount realized of $32,000). There is no income from cancellation of indebtedness because the debt was less than the value of the property.

Foreclosure proceeds less than outstanding mortgage. Where a foreclosure sale does not cancel the mortgage debt, there is a conflict of opinion on how to compute the amount realized. Take this case:

In 1982, Aizawa bought rental property for $120,000, paying $30,000 down and giving the seller a $90,000 recourse mortgage note, payable in five years. The Aizawas made timely monthly interest payments but failed to pay off the principal at the end of the fifth year. In 1987, the sellers sued and got a judgment of $133,507 for the original principal due of $90,000, attorneys' fees of $25,000, and extra interest charges. Then, at a foreclosure sale, the sellers bought back the property for $72,700. The judgment and foreclosure sale left a deficiency judgment of $60,807.

The Aizawas deducted a $70,898 loss. They claimed the deficiency judgment of $60,807 should be deducted from the mortgage of $90,000, leaving an amount realized of $29,193. The difference between this amount and the $100,091 undepreciated basis of the property gave them a $70,898 loss. The IRS claimed that the amount realized was $90,000, the amount of the mortgage principal, so that the loss was only $10,091 ($100,091 less $90,000).

The Tax Court disagreed with both sides. The court held that the amount realized was the $72,700 proceeds from the foreclosure sale, so that a loss of $27,391 ($100,091 less $72,700) was incurred. The Aizawas' approach is wrong; they reduced the amount realized by the deficiency award they had not paid. The IRS approach is wrong; it included in the amount realized part of the mortgage debt which the Aizawas still owed.

The court recognized that its approach gave the Aizawas an additional loss of $17,300 ($90,000 less $72,700) based on a debt they might not repay. However, this advantage may be eliminated by later events. If they pay off the remaining debt, they may not deduct any additional loss. If they are discharged from paying the balance of the debt, they may be required to report income on the discharge if they are solvent.

31.11 Restructuring Mortgage Debt

Rather than foreclose on a mortgage, a lender (mortgagee) may be willing to restructure the mortgage debt by canceling either all or part of the debt. As a borrower (mortgagor), do not overlook the tax consequences of the new debt arrangement. A debt cancellation or reduction is taxable unless it fits within specific exceptions, such as insolvency or bankruptcy. As discussed at *11.8,* there is no tax if the debt is restructured by the seller of the property or where a debt is reduced by a third-party lender and you are either insolvent, bankrupt, or are a qualifying farmer. These rules apply

Caution

Form 1099-A Notifies IRS

If your mortgaged property is foreclosed or repossessed, and the bank or other lender reacquires it, or if the lender knows that you have abandoned the property, you should receive from the lender Form 1099-A, which indicates foreclosure proceeds, the amount of your debt, and whether you were personally liable. The IRS may compare its copy of Form 1099-A with your return to check whether you have reported income from the foreclosure or abandonment.

If the lender also cancels your debt of $600 or more, you may instead receive Form 1099-C, on which the information about the foreclosure or repossession will be included.

also to a restructuring of a nonrecourse debt on which you are not personally liable; *see* the Jones Example below, which shows the IRS approach to figuring insolvency upon a debt cancellation.

In the case of partnership property, tax consequences of the restructuring of a third-party loan are determined at the partner level. This means that if you are a partner and are solvent (*11.8*) you may not avoid tax on the transaction, even if the partnership is insolvent.

Filing Tip

Reporting a Foreclosure or Voluntary Conveyance
You report a foreclosure sale or voluntary conveyance to a creditor on Schedule D if the property was held for personal or investment purposes. However, if a gain or loss was realized on a foreclosure (or voluntary reconveyance) of your principal residence, the "sale" is reported on Form 2119.

Foreclosures and reconveyances of business assets are reported on Form 4797.

If income from cancellation of indebtness is realized and it is not excludable under the rules of *11.8*, you report the taxable amount on Line 21, Form 1040.

EXAMPLE

In 1995, Jones borrowed $1,000,000 from Chester and signed a note payable for $1,000,000. Jones was not personally liable on the note, which was secured by an office building valued at $1,000,000 that he bought from Baker with the proceeds of Chester's loan. In 1995, when the value of the building declined to $800,000, Chester agreed to reduce the principal of the loan to $825,000. At the time, Jones held other assets valued at $100,000 and owed another person $50,000. In 1996, Jones realized income of $175,000 on the reduction of the debt, but he can avoid tax to the extent he is insolvent.

To determine the extent of Jones's insolvency, the IRS compares Jones's assets and liabilities immediately before the discharge. According to the IRS, his assets total $900,000: the building valued at $800,000 plus other assets of $100,000. His liabilities total $1,025,000: the debt of $50,000 plus the liability on the note, which the IRS considers to be $975,000, equal to the $800,000 value of the building and the $175,000 discharged debt. The difference between the assets of $900,000 and liabilities of $1,025,000 is $125,000, the amount by which Jones is insolvent. As Jones is insolvent by $125,000, only $50,000 of the $175,000 discharged debt is treated as taxable income.

Restructuring debt on business real estate. A solvent taxpayer may avoid tax on a restructuring of qualifying business real estate debt (*11.8*) by electing to reduce the basis of depreciable real property by the amount of the tax-free debt discharge. The election to reduce basis is made on Form 982.

EXAMPLE

On July 1, 1996, Grant, who is solvent, owns a building worth $150,000 used in his business. It is subject to a first mortgage of $110,000 and a second mortgage of $90,000. Grant's basis in the building is $120,000. The second mortgagee agrees to reduce the second mortgage to $30,000. This results in debt discharge of $60,000 ($90,000 – $30,000). The $60,000 is considered debt discharge income. But Grant may elect to exclude $50,000. He reports the remaining $10,000 of discharged debt as taxable income. The exclusion limit is calculated as follows:

2nd mortgage before discharge		$90,000
Less: Fair market value of building	$150,000	
Less: First mortgage	110,000	40,000
Excludable amount		$50,000

On Form 982, Grant may elect to exclude $50,000 from tax because the basis of the building is sufficient to absorb a basis reduction of $50,000.

31.12 Abandonments

On an abandonment of business or investment property, you may claim an ordinary loss for the property's adjusted basis (when abandoned) on Form 4797. However, if the abandoned property is later foreclosed or repossessed, you may realize a gain or loss under the rules of *31.10* for foreclosures or voluntary conveyances to creditors. For example, if an abandonment loss for mortgaged property is claimed in 1996 but in 1997 the property is foreclosed upon by the lender, all or part of the cancelled debt will be treated as an amount realized by you on a sale in 1997. The amount realized depends on whether you were personally liable and the value of the property. If personally liable, you may also realize ordinary income from cancellation of the debt; *see 31.10*.

Abandoning a partnership interest. Where real estate values have sharply declined, partnerships may be holding realty subject to mortgage debt that exceeds the current value of the property. Some investors in such partnerships have claimed that they can abandon their partnership interests and claim abandonment losses. In one case, an investor in a partnership holding land in Houston, Texas, argued that he abandoned his partnership interest by making an abandonment declaration at a meeting of partners, and also declaring that he would make no further payments.

He offered his interest to the others, who refused his offer. The IRS held that he failed to prove abandonment of his partnership interest or that the partnership abandoned the land. The Tax Court sided with the IRS, emphasizing his failure to show that the partnership abandoned the land. However, the appeals court for the Fifth Circuit reversed and allowed the abandonment loss. It held that the emphasis should be on the partner's actions, not the actions of the partnership. Although neither state law nor the IRS regulations described how a partnership interest is to be abandoned, the appeals court held that the partner's acts and declaration were sufficient to effect an abandonment of his partnership interest. The appeals court also held that the loss on the partnership interest could have been sustained on the basis of the worthlessness of his interest. The partnership was insolvent beyond hope of rehabilitation: (1) the partnership's only asset was land with a fair market value less than the mortgage debt; (2) the partnership had no source of income; and (3) the partners refused to contribute more funds to keep the partnership afloat.

In a subsequent case, the Tax Court held that a doctor had abandoned a movie production partnership interest when he refused to advance any more money or to participate in the venture because he disapproved of the content of the film being produced and feared it might jeopardize his position at a hospital operated by a religious organization. Also, the limited partners had voted to dissolve.

Note: If, after the year the abandoned loss is claimed, the partnership's mortgaged holdings are foreclosed upon or reconveyed to the lender, each partner's share of the cancelled debt may be treated as an amount realized on a sale, or as ordinary cancellation of debt income; *see 31.10.*

31.13 Seller's Repossession After Buyer's Default on Mortgage

When you, as a seller, repossess realty on the buyer's default of a debt which the realty secures, you may realize gain or loss. (If the realty was a personal residence, the loss is not deductible.) A debt is secured by real property whenever you have the right to take title or possession or both in the event the buyer defaults on his or her obligation under the contract.

Figuring gain on the repossession. Gain on the repossession is the excess of: (1) payments received on the original sales contract prior to and on the repossession, including payments made by the buyer for your benefit to another party; over (2) the amount of taxable gain previously reported prior to the repossession.

Gain computed under these two steps may not be fully taxable. Taxable gain is limited to the amount of original profit less gain on the sale already reported as income for periods prior to the repossession and less your repossession costs.

The limitation on gain does not apply if the selling price cannot be computed at the time of sale as, for example, where the selling price is stated as a percentage of the profits to be realized from the development of the property sold.

EXAMPLE

Assume you sell land for $25,000. You take a $5,000 down payment plus a $20,000 mortgage, secured by the property, from the buyer, with principal payable at the rate of $4,000 annually. The adjusted basis of the land was $20,000 and you elected to report the transaction on the installment basis. Your gross profit percentage is 20% ($5,000 profit over $25,000 selling price). In the year of sale, you include $1,000 in your income on the installment basis (20% of $5,000 down payment). The next year you reported profit of $800 (20% of $4,000 annual installment). In the third year, the buyer defaults, and you repossess the property. The amount of gain on repossession is computed as follows:

1. Compute gain:
   Amount of money received
   ($5,000 *plus* $4,000) $9,000
      Less: Amount of gain taxed in prior
      years ($1,000 *plus* $800)   1,800
   Gain $7,200

2. Compute limit on taxable gain, assuming cost of repossession is $500:
   Original profit $5,000
      Less:
        Gain reported as income $1,800
        Cost of repossession   500   2,300
   Taxable gain on repossession $2,700

These rules do not affect the character of the gain. Thus, if you repossess property as a dealer, the gain is subject to ordinary income rates. If you, as an investor, repossess a tract originally held long term whose gain was reported on the installment method, the gain is capital gain.

The basis of repossessed property. It is the adjusted basis of the debt (face value of the debt less the unreported profits) secured by the property, figured as of the date of repossession, increased by (1) the taxable gain on repossession, *and* (2) the legal fees and other repossession costs you paid.

EXAMPLE

Same facts as in the previous Example. The basis of the repossessed property is computed as follows:

1. Face value of debt ($20,000 note *less* $4,000 payment)		$16,000
2. *Less:* Unreported profit (20% of the $16,000 still due on the note)		3,200
3. Adjusted basis at date of repossession		$12,800
4. *Plus:* Gain on repossession	$2,700	
Cost of repossession	500	3,200
5. Basis of repossessed property		$16,000

If you treated the debt as having become worthless or partially worthless before repossession, you are considered to receive, upon the repossession of the property securing the debt, an amount equal to the amount of the debt treated as worthless. You report as income the amount of any prior bad debt deduction and increase the basis of the debt by an amount equal to the amount reported as income.

If your debt is not fully discharged as a result of the repossession, the basis of the undischarged debt is zero. No loss may be claimed if the obligations subsequently become worthless. This rule applies to undischarged debts on the original obligation of the purchaser, a substituted obligation of the purchaser, a deficiency judgment entered in a court of law into which the purchaser's obligation was merged, and any other obligations arising from the transaction.

The repossession rules do not apply if you repurchase the property by paying the buyer a sum in addition to the discharge of the debt, unless the repurchase and payment was provided for in the original sale contract, or the buyer has defaulted on his or her obligation, or default is imminent.

Personal residence. Special rules apply to repossessions and resales of a personal residence if: (1) at least some of the gain on the original sale was not taxed because you made an election to avoid tax under the exclusion for those age 55 or older or you deferred gain on the purchase of a new residence, or avoided tax on gain applying the new law exclusion discussed in Chapter 29; and (2) within a year after the repossession you resell the property.

The original sale and resale is treated as one transaction. You refigure the amount realized on the sale. You combine the selling price of the resale with the selling price of the original sale. From this total, you subtract selling expenses for both sales, the part of the original installment obligation that remains unpaid at the time of repossession, and repossession costs. The net is the amount realized on the combined sale-resale. Subtracting basis in the home from the amount realized gives the gain on the combined sale-resale before taking into account the exclusion or deferral rules.

EXAMPLE

In 1996, you, at age 60, sell a house for $250,000. You received $50,000 cash and took back a purchase money mortgage of $200,000. Selling expenses were $3,000; the adjusted basis of the house was $167,000. You realized a profit of $80,000:

Amount realized ($250,000 – $3,000)	$247,000
Less: Adjusted basis	167,000
Gain	$ 80,000

You elected to avoid tax by claiming the exclusion of for being 55 or older.

In 1997, the buyer defaulted and you repossessed the house and sold it for $300,000, incurring selling expenses of $5,000 and repossession costs of $2,000. The buyer still owed you $200,000 on his installment note. You have a $48,000 taxable gain on the combined sale-resale as follows:

Selling price on resale		$300,000
Selling price on original sale		250,000
Total selling price		$550,000
Less:		
Unpaid buyer's note	$200,000	
Repossession costs	2,000	
Combined selling expenses		
($3,000 + $5,000)	8,000	210,000
Amount realized		$340,000
Less: basis		167,000
Gain on sale-resale		$173,000
Less: $125,000 exclusion		125,000
Taxable gain		$ 48,000

31.14 Foreclosure on Mortgages Other Than Purchase Money

If you, as a mortgagee (lender), bid in on a foreclosure sale to pay off a mortgage that is *not a purchase money mortgage,* your actual financial loss is the difference between the unpaid mortgage debt and the value of the property. For tax purposes, however, you may realize a capital gain or loss and a bad debt loss which are reportable *in the year of the foreclosure sale.*

Your bid is treated as consisting of two distinct transactions:

1. The repayment of your loan. To determine whether this results in a bad debt, the bid price is matched against the face amount of the mortgage.

2. A taxable exchange of your mortgage note for the foreclosed property, which may result in a capital gain or loss. This is determined by matching the bid price against the fair market value of the property.

EXAMPLES

1. *Mortgagee's bid less than market value.* You hold a $40,000 mortgage on property having a fair market value of $30,000. You bid on the property at the foreclosure sale at $28,000. The expenses of the sale are $2,000, reducing the bid price to $26,000. The mortgagor is insolvent, so you have a bad debt loss of $14,000 ($40,000 – $26,000). You also have a $4,000 capital gain (the fair market value of the property of $30,000 – $26,000).

2. *Mortgagee's bid equal to market value.* Suppose your bid was $32,000, and had $2,000 in expenses. The difference between the net bid price of $30,000 and the mortgage of $40,000 is $10,000. As the mortgagor is insolvent, there is a bad debt loss of $10,000. Since the net bid price equals the fair market value, there is neither capital gain nor loss.

3. *Mortgagee's bid greater than market value.* Suppose your bid was $36,000 and had $2,000 in expenses. Your bad debt deduction is $6,000—the difference between the mortgage debt of $40,000 and the net bid price of $34,000. You also had a capital loss of $4,000 (the difference between the net bid price of $34,000 and the fair market value of $30,000).

Where the bid price equals the mortgage debt plus unreported but accrued interest, you report the interest as income. But where the accrued interest has been reported, the unpaid amount is added to the collection expenses.

Preserve evidence of the property's fair market value. At a later date, the IRS may claim that the property was worth more than your bid and may tax you for the difference. Furthermore, be prepared to prove the worthlessness of the debt in order to support the bad debt deduction.

Voluntary conveyance.   Instead of forcing you to foreclose, the mortgagor may voluntarily convey the property to you in consideration for your canceling the mortgage debt. Your loss is the amount by which the mortgage debt plus accrued interest exceeds the fair market value of the property. If, however, the fair market value exceeds the mortgage debt plus accrued interest, the difference is taxable gain. The gain or loss is reportable in the year you receive the property. Your basis in the property is its fair market value when you receive it.

31.15 Foreclosure Sale to Third Party

When a third party buys the property in a foreclosure, the mortgagee receives the purchase price to apply against the mortgage debt. If it is less than the debt, the mortgagee may proceed against the mortgagor for the difference. Foreclosure expenses are treated as offsets against the foreclosure proceeds and increase the bad debt loss.

You deduct your loss as a bad debt. The law distinguishes between two types of bad debt deductions: business bad debts and nonbusiness bad debts. A business bad debt is fully deductible. A nonbusiness bad debt is a short-term capital loss that can be offset only against capital gains, plus a limited amount of ordinary income (5.9). In addition, you may deduct a partially worthless business bad debt, but you may not deduct a partially worthless nonbusiness bad debt. Remember this distinction if you are thinking of forgiving part of the mortgage debt as a settlement. If the debt is a nonbusiness bad debt, you will not be able to take a deduction until the entire debt proves to be worthless. But whether you are deducting a business or a nonbusiness bad debt, your deduction will be allowed only if you show the debt to be uncollectible—for example, because a deficiency judgment is worthless or because the mortgagor is declared bankrupt.

EXAMPLE

You hold a $30,000 note and mortgage which are in default. You foreclose, and a third party buys the property for $20,000. Foreclosure expenses amount to $2,000. The deficiency is uncollectible. Your $12,000 loss is figured as follows:

Unpaid mortgage debt		$30,000
Foreclosure proceeds	$20,000	
Less: Expenses	2,000	
Net proceeds		18,000
Bad debt loss		$12,000

31.16 Transferring Mortgaged Realty

Mortgaging realty that has appreciated in value is one way of realizing cash on the appreciation without current tax consequences. The receipt of cash by mortgaging the property is not taxed; tax will generally be imposed only when the property is sold. However, there is a possible tax where the mortgage exceeds the adjusted basis of the property and the property is given away or transferred to a controlled corporation. Where the property is transferred to a controlled corporation, the excess is taxable gain. Further, if the IRS successfully charges that the transfer is part of a tax avoidance scheme, the taxable gain may be as high as the amount of the mortgage liability.

Gifts. The IRS holds that a gift of mortgaged property results in taxable income to the donor to the extent that the mortgage liability exceeds the donor's basis.

Chapter 32

Tax Pointers for Investors in Mutual Funds

Mutual-fund investments relieve you of the responsibility of making daily investment decisions for securities actively traded or affected by changing market conditions.

Mutual funds are either closed or open end.

Closed-end funds. A closed-end fund is a regular corporation that invests in securities but has issued a fixed number of shares that trade publicly like shares of any other company listed on the stock exchange. The daily price of its shares may be below or above the net value of its investment portfolio. Dividend income from a closed-end company is reported as regular dividends (*see* Chapter 4) and a sale of stock is treated as a regular sale of stock, as explained in Chapter 5.

Open-end funds. These are more popular than closed-end funds. The value and number of shares in the portfolio of the fund change daily on the purchase and redemption of shares. The more complicated tax treatment of open-end funds is discussed in this chapter.

32.1 Investing in Mutual Funds

A mutual fund is a professionally managed pool of individual investors' contributions invested in a variety of securities. Funds are designed and marketed to meet different investor objectives. Money-market mutual funds allow investors to earn a return based on swings in the short-term money market. Income funds invest in either stocks paying high current dividends or bonds paying interest. Growth funds invest in securities that are expected to appreciate over the long term. Some aggressive growth funds invest in small, developing companies with short track records. Other growth funds invest primarily in established firms. International funds invest in stocks of companies outside the United States. Sector funds specialize in specific industries, such as utilities, gold, or high technology companies. Balanced funds try to promote long-term growth by maintaining a mix of investments in bonds and stocks. Increasingly popular index funds buy the stocks that constitute a broad-based index to replicate the index's performance.

With research, try to find a fund that matches your investment objectives. Check the fund's performance over a substantial period of from five to 10 years. Keep in mind that yields fluctuate and are not guaranteed. In funds other than money markets (32.2), the value per share also fluctuates. Gain or loss may be realized when you redeem shares in growth or income mutual funds. Also consider the rate at which a fund turns over its assets. A fund with a high turnover rate will realize frequent capital gains and losses, increasing the likelihood that capital gain distributions will be short term rather than long term. Short-term capital gain distributions are taxed as ordinary income dividends. Long-term capital gain distributions are subject to the rules for long-term capital gains.

Compare sales charges and redemption fees, if any, before you buy. No-load funds do not have a sales charge. Financial sections of major newspapers list prices of mutual-fund offerings. A no-load fund has the same purchase price and redemption price for fund shares; different prices for purchases and redemptions indicate a sales charge. Funds available through a broker may have a charge for commissions.

32.2 Money-Market Mutual Funds

A money-market mutual-fund portfolio will generally include U.S. government obligations, CDs of major commercial banks, bankers acceptances, and commercial paper of prime-rated firms. Investors should check each fund's charges because they differ.

Yields, which change daily, are not guaranteed. Investments are not federally insured. Some state-chartered banks, however, offer money-market funds insured by a state insurance fund.

Gains and losses are generally not realized in money-market funds; shares are redeemed for exactly what you paid (usually $1 per share) plus accrued interest. Some funds offer limited check-writing privileges.

Tax-free money funds. These funds invest in short-term notes of state and local governments issued in anticipation of tax receipts, bond sales, and other revenues, and in "project notes" issued by local entities and backed by the federal government. The dividends paid by these funds is exempt from federal tax. The yields are lower than those of taxable funds, and are attractive only if they provide greater after-tax returns than similar taxable funds. These funds may offer check-writing privileges.

Investors in certain states may be able to invest in funds that pay dividends that are exempt from state and local, as well as federal, tax.

A tax-free interest return may also be available through unit investment trusts holding tax-exempt state and municipal bonds. These trusts mature in a specified number of years or as called.

32.3 Timing Your Investment

You may buy a tax liability if you invest in a mutual fund which has already realized significant capital gains during the year. If you invest near the end of the year and the fund shortly thereafter makes a large year-end capital gain distribution, you will in effect have to pay tax on the return of your recently invested money.

On the "record date" for determining which shareholders receive the fund's dividends and capital gain distributions, the value of the fund's shares drops by the amount of the distributions. If you buy just before that, the higher cost for your shares will be offset by the distributions you receive, but you will have to pay tax on the distributions. On the other hand, because you paid the higher pre-distribution price, your higher basis will reduce any capital gain on a later sale, or increase any capital loss.

Planning Reminder

Compare Yields

To compare fund yields, check newspaper financial sections that periodically list the yields of both taxable and tax-exempt money-market mutual funds. To increase yields, some funds temporarily waive a portion of fees and absorb expenses. Also check minimum investment requirements; some top-yielding funds require a substantial minimum balance that may be as high as $25,000.

If you want to limit your current tax and forego the basis increase, postpone your investment until after the record date for distributions. By that time, the value per share which determines the price will have been reduced by the capital gain distribution. Before investing, you may be able to find out from the fund when distributions for the year are expected; investment publications showing the distribution dates for the previous year also may be consulted.

32.4 Reinvestment Plans

Funds allow you to reinvest dividends and capital gain distributions from the fund in new fund shares instead of receiving cash. You report such distributions as if you received them in cash. Form 1099-DIV sent to you by a fund reports the gross amount of taxable distributions that you must report on Schedule B. A key to Form 1099-DIV is on the next page.

Keep track of reinvested distributions. If you reinvest your mutual-fund distributions instead of taking them in cash, keep a record of the distributions and of the shares purchased with the reinvestment. The reinvested distributions are considered your cost basis for the acquired shares. You need a record of reinvestments to figure your cost when you sell your shares; *see 32.9* for calculating gain on the sale of mutual-fund shares.

32.5 Reporting Mutual-Fund Distributions

Mutual-fund distributions are reported to you and the IRS by the fund on Form 1099-DIV or substitute statement. Distributions which you reinvested to acquire additional shares are reported and taxed in the same way as distributions which are actually paid out to you.

The Form 1099-DIV from your fund may include several types of dividend and other distributions. The gross amount shown in Box 1a must be reported on your return. The Box 1a total includes ordinary dividends from Box 1b, capital gain distributions from Box 1c, nontaxable return of capital distributions from Box 1d, and in the case of a non-publicly offered fund, your share of fund expenses from Box 1e. *Dividends that you reinvested instead of receiving in cash are included in Box 1a.*

A guide to the different distributions, and how you report them, is shown in the "Key to Reporting Mutual-Fund Distributions" on the next page.

32.6 Tax-Exempt Bond Funds

Dividend income from a tax-exempt bond fund is generally tax free, but capital gain distributions are taxable. Exempt dividends are not shown by the fund on 1099-DIV, but are reported separately by the fund. You report exempt interest on Line 8b of Form 1040. The amount on Line 8b is not taxable, but if you receive Social Security benefits, the amount may affect the amount of taxable benefits; *see 34.3.*

Capital gain distributions are shown on Form 1099-DIV and must be reported on your return.

When you redeem your shares in a tax-exempt bond fund or exchange the fund shares for other shares in a different fund, you realize taxable capital gain or deductible loss.

If you received exempt-interest dividends on mutual-fund shares held for six months or less and sold those shares at a loss, the amount of your loss is reduced by the exempt interest dividend. To reflect this adjustment, you increase the sales price reported on line 1, column (d) of Schedule D by the loss not allowed. Report the balance as a short-term capital loss.

 Filing Instruction

Year-end Dividends

Mutual funds sometimes declare dividends at the end of a calendar year but do not pay them until January of the following year. If the dividend is declared in October, November, or December, and paid in the following January, the fund will report the distribution as taxable in the year it is declared.

> **EXAMPLE**
> In January 1997, you bought a mutual-fund share for $40. In February 1997, the mutual fund paid a $5 dividend from tax-exempt interest, which is not taxable to you. In March 1996, you sold the share for $34. If it were not for the tax-exempt dividend, your loss would be $6 ($40 – 34). However, you may deduct only $1, the part of the loss that exceeds the exempt-interest dividend ($6 – 5). On Schedule D, column (d), increase the sales price from $34 to $39 (the $5 nondeductible). You may deduct $1 as a short-term capital loss.

32.7 Fund Expenses

If you own shares in a *publicly offered* mutual fund, you do not pay 1996 tax on your share of the fund expenses. There should be no entry in Box 1e of the Form 1099-DIV. However, expenses of a *non-publicly offered* fund are included in Box 1e of Form 1099-DIV and must be reported as a taxable dividend, even though the amount has not actually been distributed to you. An offsetting deduction may be claimed on Schedule A as a miscellaneous itemized deduction, subject to the 2% adjusted gross income floor; *see 19.24.*

Key To Reporting Mutual-Fund Distributions

Type of Distribution	Shown by the Fund in	Where You Report
Gross dividends. (This amount includes ordinary dividends, capital gain distributions, and return of capital distributions.)	Box 1a, Form 1099-DIV	If the total dividends received by you from all of your investments is $400 or less, ignore this box and enter information from boxes 1b to 1e. If your total dividends exceed $400, enter this amount on Schedule B, Line 5, or Line 9 of Form 1040A.
Ordinary dividends. (This includes your share of fund earnings from dividends, interest, and short-term gains.)	Box 1b, Form 1099-DIV	If *all* of your mutual-fund distributions from Forms 1099-DIV are ordinary dividends, you may report them on either Form 1040 or Form 1040A. If this total plus your other dividends from all sources is $400 or less, enter them on Line 9 of Form 1040 or Line 9 of Form 1040A. If more than $400, you should have already entered the amount on Line 5, Schedule B. *Note:* If you also have capital gain or nontaxable distributions from Form 1099-DIV, you may not use Form 1040A to report the ordinary dividends; all of your mutual-fund distributions must be reported on Form 1040 and, if necessary, Schedule B.
Capital gain distributions. (This represents your share of long-term gains realized by a fund on sales made from its portfolio.)	Box 1c, Form 1099-DIV	Capital gain distributions, if any, are included in the amount on Line 5 of Schedule B if the gross distributions from all mutual-funds plus your other dividends exceed $400. On Line 7 of Schedule B, the capital gain distributions are subtracted from the Line 6 total. Also, enter the capital gain distributions as long-term capital gain on Schedule D. Follow the instructions to Schedule B and Schedule D.
Return of capital distributions (nontaxable)	Box 1d, 1099-DIV	Return of capital distributions if any are included on Line 5 of Schedule B and then subtracted from the other dividends on Line 8. Thus, the return of capital distributions is not included in taxable income. However, if your basis for your shares has been reduced to zero by return of capital gain distributions, report additional nontaxable distributions as capital gain on Schedule D, depending on how long you held the shares. If your total dividends from all sources is less than $400, you do not have to report them on your return unless your basis has been reduced to zero. If you have received return of capital distributions exceeding basis, report any additional distributions as capital gain on Schedule D.
Exempt-interest dividends	A separate statement; not included on Form 1099-DIV. This will be sent to you within 60 days after the close of the fund's taxable year.	For informational purposes only, report along with other tax-exempt interest on Line 8b of Form 1040 or Form 1040A.
Undistributed capital gains	Undistributed gains shown on Form 2439, Line 1 Tax paid by fund shown on Form 2439, Line 2	Report the undistributed gains on Schedule D, on the line for gains from Form 2439. To get a tax credit for the tax paid by the fund, enter the tax on Line 59 of Form 1040. Increase the basis of your mutual-fund shares by the excess of the undistributed gains included on Schedule D over the tax credit claimed on Line 59 of Form 1040.
Funds expenses from non-publicly offered fund	Box 1e, Form 1099-DIV	If you itemize, the expenses are itemized deductions, subject to the 2% adjusted gross income floor *(19.1).*
Foreign taxes	Box 3, Form 1099-DIV. Box 4 shows the country imposing the tax.	The foreign taxes may be claimed as a tax credit on Form 1116 or as an itemized deduction on Schedule A of Form 1040; *see 36.14.*

For purposes of figuring gain or loss when you redeem or exchange shares, load charges (sales fees) paid after October 3, 1989, on the purchase of the shares may not be treated as part of your cost if you held the shares for 90 days or less and then reinvested the sales proceeds at a reduced load charge.

32.8 Tax Credits From Mutual Funds

Undistributed capital gains. Some mutual funds retain their long-term capital gains and pay capital gains tax on those amounts. Even though not actually received by you, you include as a capital gain distribution on your return the amount of the undistributed capital gain allocated to you by the fund. If the mutual fund paid a tax on the undistributed capital gain, you are entitled to a tax credit.

To claim the credit, check the Form 2439 sent to you by your fund, which lists your share of undistributed capital gain and the amount of tax paid on it by the fund. Enter your share of the tax the fund paid on this gain on Line 59 of Form 1040, and check the box for Form 2439. Attach Copy B of Form 2439 to your return to support your tax credit. Increase the basis of your stock by the excess of the undistributed capital gain over the amount of tax paid by the mutual fund, as reported on Form 2439.

Dividends from foreign investments. The dividends are taxable, but you may be able to claim a foreign tax credit (on Form 1116) or a deduction on Schedule A for your share of the fund's foreign taxes.

In Box 3 of Form 1099-DIV, the fund will report your share of the foreign taxes paid, and in Box 4, the name of the foreign country. The fund should give you instructions for claiming the foreign tax credit or deduction; also *see 36.14*.

32.9 Redemptions and Exchanges of Fund Shares

When you ask the fund to redeem all or part of your shares, you have transacted a sale subject to capital gain or loss rules explained in Chapter 5. Exchanges of shares of one fund for shares of another fund within the same fund "family" are treated as sales. If you owned the shares for more than one year, your gain or loss is long term; if you held them for a year or less, your gain or loss is short term. However, if you received a capital gain distribution before selling shares held six months or less at a loss, your loss must be reported as a long-term capital loss to the extent of the capital gain distribution attributable to the sold shares. Any excess loss is reported as a short-term capital loss. This restriction does not apply to dispositions under periodic redemption plans.

EXAMPLE

In June 1997, you bought mutual-fund shares for $1,000. In August, you received a capital gain distribution of $50, and you sold the shares for $850 in September. Instead of reporting a $150 short-term capital loss ($1,000 cost – $850 proceeds), you must report a long-term capital loss of $50, the amount of the capital gain distribution; the remaining $100 of the loss is a short-term capital loss.

Holding period of fund shares. You determine your holding period by using the trade dates. The *trade date* is the date on which you contract to buy or redeem the mutual-fund shares. Do not confuse the trade date with the settlement date, which is the date by which the mutual-fund shares must be delivered and payment must be made. Most mutual funds will show the trade date on your purchase and redemption confirmation statements.

Your holding period starts on the day after the day you bought the shares. (The day you bought the shares is the trade date.) This same date of each succeeding month is the start of a new month regardless of the number of days in the month before. The day you dispose of the shares (trade date) is also part of your holding period.

Keeping track of cost basis. Keep confirmation statements for purchases of shares as well as a record of distributions that are automatically reinvested in your account. These will show the cost basis for your shares. Your basis is increased by amounts reported to you by the fund on Form 2439, representing the difference between your share of undistributed capital gains which you were required to report as income and your share of the tax paid by the fund on undistributed gains. Your basis is reduced by nontaxable dividends that are a return of your investment. Keep copies of Form 2439 and information returns showing nontaxable dividends.

Basis does not include load charges (sales fees) paid after October 3, 1989, on the purchase of mutual-fund shares if you held the shares for 90 days or less and then exchanged them for shares in a different fund in the same family of funds at a reduced load charge.

EXAMPLE

You pay a $200 load charge on purchasing shares for $10,000 in Fund A. Within 90 days, you exchange the Fund A shares for Fund B shares. Because Fund A and Fund B are in the same family of funds, the $200 load charge that would otherwise be due on the purchase of the Fund B shares is waived. For purposes of figuring your gain or loss on the exchange of Fund A shares, your basis is $10,000, not $10,200. The disallowed $200 is added to the basis of the new Fund B shares, provided those shares are held more than 90 days. If the waived load charge on Fund B shares had been $100, basis for the original Fund A shares would be increased by $100, the excess of the original $200 load charge over the amount waived on the reinvestment.

32.10 Basis of Redeemed Shares

To figure gain or loss, you need to know the basis per share. Generally, your basis is the purchase price of the shares, including shares acquired by reinvesting, plus commission or load charges.

If your shares in a mutual fund were acquired at different times, you need to know the basis of the particular shares you are selling in order to determine gain or loss. There are several methods of identifying which shares you are selling:

- *Specific Identification Method*—allows you to select exactly which shares are being sold (*see* Examples 1 and 2 below).
- *Average Cost Basis Method*—averages your cost for all shares in the fund (*see* Example 3 below).
- *First-in, first-out (FIFO) Method*—applies if you do not specifically identify the shares or elect the averaging method (*see* Examples 1 and 2 below).

See the chart on the following page for details on these identification methods.

EXAMPLES

1. In 1988, you bought 100 shares of a mutual fund for $10 a share. In 1991, you bought another 200 shares for $11 a share, and in 1992, another 500 shares for $15 a share. In 1996, you sell 130 shares at $20 a share, but do not specifically identify the shares being sold. Under the IRS FIFO method, you are treated as having first sold the original 100 shares from 1988, then 30 of the shares bought in 1991. Your basis for the sold shares is $1,330:

100 shares from 1988 costing $10 each	$1,000
30 shares from 1991 costing $11 each	330
	$1,330

   Your taxable gain is $1,270 ($2,600 sales price less $1,330 basis). Had you specifically designated shares from the most recent lot, which cost you more, you would have reduced the taxable gain. For example, if you had given the fund written instructions to sell 130 of the 500 shares that you bought in 1992 at $15 per share, your basis on the sale under the specific identification method would be $1,950 (130 × $15) instead of $1,330. Gain would be reduced from $1,270 to $650 ($2,600 sales price *less* $1,950 basis).

2. Hall sold by phone part of his holdings in two mutual funds acquired over a number of years without specifying the particular shares being sold. On his return, Hall claimed a net long-term capital loss of about $2,400 using a LIFO method (last-in, first-out). However, using the FIFO method, the IRS held that he had a long-term capital gain of $163,000. In the Tax Court, Hall argued that the specific identification rule applies only to stock certificates, not noncertificate shares left on deposit with a mutual fund. The court disagreed. Without specific identification, the IRS FIFO method is reasonable. If good records are kept, you can select the specific shares being sold at the time of sale. You cannot wait until the end of the year to allot specific sales to gain a tax advantage.

   What if you give written instructions to a mutual fund that specific shares should be sold, but the fund does not acknowledge this in its written confirmation? Regulations require such a written confirmation within a reasonable time after the sale. However, the Tax Court indicates your written sale identification instructions may be acceptable without a written confirmation.

3. You bought 160 shares of the XYZ Mutual Fund on February 4, 1995, for $4,000. On August 5, 1995, you bought another 240 shares for $4,800. You obtained an additional 10 shares on December 15, 1995, when you reinvested a $300 dividend. On December 16, 1996, you obtain an additional 20 shares when you reinvested a $750 dividend. You sell 200 shares of the fund on September 23, 1997, for $8,000. Using the average basis method, your average basis is $22.91 per share, figured as follows:

   1. 2/4/95: Invest $4,000 and obtain 160 shares at $25 per share;

   2. 8/5/95: Invest $4,800 and obtain 240 shares at $20 per share;

   3. 12/15/95: Reinvest $300 dividend and obtain 10 shares at $30 per share;

   4. 12/16/96: Reinvest $750 dividend and obtain 20 shares at $35 per share.

   Your total cost basis for all 430 shares is $9,850. Dividing $9,850 by 430 gives you an average basis per share of $22.91. Thus, your basis for the 200 sold shares is $4,582 (200 × $22.91 = $4,582).

   Under the average-basis method, the shares you acquired first are the shares deemed to be sold for purposes of determining your capital gain holding period. Thus, you are deemed to have sold the 160 shares bought on February 4, 1995, and 40 of the 240 shares bought on August 5, 1995. The sold shares were held long term (see 5.2) on the sale date of September 23, 1997. You have a $3,418 long-term capital gain on the sale: $8,000 proceeds less $4,582 basis figured under the average-basis method.

Key To Identifying Mutual-Fund Shares When You Sell

Method—	Tax Effect—
Specific identification of shares sold	If you sell some of your shares that have been left on deposit with an agent for the fund, and you identify the specific lot of shares being sold in your sell order, you can fix profit or loss on the sale, depending on the cost of the shares selected. See Example 1 on page 506. You should give the fund written instructions to sell shares that you bought on a particular date and at a particular price. Ask the fund for a written confirmation that acknowledges your instructions.
FIFO (First-in, first-out)	If you do not specifically identify the sold shares as just discussed, and you do not elect to average cost basis as discussed below, the IRS requires you to compute gain or loss as if shares were sold in the order that you acquired them. If the earliest acquired shares are treated as sold, taxable gain on a current sale will generally be higher than if the specific identification method was used, assuming that your least expensive shares were bought first; see Example 1 on page 506.
Averaging your basis	You may elect to average the cost of shares acquired at different times and prices. The election applies to open-end mutual-fund shares held by an agent, usually a bank, in an account kept for the periodic acquisition or redemption of shares in the particular fund. You still need records of your total basis, but averaging avoids the difficult task of identifying the exact shares being sold. Some funds ease the record-keeping burden by providing to shareholders who have redeemed shares a statement showing their average cost basis under the single-category method. You figure the average cost per share by dividing your total basis for all shares in the account by the number of shares. For example, if you bought 100 shares of a fund in 1991 at $20 per share and another 100 shares in 1992 at $30 per share, your average basis per share is $25 ($5,000 total cost ÷ 200 shares). If you sell 50 shares in 1997 for $35 a share, your basis for the sold shares is $1,250 (50 × $25 average basis) and your gain on the sale is $500 ($1,750 sales proceeds less $1,250 basis). For holding period purposes, you are treated as having sold shares in the order you acquired them (first-in, first-out). You can use the average cost basis for sales of shares in one mutual-fund family, and use the specific identification method for sales of shares of other fund families. **Note:** Under prior law, IRS regulations allowed the use of a double-category averaging method for figuring cost basis. In light of the new law changes to the holding period rules for capital assets (see 5.2), the double-category averaging method no longer seems viable. Any revisions or alternatives must await IRS guidance.

32.11 Comparison of Basis Methods

As discussed at *32.9*, your choice of basis method can have a significant effect on the computation of capital gains and losses when you sell a portion of your shares in a mutual fund. The following example compares the single averaging method to the specific identification and FIFO methods.

Transaction history.   Assume that on February 7, 1992, you made an initial investment of $4,500 for 375 shares in ABC Mutual Fund at $12 per share. Under the dividend reinvestment plan, you reinvested a $400 dividend, received in December 1992, for an additional 40 shares at $10 per share. On June 10, 1993, you bought 350 shares at $15 per share. In December 1993 you reinvested your dividend, this time for 25 shares at $12 per share. On September 16, 1994, you bought 200 shares at $16 per share. In 1994, 1995, 1996, and 1997, you did not reinvest your dividends. On October 14, 1998, you ask ABC Mutual Fund to redeem 200 shares and you receive $20 per share. The table below illustrates your transactions.

Date	Action	Share Price	No. of Shares	Shares Owned
2/7/92	Invest $4,500	$12	375	375
12/19/92	Reinvest $400 dividend	$10	40	415
6/10/93	Invest $5,250	$15	350	765
12/14/93	Reinvest $300 dividend	$12	25	790
9/16/94	Invest $3,200	$16	200	990
10/14/98	Redeem $4,000	$20	200	790

The following are three different ways to compute the basis of the shares redeemed on October 14, 1998.

Specific identification method.   If you identify the shares you sold, you can use the adjusted basis of those shares to figure your gain or loss. You must specify the particular shares to be redeemed at the time of the sale, as well as receive confirmation of your specification in writing within a reasonable time. Depending on your situation, you may want to either maximize or minimize your gain or loss on the sale. Here, you will have a gain regardless of which shares are treated as being sold. Assuming you want to minimize your gain, then you would specify the 200 shares bought at $16 per share on September 16, 1994, as the shares sold. Since the shares were sold for $20 per share, the gain would be $4 per share, for a total of $800 of long-term capital gain ($4,000 – $3,200).

FIFO (first-in, first-out).   If you do not identify which shares you sold or choose the averaging method, you must use the basis of the shares you acquired first as the basis of the shares sold. Therefore, the oldest shares still available, the February 7, 1992, shares, are considered sold first. Thus, the basis of the 200 shares sold would be $12 per share. Your long-term capital gain is $1,600 ($4,000 – $2,400).

Average cost.   The ABC Mutual Fund may provide you with your average basis when you make the redemption. If it does not, you may compute the average basis for all shares owned at the time of disposition, regardless of how long you owned them, including shares acquired with reinvested dividends. The basis and gain is computed as follows: You total the number of shares owned prior to the sale, 990, and total your investment in these shares, which is $13,650. You divide $13,650 by 990, which gives an average cost of $13.79 per share and a total cost of $2,758 for the 200 shares. Your gain is $1,242 ($4,000 – $2,758). For holding period purposes, the shares sold are considered to be from the earliest lot in 1992, so your gain is long-term capital gain.

Result: The specific identification method gives you the lowest capital gain under this set of facts.

Chapter 33

Family Income Planning

Each additional dollar of ordinary income you receive, such as interest, dividends, and rent, is taxed in your highest bracket. If you can deflect income to a lower tax bracket of a child or other dependent relative, he or she will pay a smaller tax on the income than you would pay. However, the tax advantages of shifting income to children under age 14 are sharply reduced by the "kiddie tax"; *see* Chapter 24.

To split income, you must do more than make gifts of income. You must transfer the actual property from which the income is produced. For example, you do not avoid tax on interest by instructing your savings bank to credit interest to your children's account. Unless you actually transfer the complete ownership of the account to your children, the interest income is earned on money owned by you and must be reported by you. The same holds true with dividends, rents, and other forms of income. Unless you transfer the income-producing property, the income will be taxed to you.

You may not split earned income; income resulting from your services is taxed to you. You may not avoid this result by setting up trusts to receive your earned income.

Gift Planning

33.1 Gift Tax Basics

As family income planning generally requires the transfer of property, you must consider possible gift tax liability. The gift tax rates and credit are the same as those of the estate tax listed in Chapter 39.

Gift tax liability may be avoided by making gifts within an annual exclusion of $10,000 (or $20,000 for joint gifts). To each donee, you may give annually up to $10,000 tax free; furthermore, if your spouse joins in the gift, you may give annually tax free to each donee up to $20,000. The $20,000 exclusion is available even if the entire gift is from your or your spouse's separately owned funds. Thus, if you (with your spouse's consent) make annual gifts to four persons, you could give away without gift tax up to $80,000 (4 × $20,000 exclusion). The $10,000 (or $20,000) annual exclusion is allowed only for cash gifts or gifts of present interests in property; gifts of future interests do not qualify.

Gifts to a spouse who is a U.S. citizen are completely tax free because of the marital deduction. There also is an unlimited gift tax exclusion for paying someone else's tuition or medical expenses, if you directly pay the educational organization or care provider.

If you make an interest-free or low-interest loan to a family member, you may be subject to income tax and gift tax; see 4.31.

Filing a gift tax return. A gift tax return generally must be filed on Form 709 for a gift made to an individual other than your spouse if it exceeds $10,000 or is a gift of a future interest (regardless of value). A return does not have to be filed for gifts qualifying for the tuition or medical expense exclusion.

Married couples who consent to "split" gifts of over $10,000 but up to $20,000 must report the gifts to the IRS, although no gift tax is due under the annual exclusion. If your spouse consents to split gifts with you, you may be able to use a short form, Form 709-A, rather than Form 709; see the form instructions.

Form 709 or Form 709-A generally must be filed by April 15th of the year following the year of the gift. If you get a filing extension for your income tax return, the extension also applies to the gift tax return. An additional extension may be granted by the IRS for gift tax returns filed on Form 709 if you show good cause; further extensions are not allowed for filing Form 709-A.

> **EXAMPLE**
>
> In July 1997 Randall Johnson makes a gift of publicly traded stock to his son, Philip, and his daughter, Ann. He gives each of them 1,000 shares of stock valued at $18,500 ($18.50 per share). On Form 709-A, Randall's wife, Claire, consents to split the gifts, thereby doubling the annual exclusion for gifts to each child. Neither Randall nor Claire made any other gifts during 1997. As a result of the gift splitting, no gift tax is due.
>
> If Randall's total gifts for the year to either Philip or Ann exceeded $20,000, the gifts could not be reported on Form 709-A; the longer Form 709 would have to be used.

Even where Form 709 must be filed, gift tax liability computed on the form may be offset by the applicable credit applied to gift taxes as well as estate taxes. For example, in 1997, you and your spouse each have a credit of $192,800 that exempts up to $600,000 of lifetime taxable gifts (exceeding the annual exclusion) from gift tax, *or* transfers of up to $600,000 at death from estate tax. *See 39.5* for changes in the credit and exemption in 1998 and later years. When you report taxable gifts exceeding the annual exclusion, the applicable credit offsets the gift tax liability, so that you do not actually have to pay gift tax to the IRS. The portion of the credit used to offset gift taxes indirectly reduces the credit available for estate tax purposes upon your death; *see* the estate tax computation in Chapter 39.

33.2 Investments and Custodian Accounts for Minors

A minor generally lacks the ability to manage property. You could create a trust, but this step may be costly. Alternatively, you might set up a custodian account or select property which does not require management and which can be transferred to a minor, such as:

1. Bonds purchased and registered in a minor's name and coupons or the proceeds from the sale or maturity of the bonds deposited in a minor's name.

Law Alert

Increased Exemption and Exclusion

The $10,000 annual exclusion for gifts will be indexed annually for inflation after 1998. The effective unified credit exemption for gift tax and estate tax purposes of $600,000 is replaced by an "applicable credit amount" for gifts made after 1997 and estates of decedents dying after 1997. The amount will allow an effective exemption of $625,000 in 1998 and $650,000 in 1999. Further increases are phased in until the exemption will be fixed at $1,000,000 for 2006 and later years, *see 39.5.*

See also 30.15 for U.S. Savings Bond plan tips. Zero coupon bonds are discussed at *30.11* and *30.12.*

2. Mutual-fund custodian accounts under the Uniform Gifts (or Transfers) to Minors Act, under which shares may be registered in the name of a minor. The problem of management and reinvestment is minimized. Most funds provide for switching investments and automatic reinvestment of dividends for additional shares.

Tax consequences of college tuition prepayment plans are discussed in Chapter 38.

Custodian accounts.   Custodian accounts set up in a bank, mutual fund, or brokerage firm can achieve income splitting; the tax consequences discussed below generally apply to such accounts. Trust accounts which are considered revocable under state law are ineffective in splitting interest income.

Although custodian accounts may be opened anywhere in the United States, the rules governing the accounts may vary from state to state. The differences between the laws of the states generally do not affect federal tax consequences.

There are limitations placed on the custodian. Proceeds from the sale of an investment or income from an investment may not be used to buy additional securities on margin. While a custodian should prudently seek reasonable income and capital preservation, he or she generally is not liable for losses unless they result from bad faith, intentional wrongdoing, or gross negligence.

When the minor reaches majority age (depending on state law), property in the custodian account is turned over to him or her. No formal accounting is required. The child, now an adult, may sign a simple release freeing the custodian from any liability. But on reaching majority, the child may require a formal accounting if there are any doubts as to the propriety of the custodian's actions while acting as custodian. For this reason, and also for tax record-keeping purposes, a separate bank account should be opened in which proceeds from sales of investments and investment income are deposited pending reinvestment on behalf of the child. Such an account will furnish a convenient record of sales proceeds, investment income, and reinvestment of the same.

Income tax treatment of custodian account.   Income from a custodian account is taxable to the child as long as it is not used by the parent who set up the account to pay for the child's support. Tax-exempt income from a custodian account is not taxable to the parent even when used for child support. However, taxable income from a custodian account in excess of the annual income tax floor ($1,300 in 1997) is taxed at the parent's tax rate if the child is under age 14; computation of the "kiddie tax" is discussed in Chapter 24.

Gift tax treatment of custodian account.   When setting up a custodian account, you may have to pay a gift tax. A transfer of cash or securities to a custodian account is a gift. But you are not subject to a gift tax if you properly plan the cash contributions or purchase of securities for your children's accounts. You may make gifts of up to $10,000 per person, which is shielded from gift tax by the annual exclusion. The exclusion applies each year to each person to whom you make a gift. If your spouse consents to join with you in the gift, you may give annually tax free up to $20,000 to each person.

If the custodian account is set up at the end of December, another tax-free transfer of $20,000 may be made in the first days of January of the following year. In this way, a total of $40,000 is shifted within the two-month period.

Even if gifts exceeding the $10,000 (or $20,000) exclusion are made, gift tax liability may be offset by the unified credit applied to gift and estate taxes; *see* the Law Alert on the increased exemption and exclusion on page 510.

Estate tax treatment of custodian account.   The value of a custodian account will be taxed in your estate if you die while acting as custodian of an account before your child reaches his or her majority. However, you may avoid the problem by naming someone other than yourself as custodian. If you should decide to act as custodian, taking the risk that the account will be taxed in your estate, remember no estate tax is incurred if the tax on your estate is offset by the estate tax credit; *see* Chapter 39.

If you act as custodian and decide to terminate the custodianship, care should be taken to formally close the account. Otherwise, if you die while retaining power over the account, the IRS may try to tax the account in your estate.

33.3 Trusts in Family Planning

You establish a trust by transferring legal title to property to a trustee who manages the property for one or more beneficiaries. As the one who sets up the trust, you are called the grantor or settlor of

Planning Reminder

Custodian Securities Account
Purchase of securities through custodian accounts provides a practical method for making a gift of securities to a minor child, eliminating the need for a trust. The mechanics of opening a custodian account are simple. An adult opens a stock account for a minor child at a broker's office. He or she registers the securities in the name of a custodian for the benefit of the child. The custodian may be a parent, a child's guardian, grandparent, brother, sister, uncle, or aunt. In some states, the custodian may be any adult or a bank or trust company. The custodian has the right to sell securities in the account and collect sales proceeds and investment income, and use them for the child's benefit or reinvestment. Tax treatment of custodian accounts is discussed on this page.

Form 709-A—Worksheet

1 Donor's first name and middle initial	2 Donor's last name	3 Donor's social security number
Randall M.	Johnson	lXl : 0l : XllX

4 Address (number, street, and apartment number)	5 Legal residence (domicile)
914 State Street	State XX

6 City, state, and ZIP code	7 Citizenship
City, State 0X0X0	USA

8 Did you file any gift tax returns for prior periods? . . . . ☐ Yes ☒ No

If "Yes," state when and where earlier returns were filed ▶

9 Name of consenting spouse	10 Consenting spouse's social security number
Claire Johnson	XlZ : lX : 00lX

Note: *Do not use this form to report gifts of closely held stock, partnership interests, fractional interests in real estate, or gifts for which the value has been reduced to reflect a valuation discount. Instead, use Form 709.*

List of Gifts

(a) Donee's name and address and description of gift	(b) Donor's adjusted basis of gift	(c) Date of gift	(d) Value at date of gift
1. Philip S. Johnson, son 914 State Street, City, State 0X0X0 Gift of 1,000 shares of Central Net Corp. common stock (NYSE) at $18.50 per share on 7-10-97. Cusip No. 001005684	$10,000	7-10-97	$18,500
2. Ann C. Johnson, daughter 10 Lincoln Road, City, State 0X0X0 Gift of 1,000 shares of Central Net Corp. common stock (NYSE) at $18.50 per share on 7-10-97. Cusip No. 001005684	$10,000	7-10-97	$18,500

Consent

I consent to have the gifts made by my spouse to third parties during the calendar year considered as made one-half by each of us.

Consenting spouse's signature ▶ *Claire Johnson*   Date ▶ 3-11-98

Under penalties of perjury, I declare that I have examined this return, and to the best of my knowledge and belief it is true, correct, and complete. Declaration of preparer (other than donor) is based on all information of which preparer has any knowledge.

Donor's signature ▶ *Randall Johnson* . . . .   Date ▶ 3-11-98

Preparer's signature (other than donor's) ▶ *Jackie Alan*   Date ▶ 3-11-98

Preparer's address (other than donor's) ▶ 200 Adams Lane   City, State 0X0X0 the trust. The trustee may be one or more individuals or an institution such as a bank or a trust company.

You can create a trust during your lifetime or by your will. A trust created during your lifetime is called an *inter vivos* trust; one established in your will is a testamentary trust. An *inter vivos* trust can be revocable or irrevocable. An irrevocable trust does not allow for changes of heart; it requires a complete surrender of property. By conveying property irrevocably to a trust, you may relieve yourself of tax on the income from the trust principal. Furthermore, the property in trust usually is not subject to estate tax, although it may be subject to gift tax. A trust should be made irrevocable only if you are certain you will not need the trust property in a financial emergency.

Trust income. Where a child is a trust beneficiary, the child reports distributable net trust income as taxable income. If the child is under the age of 14, distributable net income is subject to the "kiddie tax" of *24.3*. Income that is accumulated for the benefit of a minor child is generally not taxable and, thus, not subject to the kiddie tax.

Short-term trusts. Before the tax laws were changed in 1986, 10-year (Clifford) trusts were widely used to shift income to relatives in lower tax brackets. Where a trust met the 10-year exception, trust income was taxed to the beneficiary, usually a minor child. Another type of trust used for income splitting was the spousal remainder trust set up for less than 10 years. It allowed income shifting to a child beneficiary when the trust property went to the grantor's spouse after the end of the trust period.

Under current law, both types of trust may no longer be used to shift income to the income beneficiary. Only 10-year trusts created before March 2, 1986, continue to shift income to the income beneficiary. However, tax savings may be nullified for trust beneficiaries under the age of 14 by the kiddie tax. For example, in 1997, unearned income over $1,300 of a child under age 14 is taxed to the child at the top marginal rate of the parents; *see 24.3*.

Pre-March 2, 1986, 10-year trusts continue to shift income and provide tax savings to trust beneficiaries age 14 or over.

Spousal remainder trusts have been neutralized as tax-saving techniques by current law that treats the grantor as holding a reversionary interest held by his or her spouse. This spousal attribution rule applies to a reversionary interest of a spouse who marries the grantor after the trust is created.

The current tax rules apply to trust transfers made after March 1, 1986. An exception applies to a 10-year trust created pursuant to a binding property settlement entered into before March 2, 1986, which required the taxpayer to establish a grantor trust.

Grantor trusts. The grantor of a grantor trust is taxed on the income of the trust. A trust is treated as a grantor trust where the grantor has a reversionary interest (at the time of the transfer) of more than 5% of the value of the property transferred to the trust. Under an exception, a grantor is not treated as having a reversionary interest if that interest can take effect only upon the death before age 21 of a beneficiary who is a lineal descendant of the grantor. The beneficiary must have the entire present interest in the trust or trust portion for this exception to apply.

Tax rates for trusts and estates. The following rates apply to taxable income of trusts and estates for taxable years beginning in 1997.

If Taxable Income Is Over:	The Tax Is:
$0 but not over $1,650	15% of taxable income
$1,650 but not over $3,900	$247.50 *plus* 28% of excess over $1,650
$3,900 but not over $5,950	$877.50 *plus* 31% of excess over $3,900
$5,950 but not over $8,100	$1,513 *plus* 36% of excess over $5,950
Over $8,100	$2,287 *plus* 39.6% of excess over $8,100

33.4 Gifts of Appreciated Property

Making a gift of appreciated property that will eventually be sold may reduce income tax. To shift the profit and the tax, the gift must be completed before the sale or before the donor has made a binding commitment to sell. By making a gift of interests in the property to several family members, it is possible to spread the profit and the tax among a number of taxpayers in the lowest tax bracket. Note: The IRS may claim that the gift was never completed if after sale the donor controls the sales proceeds or has the use of them.

Planning Reminder

Revocable Trusts

In a revocable trust, you retain control over the property by reserving the right to revoke the trust. As such, it is considered an incomplete gift and offers no present income tax savings. Furthermore, the trust property will be included as part of your estate. But a revocable trust minimizes delay in passing property to beneficiaries if you die while the trust is in force. When you transfer property to a trust, the property is generally not subject to probate, administration expenses, delays attendant on distributions of estates, or claims of creditors. The interests of trust beneficiaries are generally more secure than those of heirs under a will because a will may be denied probate if found invalid.

Planning Reminder

Transfers of Appreciated Property

Before making a gift of appreciated property, consider the fact that the appreciation on property passed by inheritance escapes income tax; the heir takes a basis equal to estate tax value, which is usually the fair market value at the date of death. Furthermore, appreciated property encumbered by a mortgage may result in income tax to the donor when a gift of the property is made; *see 31.16*.

Do not make a gift of property which has decreased in value if you want a deduction for the loss. Once you give the property away, the loss deduction is gone forever. Neither you nor your donee can ever take advantage of it. The better way is to first sell the property, get a loss deduction, and then make a gift of the proceeds.

33.5 Splitting Business Income With Your Family

Tax on your business income may be reduced if you can shift it to members of your family. If you keep within the annual gift tax exclusion for each donee, there will be no gift tax consequences. However, the estate tax advantages of "estate freeze" techniques has been limited, making it difficult to avoid estate tax on the appreciation in capital interests transferred to children; *see 39.7.*

Business income may be shifted by forming a family partnership or by making your family stockholders in a corporation. An S corporation in which stockholders elect to report income may be used more freely than a partnership to split income.

A minor child will not be recognized as a partner unless he or she is competent to manage his or her own property, or control of the property is exercised by another person as fiduciary for the minor's sole benefit. Here, a trust may be set up to hold the minor's partnership interest. The IRS may review not only the terms of the trust and the partnership agreement but also actual operation of the trust to make certain the grantor-partner has not retained any ownership rights over the interest he or she transferred.

Transfers of stock to a trust for a minor terminate an S election, unless the trust is a qualified trust. For this purpose, a "Subchapter S trust" may be used. Alternatively, stock may be transferred for the minor's benefit to a custodian account for which the parent may act as custodian.

In order to get the income-shifting benefits from setting up a stock custodian account, there must be a *bona fide* transfer of stock entailing a complete surrender by you of any control over the transferred stock.

With a partnership, shifting income may be more difficult, depending on whether capital is a material income-producing factor in the business. If it is, a gift or sale of a partnership interest to a family member is effective. But in a service partnership—real estate or insurance brokers, for example—a mere gift of a partnership interest to a family member will not shift partnership income unless the person actually performs services for the partnership. In one case, the Tax Court held that where substantially all of a family partnership's capital consists of borrowed funds guaranteed by family members, the family partnership interests may be disregarded on the grounds that the borrowed funds are not a material income-producing factor in the business.

In an S corporation, pass-through items must reflect the value of services rendered or capital contributed by family members of the shareholders. If a relative of an S corporation shareholder performs services for or loans money to the corporation without receiving reasonable pay or interest, the IRS may allocate income to reflect the value of the services or capital provided. The "family" of an individual includes only spouse, ancestors, lineal descendants, and any trusts for the primary benefit of such persons.

Payment of wages to your child.   Wages paid to your child are not subject to the "kiddie tax" of *24.3,* but investment income earned by the child from investing those wages is subject to the "kiddie tax." You may also deduct the wages as a business expense if the payments are reasonable. Set the wages at the scale that you would pay an outsider; keep records of the child's work; withhold tax; and provide the child with a Form W-2. If the child is age 17 or under, you do not have to withhold FICA taxes on the wages. FICA taxes are only due on wages paid to a child age 18 or over.

Life Insurance

33.6 Life Insurance Offers Tax Advantages

Insurance may provide a tax-free accumulation of cash. During the time you pay premiums, the value of your contract increases at compound interest rates. The increase is not subject to income tax. In addition, when your policy is paid at death to your beneficiaries, the proceeds are not subject to income tax; *see 33.7.*

Estate tax planning.   To shelter life insurance proceeds from estate tax, you must not have ownership rights in the policy. If you have an existing policy, you must assign your ownership rights such as the right to change beneficiaries, the right to surrender or cancel the policy, the right to assign it, and the right to borrow against it. An assignment must occur more than three years before death to exclude the proceeds from your estate.

Assigning group-term policies. Group insurance provided by an employer may be assigned. The IRS has agreed to follow a court decision holding that the power to convert a group policy into an individual policy when you leave the company will not subject the group-term insurance proceeds to estate tax. Since the conversion privilege is exercisable only by taking the economically disadvantageous step of quitting, this right is too remote to be considered a retained ownership right in the policy. If other incidents of ownership are transferred, such as the power to name beneficiaries and fix the type of benefit payable, the transfer will remove the policy from your estate.

The substitution of a new group carrier does not jeopardize assignments under a prior carrier.

When you plan to assign a policy, review your gift tax liability on such a transfer. In the case of an assignment of a group policy, the cost of the policy is determined by actuarially apportioning the employer's total premium payment among the covered employees. This is difficult for an individual employee to do, particularly where there are many employees, so the IRS generally allows employees to value the assigned policy using the same tax tables used to determine the amount of the employee's compensation where group coverage exceeds $50,000. *See* the table at *3.3*. Key employees may not use the table to determine gift tax liability.

You may want to readjust your coverage to meet new family conditions. You can exchange your policies without tax; *see 6.11*.

Using a trust to purchase insurance. If you create a trust to carry a policy on your life by transferring income-producing property the income of which is used to pay the premiums, you are taxable on the trust income. Similarly, if your spouse creates the trust to carry the policy on your life, he or she is taxable on the trust income. This tax rule does not apply to the trust funding of life insurance covering the life of a third party other than your spouse. For example, a grandparent transfers income-producing property to a trust to pay the premiums on a policy on the life of his son. His grandchildren are named trust beneficiaries. The grandparent is not taxed on the income earned by the trust on the transferred property because the trust purchased insurance on his son's life, not his own.

Insurance trust to receive proceeds. A trust may be used to receive insurance proceeds where there is concern that the beneficiary may be unable to manage a large insurance settlement. The trustee may be a bank or a person directed to invest the proceeds and pay income to beneficiaries according to standards provided in the trust. The trustee may be given the discretion to pay out more or less as circumstances warrant. He or she may be directed to terminate the trust when the beneficiaries reach a certain age, or when they demonstrate their ability to manage money. There may also be investment advantages in a trust. The trust investments may yield a higher rate of return than that of an insurance company under a settlement option.

Insurance proceeds are not subject to income tax whether paid directly to named beneficiaries or to a trust.

Single-premium policies. Single-premium policies have been touted as tax-sheltered investments. Companies offer competitive current returns and tax-free appreciation on your investment fund. The name of the policy is descriptive: You make a single-premium payment—$5,000, $10,000, $50,000, or more. Part of the premium goes for life insurance coverage and part towards an investment fund.

However, tax benefits of single-premium and other cash value policies have been cut back, as discussed below.

Universal life insurance plans. Universal life insurance offers tax-free buildup of interest income at current market rates and on death, tax-free receipt of insurance proceeds. A universal life insurance policy is made up of (1) life insurance protection, and (2) a cash reserve on which interest income accumulates without tax.

The interest rate of universal life is pegged to current bond market rates. Furthermore, a universal life policy lets you withdraw the cash reserve if you want to invest it elsewhere and to allocate how much of your premium payment is to cover insurance protection and how much is to go into the cash reserve.

The tax law sets limits on the amount of premiums that may be earmarked for the cash reserve. If these limits are violated, tax-free treatment for the proceeds may be lost. For these limits, check with the company issuing the policy.

A disadvantage of universal life is that you must incur an up-front commission payment which may be 50% or more of the first premium. There may also be a fee for withdrawing the cash reserve.

See below for restrictions on cash value policies.

 Court Decision

Policy Owned by Beneficiary
If you are buying a new policy with yourself as the insured, and you want to keep the proceeds out of your gross estate, you must buy the policy in another's name, such as in your spouse's name, or have your beneficiary buy the policy. For example, a daughter applies for a $1 million policy on her father's life and is the policy owner under the terms of the policy. Although the father pays the premiums, the proceeds paid at his death are not subject to estate tax because he never had ownership rights in the policy. In the past, the IRS contested this tax-free treatment, but now agrees to follow court decisions that allow it.

 Planning Reminder

Accelerated Death Benefits
A person who is terminally ill may withdraw without tax life insurance proceeds to pay medical bills and other living expenses. For policies lacking an accelerated benefits clause, it is possible to sell a life insurance policy without incurring tax to a viatical settlement company; *see 17.16*.

Planning Reminder

Insurance Options
Before considering a universal plan, determine the possibility that the purchase of term insurance and an investment in money-market funds or long-term bonds may be a better alternative to a universal life plan.

Tax on withdrawals from cash value modified endowment policies. Contracts entered into after June 20, 1988, may be subject to tax penalties if they are considered "modified endowment contracts." Generally, a modified endowment contract is a contract that fails to satisfy a technical "seven-year-pay test." A contract fails the "seven-year-pay test" if the premiums paid during the first seven contract years exceed the sum of the net level premiums that would have been paid by that time had the contract provided for paid-up future benefits after the payment of seven level annual premiums.

Amounts received under modified endowment contracts that are not received as an annuity, such as dividends, cash withdrawals, loans, and amounts received upon a partial surrender of the contract, are taxable to the extent the cash surrender value of the contract exceeds the policyholder's investment. Withdrawals that are greater than the excess of cash surrender value over the investment are a tax-free return of capital.

To prevent marketing of multiple contracts as a means of avoiding these tax limitations, all modified endowment contracts issued by the same insurer or its affiliates to the same policyholder within the same calendar year are aggregated to determine the amount includible in income.

For policies *other* than modified endowment contracts, non-annuity withdrawals continue to be tax free until they exceed the policyholder's investment. Assignments or pledges of a contract to cover burial or pre-arranged funeral expenses are not considered taxable distributions if the contractual death benefit is $25,000 or less.

Penalty for early withdrawals from cash value policy. A 10% premature withdrawal penalty applies to taxable distributions and loans unless the policyholder is over age 59 ½, disabled, or the distribution is one of a series of substantially equal payments over life expectancy or over joint life expectancy with a beneficiary; for further details, *see 7.14*.

33.7 How Life Insurance Proceeds Are Taxed to a Beneficiary

Life insurance proceeds received upon the death of the insured are generally tax free. However, insurance proceeds may be subject to estate tax so that the beneficiary actually receives a reduced amount; *see 39.2*.

Interest paid on proceeds left with the insurer is taxable except in this case: A surviving spouse who elects to receive installments rather than a lump sum does not pay tax on the first $1,000 of interest received each year if the decedent died before October 23, 1986.

Read the following checklist to find how your insurance receipts are taxed—

A lump-sum payment of the full face value of a life insurance policy: The proceeds are generally tax free. The tax-free exclusion also covers death benefit payments made under endowment contracts, workers' compensation insurance contracts, employers' group insurance plans, or accident and health insurance contracts. The exclusion does not apply to a policy combined with a nonrefund life annuity contract where a single premium equal to the face value of the insurance is paid.

Insurance proceeds may be taxable where the policy was transferred for valuable consideration. Exceptions to this rule are made for transfers among partners and corporations and their stockholders and officers.

Installment payments spread over your life under a policy that could have been paid in a lump sum: Part of each installment attributed to interest may be taxed. Divide the face amount of the policy by the number of years the installments are to be paid. The result is the amount which is received tax free each year.

If you are the surviving spouse of an insured who died before October 23, 1986, up to $1,000 of interest paid with the annual installment is also tax free. You are still treated as a spouse if separated from the insured at the date of his or her death, but not if divorced. (If you receive payments under a policy with a "family income rider," *see 33.8*.) The $1,000 interest exclusion is not allowed where the insured died after October 22, 1986.

> **EXAMPLE**
> Alice is the wife and beneficiary under her husband John's life insurance policy of $100,000. He died September 30, 1986. She elected to take installment payments for the rest of her life. Alice's life expectancy is 20 years. Then $5,000 ($100,000 ÷ 20) is the principal amount spread to each year. The first $6,000 received each year ($5,000 principal plus $1,000 of the spouse's special interest exclusion) is exempt from tax. If Alice lives more than 20 years, she may continue to treat up to $6,000 of annual payments as tax-free receipts.

If the policy guarantees payments to a secondary beneficiary if you should die before receiving a specified number of payments, the tax-free amount is reduced by the present value of the secondary beneficiary's interest in the policy. The insurance company can give you this figure.

Installment payments for a fixed number of years under a policy which could have been paid in a lump sum. Divide the full face amount of the policy by the number of years you are to receive the installments. The result is the amount which is received tax free each year.

> **EXAMPLE**
>
> Same facts as in the preceding Example, but Alice elects to take installment payments for 10 years. Then $10,000 ($100,000 ÷ 10) is the principal amount received tax free. So up to $11,000 per year may be received tax free by Alice, $10,000 of principal sum plus up to $1,000 of interest, under the surviving spouse's interest exclusion.

Installment payments when there is no lump-sum option in the policy: You must find the discounted value of the policy at the date of the insured's death and use that as the principal amount. The insurance company can give you that figure. After you find the discounted value, you divide it by the number of years you are to receive installments. The result is the amount that is tax free. The remainder is taxed.

> **EXAMPLE**
>
> The insured died in 1997. Under an insurance policy, the surviving wife is entitled to $5,000 a year for life. Her life expectancy is 20 years. There is no lump sum stated in the policy. Say the discounted value of the wife's rights is $60,000. The principal amount spread to each year for the wife is $3,000 ($60,000 ÷ 20). Subtracting $3,000 from each annual $5,000 payment gives her taxable income of $2,000.

Payments to you along with other beneficiaries under the same policy, by lump-sum or varying installments. *See* the following Example for the way multiple beneficiaries may be taxed.

> **EXAMPLE**
>
> Under one life insurance policy of an insured man who died in 1997, a surviving wife, daughter, and nephew are all beneficiaries. The wife is entitled to a lump sum of $60,000. The daughter and nephew are each entitled to a lump sum of $35,000. Under the installment options, the wife chooses to receive $5,000 a year for the rest of her life. (She has a 20-year life expectancy.) The daughter and the nephew each choose a yearly payment of $5,000 for 10 years. This is how each yearly installment is taxed:
>
> *Wife:* The principal amount spread to each year is $3,000. Subtracting $3,000 from the yearly $5,000 payment gives the wife taxable income of $2,000.
>
> *Daughter and Nephew:* Both are taxed the same way. The principal amount spread to each of the 10 years is $3,500. Subtracting this $3,500 from the yearly $5,000 installment gives the daughter and the nephew taxable income of $1,500 each.

Interest only option. When proceeds are left on deposit under the "interest only" option, the interest is fully taxed; the lump sum is not taxed. A surviving spouse of an insured who died before October 23, 1986, may not exclude $1,000 interest under the "interest only" option. However, if the surviving spouse later elects to receive proceeds from the policy in installments, the interest exclusion applies from the time of the election.

Universal life policy. A universal life policy allows a policyholder to apply premium payments to cash value instead of to death benefits. Death benefits may be tax free if the policies meet certain technical tests. These tests must be determined by the insurance company. Therefore, you must check with the company paying the proceeds as to whether the payments qualify as tax-free life insurance payments.

Other names applied to universal life may be "flexible premium" or "adjustable life premium" policies.

33.8   A Policy With a Family Income Rider

Payments received under a family income rider are taxed under a special rule. A family income rider provides additional term insurance coverage for a fixed number of years from the date of the basic policy. Under the terms of a rider, if the insured dies at any time during the term period, the beneficiary receives monthly payments during the balance of the term period, and then at the end of the term period, receives the lump-sum proceeds of the basic policy. If the insured dies after the end of the term period, the beneficiary receives only the lump sum from the basic policy.

When the insured dies during the term period, part of each monthly payment received during the term period includes interest on the lump-sum proceeds of the basic policy (which is held by the company until the end of the term period). That interest is fully taxed. The balance of the monthly payment consists of an installment (principal plus interest) of the proceeds from the term insurance purchased under the family income rider. You may exclude from this balance: (1) a prorated portion of the present value of the lump sum under the basic policy; and (2) an additional amount of up to $1,000 attributable to interest if you are a surviving spouse of an insured who died before October 23, 1986. The lump sum under the basic policy is tax free when you eventually receive it.

The rules here also apply to an integrated family income policy and to family maintenance policies, whether integrated or with an attached rider.

In figuring your taxable portions, ask the insurance company for its interest rate and the present value of term payments.

33.9   How Other Insurance Proceeds Are Taxed

Dividends paid by the insurance company as reduction of premiums (taken in cash, left as interest with the company, or used to accelerate the maturity of the policy) are not taxable. They serve to reduce the cost basis of your policy, thus increasing gain sometimes computed upon maturity of some policies. However, interest on such "dividends" is generally taxable, although the interest on GI insurance dividends left on deposit with the VA is tax free.

Matured endowment policies. You generally report as income the difference between the proceeds received and your investment; *see 7.24.* The payment on an endowment contract because of the insured's death is treated as the payment of tax-free life insurance proceeds provided the policy meets certain technical definitions not discussed in this book.

Sale of an endowment contract before maturity. Taxed as ordinary income; *see 7.22.*

Surrender of policy for cash. Taxed as ordinary income (not capital gain) if the cash received exceeds the premiums paid, less dividends received. If you take, instead, a paid-up policy, you may avoid tax; *see 6.11.* You get no deduction if there is a loss on the surrender of a policy.

Collection of proceeds on policy purchased by or assigned to you on the life of someone else. Where a policy is transferred for valuable consideration, only the amount paid and the premiums paid after the transfer are tax free when collected; the balance is taxed. There is no tax on life insurance proceeds paid under contracts which have been transferred to a partner or to a corporation in which the insured was a shareholder or officer.

Chapter 34

Tax Pointers for Senior Citizens

All of your Social Security benefits are tax free if your "provisional income," explained at *34.3*, is $25,000 or less if you are single, or $32,000 or less if you are married and file a joint return. No more than 50% of your benefits are subject to tax if you file a joint return and your provisional income is over $32,000 but no more than $44,000, or if you are single and your provisional income is over $25,000 but no more than $34,000. When provisional income exceeds $34,000 or $44,000 (depending on your filing status), more than 50%, but no more than 85%, of your benefits are subject to tax. If you are married and filing separately, and did not live apart for the whole year, you compute the amount of taxable benefits without considering the base amounts allowed on joint and single returns.

If you continue to earn wages or self-employed income, you must pay FICA taxes or self-employment tax on that income regardless of your age. Do not confuse this rule with the Social Security benefit rule that allows full benefits for working after you reach age 70; *see 34.5.*

Starting in 1997, new tax breaks apply to certain long-term health care expenses and benefits under qualifying policies; *see 17.15.*

34.1 Special Rules for Senior Citizens

The following special tax rules favor senior citizens:

- *Higher filing thresholds.* If you are single and age 65 or older on or before January 1, 1998, you do not have to file a 1997 return unless your gross income is $7,880 or over. This is $1,000 more than for younger taxpayers. If you are married and you and your spouse are both age 65 or older, a joint return does not have to be filed unless your gross income is $13,800 or over, or $13,000 or over if only one of you is age 65 or older; *see* the chart on page 2 for further details.
- *Higher standard deduction.* If you are age 65 or older on or before January 1, 1998, you receive an additional standard deduction allowance if you do not itemize deductions. If you are single you get an additional $1,000, $800 if you are married or a qualifying widow(er); *see 13.4.* Your 1997 standard deduction is $5,150 if you are single. If married filing jointly, it is $7,700 if one of you is age 65 or over, and $8,500 if both of you are.
- *Tax credit if age 65 or older.* This is a limited tax credit for taxpayers age 65 or older who receive little or no Social Security or Railroad Retirement benefits. The credit may also be available to persons under age 65 who are totally disabled; *see 34.7.* For example, if you are single, or married but only you are eligible, and receive more than $416 each month from Social Security, you may not claim the credit. If you are married and both you and your spouse are eligible for the credit and file a joint return, you may not claim the credit if you receive more than $625 each month from Social Security.
- *Social Security benefits may be exempt from tax.* If you are married and file jointly, none of your net Social Security benefits are taxable in 1997 if your income is not more than a base amount of $32,000, or $25,000 if your filing status is single, head of household, qualifying widow(er), or if you are married filing separately and did not live with your spouse at any time during 1997. Married persons who file separately and live together at any time during the year are not allowed any base amount; *see 34.3* for computing taxable Social Security benefits.

Social Security Benefits

34.2 Social Security Benefits Subject to Tax

If you received or repaid Social Security benefits in 1997, you should receive Form SSA-1099 by January 31, 1998. The form will show total benefits paid to you and any benefits you repaid to the government in 1997. Amounts withheld for Medicare premiums, workers' compensation offset, or attorneys' fees are itemized and included in Box 3, benefits paid in 1997. Keep Form SSA-1099 for your records; do not attach it to your return.

The *net benefit* shown in Box 5 of Form SSA-1099 (benefits paid *less* benefits repaid) is the benefit amount used to determine taxable benefits under *34.3.*

Railroad Retirement benefits.   The portion of your Tier 1 Railroad Retirement benefits which is equivalent to Social Security retirement benefits is subject to the computation at *34.3* for determining taxable benefits. If any part of your 1997 Tier 1 benefits is equivalent to Social Security benefits, you should receive Form RRB-1099 from the government by January 31, 1998. The *net* Social Security Equivalent Benefit shown on Form RRB-1099 is the amount used to determine taxable benefits under *34.3.* Other Tier 1 Railroad Retirement benefits, as well as Tier 2 benefits, are treated as pension income and not as Social Security benefits for tax purposes.

Benefits paid on behalf of child or incompetent.   If a child is entitled to Social Security benefits, such as after the death of a parent, the benefit is considered to be the child's regardless of who actually receives the payment. Whether the child's benefit is subject to tax will depend on the amount of the child's income.

Workers' compensation.   If you are receiving Social Security disability payments and workers' compensation for the same disability, your Social Security benefits may be reduced by the workers' compensation. For example, you are entitled to Social Security disability benefits of $5,000 a year. After receiving a $1,000 workers' compensation award, your disability benefits are reduced to $4,000. For purposes of the computation steps of *34.3,* you treat the full $5,000 as Social Security benefits.

Repayment of benefits.   If you lose Social Security benefits because of excessive outside income, the forfeited amount reduces your benefits subject to tax. Form SSA-1099 accounts for this reduction and you report the amount shown in Box 5.

If Box 5 shows a negative amount (a figure in parentheses), none of your benefits are taxable. If the negative amount is related to Social Security benefits included in gross income in a prior year, you may be entitled to a deduction or a credit; *see* IRS Publication 915 for further instructions on how to figure the deduction or credit when your repayments exceed your gross benefits.

Taxable Social Security benefits are not considered earnings and therefore may not be the basis of an IRA contribution *(8.2)*, earned income credit *(25.8)*, or foreign earned income exclusion *(36.2)*.

Nonresident aliens. Unless provided otherwise by tax treaty, 85% of a nonresident alien's Social Security benefits will be subject to the 30% withholding tax imposed on U.S. source income that is not connected with a U.S. trade or business. *See* IRS Publication 519 for further details.

34.3 Computing Taxable Social Security Benefits

Before reading the following tax rules, we suggest that you first fill out Worksheet I for listing your benefits and Worksheet II for determining your *provisional income*. Part of your net Social Security benefits will be subject to tax if your *provisional income* exceeds a base amount of $25,000 or $32,000.

Note that on Line 1 of Worksheet II *tax-exempt interest* reported on Line 8b of your return is included as part of provisional income for purposes of figuring the taxable part of your Social Security benefits, although this amount is not included when figuring your regular tax liability.

Worksheet I: Personal Status and Benefits Data

Check only one box:

☐ A. Single, head of household, or qualifying widow(er) with dependent child.
☐ B. Married filing a joint return.
☐ C. Married filing separately and LIVED WITH your spouse at ANY TIME during 1997.
☐ D. Married filing separately and LIVED APART from your spouse FOR ALL of 1997.

Your Social Security benefits:

1. Enter net Social Security benefits from
   Box 5 of SSA-1099 or RRB-1099.   1._____
2. 50% of Line 1.   2._____
3. 85% of Line 1.   3._____

Worksheet II: Figuring Your Provisional Income

1. From *Form 1040,* add Lines 7, 8a, 8b, 9 through 14, 15b,
   16b, 17 through 19, and Line 21. Do not include Line 20a
   (net Social Security benefits). Enter the total here.

   From *Form 1040A,* add Lines 7, 8a, 8b, 9, 10b, 11b,
   and 12. Do not include Line 13a (net Social Security
   benefits). Enter the total here.   1._____
2. *Plus:* Tax-free foreign earned income and foreign
   housing.   _____
   Other exclusions.*   _____   2._____
3. Add Lines 1 and 2.   3._____
4. *Minus:* Adjustments from Line 31 of Form 1040 other than the
   foreign housing deduction, or from Line 15 of Form 1040A.
   Do not include IRA contributions if you are covered by an
   employer retirement plan; *see* the next page for alternative
   computation.   4._____
5. Subtract Line 4 from Line 3.   5._____
6. Enter the amount from Line 2, Worksheet I (50% of net
   Social Security benefits).   6._____
7. Add Lines 5 and 6. This is provisional income.   7._____

Include exclusions for qualifying U.S. savings bond interest used for tuition, employer-provided adoption benefits, and income earned as a bona fide resident of Puerto Rico or American Samoa.

Married filing separately. If you are married filing separately and during 1997 you lived with your spouse at any time, you must include in your taxable income the *lesser* of (1) 85% of your net Social Security benefits (Line 3 of Worksheet I) *and* (2) 85% of the provisional income shown on Line 7 of Worksheet II.

IRA contributions. Do *not* use the worksheet below if you are an active participant in an employer retirement plan and you plan to make deductible IRA contributions *(8.4)*. You must use the worksheets printed in IRS Publication 590. With the worksheets, you first determine the amount of Social Security benefits that would be subject to tax, assuming you did not claim any IRA deduction. That amount is then used to figure the allowable IRA deduction, taking into account any limitations under the phase-out rules *(8.4)*, and, finally, the allowable IRA deduction is used to compute the taxable portion of your Social Security benefits.

If you are not covered by an employer retirement plan, you may use the worksheet to figure the taxable portion of your Social Security benefits.

Worksheet III: Figuring Taxable Benefits

Check only one box:

❑   A. Single, head of household, or qualifying widow(er) with dependent child.
❑   B. Married filing a joint return.
❑   C. Married filing separately and LIVED WITH your spouse at ANY TIME during 1997.
❑   D. Married filing separately and LIVED APART from your spouse FOR ALL of 1997.

1. Enter Line 7 from Worksheet II (provisional income).   1._____
2. Enter: $25,000 if you checked
   Box A or D above, or $32,000 if you checked
   Box B, or 0 if you checked Box C.
3. Subtract Line 2 from Line 1. If zero or less, enter 0.   2._____
      3._____

   • If Line 3 is zero, stop. None of your Social
     Security or Railroad Retirement benefits are taxable.
   • If Line 3 is more than zero, go to Line 4.

4. Enter 50% of Line 3.   4._____
5. Enter Line 2 of Worksheet I.   5._____
6. Enter: $34,000 if you checked
   Box A or D above, or $44,000 if you checked
   Box B, or 0 if you checked Box C.
7. Subtract Line 6 from Line 1. If zero or   6._____
   less, enter 0 and go to Line 13 now.
   If Line 7 is more than zero, go to Line 8.   7._____
8. Enter: $4,500 if you checked
   Box A or D above, or $6,000 if you checked
   Box B, or -0- if you checked Box C.
9. Enter the smallest of Line 4, Line 5, and Line 8.   8._____
10. Multiply Line 7 by 85% (.85).   9._____
11. Add Lines 9 and 10.   10._____
12. Enter Line 3 of Worksheet I.   11._____
13. **Taxable Social Security (or Railroad Retirement) benefits:**   12._____
    If Line 7 is zero, enter the *smaller* of Line 4 and Line 5. If Line 7
    is more than zero, enter the *smaller* of Line 11 and Line 12.

    Also enter this taxable amount on Line 20b of Form 1040
    or Line 13b of Form 1040A. Your net Social Security
    benefits are reported on Line 20a of Form 1040 or Line 13a
    of Form 1040A.   13._____

EXAMPLES

1. Frank Adams, who is single, has 1997 earnings of $15,000 from a part-time job, $3,000 of interest income, and $2,000 of dividends. He also receives $8,000 of net Social Security benefits (Box 5 of Form SSA-1099). Completing Worksheet II, Frank's provisional income on Line 7 is $24,000 ($15,000 + 3,000 + 2,000 + 50% of the $8,000 net Social Security benefits). Since $24,000 does not exceed the $25,000 base amount on Line 2 of Worksheet III, none of Frank's Social Security benefits are taxable.

2. Sam and Fran Baker receive in 1997 net Social Security benefits (Box 5 of Form SSA-1099) of $15,000. Their taxable interest, dividends, and capital gains are $20,000, and tax-exempt interest is $10,000. They file a joint return. Their provisional income from Line 7 of Worksheet II is $37,500 ($20,000 + 10,000 + 50% of the $15,000 net Social Security benefits). Since $37,500 exceeds the $32,000 base amount on Line 2 of Worksheet III, part of their Social Security benefits will be taxed. On Worksheet III, Sam and Fran figure that $2,750 of their benefits will be subject to tax:

Worksheet III

1.	Provisional income	$37,500
2.	Base amount for married persons filing jointly	32,000
3.	Line 1 *less* Line 2	5,500
4.	50% of Line 3	2,750
5.	50% of net Social Security benefits	7,500
6.	Adjusted base amount for married persons filing jointly	44,000
7.	Line 1 *less* Line 6	0

Since provisional income does not exceed the adjusted base amount of $44,000, the instructions for Line 13 of Worksheet III state that the taxable portion of Sam and Fran's benefits is $2,750, the lesser of Line 4 ($2,750) and Line 5 ($7,500).

34.4 Election for Lump-Sum Social Security Benefit Payment

If in 1997 you receive a lump-sum payment of benefits covering prior years, you have a choice as to how to determine the taxable portion of the benefits: (1) You may treat the entire payment as a 1997 benefit taxable under the rules of *34.3; or* (2) you may allocate the benefits between 1997 and the earlier years. Choose the method that provides the lowest required increase to income in the current year. For example, if you receive a 1997 lump-sum payment that includes benefits for 1996, you may find that an allocation of benefits is advantageous where your income over the two-year period has fluctuated and benefits allocated to 1996 would be subject to a lower taxable percentage than in 1997.

When you elect to allocate benefits to a prior year, you do not amend the return for that year. You compute the increase in income (if any) that would have resulted if the Social Security benefits had been received in that year. You then add that amount to the income of the current year.

See IRS Publication 915 for instructions on how to allocate and report the allocated income on your return.

34.5 Retiring on Social Security Benefits

Benefits are not paid automatically. You must register at the local Social Security office three months before your 65th birthday to allow time for your application to be processed and to locate all necessary information. Even if you do not plan to retire at age 65, you must register to insure your Medicare coverage.

If you retire before age 65, you may elect reduced Social Security benefits. The reduction formula is based on the number of months before age 65 that you retire. If you retire at the earliest age, 62, the reduction is about 20%.

If you delay retirement beyond age 65, your potential Social Security benefit increases for each year you delay retirement. The increase is 4½% per year for those born in 1929 or 1930, 5% for those born in 1931 or 1932, 5.5% for those born in 1933 or 1934, and 6% for those born in 1935 or 1936.

Benefits may be reduced because of earnings. If you are under age 70, Social Security benefits are reduced by earned income (wages and self-employment income). If you were age 65 or older but under age 70 in 1997, you could earn $13,500 without losing benefits. If you were under age 65 for the whole year, you could earn $8,640 without losing benefits; this ceiling is subject to

Planning Pointer

Retirement Earnings Test

For individuals age 65–69, here is the amount that may be earned without losing Social Security benefits:

In—	Earnings ceiling—
1998	$14,500
1999	15,500
2000	17,000
2001	25,000
2002	30,000

annual inflation adjustments. Once you earn more than these ceilings, benefits are reduced. If you are age 65 or over and under age 70, you lose $1 in benefits for each $3 you earn above the earnings ceiling. If you are under age 65, $1 of benefits is lost for every $2 of excess earnings. In the year of retirement, a special monthly earnings ceiling applies.

For those age 70 or over, benefits are not reduced by earnings. You can work, earn any amount, and receive full Social Security benefits.

So long as you continue to work, you pay Social Security taxes on your earnings, regardless of your age.

Regardless of your age, you may receive any amount of income from sources other than work—for example, private pensions or investments—without affecting the amount of Social Security retirement benefits.

Request an estimate of benefits and copy of earnings record. You can get an estimate of retirement benefits by sending for Form SSA-7004. After mailing in a completed Form SSA-7004, you will receive a Personal Earnings and Benefit Estimate Statement, showing your earnings history, Social Security tax payments, and an estimate of your retirement, disability, and survivor's benefits.

Form SSA-7004 is available at your local Social Security office. You can also request the form from the Social Security Administration by calling 1-800-772-1213.

34.6 How Tax on Social Security Reduces Your Earnings

There is an added tax cost of earning income if the earnings will subject your Social Security benefits to tax. Therefore, if your benefits are not currently exposed to tax, you have to figure *not only* the tax on the extra income *but also* the amount of Social Security benefits subjected to tax by those earnings. If the additional earnings will put you over the base amount *(34.3)*, then you will not only have to pay tax on the additional earnings but also on the Social Security benefits that will be subject to tax. As a result, the marginal tax rate on the extra income will be higher than the regular rate that would otherwise apply; *see* Example 2 below.

EXAMPLES

1. You are over age 70 and you and your spouse receive net Social Security benefits of $8,000. You file jointly. You have pension income of $25,000 and $3,000 in tax-exempt interest. Your provisional income *(34.3)* is $32,000. No part of your Social Security benefits is taxable because your provisional income of $32,000 does not exceed the $32,000 base amount for married persons filing jointly.

2. Same facts as in Example 1, except that you take a part-time job paying $8,000. This increases your provisional income to $40,000 and subjects $4,000 of Social Security benefits to tax.

Provisional income	$40,000
Less: Base amount	32,000
Excess	$8,000
50% of excess taxable *(34.3)*	$4,000

   The $8,000 of additional earnings increased your taxable income by $12,000, which is the $8,000 of earnings plus the $4,000 of Social Security benefits made taxable because of the increase in provisional income. Assuming a 15% tax rate, the tax on the $12,000 is $1,800 ($12,000 × 15%); the effective tax rate on the $8,000 earnings is 22.5% ($1,800 ÷ $8,000), rather than 15%. If you consider employment taxes, the effective tax rate is higher; *see* below.

When earnings result in forfeiture of Social Security benefits. If you are under 70 years of age, it is possible under the current tax structure to earn extra income and yet have only a small gain or even lose money when considering the increased tax on the earnings and on Social Security benefits, and also the forfeiture of benefits when earnings exceed the annual retirement earnings test; *see 34.5.*

Therefore, before taking on work to earn extra income, you should compute the tax cost of the extra earnings and the loss of benefits. As a rule of thumb, you may figure the extra tax cost by multiplying the earnings by your top federal tax bracket and also by the FICA tax rate of 7.65% (Social Security and Medicare withholdings) and by your top rate for state or local taxes. But be aware that this composite rate ignores the effect of the increased tax from crossing the thresholds for taxing up to 50% or 85% of Social Security benefits. Therefore, in such cases, the tax cost will be greater than the estimated composite tax rate. For greater accuracy, figure your tax position as if you were preparing two tax returns: one which does not include the extra income and the other which does include the extra income. The tax difference is the extra income tax cost of earning the extra pay. Add to this cost the FICA tax on the extra earnings and any additional state or local taxes. Then figure the amount of benefits that will be forfeited. This will give you a net gain or in some cases a net loss. If you have a tax consultant, it may be advisable to ask the consultant to make the computations.

Tax Credit for the Elderly and Disabled

34.7 Claiming the Credit for Elderly and Disabled

You may qualify for a tax credit for 1997 if you meet one of the following conditions:

- Your 65th birthday is on or before January 1, 1998; *or*
- You were under age 65 at the end of 1997, you retired before the end of 1997 because of permanent and total disability and you received taxable disability income in 1997 from your former employer's disability plan. Disability income is taxable wages or payments in lieu of wages paid to you while absent from work because of permanent and total disability. Qualifying disability income does not include payments received after reaching mandatory retirement age.

However, even if you meet one of these tests, you may not be able to claim a credit because your Social Security benefits or adjusted gross income is too high; *see 34.9.*

Disabled. You are considered permanently and totally disabled if you are unable to engage in any substantial gainful activity by reason of any medically determinable physical or mental impairment which can be expected to result in death or which has lasted or can be expected to last for a continuous period of not less than 12 months.

For the first year you claim the credit, you need a physician's certification of your disability. For later years, new certifications are generally not required.

Nonresident aliens. You may not claim the credit if you are a nonresident alien at any time during 1997, unless you are married to a citizen or resident and you have elected to be treated as a resident; *see 1.8.*

Amount of credit. The amount of the credit is 15% times the base amount after reductions. The base amount for the credit is generally $7,500, $5,000, or $3,750, as shown in *34.8*. The base amount is reduced by nontaxable Social Security and other tax-free pensions, as well as by adjusted gross income exceeding specific limits as explained in *34.9.*

How to claim the credit. You claim the credit on Schedule R if you file Form 1040. If you file Form 1040A, claim the credit on Schedule 3. You may not claim the credit on Form 1040EZ.

The credit is not refundable. That is, it is allowed only up to your tax liability. Furthermore, the credit may be limited if you have tax adjustments or preference items subject to alternative minimum tax *(23.3)*, even though you are not actually subject to AMT because of the AMT exemption. Follow the tax form instructions.

Married couples. A married couple may claim the credit only if they file a joint return. However, if a husband and wife live apart at all times during the taxable year and file separately, the credit may be claimed on a separate return.

34.8 Base Amount for the Elderly or Disabled Credit

The law fixes an initial base amount for figuring the credit. This base amount is reduced by certain tax-free benefits and excess adjusted gross income; *see 34.9.* The credit is 15% of the base amount after reductions.

The initial base amount is:

- $5,000, if you are single, head of household, or are a qualified widow(er).
- $5,000, if you file a joint return and only one spouse is eligible for the credit.
- $7,500, if you file a joint return and both spouses are eligible for the credit. The credit is figured solely on this base; a separate computation is not made for each spouse.

- $3,750, if you are married and file a separate return. The credit may be claimed on a separate return only if you and your spouse have lived apart at all times during the year.

Base amount if disabled. If you are under age 65 and permanently and totally disabled, the base amount for figuring the credit is the *lower* of your 1997 disability income and the initial base amount for your filing status shown above. For example, if you are single, under age 65, permanently and totally disabled, and received disability income of $4,800, you figure the credit on $4,800, which is less than the base of $5,000 for single persons.

Joint return and both spouses qualify for the credit. If one spouse is age 65 or over and one spouse is under age 65 and receives disability income, the initial base amount is the lesser of (1) $7,500 and (2) $5,000 *plus* the disability income of the spouse under age 65. If both spouses are under age 65 and disabled, the initial base amount is the total of their disability income, not exceeding $7,500.

34.9 Reduction of Credit Base Amount for Elderly and Disabled

The $3,750, $5,000, or $7,500 credit base amount *(34.8)* is reduced by nontaxable pensions and Social Security, and also by "excess" adjusted gross income, figured as follows:

Nontaxable Social Security and pensions. The base amount is reduced by:

- Social Security and Railroad Retirement benefits which are *not taxable* under rules of *34.3;* and

- Tax-free pension, annuity, or disability income paid under a law administered by the Veterans' Administration or under other federal laws.

   You do *not* reduce the base amount for: military disability pensions received for active service in the Armed Forces or in the Coast Guard and Geodetic Survey or Public Health Service; certain disability annuities paid under the Foreign Service Act of 1980; and workers' compensation benefits. However, if Social Security benefits are reduced by workers' compensation benefits, the amount of workers' compensation benefits is treated as Social Security benefits that reduce the base.

Excess adjusted gross income. You reduce the base amount by one-half of adjusted gross income (AGI) exceeding: $7,500 if you are single, head of household, or a qualified widow(er); $10,000 if you are married filing a joint return; or $5,000 if you are married and file a separate return. Applying these income floors, the credit is no longer available to a single person when AGI reaches $17,500, or $20,000 on a joint return where one spouse is eligible for the credit, and $25,000 where both spouses are eligible for the credit.

! *Caution*

Low Social Security Benefits Required for Credit

The tax credit for the elderly or disabled is not available to an unmarried individual who receives $5,000 or more of nontaxable Social Security benefits or nontaxable federal pensions such as from the Veterans' Administration. The $5,000 limit also applies if you are married filing jointly and only one spouse qualifies for the credit. The limit is $7,500 if you file a joint return and both spouses qualify for the credit.

EXAMPLES

1. A single person over age 65 has adjusted gross income (AGI) of $9,000 and receives Social Security benefits of $4,200 which are not taxable under *34.3*. His credit is $7.50.

Initial base amount *(34.8)*	$5,000
Less: Nontaxable Social Security	4,200
	$800
Less: 50% of AGI over $7,500	750
Credit base	$50
Credit (15%)	$7.50

2. A married couple, both spouses over age 65, file a joint return showing adjusted gross income of $12,000. They received Social Security benefits of $5,000, which are not subject to tax.

Initial base amount *(34.8)*	$7,500
Less: Nontaxable Social Security	5,000
	$2,500
Less: 50% of AGI over $10,000	1,000
Credit base	$1,500
Credit (15%)	$225

Continuing Care Communities

34.10 Tax Effects of Moving to a Continuing Care Facility

Senior citizens who move into "continuing care" or "life-care" facilities pay large upfront entrance fees upon admittance, as well as monthly fees thereafter in return for a residence, meals, and lifetime health care, including long-term skilled nursing care, should that become necessary. The payments raise several tax issues discussed in this section and in *34.11*.

Portion of monthly fees deductible as medical expense.   Part of the monthly fees to a life-care community are allocable to health care, which you may deduct as an itemized medical expense subject to the 7.5% floor; *see 17.1.* Continuing care facilities generally send a statement to the residents specifying what portion of their monthly service fees went towards health care.

What about the upfront payments required by life-care communities? Part may be allowable as a medical expense deduction if you can prove what part of the lump sum is allocable to future medical coverage. The IRS recognizes that a deduction may be based on a showing that the life-care facility historically allocates a specified percentage of the fee to future medical care. With such proof there is a current obligation to pay and the allocable medical expenses are deductible when the lump sum is paid. The IRS has allowed deductions in the situations described in the Examples at *17.11.*

Charitable contribution deductions.   Payments made to a tax-exempt organization that operates a life-care community are generally not deductible charitable contributions because you are receiving services in exchange. If you donate amounts over and above your regular monthly fees and do not receive any extra benefit as a result, you may deduct the excess payment as a charitable contribution; *see 14.16.*

In one case, an individual was allowed by the Tax Court and an appeals court to claim a charitable contribution deduction for a "sponsorship gift" paid to a life-care retirement facility where she and her husband were residents. The sponsorship gift was entirely separate from her entrance fee; it was not required for admission and did not entitle her to reduced monthly payments. She did not receive any extra benefit from her gift and was not entitled to a refund of any part of it.

34.11   Imputed Interest on Refundable Entrance Fees

You must pay a lump-sum entrance fee when you enter a continuing care community. Depending on the type of plan, a portion of the lump-sum fee may be refundable either to you if you move from the community or to your heirs upon your death. The payment of the fee may also reduce your monthly charges.

These features may result in an unexpected tax liability under the imputed interest rules. Part of the refundable entrance fee is considered a "loan" to the continuing care facility, so that imputed interest income may be charged to you under the rules of *4.31.* According to Congressional committee reports, these loan rules do *not* apply, and thus the imputed interest rules do *not* apply, to limited refund plans, under which the entrance fee is refundable on a declining pro rata basis over a relatively short number of years.

In applying the imputed interest rules, the tax law distinguishes between qualified and nonqualified continuing care facilities. The tax treatment of nonqualified facilities is currently in a state of limbo. The IRS has delayed ruling on the tax treatment of entrance fees to nonqualified facilities so that the imputed interest rules will not be applied until the IRS releases regulations requiring tax and explaining how to compute the amount of imputed interest. The tax treatment of qualified facilities is specifically covered by law and is explained in the following paragraphs. Generally, qualified care facilities provide long-term nursing care if and when a resident becomes incapacitated. A nonqualified facility provides only limited short-term care which may be as short as 30 days.

Qualified continuing care facilities.   The "loan" portion of an entrance fee of a qualified continuing care facility is not subject to imputed interest unless it exceeds an annual floor. For 1997, refundable loans of up to $131,300 are exempt from the imputed interest rules provided that (1) you or your spouse were at least age 65 during the year; and (2) the care facility provides a separate living unit, meals, maintenance, routine medical care, and, if it later becomes necessary, future long-term nursing care for no substantial additional charge. Incoming residents must not initially require long term nursing care, but such care must be provided when it becomes necessary. A traditional nursing home is not a qualified continuing care facility. The $131,300 exception is subject to increases for inflation.

Since only the refundable portion of the fee is treated as a loan, the larger the payment or refund percentage is, the greater the potential imputed interest liability is. For example, in 1997, you and your spouse paid $100,000 for a two-bedroom apartment. If your guaranteed refund percentage is 75%, the imputed interest rules would not apply in 1997 because the "loan" or $120,000 (75% of $160,000) is below the $131,300 floor. However, if the refund percentage is 85%, the loan is $136,000 (85% of $160,000), and the $4,700 excess over the $131,300 floor is subject to imputed interest.

If imputed interest applies, the care facility should give you a Form 1099 indicating the taxable amount.

Chapter 35

Tax Savings for Members of the Armed Forces

Special tax benefits are provided to Armed Forces personnel. A major tax-free benefit is the combat pay exclusion. Under this exclusion, members of the Armed Forces, including active duty reservists, may exclude from gross income all compensation for active service received for any month in which they served in a combat zone or were hospitalized as a result of any wound, injury, or disease incurred while serving in a combat zone. Commissioned officers are allowed an exclusion equal to the highest rate of basic pay at the top pay level for enlisted personnel, plus any hostile fire/imminent danger pay received for the month.

Other pay benefits may be tax free, and you may be able to get filing extensions and time extensions for home residence replacements. A list of tax-free benefits may be found at *35.2*. Filing extensions are discussed at *35.5*.

A special law designates Bosnia and Herzegovina, Croatia, and Macedonia as a qualified hazardous duty area and treats it as a combat zone for tax purposes.

35.1 Taxable Armed Forces Pay and Benefits

Armed Forces personnel report as taxable pay the following items:

- Basic pay for active duty, attendance at a designated service school, back wages, drills, reserve training, and training duty
- Special pay for aviation career incentives, diving duty, foreign duty (for serving outside the 48 contiguous states and the District of Columbia), hazardous duty, medical and dental officers, nuclear-qualified officers, and special duty assignment pay
- Enlistment and reenlistment bonuses
- Payments for accrued leave, and personal money allowances paid to high-ranking officers
- Scholarships, such as the Armed Forces Health Profession Scholarship Program (AFHPSP) and similar programs, granted after August 16, 1986
- Student loan repayment from programs such as the General Educational Loan Repayment Program

Community property. If you are married and your domicile (permanent home to which you intend to return) is in one of the following states, your military pay is subject to community property laws of that state: Arizona, California, Idaho, Louisiana, Nevada, New Mexico, Texas, Washington, and Wisconsin. *See 1.9* for community property reporting rules.

State income tax withholding. A state that makes a withholding agreement with the Secretary of the Treasury may subject members of the Armed Forces regularly stationed within that state to its payroll withholding provisions. National Guard members and reservists are not considered to be members of the Armed Forces for purposes of this section.

Where and when to file. Mail your return to the Internal Revenue Service Center for the place you are stationed. For example, you are stationed in Arizona but have a permanent home address in Missouri; you send your return to the Service Center for Arizona. For filing extensions on entering the service, *see 35.7.*

35.2 Tax-Free Armed Forces Benefits

The following benefits are *not* subject to tax:

- Combat pay; *see 35.4*
- Living allowances for: BAQ (Basic Allowance for Quarters). You may deduct mortgage interest and real estate taxes on your home even if you pay these expenses with BAQ funds.
- BAS (Basic Allowance for Subsistence) living allowances
- Housing and cost-of-living allowances abroad, whether paid by the U.S. Government or by a foreign government
- VHA (Variable Housing Allowance)
- Family allowances for educational expenses for dependents, emergencies, evacuation to a place of safety, and separation
- Death allowances for burial services, death gratuity payments to eligible survivors (not more than $3,000), and travel of dependents to burial site
- Dislocation allowance, intended to partially reimburse expenses such as lease forfeitures, temporary living charges in hotels, and other expenses incurred in relocating a household
- Temporary lodging expense allowance intended to partially offset the added living expenses of temporary lodging within the United States for up to 10 days and up to 60 days abroad
- A moving-in housing allowance, intended to defray costs, such as for rental agent fees, home-security improvements, and supplemental heating equipment, associated with occupying leased space outside the United States
- Travel allowances for annual round trip for dependent students, leave between consecutive overseas tours, reassignment in a dependent-restricted status, and transportation for you or your dependents during ship overhaul or inactivation
- Defense counseling payments
- ROTC educational and subsistence allowances
- Survivor and retirement protection plan premium payments
- Uniform allowances paid to officers and uniforms furnished to enlisted personnel
- Medical or hospital treatment provided by the United States in government hospitals
- Pay forfeited on order of a court martial
- Education, training, or subsistence allowances paid under any law administered by the Department of Veterans Affairs (VA). However, deductible education costs must be reduced by the VA allowance.
- Adjustments in pay to compensate for losses resulting from inflated foreign currency
- Payments to former prisoners of war from the U.S. Government in compensation for inhumane treatment suffered at the hands of an enemy government

- Benefits under Servicemembers' Group Life Insurance
- Dividends on GI insurance. These are a tax-free return of premiums paid.
- Interest on dividends left on deposit with the Department of Veterans Affairs (VA). The IRS has revoked a prior ruling that subjected such interest to tax.

Disability retirement pay.　Your disability retirement pay may be tax free if you are a former member of the Armed Forces of any country, the Foreign Service, the Coast Guard, the National Oceanic and Atmospheric Administration, or the Public Health Service; *see 2.13*. Tax-free treatment of disability retirement pay is retroactive to the date of the application for benefits.

35.3　Deductions for Armed Forces Personnel

Members of the Armed Services may deduct the items listed below as miscellaneous itemized deductions subject to the 2% adjusted gross income (AGI) floor; *see 19.1:*

- Board and lodging costs over those paid to you by the government while on temporary duty away from your home base
- Costs of rank insignia, collar devices, gold braids, etc. and the cost of altering rank insignia when promoted or demoted
- Contributions to a "Company" fund made according to Service regulations. But personal contributions made to stimulate interest and morale in a unit are not deductible.
- Court martial legal expenses in successfully defending against the charge of conduct unbecoming an officer
- Dues to professional societies. But you may not deduct dues for officers' and noncommissioned officers' clubs.
- Expense of obtaining increased retirement pay
- Out-of-pocket moving expenses for service-connected moves. The 50-mile test and the 39-week test generally required to deduct moving expenses do not have to be met; *see 12.3.*
- Subscriptions to professional journals
- Transportation, food, and lodging expenses while on official travel status. But you are taxed on mileage and per diem subsistence allowance.
- Travel expenses while ship or squadron is "away from home" post or base. However, you are not considered "away from home" if you are at your *permanent* duty station or you are a naval officer assigned to permanent duty aboard a ship; *see also 20.6.*
- Uniforms. The cost and cleaning of uniforms are deductible if: (1) they must be worn on duty; (2) they cannot under military regulations be worn off duty; and (3) the cost exceeds any tax-free clothing allowance.

35.4　Tax-Free Pay for Service in Combat Zone or Hazardous Duty Area

If your grade is below commissioned officer and you serve in a designated combat zone or hazardous duty area during any part of a month, *all* of your qualifying military pay (*see* below) for that month is excluded from your taxable income. You may also exclude military pay earned during any part of a month that you are hospitalized as a result of wounds, disease, or injury incurred in a combat zone or hazardous duty area. The exclusion for military pay while hospitalized does not apply to any month that begins more than two years after the end of combat activities in that combat zone or hazardous duty area. Your hospitalization does not have to be in the combat zone or hazardous duty area.

Members of the U.S. Armed Forces qualifying for the exclusion include commissioned officers and enlisted personnel in all regular and reserve units under control of the Secretaries of Defense, Army, Navy, and Air Force, and the Coast Guard. Members of the U.S. Merchant Marines or the American Red Cross are not included.

Officers.　If you are a commissioned officer, you may exclude up to the highest rate of basic pay at the highest pay grade that enlisted personnel receive per month plus any hostile fire/imminent danger pay received for each month during any part of which you served in a combat zone or hazardous duty area.

If you are a commissioned warrant officer, you are considered an enlisted person.

What is included as tax-free pay?　The following military pay qualifies for tax-free treatment: (1) active duty pay earned in any month you served in a combat zone or hazardous duty area; (2) a dislocation allowance if the move begins or ends in a month you served in a combat zone or hazardous duty area; (3) a reenlistment bonus if the voluntary extension or reenlistment occurs in a month you served in a combat zone or hazardous duty area; (4) pay for accrued leave earned in any month you served in a combat zone or hazardous duty area (the Department of Defense must determine that the unused leave was earned during that period); (5) pay received for duties as a member of the Armed Forces in clubs, messes, post and station theaters, and other nonappropriated fund activities. The pay must be earned in a month you served in a combat zone or hazardous duty area; and (6) awards for suggestions, inventions, or scientific achievements you are entitled to because of a submission you made in a month you served in a combat zone or hazardous duty area.

Service in the combat zone or hazardous duty area includes any periods you are absent from duty because of sickness, wounds, or leave. If, as a result of serving in a combat zone, you become a prisoner of war or missing in action, you are considered to be serving in the combat zone as long as you keep that status for military pay purposes.

Combat zone must be designated by President. A combat zone is any area the President of the United States designates by Executive Order as an area in which the U.S. Armed Forces are or have engaged in combat. An area becomes a combat zone and ceases to be a combat zone on the dates designated by the President.

A special law designates Bosnia and Herzegovina, Croatia, and Macedonia as a hazardous duty area.

Qualifying service outside combat zone or hazardous duty area. Military service outside a combat zone or hazardous duty area is considered to be performed in a combat zone or hazardous duty area if: (1) the service is in direct support of military operations in the combat zone or hazardous duty area, and (2) the service qualifies you for special military pay for duty subject to hostile fire or imminent danger. Military pay received for this service will qualify for the pay exclusion if the other requirements are met.

Nonqualifying service. The following military service does not qualify as service in a combat zone or hazardous duty area: (1) presence in a combat zone while on leave from a duty station located outside the combat zone; (2) passage over or through a combat zone during a trip between two points that are outside a combat zone; and (3) presence in a combat zone solely for your personal convenience.

Such service will not qualify you for the pay exclusion.

Hospitalized while serving in a combat zone or hazardous duty area. If you are hospitalized while serving in a combat zone or hazardous duty area for a wound, disease, or injury, it will be presumed to have been incurred while serving in the combat zone or hazardous duty area unless there is clear evidence to the contrary.

EXAMPLES
1. You are hospitalized for a specific disease after serving in a combat zone for three weeks, and the disease for which you are hospitalized has an incubation period of two to four weeks. The disease is presumed to have been incurred while you were serving in the combat zone. On the other hand, if the incubation period of the disease is one year, the disease would not have been incurred while you were serving in the combat zone.

Form W-2. The wages shown in Box 1 of your Form W-2 should not include combat pay. Retirement pay is not combat pay.

35.5 Tax Deadlines Extended for Combat Zone or Hazardous Duty Area Service

You are allowed an extension of at least 180 days (*see* the next column) to take care of tax matters if you are a member of the Armed Forces who served in a combat zone or hazardous duty area. The extension applies to filing tax returns, paying taxes, filing a Tax Court petition, filing refund claims, making an IRA contribution, and purchasing a new home for tax deferral purposes. The time allowed for the IRS to begin an audit or take collection actions is also extended.

Support personnel. The deadline extension also applies if you are serving in a combat zone or hazardous duty area in support of the Armed Forces. This includes Red Cross personnel, accred-

 Law Alert

Combat Zones and Hazardous Duty Area

The following locations (including airspace) were designated as combat zones beginning January 17, 1991 and retained such designation when this book went to press: the total land areas of Iraq, Kuwait, Saudi Arabia, Oman, Bahrain, Qatar, and the United Arab Emirates; the Persian Gulf; the Red Sea; the Gulf of Oman; the part of the Arabian Sea that is north of 10 degrees north latitude and west of 68 degrees east longitude; and the Gulf of Aden.

An exclusion is also available for service outside the designated areas if it was in direct support of combat zone military operations and qualified you for special hostile fire pay. At the time this book went to press, the Persian Gulf area continued to be a combat zone.

By law, Bosnia and Herzegovina, Croatia, and Macedonia were designated as a qualified hazardous duty area, service in which entitles service personnel to combat pay tax benefits.

ited correspondents, and civilian personnel acting under the direction of the Armed Forces in support of those forces.

Extension is minimum of 180 days.   Your deadline for taking actions with the IRS is extended for at least 180 days after the later of: (1) the last day you are in a combat zone or hazardous duty area (or the last day it qualifies as a combat zone or hazardous duty area), and (2) the last day of any continuous qualified hospitalization for injury from service in the combat zone or hazardous duty area. Hospitalization may be outside the United States, or up to five years of hospitalization in the United States.

Time in a missing status (missing in action or prisoner of war) counts as time in a combat zone or hazardous duty area.

In addition to the 180 days, your deadline is also extended by the number of days you had left to file with the IRS when you entered a combat zone or hazardous duty area. If you entered the combat zone or hazardous duty area before the time to file began, the deadline is extended by the entire filing time.

Spouses of combat zone personnel.   If your spouse serves in a combat zone or hazardous duty area, you are generally entitled to the same deadline extension as he or she is. However, any extra extension for your spouse's hospitalization within the United States is not available to you. Further, a spouse's extension does not apply to any year beginning more than two years after the end of combat or hazardous duty activities.

35.6 Tax Forgiveness for Combat Zone or Hazardous Duty Area Deaths

If a member of the Armed Forces is killed in a combat zone or hazardous duty area or dies from wounds or disease incurred while in these zones or areas, any income tax liability for the year of death or any earlier year including service in such zones or areas is waived. In addition, the service member's estate is entitled to a refund for income tax paid while serving there.

If a member of the Armed Forces was a resident of a community property state and his or her spouse reported half of the military pay on a separate return, the spouse may get a refund of taxes paid on his or her share of the combat zone or hazardous duty area pay.

Forgiveness benefits apply to an Armed Forces member serving outside the zone or area if service: (1) was in direct support of military operations there, and (2) qualified the member for special military pay for duty subject to hostile fire or imminent danger.

Missing status.   The date of death for a member of the Armed Forces who was in a missing status (missing in action or prisoner of war) is the date his or her name is removed from missing status for military pay purposes. This is true even if death occurred earlier.

How tax forgiveness is claimed.   If the individual died in a combat zone or in a terroristic or military action, you file as the individual's representative: (1) Form 1040 if a U.S. individual income tax return (Form 1040, 1040A, or 1040EZ) has not been filed for the tax year. Form W-2, Wage and Tax Statement, must accompany the return. (2) Form 1040X if a U.S. individual income tax return has been filed. A separate Form 1040X must be filed for each year in question.

Check with your local IRS office for the address of the IRS office to which the return is filed.

An attachment should accompany any return or claim and should include a computation of the decedent's tax liability before any amount is forgiven and the amount that is to be forgiven.

The following documents must also accompany all returns and claims for refund: (1) Form 1310, Statement of Person Claiming Refund Due a Deceased Taxpayer; and (2) a certification from the Department of Defense. Department of State certification is required if the decedent was a civilian employee of an agency other than the Department of Defense.

Tax abatement for civilian or military personnel killed in terroristic or military action.   Tax liability is waived for civilian or military U.S. employees killed in terroristic or military actions outside the U.S., even if the President has not designated the area as a combat zone and it is not a hazardous duty area. Tax liability is waived for the period beginning with the taxable year before the year in which the injuries were incurred and ending with the year of death. Refund claims for prior years must generally be filed on Form 1040X by the later of three years from the time the original return was filed or two years from the time the tax was paid. However, if death occurred in a combat zone, the filing period is extended by the time served in the combat zone, plus the period of continuous hospitalization outside the U.S., plus an additional 180 days. The individual must also be a U.S. employee both on the date of injury and date of death.

Tax abatement does not apply to a U.S. civilian or military employee who dies as a result of an accident or a training exercise. Abatement also does not apply to terroristic action within the United States. However, abatement does apply if the individual dies in the U.S. from a wound or injury incurred in a terroristic or military action outside the United States.

Determination of death for Vietnam MIAs.   Under prior law, MIAs were generally presumed dead as of December 31, 1982. Under current law, the date of death of service members missing in action in Vietnam is the date determined by the Armed Forces. Thus, under current law, tax abatement may be available for years after 1982. Furthermore, the date of death, as determined by the Armed Forces, also applies for such rules as whether to file as a surviving spouse, and for postponing the due date for filing returns and paying taxes.

35.7 Extension To Pay Your Tax When Entering the Service

If you are unable to pay your tax when you enter the Armed Forces, you may get an extension until six months after your initial period of service ends. Get a form at the IRS office of your District Director or write a letter to the District Director or to the IRS office requesting payment (your spouse or parent may do it for you). An extension, without interest, may be given if your income dropped after entering the military *and* you actually apply for the extension.

The extension does not cover your spouse, who must file a separate return and pay the tax due. But you and your spouse may file a joint return before the postponement period expires even though your spouse filed a separate return for that particular year. No interest is charged on this postponement of your tax.

Automatic extension of time to file your return.   If you are on duty outside the U.S. or Puerto Rico on April 15, 1998, you get an automatic two-month extension to file your 1997 return; *see* page 5.

Interest charged on back taxes.   If you do not show hardship qualifying you for the above interest-free payment extension, the IRS may reduce its interest rate on the deficiency. The maximum interest rate the IRS may charge for taxes incurred prior to your entry into active service is 6%. This reduced rate applies only to the period of your active duty.

35.8 Tax Information for Reservists

Transportation costs to reservist meetings generally are not deductible. A possible exception is the cost of traveling from your regular job location to a meeting held on a regular workday. The cost would be deductible, subject to the 2% adjusted gross income (AGI) floor for miscellaneous itemized deductions; *see 19.1*.

If you travel overnight away from your tax home *(20.6)* to a meeting or training camp, you may deduct expenses for transportation, lodging, and meals subject to the 50% reduction.

If you are called for active duty away from your tax home, you may deduct travel expenses provided you keep your regular job while on active duty, return to it after you are released, and pay for those expenses at the military post. To the extent they exceed BAQ (quarters) and BAS (subsistence) allowances, the expenses are deductible only as a miscellaneous itemized deduction subject to the 2% AGI floor.

Uniform costs.   The cost and upkeep of uniforms is deductible only if you are prohibited from wearing them when off duty; *see 19.6*. A deduction allowed under this test must be reduced by any uniform allowance you receive, and the unreimbursed cost is subject to the 2% adjusted gross income (AGI) floor for miscellaneous itemized deductions.

Deferring tax payments and reduction of IRS interest rate.   If you owed a tax deficiency to the IRS before being called to active duty, the IRS may defer payment, without interest, if your ability to pay has been severely impaired by your call-up. If you are not allowed a deferment, the IRS will reduce its interest charge to 6% on the taxes you owed before your call-up.

Chapter 36

How To Treat Foreign Earned Income

There is a tax incentive for working abroad—in 1997 up to $70,000 of income earned abroad may escape U.S. income taxes and you may be entitled to an exclusion or deduction for certain housing costs. In 1998, you may earn up to $72,000 tax free, $74,000 in 1999, $76,000 in 2000, $78,000 in 2001, and $80,000 after 2001. In measuring the economic value of this tax savings, consider the extra cost of living abroad. In some areas, the high cost of living and currency exchange rates will erode your tax savings and may make the position economically unfeasible.

The exclusion does not apply to investment income or to any other earned income that does not meet the exclusion tests.

To claim a foreign income exclusion you must satisfy a foreign residence or physical presence test.

Employees of the U.S. Government may not claim an exclusion based on the government pay earned abroad.

36.1 Claiming the Foreign Earned Income Exclusion

You must file a U.S. return if your gross income *exceeds* the filing threshold for your personal status, even though all or part of your foreign earned income may be tax free. The exclusion is not automatic; you must elect it. You elect the foreign earned income exclusion on Form 2555, which you attach to Form 1040. The housing cost exclusion *(36.3)* is also elected on Form 2555.

You may file simplified Form 2555-EZ if your 1997 foreign wages are $70,000 or less, you do not have self-employment income, and you do not claim the foreign housing exclusion, housing deduction, and business or moving expenses.

A separate exclusion is allowed for the value of meals and lodging received by employees living in qualified camps; *see 36.8.*

If you claim the foreign earned income exclusion of $70,000, you may not:

- Claim business deductions allocable to the excluded income;
- Make a deductible IRA contribution based on the excluded income; or
- Claim foreign taxes, paid on excluded income, as a credit or deduction.

In deciding whether to claim the exclusion, compare the overall tax (1) with the exclusion; and (2) without the exclusion but with the full foreign tax credit and allocable deductions. Choose whichever gives you the lower tax; *see 36.2 and 36.6.*

Once you elect the exclusion, that election remains in effect for all future years unless you revoke it. If you revoke the election, you cannot elect the exclusion again during the next five years without IRS consent. A revocation is made in a statement attached to your return for the year you want it to take effect. The foreign earned income exclusion and the housing cost exclusion must be revoked separately.

36.2 Qualifying for the Foreign Earned Income Exclusion

You may elect the exclusion for foreign earned income only if your tax home is in a foreign country *and* you meet either the foreign residence test *or* the foreign physical presence test of 330 days. The tests are discussed at *36.5.* Tax home is discussed at *20.6.* If your tax home is in the U.S., you may not claim the exclusion but may claim the foreign tax credit and your living expenses while away from home if you meet the rules at *20.9* for temporary assignments *expected* to last one year or less. U.S. government employees may not claim either the earned income exclusion or housing exclusion based on government pay.

Exclusion prorated on a daily basis. If you qualify under the foreign residence or physical presence test for only part of 1997, the $70,000 exclusion limit is reduced on a daily basis.

EXAMPLES
1. You were a resident of France from February 20, 1995, until June 30, 1997. On July 1 you returned to the U.S. Since your period of foreign residency included all of 1996, thereby satisfying the foreign residence test, you may claim a prorated exclusion for 1997. As you were abroad for 181 of the 365 days in 1997, you exclude earnings up to $\frac{182}{366}$ of the $70,000 maximum exclusion. If you earned $60,000 from January through June 1997, you would exclude $34,712 ($70,000 × $\frac{182}{366}$).
2. You worked in France from June 1, 1996, through September 30, 1997. Your only days outside France were a 15-day vacation to the U.S. in December 1996. You do not qualify for an exclusion under the foreign residence test because you were not abroad for a full taxable year; you were not abroad for either the full year of 1996 or 1997. However, you do qualify under the physical presence test; you were physically present abroad for at least 330 full days during a 12-month period. The 12-month period giving you the largest 1997 exclusion is the 12-month period starting October 21, 1996, and ending October 20, 1997. *See 36.5* for figuring the 12-month period. Since you were abroad for at least 330 full days during that 12-month period, you may claim an exclusion. In 1997, you were abroad for 293 days within the 12-month period (January 1 to October 20, 1997, is 293 days). Thus, you exclude earnings up to $\frac{294}{366}$ of the maximum exclusion. If your earnings in France for 1997 were $80,000, your exclusion is limited to $56,192 ($70,000 × $\frac{294}{366}$).

If you are married and you and your spouse each have foreign earned income and meet the foreign residence or physical presence test, you may each claim a separate exclusion. If your permanent home is in a community property state, your earned income is not considered community property for purposes of the exclusion.

Caution

Claiming Foreign Tax Credit Revokes Prior Election

If you have been claiming the $70,000 exclusion and decide that it would be advantageous this year to forego the exclusion and instead claim the foreign tax credit for foreign earned income, be aware that claiming the credit is treated by the IRS as a revocation of the prior exclusion election. You cannot claim a credit for the next five years unless the IRS allows you to reelect the exclusion.

Claiming a foreign tax credit also may revoke a prior election to claim the housing cost exclusion. Depending on the foreign earned income in the year the credit is claimed, the credit may be considered a revocation of a prior earned income exclusion election and also a prior housing cost exclusion election, or as a revocation of only one of the elections.

A good faith error in calculating foreign earned income that leads to claiming a foreign credit will not be treated as a revocation of prior elections.

Foreign earnings from a prior year. Foreign income earned in a prior year but paid in 1997 does not qualify for the 1997 exclusion. However, if the income was attributable to foreign services performed in 1996, the pay is tax free in 1997 provided you did not use the full 1996 exclusion of $70,000. Under another exception, payments received in 1997 for 1996 services are treated as 1997 income if the payment was within a normal payroll period of 16 days or less that included the last day of 1996. If the services were performed before 1996, no exclusion is available to shelter the pay.

Income for services performed in the U.S. does not qualify for the exclusion, even though it is paid to you while you are abroad.

Foreign tax credit. Foreign taxes paid on tax-free foreign earned income do not qualify for a credit or deduction. But if your foreign pay exceeds $70,000, you may claim a foreign tax credit or deduction for the foreign taxes allocated to taxable income. The instructions to Forms 2555 and 1116 and IRS Publication 514 provide details for making the computation.

Countries subject to travel restrictions. You may not claim the exclusion if you work in a country subject to U.S. government travel restrictions. You are not treated as a bona fide resident of, or as present in, a country subject to the travel ban. Libya, Cuba, and Iraq are within this ban. Check Form 2555 for changes to this list.

36.3 How To Treat Housing Costs

The housing costs of employees and self-employed persons are treated differently by the tax law. Employees get a housing exclusion; self-employed persons get a deduction from *taxable* foreign earned income. If you live in a special camp provided by your employer, all housing costs are excluded; *see* 36.8.

Exclusion for employer-financed housing costs. If you qualify for the exclusion for all of 1997 and your foreign wage or salary income plus the value of employer-financed housing costs in 1997 does not exceed $70,000, both parts of your pay package are tax free. Your housing costs are considered to be employer-financed as long as they are covered by salary, employer reimbursements, a housing allowance, or if they are paid directly by your employer. If wages plus employer-financed housing exceed $70,000, a special housing exclusion will shelter part of your housing costs from tax. The housing exclusion is the difference between the employer's payment of reasonable housing expenses and a "base housing amount." The base housing amount is 16% of the salary for a U.S. government employee at the GS-14, Step 1 level as of the beginning of the year (the 1997 base amount may be found in Form 2555). If you qualify under the foreign residence or physical presence test for only part of 1997, the base housing amount is reduced on a daily basis. Follow instructions to Form 2555. The housing cost exclusion is elected on Form 2555. Employer-financed housing payments exceeding this housing cost exclusion may also escape tax if your foreign salary is below the maximum foreign earned income exclusion. That part of the foreign earned income exclusion not applied to your salary may be applied to housing costs; *see* Example 1 below.

On Form 2555, you figure the housing exclusion before the foreign income exclusion. The income exclusion is limited to the excess of foreign earned income over the housing exclusion.

EXAMPLES
(Assume qualification for full-year exclusion)
1. In 1997, your salary for work abroad is $57,808 and your employer pays $13,076 for your housing. On Form 2555, you list $70,884 (salary *plus* housing) as your foreign earned income. Assume that the housing cost exclusion is $3,650 (housing costs of $13,076 exceeding a base housing amount of $9,426). Your earned income exclusion is $67,234: $70,884 earned income *less* $3,650 housing exclusion.

2. In 1997, you earn a salary of $60,325 abroad and your employer pays $13,076 for your housing. Assume the housing exclusion is $3,650 (housing costs of $13,076 exceeding a base housing amount of $9,426). All of your salary plus the full amount of the housing costs avoids tax: the housing cost exclusion of $3,650 and an earned income exclusion of $69,751 ($73,401 foreign earned income *less* $3,650 housing exclusion).

3. Same as Example 2 above, except that you earn $64,325. Foreign earned income is $77,401 ($64,325 *plus* $13,076), but the total amount of income not subject to tax is $73,650. The total tax-free amount is made up of the housing cost exclusion of $3,650 and the maximum foreign earned income exclusion of $70,000.

Reasonable housing expenses.   Include rent, utilities other than telephone costs, insurance, parking, furniture rentals, and repairs for yourself, your spouse, and dependents living with you. The following expenses do not qualify: cost of purchasing a home, furniture, or accessories; home improvements; payments of mortgage principal; domestic labor; and depreciation on a home or on improvements to leased housing. Furthermore, interest and taxes which are otherwise deductible do not qualify for the exclusion.

You may include the costs of a separate household that you maintain outside the U.S. for your spouse and dependents because living conditions at your foreign home are adverse.

Self-employed persons.   On Form 2555, self-employed individuals may claim a limited deduction for housing costs exceeding the base housing amount. You may claim this deduction only to the extent it offsets taxable foreign earned income. The deduction is claimed as an "adjustment to income" on Line 31 of Form 1040, even if you do not itemize deductions.

Where you may not deduct expenses because you do not have taxable foreign earned income, expenses may be carried forward one year and deducted in the next year to the extent of taxable foreign earned income.

If you are an employee and self-employed during the same year.   Housing expenses above the base amount are partly excludable and partly deductible. For example, if half of your foreign earned income is from services as an employee, half of the excess housing expenses over the base amount are excludable. The remaining excess housing costs are deductible to the extent of taxable foreign earned income. Follow the instructions to Form 2555.

Countries ineligible for tax benefits.   Housing expenses incurred in a country subject to a U.S. government travel restriction are not eligible for the tax benefits explained in this section. *See* Form 2555 instructions for a list of countries to which travel restrictions apply.

36.4   What Is Foreign Earned Income?

Earned income includes salaries, wages, commissions, professional fees, and bonuses. Earned income also includes allowances from your employer for housing or other expenses, as well as the value of housing or a car provided by the employer. It may also include business profits, royalties, and rents, provided this income is tied to the performance of services. Earned income does not include pension or annuity income, payments for nonqualified employee trusts or nonqualified annuities, dividends, interest, capital gains, gambling winnings, alimony, or the value of tax-free meals or lodging under the rules at *3.11*. Foreign earned income does not include amounts earned in countries subject to U.S. government travel restrictions.

Foreign earned income eligible for the exclusion must be received no later than the taxable year after the year in which you perform the services. Pay is excludable in the year of receipt if you did not use the full exclusion in the year of the services.

U.S. government pay ineligible.   If you are an employee of the U.S. government or its agencies, you may *not* exclude any part of your pay from your government employer. Courts have agreed with the IRS that U.S. government workers were U.S. employees even though they were paid from sources other than Congressionally appropriated funds. If you are not an employee of the U.S. government or any of its agencies, your pay is excludable even if paid by a government source. You are not an employee of the U.S. if you work under a contract made between your employer and the government.

Under a special law, tax liability is waived for a civilian or military employee of the U.S. government killed in a military action overseas; *see 35.6*.

Profits from sole proprietorship or partnership.   If your business consists solely of services (no capital investment), 100% of gross income is considered earned income. If services and capital are both income-producing factors, no more than 30% of your net profit may be considered earned income.

If you do not contribute any services to a business (for example, you are a "silent partner"), your share of the net profits is *not* earned income.

EXAMPLES

1. A U.S. citizen resides in England. He invests in an English partnership that sells manufactured goods outside the U.S. He performs no services for the business. His share of net profits does not qualify as earned income.

2. Same facts as in Example 1, except he devotes his full time to the partnership business. Then 30% of his share of the net profits qualifies as earned income. Thus, if his

share of profits is $50,000, earned income is $15,000 (30% of $50,000), assuming the value of his services is at least $15,000.

3. You and another person are consultants, operating as a partnership in Europe. Since capital is not an income-producing element, the entire gross income of the business is earned income.

The partnership agreement generally determines the tax status of partnership income in a U.S. partnership with a foreign branch. Thus, if the partnership agreement allocates foreign earnings to partners abroad, the allocation will be recognized unless it lacks substantial economic effect.

Fringe benefits.   The value of fringe benefits, such as the right to use company property and facilities, is added to your compensation when figuring the amount of your earned income.

Royalties.   Royalties from articles or books are earned income if you receive them for transferring all of your rights to your work, or you have contracted to write the articles or book for an amount in cash plus a royalty on sales.

Royalties from the leasing of oil and mineral lands and from patents are not earned income.

Rental income.   Rental income is generally not earned income. However, if you perform personal services, for example as an owner-manager of a hotel or rooming house in a foreign country, then up to 30% of your net rents may be earned income.

Reimbursement of employee expenses.   Do not include reimbursement of expenses as earned income to the extent they equal expenses which you adequately accounted for to your employer; *see 20.31*. If your expenses exceed reimbursements, the excess is allocated according to the rules in *36.6*. If reimbursements exceed expenses, the excess is treated as earned income.

Straight commission salespersons or other employees who arrange with their employers, for withholding purposes, to consider a percentage of their commissions as attributable to their expenses treat such amounts as earned income.

Reimbursed moving expenses.   Reimbursements of moving expenses are not reported as income if you adequately account to your employer for the expenses; *see 12*.8.

A reimbursement is taxable if received under a nonaccountable plan or for moving expenses that are not deductible *(12.3)* or that you deducted in an earlier year. However, for purposes of claiming the earned income exclusion, the reimbursement may be considered to have been earned in a year other than the year of receipt. This is important because an exclusion is allowed only for the year income is earned. If the move is from the U.S. to a foreign country, the reimbursement is considered foreign earned income in the year of the move if you qualify under the foreign residence or physical presence test for at least 120 days during that tax year. Reimbursement of moving expenses from one foreign country to another is considered foreign earned income in the year of the move, if you qualify under the residency or physical presence test at the new location for at least 120 days during the tax year. If you do not meet one of these tests in the year of the move, the reimbursements are earned income which must be allocated between the year of the move and the following tax year.

A taxable reimbursement for a move back to the U.S. is considered income from U.S. sources if you continue to work for the same employer. If you move back to the U.S. and take a job with a new employer *or* if you retire and move back to the U.S. and your old employer reimburses your moving expenses under a prior written agreement or company policy, the reimbursement is considered to be for past services in the foreign country and qualifies as foreign earned income eligible for the exclusion. The reimbursement is considered earned in the year of the move if you qualified under the residency or physical presence test *(36.5)* for at least 120 days during the tax year. Otherwise, the reimbursement is allocated between the year of the move and the year preceding the move. *See* IRS Publication 54 for details.

36.5 Meeting the Foreign Residence or Physical Presence Test

To qualify for the foreign earned income exclusion, you must be either a U.S. citizen (or U.S. resident entitled to tax treaty benefits)meeting the foreign residence test or a U.S. citizen or resident meeting the physical presence test in a foreign country. The following areas are not considered foreign countries: Puerto Rico, Virgin Islands, Guam, Commonwealth of the Northern Mariana Islands, American Samoa, or the Antarctic region.

If war or civil unrest prevented you from meeting the foreign residence or physical presence test, you may claim the exclusion for the period you actually were a resident or physically present abroad. Foreign locations and the time periods which qualify for the waiver of the residency and physical presence tests are listed in the instructions to Form 2555.

If, by the due date of your 1997 return (April 15, 1998), you have not yet satisfied the foreign residence or physical presence test, but you expect to meet either test after the filing date, you may either file on the due date and report your earnings or ask for a filing extension under the rules at *36.7*.

Foreign residence test.   You must be a U.S. citizen who is a bona fide resident of a foreign country for an uninterrupted period that includes one full tax year; a full tax year is from January 1 through December 31 for individuals who file on a calendar-year basis. Business or vacation trips to the U.S. or another country will not disqualify you from satisfying the foreign residence test. If you are abroad more than one year but less than two, the entire period qualifies if it includes one full tax year.

> **EXAMPLE**
>
> You are a bona fide foreign resident from September 30, 1996, to March 25, 1998. The period includes your entire 1997 tax year. Therefore, up to $70,000 of your 1997 earnings is excludable. Your overseas earnings in 1996 and 1998 will qualify for a proportionate part of the exclusion of $70,000 allowed for 1996 and $72,000 for 1998.

To prove you are a foreign resident, you must show your intention to be a resident of the foreign country. Evidence tending to confirm your intention to stay in a foreign country is: (1) your family accompanies you; (2) you buy a house or rent an apartment rather than a hotel room; (3) you participate in the foreign community activities; (4) you can speak the foreign language; (5) you have a permanent foreign address; (6) you join clubs there; or (7) you open charge accounts in stores in the foreign country.

Residence does not have the same meaning as *domicile*. Your domicile is a permanent place of abode; it is the place to which you eventually plan to return wherever you go. You may have a residence in a place other than your domicile. Thus, you may go, say, to Amsterdam, and take up residence there and still intend to return to your domicile in the U.S. But your leaving your domicile does not, by itself, establish a bona fide residence in a new place. You must intend to make a new place your residence.

You will not qualify if you take inconsistent positions toward your foreign residency. That is, you will *not* be treated as a bona fide resident of a foreign country if you have earned income from sources within that country, filed a statement with the authorities of that country that you are not a resident there, and have been held not subject to the income tax of that country. However, this rule does not prevent you from qualifying under the physical presence test.

If you cannot prove that you are a resident, check to determine if your stay qualifies under the physical presence test.

Physical presence test.   To qualify under this test, you must show you were on foreign soil 330 days (about 11 months) during a 12-month period. Whether you were a resident or a transient is of no importance. You have to show you were physically present in a foreign country or countries for 330 full days during any 12-consecutive-month period. The 12-month period may begin with any day. There is no requirement that it begin with your first full day abroad. It may begin before or after arrival in a foreign country and may end before or after departure from a foreign country. A *full* day is from midnight to midnight (24 consecutive hours). You must spend each of the 330 days on foreign soil. In departing from U.S. soil to go directly to the foreign country, or in returning directly to the U.S. from a foreign country, the time you spend on or over international waters does not count toward the 330-day total.

> **EXAMPLES**
> 1. On August 9, you fly from New York City to Paris. You arrive there at 10 a.m. August 10. Your first full qualifying day toward the 330-day period is August 11.
>   You may count in your 330-day period:
>   - Time spent traveling between foreign countries.
>   - Time spent on a vacation in foreign countries. There is no requirement that the 330 days must be spent on a job.
>   - Time spent in a foreign country while employed by the U.S. government counts towards the 330-day test, even though pay from the government does not qualify for the earned income exclusion.

- Time in foreign countries, territorial waters, or travel in the air over a foreign country. However, you will lose qualifying days if any part of such travel is on or over international waters and takes 24 hours or more, or any part of such travel is within the U.S. or its possessions.

2. You depart from Naples, Italy, by ship on June 10 at 6:00 p.m. and arrive at Haifa, Israel, at 7:00 a.m. on June 14. The trip exceeded 24 hours and passed through international waters. Therefore, you lose as qualifying days June 10, 11, 12, 13, and 14. Assuming you remain in Haifa, Israel, the next qualifying day is June 15.

Choosing the 12-month period. You qualify under the physical presence test if you were on foreign soil 330 days during any period of 12 consecutive months. Since there may be several 12-month periods during which you meet the 330-day test, you should choose the 12-month period allowing you the largest possible exclusion if you qualify under the physical presence test for only part of 1997.

EXAMPLE

You worked in France from June 1, 1996, through September 30, 1997, and the next day you left the country. During this period, you left France only for a 15-day vacation to the U.S. during December 1996. You earned $80,000 for your work in France during 1997. Your maximum 1997 exclusion is $56,192, figured as follows:

1. Start with your last full day, September 30, 1997, and count back 330 full days during which you were abroad. Not counting the vacation days, the 330th day is October 21, 1996. This is the first day of your 12-month period.
2. From October 21, 1996, count forward 12 months to October 20, 1997, which is the last day of your 12-month period.
3. Count the number of days in 1997 which fall within the 12-month period ending October 20, 1997. Here, the number of qualifying days is 293, from January 1 through October 20, 1997.
4. The maximum 1997 exclusion is $70,000 \times {}^{293}/_{365}$, or $56,192. You may exclude $56,192, the lesser of the maximum exclusion and your actual earnings of $80,000.

36.6 Claiming Deductions

You may not deduct expenses that are allocable to the foreign earned income and housing exclusions. If you elect the earned income exclusion, you deduct expenses as follows:

Personal or nonbusiness deductions, such as medical expenses, mortgage interest, and real estate taxes paid on a personal residence, are deductible if you itemize deductions. Business expenses that are attributable to earning excludable income are not deductible. Dependency exemptions are fully deductible; *see* Example 1 below.

If your foreign earnings exceed the exclusion ceiling, you allocate expenses between taxable and excludable income and deduct the amount allocated to taxable earned income; *see* Example 2 below.

EXAMPLES

1. You were a resident of Denmark and elect to exclude your wages of $70,000 from income. You also incurred unreimbursed travel expenses of $2,000. You may not deduct the travel expenses, since the amount is attributable to the earning of tax-free income.
2. You earn wages of $100,000 and satisfy the physical presence test. Your unreimbursed travel expenses for 1997 are $5,000, after reducing meals and entertainment by 50%. If you elect the $70,000 exclusion, 30% of the travel expenses, or $1,500, attributable to the taxable 30% of earnings, may be claimed as a miscellaneous itemized deduction subject to the 2% AGI floor.

If your job expenses are reimbursed and the expenses are adequately accounted for to your employer *(20.30)*, the reimbursements are not reported as income on your Form W-2. If the reimbursement is less than expenses, the excess expenses are allocated as in Example 2 above.

You may have to allocate state income taxes paid on your income.

If either you or your spouse elects the earned income or housing exclusion, you may not claim an IRA deduction based on excluded income.

Overseas moving expenses. These expenses are generally treated as related to your foreign earnings. Thus, if you move to a foreign country and exclude your income, you may not deduct your moving expenses. If your earned income exceeds the exclusion limit, you allocate moving expenses between your tax-free and taxable earned income.

If you were reimbursed by your employer under a nonaccountable plan, or if the reimbursement is for expenses that you deducted in an earlier year, the reimbursement is considered earned income in the year of receipt and is added to other earned income before taking the exclusion and making the allocation. *See 36.4* for allocating reimbursements between the year of the move and the following year for purposes of claiming the exclusion.

If, after working in a foreign country, your employer transfers you back to the U.S. or you move back to the U.S. to take a different job, your moving expenses are deductible under the general rules of *12.3*. If your residence and principal place of work was outside the U.S. and you retire and move back to the U.S., your moving expenses are also deductible, except that you do not have to meet the 39-week test for employees or the 78-week test for the self-employed and partners.

Survivors of workers abroad returning to U.S. If you are the spouse or dependent of a worker who died while his or her principal place of work was outside the U.S., you may deduct your moving expenses back to the U.S. For the costs to be deductible, the move must begin within six months of the worker's death. The requirements for deducting moving expenses apply, except for the 39-week test for employees or the 78-week test for the self-employed and partners.

Compulsory home leave. Foreign service officers stationed abroad must periodically return to the U.S. to reorient themselves to American ways of life. Because the home leave is compulsory, foreign service officers may deduct their travel expenses; travel expenses of the officer's family are not deductible.

36.7 Exclusion Not Established When Your Return Is Due

When your 1997 return is due, you may not have been abroad long enough to qualify for the exclusion. If you expect to qualify under either the residence or physical presence test after the due date for your 1997 return, you may either (1) ask for an extension of time for filing your return on Form 2350 until after you qualify under either rule; or (2) file your return on the due date, reporting the foreign income in the return, pay the full tax, and then file for a refund when you qualify.

If you will have tax to pay even after qualifying for the exclusion—for example, your earned income exceeds the exclusion—you may file for an extension to file but you will owe interest on the tax due. To avoid interest charges on the tax, you may take one of the following steps:

1. File a timely return and pay the total tax due without the application of the exclusion. When you do qualify, make sure you file a refund claim within the time limits discussed at Chapter 38; *or*
2. Pay the estimated tax liability when you apply for the extension to file on Form 2350. If the extension is granted, the payment is applied to the tax shown on your return when you file.

36.8 Tax-Free Meals and Lodging for Workers in Camps

If you must live in a camp provided by your employer, you may exclude from income the value of the lodging and meals furnished if the camp is (1) provided because you work in a remote area where satisfactory housing is not available; (2) located as near as is practical to the worksite; and (3) a common area not open to the public normally accommodating at least 10 employees.

You also may qualify for the earned income exclusion.

36.9 Virgin Islands, Samoa, Guam, Northern Marianas

The Virgin Islands, Guam, American Samoa, and the Commonwealth of the Northern Mariana Islands have their own independent tax departments. Therefore, contact the particular tax authority for the proper treatment of your income and ask the IRS for the 1997 edition of Publication 570, *Tax Guide for Individuals With Income From U.S. Possessions*. If you have a mailing address overseas, get Publication 570 by writing to the Eastern Area Distribution Center, P.O. Box 25866, Richmond, VA 23286-8107.

For tax information from Guam, write to Department of Revenue and Taxation, P.O. Box 23607, GMF, Guam 96921. For information from the Commonwealth of the Northern Mariana Islands, write to the Division of Revenue and Taxation, Commonwealth of the Northern Mariana Islands, P.O. Box 5234, CHRB, Saipan, Northern Mariana Islands 96950. For information from Ameri-

 Filing Tip

Extension of Time To File

If you are living and working abroad on April 15, 1998, you have an automatic extension to June 15, 1998. For an additional two months, file Form 4868 by June 15, 1998, and pay an estimated tax. For a longer extension, in anticipation of owing no tax on your foreign income, you may file Form 2350 either with the Internal Revenue Service, Philadelphia, Pennsylvania 19255, or with a local IRS representative. File Form 2350 before the due date for filing your 1997 return, which is June 15, 1998, if you are abroad and are on a calendar year. If you cannot get Form 2350, apply for the extension on your own stationery. State the facts you rely on to justify the extension and the earliest date you expect to be in a position to determine under which rule you will qualify. You will receive an official letter and copy granting the extension. Generally, you will be granted an extension for a period ending 30 days after the date you expect to qualify for the foreign earned income exclusion.

can Samoa, write to the Tax Division, Government of American Samoa, Pago Pago, American Samoa 96799. Also *see* IRS Publication 570.

For information about tax liability in the Virgin Islands, write to Virgin Islands Bureau of Internal Revenue, 9601 Estate Thomas, Charlotte Amalie, St. Thomas, U.S. Virgin Islands 00802. Also *see* IRS Publication 570.

Possession exclusion.   At the time this book went to press, a possession exclusion applied to bona fide residents of American Samoa. On Form 4563, such residents may exclude for U.S. tax purposes their income from sources in American Samoa, Guam, and the Commonwealth of the Northern Marianas and income effectively connected with a business in these possessions.

36.10   Earnings in Puerto Rico

If you are a U.S. citizen who is also a resident of Puerto Rico for the entire year, you generally report all of your income on your Puerto Rico tax return. Where you report income from U.S. sources on the Puerto Rico tax return, a credit against the Puerto Rico tax may be claimed for income taxes paid to the United States.

If you are not a resident of Puerto Rico, you report on a Puerto Rico return only income from Puerto Rican sources. Wages earned for services performed in Puerto Rico for the U.S. government or for private employers are treated as income from Puerto Rican sources.

Information on Puerto Rico tax returns may be requested from Department of the Treasury Bureau of Income Tax, Consulting and Legislation Office, P.O. Box 2501, San Juan, Puerto Rico 00902-2501.

U.S. tax returns.   As a U.S. citizen, you must file a U.S. tax return reporting income from all sources. But if you are a bona fide resident of Puerto Rico for an entire tax year, you do not report on a U.S. tax return any income earned in Puertc Rico during your residence there, except amounts received for services performed in Puerto Rico as an employee of the U.S. government. Similar rules apply if you have been a bona fide resident of Puerto Rico for at least two years before changing your residence from Puerto Rico. On a U.S. tax return, you may not deduct expenses or claim tax credits allocable to the excludable income. Personal exemptions are fully deductible.

If you are not a bona fide resident of Puerto Rico for the entire tax year, or were not a bona fide resident for two years prior to the tax year, you report on your U.S. tax return all income you earned in Puerto Rico, as well as all income from other sources. If you are required to report income earned in Puerto Rico on your U.S. tax return, you may claim a credit for income tax paid to Puerto Rico. You figure the credit on Form 1116.

EXAMPLE

You and your spouse are bona fide residents of Puerto Rico during the entire year of 1997. You receive $25,000 in wages as an employee of the U.S. government working in Puerto Rico, a $100 dividend from a Puerto Rican corporation that does business in Puerto Rico, and a $500 dividend from a U.S. corporation that does business in the U.S. Your spouse earned $18,000 in wages from a Puerto Rican corporation for services performed in Puerto Rico. Your exempt and taxable income for U.S. federal tax purposes is as follows:

	Taxable	Exempt
Your wages	$25,000	
Your spouse's wages		$18,000
Puerto Rican corporation dividend		100
U.S. corporation dividend	500	
Totals	$25,500	$18,100

You file tax returns with both Puerto Rico and the U.S. You have gross income of $25,500 for U.S. tax purposes and $43,600 for Puerto Rican tax purposes. A tax credit may be claimed on the U.S. tax return for income taxes paid to Puerto Rico and on your Puerto Rico return for income taxes paid to the U.S on U.S. source income.

36.11   Tax Treaties with Foreign Countries

Tax treaties between the United States and foreign countries modify some of the rules discussed in this chapter. The purpose of the treaties is to avoid double taxation. Consult your tax advisor about the effect of these treaties on your income. IRS Publication 54 contains a list of tax treaties.

36.12 Exchange Rates and Blocked Currency

Income reported on your federal income tax return must be stated in U.S. dollars. Where you are paid in foreign currency, you report your pay in U.S. dollars on the basis of the exchange rates prevailing at the time the income is actually or constructively received. You use the rate that most closely reflects the value of the foreign currency—the official rate, the open market rate, or any other relevant rate. You may even be required to use the black market rate if that is the most accurate measure of the actual purchasing power of U.S. dollars in the foreign country. Be prepared to justify the rate you use.

Currency gains and losses. A special statute, Section 988, governs the treatment of gain or loss on currency transactions. After 1997, an individual who disposes of foreign currency in a personal transaction is not subject to tax under Section 988 on gain resulting from fluctuating exchange rates if the gain on the transaction is $200 or less.

Fulbright grants. If 70% of a Fulbright grant is paid in nonconvertible foreign currency, U.S. tax may be paid in the foreign currency. *See* IRS Publication 520 for details.

Blocked currency. A citizen or resident alien may be paid in a foreign currency that cannot be converted into American dollars and removed from the foreign country. If your income is in blocked currency, you may elect to defer the reporting of that income until (1) The currency becomes convertible into dollars. (2) You actually convert it into dollars. (3) You use it for personal expenses (for example, in the foreign country when you go there). Purchase of a business or investment in the foreign country is not the kind of use that is treated as a conversion. (4) You make a gift of it or leave it in your will. (5) You are a resident alien and you give up your U.S. residence.

If you use this method to defer the income, you may not deduct the expenses of earning it until you report it. You must continue to use this method after you choose it. You may only change with permission of the IRS.

You do not defer the reporting of capital losses incurred in a country having a blocked currency. There may be these disadvantages in deferring income:

- Many years' income may accumulate and all be taxed in one year.
- You have no control over the year in which the blocked income becomes taxable. You usually cannot control the events that cause the income to become unblocked.

You choose to defer income in blocked currency by filing a tentative tax return reporting your blocked taxable income and explain that you are deferring the payment of income tax because your income is not in dollars or in property or currency which is readily convertible into dollars. You must attach to your tentative return a regular return, reporting any unblocked taxable income received during the year or taxable income which became unblocked during the year. When the currency finally becomes unblocked or convertible into a currency or property convertible to dollars, you pay tax on the earnings at the rate prevailing in the year the currency became unblocked or convertible. On the tentative return, note at the top: "Report of Deferrable Foreign Income, pursuant to Revenue Ruling 74-351." File separate returns for each country from which blocked currency is received. The election must be made by the due date for filing a return for the year in which an election is sought.

36.13 Information Returns on Foreign Currency

If you have a financial interest in, signature, or other authority over a foreign bank account, a foreign securities account, or any other foreign financial account, you must report this fact on Form TDF 90-22.1 (Report of Foreign Bank and Financial Accounts) if the aggregate value of the accounts at any time during the year exceeds $10,000. The form does not have to be filed if the accounts were with a U.S. military banking facility operated by a U.S. financial institution. Taxpayers filing Form 1040 must also indicate on Schedule B whether they had an interest in a foreign account during the year. Form TDF 90-22.1 is not filed with your income tax return. The form must be filed by June 30 of the year following the year in which you had this financial interest. Foreign accounts for 1997 must be reported by June 30, 1998.

Treasury regulations impose reporting and record-keeping requirements for currency transfers to and from the U.S. Generally, transactions involving a physical transfer of funds or monetary instruments into or outside the U.S. must be reported if the amount involved exceeds $10,000 on any one occasion; *see* Form 4790.

Financial institutions must file a Form 4789 for each deposit, withdrawal, exchange of currency, or any other currency transaction of more than $10,000.

Filing Tip

Choosing Credit or Deduction

If you qualify for a credit or deduction, you will generally receive a larger tax reduction by claiming a tax credit rather than a deduction. A deduction is only a partial offset against your tax, whereas a credit is deducted in full from your tax. Also, taking a deduction may bar you from carrying back an excess credit from a later year. However, a deduction may give you a larger tax saving if the foreign tax is levied at a high rate and the proportion of foreign income to U.S. income is small. Compute your tax under both methods and choose the one providing the larger tax reduction.

36.14 Foreign Tax Credit

You may claim an itemized deduction for qualified foreign taxes or you may claim a foreign tax credit. You must file Form 1116 to compute your credit. You may not claim a foreign tax credit or deduction for taxes paid on income not subject to U.S. tax. If all of your foreign earned income is excluded, none of the foreign taxes paid on such income may be taken as a credit or deduction on your U.S. return. If you exclude only part of your foreign pay, you determine which foreign taxes are attributable to excluded income and thus barred as foreign tax credits by applying the fractional computation provided in the instructions to Form 1116 and IRS Publication 514.

In one tax year, you may not elect to deduct some foreign taxes and claim others as a credit. One method must be applied to all taxes paid or accrued during the tax year. If you are a cash basis taxpayer, you may claim a credit for accrued foreign taxes, but you must consistently follow this method once elected.

The credit is the amount of foreign taxes paid or accrued, not to exceed the effective U.S. tax on foreign income multiplied by a ratio of foreign taxable income over total taxable income.

Credit disallowed. The credit may *not* be claimed if:

- You are a nonresident alien. However, under certain circumstances, an alien who is a bona fide resident for an entire taxable year in Puerto Rico may claim the credit. Also, a nonresident alien engaged in a U.S. trade or business may claim a credit if he or she receives income *effectively connected* to that business.
- You are a citizen of a U.S. possession (except Puerto Rico) but not a U.S. citizen or resident.

No credit is allowed for taxes imposed by a country designated by the government as engaging in terroristic activities; *see* IRS Publication 514 for a list of these countries.

Taxes qualifying for the credit. The credit is allowed only for foreign income tax, excess profits taxes, and similar taxes in the nature of an income tax. It is not allowed for any taxes paid to foreign countries on sales, gross receipts, production, the privilege to do business, personal property, or export of capital. But it may apply to a:

- Tax similar to a U.S. tax on income
- Tax paid by a domestic taxpayer in lieu of the tax upon income, which would otherwise be imposed by any foreign country or by any U.S. possession
- Tax of a foreign country imposing income tax, where for reasons growing out of the administrative difficulties of determining net income or basis within that country, the tax is measured by gross income, sales, and number of units produced
- Pension, unemployment, or disability funds of a foreign country; certain foreign social security taxes do not qualify.

Reporting foreign income on your return. You report the gross amount of your foreign income in terms of United States currency. You also attach a schedule showing how you figured the foreign income in United States currency.

> **EXAMPLE**
> You earn Canadian dividends of $100 (Canadian dollars), from which $15 of Canadian taxes were withheld. When the dividends were declared, a Canadian dollar could be exchanged for $.78 of United States currency. Therefore, the dividend of $100 (in Canadian dollars) is reported on your return as $78 ($100 × .78). The tax withheld which may be taken as a credit is $11.70 ($15 × .78).

36.15 Computing the Foreign Tax Credit

The foreign tax credit is based on the amount of foreign taxes you paid or accrued, subject to this overall limitation which is figured on Form 1116:

$$\text{U.S. Tax} \times \frac{\text{Taxable income from all foreign countries}}{\text{Taxable income from all sources}}$$

Separate limitation categories. The above fractional limitation must be figured separately for specific categories of foreign income. These categories are (1) passive income (such as dividends, interest, rents, royalties, and gains on certain commodity transactions; (2) foreign interest income subject to withholding at a rate of 5% or more; (3) shipping and aircraft related income; (4) lump-sum retirement distributions from foreign sources subject to special averaging; (5) certain income derived in banking, insurance, or financing businesses. Taxable income for each category must be

Law Alert

Deminimis Foreign Tax Credits

Starting in 1998, an individual with $300 or less of creditable foreign taxes, $600 for married persons filing jointly, may elect to be exempt from the overall limitation shown at the beginning of 36.15, provided that the only foreign source income is qualified passive income. If the election is made, a foreign tax credit may be claimed without having to file Form 1116.

separately computed and the overall limitation fraction applied. A separate computation also must be made for all other foreign income not within these categories; this "other" income group is called general limitation income. Follow the instructions to Form 1116 and *see* IRS Publication 514 for further details.

Recapture of foreign losses.   If you sustain an "overall foreign loss" for any taxable year, a recapture provision treats part of foreign income realized in a later year as income from U.S. sources. By treating part of the later year's foreign income as U.S. income, the numerator of the fraction used to compute the overall limitation (see above) is reduced and this in turn reduces the maximum foreign tax credit that may be claimed in the later year. More specifically, the portion of foreign income in succeeding years which is treated as U.S. income equals the lower of (1) the amount of the loss, and (2) 50% (or a larger percentage, as you may choose) of taxable income from foreign sources. An "overall foreign loss" means the amount by which the gross income for the taxable year from foreign sources for that year is exceeded by the sum of allocated deductions. For this purpose, the following deductions are not subject to recapture: operating loss deductions, any uncompensated foreign expropriation, and casualty loss. Special rules apply to dispositions of property if used predominantly outside the United States in a trade or business. *See* IRS Publication 514 for recapture details.

Taxable income.   Income which is tax free under the foreign earned income exclusion is not taken into account when figuring taxable income. Foreign taxable income, for purposes of computing the ratio, is reduced by all expenses directly related to earning the income. Itemized deductions, such as medical expenses, that are not directly related to foreign sources are allocated to foreign income according to relative gross incomes from foreign and U.S. sources. You do not consider personal exemptions when figuring foreign or total taxable income.

The foreign tax credit may not exceed foreign taxes actually paid or accrued. Where a joint return is filed, the limitation is applied to the aggregate taxable income of both spouses.

A limited foreign tax credit may be applied against the alternative minimum tax; *see* Chapter 23.

Capital gains.   In figuring the overall limitation, taxable income from foreign countries (the numerator) includes gain from the sale of capital assets only to the extent of foreign source capital gain net income, which is the lower of net capital gain from foreign sources or net capital gain from all sources. If you are entitled to a preferential capital gains rate, you must make an adjustment to account for the rate differential when figuring the credit. Gain on the sale of nondepreciable personal property sold outside the country of your residence may be treated as gain from U.S. sources, unless the gain is subject to a foreign income tax at a rate of 10% or more of the gain. *See* instructions to Form 1116.

36.16 Carryback and Carryover of Excess Foreign Tax Credit

Where the amount allowable as a credit under the overall basis is restricted, the excess may be carried back to the two preceding years and then carried forward to the five succeeding taxable years. The carryback or carryover will not be allowed in a year for which you have no income from foreign sources or the credit limitation already applies to taxes of that year. For further details, *see* IRS Publication 514.

Chapter 37

Planning Alimony and Marital Settlements

Alimony payments that meet tax law tests of this chapter are deductible if you pay them, and taxable if you receive them. Payments are not deductible by the payer unless taxable to the recipient.

You claim a deduction for deductible alimony that you pay on Line 30a of Form 1040. You deduct the payments even if you claim the standard deduction rather than itemizing deductions. You must enter the Social Security number of your ex-spouse. Otherwise, your deduction may be disallowed and you may have to pay a $50 penalty. If you pay deductible alimony to more than one ex-spouse, enter the Social Security number of one of them and provide similar information for the others on a separate statement attached to your return.

If you receive taxable alimony, report the payments on Line 11 of Form 1040. You must give your ex-spouse your Social Security number and could be subject to a $50 penalty if you fail to do so.

37.1 Planning Alimony Agreements

You can arrange beforehand the way in which the costs of a divorce are to be borne. You may specifically state in the decree or agreement that the alimony is neither taxable to the payee-spouse (under IRC Section 71), nor deductible by the payer-spouse (under IRC section 215). Such a statement effectively disqualifies payments that otherwise would be taxable to the payee-spouse and deductible by the payer-spouse. A copy of the agreement that contains the statement must be attached to the tax return of the payee-spouse for each year the statement is applicable.

The first step in planning the after-tax consequences of alimony is convincing a couple that they may have a common financial interest; the second is projecting future tax consequences.

For example, assume that the husband is to make payments to the wife. If tax planning is approached from the viewpoint of each spouse separately, the tax deduction is an advantage for the husband; tax-free income is an advantage for the wife. However, both advantages cannot be achieved, and the couple must face the reality of the tax law, which allows the husband to deduct payments only if they are taxed as alimony to the wife. They must compromise by setting amounts and tax consequences that balance their interests.

One approach is to view both spouses as a single economic tax unit. If this is done and the husband will be in a higher tax bracket during the payout period than the wife, an agreement should generally provide for taxable and deductible alimony. The tax savings provided by the deduction can conserve more of the husband's assets while providing funds required by the wife. The final amount of alimony to be paid depends on the spouses' tax brackets. Where tax brackets do not differ, there may be no advantage in making an agreement for taxable and deductible alimony when viewing the two parties as a unit.

If you agree that one spouse is to pay deductible alimony and the other spouse is to report the alimony as income, these rules must be met:

- The alimony must be paid under the decree of divorce or legal separation agreement or decree of support; *see 37.2.*
- The agreement must provide for cash payments; *see 37.3.* There is no minimum payout period for annual alimony payments of $15,000 or less. One payment of $15,000 can qualify as deductible and taxable alimony. There is also no minimum payout period for annual alimony payments exceeding $15,000. However, recapture of alimony deductions claimed in the first or second year may occur where annual payments of over $15,000 are scheduled and paid, but in the second or third year a reduced payment is made. To avoid recapture of deductions for payments over $15,000, carefully plan schedules of declining payments within the rules of *37.7.*
- In providing for the support of children, a specific allocation to their support or the setting of certain contingencies disqualifies payments as deductible and alimony as taxable; *see 37.5.*
- Divorced and legally separated parties may not live in the same household. If they live in the same household, alimony payments are not deductible or taxable. However, there are these exceptions: A spouse who makes payments while preparing to leave the common residence may deduct payments made within one month before the departure. Also, where you are separated under a written agreement, but not legally separated under a decree of divorce or separate maintenance, you may deduct alimony payments even if you both are members of the same household.
- The payer spouse's liability to pay alimony must end on the death of the payee spouse. The alimony agreement does not have to state expressly that payments end on death if liability ends under state law; *see 37.4.*

37.2 Decree or Agreement Required

Alimony, to be deductible and taxable, must be required by one of the following: (1) a decree of divorce or legal separation; (2) a written separation agreement; or (3) a decree of support. This rule applies to both pre-1985 and post-1984 decrees and agreements. Voluntary payments are not deductible.

Divorced or legally separated. The obligation to pay alimony must be imposed by the decree of divorce or separate maintenance or a written agreement incident to the divorce or separation.

Alimony paid under a Mexican divorce decree qualifies. Payments under a Mexican or state decree declared invalid by another jurisdiction do not qualify according to the IRS. Two appeals courts have rejected the IRS position.

Support payments ordered by a court in a wife's home state qualify as alimony, even though not provided for by an *ex parte* divorce decree obtained by the husband in another state. Similarly, payments qualified when a state court increased support originally ordered before the husband obtained an uncontested Mexican divorce.

 Filing Instruction

Reporting Alimony
If you paid alimony in 1997 meeting the deductible tests, claim your deduction on Line 30a of Form 1040, and enter the recipient's Social Security number. If you receive qualifying alimony payments, report them on Line 11 of Form 1040.

Payments made under a separation approved by a Roman Catholic ecclesiastical board do not qualify.

When a decree of divorce or separate maintenance fails to mention alimony, payments qualify as long as they are made under a written agreement considered "incident to" the decree.

Payments made under an agreement *amended* after a divorce or legal separation may also qualify, if the amendment is considered "incident" to the divorce or separation. For example, the IRS agrees that a *written* amendment changing the amount of alimony payments is incident to the divorce where the legal obligation to support under the original agreement survived the divorce. However, payments under an amended agreement did not qualify where the original agreement settled all rights between the husband and wife and made no provision for future support. The legal obligation to support the wife did not survive the divorce and could not be revived by the new agreement.

Annulments.   Payments made under an annulment decree qualify as deductible (and taxable) alimony.

Where a couple is separated and living apart, alimony is deductible by the payer-spouse and taxable to the payee-spouse provided it is paid under either a written separation agreement or decree of support.

A decree of support.   Any court decree or order requiring support payments qualifies, including alimony *pendente lite* (temporary alimony while the action is pending) and an interlocutory (not final) divorce decree.

In certain community property states, payments under a decree of alimony *pendente lite* which do not exceed the wife's interest in community income are neither deductible by the husband nor taxable to the wife; payments exceeding the wife's interest are taxable to her and deductible by the husband.

37.3 Cash Payments Requied

Only payments of cash, checks, and money orders payable on demand qualify as taxable and deductible alimony.

Providing services or transferring or providing property does not qualify. For example, you may not deduct as alimony your note, the assignment of a third party note, or an annuity contract.

Your cash payment to a third party for a spouse qualifies if made under the terms of a divorce decree or separation instrument. For example, you pay the rent, mortgage, tax, medical expenses, or tuition liabilities of your former spouse. The payments qualify if made under the terms of the divorce or separation instrument. If taxable as alimony, your former spouse may deduct your payment of real estate taxes, mortgage interest, or medical expenses if he or she claims itemized deductions. You may not deduct payments to maintain property owned by you but used by your spouse. For example, you pay the mortgage expenses, real estate taxes, and insurance premiums for a house which you own and in which your former spouse lives. You may not deduct those payments as alimony even if required by a decree or agreement.

Premiums paid for term or whole life insurance on your life made under a divorce or separation instrument qualify as deductible alimony to the extent your former spouse owns the policy.

37.4 Payments Must Stop at Death

Payments must stop on the death of the payee-spouse. If not, none of the payments, whether made before or after the payee's death, qualify as taxable or deductible alimony.

The divorce decree or separation agreement does not have to specifically state that payments end at death, if under state law the liability to pay ends on the death of the payee-spouse.

To the extent that one or more payments are to begin, increase in amount, or accelerate after the death of the payee-spouse, such payments may be treated as a substitute for the continuation of payments terminating on the death of the payee-spouse.

EXAMPLES
1. Under the terms of a divorce decree, Smith is obligated to make annual alimony payments of $30,000, terminating on the earlier of the end of six years or the death of Mrs. Smith. She also is to keep custody of their two minor children. The decree also provides that if on her death the children are still minors, Jones is to pay annually $10,000 to a trust each year. The trust income and corpus are to be used for the children until the youngest child reaches the age of majority. Under these facts, Smith's possible liability to make annual $10,000 payments to the trust is treated as a substitute for $10,000 of the $30,000 annual payments. $10,000 of each of the $30,000 annual payments does not qualify as alimony.

Planning Reminder

Payments to a Third Party

Cash payments to a third party may be deducted as alimony if they are under the terms of a divorce decree or separation instrument, as just discussed. You may also deduct as alimony payments made to a third party at the written request of the payee spouse. For example, your former wife asks you to make a cash donation to a charitable organization instead of paying alimony installments to her. Her request must be in writing and state that both she and you intend the payment to be treated as alimony. You must receive the written request before you file your return for the taxable year in which the payment was made. Your former wife may deduct the payment as a charitable contribution if she claims itemized deductions.

Key to Alimony and Marital Settlement Issues

Item—	Comments—
Alimony	The same rules determine whether alimony is deductible and taxable. For example, if a husband makes deductible alimony payments to his ex-wife, the payments are taxable to her. He may not deduct payments that are not taxable to her. If you are currently planning an alimony agreement, consider the tax consequences to both spouses. As current tax rates may be as high as 39.6% for one spouse and as low as 15% for the other, there may be a substantial tax savings to the couple, when considered as an economic unit, in negotiating an agreement that qualifies the payments as deductible alimony; *see 37.1*. *Note*: Prior tax rules that apply to pre-1985 agreements are not discussed in this chapter. If you have a problem involving a payment of alimony under a pre-1985 agreement, refer to a past issue of *Your Income Tax* or to IRS Publication 504.
Child support agreements	A payment fixed as payable for the support of your child may not qualify as deductible or taxable alimony; *see 37.5*.
Property settlements	Transfers of property between a couple that are incident to a divorce are treated as a tax-free exchange. There is no recognition of gain or loss. Future tax consequences should be considered by the spouse receiving appreciated property. When the property is sold, that spouse will be taxed on the appreciation. If this is so, that spouse may want to bargain for larger alimony payments or additional property to compensate for the projected future tax; *see 6.6*.
Alimony to nonresident alien	If you pay alimony payments to a nonresident alien, and you are a U.S. citizen or resident, you must withhold 30% (or a lower rate as set by treaty) on each payment for income tax purposes. *See* IRS Publications 504 and 515 for more information.
Exemptions for children	Exemptions for children of a divorced couple are governed by the rules explained at *21.11*. Further, where a spouse is in the income range requiring the phaseout or disallowance of personal exemptions *(21.15)*, there may be no advantage in providing the exemption to that spouse. The exemption should be given to the spouse who may claim a full deduction for the exemption.
Annuity or endowment policy	Funds for payments of alimony may be provided through the purchase of an annuity or endowment policy. You may not deduct payments made under the policies assigned or purchased for your spouse. For example, to meet an alimony obligation of $500 a month, you buy your spouse a commercial annuity contract. The full $500 a month received by him or her is taxable. You may not deduct these payments.
Trust to pay alimony	To meet your alimony obligations, you may transfer income-producing property to a trust that is to pay the income to your spouse. You may not deduct payments made by the trust. You are not taxable on the income earned by the trust, even though it meets your alimony obligations. This tax treatment is the equivalent of receiving a tax deduction for paying alimony. If you receive alimony from a trust, ask the trustee how to report such income. Tax treatment may depend on whether the trust was created before 1985 or after 1984. If the trust was set up after 1984, as a beneficiary you generally report trust income under the general trust reporting rules in Chapter 11. These general trust rules may not apply to certain alimony trusts created before 1985 that were subject to the prior alimony rules. Distributions from such trusts may be treated as taxable alimony regardless of whether the distributions are from income or principal. In any event, the trustee should provide you with the necessary tax information.
Retirement plans	A state court can allocate your interest in a qualified retirement plan to a former spouse in a qualified domestic relations order. The benefits are taxed to your former spouse when they are paid to her or him. Benefits paid to another beneficiary, such as a child, are taxable to you; *see 7.12*.
Remarriage's effect on pre-1985 agreement	The tax deduction allowed for alimony payments made under a pre-1985 decree or agreement hinges on the obligation to support. Once the spouse receiving alimony remarries, the obligation to support generally ends under state law. In these states, any payment after remarriage is not considered alimony and is not deductible. For example, payments to a former wife made after remarriage are considered tax-free gifts if the former husband knows of the remarriage and that he is no longer obligated to pay. If she does not inform him of her remarriage, his payments are taxable to her but are not deductible by him.
Voluntary payments in excess of required alimony	Voluntary payments in excess of required alimony are not deductible or taxable as alimony. Amending the decrees retroactively to cover an increase does not qualify the increase as deductible and taxable alimony. The increase has to be approved by the court before the increased payments are made.

2. Same facts as in Example 1, but the alimony is to end on the earlier of the expiration of 15 years and the death of Mrs. Smith. Further, if Mrs. Smith dies before the end of the 15-year period, Smith will pay her estate the difference between the total amount that he would have paid had she survived and the amount actually paid. For example, if she dies at the end of the tenth year, he will pay her estate $150,000 ($450,000 – $300,000). Under these facts, his liability to make a lump-sum payment to the estate is a substitute for the full amount of each of the annual $30,000 payments. Accordingly, none of the annual $30,000 payments qualifies as alimony.

37.5 Child Support Payments Are Not Alimony

A payment is fixed as payable for child support if the divorce or separation instrument specifically fixes an amount payable for support. That amount is not deductible or taxable as alimony.

Even if there is not a specific allocation to child support, a payment will be treated as payable for child support if it is to be reduced on the happening of a contingency relating to the child, such as: the child reaches a specific age or income level, or the child leaves school, marries, leaves the parent's household, or begins to work.

Caution

Alimony Reductions Tied to Child's Age

If a reduction in your payments is not specifically tied to your child's reaching majority age but the scheduled date for the reduction is within six months before or after your child reaches age 18 or 21 (or other age of majority under local law), the IRS holds that the reduction is tied to the child's age. The reduction amount will be treated as child support unless you can prove that the reduction is for some other purpose. The IRS makes the same presumption if you have more than one child and your alimony payments are to be reduced at least twice and each reduction is within one year of a different child's reaching a particular age between ages 18 and 24; *see* the Example below.

EXAMPLE

On July 1, 1992, a couple is divorced when their children, John (born July 15, 1977) and Jane (born September 23, 1979), are ages 14 and 12. Under the divorce decree, the husband is to make monthly alimony payments of $2,000. The monthly payments are to be reduced to $1,500 on January 1, 1998, and to $1,000 on January 1, 2002. On January 1, 1998, the date of the first reduction, John will be 20 years, 5 months, and 17 days old. On January 1, 2002, the date of the second reduction, Jane will be 22 years, 3 months, and 9 days old. As each reduction is to occur not more than one year before or after each child reaches the age of 21 years and four months, the IRS will presume that the deductions are associated with the happening of a contingency relating to the children. The two reductions total $1,000 per month and are treated as the amount fixed for the support of the children. Thus, $1,000 of the $2,000 monthly payment does not qualify as alimony. To avoid this result, the husband must prove that the reductions were not related to the support of the children.

If both alimony and child support are specified and a payment is less than the total of the two amounts, then the payment is first allocated to child support.

Tax refund diversion for delinquent child support.   The IRS can give your tax refund to a state which is paying support to your child if you fail to make support payments. For past-due support of a child in a family receiving AFDC welfare (or successor program) payments, the IRS has the authority to make the diversion where the delinquency is $150 or more and is overdue for at least three months. The IRS will not notify you of the diversion until it is made to the state. However, a federal court has held that a state must provide notice to all those whose refunds may be intercepted, specifying possible defenses and how to challenge the diversion before it is made; judicial review of the state's administrative decision must also be available.

For support of non-AFDC families, the IRS may divert your refund if you owe child support of $500 or more; the state agency must provide prior notice of the proposed offset and procedures for contesting it.

Minimum Payments and Recapture of Alimony

37.6 No Minimum Payment Period for Alimony

There is no minimum payment period, but a recapture rule applies where payments fall by more than $15,000 within the first three years; *see 37.7.*

37.7 3rd Year Recapture If Alimony Drops $15,000 or More

The recapture rules are designed to prevent the so-called "front loading" of property settlement payments disguised as alimony. However, the rules apply even where no property settlement was intended if you come within its terms. Here are the rules: Deductible payments made in the first year or second year may be recaptured (that is, reported as income) in the third year where payments within the first three years decline by more than $15,000. The three years are called "post-separation years." The first post-separation year is the first calendar year in which you pay alimony under a decree of divorce or separation agreement. The period does not begin with the year of the decree or agreement if no payments are made. Recapture does not apply to temporary support payments made before the final decree or agreement. The second and third post-separation years are the next two calendar years after the first post-separation year whether or not payments are made during those years.

Payments made in the second post-separation year are recaptured if the payments exceed the payments made in the third post-separation year by more than $15,000. Payments made in the first post-separation year are recaptured if they exceed the average payments made in the second post-separation year and the third post-separation year by more than $15,000. The following Examples illustrate how to make these computations.

When recapture does not apply.   Recapture is not triggered if payments in both the first and second post-separation years do not exceed $15,000. Recapture also does not apply to:

- Payments made under a continuing liability to pay for at least three years a fixed part of your income from a business or property or from a job or self-employed business or profession, or
- Payments that end because of your death or the death of your former spouse or the remarriage of your former spouse at any time before the end of the third post-separation year.

Reporting recapture on your return.   The payer-spouse reports the recaptured amount as income in the third year and the payee-spouse claims a deduction for the same amount. The payer reports the recaptured amount on Form 1040, Line 11 (alimony received); cross out "received" and write "recapture" along with the payee-spouse's Social Security number.

The payee-spouse deducts the recaptured amount on Form 1040, Line 30a (alimony paid). He or she crosses out the word "paid" and writes "recapture," and also enters on that line the payer-spouse's Social Security number.

Steps of recapture:

Step 1.   Recapture for the second-year payment is computed first. This is the excess, if any, of the second-year payment over the third-year payment, *minus* $15,000.

Step 2.   Recapture for the first-year payment is computed next. There is recapture if the first-year payment exceeds by more than $15,000 the average payment made in the second and third years. In figuring the average payment, reduce the second-year payment by any recapture amount for the second year figured under Step 1.

EXAMPLES

1. In 1995, Jones obtains a divorce and pays deductible alimony of $50,000. His wife reports $50,000 as income. In 1996 and 1997, he makes no payments. On his 1997 return, $35,000 of the first year 1995 deduction is recaptured ($50,000 – $15,000) and reported as income by Jones. His ex-spouse deducts $35,000.

2. In 1995, Smith makes his first alimony payment of $50,000; in 1996 he pays $20,000 and, in 1997, he pays nothing. On his 1997 return, $32,500 is recaptured as follows:

Recapture of second-year payment:		
Payment in 2nd year		$20,000
Less: 3rd-year payment	$0	
Less: allowance	15,000	15,000
Recapture for second year		$ 5,000
Recapture of first-year payment:		
Average calculation:		
Payment over the 2nd and 3rd years	$20,000	
Less: recapture in the 2nd year	$ 5,000	
	$15,000	
Average ($15,000 ÷ 2)	$ 7,500	
Payment in first year		$50,000
Less: Average	$ 7,500	
Less: Allowance	15,000	22,500
Recapture for first year		$27,500
Total recaptured in 1997:		
For second year		$ 5,000
For first year		$27,500
Total:		$32,500

37.8 Legal Fees of Marital Settlements

If you are receiving taxed alimony, you may deduct part of your legal fees. Ask your attorney to divide his or her fees into charges for arranging: (1) the divorce or separation; and (2) details of the alimony payments.

You may deduct the legal fees allocated to (2), but you may not deduct the fee attributed to the divorce or separation negotiation. The deduction is subject to the 2% adjusted gross income (AGI) floor on miscellaneous itemized deductions (*see* Chapter 19). If the alimony is not taxed to you, you may not deduct any part of the fee. However, part of a fee allocated to a property settlement may be added to the basis of the property.

If you are paying deductible alimony, you may not deduct legal fees paid for arranging a divorce or for resisting your spouse's demands for alimony. Furthermore, you may not deduct legal fees incurred in resisting your spouse's claims to income-producing property the loss of which would affect your earnings. However, these rules do not bar you from deducting that part of your legal fee that is identified as being paid for tax advice. The following types of proof may support a deduction:

- The fee is charged by a firm that limits its practice to state and federal matters and is engaged to advise on the consequences of a property settlement involving the transfer of property in exchange for other property and the release of the other spouse's marital rights in the property.
- The fee is charged by a firm engaged in general practice which assigns tax problems, such as the tax consequences of creating an alimony trust, to its special tax department. On the bill, an allocation is made for tax advice based on time, complexity of the case, and the amount of tax involved.
- An attorney handles the divorce for a fixed fee and also gives advice on the right to claim exemptions for the children following the divorce. The bill allocates part of the fee to the tax advice, based on time, and fees customarily charged in the locality for similar services.

You may not deduct your payment of your spouse's legal fees as a miscellaneous itemized deduction, even if the fees are only for tax advice. However, the fees may be deductible as alimony under the rules of *37.3* for payments to third parties.

Chapter 38

Educational Tax Benefits

The tax law provides several tax benefits for people attending school. If you can take advantage of them, you are in effect receiving a government subsidy that will lower the cost of education.

The 1997 tax law has broadened the base for educational benefits by providing new tax benefits that you can take advantage of starting in 1998.

Scholarships, Fellowships, Grants, and Tuition Plans

38.1 Scholarships and Grants

Scholarships and fellowships of a degree candidate are tax free to the extent that the grant pays for tuition and course-related fees, books, supplies, and equipment that are required for courses. Amounts for room, board, and incidental expenses are taxable. If you are not a candidate for a degree (see the Degree test below), your entire grant is taxable.

You must pay tax on grants or tuition reductions that pay for teaching or other services required as a condition of receiving the grant. This is true even if all degree candidates are required to perform the services. Thus, if you are a graduate student and receive a stipend for teaching, those payments are taxable, subject to withholding, and reported by the school on Form W-2. Similarly, no tax-free exclusion is allowed for federal grants where the recipient agrees to do future work with the federal government.

Degree test. Scholarships given to students attending a primary or secondary school, or to those pursuing a degree at a college or university, meet the degree test. Also qualifying are full-time or part-time scholarships for study at an educational institution that (1) provides an educational program acceptable for full-time credit towards a higher degree or offers a program of training to prepare students for gainful employment in a recognized occupation; and (2) is authorized under federal or state law to provide such a program and is accredited by a nationally recognized accreditation agency.

38.2 Tuition Plans for College Employees

Free or partially free tuition for *undergraduate* studies provided to a faculty member or school employee is generally not taxable. The tuition reduction may be for education at his or her own school or at a similar school. Tuition benefits may be taxable to highly compensated employees if the tuition plan discriminates in their favor.

Tax-free tuition benefits may also be provided to the employee's spouse, dependent child, a former employee who retired or left on disability, a widow or widower of an individual who died while employed by the school, or a widow or widower of a retired or disabled employee.

A child under the age of 25 qualifies for tuition reduction if both parents have died and one of the parents qualified for tax-free tuition benefits. If the child is age 25 or over, tuition reductions are taxed even if both parents are deceased.

Tuition reduction for teaching and research assistants. If you must teach, do research, or provide other services to obtain a tuition reduction for *graduate or undergraduate* studies, a tuition reduction from the school is tax free if it is in addition to regular pay for the services. If the tuition reduction is your compensation, it is taxable.

38.3 How Fulbright Awards Are Taxed

Fulbright awards for teaching, lecturing, or research are taxable unless you can claim the foreign earned income exclusion to avoid tax on the grant (Chapter 36). If you do not qualify for the exclusion and if your overseas stay is temporary and you intend to return to your regular teaching position in the United States, you may deduct the cost of your travel, meals, and lodgings overseas.

38.4 U.S. Savings Bond Tuition Plans

Consider the use of EE bonds to fund part of a college savings program. You can defer the interest until final maturity (30 years) or report the interest annually. The interest is not subject to state or local tax. For bonds purchased in your child's name, having your child report the interest annually may be advisable where it can be offset by the child's standard deduction or itemized deductions. To the extent interest is offset each year, it escapes tax; see 4.29.

Interest exclusion may be available if you redeem EE bonds issued after 1989. If you purchased bonds after 1989 in your name, or in the joint names of you and your spouse, you may be able to exclude accumulated interest from federal tax in the year you redeem the bonds if in that year you pay tuition and similar education fees.

Who qualifies for the exclusion. You must be age 24 or over before the month in which the bonds are purchased, and the bonds must be issued solely in your name or in the joint names of you and your spouse. You may not claim the exclusion for bonds bought in your child's name, or which you own jointly with your child. In the year the bonds are redeemed you must pay tuition and similar educational fees for yourself, your spouse, or your dependents. Thus, grandparents may not claim the exclusion if they buy savings bonds to fund the college education of grandchildren unless the children are dependents of the grandparents in the year the bonds are cashed. Tuition and fees must be for a college, university, or vocational school that meets federal financial aid standards. Room and board are not eligible expenses.

Excludable amount and phase-out rule. The tax-free amount of interest is figured on Form 8815. It depends on the educational expenses and your modified adjusted gross income (MAGI) in the year of redemption. However, no exclusion is allowed to a married person who files separately, regardless of income or amount of tuition paid.

Educational expenses must be reduced by nontaxable scholarship or fellowship grants, by education benefits paid from a qualifying state tuition plan *(see 38.5)*, or by educational expenses for which the Hope/Lifetime Learning Credit is claimed *(see 38.6)*. Starting in 1998, if qualifying savings bonds are redeemed and contributed to a qualifying state tuition plan *(38.5)*, the transfer is treated as an education expense eligible for the exclusion. If the redemption amount exceeds the educational expenses, the excludable amount is based on the ratio of expenses to redemption amount. For example, you redeem a $10,000 EE bond and receive $7,344, $5,000 principal and $2,344 interest. If you paid educational expenses of $6,000, the excludable percentage of interest is 82% ($6,000 divided by $7,344). Thus, $1,922 (82% X $2,344) of the interest is potentially excludable from income, subject to the phase-out rules.

A full interest exclusion is allowed only to persons with MAGI below a phase-out threshold. For 1997, the MAGI phase-out ranges are $76,250 to $106,250 for married persons filing jointly and $50,850 to $65,850 for unmarried persons. Married persons filing separately do not qualify. For purposes of applying the phaseout, MAGI is generally your regular adjusted gross income plus the interest on the redeemed EE bonds and foreign income items which you excluded from income. *See* the Form 8815 instructions.

38.5 State-Sponsored College Savings Plans

Many states now have a state-sponsored college savings plan in place or are in the process of approving one. Each state has its own variation, so it is important to look at the details of the program in the state in which you live.

There are currently two basic types of state-sponsored college savings plans: (1) savings plan trusts and (2) college tuition prepayment plans. Much more widely used is the state-sponsored college tuition prepayment plan, discussed below, but the same income tax and gift tax rules apply to savings plan trusts.

State sponsored college tuition prepayment plans. A typical plan allows a parent to prepay tuition costs, even though the child will not start college for 10 or more years. Prepayments are made to a state trust which holds and invests the fund until the child reaches college age. The parent's prepayment covers the tuition, regardless of how much tuition has increased in the interim. A refund, less an administrative fee, is allowed if the state ends the plan or the child is not admitted, decides not to attend college, or dies. Some plans allow part of the prepayment to be used for out-of-state colleges.

Earnings are not taxed while the fund accumulates. Upon entering college, the student is taxed on the earnings attributed to withdrawals from the plan to pay tuition, fees, books, supplies, and qualified room and board expenses. If the child does not enter college and a refund is made to the parent or other contributor, the refund to the extent of earnings is taxable and subject to a penalty.

Contributions to the plan by a parent or other relative before August 6, 1997, were treated as incomplete gifts, with gift tax consequences, if any, determined when distributions were made from the plan. Contributions after August 5, 1997, are subject to the following gift tax rules. A contribution to a qualified state tuition program is treated as a completed gift of a present interest from the contributor to the beneficiary at the time of contribution. Annual contributions are eligible for the gift tax exclusion. If your contribution exceeds the annual exclusion, you may elect to treat the contribution as if made ratably over five years. A gift tax return must be filed for any contribution in excess of the gift tax exclusion limit. If a contributor making a contribution in excess of the gift tax exclusion limit dies during the five-year period, the portion of the contribution which has

 Law Alert

Tuition Prepayment Plans
A new law allows a tuition prepayment plan to include room and board expenses as well as tuition. The room and board amount is determined under a formula applied to federal financial aid programs. This break applies retroactively to tax years ending after August 20, 1996.

not yet been allocated is included in the contributor's estate. If a beneficiary's interest is rolled over to another beneficiary or there is a change in beneficiary, no gift or generation-skipping transfer tax consequences result, provided that the two beneficiaries are of the same generation. If a beneficiary's interest is rolled over to a beneficiary in a lower generation (*e.g.,* parent to child or aunt to niece), the five-year averaging rule may exempt up to $50,000 of the transfer.

Parent's legal obligation to provide college education. Under grantor trust rules, a parent making a tuition prepayment could be taxed on trust income if under state law there is a legal obligation to provide the children with a college education. To date the IRS has not addressed this issue.

1998 Education Benefits

38.6 Higher Education Tax Credits in 1998

The 1997 Tax Act created new higher education credits. There are two types of credits: (1) Hope Scholarship Credit for the first two years of college and (2) Lifetime Learning Credit for a broader range of schooling.

Hope Scholarship Credit. This is a tax credit for the expenses incurred in the first two years of post-secondary education. It is effective for expenses paid in 1998 for an academic period starting in 1998. The credit is a maximum of $1,500 per student per year. The credit is structured on 100% of the first $1,000 of tuition costs and 50% of the second $1,000. This credit is allowable only for the first two years of post-secondary education, regardless of how long the student attends school to complete two years of credits.

The credit applies to qualified tuition and related expenses, such as registration fees in a degree or certificate program. Room and board are not included. The student must have a high school diploma or its equivalent to receive the credit and the student must carry at least one-half the normal full-time course load for one academic period in the year. The credit is not available for a student who has been convicted of a federal or state felony drug offense.

Lifetime Learning Credit. This credit covers qualified education expenses paid after June 30, 1998, for an academic period beginning after that date. It applies to tuition costs of undergraduates, graduate students, and those acquiring or improving their job skills through a training program. Students who are learning job skills may claim the credit even for part-time attendance. The credit is based on 20% of up to $5,000 of qualified expenses. Starting in 2002, the credit increases to 20% up to $10,000 of qualified expenses. There is no limit on the number of years the credit can be claimed. However, the Lifetime Learning Credit and the Hope Credit may not be claimed in the same year or in any year that funds are withdrawn from an Educational IRA. You may not claim the credit for any educational expenses if you cashed in EE bonds to pay those same expenses.

Eligibility for credits. Both credits are restricted to expenses paid for the education of the taxpayer, his or her spouse, or a dependent for whom a personal exemption is allowed. If you are a dependent, you may not claim either credit yourself. Parents who claim a student as a dependent may treat any amount paid by the student as paid by them for credit purposes.

The Lifetime Learning and the Hope Credits both start to phase out ratably at modified adjusted gross income (MAGI) of $40,000 for single persons and $80,000 for joint filers. The credits are reduced to zero at MAGI of $50,000 for single persons and $100,000 for joint filers. Married persons must file a joint return to claim either credit. *See* the Supplement for further details on the tax credits for higher education.

38.7 Student Loan Interest Deduction in 1998

Starting in 1998, a student paying interest on a student loan may claim an above-the-line deduction (directly from gross income) of up to $1,000. This amount will increase to $1,500 in 1999, $2,000 in 2000, and finally caps at $2,500 in 2001.

Qualifying loans include any debt incurred to pay higher education expenses for oneself, a spouse, or a dependent at the time the debt was incurred. The educational loan must relate to a time when the student was enrolled at least half-time.

The deduction is allowed only for the first 60 months in which interest payments are required; thus, interest is not deductible after the expiration of the 60-month period. Refinancing of a loan after the 60-month period will not extend the deductible period, but the deduction does apply to refinancing within the 60-month limit.

The deduction phases out ratably for single persons with modified adjusted gross income (MAGI) of $40,000–$55,000, and $60,000–$75,000 for married persons filing jointly. Individuals with MAGI over $55,000 and joint filers with MAGI over $75,000 may not claim any deduction. A student who is claimed as a dependent may not claim the deduction.

38.8 Educational IRA in 1998

You may be able to accumulate a limited amount of tax-free savings for education expenses in an Educational IRA. Starting in 1998, you may make nondeductible annual contributions of up to $500 per child to an Educational IRA.

Contributions must be made in cash and may not be made after the beneficiary reaches 18. Contributions to an Educational IRA do not count against contributions to other IRAs. The $500 contribution limit is phased out starting at modified adjusted gross income (MAGI) of $95,000 for single filers and $150,000 for joint filers. Single persons who have MAGI of more than $110,000 and joint filers who have MAGI of more than $160,000 may not make contributions to an Educational IRA. You also may not make a contribution to a child's Education IRA in the same year that you or anyone else funds a state-sponsored tuition plan for that child.

Distributions from an Educational IRA *not* used to pay education expenses are subject to tax to the extent of income earned on the contributions. A 10% penalty also generally applies to taxable distributions. For tax-free treatment, the money must generally be used to pay for post-secondary school tuition and expenses for room, board, books, and supplies. It may not be used for elementary and secondary schooling. According to Committee Reports, if the child does not go to college by age 30, the fund must be withdrawn and earnings are taxed and subject to a 10% penalty. Through an oversight the 30-year cap was left out of the statute, and further legislation will be needed to correct the statute.

A distribution from an Educational IRA is not taxable if it is paid into another Education IRA for the beneficiary or a member of the beneficiary's family within 60 days of the distribution. Only one distribution from an Educational IRA may be rolled over to another one in a 12-month period.

Contributions to an Educational IRA for the benefit of a beneficiary are treated as completed gifts of a present interest at the time of contribution and thus eligible for the gift tax exclusion *(33.1)*.

Note: See 8.12 for discussion of penalty-free withdrawals from regular IRAs for education costs.

Chapter 39

A Guide To Estate Taxes and Planning

The federal estate tax is a tax on the transfer of property at death. In 1997, the tax applies to net taxable estates over $600,000, after taking into account allowable deductions, such as deductions for charitable bequests and property passing to a surviving spouse.

By following the guidelines in this chapter, you can estimate your potential estate. If your estate may be subject to tax, you may want to start thinking about property transfers that may reduce or avoid the estate tax. A brief review of estate tax plans is at *39.6*, and gift tax plans are discussed in Chapter 33.

39.1 What Is the Estate Tax?

The estate you built up may not be entirely yours to give away. The federal government and, in most cases, at least one state government stand ready to claim their shares.

Do you know what will remain for your family, your favorite charities, and your other beneficiaries? If you do not, you cannot intelligently estimate what you can give to each. To help you make such an estimate, we offer this general guide to federal estate taxation. It will alert you to the extent of estate tax costs, and help you plan for estate tax savings that you may discuss with your attorney.

The federal estate tax is a tax on the act of transferring property at death. It is not a tax on the right of the beneficiary to receive the property; the estate and the estate alone pays the tax, although the property passing to individual beneficiaries may be diminished by the tax.

Understand what the word *estate* means in estate tax law so that you do not underestimate the value of your taxable estate. The estate includes not only your real estate (foreign and domestic), bank deposits, securities, and personal property such as art objects, but can also include insurance, your interest in trusts or jointly held property, and certain interests you have in other estates.

39.2 Take Inventory

The first step in estate tax planning follows a simple business practice of taking inventory of everything you own. Listing your belongings takes thought, time, and a surprising amount of work. On your list you should include records of purchases, fire and theft insurance inventories, bankbooks, brokers' statements, etc. You should also include your cash, real estate (here and abroad), securities, mortgages, rights in property, trust accounts, personal effects, collections, and art works. Life insurance is includible if: (1) payable to your estate; (2) payable to others and you have kept "incidents of ownership" such as the right to change beneficiaries, surrender or assign the policy, or pledge it for a loan; or (3) you assign the policy and die within three years *(33.6)*.

If you own property jointly with your spouse, your estate includes only one-half its value.

If you had appraisals made of specially treasured items or collections, or property of substantial value, file such appraisals with your estate papers and then enter the value on your inventory.

There are some assets that you might not ordinarily consider as part of your estate. Nevertheless, include in your inventory any trust arrangements created by you in which you have: (1) a life estate (the income or other use of property for life); (2) income that is to be used to pay your legal obligations (support of a child, for example); (3) the right to change the beneficiary or his or her interest (a power of appointment); (4) the right to revoke a trust transfer or gift; and (5) a reversionary interest (the possibility that the property can come back to you).

Retirement benefits. The taxable estate generally includes benefits payable at your death from any of the following retirement plans: pension plan, profit-sharing plan, Keogh plan, individual retirement account, or annuity. However, the value of an annuity from an IRA or employer plan that is payable to a beneficiary other than your estate may qualify for a full or partial exclusion if IRA distributions began before 1985 or you separated from service before 1985; no exclusion is allowed to the extent of your own nondeductible contributions to the plan.

A full exclusion is allowed for IRA funds if you began taking distributions from the account before 1983 under a schedule that irrevocably set the form of benefits. If IRA distributions began in 1983 or 1984 and you irrevocably elected the form of benefits before July 18, 1984, a $100,000 exclusion is allowed.

If you began receiving distributions from an employer plan before 1983 under a schedule that irrevocably set the form of benefits, a full estate tax exclusion is allowed. If you separated from service in 1983 or 1984, a $100,000 exclusion is allowed if the form of benefits is not changed before death; this is true even if distributions did not begin until after 1984.

39.3 Finding the Value of Your Estate

When you have completed your inventory, assign to each asset what you consider to be its fair market value. This may be difficult to do for some assets. Resist the tendency to overvalue articles which arouse feelings of pride or sentiment and undervalue some articles of great intrinsic worth. For purposes of your initial estimate, it is better to err on the side of overvaluation. You can list ordinary personal effects at nominal value.

If you have a family business, your idea of its value and that of the IRS may vary greatly. Estate plans have been upset by the higher value placed on such a business by the IRS. You can protect your estate by anticipating and solving this problem with your business associates and counselors.

If your business is owned by a closely held corporation, and there is no ready or open market in which the stock can be valued, get some factual basis for a figure that will be reported on the estate tax return. One of the ways to do this is by arranging a buy-sell agreement with a potential purchaser. This agreement must fix the value of the stock. Generally, an agreement that binds both the estate and the purchaser and which restricts lifetime sales of the stock will effectively fix the value of the stock for estate tax purposes. Another way would be to make a gift of some shares to a family member and have value established in gift tax proceedings.

If a substantial part of your estate is real estate used in farming or a closely held business, your executor may be able to elect, with the consent of heirs having an interest in the property, to value the property on the basis of its farming or business use, rather than its highest and best use. The special use valuation, however, may not reduce the gross estate by more than $750,000, subject to adjustment for inflation. This savings may be recaptured from your heir if he or she stops using the property in farming or business within 10 years of your death.

39.4 How the Estate Tax Is Applied

A single unified rate schedule applies to a decedent's estate and all post-1976 lifetime gifts *over* the annual gift tax exclusion. Under the unified gift and estate tax rate, the overall tax on your property holdings is theoretically the same whether or not you make lifetime gifts. In actual cases, however, lifetime gifts may reduce the potential overall tax because of the annual gift tax exclusion.

If you make no taxable gifts during your life, estimating estate tax on Form 706 is fairly easy. You start with the total market value of the property in the estate. This is called the gross estate. From the gross estate you subtract certain deductions. For example, charitable bequests are deductible. An unlimited marital deduction is allowed for bequests to a surviving spouse who is a U.S. citizen; *see 39.5* for noncitizen surviving spouses. The net amount after deductions is your taxable estate. A unified or applicable credit is subtracted from the tax calculated on the taxable estate; *see 39.5*. Other credits, including the state death tax credit, further reduce the federal estate tax on your estate. *See 39.5* for a sample computation of estate tax.

If you make taxable gifts after 1976, estimating your estate tax is more complicated. The estate tax and gift tax are cumulative. That is, the tax rate is applied to the sum of (1) your taxable estate at death, and (2) taxable lifetime gifts made after 1976 (other than gifts included in your estate). The tax you figure on both (1) and (2) is reduced by gift taxes payable on gifts made after 1976. The unified or applicable credit and other credits are then subtracted from the remaining amount.

Generation-skipping transfers. Transfers that "skip" a generation, such as a gift to a grandchild, are subject to a special tax (computed on Schedule R of Form 706) if they exceed a lifetime exemption of $1 million per transferor, subject to inflation adjustments. Because of other exceptions and the complexity of these rules, you should consult an experienced tax practitioner if planning "skip" transfers.

39.5 Unified Tax Rates and Credit

For estates of individuals dying before 1998, a unified tax credit of $192,800 based on an exemption of $600,000 eliminated tax on estates of $600,000 or less, assuming the decedent did not make any taxable gifts and the taxable estate was gross estate less allowable deductions. Estates of individuals dying after 1997 may benefit from an increased credit called the "applicable credit amount," which will increase according to the following scheduled increases in the applicable exclusion amount:

Individual dying in—	Exclusion amount—
1998	$625,000
1999	$650,000
2000–2001	$675,000
2002–2003	$700,000
2004	$850,000
2005	$950,000
2006 and later years	$1,000,000

For an estate of an individual dying in 1998, the applicable credit amount is $202,050, based on the applicable exclusion amount of $625,000.

 Law Alert

Family-Owned Business

For individuals dying after 1997, a tax exclusion for a family business will reduce estate tax. For example, where an individual owning a qualified business dies in 1998, up to $675,000 of the adjusted value of the business may be excluded. Further exclusion details will be in the Supplement.

Phaseout of credit and graduated rates. The benefit of the credit and graduated rates is phased out for cumulative transfers (taxable gifts plus estates) above $10 million. For estates of individuals dying before 1998, the tentative estate tax liability figured on Form 706 is increased for estates between $10 million and $21,040,000. The increase is 5% of the excess of the estate over $10 million. Estates over $21,040,000 are taxed at a flat 55%. Taxable gifts after 1976 are added to the estate for purposes of computing the 5% adjustment.

You Are Now Ready To Estimate the Federal Estate Tax

Gross estate (your estimated inventory) $_____

Less:

1. Administration expenses (executor's commissions, attorneys' fees, etc.; estimate about 5% to 10% of your estate) $_____
2. Debts, mortgages, liens   _____
3. Funeral expenses   _____
4. Marital deduction   _____
5. Charitable deductions   _____

Total of Lines 1–5 $_____

Your taxable estate $_____

   Plus: Post-1976 taxable gifts (over the annual exclusion) $_____

Total taxable amount $_____

Tentative tax on total   _____

   Less:

1. Gift tax payable on post-1976 gifts $_____
2. Credit (unified or applicable) $_____
3. State death taxes credit and other credits $_____   _____

Estate tax due $_____

EXAMPLE

Assume an unmarried person who made no taxable gifts after 1976 leaves a gross estate of $700,000 in 1997. Debts, administration, and funeral expenses total $60,000. The decedent bequeaths $160,000 to charity.

Gross estate		$700,000
Less: Debts, administration, and funeral expenses		60,000
		$640,000
Less: Charitable deduction		160,000
Taxable estate		$480,000
Tentative tax	$149,000	
Less: Unified credit	192,800	
Estate tax due		None

If there was an estate tax due after applying the unified credit, the tax may be reduced by the credit for state death taxes. There are also credits for foreign death taxes, gift taxes paid on gifts before 1977, and federal estate taxes paid on certain prior transfers.

Nonresident alien decedents and surviving spouses. For nonresident aliens, estate tax applies only to the part of the gross estate located in the United States. The estate and gift tax rates applied to U.S. citizens and residents also apply to nonresident aliens. However, the unified credit is limited to $13,000, exempting the first $60,000 of the estate from estate tax. Where required by a tax treaty, a proportionate part of the regular unified credit or applicable credit amount is allowed, based on the percentage of the total gross estate that is situated in the U.S. Estates of certain residents of U.S. possessions are allowed a credit equal to the greater of $13,000, and $46,800 multiplied by the proportion of the gross estate situated in the U.S. to the total gross estate.

Unified Gift and Estate Tax Rates

If taxable amount is:

Over—	But not over—	The tax is—	Plus%—	Of the amount over—
$0	$10,000	$0	18	$0
10,000	20,000	1,800	20	10,000
20,000	40,000	3,800	22	20,000
40,000	60,000	8,200	24	40,000
60,000	80,000	13,000	26	60,000
80,000	100,000	18,200	28	80,000
100,000	150,000	23,800	30	100,000
150,000	250,000	38,800	32	150,000
250,000	500,000	70,800	34	250,000
500,000	750,000	155,800	37	500,000
750,000	1,000,000	248,300	39	750,000
1,000,000	1,250,000	345,800	41	1,000,000
1,250,000	1,500,000	448,300	43	1,250,000
1,500,000	2,000,000	555,800	45	1,500,000
2,000,000	2,500,000	780,800	49	2,000,000
2,500,000	3,000,000	1,025,800	53	2,500,000
3,000,000		1,290,800	55*	3,000,000

*See also *(the phase-out rule on the preceding page.)*

39.6 Reducing or Eliminating a Potential Estate Tax

Here are general approaches to eliminating or reducing a potential estate tax: You can make direct lifetime gifts. Any appreciation on the property transferred will be removed from your estate. Furthermore, each gift, to the extent of the $10,000 per donee annual exclusion, reduces your gross estate; *see 33.1* and *33.2.* Life insurance can be assigned to avoid estate tax, provided the assignment takes place more than three years before death; *see 33.6.* You can provide in your will for bequests that will qualify for the marital and charitable deductions.

The marital deduction.   A married person may greatly reduce or eliminate estate tax by using the marital deduction. Property passing to a spouse is generally free from estate or gift tax because of an unlimited marital deduction.

Weigh carefully the tax consequences of leaving your spouse all of your property. For maximum tax savings, you may want to give your spouse only enough property to reduce your taxable estate to the exclusion floor *(see 39.5).* The applicable credit amount will then eliminate tax on that amount at the time of your death. By leaving your spouse less than the maximum deductible amount, you may be able to reduce the estate tax at the time of his or her death.

To qualify for the marital deduction, the property must generally be given to the spouse outright or by other arrangements that are the legal equivalent to outright ownership. There is an exception for income interests in charitable remainder annuity or unitrusts and certain other qualified terminable interest property (QTIP) for which the executor makes an election.

Life insurance proceeds may qualify as marital deduction property. Name your spouse the unconditional beneficiary of the proceeds with unrestricted control over any unpaid proceeds. If your spouse is not given this control or general power of appointment, and there is no requirement that proceeds remaining on your spouse's death be payable to his or her estate, the insurance proceeds will not qualify for the marital deduction.

What should be done if you believe your spouse cannot manage property? You will not want to give complete and personal control. The law permits you to put the property in certain trust arrangements that are considered equivalent to complete ownership. Your attorney can explain how you can protect your spouse's interest and qualify the trust property for the marital deduction.

Marital deduction restrictions for noncitizen spouses.   A marital deduction may not be claimed for property passing outright to a surviving spouse who is not a U.S. citizen. However, the marital deduction is allowed if the surviving spouse's interest is in a qualifying domestic trust (QDOT). At least one trustee must be an individual U.S. citizen or domestic corporation with power to withhold estate tax due from distributions of trust corpus. The trust must maintain sufficient assets as required by IRS regulations. For the marital deduction to apply, the executor must make an irrevocable election on the decedent's estate tax return. On Form 706-QDT, estate tax will apply to certain distributions of trust corpus made prior to the surviving spouse's death, and to the value of the QDOT property remaining at the surviving spouse's death. You should consult an experienced tax practitioner to set up a QDOT trust and plan for distribution provisions.

The estate of a nonresident alien is subject to estate tax only to the extent that the estate is located in the United States. A marital deduction may be claimed by the estate of a nonresident alien for property passing to a surviving spouse who is a U.S. citizen. If the surviving spouse is not a U.S. citizen, then the transferred interest must be in the form of a QDOT.

Periodically review your estate plan.   You are now aware of the costs of transferring an estate and of the amount of tax that may be levied. But no estate plan is ever really final. Economic conditions and inflation constantly change values. For this reason, your plan must be reviewed periodically as changes occur in your family and business, as when a birth or death occurs; when you receive a substantial increase or decrease in income; when you enter a new business venture or resign from an old one; or when you sell, retire from, or bring new persons into business. A member of your family may no longer need any part of your estate, while others may need more. Estate or gift tax laws may be revised, or material changes may occur in the health or life expectancy of one of your beneficiaries.

A final word of caution: Estate tax planning is not a do-it-yourself activity. We suggest you contact experienced counsel for help.

39.7 Estate Tax Freeze Advisory

The object of an estate tax freeze is to reduce or eliminate estate tax on the inheritance of property by fixing the value through certain property arrangements. A complicated gift and estate tax law (IRC §§2701–2704) attempts to discourage such plans by applying special valuation rules. The rules cover not only common and preferred stock holdings within the family but also partnership interests, the deferral of dividend payments on preferred stock, life and remainder interests, and buy-sell agreements in family businesses.

The estate freeze rules impose gift tax and estate tax values for property transfers subject to the law. Because of the complexity of these rules and their effect on gift and estate values, we suggest that you seek professional advice in the following situations:

- As an owner of a family business, you plan to give common stock to family members while retaining preferred stock or recapitalize with common and preferred stock.
- You plan to give up a voting interest or liquidating rights attached to preferred stock in a family business.
- You defer payment of dividends in preferred stock in a family business.
- You plan to retain an interest for life in a transfer or purchase of property.
- You plan to give stock to a family member in a company in which you have a buy-sell agreement.

Part 6

Business Tax Planning

In this part, you will learn how to report your income from a business or profession, and how to reduce your tax liability by claiming expense deductions. Pay special attention to—

- Reporting rules for income and expenses on Schedule C (Chapter 40).
- Restrictions on deducting home office expenses. Your deduction may be limited by a restrictive income test (Chapter 40).
- Keogh, SEP, and SIMPLE retirement plan rules if you are self-employed. These plans offer tax deductions for contributions and tax-free accumulation of income within the plan. In some cases, special averaging for lump-sum distributions from a Keogh plan is allowed (Chapter 41).
- First-year expensing and depreciation write-offs for business assets (Chapter 42).
- The IRS mileage allowance as an alternative to claiming operating expenses and depreciation for your business automobile (Chapter 43).
- Computing and paying self-employment tax on self-employment earnings from a business or profession (Chapter 45).

Chapter 40

Income or Loss From Your Business or Profession

As a self-employed person, you report income and expenses from your business or profession separately from your other income, such as income from wages. On Schedule C, you report your business income and itemize your expenses. Any net profit is subject to self-employment tax, as well as regular tax. A net profit can also be the basis of deductible contributions to a SEP or Keogh retirement plan, as discussed in Chapter 41.

If you work out of your home, you may deduct home office expenses.

If you claim a loss on Schedule C, be prepared to show that you regularly and substantially participate in the business. Otherwise, your loss may be considered a passive loss deductible only from passive income, as discussed in Chapter 10.

If you have a 1997 business loss that exceeds your other income, you may carry back the loss to three prior years and claim a refund.

If you have no employees and business expenses of $2,500 or less, you may be able to file a simplified schedule called Schedule C-EZ; *see 40.5.*

40.1 Forms of Doing Business

Before doing business, it is important to decide the legal form of your business. This decision will determine the way you report business income and loss, the taxes you pay, the ability of the business to accumulate capital, and the extent of your personal liability. It is beyond the scope of this book to discuss the pros and cons of each form. The decision should be made with the services of a professional experienced in both the legal and tax consequences of doing business in a particular form as it applies to your current and future business prospects.

If you are going into business alone, your choices are: operating as a sole proprietor, incorporating, and forming a limited liability company (LLC), if the law in your state permits. If you are going to operate with associates, you may choose to operate as a partnership, a corporation, or an LLC. If you are concerned with limiting your personal liability, your choice is between a corporation or an LLC. An LLC is a relatively new form of business. It gives you the advantage of limited liability without having to incorporate.

As a sole proprietor, you report business profit or loss on your personal tax return, as explained in this chapter. If you are a partner, you report your share of partnership profit and loss as explained in Chapter 11. If you incorporate, the corporation pays tax on business income. You are taxable on salaries and dividends paid to you by the corporation. You may avoid this double corporate tax by making an S corporation election, which allows you to report corporate income and loss; *see 11.14*.

If you operate through an LLC as an individual, you report income and loss as a sole proprietor. If you operate an LLC with associates, the LLC reports as a partnership and you report your share of income and loss. However, under the current check-the-box rules, the LLC may elect to report as an association taxable as a corporation on Form 8832.

40.2 Reporting Self-Employed Income

You file a separate Schedule C along with Form 1040 if you are a sole proprietor of a business or a professional in your own practice. If you are an employee with a sideline business, report the self-employment income from that business on Schedule C. Do not file Schedule C if your business is operated through a partnership or corporation. A guide to Schedule C is in *40.6*.

Net business profit (or loss) figured on Schedule C is entered on Line 12, Page 1 of Form 1040. Thus, business profit (or loss) is added to (or subtracted from) nonbusiness income on Form 1040. This procedure gives you the chance to deduct your business expenses, whether or not you claim itemized deductions.

On Schedule C, you deduct all of your business expenses from your business income. Then, after adding your business profit to, or subtracting a business loss from, nonbusiness income on Form 1040, you may itemize nonbusiness deductions on Schedule A, such as charitable contributions, taxes, and medical expenses—provided the total of itemized deductions exceeds the standard deduction; *see 13.2*.

You may be able to file a simplified schedule, Schedule C-EZ, if your income and expenses are below certain limits; *see 40.6*.

Passive loss restrictions. Pay special attention to the passive loss restrictions discussed in Chapter 10. Generally, if you do not regularly and substantially participate in your business, losses are considered passive and are deductible only against other passive income.

Accounting for Business Income

40.3 Accounting Methods for Reporting Business Income

Business income is reported on either the accrual or cash basis. If you have more than one business, you may have a different accounting method for each business.

Inventories. If you have inventories, you *must* use the accrual basis.

Cash basis. You report income items in the taxable year in which they are received; you deduct all expenses in the taxable year in which they are paid. Under the cash basis, income is also reported if it is "constructively" received. You have "constructively" received income when an amount is credited to your account, subject to your control, or set apart for you and may be drawn by you at any time. For example, in 1997 you receive a check in payment of services, but you do not cash it until 1998. You have constructively received the income in 1997, and it is taxable in 1997.

On the cash basis, you deduct expenses in the year of payment. Expenses paid by credit card are deducted in the year they are charged. Expenses paid through a "pay by phone" account with a

Filing Tip

Did You Suffer a Loss?
Business persons and professionals with a 1997 net operating loss may get a refund of taxes paid in three prior tax years. If the loss is not fully eliminated by the income of the three prior years, the balance of the loss may be used to reduce your business income for up to 15 of the following years. *See 40.18* for details.

Key To Reporting Business and Professional Income and Loss

Item—	Comments—
Tax return to file	If you are self-employed, prepare Schedule C to report business or professional income. If your business expenses are $2,500 or less, and you have no employees, you may be able to file a simplified Schedule C-EZ; *see 40.6*. If you are a farmer, use Schedule F. You attach Schedule C and/or F to Form 1040. If you operate as a partnership, use Form 1065; if you operate as a corporation, use Form 1120S or Form 1120.
Method of reporting income	The cash or accrual accounting rules determine when you report income and expenses. You must use the accrual basis if you sell a product that must be inventoried. The cash-basis and accrual-basis methods are discussed at *40.3*.
Tax reporting year	There are two general tax reporting years: calendar years which end on December 31 and fiscal years which end on the last day of any month other than December. Your taxable year must be the same for both your business and nonbusiness income. Most business income must be reported on a calendar-year basis. If, as a self-employed person, you report your business income on a fiscal-year basis, you must also report your nonbusiness income on a fiscal-year basis. Use of a fiscal year is restricted for partnerships and S corporations.
Office in home	To claim home office expenses as a self-employed person, you must use the home area exclusively and on a regular basis either as a place of business to meet or deal with patients, clients, or customers in the normal course of your business or as your principal place of business. Form 8829 must be used to compute the deduction; *see 40.12*.
Social Security coverage	If you have self-employed income, you may have to pay self-employment tax, which goes to financing Social Security benefits; *see* Chapter 45.
Passive participation in a business	If you do not regularly, continuously, and substantially participate in the business, your business income or loss is subject to passive activity restrictions. A loss is deductible only against other passive activity income. The passive activity restrictions are discussed in detail in Chapter 10.
Self-employed Keogh plan	You may set up a retirement plan based on business or professional income. Individuals who are self-employed may contribute to a self-employed retirement plan, according to the rules of Chapter 41.
Depreciation	Business assets other than real estate placed in service in 1997 are depreciable over three, five, seven, 10, 15, or 20 years. Automobiles and light trucks, computers, and office equipment are in the five-year class. Property in the three-, five-, seven-, and 10-year classes is depreciable using the double declining balance method, switching to the straight-line method so as to maximize the deduction; *see* Chapter 42 for details. Instead of depreciating equipment, you may claim the first-year expensing deduction. You may generally deduct up to $18,000 in 1997; *see 42.3*.
Health insurance	In 1997, you may deduct 40% of premium costs of health insurance coverage for yourself, spouse, and dependents. You may also take advantage of a medical savings account plan as explained in *17.17*.
Net operating losses	A loss incurred in your profession or business is deducted from other income reported on Form 1040. If the 1997 loss (plus any casualty loss) exceeds income, the excess may be first carried back to 1994, 1995, and 1996, and then forward 15 years to 1998 through 2012 until it is used up. A loss carried back to a prior year reduces income of that year and entitles you to a refund. A loss applied to a later year reduces income for that year. You may elect to carry forward your 1997 loss for 15 years, foregoing the three-year carryback; *see 40.22*.
Sideline business	You report business income of a sideline business following the rules that apply to full-time business. For example, if you are self-employed, you report business income on Schedule C or C-EZ. You may also have to pay self-employment tax on this income; *see* Chapter 45. You may also set up a self-employment retirement plan based on such income. If you incur losses over several years, the hobby loss rules of *40.10* may limit your loss deduction.

Planning Reminder

Advantage of Cash-Basis Accounting

The cash basis has this advantage over other accounting methods: You may defer reporting income by postponing the receipt of income. For example, if 1997 is a high income year or income tax rates will be lower in 1998, you might extend the date of payment of some of your customers' bills until 1998. But make certain that you avoid the constructive receipt rule. You may also postpone the payment of presently due expenses to a year in which the deduction gives you a greater tax savings.

bank are deducted in the year the bank sends the check. This date is reported by the bank on its monthly statement.

Advance payments. On the cash basis, you may not deduct advance rent payments covering charges of a later tax year. The IRS applies a similar rule to advance payments of insurance premiums; however, an appeals court has allowed an immediate deduction.

Cash method of accounting limited. The following may not use the cash method: a regular C corporation, a partnership with a C corporation as a partner, a tax shelter, or a tax-exempt trust with unrelated business income. Exceptions: The cash method may be used by personal service corporations in the fields of medicine, law, engineering, accounting, architecture, performing arts, actuarial science, or consulting. To qualify, substantially all of the stock must be owned directly or indirectly (through partnerships, S corporations, or personal service corporations) by employees. The cash method may also be used by other businesses with average annual gross receipts of $5 million or less, and farming and timber businesses. Tax shelters may not use the cash method; the $5 million gross receipts exception is not available.

Accrual basis. On the accrual basis, report income that has been earned, whether or not received, unless your right to collect the income is unsure because a substantial contingency may prevent payment; *see* the Example below.

EXAMPLE

You report business income as a calendar-year accrual taxpayer. You sell several products on December 27, 1997, and bill the customer in January 1998. You report the sales income on your 1997 Schedule C, even though payment is not made until 1998. Under the accrual method, you are considered to earn the income when the products are sold and delivered to the customer.

Where you are prepaid for future services that must be completed by the end of the next tax year, you report the income in the year that services are performed; *see* the following Example.

EXAMPLE

In 1997, you receive full payment under a one-year contract requiring you to provide 48 music lessons. In 1997, you give eight lessons, and report one-sixth ($\frac{8}{48}$) of the payment as income. In 1998, the remaining five-sixths of the payment must be reported, even if you do not actually give the required number of lessons.

Planning Reminder

Advantage of Accrual-Basis Accounting

The accrual basis has this advantage over the cash basis: It generally gives a more even and balanced financial report.

Expenses under the accrual method are deductible in the year your liability for payment is fixed, even though payment is made in a later year. To prevent manipulation of expense deductions, there are tax law tests for fixing the timing of accrual method expense deductions. The tests generally require that *economic performance* must occur before a deduction may be claimed, but there are exceptions, such as for "recurring expenses." These rules are discussed in IRS Publication 538, which is available without charge from the IRS. However, the basic application of the accrual expense rule can be understood from the following Examples.

EXAMPLES

1. You report business income as a calendar-year accrual taxpayer. In December 1997, you order and receive supplies with an invoice for payment. You pay the bill in 1998. You deduct the expenses on your 1997 Schedule C. Liability was fixed in 1997, and the supplies were delivered in 1997. What if delivery was not until 1998? The expense is deductible in 1997 if the timing of the order and the delivery follows your normal business practice.

2. In 1997, you pay rent for December 1997 and January 1998. You deduct the rent for December on your 1997 return. You defer the deduction of the January rent to your 1998 return.

Expenses owed to a related cash-basis taxpayer. A business expense owed to your spouse, brother, sister, parent, child, grandparent, or grandchild who reports on the cash basis may not be deducted by you until you make the payment and the relative includes it as income. The same rule applies to amounts owed to a controlled corporation (more than 50% ownership) and other related entities.

Long-term contracts.   Section 460 of the Internal Revenue Code has a special percentage of completion method of accounting for long-term construction contractors.

Capitalize costs of business property you produce or buy for resale.   A complicated statute (Code Section 263A) requires manufacturers and builders to capitalize certain indirect costs (such as administrative costs, interest expenses, storage fees, and insurance), as well as direct production expenses, by including them in inventory costs.

Retailers and wholesalers who acquire real estate for resale also are subject to the uniform capitalization requirements. Purchasers of personal property (not real estate) for resale are exempt from the capitalization rules, unless average annual gross receipts from all businesses for the three prior tax years exceeded $10 million.

Different capitalization methods apply to resellers and manufacturers. Special exceptions apply for farm products. A special production period rule applies to capitalization of interest expenses. Inventory adjustments may be spread over four years. Authors, artists, and photographers are generally exempt from the capitalization requirements; *see 40.8*. For further details, *see* IRS Publication 538, Form 3115, and the regulations to Code Section 263A.

Accrual deferral of service income.   If, on the basis of your experience, a percentage of billings due for your services will not be collected in that year, you do not have to report that "uncollectible" amount until the year you actually receive it.

However, if interest or a penalty is charged for a failure to make a timely payment, income is reported when the amount is billed. Furthermore, if discounts for early payments are offered, the full amount of the bill must be accrued; the discount for early payment is treated as an adjustment to income in the year payment is made.

The amount of income to be deferred is based on a percentage that considers billing and uncollectibles over the past five most recent years. The percentage is found by dividing the uncollectible amounts by the total billings during the five-year period. That percentage applied to the total billings during the tax year may be deferred. For example, if $200,000 was billed during the five-year period and $20,000 was uncollectible, the percentage is 10% and 10% of the current billings may be deferred. If you do not have a five-year experience, you use the period during which you were in business.

40.4 Tax Reporting Year for Self-Employed

Your taxable year must be the same for both your business and nonbusiness income. If you report your business income on a fiscal-year basis, you must also report your nonbusiness income on a fiscal-year basis.

Generally, you report the tax consequences of transactions that have occurred during a 12-month period. If the period ends on December 31, it is called a calendar year. If it ends on the last day of any month other than December, it is called a fiscal year. A reporting period, technically called a *taxable year*, can never be longer than 12 months unless you report on a 52-to-53-week fiscal-year basis, details of which can be found in IRS Publication 538. A reporting period may be less than 12 months whenever you start or end your business in the middle of your regular taxable year, or change your taxable year.

To change from a calendar year to fiscal-year reporting for self-employment income, you must ask the IRS for permission by filing Form 1128. Support your request with a business reason such as that the use of the fiscal year coincides with your business cycle. To use a fiscal year basis, you must keep your books and records following that fiscal year period.

Fiscal year restrictions.   Restrictions on fiscal years for partnerships, personal service corporations, and S corporations are discussed in Chapter 45.

40.5 Reporting Business Cash Receipts to the IRS

Cash receipts of more than $10,000 in one business transaction or two or more related transactions must be reported on Form 8300. There are penalties for failure to file.

File Form 8300 with the IRS within 15 days of each cash transaction of over $10,000. Only cash payments are reported; do not report funds received by bank check or wire transfer where cash was not physically transferred. Foreign currency is considered cash. If multiple payments from a single payer (or a payer's agent) are received within a 24-hour period, the payments are aggregated, and the total must be reported if over $10,000.

 Filing Tip

Changing Your Accounting Method

Generally, you must obtain the consent of the Internal Revenue Service prior to any change in accounting method. Apply for consent by filing Form 3115 within 180 days after the beginning of the tax year in which you wish to make the change. Thus, if you report on the calendar-year basis and want to change from the cash method to the accrual method for 1998, file by June 30, 1998. You may also get a 90-day extension to file Form 3115 if you need extra time.

The reporting requirement applies to individuals, corporations, partnerships, trusts, and estates, except for certain financial institutions that are already required to report cash transactions to the Treasury. Cash received in transactions occurring entirely outside the U.S. does not have to be reported.

The filing requirement applies to cash received for providing goods or services. Thus, an attorney, doctor, or other professional must report cash payments of over $10,000 from a client. Furthermore, cash received for setting up a trust of more than $10,000 for a client must be reported. The IRS has a program to assess penalties against attorneys who have disregarded the cash reporting rules. Courts have held that an attorney may not refuse to report large cash fees by invoking the attorney-client privilege. However, one appeals court held that disclosure of the name of a client who paid cash exceeding $10,000 was not required where disclosure would implicate the client or would reveal confidential communications made by the client to the attorney. The trial court in a closed hearing heard the attorney's claim and ruled against him, but the appeals court ruled in his favor; the circumstances were not disclosed because of their confidential nature.

On an installment sale of business property, you report each payment exceeding $10,000 within 15 days of receipt. If the initial installment is $10,000 or less, you aggregate it plus all payments received within one year of the initial payment. If the total exceeds $10,000, report the total within 15 days after the receipt of the payment that raised the total to over $10,000. In addition, if—after receiving single or aggregated reportable payments—subsequent payments within one year exceed $10,000 individually or in the aggregate, you must report the payments within 15 days.

Caution

Splitting Up a Transaction

The reporting requirement may not be avoided by splitting up a single transaction into separate transactions. Thus, a sale of property for $36,000 may not be broken down into four separate sales of $9,000 to avoid reporting. Similarly, an attorney who represents a client in a case must aggregate all cash payments by the client, although payments may be spread over several months. If the total exceeds $10,000, it must be reported.

EXAMPLE

On February 8, 1998, you receive an initial cash payment of $11,000. For the same transaction, you also receive cash of $4,000 on March 15, 1998; $6,000 on April 19, 1998; and $12,000 on June 13, 1998. You report the February payment by February 23, 1998. You also report the payments totaling $22,000 received from March 15, 1998, through June 13, 1998, by June 28, 1998, that is, within 15 days of the date (June 13) that the later payments, all received within a one-year period, exceeded $10,000.

Cash equivalents of $10,000 or less. Cash equivalents such as money orders, traveler's checks, cashier's checks, and bank drafts with a face value of $10,000 or less are treated as cash in sales of consumer durables, collectibles, and travel or entertainment services costing $10,000 or more. Common examples of consumer durables are autos, boats, and jewelry.

For example, if jewelry costing $12,000 is bought with $2,400 cash and traveler's checks of $9,600, the jeweler must file Form 8300 reporting the transaction. If the $2,400 were paid by personal check, the transaction would not have to be reported because personal checks are not treated as cash. Reporting exceptions are also allowed where the cash equivalent constitutes the proceeds of a bank loan, or where it is used as a down payment or promissory note payment under a payment plan used for all retail sales by the seller.

Form 8300. On Form 8300, you must provide the payer's home address and tax identification number to the IRS. You also must provide the payer with a copy of the form or a similar statement by January 31 of the following year.

A $50 penalty may be imposed for each failure to file a properly completed Form 8300 or provide the payer with a statement, unless reasonable cause is shown. The penalty may be reduced if a timely correction is made. For small businesses meeting a $5 million average gross receipts test, the maximum penalty for failure to file with the IRS is $100,000 per calendar year; otherwise, the maximum is $250,000.

If failure to file is intentional, the penalty for each failure is the *greater* of $25,000 and the cash received in the transaction, but the maximum penalty is $100,000. Criminal penalties apply for willful failure to file Form 8300 or for filing a fraudulent form.

There is an exception to the reporting requirement for persons who act as agents if they receive cash of over $10,000 from their principal and use it within 15 days in a cash transaction, provided they identify the principal to the payee in the cash transaction.

You must keep a copy of each Form 8300 you file with the IRS for five years from the date of filing.

Reporting Income and Expenses on Schedule C

40.6 How To File Schedule C

In this section are explanations of how a sole proprietor reports income and expenses on Schedule C, a sample of which is on page 571.

Schedule C-EZ. This simple form is designed for persons on the cash basis who do not have a net business loss and have:

- Business expenses of $2,500 or less;
- No inventory at any time during the year;
- Only one sole proprietorship;
- No employees;
- No home office expense deduction;
- No prior-year suspended passive activity losses from this business; and
- No depreciation to be reported on Form 4562.

Statutory employees: Full-time life insurance salespersons, commission drivers, and full-time outside salespersons. Statutory employees report income and expenses on Schedule C. Thus, expenses may be deducted in full on Schedule C rather than as a miscellaneous itemized deduction *(19.1)*, subject to the 2% adjusted gross income (AGI) floor on Schedule A.

Statutory employees are full-time life insurance salespersons, agent or commission drivers distributing certain foods and beverages, pieceworkers, and full-time traveling or city salespersons who solicit on behalf of and transmit to their principals orders from wholesalers and retailers for merchandise for resale or for supplies.

The term *full time* refers to an exclusive or principal business activity for a single company or person and not to the time spent on the job. If your principal activity is soliciting orders for one company, but you also solicit incidental orders for another company, you are a full-time salesperson for the primary company. Solicitations of orders are considered incidental to a principal business activity if you devote 20% or less of your time to the solicitation activity. A city or traveling salesperson is presumed to meet the principal business activity test in a calendar year in which he or she devotes 80% or more of working time to soliciting orders for one principal.

IRS regulations give this example: A salesman's principal activity is getting orders from retail pharmacies for a wholesale drug company called Que Company. He occasionally takes orders for two other companies. He is a statutory employee only for Que Company.

If you are a statutory employee, your company checks Box 15 on Form W-2, identifying you as a statutory employee. Although a statutory employee may treat job expenses as business expenses, the employer withholds FICA (Social Security and Medicare) taxes on wages and commissions. However, a statutory employee has the option of allowing his or her employer to withhold federal income taxes or to meet the employee's tax liability through the payment of estimated tax.

You must check a box on Line 1 of Schedule C (or C-EZ) to indicate statutory employee status. If you also have self-employment earnings from another business, you must report the self-employment earnings and statutory employee income on separate Schedules C. If both types of income are earned in the same business, allocate the expenses between the two activities on the separate schedules.

Gross receipts or sales on Schedule C (Line 1). If you do not produce or sell goods, but provide only services, you do not determine cost of goods sold, but report only your receipts from services on Line 1. (A sample of Schedule C in the Supplement illustrates the case of a retail business selling merchandise that is required to determine the cost of goods sold using Part III of Schedule C.)

Do not report as receipts on Schedule C the following items:

- Gains or losses on the sale of property used in your business or profession. These transactions are reported on Schedule D and Form 4797.
- Dividends from stock held in the ordinary course of your business. These are reported as dividends from stocks that are held for investment.

Deductions on Schedule C. Deductible business expenses are claimed in Part II; the descriptive breakdown of items is generally self-explanatory. However, note these points:

Bad debts (Line 9): Business bad debt rules are discussed at *5.9.* Cash-basis taxpayers may not claim a business bad debt for payments that have not been received or which are uncollectible, where the payments have not been reported as income.

Caution

Doctor's Malpractice Insurance
A self-employed doctor may deduct the premium costs of malpractice insurance. However, a doctor who is not self-employed but employed by someone else, say a hospital, may deduct the premium costs only as an itemized deduction. Whether malpractice premiums paid to a physician-owned carrier are deductible depends on how the carrier is organized. If there is a sufficient number of policyholders who are not economically related and none of whom owns a controlling interest in the insuring company, a deduction is allowed provided the premiums are reasonable and are based on sound actuarial principles.

In one case, physicians set up a physician-owned carrier which was required by state insurance authorities to set up a surplus fund. The physicians contributed to the fund and received nontransferable certificates that were redeemable only if they retired, moved out of the state, or died. The IRS and Tax Court held the contributions to the fund were nondeductible capital expenses.

In another case, a professional corporation of anesthesiologists set up a trust to pay malpractice claims, up to specified limits. The IRS and Tax Court disallowed deductions for the trust contributions on the grounds that the PC remained potentially liable. Malpractice claims within the policy limits might exceed trust funds and the PC would be liable for the difference. Since risk of loss was not shifted to the trust, the trust was not a true insurance arrangement.

Car and truck expenses (Line 10): In the year you place a car in service, you may choose between the IRS mileage allowance and deducting actual expenses, plus depreciation. You must also attach Form 4562 to support the deduction; *see* Chapter 43.

Depreciation (Line 13): Enter here the amount of your annual depreciation deduction. A complete discussion of depreciation may be found in Chapter 42. You must figure your depreciation deduction on Form 4562 for assets placed in service in 1997, or for cars, computers, or other "listed property," regardless of when the assets were placed in service.

Employee benefit programs (Line 14): Enter your cost for the following programs you provide for your employees: accident or health plans; wage continuation; self-insured medical reimbursement plans; educational assistance programs; supplemental unemployment benefits; and prepaid legal expenses. Retirement plans, such as pension and profit-sharing plans, are reported separately on Line 19.

Insurance other than health insurance (Line 15): Insurance policy premiums for the protection of your business, such as accident, burglary, embezzlement, marine risks, plate glass, public liability, workers' compensation, fire, storm, or theft, and indemnity bonds upon employees, are deductible. State unemployment insurance payments are deducted here or as taxes if they are considered taxes under state law.

Premiums paid on an insurance policy on the life of an employee or one financially interested in a business, for the purpose of protecting you from loss in the event of the death of the insured, are not deductible.

Prepaid insurance premiums are deducted ratably over the term covered by the policy, whether you are on a cash or accrual basis. However, an appeals court allowed a cash-basis taxpayer to take an immediate deduction for premiums paid on a policy covering more than a year.

Premiums for disability insurance to cover loss of earnings when out ill or injured are nondeductible personal expenses. But you may deduct premiums covering business overhead expenses.

Note: You do not claim on Schedule C the deduction of 40% of health insurance costs for yourself, your spouse, and your dependents. You take the deduction on Line 27, Form 1040. See also 17.17 for the way to claim MSA account contributions on Line 24 of Form 1040.

Interest (Line 16): Include interest on business debts, but prepaid interest that applies to future years is not deductible.

Deductible interest on an insurance loan is limited if you borrow against a life insurance policy covering yourself as an employee or the life of any other employee, officer, or other person financially interested in your business. Interest on such a loan is deductible only if the loan is no more than $50,000 per employee or other covered person. If you own policies covering the same employees (or other persons) in more than one business, the $50,000 limit applies on an aggregate basis to all the policies. The interest deduction limit applies even if a sole proprietor borrows against a policy on his or her own life and uses the proceeds in a business; interest is not deductible to the extent the loan exceeds $50,000.

Pension and profit-sharing plans (Line 19): Keogh plan or SEP contributions made for your employees are entered here; contributions made for your account are entered directly on Form 1040 as an adjustment to income. In addition, you may have to file an information return by the last day of the seventh month following the end of the plan year; *see 41.8.*

Rent on business property (Line 20): Rent paid for the use of lofts, buildings, trucks, and other equipment is deductible. However, you may not deduct the entire amount of an advance rental in the year of its payment. This is true even if you are on the cash basis. You deduct only that portion of the payment attributed to the use of the property in the taxable year. For example, you sign a 10-year lease calling for yearly rental payments of $2,000. You pay the first year's rent on July 1. In your tax return for the calendar year, you may deduct only $1,000 ($6/12$ of $2,000). However, an appeals court allowed a calendar-year cash-basis lessee to deduct advance rentals where the rental payments covered a period of a year or less. For example, on December 1, 1997, the lessee pays the entire rental due for the lease ending November 30, 1998. While the IRS would allow only $1/12$ of the payment to be deductible in 1997, the appeals court would allow a deduction for the entire payment. The court believes this approach is within the spirit of the cash-basis rule. In the case of a long-term lease where advance rental payments cover no more than a year beyond the year of payment, the IRS proration rule sacrifices the simplicity of the cash-basis method without a meaningful change in the timing of deductions, according to the appeals court.

Taxes on leased property that you pay to the lessor are deductible as additional rent.

Repairs (Line 21): The cost of repairs and maintenance is deductible provided they do not materially add to the value of the property or appreciably prolong its life. Expenses of replacements

Schedule C—Worksheet

Part I   Income

1	Gross receipts or sales. **Caution:** *If this income was reported to you on Form W-2 and the "Statutory employee" box on that form was checked, see page C-2 and check here* . . . . ▶ ☐	1	
2	Returns and allowances	2	
3	Subtract line 2 from line 1	3	
4	Cost of goods sold (from line 42 on page 2)	4	
5	**Gross profit.** Subtract line 4 from line 3	5	
6	Other income, including Federal and state gasoline or fuel tax credit or refund (see page C-2) . . .	6	
7	**Gross income.** Add lines 5 and 6 . . . . ▶	7	

Part II   Expenses. Enter expenses for business use of your home **only** on line 30.

8	Advertising	8		19 Pension and profit-sharing plans	19	
9	Bad debts from sales or services (see page C-3) . .	9		20 Rent or lease (see page C-4):		
				a Vehicles, machinery, and equipment .	20a	
10	Car and truck expenses (see page C-3)	10		b Other business property . .	20b	
11	Commissions and fees . .	11		21 Repairs and maintenance . .	21	
12	Depletion	12		22 Supplies (not included in Part III) .	22	
13	Depreciation and section 179 expense deduction (not included in Part III) (see page C-3) . .	13		23 Taxes and licenses	23	
				24 Travel, meals, and entertainment:		
				a Travel	24a	
14	Employee benefit programs (other than on line 19) . . .	14		b Meals and entertainment .		
15	Insurance (other than health) .	15		c Enter 50% of line 24b subject to limitations (see page C-4) .		
16	Interest:					
a	Mortgage (paid to banks, etc.) .	16a		d Subtract line 24c from line 24b	24d	
b	Other	16b		25 Utilities	25	
17	Legal and professional services	17		26 Wages (less employment credits) .	26	
18	Office expense	18		27 Other expenses (from line 48 on page 2)	27	

28	**Total expenses** before expenses for business use of home. Add lines 8 through 27 in columns . ▶	28	
29	Tentative profit (loss). Subtract line 28 from line 7	29	
30	Expenses for business use of your home. Attach **Form 8829**	30	
31	**Net profit or (loss).** Subtract line 30 from line 29.		
	• If a profit, enter on **Form 1040, line 12,** and ALSO on **Schedule SE, line 2** (statutory employees, see page C-5). Estates and trusts, enter on Form 1041, line 3.	31	
	• If a loss, you MUST go on to line 32.		

32   If you have a loss, check the box that describes your investment in this activity (see page C-5).

   • If you checked 32a, enter the loss on **Form 1040, line 12,** and ALSO on **Schedule SE, line 2** (statutory employees, see page C-5). Estates and trusts, enter on Form 1041, line 3.

     32a ☐ All investment is at risk.
     32b ☐ Some investment is not at risk.

   • If you checked 32b, you MUST attach **Form 6198.**

that arrest deterioration and appreciably increase the value of the property are capitalized and their cost recovered through depreciation.

Taxes (Line 23): Deduct real estate and personal property taxes on business assets here. Also deduct your share of Social Security and Medicare taxes paid on behalf of employees and payments of federal unemployment tax. Federal highway use tax is deductible. Federal import duties and excise and stamp taxes normally not deductible as itemized deductions are deductible as business taxes if incurred by the business. Taxes on business property, such as an *ad valorem* tax, must be deducted here; they are not to be treated as itemized deductions. However, the IRS holds that you may not deduct state income taxes on business income as a business expense. Its reasoning: Income taxes are personal taxes even when paid on business income. As such, you may deduct state income tax only as an itemized deduction on Schedule A. The Tax Court supports the IRS rule on the grounds that it reflects Congressional intent toward the treatment of state income taxes in figuring taxable income.

For purposes of computing a net operating loss, state income tax on business income is treated as a business deduction.

If you pay or accrue sales tax on the purchase of nondepreciable business property, the sales tax is a deductible business expense. If the property is depreciable, add the sales tax to the cost basis for purposes of computing depreciation deductions.

Interest on a tax deficiency was held to be a deductible business expense by a majority of the Tax Court in a dispute involving a change of accounting method. The Tax Court majority rejected an IRS regulation that holds that interest on a tax deficiency is always nondeductible personal interest. However, the majority warned that not all business tax deficiencies would support a deduction of interest. For example, in the case of disallowed expenses, the dispute must involve the issue of whether they were ordinary and necessary business expenses. A deficiency arising from a tax avoidance transaction would not support a deduction of interest. Dissenting Tax Court judges argued that interest on a tax deficiency is a nondeductible personal expense and never a business expense because the obligation to pay income taxes is based on the concept of personal income.

A federal appeals court (Eighth Circuit) has upheld the IRS position denying a business expense deduction for interest on a tax deficiency.

Travel, meals, and entertainment (Line 24): Travel expenses on overnight business trips while "away from home" *(20.6)* and 50% of meals and entertainment for business are deductible. Total meals and entertainment expenses are listed on Line 24b and then reduced by 50% on Line 24c. The total amount after figuring the 50% reduction is reported on Line 24d.

Self-employed persons may use the IRS meal allowance rates discussed at *20.4,* instead of claiming actual expenses. *See also 20.28* for record-keeping requirements for travel and entertainment expenses.

Utilities (Line 25): Deduct utilities such as gas, electric, and telephone expenses incurred in your business. However, if you have a home office *(40.12),* you may *not* deduct the base rate (including taxes) of the *first* phone line into your home; see *19.14.*

Wages (Line 26): You do not deduct wages paid to yourself. You may deduct reasonable wages paid to family members who work for you. If you have an employee who works in your office and also in your home, such as a domestic, you deduct that part of the salary allocated to the work in your office. If you take a targeted jobs credit, the wage deduction is reduced by the credit.

Other expenses (Line 27): In Part V of Schedule C, you list deductible expenses not reported in Part II, such as amortizable business start-up costs.

40.7 Deductions for Professionals

The following expenses incurred by self-employed professionals in the course of their work are generally allowed as deductions from income when figuring profit (or loss) from their professional practices on Schedule C:

- Dues to professional societies
- Operating expenses and repairs of car used on professional calls
- Supplies
- Subscriptions to professional journals
- Rent for office space
- Cost of fuel, light, water, and telephone used in the office
- Salaries of assistants
- Malpractice insurance; *see 40.6*

- Cost of books, information services, professional instruments, and equipment with a useful life of one year or less. Professional libraries are depreciable if their value decreases with time. Depreciation rules are discussed at *42.1*.
- Fees paid to a tax preparer for preparing Schedule C and related business forms

Professionals as employees. Professionals who are not in their own practice may not deduct professional expenses on Schedule C. Salaried professionals may deduct professional expenses only as miscellaneous itemized deductions on Schedule A, subject to the 2% adjusted gross income (AGI) floor; *see 19.1*. However, "statutory" employees may use Schedule C; *see 40.6*.

The cost of preparing for a profession. You may not deduct the cost of a professional education; *see 19.16*.

The IRS does not allow a deduction for the cost of a license to practice. However, the Tax Court has allowed attorneys to amortize over their life expectancy bar admission fees paid to state authorities; *see 19.17*.

Continuing education courses. The costs of courses taken to keep current with professional developments are usually deductible; *see 19.16*.

Payment of clients' expenses. An attorney may follow a practice of paying his or her clients' expenses in pending cases. The IRS will disallow a deduction claimed for these payments on the grounds that the expenses are those of the client, not the attorney. The courts agree with the IRS position where there is a net fee agreement. In a net fee agreement, expenses first reduce the recovery before the attorney takes a fee. However, where the attorney is paid under a gross fee agreement, an appeals court has reversed a Tax Court decision that disallowed the deduction of the attorney's payment of client expenses. Under a gross fee agreement, the attorney's fee is based on the gross award; the prior payment of expenses does not enter into the fee agreement and so is not reimbursed. Because he would not be reimbursed, an attorney claimed his payment of client expenses was deductible. An appeals court accepted this argument and allowed the deduction. The court allowed the deduction although California law disapproved of the practice of paying client expenses without a right of reimbursement. The court believed that there is no ethical difficulty with the practice and other jurisdictions approve of it. It is necessary for and it is the practice of personal injury firms to pay the costs of many of their clients.

If you are not allowed a current deduction for payment of clients' expenses, you may deduct your advance as a bad debt if the claim is worthless in another year; *see 5.10*.

An attorney might deduct a payment to a client reimbursing the client for a bad investment recommended by the attorney. A court upheld the deduction on the grounds that the reimbursement was required to protect the reputation of an established law practice. However, no deduction is allowed when malpractice insurance reimbursement is available but the attorney fails to make a claim.

Daily business lunches with associates have been held to lack business purpose. Courts agree with the IRS that professionals do not need to have lunch together every day to talk shop. The cost of the meals is therefore not deductible.

EXAMPLES
1. A law partnership deducted the meal costs of the staff attorneys who lunched every day at the same restaurant to discuss cases and court assignments. The deductions were disallowed as personal expenses. The Tax Court and an appeals court agreed with the IRS that daily lunches are not necessary. Co-workers generally do not need luncheons to provide social lubrication for business talk, as is true with clients.
2. A physician held luncheon meetings three or four times a week with other physicians. He argued that the purpose of the luncheons was to generate referrals. A court held that such frequent luncheons became a routine personal event not tied to specific business. The cost of the meals was not deductible.
3. A medical professional corporation (PC) deducted the cost of meals taken by its physician-stockholders at a hospital cafeteria. It argued that the doctors discussed patients and met other doctors who made referrals to them. The Tax Court agreed with the IRS that the meal costs were not deductible; doctors ate in the cafeteria for their personal convenience. Furthermore, the payments were taxed to the doctors as dividends. The court noted that the PC might have been able to claim a deduction had it treated the meal payments as taxable pay; however, the PC refused to take this position, unsuccessfully gambling that it could claim the costs as business deductions.

40.8 Nondeductible Expense Items

Capital expenditures may not be deducted. Generally, the cost of acquiring an asset or of prolonging its life is a capital expenditure that must be amortized over its expected life.

> **EXAMPLE**
>
> A new roof is installed on your office building. If the roof increases the life of the building, its cost is a capital expenditure recovered by depreciation deductions. The cost of repairing a leak in the roof is a deductible operating expense. A deduction was allowed for the cost of a major roof renovation on evidence that the work was not designed to increase the value of the building but to correct the defect.

If the useful life of an item is less than a year, its cost, including sales tax on the purchase, is deductible. Otherwise, you may recover your cost only through depreciation except to the extent first-year expensing applies; *see 42.3.*

Expenses while you are not in business.   You are not allowed to deduct business expenses incurred during the time you are not engaged in your business or profession.

> **EXAMPLE**
>
> A lawyer continued to maintain his office while he was employed by the government. During that time he did no private law work. He only kept the office to have it ready at such time as he quit the government job and returned to practice. His costs of keeping up his office while he was working for the government were not deductible.

Payments of fines.   You may not deduct the payment of a fine, even if your violation was unintentional.

Bribes and kickbacks.   Bribes and kickbacks are not deductible if they are illegal under a federal or a generally enforced state law which subjects the payer to a criminal penalty or provides for the loss of license or privilege to engage in business. A kickback, even if not illegal, is not deductible by a physician or other person who has furnished items or services that are payable under the Social Security Act (including state programs). A kickback includes payments for referral of a client, patient, or customer.

In one case, the IRS, with support from the Tax Court and a federal appeals court, disallowed a deduction for legal kickbacks paid by a subcontractor. The courts held that the kickbacks were not a "necessary" business expense because the contractor had obtained nearly all of its other contracts without paying kickbacks, including contracts from the same general contractor bribed here.

40.9 How Authors and Artists May Write Off Expenses

Self-employed authors, artists, photographers, and other qualifying creative professionals may write off business expenses as they are paid. The law (Code Section 263A) that requires expenses to be amortized over the period income is received does not apply to freelancers who personally create literary manuscripts, musical or dance scores, paintings, pictures, sculptures, drawings, cartoons, graphic designs, original print editions, photographs, or photographic negatives or transparencies. Furthermore, expenses of a personal service corporation do not have to be amortized if they directly relate to expenses of a qualifying author, artist, or photographer who owns (or whose relatives own) substantially all of the corporation's stock.

Current deductions are *not* allowed for expenses relating to motion picture films, videotapes, printing, photographic plates, or similar items.

An author or artist with expenses exceeding income may be barred by the IRS from claiming a loss under a profit motive test; in that case, the profit-presumption rule of *40.10* may allow a deduction of the loss.

40.10 Deducting Expenses of a Sideline Business or Hobby

There is a one-way tax rule for hobbies: Income from a hobby is taxable; expenses are deductible only to the extent you have income, and the deduction is limited on Schedule A by the 2% adjusted gross income (AGI) floor for miscellaneous itemized deductions. Hobby losses are considered nondeductible personal losses. A profitable sale of a hobby collection or activity held long term is taxable as capital gain; losses are not deductible.

How to deduct hobby expenses. If the profit presumption discussed later does *not* apply and the activity is held *not* to be engaged in for profit, expenses are deductible only as itemized deductions and only up to the extent of income from the activity; a deduction for expenses exceeding the income is disallowed.

A special sequence is followed in determining which expenses are deductible from income. Deducted first on Schedule A are amounts allowable without regard to whether the activity is a business engaged in for profit, such as mortgage interest and state and local taxes, as well as casualty losses. If any income remains, first deduct "business" operating expenses such as wages, utilities, advertising, repairs, and maintenance. Then deduct depreciation to the extent of remaining income. The "business" expenses and depreciation are allowed only as miscellaneous itemized deductions subject to the 2% AGI floor; *see 19.1*. Thus, even if the expenses offset income from the activity, the expenses will not be deductible unless your total miscellaneous expenses (including those from the activity) exceed 2% of your adjusted gross income.

Presumption of profit-seeking motive. You are *presumed* to be engaged in an activity for profit if you can show a profit in at least three of the last five years, including the current year. If the activity is horse breeding, training, racing, or showing, the profit presumption applies if you show profits in two of seven consecutive years. The presumption does not necessarily mean that losses will automatically be allowed; the IRS may try to rebut the presumption. You would then have to prove a profit motive by showing these types of facts: You spend considerable time in the activity; you keep businesslike records; you relied on expert advice; you expect the assets to appreciate in value; and losses are common in the start-up phase of your type of business.

Election postpones determination of profit presumption. If you have losses in the first few years of an activity and the IRS tries to disallow them as hobby losses, you have this option: You may make an election on Form 5213 to postpone the determination of whether the above profit presumption applies. The postponement is until after the end of the fourth taxable year (sixth year for a horse breeding, training, showing, or racing activity) following the first year of the activity. For example, if you enter a farming activity in 1994, you can elect to postpone the profit motive determination until after 1998. Then, if you have realized profits in at least three of the five years (1994 to 1998), the profit presumption applies. When you make the election on Form 5213, you agree to waive the statute of limitations for all activity-related items in the taxable years involved. The waiver generally gives the IRS an additional two years after the filing due date for the last year in the presumption period to issue deficiencies related to the activity.

To make the election, you must file Form 5213 within three years of the due date of the return for the year you started the activity. Thus, if you started your activity during 1997, you have until April 15, 2001, to make the election. If before the end of this three-year period you receive a deficiency notice from the IRS disallowing a loss from the activity and you have not yet made the election, you can still do so within 60 days of receiving the notice. These election rules apply to individuals, partnerships, and S corporations. An election by a partnership or S corporation is binding on all partners or S corporation shareholders holding interests during the presumption period.

40.11 Deducting Expenses of Looking for a New Business

When you are planning to invest in a business, you may incur preliminary expenses for traveling to look at the property and for legal or accounting advice. Expenses incurred during a general search or preliminary investigation of a business are not deductible, including expenses related to the decision whether or not to enter a transaction. However, when you go beyond a general search and focus on acquiring a particular business, you may deduct the start-up expenses. The timing of the deduction depends on whether or not you actually go into the business.

Amortizable expenses if you go into business. When you go into a business, you may elect to amortize over at least a 60-month period the costs of investigating and setting up the business, such as expenses of surveying potential markets, products, labor supply, and transportation facilities; travel and other expenses incurred in lining up prospective distributors, suppliers, or customers; salaries or fees paid to consultants or attorneys, and fees for similar professional services. The business may be one you acquire from someone else or a new business you create. The amortization period starts when you actually begin or acquire a going business.

Organizational costs for a partnership or corporation. Costs incident to the creation of a partnership or corporation are also amortizable over a period of at least 60 months. For a partnership, qualifying expenses include legal fees for negotiating and preparing a partnership agree-

Planning Reminder

Hobby or Sideline Business
The question of whether an activity, such as dog breeding or collecting and selling coins and stamps, is a hobby or sideline business arises when losses are incurred. As long as you show a profit, you may deduct the expenses of the activity. But when expenses exceed income and your return is examined, an agent may allow expenses only up to the amount of your income and disallow the remaining expenses that make up your loss. At this point, to claim the loss, you may be able to take advantage of a "profit presumption" discussed in *40.10*, or you may have to prove that you are engaged in the activity to make a profit.

Filing Tip

How To Claim Amortization
The election to amortize start-up expenses is made by claiming the deduction on Form 4562, and by attaching a statement to the return for the first year you are in business. In the statement, describe the expenses, when they were incurred, the date the business began, and the number of months (not less than 60) in the amortization period.

ment, and management, consulting or accounting fees in setting up the partnership. Amortization is not allowed for syndication costs of issuing and marketing partnership interests such as brokerage and registration fees, fees of an underwriter, and costs of preparing a prospectus.

For a corporation, amortizable expenses include the cost of organizational meetings, incorporation fees, and accounting and legal fees for drafting corporate documents. Costs of selling stock or securities, such as commissions, do not qualify.

The election to amortize is made on Form 4562 for the first year the partnership or corporation is in business. A statement attached to the return must describe the expenses and the amortization period.

Nonamortizable expenses. Amortizable expenses are restricted to expenses incurred in investigating the acquisition or creation of an active business, and setting up such an active business. They do not include taxes, interest, research, or experimental costs deductible under Code Section 174. Expenses of looking for investment property may not be amortized. For rental activities to qualify as an active business, there must be significant furnishing of services incident to the rentals. For example, the operation of an apartment complex, an office building, or a shopping center would generally be considered an active business.

You may *not* amortize the expenses incurred in acquiring or selling securities or partnership interests such as securities registration expenses or underwriters' commissions. You may *not* amortize the costs of acquiring property to be held for sale or property which may be depreciated or amortized, including expenses incident to a lease and leasehold improvements.

You may not claim any deduction for start-up expenses if you do not elect to amortize. For example, if you incur expenses prior to completion of a building to be used in an active rental business, such as rental payments for leasing the land on which the building is to be constructed, you must elect to amortize the expenses or you will lose the deduction. If you do not elect to amortize, you treat the expenses as follows:

- Costs connected with the acquisition of capital assets are capitalized and depreciated; and
- Costs related to assets with unlimited or indeterminable useful lives are recovered only on the future sale or liquidation of the business.

If the acquisition fails. Where you have gone beyond a general search and have focused on the acquisition of a particular business, but the acquisition falls through, you may deduct the expenses as a capital loss.

EXAMPLES

1. In search of a business, you place newspaper advertisements and travel to investigate various prospective ventures. You pay for audits to evaluate the potential of some of the ventures. You then decide to purchase a specific business and hire a law firm to draft necessary documents. However, you change your mind and later abandon your plan to acquire the business. According to the IRS, you may not deduct the related expenses for advertisements, travel, and audits. These are considered investigatory. You may deduct the expense of hiring the law firm.

2. Domenie left his job to invest in a business. He advertised and was contacted by a party who wished to sell. He agreed to buy, hired an attorney, transferred funds to finance the business, and worked a month with the company manager to familiarize himself with the business. Discovering misrepresentations, he refused to buy the company and deducted over $5,000 for expenses, including travel and legal fees. The IRS disallowed the deduction as incurred in a business search. The Tax Court disagreed. Domenie thought he had found a business and acted as such in transferring funds and drawing legal papers for a takeover.

Job-hunting costs. For deducting the expenses of looking for a new job, *see 19.7.*

Business Use of a Home

40.12 Exclusive and Regular Use of a Home Office

If you operate your business from your home, using a room or other space as an office or area to assemble or prepare items for sale, you may be able to deduct expenses such as utilities, insurance, repairs, and depreciation allocated to your business use of the area. However, there are several obstacles to deducting the expenses allocated to the business area. The fact that there is a business purpose for your use of an office at your home is not a sufficient basis for deducting expenses of a home office. To deduct home office expenses, you must prove that you use the home area *exclusively* and on a *regular basis* either as:

1. *A place of business to meet or deal with patients, clients, or customers in the normal course of your business, or*
2. *Your principal place of business.* Your home office will qualify as your principal place of business if you spend most of your working time there and most of your business income is attributable to your activities there.

Two steps are followed to determine whether a home office is the principal place of business: (1) A review of the activity at each business location and the relative importance of each. The place where a person is required to meet with clients or patients, deliver goods, or perform services is generally the principal place of business, especially if that place has unique or special characteristics, as a hospital does. (2) A review of the time spent at each location if it is difficult to make a determination under Step 1. Under these tests, an anesthesiologist's home office expenses are not deductible because the principal place of his business as an anesthesiologist is at the hospitals where he works. That he needs the home office to do administrative work because he had no office space at the hospitals does not make the home office his principal place of business. However, under a new law effective in 1999, an office used for administrative work may qualify as the principal place of business; *see* the Law Alert below.

Similarly, a self-employed plumber may not deduct home office expenses where he spends 40 hours a week at customers' homes and 10 hours a week in a home office talking with customers over the phone, ordering supplies, and scheduling appointments, assisted by a full-time employee who works in the home office. According to the IRS, the activities at the home office may be important, but not as important as the service calls to customers. Therefore, the home office is not the plumber's principal place of business. On the other hand, a deduction was allowed to a self-employed retailer of costume jewelry who spends 25 hours a week at a home office filling and shipping orders, ordering supplies, and keeping the business books, while spending 15 hours a week at craft shows and consignment sale locations. Here, the IRS says that since sales to customers, the most important part of the business, occur inside and outside the home, the "relative importance" test is inconclusive. However, since more time is spent at the home office than on the road, the home office qualifies as the principal place of business.

Exclusive and regular business use of home area required. If you use a room, such as a den, both for business and family purposes, be prepared to show that a specific section of the den is used *exclusively* as office space. For example, a real estate operator was not allowed to deduct the cost of a home office, on evidence that he also used the office area for nonbusiness purposes. A partition or other physical separation of the office area is helpful but not required.

Under the regular basis test, expenses attributable to incidental or occasional trade or business use are not deductible, even if the room is used for no other purpose but business.

Even if you meet these tests, your deduction for allocable office expenses may be substantially limited or barred by a restrictive rule that limits deductions to the income from the office activity. This computation is made on Form 8829 and is illustrated in *40.15*.

Multiple business use of home office. If you use a home office for more than one business, make sure that the home office tests are met for all businesses before you claim deductions. If one business use qualifies and another use does not, the IRS will disallow deductions even for the qualifying use.

Employee with sideline business. Employees who use a home office for their job and for a sideline business also should be aware of this problem. Most employees are unable to show that their home office is the principal place of their work. Claiming an unallowable deduction for employee home office use will jeopardize the deduction for sideline business use. This happened to Hamacher, who as a self-employed actor earned $24,600 over a two-year period from an Atlanta theater and a few radio and television commercials. He also earned $18,000 each year as the administrator of an acting school at the theater. For his job as administrator, Hamacher shared an office at the theater with other employees. He had access to this office during nonbusiness hours. He also used one of the six rooms in his apartment for an office. Because of interruptions at the theater, he used the home office to work on the school curriculum and select plays for the theater. In connection with his acting business, he used the home office to receive phone calls, to prepare for auditions, and rehearse for acting roles.

Caution

Principal Place of Business Test

The tests for deducting office expenses will generally not present problems where the home area is the principal place of business or professional activity. For example, you are a doctor and see most of your patients at an office set aside in your home. A tax dispute may arise where you have a principal place of business elsewhere and use a part of your home for occasional work or administrative paperwork. Occasional use is not sufficient. If your deduction is questioned, you must prove that the area is used regularly and exclusively to meet with customers, clients, or patients. Have evidence that you have actual office facilities. Furnish the room as an office—with a desk, files, and a phone used only for business calls. Also keep a record of work done and business visitors.

Under current law, you may not deduct the cost of a home office if you use the office only to do administrative paperwork. However, *see* the Law Alert below.

Law Alert

Administrative Office Deductions Allowed Starting in 1999

For tax years beginning after December 31, 1998, a home office will meet the principal place of business test if it is used to conduct administrative or management activities and you can show that there is no other fixed location where you conduct substantial administrative or managerial activities for your business.

40.13 • What Home Office Expenses Are Deductible

The IRS disallowed his deduction for both self-employment and employee purposes because Hamacher's office use as an employee did not qualify. The Tax Court agreed. A single-office space may be used for different business activities, but all of the uses must qualify for a deduction. Here, Hamacher's use of the home office as an employee did not qualify. He had suitable office space at the theater. He was not expected or required to do work at home. As the employee use of the home office did not qualify, the Tax Court did not have to determine if the sideline business use qualified. Even if it had qualified, no allocation of expenses between the two uses would have been made. By requiring that a home office be used "exclusively" as a principal place of business or place for seeing clients, patients, or customers, the law imposes an all-or-nothing test.

Separate structure.   If in your business you use a separate structure not attached to your home, such as a studio adjacent but unattached to your home, the expenses are generally deductible if you satisfy the exclusive use and regular basis tests discussed earlier. A separate structure does not have to qualify as your principal place of business or a place for meeting patients, clients, or customers. However, the income limitation discussed at *40.15* applies. In one case, a taxpayer argued that an office located in a separate building in his backyard was not subject to the exclusive and regular business use tests and the gross income limitation. However, the IRS and Tax Court held that it was. The office building was "appurtenant" to the home and thus part of it, based on these facts: The office building was 12 feet away from the house and within the same fenced-in residential area; it did not have a separate address; it was included in the same title and subject to the same mortgage as the house, and all taxes, utilities, and insurance were paid as a unit for both buildings.

Day-care services.   The exclusive-use test does not have to be met for business use of a home to provide day-care services for children and handicapped persons, or persons age 65 or older, provided certain state licensing requirements are met. If part of your home is *regularly* but not exclusively used to provide day-care services, you may deduct an allocable part of your expenses. You allocate expenses by multiplying the total costs by two fractions: (1) The total square footage in the home that is available for day-care use throughout each business day and regularly so used, divided by the total square footage for the home. (2) The total hours of operation divided by the total number of hours in a year (8,760).

If the area *is* exclusively used for day-care services, only fraction (1) applies.

> ### EXAMPLE
> Alice Jones operates a day-care center at home from 7 a.m. to 6 p.m., five days a week, 250 days a year for a total of 2,750 business-use hours during the year. Her family uses the area the rest of the time. Annual home expenses total $10,000 ($5,000 for interest and taxes; $4,000 for electricity, gas, water, trash collection, maintenance, and insurance; and $1,000 for depreciation). The total floor area of the home is 2,000 square feet; 1,500 square feet are used for day-care purposes. Alice multiplies her $10,000 of expenses by 75%, the part of the home used for daycare purposes (1,500 square feet ÷ 2,000 square feet), and also by 31.39%, the percentage of business-use time (2,750 hours ÷ 8,760 hours). Thus, she may deduct $2,354: $10,000 × 75% × 31.39%. The full $2,354 is deductible only if net income generated from the day-care facility is at least that much.

In one case, the Tax Court held that utility rooms, such as a laundry and storage room and garage, may be counted as part of the day-care business area. The IRS had argued that because the children were not allowed in these areas, the space could not be considered as used for business. The Tax Court disagreed. The laundry room was used to wash the children's clothes; the storage room and garage were used to store play items and equipment. Thus, the space was considered as used for child care even though the rooms were off limits to the children.

Storage space and inventory.   If your home is the only location of a business selling products, you may deduct expenses allocated to space regularly used for inventory storage, including product samples, if the space is separately identifiable and suitable for storage.

40.13   What Home Office Expenses Are Deductible

Depending on your income *(40.15)*, a deduction for home business use may include real estate taxes, mortgage interest, operating expenses (such as home insurance premiums and utility costs), and depreciation allocated to the area used for business.

The deduction is figured on Form 8829 and entered on Line 30 of Schedule C.

Filing Instruction

Form 8829
You must report deductible 1997 home office expenses on Form 8829. Part I is used for showing the space allocated to business use *(40.14)*; Part II for reporting deductible expenses allocated to business use *(40.15)*; Part III for figuring depreciation on the business area *(40.13)*; and Part IV for carryover of expenses not allowed in 1996 because of income limitations applied in Part II *(40.15)*. A sample copy of Form 8829 is on page 580.

Filing Tip

If You Rent Your Home
If you rent rather than own your home, and you meet the home office tests of *40.12*, enter the rent you paid during the year on Line 20 (Other Expenses) of Form 8829.

578

Household expenses and repairs that do not benefit that space are not deductible. However, a pro rata share of the cost of painting the outside of a house or repairing a roof is deductible. Costs of lawn care and landscaping are not deductible.

If you install a security system for all your home's windows and doors, the portion of your monthly maintenance fee that is allocable to the office area is a deductible operating expense. Furthermore, the business portion of your cost for the system is depreciable. Thus, if the office takes up 20% of your home (40.14) you may deduct, subject to the income limitation of 40.15, 20% of the maintenance fee and a 20% depreciation deduction.

Figuring depreciation. For depreciation purposes, the cost basis of the house is the lower of the fair market value of the house at the time you started to use a part of it for business, and its adjusted basis, exclusive of the land. Only that part of the cost basis allocated to the office is depreciable. Form 8829 has a special section, Part III, for making this computation.

EXAMPLE

In April 1997, you start to use one room in your house exclusively and on a regular basis to meet with clients. This room is 10% of the square footage of your home. In 1984, you bought the property for $100,000, of which $90,000 was allocated to the house. The house now has a fair market value of $185,000. You compute depreciation on the cost basis of $90,000, which is lower than the value. You multiply $90,000 by 10% (business-use percentage), which gives you $9,000 as the depreciable basis of the business part of the house. As you started business use in the fourth month of 1997, you multiply the depreciable basis of $9,000 by 1.819%. This percentage is listed for the fourth month in the depreciation rate table for 39-year property shown below. Your depreciation deduction is $163.71 (9,000 × 1.819%).

Nonresidential Real Property (31.5 years—For property placed in service after 1986 and before May 13, 1993)

Use the column for the month of taxable year placed in service.

	1	2	3	4	5	6	7	8	9	10	11	12
Year												
1	3.042%	2.778%	2.513%	2.249%	1.984%	1.720%	1.455%	1.190%	0.926%	0.661%	0.397%	0.132%
2–7	3.175	3.175	3.175	3.175	3.175	3.175	3.175	3.175	3.175	3.175	3.175	3.175
8	3.175	3.174	3.175	3.174	3.175	3.174	3.175	3.175	3.175	3.175	3.175	3.175
9	3.174	3.175	3.174	3.175	3.174	3.175	3.174	3.175	3.174	3.175	3.174	3.175
10	3.175	3.174	3.175	3.174	3.175	3.174	3.175	3.174	3.175	3.174	3.175	3.174
11	3.174	3.175	3.174	3.175	3.174	3.175	3.174	3.175	3.174	3.175	3.174	3.175
12	3.175	3.174	3.175	3.174	3.175	3.174	3.175	3.174	3.175	3.174	3.175	3.174

Nonresidential Real Property (39 years—For property placed in service after May 12, 1993)

Use the column for the month of taxable year placed in service.

	1	2	3	4	5	6	7	8	9	10	11	12
Year												
1	2.461%	2.247%	2.033%	1.819%	1.605%	1.391%	1.177%	0.963%	0.749%	0.535%	0.321%	0.107%
2–39	2.564	2.564	2.564	2.564	2.564	2.564	2.564	2.564	2.564	2.564	2.564	2.564
40	0.107	0.321	0.535	0.749	0.963	1.177	1.391	1.605	1.819	2.033	2.247	2.461

Form 8829—Worksheet

Name(s) of proprietor(s) Gerard Smith			Your social security number XIX 01 1111

Part I — Part of Your Home Used for Business

1	Area used regularly and exclusively for business, regularly for day care, or for inventory storage. See instructions	1	500 sq. ft.
2	Total area of home	2	2,500 sq. ft.
3	Divide line 1 by line 2. Enter the result as a percentage	3	.20 %

• **For day-care facilities not used exclusively for business, also complete lines 4–6.**

• **All others, skip lines 4–6 and enter the amount from line 3 on line 7.**

4	Multiply days used for day care during year by hours used per day	4		hr.
5	Total hours available for use during the year (365 days × 24 hours). See instructions	5	8,760 hr.	
6	Divide line 4 by line 5. Enter the result as a decimal amount	6	.	
7	Business percentage. For day-care facilities not used exclusively for business, multiply line 6 by line 3 (enter the result as a percentage). All others, enter the amount from line 3 ▶	7	.20 %	

Part II — Figure Your Allowable Deduction

8	Enter the amount from Schedule C, line 29, **plus** any net gain or (loss) derived from the business use of your home and shown on Schedule D or Form 4797. If more than one place of business, see instructions			8	3,400

See instructions for columns (a) and (b) before completing lines 9–20.

		(a) Direct expenses	(b) Indirect expenses		
9	Casualty losses. See instructions	9			
10	Deductible mortgage interest. See instructions	10		10,000	
11	Real estate taxes. See instructions	11		4,000	
12	Add lines 9, 10, and 11	12		14,000	
13	Multiply line 12, column (b) by line 7	13		2,800	
14	Add line 12, column (a) and line 13			14	2,800
15	Subtract line 14 from line 8. If zero or less, enter -0-			15	600
16	Excess mortgage interest. See instructions	16			
17	Insurance	17		1,200	
18	Repairs and maintenance	18			
19	Utilities	19		1,800	
20	Other expenses. See instructions	20			
21	Add lines 16 through 20	21		3,000	
22	Multiply line 21, column (b) by line 7	22	600		
23	Carryover of operating expenses from 1996 Form 8829, line 41	23			
24	Add line 21 in column (a), line 22, and line 23			24	600
25	Allowable operating expenses. Enter the **smaller** of line 15 or line 24			25	600
26	Limit on excess casualty losses and depreciation. Subtract line 25 from line 15			26	0
27	Excess casualty losses. See instructions	27			
28	Depreciation of your home from Part III below	28	1,200		
29	Carryover of excess casualty losses and depreciation from 1996 Form 8829, line 42	29			
30	Add lines 27 through 29			30	1,200
31	Allowable excess casualty losses and depreciation. Enter the **smaller** of line 26 or line 30			31	0
32	Add lines 14, 25, and 31			32	3,400
33	Casualty loss portion, if any, from lines 14 and 31. Carry amount to **Form 4684**, Section B			33	0
34	Allowable expenses for business use of your home. Subtract line 33 from line 32. Enter here and on Schedule C, line 30. If your home was used for more than one business, see instructions ▶			34	3,400

Part III — Depreciation of Your Home

35	Enter the **smaller** of your home's adjusted basis or its fair market value. See instructions	35	238,975
36	Value of land included on line 35	36	50,000
37	Basis of building. Subtract line 36 from line 35	37	188,975
38	Business basis of building. Multiply line 37 by line 7	38	37,795
39	Depreciation percentage. See instructions	39	3.175 %
40	Depreciation allowable. Multiply line 38 by line 39. Enter here and on line 28 above. See instructions	40	1,200

Part IV — Carryover of Unallowed Expenses to 1998

41	Operating expenses. Subtract line 25 from line 24. If less than zero, enter -0-	41	0
42	Excess casualty losses and depreciation. Subtract line 31 from line 30. If less than zero, enter -0-	42	1,200

40.14 Allocating Expenses to Business Use

You may allocate to home office use qualifying expenses *(40.13)* as follows: If the rooms are not equal or approximately equal in size, compare the number of square feet of space used for business with the total number of square feet in the home and then apply the resulting percentage to the total deductible expenses.

If all rooms in your home are approximately the same size, you may base the allocation on a comparison of the number of rooms used as an office to the total number of rooms.

EXAMPLE

A doctor rents a apartment using three rooms for his office and seven rooms for his residence. The rooms are not equal in size. The apartment has 2,000 square feet; the office has 600. He allocated 30% ($^{600}/_{2,000}$) of the following expenses to his office:

	Total	Office	Residence
Rent	$7,200	$2,160	$5,040
Light	600	180	420
Heat	1,000	300	700
Wages of domestic	2,000	600	1,400
	$10,800	$3,240	$7,560

Thus, $3,240 is deductible as office expenses, subject to the income limitation of *40.15*.

40.15 Business Income May Limit Home Office Deductions

Even if your home business use satisfies the deduction tests of *40.12*, deductions for the business portion *(40.14)* of utilities, maintenance, and insurance costs, as well as depreciation or rent deductions, may not exceed net income derived from the office use after allocable mortgage interest, real estate taxes, and casualties are subtracted. To make sure that deductible expenses do not exceed income, the IRS requires you to use Form 8829. If you do not realize income during the year, no deduction is allowed. For example, you are a full-time writer and use an office in your home. You do not sell any of your work this year or receive any advances or royalties. Therefore, you may not claim a home office deduction for this year. *See also 40.9* on rules for writers and artists.

Part II of Form 8829 limits the deduction of home office expenses to net income derived from office use. You start with the tentative profit from Schedule C. If you sold your home during the year, increase the tentative profit by any net gain (or decrease tentative profit by any net loss) that is allocable to the office area and reported on Schedule D or Form 4797. The following expenses are listed in Part II of Form 8829 for purposes of applying the income limit: Casualty losses affecting the residence, deductible mortgage interest, real estate taxes, home insurance premiums, repair and maintenance expenses for the residence, utility expenses, rent, and depreciation. Business expenses not related to the home are deducted on the appropriate lines of Schedule C. For example, a salary paid to a secretary is deducted on Line 26 of Schedule C; the cost of depreciable business equipment used in your home is deducted on Line 13 of Schedule C.

Expenses disallowed because of the income limitation may be carried forward and treated as home office expenses in a later tax year (Part IV, Form 8829). The carryover as well as the expenses of the later year are subject to the income limitation of that year. For example, tentative net profit on Line 29, Schedule C, is $1,000. Rent and other expenses allocated to home office business are $2,000. Only $1,000 of the expenses are deductible; $1,000 is carried over to 1998.

The amount of real estate taxes, mortgage interest, or casualty losses not allocated to home office use may be claimed as itemized deductions on Schedule A.

EXAMPLE

Smith does sideline business consulting from a home office which he uses exclusively for business for all of 1997. His income in 1997 from consulting services is $12,400. He paid $3,600 for a photocopy machine and $4,000 for a computer, and had office telephone expenses of $600 and office supply costs of $800.

In addition, his home costs are:

Mortgage interest	$10,000
Real estate taxes	4,000
Insurance	1,200
Utilities	1,800

His office space took up 20% of the area of his home, and he figured depreciation allocated to business use was $1,200.

On Schedule C he claims first-year expensing for the copier and the computer, and deducts the cost of the business phone and supplies on Schedule C. This gives a tentative profit of $3,400 ($12,400 – $9,000) on Line 29, Schedule C.

In Part I of Form 8829, he lists the total area of the home and the area used for business, showing 20% business use.

In Part II, he enters the home costs listed above. We have taken only the relevant lines of the Form 8829 as an illustration. A sample Form 8829 is on page 580.

Line—			Column B Entries—
8.	Tentative profit from Schedule C, Line 29		$3,400
10.	Mortgage interest	$10,000	
11.	Real estate taxes	4,000	
12.	Total	$14,000	
13. & 14.	Business portion of Line 12		2,800
15.	Remaining tentative profit		600
17.	Insurance	1,200	
19.	Utilities	1,800	
21.	Total	3,000	
22., 24., & 25.	Business portion of Line 21		600
26.	Remaining tentative profit		0

No depreciation is deductible because there is no remaining business income and excess home office expenses may not generate a loss deduction. The depreciation is carried over to 1998. Home office expenses of $3,400 from Lines 14 and 25 are deducted on Line 30, Schedule C.

40.16 Home Office for Sideline Business

You may have an occupation and also run a sideline business from an office in your home. The home office expenses are deductible on Form 8829 if the office is a principal place of operating the sideline business or a place to meet with clients, customers, or patients. *See* the deduction tests at *40.12* and the income limit computation at *40.15*. Managing rental property may qualify as a business.

EXAMPLE

A doctor is employed full time by a hospital. He also owns six rental properties which he personally manages. He uses one bedroom in his two-bedroom home exclusively as an office to manage the properties. The room is furnished with a desk, bookcase, filing cabinet, calculators, and answering service; furnishings and other materials for preparing rental units for tenants are stored there. He may deduct expenses allocable to the home office.

Substantiating the sideline business. In claiming home office expenses of a sideline business, it is important to be ready to prove that you are actually in business; *see 40.10*. The Tax Court has held that activities in seeking new tenants, supplying furnishings, and cleaning and preparing six units for tenants are sufficiently systematic and continuous to put a person in the rental real estate business. In some cases, the rental of even a single piece of real property may be a business if additional services are provided such as cleaning or maid service.

Managing your own securities portfolio. Investors managing their own securities portfolios may find it difficult to convince a court that investment management is a business activity. According to Congressional committee reports, a home office deduction should be denied to an investor who uses a home office to read financial periodicals and reports, clip bond coupons, and perform similar activities. In one case, the Claims Court allowed a deduction to Moller, who spent about 40 hours a week at a home office managing a substantial stock portfolio. The Claims Court held these activities amounted to a business. However, an appeals court reversed the decision. According to the appeals court, the test is whether or not a person is a trader. A trader is in a business; an investor is not. A trader buys and sells frequently to catch daily market swings. An investor buys securities for capital appreciation and income without regard to daily market developments. Therefore, to be a trader, one's activities must be directed to short-term trading, not the long-term holding of investments. Here, Moller was an investor; he was primarily interested in the long-term growth potential of stock. He did not earn his income from the short-term turnovers of stocks. He had no significant trading profits. His interest and dividend income was 98% of his income.

40.17 Depreciation of Office in Cooperative Apartment

If your home office meets the tests of *40.12*, you may deduct depreciation on your stock interest in the cooperative. The basis for depreciation may be your share of the cooperative corporation's basis for the building or an amount computed from the price you paid for the stock. The method you use depends on whether you are the first or a later owner of the stock.

You are the first owner. In figuring your depreciation, you start with the cooperative's depreciable basis of the building. You then take your share of depreciation according to the percentage of stock interest you own. The cooperative can provide the details needed for the computation.

If space in the building is rented to commercial tenants who do not have stock interests in the corporation, the total allowable depreciation is reduced by the amount allocated to the space used by the commercial tenants.

You are a later owner of the cooperative's stock. When you buy stock from a prior owner, your depreciable basis is determined by the price of your stock and your share of the coop's outstanding mortgage, reduced by amounts allocable to land and to commercial space.

Figuring Net Operating Losses for Refund of Prior Taxes

40.18 Net Operating Losses for Refund of Prior Taxes

A loss incurred in your profession or unincorporated business is deducted from other income reported on Form 1040. If a 1997 loss (plus any casualty loss) exceeds income, the excess may be first carried back to 1994, 1995, or 1996, and *then* forward 15 years to 1998 through 2012 until it is used up. A loss carried back to a prior year reduces income of that year and entitles you to a refund. A loss applied to a later year reduces income for that year. You may elect to carry forward your 1997 loss for 15 years, foregoing the three-year carryback; *see 40.22. See* the Law Alert on page 584.

The rules below apply not only to self-employed individuals, farmers, and professionals, but also to individuals whose casualty losses exceed income, stockholders in S corporations, and partners whose partnerships have suffered losses. Each partner claims his or her share of the partnership loss.

Carryover of loss from prior year to 1997. If you had a net operating loss in an earlier year which is being carried forward to 1997, the loss carryover is reported as a minus figure on Line 21 of Form 1040. You must attach a detailed statement showing how you figured the carryover. The Example below shows you how a 1997 loss could be carried back and forward.

EXAMPLE

You have a 1997 business net operating loss of $650.

Year	Income	Loss	Loss carried back or forward to income
1994	$50		($50)
1995	80		(80)
1996	60		(60)
1997		($650)	
1998	20		(20)
1999	40		(40)
2000	50		(50)
2001	100		(100)
2002	100		(100)
2003	125		(125)
2004	150		(25)

Change in marital status. If you incur a net operating loss while single but are married filing jointly in a carryback or carryforward year, the loss may be used only to offset your own income on the joint return.

If the net operating loss was claimed on a joint return and in the carryback or carryforward year you are not filing jointly with that same spouse, only your allocable share of the original loss may be claimed; *see* IRS Publication 536.

Passive activity limitation. Losses subject to passive activity rules of Chapter 10 are not deductible as net operating losses. However, losses of rental operations coming within the $25,000 allowance of *10.2* may be treated as a net operating loss if the loss exceeds passive and other income.

Restrictions on loss after accounting method change. You may realize a net operating loss for a short taxable year created by the accounting change. As a condition of allowing the accounting method change, the IRS may require you to forego the right to a loss carryback and agree to a six-year carryforward period.

> **EXAMPLE**
>
> You want to change from a calendar year to a fiscal year ending April 30. Assume further that May through October is your peak selling period. Thus, you may have a net operating loss for the short taxable year January 1–April 30 because of slack business. According to the IRS, if the net operating loss is $10,000 or less, you may apply the regular net operating loss rules that allow you to carry back the loss three years and then forward 15 years. But if the net operating loss exceeds $10,000 and the short period is less than nine months, the operating loss must be deducted ratably over a six-year period starting with the first tax year after the short period.

40.19 Your Net Operating Loss

A net operating loss is generally the excess of deductible business expenses over business income. The net operating loss may also include the following losses and deductions:

- Casualty and theft losses, even if the property was used for personal purposes; *see* Chapter 18.
- Expenses of moving to a new job location; *see* Chapter 21.
- Deductible job expenses such as travel expenses, work clothes, costs, and union dues; *see* 19.3.
- Your share of a partnership or S corporation operating loss.
- Loss on the sale of Small Business Investment Company stock.
- Loss incurred on Section 1244 stock.

An operating loss may *not* include:

- Net operating loss carryback or carryover from any year.
- Capital losses that exceed capital gain.
- Excess of nonbusiness deductions over nonbusiness income plus nonbusiness net capital gain.
- Deductions for personal exemptions.
- A self-employed person's contribution to a Keogh plan.
- An IRA deduction.

Income from other sources may eliminate or reduce your net operating loss.

> **EXAMPLE**
>
> You are self-employed and incur a business loss of $10,000. Your spouse earns a salary of $10,000. When you file a joint return, your business loss will be eliminated by your spouse's salary. Similarly, if you also had salary from another position, the salary would reduce your business loss.

40.20 Form 1045

You compute your net operating loss deduction on Form 1045. You start with adjusted gross income and personal deductions shown on your tax return. As these figures include items not allowed for net operating loss purposes, you follow the line-by-line steps of Form 1045 to eliminate them. That is, you reduce the loss by the nonallowed items such as deductions for personal exemptions, net capital loss, and nonbusiness deductions exceeding nonbusiness income. On the schedule, the reductions are described as adjustments. The Example at the end of this section illustrates the steps in the schedule.

Law Alert

New Net Operating Loss Carryback and Carryforward Periods for Tax Years Beginning After August 5, 1997

The new carryback period is two years; the new carryforward period is 20 years. However, the three-year carryback still applies to net operating losses attributable to presidentially declared disasters that are incurred by a farming or qualifying small business. A small business qualifies if it has average gross receipts over a three-year period of $5 million or less.

For individual taxpayers, the three-year carryback still applies for net operating losses attributable to casualty and theft losses.

Adjustment for nonbusiness deductions. Nonbusiness expenses that exceed nonbusiness income may not be included in a net operating loss deduction. Nonbusiness deductions include deductions for IRA and Keogh plans and itemized deductions such as charitable contributions, interest expense, state taxes, and medical expenses. Do not include in this non-allowed group deductible casualty and theft losses, which for net operating loss purposes are treated as business losses. If you do not claim itemized deductions in the year of the loss, you must treat the standard deduction as a nonbusiness deduction.

Nonbusiness income is income that is *not* from a trade or business—such as dividends, interest, and annuity income. The excess of nonbusiness capital gains over nonbusiness capital losses is also treated as part of nonbusiness income.

EXAMPLE

Income from dividends and interest is $6,000 and nonbusiness deductions are $6,500. The excess deduction of $500 is an adjustment that reduces your loss on Form 1045.

Adjustment for capital losses. A net nonbusiness capital loss may not be included in a net operating loss. If nonbusiness capital losses exceed nonbusiness capital gains, the excess is an adjustment that reduces your loss on Form 1045. In figuring your loss, you may take into account business capital losses only up to the total of business capital gains plus any nonbusiness capital gains remaining after the nonbusiness deduction adjustment discussed earlier.

At-risk loss limitations. The loss used to figure your net operating loss deduction is subject to the at-risk rules discussed at *10.17*. If part of your investment is in nonrecourse loans or is otherwise not at risk, you must compute your deductible loss on Form 6198, which you attach to Form 1040. The deductible loss from Form 6198 is reflected in the income and deduction figures you enter on the Form 1045 schedule to compute your net operating loss deduction.

EXAMPLE

You are single and in 1997 you have a salary of $3,000, interest of $1,200, a net business loss of $10,000 (income of $50,000 and expenses of $60,000), itemized Schedule A deductions of $6,000, and a net nonbusiness capital gain of $1,000. Your net operating loss is $7,000. The following computation approximates the steps of the Form 1045 computation schedule starting from the line showing your negative adjusted gross income of $4,800.

Salary		$3,000
Interest		1,200
Capital gain income		1,000
Business loss		($10,000)
Adjusted gross income		($4,800)
Add: Exemption and itemized deductions		(8,650)
		($13,450)
Adjustments:		
Exemption	$2,650	
Excess nonbusiness deduction*	3,800	6,450
Net operating loss		($7,000)

The excess nonbusiness expenses deduction was figured as follows:

Itemized deductions		$6,000
Net capital gain income	$1,000	
Interest income	1,200	2,200
Excess		$3,800

40.21 How To Carry Back Your Net Operating Loss

Tax year 1994 is the first year to which you may carry back your 1997 net operating loss. When you carry back the loss to 1994, you recompute your 1994 tax on Form 1045 by deducting the 1997 net operating loss. The net operating loss is deducted from the amount of your original 1994 adjusted gross income. Because of the reduction to adjusted gross income, you have to increase any 1994 medical expense and casualty loss deduction when recomputing 1994 income. You do not have to change the amount of your 1994 charitable deduction. *See* the instructions to Form 1045 and also IRS Publication 536 for details of the recomputation calculation.

Planning Reminder

Advantage of Relinquishing the Carryback

You will generally make the election to relinquish the carryback if you expect greater tax savings by carrying the loss forward. You might also make the election if you are concerned you might be audited for earlier years if you carry back a loss for a refund. You make the election by attaching a statement to this effect to your return for the year of the loss, which must be filed by the due date plus extensions. The IRS refuses to allow a late election and received court approval for its position.

After recomputing the 1994 tax on Form 1045, your refund is the difference between the tax originally paid for 1994 and the lower tax figured after deducting the net operating loss deduction.

Use Form 1045 as a "quick refund" claim. The IRS will usually allow or reject your claim within 90 days from the time you file Form 1045. Do not attach Form 1045 to your 1997 Form 1040. File Form 1045 separately, together with a copy of your return. You may file Form 1045 within 12 months after the end of your tax year. Thus, if you are a calendar-year taxpayer, you have until December 31, 1998, to carry back a 1997 loss to 1994 on Form 1045. If the IRS allows the refund, it may still determine later that the refund was excessive and assess additional tax.

Although using Form 1045 is the quickest way to obtain the refund, you may instead file an amended return on Form 1040X to claim the refund. You have three years after the due date (including extensions) of your 1997 tax return to file Form 1040X. Thus, to claim a refund on Form 1040X for 1994, because of a net operating loss carried back three years from 1997, you have until April 15, 2001, to file. On Form 1040X, you must attach a statement detailing how the loss carryback was figured; the schedule from Form 1045 for computing the loss may be used.

Operating losses from more than one year.   If you have more than one year net operating loss to be carried to the same taxable year, you apply the loss from the earliest year first.

> **EXAMPLE**
>
> You had net operating losses in both 1996 and 1997 of $6,000 and $10,000, respectively. Your taxable income in 1992 was $5,000. You carried the $6,000 loss from 1996 to 1993, leaving an unused portion of $1,000 to be carried to 1994. Therefore, you have two losses to be applied against 1994 income—the unused portion of the 1996 loss and the 1997 loss. First apply the unused portion of the 1996 loss, and then apply the 1997 loss. On Form 1045 or 1040X, attach a detailed schedule showing the net operating loss computation for each year.
>
> Any part of the loss that may not be deducted in 1994 is carried to 1995. *See* the instructions to Form 1045 and also IRS Publication 536 for details of this computation.

40.22 Election To Carry Forward Losses

Instead of carrying back your 1997 net operating loss under the rules of *40.21*, you may elect to forego the carryback. Instead, you just carry forward losses. The carryforward period is still 15 years under the election. The election is irrevocable.

If you are carrying forward a net operating loss from an earlier year to 1997, report the loss carryover as a minus figure on Line 21 of Form 1040 and attach a statement explaining how the carryover was computed.

Business Tax Credits

40.23 General Business Credit

The general business credit includes the following credits:

* The work opportunity credit on Form 5884;
* The investment credit on Form 3468, consisting of the rehabilitation property credit, the energy credit, and the reforestation credit;
* The alcohol fuels credit on Form 6478;
* The research credit on Form 6765;
* The low-income housing credit on Form 8586;
* The enhanced oil recovery credit on Form 8830;
* The disabled access credit on Form 8826;
* The renewable electricity production credit on Form 8835;
* The credit for wages paid in an empowerment zone on Form 8844;
* The Indian employment credit on Form 8845;
* The credit for employer-paid Social Security and Medicare taxes on certain tips received by employees of food and beverage establishments on Form 8846; and
* The credit for contributions to certain community development corporations on Form 8847.

The 1997 tax law added a welfare-to-work credit for wages paid to long-term family assistance recipients who begin work after 1997.

The low-income housing credit and the rehabilitation tax credit are discussed at *31.9*.

Computing the general business credit. You compute each credit separately. If you claim only one credit, that credit is considered your *general business credit* for 1997. The credit is subject to a limitation based on tax liability which is figured on the form used to compute that particular credit. You then enter the allowable credit as your general business credit on Form 1040.

If you claim more than one credit, the credits are combined into one general business credit on Form 3800, except for the empowerment zone wages credit, which is figured on Form 8844 and not carried to Form 3800. Each of the other credits is first computed separately and then listed on Form 3800. The combined credit is subject to a limitation based on tax liability. To figure the limit, you must compute tentative alternative minimum tax (AMT) on Form 6251 even if the complete computation on Form 6251 shows that you do not have an actual AMT liability for the year. Your limit for the general business credit on Form 3800 is your regular tax liability (after tax credits other than the general business credit), *plus* actual AMT liability from Form 6251 (if any), *minus* whichever of the following is larger: either (1) tentative AMT from Form 6251; or (2) 25% of your regular income tax liability (after other credits) over $25,000.

Keep separate records of each of the component credits making up the general business credit. The credits are considered to be used up in a specific order; *see* the instructions to Form 3800.

If your full 1997 general business credit may not be claimed because of the tax liability limitation, you may be able to *carry back* the excess three years, starting with the earliest year. Check the Form 3800 instructions for restrictions on carrying back certain credits. After the carryback, any remaining credit may be *carried forward* 15 years until used up. The carrybacks and carryforwards are listed on Form 3800.

For credits arising in tax years beginning after 1997, the carryback period has been reduced from three years to one year; the carryforward period extended from 15 years to 20 years.

If you have business credits from a passive activity under the rules of Chapter 10, you must figure the credits on Form 8582-CR; generally, the credits are limited to the tax liability from passive activities.

40.24 Other Fuel-Related Credits

For a qualified business use, a refundable credit may be claimed for *gasoline or special fuels.* For example, a credit applies for fuel used in non-highway vehicles (other than motorboats), including generators, compressors, fork-lift trucks, and bulldozers. A credit may also be claimed for aviation fuel used for farming or commercial aviation. Different credit rates apply depending on the type of fuel. You must claim the credit on a timely filed income tax return, including extensions. You compute the credit on Form 4136, which you attach to Form 1040. For further details, *see* IRS Publication 378; farmers should *see* IRS Publication 225.

Electric vehicles. A credit for 10% of the cost of a qualified electric motor vehicle may be claimed on Form 8834. The maximum credit is $4,000 per vehicle. On Form 3800 you include the qualified electric motor vehicle credit in the total of other credits that reduce regular tax before the general business credit limit *(40.21)* is figured.

Chapter 41

Retirement Plans for Self-Employed

Self-employed persons and partners can take advantage of tax-sheltered Keogh retirement plans or simplified employee pension plans (SEP).

Advantages flow from: (1) tax deductions allowed for contributions to the plan (a form of forced savings); (2) tax-free accumulations of income earned on assets held by the plan; and (3) in some cases, special averaging for lump-sum benefits paid from a Keogh plan on retirement.

If you have employees, you must consider the cost of covering them when setting up your plan.

If you do not have any other retirement plan and have no more than 100 employees, you may set up a salary-reduction SIMPLE plan.

41.1 Who May Set Up a Keogh Plan

You may set up a self-employed retirement plan called a Keogh plan if you earn self-employment income from personal services and have *net earnings* (gross business or professional income less allowable business deductions). Income earned abroad and excluded from federal income tax is not considered earned income for purposes of the plan. If you are an inactive owner, such as a limited partner, you do not qualify to set up a Keogh plan—unless you receive guaranteed payments for services which are treated as earnings from self-employment.

Partnership plans. An individual partner or partners, although self-employed, may not set up a Keogh plan. The plan must be established by the partnership. Partnership deductions for contributions to an individual partner's account are reported on the partner's Schedule K-1 (Form 1065) and deducted by the partner as an adjustment to income on Line 28 of Form 1040.

Including employees in your plan. You must include in your plan all employees who have reached age 21 with at least one year of service. An employee may be required to complete two years of service before participating if your plan provides for full and immediate vesting after no more than two years. You generally are not required to cover seasonal or part-time employees who work less than 1,000 hours during a 12-month period.

Your plan may not exclude employees who are over a certain age.

A plan may not discriminate in favor of officers or other highly compensated personnel. Benefits must be for the employees and their beneficiaries, and their plan rights may not be subject to forfeiture. A plan may not allow any of its funds to be diverted for purposes other than pension benefits. Contributions made on your behalf may not exceed the ratio of contributions made on behalf of employees.

41.2 Choosing a Keogh Plan

There are two types of Keogh plans: defined-benefit plans and defined-contribution plans, and different rules apply to each. A defined-benefit plan provides in advance for a specific retirement benefit funded by quarterly contributions based on an IRS formula and actuarial assumptions. A defined-contribution plan does not fix a specific retirement benefit, but rather sets the amount of annual contributions so that the amount of retirement benefits depends on contributions and income earned on those contributions. If contributions are geared to profits, the plan is a profit-sharing plan. A plan that requires fixed contributions regardless of profits is a money-purchase plan.

A defined-benefit plan may prove costly if you have older employees who also must be provided with proportionate defined benefits. Furthermore, a defined-benefit plan requires you to contribute to their accounts even if you do not have profits. The maximum annual retirement benefit for basing 1997 plan year contributions may not exceed $125,000 and the $125,000 limit may have to be reduced if benefits begin before the Social Security age, which is currently age 65. The $125,000 limit is subject to annual inflation adjustments. All plans of a controlled group of businesses are aggregated for purposes of the limitations applied to defined benefits. A defined-benefit plan or defined-contribution plan may take into account Social Security benefits for employees subject to technical nondiscrimination limitations.

A minimum coverage rule requiring that a plan must include at least 40% of all employees (or 50 employees if that is less) applies only to defined benefit plans for years beginning after 1996.

Setting up a trust for investing in Keoghs. If you are interested in following an aggressive investment policy for funds in your Keogh plan, you will set up a trust to receive Keogh contributions. You may name yourself or an independent trustee to oversee the plan.

If you use funds to buy nontransferable annuity contracts from an insurance company, use of a trust is optional. Premium payments may be made directly to the insurance company. The annuity contract may pay a fixed monthly income for life or for a fixed period of years, or may be a variable annuity contract. Life insurance can be included only if it is incidental to retirement benefits.

If you are investing in savings certificates, you need not set up a trust; you may use a custodial account with the bank.

41.3 Top-Heavy Plan Restrictions

"Top-heavy" plan rules, which apply to corporate plans favoring "key employees," may also apply to a Keogh plan of a self-employed person. The top-heavy rules apply if more than 60% of the account balances or accrued benefits are for key employees; *see* the next column for the definition of key employees. Even if your Keogh plan is not currently considered top heavy, your plan may be disqualified, unless it includes provisions that would automatically take effect if the plan becomes

Planning Reminder

Employees Who Are Self-Employed on the Side

If you are an employee-member of a company retirement plan, you may set up a Keogh plan if you carry on a self-employed enterprise or profession on the side. For example, you are employed by a company that has a qualified 401(k) plan to which you make salary deferrals. At the same time, you have a sideline consulting business. You may set up a Keogh plan based on your consultant earnings. Each plan is independent of the other. As an alternative to a Keogh plan, you may contribute to a simplified employee pension plan (SEP) as discussed in *41.4*, or a SIMPLE IRA, discussed in *41.11*.

Caution

Prohibited Transactions

As an owner-employee (owning more than 10% of the business), your dealings with the Keogh trust are subject to restrictions. You are generally subject to penalties if you borrow funds from the trust *(41.9)*; buy property from or sell property to the trust; or charge any fees for services you render to the trust. These restrictions also apply to any member of your immediate family and any corporation in which you own more than half the voting stock, either directly or indirectly.

top heavy. The major top-heavy restriction requires an accelerated vesting schedule. There is also a lower limit on benefits where a key employee participates in both a defined-contribution plan and defined-benefit plan.

Vesting.   A top-heavy plan must provide either 100% vesting after three years of service or graded vesting at the rate of at least 20% after two years of service, 40% after three years of service, 60% after four years of service, 80% after five years of service, and 100% after six years of service. There may be an advantage in electing three-year vesting if you have a high turnover of employees.

The $160,000 pay limit.   The first $160,000 of a self-employed person's net earnings in 1997 is considered in determining deductible contributions, whether or not the plan is top heavy. The $160,000 limit may be adjusted for inflation.

Distributions before age 59 $\frac{1}{2}$.   The 10% penalty for distributions before age 59 $\frac{1}{2}$ *(7.14)* applies whether or not the plan is top heavy. The penalty does not apply to distributions made because you are disabled. Other exceptions to the penalty are listed at *7.14*.

The IRS has ruled that a tax-free rollover may be made when the Keogh plan is terminated. A timely rollover will avoid the 10% penalty on premature distributions if the recipient is under age 59 $\frac{1}{2}$.

Retirement plan bonds.   If you invested Keogh plan funds in Treasury Department Retirement Plan Bonds before May 1, 1982, you may redeem them at any time, even if you are under age 59 $\frac{1}{2}$. To avoid immediate tax, a rollover may be made within 60 days to an IRA or qualified pension or profit-sharing plan.

Who are key employees?   The above top-heavy restrictions apply if more than 60% of a defined-contribution plan account balances or more than 60% of the accrued benefits of a defined-benefit plan are for key employees. For the 1997 plan year, key employees are employees who at any time during the plan year own: (1) one of the 10 largest ownership interests and have compensation exceeding $30,000; (2) more than a 5% interest; or (3) more than a 1% interest and also earn compensation of more than $150,000. Officers are considered key employees for 1997 if they have compensation exceeding $62,500 (subject to annual inflation adjustments). Key employee treatment also applies if the employee was a key employee in any of the four preceding years under the applicable compensation limit for such year.

41.4 Choosing a SEP

Under a SEP (simplified employee pension plan), you may contribute to a special type of IRA more than is allowed under the regular IRA rules. Contributions do not have to be made every year. When you do make contributions, they must be based on a written allocation formula and must not discriminate in favor of yourself, other owners with more than a 5% interest, or highly compensated employees. Coverage requirements for employees are at *8.16*. A salary-reduction arrangement for employees may be provided under a qualifying SEP established before 1997, or under a SIMPLE plan established after 1996; *see 8.17.*

Deductible contributions to your personal SEP account may not exceed 13.0435% of your net earnings (less 50% of self-employment tax liability), as discussed at *41.5*.

The deadline for both setting up and contributing to a SEP is the due date for your return, *including extensions*. Thus, if you have not set up a Keogh plan by the end of the taxable year *(41.1)*, you may still make a deductible retirement contribution for the year by contributing to a SEP by the due date of your return.

41.5 Deductible Keogh or SEP Contributions

The deductible limit for a Keogh plan depends on whether you have a defined-contribution plan (profit-sharing or money-purchase pension plan) or a defined-benefit plan. A SEP is treated as a profit-sharing plan for purposes of the deduction computation rules.

If you have a defined-benefit plan, you generally may deduct contributions needed to produce the accrued benefits provided for by the plan. This is a complicated calculation requiring actuarial computations that call for the services of a pension expert.

Deductible contribution rate for a defined-contribution Keogh Plan or a SEP.   Before figuring the deductible contribution you can make for 1997 to a profit-sharing Keogh or SEP account, or to a money-purchase pension plan, you must first figure your self-employment tax liability on Schedule SE and the 50% deduction for self-employment tax to be claimed on Line 26 of Form 1040. In computing your deductible plan contribution, your net profit from Line 31 of Schedule C, Line 3 of Schedule C-EZ, or Line 36 of Schedule F is *reduced* by the deduction for 50% of self-employment tax; *see* the Example on the next page.

As a self-employed person, you are not allowed to figure the deductible contribution for yourself by applying the contribution rate stated in your plan. The rate must be reduced, as required by law, to reflect the reduction of net earnings by the deductible contribution itself. If your plan rate is a whole number, you need not make the computation. Use the table below, which provides an adjusted decimal to apply to net earnings to figure the deductible contribution.

Self-Employed Person's Rate Table

If plan rate is—	The adjusted decimal rate is—
1%	.009901
2	.019608
3	.029126
4	.038462
5	.047619
6	.056604
7	.065421
8	.074074
9	.082569
10	.090909
11	.099099
12	.107143
13	.115044
14	.122807
15*	.130435*
16	.137931
17	.145299
18	.152542
19	.159664
20	.166667
21	.173554
22	.180328
23	.186992
24	.193548
25**	.200000**

The maximum deduction percentage for contributions to your own profit-sharing Keogh account or to your own SEP account is 13.0435%. For your employees, the maximum rate is 15%.
**The maximum deduction percentage for contributions to your own money-purchase Keogh plan is 20%; for employees it is 25%.*

Fractional rates. If the plan rate is fractional and thus not listed in the table above, figure your deductible percentage this way:

1. Write the plan rate as a decimal. For example, if the plan rate is 10.5%, write .105 as the decimal amount.
2. Add 1 to the decimal rate. For example, if the rate is .105, the result is 1.105.
3. Divide Step 1 by Step 2. This gives you the deductible percentage. If the plan rate is .105, the deductible percentage is .095023 (.105 ÷ 1.105).

Figuring your maximum deductible contribution. After figuring your net earnings and reducing that amount by 50% of your self-employment tax liability, you multiply the balance by the adjusted rate from the Self-Employed Person's Rate Table or the fractional rate discussed above. This is generally your maximum deductible contribution. However, your deduction for 1997 contributions may not exceed the *lesser* of (1) $30,000 and (2) $160,000 multiplied by the stated plan contribution rate shown in the left column of the above Self-Employed Person's Rate Table. The maximum amount of compensation that can be taken into account for 1997 is $160,000.

The following Example illustrates the computation of the maximum deductible contribution.

EXAMPLE

You are a sole proprietor with no employees and have a profit-sharing plan which provides for a 15% contribution rate. Your net self-employment earnings for 1997 from Line 31 of Schedule C are $147,000. On Schedule SE, you figure your self-employment tax liability of $12,046, and you claimed a 50% deduction for self-employment taxes of $6,023 ($\frac{1}{2}$ of $12,046, self-employment tax from Schedule SE) on Line 26 of Form 1040. Your maximum deductible profit-sharing contribution is $18,388:

Step 1.	Net earnings reduced by 50% of self-employment tax liability ($147,000 – $6,023)	$140,977
Step 2.	Decimal rate from the table in the right column	.130435
Step 3.	Decimal rate multiplied by reduced net earnings ($140,977 × .130435)	$18,388
Step 4.	Overall contribution limit: $160,000 multiplied by 15% plan rate, but no more than $30,000	$24,000
Step 5.	Lesser of Step 3 and Step 4. This is your maximum deductible contribution	$18,388

Money-purchase plan may supplement profit-sharing plan. A money-purchase plan requires an employer to make fixed contributions each year, without regard to profit.

As shown in the table on the preceding page, the maximum deduction percentage for a self-employed person's money-purchase plan is 20% (25% for regular employees).

To maximize your deductible contributions, you may establish a separate money-purchase plan to supplement a profit-sharing plan. A bank or other plan trustee can help you set up separate plans and stay within the overall contribution limit of 20% of net earnings.

Contributions for your employees. The deduction complications that apply to your own contributions do not apply to contributions for employees. You make contributions for your employees at the rate specified in your plan, based upon their 1997 compensation (but not to exceed the lesser of $30,000 and $160,000 multiplied by the plan contribution rate). Thus, in the Example above, you would contribute 15% of your employees' pay to the plan. You deduct contributions for employees when figuring your net earnings from self-employment on Schedule C or Schedule F before figuring your own deductible contribution using the steps shown on the Example above.

Contributions after age 70 $\frac{1}{2}$. You may continue to make contributions for yourself as long as you have self-employment income. If you have reached age 70 $\frac{1}{2}$, you generally do not have to begin to receive minimum distributions from the plan until April 1 of the year following the year in which you retire; *see 7.13*. A penalty may be imposed if the minimum distribution is not received. The minimum distribution must be based on your life expectancy. If you are married, withdrawals may be spread over the joint lives of you and your spouse. Use the IRS actuarial tables to figure life expectancy, as explained at *7.23*.

The same minimum distribution rules apply to your employees.

Excess contributions. Contributions to a profit-sharing plan exceeding the 13.0435% deduction ceiling (15% for your employees) may be carried over and deducted in later years subject to the ceiling for those years. However, if contributions exceed the deductible amount, you are generally subject to a 10% penalty on nondeductible contributions that are not returned by the end of your tax year. The penalty is computed on Form 5330, which must be filed with the IRS by the end of the seventh month following the end of the tax year.

41.6 How To Claim the Keogh or SEP Deduction

Contributions made to your Keogh or SEP account as a self-employed person are deducted as an adjustment to gross income on Line 28 of Form 1040. A deduction for a contribution made for your benefit may not be part of a net operating loss.

Contributions for your employees are entered as deductions on Schedule C (or Schedule F) for purposes of computing profit or loss from your business. Trustees' fees not provided for by contributions are deductible in addition to the maximum contribution deduction.

Deductible Keogh plan contributions may generally be made at any time up to the due date of your return, including any extension of time. However, the plan itself must be set up before the close of the taxable year for which the deduction is sought. If you miss the December 31 deadline for setting up a Keogh plan, you have at least up to April 15, 1998, to set up a SEP for 1997. If you have a filing extension, you have until the extended due date to set up a SEP and make your contribution.

41.7 How To Qualify a Keogh Plan or SEP Plan

You may set up a Keogh plan and contribute to it without advance approval. But, since advance approval is advisable, you may, in a determination letter, ask the IRS to review your plan. Approval requirements depend on whether you set up your own administered plan or join a master plan administered by a bank, insurance company, mutual fund, or a prototype plan sponsored by a trade or professional association. If you start your own individually designed plan, you apply for a determination letter on Form 5300 whether the plan is a defined-benefit plan or defined-contribution plan. You must pay a fee to the IRS when you apply for a determination letter. File Form 8717 showing your fee, together with Form 5300.

If you join a master or prototype plan, the sponsoring organization applies to the IRS for approval of its plan. You should then be given a copy of the approved plan and copies of any subsequent amendments.

To set up a SEP with a bank, broker, or other financial institution, you do not need IRS approval. If you do not maintain any other qualified retirement plan and other tests are met, a model SEP may be adopted using Form 5305-SEP. To adopt a SEP with a qualifying salary-reduction arrangement (8.16), you may be able to use Form 5305A-SEP.

41.8 Annual Keogh Plan Return

Partial relief from one burdensome IRS paperwork requirement may be available if your pension or profit-sharing Keogh plan covers only yourself, or you and your spouse, or you and your business partners and spouses. Such plans are treated as one-participant plans by the IRS.

One-participant plans that hold more than $100,000 at the end of any plan year beginning on or after January 1, 1994, must file a Form 5500-EZ for the first year the assets exceed $100,000 and for each year thereafter, even if total plan assets are reduced to $100,000 or less. For example, if plan assets in a plan that otherwise satisfies the requirements for filing the Form 5500-EZ totaled $110,000 at the end of the 1994 plan year, and a distribution occurred in 1997 so that plan assets totaled $85,000 at the end of the 1997 plan year, a Form 5500-EZ must be filed for the 1997 plan year.

The Form 5500-EZ due date for a 1997 calendar-year plan is July 31, 1998, unless an extension is obtained from the IRS.

The $100,000 exception applies if you, or you and your spouse, are sole proprietors or sole shareholders of a corporation maintaining the plan. The exception also applies if your business is operated as a partnership and the only plan participants are partners and their spouses.

You must file Form 5500-EZ for the final plan year regardless of the amount of plan assets.

If you cannot use Form 5500-EZ, you must file Form 5500-C/R if there are fewer than 100 plan participants (Form 5500 if 100 or more participants). On Form 5500-C/R, you check a box indicating whether the form is being filed as a Form 5500-C or Form 5500-R. Form 5500-R is a shorter form that may be used for a plan year that is *not* the first plan year or final plan year, provided that you used the longer Form 5500-C for at least one of the two prior plan years. Thus, after the first year, Form 5500-R may be filed in two of every three years. Only some of the Form 5500-C/R pages are filled in by Form 5500-R filers; follow the form instructions. The form must be filed by the end of the seventh month following the end of the plan year. There are penalties for late filing, unless you show reasonable cause or an extension is obtained; follow the Form 5500-C/R instructions for extension rules.

Electronic filing allowed. Forms 5500-EZ and 5500-C/R may be filed electronically or on magnetic tape by qualifying tax return filers. To file electronically or on magnetic tape, the plan administrator must provide a signed declaration on Form 8453-E.

41.9 Restrictions on Loans

Keogh plan loans to an owner-employee (more than 10% ownership) are subject to prohibited transaction penalties. There are two penalties: (1) a 10% or 15% penalty, and (2) a 100% penalty. The first-tier penalty is 10% for transactions before August 6, 1997, and 15% for transactions after August 5, 1997.

The 10% or 15% penalty applies in the year of the loan and in later years until the loan is repaid with interest. The penalty is figured on a fair market interest factor which is explained in the instructions to Form 5330. You are required to report loans to the IRS on Form 5330 and pay the 10% or 15% penalty when you file the form. Form 5330 must be filed within seven months after the end of the taxable year; *see* Form 5330 instructions for filing extension rules.

The 100% penalty is imposed if the loan is not repaid. The penalty may be avoided by repaying the loan within 90 days after the IRS sends a deficiency notice for the 100% tax. The 90-day period may be extended by the IRS to allow you a reasonable time for repayment.

Exception. If you are an owner-employee, you may apply to the Department of Labor for a special exemption from the prohibited transaction penalties.

Loans treated as taxable distributions. Self-employed individuals are taxable on certain loans from their Keogh plan under the same rules applied to regular employees, as discussed at *7.16*.

Loans from SEP are prohibited. Borrowing from a SEP is a prohibited transaction under the IRA rules and will result in the loss of the account's tax-exempt status. The account will be treated as if it were distributed to you on the first day of the year; *see 8.8*.

41.10 How Keogh Plan Distributions Are Taxed

Distributions from a Keogh plan generally may not be received without penalty before age $59 \frac{1}{2}$ unless you are disabled or meet the other exceptions listed at *7.14*. You generally must begin to receive distributions by April 1 of the year following the later of (1) the year in which you reach age $70 \frac{1}{2}$ and (2) the year in which you retire. Penalties may apply if an insufficient distribution is received; *see 7.13*.

Qualifying lump-sum distributions are taxable under special averaging methods, or may be rolled over tax free to an IRA or other qualified plan; *see 7.2* for details. Pension distributions from a Keogh are taxed under the annuity rules of *7.25*, but for purposes of figuring your cost investment, include only nondeductible voluntary contributions; deductible contributions made on your behalf are not part of your investment.

The excess distribution penalty that had applied prior to 1997 has been repealed for distributions received after 1996.

If you receive amounts in excess of the benefits provided for you under the plan formula and you own more than a 5% interest in the employer, the excess benefit is subject to a 10% penalty. The penalty also applies if you were a more-than-5% owner at any time during the five plan years preceding the plan year that ends within the year of an excess distribution.

Other rules discussed at *7.1* to *7.16* apply to Keogh plans as well as qualified corporate plans.

After the death of a Keogh plan owner, distributions to beneficiaries may be spread over the periods discussed at *7.13*.

SEP distributions. Distributions from a SEP are subject to the IRA rules at *8.8*.

41.11 SIMPLE Retirement Plans

If you do not maintain any other retirement plan and have 100 or fewer employees, you may set up a salary-reduction type plan for yourself and your employees. The SIMPLE IRA contribution rules are discussed at *8.19*. A SIMPLE plan may also be made as part of a 401(k) plan; *see 7.17*.

Under a SIMPLE IRA, you may contribute to your own account $6,000 of net earnings. You may also make a "matching" contribution of up to 3% of your net earnings.

If you have employees, they generally may make elective salary-reduction contributions up to $6,000. You must make a 3% matching contribution unless you choose to make a 2% non-elective contribution.

See 8.18 and *8.19* for further details on SIMPLE IRAs.

Chapter 42

Claiming Depreciation Deductions

There are two methods of claiming expense deductions for your purchases of equipment, fixtures, autos, and trucks used in your business:

- First-year expensing (Section 179 deduction), which allows a deduction of up to $18,000 in 1997. In 1998, the limit will be $18,500.
- Regular depreciation, which allows a prorated deduction over a period of years. Most business equipment is depreciable under MACRS over a six-year period. The objective of MACRS is to provide rapid depreciation and to eliminate disputes over useful life, salvage value, and depreciation methods. Useful life and depreciation methods are fixed by law; salvage value is treated as zero. If you do not want to use MACRS accelerated rates, you may elect the straight-line method. MACRS applies to new and used property.

Capital investments in buildings are depreciable using the straight-line method; residential buildings are depreciated over 27.5 years; nonresidential real property placed in service after May 12, 1993, is depreciated over 39 years; *see 42.13*. Specific annual rates for each class of property are provided by IRS tables.

42.1 What Property May Be Depreciated

Depreciation deductions may be claimed only for property used in your business or other income-producing activity.

Depreciation may not be claimed on property held for personal purposes such as a personal residence or pleasure car. If property, such as a car, is used both for business and pleasure, only the business portion may be depreciated.

Property bought for income-producing purposes, although yielding no current income, may be depreciated.

EXAMPLES

1. An anesthesiologist suspended his practice indefinitely because of malpractice premium rate increases. He continued to maintain his professional competence by taking courses and keeping up his equipment. The IRS ruled that he could not take depreciation on his equipment. Since he was no longer practicing, the depreciation did not relate to a current trade or business.

2. An electrician spent $1,325 on a trailer to carry his tools and protective clothing. Based on a useful life of three years less salvage value of $25, annual depreciation deductions came to $433. However, the IRS claimed that he could not claim depreciation during the months he was unemployed and the trailer was not used. The Tax Court disagrees. Depreciation is allowed as long as the asset is held for use in a trade or business, even though the asset is idle or its use is temporarily suspended due to business conditions.

Nondepreciable assets.   Not all assets used in your business or for the production of income may be depreciable. Land is not depreciable, but the cost of landscaping business property may be depreciated if the landscaping is so closely associated with a building that the landscaping would have to be destroyed if the building were replaced. Qualifying trees and bushes are depreciable over 15 years.

Property held primarily for sale to customers or property includible in inventory is not depreciable, regardless of its useful life.

Amortization for business intangibles.   The cost of goodwill, going concern value, and other intangibles including covenants not to compete, information bases, customer lists, franchises, licenses, and trademarks is amortizable over a 15-year period.

The amortization rule generally applies to property acquired after August 10, 1993. *See 42.18* for further details.

Residences.   For depreciation of rented residences, *see 9.5.*

For depreciation of a sublet cooperative apartment or one used in business, *see 40.17.*

Farm property.   Farmland is not depreciable; farm machinery and buildings are. Livestock acquired for work, breeding, or dairy purposes and not included in inventory may also be depreciated. For a detailed explanation of the highly technical rules for depreciating farm property and livestock, *see* IRS Publication 225, Farmer's Tax Guide.

Prior-year returns.   You may not deduct unclaimed depreciation for a prior year by increasing your present depreciation deduction. If the prior year is not yet closed by the statute of limitations, you may file an amended return to claim the depreciation deduction for that year. If the year is open or closed, you may request an accounting method change. *See also 5.24* for adjustments of unclaimed depreciation taken in prior years.

Dispute over importance of useful life.   Before 1981, useful life was basic to determining depreciation, and there were two applications of useful life: (1) whether an asset had a determinable life—if the asset, such as land, had an indefinite or indeterminable useful life, depreciation was not allowable—and (2) if it had a useful life, what the period of useful life was. This two-part approach of useful life has become blurred in recent cases involving depreciation of antique musical instruments and exotic display automobiles. No one disputes that Congress in passing ACRS and MACRS intended to do away with factual disputes in determining the useful life of a depreciable asset. But the IRS has argued that Congress did not intend to do away with the basic issue posed by (1), whether an asset with an indeterminable life is entitled to depreciation at all. The IRS has failed to convince the Tax Court of its position. According to the Tax Court, under ACRS (1981–86) and current MACRS law, useful life is irrelevant for claiming depreciation if you can show that an asset is subject to exhaustion, wear and tear, or obsolescence. Thus, in the case of antique musical instruments played by professional musicians, depreciation is allowable because of wear and tear, even though the instruments have an indeterminable useful life. Two federal appeals courts have agreed, allowing professional violinists to deduct ACRS depreciation for their instruments.

In a case involving exotic cars that were not used for transportation but for exhibition, MACRS depreciation was allowed because the owner showed that they were subject to obsolescence. The autos were purchased solely for exhibition. The three state-of-the-art autos were a 1987 Lotus Pantera costing $63,000, a Lotus Espirit costing $48,000, and a Ferrari Testarossa costing $290,453. Over a four-year period, the owner deducted depreciation of over $298,000 while reporting gross income from exhibition fees of $96,630. The IRS disallowed the depreciation because the cars had no determinable useful life. The Tax Court allowed the depreciation because such cars are subject to obsolescence in the car-show business when new models appear with newer designs and high-tech features. One witness testified this could occur in some cases within a year.

The Tax Court warned that such exotic cars should not be confused with museum pieces. If they had been museum pieces, such as antique cars, no depreciation would have been allowed because in the case of art objects and antiques used as business assets, the finding of useful life remains relevant because such assets are not subject to exhaustion, wear or tear, or obsolescence.

The IRS has announced that it will continue to dispute and litigate cases in which depreciation is claimed on assets with indeterminable useful lives.

42.2 Claiming Depreciation on Your Tax Return

If you report business or professional self-employed income, use Form 4562 for assets placed in service during 1997 and enter the total deduction on Line 13, Schedule C. For claiming depreciation on "listed property" such as cars, computers, and cellular phones, you use Form 4562, regardless of the year placed in service. Listed property is explained at *42:10*. If your only depreciation deduction is for pre-1997 assets, none of which is listed property, you do not need to use Form 4562; figure the deduction on your own worksheet, and enter it on Line 13, Schedule C.

If you are an employee claiming auto expenses, you must use Form 2106 to claim depreciation on an automobile used for business purposes.

If you report rental income on Schedule E, you must use Form 4562 for claiming depreciation on buildings placed in service in 1997. For buildings placed in service before 1997, enter the depreciation deduction directly on Schedule E. If you have a rental loss on Schedule E, your deduction for depreciation and other expenses may have to be included on Form 8582 to figure net passive activity income or loss; *see* Chapter 10.

See the sample Schedule E in Part 8 of this book.

42.3 First-Year Expensing Deduction

For qualifying business equipment purchased and placed in service in 1997, you may elect to deduct up to $18,000 of the cost. For equipment placed in service by a business in an "enterprise zone," the deduction may be as high as $38,000. For an automobile, the maximum expensing deduction in 1997 is $3,160; *see 43.4*. The portion of cost not eligible for first-year expensing may be recovered by depreciation under the regular MACRS rules. The first-year expensing deduction is technically called the "Section 179 deduction."

In 1998, the deduction will have a cap of $18,500.

You may *not* elect first-year expensing for property purchased before 1997, even if 1997 is the first year you use it for business.

The election is limited to tangible personal property bought in 1997 for business use, such as machinery, office equipment, a computer, car, or truck acquired from non-related parties. The deduction is not allowed for buildings, structural components of buildings, furniture or refrigerators used in operating apartment buildings, property held for the production of income, or equipment previously used for personal purposes, such as an automobile bought for pleasure but later used for business.

To claim the first-year expensing deduction on Form 4562, which you attach to your Form 1040, you must make the election on an *original* return for the year the property is placed in service (whether or not the return is timely filed). First-year expensing may *not* be claimed on an amended return unless it is filed within the due date for the original return (including extensions). If you fail to make the election on an original return (or on an amended return filed by the due date including extensions) the election is lost. You may not revoke the expensing election without consent from the IRS.

Partial business use.   If you use the equipment for both business and personal use, business use must exceed 50% in the year the equipment is first placed into service to claim a first-year expensing deduction. The expensing deduction may be claimed for the cost allocated to business use up to the $18,000 limit; the 1997 limit for a car is $3,160 *(43.4)*.

To elect first-year expensing for "listed property" such as a computer or car *(42.10)*, business use in the first year you use it must exceed 50%. If it does, you show the amount eligible for expensing in the section for "Listed Property" on Form 4562 and then transfer the amount to the part of Form 4562 where the expensing election is claimed.

Figuring the deduction.   The maximum annual deduction in 1997 is $18,000 of the cost of qualifying property and $3,160 for a car *(43.4)*. For business use of less than 100% (but more than 50%), the expensing deduction is limited to the business portion of the cost. As discussed below, the $18,000 limit may have to be reduced because your taxable income is lower than $18,000, eligible purchases exceed $200,000, or you are married filing separately.

If you qualify for the full $18,000 limit, you do not have to claim the entire amount. If in 1997 you place in service more than one item of property, you may allocate the $18,000 deduction between the items. If you placed in service only one item of qualifying property which cost less than $18,000, your deduction is limited to that cost.

If you acquire property in a trade-in, the cost eligible for expensing is limited to the cash you paid. You may not include the adjusted basis of the property traded in, although your basis for the new property includes that amount.

Effect on regular depreciation.   If the cost basis of the property exceeds the first-year expensing limit, you compute depreciation on the cost of the property less the amount of the first-year deduction.

EXAMPLE

In 1997, you placed in service a $30,000 machine and a $2,000 lathe. You elect to deduct as a first-year expense $2,000 for the lathe and $16,000 for the machine, a total of $18,000, the maximum first-year deduction. The $2,000 deduction has completely recovered the cost of the lathe. The cost of the machine is reduced by $16,000, giving a depreciable basis of $14,000 ($30,000 – 16,000).

$18,000 limit reduced if taxable income is lower.   Your expensing deduction may not exceed net income from all your active businesses; *see* the Caution on this page.

$18,000 limit reduced if qualifying purchases exceed $200,000.   If the total cost of qualifying property placed in service during a taxable year is over $200,000, the $18,000 expensing limit is reduced dollar for dollar by the cost of qualifying property exceeding $200,000. For example, if you place in service machinery costing $206,000, the $18,000 limit is reduced by $6,000. The reduced limit of $12,000 is shown on Form 4562 on the line labeled "Dollar limitation for tax year." If the total cost is $218,000 or more, no first-year expensing deduction is allowed.

$18,000 limit reduced if married filing separately.   If you and your spouse file separate returns, the expensing limit for both of you is $18,000. Unless you agree to a different allocation, you are each allowed only a $9,000 expensing limit. The $200,000 cost threshold also applies to both of you as a unit. For example, if you place in service qualifying property costing $195,000 and your spouse places $9,000 of property in service, the total cost of $204,000 reduces the $18,000 limit by $4,000 to $14,000. The reduced limit for each of you on separate returns is $7,000.

Partners and S corporation stockholders.   For property bought by a partnership or an S corporation, the $18,000 limit and taxable income limit applies to the business, as well as the owners as individual taxpayers. The partnership or S corporation determines its expensing deduction subject to the limits and allocates the deduction, if any, among the partners or shareholders. The allocated deduction may not exceed the net taxable income of the partnership or S corporation from actively conducted businesses.

An individual partner's expensing deduction may not exceed $18,000, regardless of how many partnership interests he or she has. However, the partner must reduce the basis of each partnership interest by the full allocable share of each partnership's expensing deduction, even if that amount is not deductible because of the $18,000 limit.

Caution

Losses and Low Income May Limit Deduction

The expensing deduction may not exceed the net taxable income from all businesses which you actively conduct. Net income from active businesses is figured without regard to expensing, the deduction for 50% of self-employment liability, or any net operating loss carryback or carryforward. You may include wage or salary income as active business income and if you are married filing jointly, also include your spouse's net taxable income.

If you have an overall net loss from all actively conducted businesses, you may not claim a 1997 expensing deduction. If net income is less than the cost of qualifying assets, expensing is limited to the income. However, the cost over the income limit is carried forward to 1998 on Form 4562 provided you complete the expensing section of Form 4562 for 1997. You do *not* get a carryover unless the deduction is claimed on the return for the first year the property is placed in service.

Planning Reminder

Year-End Purchases

Equipment placed in service on the last day of the taxable year may qualify for the entire $18,000 first-year expensing deduction. You do not have to prorate the $18,000 limit for the amount of time you held the property.

Disqualified acquisitions from related parties. Property does not qualify for the expense election if:

1. It is acquired from a spouse, ancestor or lineal descendant, or from non-family-related parties subject to the loss disallowance rule of *5.5*. For purposes of the expensing election, a corporation is controlled by you and thus subject to the loss disallowance rule of *5.5* if 50% or more of the stock is owned by you, your spouse, your ancestors, or your descendants.
2. The property is acquired by a member of the same controlled group (using a 50% control test).
3. The basis of the property is determined in whole or in part (a) by reference to the adjusted basis of the property of the person from whom you acquired it or (b) under the stepped-up basis rules for inherited property.

Recapture of expensing deduction. Recapture of the first-year expensing deduction may occur on a disposition of the asset or if business use falls to 50% or less. If the business use falls to 50% or less after the year the property is placed in service but before the end of the depreciable recovery period *(42.4, 42.10)* you must "recapture" the benefit from the first-year expensing deduction. The amount recaptured is the excess of the expensing deduction over the amount of depreciation that would have been claimed (through the year of recapture) without expensing; *see 42.10*. Recaptured amounts are reported as ordinary income on Form 4797.

When you sell or dispose of the property, the first-year expensing deduction is treated as depreciation for purposes of the recapture rules *(44.1)* that treat gain realized as ordinary income to the extent of depreciation claimed.

42.4 MACRS Class Lives

Depreciable assets other than buildings fall within a three-, five-, seven-, 10-, 15-, or 20-year class life. For property in the three-, five-, seven-, and 10-year classes, the depreciation method is 200% declining balance, with a switch to straight line. Instead of the 200% rate, you may elect a 150% rate; *see 42.8*. For 15- and 20-year property, the 150% declining balance method is used with a switch to straight line. The conversion to straight line is made when larger annual deductions may be claimed over the remaining life.

Straight-line recovery for buildings is discussed at *42.13*.

Note: The actual write-off period of depreciation for an asset is one year longer than the class life because of the convention rules explained in the following sections.

Three-year property. This class includes property with a class life of four years or less, other than cars and light-duty trucks which are in the five-year class.

This class includes: special handling devices for the manufacture of food and beverages; special tools and devices for the manufacture of rubber products; special tools for the manufacture of finished plastic products, fabricated metal products, or motor vehicles; and breeding hogs. By law, racehorses more than two years old when placed in service and other horses more than 12 years old when placed in service are also in the three-year class.

Five-year class. This class includes property with a class life of more than four years and less than 10 years such as computers *(42.10)*, typewriters, copiers, duplicating equipment, heavy general-purpose trucks, trailers, cargo containers, and trailer-mounted containers. Also included by law in the five-year class are cars, light-duty trucks (actual unloaded weight less than 13,000 pounds), computer-based telephone central office switching equipment, computer-related peripheral equipment, semiconductor manufacturing equipment, and property used in research and experimentation.

Seven-year class. This class includes any property with a class life of 10 years or more but less than 16 years. This is also a catch-all category for assets with no class life that have not been assigned by law to another class. Included in the seven-year class are: office furniture and fixtures, such as desks and files; cellular phones; fax machines; refrigerators; dishwashers; and machines used to produce jewelry, musical instruments, toys, and sporting goods. Single-purpose agricultural or horticultural structures placed in service in 1987 or 1988 are in the seven-year class; they are in the 10-year class if placed in service after 1988.

Ten-year property. This includes property with a class life of 16 years or more and less than 20 years, such as vessels and water transportation equipment, and assets used in petroleum refining or in the manufacture of tobacco products and certain food products.

 Law Alert

Expensing Limit Increases After 1997

In 1998, the deduction limit will increase to $18,500; in 1999, to $19,000; in 2000, to $20,000; in 2001 and 2002 to $24,000; and after 2002 to $25,000.

The 10-year class includes single-purpose agricultural and horticultural structures, and trees or vines bearing fruit or nuts, if placed in service after 1988. Under a transition rule, the seven-year period will apply to single purpose agricultural or horticultural structures under construction on July 14, 1988, or acquired pursuant to a written contract binding on that date.

Fifteen-year property. This includes land improvements such as fences, shrubbery, roads and bridges. It also includes other property with a class life of 20 years or more but less than 25 years, such as municipal sewage plants and telephone distribution plants. Gas station convenience stores are in the 15-year class if the property is no more than 1,400 square feet, or at least 50% of the floor space is devoted to selling petroleum products, or at least 50% of revenues are from petroleum sales. The owner of the gas station property does not have to be the operator of businesses on the property.

Twenty-year property. This class includes property with a class life of 25 years or more, such as farm buildings and municipal sewers, except that residential and nonresidential real estate is excluded; *see 42.13*.

42.5 MACRS Rates

The MACRS rate depends on the recovery period *(42.4)* for the property and whether the half-year or mid-quarter convention applies. The 200% declining rate for three-year property is 66.67%; for five-year property, 40%; and for seven-year property it is 28.57%. *See 42.8* for the 150% rate election. These rates are adjusted for the convention rules explained below. When the double declining rate provides a lower annual deduction than the straight-line rate, the double declining rate is replaced by the straight-line rate. The rates in the tables at the end of this section reflect the applicable convention and the change to a straight-line recovery.

Conventions. Under the half-year convention, all property acquired during the year, regardless of when acquired during the year, is treated as acquired in the middle of the year. As a result, only one-half of the full first-year depreciation is deductible and in the year after the last class life year, the balance of the depreciation is written off. Furthermore, in the year property is sold, only half of the full depreciation for that year is deductible; *see 42.6*.

The half-year convention applies unless the total cost bases of depreciable assets placed in service during the last three months of the taxable year exceed 40% of the total bases of all property placed in service during the entire year. If this 40% test applies, you must use a mid-quarter convention to figure your annual depreciation deduction, as explained at *42.7*.

Buildings are depreciated using a mid-month convention; *see 42.13*.

Depreciation tables. The following table provides year-by-year rates for property in the three, five-, and seven-years class. The rates incorporate the adjustment for the half-year or mid-quarter convention and the switch from the 200% declining rate to the straight-line method. Use the rate shown in the table under the convention for your asset. The rate is applied to original basis, minus any first-year expensing deduction; *see 42.3*. You claim the deduction from the table in the section of Form 4562 labeled "General Depreciation System" (GDS).

You use the tables for the entire recovery period unless you claim a deductible casualty loss that reduces your basis in the property. For the year of the casualty loss and later years, depreciation must be based on the adjusted basis of the property at the end of the year. The tables may no longer be used; *see* IRS Publication 946 for further details.

MACRS Depreciation Rates

Year	Half-Year Convention	Mid-Quarter Convention			
		1st	2nd	3rd	4th (Quarter)
3-Year Property					
1	33.33%	58.33%	41.67%	25.00%	8.33%
2	44.45	27.78	38.89	50.00	61.11
3	14.81	12.35	14.14	16.67	20.37
4	7.41	1.54	5.30	8.33	10.19

MACRS Depreciation Rates

| Year | Half-Year Convention | Mid-Quarter Convention | | | |
		1st	2nd	3rd	4th (Quarter)
5-Year Property					
1	20.00%	35.00%	25.00%	15.00%	5.00%
2	32.00	26.00	30.00	34.00	38.00
3	19.20	15.60	18.00	20.40	22.80
4	11.52	11.01	11.37	12.24	13.68
5	11.52	11.01	11.37	11.30	10.94
6	5.76	1.38	4.26	7.06	9.58
7-Year Property					
1	14.29%	25.00%	17.85%	10.71%	3.57%
2	24.49	21.43	23.47	25.51	27.55
3	17.49	15.31	16.76	18.22	19.68
4	12.49	10.93	11.97	13.02	14.06
5	8.93	8.75	8.87	9.30	10.04
6	8.92	8.74	8.87	8.85	8.73
7	8.93	8.75	8.87	8.86	8.73
8	4.46	1.09	3.33	5.53	7.64

EXAMPLE

During June 1997, you place in service a machine costing $20,000. It is your only acquisition in 1997. The machine is in the five-year class and subject to the half-year convention. The depreciation rate for the first year is 20% (see the above table of MACRS rates). Your 1997 depreciation deduction is $4,000 ($20,000 × 20%).

Summary of Deductions

Year	Deduction
1	$4,000
2	6,400
3	3,840
4	2,304
5	2,304
6	1,152
Total	$20,000

42.6 Half-Year Convention for MACRS

The half-year convention treats all business equipment placed in service during a tax year as placed in service in the midpoint of that tax year. The same rule applies in the year in which the property is disposed of. The effect of this rule is as follows: A half-year of depreciation is allowed in the first year property is placed in service, regardless of when the property is placed in service during the tax year. For each of the remaining years of the recovery period, a full year of depreciation is claimed. If you hold the property for the entire recovery period, a half-year of depreciation is claimed for the year following the end of the recovery period. If you dispose of the property before the end of the recovery period, a half-year of depreciation is allowable for the year of disposition.

See the Table of MACRS Depreciation Rates in *42.5* for year-by-year rates under the half-year convention. Apply the rate from the table to the original basis, minus any first-year expensing *(42.3)* deduction claimed.

The Example in *42.5* shows the year-by-year deduction computation for five-year property under the half-year convention. If you dispose of the property before the end of the recovery period shown in *42.5*, your deduction for the year of disposition is one-half of the deduction that would be allowed for the full year using the rate shown in the table.

42.7 Last Quarter Placements—Mid-Quarter Convention

A mid-quarter convention applies if the total cost bases of business equipment placed in service during the last three months of the tax year exceed 40% of the total bases of all the property placed in service during the year. You must use a mid-quarter convention for all property (other than nonresidential real property and residential rental property) placed in service during the year. In applying the 40% rule, you do not count residential rental property, nonresidential realty, and assets that were placed in service and disposed of during the same year.

Under the mid-quarter convention, the first-year depreciation allowance is based on the number of quarters that the asset was in service. Property placed in service at any time during a quarter is treated as having been placed in service in the middle of the quarter. The mid-quarter convention also applies to sales and disposals of property. The disposal is treated as occurring in the midpoint of the quarter.

To figure your MACRS deduction for property subject to the mid-quarter convention, use the rate shown in the table in *42.5* for the quarter of the tax year the property is placed in service. In using the table, multiply the original basis, minus any first-year expensing deduction, by the applicable rate.

EXAMPLE

During August 1997, you place in service office furniture costing $1,000, and in October, a computer costing $5,000. You are on the calendar year. The total basis of all property placed in service in 1996 is $6,000. As the basis of the computer of $5,000 placed in service in the last quarter exceeds 40% of the total basis of all property placed in service during 1997, you must use the mid-quarter convention for the furniture and the computer. The office furniture, which is seven-year property, and the computer, which is five-year property, are depreciated using MACRS and a mid-quarter convention.

You first multiply the $1,000 basis of the furniture by 10.71%—the seven-year property mid-quarter convention rate for the third quarter (*see* the table in *42.5*). The depreciation deduction is $107. You then multiply the $5,000 basis of the computer by 5%—the five-year property mid-quarter convention rate for the fourth quarter (*see* the table in *42.5*). The deduction is $250. Total depreciation is $357.

42.8 150% Rate Election

Instead of using the 200% rate for property in the three-, five-, seven-, and 10-year classes, you may elect a 150% rate. You may prefer the 150% rate when you are subject to the alternative minimum tax (AMT). For AMT purposes, you must use the 150% rate and adjust your taxable income if the 200% rate was used for regular tax purposes; *see 23.2*. You may elect to apply the 150% rate for regular tax purposes. The 150% rate is applied over the alternative depreciation system (ADS) recovery period; *see 42.9*. Thus, the recovery period is five years for cars and computers and 10 years for furniture and fixtures. If a half-year convention applies, the first-year rate for the five-year class is 15%, and 7.50% for the 10-year class; *see* the table below. Apply the rate from the table to your original basis, minus any first-year expensing deduction claimed. If you are subject to the mid-quarter convention, *see* IRS Publication 946 for the tables showing mid-quarter convention rates.

The election to use the 150% rate must be made for all property within a given class placed in service in the same year. The election is irrevocable.

Half-Year Convention—150% Rate

Year—	Property Class	
	5-Year—	10-Year—
1	15.00%	7.50%
2	25.50	13.88
3	17.85	11.79
4	16.66	10.02
5	16.66	8.74
6	8.33	8.74
7		8.74
8		8.74
9		8.74
10		8.74
11		4.37

42.9 Straight-Line Depreciation

You may not want an accelerated rate and may prefer to write off depreciation at an even pace. There are two straight-line methods. You may make an irrevocable election to use the straight-line method over the regular MACRS recovery period (42.4) under the general depreciation system (GDS), or you may elect straight-line recovery over the designated recovery period for the class life under the alternative depreciation system (ADS). For some assets, such as cars, the GDS and ADS recovery periods are the same (five years for a car).

Half-year and quarter-year conventions apply to both straight-line methods; see 42.6 and 42.7. A mid-month convention applies under the straight-line rule for buildings; see 42.13.

Straight-line over regular recovery period (GDS). You make this election in the section of Form 4562 labeled "General Depreciation System" (GDS). To elect this method for one asset, you must also use it for all other assets in the same class that are placed in service during the year. The straight-line election is irrevocable.

Straight-line under the alternative depreciation system (ADS). Under the alternative depreciation system (ADS), the straight-line recovery period for cars, light trucks, and computers is five years, the same as under the regular MACRS method. For business furniture and fixtures, the ADS straight-line recovery period is 10 years, but, as discussed above, you may instead elect to use straight-line recovery over the regular seven-year MACRS recovery period (GDS). The ADS recovery period for personal property with no class life is 12 years. For nonresidential real and residential rental property, you may elect ADS straight-line recovery over 40 years. See IRS Publication 946 for other ADS class lives.

Except for real estate, the ADS election applies to all property within the same class placed in service during the taxable year. For real estate, the election to use the alternative depreciation method may be made on a property-by-property basis. The election is irrevocable.

The deduction is claimed in the section of Form 4562 labeled "Alternative Depreciation System" (ADS).

Should you elect straight-line recovery? Accelerated rates of MACRS merely give you an opportunity to advance the time of taking your deduction. This may be a decided advantage where the higher deductions in the first few years will provide you with cash for working capital or for investments in other income-producing sources. That is, by accelerating the deductions, you defer the payment of taxes that would be due if you claimed smaller depreciation deductions, using more conservative straight-line rates. The tax deferral lasts until the rapid method provides less depreciation deductions than would the more conservative method. Your ability to receive the benefits of MACRS generally is more feasible in an ongoing business.

If you are starting a new business in which you expect losses or low income at the start, accelerated MACRS may waste depreciation deductions that could be used in later years when your income increases. Therefore, before deciding to use the faster write-offs of MACRS, consider your income prospects.

Straight-line rate table. The table below shows straight-line rates for five-year, seven-year, and 10-year property under the half-year convention. As discussed earlier, the recovery period depends on whether the GDS or ADS straight-line method is used. If you are subject to the mid-quarter convention (42.7), see IRS Publication 946 for tables showing the applicable rates.

Half-Year Convention—Straight-Line Rate

Year—	5-Year—	7-Year—	10-Year—
1	10.00%	7.14%	5.00%
2	20.00	14.29	10.00
3	20.00	14.29	10.00
4	20.00	14.28	10.00
5	20.00	14.29	10.00
6	10.00	14.28	10.00
7		14.29	10.00
8		7.14	10.00
9			10.00
10			10.00
11			5.00

AMT depreciation.   For alternative minimum tax (AMT) purposes, depreciation is figured using the 150% declining rate if double declining MACRS rates were used for regular tax purposes; *see 23.2.* If straight-line depreciation was used for regular tax purposes, AMT depreciation is figured using the straight-line alternative depreciation system (ADS) over the class life recovery period. For real estate placed in service after 1986, AMT depreciation is figured using the 40-year ADS straight-line method.

Mandatory straight-line depreciation.   You are required to use the alternative depreciation system for automobiles *(43.3)* and certain computers *(42.10)* used 50% or less for business.

Alternative MACRS depreciation must also be used for:

- Figuring earnings and profits;
- Tangible property which, during the taxable year, is used predominantly outside the United States;
- Tax-exempt use property;
- Tax-exempt bond financed property; and
- Imported property covered by an executive order.

42.10   Computers and Other Listed Property

"Listed property" is a term applied to certain equipment that may be used for personal and business purposes. For such property, the law allows first-year expensing *(42.3)* or accelerated MACRS *(42.5)* deductions only if business use exceeds 50%. For business use of 50% or less, you must use ADS straight-line depreciation; *see 42.9.* Deductions for listed property are claimed on Form 4562. If the more-than-50% business-use test is met in the first year and first-year expensing or accelerated MACRS is claimed, but business use of listed property falls to 50% or less during the ADS straight-line recovery period *(42.9)*, you must "recapture" first-year expensing and accelerated MACRS deductions; *see* Example 2 below.

What is "listed property"?   Listed property includes passenger autos weighing 6,000 pounds or less, trucks *(see 43.3* for exceptions), cellular phones, computers and peripheral equipment, boats, airplanes, and any photographic, sound, or video recording equipment that could be used for entertainment or recreational purposes. However, exceptions remove some items from the listed property class for many businesses. Listed property does not include (1) any computer or peripheral equipment used exclusively at a regular business establishment owned or leased by you, and (2) photographic, phonographic, communications, or video equipment used exclusively and regularly in your business or regular business establishment. A home office that meets the rules of *40.11* is considered a business establishment.

> **EXAMPLES**
> 1. You buy a computer in 1997 and use it exclusively in your regular business office. The computer is not listed property. You may claim either first-year expensing *(42.3)* or accelerated MACRS depreciation *(42.5)* for your investment on Form 4562. If business use falls to 50% or less after 1997, the only deduction subject to recapture is the first-year deduction; *see 42.3.*
> 2. You have no regular business establishment and use a computer bought in 1997 as a freelance consultant. The computer is listed property and you may claim MACRS and/or first-year expensing only if you use the computer more than 50% for business. If business use does not exceed 50%, you may only claim ADS straight-line depreciation *(42.9)*. Your deductions are claimed in the section for "Listed Property" on Form 4562.
>
> If business use exceeds 50% in the first year but in a later year drops to 50% or less, MACRS and any first-year depreciation are subject to "recapture." In the year in which business use drops to 50% or less, you recapture the excess of (1) the MACRS and first-year expensing deductions claimed in prior years over (2) the deduction that would have been allowed using the straight-line alternative depreciation rates of *42.9.* For the rest of the recovery period, you continue to use the alternative straight-line rate.
> Recapture is figured on Form 4797. The recapture computation follows the steps shown in *43.9* for recapture of excess depreciation on an automobile.

Investor's use of computer.   For an investor who uses a home computer for managing an investment portfolio, the computer is treated as listed property. Unless the computer is also used for business, and the computer time spent on business work exceeds 50% of the total, only straight-line depreciation may be claimed; neither first-year expensing nor accelerated MACRS is allowed.

Although the investment use is disregarded for purposes of the more-than-50% business-use test, the investment use is combined with the business use for purposes of determining the percentage of depreciable cost. Depreciable investment use must relate to managing investments that produce taxable income. *See* the Examples below.

EXAMPLES

1. In 1997, Jane Adams buys a computer; she uses it 50% of the time to manage her stock investments and 40% in a part-time research business. The more-than-50% business-use test is not met for claiming first-year expensing or accelerated MACRS deductions. She must use ADS straight-line depreciation over five years *(42.9)*; her depreciable basis is 90% of cost.

2. Assume that Jane used the computer 60% of the time for business and 30% for investment. As business use exceeds 50%, she may claim first-year expensing under the rules of *42.3*. If she instead claims accelerated MACRS, the MACRS rate is applied to 90% of her cost.

Leasing a computer or cellular phone.   You may deduct the portion of your lease payments attributable to business use. However, if business use is 50% or less for any year, you must report as income an amount based on the fair market value of the unit, the percentage of business plus investment use, and percentages from two IRS tables shown in Publication 534.

Computer software.   Software purchased "off the shelf" and used for business or investment purposes is depreciable over a three-year period provided it has a useful life exceeding one year. If the useful life does not exceed one year, the cost is immediately deductible. Also *see 42.19*.

42.11   ACRS Recovery for Assets in Service Before 1987

Assets other than real estate placed in service after 1980 and before 1987 fell within one of the following ACRS classes: three-, five-, or 10-year property.

Three-year property.   This class included automobiles, taxis, light-duty trucks (actual unloaded weight of less than 13,000 pounds), equipment used for research and experimentation, hogs used for breeding, racehorses more than two years old, and any other horse more than 12 years old when placed in service.

   With the exception of certain automobiles *(43.6)*, three-year property is no longer depreciable unless straight-line recovery over 12 years was elected, *see 42.12*.

Five-year property.   All tangible personal property had a five-year recovery period, unless specifically included in the three-year or 10-year class. Thus, most equipment and other business assets qualified for a five-year write-off, including office furniture, typewriters, computers, calculators, copiers, and single-purpose agricultural structures. Facilities used for storage of petroleum and its primary products also fell within the five-year class.

   Five-year property is no longer depreciable unless you elected straight-line recovery over a period of 12 years or 25 years; *see 42.12*.

Ten-year property.   This is a limited category covering assets in residential mobile homes, theme and amusement parks, railroad tank cars, public utility equipment with an ADR class life of more than 18 but not more than 25 years (except research and experimentation equipment included in the three-year class), and public utility equipment used in coal conversions. If a straight-line recovery over 25 or 35 years was elected, *see 42.12*.

Dispositions.   No depreciation deduction is allowed in the year you dispose of three-year, five-year, or 10-year ACRS property.

Real estate.   *See 42.16* for ACRS rates.

Pre-ACRS assets.   For assets placed in service before 1981, the straight-line and declining balance methods are discussed in IRS Publication 534.

42.12   Straight-Line Recovery for Equipment in Service Before 1987

You may still be able to claim straight-line deductions for three-year ACRS property if you elected a recovery period of 12 years, or for five-year property if a recovery period of 12 or 25 years was elected. For 10-year property, an election could have been made to elect straight-line depreciation over 10, 25, or 35 years.

If you made the straight-line election, the straight-line rate to be used on your 1997 return is as follows:

Recovery Period—	Rate—
12 years	8.333%
25 years	4.000%
35 years	2.857%

Because of the half-year convention, only 50% of the above percentages was allowed in the year the property was placed in service. If the property is held for the entire elected recovery period, another half-year of depreciation is allowed for the year following the end of the recovery period. If property is disposed of prior to the end of the recovery period, no cost recovery is allowable in the year of disposition. *See* IRS Publication 534 for further details.

42.13 MACRS for Real Estate Placed in Service After 1986

The recovery period for residential rental property placed in service after December 31, 1986, is 27.5 years. The recovery period for nonresidential real property depends on when the property was placed in service.

The method of recovery for nonresidential or residential property is the straight-line method using a mid-month convention. *See* page 607 for rate tables for each class of property.

For nonresidential real property placed in service after December 31, 1986, but before May 13, 1993, the depreciation recovery period is 31.5 years.

For nonresidential real property placed in service after May 12, 1993, the recovery period is 39 years. Under a transition rule, the 31.5-year recovery period rather than the 39-year recovery period applies to a building placed in service before 1994 if before May 13, 1993, you had entered into a binding, written contract to buy or build it, or if, before that date, you had begun construction. The transition rule also applies if you obtained the contract or property from someone else who satisfied the pre-May 13, 1993, contract or construction requirement, provided he or she never put the building in service and you did so before 1994.

Residential rental property is a rental building or structure for which 80% or more of the gross rental income for the tax year is rental income from dwelling units. If you occupy any part of the building, the gross rental income includes the fair rental value of the part you occupy.

A dwelling unit is a house or an apartment used to provide living accommodations in a building or structure, but not a unit in a hotel, motel, inn, or other establishment where more than one-half of the units are used on a transient basis.

Mid-month convention. Under a mid-month convention, all property placed in service or disposed of during any month is treated as placed in service or disposed of on the midpoint of that month. You may determine the first-year deduction for residential rental property by applying the percentage from the table on the next page to the original depreciable basis. In later years, use the same column of the table to figure your deduction.

> **EXAMPLE**
>
> In February 1997, you buy and place in service an apartment building for $100,000. You use the calendar year. The table on the next page gives a first-year depreciation rate of 3.182% for 27.5- year residential rental property placed in service during February. Applying this rate, you get a deduction of $3,182.
>
> For 1998, the rate will be 3.636%, for a deduction of $3,636.

Additions or improvements to property. The depreciation deduction for any additions to, or improvement of, any property is figured in the same way as the deduction for the property would be figured if the property had been placed in service at the same time as the addition or improvement.

The MACRS class for the addition or improvement is determined by the MACRS class of the property to which the addition or improvement is made. The period for figuring depreciation begins on the date that the addition or improvement is placed in service, or, if later, the date that the property to which the addition or improvement was made is placed in service.

Residential Rental Property (27.5 years; *see 42.13*)

Use the column for the month of taxable year placed in service.

Month	1	2	3	4	5	6	7	8	9	10	11	12
Year												
1	3.485%	3.182%	2.879%	2.576%	2.273%	1.970%	1.667%	1.364%	1.061%	0.758%	0.455%	0.152%
2–9	3.636	3.636	3.636	3.636	3.636	3.636	3.636	3.636	3.636	3.636	3.636	3.636
10	3.637	3.637	3.637	3.637	3.637	3.637	3.636	3.636	3.636	3.636	3.636	3.636
11	3.636	3.636	3.636	3.636	3.636	3.636	3.637	3.637	3.637	3.637	3.637	3.637
12	3.637	3.637	3.637	3.637	3.637	3.637	3.636	3.636	3.636	3.636	3.636	3.636

Nonresidential Real Property (31.5 years—placed in service before May 13, 1993; *see 42.13*)

Use the column for the month of taxable year placed in service.

Month	1	2	3	4	5	6	7	8	9	10	11	12
Year												
1	3.042%	2.778%	2.513%	2.249%	1.984%	1.720%	1.455%	1.190%	0.926%	0.661%	0.397%	0.132%
2–7	3.175	3.175	3.175	3.175	3.175	3.175	3.175	3.175	3.175	3.175	3.175	3.175
8	3.175	3.174	3.175	3.174	3.175	3.174	3.175	3.175	3.175	3.175	3.175	3.175
9	3.174	3.175	3.174	3.175	3.174	3.175	3.174	3.175	3.174	3.175	3.174	3.175
10	3.175	3.174	3.175	3.174	3.175	3.174	3.175	3.174	3.175	3.174	3.175	3.174
11	3.174	3.175	3.174	3.175	3.174	3.175	3.174	3.175	3.174	3.175	3.174	3.175
12	3.175	3.174	3.175	3.174	3.175	3.174	3.175	3.174	3.175	3.174	3.175	3.174

Nonresidential Real Property (39 years—placed in service on or after May 13, 1993; *see 42.13*)

Use the column for the month of taxable year placed in service.

Month	1	2	3	4	5	6	7	8	9	10	11	12
Year												
1	2.461%	2.247%	2.033%	1.819%	1.605%	1.391%	1.177%	0.963%	0.749%	0.535%	0.321%	0.107%
2–39	2.564	2.564	2.564	2.564	2.564	2.564	2.564	2.564	2.564	2.564	2.564	2.564

42.14 Demolishing a Building

When you buy improved property, the purchase price is allocated between the land and the building; only the building may be depreciated. The land may not; *see 42.2*. If you later demolish the building, you may not deduct the cost of the demolition or the undepreciated basis of the building as a loss in the year of demolition. Expenses or losses in connection with the demolition of any structure, including certified historic structures, are not deductible. They must be capitalized and added to the basis of the land on which the structure is located.

Major rehabilitation. Where you are considering a major rehabilitation of a building which involves some demolition of the building, IRS guidelines may allow you to deduct the costs of demolition and a removal of part of the structure. Under the IRS rules, the costs of structural modification do not have to be capitalized if 75% or more of the existing external walls are retained as internal or external walls and 75% or more of the existing internal framework is also retained. For certified historic structures, the modification must also be part of a certified rehabilitation. The 75% tests are effective for work starting after June 5, 1995, and also for open taxable years, if an election is made for those years.

42.15 Leasehold Improvements

Lessee improvements. Leasehold improvements placed in service after 1986 by a lessee are depreciated under MACRS real estate rates listed at *42.13*. You ignore the term of the lease. If the lease term is shorter than the MACRS life and you do not retain the improvements at the end of the term, the remaining undepreciated basis is considered in computing gain or loss at that time.

Pre-1987 improvements. For leasehold improvements placed in service before 1987, the cost of improvements is deductible over the *shorter* of the following periods:

1. The useful life of the improvement if the improvement was before 1981, or the ACRS recovery period if after 1980 but before 1987, *and*
2. The remaining term of the lease.

If (1) is the shorter period, the cost of the improvement is depreciated. If (2) is the shorter period, the cost is amortized ratably.

In determining the shorter period, you must add optional lease renewals to the remaining lease term under (2) if, at the completion of the improvement, the remaining term of the original lease (excluding unexercised renewal options) is less than 60% of the useful life (or ACRS recovery period) of the improvement. Renewals do not have to be taken into account under the 60% test if the lessee can show that it is more probable that the lease would not be renewed than that it would be renewed.

If the lessee and lessor are related, the term of the lease is treated as being equal to the remaining useful life (or recovery period) of the improvement. Related parties include spouses, children, grandchildren, parents, grandparents, brothers, sisters, and certain controlled corporations, partnerships, and trusts.

Abandonment of leasehold improvements. Upon the termination of a lease, the adjusted basis of a lessee's leasehold improvements that are abandoned may be claimed as a loss.

For dispositions after June 12, 1996, a lessor may follow the rule applied to lessees if the improvements are irrevocably disposed of or abandoned at the termination of the lease. The lessor may recognize loss for the remaining adjusted basis of the improvements. For dispositions on or before June 12, 1996, the IRS has held that leasehold improvements made by a lessor that are considered structural components of a building must be continued to be depreciated in the same manner as the underlying real property, even if such improvements are retired at the end of the lease term.

42.16 Depreciating Real Estate Placed in Service After 1980 and Before 1987

The ACRS recovery period of a building that does not qualify as low-income housing depends on the year in which the building was placed in service:

- For buildings placed in service after May 8, 1985, and before 1987, the recovery period is 19 years.
- For buildings placed in service after March 15, 1984, and before May 9, 1985, the recovery period is 18 years.
- For buildings placed in service before March 16, 1984, and for all low-income housing, the recovery period is 15 years.

Mobile homes and theme parks are in a 10-year class and agricultural, horticultural, and petroleum storage structures are in the five-year class.

Under transitional rules, some 19-year buildings may be depreciated over 18 years, and some 18-year buildings over 15 years if placed in service before 1987. Specifically, recovery over 18 years is allowed for a building placed in service after May 8, 1985, provided that before May 9, 1985, (1) you began construction or had a binding contract to buy the building, and (2) you placed the building in service before the end of 1986. The 18-year period also applies if construction was begun, or a contract entered into by a person who transferred the rights to you and you placed the building in service before 1987. Recovery over 15 years is allowed for a building that you (or a prior owner who transferred the right to you) began constructing or contracted for before March 16, 1984, provided you placed it in service before the end of 1986.

Election to use straight-line depreciation. You may have elected to use the straight-line method over the regular recovery period: 19 years for 19-year property, 18 years for 18-year property, and 15 years for 15-year property. Furthermore, for any building, a longer recovery period of either 35 or 45 years was available. An election of the straight-line method for real property had to be made on a property-by-property basis, by the return due date, plus extensions, for the year the property was placed in service.

Rate of recovery.   The rate of recovery is listed in Treasury tables which are available in IRS Publication 534. The specific rates are adjusted according to the month in the first year in which a building or improvement is placed in service.

Substantial improvements.   Substantial improvements made after 1986 to an ACRS building are depreciable under MACRS *(42.13)*, not ACRS.

Dispositions.   If you dispose of 15-year real property, the ACRS deduction for the year of disposition is based on the number of full months in use. However, no deduction is allowed for the month of disposition.

The same full-month convention rule applies to dispositions of 18-year property placed in service before June 23, 1984.

If you dispose of other 18-year or 19-year real property, the ACRS deduction for the year of disposition is based on the number of months in use determined under a mid-month convention. Under the mid-month convention, real property disposed of any time during a month is treated as disposed of in the middle of that month. You count the month of disposition as one-half of a month of use.

See 44.1 for recapture rules on the sale of ACRS property.

42.17 When MACRS Is Not Allowed

If you place in service personal property which you previously used or which was previously owned by a related taxpayer before 1987, you may not be able to apply MACRS rules. This anti-churning restriction is designed to discourage asset transfers between related persons to take advantage of MACRS deductions that exceed the deductions allowed before 1987 under ACRS. The anti-churning restriction does not apply to personal property if, for the first full taxable year of service, the deduction allowable under ACRS would be greater than the deduction allowable under MACRS.

The anti-churning rule also does not bar MACRS rules for real estate acquired after 1986, unless you lease back the real estate to a related party who owned it before 1987.

Special rules also apply to the transfer of property in certain tax-free corporate or partnership transactions where the property was used before 1987. If you receive property in a tax-free exchange, you may have to use the method used by the transferor in computing the ACRS deduction for that part of basis that does not exceed what was the transferor's basis in the property. To the extent that basis exceeds the transferor's, the MACRS rules may apply; for example, when you paid boot in addition to transferring property.

Where property is disposed of and reacquired, the depreciation deduction is computed as if the disposition had not occurred.

42.18 Amortizing Goodwill and Other Intangibles (Section 197)

The costs of intangibles coming within Section 197 are amortized over a 15-year period. The 15-year period applies regardless of the actual useful life of "Section 197 intangibles" acquired after August 10, 1993, and held in connection with a business or income-producing activity.

Generally, the amount subject to amortization is cost. Annual amortization is reported on Form 4562. The 15-year period starts with the month the intangible was acquired.

A "Section 197 intangible" is: (1) goodwill; (2) going-concern value; (3) workforce in place; (4) information base; (5) know-how, but *see* exceptions below; (6) any customer-based intangible; (7) any supplier-based intangible; (8) any license, permit, or other right granted by a governmental unit or agency; (9) any covenant not to compete made in the acquisition of a business; and (10) any franchise, trademark, or trade name.

Goodwill.   Goodwill is the value of a business attributable to the expectancy of continued customer patronage, due to the name or reputation of a business or any other factor.

Covenants not to compete.   A covenant not to compete is a Section 197 intangible if paid for in connection with the acquisition of a business. Excessive compensation or rental paid to a former owner of a business for continuing to perform services or provide the use of property is considered an amount paid for a covenant not to compete if the services or property benefits the trade or business. But an amount paid under a covenant not to compete which actually represents additional consideration for corporate stock is not a Section 197 intangible and must be added to the basis of the acquired stock.

Franchises, trademarks, and trade names.   A franchise (excluding sports franchises), trademark, or trade name is a Section 197 intangible. Amounts, whether fixed or contingent, paid on the transfer of a trademark, trade name, or franchise are chargeable to capital account and must be ratably amortized over a 15-year period. The renewal of a franchise, trademark, or trade name is treated as an acquisition of the franchise, trademark, or trade name. Renewal costs are amortized over 15 years beginning in the month of renewal.

Know-how.   A patent, copyright, formula, process, design, pattern, format, or similar item may be a Section 197 intangible. However, the following interests are not Section 197 intangibles unless acquired as part of the acquisition of a business: patents, copyrights, and interests in films, sound recordings, videotapes, books, or other similar property.

Customer-based intangibles.   Customer-based intangibles include the portion of an acquired trade or business attributable to a customer base, circulation base, undeveloped market or market growth, insurance in force, investment management contracts, or other relationships with customers that involve the future provision of goods or services.

Supplier-based intangibles.   The portion of the purchase price of an acquired business attributable to a favorable relationship with persons who provide distribution services, such as favorable shelf or display space at a retail outlet, the existence of a favorable credit rating, or the existence of favorable supply contracts, are Section 197 intangibles.

Going-concern value.   This is the additional value that attaches to property because it is an integral part of a going concern. This includes the value attributable to the ability of a trade or business to continue to operate and generate sales without interruption in spite of a change in ownership.

Workforce in place.   The portion of the purchase price of an acquired business attributable to a highly skilled workforce is amortizable over 15 years. Similarly, the cost of acquiring an existing employment contract is amortizable over 15 years.

Information base.   This includes the cost of acquiring customer lists; subscription lists; insurance expirations; patient or client files; lists of newspaper, magazine, radio, or television advertisers; business books and records; and operating systems. The intangible value of technical manuals, training manuals or programs, data files, and accounting or inventory control systems is also a Section 197 intangible.

Self-created intangibles.   A Section 197 intangible created by a taxpayer is generally not amortizable, unless created in connection with a transaction that involves the acquisition of assets of a business. However, this deduction bar for self-created intangibles does not apply to the following: (1) any license, permit, or other right granted by a governmental unit or agency; (2) a covenant not to compete entered into on the acquisition of a business; or (3) any franchise, trademark, or trade name. For example, the 15-year amortization period may apply to the capitalized costs of registering or developing a trademark or trade name.

A person who contracts for or renews a contract for the use of a Section 197 intangible may not be considered to have created that intangible. For example, a licensee who contracts for the use of know-how may amortize capitalized costs over 15 years.

The following intangible assets are not Section 197 intangibles: (1) interests in a corporation, partnership, trust, or estate; (2) interests under certain financial contracts; (3) interests in land; (4) certain computer software; (5) certain separately acquired rights and interests; (6) interests under existing leases of tangible property; (7) interests under existing indebtedness; (8) sports franchises; (9) certain residential mortgage servicing rights; and (10) certain corporate transaction costs.

Computer software.   Computer software is *not* a Section 197 intangible if it: (1) is readily available to the general public; (2) is not subject to an exclusive license; and (3) has not been substantially changed. Furthermore, even computer software falling outside of this exception is considered a Section 197 intangible only if acquired in the acquisition of a business. For software excluded from Section 197 treatment, *see 42.19.*

Loss limitations.   A person who disposes of an amortizable Section 197 intangible at loss and at the same time retains other Section 197 intangibles acquired in the same transaction may not deduct the loss. The disallowed loss is added to the basis of the retained Section 197 intangibles. The same rule applies if a Section 197 intangible is abandoned or becomes worthless and other Section 197 intangibles acquired in the same transaction are kept. The basis of the remaining intangibles is increased by the disallowed loss.

You may not treat a covenant not to compete as worthless any earlier than the disposition or worthlessness of the entire interest in a business.

Anti-churning rule. No deduction is allowed for goodwill, going-concern value, or any other Section 197 intangibles acquired by a taxpayer after August 10, 1993, if:

1. The taxpayer or a related person held or used the intangible at any time on or after July 25, 1991, and on or before August 10, 1993;

2. The taxpayer acquired the intangible from a person who held it at any time on or after July 25, 1991, and on or before August 10, 1993, and, as part of the transaction, the user of the intangible does not change; or

3. The taxpayer grants the right to use the intangible to a person or a related person who held or used the intangible at any time on or after July 25, 1991, and on or before August 10, 1993.

Who are related persons? A person may be treated as related to another person if engaged in businesses under common control. A 20% ownership test is used to determine the stock and partnership percentages.

An exception to the "anti-churning" rule may apply if the person from whom the intangible is acquired elects to recognize gain on its disposition and pay a tax on the gain which, when added to other income taxes imposed on the gain, equals the product of the gain and the highest rate of income tax applicable to the person. If the election is made, the anti-churning rules apply to the intangible only to the extent that adjusted basis in the intangible exceeds the recognized gain.

The anti-churning rules do not apply to a Section 197 intangible acquired from a decedent if the basis of the intangible is stepped up to fair market value.

Dispositions. An amortizable Section 197 intangible is not a capital asset. It is treated as depreciable property, and if held for more than one year, it will generally qualify as a Section 1231 asset; *see 44.1*. Amortization claimed on a Section 197 intangible is subject to recapture under Section 1245 and gain on its sale to certain related persons is subject to ordinary income treatment under Section 1239.

42.19 Deducting the Cost of Computer Software

The cost of software installed in a computer that you buy and use in your business is not deducted separately, unless the software cost is separately stated. In most cases, the cost of software bundled with a computer is not separately stated. The cost of the computer including such software is depreciable under the rules of *42.10*.

If you buy software for business use, such as a database or spreadsheet program, the treatment of the cost depends on your use of the program. If you use it for a year or less, such as an annual tax program, you may deduct the cost as a business expense for that year. If the useful life in your business exceeds a year, you may depreciate the cost over 36 months.

See *42.18* for 15-year amortization of certain software acquired in the acquisition of a business.

Chapter 43

Deducting Automobile Expenses

The costs of buying and operating a car for business are deductible under rules hedged with restrictions. The maximum depreciation deduction for a car placed in service in 1997 may not exceed $3,160, and this limit is reduced further by the percentage of your personal use. If you do not use your car more than 50% of the time for business, depreciation must be based on the straight-line method.

To avoid accounting for actual auto expenses and depreciation, you may claim an IRS mileage allowance of 31.5 cents per mile. Whatever choice you make, keep a record of business trip mileage.

If you are self-employed, you deduct your automobile expenses on Schedule C or Schedule C-EZ if eligible; *see 40.6.* Use Form 4562 to compute depreciation if you claim actual operating costs instead of the IRS mileage allowance. If you are an employee, use Form 2106 to claim unreimbursed automobile expenses, which are deductible only to the extent that together with other miscellaneous itemized deductions they exceed 2% of your adjusted gross income.

43.1 IRS Automobile Allowance

If you start to use your car for business in 1997, you have a choice of either deducting the actual operating costs of your car during business trips or deducting a flat IRS allowance of 31.5 cents per mile for all business mileage traveled during 1997.

If you placed a business car in service before 1997 and have always used the IRS mileage allowance, you may apply the 31.5 cents per mile rate to your 1997 business mileage or deduct your actual operating costs plus straight-line depreciation (assuming the car is not considered fully depreciated).

The mileage rate also applies to business trips in a van or pickup or panel truck as if it were a car.

The rate may not be used to deduct the costs of an automobile used for nonbusiness income-producing activities such as looking after investment property.

The choice of the allowance must be made in the first year you place an auto in service for business travel. If you do not use the allowance in the year you first use the car for business, you may not use the allowance for that car in any other year. Thus, if you bought a car for business in 1996 and on your 1996 return you deducted actual operating costs plus depreciation, you may not use the mileage allowance on your 1997 return or in any later year.

The allowance takes the place of fixed operating costs such as gasoline (including state and local taxes), oil, repairs, license tags, insurance, and depreciation. You may not take the allowance and deduct your actual outlays for these expenses. Parking fees and tolls during business trips are allowed in addition to the mileage allowance. The IRS will not disallow a deduction based on the allowance even though it exceeds your actual car costs.

EXAMPLE

You buy a car in 1997 and drive it on business trips. You keep a record of your business mileage. You traveled 20,000 miles on business. You may deduct $6,300 (20,000 × 31.5 cents). In addition, you spend $300 on tolls and parking. You may deduct a total of $6,600.

You may decide to use the allowance if you do not keep accurate records of operating costs. However, you must keep a record of your business trips, dates, customers or clients visited, business purpose of the trips, your total mileage during the year, and the number of miles traveled on business. An IRS agent may attempt to verify mileage by asking for repair bills near the beginning and end of the year if the bills note mileage readings.

Interest on a car loan and taxes.   *See 43.2* for when a deduction is allowed.

Mileage allowance disallowed.   You may not claim the 31.5-cents-a-mile allowance if:

- You have depreciated your car using the ACRS or MACRS method, including straight-line MACRS, or you claimed first-year expensing.
- You use in your business two or more cars simultaneously, such as in a fleet operation.
- You use your car for hire—that is, you use it as a taxicab, carrying passengers for a fare.
- You lease the car.

EXAMPLES

1. In 1997, you place in service a new auto costing $20,000 and use it only for business. You travel 20,000 miles on business trips. If you claim the allowance, your deduction is $6,300 (20,000 × 31.5 cents). If you claim actual costs, your depreciation deduction is limited to $3,160; *see 43.3.* To match the IRS allowance, you need actual operating costs (such as gas, oil, and maintenance) of at least $3,140. If these costs exceed $3,140, it is advisable to claim your actual expenses plus depreciation. Moreover, in 1998, you may deduct depreciation of up to $5,000 in addition to operating costs. The $5,000 represents the second year depreciation limit on cars placed in service in 1997.

2. Same facts as in Example 1, but you travel only 9,600 business miles. If you elect the allowance, you may deduct only $3,024 (9,600 × 31.5 cents). If you elect to deduct actual costs, your depreciation deduction of $3,160 by itself exceeds the allowance. Assume your operating costs are $1,500. Your total deduction of $4,660 exceeds the allowance.

 Planning Reminder

First-Year Election Affects Later Years

In deciding whether to elect the allowance in the first year, consider not only whether you will get a bigger first-year deduction using the allowance, or deducting actual operating costs plus depreciation, but also project your mileage, operating expenses, and depreciation expenses over the years you expect to use the car. If in the first year you elect to deduct actual costs, including accelerated MACRS or straight-line MACRS depreciation, you may not use the IRS auto allowance for *that car* in a later year. On the other hand, claiming the IRS allowance in the first year you put a car in service forfeits your privilege to use MACRS and first-year expensing. If you switch from the allowance to deducting actual expenses in later years, you may claim straight-line depreciation if the car is not considered fully depreciated.

Key To Deducting Automobile Expenses

Item—	Tax Rule—

IRS mileage allowance

You may avoid the trouble of keeping a record of actual auto expenses and calculating depreciation by electing the IRS mileage allowance of 31.5 cents a mile. The allowance may give you a larger deduction than your actual outlays plus depreciation. You must elect the allowance in the first year you use the car for business. If you do not, you may not use the allowance for that car in any other year.

If business mileage is—	Your mileage allowance is—	If business mileage is—	Your mileage allowance is—
5,000	$1,575	16,000	$5,040
8,000	2,520	17,000	5,355
10,000	3,150	18,000	5,670
11,000	3,465	19,000	5,985
12,000	3,780	20,000	6,300
13,000	4,095	22,000	6,930
14,000	4,410	25,000	7,875
15,000	4,725	30,000	9,450

To claim the allowance, you must be ready to prove business use of the auto and keep a record of your mileage. Of course, if your actual operating costs plus depreciation exceed the allowance, claim your actual operating expenses and depreciation.

Depreciation

If you claim actual operating expenses for a new car, such as gasoline, repairs, and insurance costs, you may also claim depreciation. There is a cap on the annual depreciation deduction. If you placed a car in service in 1997 your top deduction may not exceed $3,160. The amount is reduced if business use is less than 100%. Furthermore, accelerated MACRS depreciation is allowed only for autos used more than 50% of the time for business driving. Where business driving is 50% or less, straight-line depreciation must be used. MACRS depreciation deductions claimed in prior years may be recaptured if business use declines to 50% or less; see 43.9. If the car was placed in service before 1997, see 43.4 for the maximum depreciation you can take for 1997.

First-year expensing

Whether you choose regular depreciation or first-year expensing, the limit for 1997 is $3,160. If the cost of your car is $15,800 or greater, then you are subject to the $3,160 limit. Regular depreciation under the half-year convention at the 20% first-year MACRS rate (43.5) will be at least $3,160 ($15,800 × 20%). Thus, if the cost of your car is more than $15,800, it makes no difference whether you expense or depreciate because the result is the maximum $3,160 either way. If the cost of your car is less than $15,800, you are better off taking first-year expensing. First-year expening may also provide a larger deduction if the mid-quarter convention applies; see 43.5. The first-year expensing rules are discussed in 42.3. To claim first-year expensing, the auto must be used more than 50% for business travel. If business use is less than 100% but more than 50%, the $3,160 limit is reduced. For example, if you use the auto 80% for business, the top deduction is $2,528 ($3,160 × 80%). If you elect first-year expensing in 1997, you may not use the IRS mileage allowance in later years for travel in that car. In 1998, you may claim MACRS depreciation, applying the second-year MACRS rate to your original basis reduced by the first-year deduction claimed in 1997; see 43.5.

Auto used for business and personal driving

You may deduct only the amount allocated to business mileage. For example, total mileage is 20,000 in 1997 and your business mileage is 15,000. You may claim only 75% of your deductible costs (15,000 ÷ 20,000).

Tax return reporting

If you are an *employee*, you claim actual auto expenses or the IRS allowance on Form 2106. Form 2106 requires you to list mileage for business, commuting, and other personal trips. If your auto costs are not reimbursed by your employer, you must deduct them as miscellaneous deductions subject to the 2% AGI floor on Schedule A.

If you are *self-employed*, you deduct business costs on Schedule C and use Form 4562 to compute depreciation if you claim actual operating costs. Costs deducted on Schedule C are not limited by the 2% adjusted gross income (AGI) floor.

If you use more than one automobile in your business travel and elect the allowance, total the business mileage traveled in both cars.

> ### EXAMPLE
> You use one car primarily for business and occasionally your spouse's car for business trips. During the taxable year, on business trips, you drove your car 10,000 miles and your spouse's car 2,000 miles. Total business mileage is 12,000 miles for purposes of the 31.5-cents-a-mile allowance.

Rural mail carriers allowed higher auto mileage rate.   U.S. Postal Service mail carriers who use their cars to deliver and collect mail on rural routes may deduct a mileage rate equal to 150% of the basic rate. As the basic rate for 1997 is 31.5 cents per mile, the special allowance for 1997 is 47.25 cents per mile and applies to all rural delivery mileage. *See* the Law Alert below.

Employer reimbursements.   If your employer reimburses your auto costs at a rate lower than the IRS allowance, you may use the IRS rate to deduct the excess over your employer's reimbursement; *see* Example 3 at *20.33*.

IRS allowance includes depreciation.   When you use the IRS allowance, you may not claim a separate depreciation deduction. The IRS mileage allowance includes an estimate for depreciation. However, for purposes of figuring gain or loss on a disposition, you must reduce the basis of the car according to the following rates: 7 cents per business mile for 1980–1981; 7.5 cents per mile for 1982; 8 cents per mile for 1983, 1984, and 1985; 9 cents per mile for 1986; 10 cents per mile for 1987; 10.5 cents per mile for 1988; 11 cents per mile for 1989, 1990, and 1991; 11.5 cents per mile for 1992 and 1993; and 12 cents per mile for 1994, 1995, 1996, and 1997. For years before 1990, the annual cents-per-mile reduction applies only to the first 15,000 miles of business use per year for which the IRS allowance was claimed.

Depreciation when switching from allowance to actual costs.   If you use the IRS mileage allowance in the first year, you may switch to the actual-cost method in a later year, but depreciation must be based on the straight-line method over the remaining estimated useful life. However, no depreciation may be claimed if basis has been reduced to zero under the annual cents-per-mile reduction rule just discussed.

 Law Alert

Rural Mail Carriers
Beginning in 1998, U.S. postal workers who use their personal vehicles on rural routes may deduct an amount equal to the reimbursement received from the government.

43.2 Auto Expense Allocations

If you do not claim the IRS mileage allowance, you may deduct car expenses on business trips such as the cost of gas and oil (including state and local taxes), repairs, parking, and tolls.

If you use your car exclusively for business, all of your operating expenses are deductible. However, if you are an employee, the deduction is limited by the 2% adjusted gross income (AGI) floor; *see 19.1*.

Apportioning car expenses between business and personal use.   For a car used for business and personal purposes, deduct only the depreciation and expenses allocated to your business use of the car. Depreciation is discussed at *43.3*, *43.4*, and *43.5*.

The business portion of car expenses is determined by the percentage of mileage driven on business trips during the year.

> ### EXAMPLE
> In 1997, you drove your car 15,000 miles. Of this, 12,000 miles was on business trips. The percentage of business use is 80%:
>
> $$\frac{\text{Business mileage}}{\text{Total mileage}} = {12,000}/{15,000} = 80\%$$
>
> Your actual car expenses (gas, oil, repairs, etc.) for the year were $1,000, of which $800 ($1,000 × 80%) is deductible. If you are an employee, the $800 is deductible as a miscellaneous itemized deduction subject to the 2% AGI floor; *see 19.1*.

Interest on car loan.   If you are an *employee*, all of the interest is considered personal interest and is not deductible even if you use the car 100% for your job. If you are *self-employed*, the allocated business percentage of the interest is fully deductible on Schedule C; the personal percentage is not deductible.

Taxes on purchase.   Sales tax is not deductible whether you are an employee or self-employed; the tax is added to the basis of the auto for depreciation purposes; *see 43.3.* State and local property taxes are deductible as itemized deductions on Schedule A if you are an employee. If you are self-employed, deduct the business portion of the property taxes on Schedule C and the personal percentage on Schedule A if you itemize.

Leased car.   If you lease a car for business use, you deduct the rental fee plus other costs of operating the car. If the car is also used for personal driving, the rental fee must be allocated between business and personal mileage. *See also 43.11* for rules requiring the reporting of extra income attributable to the lease.

43.3 Auto Depreciation Restrictions

The law contains restrictions that limit and, in some cases, deny depreciation deductions for a business car. Employees may be unable to claim any deduction at all under an employer convenience test. Employees meeting that test and self-employed individuals must determine if they can use accelerated MACRS rates or must use straight-line rates. Finally, regardless of which depreciation method is used, the annual deduction may not exceed a ceiling set by law. For a car placed in service in 1997, the ceiling is $3,160; *see 43.4* for details on the annual ceilings.

Employer convenience test.   If you are an employee and use your own car for work, you must be ready to prove that you use a car for the *convenience of your employer* who requires you to use it in your job. If you do not meet this employer convenience test, you may not claim depreciation or first-year expensing. A letter from your employer stating you need the car for business will not meet this test.

The facts and circumstances of your use of the car may show that it is a condition of employment. For example, an inspector for a construction company uses his automobile to visit construction sites over a scattered area. The company reimburses him for his expenses. According to the IRS, the inspector's use of the car is for the convenience of the company and is a condition of the job. However, if a company car were available to the inspector, the use of his own car would not meet the condition of employment and convenience of the employer tests.

More-than-50% business-use test for claiming expensing or accelerated MACRS depreciation.   An automobile is considered "listed property," as explained in *42.10,* whether you are an employee or are self-employed. As such, you may claim first-year expensing *(42.3)* or accelerated MACRS *(43.5)* for a car placed in service during 1997 only if you use it in 1997 more than 50% of the time for business. The same annual ceiling applies to the expensing and MACRS deductions; *see 43.4.*

If business use is *50% or less* in the year the auto is placed in service, first-year expensing and accelerated MACRS are barred; the auto is depreciable over a six-year period under the straight-line method. Technically, the recovery period is five years but the period is extended to six years because, in the first year, a convention rule limits the deductible percentage. *See* the straight-line rate tables at *43.6.* The straight-line method must also be used in future years, even if business use in those years exceeds 50%.

If a car is used for both business and investment purposes, only business use is considered in determining whether you meet the more than 50% business-use test and therefore qualify for MACRS. However, if your business use does exceed 50%, investment use is added to business use in determining your actual deduction.

> **EXAMPLE**
>
> Brown buys an automobile for $30,000 and places it in service in 1997. He uses it 40% for business and 20% for investment activity. Because he does not use his car more than 50% in his business, he may not claim first-year expensing or accelerated MACRS. He figures depreciation using the straight-line method. The business use allocation rate for depreciation is 60% (40% for business use plus 20% investment use).

Trucks and other vehicles.   The more-than-50% business-use test generally applies to vehicles other than automobiles such as trucks, vans, boats, motorcycles, airplanes, and buses. However, the test does not apply to taxicabs and other vehicles used substantially all of the time to transport persons or property for hire. The test also does not apply to vehicles that are exempt from record-keeping requirements under *43.10* such as a school bus, dump truck, farm tractor or other specialized farm vehicle, delivery truck with seating only for the driver or with a folding jump seat, flat bed truck, garbage truck, passenger bus with capacity of at least 20, refrigerated truck, combine, specialized utility repair truck, unmarked law enforcement vehicle officially authorized for use, and a moving van if personal use is limited by the employer to travel from the employee's home to a move site.

A vehicle not in the exempt list is subject to the more-than-50% test for claiming accelerated MACRS depreciation or first-year expensing. If you do not satisfy the more-than-50% test, you must apply the straight-line recovery rates shown at *43.6*.

Do your employees use the car?   In certain cases, an employer who provides a company car to employees as part of their compensation may be unable to count the employee's use as qualified business use, thereby preventing the employer from meeting the more-than-50% business-use test for claiming MACRS. An employer is allowed to treat the employee's use as qualified business use only if: (1) the employee is not a relative and does not own more than 5% of the business; and (2) the employer treats the fair market value of the employee's personal use of the car as wage income and withholds tax on that amount. If such income is reported, all of the employee's use, including personal use, may be counted by an employer as qualified business use.

If an employee owning more than a 5% interest is allowed use of a company car as part of his or her compensation, the employer may not count that use as qualified business use, even if the personal use is reported as income. The same strict rule applies if the car is provided to a person who is related to the employer.

43.4   Annual Ceilings on Depreciation

For cars placed in service after 1986, annual ceilings limit the amount of depreciation you may deduct. The ceilings apply both to self-employed individuals and employees. As a result of the ceilings, the actual write-off period for your car may be several years longer than the minimum recovery period of six years; *see 43.5*.

If the ceiling is less than the amount of depreciation figured under the regular MACRS rules, you are limited to the ceiling amount. For example, if in 1997 you bought a car for $20,000 which you used 100% for business, the regular MACRS rules would allow a deduction of $4,000 in 1997 (20% × $20,000), assuming the half-year convention applied; *see 43.5*. However, your 1997 depreciation deduction is limited to $3,160, the ceiling for cars placed in service during 1997. The ceiling is reduced if you use the car for both personal and business driving as discussed below.

You may not exceed the ceiling by claiming first-year expensing *(42.3)*. The $3,160 limit for cars placed in service in 1997 also applies to the first-year expensing deduction. Thus, the first-year expensing deduction in 1997 may not exceed $3,160. If you claim first-year expensing of $3,160, you may not deduct any other depreciation. Claiming first-year expensing on Form 4562 (if self-employed) or Form 2106 (if an employee) may provide a larger deduction than regular MACRS depreciation where your deduction is subject to the mid-quarter convention; *see 43.5*.

The table on the next page shows the year-by-year ceilings for cars placed in service between 1988 and 1997.

Personal driving reduces the annual ceiling.   The annual ceilings are reduced if you use a car for both personal and business use. The reduced ceiling is equal to the regular ceiling multiplied by the percentage of business use. For example, in 1997, you buy a car costing $40,000. You use the car 70% for business travel. The MACRS or first-year expensing deduction is limited to $2,212 ($3,160 × 70%). Furthermore, for purposes of figuring whether depreciation is allowed after the end of the recovery period, the basis of the car is reduced by the amount of the depreciation that would have been allowed if you had used the car 100% for business travel; *see 43.7*.

Ceilings for cars placed in service before 1987.   The luxury car ceilings for cars placed in service after June 18, 1984, and before 1987, vary depending on when the car was placed in service.

For cars placed in service—	Current ceiling—
Before 6/19/84	None
After 6/18/84 and before 1985	$6,000
After 1984 and before 4/3/85	$6,200
After 4/2/85 and before 1987	$4,800

Caution

Recapture of MACRS Deductions
If you meet the more-than-50% test in the year the car or other vehicle is placed in service but business use falls to 50% or less in a later year, the recapture rules discussed at *43.9* apply.

Light trucks and vans subject to the ceilings. The annual depreciation ceilings apply only to "passenger automobiles." For this purpose, a passenger automobile is generally considered to be any four-wheeled vehicle that is manufactured primarily for use on public streets, roads, and highways and that is weight-rated by the manufacturer at 6,000 pounds or less when unloaded (without passengers or cargo). However, a light truck or van that is weight-rated by the manufacturer at 6,000 pounds or less when loaded (gross vehicle weight) is treated as a passenger automobile.

The following are not considered "passenger" automobiles and thus are exempt from the annual ceilings: (1) an ambulance, hearse, or combination ambulance-hearse used directly in a business; and (2) a vehicle such as a taxicab used directly in the business of transporting persons or property for compensation or hire.

Sport utility vehicles. Owners of certain sport utility vehicles (SUVs) that are used for business purposes and that have a gross vehicle weight (loaded) of more than 6,000 pounds are not subject to the ceiling on depreciation deductions. This means the owner is entitled to the full depreciation deduction using the MACRS rate shown in 43.5.

SUV owners should check the manufacturers' specifications for their vehicles to see if the weight exceeds the 6,000 limit.

Annual Depreciation Ceiling for Cars Placed in Service After 1986

For auto placed in service in—

Ceiling in—	1988	1989	1990	1991	1992	1993	1994	1995	1996	1997
1988	$2,560									
1989	4,100	$2,660								
1990	2,450	4,200	$2,660							
1991	1,475	2,550	4,200	$2,660						
1992	1,475	1,475	2,550	4,300	$2,760					
1993	1,475	1,475	1,475	2,550	4,400	$2,860				
1994	1,475	1,475	1,475	1,575	2,650	4,600	$2,960			
1995	1,475	1,475	1,475	1,575	1,575	2,750	4,700	$3,060		
1996	1,475	1,475	1,475	1,575	1,575	1,675	2,850	4,900	$3,060	
1997	1,475	1,475	1,475	1,575	1,575	1,675	1,675	2,950	4,900	3,160
1998	1,475	1,475	1,475	1,575	1,575	1,675	1,675	1,775	2,950	5,000
1999	1,475	1,475	1,475	1,575	1,575	1,675	1,675	1,775	1,775	3,050
2000 and later years	1,475	1,475	1,475	1,575	1,575	1,675	1,675	1,775	1,775	1,775

43.5 MACRS Rates for Cars

Business autos placed in service in 1987 and later years are technically in a five-year MACRS class (42.4), but because of the half-year or mid-quarter convention and the annual deduction ceilings, the minimum depreciation period is six years.

MACRS rate. To use accelerated MACRS or first-year expensing, you must meet the more-than-50% business-use test explained at 43.3. If you do, the MACRS rate is based on the 200% declining balance method with a switchover to straight line. The declining balance rate for a car that is five-year property is 40%. However, the full amount of the deduction is not allowed, because of the convention rules and the annual car limits discussed in this section. As explained in 42.5, each year the declining balance rate of 40% is applied against the declining balance of the basis of property.

As a shortcut, you may apply the half-year convention rates or the mid-quarter convention rates shown on this page and page 620, whichever applies in your case. The rates are applied against unadjusted basis, which is your cost minus any first-year expensing deduction. The deduction may not exceed the annual ceiling for auto depreciation, multiplied by the percentage of business use; *see* the Example at the top of page 620.

Straight-line election for car if business use exceeds 50%.   If business use of your car exceeds 50%, you may elect to write off your cost under the straight-line method instead of using the regular MACRS 200% declining balance method. The straight-line rates are shown in *43.6.* The straight-line deduction is limited by the annual ceilings shown in *43.4.* By electing straight-line depreciation, you avoid the recapture of excess MACRS deductions if business use drops to 50% or less in a later year; *see 43.9.* If the election is made, you must also use the straight-line method for all other five-year property placed in service during the same year as the car.

Electing 150% rate.   The rates shown in this section for the half-year and mid-quarter convention are based on the 200% declining balance method. You may instead elect to apply a 150% declining balance rate. The 150% rate may be advantageous when you are subject to alternative minimum tax (AMT); *see 42.8.*

Half-year or mid-quarter convention.   Regardless of the time of year you bought the car in 1997, your deduction is limited by a convention rule. If the only business equipment bought in 1997 was the car, then the half-year convention applies, unless you bought the car in the last quarter of 1997 (October, November, or December). Under the half-year convention, the car is treated as if it were placed in service in the middle of the year and the 40% declining balance rate is reduced to 20%. Use the table below to determine your deduction under the half-year convention.

If the only business equipment bought in 1997 was a car bought in the last quarter (October, November, or December), the mid-quarter convention applies. Under the table for mid-quarter convention rates on the next page, a 5% rate applies for fourth-quarter property, subject to the $3,160 deduction ceiling in 1997.

If you bought other business equipment in addition to the car, you must consider the total cost bases of property placed in service during the last quarter of 1997. If the total bases of such acquisitions (other than realty) exceed 40% of the total bases of all property placed in service during the year, then a mid-quarter rate applies to all property (other than realty). The mid-quarter rate for each asset then depends on the quarter the asset was placed in service. If the 40% test is not met, then the half-year convention applies to all the property acquisitions. As shown in the mid-quarter convention table on the next page, mid-quarter rates for each year of the recovery period depend on the quarter the property is placed in service.

MACRS Deduction: Half-Year Convention

Year—	Lower of percentage below or annual ceiling*—
1	20.00%
2	32.00
3	19.20
4	11.52
5	11.52
6	5.76

The annual ceiling for the year depends on the year the car was placed in business service. For cars placed in service in 1997, the ceiling on 1997 returns is $3,160. The table on the previous page shows the ceiling for other years of service.

If your car is not used 100% for business in 1997, multiply the business-use percentage by the applicable ceiling and compare the result to the deduction figured by multiplying the business-use portion of the unadjusted basis (cost minus first-year expensing) of the car by the rate in the above table. Your deduction is the lower amount; see the following Example.

Filing Tip

Mid-Quarter Rate Limitation

If the application of the mid-quarter convention limits your deduction to less than $3,160 for a car placed in service during 1997, consider an election to claim the first-year expensing deduction at *42.3* if your business-use percentage exceeds 50%. This may allow you to deduct up to $3,160.

EXAMPLE

In May 1997, you place in service a car used 100% for business. The car cost $20,000. Here is the depreciation schedule assuming the car is kept for the period shown below and is used 100% for business trips:

1997	3,160
1998	5,000
1999	3,050
2000	1,775
2001	1,775
2002*	1,152
2003	1,775
2004	1,775
2005	538

* Note that in year 6 (2002), the depreciation deduction is $1,152 and not $1,775. The $1,152 represents the year 6 MACRS depreciation deduction of 5.76% of $20,000. Since you take the lower of the MACRS percentage and the annual ceiling, the $1,152 is used because it is less than $1,175. In years 7 and 8 (2003 and 2004), the annual ceiling of $1,775 is used as the 6-year MACRS recovery period has run. In year 9 (2005), the balance left to be depreciated, or $538, is deducted.

Assume that in 1997 you use the car only 60% rather than 100% for business. You deduct $1,896 in 1997 (60% of the annual limit of $3,160). Your deduction may not be based on 60% of depreciable basis; this would give a larger deduction of $2,400 ($20,000 × 60% business use × 20% first-year depreciation rate) without considering the first-year deduction limit.

MACRS Deduction: Mid-Quarter Convention*

	Placed in service in—			
Year—	First Quarter	Second Quarter	Third Quarter	Fourth Quarter
1	35.00%	25.00%	15.00%	5.00%
2	26.00	30.00	34.00	38.00
3	15.60	18.00	20.40	22.80
4	11.01	11.37	12.24	13.68
5	11.01	11.37	11.30	10.94
6	1.38	4.26	7.06	9.58

If business use is 100%, you deduct the lower of the annual ceiling (see table on page 618) and the applicable mid-quarter rate multiplied by the unadjusted basis (cost less any first-year expensing deduction). If business use is less than 100%, multiply the lower amount by the business-use percentage to get the allowable deduction.

EXAMPLES

1. In November 1997, you buy a car for $23,000 that you use 100% for business. Applying the 5% rate for the fourth quarter from the table above, your deduction is $1,150 ($23,000 × 5%). This is less than the ceiling of $3,160.

   If the car had been bought in May 1997, the 25% rate for the second quarter would give a deduction of $5,750 ($23,000 × 25%). However, your deduction would be limited to the $3,160 ceiling.

2. In December 1997, you place in service an auto used solely for business. It costs $25,000. Applying the fourth-quarter rate of 5% from the mid-quarter convention table above gives a depreciation deduction of only $1,250. If you elect first-year expensing, the deduction is $3,160.

Capital improvements. A capital improvement to a business auto is depreciable under MACRS in the year the improvement is made. The MACRS deductions for the improvement and the auto are considered as a unit for purposes of applying the limits on the annual MACRS depreciation deduction.

Basis reduced by depreciation. The basis of a car is reduced by the full amount of depreciation that is allowable, whether or not a full deduction is actually claimed. For example, in 1997 you place in service a car costing $25,000, used 80% for business. Assuming the half-year convention applies, the unadjusted basis of the car is reduced by $3,160, the depreciation that would have been allowed in 1997 for 100% business use and not by the $2,528 depreciation deduction actually allowed (80% of business use × $3,160 maximum limit for 1997).

Converting a pleasure car to business use. The basis for depreciation is the lower of the market value of the car at the time of conversion and its adjusted basis, which is your original cost plus any substantial improvements and minus any deductible casualty losses or diesel fuel tax credit claimed for the car. In most cases, the value of the car will be lower than adjusted basis, and thus the value will be your depreciable basis. For a car converted to business use in 1997, the MACRS rate is applied to basis allocated to business travel. Unless you have mileage records for the entire year, you should base your business-use percentage on driving after the conversion. For example, in April 1997, you started to use your car for business and in the last nine months of the year you drove 10,000 miles, 8,000 of which were for business. This business percentage of 80% is multiplied by the fraction $\frac{9}{12}$ (months used for business divided by 12) to give you a business-use percentage for the year of 60% ($\frac{9}{12}$ of 80%).

43.6 Straight-Line Rate for Business Use of 50% or Less

You may not use accelerated MACRS if your business use of your car is 50% or less. Mandatory straight-line recovery rates for business use of 50% or less using the half-year or mid-quarter convention are shown below. These straight-line rates are also used if you elect straight-line recovery *(43.5)* instead of the regular MACRS method. Because of the half-year convention, the straight-line recovery period is extended from five to six years.

The annual depreciation ceilings of *43.4* apply.

Straight-line year—	Half-year convention rate—
1	10%
2	20
3	20
4	20
5	20
6	10

EXAMPLE

In April 1997, you place in service an automobile which cost $15,000. You used it 40% for business. The depreciable basis is $6,000 (40% of $15,000). The depreciation deduction in 1997 is $600 (10% of $6,000) if the half-year convention applies.

If the mid-quarter convention applies *(43.5)*, the depreciation deduction depends on the quarter the car was placed in service.

Straight-Line Mid-Quarter Convention*

Year	First Quarter	Second Quarter	Third Quarter	Fourth Quarter
			Placed in service in—	
1	17.50%	12.50%	7.50%	2.50%
2	20.00	20.00	20.00	20.00
3	20.00	20.00	20.00	20.00
4	20.00	20.00	20.00	20.00
5	20.00	20.00	20.00	20.00
6	2.50	7.50	12.50	17.50

The deduction may not exceed the annual deduction ceiling; see page 618.

EXAMPLE

In 1997, you place in service a car costing $15,000 used 40% for business. Assume the mid-quarter convention applies. Depending on the applicable quarter, the deduction is listed below, figured on a basis of $6,000 ($15,000 × 40%). The first-year ceiling at 40% business use is $1,264 ($3,160 × 40%). The ceiling does not apply because the mid-quarter rates provide a lower deduction.

Quarter	Deduction
1	$1,050 ($6,000 × 17.5%)
2	750 ($6,000 × 12.5%)
3	450 ($6,000 × 7.5%)
4	150 ($6,000 × 2.5%)

43.7 Depreciation After Recovery Period Ends

If your business use of a car during the recovery period is 100% and your deductions are limited by the annual ceilings *(43.4)*, any remaining basis that was not deducted because of the ceilings may be depreciated in the years after the end of the recovery period.

If the car was used less than 100% for business, any unrecovered basis may be deductible, but to determine unrecovered basis, original basis must be reduced by the depreciation that would have been allowed had the car been used 100% for business.

EXAMPLE

In 1991 you bought a car costing $28,600 which you used 100% for business every year from 1991 through 1996. Your depreciation deductions for the six-year recovery period were limited to a total of $14,235 by the annual ceilings. You deducted the ceiling amounts (*see* the table on page 618) of $2,660 in 1991, $4,300 in 1992, $2,550 in 1993, and $1,575 in each of 1994, 1995, and 1996, for a total of $14,235.

At the beginning of 1997, your unrecovered basis in the car is $14,365 (the original basis of $28,600 *minus* the $14,235 of depreciation deductions allowed from 1991 through 1996). If you continue to use the car 100% for business in 1997 and later years, you can deduct $1,575 in 1997 and also in later years until the $14,365 of unrecovered basis is used up.

If you had *not* used the car for business 100% of the time in all prior years, your unrecovered basis would still be $14,365. That is because for purposes of figuring unrecovered basis, you must reduce original basis by the depreciation that would have been allowed based on 100% business use. For years after 1996 in which business use is 100%, deductions of $1,575 are allowed until the unrecovered basis is used up. In years of partial business use, the deduction is limited to $1,575 multiplied by the business-use percentage.

43.8 Trade-in of Business Auto

No gain or loss is recognized on a trade-in of a business auto. Generally, the basis of the new auto the car that was traded in, add any cash paid on the trade-in, and reduce the total by the excess, if any, of (1) the total depreciation that would have been allowable if the old auto had been used solely for business or investment, over (2) the total of the depreciation actually allowed.

EXAMPLES

1. You traded in a car with an adjusted basis of $5,000 for a new car and, in addition, paid $8,000 cash for the new car. Both cars are used 100% for business. The unadjusted basis of the new car is $13,000 ($5,000 adjusted basis of the old car plus the $8,000 cash paid).

2. In 1995, you bought a car for $20,000 and used it 80% for business in 1995 and 1996. In January 1997, you traded it in for a new car and paid an additional $11,000. In 1995, you deducted MACRS depreciation of $2,448 (80% of $3,060 ceiling) and in 1996, $3,920 (80% of $4,900 ceiling). Your basis for purposes of figuring 1997 MACRS depreciation is $23,040, figured as follows:

Adjusted basis of old car	
Cost	$20,000
Less: depreciation for 1995 and 1996	6,368
Adjusted basis of old car	$13,632
Basis of new car	
Adjusted basis of old car	$13,632
Cash paid for new car	11,000
	$24,632
Less: depreciation adjustment (*see* below)	1,592
Basis of new car	$23,040
Depreciation adjustment for partial use:	
Depreciation if 100% business use	
1995	$3,060
1996	4,900
Total	$7,960
Less: actual depreciation for 1995 and 1996*	6,368
Adjustment	$1,592

Actual depreciation for 80% business use is $2,448 in 1995 and $3,900 in 1996.

43.9 Recapture of Deductions on Business Auto

If you use your car more than 50% for business in the year you place it in service, you may use MACRS accelerated rates; *see 43.5*. If business use drops to 50% or less in the second, third, fourth, fifth, or sixth year, earlier MACRS deductions must be recaptured and reported as ordinary income. In the year in which business use drops to 50% or less, you must recapture excess depreciation for all prior years. Excess depreciation is the difference between: (1) the MACRS deductions allowed in previous years, including the first-year expensing deduction, if any; and (2) the amount of depreciation that would have been allowed if you claimed straight-line depreciation based on a six-year recovery period. *See 43.6* for straight-line rates.

The recapture rules do not apply if you elected straight-line recovery instead of applying accelerated MACRS rates.

Recapture is computed on Form 4797, which must be attached to Form 1040. The 50% business-use test and recapture rule applies to trucks and airplanes in addition to cars, but see the list of exceptions for taxicabs and other specialty vehicles at *43.3*.

Any recaptured amount increases the basis of the property. To compute depreciation for the year in which business use drops to 50% or less and for later years within the six-year straight-line recovery period, you apply the straight-line rates shown at *43.6*.

EXAMPLE

On June 25, 1994, you bought a car for $11,000 which you used exclusively for business in 1994, 1995, and 1996. During 1997, you used it 40% for business and 60% for personal purposes. In 1997, as you did not meet the more-than-50% business-use test, excess depreciation of $2,332 is recaptured and reported on Form 4797:

Total MACRS depreciation claimed (1994–1996)		$7,832
Total straight-line depreciation allowable:		
1994—10% of $11,000	$1,100	
1995—20% of $11,000	2,200	
1996—20% of $11,000	2,200	5,500
Excess depreciation recaptured		$2,332

Your 1997 depreciation deduction is $880 ($11,000 × 20% straight-line rate in fourth year × 40% business use).

The amount of recaptured depreciation increases the adjusted basis for purposes of computing gain or loss on a disposition of the automobile.

43.10 Keeping Records of Business Use

Keep a log or diary or similar record of the business use of a car. Record the purpose of the business trips and mileage covered for business travel. In the record book, also note the odometer reading for the beginning and end of the taxable year. You need this data to prove business use. If you do not keep written records of business mileage and your return is examined, you will have to convince an IRS agent of your business mileage through oral testimony. Without written evidence, you may be unable to convince an IRS agent that you use the car for business travel or that you meet the business use tests for claiming MACRS. You may also be subject to general negligence penalties for claiming deductions that you cannot prove you incurred.

Mileage records are not required for vehicles that are unlikely to be used for personal purposes, such as delivery trucks with seating only for the driver.

Employees using company cars are not required to keep mileage records if (1) a written company policy allows them to use the car for commuting and no other personal driving other than personal errands while commuting home, or (2) a written company policy bars all personal driving except for minor stops, such as for lunch, between business travel. Owners, directors, and officers of the company generally do not qualify for exception (1).

43.11 Leased Business Autos: Deductions and Income

If you lease rather than purchase a car for business use, you may deduct the lease charges as a business expense deduction if you use the car exclusively for business. If you also use the car for personal driving, you may deduct only the lease payments allocated to business travel. Also keep a record of business use; *see 43.10.*

Added income. If in 1997 you lease a car for 30 days or more and the fair market value of the car at the beginning of the lease was over $15,800, you may have to report as income an amount based on an IRS table. This income rule indirectly limits deductions of lease payments to the amounts that would be deductible as depreciation if you had bought the car outright. The income amount is reduced where you leased the car for less than the entire year or business use is less than 100%.

The lease tables, which are in IRS Publication 463, show income amounts for each year or the lease. Publication 463 also has tables showing income amounts for cars leased before 1997.

Chapter 44

Sales of Business Property

The tax treatment of business assets depends on the type of asset sold.

Inventory items: Profits are taxable as ordinary income; losses are fully deductible. Sales of merchandise are reported on Schedule C if you are self-employed or Schedule F if you are a farmer.

Depreciable property, such as buildings, machinery, and equipment: If you sell at a gain, the gain is taxable as ordinary income to the extent depreciation is recaptured under *44.1*. Any remaining gain may be treated as capital gain or ordinary income, depending on the Section 1231 computation at *44.8*. Losses may be deductible as ordinary losses; *see 44.8*. Sales are reported on Form 4797. Depreciable business equipment subject to recapture is described as Section 1245 assets. Depreciable livestock are also Section 1245 assets. Depreciable realty is generally described as Section 1250 assets. In 1997, different recapture rules apply to depreciable realty because of a new law change; *see 44.2*.

Land: If used in your business, capital gain or ordinary income may be realized under the rules of Section 1231; *see 44.8*. If land owned by your business is held for investment, gain or loss is subject to capital gain treatment. Schedule D is used to report the sale of capital assets.

44.1 Recapture of Depreciation on Sale of Property

On Form 4797, you report gain or loss on depreciable property. Gain realized on the sale of depreciable *personal property* is treated as ordinary income to the extent the gain is attributed to depreciation deductions that reduced basis. In other words, the depreciation deductions are "recaptured" as ordinary income. If gain exceeds the amount of depreciation subject to recapture, the excess may be capital gain under Section 1231; *see 44.8.*

Gain on the sale of real estate placed in service before 1987 may be subject to depreciation recapture as discussed in *44.2.*

Gain subject to recapture for Section 1245 property is limited to the lower of (1) the amount realized less adjusted basis; and (2) recomputed basis less the adjusted basis. Recomputed basis is adjusted basis increased by depreciation deductions allowed or allowable. Generally, the depreciation deduction taken into account for each year is the amount allowed or allowable, whichever is greater. However, for purposes of figuring what portion of the gain is treated as ordinary income under the recapture rules (but not for purposes of figuring gain or loss), the depreciation taken into account for any year will be the amount actually "allowed" on your prior returns under a proper depreciation method, rather than the amount "allowable," if the allowed deduction is smaller and you can prove its amount.

The adjusted basis of personal property depreciable under ACRS, such as business equipment and machinery, is fixed as of the beginning of the year of disposition. However, property depreciated under MACRS is subject to the convention rules so that partial depreciation under the applicable convention is allowed in the year of sale; this year of sale depreciation reduces adjusted basis.

Where basis was reduced by an investment credit for property placed in service after 1982, the basis reduction is treated as a depreciation deduction when figuring recapture; *see* Form 4797.

EXAMPLE

In 1995, you placed in service equipment (five-year property) costing $10,000. In 1995 you deducted depreciation of $2,000 and in 1996 you deducted $3,200. In January 1997, you sell it for $6,000. The MACRS deduction allowed for 1997, the year of sale, is $960 (19.20% × $10,000 ÷ 2). The adjusted basis is $3,840 ($10,000 − $6,160 total depreciation). Recomputed basis is $10,000 ($3,840 + $6,160). The amount of recapture is the lower of—

1. $6,160, the recomputed basis of $10,000 *less* adjusted basis of $3,840; *and*

2. $2,160, the amount realized of $6,000 *less* adjusted basis of $3,840.

The lower amount of $2,160 is recaptured as ordinary income on Part III of Form 4797.

Dispositions other than sales. Exchanges of property *(6.1)* and involuntary conversions *(18.19)* may result in recapture of depreciation. For distributions which are not sales, exchanges, or involuntary conversions, the amount of recapture is all depreciation claimed, but not in excess of the difference between fair market value at disposition or original cost, whichever is less, and adjusted basis.

44.2 Recapture on Depreciable Realty

Sales of depreciable realty are subject to different tax rules in 1997. Sales before May 7, 1997, are subject to the following recapture rules depending on when the property was placed in service, its use, and the method of depreciation. These rules no longer apply to sales of depreciable realty after May 6, 1997.

Sales of depreciable realty before May 7, 1997

There is no recapture of straight-line MACRS depreciation *(42.13)* for buildings placed in service after 1986.

Recapture may apply to Section 1250 realty placed in service before 1987. Section 1250 property includes buildings and structural components, *except* for elevators and escalators or other tangible property used as an integral part of manufacturing, production, or extraction, or of furnishing transportation, electrical energy, water, gas, sewage disposal services, or communications. Property may initially be Section 1250 property and then, on a change of use, become Section 1245 property *(44.1)*. Such property may not be reconverted to Section 1250 property.

Depreciation claimed on realty during the years 1964 through 1969.   Depreciation claimed during this period is not recaptured.

Depreciation claimed after 1969 for realty placed in service before 1981.   For nonresidential realty, 100 percent of the depreciation claimed after 1969 in excess of straight-line recovery is subject to recapture, but not in excess of the actual gain.

For residential rental property, there is no recapture of excess depreciation (over straight-line) claimed after 1969 and before 1976. Real property is considered residential rental property if 80% or more of gross income is from dwelling units. One hundred percent of the excess depreciation claimed after 1975 is subject to recapture. Part III of Form 4797 is used to compute the amount of depreciation recapture that is to be reported as ordinary income.

Depreciation claimed on realty placed in service after 1980 and before 1987.   For real property placed in service after 1980 and before 1987 that was subject to ACRS, adjusted basis for computing gain or loss is the adjusted basis at the start of the year reduced by the ACRS deduction allowed for the number of months the realty is in service in the year of disposition; *see 42.16.*

If the prescribed accelerated method is used to recover the cost of *nonresidential* property, all gain on the disposition of the realty is recaptured as ordinary income to the extent of recovery allowances previously taken. Thus, nonresidential realty will be treated in the same way as personal property *(44.1)* for purposes of recapture if the accelerated recovery allowance was claimed. If the straight-line method was elected, there is no recapture; all gain is capital gain subject to the netting rules of Section 1231; *see 44.8.*

If accelerated cost recovery is used for a nonresidential building and straight-line depreciation is used for a substantial improvement to that building which you are allowed to depreciate separately *(42.16)*, all gain on a disposition of the entire building is treated as ordinary income to the extent of the accelerated cost recovery claimed; remaining gain is capital gain taxed under the rules for Section 1231 assets *(44.8).*

For *residential* real estate, gain is ordinary income to the extent the depreciation allowed under the prescribed accelerated method exceeds the recovery that would have been allowable if the straight-line method over the ACRS recovery period had been used. If the straight-line method was elected, there is no recapture. All gain is capital gain, subject to Section 1231 netting; *see 44.8.*

For *low-income rental housing,* the same rule as for residential realty applies except that recapture is phased out at the rate of one percentage point per month for property held at least 100 months, so that there is no recapture of cost recovery deductions for property held at least 200 months (16 years, 8 months).

Sales of depreciable realty after May 6, 1997

Sales of depreciable realty after May 6, 1997, are subject to new recapture rules. Gain attributed to prior depreciation deductions may qualify for a 25% maximum tax rate. The method of allocating gain to depreciation is explained in IRS instructions to Schedule D and Form 4797, which were not released when this book went to press. *See* the Supplement for further details.

44.3   Recapture of First-Year Expensing

On Form 4797, the first-year expensing deduction (Section 179) is treated as depreciation for purposes of recapture. When expensed property is sold or exchanged, gain is ordinary income to the extent of the first-year expense deduction plus ACRS or MACRS deductions, if any; *see 44.1.*

Expensing deductions are also subject to recapture if property placed in service after 1986 is not used more than 50% of the time for business in any year before the end of the recovery period. The amount recaptured is the excess of the first-year *expensing* deduction over the amount of depreciation that would have been claimed in prior years and in the recapture year without expensing.

Automobiles and other "listed property."   If the more-than-50% business-use test for a business automobile or other "listed property" such as certain computers *(see 42.10)* is not met in a year after the auto or other "listed property" is placed in service and before the end of the recovery period, any first-year expensing deduction is subject to recapture on Form 4797; *see* the Example at *43.9.*

Installment sale.   If you sell property on the installment basis, the first-year expensing deduction claimed for the property in a prior year is recaptured in the year of sale on Form 4797. An installment sale does not defer recapture of the first-year deduction.

44.4 Gifts and Inheritances of Depreciable Property

Gifts and charitable donations of depreciable property may be affected by the recapture rules. On the gift of depreciable property, the ordinary income potential of the depreciation carries over into the hands of the donee. When the donee later sells the property at a profit, he or she will realize ordinary income to the extent described in *44.1*. A person receiving a gift of low-income housing property includes in the holding period the period for which the donor held the property for purposes of applying the 200-month phaseout of recapture rule *(44.2)*.

On the donation of depreciable property, the amount of the contribution deduction is reduced by the amount which would be taxed as ordinary income had the donor sold the equipment at its fair market value.

On the death of a decedent, the transfer of depreciable property to an heir through inheritance is not a taxable event for recapture purposes. The ordinary income potential does not carry over to the heir because his or her basis is usually fixed as of the date of the decedent's death.

Important: A gift of depreciable property subject to a mortgage may be taxed to the extent that the liability exceeds the basis of the property; *see 14.6* and *31.16*.

44.5 Involuntary Conversions and Tax-Free Exchanges

Involuntary conversions.   Gain may be taxed as ordinary income in either of the following two cases: (1) You do not buy qualified replacement property; *or* (2) you buy a qualified replacement, but the cost of the replacement is less than the amount realized on the conversion; *see 18.23.* The amount taxable as ordinary income may not exceed the amount of gain that is normally taxed under involuntary conversion rules when the replacement cost is less than the amount realized on the conversion. Also, the amount of ordinary income is increased by the value of any nondepreciable property which is bought as qualified replacement property, such as the purchase of 80% or more of stock in a company that owns property similar to the converted property.

Tax–free exchanges.   Ordinary income generally is not realized on a tax-free exchange or trade-in (unless some gain is taxed because the exchange is accompanied by "boot" *(6.3)* such as money). The ordinary income potential is assumed in the basis of the new property.

Distributions by a partnership to a partner.   A distribution of depreciable property by a partnership to a partner does not result in ordinary income to the distributee at the time of the distribution. But the partner assumes the ordinary income potential of the depreciation deduction taken by the partnership on the property. When he or she later disposes of the property, ordinary income may be realized.

44.6 Installment Sale of Depreciable Property

All recaptured ordinary income is fully taxable in the year of sale, without regard to the time of payment. This rule does not apply to installment sales made after June 6, 1984, under a contract binding on March 22, 1984, and all times thereafter.

If you are reporting on an installment basis a profitable sale of depreciable property made before June 7, 1984, "recaptured" ordinary income is reported before any of the capital gain is reported. You do not allocate the profit element of each installment payment between ordinary income and capital gain. As installments are received, you report all of the ordinary income until that amount is exhausted.

Recapture is figured on Form 4797.

44.7 Sale of a Proprietorship

The sale of a sole proprietorship is not considered as the sale of a business unit but as sales of individual business assets. Each sale is reported separately on your tax return.

A purchase of a business involves the purchase of various individual business assets of the business. To force buyers and sellers to follow the same allocation rules, current law requires both the buyer and the seller to allocate the purchase price of a business among the transferred assets using a residual method formula. Allocations are based on the proportion of sales price to an asset's fair market value and they are made in a specific order set out on Form 8594.

44.8 Property Used in a Business (Section 1231 Assets)

Form 4797 is used to report the sale or exchange of Section 1231 assets. The following properties used in a business are considered "Section 1231 assets":

- Depreciable assets such as buildings, machinery, and other equipment held more than one year. Depreciable rental property fits in this category if held more than one year.
- Land (including growing crops and water rights underlying farmland) held more than one year.
- Timber, coal, or domestic iron ore subject to special capital gain treatment.
- Leaseholds held more than one year.
- An unharvested crop on farmlands, if the crop and land are sold, exchanged, or involuntarily converted at the same time and to the same person and the land has been held more than one year. Such property is not included here if you retain an option to reacquire the land.
- Cattle and horses held for draft, breeding, dairy, or sporting purposes for at least 24 months.
- Livestock (other than cattle and horses) held for draft, breeding, dairy, or sporting purposes for at least 12 months. Poultry is *not* treated as livestock for purposes of Section 1231.

Section 1231 netting. On Form 4797, you combine all losses and gains, except gains allocated to depreciation recapture, from:

- Sale of Section 1231 assets (from the list at the beginning of this section).
- The involuntary conversion of Section 1231 assets and capital assets held for more than one year for business or investment purposes. You include casualty and theft losses incurred on business or investment property held for more than one year. However, there is an exception if losses exceed gains from casualties or thefts in one taxable year.

Involuntary conversions of capital assets held for personal purposes are not subject to a Section 1231 computation but are subject to a separate computation; see 18.25.

Result of netting. A net gain on Section 1231 assets from Form 4797 is entered on Schedule D as a long-term capital gain unless the recapture rule discussed below for net ordinary losses applies. A net loss on Section 1231 assets is combined on Form 4797 with ordinary income from depreciation recapture (44.1) and with ordinary gains and losses from the sale of business property that does not qualify for Section 1231 netting.

Recapture of net ordinary losses. Net Section 1231 gain is not treated as capital gain but as ordinary income to the extent of net Section 1231 losses realized in the five most recent prior taxable years. Losses are recaptured in chronological order on Form 4797. Losses that have already been "recaptured" under this rule in prior years are not taken into account.

Installment sale. Gain realized on the installment sale of business or income-producing property held for more than a year may be capital gain one year and ordinary income another year. Actual treatment in each year depends on the net result of all sales, including installment payments received in that year; also see 44.6.

Caution

Capital Gain or Ordinary Loss
Profitable sales and involuntary conversions of Section 1231 assets are generally taxed as capital gain, except for profits on equipment and real estate allocated to recaptured depreciation (44.1), and losses are deducted as ordinary loss. However, the exact tax result depends on the net profit and loss realized for all sales of such property made during the tax year. Under the netting rules explained on the left, the net result of these sales determines the tax treatment of each individual sale. In making the computation on Form 4797, you must also consider losses and gains from casualty, theft, and other involuntary conversions involving business and investment property held more than one year. Follow the Form 4797 instructions.

EXAMPLES

1. You realize these 1997 gains and losses:

	Gain	Loss
Gain on sale of rental property held two years	$5,000	
Loss on sale of business assets held four years		$3,000
	$5,000	$3,000
Net gain subject to capital gain rates	$2,000	

   As your gain exceeded the loss, each sale is treated as a sale of a capital asset held for a long-term period. The net gain is included in Schedule D as a long-term gain. The effect of this treatment is to give you a $2,000 long-term capital gain unless you realized a net Section 1231 loss in 1992, 1993, 1994, 1995, or 1996.

2. Assume the same facts as above, but your gain on the sale of rental property was $2,500. Since the gain does not exceed the loss and a net loss of $500 was realized, all of the transactions are treated as dispositions of noncapital assets. The net result is an ordinary loss of $500.

Losses exceed gains from casualties or thefts.   You must compute the net financial result from all involuntary conversions arising from fire, storm, or other casualty or theft of assets used in your business and capital assets held for business or income-producing purposes and held more than one year. The purpose of the computation is to determine whether these involuntary conversions enter into the above Section 1231 computation. If the net result is a gain, all of the assets enter into the Section 1231 computation. If the net result is a loss, then these assets do not enter into the computation; the losses are deducted separately as casualty losses, and the gains reported separately as ordinary income. If you incur only losses, the losses similarly do not enter into the Section 1231 computation.

> ### EXAMPLE
> You suffer an uninsured fire loss of $2,000 on business equipment and gain of $1,000 on other insured investment property damaged by a storm. All of the property was held more than one year. Because loss exceeds gain, neither transaction enters into a Section 1231 computation. The gain is reported as ordinary income and the loss is deducted as an ordinary loss. The effect is a net $1,000 loss deduction. If the figures were reversed, that is, if the gain were $2,000 and the loss $1,000, both assets would enter into the Section 1231 computation. If only the fire loss occurred, the loss would be treated as a casualty loss and would not enter into the Section 1231 computation.

44.9 Sale of Property Used for Business and Personal Purposes

One sale will be reported as two separate sales for tax purposes when you sell a car or any other equipment used for business and personal purposes, or in some cases (*see* IRS Form 2119) where a sold residence was used partly as a residence and partly as a place of business or to produce rent income.

You allocate the sales price and the basis of the property between the business portion and the personal portion. The allocation is based on use. For example, with a car, the allocation is based on mileage used in business and personal driving.

> ### EXAMPLE
> Two partners bought an airplane for about $54,000. They used approximately 75% of its flying time for personal flights and 25% for business flights. After using the plane for eight years, they sold it for about $35,000. Depreciation taken on the business part of the plane amounted to $13,000. The partners figured they incurred a loss of $6,000 on the sale. The IRS, allocating the proceeds and basis between business and personal use, claimed they realized a profit of $8,250 on the business part of the plane and a nondeductible loss of $14,250 on the personal part. The allocation was as follows:
>
> | | Partners' claim | IRS Position Business (25%) | Personal (75%) |
> |---|---|---|---|
> | Original cost | $54,000 | $13,500 | $40,500 |
> | Depreciation | 13,000 | 13,000 | |
> | Adjusted basis | 41,000 | 500 | 40,500 |
> | Selling price | 35,000 | 8,750 | 26,250 |
> | Gain (Nondeductible loss) | ($6,000) | $8,250 | ($14,250) |
>
> The partners argued that the IRS could not split the sale into two separate sales. They sold only one airplane and therefore there was only one sale. A federal district court and appeals court disagreed and held that the IRS method of allocation is practical and fair.

44.10 Should You Trade in Business Equipment?

The purchase of new business equipment is often partially financed by trading in old equipment. For tax purposes, a trade-in may not be a good decision. If the market value of the equipment is below its adjusted basis, it may be preferable to sell the equipment to realize an immediate deductible loss. You may not deduct a loss on a trade-in. However, if you do trade, the potential deduction reflected in the cost basis of the old equipment is not forfeited. The undepreciated basis of the old property becomes part of the basis of the new property and may be depreciated. Therefore, in deciding whether to trade or sell where a loss may be realized, determine whether you will get a greater tax reduction by taking an immediate loss on a sale or by claiming larger depreciation deductions.

If the fair market value of the old equipment exceeds its adjusted basis, you have a potential gain. To defer tax on this gain, you may want to trade the equipment in for new equipment. Your decision to sell or trade will generally be based on a comparison between (1) tax imposed on an immediate sale and larger depreciation deductions taken on the cost basis of the new property, and (2) the tax consequences of a trade-in in which the tax is deferred but reduced depreciation deductions are taken on a lower cost basis of the property. In making this comparison, you will have to estimate your future income and tax rates. Also pay attention to the possibility that gain on a sale may be taxed as ordinary income under the depreciation recapture rules; *see 44.1.*

The tax consequences of a trade-in may not be avoided by first selling the used property to the dealer who sells you the new property. The IRS will disregard the sale made to the same dealer from whom you purchase the new equipment. The two transactions will be treated as one trade-in.

When you trade in a car used partly for business and partly for pleasure, treat the deal as if you had exchanged and received two different types of assets: a personal asset and a business asset. Allocate part of the costs of the old and new car to your business use and part to your personal use. Figure the results on each part. Trade-in rules for a business auto are discussed at *43.8.*

44.11 Corporate Liquidation

Liquidation of a corporation and distribution of its assets for your stock is generally subject to capital gain or loss treatment. For example, on a corporate liquidation, you receive property worth $10,000 from the corporation. Assume the basis of your shares, which you have held long term, is $6,000. You have realized a long-term gain of $4,000.

If you incur legal expenses in pressing payment of a claim, you treat the fee as a capital expense, according to the IRS. The Tax Court and an appeals court hold that the fee is deductible as an expense incurred to earn income; the deduction is subject to the 2% adjusted gross income (AGI) floor discussed at *19.1.*

If you recover a judgment against the liquidator of a corporation for misuse of corporate funds, the judgment is considered part of the amount you received on liquidation and gives you capital gain, not ordinary income.

If you paid a corporate debt after liquidation, the payment reduces the gain realized on the corporate liquidation in the earlier year; thus, in effect, it is a capital loss.

If the corporation distributes liquidating payments over a period of years, gain is not reported until the distributions exceed the adjusted basis of your stock.

Chapter 45

Figuring Self-Employment Tax

Self-employment tax provides funds for Social Security and Medicare benefits. The self-employment tax is calculated on Schedule SE. You are required to prepare Schedule SE if you have self-employment earnings of $400 or more in 1997, but you will not incur the tax unless your self-employment earnings exceed $433.13. The tax is added to you income tax liability. When preparing your estimated tax liability, you must also include an estimate of self-employment tax; *see* Chapter 27.

On Schedule SE, self-employment income is reduced by a deduction reflected in the decimal of .9235 listed on the form. You also deduct 50% of the self-employment tax on Line 26 of Form 1040.

For 1997, the self-employment tax of 15.3% consists of the following two rates: 12.4% for Social Security and 2.9% for Medicare. After multiplying the net earnings by .9235, the 15.3% rate applies to a taxable earnings base of $65,400 or less; the 2.9% rate applies to all taxable earnings exceeding $65,400. For example, if net earnings after the .9235 adjustment are $65,400, the self-employment tax is $10,006.20 (65,400 × 15.3%). If the earnings (after the .9235 adjustment) are $100,000, the self-employment tax would be $11,009.60: $10,006.20 on the first $65,400 of taxable self-employment earnings at 15.3%, *plus* $1,003.40 on the excess $34,600 at 2.9%.

You are required to pay self-employment tax on self-employment income even after you retire and receive Social Security benefits.

45.1 What Is Self-Employment Income?

On Schedule SE, your self-employment income is generally your net profit from your business or profession whether you participate in its activities full or part time. Net profit is generally the amount shown on Line 31 of Schedule C (or Line 3 of Schedule C-EZ) if you are a sole proprietor. If you are a partner, net earnings subject to self-employment tax are taken from Line 15a, Schedule K-1 of Form 1065. If you are a farmer, net farm profit is shown on Line 36, Schedule F.

If you have more than one self-employed operation, your net profit from all the operations is combined. A loss in one self-employed business will reduce the income from another business. You file separate Schedules C for each operation and one Schedule SE showing the combined income (less losses, if any). Contributions to your *own* Keogh plan or SEP retirement account do not reduce the net earnings subject to self-employment tax.

Married couples. Where you and your spouse *each* have self-employment income, each spouse must figure separate self-employment income on a separate schedule. Each pays the tax on the separate self-employment income. Both schedules are attached to the joint return.

If you live in a community property state, business income is not treated as community property for self-employment tax purposes. The spouse who is actually carrying on the business is subject to self-employment tax on the earnings.

Exceptions. The following types of income or items are *not* included as self-employment income on Schedule SE:

1. Rent from real estate is not self-employment income, *unless* it is the business income of a real estate dealer or income in a business where substantial services are rendered to the occupant, as in the leasing of—

- Rooms in a hotel or in a boardinghouse.
- Apartments, but only if extra services for the occupants' convenience, such as maid service or changing linens, are provided.
- Cabins or cabanas in tourist camps where you provide maid services, linens, utensils, and swimming, boating, fishing, and other facilities, for which you do not charge separately.
- Farmland in which the landlord materially participates in the actual production of the farm or in the management of production. For purposes of "material participation," the activities of a landlord's agent are not counted, only the landlord's actual participation.

2. Dividends and interest are not self-employment income. However, dividends earned by a dealer in securities and interest on accounts receivable are treated as self-employment income. A dealer is one who buys stock as inventory to sell to customers.

3. Capital gains are not self-employment income. Similarly, not treated as self-employment income are gains from the sale of property which is not inventory or held for sale to customers in the ordinary course of business. There is an exception for dealers in commodities and options; *see* the chart in *45.6*.

Net operating loss deduction. A loss carryover from past years does not reduce business income for self-employment tax purposes. Similarly, the personal exemption may not be used to reduce self-employment income.

Statutory employees. Wages of a statutory employee, such as a full-time life insurance salesperson *(40.6)*, are not subject to self-employment tax, as Social Security and Medicare tax have been withheld.

Farmers. Cash or a payment in kind under the "Payment-in-Kind" program is considered earned income subject to self-employment tax.

Business interruption proceeds. The IRS and the Tax Court disagree over whether business interruption insurance proceeds must be reported as earnings subject to self-employment tax. The Tax Court held that insurance payments made to a grocer as compensation for lost earnings due to a fire were not subject to self-employment tax because the payment was not for actual services. The IRS refuses to follow the decision, holding that such payments represented income that would have been earned had business operations not been interrupted.

45.2 Partners Pay Self-Employment Tax

A general partner includes his or her share of partnership income or loss in net earnings from self-employment, including guaranteed payments. If your personal tax year is different from the partnership's tax year, you include your share of partnership income or loss for the partnership tax year ending within 1997.

Filing Tip

Real Estate Investor
The owner of one office building who holds it for investment (rather than for sale in the ordinary course of business) is not a real estate dealer, but a real estate investor. The rent income is not self-employment income. Furnishing heat, light, water, and trash and garbage collection to tenants does not produce self-employment income.

A limited partner is not subject to self-employment tax on his or her share of partnership income except for guaranteed payments for services performed, which are subject to the tax. However, the IRS proposed regulations that would have imposed self-employment tax on a limited partner who (1) participates in the business more than 500 hours during the tax year, (2) has personal liability for partnership debts, or, (3) has authority to contract on the partnership's behalf. Furthermore, limited partners who provide any services in a service business, such as law, accounting, medicine, or consulting, would always be subject to self-employment tax on their distributive share of partnership income.

Critics argued that the proposal was an unauthorized tax increase on limited partners who were not previously subject to self-employment tax and that the proposal wrongly assumed that all income from a service partnership is attributable to that partner's personal services.

The IRS has been prohibited by the 1997 Tax Act from imposing this rule until July 1, 1998. It is possible that the IRS may modify the proposed regulation before that date, or that Congress may enact legislation on this issue.

If a general partner dies within the partnership's tax year, self-employment income includes his or her distributive share of the income earned by the partnership through the end of the month in which the death occurs. This is true even though his or her heirs or estate succeeds to the partnership rights. For this purpose, partnership income for the year is considered to be earned ratably each month.

Partnership's retirement payments.   Retirement payments you receive from your partnership are *not* subject to self-employment tax if the following conditions are met:

1. The payments are made under a qualified written plan providing for periodic payments on retirement of partners with payments to continue until death.

2. You rendered no services in any business conducted by the partnership during the tax year of the partnership ending within or with your tax year.

3. By the end of the partnership's tax year, your share in the partnership's capital has been paid to you in full, and there is no obligation from the other partners to you other than with respect to the retirement payments under the plan.

LLCs. The IRS planned to impose self-employment tax on a member of an LLC under the proposed regulations for limited partners discussed above. The IRS has been prevented by law from imposing such rules until July 1, 1998.

Worksheet—Short Schedule SE

Section A—Short Schedule SE. Caution: *Read above to see if you can use Short Schedule SE.*

1	Net farm profit or (loss) from Schedule F, line 36, and farm partnerships, Schedule K-1 (Form 1065), line 15a	**1**	
2	Net profit or (loss) from Schedule C, line 31; Schedule C-EZ, line 3; and Schedule K-1 (Form 1065), line 15a (other than farming). Ministers and members of religious orders see page SE-1 for amounts to report on this line. See page SE-2 for other income to report	**2**	100,000 —
3	Combine lines 1 and 2	**3**	100,000 —
4	**Net earnings from self-employment.** Multiply line 3 by 92.35% (.9235). If less than $400, **do not** file this schedule; you do not owe self-employment tax . . . . ▶	**4**	92,350 —
5	**Self-employment tax.** If the amount on line 4 is: • $65,400 or less, multiply line 4 by 15.3% (.153). Enter the result here and on **Form 1040, line 47** • More than $65,400 multiply line 4 by 2.9% (.029). Then, add $8,109.60 to the result. Enter the total here and on **Form 1040, line 47**	**5**	10,787 75
6	**Deduction for one-half of self-employment tax.** Multiply line 5 by 50% (.5). Enter the result here and on **Form 1040, line 26**	**6**	5393 88

45.3 Schedule SE

Schedule SE has an introductory "road map" designed to lead you to either the short or long version of Schedule SE. Once you pass through the road map, the preparation of either the short or long schedule is not difficult. In both versions, you multiply your net earnings by a decimal of .9235. Only 92.35% of net earnings is subject to the self-employment tax. The .9235 adjustment is the equivalent of a 7.65% reduction to net earnings, which along with the income tax deduction for 50% of self-employment tax on Line 26 of Form 1040, attempts to place self-employed individuals on the same level as employees subject to FICA taxes.

The .9235 adjustment is made on Line 4 of either the short or long Schedule SE. For example, if your net profit reported on Line 31 of Schedule C is $100,000, the amount subject to self-employment tax after the adjustment is $92,350; *see* the filled-in short Schedule SE worksheet below, and *see* 45.4 for the long Schedule SE.

45.4 How Wages Affect Self-Employment Tax

If you have both a net profit from self-employment and also wage and/or tip income subject to FICA taxes (Social Security and Medicare), the amount of such FICA earnings will affect the self-employment tax rate applied to your net profit.

If your 1997 FICA wages or tips were $65,400 or over, your net self-employment profit is subject only to the 2.9% Medicare rate.

If your 1997 FICA wages or tips were under the $65,400 limit for the 12.4% Social Security rate, your net self-employment earnings on Line 6 of long Schedule SE (after the .9235 adjustment) are subject to the 12.4% rate to the extent of the excess of $65,400 over your FICA wages or

Worksheet—Long Schedule SE

Section B—Long Schedule SE

Part I Self-Employment Tax

Note: If your only income subject to self-employment tax is **church employee income,** skip lines 1 through 4b. Enter -0- on line 4c and go to line 5a. Income from services you performed as a minister or a member of a religious order **is not** church employee income. See page SE-1.

A If you are a minister, member of a religious order, or Christian Science practitioner **and** you filed Form 4361, but you had $400 or more of **other** net earnings from self-employment, check here and continue with Part I . . . . . ▶ ☐

1	Net farm profit or (loss) from Schedule F, line 36, and farm partnerships, Schedule K-1 (Form 1065), line 15a. Note: Skip this line if you use the farm optional method. See page SE-3	1	
2	Net profit or (loss) from Schedule C, line 31; Schedule C-EZ, line 3; and Schedule K-1 (Form 1065), line 15a (other than farming). Ministers and members of religious orders see page SE-1 for amounts to report on this line. See page SE-2 for other income to report. Note: Skip this line if you use the nonfarm optional method. See page SE-3	2	35,000 —
3	Combine lines 1 and 2	3	35,000 —
4a	If line 3 is more than zero, multiply line 3 by 92.35% (.9235). Otherwise enter amount from line 3	4a	32,322 50
b	If you elected one or both of the optional methods, enter the total of lines 15 and 17 here	4b	
c	Combine lines 4a and 4b. If less than $400, **do not** file this schedule; you do not owe self-employment tax. **Exception.** If less than $400 and you had **church employee income,** enter -0- and continue ▶	4c	32,322 50
5a	Enter your **church employee income** from Form W-2. Caution: See page SE-1 for definition of church employee income	5a	
b	Multiply line 5a by 92.35% (.9235). If less than $100, enter -0-	5b	0
6	**Net earnings from self-employment.** Add lines 4c and 5b	6	32,322 50
7	Maximum amount of combined wages and self-employment earnings subject to social security tax or the 6.2% portion of the 7.65% railroad retirement (tier 1) tax for 1997	7	65,400 00
8a	Total social security wages and tips (total of boxes 3 and 7 on Form(s) W-2) and railroad retirement (tier 1) compensation . . . . 8a 30,000 —		
b	Unreported tips subject to social security tax (from Form 4137, line 9) 8b		
c	Add lines 8a and 8b	8c	30,000 —
9	Subtract line 8c from line 7. If zero or less, enter -0- here and on line 10 and go to line 11 ▶	9	32,700 —
10	Multiply the **smaller** of line 6 or line 9 by 12.4% (.124)	10	4,007 99
11	Multiply line 6 by 2.9% (.029)	11	937 35
12	**Self-employment tax.** Add lines 10 and 11. Enter here and on **Form 1040, line 47**	12	4,945 34
13	**Deduction for one-half of self-employment tax.** Multiply line 12 by 50% (.5). Enter the result here and on **Form 1040, line 26** . . . 13	2,472 67	

tips. The 2.9% Medicare rate applies to the entire amount of net self-employment earnings. *See* the following Example and the filled-in long Schedule SE worksheet on the previous page.

EXAMPLE

You earn a salary of $30,000 and have a net profit from self-employment of $35,000. As shown on the long Schedule SE worksheet below, the 12.4% rate applies to the smaller of Line 6 and Line 9. Here, the smaller amount is the Line 6 net earnings (after .9235 adjustment)of $32,322.50.

12.4% × $32,322.50	$4,007.99
2.9% × $32,322.50	
	+937.35
	4,945.34

45.5 Optional Method If 1997 Was a Low-Income or Loss Year

The law provides a small increased tax base for Social Security coverage if you have a low net profit or loss.

Electing the optional method may also increase earned income for dependent care and earned income credit purposes.

The increased tax base is called the optional method. One optional method is for nonfarm self-employment and another for farm income. You may not use the optional method to report an amount less than your actual net earnings from self-employment.

Nonfarm method. You may use the nonfarm optional method for 1997 if you meet all the following tests:

Test 1. Your net earnings (profit) from nonfarm self-employment on Line 31 of Schedule C, Line 3 of Schedule C-EZ, or Line 15a of Schedule K-1 (Form 1065) are less than $1,733 (.9235 × $1,733 = $1,600 maximum income subject to the optional method).

Test 2. Your net earnings from nonfarm self-employment are less than 72.189% of the total gross income you made from nonfarm self-employment.

Test 3. You had net earnings from self-employment of $400 or more in at least two of the following years: 1994, 1995, and 1996.

Test 4. You have not previously used this method for more than four years. There is a five-year lifetime limit for use of the nonfarm optional base. The years do not have to be consecutive.

Income of $2,400 or less. If your gross income from all nonfarm trades or businesses is $2,400 or less and you meet the four tests just discussed, you may report two-thirds of the gross income from your nonfarm business as net earnings from self-employment.

EXAMPLES

1. Brown had net earnings from self-employment of $800 in 1995 and $900 in 1996 and so meets Test 3 above. In 1997, she has gross nonfarm self-employment income of $2,100 and net nonfarm self-employment earnings of $1,200. Net earnings from self-employment of $1,200 are less than $1,733 (Test 1 above) and also less than $1,516 (under Test 2, 72.189% of $2,100 gross income is $1,516). Brown may either figure self-employment tax on actual net earnings of $1,200 or on $1,400 ($\frac{2}{3}$ of $2,100).

2. Same facts as in Example 1 but Brown has a net self-employment loss of $700. She may elect to report $1,400 ($\frac{2}{3}$ of $2,100) as net earnings under the optional method.

3. Smith had gross nonfarm income of $1,000 and net nonfarm self-employment earnings of $800. He may not use the optional method because net earnings of $800 are not less than $722 (72.189% of gross income of $1,000).

4. Jones has gross nonfarm income of $525 and net nonfarm self-employment earnings of $175. Jones may not use the optional method because two-thirds of his gross income, or $350, is less than the minimum income of $400 required to be subject to the tax.

Income over $2,400. If your gross income from all nonfarm businesses exceeds $2,400, and you meet the four tests just discussed, you may report $1,600 as your net earnings from nonfarm self-employment.

EXAMPLES

1. White had net earnings from self-employment in 1994 of $8,500; in 1995, $10,500; and in 1996, $9,500. His 1997 gross nonfarm income is $12,000 and net nonfarm earnings are $1,200. Because his net earnings of $1,200 from self-employment are less than $1,733 and also less than 72.189% of his gross income, he may report either $1,600 or $1,200 as his net earnings from self-employment.

2. Same facts as in Example 1, but assume net earnings for 1997 are $1,800. White may not use the optional method because his actual net earnings of $1,800 from self-employment are not less than $1,733. He reports $1,800 as net earnings using the regular method.

3. Assume White has a net loss of $700 in 1997. He may use the optional method to report $1,600 of net earnings from self-employment.

Optional farm method.   If you have farming income (other than as a limited partner) you may use the farm optional method to figure your net earnings from farm self-employment.

The nonfarm optional method does *not* have a two-year self-employment test (Test 3) or a requirement that actual net earnings be less than 72.189% of gross income (Test 2). There is also no limitation on the number of years you may use this method (Test 4).

If your gross income from farming is $2,400 or less, you may report two-thirds of your gross income as your net earnings from farm self-employment. If your gross income from farming exceeds $2,400 and your net earnings from farm self-employment are less than $1,733, you may report $1,600 as your net earnings from farm self-employment. If your gross income from farming exceeds $2,400 and your net earnings from farm self-employment are $1,733 or more, you may not use the optional method.

Farm income includes income from cultivating the soil or harvesting any agricultural commodities. It also includes income from the operation of livestock, dairy, poultry, bee, fish, fruit or truck farm, or plantation, ranch, nursery, range, orchard, or oyster bed, as well as income in the form of crop shares if you materially participate in production or management of production.

45.6   Self-Employment Tax Rules for Certain Positions

If you are—	Tax rule—
Babysitter	Where you perform services in your own home and determine the nature and manner of the services to be performed, you are considered to have self-employment income. However, where services are performed in the parent's home according to instructions by the parents, you are an employee of the parents and do not have self-employment earnings.
Clergy	If you are an ordained minister, priest, or rabbi (other than a member of a religious order who has taken a vow of poverty), you are subject to self-employment tax, unless you elect not to be covered on the grounds of conscientious or religious objection to Social Security benefits. Before 1968, a minister had to elect Social Security coverage.
	An application for exemption from Social Security coverage must be filed on or before the due date of your income tax return for the second taxable year for which you have net earnings from services as a minister of $400 or more (Form 4361).
	An exemption, once granted, is generally irrevocable. However, a law did allow revocation of the exemption for 1977 or 1978. An exemption will not be granted to a minister who elected coverage under prior law.
	Self-employment tax does not apply to the rental value of any parsonage or parsonage allowance provided after retirement. Other retirement benefits from a church plan are also exempted. The exemptions are allowed retroactively for years beginning on, before, or after December 31, 1994, so a refund opportunity is available if self-employment tax was paid on such amounts in a prior year not closed by the statute of limitations.
Consultant	The IRS generally takes the position that income earned by a consultant is subject to self-employment tax. The IRS has also held that a retired executive hired as a consultant by his former firm received self-employment income, even though he was subject to an agreement prohibiting him from giving advice to competing companies. According to the IRS, consulting for one firm is a business; it makes no difference that you act as a consultant only with your former company. The IRS has also imposed self-employment tax on consulting fees, although no services were performed for them. The courts have generally approved the IRS position.

If you are—	Tax rule—
Dealer in commodities and options	Registered options dealers and commodities dealers are subject to self-employment tax on net gains from trading in Section 1256 contracts, which include regulated futures contracts, foreign currency contracts, dealer equity options, and non-equity options. Self-employment tax also applies to net gains from trading property related to such contracts, like stock used to hedge options.
Director	You are taxed as a self-employed person if you are not an employee of the company. Fees for attendance at meetings are self-employment income. If the fees are not received until after the year you provide the services, you treat the fees as self-employment earnings in the year they are received.
Employee of foreign government or international organization	If you are a U.S. citizen and you work in the United States for a foreign government or its wholly owned instrumentality, or an international organization, you pay self-employment tax if Social Security and Medicare taxes are not withheld from your pay.
Executor or guardian	If you are a professional fiduciary, you will always be treated as having self-employment income, regardless of the assets held by the estate. But if you serve as a nonprofessional executor or administrator for the estate of a deceased friend or relative, you will not be treated as having self-employment income unless all of the following tests are met: (1) the estate includes a business; (2) you actively participate in the operation of the business; and (3) all or part of your fee is related to your operation of the business. The IRS applied similar business tests to deny self-employment treatment for a guardian who was appointed by a court to care for a disabled cousin. The guardian negotiated sales of the cousin's property and invested the proceeds, but these activities were not extensive enough to be considered management of a business.
Lecturer	You are not taxed as a self-employed person if you give only occasional lectures. If, however, you seek lecture engagements and get them with reasonable regularity, your lecture fees are treated as self-employment income.
Nonresident alien	You do not pay Social Security tax on your self-employment income derived from a trade, business, or profession. This is so even though you pay income tax. Your exemption from self-employment tax is not influenced by the fact that your business in the United States is carried on by an agent, employee, or partnership of which you are a member. However, if you live in Puerto Rico, the Virgin Islands, American Samoa, or Guam, you are not considered a nonresident alien and are subject to self-employment tax.
Nurse	If you are a registered nurse or licensed practical nurse who is hired directly by clients for private nursing services, you are considered self-employed. You are an employee if hired directly by a hospital or a private physician and work for a salary following a strict routine during fixed hours, or if you provide primarily domestic services in the home of a client. Where registered or licensed practical nurses are assigned nursing jobs by an agency which pays them, the IRS, in several rulings, has treated such nurses as employees of the agency. Nurses' aides, domestics, and other unlicensed individuals who classify themselves as practical nurses are treated by the IRS as employees, regardless of whether they work for a medical institution, a private physician, or a private household.
Real estate agent or door-to-door salesperson	Licensed real estate agents are considered self-employed if they have a contract specifying that they are not to be treated as employees and if substantially all of their pay is related to sales rather than number of hours worked. The same rule also applies to door-to-door salespeople with similar contracts who work on a commission basis selling products in homes or other non-retail establishments.
Technical service contractor	Consulting engineers and computer technicians who receive assignments from technical service agencies are generally treated as employees and do not pay self-employment tax. The IRS distinguishes between (1) technicians who in three-party arrangements are assigned clients by a technical services agency, and (2) those who directly enter into contracts with clients. Employee status covers only technicians in Group 1. Technical specialists who contract directly with clients may be classified as independent contractors by showing that they have been consistently treated as independent contractors by the client, and that other workers in similar positions have also been treated as independent contractors. Thus, they may treat their income as self-employment income. Firms that are treated as employers of technical specialists are responsible for withholding and payroll taxes.
Writer	Royalties from writing books are self-employment income to a writer. Royalties on books by a professor employed by a university may also be self-employment income despite employment as a professor.

Part 7

Filing Your Return and What Happens After You File

This part is designed to help you —

• Organize your tax data. Whether you plan to prepare your own tax return or have someone else prepare it, you must first gather and organize your tax information. In Chapter 46, you will find record-keeping guides for income items and expense deductions.

• Understand how the IRS reviews your return and initiates audit procedures, including information on how the IRS matches your return with reports of distributions to you from banks, corporations, and government agencies.

• Avoid penalties for underpaying your tax. You may avoid penalties for positions taken on your tax return by making certain disclosures, obtaining authoritative support for your position, or showing reasonable cause for a tax underpayment; see 47.5.

• Understand the factors that might lead to an audit. Your chances of being selected for an examination depend on your income, profession, deductions claimed, and even where you live; see 48.1.

• Prepare for an audit. Advance preparations and knowing your rights can help support your position; see 48.3.

• Dispute adverse IRS determinations. You can appeal within the IRS and go to court if you disagree with the IRS audit results. If you win, you may receive attorneys' fees and other expenses; see 48.7 and 48.8.

• File a timely refund claim if you have overpaid your tax; see 49.1.

Chapter 46

Filing Your Return

Whether you prepare your return yourself or retain a professional preparer, you must first collect and organize your tax records. You cannot prepare your return unless you get your personal tax data in order. Good records will help you figure your income and deductions and will serve as a written record to present to the IRS in the event that you are audited.

Review income statements from banks, employers, brokers, and governmental agencies on their respective Form 1099s. Check for miscalculations, additions, and omissions.

Survey Chapters 12–20 of *Your Income Tax 1998* for deductions you can claim directly from gross income and itemized deductions you can claim on Schedule A of Form 1040.

Reviewing your tax return from prior years will help refresh your memory as to how you handled income and expenses in prior years. This review will also remind you of deductions, carryover losses, and other items you might otherwise have overlooked that you might be eligible for.

You may obtain copies of prior-year tax returns by filing Form 4506 with the IRS and paying a nominal fee. In this Chapter you will find a checklist of steps to take when preparing and checking your return. If you need an extension to file, see *46.3*.

Preparing Your Return

46.1 Keeping Tax Records

Tax saving requires keeping records. Good record-keeping makes it easier to prepare your return, reduces errors, and provides a defense to any challenge from the IRS.

- Make a habit of jotting down deductible items as they come along.
- Keep a calender or diary of expenses to record deductible items.
- Keep a file of bills. This can be an ordinary folder in which you arrange your bills and receipts alphabetically. This will remind you of deductible items and provide you with supporting evidence to present to the IRS if audited.
- Use your checkbook stubs as a record. If you own a business, you must keep a complete set of account books for it.

IRA records. If you make nondeductible IRA contributions, keep a record of both your nondeductible and deductible contributions. This will help you when you withdraw IRA money to figure the tax-free and taxed parts of the withdrawal. For this purpose you should also keep copies of Form 8606 and Form 5498; *see 8.8.*

Passive losses. If you have losses that are suspended and carried forward to future years under the passive loss restrictions *(10.13)*, keep the worksheets to Form 8582 as a record of the carry-forward losses.

Home mortgage interest. Keep your bank statements and canceled checks. If a loan secured by a first or second home is used to make substantial home improvements, keep records of the improvement costs to support your home interest deduction; *see 15.5.*

How long should you keep your records? Your records should be kept for a minimum of three years after the year to which they are applicable. Some authorities advise keeping them for six years, since in some cases where income has not been reported, the IRS may go back as far as six years to question a tax return. In cases of suspected tax fraud, there is no time limitation at all.

Keep records of transactions relating to the *basis* of property for as long as they are important in figuring the basis of the original or replacement property. For example, records of the purchase of a residence or improvements must be held as long as you own the house.

As mentioned above, if you have made any nondeductible IRA contributions, records of IRA contributions and distributions must be kept until all funds have been withdrawn. Similarly, you should save mutual-fund confirmations or other records showing reinvested dividends and cash purchases of shares; these are part of your cost basis and will reduce taxable gain when you sell shares in the fund.

46.2 Getting Ready To File Your Return

You must collect your tax records before you can start the preparation of your return. Even if you employ a tax professional to prepare your return, organizing your tax data is essential. *See* the Tax Record and Return Directories at the end of this chapter for the records you need to report income and expenses and where on your return to report them. If you are using a tax return preparer, *see 46.7.* Once you have compiled all your return information and your records are complete, decide whether to use Form 1040EZ, 1040A, or 1040 with the aid of the checklist at the front of this book on page 6. After you have decided which return to file, review the form to familiarize yourself with its details.

You may use the sample forms in Part 8 to prepare a draft copy of your return. The Supplement will contain forms suitable for filing, or you can obtain forms by phone from the IRS by calling (800) 809-3676. If you have a computer with a modem, you may obtain forms from the IRS Internet Website at http://www.irs.ustreas.gov or by dialing directly by modem to the IRS bulletin board at (703) 321-8020.

Checking for possible errors. After you have completed your return, put it aside and postpone checking your completed return for several hours or even a day so that you can review it in a fresh state of mind. *See* below for common errors that might delay a refund or result in a tax deficiency and interest costs.

Check your return to ensure the following *before* mailing it to the IRS:

- Your arithmetic is correct.
- Your Social Security number is recorded correctly on each form and schedule.

Planning Reminder

Keep Copies

Photocopy your signed return and keep the copy along with copies of Form W-2 and other income statements, receipts, cancelled checks, and other items to substantiate your deductions.

- You have filled in the proper boxes that state your filing status and exemption claims, and reported the Social Security number of each dependent born before December 1, 1997; *see 21.14*.

- You have claimed the full standard deduction you are entitled to if you are age 65 or older, or blind; *see 13.4*.

- You have claimed the earned income credit if you have one qualifying child and either your earned income or your modified adjusted gross income is less than $25,760, or less than $29,290 if you have more than one qualifying child; *see 25.10*.

- You have used the tax table or schedule applicable to your tax status; *see* Part 8 for the tax tables and the rate schedules. Use the tables if your taxable income is less than $100,000.

- You have put the refund due you or your tax payable on the correct line.

- If you owe any tax, your check should be made out to the Internal Revenue Service (*not* IRS) for the correct amount due and your Social Security number should be on the check. The IRS encourages, but does not require, that you send payment voucher Form 1040-V along with your Form 1040 payment.

- You have signed your return and, if you are filing a joint return, your spouse has also signed; *see 1.3*.

- You have attached the correct copy of your Form W-2 and all appropriate forms and schedules to your return.

- If you have elected to have your refund directly deposited, verify that you have provided the IRS with the correct information on Line 62 of Form 1040, Line 31 of Form 1040A, or Line 11 of Form 1040EZ.

- You have correctly addressed the envelope and affixed proper postage; *see 46.4*.

Using a computer to prepare your return. Tax return software has reached a high state of proficiency. If you have a personal computer, any one of the leading software programs will aid you in preparing your return by facilitating the calculation of sums, percentages, and tax liabilities. However, do not rely entirely on the computer program if you are preparing your return by yourself. You may inadvertently make an error by inputting the wrong information or there might be a quirk in the software itself. A suggestion: prepare a return by hand and then prepare a return using the computer program; each will act as a check for the other.

Form 1040 PC. Some commercially available tax preparation software programs allow you to generate a Form 1040 PC, a condensed tax form that prints only the lines for which you have entries. A paid tax preparer can also produce a Form 1040 PC for you. Form 1040 PC is easier for the IRS to process than a regular return, and allows for a direct deposit of a refund into your personal account.

46.3 Applying for an Extension

If you cannot file your return on time, apply by the due date for an extension of time to file. Send the extension request to the Internal Revenue Service office with which you file your return.

Automatic filing extension. You may get an extension without waiting for the IRS to act on your request. You receive an automatic four-month extension for your 1997 return if you file Form 4868 by April 15, 1998. The extension gives you until August 17, 1998, to file your return. A late *filing* penalty will not be imposed if you fail to submit a payment with Form 4868 provided you make a good faith estimate of your liability based upon available information at the time of filing. Although the extension will be allowed without a payment, you will be subject to interest charges and possible penalties on taxes due after April 15.

If paying the tax due would cause you to suffer a severe hardship you may apply for a special payment extension on Form 1127. This extension is generally limited to six months. Even if the IRS allows the extension, you will still owe interest on the late payment.

Abroad on April 15, 1998. You do not get an automatic extension for filing and paying your tax merely because you are out of the country on the filing due date. If you plan to be traveling abroad on April 15, 1998, and want to get a filing extension, you must submit a claim for the automatic four-month filing extension on Form 4868.

The only exception is for U.S. citizens or residents who live and have their main place of business outside the U.S. or Puerto Rico, or military personnel stationed outside the U.S. or Puerto Rico, on April 15, 1998. Such taxpayers qualify for an automatic two-month extension, until June 15, 1998. Such taxpayers may receive an additional two-month extension by filing Form 4868 by June 15 and making a proper estimate of the taxes due; as just discussed, payment of the estimated liability is not required to avoid a late *filing* penalty. However, you will still be subject to interest charges and possible penalties on taxes due after April 15, 1998.

Interest and penalty for underpayment. If, on filing Form 4868, you pay less than the balance of the final tax you owe, you will be charged interest on the unpaid amount. If the tax paid with Form 4868, plus withholdings and estimated tax payments during 1997, is less than 90% of the amount due, you may also be subject to a late-payment penalty (equal to $\frac{1}{2}$ of 1% of the unpaid tax per month)—unless you can show reasonable cause.

When you file your return within the extension period, you attach a duplicate of Form 4868 and include the balance of the unpaid tax, if any.

While the extension is automatically obtained by a proper filing on Form 4868, the IRS may terminate the extension on 10 days' notice to you.

Installment arrangements. If you cannot pay the tax due by the August 17 extension date, you should file your return and attach Form 9465 to request an installment arrangement. On Form 9465, you may request a monthly payment plan. The IRS will inform you within 30 days if your proposed payment plan is accepted. If it is, you will have to pay a processing fee. Even if the IRS agrees to an installment arrangement, you will have to pay interest and possibly a late-payment penalty (see above) on the amount not paid by the due date.

Filing extensions beyond August 17, 1998. Filing extensions beyond the automatic four-month period are allowed only if you file Form 2688 and show good cause, such as illness of yourself or a family member, or lack of information returns, such as a Form W-2 or Form 1099, needed to complete your return. Form 2688 must be filed before the end of the original four-month extension period. If the IRS agrees to your request, an additional two-month filing extension will be allowed, until October 15, 1998.

46.4 Where To Send Your Return

If your tax package includes a pre-printed address label and envelope, use them if you have not moved. Make sure you attach sufficient postage, or the envelope will be returned to you by the Post Office. If you moved or do not have a pre-addressed envelope, address the envelope containing your return to the Internal Revenue Service Center for the area where you live. No street address is needed. *See* the chart on the next page for filing addresses. Check the instructions in the IRS booklet for any address changes.

46.5 Electronic Filing

Electronic filing simply involves the transmission of data on your return from the computer of a tax preparer to an IRS computer via telephone wires. To file electronically, you must use an authorized service. Many tax preparers now offer this service. You also fill out and sign Form 8453 (U.S. Individual Income Tax Declaration for Electronic Filing) to authorize the electronic transmission. When filing jointly, both you and your spouse must sign the form. If you report salary income, Forms W-2 are attached to Form 8453, which is mailed to the IRS.

For a price, electronic filing offers a faster refund—a check mailed within three weeks or a direct deposit to your bank account. You authorize a direct deposit by writing your savings or checking account number and the "routing transit number" of your bank on Form 8453. The routing transit number is the electronic mailing address of your bank that directs the refund to the correct account. The number is on your checks or other account statements. Before naming a bank, first ask if it accepts direct deposits and what its conditions are for receiving a deposit.

You must decide whether the faster refund is worth the fee charged. Keep in mind that even without electronic filing, you may instruct the IRS to directly deposit your refund to an account that you designate on your return. If you file electronically and owe taxes, you must pay by mail. In this case, you file Form 1040-V (Payment Voucher) with your payment before April 15, 1998.

Refund anticipation loans. An electronic tax filing service may offer refund anticipation loans. These are loans on expected refunds from lenders affiliated with the electronic filing service. This service is strictly an agreement between you and the preparer; the IRS is not a party to the arrangement. Before agreeing to such a loan, consider the additional cost and whether it is worthwhile in light of the short refund payment period.

Planning Reminder

Last Minute Mailing

Last minute filers may use specified services from *DHL, Airborne, Federal Express,* and *UPS* as well as the *U.S. Postal Service.* Do not forget to get a receipt to verify a timely postmark. If your return is postmarked on or before the filing due date (April 15, 1998, for 1997 returns) it is considered timely filed under a "timely marked, timely filed" rule, even if the IRS receives it after the due date.

Where To File

ALABAMA—Memphis, TN 37501-0002

ALASKA—Ogden, UT 84201-0002

ARIZONA—Ogden, UT 84201-0002

ARKANSAS—Memphis, TN 37501-0002

CALIFORNIA—File with the IRS Service Center at Ogden, UT 84201-0002, if you live in the counties of Alpine, Amador, Butte, Calaveras, Colusa, Contra Costa, Del Norte, El Dorado, Glenn, Humboldt, Lake, Lassen, Marin, Mendocino, Modoc, Napa, Nevada, Placer, Plumas, Sacramento, San Joaquin, Shasta, Sierra, Siskiyou, Solano, Sonoma, Sutter, Tehama, Trinity, Yolo, and Yuba. All other California residents file at Fresno, CA 93888-0002

COLORADO—Ogden, UT 84201-0002

CONNECTICUT—Andover, MA 05501-0002

DELAWARE—Philadelphia, PA 19255-0002

DISTRICT OF COLUMBIA—Philadelphia, PA 19255-0002

FLORIDA—Atlanta, GA 39901-0002

GEORGIA—Atlanta, GA 39901-0002

HAWAII—Fresno, CA 93888-0002

IDAHO—Ogden, UT 84201-0002

ILLINOIS—Kansas City, MO 64999-0002

INDIANA—Cincinnati, OH 45999-0002

IOWA—Kansas City, MO 64999-0002

KANSAS—Austin, TX 73301-0002

KENTUCKY—Cincinnati, OH 45999-0002

LOUISIANA—Memphis, TN 37501-0002

MAINE—Andover, MA 05501-0002

MARYLAND—Philadelphia, PA 19255-0002

MASSACHUSETTS—Andover, MA 05501-0002

MICHIGAN—Cincinnati, OH 45999-0002

MINNESOTA—Kansas City, MO 64999-0002

MISSISSIPPI—Memphis, TN 37501-0002

MISSOURI—Kansas City, MO 64999-0002

MONTANA—Ogden, UT 84201-0002

NEBRASKA—Ogden, UT 84201-0002

NEVADA—Ogden, UT 84201-0002

NEW HAMPSHIRE—Andover, MA 05501-0002

NEW JERSEY—Holtsville, NY 00501-0002

NEW MEXICO—Austin, TX 73301-0002

NEW YORK—New York City and counties of Nassau, Rockland, Suffolk, and Westchester—Holtsville, NY 00501-0002

All Other Counties—Andover, MA 05501-0002

NORTH CAROLINA—Memphis, TN 37501-0002

NORTH DAKOTA—Ogden, UT 84201-0002

OHIO—Cincinnati, OH 45999-0002

OKLAHOMA—Austin, TX 73301-0002

OREGON—Ogden, UT 84201-0002

PENNSYLVANIA—Philadelphia, PA 19255-0002

RHODE ISLAND—Andover, MA 05501-0002

SOUTH CAROLINA—Atlanta, GA 39901-0002

SOUTH DAKOTA—Ogden, UT 84201-0002

TENNESSEE—Memphis, TN 37501-0002

TEXAS—Austin, TX 73301-0002

UTAH—Ogden, UT 84201-0002

VERMONT—Andover, MA 05501-0002

VIRGINIA—Philadelphia, PA 19255-0002

WASHINGTON—Ogden, UT 84201-0002

WEST VIRGINIA—Cincinnati, OH 45999-0002

WISCONSIN—Kansas City, MO 64999-0002

WYOMING—Ogden, UT 84201-0002

FOREIGN COUNTRY: U.S. citizens or dual-status aliens and those filing Form 2555, Form 2555-EZ, or Form 4563, even if you have an A.P.O. or F.P.O. address—Philadelphia, PA 19255-0002

A.P.O. or F.P.O. addresses—Philadelphia, PA 19255-0002

PUERTO RICO (or if excluding income under Section 933)—Philadelphia, PA 19255-0002

VIRGIN ISLANDS—Nonpermanent residents file with the IRS Service Center in Philadelphia, PA 19255-0002; permanent residents file with the V.I. Bureau of Internal Revenue, 9601 Estate Thomas, St. Thomas, VI 00802

GUAM—Nonpermanent residents file with the IRS Service Center in Philadelphia, PA 19255-0002; permanent residents file with the Department of Revenue and Taxation, Government of Guam, P.O. Box 23607, GMF, GU 96921

AMERICAN SAMOA—Philadelphia, PA 19255-0002

46.6 Calling the IRS About Your Refund

You can call the IRS to check on the status of an expected refund. When you call the IRS automated phone service, you must provide the Social Security number shown on the return (or the first Social Security number if you filed jointly), filing status, and the amount of the refund.

The general IRS phone number is 1-800-829-4477. However, in the following areas, you must dial a different number.

Arizona, Phoenix: (602) 640-3933; *California*, Oakland: (510) 839-4245; *Colorado*, Denver: (303) 592-1118; *District of Columbia*, (202) 628-2929; *Florida*, Jacksonville: (904) 355-2000; *Georgia*, Atlanta: (404) 331-6572; *Illinois*, Chicago: (312) 886-9614; *Indiana*, Indianapolis: (317) 377-0001; *Maryland*, Baltimore: (410) 244-7306; *Massachusetts*, Boston: (617) 536-0709; *Missouri*, St. Louis: (314) 241-4700; *New York*, Buffalo: (716) 685-5533; *Ohio*, Cincinnati: (513) 421-0329; Cleveland: (216) 522-3037; *Oregon*, Portland: (503) 294-5363; *Pennsylvania*, Philadelphia: (215) 627-1040; Pittsburgh: (412) 261-1040; *Tennessee*, Nashville: (615) 781-5040; *Texas*, Dallas: (214) 767-1792; Houston: (713) 541-3400; *Virginia*, Richmond: (804) 783-1569; *Washington*, Seattle: (206) 343-7221.

Any late changes to these numbers will be in the Supplement.

46.7 Choosing a Tax Return Preparer

There are two phases in preparing your tax return: (1) collecting your tax data and (2) converting that data into entries on your tax return. You must perform the first step yourself, as discussed at *46.1*. Once this is done, the second step of preparing your return may not be troublesome, especially if your return merely requires several entries on Form 1040A or Form 1040EZ. If you think tax return preparation is troublesome, or if you do not have the time to prepare your return, ask acquaintances about their knowledge and experience with qualified tax preparers in your area. If they are satisfied, you may want to contact their recommendations. If you cannot get recommendations, visit the offices of established franchised tax preparers.

Fees for tax return preparation depend on the complexity of the return to be filed and the preparer's professional standing. A preparer is not necessarily a trained accountant. Shop around; visit offices of preparers in your locality. This way you will get a firsthand idea of the cost of services. A preparation fee of a single form, such as Form 1040A or Form 1040EZ, may be around $50. Fees will be higher for more complicated returns.

Finally, do not rely on a preparer for tax planning advice. A person who can prepare a return may not have the experience or training to give tax planning advice. Consult a qualified professional, such as an accountant, CPA, tax attorney, or enrolled agent, who will charge more for services than a person who merely prepares returns during the tax season.

If you are concerned about a possible IRS audit of your return, consider hiring a preparer who is qualified to represent taxpayers before the IRS. Only CPAs, attorneys, and enrolled agents may represent taxpayers before the IRS, at the appeals as well as at the audit level. Attorneys or CPAs automatically qualify to practice before the IRS because of their professional licenses. An enrolled agent qualifies to practice before the IRS after passing an IRS examination or after completing five years of audit-level service as an IRS employee. Enrolled agents are also required by IRS regulations to complete continuing education courses every year.

Preparer Responsibilities

Tax preparers are subject to IRS regulations. They may be subject to penalties for understating the tax on a return or failing to keep proper records. Anyone who prepares a return or refund claim for a fee is considered a preparer under the tax law. When more than one person works on the return or claim, each schedule or entry is reviewed separately to determine the preparer of that schedule or item. A practitioner who gives advice directly relevant to a determination of the existence, characterization, or amount of an entry on a return is considered the preparer of that item.

A practitioner who prepares entries on a return that affect entries on the return of another taxpayer may also be considered the preparer of the other return if the entries are directly reflected on the other return and constitute a substantial portion of that return. For example, a practitioner preparing a partnership return may be considered the preparer of a partner's return if the entries that are picked up from the partnership return constitute a substantial portion of the partner's individual tax return. Regulations provide tests for determining whether a part of a return is considered substantial. Under the regulations, an entry is not considered substantial if it is (1) less than $2,000, or (2) less than $100,000 and also less than 20% of adjusted gross income.

You are not a preparer if you merely type or reproduce a return or claim, or prepare a return for your employer or an officer of your employer or a fellow employee.

Preparer Penalties

A $250 penalty may be imposed on a preparer for a tax understatement if: (1) the preparer knew (or reasonably should have known) that the understatement was based on a taxpayer position that did not have a realistic possibility of being sustained on its merits; and (2) the taxpayer position was frivolous or, if not frivolous, was not adequately disclosed. If the preparer can show good faith and a reasonable cause for the understatement, the $250 penalty will not be imposed. If a tax understatement is willful, or due to reckless disregard of IRS rules, a $1,000 penalty may be imposed; the penalty is $750 if the $250 penalty also applies to the return.

According to the IRS, a taxpayer position has a "realistic possibility" of being sustained on its merits if a person who is knowledgeable in the tax law would conclude, after a well-informed analysis, that there is at least a one-in-three likelihood that the position will be sustained.

For purposes of the $250 or $1,000 penalty, IRS regulations provide that only one person associated with a firm is considered to be the preparer of the return. The practitioner who signs the return is considered to be the preparer. If none of the persons considered to be preparers under IRS rules signs the return, then the person with overall supervisory responsibility is treated as the preparer for tax penalty purposes.

Note: a nonsigning preparer may also be subject to a $1,000 penalty for knowingly aiding and abetting the understatement of tax liability on a return ($10,000 for corporate returns).

Preparers must satisfy the following requirements:

1. Retain a record of the name, Social Security number, and place of work of each preparer whom he or she employs. The records must be kept for three years following the close of the return period and must be made available for inspection upon request of the district director. There is a $50 penalty for each failure to keep and make available a proper record and a $50 penalty for each required item that is missing from the record. The maximum penalty for any return period is $25,000.

2. Furnish a completed copy of the return or refund claim to the taxpayer not later than when it is presented to the taxpayer for signature. There is a $50 penalty for each failure, up to a maximum of $25,000, for documents filed during any one calendar year.

3. Keep for three years and have available for inspection by the IRS a completed copy of each return or claim prepared, or a list of the names and identification numbers of taxpayers for whom returns or claims were prepared. A $50 penalty is imposed for each failure, up to a maximum of $25,000, for any return period. A preparer who sells his or her business is not relieved of the requirement of retaining these records.

4. Sign the return and include his or her identifying number or the identifying number of his or her employer. A $50 penalty is imposed for each failure, up to a maximum of $25,000, for documents filed during any calendar year. Where more than one practitioner has worked on a return, the individual with primary responsibility for overall accuracy must sign the return.

The penalty for failure to meet these four requirements may be avoided by showing reasonable cause for the failure.

Tax preparers are subject to a $500 penalty if they endorse or negotiate a refund check issued to a taxpayer whose return they have prepared. Business managers for athletes, actors, or other professionals who prepare their clients' tax returns and handle their tax refunds may also be subject to the penalty. To avoid the penalty, the manager must act only as an agent in depositing the client's refund check.

In addition to the penalties imposed, the IRS may also seek to enjoin a preparer from engaging in fraudulent or deceptive practices or from acting as an income tax return preparer. The IRS may also seek an injunction against a preparer for "aiding and abetting" a taxpayer to underpay tax. A list of enjoined preparers is published by the IRS in the Internal Revenue Bulletin.

Note: For additional details regarding income tax return preparers, *see* the Professional Edition of *Your Income Tax.*

Tax Record and Return Directory

The following table lists tax records you need for specific items of income and expense and directs you to the return, schedule, and line on which to report the items. The items are listed in the order in which they appear on Forms 1040, 1040A, and 1040EZ.

Item	Records Needed	Reporting
Exemptions for dependents	Records of support contribution for food, lodging, medical expenses, such as cancelled checks, diary entries. Birth certificates in case age of a child is questioned. School attendance record if student status is questioned. Form 8332 allowing noncustodial parent to claim the exemption. This form must also be attached to return by noncustodial parent claiming exemption; *see 22.11.* Forms 2120 if dependent's support is shared by other persons; *see 22.10.*	Form 1040A, Line 6(c) Form 1040, Line 6(c)
Wages and salaries	Form W-2. Your employer must send your 1996 Form W-2 by January 31, 1997. Attach Copy B to your federal return. Keep Copy C for your records. If you worked for more than one employer during 1996, attach all Copy B forms to your return.	Form 1040EZ, Line 1 Form 1040A, Line 7 Form 1040, Line 7
Tip income	Form 4070 or other record showing your monthly reports of cash tips of $20 or more. Form W-2. Also *see 26.8* for reporting FICA taxes on unreported tips.	Form 1040EZ, Line 1 Form 1040A, Line 7 Form 1040, Line 7
Interest income	Form 1099-INT Form 1099-OID Deposit slips of interest received on money you loaned to others	Form 1040EZ, Line 2 ($400 or less) Form 1040A, Line 8(a); Schedule 1, Part I (over $400) Form 1040, Line 8(a); Schedule B, Part I (over $400)
Dividend income	Form 1099-DIV Company statements of dividend payments, especially if stock dividends have been paid	Form 1040A, Line 9; Schedule 1, Part II (over $400) Form 1040, Line 9; Schedule B, Part II (over $400)

Tax Record and Return Directory (continued)

Item	Records Needed	Reporting
Taxable refund of state and local income tax	Form 1099-G	Form 1040, Line 10
Alimony received	Deposit slips of alimony received and ex-spouse's Social Security number Copy of divorce or separation decree or agreements	Form 1040, Line 11 if taxable
Business income or loss	Business accounting records, deposit slips Business checkbook, deposit slips, invoice receipts, cancelled checks, bank statements Form 1099-MISC	Form 1040, Line 12; Schedule C or C-EZ Form 8582 if passive activity rules apply; *see* Chapter 10
Sale of stocks and bonds	Form 1099-B and broker confirmation statements	Schedule D Form 1040, Line 13
Sale of personal residence	Closing papers, records of purchase, improvements; *see 29.6.*	Schedule D Form 2119 Form 1040, Line 13 if gain is reported; losses are not deductible
Sale of real estate	Closing statement, records of cost and improvements Records of depreciation	Form 4797 Schedule D Form 1040, Line 13
IRA distributions	Form 1099-R	Form 1040A, Line 10 Form 1040, Line 15
Pensions and annuities	Form 1099-R if you receive annuity payments or lump-sum distributions	Form 1040A, Line 11 Form 1040, Line 16
Commercial annuity income	Form 1099-R	Form 1040A, Line 11 Form 1040, Line 16
Rent income	Account records, checkbook, cancelled checks, and receipts	Schedule E Form 1040, Line 17 Form 8582 if passive activity rules apply
Royalty income	Form 1099-MISC	Schedule E Form 1040, Line 17
Partnership income	Schedule K-1, Form 1065	Schedule E Form 1040, Line 17
Beneficiary of trust or estate	Schedule K-1, Form 1041	Schedule E Form 1040, Line 17
S corporation	Schedule K-1, Form 1120S	Schedule E Form 1040, Line 17
Unemployment compensation	Form 1099-G	Form 1040A, Line 12 Form 1040, Line 19
Social Security benefits	Form SSA-1099	Form 1040A, Line 13 Form 1040, Line 20
Gambling income	Form W-2G, diary or other record showing wins and losses, losing tickets	Form 1040, Line 21
Other income	Form 1099-MISC, records of amounts received, date received	Form 1040, Line 21

Tax Record and Return Directory (continued)

Item	Records Needed	Reporting
IRA deductible contribution	Trustee's statements of contribution, copy of plan	Form 1040A, Lines 15(a) and 15(b) Form 1040, Lines 23(a) and 23(b)
Moving expenses	Cancelled checks or receipts for expenses incurred, diary or log	Form 1040, Line 25 Form 3903
Deduction for self-employment tax	Schedule SE, Form 1040	Form 1040, Line 26
Self-employed health insurance premium	Cancelled check of payment, copy of contract, insurance statement	Form 1040, Line 27
Keogh or SEP contribution for yourself	Trustee statement, copy of plan	Form 1040, Line 28
Penalty on early withdrawal of savings	Form 1099-INT	Form 1040, Line 29
Alimony deduction	Cancelled checks, copy of divorce or separation decree, written separation agreement, ex-spouse's Social Security number	Form 1040, Line 30
Employee expenses	Diary logs, receipts, copy of accounting to employer	Form 2106 Schedule A, Line 20
Home office expenses	Records of expenses, business use, and allocation	Form 2106 if an employee; Schedule A, Line 20 Form 8829 if self-employed; Schedule C, Line 30
Medical and dental expenses	Cancelled checks, statements, prescriptions; log of travel expenses and lodging costs	Form 1040 Schedule A, Lines 1–4
Taxes—state and local income, personal property, real estate	Form W-2 for withholding of income tax Cancelled checks Bank statements of property taxes paid by bank (mortgages) Form 1099-DIV for foreign tax Form 1099-INT or tax receipt for foreign tax withheld at source	Form 1040 Schedule A, Lines 5–9
Mortgage interest	Bank statement showing interest paid Form 1098	Form 1040 Schedule A, Line 10
Points	Copy of bank statements, canceled checks	Form 1040 Schedule A, Lines 10 and 12
Cash donations	Cancelled checks, receipt from charity	Form 1040; Schedule A, Line 15
Volunteer expenses for charitable organizations	Log of travel, cancelled checks showing purpose	Form 1040 Schedule A, Line 15
Property donation	Description of property, records of fair market value and cost. Receipt from organization. If at least $250, a written receipt from organization to substantiate donation. Cancelled check is not sufficient. If in excess of $5,000, qualified appraisal report and statement from organization.	Form 1040 Schedule A, Line 16
Casualty losses	The records and steps are detailed at *18.11* and *18.12*.	Form 1040; Schedule A, Line 19 Form 4684

Tax Record and Return Directory (continued)

Item	Records Needed	Reporting
Theft losses	Statements from witnesses who saw the theft or police records of a breaking into your house or car. A newspaper account of the crime might also help.	Form 1040 Form 4684 Schedule A, Line 19
Gambling losses	Losing tickets or receipts, diary showing daily wagers, wins, and losses	Form 1040 Schedule A, Line 27
Union dues	Wage statements showing withholding for dues or canceled checks	Form 1040 Schedule A, Line 20
Unreimbursed travel and entertainment expenses	Diary log and receipts kept according to the rules of *20.26*	Form 2106 Form 1040; Schedule A, Line 20
Unreimbursed auto expenses if you are employed	Statement from employer requiring use of car Mileage log Receipts of expenses if actual costs are claimed Cost records of auto if depreciation is claimed	Form 2106 Form 1040 Schedule A, Line 20
Investment expenses	Cancelled checks	Form 1040; Schedule A, Line 22
Bank deposit boxes	Bank statements	Form 1040; Schedule A, Line 22
Tax preparation fees	Cancelled checks	Form 1040; Schedule A, Line 21
"Kiddie" tax	Child's Forms 1099-INT, 1099-DIV, and 1099-OID	Form 1040A, Line 23 Form 1040, Line 38 Form 8615 if income is reported on child's return Form 8814 if parent elects to report child's income on Form 1040
Child and dependent care expenses	Cancelled checks for amounts paid to care for child	Form 1040A, Line 24(a); Schedule 2 Form 1040, Line 40 Form 2441
Credit for the elderly or the disabled	Physician's statement of condition	Form 1040A, Line 24(b); Schedule 3 Form 1040, Line 41; Schedule R
Advanced earned income credit payments	Form W-2	Form 1040A, Line 26 Form 1040, Line 51
Federal taxes withheld	Form 1099 Form W-2	Form 1040EZ, Line 7 Form 1040A, Line 29(a) Form 1040, Line 54
Estimated tax payments	Cancelled checks and copy of Form 1040-ES	Form 1040A, Line 29(b) Form 1040, Line 55
Earned income credit	Form W-2 if an employee, Schedule SE if self-employed, to show earnings Form W-5 if advanced payment of credit was received	Form 1040EZ, Line 8 Form 1040A, Line 29(c); Schedule EIC Form 1040, Line 56(a); Schedule EIC
Foreign tax credit	Form 1099-DIV; foreign tax returns or statements	Form 1116 Form 1040, Line 43
Prior alternative minimum tax credit	Copy of prior year's Form 6251	Form 8801 Form 1040, Line 44(c)

Chapter 47

How Tax Data Is Processed by the IRS

Data from filed tax returns and information returns is recorded in computers on magnetic tape which is sent to the National Computer Center in Martinsburg, West Virginia, for posting to the master list of taxpayers arranged by account number. Failure to file returns, duplicate or multiple filings, and other discrepancies can be detected. Data from information returns is matched with the entries on individual returns.

You are required to put your Social Security number on your tax return. Your number also appears on information returns sent to the IRS reporting the wages, interest, dividends, royalties, etc., paid to you. Your number serves as a basis for posting and cross-referencing data to your account in the master IRS file.

You may incur penalties and interest charges if you fail to comply with reporting requirements or fail to pay your taxes on time.

47.1 IRS Preliminary Review

Your return is first checked for arithmetic accuracy by the IRS. If an error is found, you receive either a refund or a bill for additional taxes. Special IRS screening also spots the following types of errors:

- Incorrectly reporting income shown on Forms W-2 or Forms 1099.
- Incorrectly applying the adjusted gross income limitations for medical expenses, casualty and theft losses, and miscellaneous itemized deductions.
- Using an auto mileage rate for business travel exceeding the IRS rate.
- Claiming of the dependent care credit by a married person filing separately; *see 25.1.*
- Using head of household rates without noting the name of a qualifying child who is not your dependent.
- Not supplying the Social Security number of a dependent.

If you make errors of this type, you will probably be advised by mail of the corrections and of additional tax due, or you may be asked to provide additional information to substantiate tax deductions or credits. If you disagree with an IRS assessment of additional tax, you may request an interview or submit additional information. If you file early for 1997 and the correction is made before April 15, 1998, interest is not charged.

If you fail to provide a dependent's Social Security number, the IRS may give you an opportunity to provide the number. If the IRS disallows the exemption, it may use an immediate assessment procedure. You have 60 days to object to an immediate assessment.

If your return is selected for a more thorough review, you are notified by letter. This may not happen for a year or two. How to handle an audit if your return is selected for examination is discussed in Chapter 48.

If you are due a refund on your 1997 return, the IRS follows a practice of expediting refunds to avoid interest costs. Interest is not required to be paid on refunds before May 31, 1998, which is 46 days after April 15, the day the tax was due. If the overpayment is not refunded within 45 days, interest is paid from the date the tax was overpaid up to a date determined by the IRS that can be as much as 30 days before the date of the refund check.

47.2 Information Returns Required by the IRS

The IRS matches tax returns with information returns from employers, payers of interest and dividends, brokers, and others to check whether income has been omitted from an individual's tax return. The IRS processes more than one billion information returns, primarily Forms W-2 and Forms 1099. By matching these information returns against individual tax returns, the IRS assesses billions in additional tax and penalties.

Here is a list of items for which an information return will be sent to the IRS:

Wages.   Employers report wage income on Form W-2.

Dividends.   Dividend payments of $10 or more during the calendar year are reported to the IRS on Form 1099-DIV. Each payer must furnish you by February 2, 1998, a statement showing the dividend payments made in 1997. Corporations, banks, and other payers, as well as persons or firms who receive such payments for you as nominee, report annually the dividend payments totaling $10 or more per person. Dividends, for reporting purposes, include dividends paid by corporations, and "dividend equivalents" paid to you while your stock is on loan for a short sale. Nontaxable distributions paid to shareholders are reported to the IRS on Form 5452.

Interest.   Interest payments of $10 or more during the calendar year are reported to the IRS on Form 1099-INT. Each payer must furnish you by February 2, 1998, a statement showing the interest payments made in 1997. Interest for reporting purposes includes interest on registered corporate bonds, debentures, notes, and certificates, as well as interest on deposits with savings banks, savings and loan associations, stockbrokers, and insurance companies. No returns are required for tax-free interest.

Original issue discount (OID).   The discount on time deposits and certificates maturing in more than one year is reported to the IRS on Form 1099-OID if it is at least $10. You should receive a copy of the Form 1099-OID for 1997 by February 2, 1998.

Interest and dividend income information disclosed to Social Security and other agencies.   To verify your eligibility for certain government benefits, agencies such as the Social Security Administration, state unemployment compensation agencies, and state welfare agencies may obtain from the IRS information on the interest and dividend income that is shown on your tax return.

Rents or royalties. Royalty payments of $10 or more are reported on intangible property, such as copyrights and interests in oil, gas, and other natural resources, on Form 1099-MISC. Rents collected by a real estate agent on behalf of the property owner of $600 or more also are reported on Form 1099-MISC.

State income tax refunds. States are required to report income tax refunds of $10 or more on Form 1099-G.

Unemployment compensation. Unemployment payments of $10 or more during the year are reported to the IRS on Form 1099-G, a copy of which will be furnished to unemployment benefit recipients.

Proceeds from real estate transactions. Real estate sales are generally reported on Form 1099-S to the IRS by the attorney or other party who is responsible for closing the transaction. On the sale of a home, the form must also show the portion of real property taxes imposed on the buyer. However, *see* the Law Alert at right.

Proceeds from sales of securities. Brokers are required to report to the IRS on Form 1099-B gross proceeds from sales of stocks, bonds, commodities, regulated futures, and forward contracts. Commodity options are not covered by this reporting rule.

Miscellaneous income. Persons who, in the course of business, make payments totaling $600 or more in the calendar year must file Form 1099-MISC with the IRS if the payments are in the form of:

1. Compensation for personal services (including salaries, wages, commissions, and professional fees) from which no tax is withheld. However, no information return is required for payments to a domestic or other household employee.

2. Prizes and awards that are not for services, such as winnings on TV shows (gambling winnings are reported on Form W-2G); *or*

3. Payments of fees to physicians by insurance companies, such as Blue Cross, or by a government agency under Medicare or Medicaid. The physician or other health care provider must receive a copy of Form 1099-MISC by February 2, 1998, for inclusion of the amount on his or her 1997 return.

Retirement plan distributions. Distributions from pension, profit-sharing and annuity plans, IRAs, or simplified employee pension plans (SEPs) are reported on Form 1099-R. Contributions to an IRA and the year-end value of an IRA or SEP account are reported on Form 5498.

Mortgage interest. Banks, government agencies, and businesses receiving mortgage interest and points of $600 or more for any calendar year report the payment to the IRS on Form 1098. The reporting requirement applies to interest on all obligations secured by real property. The lender must provide you with a statement of the interest reported to the IRS for 1997 by February 2, 1998.

Foreclosures and abandonments of property. If a business or government agency lends you money and later forecloses on your property or knows that you have abandoned property secured by the loan, the lender must file a report with the IRS on Form 1099-A. The purpose of the reporting requirement is to help the IRS check whether you have realized income from the discharge of indebtedness or gain on foreclosure, or whether you must recapture a previously claimed investment credit. If a report to the IRS has been made, you will be sent a statement by the lender by January 31 following the year of the foreclosure or abandonment.

Tax shelters. A new tax-shelter offering may be required to register with the IRS. If registration is required, the IRS assigns the tax shelter an identification number that must be furnished to investors. As an investor, you must report the registration number on Form 8271. Form 8271 must be attached to your tax return if you report any income or claim any deductions or credits from the shelter. Promoters of registered tax shelters and any other tax-shelter arrangements which the IRS considers potentially abusive must also keep a list of investors for seven years and provide the list to the IRS upon request. Furthermore, an investor who sells his interest in such a tax shelter to another investor must keep records identifying the buyer.

Cooperatives. Cooperatives must file annual information returns for patronage dividends totaling $10 or more during the calendar year. A statement showing the amount reported must be furnished to the patron by the end of January of the following year; *see* Form 1099-PATR.

Partnerships. A partnership does not pay income taxes, but must file an annual information return (Form 1065), stating all items of income and deductions. Also included in the return are the

 Law Alert

Reporting Requirement for Home Sales After May 6, 1997

Sales of principal residences with a gross sales price of $250,000 or less ($500,000 or less for married sellers) are exempt from the real estate reporting requirement if the seller provides the person responsible for closing the sale written assurance that the full gain on the sale is excludable from income under the new law rules of *29.2.*

names and addresses of all partners, and the amount of each partner's distributive share. The return is filed at the close of the partnership's tax year, whether or not it coincides with that of its partners. Failure to file the return will result in a penalty assessable against the partnership. If a partner sells or exchanges a partnership interest and payment is partly attributable to the partner's share of unrealized receivables or substantially appreciated inventory, the partnership must be notified of the transaction and the partnership must then file an information return with the IRS, Form 8308. The purpose of the reporting requirement is to enable the IRS to verify the income attributable to the receivables and inventory, which is taxable as ordinary income. Statements to the transferor and transferee of the partnership interest must also be provided.

Barter transactions.   The value of the trades by members of a barter club is subject to income tax. If you exchanged services or goods through a barter exchange during 1997, you should receive Form 1099-B from the exchange by February 2, 1998, showing the value received during 1997. The IRS also gets a copy.

Cancelled debts.   If a financial institution or federal agency cancels or forgives a debt you owe of $600 or more, the cancellation will be reported to the IRS on Form 1099-C and a copy sent to you. A cancellation of a debt is generally taxable, but *see* exceptions in *11.8*.

47.3 When the IRS Can Assess Additional Taxes

Three-year statute of limitations.   The IRS has three years after the date on which your return is filed to assess additional taxes. When you file a return before the due date, however, the three-year period starts from the due date, generally April 15.

Where the due date of a return falls on a Saturday, Sunday, or legal holiday, the due date is postponed to the next business day.

> **EXAMPLES**
> 1. You filed your 1994 return on February 4, 1995. The last day on which the IRS can make an assessment on your 1994 return is April 15, 1998.
> 2. You file your 1997 return on May 27, 1998. The IRS has until May 27, 2001, to assess a deficiency.

Amended returns.   If you file an amended return shortly before the three-year limitations period is about to expire and the return shows that you owe additional tax, the IRS has 60 days from the date it receives the return to assess the additional tax, even though the regular limitations period would expire before the 60-day period.

Six-year statute.   When you fail to report an item of gross income which is more than 25% of the gross income reported on your return, the IRS has six years after the return is filed to assess additional taxes.

Where a false or fraudulent return is filed with intent to evade the tax, or where no return is filed, there is no limitation on when the tax may be assessed.

IRS request for audit extension.   If the IRS cannot complete an audit within three years, it may request that you sign Form 872 to extend the time for assessing the tax. However, where an individual was "scared" into signing such an agreement, it was held invalid. See the following Example.

> **EXAMPLE**
> Robertson, a plumber, won $30,000 in a sweepstakes. An IRS agent asked him to sign an extension agreement. Robertson never had any prior dealings with the IRS, he did not know that his return was under examination, and he was not in touch with the lawyer who prepared the return on which his sweepstakes winnings were averaged.
> Robertson wanted to see his lawyer before signing Form 872, but the agent pressed hard for the signature, phoning him and his wife at home and at work 20 times in a week. The agent did not tell him the amount of additional tax that might be involved, or explain that if he refused to sign he would have an opportunity before the IRS and the courts to contest any additional tax. Instead, the agent's comments gave him the impression that his home could be confiscated if he refused to sign. Robertson signed and the IRS later increased his tax.

Robertson argued that the agreement was not valid. He signed under duress. The Tax Court agreed. He convinced the court that he really believed he could lose his house and property if he did not comply. No adequate explanation of the real consequences of refusal to sign was made, although Robertson asked. Since he signed Form 872 under duress, the IRS could not increase his tax after the three-year period.

47.4 Interest on Deficiencies

Interest is charged on a deficiency at rates listed in the following table. Interest begins to accrue from the due date of the return. As of January 1, 1983, interest is compounded daily except for estimated tax penalties. IRS tables on compound interest may be found in IRS Revenue Procedure 95-17. Where a taxpayer has relied on IRS assistance in preparing a return, and taxes are owed because of a mathematical or clerical error, interest does not begin to accrue until 30 days from a formal demand by the IRS for the payment of additional taxes.

IRS interest rates on taxes owed are as follows:

From—	To—	Deficiency Rate—
7/1/96	9/30/97	9%
4/1/96	6/30/96	8
7/1/95	3/31/96	9
4/1/95	6/30/95	10
10/1/94	3/31/95	9
7/1/94	9/30/94	8
10/1/92	6/30/94	7
4/1/92	9/30/92	8
1/1/92	3/31/92	9
4/1/91	12/31/91	10
10/1/89	3/31/91	11

Refunds. The interest rate on refunds is 1% less than the rate on deficiencies. Generally, no interest is paid on a refund made within 45 days of the due date of the return (disregarding extensions). If you file after the due date, no interest is paid on a refund made within 45 days of the actual filing date. *See 49.5.*

47.5 Tax Penalties

Late payments. If you are late in paying your taxes, a nondeductible monthly penalty of 0.5% (½ of 1%) is imposed on the net amount of tax due and not paid by the due date. The maximum penalty is 25% of the tax due. The penalty is in addition to the regular interest charge. The penalty does not apply if you can show that the failure to pay is due to reasonable cause and not to willful neglect. The penalty does not apply to the estimated tax.

A similar penalty applies for failure to pay a tax deficiency within 21 calendar days of the date of notice and demand for payment if the tax due is less than $100,000. If the tax is $100,000 or more, the penalty-free payment period is 10 business days.

The monthly penalty may be doubled to 1%, if, after repeated requests to pay and a notice of levy, you do not pay. The increased penalty applies starting in the month that begins after the earlier of the following IRS notices: (1) a notice that the IRS will levy upon your assets within 10 days unless payment is made and (2) a notice demanding immediate payment where the IRS believes collection of the tax is in jeopardy. If the tax is not paid after such a demand for immediate payment, the IRS may levy upon your assets without waiting 10 days.

Late filing. If your return is filed late without reasonable cause, the IRS may impose a penalty of 5% of the net tax due for each month the return is late, with a maximum penalty of 25%. If the return is more than 60 days late, the penalty will not be less than the smaller of $100 and 100% of the tax due. In one case, the IRS tried to impose the $100 minimum penalty on a taxpayer who did not owe any tax because her withholdings exceeded her liability. However, the Tax Court held that the minimum $100 penalty does not apply unless tax is underpaid. The IRS has agreed to follow the decision.

If failure to file is fraudulent, the monthly penalty is 15% of the net tax due, with a maximum penalty of 75%.

If you are subject to penalties for both late payment and late filing, the 0.5% penalty for late payment (but not the 1% penalty) offsets the penalty for late filing.

Penalties for inaccurate returns. A 20% penalty generally applies to the portion of any tax underpayment attributable to (1) negligence or disregard of IRS rules and regulations; (2) substantial understatement of tax liability; (3) overvaluation of property; or (4) undervaluation of property on a gift tax or estate tax return. These penalties may be avoided by showing good faith and reasonable cause for the underpayment; a stricter version of this exception applies to charitable contribution overvaluations as discussed later in this section.

Negligence or disregard of IRS rules or regulations. The 20% penalty applies to the portion of the underpayment attributable to negligence. Negligence is defined as failing to make a reasonable attempt to comply with the law. Failure to report income shown on an information return, such as interest or dividends, is considered strong evidence of negligence, but negligence is not presumed as it was under prior law. For returns with an original due date before 1990, a 5% negligence penalty is applied to the entire underpayment where any part of it was attributable to negligence.

The 20% penalty may also apply if you take a position on a return which is contrary to IRS revenue rulings, notices, or regulations. This penalty for disregarding IRS rules or regulations may be avoided if you have a reasonable basis for your position and you disclose that position on Form 8275 or on Form 8275-R in the case of a good faith position contrary to a regulation. Thus, disclosure will not avoid a penalty for a position that does not have a reasonable basis.

Substantial underpayment of tax. If you understate tax liability on a return by the greater of $5,000 and 10% of the proper tax, you may be subject to a penalty equal to 20% of the underpayment attributable to the understatement on returns due after 1989.

The penalty may be avoided if you have a reasonable basis for your position and you disclose the position to the IRS on Form 8275, or on Form 8275-R in the case of a position that is contrary to an IRS regulation.

The penalty also may be avoided if you can show that your position was supported by "substantial authority" such as statutes, court decisions, final, temporary, or proposed IRS regulations, IRS revenue rulings and procedures, and press releases or notices published by the IRS in the weekly Internal Revenue Bulletin. You may also rely on IRS private letter rulings and technical advice memoranda issued after October 31, 1976, and IRS actions on decisions and general counsel memoranda issued after March 12, 1981. However, according to the IRS, such rulings and internal IRS memoranda that are more than 10 years old should be accorded very little weight. Congressional committee reports and the tax law explanations prepared by Congress's Joint Committee on Taxation, known as the "Blue Book," may be relied on as authority for your position.

However, if an understatement of tax is due to tax-shelter items, having substantial authority for your position is not enough to avoid the penalty; you must also reasonably believe that your position was "more likely than not" correct. Disclosure does not avoid a penalty for tax-shelter items.

Overvaluing property or basis. The 20% penalty for overvaluing property, such as where inflated charitable contribution deductions are claimed or where the basis of depreciable property is inflated, applies *only* if the claimed value or basis is 200% or more of the correct amount. Furthermore, there is no penalty unless the tax underpayment attributable to the overvaluation exceeds $5,000. The penalty rate is doubled to 40% if the overvaluation is 400% or more of the correct value. To avoid the penalty for donated property on the grounds that you had reasonable cause, the value must be based on a qualified appraisal *(14.12)* and your own good faith investigation of value.

Undervaluation on gift or estate tax return. If property is undervalued on a gift tax return or estate tax return by 50% or more, and if the tax underpayment attributed to the undervaluation exceeds $5,000, a 20% penalty applies. The penalty doubles to 40% if the undervaluation is 75% or more.

Fraud penalty. A 75% penalty applies to the portion of any tax underpayment due to fraud. If the IRS establishes that any part of an underpayment is due to fraud, the entire underpayment will be attributed to fraud, unless you prove otherwise.

Caution

Too Good to Be True
If you claim a deduction, credit, or exclusion on your return that would seem to a reasonable person to be "too good to be true" under the circumstances, the IRS is likely to consider you negligent unless you show you made an attempt to verify the correctness of the position.

Interest on penalties. A higher interest cost is imposed on individuals subject to the following penalties: failure to file a timely return, negligence or fraud, overvaluation of property, undervaluation of gift or estate tax property, *or* substantial understatement of tax liability. Interest starts to run from the due date of the return (including extensions) until the date the penalty is paid. For other penalties, interest is not imposed, unless the penalty is not paid within 10 days of an IRS demand for payment made before 1997. If the demand is after 1996, and the penalty is less than $100,000, the interest-free period is 21 calendar days, or 10 business days if the penalty is $100,000 or more.

Acting on wrong IRS advice. A penalty will not be imposed if you rely on erroneous advice provided in writing by IRS officials. It is necessary for you to show that you provided accurate information when asking for advice.

47.6 Notify the IRS of Address Changes

If the IRS does not have your current address, payment of a refund due you may be delayed. If you owe taxes, the IRS may enforce a deficiency notice sent to the address on your most recently filed tax return, even if you never receive the IRS notice.

To avoid these problems, file Form 8822 with the IRS to provide notice of an address change. Alternatively, you may send a signed written statement to the IRS Service Center covering your old residence. The statement should state the new and old address, your full name, and your Social Security or employer identification number.

If you and your spouse separate after filing a joint return, you should each notify the IRS of your current address.

If after you move you receive an IRS correspondence that has been forwarded by the Post Office, you may correct the address shown on the letter and mail it back to the IRS. Your correction is considered notice of an address change.

Chapter 48

IRS Tax Audits

Because the IRS is unable to examine every return, it follows a policy of examining returns which, upon preliminary inspection, indicate the largest possible source of potential tax deficiency.

Returns are rated for audit according to a mathematical formula called the discriminant function system (DIF). Various weights are assigned to separate items on each tax return, thus permitting the ranking of returns for the greatest potential error. The method is based on data the IRS compiled from extensive audits of taxpayers under the Taxpayer Compliance Measurement Program (TCMP). The specific factors entering into the DIF formula are not disclosed by the IRS. However, its general procedure for selecting returns for audit may be found in an IRS classification handbook which is part of the Internal Revenue Manual (Part IV, Audit).

This chapter discusses what may trigger an audit and how you can handle an audit if your return is selected for examination.

48.1 Odds of Being Audited

The odds are low that your return will be picked for an audit. The IRS does not have the personnel and resources to examine every return, so it selects those returns which upon preliminary inspection have a high audit potential—those that are most likely to result in a substantial tax deficiency.

Audit odds vary depending on your income, profession, type of return, type of transactions reported, and where you live. Individual returns are classified by all income items on the return without regard to losses. Professional or business income reported on Schedule C and farm income reported on Schedule F is classified by total gross receipts, and corporate returns are classified by total assets.

Your return may command special IRS scrutiny because of your profession, the type of transactions reported, or the deductions claimed. The chances of being audited are greater under the following circumstances:

- Your itemized deductions exceed IRS targets.
- You claim tax-shelter losses.
- You report complex investment or business transactions without clear explanations.
- You receive cash payments in your work that the IRS thinks are easy to conceal, such as cash fees received by doctors or tips received by cab drivers and waiters.
- Business expenses are large in relation to income.
- Cash contributions to charity are large in relation to income.
- You are a shareholder of a close corporation whose return has been examined.
- A prior audit resulted in a tax deficiency.
- An informer gives the IRS grounds to believe that you are omitting income from your return.

Itemized deductions. If your itemized deductions exceed target ranges set by the IRS, the chances of being audited increase. The IRS does not publicize its audit criteria for excessive deductions, but it does release statistics showing the average amount of deductions claimed according to reported income. Here are IRS figures based on deductions claimed on 1995 returns.

Average Itemized Deductions

Adjusted gross income (thousands)—	Taxes—	Interest—	Medical and dental—	Charitable donations—
0–15	$2,555	$7,463	$8,379	$1,097
15–30	2,270	5,442	5,390	1,338
30–50	3,112	5,715	4,226	1,465
50–75	4,429	6,587	4,722	1,768
75–100	6,171	8,063	6,544	2,286
100–200	9,758	11,107	12,277	3,433
200+	36,076	25,046	32,113	16,882

48.2 Types of Audits

An examination may be held by correspondence, at a local IRS office, or at the taxpayer's place of business, office, or home. An examination at an IRS office is called a desk or office examination; an examination at a place of business or home is called a field examination. When you are contacted by the IRS, you should receive an explanation of the examination process.

In a correspondence audit, the IRS sends you a letter asking for additional information about an item on your return. For example, the IRS may ask you to document a claimed deduction for charitable contributions or medical expenses. If the IRS is not satisfied with your response, you may be called in for an office audit. The IRS also notifies you by letter of mathematical or clerical errors you have made on your return, or if you have failed to report income, such as interest or dividends, that are shown by payers on information returns and matched to taxpayer returns by IRS computers.

The complexity of the transactions reported on a return generally determines whether a return will be reviewed at an office or field examination.

Most audits of individual returns, except for the self-employed, are conducted at IRS offices. An office audit usually covers only a few specific issues which the IRS specifies in its notice to you. For example, the examining agent may only be interested in seeing proof for travel expense deductions or educational expenses.

Field audits generally involve business returns; they are more extensive and time-consuming than office audits and are handled by more experienced IRS agents. For self-employed individuals, most examinations are field audits at their place of business. It is advisable to have a tax professional go over the potential weak spots in your return and represent you at the examination.

48.3 Preparing for the Audit

After an office audit is scheduled, the first thing to do is look over your return. Refresh your memory. Examine the items the IRS questioned in its notice of audit, and organize your records accordingly. Also check the rest of your return and gather proof for items you are unsure of. At this point, you should take a broad view of your return to anticipate problems you may encounter. Before the actual examination begins, consider possible settlement terms. Assume that the agent will assess additional tax, but establish the range you will consider reasonable. You can always change your mind, but giving some thought beforehand to possible settlement terms will help you later when settlements are actually discussed.

You may authorize an attorney, CPA, enrolled agent, or other individual recognized to practice before the IRS to represent you at the examination without your being there. To do so, give your representative authorization on Form 2848. An attorney or other representative authorized on Form 2848 can perform any acts that you could, including entering into a binding settlement agreement; *see* the Sample Form 2848 at the end of this chapter.

If you attend the audit, take only the records related to the items questioned in the IRS notice. Do not volunteer extra records; if the agent sees them, it might suggest new areas for investigation.

If you are concerned that there may be a problem of negligence or fraud, see a qualified attorney before you come into contact with an IRS official. The attorney can put your actions in perspective and help protect your legal rights. Besides, what you tell an attorney is privileged information; he or she cannot divulge or be forced to divulge data you have provided, so you need not be concerned that disclosures to an attorney will jeopardize your position.

A field audit of your business return is likely to involve a comprehensive examination and requires careful preparation. Together with your tax adviser, go over your return for potential areas of weakness. For example, the agent is likely to question deductions you have claimed for business travel. If you are an incorporated professional, the corporation's deductions for expenses of company-owned cars or planes will probably be reviewed. The agent may suspect that a portion of these business deductions are actually nondeductible personal travel costs; be prepared to substantiate the business portion of your total mileage and operating expenses.

Under the Taxpayer Bill of Rights *(48.8)*, the IRS is generally required to hold an office audit at the office located nearest to your home. The IRS generally may not conduct a field audit at the site of a small business if the audit would essentially require the shutting down of the business, unless a direct visit is necessary to determine inventory or verify assets.

48.4 Handling the Audit

If you have authorized someone to represent you at the examination, your representative may appear at the examination without you. If the IRS wants to question you, it must issue you an administrative summons. If you are present and questioned, you may stop the examination to consult with counsel, unless the examination is pursuant to an administrative summons.

Audits conducted at an IRS office may conclude quickly because they usually involve only a few specific issues. In some cases, the audit may take less than an hour. The key to handling the audit is advance preparation. When you arrive at the IRS office, be prepared to produce your records quickly. Records should be organized by topic so that you do not waste time leafing through pages for a receipt or other document.

If the agent decides to question an item not mentioned in the notice of audit, refuse politely but firmly to answer the questions. Tell the agent that you must first review your records. If the agent insists on pursuing the matter, another meeting will have to be scheduled. The agent might decide it is not worth the time and drop the issue.

Common sense rules of courtesy should be your guide in your contacts with the agent. Avoid personality clashes; they can only interfere with a speedy and fair resolution of the examination.

Planning Reminder

Audit Scheduling

Make sure that the examination is scheduled far enough in advance for you to get ready. Do not let the IRS hurry you into an examination until you are prepared. In some localities, particularly rural areas, the IRS may give short notice in scheduling a field audit. An agent may even appear at your home or place of business and try to begin the audit immediately. Resist this pressure and reschedule the meeting at your convenience.

However, be firm in your approach and, if the agent appears to be unreasonable in his or her approach, make it clear that—if necessary—you will go all the way to court to win your point. A vacillating approach may weaken your position in reaching a settlement.

If the IRS has scheduled a field audit, ask that the examination be held at your representative's office. If you have not retained professional help and the examination takes place on your business premises, do not allow the agent free run of the area: Provide the agent with a comfortable work area for examining your records. If possible, the workplace should be isolated so that the agent can concentrate on the examination without being distracted by office operations that might spark questions. Tell your employees not to answer questions about your business or engage in small talk with the agent. As with an office audit, help speed along the field examination by having prepared your records so that requested information can be quickly produced.

Recording the examination.   You have the right to make an audio recording of any interview with an IRS official. Video recordings are not permitted. No later than 10 calendar days before the interview, give written notice to the agent conducting the interview that you will make a recording. Later requests are at the discretion of the IRS. You must pay for all recording expenses and supply the equipment. The IRS may also make a recording of the interview, upon giving notice of at least 10 calendar days. However, IRS notice is not necessary if you have already submitted a request to make a recording. You have the right to obtain a transcript, at your own expense, of any recording made by the IRS. Generally, a request for a copy must be received by the IRS agent within 30 calendar days after the recording, although later requests may be honored.

48.5   Agreeing to Audit Changes

After the audit, the agent will discuss proposed changes either with you or your representative.

If you agree with the agent's proposed changes, you will be asked to sign a Form 870, which, when signed, permits an immediate assessment of a deficiency plus penalties and interest, if due. The Form 870 is called "Waiver of Restrictions on Assessment and Collection of Deficiency in Tax and Acceptance of Overassessment."

Before deciding whether to sign the Form 870, consider that, by signing, you are giving up your right of appeal to both an IRS Appellate Conference and the Tax Court. However, you may still file a refund suit in a federal district court or in the Court of Federal Claims unless you have agreed not to do so on the Form 870.

If you believe that you have done as well or better than expected regarding the proposed deficiency, you can bring the case to a close by signing the Form 870, but the agent's supervisor must also approve the assessment.

By signing the form, you limit the amount of interest charges added to the deficiency; interest stops running within 30 days after the date it is signed. A signed Form 870 does not prevent the IRS from reopening the case to assess an additional deficiency. If on review the deficiency is increased, you will receive a revised Form 870. You can refuse to sign the form. The signed first form has the effect of stopping the interest on the original deficiency. As a matter of practice, however, waivers of acceptances ordinarily result in closing of the case.

It is possible, although unlikely, that upon examining your return, the agent will determine that you are due a refund. In this situation, a signed Form 870 is considered a valid refund claim. You should file a protective refund claim even if you sign the Form 870 acknowledging the overpayment. Generally, the agent will process the refund, but if he or she fails to do so or the review staff puts it aside for some reason and the limitations period expires, the refund will be lost. The refund claim will protect you from such a mishap.

The payment of tax before the deficiency notice (90-day letter) is mailed is, in effect, a waiver of the restrictions on assessment and collection. If the payment satisfies your entire tax liability for that year, you cannot appeal to the Tax Court. You must sue for a refund in either federal district court or the Court of Federal Claims.

48.6   Disputing the Audit Changes

If you disagree with the agent and the examination takes place in an IRS office, you may ask for an immediate meeting with a supervisor to argue your side of the dispute. If an agreement is not reached at this meeting or the audit is at your office or home, the agent prepares a report of the proposed adjustments. You will receive a 30-day letter in which you are given the opportunity to request a conference. You may decide not to ask for a conference and await a formal notice of deficiency.

Caution

Penalty for Frivolous Court Action

If you bring a frivolous case to the Tax Court or unreasonably failed to discuss your position within the IRS audit procedures, the Tax Court may impose a penalty of up to $25,000. If an attorney unreasonably multiplies Tax Court proceedings, the attorney may be required to pay excess court costs or attorneys' fees incurred because of the resulting delay. Furthermore, if you appeal a Tax Court decision and the appeals court finds that the appeal was frivolous, you may be penalized.

If your examination was conducted as an office audit or by correspondence, or the disputed amount does not exceed $2,500, you do not have to prepare a written protest for a conference. The written protest presents your reason for disagreeing with the agent's report. *See* IRS Publication 5, "Appeal Rights and Preparation of Protests for Unagreed Cases."

At the conference you may appear for yourself or be represented by an attorney or other agent, and you may bring witnesses. The conference is held in an informal manner and you are given ample opportunity to present your case.

If you cannot reach a settlement, you will receive a Notice of Deficiency, commonly called a 90-day letter. In it, you are notified that at the end of 90 days from the date it was mailed, the government will assess the additional tax.

Going to court. When you receive a 90-day letter, if you are still convinced that your position is correct, you may take your case to one of three courts. You may within 90 days file a petition with the Tax Court; *or* you may pay the additional tax, file a refund claim for it, and—after the refund claim is denied—sue for a refund in a federal district court or the U.S. Court of Federal Claims.

Generally, the decision to litigate should be considered by an experienced tax practitioner.

The Tax Court has a small tax case procedure for deficiencies of $10,000 or less. Such cases are handled expeditiously and informally. Cases may be heard by appointed special trial judges. A small claim case may be discontinued at any time before a decision, but the decision when made is final. No appeal may be taken.

48.7 Recovering Legal Fees

In a tax dispute, you may feel that the IRS has taken an unreasonable position that forced you to incur legal fees and other expenses to win your case. You may be able to recover all or part of your costs under the following rules in a civil tax case.

Cases commenced after July 30, 1996. Generally, taxpayers who win their cases in the Tax Court or any other federal court may recover up to $110 an hour for attorneys' fees plus related litigation expenses. After 1997, the $110 hourly limit may be increased by an inflation factor. If the following requirements are satisfied, attorneys' fees in a declaratory judgment proceeding may be recovered.

All administrative remedies with the IRS must be exhausted to recover litigation and administrative costs, but this does not include having to agree to an extension of time for the assessment of tax. An award may be based on unjustified conduct by the IRS during pretrial administrative proceedings as well as on IRS conduct after litigation begins.

If you prevail in an IRS proceeding commenced after August 5, 1997, you must apply to the IRS for administrative costs before the 91st day after the date on which the final IRS determination of tax, interest, or penalty is mailed to you. To appeal a denial of your application for costs, you must petition the Tax Court within 90 days from the date the IRS mails the denial.

Individuals *may not* recover legal fees if their net worth at the time the action begins exceeds $2 million. For proceedings commenced after August 5, 1997, the $2 million net worth limit applies separately to each spouse in determining whether a married couple filing jointly is entitled to recover legal fees. No recovery is allowed to sole proprietors, partnerships, and corporations if their net worth exceeds $7 million or they have more than 500 employees.

The $110 per hour recovery for fees of an attorney or other qualified representative may be increased if the court determines that a higher rate is justified. A higher rate may be based on the high cost of attorneys in urban areas, or the limited availability of attorneys.

To recover administrative or litigation costs, you must "substantially prevail" as to the key issues in the case or the amount of tax involved. If you do, you will be entitled to a recovery unless the IRS proves that it was "substantially justified" in maintaining the position that it did. The Tax Court and other courts have interpreted "substantially justified" to be a reasonableness standard. The IRS is presumed not to be "substantially justified" if it does not follow its own published regulations, revenue rulings, or procedures, notices, announcements, or a private ruling issued to the taxpayer. The IRS may try to rebut the presumption. The reasonableness of an IRS position at the administrative stage is determined as of the earlier of two dates: (1) the date you received notice of an IRS decision from its appeals office, and (2) the date of the deficiency notice. If the IRS position as of the earlier date was not justified and you win your case in Tax Court or other federal court, the court may award the following costs incurred on or after that date: (1) administrative fees or similar charges imposed by the IRS; (2) reasonable expenses of expert witnesses; (3) the reasonable cost of any study, analysis, engineering report, test, or project that is necessary for the preparation of the case; and (4) reasonable fees (generally not to exceed $110 per hour) paid or incurred for the services of a qualified representative in connection with the administrative action.

If your case is settled with the IRS before going to court, the IRS may settle your claim for administrative expenses. If it denies or limits your claim, you may appeal to the Tax Court under the informal "small" case procedures.

An award for litigation expenses may also include court costs and other reasonable fees based on prevailing market rates for expert witnesses and special reports, such as an engineer's report necessary to the preparation of your court case. However, the recovery for expert witnesses may not exceed the amount paid by the government to its own expert witnesses. Litigation expenses are recoverable only if you have exhausted administrative remedies within the IRS.

Cases commenced after November 10, 1988, but before July 31, 1996.

The rules for recovering attorneys' fees and related litigation and administrative proceeding costs are similar to those previously discussed for cases begun after July 30, 1996, but there are some key differences.

The maximum recovery for attorneys' fees is $75 per hour, unless the court finds that a higher rate is justified. In one case, an award of $180 per hour was approved by a federal court because of the attorney's specialized skills and the complexity of corporate tax issues involved in the case. However, in another case, the Tax Court refused to allow fees of $150 per hour, which was the going rate for tax litigation experts in Albuquerque.

To receive attorneys' fees or other litigation or administrative proceeding costs, the burden is on you to prove that the IRS's position was *not* substantially justified. There is no presumption, as there is in cases starting after July 30, 1996, that the IRS was not substantially justified if it did not follow its published rulings or other guidance.

Suing the IRS for unauthorized collection action.

If an IRS employee recklessly or intentionally disregards the law or IRS regulations when making a tax assessment or taking some other collection action, you may sue the IRS in federal district court for actual economic damages resulting from the IRS employee's misconduct plus certain costs of bringing the action. The lawsuit must be filed within two years of the date your right to sue accrued.

The maximum damage award is $1 million for actions by IRS officers or employees after July 30, 1996. An award may be reduced if administrative remedies before the IRS are not exhausted. If the IRS action was after November 10, 1988, but before July 31, 1996, the maximum award is $100,000, and no amount will be awarded if the court determines that administrative remedies were not exhausted. No suit may be brought for IRS actions before November 11, 1988.

According to IRS regulations, actual economic damages that may be recovered are monetary losses you suffer as a direct result of the IRS's unlawful action. For example, a business may lose loyal customers and suffer an actual cash loss if the IRS's action damages the business's reputation. Other actual expenses could include the cost of renting a house or a car if the IRS puts a lien on or seizes your property, or loss of income due to the garnishment of your paycheck. Damages from the IRS for loss of reputation, inconvenience, or emotional distress are allowed only to the extent that they result in such actual monetary loss.

The IRS defines "costs of action" that you may recover as (1) fees of the clerk and marshall; (2) fees of the court reporter; (3) fees and disbursements for printing and witnesses; (4) copying fees; (5) docket fees; and (6) compensation for court-appointed experts and interpreters.

Litigation costs and administrative proceeding costs are not treated as "costs of the action." However, if the IRS denies your administrative claim for damages and you successfully sue in federal district court, you are considered a "prevailing party" and may recover attorneys' fees, related litigation expenses, and administrative costs before the IRS as previously discussed.

Warning: If you start a court action and the court holds that it is frivolous, you may be penalized up to $10,000.

IRS failure to release lien.

A suit for damages may also be brought in federal district court against the IRS if IRS employees improperly fail to release a lien on your property. Before you sue, you must file an administrative claim for damages. The lawsuit must be filed within two years after your claim arose. You may sue for actual economic damages plus costs of the action; the types of damages that may be recovered are similar to those previously discussed for suing the IRS for unauthorized collection actions.

48.8 Taxpayer Bill of Rights

The provisions of the Taxpayer Bill of Rights are generally intended to protect taxpayers during IRS examinations and tax collection procedures. Key provisions are in the following list and in the table below.

- The Taxpayer Advocate helps individuals resolve problems with the IRS. and is responsible for identifying problem areas and reporting them to tax-writing committees that propose administrative and legislative changes to correct these problems. The Taxpayer Advocate has broad authority to take action for taxpayers who would otherwise suffer a significant hardship as a result of IRS administration of the tax laws.
- The IRS must notify taxpayers 30 days before altering, modifying, or terminating any installment agreement for any reason, except when tax collection is in jeopardy.
- The IRS may abate interest charged to a taxpayer if unreasonable errors or delays were caused by IRS employees performing "managerial or ministerial" acts. The Tax Court has jurisdiction to review whether IRS failure to abate interest for an eligible taxpayer was an abuse of discretion.
- The interest-free payment deadline for taxpayers to pay tax after receiving notice and demand is 21 calendar days if the deficiency is less than $100,000 and 10 business days if the deficiency is at least $100,000.

Item—	Taxpayer Bill of Rights Rule—
Being informed of your rights	If the IRS sends you notice of a deficiency or collection action, it must include a nontechnical statement of your rights during an audit and an explanation of IRS collection procedures and appeals procedures within the IRS and the courts.
Having a representative handle your case	To represent you at an examination, you may give a written power of attorney to a lawyer, CPA, or enrolled agent or actuary qualified to practice before the IRS. You do not have to attend the examination unless the IRS issues an administrative summons requesting your presence.
Recording your examination	As discussed at 48.4, you may, at your own expense, make an audio recording of an interview if you give advance notice to the IRS. The IRS may also record an interview; you must be given prior notice and an opportunity to obtain a transcript by reimbursing the IRS for the printing costs.
Getting hardship relief from the IRS	If the IRS is threatening to seize your property or take some other collection measure that could cause you significant hardship, you may apply for a Taxpayer Assistance Order by filing Form 911 with the Problem Resolution Office in the IRS district where you live. While the Problem Resolution Officer or the IRS Taxpayer Advocate reviews your application, enforcement actions are suspended.
Relying on erroneous IRS advice	You may avoid penalties but not tax or interest if you rely on written IRS advice when preparing a return and the advice turns out to be erroneous. You must provide specific information to the IRS in writing when making a request for advice. You may no longer rely on the advice if the IRS gives you written notice that the advice is no longer the IRS position; if it takes a contrary position in regulations or in a published revenue ruling, procedure, or notice; or if the law is changed by a Supreme Court decision or tax treaty. If you have not been notified of a change in IRS position but a penalty is nevertheless assessed, file Form 843 for an abatement of the penalty and attach copies of your request for advice and the IRS's erroneous advice. Write at the top of Form 843: "Abatement of penalty or addition to tax pursuant to Section 6404(f)." If the penalty has been paid, file Form 843 as a refund claim.
Property exempt from IRS seizure	The weekly amount of wages exempt from IRS levy (seizure) is equal to your standard deduction plus allowable personal exemptions divided by 52.
	Property exempt from levy after 1996 is $2,500 for personal property and $1,250 for books and business tools.
	A personal residence is exempt from IRS levy, unless an IRS district director or assistant district director personally authorizes it in writing or the Treasury Secretary finds that collection of the tax would be jeopardized if the residence is not seized.
	Before the IRS may seize property, it must give 30 days' notice. The notice must clearly describe the levy procedures, your options to avoid the levy, such as beginning installment payments for overdue tax, and steps for redeeming property if property is seized by the IRS.
	A bank will hold your account for 21 days after receiving notice of an IRS levy before turning over the money to the IRS. The 21-day freeze allows you time to contact the IRS.
	If the IRS attempts to levy your property after you have paid the underlying tax liability, the statute of limitations has expired, or if the property is exempt under bankruptcy rules, you should appeal to the IRS to release the levy. Send a written statement to the District Director of the IRS district in which the lien was filed, explaining your grounds for appeal.

Chapter 49

Filing Refund Claims, and Amended Returns

File a refund claim on Form 1040X if you want to take advantage of a retroactive change in the law or if you have overpaid your tax because you failed to take allowable deductions or credits, or overstated your income. *See* the sample Form 1040X at the end of this chapter.

File a refund claim on time. The time limits discussed at *49.1* must be strictly observed; otherwise, even if you file a valid refund claim, it will be denied because of late filing.

Before filing a refund claim for a prior year, carefully review the return of that year for accuracy. A refund claim may subject the return to an examination in which the IRS may find errors that reduce or completely eliminate the refund claim, or may even lead to the assessment of a deficiency.

Income tax overwithholding. You do not have to file a refund claim if you have overpaid your tax due to excessive withholding of taxes on your wages or salary, or if you have overestimated your estimated tax. You get a refund on these overpayments by filing your tax return and requesting a refund for these amounts. You may not recover an overpayment of estimated tax until you file your final return.

For a refund of an overpayment of FICA taxes, *see* 26.10 for how to claim a refund on your tax return. If you are not required to file a tax return, you file a refund claim on Form 843.

Earned income credit. If you are entitled to a refund due to the earned income credit for certain low-income working families, you must file your tax return to get your refund, even though your income and filing status would not otherwise require that a return be filed. *See* Chapter 25.

49.1 When To File a Refund Claim

You may file a refund claim on Form 1040X within three years from the time your return was filed, or within two years from the time you paid your tax, whichever is later. A return filed before its due date is treated as having been filed on the due date.

A refund claim based on a bad debt or worthless securities may be made within seven years of the due date of the return for the year in which the debt or security became worthless.

The time for filing refund claims based on carrybacks of net operating losses or general business credits is within three years of the due date (including extensions) of the return for the year the loss or credit arose.

A refund claim based on your share of a joint return refund withheld by the IRS to pay your spouse's debts *(49.2)* may be made within six years of the date you received the IRS notice that the refund had been withheld.

If you filed an agreement giving the IRS an extended period of time in which to assess a tax against you, you are allowed an additional period in which to file a claim for refund. The claim, up to certain amounts, may be filed through the extension period and for six months afterwards.

Armed Forces service members and veterans. In determining the time limits within which a refund claim may be filed, you disregard intervening periods of service in a combat zone or hazardous duty area, plus periods of continuous hospitalization outside the United States as a result of combat zone injury, and the next 180 days thereafter.

49.2 Joint Refund Claims

If a joint return was filed for a year in which a refund is due, both spouses are entitled to recover jointly and both must file a joint refund claim. Where separate returns were filed, each spouse is a separate taxpayer and may not file a claim to recover a refund based on the other spouse's return, except if that spouse becomes the fiduciary when one spouse becomes incompetent or dies. If you are divorced and incur a net operating loss or credit that may be carried back to a year in which you were married, you may file a refund claim with your signature alone and the refund check will be made out only to you; *see 40.18.*

Refund withheld to pay spouse's debts. If you showed a refund due on a joint return filed with a spouse who owed child support or federal student loans, the IRS may have withheld payment of the refund to cover the obligations. If you are not liable for the past-due payments, and your tax payments (withholdings or estimated tax installments) exceed your income reported on the joint return, you may file Form 8379 to get back your share of the refund.

49.3 Stating the Reasons for Refund Claims

The most important part of a refund claim is a statement of the "reasons" for the refund. A general claim simply noting an overpayment, without supporting facts and grounds, is not sufficient. If a claim is denied by the IRS, it may become the basis of a court suit. If you have not stated all the grounds, you may not be allowed to argue them in court. You must make a claim showing all the:

- Facts that support the claim. Attach all supporting documents and tax forms supporting your claim.
- Grounds for the claim. If you are uncertain about the exact legal grounds, alternate and even inconsistent grounds may be given. For example: "The loss was incurred from an embezzlement; if not, from a bad debt." To protect against understating the amount of the claim, you might preface the claim with this phrase: "The following or such greater amounts, as may be legally refunded."

49.4 Quick Refund Claims

Form 1045 may be used for filing refunds due to carrybacks from net operating losses, and the general business credit. Form 1045 also may be used for a quick refund based on a repayment exceeding $3,000 of income reported in an earlier year. Form 1045 must be filed within 12 months after the loss year. The IRS must act on the claim within 90 days. Payment of quick refund claims is not a final settlement of your return; the IRS may still audit and then disallow the refund claim. Note that the filing of a quick refund, if rejected, may not be the basis of a suit for refund; a regular refund claim must be filed.

Tax-shelter claims. If you file a quick refund claim on Form 1045 and the IRS determines it is likely that you claimed excessive tax-shelter benefits, the IRS will offset the quick refund claim by a deficiency attributable to the tax-shelter items. You will receive the balance and receive a notice of the tax-shelter deficiency.

Caution

Time Limits Must Be Observed

Failure to file a timely refund claim is fatal, regardless of its merits. Even if you expect that your claim will have to be pursued in court, you must still file a timely refund claim. Mailing a return so that it is postmarked by the due date (including extensions) qualifies as a timely filing if you use the U.S. Postal Service. The timely mailing rule also applies to returns that are timely deposited with private delivery services that have been designated by the IRS.

49.5 Interest Paid on Refunds

If you file for 1997 on or before the April 15, 1998, filing deadline, interest is not paid by the IRS on refunds made within 45 days of the April 15 due date. For example, you file your 1997 return on April 1, 1998, claiming an overpayment due to overwithholding on your wages. Interest does not have to be paid on refunds before May 31, which is 46 days after April 15, the day the tax was due. A return filed before its due date is treated as having been filed on the due date. If the overpayment is not refunded within 45 days, interest is paid from the date the tax was overpaid up to a date determined by the IRS that can be as much as 30 days before the date of the refund check.

If you get a filing extension or otherwise file after the due date of the return (without regard to extensions of time), no interest is paid if the refund is made within 45 days after the date you filed.

Refund claims.   Interest on a refund claim filed within the time limits of *49.1* is paid from the date of overpayment to the date the claim was filed if the IRS pays the refund within 45 days. If the refund is not made within the 45-day period, interest is paid from the date of overpayment to a date set by the IRS that is not more than 30 days before the date of the refund check.

The IRS does not have to pay interest on overpayments resulting from net operating loss carrybacks, or business credit carrybacks if a refund is paid within 45 days of the filing of the refund claim. If a refund claim based on a loss or credit carryback is filed and subsequently a quick refund claim is filed on Form 1045 for the same refund, the 45-day period starts to run on the date Form 1045 is filed.

Interest rates applied to overpayments are as follows:

Amounts outstanding between—	Rate is—
10/1/92 – 6/30/94	6%
7/1/94 – 9/30/94	7
10/1/94 – 3/31/95	8
4/1/95 – 6/30/95	9
7/1/95 – 3/31/96	8
4/1/96 – 6/30/96	7
7/1/96 – 9/30/97	8

49.6 Refunds Withheld by the IRS

The IRS may withhold all or part of your refund if you owe child support or federal debts such as student loans. If you file a joint return with a spouse who owes child support or federal debts, you may be able to obtain your share of a refund due on the joint return; for further details, *see 49.2.*

Tax-shelter claims.   The IRS may withhold refunds based on questionable tax-shelter claims. This rule applies to original tax returns showing a refund due as well as to refund claims. In each IRS Service Center, returns of tax-shelter investors are screened to determine if the tax shelter has fraudulently misrepresented tax benefits or grossly overvalued assets or services. If the tax shelter is considered to be abusive and if claimed deductions or tax credits are disallowed, refunds attributable to the tax-shelter items will not be paid. The balance of your refund claim will be paid.

A refund will also be frozen if you file your return after receiving a pre-filing notification letter from the IRS warning you not to claim certain tax-shelter writeoffs.

49.7 Amended Returns Showing Additional Tax

If, after filing your 1997 return, you find that you did not report some income or claimed excessive deductions, you should file an amended return on Form 1040X to limit interest charges and possible tax penalties.

If you filed early and then file an amended return by the filing due date (including any extensions) that shows additional tax due, you will not be charged interest or penalties based on the original return; the amended return is considered a substitute for the original.

You must pay the additional tax due as shown on Form 1040X. Even if you expect a refund on your original return, the IRS will not reduce the refund check to cover the additional tax. You must pay it and you will receive the original refund separately.

Part 8

Sample Tax Forms, Tax Tables, and Tax Rate Schedules

In the following pages, you will find sample tax forms that you can use as worksheets. However, the final version of the tax forms may vary. The Supplement to this book will provide final blank forms suitable for filing.

Use the tax tables starting on page 709 to look up your tax liability if your taxable income is less than $100,000. If your taxable income is $100,000 or more, use the tax rate schedules on page 721.

*All the forms in this section are based on IRS advance proofs that are subject to change. Use the IRS final version for filing your tax return. Note that at the time this book went to press, the IRS was in the process of revising Schedule D in light of the new capital gain rules. Schedule D, as well as other final blank forms suitable for filing, will be available in the Supplement. Use the card at the front of this book to send for the free Suupplement. If you visit the J.K. Lasser homepage located on the World Wide Web at *http://www.jklasser.com* you may link to the IRS web site to obtain final forms. The IRS web site is *http://www.irs.ustreas.gov/*.

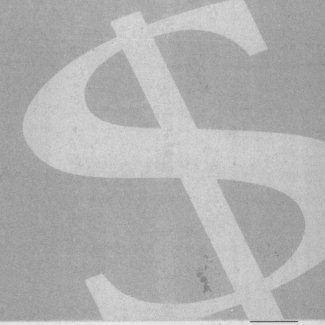

Form **1040EZ**

Department of the Treasury—Internal Revenue Service

Income Tax Return for Single and Joint Filers With No Dependents (99) **1997**

OMB No. 1545-0675

Use the IRS label here

Your first name and initial | Last name

If a joint return, spouse's first name and initial | Last name

Home address (number and street). If you have a P.O. box, see page 7. | Apt. no.

City, town or post office, state, and ZIP code. If you have a foreign address, see page 7.

Your social security number

Spouse's social security number

Presidential Election Campaign (See page 7.)

Note: *Checking "Yes" will not change your tax or reduce your refund.*

Do you want $3 to go to this fund? ▶ Yes ☐ No ☐

If a joint return, does your spouse want $3 to go to this fund? ▶ Yes ☐ No ☐

Dollars | **Cents**

Income

Attach Copy B of Form(s) W-2 here. Enclose, but do not attach, any payment with your return.

1 Total wages, salaries, and tips. This should be shown in box 1 of your W-2 form(s). Attach your W-2 form(s). **1**

2 Taxable interest income. If the total is over $400, you cannot use Form 1040EZ. **2**

3 Unemployment compensation (see page 9). **3**

4 Add lines 1, 2, and 3. This is your **adjusted gross income.** If under $9,770, see page 9 to find out if you can claim the earned income credit on line 8a. **4**

Note: *You* **must** *check Yes or No.*

5 Can your parents (or someone else) claim you on their return?

Yes. Enter amount from worksheet on back. ☐

No. If **single,** enter 6,800.00. If **married,** enter 12,200.00. See back for explanation. **5**

6 Subtract line 5 from line 4. If line 5 is larger than line 4, enter 0. This is your **taxable income.** ▶ **6**

Payments and tax

7 Enter your Federal income tax withheld from box 2 of your W-2 form(s). **7**

8a **Earned income credit** (see page 9).

b Nontaxable earned income: enter type and amount below.

Type | $ | **8a**

9 Add lines 7 and 8a. These are your **total payments.** **9**

10 **Tax.** Use the amount on **line 6** to find your tax in the tax table on pages 20–24 of the booklet. Then, enter the tax from the table on this line. **10**

Refund

Have it directly deposited! See page 13 and fill in 11b, 11c, and 11d.

11a If line 9 is larger than line 10, subtract line 10 from line 9. This is your **refund.** **11a**

▶ **b** Routing number

▶ **c** Type: Checking ☐ Savings ☐

d Account number

Amount you owe

12 If line 10 is larger than line 9, subtract line 9 from line 10. This is the **amount you owe.** See page 13 for details on how to pay. **12**

1 2 3 4 5

I have read this return. Under penalties of perjury, I declare that to the best of my knowledge and belief, the return is true, correct, and accurately lists all amounts and sources of income I received during the tax year.

Sign here

Keep copy for your records.

Your signature | Spouse's signature if joint return

Date | Your occupation | Date | Spouse's occupation

For Official Use Only

6 7 8 9 10

For Privacy Act and Paperwork Reduction Act Notice, see page 5.

Cat. No. 11329W

1997 Form 1040EZ

Use this form if

- Your filing status is single or married filing jointly.
- You do not claim any dependents.
- You had **only** wages, salaries, tips, taxable scholarship or fellowship grants, unemployment compensation, or Alaska Permanent Fund dividends, and your taxable interest income was not over $400. **But** if you earned tips, including allocated tips, that are not included in box 5 and box 7 of your W-2, you may not be able to use Form 1040EZ. See page 8.
- You did not receive any advance earned income credit payments.

- You (and your spouse if married) were under 65 on January 1, 1998, and not blind at the end of 1997.
- Your taxable income (line 6) is less than $50,000.

If you are not sure about your filing status, see page 7. If you have questions about dependents, use TeleTax topic 354 (see page 18). If you **cannot use this form,** use TeleTax topic 352 (see page 18).

Filling in your return

For tips on how to avoid common mistakes, see page 3.

Because this form is read by a machine, please print your numbers inside the boxes like this:

9876543210

Do not type your numbers. Do not use dollar signs.

If you received a scholarship or fellowship grant or tax-exempt interest income, such as on municipal bonds, see the booklet before filling in the form. Also, see the booklet if you received a Form 1099-INT showing income tax withheld or if tax was withheld from your Alaska Permanent Fund dividends.

Remember, you must report all wages, salaries, and tips even if you do not get a W-2 form from your employer. You must also report all your taxable interest income, including interest from banks, savings and loans, credit unions, etc., even if you do not get a Form 1099-INT.

Worksheet for dependents who checked "Yes" on line 5

Use this worksheet to figure the amount to enter on line 5 if someone can claim you (or your spouse if married) as a dependent, even if that person chooses not to do so. To find out if someone can claim you as a dependent, use TeleTax topic 354 (see page 18).

A. Enter the amount from line 1 on the front. A. _____

B. Minimum standard deduction. B. _____ 650.00

C. Enter the LARGER of line A or line B here. C. _____

D. Maximum standard deduction. If single, enter 4,150.00; if married, enter 6,900.00. D. _____

E. Enter the SMALLER of line C or line D here. This is your standard deduction. E. _____

F. Exemption amount.
- If single, enter 0.
- If married and—
  —both you and your spouse can be claimed as dependents, enter 0.
  —only one of you can be claimed as a dependent, enter 2,650.00. F. _____

G. Add lines E and F. Enter the total here and on line 5 on the front. G. _____

If you checked "No" on line 5 because no one can claim you (or your spouse if married) as a dependent, enter on line 5 the amount shown below that applies to you.

- Single, enter 6,800.00. This is the total of your standard deduction (4,150.00) and your exemption (2,650.00).
- Married, enter 12,200.00. This is the total of your standard deduction (6,900.00), your exemption (2,650.00), and your spouse's exemption (2,650.00).

Mailing your return

Mail your return by **April 15, 1998.** Use the envelope that came with your booklet. If you do not have that envelope, see page 28 for the address to use.

Paid preparer's use only

See page 14.

Under penalties of perjury, I declare that I have examined this return, and to the best of my knowledge and belief, it is true, correct, and accurately lists all amounts and sources of income received during the tax year. This declaration is based on all information of which I have any knowledge.

Preparer's signature	Date	Check if self-employed ☐	Preparer's SSN
Firm's name (or yours if self-employed) and address		EIN	
		ZIP code	

Form
1040A (99)
Department of the Treasury—Internal Revenue Service
U.S. Individual Income Tax Return **1997** IRS Use Only—Do not write or staple in this space.

Label (See page 15.) **Use the IRS label.** Otherwise, please print in **ALL CAPITAL LETTERS.**

OMB No. 1545-0085

L A B E L — H E R E

Your first name	Init.	Last name

Your social security number

If a joint return, spouse's first name	Init.	Last name

Spouse's social security number

Home address (number and street). If you have a P.O. box, see page 15. | Apt. no.

City, town or post office. If you have a foreign address, see page 15. | State | ZIP code

For Privacy Act and Paperwork Reduction Act Notice, see page 9.

Presidential Election Campaign Fund (See page 15.)

Yes | No

Do you want $3 to go to this fund? . . . .

If a joint return, does your spouse want $3 to go to this fund? . . . .

Note: *Checking "Yes" will not change your tax or reduce your refund.*

1 ☐ Single

2 ☐ Married filing joint return (even if only one had income)

3 ☐ Married filing separate return. Enter spouse's social security number above and full name here. ▶ _____

4 ☐ Head of household (with qualifying person). (See page 16.) If the qualifying person is a child but not your dependent, enter this child's name here. ▶ _____

5 ☐ Qualifying widow(er) with dependent child (year spouse died ▶ 19   ). (See page 16.)

6a ☐ **Yourself.** If your parent (or someone else) can claim you as a dependent on his or her tax return, **do not** check box 6a.

b ☐ **Spouse**

No. of boxes checked on 6a and 6b ☐

c Dependents. If more than six dependents, see page 17.

(1) First name Last name	(2) Dependent's social security number	(3) Dependent's relationship to you	(4) No. of months lived in your home in 1997

No. of your children on 6c who:
• lived with you ☐
• did not live with you due to divorce or separation (see page 18) ☐
Dependents on 6c not entered above ☐

d Total number of exemptions claimed . . . . ▶

Add numbers entered in boxes above ☐

		Dollars	Cents
7	Wages, salaries, tips, etc. Attach Form(s) W-2.	**7**	
8a	**Taxable** interest income. Attach Schedule 1 if required.	**8a**	
b	**Tax-exempt** interest. DO NOT include on line 8a.	**8b**	
9	Dividends. Attach Schedule 1 if required.	**9**	

10a Total IRA distributions.	**10a**		**10b** Taxable amount (see page 20).	**10b**	
11a Total pensions and annuities.	**11a**		**11b** Taxable amount (see page 20).	**11b**	
12 Unemployment compensation.				**12**	
13a Social security benefits.	**13a**		**13b** Taxable amount (see page 22).	**13b**	

14 Add lines 7 through 13b (far right column). This is your **total income.** ▶ **14**

15 IRA deduction (see page 22). **15**

16 Subtract line 15 from line 14. This is your **adjusted gross income.** If under $29,290 (under $9,770 if a child did not live with you), see the EIC instructions on page 28. ▶ **16**

Attach Copy B of W-2 and 1099-R here.

Cat. No. 11327A

1997 Form 1040A

17 Enter the amount from line 16.   **17**

18a Check if: ☐ **You** were 65 or older   ☐ Blind   ☐ **Spouse** was 65 or older   ☐ Blind   **Enter number of boxes checked ▶** 18a

b If you are married filing separately and your spouse itemizes deductions, see page 24 and check here . . . . ▶ 18b ☐

19 Enter the **standard deduction** for your filing status. **But** see page 24 if you checked any box on line 18a or 18b **OR** someone can claim you as a dependent.
- Single—4,150   • Married filing jointly or Qualifying widow(er)—6,900
- Head of household—6,050   • Married filing separately—3,450   **19**

20 Subtract line 19 from line 17. If line 19 is more than line 17, enter 0.   **20**

21 Multiply $2,650 by the total number of exemptions claimed on line 6d.   **21**

22 Subtract line 21 from line 20. If line 21 is more than line 20, enter 0. This is your **taxable income. If you want the IRS to figure your tax, see page 24.** ▶ **22**

23 Find the tax on the amount on line 22 (see page 25).   **23**

24a Credit for child and dependent care expenses. Attach Schedule 2.   **24a**

b Credit for the elderly or the disabled. Attach Schedule 3.   **24b**

c Adoption credit. Attach Form 8839.   **24c**

d Add lines 24a, 24b, and 24c. These are your **total credits.**   **24d**

25 Subtract line 24d from line 23. If line 24d is more than line 23, enter 0.   **25**

26 Advance earned income credit payments from Form(s) W-2.   **26**

27 Household employment taxes. Attach Schedule H.   **27**

28 Add lines 25, 26, and 27. This is your **total tax.** ▶ **28**

29a Total Federal income tax withheld from Forms W-2 and 1099.   **29a**

b 1997 estimated tax payments and amount applied from 1996 return.   **29b**

c **Earned income credit.** Attach Schedule EIC if you have a qualifying child.   **29c**

d Nontaxable earned income: amount ▶   and type ▶

e Add lines 29a, 29b, and 29c. These are your **total payments.** ▶ **29e**

30 If line 29e is more than line 28, subtract line 28 from line 29e. This is the amount you **overpaid.**   **30**

31a Amount of line 30 you want **refunded to you.** If you want it directly deposited, see page 34 and fill in 31b, 31c, and 31d.   **31a**

b Routing number

c Type: ☐ Checking ☐ Savings

d Account number

32 Amount of line 30 you want **applied to your 1998 estimated tax.** **32**

33 If line 28 is more than line 29e, subtract line 29e from line 28. This is the **amount you owe.** For details on how to pay, see page 34.   **33**

34 Estimated tax penalty (see page 35).   **34**

Sign here

Under penalties of perjury, I declare that I have examined this return and accompanying schedules and statements, and to the best of my knowledge and belief, they are true, correct, and accurately list all amounts and sources of income I received during the tax year. Declaration of preparer (other than the taxpayer) is based on all information of which the preparer has any knowledge.

Keep a copy of this return for your records.

Your signature	Date	Your occupation
Spouse's signature. If joint return, BOTH must sign.	Date	Spouse's occupation

Paid preparer's use only

Preparer's signature	Date		Check if self-employed ☐	Preparer's SSN
Firm's name (or yours if self-employed) and address			EIN	
			ZIP code	

Schedule 1
(Form 1040A)

(99)

Department of the Treasury—Internal Revenue Service

Interest and Dividend Income for Form 1040A Filers

1997

OMB No. 1545-0085

Name(s) shown on Form 1040A: First and initial(s)	Last	Your social security number

Part I — Interest Income (See pages 19 and 49.)

Note: *If you received a Form 1099–INT, Form 1099–OID, or substitute statement from a brokerage firm, enter the firm's name and the total interest shown on that form.*

1 List name of payer. If any interest is from a seller-financed mortgage and the buyer used the property as a personal residence, see page 49 and list this interest first. Also, show that buyer's social security number and address.

Dollars — Cents

1

2 Add the amounts on line 1. **2**

3 Excludable interest on series EE U.S. savings bonds issued after 1989 from Form 8815, line 14. You **must** attach Form 8815 to Form 1040A. **3**

4 Subtract line 3 from line 2. Enter the result here and on Form 1040A, line 8a. **4**

Part II — Dividend Income (See pages 20 and 49.)

Note: *If you received a Form 1099–DIV or substitute statement from a brokerage firm, enter the firm's name and the total dividends shown on that form.*

5 List name of payer

Dollars — Cents

5

6 Add the amounts on line 5. Enter the total here and on Form 1040A, line 9. **6**

For Paperwork Reduction Act Notice, see Form 1040A instructions.

Cat. No. 12075R

1997 Schedule 1 (Form 1040A)

Schedule 2
(Form 1040A)

Department of the Treasury—Internal Revenue Service

Child and Dependent Care
Expenses for Form 1040A Filers   1997

OMB No. 1545-0085

Name(s) shown on Form 1040A: First and initial(s)	Last	Your social security number

Before you begin, you need to understand the following terms. See **Definitions** on page 50.

- **Dependent Care Benefits**   • **Qualifying Person(s)**   • **Qualified Expenses**   • **Earned Income**

Part I   Persons or Organizations Who Provided the Care—You **must** complete this part.
(If you need more space, use the bottom of page 2.)

	(a) Care provider's name	**(b)** Address (number, street, apt. no., city, state, and ZIP code)	**(c)** Identifying number (SSN or EIN)	**(d)** Amount paid (see page 51)
1				

Did you receive **dependent care benefits?**

— **No** ——→ Complete only Part II below.

— **Yes** ——→ Complete Part III on the back next.

Caution: *If the care was provided in your home, you may owe employment taxes. See the instructions for Form 1040A, line 27, on page 26.*

Part II   Credit for Child and Dependent Care Expenses

2 Information about your **qualifying person(s).** If you have more than two qualifying persons, see page 52.

(a) Qualifying person's name		**(b)** Qualifying person's social security number	**(c) Qualified expenses** you incurred and paid in 1997 for the person listed in column (a)
First	Last		

3 Add the amounts in column (c) of line 2. DO NOT enter more than 2,400 for one qualifying person or 4,800 for two or more persons. If you completed Part III, enter the amount from line 24.   **3**

4 Enter YOUR **earned income.**   **4**

5 If married filing a joint return, enter YOUR SPOUSE'S earned income (if student or disabled, see page 52); **all others,** enter the amount from line 4.   **5**

6 Enter the **smallest** of line 3, 4, or 5.   **6**

7 Enter the amount from Form 1040A, line 17.   **7**

8 Enter on line 8 the decimal amount shown below that applies to the amount on line 7.

If line 7 is—		Decimal amount is	If line 7 is—		Decimal amount is
Over	But not over		Over	But not over	
$0—10,000		.30	$20,000—22,000		.24
10,000—12,000		.29	22,000—24,000		.23
12,000—14,000		.28	24,000—26,000		.22
14,000—16,000		.27	26,000—28,000		.21
16,000—18,000		.26	28,000—No limit		.20
18,000—20,000		.25			

8   ×

9 Multiply **line 6** by the decimal amount on line 8. Enter the result. Then, see page 52 for the amount of credit to enter on Form 1040A, line 24a.   **9**

For Paperwork Reduction Act Notice, see Form 1040A instructions.   Cat. No. 10749I   **1997 Schedule 2 (Form 1040A)**

Part III   Dependent Care Benefits

10 Enter the total amount of **dependent care benefits** you received for 1997. This amount should be shown in box 10 of your W-2 form(s). DO NOT include amounts that were reported to you as wages in box 1 of Form(s) W-2.   **10**

11 Enter the amount forfeited, if any. See page 52.   **11**

12 Subtract line 11 from line 10.   **12**

13 Enter the total amount of **qualified expenses** incurred in 1997 for the care of the qualifying person(s).   **13**

14 Enter the **smaller** of line 12 or 13.   **14**

15 Enter YOUR **earned income.**   **15**

16 If married filing a joint return, enter YOUR SPOUSE'S earned income (if student or disabled, see the line 5 instructions); if married filing a separate return, see the instructions for the amount to enter; **all others,** enter the amount from line 15.   **16**

17 Enter the **smallest** of line 14, 15, or 16.   **17**

18 **Excluded benefits.** Enter here the **smaller** of the following:
- The amount from line 17, or
- 5,000 (2,500 if married filing a separate return **and** you were required to enter your spouse's earned income on line 16).   **18**

19 **Taxable benefits.** Subtract line 18 from line 12. Also, include this amount on Form 1040A, line 7. In the space to the left of line 7, print "DCB."   **19**

To claim the child and dependent care credit, complete lines 20–24 below.

20 Enter 2,400 (4,800 if two or more qualifying persons).   **20**

21 Enter the amount from line 18.   **21**

22 Subtract line 21 from line 20. If zero or less, **STOP.** You cannot take the credit. **Exception.** If you paid 1996 expenses in 1997, see the line 9 instructions.   **22**

23 Complete line 2 on the front of this schedule. DO NOT include in column (c) any excluded benefits shown on line 18 above. Then, add the amounts in column (c) and enter the total here.   **23**

24 Enter the **smaller** of line 22 or 23. Also, enter this amount on line 3 on the front of this schedule and complete lines 4–9.   **24**

Schedule 3
(Form 1040A)

Department of the Treasury—Internal Revenue Service

Credit for the Elderly or the Disabled
for Form 1040A Filers

1997

OMB No. 1545-0085

Name(s) shown on Form 1040A: First and initial(s)	Last	Your social security number

You may be able to take this credit and reduce your tax if by the end of 1997:
- You were age 65 or older, **OR** • You were under age 65, you retired on **permanent and total** disability, and you received taxable disability income.

But you must also meet other tests. See the separate instructions for Schedule 3.

Note: *In most cases, the IRS can figure the credit for you. See the instructions.*

Part I   Check the Box for Your Filing Status and Age

If your filing status is:	And by the end of 1997:	Check only one box:
Single, Head of household, or Qualifying widow(er) with dependent child	**1** You were 65 or older	1 ☐
	2 You were under 65 and you retired on permanent and total disability .	2 ☐
Married filing a joint return	**3** Both spouses were 65 or older	3 ☐
	4 Both spouses were under 65, but only one spouse retired on permanent and total disability	4 ☐
	5 Both spouses were under 65, and both retired on permanent and total disability	5 ☐
	6 One spouse was 65 or older, and the other spouse was under 65 and retired on permanent and total disability	6 ☐
	7 One spouse was 65 or older, and the other spouse was under 65 and **NOT** retired on permanent and total disability	7 ☐
Married filing a separate return	**8** You were 65 or older and you lived apart from your spouse for all of 1997	8 ☐
	9 You were under 65, you retired on permanent and total disability, and you lived apart from your spouse for all of 1997	9 ☐

Did you check box 1, 3, 7, or 8? —— **Yes** ——▶ Skip Part II and complete Part III on the back.

—— **No** ——▶ Complete Parts II and III.

Part II   Statement of Permanent and Total Disability (Complete **only** if you checked box 2, 4, 5, 6, or 9 above.)

IF: **1** You filed a physician's statement for this disability for 1983 or an earlier year, or you filed a statement for tax years after 1983 and your physician signed line B on the statement, **AND**

2 Due to your continued disabled condition, you were unable to engage in any substantial gainful activity in 1997, check this box . . . . ▶ ☐

- If you checked this box, you do not have to file another statement for 1997.
- If you **did not** check this box, have your physician complete the statement below.

Physician's Statement (See instructions at bottom of page 2.)

I certify that _____
                                        Name of disabled person

was permanently and totally disabled on January 1, 1976, or January 1, 1977, **OR** was permanently and totally disabled on the date he or she retired. If retired after 1976, enter the date retired . . . . ▶ [   ]

Physician: Sign your name on **either** line A or B below.

A The disability has lasted or can be expected to last continuously for at least a year . . . .
_____ _____
Physician's signature   Date

B There is no reasonable probability that the disabled condition will ever improve . . . . .
_____ _____
Physician's signature   Date

Physician's name	Physician's address

For Paperwork Reduction Act Notice, see Form 1040A instructions.   Cat. No. 12064K   **1997 Schedule 3 (Form 1040A)**

Part III   Figure Your Credit

10 If you checked (in Part I):   Enter:
   Box 1, 2, 4, or 7   5,000
   Box 3, 5, or 6   7,500   **10**
   Box 8 or 9   3,750

Did you check box 2, 4, 5, 6, or 9 in Part I?	— Yes ➤	You **must** complete line 11.
	— No ➤	Enter the amount from line 10 on line 12 and go to line 13.

11 • If you checked box 6 in Part I, add $5,000 to the taxable disability income of the spouse who was under age 65. Enter the total.
   • If you checked box 2, 4, or 9 in Part I, enter your taxable disability income.
   • If you checked box 5 in Part I, add your taxable disability income to your spouse's taxable disability income. Enter the total.
   TIP: For more details on what to include on line 11, see the instructions.   **11**

12 If you completed line 11, enter the **smaller** of line 10 or line 11; **all others,** enter the amount from line 10.   **12**

13 Enter the following pensions, annuities, or disability income that you (and your spouse if filing a joint return) received in 1997:
   a Nontaxable part of social security benefits, and Nontaxable part of railroad retirement benefits treated as social security. See instructions.   **13a**
   b Nontaxable veterans' pensions and any other pension, annuity, or disability benefit that is excluded from income under any other provision of law. See instructions.   **13b**
   c Add lines 13a and 13b. (Even though these income items are not taxable, they **must** be included here to figure your credit.) If you did not receive any of the types of nontaxable income listed on line 13a or 13b, enter 0 on line 13c.   **13c**

14 Enter the amount from Form 1040A, line 17.   **14**

15 If you checked (in Part I):   Enter:
   Box 1 or 2   7,500
   Box 3, 4, 5, 6, or 7   10,000
   Box 8 or 9   5,000   **15**

16 Subtract line 15 from line 14. If zero or less, enter 0.   **16**

17 Enter one-half of line 16.   **17**

18 Add lines 13c and 17.   **18**

19 Subtract line 18 from line 12. If zero or less, **stop;** you **cannot** take the credit. Otherwise, go to line 20.   **19**

20 Multiply line 19 by 15% (.15). Enter the result here and on Form 1040A, line 24b.   **20**

Instructions for Physician's Statement

Taxpayer

If you retired after 1976, enter the date you retired in the space provided in Part II.

Physician

A person is permanently and totally disabled if **both** of the following apply:

   1. He or she cannot engage in any substantial gainful activity because of a physical or mental condition, and

2. A physician determines that the disability has lasted or can be expected to last continuously for at least a year or can lead to death.

Form **1040**

Department of the Treasury—Internal Revenue Service

U.S. Individual Income Tax Return 1997

(99)   IRS Use Only—Do not write or staple in this space.

For the year Jan. 1–Dec. 31, 1997, or other tax year beginning   1997, ending   , 19   OMB No. 1545-0074

Label

(See instructions on page 10.)

Use the IRS label. Otherwise, please print or type.

L A B E L   H E R E

Your first name and initial   Last name

If a joint return, spouse's first name and initial   Last name

Home address (number and street). If you have a P.O. box, see page 10.   Apt. no.

City, town or post office, state, and ZIP code. If you have a foreign address, see page 10.

Your social security number

Spouse's social security number

For help in finding line instructions, see pages 2 and 3 in the booklet.

Presidential Election Campaign ▶
(See page 10.)

Do you want $3 to go to this fund? . . . .

If a joint return, does your spouse want $3 to go to this fund? . . . .

	Yes	No

Note: Checking "Yes" will not change your tax or reduce your refund.

Filing Status

Check only one box.

1. ☐ Single
2. ☐ Married filing joint return (even if only one had income)
3. ☐ Married filing separate return. Enter spouse's social security no. above and full name here. ▶ _____
4. ☐ Head of household (with qualifying person). (See page 10.) If the qualifying person is a child but not your dependent, enter this child's name here. ▶ _____
5. ☐ Qualifying widow(er) with dependent child (year spouse died ▶ 19   ). (See page 10.)

Exemptions

If more than six dependents, see page 10.

6a ☐ **Yourself.** If your parent (or someone else) can claim you as a dependent on his or her tax return, **do not** check box 6a . . . . . .

b ☐ **Spouse** . . . .

c **Dependents:**

(1) First name Last name	(2) Dependent's social security number	(3) Dependent's relationship to you	(4) No. of months lived in your home in 1997

d Total number of exemptions claimed . . . .

No. of boxes checked on 6a and 6b _____

No. of your children on 6c who:
- lived with you _____
- did not live with you due to divorce or separation (see page 11) _____

Dependents on 6c not entered above _____

Add numbers entered on lines above ▶ ☐

Income

Attach Copy B of your Forms W-2, W-2G, and 1099-R here.

If you did not get a W-2, see page 12.

Enclose but do not attach any payment. Also, please use **Form 1040-V.**

7	Wages, salaries, tips, etc. Attach Form(s) W-2	**7**
8a	**Taxable** interest. Attach Schedule B if required	**8a**
b	**Tax-exempt** interest. DO NOT include on line 8a . . . **8b**	
9	Dividend income. Attach Schedule B if required	**9**
10	Taxable refunds, credits, or offsets of state and local income taxes (see page 12) . .	**10**
11	Alimony received	**11**
12	Business income or (loss). Attach Schedule C or C-EZ	**12**
13	Capital gain or (loss). Attach Schedule D if required	**13**
14	Other gains or (losses). Attach Form 4797	**14**
15a	Total IRA distributions . **15a** **b** Taxable amount (see page 13)	**15b**
16a	Total pensions and annuities **16a** **b** Taxable amount (see page 13)	**16b**
17	Rental real estate, royalties, partnerships, S corporations, trusts, etc. Attach Schedule E	**17**
18	Farm income or (loss). Attach Schedule F	**18**
19	Unemployment compensation	**19**
20a	Social security benefits . **20a** **b** Taxable amount (see page 15)	**20b**
21	Other income. List type and amount—see page 15 _____	**21**
22	Add the amounts in the far right column for lines 7 through 21. This is your **total income** ▶	**22**

Adjusted Gross Income

If line 32 is under $29,290 (under $9,770 if a child did not live with you), see EIC on page 22.

23	IRA deduction (see page 16) **23**	
24	Medical savings account deduction. Attach Form 8853 . **24**	
25	Moving expenses. Attach Form 3903 or 3903-F . . **25**	
26	One-half of self-employment tax. Attach Schedule SE . **26**	
27	Self-employed health insurance deduction (see page 17) **27**	
28	Keogh and self-employed SEP and SIMPLE plans . **28**	
29	Penalty on early withdrawal of savings . . **29**	
30a	Alimony paid **b** Recipient's SSN ▶ _____ **30a**	
31	Add lines 23 through 30a	**31**
32	Subtract line 31 from line 22. This is your **adjusted gross income** . . . ▶	**32**

For Privacy Act and Paperwork Reduction Act Notice, see page 38.   Cat. No. 11320B   Form **1040** (1997)

Tax Compu-tation	33	Amount from line 32 (adjusted gross income)	33	
	34a	Check if: ☐ **You** were 65 or older, ☐ Blind; ☐ **Spouse** was 65 or older, ☐ Blind. Add the number of boxes checked above and enter the total here . . . . ▶ **34a**		
	b	If you are married filing separately and your spouse itemizes deductions or you were a dual-status alien, see page 18 and check here . . . . . . ▶ **34b** ☐		
	35	Enter the **larger** of your: { **Itemized deductions** from Schedule A, line 28, **OR** **Standard deduction** shown below for your filing status. **But** see page 18 if you checked any box on line 34a or 34b **or** someone can claim you as a dependent. ● Single—$4,150 ● Married filing jointly or Qualifying widow(er)—$6,900 ● Head of household—$6,050 ● Married filing separately—$3,450 }	35	
If you want the IRS to figure your tax, see page 18.	36	Subtract line 35 from line 33	36	
	37	If line 33 is $90,900 or less, multiply $2,650 by the total number of exemptions claimed on line 6d. If line 33 is over $90,900, see the worksheet on page 19 for the amount to enter .	37	
	38	**Taxable income.** Subtract line 37 from line 36. If line 37 is more than line 36, enter -0- .	38	
	39	**Tax.** See page 19. Check if any tax from **a** ☐ Form(s) 8814 **b** ☐ Form 4972 . . ▶	39	
Credits	40	Credit for child and dependent care expenses. Attach Form 2441	40	
	41	Credit for the elderly or the disabled. Attach Schedule R .	41	
	42	Adoption credit. Attach Form 8839	42	
	43	Foreign tax credit. Attach Form 1116	43	
	44	Other. Check if from **a** ☐ Form 3800 **b** ☐ Form 8396 **c** ☐ Form 8801 **d** ☐ Form (specify) _____	44	
	45	Add lines 40 through 44	45	
	46	Subtract line 45 from line 39. If line 45 is more than line 39, enter -0-. . . . . ▶	46	
Other Taxes	47	Self-employment tax. Attach Schedule SE	47	
	48	Alternative minimum tax. Attach Form 6251	48	
	49	Social security and Medicare tax on tip income not reported to employer. Attach Form 4137 .	49	
	50	Tax on qualified retirement plans (including IRAs) and MSAs. Attach Form 5329 if required	50	
	51	Advance earned income credit payments from Form(s) W-2	51	
	52	Household employment taxes. Attach Schedule H	52	
	53	Add lines 46 through 52. This is your **total tax** . . . . ▶	53	
Payments Attach Forms W-2, W-2G, and 1099-R on the front.	54	Federal income tax withheld from Forms W-2 and 1099 . .	54	
	55	1997 estimated tax payments and amount applied from 1996 return .	55	
	56a	**Earned income credit.** Attach Schedule EIC if you have a qualifying child **b** Nontaxable earned income: amount ▶ _____ and type ▶ _____	56a	
	57	Amount paid with Form 4868 (request for extension) . . .	57	
	58	Excess social security and RRTA tax withheld (see page 27)	58	
	59	Other payments. Check if from **a** ☐ Form 2439 **b** ☐ Form 4136	59	
	60	Add lines 54, 55, 56a, 57, 58, and 59. These are your **total payments** . . . . . ▶	60	
Refund Have it directly deposited! See page 27 and fill in 62b, 62c, and 62d.	61	If line 60 is more than line 53, subtract line 53 from line 60. This is the amount you **OVERPAID**	61	
	62a	Amount of line 61 you want **REFUNDED TO YOU**. . . . . ▶	62a	
	▶ b	Routing number _____ ▶ **c** Type: ☐ Checking ☐ Savings		
	▶ d	Account number _____		
	63	Amount of line 61 you want **APPLIED TO YOUR 1998 ESTIMATED TAX** ▶	63	
Amount You Owe	64	If line 53 is more than line 60, subtract line 60 from line 53. This is the **AMOUNT YOU OWE**. For details on how to pay, see page 27 . . . . ▶	64	
	65	Estimated tax penalty. Also include on line 64	65	

Sign Here

Keep a copy of this return for your records.

Under penalties of perjury, I declare that I have examined this return and accompanying schedules and statements, and to the best of my knowledge and belief, they are true, correct, and complete. Declaration of preparer (other than taxpayer) is based on all information of which preparer has any knowledge.

▶ Your signature	Date	Your occupation
▶ Spouse's signature. If a joint return, BOTH must sign.	Date	Spouse's occupation

Paid Preparer's Use Only

Preparer's ▶ signature	Date	Check if self-employed ☐	Preparer's social security no.
Firm's name (or yours if self-employed) and ▶ address		EIN	
			ZIP code

SCHEDULES A&B
(Form 1040)

Department of the Treasury
Internal Revenue Service (99)

Schedule A—Itemized Deductions

(Schedule B is on back)

▶ **Attach to Form 1040.** ▶ **See Instructions for Schedules A and B (Form 1040).**

OMB No. 1545-0074

19**97**

Attachment
Sequence No. **07**

Name(s) shown on Form 1040

Your social security number

Medical and Dental Expenses		Caution: *Do not include expenses reimbursed or paid by others.*		
	1	Medical and dental expenses (see page A-1)	1	
	2	Enter amount from Form 1040, line 33 . `2`		
	3	Multiply line 2 above by 7.5% (.075)	3	
	4	Subtract line 3 from line 1. If line 3 is more than line 1, enter -0-	4	
Taxes You Paid (See page A-1.)	5	State and local income taxes	5	
	6	Real estate taxes (see page A-2)	6	
	7	Personal property taxes	7	
	8	Other taxes. List type and amount ▶ _____ _____	8	
	9	Add lines 5 through 8	9	
Interest You Paid (See page A-2.) **Note:** Personal interest is not deductible.	10	Home mortgage interest and points reported to you on Form 1098	10	
	11	Home mortgage interest not reported to you on Form 1098. If paid to the person from whom you bought the home, see page A-3 and show that person's name, identifying no., and address ▶ _____ _____	11	
	12	Points not reported to you on Form 1098. See page A-3 for special rules	12	
	13	Investment interest. Attach Form 4952, if required. (See page A-3.)	13	
	14	Add lines 10 through 13	14	
Gifts to Charity If you made a gift and got a benefit for it, see page A-3.	15	Gifts by cash or check. If you made any gift of $250 or more, see page A-3	15	
	16	Other than by cash or check. If any gift of $250 or more, see page A-3. You **MUST** attach Form 8283 if over $500	16	
	17	Carryover from prior year	17	
	18	Add lines 15 through 17	18	
Casualty and Theft Losses	19	Casualty or theft loss(es). Attach Form 4684. (See page A-4.)	19	
Job Expenses and Most Other Miscellaneous Deductions (See page A-5 for expenses to deduct here.)	20	Unreimbursed employee expenses—job travel, union dues, job education, etc. You **MUST** attach Form 2106 or 2106-EZ if required. (See page A-4.) ▶ _____ _____ _____	20	
	21	Tax preparation fees	21	
	22	Other expenses—investment, safe deposit box, etc. List type and amount ▶ _____ _____	22	
	23	Add lines 20 through 22	23	
	24	Enter amount from Form 1040, line 33 . `24`		
	25	Multiply line 24 above by 2% (.02)	25	
	26	Subtract line 25 from line 23. If line 25 is more than line 23, enter -0-	26	
Other Miscellaneous Deductions	27	Other—from list on page A-5. List type and amount ▶ _____ _____	27	
Total Itemized Deductions	28	Is Form 1040, line 33, over $121,200 (over $60,600 if married filing separately)? **NO.** Your deduction is not limited. Add the amounts in the far right column for lines 4 through 27. Also, enter on Form 1040, line 35, the **larger** of this amount or your standard deduction. **YES.** Your deduction may be limited. See page A-5 for the amount to enter. ▶	28	

Name(s) shown on Form 1040. Do not enter name and social security number if shown on other side. | **Your social security number**

Schedule B—Interest and Dividend Income

Attachment
Sequence No. **08**

Part I
Interest
Income

(See pages 13
and B-1.)

Note: *If you had over $400 in taxable interest income, you must also complete Part III.*

1 List name of payer. If any interest is from a seller-financed mortgage and the buyer used the property as a personal residence, see page B-1 and list this interest first. Also, show that buyer's social security number and address ▶

	Amount

Note: If you received a Form 1099-INT, Form 1099-OID, or substitute statement from a brokerage firm, list the firm's name as the payer and enter the total interest shown on that form.

1 | |

2 Add the amounts on line 1	**2**
3 Excludable interest on series EE U.S. savings bonds issued after 1989 from Form 8815, line 14. You MUST attach Form 8815 to Form 1040	**3**
4 Subtract line 3 from line 2. Enter the result here and on Form 1040, line 8a ▶	**4**

Part II
Dividend
Income

(See pages 13
and B-1.)

Note: *If you had over $400 in gross dividends and/or other distributions on stock, you must also complete Part III.*

5 List name of payer. Include gross dividends and/or other distributions on stock here. Any capital gain distributions and nontaxable distributions will be deducted on lines 7 and 8 ▶

	Amount

Note: If you received a Form 1099-DIV or substitute statement from a brokerage firm, list the firm's name as the payer and enter the total dividends shown on that form.

5 | |

6 Add the amounts on line 5		**6**
7 Capital gain distributions. Enter here and on Schedule D, line 14*	**7**	
8 Nontaxable distributions. (See the inst. for Form 1040, line 9.)	**8**	
9 Add lines 7 and 8		**9**
10 Subtract line 9 from line 6. Enter the result here and on Form 1040, line 9 . ▶		**10**

If you don't need Schedule D to report any other gains or losses, see the instructions for Form 1040, line 13, on page 14.

Part III
Foreign
Accounts
and
Trusts

(See
page B-2.)

You must complete this part if you **(a)** had over $400 of interest or dividends; **(b)** had a foreign account; or **(c)** received a distribution from, or were a grantor of, or a transferor to, a foreign trust. | **Yes** | **No**

11a At any time during 1997, did you have an interest in or a signature or other authority over a financial account in a foreign country, such as a bank account, securities account, or other financial account? See page B-2 for exceptions and filing requirements for Form TD F 90-22.1 . . . . .

b If "Yes," enter the name of the foreign country ▶ ----------------------------------

12 During 1997, did you receive a distribution from, or were you the grantor of, or transferor to, a foreign trust? If "Yes," you may have to file Form 3520 or 926. See page B-2 . . . .

For Paperwork Reduction Act Notice, see Form 1040 instructions. ✱ **Schedule B (Form 1040) 1997**

SCHEDULE C
(Form 1040)

Department of the Treasury
Internal Revenue Service   (99)

Profit or Loss From Business
(Sole Proprietorship)
▶ Partnerships, joint ventures, etc., must file Form 1065.
▶ Attach to Form 1040 or Form 1041.   ▶ See Instructions for Schedule C (Form 1040).

OMB No. 1545-0074

1997

Attachment
Sequence No. **09**

Name of proprietor

Social security number (SSN)

A	Principal business or profession, including product or service (see page C-1)	**B Enter principal business code** (see page C-6) ▶

C	Business name. If no separate business name, leave blank.	**D Employer ID number (EIN), if any**

E Business address (including suite or room no.) ▶
City, town or post office, state, and ZIP code

F Accounting method: (1) ☐ Cash   (2) ☐ Accrual   (3) ☐ Other (specify) ▶

G Did you "materially participate" in the operation of this business during 1997? If "No," see page C-2 for limit on losses.   ☐ Yes   ☐ No

H If you started or acquired this business during 1997, check here . . . . ▶ ☐

Part I   Income

1	Gross receipts or sales. **Caution:** If this income was reported to you on Form W-2 and the "Statutory employee" box on that form was checked, see page C-2 and check here . . . . . . ▶ ☐	1	
2	Returns and allowances	2	
3	Subtract line 2 from line 1	3	
4	Cost of goods sold (from line 42 on page 2)	4	
5	**Gross profit.** Subtract line 4 from line 3	5	
6	Other income, including Federal and state gasoline or fuel tax credit or refund (see page C-2) . . .	6	
7	**Gross income.** Add lines 5 and 6 . . . . ▶	7	

Part II   Expenses. Enter expenses for business use of your home **only** on line 30.

8	Advertising	8		19	Pension and profit-sharing plans	19	
9	Bad debts from sales or services (see page C-3) . .	9		20	Rent or lease (see page C-4):		
				a	Vehicles, machinery, and equipment .	20a	
10	Car and truck expenses (see page C-3)	10		b	Other business property . .	20b	
11	Commissions and fees . .	11		21	Repairs and maintenance . .	21	
12	Depletion	12		22	Supplies (not included in Part III) .	22	
13	Depreciation and section 179 expense deduction (not included in Part III) (see page C-3) . .	13		23	Taxes and licenses	23	
				24	Travel, meals, and entertainment:		
				a	Travel	24a	
14	Employee benefit programs (other than on line 19) . . .	14		b	Meals and entertainment .		
15	Insurance (other than health) .	15		c	Enter 50% of line 24b subject to limitations (see page C-4) .		
16	Interest:						
a	Mortgage (paid to banks, etc.) .	16a		d	Subtract line 24c from line 24b .	24d	
b	Other	16b		25	Utilities	25	
17	Legal and professional services	17		26	Wages (less employment credits) .	26	
18	Office expense	18		27	Other expenses (from line 48 on page 2)	27	

28	**Total expenses** before expenses for business use of home. Add lines 8 through 27 in columns . ▶	28	

29	Tentative profit (loss). Subtract line 28 from line 7	29	
30	Expenses for business use of your home. Attach **Form 8829**	30	
31	**Net profit or (loss).** Subtract line 30 from line 29.		
	• If a profit, enter on **Form 1040, line 12,** and ALSO on **Schedule SE, line 2** (statutory employees, see page C-5). Estates and trusts, enter on Form 1041, line 3.	31	
	• If a loss, you MUST go on to line 32.		

32 If you have a loss, check the box that describes your investment in this activity (see page C-5).

• If you checked 32a, enter the loss on **Form 1040, line 12,** and ALSO on **Schedule SE, line 2** (statutory employees, see page C-5). Estates and trusts, enter on Form 1041, line 3.

32a ☐ All investment is at risk.

32b ☐ Some investment is not at risk.

• If you checked 32b, you MUST attach **Form 6198.**

For Paperwork Reduction Act Notice, see Form 1040 instructions.   Cat. No. 11334P   **Schedule C (Form 1040) 1997**

Part III   Cost of Goods Sold (see page C-5)

33 Method(s) used to
value closing inventory: **a** ☐ Cost   **b** ☐ Lower of cost or market   **c** ☐ Other (attach explanation)

34 Was there any change in determining quantities, costs, or valuations between opening and closing inventory? If
"Yes," attach explanation . . . . ☐ **Yes**   ☐ **No**

35 Inventory at beginning of year. If different from last year's closing inventory, attach explanation . .	**35**	
36 Purchases less cost of items withdrawn for personal use	**36**	
37 Cost of labor. Do not include salary paid to yourself	**37**	
38 Materials and supplies	**38**	
39 Other costs	**39**	
40 Add lines 35 through 39	**40**	
41 Inventory at end of year	**41**	
42 **Cost of goods sold.** Subtract line 41 from line 40. Enter the result here and on page 1, line 4 . .	**42**	

Part IV   Information on Your Vehicle. Complete this part ONLY if you are claiming car or truck expenses on line 10 and are not required to file Form 4562 for this business. See the instructions for line 13 on page C-3 to find out if you must file.

43 When did you place your vehicle in service for business purposes? (month, day, year) ▶ ..../.............../............. .

44 Of the total number of miles you drove your vehicle during 1997, enter the number of miles you used your vehicle for:

a Business ....   **b** Commuting ....   **c** Other ....

45 Do you (or your spouse) have another vehicle available for personal use? . . . . ☐ **Yes**   ☐ **No**

46 Was your vehicle available for use during off-duty hours? . . . . ☐ **Yes**   ☐ **No**

47a Do you have evidence to support your deduction? . . . . ☐ **Yes**   ☐ **No**

  b If "Yes," is the evidence written? . . . . ☐ **Yes**   ☐ **No**

Part V   Other Expenses. List below business expenses not included on lines 8–26 or line 30.

....		
....		
....		
....		
....		
....		
....		
....		
....		
48 **Total other expenses.** Enter here and on page 1, line 27	**48**	

Net Profit From Business

(Sole Proprietorship)

▶ **Partnerships, joint ventures, etc., must file Form 1065.**

▶ **Attach to Form 1040 or Form 1041.** ▶ **See instructions on back.**

OMB No. 1545-0074

19**97**

Attachment
Sequence No. **09A**

Name of proprietor | Social security number (SSN)

Part I   General Information

**You May Use
This Schedule
Only If You:**

- Had business expenses of $2,500 or less.
- Use the cash method of accounting.
- Did not have an inventory at any time during the year.
- Did not have a net loss from your business.
- Had only one business as a sole proprietor.

And You:

- Had no employees during the year.
- Are not required to file **Form 4562,** Depreciation and Amortization, for this business. See the instructions for Schedule C, line 13, on page C-3 to find out if you must file.
- Do not deduct expenses for business use of your home.
- Do not have prior year unallowed passive activity losses from this business.

A Principal business or profession, including product or service

B Enter principal business code
(see page C-6) ▶

C Business name. If no separate business name, leave blank.

D Employer ID number (EIN), if any

E Business address (including suite or room no.). Address not required if same as on Form 1040, page 1.

City, town or post office, state, and ZIP code

Part II   Figure Your Net Profit

1 **Gross receipts.**
Caution: *If this income was reported to you on Form W-2 and the "Statutory employee" box on that form was checked, see **Statutory Employees** in the instructions for Schedule C, line 1, on page C-2 and check here* . . . . ▶ ☐ | **1**

2 **Total expenses.** If more than $2,500, you **must** use Schedule C. See instructions . . . . . | **2**

3 **Net profit.** Subtract line 2 from line 1. If less than zero, you **must** use Schedule C. Enter on **Form 1040, line 12,** and ALSO on **Schedule SE, line 2.** (Statutory employees **do not** report this amount on Schedule SE, line 2. Estates and trusts, enter on Form 1041, line 3.) . . . . . | **3**

Part III   Information on Your Vehicle. Complete this part ONLY if you are claiming car or truck expenses on line 2.

4 When did you place your vehicle in service for business purposes? (month, day, year) ▶ ..... / ..... / ..... .

5 Of the total number of miles you drove your vehicle during 1997, enter the number of miles you used your vehicle for:

a Business .... **b** Commuting .... **c** Other ....

6 Do you (or your spouse) have another vehicle available for personal use? . . . . ☐ **Yes** ☐ **No**

7 Was your vehicle available for use during off-duty hours? . . . . ☐ **Yes** ☐ **No**

8a Do you have evidence to support your deduction? . . . . ☐ **Yes** ☐ **No**

b If "Yes," is the evidence written? . . . . ☐ **Yes** ☐ **No**

For Paperwork Reduction Act Notice, see Form 1040 instructions.   Cat. No. 14374D   **Schedule C-EZ (Form 1040) 1997**

Instructions

You may use Schedule C-EZ instead of Schedule C if you operated a business or practiced a profession as a sole proprietorship and you have met all the requirements listed in Part I of Schedule C-EZ.

Line A

Describe the business or professional activity that provided your principal source of income reported on line 1. Give the general field or activity and the type of product or service.

Line B

Enter on this line the four-digit code that identifies your principal business or professional activity. See page C-6 for the list of codes.

Line D

You need an employer identification number (EIN) only if you had a Keogh plan or were required to file an employment, excise, estate, trust, or alcohol, tobacco, and firearms tax return. If you need an EIN, file **Form SS-4,** Application for Employer Identification Number. If you do not have an EIN, leave line D blank. **Do not** enter your SSN.

Line E

Enter your business address. Show a street address instead of a box number. Include the suite or room number, if any.

Line 1—Gross Receipts

Enter gross receipts from your trade or business. Be sure to include any amount you received in your trade or business that was reported on Form(s) 1099-MISC. You must show all items of taxable income actually or constructively received during the year (in cash, property, or services). Income is constructively received when it is credited to your account or set aside for you to use. Do not offset this amount by any losses.

Line 2—Total Expenses

Enter the total amount of all deductible business expenses you actually paid during the year. Examples of these expenses include advertising, car and truck expenses, commissions and fees, insurance, interest, legal and professional services, office expense, rent or lease expenses, repairs and maintenance, supplies, taxes, travel, 50% of business meals and entertainment, and utilities (including telephone). For details, see the instructions for Schedule C, Parts II and V, on pages C-2 through C-5. If you wish, you may use the optional worksheet below to record your expenses.

 If you claim car or truck expenses, be sure to complete Part III of Schedule C-EZ.

Optional Worksheet for Line 2 (keep for your records)

a Business meals and entertainment	**a**		
b Less: 50% of business meals and entertainment subject to limitations (see the instructions for lines 24b and 24c on page C-4)	**b**		
c Deductible business meals and entertainment. Subtract line **b** from line **a**	**c**		
d	**d**		
e	**e**		
f	**f**		
g	**g**		
h	**h**		
i	**i**		
j **Total.** Add lines c through i. Enter here and on line 2	**j**		

Self-Employment Tax

▶ See Instructions for Schedule SE (Form 1040).

▶ Attach to Form 1040.

OMB No. 1545-0074

1997

Attachment
Sequence No. **17**

Name of person with **self-employment** income (as shown on Form 1040)	Social security number of person with **self-employment** income ▶

Who Must File Schedule SE

You must file Schedule SE if:

- You had net earnings from self-employment from **other than** church employee income (line 4 of Short Schedule SE or line 4c of Long Schedule SE) of $400 or more, **OR**

- You had church employee income of $108.28 or more. Income from services you performed as a minister or a member of a religious order **is not** church employee income. See page SE-1.

Note: *Even if you had a loss or a small amount of income from self-employment, it may be to your benefit to file Schedule SE and use either "optional method" in Part II of Long Schedule SE. See page SE-3.*

Exception. If your only self-employment income was from earnings as a minister, member of a religious order, or Christian Science practitioner **and** you filed Form 4361 and received IRS approval not to be taxed on those earnings, **do not** file Schedule SE. Instead, write "Exempt–Form 4361" on Form 1040, line 47.

May I Use Short Schedule SE or MUST I Use Long Schedule SE?

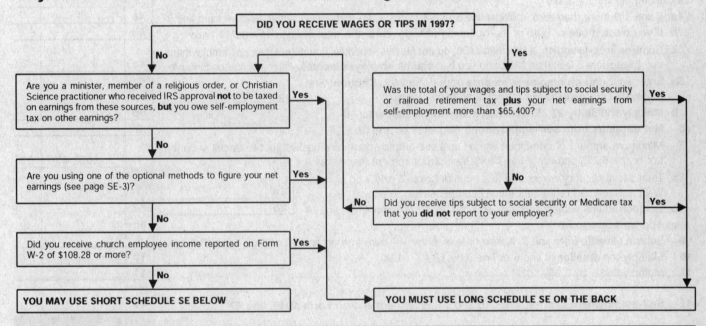

Section A—Short Schedule SE. Caution: *Read above to see if you can use Short Schedule SE.*

1	Net farm profit or (loss) from Schedule F, line 36, and farm partnerships, Schedule K-1 (Form 1065), line 15a	**1**	
2	Net profit or (loss) from Schedule C, line 31; Schedule C-EZ, line 3; and Schedule K-1 (Form 1065), line 15a (other than farming). Ministers and members of religious orders, see page SE-1 for amounts to report on this line. See page SE-2 for other income to report	**2**	
3	Combine lines 1 and 2	**3**	
4	**Net earnings from self-employment.** Multiply line 3 by 92.35% (.9235). If less than $400, **do not** file this schedule; you do not owe self-employment tax . . . . ▶	**4**	
5	**Self-employment tax.** If the amount on line 4 is: • $65,400 or less, multiply line 4 by 15.3% (.153). Enter the result here and on **Form 1040, line 47.** • More than $65,400, multiply line 4 by 2.9% (.029). Then, add $8,109.60 to the result. Enter the total here and on **Form 1040, line 47.**	**5**	
6	**Deduction for one-half of self-employment tax.** Multiply line 5 by 50% (.5). Enter the result here and on **Form 1040, line 26**	**6**		

For Paperwork Reduction Act Notice, see Form 1040 instructions.   Cat. No. 11358Z   Schedule SE (Form 1040) 1997

Name of person with **self-employment** income (as shown on Form 1040)	Social security number of person with **self-employment** income ▶		

Section B—Long Schedule SE

Part I   Self-Employment Tax

Note: *If your only income subject to self-employment tax is **church employee income,** skip lines 1 through 4b. Enter -0- on line 4c and go to line 5a. Income from services you performed as a minister or a member of a religious order **is not** church employee income. See page SE-1.*

A   If you are a minister, member of a religious order, or Christian Science practitioner **and** you filed Form 4361, but you had $400 or more of **other** net earnings from self-employment, check here and continue with Part I . . . . . . ▶ ☐

1	Net farm profit or (loss) from Schedule F, line 36, and farm partnerships, Schedule K-1 (Form 1065), line 15a. **Note:** *Skip this line if you use the farm optional method. See page SE-3* . .	**1**		
2	Net profit or (loss) from Schedule C, line 31; Schedule C-EZ, line 3; and Schedule K-1 (Form 1065), line 15a (other than farming). Ministers and members of religious orders, see page SE-1 for amounts to report on this line. See page SE-2 for other income to report. **Note:** *Skip this line if you use the nonfarm optional method. See page SE-3.*	**2**		
3	Combine lines 1 and 2	**3**		
4a	If line 3 is more than zero, multiply line 3 by 92.35% (.9235). Otherwise, enter amount from line 3	**4a**		
b	If you elected one or both of the optional methods, enter the total of lines 15 and 17 here . .	**4b**		
c	Combine lines 4a and 4b. If less than $400, **do not** file this schedule; you do not owe self-employment tax. **Exception.** If less than $400 and you had **church employee income,** enter -0- and continue ▶	**4c**		
5a	Enter your **church employee income** from Form W-2. **Caution:** *See page SE-1 for definition of church employee income* **5a**			
b	Multiply line 5a by 92.35% (.9235). If less than $100, enter -0-	**5b**		
6	**Net earnings from self-employment.** Add lines 4c and 5b	**6**		
7	Maximum amount of combined wages and self-employment earnings subject to social security tax or the 6.2% portion of the 7.65% railroad retirement (tier 1) tax for 1997	**7**	65,400	00
8a	Total social security wages and tips (total of boxes 3 and 7 on Form(s) W-2) and railroad retirement (tier 1) compensation **8a**			
b	Unreported tips subject to social security tax (from Form 4137, line 9) **8b**			
c	Add lines 8a and 8b	**8c**		
9	Subtract line 8c from line 7. If zero or less, enter -0- here and on line 10 and go to line 11 . ▶	**9**		
10	Multiply the **smaller** of line 6 or line 9 by 12.4% (.124)	**10**		
11	Multiply line 6 by 2.9% (.029)	**11**		
12	**Self-employment tax.** Add lines 10 and 11. Enter here and on **Form 1040, line 47**	**12**		
13	**Deduction for one-half of self-employment tax.** Multiply line 12 by 50% (.5). Enter the result here and on **Form 1040, line 26** **13**			

Part II   Optional Methods To Figure Net Earnings (See page SE-3.)

Farm Optional Method. You may use this method **only** if:
- Your gross farm income[1] was not more than $2,400, **or**
- Your gross farm income[1] was more than $2,400 and your net farm profits[2] were less than $1,733.

14	Maximum income for optional methods	**14**	1,600	00
15	Enter the **smaller** of: two-thirds (⅔) of gross farm income[1] (not less than zero) **or** $1,600. Also, include this amount on line 4b above	**15**		

Nonfarm Optional Method. You may use this method **only** if:
- Your net nonfarm profits[3] were less than $1,733 and also less than 72.189% of your gross nonfarm income,[4] **and**
- You had net earnings from self-employment of at least $400 in 2 of the prior 3 years.

Caution: *You may use this method no more than five times.*

16	Subtract line 15 from line 14	**16**		
17	Enter the **smaller** of: two-thirds (⅔) of gross nonfarm income[4] (not less than zero) **or** the amount on line 16. Also, include this amount on line 4b above	**17**		

[1]From Schedule F, line 11, and Schedule K-1 (Form 1065), line 15b.   [3]From Schedule C, line 31; Schedule C-EZ, line 3; and Schedule K-1 (Form 1065), line 15a.
[2]From Schedule F, line 36, and Schedule K-1 (Form 1065), line 15a.   [4]From Schedule C, line 7; Schedule C-EZ, line 1; and Schedule K-1 (Form 1065), line 15c.

| SCHEDULE E
(Form 1040)

Department of the Treasury
Internal Revenue Service (99) | **Supplemental Income and Loss**
(From rental real estate, royalties, partnerships,
S corporations, estates, trusts, REMICs, etc.)
▶ **Attach to Form 1040 or Form 1041.** ▶ **See Instructions for Schedule E (Form 1040).** | OMB No. 1545-0074
19**97**
Attachment
Sequence No. **13** |

Name(s) shown on return | Your social security number

Part I — Income or Loss From Rental Real Estate and Royalties **Note:** *Report income and expenses from your business of renting personal property on **Schedule C** or **C-EZ** (see page E-1). Report farm rental income or loss from **Form 4835** on page 2, line 39.*

1 Show the kind and location of each **rental real estate property:**

A ....

B ....

C ....

2 For each rental real estate property listed on line 1, did you or your family use it during the tax year for personal purposes for more than the greater of:
- 14 days, **or**
- 10% of the total days rented at fair rental value?

(See page E-1.)

	Yes	No
A		
B		
C		

Income:

			Properties			**Totals** (Add columns A, B, and C.)
			A	**B**	**C**	
3	Rents received	**3**				**3**
4	Royalties received	**4**				**4**

Expenses:

			A	B	C	
5	Advertising	**5**				
6	Auto and travel (see page E-2)	**6**				
7	Cleaning and maintenance	**7**				
8	Commissions	**8**				
9	Insurance	**9**				
10	Legal and other professional fees	**10**				
11	Management fees	**11**				
12	Mortgage interest paid to banks, etc. (see page E-2)	**12**				**12**
13	Other interest	**13**				
14	Repairs	**14**				
15	Supplies	**15**				
16	Taxes	**16**				
17	Utilities	**17**				
18	Other (list) ▶	**18**				
19	Add lines 5 through 18	**19**				**19**
20	Depreciation expense or depletion (see page E-2)	**20**				**20**
21	Total expenses. Add lines 19 and 20	**21**				
22	Income or (loss) from rental real estate or royalty properties. Subtract line 21 from line 3 (rents) or line 4 (royalties). If the result is a (loss), see page E-2 to find out if you must file **Form 6198**	**22**				
23	Deductible rental real estate loss. **Caution:** *Your rental real estate loss on line 22 may be limited. See page E-3 to find out if you must file **Form 8582**. Real estate professionals must complete line 42 on page 2*	**23**	( )	( )	( )	( )
24	**Income.** Add positive amounts shown on line 22. **Do not** include any losses					**24**
25	**Losses.** Add royalty losses from line 22 and rental real estate losses from line 23. Enter total losses here				**25**	( )
26	Total rental real estate and royalty income or (loss). Combine lines 24 and 25. Enter the result here. If Parts II, III, IV, and line 39 on page 2 do not apply to you, also enter this amount on Form 1040, line 17. Otherwise, include this amount in the total on line 40 on page 2					**26**

For Paperwork Reduction Act Notice, see Form 1040 instructions.   Cat. No. 11344L   **Schedule E (Form 1040) 1997**

Name(s) shown on return. Do not enter name and social security number if shown on other side.   **Your social security number**

Note: *If you report amounts from farming or fishing on Schedule E, you must enter your gross income from those activities on line 41 below. Real estate professionals must complete line 42 below.*

Part II   **Income or Loss From Partnerships and S Corporations**   **Note:** *If you report a loss from an at-risk activity, you MUST check either column (e) or (f) on line 27 to describe your investment in the activity. See page E-4. If you check column (f), you must attach Form 6198.*

27	(a) Name	(b) Enter P for partnership; S for S corporation	(c) Check if foreign partnership	(d) Employer identification number	Investment At Risk? (e) All is at risk	(f) Some is not at risk
A						
B						
C						
D						
E						

	Passive Income and Loss		Nonpassive Income and Loss		
	(g) Passive loss allowed (attach **Form 8582** if required)	(h) Passive income from **Schedule K-1**	(i) Nonpassive loss from **Schedule K-1**	(j) Section 179 expense deduction from **Form 4562**	(k) Nonpassive income from **Schedule K-1**
A					
B					
C					
D					
E					
28a Totals					
b Totals					

29	Add columns (h) and (k) of line 28a	29	
30	Add columns (g), (i), and (j) of line 28b	30 (	)
31	Total partnership and S corporation income or (loss). Combine lines 29 and 30. Enter the result here and include in the total on line 40 below	31	

Part III   **Income or Loss From Estates and Trusts**

32	(a) Name	(b) Employer identification number
A		
B		

	Passive Income and Loss		Nonpassive Income and Loss	
	(c) Passive deduction or loss allowed (attach **Form 8582** if required)	(d) Passive income from **Schedule K-1**	(e) Deduction or loss from **Schedule K-1**	(f) Other income from **Schedule K-1**
A				
B				
33a Totals				
b Totals				

34	Add columns (d) and (f) of line 33a	34	
35	Add columns (c) and (e) of line 33b	35 (	)
36	Total estate and trust income or (loss). Combine lines 34 and 35. Enter the result here and include in the total on line 40 below	36	

Part IV   **Income or Loss From Real Estate Mortgage Investment Conduits (REMICs)—Residual Holder**

37	(a) Name	(b) Employer identification number	(c) Excess inclusion from **Schedules Q**, line 2c (see page E-4)	(d) Taxable income (net loss) from **Schedules Q**, line 1b	(e) Income from **Schedules Q**, line 3b

38	Combine columns (d) and (e) only. Enter the result here and include in the total on line 40 below	38	

Part V   **Summary**

39	Net farm rental income or (loss) from **Form 4835**. Also, complete line 41 below	39	
40	TOTAL income or (loss). Combine lines 26, 31, 36, 38, and 39. Enter the result here and on Form 1040, line 17 ▶	40	

41   **Reconciliation of Farming and Fishing Income.** Enter your **gross** farming and fishing income reported on Form 4835, line 7; Schedule K-1 (Form 1065), line 15b; Schedule K-1 (Form 1120S), line 23; and Schedule K-1 (Form 1041), line 13 (see page E-4) . . . . | **41** | |

42   **Reconciliation for Real Estate Professionals.** If you were a real estate professional (see page E-3), enter the net income or (loss) you reported anywhere on Form 1040 from all rental real estate activities in which you materially participated under the passive activity loss rules . . . | **42** | |

SCHEDULE F
(Form 1040)

Department of the Treasury
Internal Revenue Service (99)

Profit or Loss From Farming

▶ Attach to Form 1040, Form 1041, or Form 1065.

▶ See Instructions for Schedule F (Form 1040).

OMB No. 1545-0074

1997

Attachment
Sequence No. **14**

Name of proprietor

Social security number (SSN)

A Principal product. Describe in one or two words your principal crop or activity for the current tax year.

B Enter principal agricultural activity code (from page 2) ▶

D Employer ID number (EIN), if any

C Accounting method: **(1)** ☐ Cash **(2)** ☐ Accrual

E Did you "materially participate" in the operation of this business during 1997? If "No," see page F-2 for limit on passive losses. ☐ Yes ☐ No

Part I — Farm Income—Cash Method. Complete Parts I and II (Accrual method taxpayers complete Parts II and III, and line 11 of Part I.)
Do not include sales of livestock held for draft, breeding, sport, or dairy purposes; report these sales on Form 4797.

1	Sales of livestock and other items you bought for resale	**1**	
2	Cost or other basis of livestock and other items reported on line 1	**2**	
3	Subtract line 2 from line 1		**3**
4	Sales of livestock, produce, grains, and other products you raised		**4**
5a	Total cooperative distributions (Form(s) 1099-PATR) **5a**	**5b** Taxable amount	**5b**
6a	Agricultural program payments (see page F-2) **6a**	**6b** Taxable amount	**6b**
7	Commodity Credit Corporation (CCC) loans (see page F-2):		
a	CCC loans reported under election		**7a**
b	CCC loans forfeited **7b**	**7c** Taxable amount	**7c**
8	Crop insurance proceeds and certain disaster payments (see page F-2):		
a	Amount received in 1997 **8a**	**8b** Taxable amount	**8b**
c	If election to defer to 1998 is attached, check here ▶ ☐	**8d** Amount deferred from 1996	**8d**
9	Custom hire (machine work) income		**9**
10	Other income, including Federal and state gasoline or fuel tax credit or refund (see page F-2)		**10**
11	**Gross income.** Add amounts in the right column for lines 3 through 10. If accrual method taxpayer, enter the amount from page 2, line 51 ▶		**11**

Part II — Farm Expenses—Cash and Accrual Method. Do not include personal or living expenses such as taxes, insurance, repairs, etc., on your home.

12	Car and truck expenses (see page F-3—also attach **Form 4562**)	**12**	25	Pension and profit-sharing plans	**25**	
13	Chemicals	**13**	26	Rent or lease (see page F-4):		
14	Conservation expenses (see page F-3)	**14**	a	Vehicles, machinery, and equipment	**26a**	
15	Custom hire (machine work)	**15**	b	Other (land, animals, etc.)	**26b**	
16	Depreciation and section 179 expense deduction not claimed elsewhere (see page F-4)	**16**	27	Repairs and maintenance	**27**	
			28	Seeds and plants purchased	**28**	
			29	Storage and warehousing	**29**	
17	Employee benefit programs other than on line 25	**17**	30	Supplies purchased	**30**	
18	Feed purchased	**18**	31	Taxes	**31**	
19	Fertilizers and lime	**19**	32	Utilities	**32**	
20	Freight and trucking	**20**	33	Veterinary, breeding, and medicine	**33**	
21	Gasoline, fuel, and oil	**21**	34	Other expenses (specify):		
22	Insurance (other than health)	**22**	a	_____	**34a**	
23	Interest:		b	_____	**34b**	
a	Mortgage (paid to banks, etc.)	**23a**	c	_____	**34c**	
b	Other	**23b**	d	_____	**34d**	
24	Labor hired (less employment credits)	**24**	e	_____	**34e**	
			f	_____	**34f**	

35	**Total expenses.** Add lines 12 through 34f ▶	**35**
36	**Net farm profit or (loss).** Subtract line 35 from line 11. If a profit, enter on **Form 1040, line 18,** and ALSO on **Schedule SE, line 1.** If a loss, you MUST go on to line 37 (estates, trusts, and partnerships, see page F-5).	**36**
37	If you have a loss, you MUST check the box that describes your investment in this activity (see page F-5). If you checked 37a, enter the loss on **Form 1040, line 18,** and ALSO on **Schedule SE, line 1.** If you checked 37b, you MUST attach **Form 6198.**	**37a** ☐ All investment is at risk. **37b** ☐ Some investment is not at risk.

For Paperwork Reduction Act Notice, see Form 1040 instructions.

Cat. No. 11346H

Schedule F (Form 1040) 1997

Part III　**Farm Income—Accrual Method** (see page F-5)

Do not include sales of livestock held for draft, breeding, sport, or dairy purposes; report these sales on Form 4797 and do not include this livestock on line 46 below.

38	Sales of livestock, produce, grains, and other products during the year	38	
39a	Total cooperative distributions (Form(s) 1099-PATR) **39a** _____ **39b** Taxable amount	39b	
40a	Agricultural program payments . . . . . **40a** _____ **40b** Taxable amount	40b	
41	Commodity Credit Corporation (CCC) loans:		
a	CCC loans reported under election	41a	
b	CCC loans forfeited . . . . . **41b** _____ **41c** Taxable amount	41c	
42	Crop insurance proceeds	42	
43	Custom hire (machine work) income	43	
44	Other income, including Federal and state gasoline or fuel tax credit or refund	44	
45	Add amounts in the right column for lines 38 through 44	45	

46	Inventory of livestock, produce, grains, and other products at beginning of the year	46		
47	Cost of livestock, produce, grains, and other products purchased during the year	47		
48	Add lines 46 and 47	48		
49	Inventory of livestock, produce, grains, and other products at end of year	49		
50	Cost of livestock, produce, grains, and other products sold. Subtract line 49 from line 48*	50		
51	**Gross income.** Subtract line 50 from line 45. Enter the result here and on page 1, line 11 . . . . ▶	51		

*If you use the unit-livestock-price method or the farm-price method of valuing inventory and the amount on line 49 is larger than the amount on line 48, subtract line 48 from line 49. Enter the result on line 50. Add lines 45 and 50. Enter the total on line 51.

Part IV　**Principal Agricultural Activity Codes**

Caution: File **Schedule C** (Form 1040), Profit or Loss From Business, or **Schedule C-EZ** (Form 1040), Net Profit From Business, instead of Schedule F if:

● Your principal source of income is from providing agricultural services such as soil preparation, veterinary, farm labor, horticultural, or management for a fee or on a contract basis, or

● You are engaged in the business of breeding, raising, and caring for dogs, cats, or other pet animals.

Select one of the following codes and write the 3-digit number on page 1, line B:

120 **Field crop,** including grains and nongrains such as cotton, peanuts, feed corn, wheat, tobacco, Irish potatoes, etc.

160 **Vegetables and melons,** garden-type vegetables and melons, such as sweet corn, tomatoes, squash, etc.

170 **Fruit and tree nuts,** including grapes, berries, olives, etc.

180 **Ornamental floriculture and nursery products**

185 **Food crops grown under cover,** including hydroponic crops

211 **Beefcattle feedlots**

212 **Beefcattle,** except feedlots

215 **Hogs, sheep, and goats**

240 **Dairy**

250 **Poultry and eggs,** including chickens, ducks, pigeons, quail, etc.

260 **General livestock,** not specializing in any one livestock category

270 **Animal specialty,** including bees, fur-bearing animals, horses, snakes, etc.

280 **Animal aquaculture,** including fish, shellfish, mollusks, frogs, etc., produced within confined space

290 **Forest products,** including forest nurseries and seed gathering, extraction of pine gum, and gathering of forest products

300 **Agricultural production,** not specified

<table>
<tr><td>**SCHEDULE H**
(Form 1040)

Department of the Treasury
Internal Revenue Service   (99)</td><td>**Household Employment Taxes**
(For Social Security, Medicare, Withheld Income, and Federal Unemployment (FUTA) Taxes)
▶ **Attach to Form 1040, 1040A, 1040NR, 1040NR-EZ, 1040-SS, or 1041.**
▶ **See separate instructions.**</td><td>OMB No. 1545-0074
19**97**
Attachment
Sequence No. **44**</td></tr>
</table>

Name of employer

Social security number

Employer identification number

A   Did you pay **any one** household employee cash wages of $1,000 or more in 1997? (If any household employee was your spouse, your child under age 21, your parent, or anyone under age 18, see the line A instructions on page 3 before you answer this question.)

     ☐ **Yes.**   Skip questions B and C and go to Part I.
     ☐ **No.**   Go to question B.

B   Did you withhold Federal income tax during 1997 for any household employee?

     ☐ **Yes.**   Skip question C and go to Part I.
     ☐ **No.**   Go to question C.

C   Did you pay **total** cash wages of $1,000 or more in **any** calendar **quarter** of 1996 or 1997 to household employees? (**Do not** count cash wages paid in 1996 or 1997 to your spouse, your child under age 21, or your parent.)

     ☐ **No.**   **Stop.** Do not file this schedule.
     ☐ **Yes.**   Skip Part I and go to Part II on the back.

Part I   **Social Security, Medicare, and Income Taxes**

1	Total cash wages subject to social security taxes (see page 3) . . . **1**	
2	Social security taxes. Multiply line 1 by 12.4% (.124)	**2**
3	Total cash wages subject to Medicare taxes (see page 3) **3**	
4	Medicare taxes. Multiply line 3 by 2.9% (.029)	**4**
5	Federal income tax withheld, if any	**5**
6	Add lines 2, 4, and 5	**6**
7	Advance earned income credit (EIC) payments, if any	**7**
8	**Total social security, Medicare, and income taxes.** Subtract line 7 from line 6	**8**

9   Did you pay **total** cash wages of $1,000 or more in **any** calendar **quarter** of 1996 or 1997 to household employees? (**Do not** count cash wages paid in 1996 or 1997 to your spouse, your child under age 21, or your parent.)

     ☐ **No.**   **Stop.** Enter the amount from line 8 above on Form 1040, line 52, or Form 1040A, line 27. If you are not required to file Form 1040 or 1040A, see the line 9 instructions on page 4.

     ☐ **Yes.**   Go to Part II on the back.

For Paperwork Reduction Act Notice, see Form 1040 instructions.   Cat. No. 12187K   **Schedule H (Form 1040) 1997**

Part II   Federal Unemployment (FUTA) Tax

		Yes	No
10	Did you pay unemployment contributions to only one state?		
11	Did you pay all state unemployment contributions for 1997 by April 15, 1998? Fiscal year filers, see page 4 . .		
12	Were all wages that are taxable for FUTA tax also taxable for your state's unemployment tax?		

Next: If you answered **"Yes"** to **all** of the questions above, complete Section A.

If you answered **"No"** to **any** of the questions above, skip Section A and complete Section B.

Section A

13	Name of the state where you paid unemployment contributions ▶		
14	State reporting number as shown on state unemployment tax return ▶		
15	Contributions paid to your state unemployment fund (see page 4) .	**15**	
16	Total cash wages subject to FUTA tax (see page 4)	**16**	
17	**FUTA tax.** Multiply line 16 by .008. Enter the result here, skip Section B, and go to Part III . .	**17**	

Section B

18 Complete all columns below that apply (if you need more space, see page 4):

(a) Name of state	(b) State reporting number as shown on state unemployment tax return	(c) Taxable wages (as defined in state act)	(d) State experience rate period		(e) State experience rate	(f) Multiply col. (c) by .054	(g) Multiply col. (c) by col. (e)	(h) Subtract col. (g) from col. (f). If zero or less, enter -0-.	(i) Contributions paid to state unemployment fund
			From	To					

19	Totals	**19**		
20	Add columns (h) and (i) of line 19	**20**	**21**	
21	Total cash wages subject to FUTA tax (see the line 16 instructions on page 4)		**21**	
22	Multiply line 21 by 6.2% (.062)		**22**	
23	Multiply line 21 by 5.4% (.054)	**23**		
24	Enter the **smaller** of line 20 or line 23		**24**	
25	**FUTA tax.** Subtract line 24 from line 22. Enter the result here and go to Part III		**25**	

Part III   Total Household Employment Taxes

26	Enter the amount from line 8	**26**	
27	Add line 17 (or line 25) and line 26	**27**	
28	Are you required to file Form 1040 or 1040A?		

☐ **Yes.** **Stop.** Enter the amount from line 27 above on Form 1040, line 52, or Form 1040A, line 27. **Do not** complete Part IV below.

☐ **No.** You may have to complete Part IV. See page 4 for details.

Part IV   Address and Signature—Complete this part **only** if required. See the line 28 instructions on page 4.

Address (number and street) or P.O. box if mail is not delivered to street address

Apt., room, or suite no.

City, town or post office, state, and ZIP code

Under penalties of perjury, I declare that I have examined this schedule, including accompanying statements, and to the best of my knowledge and belief, it is true, correct, and complete. No part of any payment made to a state unemployment fund claimed as a credit was, or is to be, deducted from the payments to employees.

▶ _____   ▶ _____
Employer's signature   Date

Schedule R
(Form 1040)

Department of the Treasury
Internal Revenue Service   (99)

Credit for the Elderly or the Disabled

▶ **Attach to Form 1040.**   ▶ **See separate instructions for Schedule R.**

OMB No. 1545-0074

1997

Attachment
Sequence No. **16**

Name(s) shown on Form 1040

Your social security number

You may be able to take this credit and reduce your tax if by the end of 1997:

- You were age 65 or older,   **OR**   • You were under age 65, you retired on **permanent and total** disability, and you received taxable disability income.

But you must also meet other tests. See the separate instructions for Schedule R.

Note: *In most cases, the IRS can figure the credit for you. See the instructions.*

Part I   Check the Box for Your Filing Status and Age

If your filing status is:	And by the end of 1997:	Check only one box:
Single, Head of household, or Qualifying widow(er) with dependent child	**1** You were 65 or older **1**	☐
	2 You were under 65 and you retired on permanent and total disability . . . **2**	☐
Married filing a joint return	**3** Both spouses were 65 or older **3**	☐
	4 Both spouses were under 65, but only one spouse retired on permanent and total disability **4**	☐
	5 Both spouses were under 65, and both retired on permanent and total disability **5**	☐
	6 One spouse was 65 or older, and the other spouse was under 65 and retired on permanent and total disability **6**	☐
	7 One spouse was 65 or older, and the other spouse was under 65 and **NOT** retired on permanent and total disability **7**	☐
Married filing a separate return	**8** You were 65 or older and you lived apart from your spouse for all of 1997 . . **8**	☐
	9 You were under 65, you retired on permanent and total disability, and you lived apart from your spouse for all of 1997 . . . . **9**	☐

Did you check box 1, 3, 7, or 8?	**Yes** ───▶ Skip Part II and complete Part III on back.
	No ───▶ Complete Parts II and III.

Part II   Statement of Permanent and Total Disability (Complete **only** if you checked box 2, 4, 5, 6, or 9 above.)

IF: 1 You filed a physician's statement for this disability for 1983 or an earlier year, or you filed a statement for tax years after 1983 and your physician signed line B on the statement, **AND**

    2 Due to your continued disabled condition, you were unable to engage in any substantial gainful activity in 1997, check this box . . . . ▶ ☐

- If you checked this box, you do not have to file another statement for 1997.
- If you **did not** check this box, have your physician complete the statement below.

Physician's Statement (See instructions at bottom of page 2.)

I certify that _____
Name of disabled person

was permanently and totally disabled on January 1, 1976, or January 1, 1977, **OR** was permanently and totally disabled on the date he or she retired. If retired after 1976, enter the date retired. ▶ _____

Physician: Sign your name on **either** line A or B below.

A The disability has lasted or can be expected to last continuously for at least a year . . . .
_____   _____
Physician's signature   Date

B There is no reasonable probability that the disabled condition will ever improve . . . .
_____   _____
Physician's signature   Date

Physician's name _____   Physician's address _____

For Paperwork Reduction Act Notice, see Form 1040 instructions.   Cat. No. 11359K   Schedule R (Form 1040) 1997

699

Part III **Figure Your Credit**

10 If you checked (in Part I):

    Enter:

Box 1, 2, 4, or 7 . . . . $5,000 ⎫

Box 3, 5, or 6 . . . . $7,500 ⎬ **10**

Box 8 or 9 . . . . $3,750 ⎭

Did you check box 2, 4, 5, 6, or 9 in Part I?	Yes ──────▶	You **must** complete line 11.
	No ──────▶	Enter the amount from line 10 on line 12 and go to line 13.

11 If you checked:

• Box 6 in Part I, add $5,000 to the taxable disability income of the spouse who was under age 65. Enter the total.

• Box 2, 4, or 9 in Part I, enter your taxable disability income.

• Box 5 in Part I, add your taxable disability income to your spouse's taxable disability income. Enter the total.

⎫⎬⎭ **11**

TIP: For more details on what to include on line 11, see the instructions.

12 If you completed line 11, enter the **smaller** of line 10 or line 11; **all others,** enter the amount from line 10 . . . . **12**

13 Enter the following pensions, annuities, or disability income that you (and your spouse if filing a joint return) received in 1997:

  a Nontaxable part of social security benefits, and

Nontaxable part of railroad retirement benefits treated as social security. See instructions. ⎬ . . . **13a**

  b Nontaxable veterans' pensions, and

Any other pension, annuity, or disability benefit that is excluded from income under any other provision of law. See instructions. ⎬ . . . **13b**

  c Add lines 13a and 13b. (Even though these income items are not taxable, they **must** be included here to figure your credit.) If you did not receive any of the types of nontaxable income listed on line 13a or 13b, enter -0- on line 13c **13c**

14 Enter the amount from Form 1040, line 33 **14**

15 **If you checked (in Part I):** **Enter:**

Box 1 or 2 . . . . $7,500 ⎫

Box 3, 4, 5, 6, or 7 . . . . $10,000 ⎬ **15**

Box 8 or 9 . . . . $5,000 ⎭

16 Subtract line 15 from line 14. If zero or less, enter -0- **16**

17 Enter one-half of line 16 . . . . **17**

18 Add lines 13c and 17 . . . . **18**

19 Subtract line 18 from line 12. If zero or less, **stop;** you **cannot** take the credit. Otherwise, go to line 20 . . . . **19**

20 Multiply line 19 by 15% (.15). Enter the result here and on Form 1040, line 41. **Caution:** *If you file Schedule C, C-EZ, D, E, or F (Form 1040), your credit may be limited. See the instructions for line 20 for the amount of credit you can claim* **20**

Instructions for Physician's Statement

Taxpayer

If you retired after 1976, enter the date you retired in the space provided in Part II.

Physician

A person is permanently and totally disabled if **both** of the following apply:

  1. He or she cannot engage in any substantial gainful activity because of a physical or mental condition, and

2. A physician determines that the disability has lasted or can be expected to last continuously for at least a year or can lead to death.

Form **2441**	Child and Dependent Care Expenses	OMB No. 1545-0068

Form 2441

Department of the Treasury
Internal Revenue Service (99)

► Attach to Form 1040.

► See separate instructions.

1997

Attachment
Sequence No. **21**

Name(s) shown on Form 1040

Your social security number

Before you begin, you need to understand the following terms. See **Definitions** on page 1 of the instructions.

- **Dependent Care Benefits**
- **Qualifying Person(s)**
- **Qualified Expenses**
- **Earned Income**

Part I | **Persons or Organizations Who Provided the Care—You must complete this part.**
(If you need more space, use the bottom of page 2.)

1

(a) Care provider's name	(b) Address (number, street, apt. no., city, state, and ZIP code)	(c) Identifying number (SSN or EIN)	(d) Amount paid (see instructions)

Did you receive **dependent care benefits?**

— NO ——→ Complete only Part II below.

— YES ——→ Complete Part III on the back next.

Caution: *If the care was provided in your home, you may owe employment taxes. See the instructions for Form 1040, line 52.*

Part II | **Credit for Child and Dependent Care Expenses**

2 Information about your **qualifying person(s).** If you have more than two qualifying persons, see the instructions.

(a) Qualifying person's name		(b) Qualifying person's social security number	(c) **Qualified expenses** you incurred and paid in 1997 for the person listed in column (a)
First	Last		

3 Add the amounts in column (c) of line 2. DO NOT enter more than $2,400 for one qualifying person or $4,800 for two or more persons. If you completed Part III, enter the amount from line 24 . . . . | **3** | |

4 Enter YOUR **earned income** . . . . | **4** | |

5 If married filing a joint return, enter YOUR SPOUSE'S earned income (if student or disabled, see the instructions); **all others,** enter the amount from line 4 . . . . . . | **5** | |

6 Enter the **smallest** of line 3, 4, or 5 . . . . | **6** | |

7 Enter the amount from Form 1040, line 33 . . . . . | **7** | |

8 Enter on line 8 the decimal amount shown below that applies to the amount on line 7

If line 7 is—		Decimal amount is	If line 7 is—		Decimal amount is
Over	But not over		Over	But not over	
$0—10,000		.30	$20,000—22,000		.24
10,000—12,000		.29	22,000—24,000		.23
12,000—14,000		.28	24,000—26,000		.22
14,000—16,000		.27	26,000—28,000		.21
16,000—18,000		.26	28,000—No limit		.20
18,000—20,000		.25			

8 | X .

9 Multiply **line 6** by the decimal amount on line 8. Enter the result. Then, see the instructions for the amount of credit to enter on Form 1040, line 40 . . . . | **9** | |

For Paperwork Reduction Act Notice, see page 3 of the instructions.   Cat. No. 11862M   Form **2441** (1997)

Part III Dependent Care Benefits

10	Enter the total amount of **dependent care benefits** you received for 1997. This amount should be shown in box 10 of your W-2 form(s). DO NOT include amounts that were reported to you as wages in box 1 of Form(s) W-2	**10**		
11	Enter the amount forfeited, if any. See the instructions	**11**		
12	Subtract line 11 from line 10	**12**		
13	Enter the total amount of **qualified expenses** incurred in 1997 for the care of the qualifying person(s) . . .	**13**		
14	Enter the **smaller** of line 12 or 13	**14**		
15	Enter YOUR **earned income**	**15**		
16	If married filing a joint return, enter YOUR SPOUSE'S earned income (if student or disabled, see the line 5 instructions); if married filing a separate return, see the instructions for the amount to enter; **all others,** enter the amount from line 15	**16**		
17	Enter the **smallest** of line 14, 15, or 16	**17**		
18	**Excluded benefits.** Enter here the **smaller** of the following: • The amount from line 17, or • $5,000 ($2,500 if married filing a separate return **and** you were required to enter your spouse's earned income on line 16).	**18**		
19	**Taxable benefits.** Subtract line 18 from line 12. Also, include this amount on Form 1040, line 7. On the dotted line next to line 7, write "DCB"	**19**		

To claim the child and dependent care
credit, complete lines 20–24 below.

20	Enter $2,400 ($4,800 if two or more qualifying persons)	**20**		
21	Enter the amount from line 18	**21**		
22	Subtract line 21 from line 20. If zero or less, **STOP.** You cannot take the credit. **Exception.** If you paid 1996 expenses in 1997, see the line 9 instructions	**22**		
23	Complete line 2 on the front of this form. DO NOT include in column (c) any excluded benefits shown on line 18 above. Then, add the amounts in column (c) and enter the total here	**23**		
24	Enter the **smaller** of line 22 or 23. Also, enter this amount on line 3 on the front of this form and complete lines 4–9	**24**		

Form **5329**

Department of the Treasury
Internal Revenue Service

Additional Taxes Attributable to Qualified Retirement Plans (Including IRAs), Annuities, Modified Endowment Contracts, and MSAs

(Under Sections 72, 4973, 4974, and 4980A of the Internal Revenue Code)
▶ Attach to Form 1040. See separate instructions.

OMB No. 1545-0203

1997

Attachment
Sequence No. **29**

Name of individual subject to additional tax. (If married filing jointly, see page 2 of the instructions.) | Your social security number

Fill in Your Address Only If You Are Filing This Form by Itself and Not With Your Tax Return ▷

Home address (number and street), or P.O. box if mail is not delivered to your home | Apt. no.

City, town or post office, state, and ZIP code | If this is an amended return, check here ▶ ☐

If you are subject to the 10% tax on early distributions **only,** see **Who Must File** in the instructions before continuing. You may be able to report this tax directly on Form 1040 without filing Form 5329.

Part I Tax on Early Distributions

Complete this part if a taxable distribution was made from your qualified retirement plan (including an IRA), annuity contract, or modified endowment contract before you reached age 59½ (or was incorrectly indicated as such on your Form 1099-R—see instructions). **Note:** *You must include the amount of the distribution on line 15b or 16b of Form 1040.*

1	Early distributions included in gross income (see page 2 of the instructions)	1	
2	Distributions excepted from additional tax (see page 2 of the instructions). Enter appropriate exception number from instructions ▶ _____	2	
3	Amount subject to additional tax. Subtract line 2 from line 1	3	
4	**Tax due.** Multiply line 3 by 10% (.10). Enter here and on Form 1040, line 50	4	

Caution: *If any amount on line 3 was a distribution from a SIMPLE retirement plan, you must multiply that distribution by 25% (.25) instead of 10%. See instructions for more information.*

Part II Tax on Excess Contributions to Individual Retirement Arrangements

Complete this part if, either in this year or in earlier years, you contributed more to your IRA than is or was allowable and you have an excess contribution subject to tax.

5	Excess contributions for 1997 (see page 3 of the instructions). Do not include this amount on Form 1040, line 23		5	
6	Earlier year excess contributions not previously eliminated (see page 3 of the instructions)	6		
7	Contribution credit. If your actual contribution for 1997 is less than your maximum allowable contribution, see page 3 of the instructions; otherwise, enter -0-	7		
8	1997 distributions from your IRA account that are includible in taxable income	8		
9	1996 tax year excess contributions (if any) withdrawn after the due date (including extensions) of your 1996 income tax return, and 1995 and earlier tax year excess contributions withdrawn in 1997 . . .	9		
10	Add lines 7, 8, and 9	10		
11	Adjusted earlier year excess contributions. Subtract line 10 from line 6. Enter the result, but not less than zero		11	
12	Total excess contributions. Add lines 5 and 11		12	
13	**Tax due.** Enter the **smaller** of 6% (.06) of line 12 or 6% (.06) of the value of your IRA on the last day of 1997. Also enter this amount on Form 1040, line 50		13	

For Paperwork Reduction Act Notice, see page 4 of separate instructions.

Cat. No. 13329Q

Form **5329** (1997)

Part III	**Tax on Excess Contributions to Medical Savings Accounts**		
14	Excess contributions for 1997 (see page 3 of the instructions). Do not include this amount on Form 1040, line 24	**14**	
15	**Tax due.** Enter the **smaller** of 6% (.06) of line 14 or 6% (.06) of the value of your MSA on the last day of 1997. Also enter this amount on Form 1040, line 50	**15**	

Part IV	**Tax on Excess Accumulation in Qualified Retirement Plans (Including IRAs)**	
16	Minimum required distribution (see page 3 of the instructions)	**16**
17	Amount actually distributed to you	**17**
18	Subtract line 17 from line 16. If line 17 is more than line 16, enter -0-	**18**
19	**Tax due.** Multiply line 18 by 50% (.50). Enter here and on Form 1040, line 50	**19**

Part V	**Tax on Excess Distributions From Qualified Retirement Plans (Including IRAs)**

This tax does not apply to distributions during years beginning after December 31, 1996, and before January 1, 2000. See instructions.

Acceleration Election (see instructions)

If you previously made an acceleration election and wish to revoke that election, check here . . . . ▶ ☐

Signature. *Complete **ONLY** if you are filing this form by itself and not with your tax return.*

Please Sign Here	Under penalties of perjury, I declare that I have examined this form, including accompanying schedules and statements, and to the best of my knowledge and belief, it is true, correct, and complete. Declaration of preparer (other than taxpayer) is based on all information of which preparer has any knowledge.		
	▶ _____ Your signature		▶ _____ Date

Paid Preparer's Use Only	Preparer's signature ▶	Date	Check if self-employed ▶ ☐	Preparer's social security no.
	Firm's name (or yours, if self-employed) and address ▶		EIN ▶	
			ZIP code ▶	

⊛

Form **8839**

Department of the Treasury
Internal Revenue Service

Qualified Adoption Expenses

▶ Attach to Form 1040 or 1040A.

▶ See separate instructions.

OMB No. 1545-xxxx

1997

Attachment
Sequence No. **38**

Name(s) shown on return

Your social security number

Before you begin, you need to understand the following terms. See **Definitions** on page 1 of the instructions.

- **Eligible Child**
- **Employer-Provided Adoption Benefits**
- **Qualified Adoption Expenses**

Part I   Information About Your Eligible Child or Children—You **must** complete this part. See the instructions for details, including what to do if you need more space.

1	(a) Child's name		(b) Child's year of birth	Check if child was—			(f) Child's identifying number
	First	Last		(c) born **before 1979** and was disabled	(d) a child with special needs	(e) a foreign child	
Child 1			**19**	☐	☐	☐	
Child 2			**19**	☐	☐	☐	

Caution: *If you received employer-provided adoption benefits, complete Part III on the back next.*

Part II   Adoption Credit—Complete this part **only** if the adoption was final in 1997.

			Child 1	Child 2	
2	Enter $5,000 ($6,000 if a child with special needs)	2			
3	Enter the total **qualified adoption expenses** you paid in 1997	3			
4	Enter the **smaller** of line 2 or line 3 . .	4			
5	Add the amounts on line 4			5	
6	Enter your modified adjusted gross income (see the instructions)	6			
7	Is line 6 more than $75,000?				
	No. Skip lines 7 and 8 and enter -0- on line 9.				
	Yes. Subtract $75,000 from the amount on line 6	7			
8	Divide line 7 by $40,000. Enter the result as a decimal (rounded to two places). Do not enter more than "1.00"		8	✕	.
9	Multiply line 5 by line 8			9	
10	Subtract line 9 from line 5. Enter the result. Then, see the instructions for the amount of credit to enter on Form 1040, line 42, or on Form 1040A, line 24c			10	
11	1997 credit carryforward, if any, to 1998 (see the instructions) .	11			

For Paperwork Reduction Act Notice, see page 4 of instructions.   Cat. No. 22843L   Form **8839** (1997)

705

Part III Employer-Provided Adoption Benefits

Caution: *If the eligible child is a foreign child, see the instructions for line 1, column (e), before completing this part.*

		Child 1	Child 2	
12	Enter $5,000 ($6,000 if a child with special needs)	**12**		
13	Enter the total amount of your **employer-provided adoption benefits** received in 1997. This amount should be shown in box 13 of your 1997 W-2 form(s) with code "T" . .	**13**		
14	Add the amounts on line 13			**14**
15	Enter the **smaller** of line 12 or line 13	**15**		
16	Add the amounts on line 15		**16**	
17	Enter your modified adjusted gross income (from the worksheet in the instructions)	**17**		
18	Is line 17 more than $75,000? **No.** Skip lines 18–20 and enter the amount from line 16 on line 21. **Yes.** Subtract $75,000 from the amount on line 17	**18**		
19	Divide line 18 by $40,000. Enter the result as a decimal (rounded to two places). Do not enter more than "1.00"	**19**	✕ .	
20	Multiply line 16 by line 19	**20**		
21	Subtract line 20 from line 16	**21**		
22	**Excluded benefits.** Enter the **smaller** of line 16 or line 21			**22**
23	**Taxable benefits.** Subtract line 22 from line 14. Also, include this amount on Form 1040, line 7, or Form 1040A, line 7. On the line next to line 7, write "AB"			**23**

Next, complete Form 1040 through line 41 or Form 1040A through line 24b.
Then, if the total adoption expenses you paid in 1997 were not fully reimbursed by your employer **AND** the adoption was final in 1997, you may be able to claim the adoption credit. Fill in Part II on the front of this form to see if you can.

1997 Earned Income Credit (EIC) Table

Caution: This is **not** a tax table.

To find your credit: First, read down the "At least — But less than" columns and find the line that includes the amount you entered on line 6 or line 8 of the **Earned Income Credit Worksheet** on page 23. Next, read across to the column that includes the number of qualifying children you have. Then, enter the credit from that column on line 7 or line 9 of that worksheet, whichever applies.

If the amount on line 6 or line 8 of the worksheet on page 23 is—		And you have—		
At least	But less than	No children	One child	Two children
		Your credit is—		
$1	$50	$2	$9	$10
50	100	6	26	30
100	150	10	43	50
150	200	13	60	70
200	250	17	77	90
250	300	21	94	110
300	350	25	111	130
350	400	29	128	150
400	450	33	145	170
450	500	36	162	190
500	550	40	179	210
550	600	44	196	230
600	650	48	213	250
650	700	52	230	270
700	750	55	247	290
750	800	59	264	310
800	850	63	281	330
850	900	67	298	350
900	950	71	315	370
950	1,000	75	332	390
1,000	1,050	78	349	410
1,050	1,100	82	366	430
1,100	1,150	86	383	450
1,150	1,200	90	400	470
1,200	1,250	94	417	490
1,250	1,300	98	434	510
1,300	1,350	101	451	530
1,350	1,400	105	468	550
1,400	1,450	109	485	570
1,450	1,500	113	502	590
1,500	1,550	117	519	610
1,550	1,600	120	536	630
1,600	1,650	124	553	650
1,650	1,700	128	570	670
1,700	1,750	132	587	690
1,750	1,800	136	604	710
1,800	1,850	140	621	730
1,850	1,900	143	638	750
1,900	1,950	147	655	770
1,950	2,000	151	672	790
2,000	2,050	155	689	810
2,050	2,100	159	706	830
2,100	2,150	163	723	850
2,150	2,200	166	740	870
2,200	2,250	170	757	890
2,250	2,300	174	774	910
2,300	2,350	178	791	930
2,350	2,400	182	808	950
2,400	2,450	186	825	970
2,450	2,500	189	842	990
2,500	2,550	193	859	1,010
2,550	2,600	197	876	1,030
2,600	2,650	201	893	1,050
2,650	2,700	205	910	1,070
2,700	2,750	208	927	1,090
2,750	2,800	212	944	1,110
2,800	2,850	216	961	1,130
2,850	2,900	220	978	1,150
2,900	2,950	224	995	1,170
2,950	3,000	228	1,012	1,190
3,000	3,050	231	1,029	1,210
3,050	3,100	235	1,046	1,230
3,100	3,150	239	1,063	1,250
3,150	3,200	243	1,080	1,270

If the amount on line 6 or line 8 of the worksheet on page 23 is—		And you have—		
At least	But less than	No children	One child	Two children
		Your credit is—		
3,200	3,250	247	1,097	1,290
3,250	3,300	251	1,114	1,310
3,300	3,350	254	1,131	1,330
3,350	3,400	258	1,148	1,350
3,400	3,450	262	1,165	1,370
3,450	3,500	266	1,182	1,390
3,500	3,550	270	1,199	1,410
3,550	3,600	273	1,216	1,430
3,600	3,650	277	1,233	1,450
3,650	3,700	281	1,250	1,470
3,700	3,750	285	1,267	1,490
3,750	3,800	289	1,284	1,510
3,800	3,850	293	1,301	1,530
3,850	3,900	296	1,318	1,550
3,900	3,950	300	1,335	1,570
3,950	4,000	304	1,352	1,590
4,000	4,050	308	1,369	1,610
4,050	4,100	312	1,386	1,630
4,100	4,150	316	1,403	1,650
4,150	4,200	319	1,420	1,670
4,200	4,250	323	1,437	1,690
4,250	4,300	327	1,454	1,710
4,300	4,350	332	1,471	1,730
4,350	4,400	332	1,488	1,750
4,400	4,450	332	1,505	1,770
4,450	4,500	332	1,522	1,790
4,500	4,550	332	1,539	1,810
4,550	4,600	332	1,556	1,830
4,600	4,650	332	1,573	1,850
4,650	4,700	332	1,590	1,870
4,700	4,750	332	1,607	1,890
4,750	4,800	332	1,624	1,910
4,800	4,850	332	1,641	1,930
4,850	4,900	332	1,658	1,950
4,900	4,950	332	1,675	1,970
4,950	5,000	332	1,692	1,990
5,000	5,050	332	1,709	2,010
5,050	5,100	332	1,726	2,030
5,100	5,150	332	1,743	2,050
5,150	5,200	332	1,760	2,070
5,200	5,250	332	1,777	2,090
5,250	5,300	332	1,794	2,110
5,300	5,350	332	1,811	2,130
5,350	5,400	332	1,828	2,150
5,400	5,450	332	1,845	2,170
5,450	5,500	329	1,862	2,190
5,500	5,550	325	1,879	2,210
5,550	5,600	321	1,896	2,230
5,600	5,650	317	1,913	2,250
5,650	5,700	313	1,930	2,270
5,700	5,750	309	1,947	2,290
5,750	5,800	306	1,964	2,310
5,800	5,850	302	1,981	2,330
5,850	5,900	298	1,998	2,350
5,900	5,950	294	2,015	2,370
5,950	6,000	290	2,032	2,390
6,000	6,050	286	2,049	2,410
6,050	6,100	283	2,066	2,430
6,100	6,150	279	2,083	2,450
6,150	6,200	275	2,100	2,470
6,200	6,250	271	2,117	2,490
6,250	6,300	267	2,134	2,510
6,300	6,350	264	2,151	2,530
6,350	6,400	260	2,168	2,550

If the amount on line 6 or line 8 of the worksheet on page 23 is—		And you have—		
At least	But less than	No children	One child	Two children
		Your credit is—		
6,400	6,450	256	2,185	2,570
6,450	6,500	252	2,202	2,590
6,500	6,550	248	2,210	2,610
6,550	6,600	244	2,210	2,630
6,600	6,650	241	2,210	2,650
6,650	6,700	237	2,210	2,670
6,700	6,750	233	2,210	2,690
6,750	6,800	229	2,210	2,710
6,800	6,850	225	2,210	2,730
6,850	6,900	221	2,210	2,750
6,900	6,950	218	2,210	2,770
6,950	7,000	214	2,210	2,790
7,000	7,050	210	2,210	2,810
7,050	7,100	206	2,210	2,830
7,100	7,150	202	2,210	2,850
7,150	7,200	199	2,210	2,870
7,200	7,250	195	2,210	2,890
7,250	7,300	191	2,210	2,910
7,300	7,350	187	2,210	2,930
7,350	7,400	183	2,210	2,950
7,400	7,450	179	2,210	2,970
7,450	7,500	176	2,210	2,990
7,500	7,550	172	2,210	3,010
7,550	7,600	168	2,210	3,030
7,600	7,650	164	2,210	3,050
7,650	7,700	160	2,210	3,070
7,700	7,750	156	2,210	3,090
7,750	7,800	153	2,210	3,110
7,800	7,850	149	2,210	3,130
7,850	7,900	145	2,210	3,150
7,900	7,950	141	2,210	3,170
7,950	8,000	137	2,210	3,190
8,000	8,050	133	2,210	3,210
8,050	8,100	130	2,210	3,230
8,100	8,150	126	2,210	3,250
8,150	8,200	122	2,210	3,270
8,200	8,250	118	2,210	3,290
8,250	8,300	114	2,210	3,310
8,300	8,350	111	2,210	3,330
8,350	8,400	107	2,210	3,350
8,400	8,450	103	2,210	3,370
8,450	8,500	99	2,210	3,390
8,500	8,550	95	2,210	3,410
8,550	8,600	91	2,210	3,430
8,600	8,650	88	2,210	3,450
8,650	8,700	84	2,210	3,470
8,700	8,750	80	2,210	3,490
8,750	8,800	76	2,210	3,510
8,800	8,850	72	2,210	3,530
8,850	8,900	68	2,210	3,550
8,900	8,950	65	2,210	3,570
8,950	9,000	61	2,210	3,590
9,000	9,050	57	2,210	3,610
9,050	9,100	53	2,210	3,630
9,100	9,150	49	2,210	3,656
9,150	9,200	46	2,210	3,656
9,200	9,250	42	2,210	3,656
9,250	9,300	38	2,210	3,656
9,300	9,350	34	2,210	3,656
9,350	9,400	30	2,210	3,656
9,400	9,450	26	2,210	3,656
9,450	9,500	23	2,210	3,656
9,500	9,550	19	2,210	3,656
9,550	9,600	15	2,210	3,656

If the amount on line 6 or line 8 of the worksheet on page 23 is—		And you have—		
At least	But less than	No children	One child	Two children
		Your credit is—		
9,600	9,650	11	2,210	3,656
9,650	9,700	7	2,210	3,656
9,700	9,750	3	2,210	3,656
9,750	9,800	*	2,210	3,656
9,800	11,950	0	2,210	3,656
11,950	12,000	0	2,203	3,647
12,000	12,050	0	2,195	3,636
12,050	12,100	0	2,187	3,625
12,100	12,150	0	2,179	3,615
12,150	12,200	0	2,171	3,604
12,200	12,250	0	2,163	3,594
12,250	12,300	0	2,155	3,583
12,300	12,350	0	2,147	3,573
12,350	12,400	0	2,139	3,562
12,400	12,450	0	2,131	3,552
12,450	12,500	0	2,123	3,541
12,500	12,550	0	2,115	3,531
12,550	12,600	0	2,107	3,520
12,600	12,650	0	2,099	3,510
12,650	12,700	0	2,091	3,499
12,700	12,750	0	2,083	3,489
12,750	12,800	0	2,075	3,478
12,800	12,850	0	2,067	3,468
12,850	12,900	0	2,059	3,457
12,900	12,950	0	2,051	3,446
12,950	13,000	0	2,043	3,436
13,000	13,050	0	2,035	3,425
13,050	13,100	0	2,027	3,415
13,100	13,150	0	2,019	3,404
13,150	13,200	0	2,011	3,394
13,200	13,250	0	2,003	3,383
13,250	13,300	0	1,995	3,373
13,300	13,350	0	1,987	3,362
13,350	13,400	0	1,979	3,352
13,400	13,450	0	1,971	3,341
13,450	13,500	0	1,963	3,331
13,500	13,550	0	1,955	3,320
13,550	13,600	0	1,947	3,310
13,600	13,650	0	1,939	3,299
13,650	13,700	0	1,931	3,289
13,700	13,750	0	1,923	3,278
13,750	13,800	0	1,915	3,267
13,800	13,850	0	1,907	3,257
13,850	13,900	0	1,899	3,246
13,900	13,950	0	1,891	3,236
13,950	14,000	0	1,883	3,225
14,000	14,050	0	1,875	3,215
14,050	14,100	0	1,867	3,204
14,100	14,150	0	1,859	3,194
14,150	14,200	0	1,851	3,183
14,200	14,250	0	1,843	3,173
14,250	14,300	0	1,835	3,162
14,300	14,350	0	1,827	3,152
14,350	14,400	0	1,819	3,141
14,400	14,450	0	1,811	3,131
14,450	14,500	0	1,803	3,120
14,500	14,550	0	1,795	3,109
14,550	14,600	0	1,787	3,099
14,600	14,650	0	1,779	3,088
14,650	14,700	0	1,771	3,078
14,700	14,750	0	1,763	3,067
14,750	14,800	0	1,755	3,057
14,800	14,850	0	1,747	3,046
14,850	14,900	0	1,739	3,036

* If the amount on line 6 or line 8 of the worksheet is at least $9,750 but less than $9,770, your credit is $1. Otherwise you **cannot** take the credit.

1997 Earned Income Credit (EIC) Table Continued (Caution: This is **not** a tax table.)

If the amount on line 6 or line 8 of the worksheet on page 23 is— At least	But less than	No children	One child	Two children
14,900	14,950	0	1,731	3,025
14,950	15,000	0	1,723	3,015
15,000	15,050	0	1,715	3,004
15,050	15,100	0	1,707	2,994
15,100	15,150	0	1,699	2,983
15,150	15,200	0	1,691	2,973
15,200	15,250	0	1,683	2,962
15,250	15,300	0	1,675	2,952
15,300	15,350	0	1,667	2,941
15,350	15,400	0	1,659	2,930
15,400	15,450	0	1,651	2,920
15,450	15,500	0	1,644	2,909
15,500	15,550	0	1,636	2,899
15,550	15,600	0	1,628	2,888
15,600	15,650	0	1,620	2,878
15,650	15,700	0	1,612	2,867
15,700	15,750	0	1,604	2,857
15,750	15,800	0	1,596	2,846
15,800	15,850	0	1,588	2,836
15,850	15,900	0	1,580	2,825
15,900	15,950	0	1,572	2,815
15,950	16,000	0	1,564	2,804
16,000	16,050	0	1,556	2,794
16,050	16,100	0	1,548	2,783
16,100	16,150	0	1,540	2,773
16,150	16,200	0	1,532	2,762
16,200	16,250	0	1,524	2,751
16,250	16,300	0	1,516	2,741
16,300	16,350	0	1,508	2,730
16,350	16,400	0	1,500	2,720
16,400	16,450	0	1,492	2,709
16,450	16,500	0	1,484	2,699
16,500	16,550	0	1,476	2,688
16,550	16,600	0	1,468	2,678
16,600	16,650	0	1,460	2,667
16,650	16,700	0	1,452	2,657
16,700	16,750	0	1,444	2,646
16,750	16,800	0	1,436	2,636
16,800	16,850	0	1,428	2,625
16,850	16,900	0	1,420	2,615
16,900	16,950	0	1,412	2,604
16,950	17,000	0	1,404	2,594
17,000	17,050	0	1,396	2,583
17,050	17,100	0	1,388	2,572
17,100	17,150	0	1,380	2,562
17,150	17,200	0	1,372	2,551
17,200	17,250	0	1,364	2,541
17,250	17,300	0	1,356	2,530
17,300	17,350	0	1,348	2,520
17,350	17,400	0	1,340	2,509
17,400	17,450	0	1,332	2,499
17,450	17,500	0	1,324	2,488
17,500	17,550	0	1,316	2,478
17,550	17,600	0	1,308	2,467
17,600	17,650	0	1,300	2,457
17,650	17,700	0	1,292	2,446
17,700	17,750	0	1,284	2,436
17,750	17,800	0	1,276	2,425
17,800	17,850	0	1,268	2,415
17,850	17,900	0	1,260	2,404
17,900	17,950	0	1,252	2,393
17,950	18,000	0	1,244	2,383
18,000	18,050	0	1,236	2,372
18,050	18,100	0	1,228	2,362
18,100	18,150	0	1,220	2,351
18,150	18,200	0	1,212	2,341
18,200	18,250	0	1,204	2,330
18,250	18,300	0	1,196	2,320
18,300	18,350	0	1,188	2,309
18,350	18,400	0	1,180	2,299
18,400	18,450	0	1,172	2,288
18,450	18,500	0	1,164	2,278

If the amount on line 6 or line 8 of the worksheet on page 23 is— At least	But less than	No children	One child	Two children
18,500	18,550	0	1,156	2,267
18,550	18,600	0	1,148	2,257
18,600	18,650	0	1,140	2,246
18,650	18,700	0	1,132	2,236
18,700	18,750	0	1,124	2,225
18,750	18,800	0	1,116	2,214
18,800	18,850	0	1,108	2,204
18,850	18,900	0	1,100	2,193
18,900	18,950	0	1,092	2,183
18,950	19,000	0	1,084	2,172
19,000	19,050	0	1,076	2,162
19,050	19,100	0	1,068	2,151
19,100	19,150	0	1,060	2,141
19,150	19,200	0	1,052	2,130
19,200	19,250	0	1,044	2,120
19,250	19,300	0	1,036	2,109
19,300	19,350	0	1,028	2,099
19,350	19,400	0	1,020	2,088
19,400	19,450	0	1,012	2,078
19,450	19,500	0	1,004	2,067
19,500	19,550	0	996	2,056
19,550	19,600	0	988	2,046
19,600	19,650	0	980	2,035
19,650	19,700	0	972	2,025
19,700	19,750	0	964	2,014
19,750	19,800	0	956	2,004
19,800	19,850	0	948	1,993
19,850	19,900	0	940	1,983
19,900	19,950	0	932	1,972
19,950	20,000	0	924	1,962
20,000	20,050	0	916	1,951
20,050	20,100	0	908	1,941
20,100	20,150	0	900	1,930
20,150	20,200	0	892	1,920
20,200	20,250	0	884	1,909
20,250	20,300	0	876	1,899
20,300	20,350	0	868	1,888
20,350	20,400	0	860	1,877
20,400	20,450	0	852	1,867
20,450	20,500	0	845	1,856
20,500	20,550	0	837	1,846
20,550	20,600	0	829	1,835
20,600	20,650	0	821	1,825
20,650	20,700	0	813	1,814
20,700	20,750	0	805	1,804
20,750	20,800	0	797	1,793
20,800	20,850	0	789	1,783
20,850	20,900	0	781	1,772
20,900	20,950	0	773	1,762
20,950	21,000	0	765	1,751
21,000	21,050	0	757	1,741
21,050	21,100	0	749	1,730
21,100	21,150	0	741	1,720
21,150	21,200	0	733	1,709
21,200	21,250	0	725	1,698
21,250	21,300	0	717	1,688
21,300	21,350	0	709	1,677
21,350	21,400	0	701	1,667
21,400	21,450	0	693	1,656
21,450	21,500	0	685	1,646
21,500	21,550	0	677	1,635
21,550	21,600	0	669	1,625
21,600	21,650	0	661	1,614
21,650	21,700	0	653	1,604
21,700	21,750	0	645	1,593
21,750	21,800	0	637	1,583
21,800	21,850	0	629	1,572
21,850	21,900	0	621	1,562
21,900	21,950	0	613	1,551
21,950	22,000	0	605	1,541
22,000	22,050	0	597	1,530
22,050	22,100	0	589	1,519

If the amount on line 6 or line 8 of the worksheet on page 23 is— At least	But less than	No children	One child	Two children
22,100	22,150	0	581	1,509
22,150	22,200	0	573	1,498
22,200	22,250	0	565	1,488
22,250	22,300	0	557	1,477
22,300	22,350	0	549	1,467
22,350	22,400	0	541	1,456
22,400	22,450	0	533	1,446
22,450	22,500	0	525	1,435
22,500	22,550	0	517	1,425
22,550	22,600	0	509	1,414
22,600	22,650	0	501	1,404
22,650	22,700	0	493	1,393
22,700	22,750	0	485	1,383
22,750	22,800	0	477	1,372
22,800	22,850	0	469	1,362
22,850	22,900	0	461	1,351
22,900	22,950	0	453	1,340
22,950	23,000	0	445	1,330
23,000	23,050	0	437	1,319
23,050	23,100	0	429	1,309
23,100	23,150	0	421	1,298
23,150	23,200	0	413	1,288
23,200	23,250	0	405	1,277
23,250	23,300	0	397	1,267
23,300	23,350	0	389	1,256
23,350	23,400	0	381	1,246
23,400	23,450	0	373	1,235
23,450	23,500	0	365	1,225
23,500	23,550	0	357	1,214
23,550	23,600	0	349	1,204
23,600	23,650	0	341	1,193
23,650	23,700	0	333	1,183
23,700	23,750	0	325	1,172
23,750	23,800	0	317	1,161
23,800	23,850	0	309	1,151
23,850	23,900	0	301	1,140
23,900	23,950	0	293	1,130
23,950	24,000	0	285	1,119
24,000	24,050	0	277	1,109
24,050	24,100	0	269	1,098
24,100	24,150	0	261	1,088
24,150	24,200	0	253	1,077
24,200	24,250	0	245	1,067
24,250	24,300	0	237	1,056
24,300	24,350	0	229	1,046
24,350	24,400	0	221	1,035
24,400	24,450	0	213	1,025
24,450	24,500	0	205	1,014
24,500	24,550	0	197	1,003
24,550	24,600	0	189	993
24,600	24,650	0	181	982
24,650	24,700	0	173	972
24,700	24,750	0	165	961
24,750	24,800	0	157	951
24,800	24,850	0	149	940
24,850	24,900	0	141	930
24,900	24,950	0	133	919
24,950	25,000	0	125	909
25,000	25,050	0	117	898
25,050	25,100	0	109	888
25,100	25,150	0	101	877
25,150	25,200	0	93	867
25,200	25,250	0	85	856
25,250	25,300	0	77	846
25,300	25,350	0	69	835
25,350	25,400	0	61	824
25,400	25,450	0	53	814
25,450	25,500	0	46	803
25,500	25,550	0	38	793
25,550	25,600	0	30	782
25,600	25,650	0	22	772
25,650	25,700	0	14	761

If the amount on line 6 or line 8 of the worksheet on page 23 is— At least	But less than	No children	One child	Two children
25,700	25,750	0	6	751
25,750	25,800	0	*	740
25,800	25,850	0	0	730
25,850	25,900	0	0	719
25,900	25,950	0	0	709
25,950	26,000	0	0	698
26,000	26,050	0	0	688
26,050	26,100	0	0	677
26,100	26,150	0	0	667
26,150	26,200	0	0	656
26,200	26,250	0	0	645
26,250	26,300	0	0	635
26,300	26,350	0	0	624
26,350	26,400	0	0	614
26,400	26,450	0	0	603
26,450	26,500	0	0	593
26,500	26,550	0	0	582
26,550	26,600	0	0	572
26,600	26,650	0	0	561
26,650	26,700	0	0	551
26,700	26,750	0	0	540
26,750	26,800	0	0	530
26,800	26,850	0	0	519
26,850	26,900	0	0	509
26,900	26,950	0	0	498
26,950	27,000	0	0	488
27,000	27,050	0	0	477
27,050	27,100	0	0	466
27,100	27,150	0	0	456
27,150	27,200	0	0	445
27,200	27,250	0	0	435
27,250	27,300	0	0	424
27,300	27,350	0	0	414
27,350	27,400	0	0	403
27,400	27,450	0	0	393
27,450	27,500	0	0	382
27,500	27,550	0	0	372
27,550	27,600	0	0	361
27,600	27,650	0	0	351
27,650	27,700	0	0	340
27,700	27,750	0	0	330
27,750	27,800	0	0	319
27,800	27,850	0	0	309
27,850	27,900	0	0	298
27,900	27,950	0	0	287
27,950	28,000	0	0	277
28,000	28,050	0	0	266
28,050	28,100	0	0	256
28,100	28,150	0	0	245
28,150	28,200	0	0	235
28,200	28,250	0	0	224
28,250	28,300	0	0	214
28,300	28,350	0	0	203
28,350	28,400	0	0	193
28,400	28,450	0	0	182
28,450	28,500	0	0	172
28,500	28,550	0	0	161
28,550	28,600	0	0	151
28,600	28,650	0	0	140
28,650	28,700	0	0	130
28,700	28,750	0	0	119
28,750	28,800	0	0	108
28,800	28,850	0	0	98
28,850	28,900	0	0	87
28,900	28,950	0	0	77
28,950	29,000	0	0	66
29,000	29,050	0	0	56
29,050	29,100	0	0	45
29,100	29,150	0	0	35
29,150	29,200	0	0	24
29,200	29,250	0	0	14
29,250	29,290	0	0	4
29,290 or more		0	0	0

*If the amount on line 6 or line 8 of the worksheet is at least $25,750 but less than $25,760, your credit is $1. Otherwise, you cannot take the credit.

Section 5.

1997 Tax Table

**Use if your taxable income is less than $100,000.
If $100,000 or more, use the Tax Rate Schedules.**

Example. Mr. and Mrs. Brown are filing a joint return. Their taxable income on line 38 of Form 1040 is $25,300. First, they find the $25,300–25,350 income line. Next, they find the column for married filing jointly and read down the column. The amount shown where the income line and filing status column meet is $3,799. This is the tax amount they should enter on line 39 of their Form 1040.

Sample Table

At least	But less than	Single	Married filing jointly *	Married filing separately	Head of a house-hold
			Your tax is—		
25,200	25,250	3,859	3,784	4,385	3,784
25,250	25,300	3,873	3,791	4,399	3,791
25,300	25,350	3,887	(3,799)	4,413	3,799
25,350	25,400	3,901	3,806	4,427	3,806

If line 38 (taxable income) is— At least	But less than	Single	Married filing jointly *	Married filing separately	Head of a house-hold
			Your tax is—		
$0	$5	$0	$0	$0	$0
5	15	2	2	2	2
15	25	3	3	3	3
25	50	6	6	6	6
50	75	9	9	9	9
75	100	13	13	13	13
100	125	17	17	17	17
125	150	21	21	21	21
150	175	24	24	24	24
175	200	28	28	28	28
200	225	32	32	32	32
225	250	36	36	36	36
250	275	39	39	39	39
275	300	43	43	43	43
300	325	47	47	47	47
325	350	51	51	51	51
350	375	54	54	54	54
375	400	58	58	58	58
400	425	62	62	62	62
425	450	66	66	66	66
450	475	69	69	69	69
475	500	73	73	73	73
500	525	77	77	77	77
525	550	81	81	81	81
550	575	84	84	84	84
575	600	88	88	88	88
600	625	92	92	92	92
625	650	96	96	96	96
650	675	99	99	99	99
675	700	103	103	103	103
700	725	107	107	107	107
725	750	111	111	111	111
750	775	114	114	114	114
775	800	118	118	118	118
800	825	122	122	122	122
825	850	126	126	126	126
850	875	129	129	129	129
875	900	133	133	133	133
900	925	137	137	137	137
925	950	141	141	141	141
950	975	144	144	144	144
975	1,000	148	148	148	148

1,000

At least	But less than	Single	Married filing jointly	Married filing separately	Head of a house-hold
1,000	1,025	152	152	152	152
1,025	1,050	156	156	156	156
1,050	1,075	159	159	159	159
1,075	1,100	163	163	163	163
1,100	1,125	167	167	167	167
1,125	1,150	171	171	171	171
1,150	1,175	174	174	174	174
1,175	1,200	178	178	178	178
1,200	1,225	182	182	182	182
1,225	1,250	186	186	186	186
1,250	1,275	189	189	189	189
1,275	1,300	193	193	193	193

At least	But less than	Single	Married filing jointly	Married filing separately	Head of a house-hold
			Your tax is—		
1,300	1,325	197	197	197	197
1,325	1,350	201	201	201	201
1,350	1,375	204	204	204	204
1,375	1,400	208	208	208	208
1,400	1,425	212	212	212	212
1,425	1,450	216	216	216	216
1,450	1,475	219	219	219	219
1,475	1,500	223	223	223	223
1,500	1,525	227	227	227	227
1,525	1,550	231	231	231	231
1,550	1,575	234	234	234	234
1,575	1,600	238	238	238	238
1,600	1,625	242	242	242	242
1,625	1,650	246	246	246	246
1,650	1,675	249	249	249	249
1,675	1,700	253	253	253	253
1,700	1,725	257	257	257	257
1,725	1,750	261	261	261	261
1,750	1,775	264	264	264	264
1,775	1,800	268	268	268	268
1,800	1,825	272	272	272	272
1,825	1,850	276	276	276	276
1,850	1,875	279	279	279	279
1,875	1,900	283	283	283	283
1,900	1,925	287	287	287	287
1,925	1,950	291	291	291	291
1,950	1,975	294	294	294	294
1,975	2,000	298	298	298	298

2,000

At least	But less than	Single	Married filing jointly	Married filing separately	Head of a house-hold
2,000	2,025	302	302	302	302
2,025	2,050	306	306	306	306
2,050	2,075	309	309	309	309
2,075	2,100	313	313	313	313
2,100	2,125	317	317	317	317
2,125	2,150	321	321	321	321
2,150	2,175	324	324	324	324
2,175	2,200	328	328	328	328
2,200	2,225	332	332	332	332
2,225	2,250	336	336	336	336
2,250	2,275	339	339	339	339
2,275	2,300	343	343	343	343
2,300	2,325	347	347	347	347
2,325	2,350	351	351	351	351
2,350	2,375	354	354	354	354
2,375	2,400	358	358	358	358
2,400	2,425	362	362	362	362
2,425	2,450	366	366	366	366
2,450	2,475	369	369	369	369
2,475	2,500	373	373	373	373
2,500	2,525	377	377	377	377
2,525	2,550	381	381	381	381
2,550	2,575	384	384	384	384
2,575	2,600	388	388	388	388
2,600	2,625	392	392	392	392
2,625	2,650	396	396	396	396
2,650	2,675	399	399	399	399
2,675	2,700	403	403	403	403

At least	But less than	Single	Married filing jointly	Married filing separately	Head of a house-hold
			Your tax is—		
2,700	2,725	407	407	407	407
2,725	2,750	411	411	411	411
2,750	2,775	414	414	414	414
2,775	2,800	418	418	418	418
2,800	2,825	422	422	422	422
2,825	2,850	426	426	426	426
2,850	2,875	429	429	429	429
2,875	2,900	433	433	433	433
2,900	2,925	437	437	437	437
2,925	2,950	441	441	441	441
2,950	2,975	444	444	444	444
2,975	3,000	448	448	448	448

3,000

At least	But less than	Single	Married filing jointly	Married filing separately	Head of a house-hold
3,000	3,050	454	454	454	454
3,050	3,100	461	461	461	461
3,100	3,150	469	469	469	469
3,150	3,200	476	476	476	476
3,200	3,250	484	484	484	484
3,250	3,300	491	491	491	491
3,300	3,350	499	499	499	499
3,350	3,400	506	506	506	506
3,400	3,450	514	514	514	514
3,450	3,500	521	521	521	521
3,500	3,550	529	529	529	529
3,550	3,600	536	536	536	536
3,600	3,650	544	544	544	544
3,650	3,700	551	551	551	551
3,700	3,750	559	559	559	559
3,750	3,800	566	566	566	566
3,800	3,850	574	574	574	574
3,850	3,900	581	581	581	581
3,900	3,950	589	589	589	589
3,950	4,000	596	596	596	596

4,000

At least	But less than	Single	Married filing jointly	Married filing separately	Head of a house-hold
4,000	4,050	604	604	604	604
4,050	4,100	611	611	611	611
4,100	4,150	619	619	619	619
4,150	4,200	626	626	626	626
4,200	4,250	634	634	634	634
4,250	4,300	641	641	641	641
4,300	4,350	649	649	649	649
4,350	4,400	656	656	656	656
4,400	4,450	664	664	664	664
4,450	4,500	671	671	671	671
4,500	4,550	679	679	679	679
4,550	4,600	686	686	686	686
4,600	4,650	694	694	694	694
4,650	4,700	701	701	701	701
4,700	4,750	709	709	709	709
4,750	4,800	716	716	716	716
4,800	4,850	724	724	724	724
4,850	4,900	731	731	731	731
4,900	4,950	739	739	739	739
4,950	5,000	746	746	746	746

Continued on next page

* This column must also be used by a qualifying widow(er).

- 39 -

709

If line 38 (taxable income) is—		And you are—				If line 38 (taxable income) is—		And you are—				If line 38 (taxable income) is—		And you are—			
At least	But less than	Single	Married filing jointly *	Married filing separately	Head of a house-hold	At least	But less than	Single	Married filing jointly *	Married filing separately	Head of a house-hold	At least	But less than	Single	Married filing jointly *	Married filing separately	Head of a house-hold
		Your tax is—						Your tax is—						Your tax is—			

5,000 / 8,000 / 11,000

At least	But less than	Single	MFJ	MFS	HoH	At least	But less than	Single	MFJ	MFS	HoH	At least	But less than	Single	MFJ	MFS	HoH
5,000	5,050	754	754	754	754	8,000	8,050	1,204	1,204	1,204	1,204	11,000	11,050	1,654	1,654	1,654	1,654
5,050	5,100	761	761	761	761	8,050	8,100	1,211	1,211	1,211	1,211	11,050	11,100	1,661	1,661	1,661	1,661
5,100	5,150	769	769	769	769	8,100	8,150	1,219	1,219	1,219	1,219	11,100	11,150	1,669	1,669	1,669	1,669
5,150	5,200	776	776	776	776	8,150	8,200	1,226	1,226	1,226	1,226	11,150	11,200	1,676	1,676	1,676	1,676
5,200	5,250	784	784	784	784	8,200	8,250	1,234	1,234	1,234	1,234	11,200	11,250	1,684	1,684	1,684	1,684
5,250	5,300	791	791	791	791	8,250	8,300	1,241	1,241	1,241	1,241	11,250	11,300	1,691	1,691	1,691	1,691
5,300	5,350	799	799	799	799	8,300	8,350	1,249	1,249	1,249	1,249	11,300	11,350	1,699	1,699	1,699	1,699
5,350	5,400	806	806	806	806	8,350	8,400	1,256	1,256	1,256	1,256	11,350	11,400	1,706	1,706	1,706	1,706
5,400	5,450	814	814	814	814	8,400	8,450	1,264	1,264	1,264	1,264	11,400	11,450	1,714	1,714	1,714	1,714
5,450	5,500	821	821	821	821	8,450	8,500	1,271	1,271	1,271	1,271	11,450	11,500	1,721	1,721	1,721	1,721
5,500	5,550	829	829	829	829	8,500	8,550	1,279	1,279	1,279	1,279	11,500	11,550	1,729	1,729	1,729	1,729
5,550	5,600	836	836	836	836	8,550	8,600	1,286	1,286	1,286	1,286	11,550	11,600	1,736	1,736	1,736	1,736
5,600	5,650	844	844	844	844	8,600	8,650	1,294	1,294	1,294	1,294	11,600	11,650	1,744	1,744	1,744	1,744
5,650	5,700	851	851	851	851	8,650	8,700	1,301	1,301	1,301	1,301	11,650	11,700	1,751	1,751	1,751	1,751
5,700	5,750	859	859	859	859	8,700	8,750	1,309	1,309	1,309	1,309	11,700	11,750	1,759	1,759	1,759	1,759
5,750	5,800	866	866	866	866	8,750	8,800	1,316	1,316	1,316	1,316	11,750	11,800	1,766	1,766	1,766	1,766
5,800	5,850	874	874	874	874	8,800	8,850	1,324	1,324	1,324	1,324	11,800	11,850	1,774	1,774	1,774	1,774
5,850	5,900	881	881	881	881	8,850	8,900	1,331	1,331	1,331	1,331	11,850	11,900	1,781	1,781	1,781	1,781
5,900	5,950	889	889	889	889	8,900	8,950	1,339	1,339	1,339	1,339	11,900	11,950	1,789	1,789	1,789	1,789
5,950	6,000	896	896	896	896	8,950	9,000	1,346	1,346	1,346	1,346	11,950	12,000	1,796	1,796	1,796	1,796

6,000 / 9,000 / 12,000

At least	But less than	Single	MFJ	MFS	HoH	At least	But less than	Single	MFJ	MFS	HoH	At least	But less than	Single	MFJ	MFS	HoH
6,000	6,050	904	904	904	904	9,000	9,050	1,354	1,354	1,354	1,354	12,000	12,050	1,804	1,804	1,804	1,804
6,050	6,100	911	911	911	911	9,050	9,100	1,361	1,361	1,361	1,361	12,050	12,100	1,811	1,811	1,811	1,811
6,100	6,150	919	919	919	919	9,100	9,150	1,369	1,369	1,369	1,369	12,100	12,150	1,819	1,819	1,819	1,819
6,150	6,200	926	926	926	926	9,150	9,200	1,376	1,376	1,376	1,376	12,150	12,200	1,826	1,826	1,826	1,826
6,200	6,250	934	934	934	934	9,200	9,250	1,384	1,384	1,384	1,384	12,200	12,250	1,834	1,834	1,834	1,834
6,250	6,300	941	941	941	941	9,250	9,300	1,391	1,391	1,391	1,391	12,250	12,300	1,841	1,841	1,841	1,841
6,300	6,350	949	949	949	949	9,300	9,350	1,399	1,399	1,399	1,399	12,300	12,350	1,849	1,849	1,849	1,849
6,350	6,400	956	956	956	956	9,350	9,400	1,406	1,406	1,406	1,406	12,350	12,400	1,856	1,856	1,856	1,856
6,400	6,450	964	964	964	964	9,400	9,450	1,414	1,414	1,414	1,414	12,400	12,450	1,864	1,864	1,864	1,864
6,450	6,500	971	971	971	971	9,450	9,500	1,421	1,421	1,421	1,421	12,450	12,500	1,871	1,871	1,871	1,871
6,500	6,550	979	979	979	979	9,500	9,550	1,429	1,429	1,429	1,429	12,500	12,550	1,879	1,879	1,879	1,879
6,550	6,600	986	986	986	986	9,550	9,600	1,436	1,436	1,436	1,436	12,550	12,600	1,886	1,886	1,886	1,886
6,600	6,650	994	994	994	994	9,600	9,650	1,444	1,444	1,444	1,444	12,600	12,650	1,894	1,894	1,894	1,894
6,650	6,700	1,001	1,001	1,001	1,001	9,650	9,700	1,451	1,451	1,451	1,451	12,650	12,700	1,901	1,901	1,901	1,901
6,700	6,750	1,009	1,009	1,009	1,009	9,700	9,750	1,459	1,459	1,459	1,459	12,700	12,750	1,909	1,909	1,909	1,909
6,750	6,800	1,016	1,016	1,016	1,016	9,750	9,800	1,466	1,466	1,466	1,466	12,750	12,800	1,916	1,916	1,916	1,916
6,800	6,850	1,024	1,024	1,024	1,024	9,800	9,850	1,474	1,474	1,474	1,474	12,800	12,850	1,924	1,924	1,924	1,924
6,850	6,900	1,031	1,031	1,031	1,031	9,850	9,900	1,481	1,481	1,481	1,481	12,850	12,900	1,931	1,931	1,931	1,931
6,900	6,950	1,039	1,039	1,039	1,039	9,900	9,950	1,489	1,489	1,489	1,489	12,900	12,950	1,939	1,939	1,939	1,939
6,950	7,000	1,046	1,046	1,046	1,046	9,950	10,000	1,496	1,496	1,496	1,496	12,950	13,000	1,946	1,946	1,946	1,946

7,000 / 10,000 / 13,000

At least	But less than	Single	MFJ	MFS	HoH	At least	But less than	Single	MFJ	MFS	HoH	At least	But less than	Single	MFJ	MFS	HoH
7,000	7,050	1,054	1,054	1,054	1,054	10,000	10,050	1,504	1,504	1,504	1,504	13,000	13,050	1,954	1,954	1,954	1,954
7,050	7,100	1,061	1,061	1,061	1,061	10,050	10,100	1,511	1,511	1,511	1,511	13,050	13,100	1,961	1,961	1,961	1,961
7,100	7,150	1,069	1,069	1,069	1,069	10,100	10,150	1,519	1,519	1,519	1,519	13,100	13,150	1,969	1,969	1,969	1,969
7,150	7,200	1,076	1,076	1,076	1,076	10,150	10,200	1,526	1,526	1,526	1,526	13,150	13,200	1,976	1,976	1,976	1,976
7,200	7,250	1,084	1,084	1,084	1,084	10,200	10,250	1,534	1,534	1,534	1,534	13,200	13,250	1,984	1,984	1,984	1,984
7,250	7,300	1,091	1,091	1,091	1,091	10,250	10,300	1,541	1,541	1,541	1,541	13,250	13,300	1,991	1,991	1,991	1,991
7,300	7,350	1,099	1,099	1,099	1,099	10,300	10,350	1,549	1,549	1,549	1,549	13,300	13,350	1,999	1,999	1,999	1,999
7,350	7,400	1,106	1,106	1,106	1,106	10,350	10,400	1,556	1,556	1,556	1,556	13,350	13,400	2,006	2,006	2,006	2,006
7,400	7,450	1,114	1,114	1,114	1,114	10,400	10,450	1,564	1,564	1,564	1,564	13,400	13,450	2,014	2,014	2,014	2,014
7,450	7,500	1,121	1,121	1,121	1,121	10,450	10,500	1,571	1,571	1,571	1,571	13,450	13,500	2,021	2,021	2,021	2,021
7,500	7,550	1,129	1,129	1,129	1,129	10,500	10,550	1,579	1,579	1,579	1,579	13,500	13,550	2,029	2,029	2,029	2,029
7,550	7,600	1,136	1,136	1,136	1,136	10,550	10,600	1,586	1,586	1,586	1,586	13,550	13,600	2,036	2,036	2,036	2,036
7,600	7,650	1,144	1,144	1,144	1,144	10,600	10,650	1,594	1,594	1,594	1,594	13,600	13,650	2,044	2,044	2,044	2,044
7,650	7,700	1,151	1,151	1,151	1,151	10,650	10,700	1,601	1,601	1,601	1,601	13,650	13,700	2,051	2,051	2,051	2,051
7,700	7,750	1,159	1,159	1,159	1,159	10,700	10,750	1,609	1,609	1,609	1,609	13,700	13,750	2,059	2,059	2,059	2,059
7,750	7,800	1,166	1,166	1,166	1,166	10,750	10,800	1,616	1,616	1,616	1,616	13,750	13,800	2,066	2,066	2,066	2,066
7,800	7,850	1,174	1,174	1,174	1,174	10,800	10,850	1,624	1,624	1,624	1,624	13,800	13,850	2,074	2,074	2,074	2,074
7,850	7,900	1,181	1,181	1,181	1,181	10,850	10,900	1,631	1,631	1,631	1,631	13,850	13,900	2,081	2,081	2,081	2,081
7,900	7,950	1,189	1,189	1,189	1,189	10,900	10,950	1,639	1,639	1,639	1,639	13,900	13,950	2,089	2,089	2,089	2,089
7,950	8,000	1,196	1,196	1,196	1,196	10,950	11,000	1,646	1,646	1,646	1,646	13,950	14,000	2,096	2,096	2,096	2,096

* This column must also be used by a qualifying widow(er).

Continued on next page

* This column must also be used by a qualifying widow(er).

14,000

At least	But less than	Single	Married filing jointly *	Married filing separately	Head of a household
14,000	14,050	2,104	2,104	2,104	2,104
14,050	14,100	2,111	2,111	2,111	2,111
14,100	14,150	2,119	2,119	2,119	2,119
14,150	14,200	2,126	2,126	2,126	2,126
14,200	14,250	2,134	2,134	2,134	2,134
14,250	14,300	2,141	2,141	2,141	2,141
14,300	14,350	2,149	2,149	2,149	2,149
14,350	14,400	2,156	2,156	2,156	2,156
14,400	14,450	2,164	2,164	2,164	2,164
14,450	14,500	2,171	2,171	2,171	2,171
14,500	14,550	2,179	2,179	2,179	2,179
14,550	14,600	2,186	2,186	2,186	2,186
14,600	14,650	2,194	2,194	2,194	2,194
14,650	14,700	2,201	2,201	2,201	2,201
14,700	14,750	2,209	2,209	2,209	2,209
14,750	14,800	2,216	2,216	2,216	2,216
14,800	14,850	2,224	2,224	2,224	2,224
14,850	14,900	2,231	2,231	2,231	2,231
14,900	14,950	2,239	2,239	2,239	2,239
14,950	15,000	2,246	2,246	2,246	2,246

15,000

At least	But less than	Single	Married filing jointly *	Married filing separately	Head of a household
15,000	15,050	2,254	2,254	2,254	2,254
15,050	15,100	2,261	2,261	2,261	2,261
15,100	15,150	2,269	2,269	2,269	2,269
15,150	15,200	2,276	2,276	2,276	2,276
15,200	15,250	2,284	2,284	2,284	2,284
15,250	15,300	2,291	2,291	2,291	2,291
15,300	15,350	2,299	2,299	2,299	2,299
15,350	15,400	2,306	2,306	2,306	2,306
15,400	15,450	2,314	2,314	2,314	2,314
15,450	15,500	2,321	2,321	2,321	2,321
15,500	15,550	2,329	2,329	2,329	2,329
15,550	15,600	2,336	2,336	2,336	2,336
15,600	15,650	2,344	2,344	2,344	2,344
15,650	15,700	2,351	2,351	2,351	2,351
15,700	15,750	2,359	2,359	2,359	2,359
15,750	15,800	2,366	2,366	2,366	2,366
15,800	15,850	2,374	2,374	2,374	2,374
15,850	15,900	2,381	2,381	2,381	2,381
15,900	15,950	2,389	2,389	2,389	2,389
15,950	16,000	2,396	2,396	2,396	2,396

16,000

At least	But less than	Single	Married filing jointly *	Married filing separately	Head of a household
16,000	16,050	2,404	2,404	2,404	2,404
16,050	16,100	2,411	2,411	2,411	2,411
16,100	16,150	2,419	2,419	2,419	2,419
16,150	16,200	2,426	2,426	2,426	2,426
16,200	16,250	2,434	2,434	2,434	2,434
16,250	16,300	2,441	2,441	2,441	2,441
16,300	16,350	2,449	2,449	2,449	2,449
16,350	16,400	2,456	2,456	2,456	2,456
16,400	16,450	2,464	2,464	2,464	2,464
16,450	16,500	2,471	2,471	2,471	2,471
16,500	16,550	2,479	2,479	2,479	2,479
16,550	16,600	2,486	2,486	2,486	2,486
16,600	16,650	2,494	2,494	2,494	2,494
16,650	16,700	2,501	2,501	2,501	2,501
16,700	16,750	2,509	2,509	2,509	2,509
16,750	16,800	2,516	2,516	2,516	2,516
16,800	16,850	2,524	2,524	2,524	2,524
16,850	16,900	2,531	2,531	2,531	2,531
16,900	16,950	2,539	2,539	2,539	2,539
16,950	17,000	2,546	2,546	2,546	2,546

17,000

At least	But less than	Single	Married filing jointly *	Married filing separately	Head of a household
17,000	17,050	2,554	2,554	2,554	2,554
17,050	17,100	2,561	2,561	2,561	2,561
17,100	17,150	2,569	2,569	2,569	2,569
17,150	17,200	2,576	2,576	2,576	2,576
17,200	17,250	2,584	2,584	2,584	2,584
17,250	17,300	2,591	2,591	2,591	2,591
17,300	17,350	2,599	2,599	2,599	2,599
17,350	17,400	2,606	2,606	2,606	2,606
17,400	17,450	2,614	2,614	2,614	2,614
17,450	17,500	2,621	2,621	2,621	2,621
17,500	17,550	2,629	2,629	2,629	2,629
17,550	17,600	2,636	2,636	2,636	2,636
17,600	17,650	2,644	2,644	2,644	2,644
17,650	17,700	2,651	2,651	2,651	2,651
17,700	17,750	2,659	2,659	2,659	2,659
17,750	17,800	2,666	2,666	2,666	2,666
17,800	17,850	2,674	2,674	2,674	2,674
17,850	17,900	2,681	2,681	2,681	2,681
17,900	17,950	2,689	2,689	2,689	2,689
17,950	18,000	2,696	2,696	2,696	2,696

18,000

At least	But less than	Single	Married filing jointly *	Married filing separately	Head of a household
18,000	18,050	2,704	2,704	2,704	2,704
18,050	18,100	2,711	2,711	2,711	2,711
18,100	18,150	2,719	2,719	2,719	2,719
18,150	18,200	2,726	2,726	2,726	2,726
18,200	18,250	2,734	2,734	2,734	2,734
18,250	18,300	2,741	2,741	2,741	2,741
18,300	18,350	2,749	2,749	2,749	2,749
18,350	18,400	2,756	2,756	2,756	2,756
18,400	18,450	2,764	2,764	2,764	2,764
18,450	18,500	2,771	2,771	2,771	2,771
18,500	18,550	2,779	2,779	2,779	2,779
18,550	18,600	2,786	2,786	2,786	2,786
18,600	18,650	2,794	2,794	2,794	2,794
18,650	18,700	2,801	2,801	2,801	2,801
18,700	18,750	2,809	2,809	2,809	2,809
18,750	18,800	2,816	2,816	2,816	2,816
18,800	18,850	2,824	2,824	2,824	2,824
18,850	18,900	2,831	2,831	2,831	2,831
18,900	18,950	2,839	2,839	2,839	2,839
18,950	19,000	2,846	2,846	2,846	2,846

19,000

At least	But less than	Single	Married filing jointly *	Married filing separately	Head of a household
19,000	19,050	2,854	2,854	2,854	2,854
19,050	19,100	2,861	2,861	2,861	2,861
19,100	19,150	2,869	2,869	2,869	2,869
19,150	19,200	2,876	2,876	2,876	2,876
19,200	19,250	2,884	2,884	2,884	2,884
19,250	19,300	2,891	2,891	2,891	2,891
19,300	19,350	2,899	2,899	2,899	2,899
19,350	19,400	2,906	2,906	2,906	2,906
19,400	19,450	2,914	2,914	2,914	2,914
19,450	19,500	2,921	2,921	2,921	2,921
19,500	19,550	2,929	2,929	2,929	2,929
19,550	19,600	2,936	2,936	2,936	2,936
19,600	19,650	2,944	2,944	2,944	2,944
19,650	19,700	2,951	2,951	2,951	2,951
19,700	19,750	2,959	2,959	2,959	2,959
19,750	19,800	2,966	2,966	2,966	2,966
19,800	19,850	2,974	2,974	2,974	2,974
19,850	19,900	2,981	2,981	2,981	2,981
19,900	19,950	2,989	2,989	2,989	2,989
19,950	20,000	2,996	2,996	2,996	2,996

20,000

At least	But less than	Single	Married filing jointly *	Married filing separately	Head of a household
20,000	20,050	3,004	3,004	3,004	3,004
20,050	20,100	3,011	3,011	3,011	3,011
20,100	20,150	3,019	3,019	3,019	3,019
20,150	20,200	3,026	3,026	3,026	3,026
20,200	20,250	3,034	3,034	3,034	3,034
20,250	20,300	3,041	3,041	3,041	3,041
20,300	20,350	3,049	3,049	3,049	3,049
20,350	20,400	3,056	3,056	3,056	3,056
20,400	20,450	3,064	3,064	3,064	3,064
20,450	20,500	3,071	3,071	3,071	3,071
20,500	20,550	3,079	3,079	3,079	3,079
20,550	20,600	3,086	3,086	3,086	3,086
20,600	20,650	3,094	3,094	3,097	3,094
20,650	20,700	3,101	3,101	3,111	3,101
20,700	20,750	3,109	3,109	3,125	3,109
20,750	20,800	3,116	3,116	3,139	3,116
20,800	20,850	3,124	3,124	3,153	3,124
20,850	20,900	3,131	3,131	3,167	3,131
20,900	20,950	3,139	3,139	3,181	3,139
20,950	21,000	3,146	3,146	3,195	3,146

21,000

At least	But less than	Single	Married filing jointly *	Married filing separately	Head of a household
21,000	21,050	3,154	3,154	3,209	3,154
21,050	21,100	3,161	3,161	3,223	3,161
21,100	21,150	3,169	3,169	3,237	3,169
21,150	21,200	3,176	3,176	3,251	3,176
21,200	21,250	3,184	3,184	3,265	3,184
21,250	21,300	3,191	3,191	3,279	3,191
21,300	21,350	3,199	3,199	3,293	3,199
21,350	21,400	3,206	3,206	3,307	3,206
21,400	21,450	3,214	3,214	3,321	3,214
21,450	21,500	3,221	3,221	3,335	3,221
21,500	21,550	3,229	3,229	3,349	3,229
21,550	21,600	3,236	3,236	3,363	3,236
21,600	21,650	3,244	3,244	3,377	3,244
21,650	21,700	3,251	3,251	3,391	3,251
21,700	21,750	3,259	3,259	3,405	3,259
21,750	21,800	3,266	3,266	3,419	3,266
21,800	21,850	3,274	3,274	3,433	3,274
21,850	21,900	3,281	3,281	3,447	3,281
21,900	21,950	3,289	3,289	3,461	3,289
21,950	22,000	3,296	3,296	3,475	3,296

22,000

At least	But less than	Single	Married filing jointly *	Married filing separately	Head of a household
22,000	22,050	3,304	3,304	3,489	3,304
22,050	22,100	3,311	3,311	3,503	3,311
22,100	22,150	3,319	3,319	3,517	3,319
22,150	22,200	3,326	3,326	3,531	3,326
22,200	22,250	3,334	3,334	3,545	3,334
22,250	22,300	3,341	3,341	3,559	3,341
22,300	22,350	3,349	3,349	3,573	3,349
22,350	22,400	3,356	3,356	3,587	3,356
22,400	22,450	3,364	3,364	3,601	3,364
22,450	22,500	3,371	3,371	3,615	3,371
22,500	22,550	3,379	3,379	3,629	3,379
22,550	22,600	3,386	3,386	3,643	3,386
22,600	22,650	3,394	3,394	3,657	3,394
22,650	22,700	3,401	3,401	3,671	3,401
22,700	22,750	3,409	3,409	3,685	3,409
22,750	22,800	3,416	3,416	3,699	3,416
22,800	22,850	3,424	3,424	3,713	3,424
22,850	22,900	3,431	3,431	3,727	3,431
22,900	22,950	3,439	3,439	3,741	3,439
22,950	23,000	3,446	3,446	3,755	3,446

Continued on next page

- 41 -

If line 38 (taxable income) is— At least	But less than	And you are— Single	Married filing jointly *	Married filing separately	Head of a household
					Your tax is—
23,000					
23,000	23,050	3,454	3,454	3,769	3,454
23,050	23,100	3,461	3,461	3,783	3,461
23,100	23,150	3,469	3,469	3,797	3,469
23,150	23,200	3,476	3,476	3,811	3,476
23,200	23,250	3,484	3,484	3,825	3,484
23,250	23,300	3,491	3,491	3,839	3,491
23,300	23,350	3,499	3,499	3,853	3,499
23,350	23,400	3,506	3,506	3,867	3,506
23,400	23,450	3,514	3,514	3,881	3,514
23,450	23,500	3,521	3,521	3,895	3,521
23,500	23,550	3,529	3,529	3,909	3,529
23,550	23,600	3,536	3,536	3,923	3,536
23,600	23,650	3,544	3,544	3,937	3,544
23,650	23,700	3,551	3,551	3,951	3,551
23,700	23,750	3,559	3,559	3,965	3,559
23,750	23,800	3,566	3,566	3,979	3,566
23,800	23,850	3,574	3,574	3,993	3,574
23,850	23,900	3,581	3,581	4,007	3,581
23,900	23,950	3,589	3,589	4,021	3,589
23,950	24,000	3,596	3,596	4,035	3,596
24,000					
24,000	24,050	3,604	3,604	4,049	3,604
24,050	24,100	3,611	3,611	4,063	3,611
24,100	24,150	3,619	3,619	4,077	3,619
24,150	24,200	3,626	3,626	4,091	3,626
24,200	24,250	3,634	3,634	4,105	3,634
24,250	24,300	3,641	3,641	4,119	3,641
24,300	24,350	3,649	3,649	4,133	3,649
24,350	24,400	3,656	3,656	4,147	3,656
24,400	24,450	3,664	3,664	4,161	3,664
24,450	24,500	3,671	3,671	4,175	3,671
24,500	24,550	3,679	3,679	4,189	3,679
24,550	24,600	3,686	3,686	4,203	3,686
24,600	24,650	3,694	3,694	4,217	3,694
24,650	24,700	3,705	3,701	4,231	3,701
24,700	24,750	3,719	3,709	4,245	3,709
24,750	24,800	3,733	3,716	4,259	3,716
24,800	24,850	3,747	3,724	4,273	3,724
24,850	24,900	3,761	3,731	4,287	3,731
24,900	24,950	3,775	3,739	4,301	3,739
24,950	25,000	3,789	3,746	4,315	3,746
25,000					
25,000	25,050	3,803	3,754	4,329	3,754
25,050	25,100	3,817	3,761	4,343	3,761
25,100	25,150	3,831	3,769	4,357	3,769
25,150	25,200	3,845	3,776	4,371	3,776
25,200	25,250	3,859	3,784	4,385	3,784
25,250	25,300	3,873	3,791	4,399	3,791
25,300	25,350	3,887	3,799	4,413	3,799
25,350	25,400	3,901	3,806	4,427	3,806
25,400	25,450	3,915	3,814	4,441	3,814
25,450	25,500	3,929	3,821	4,455	3,821
25,500	25,550	3,943	3,829	4,469	3,829
25,550	25,600	3,957	3,836	4,483	3,836
25,600	25,650	3,971	3,844	4,497	3,844
25,650	25,700	3,985	3,851	4,511	3,851
25,700	25,750	3,999	3,859	4,525	3,859
25,750	25,800	4,013	3,866	4,539	3,866
25,800	25,850	4,027	3,874	4,553	3,874
25,850	25,900	4,041	3,881	4,567	3,881
25,900	25,950	4,055	3,889	4,581	3,889
25,950	26,000	4,069	3,896	4,595	3,896

If line 38 (taxable income) is— At least	But less than	And you are— Single	Married filing jointly *	Married filing separately	Head of a household
					Your tax is—
26,000					
26,000	26,050	4,083	3,904	4,609	3,904
26,050	26,100	4,097	3,911	4,623	3,911
26,100	26,150	4,111	3,919	4,637	3,919
26,150	26,200	4,125	3,926	4,651	3,926
26,200	26,250	4,139	3,934	4,665	3,934
26,250	26,300	4,153	3,941	4,679	3,941
26,300	26,350	4,167	3,949	4,693	3,949
26,350	26,400	4,181	3,956	4,707	3,956
26,400	26,450	4,195	3,964	4,721	3,964
26,450	26,500	4,209	3,971	4,735	3,971
26,500	26,550	4,223	3,979	4,749	3,979
26,550	26,600	4,237	3,986	4,763	3,986
26,600	26,650	4,251	3,994	4,777	3,994
26,650	26,700	4,265	4,001	4,791	4,001
26,700	26,750	4,279	4,009	4,805	4,009
26,750	26,800	4,293	4,016	4,819	4,016
26,800	26,850	4,307	4,024	4,833	4,024
26,850	26,900	4,321	4,031	4,847	4,031
26,900	26,950	4,335	4,039	4,861	4,039
26,950	27,000	4,349	4,046	4,875	4,046
27,000					
27,000	27,050	4,363	4,054	4,889	4,054
27,050	27,100	4,377	4,061	4,903	4,061
27,100	27,150	4,391	4,069	4,917	4,069
27,150	27,200	4,405	4,076	4,931	4,076
27,200	27,250	4,419	4,084	4,945	4,084
27,250	27,300	4,433	4,091	4,959	4,091
27,300	27,350	4,447	4,099	4,973	4,099
27,350	27,400	4,461	4,106	4,987	4,106
27,400	27,450	4,475	4,114	5,001	4,114
27,450	27,500	4,489	4,121	5,015	4,121
27,500	27,550	4,503	4,129	5,029	4,129
27,550	27,600	4,517	4,136	5,043	4,136
27,600	27,650	4,531	4,144	5,057	4,144
27,650	27,700	4,545	4,151	5,071	4,151
27,700	27,750	4,559	4,159	5,085	4,159
27,750	27,800	4,573	4,166	5,099	4,166
27,800	27,850	4,587	4,174	5,113	4,174
27,850	27,900	4,601	4,181	5,127	4,181
27,900	27,950	4,615	4,189	5,141	4,189
27,950	28,000	4,629	4,196	5,155	4,196
28,000					
28,000	28,050	4,643	4,204	5,169	4,204
28,050	28,100	4,657	4,211	5,183	4,211
28,100	28,150	4,671	4,219	5,197	4,219
28,150	28,200	4,685	4,226	5,211	4,226
28,200	28,250	4,699	4,234	5,225	4,234
28,250	28,300	4,713	4,241	5,239	4,241
28,300	28,350	4,727	4,249	5,253	4,249
28,350	28,400	4,741	4,256	5,267	4,256
28,400	28,450	4,755	4,264	5,281	4,264
28,450	28,500	4,769	4,271	5,295	4,271
28,500	28,550	4,783	4,279	5,309	4,279
28,550	28,600	4,797	4,286	5,323	4,286
28,600	28,650	4,811	4,294	5,337	4,294
28,650	28,700	4,825	4,301	5,351	4,301
28,700	28,750	4,839	4,309	5,365	4,309
28,750	28,800	4,853	4,316	5,379	4,316
28,800	28,850	4,867	4,324	5,393	4,324
28,850	28,900	4,881	4,331	5,407	4,331
28,900	28,950	4,895	4,339	5,421	4,339
28,950	29,000	4,909	4,346	5,435	4,346

If line 38 (taxable income) is— At least	But less than	And you are— Single	Married filing jointly *	Married filing separately	Head of a household
					Your tax is—
29,000					
29,000	29,050	4,923	4,354	5,449	4,354
29,050	29,100	4,937	4,361	5,463	4,361
29,100	29,150	4,951	4,369	5,477	4,369
29,150	29,200	4,965	4,376	5,491	4,376
29,200	29,250	4,979	4,384	5,505	4,384
29,250	29,300	4,993	4,391	5,519	4,391
29,300	29,350	5,007	4,399	5,533	4,399
29,350	29,400	5,021	4,406	5,547	4,406
29,400	29,450	5,035	4,414	5,561	4,414
29,450	29,500	5,049	4,421	5,575	4,421
29,500	29,550	5,063	4,429	5,589	4,429
29,550	29,600	5,077	4,436	5,603	4,436
29,600	29,650	5,091	4,444	5,617	4,444
29,650	29,700	5,105	4,451	5,631	4,451
29,700	29,750	5,119	4,459	5,645	4,459
29,750	29,800	5,133	4,466	5,659	4,466
29,800	29,850	5,147	4,474	5,673	4,474
29,850	29,900	5,161	4,481	5,687	4,481
29,900	29,950	5,175	4,489	5,701	4,489
29,950	30,000	5,189	4,496	5,715	4,496
30,000					
30,000	30,050	5,203	4,504	5,729	4,504
30,050	30,100	5,217	4,511	5,743	4,511
30,100	30,150	5,231	4,519	5,757	4,519
30,150	30,200	5,245	4,526	5,771	4,526
30,200	30,250	5,259	4,534	5,785	4,534
30,250	30,300	5,273	4,541	5,799	4,541
30,300	30,350	5,287	4,549	5,813	4,549
30,350	30,400	5,301	4,556	5,827	4,556
30,400	30,450	5,315	4,564	5,841	4,564
30,450	30,500	5,329	4,571	5,855	4,571
30,500	30,550	5,343	4,579	5,869	4,579
30,550	30,600	5,357	4,586	5,883	4,586
30,600	30,650	5,371	4,594	5,897	4,594
30,650	30,700	5,385	4,601	5,911	4,601
30,700	30,750	5,399	4,609	5,925	4,609
30,750	30,800	5,413	4,616	5,939	4,616
30,800	30,850	5,427	4,624	5,953	4,624
30,850	30,900	5,441	4,631	5,967	4,631
30,900	30,950	5,455	4,639	5,981	4,639
30,950	31,000	5,469	4,646	5,995	4,646
31,000					
31,000	31,050	5,483	4,654	6,009	4,654
31,050	31,100	5,497	4,661	6,023	4,661
31,100	31,150	5,511	4,669	6,037	4,669
31,150	31,200	5,525	4,676	6,051	4,676
31,200	31,250	5,539	4,684	6,065	4,684
31,250	31,300	5,553	4,691	6,079	4,691
31,300	31,350	5,567	4,699	6,093	4,699
31,350	31,400	5,581	4,706	6,107	4,706
31,400	31,450	5,595	4,714	6,121	4,714
31,450	31,500	5,609	4,721	6,135	4,721
31,500	31,550	5,623	4,729	6,149	4,729
31,550	31,600	5,637	4,736	6,163	4,736
31,600	31,650	5,651	4,744	6,177	4,744
31,650	31,700	5,665	4,751	6,191	4,751
31,700	31,750	5,679	4,759	6,205	4,759
31,750	31,800	5,693	4,766	6,219	4,766
31,800	31,850	5,707	4,774	6,233	4,774
31,850	31,900	5,721	4,781	6,247	4,781
31,900	31,950	5,735	4,789	6,261	4,789
31,950	32,000	5,749	4,796	6,275	4,796

* This column must also be used by a qualifying widow(er).

Continued on next page

If line 38 (taxable income) is—		And you are—				If line 38 (taxable income) is—		And you are—				If line 38 (taxable income) is—		And you are—			
At least	But less than	Single	Married filing jointly *	Married filing separately	Head of a household	At least	But less than	Single	Married filing jointly *	Married filing separately	Head of a household	At least	But less than	Single	Married filing jointly *	Married filing separately	Head of a household
		Your tax is—						Your tax is—						Your tax is—			
32,000						**35,000**						**38,000**					
32,000	32,050	5,763	4,804	6,289	4,804	35,000	35,050	6,603	5,254	7,129	5,511	38,000	38,050	7,443	5,704	7,969	6,351
32,050	32,100	5,777	4,811	6,303	4,811	35,050	35,100	6,617	5,261	7,143	5,525	38,050	38,100	7,457	5,711	7,983	6,365
32,100	32,150	5,791	4,819	6,317	4,819	35,100	35,150	6,631	5,269	7,157	5,539	38,100	38,150	7,471	5,719	7,997	6,379
32,150	32,200	5,805	4,826	6,331	4,826	35,150	35,200	6,645	5,276	7,171	5,553	38,150	38,200	7,485	5,726	8,011	6,393
32,200	32,250	5,819	4,834	6,345	4,834	35,200	35,250	6,659	5,284	7,185	5,567	38,200	38,250	7,499	5,734	8,025	6,407
32,250	32,300	5,833	4,841	6,359	4,841	35,250	35,300	6,673	5,291	7,199	5,581	38,250	38,300	7,513	5,741	8,039	6,421
32,300	32,350	5,847	4,849	6,373	4,849	35,300	35,350	6,687	5,299	7,213	5,595	38,300	38,350	7,527	5,749	8,053	6,435
32,350	32,400	5,861	4,856	6,387	4,856	35,350	35,400	6,701	5,306	7,227	5,609	38,350	38,400	7,541	5,756	8,067	6,449
32,400	32,450	5,875	4,864	6,401	4,864	35,400	35,450	6,715	5,314	7,241	5,623	38,400	38,450	7,555	5,764	8,081	6,463
32,450	32,500	5,889	4,871	6,415	4,871	35,450	35,500	6,729	5,321	7,255	5,637	38,450	38,500	7,569	5,771	8,095	6,477
32,500	32,550	5,903	4,879	6,429	4,879	35,500	35,550	6,743	5,329	7,269	5,651	38,500	38,550	7,583	5,779	8,109	6,491
32,550	32,600	5,917	4,886	6,443	4,886	35,550	35,600	6,757	5,336	7,283	5,665	38,550	38,600	7,597	5,786	8,123	6,505
32,600	32,650	5,931	4,894	6,457	4,894	35,600	35,650	6,771	5,344	7,297	5,679	38,600	38,650	7,611	5,794	8,137	6,519
32,650	32,700	5,945	4,901	6,471	4,901	35,650	35,700	6,785	5,351	7,311	5,693	38,650	38,700	7,625	5,801	8,151	6,533
32,700	32,750	5,959	4,909	6,485	4,909	35,700	35,750	6,799	5,359	7,325	5,707	38,700	38,750	7,639	5,809	8,165	6,547
32,750	32,800	5,973	4,916	6,499	4,916	35,750	35,800	6,813	5,366	7,339	5,721	38,750	38,800	7,653	5,816	8,179	6,561
32,800	32,850	5,987	4,924	6,513	4,924	35,800	35,850	6,827	5,374	7,353	5,735	38,800	38,850	7,667	5,824	8,193	6,575
32,850	32,900	6,001	4,931	6,527	4,931	35,850	35,900	6,841	5,381	7,367	5,749	38,850	38,900	7,681	5,831	8,207	6,589
32,900	32,950	6,015	4,939	6,541	4,939	35,900	35,950	6,855	5,389	7,381	5,763	38,900	38,950	7,695	5,839	8,221	6,603
32,950	33,000	6,029	4,946	6,555	4,946	35,950	36,000	6,869	5,396	7,395	5,777	38,950	39,000	7,709	5,846	8,235	6,617
33,000						**36,000**						**39,000**					
33,000	33,050	6,043	4,954	6,569	4,954	36,000	36,050	6,883	5,404	7,409	5,791	39,000	39,050	7,723	5,854	8,249	6,631
33,050	33,100	6,057	4,961	6,583	4,965	36,050	36,100	6,897	5,411	7,423	5,805	39,050	39,100	7,737	5,861	8,263	6,645
33,100	33,150	6,071	4,969	6,597	4,979	36,100	36,150	6,911	5,419	7,437	5,819	39,100	39,150	7,751	5,869	8,277	6,659
33,150	33,200	6,085	4,976	6,611	4,993	36,150	36,200	6,925	5,426	7,451	5,833	39,150	39,200	7,765	5,876	8,291	6,673
33,200	33,250	6,099	4,984	6,625	5,007	36,200	36,250	6,939	5,434	7,465	5,847	39,200	39,250	7,779	5,884	8,305	6,687
33,250	33,300	6,113	4,991	6,639	5,021	36,250	36,300	6,953	5,441	7,479	5,861	39,250	39,300	7,793	5,891	8,319	6,701
33,300	33,350	6,127	4,999	6,653	5,035	36,300	36,350	6,967	5,449	7,493	5,875	39,300	39,350	7,807	5,899	8,333	6,715
33,350	33,400	6,141	5,006	6,667	5,049	36,350	36,400	6,981	5,456	7,507	5,889	39,350	39,400	7,821	5,906	8,347	6,729
33,400	33,450	6,155	5,014	6,681	5,063	36,400	36,450	6,995	5,464	7,521	5,903	39,400	39,450	7,835	5,914	8,361	6,743
33,450	33,500	6,169	5,021	6,695	5,077	36,450	36,500	7,009	5,471	7,535	5,917	39,450	39,500	7,849	5,921	8,375	6,757
33,500	33,550	6,183	5,029	6,709	5,091	36,500	36,550	7,023	5,479	7,549	5,931	39,500	39,550	7,863	5,929	8,389	6,771
33,550	33,600	6,197	5,036	6,723	5,105	36,550	36,600	7,037	5,486	7,563	5,945	39,550	39,600	7,877	5,936	8,403	6,785
33,600	33,650	6,211	5,044	6,737	5,119	36,600	36,650	7,051	5,494	7,577	5,959	39,600	39,650	7,891	5,944	8,417	6,799
33,650	33,700	6,225	5,051	6,751	5,133	36,650	36,700	7,065	5,501	7,591	5,973	39,650	39,700	7,905	5,951	8,431	6,813
33,700	33,750	6,239	5,059	6,765	5,147	36,700	36,750	7,079	5,509	7,605	5,987	39,700	39,750	7,919	5,959	8,445	6,827
33,750	33,800	6,253	5,066	6,779	5,161	36,750	36,800	7,093	5,516	7,619	6,001	39,750	39,800	7,933	5,966	8,459	6,841
33,800	33,850	6,267	5,074	6,793	5,175	36,800	36,850	7,107	5,524	7,633	6,015	39,800	39,850	7,947	5,974	8,473	6,855
33,850	33,900	6,281	5,081	6,807	5,189	36,850	36,900	7,121	5,531	7,647	6,029	39,850	39,900	7,961	5,981	8,487	6,869
33,900	33,950	6,295	5,089	6,821	5,203	36,900	36,950	7,135	5,539	7,661	6,043	39,900	39,950	7,975	5,989	8,501	6,883
33,950	34,000	6,309	5,096	6,835	5,217	36,950	37,000	7,149	5,546	7,675	6,057	39,950	40,000	7,989	5,996	8,515	6,897
34,000						**37,000**						**40,000**					
34,000	34,050	6,323	5,104	6,849	5,231	37,000	37,050	7,163	5,554	7,689	6,071	40,000	40,050	8,003	6,004	8,529	6,911
34,050	34,100	6,337	5,111	6,863	5,245	37,050	37,100	7,177	5,561	7,703	6,085	40,050	40,100	8,017	6,011	8,543	6,925
34,100	34,150	6,351	5,119	6,877	5,259	37,100	37,150	7,191	5,569	7,717	6,099	40,100	40,150	8,031	6,019	8,557	6,939
34,150	34,200	6,365	5,126	6,891	5,273	37,150	37,200	7,205	5,576	7,731	6,113	40,150	40,200	8,045	6,026	8,571	6,953
34,200	34,250	6,379	5,134	6,905	5,287	37,200	37,250	7,219	5,584	7,745	6,127	40,200	40,250	8,059	6,034	8,585	6,967
34,250	34,300	6,393	5,141	6,919	5,301	37,250	37,300	7,233	5,591	7,759	6,141	40,250	40,300	8,073	6,041	8,599	6,981
34,300	34,350	6,407	5,149	6,933	5,315	37,300	37,350	7,247	5,599	7,773	6,155	40,300	40,350	8,087	6,049	8,613	6,995
34,350	34,400	6,421	5,156	6,947	5,329	37,350	37,400	7,261	5,606	7,787	6,169	40,350	40,400	8,101	6,056	8,627	7,009
34,400	34,450	6,435	5,164	6,961	5,343	37,400	37,450	7,275	5,614	7,801	6,183	40,400	40,450	8,115	6,064	8,641	7,023
34,450	34,500	6,449	5,171	6,975	5,357	37,450	37,500	7,289	5,621	7,815	6,197	40,450	40,500	8,129	6,071	8,655	7,037
34,500	34,550	6,463	5,179	6,989	5,371	37,500	37,550	7,303	5,629	7,829	6,211	40,500	40,550	8,143	6,079	8,669	7,051
34,550	34,600	6,477	5,186	7,003	5,385	37,550	37,600	7,317	5,636	7,843	6,225	40,550	40,600	8,157	6,086	8,683	7,065
34,600	34,650	6,491	5,194	7,017	5,399	37,600	37,650	7,331	5,644	7,857	6,239	40,600	40,650	8,171	6,094	8,697	7,079
34,650	34,700	6,505	5,201	7,031	5,413	37,650	37,700	7,345	5,651	7,871	6,253	40,650	40,700	8,185	6,101	8,711	7,093
34,700	34,750	6,519	5,209	7,045	5,427	37,700	37,750	7,359	5,659	7,885	6,267	40,700	40,750	8,199	6,109	8,725	7,107
34,750	34,800	6,533	5,216	7,059	5,441	37,750	37,800	7,373	5,666	7,899	6,281	40,750	40,800	8,213	6,116	8,739	7,121
34,800	34,850	6,547	5,224	7,073	5,455	37,800	37,850	7,387	5,674	7,913	6,295	40,800	40,850	8,227	6,124	8,753	7,135
34,850	34,900	6,561	5,231	7,087	5,469	37,850	37,900	7,401	5,681	7,927	6,309	40,850	40,900	8,241	6,131	8,767	7,149
34,900	34,950	6,575	5,239	7,101	5,483	37,900	37,950	7,415	5,689	7,941	6,323	40,900	40,950	8,255	6,139	8,781	7,163
34,950	35,000	6,589	5,246	7,115	5,497	37,950	38,000	7,429	5,696	7,955	6,337	40,950	41,000	8,269	6,146	8,795	7,177

* This column must also be used by a qualifying widow(er).

Continued on next page

41,000

At least	But less than	Single	Married filing jointly *	Married filing separately	Head of a household
41,000	41,050	8,283	6,154	8,809	7,191
41,050	41,100	8,297	6,161	8,823	7,205
41,100	41,150	8,311	6,169	8,837	7,219
41,150	41,200	8,325	6,176	8,851	7,233
41,200	41,250	8,339	6,187	8,865	7,247
41,250	41,300	8,353	6,201	8,879	7,261
41,300	41,350	8,367	6,215	8,893	7,275
41,350	41,400	8,381	6,229	8,907	7,289
41,400	41,450	8,395	6,243	8,921	7,303
41,450	41,500	8,409	6,257	8,935	7,317
41,500	41,550	8,423	6,271	8,949	7,331
41,550	41,600	8,437	6,285	8,963	7,345
41,600	41,650	8,451	6,299	8,977	7,359
41,650	41,700	8,465	6,313	8,991	7,373
41,700	41,750	8,479	6,327	9,005	7,387
41,750	41,800	8,493	6,341	9,019	7,401
41,800	41,850	8,507	6,355	9,033	7,415
41,850	41,900	8,521	6,369	9,047	7,429
41,900	41,950	8,535	6,383	9,061	7,443
41,950	42,000	8,549	6,397	9,075	7,457

42,000

At least	But less than	Single	Married filing jointly *	Married filing separately	Head of a household
42,000	42,050	8,563	6,411	9,089	7,471
42,050	42,100	8,577	6,425	9,103	7,485
42,100	42,150	8,591	6,439	9,117	7,499
42,150	42,200	8,605	6,453	9,131	7,513
42,200	42,250	8,619	6,467	9,145	7,527
42,250	42,300	8,633	6,481	9,159	7,541
42,300	42,350	8,647	6,495	9,173	7,555
42,350	42,400	8,661	6,509	9,187	7,569
42,400	42,450	8,675	6,523	9,201	7,583
42,450	42,500	8,689	6,537	9,215	7,597
42,500	42,550	8,703	6,551	9,229	7,611
42,550	42,600	8,717	6,565	9,243	7,625
42,600	42,650	8,731	6,579	9,257	7,639
42,650	42,700	8,745	6,593	9,271	7,653
42,700	42,750	8,759	6,607	9,285	7,667
42,750	42,800	8,773	6,621	9,299	7,681
42,800	42,850	8,787	6,635	9,313	7,695
42,850	42,900	8,801	6,649	9,327	7,709
42,900	42,950	8,815	6,663	9,341	7,723
42,950	43,000	8,829	6,677	9,355	7,737

43,000

At least	But less than	Single	Married filing jointly *	Married filing separately	Head of a household
43,000	43,050	8,843	6,691	9,369	7,751
43,050	43,100	8,857	6,705	9,383	7,765
43,100	43,150	8,871	6,719	9,397	7,779
43,150	43,200	8,885	6,733	9,411	7,793
43,200	43,250	8,899	6,747	9,425	7,807
43,250	43,300	8,913	6,761	9,439	7,821
43,300	43,350	8,927	6,775	9,453	7,835
43,350	43,400	8,941	6,789	9,467	7,849
43,400	43,450	8,955	6,803	9,481	7,863
43,450	43,500	8,969	6,817	9,495	7,877
43,500	43,550	8,983	6,831	9,509	7,891
43,550	43,600	8,997	6,845	9,523	7,905
43,600	43,650	9,011	6,859	9,537	7,919
43,650	43,700	9,025	6,873	9,551	7,933
43,700	43,750	9,039	6,887	9,565	7,947
43,750	43,800	9,053	6,901	9,579	7,961
43,800	43,850	9,067	6,915	9,593	7,975
43,850	43,900	9,081	6,929	9,607	7,989
43,900	43,950	9,095	6,943	9,621	8,003
43,950	44,000	9,109	6,957	9,635	8,017

44,000

At least	But less than	Single	Married filing jointly *	Married filing separately	Head of a household
44,000	44,050	9,123	6,971	9,649	8,031
44,050	44,100	9,137	6,985	9,663	8,045
44,100	44,150	9,151	6,999	9,677	8,059
44,150	44,200	9,165	7,013	9,691	8,073
44,200	44,250	9,179	7,027	9,705	8,087
44,250	44,300	9,193	7,041	9,719	8,101
44,300	44,350	9,207	7,055	9,733	8,115
44,350	44,400	9,221	7,069	9,747	8,129
44,400	44,450	9,235	7,083	9,761	8,143
44,450	44,500	9,249	7,097	9,775	8,157
44,500	44,550	9,263	7,111	9,789	8,171
44,550	44,600	9,277	7,125	9,803	8,185
44,600	44,650	9,291	7,139	9,817	8,199
44,650	44,700	9,305	7,153	9,831	8,213
44,700	44,750	9,319	7,167	9,845	8,227
44,750	44,800	9,333	7,181	9,859	8,241
44,800	44,850	9,347	7,195	9,873	8,255
44,850	44,900	9,361	7,209	9,887	8,269
44,900	44,950	9,375	7,223	9,901	8,283
44,950	45,000	9,389	7,237	9,915	8,297

45,000

At least	But less than	Single	Married filing jointly *	Married filing separately	Head of a household
45,000	45,050	9,403	7,251	9,929	8,311
45,050	45,100	9,417	7,265	9,943	8,325
45,100	45,150	9,431	7,279	9,957	8,339
45,150	45,200	9,445	7,293	9,971	8,353
45,200	45,250	9,459	7,307	9,985	8,367
45,250	45,300	9,473	7,321	9,999	8,381
45,300	45,350	9,487	7,335	10,013	8,395
45,350	45,400	9,501	7,349	10,027	8,409
45,400	45,450	9,515	7,363	10,041	8,423
45,450	45,500	9,529	7,377	10,055	8,437
45,500	45,550	9,543	7,391	10,069	8,451
45,550	45,600	9,557	7,405	10,083	8,465
45,600	45,650	9,571	7,419	10,097	8,479
45,650	45,700	9,585	7,433	10,111	8,493
45,700	45,750	9,599	7,447	10,125	8,507
45,750	45,800	9,613	7,461	10,139	8,521
45,800	45,850	9,627	7,475	10,153	8,535
45,850	45,900	9,641	7,489	10,167	8,549
45,900	45,950	9,655	7,503	10,181	8,563
45,950	46,000	9,669	7,517	10,195	8,577

46,000

At least	But less than	Single	Married filing jointly *	Married filing separately	Head of a household
46,000	46,050	9,683	7,531	10,209	8,591
46,050	46,100	9,697	7,545	10,223	8,605
46,100	46,150	9,711	7,559	10,237	8,619
46,150	46,200	9,725	7,573	10,251	8,633
46,200	46,250	9,739	7,587	10,265	8,647
46,250	46,300	9,753	7,601	10,279	8,661
46,300	46,350	9,767	7,615	10,293	8,675
46,350	46,400	9,781	7,629	10,307	8,689
46,400	46,450	9,795	7,643	10,321	8,703
46,450	46,500	9,809	7,657	10,335	8,717
46,500	46,550	9,823	7,671	10,349	8,731
46,550	46,600	9,837	7,685	10,363	8,745
46,600	46,650	9,851	7,699	10,377	8,759
46,650	46,700	9,865	7,713	10,391	8,773
46,700	46,750	9,879	7,727	10,405	8,787
46,750	46,800	9,893	7,741	10,419	8,801
46,800	46,850	9,907	7,755	10,433	8,815
46,850	46,900	9,921	7,769	10,447	8,829
46,900	46,950	9,935	7,783	10,461	8,843
46,950	47,000	9,949	7,797	10,475	8,857

47,000

At least	But less than	Single	Married filing jointly *	Married filing separately	Head of a household
47,000	47,050	9,963	7,811	10,489	8,871
47,050	47,100	9,977	7,825	10,503	8,885
47,100	47,150	9,991	7,839	10,517	8,899
47,150	47,200	10,005	7,853	10,531	8,913
47,200	47,250	10,019	7,867	10,545	8,927
47,250	47,300	10,033	7,881	10,559	8,941
47,300	47,350	10,047	7,895	10,573	8,955
47,350	47,400	10,061	7,909	10,587	8,969
47,400	47,450	10,075	7,923	10,601	8,983
47,450	47,500	10,089	7,937	10,615	8,997
47,500	47,550	10,103	7,951	10,629	9,011
47,550	47,600	10,117	7,965	10,643	9,025
47,600	47,650	10,131	7,979	10,657	9,039
47,650	47,700	10,145	7,993	10,671	9,053
47,700	47,750	10,159	8,007	10,685	9,067
47,750	47,800	10,173	8,021	10,699	9,081
47,800	47,850	10,187	8,035	10,713	9,095
47,850	47,900	10,201	8,049	10,727	9,109
47,900	47,950	10,215	8,063	10,741	9,123
47,950	48,000	10,229	8,077	10,755	9,137

48,000

At least	But less than	Single	Married filing jointly *	Married filing separately	Head of a household
48,000	48,050	10,243	8,091	10,769	9,151
48,050	48,100	10,257	8,105	10,783	9,165
48,100	48,150	10,271	8,119	10,797	9,179
48,150	48,200	10,285	8,133	10,811	9,193
48,200	48,250	10,299	8,147	10,825	9,207
48,250	48,300	10,313	8,161	10,839	9,221
48,300	48,350	10,327	8,175	10,853	9,235
48,350	48,400	10,341	8,189	10,867	9,249
48,400	48,450	10,355	8,203	10,881	9,263
48,450	48,500	10,369	8,217	10,895	9,277
48,500	48,550	10,383	8,231	10,909	9,291
48,550	48,600	10,397	8,245	10,923	9,305
48,600	48,650	10,411	8,259	10,937	9,319
48,650	48,700	10,425	8,273	10,951	9,333
48,700	48,750	10,439	8,287	10,965	9,347
48,750	48,800	10,453	8,301	10,979	9,361
48,800	48,850	10,467	8,315	10,993	9,375
48,850	48,900	10,481	8,329	11,007	9,389
48,900	48,950	10,495	8,343	11,021	9,403
48,950	49,000	10,509	8,357	11,035	9,417

49,000

At least	But less than	Single	Married filing jointly *	Married filing separately	Head of a household
49,000	49,050	10,523	8,371	11,049	9,431
49,050	49,100	10,537	8,385	11,063	9,445
49,100	49,150	10,551	8,399	11,077	9,459
49,150	49,200	10,565	8,413	11,091	9,473
49,200	49,250	10,579	8,427	11,105	9,487
49,250	49,300	10,593	8,441	11,119	9,501
49,300	49,350	10,607	8,455	11,133	9,515
49,350	49,400	10,621	8,469	11,147	9,529
49,400	49,450	10,635	8,483	11,161	9,543
49,450	49,500	10,649	8,497	11,175	9,557
49,500	49,550	10,663	8,511	11,189	9,571
49,550	49,600	10,677	8,525	11,203	9,585
49,600	49,650	10,691	8,539	11,217	9,599
49,650	49,700	10,705	8,553	11,231	9,613
49,700	49,750	10,719	8,567	11,245	9,627
49,750	49,800	10,733	8,581	11,259	9,641
49,800	49,850	10,747	8,595	11,274	9,655
49,850	49,900	10,761	8,609	11,289	9,669
49,900	49,950	10,775	8,623	11,305	9,683
49,950	50,000	10,789	8,637	11,320	9,697

* This column must also be used by a qualifying widow(er).

Continued on next page

50,000 – 52,000

At least	But less than	Single	Married filing jointly*	Married filing separately	Head of a household
50,000					
50,000	50,050	10,803	8,651	11,336	9,711
50,050	50,100	10,817	8,665	11,351	9,725
50,100	50,150	10,831	8,679	11,367	9,739
50,150	50,200	10,845	8,693	11,382	9,753
50,200	50,250	10,859	8,707	11,398	9,767
50,250	50,300	10,873	8,721	11,413	9,781
50,300	50,350	10,887	8,735	11,429	9,795
50,350	50,400	10,901	8,749	11,444	9,809
50,400	50,450	10,915	8,763	11,460	9,823
50,450	50,500	10,929	8,777	11,475	9,837
50,500	50,550	10,943	8,791	11,491	9,851
50,550	50,600	10,957	8,805	11,506	9,865
50,600	50,650	10,971	8,819	11,522	9,879
50,650	50,700	10,985	8,833	11,537	9,893
50,700	50,750	10,999	8,847	11,553	9,907
50,750	50,800	11,013	8,861	11,568	9,921
50,800	50,850	11,027	8,875	11,584	9,935
50,850	50,900	11,041	8,889	11,599	9,949
50,900	50,950	11,055	8,903	11,615	9,963
50,950	51,000	11,069	8,917	11,630	9,977
51,000					
51,000	51,050	11,083	8,931	11,646	9,991
51,050	51,100	11,097	8,945	11,661	10,005
51,100	51,150	11,111	8,959	11,677	10,019
51,150	51,200	11,125	8,973	11,692	10,033
51,200	51,250	11,139	8,987	11,708	10,047
51,250	51,300	11,153	9,001	11,723	10,061
51,300	51,350	11,167	9,015	11,739	10,075
51,350	51,400	11,181	9,029	11,754	10,089
51,400	51,450	11,195	9,043	11,770	10,103
51,450	51,500	11,209	9,057	11,785	10,117
51,500	51,550	11,223	9,071	11,801	10,131
51,550	51,600	11,237	9,085	11,816	10,145
51,600	51,650	11,251	9,099	11,832	10,159
51,650	51,700	11,265	9,113	11,847	10,173
51,700	51,750	11,279	9,127	11,863	10,187
51,750	51,800	11,293	9,141	11,878	10,201
51,800	51,850	11,307	9,155	11,894	10,215
51,850	51,900	11,321	9,169	11,909	10,229
51,900	51,950	11,335	9,183	11,925	10,243
51,950	52,000	11,349	9,197	11,940	10,257
52,000					
52,000	52,050	11,363	9,211	11,956	10,271
52,050	52,100	11,377	9,225	11,971	10,285
52,100	52,150	11,391	9,239	11,987	10,299
52,150	52,200	11,405	9,253	12,002	10,313
52,200	52,250	11,419	9,267	12,018	10,327
52,250	52,300	11,433	9,281	12,033	10,341
52,300	52,350	11,447	9,295	12,049	10,355
52,350	52,400	11,461	9,309	12,064	10,369
52,400	52,450	11,475	9,323	12,080	10,383
52,450	52,500	11,489	9,337	12,095	10,397
52,500	52,550	11,503	9,351	12,111	10,411
52,550	52,600	11,517	9,365	12,126	10,425
52,600	52,650	11,531	9,379	12,142	10,439
52,650	52,700	11,545	9,393	12,157	10,453
52,700	52,750	11,559	9,407	12,173	10,467
52,750	52,800	11,573	9,421	12,188	10,481
52,800	52,850	11,587	9,435	12,204	10,495
52,850	52,900	11,601	9,449	12,219	10,509
52,900	52,950	11,615	9,463	12,235	10,523
52,950	53,000	11,629	9,477	12,250	10,537

53,000 – 55,000

At least	But less than	Single	Married filing jointly*	Married filing separately	Head of a household
53,000					
53,000	53,050	11,643	9,491	12,266	10,551
53,050	53,100	11,657	9,505	12,281	10,565
53,100	53,150	11,671	9,519	12,297	10,579
53,150	53,200	11,685	9,533	12,312	10,593
53,200	53,250	11,699	9,547	12,328	10,607
53,250	53,300	11,713	9,561	12,343	10,621
53,300	53,350	11,727	9,575	12,359	10,635
53,350	53,400	11,741	9,589	12,374	10,649
53,400	53,450	11,755	9,603	12,390	10,663
53,450	53,500	11,769	9,617	12,405	10,677
53,500	53,550	11,783	9,631	12,421	10,691
53,550	53,600	11,797	9,645	12,436	10,705
53,600	53,650	11,811	9,659	12,452	10,719
53,650	53,700	11,825	9,673	12,467	10,733
53,700	53,750	11,839	9,687	12,483	10,747
53,750	53,800	11,853	9,701	12,498	10,761
53,800	53,850	11,867	9,715	12,514	10,775
53,850	53,900	11,881	9,729	12,529	10,789
53,900	53,950	11,895	9,743	12,545	10,803
53,950	54,000	11,909	9,757	12,560	10,817
54,000					
54,000	54,050	11,923	9,771	12,576	10,831
54,050	54,100	11,937	9,785	12,591	10,845
54,100	54,150	11,951	9,799	12,607	10,859
54,150	54,200	11,965	9,813	12,622	10,873
54,200	54,250	11,979	9,827	12,638	10,887
54,250	54,300	11,993	9,841	12,653	10,901
54,300	54,350	12,007	9,855	12,669	10,915
54,350	54,400	12,021	9,869	12,684	10,929
54,400	54,450	12,035	9,883	12,700	10,943
54,450	54,500	12,049	9,897	12,715	10,957
54,500	54,550	12,063	9,911	12,731	10,971
54,550	54,600	12,077	9,925	12,746	10,985
54,600	54,650	12,091	9,939	12,762	10,999
54,650	54,700	12,105	9,953	12,777	11,013
54,700	54,750	12,119	9,967	12,793	11,027
54,750	54,800	12,133	9,981	12,808	11,041
54,800	54,850	12,147	9,995	12,824	11,055
54,850	54,900	12,161	10,009	12,839	11,069
54,900	54,950	12,175	10,023	12,855	11,083
54,950	55,000	12,189	10,037	12,870	11,097
55,000					
55,000	55,050	12,203	10,051	12,886	11,111
55,050	55,100	12,217	10,065	12,901	11,125
55,100	55,150	12,231	10,079	12,917	11,139
55,150	55,200	12,245	10,093	12,932	11,153
55,200	55,250	12,259	10,107	12,948	11,167
55,250	55,300	12,273	10,121	12,963	11,181
55,300	55,350	12,287	10,135	12,979	11,195
55,350	55,400	12,301	10,149	12,994	11,209
55,400	55,450	12,315	10,163	13,010	11,223
55,450	55,500	12,329	10,177	13,025	11,237
55,500	55,550	12,343	10,191	13,041	11,251
55,550	55,600	12,357	10,205	13,056	11,265
55,600	55,650	12,371	10,219	13,072	11,279
55,650	55,700	12,385	10,233	13,087	11,293
55,700	55,750	12,399	10,247	13,103	11,307
55,750	55,800	12,413	10,261	13,118	11,321
55,800	55,850	12,427	10,275	13,134	11,335
55,850	55,900	12,441	10,289	13,149	11,349
55,900	55,950	12,455	10,303	13,165	11,363
55,950	56,000	12,469	10,317	13,180	11,377

56,000 – 58,000

At least	But less than	Single	Married filing jointly*	Married filing separately	Head of a household
56,000					
56,000	56,050	12,483	10,331	13,196	11,391
56,050	56,100	12,497	10,345	13,211	11,405
56,100	56,150	12,511	10,359	13,227	11,419
56,150	56,200	12,525	10,373	13,242	11,433
56,200	56,250	12,539	10,387	13,258	11,447
56,250	56,300	12,553	10,401	13,273	11,461
56,300	56,350	12,567	10,415	13,289	11,475
56,350	56,400	12,581	10,429	13,304	11,489
56,400	56,450	12,595	10,443	13,320	11,503
56,450	56,500	12,609	10,457	13,335	11,517
56,500	56,550	12,623	10,471	13,351	11,531
56,550	56,600	12,637	10,485	13,366	11,545
56,600	56,650	12,651	10,499	13,382	11,559
56,650	56,700	12,665	10,513	13,397	11,573
56,700	56,750	12,679	10,527	13,413	11,587
56,750	56,800	12,693	10,541	13,428	11,601
56,800	56,850	12,707	10,555	13,444	11,615
56,850	56,900	12,721	10,569	13,459	11,629
56,900	56,950	12,735	10,583	13,475	11,643
56,950	57,000	12,749	10,597	13,490	11,657
57,000					
57,000	57,050	12,763	10,611	13,506	11,671
57,050	57,100	12,777	10,625	13,521	11,685
57,100	57,150	12,791	10,639	13,537	11,699
57,150	57,200	12,805	10,653	13,552	11,713
57,200	57,250	12,819	10,667	13,568	11,727
57,250	57,300	12,833	10,681	13,583	11,741
57,300	57,350	12,847	10,695	13,599	11,755
57,350	57,400	12,861	10,709	13,614	11,769
57,400	57,450	12,875	10,723	13,630	11,783
57,450	57,500	12,889	10,737	13,645	11,797
57,500	57,550	12,903	10,751	13,661	11,811
57,550	57,600	12,917	10,765	13,676	11,825
57,600	57,650	12,931	10,779	13,692	11,839
57,650	57,700	12,945	10,793	13,707	11,853
57,700	57,750	12,959	10,807	13,723	11,867
57,750	57,800	12,973	10,821	13,738	11,881
57,800	57,850	12,987	10,835	13,754	11,895
57,850	57,900	13,001	10,849	13,769	11,909
57,900	57,950	13,015	10,863	13,785	11,923
57,950	58,000	13,029	10,877	13,800	11,937
58,000					
58,000	58,050	13,043	10,891	13,816	11,951
58,050	58,100	13,057	10,905	13,831	11,965
58,100	58,150	13,071	10,919	13,847	11,979
58,150	58,200	13,085	10,933	13,862	11,993
58,200	58,250	13,099	10,947	13,878	12,007
58,250	58,300	13,113	10,961	13,893	12,021
58,300	58,350	13,127	10,975	13,909	12,035
58,350	58,400	13,141	10,989	13,924	12,049
58,400	58,450	13,155	11,003	13,940	12,063
58,450	58,500	13,169	11,017	13,955	12,077
58,500	58,550	13,183	11,031	13,971	12,091
58,550	58,600	13,197	11,045	13,986	12,105
58,600	58,650	13,211	11,059	14,002	12,119
58,650	58,700	13,225	11,073	14,017	12,133
58,700	58,750	13,239	11,087	14,033	12,147
58,750	58,800	13,253	11,101	14,048	12,161
58,800	58,850	13,267	11,115	14,064	12,175
58,850	58,900	13,281	11,129	14,079	12,189
58,900	58,950	13,295	11,143	14,095	12,203
58,950	59,000	13,309	11,157	14,110	12,217

* This column must also be used by a qualifying widow(er).

Continued on next page

Column group 1

If line 38 (taxable income) is—		And you are—			
At least	But less than	Single	Married filing jointly *	Married filing separately	Head of a household
		Your tax is—			
59,000					
59,000	59,050	13,323	11,171	14,126	12,231
59,050	59,100	13,337	11,185	14,141	12,245
59,100	59,150	13,351	11,199	14,157	12,259
59,150	59,200	13,365	11,213	14,172	12,273
59,200	59,250	13,379	11,227	14,188	12,287
59,250	59,300	13,393	11,241	14,203	12,301
59,300	59,350	13,407	11,255	14,219	12,315
59,350	59,400	13,421	11,269	14,234	12,329
59,400	59,450	13,435	11,283	14,250	12,343
59,450	59,500	13,449	11,297	14,265	12,357
59,500	59,550	13,463	11,311	14,281	12,371
59,550	59,600	13,477	11,325	14,296	12,385
59,600	59,650	13,491	11,339	14,312	12,399
59,650	59,700	13,505	11,353	14,327	12,413
59,700	59,750	13,519	11,367	14,343	12,427
59,750	59,800	13,533	11,381	14,358	12,441
59,800	59,850	13,549	11,395	14,374	12,455
59,850	59,900	13,564	11,409	14,389	12,469
59,900	59,950	13,580	11,423	14,405	12,483
59,950	60,000	13,595	11,437	14,420	12,497
60,000					
60,000	60,050	13,611	11,451	14,436	12,511
60,050	60,100	13,626	11,465	14,451	12,525
60,100	60,150	13,642	11,479	14,467	12,539
60,150	60,200	13,657	11,493	14,482	12,553
60,200	60,250	13,673	11,507	14,498	12,567
60,250	60,300	13,688	11,521	14,513	12,581
60,300	60,350	13,704	11,535	14,529	12,595
60,350	60,400	13,719	11,549	14,544	12,609
60,400	60,450	13,735	11,563	14,560	12,623
60,450	60,500	13,750	11,577	14,575	12,637
60,500	60,550	13,766	11,591	14,591	12,651
60,550	60,600	13,781	11,605	14,606	12,665
60,600	60,650	13,797	11,619	14,622	12,679
60,650	60,700	13,812	11,633	14,637	12,693
60,700	60,750	13,828	11,647	14,653	12,707
60,750	60,800	13,843	11,661	14,668	12,721
60,800	60,850	13,859	11,675	14,684	12,735
60,850	60,900	13,874	11,689	14,699	12,749
60,900	60,950	13,890	11,703	14,715	12,763
60,950	61,000	13,905	11,717	14,730	12,777
61,000					
61,000	61,050	13,921	11,731	14,746	12,791
61,050	61,100	13,936	11,745	14,761	12,805
61,100	61,150	13,952	11,759	14,777	12,819
61,150	61,200	13,967	11,773	14,792	12,833
61,200	61,250	13,983	11,787	14,808	12,847
61,250	61,300	13,998	11,801	14,823	12,861
61,300	61,350	14,014	11,815	14,839	12,875
61,350	61,400	14,029	11,829	14,854	12,889
61,400	61,450	14,045	11,843	14,870	12,903
61,450	61,500	14,060	11,857	14,885	12,917
61,500	61,550	14,076	11,871	14,901	12,931
61,550	61,600	14,091	11,885	14,916	12,945
61,600	61,650	14,107	11,899	14,932	12,959
61,650	61,700	14,122	11,913	14,947	12,973
61,700	61,750	14,138	11,927	14,963	12,987
61,750	61,800	14,153	11,941	14,978	13,001
61,800	61,850	14,169	11,955	14,994	13,015
61,850	61,900	14,184	11,969	15,009	13,029
61,900	61,950	14,200	11,983	15,025	13,043
61,950	62,000	14,215	11,997	15,040	13,057

Column group 2

If line 38 (taxable income) is—		And you are—			
At least	But less than	Single	Married filing jointly *	Married filing separately	Head of a household
		Your tax is—			
62,000					
62,000	62,050	14,231	12,011	15,056	13,071
62,050	62,100	14,246	12,025	15,071	13,085
62,100	62,150	14,262	12,039	15,087	13,099
62,150	62,200	14,277	12,053	15,102	13,113
62,200	62,250	14,293	12,067	15,118	13,127
62,250	62,300	14,308	12,081	15,133	13,141
62,300	62,350	14,324	12,095	15,149	13,155
62,350	62,400	14,339	12,109	15,164	13,169
62,400	62,450	14,355	12,123	15,180	13,183
62,450	62,500	14,370	12,137	15,195	13,197
62,500	62,550	14,386	12,151	15,211	13,211
62,550	62,600	14,401	12,165	15,226	13,225
62,600	62,650	14,417	12,179	15,242	13,239
62,650	62,700	14,432	12,193	15,257	13,253
62,700	62,750	14,448	12,207	15,273	13,267
62,750	62,800	14,463	12,221	15,288	13,281
62,800	62,850	14,479	12,235	15,304	13,295
62,850	62,900	14,494	12,249	15,319	13,309
62,900	62,950	14,510	12,263	15,335	13,323
62,950	63,000	14,525	12,277	15,350	13,337
63,000					
63,000	63,050	14,541	12,291	15,366	13,351
63,050	63,100	14,556	12,305	15,381	13,365
63,100	63,150	14,572	12,319	15,397	13,379
63,150	63,200	14,587	12,333	15,412	13,393
63,200	63,250	14,603	12,347	15,428	13,407
63,250	63,300	14,618	12,361	15,443	13,421
63,300	63,350	14,634	12,375	15,459	13,435
63,350	63,400	14,649	12,389	15,474	13,449
63,400	63,450	14,665	12,403	15,490	13,463
63,450	63,500	14,680	12,417	15,505	13,477
63,500	63,550	14,696	12,431	15,521	13,491
63,550	63,600	14,711	12,445	15,536	13,505
63,600	63,650	14,727	12,459	15,552	13,519
63,650	63,700	14,742	12,473	15,567	13,533
63,700	63,750	14,758	12,487	15,583	13,547
63,750	63,800	14,773	12,501	15,598	13,561
63,800	63,850	14,789	12,515	15,614	13,575
63,850	63,900	14,804	12,529	15,629	13,589
63,900	63,950	14,820	12,543	15,645	13,603
63,950	64,000	14,835	12,557	15,660	13,617
64,000					
64,000	64,050	14,851	12,571	15,676	13,631
64,050	64,100	14,866	12,585	15,691	13,645
64,100	64,150	14,882	12,599	15,707	13,659
64,150	64,200	14,897	12,613	15,722	13,673
64,200	64,250	14,913	12,627	15,738	13,687
64,250	64,300	14,928	12,641	15,753	13,701
64,300	64,350	14,944	12,655	15,769	13,715
64,350	64,400	14,959	12,669	15,784	13,729
64,400	64,450	14,975	12,683	15,800	13,743
64,450	64,500	14,990	12,697	15,815	13,757
64,500	64,550	15,006	12,711	15,831	13,771
64,550	64,600	15,021	12,725	15,846	13,785
64,600	64,650	15,037	12,739	15,862	13,799
64,650	64,700	15,052	12,753	15,877	13,813
64,700	64,750	15,068	12,767	15,893	13,827
64,750	64,800	15,083	12,781	15,908	13,841
64,800	64,850	15,099	12,795	15,924	13,855
64,850	64,900	15,114	12,809	15,939	13,869
64,900	64,950	15,130	12,823	15,955	13,883
64,950	65,000	15,145	12,837	15,970	13,897

Column group 3

If line 38 (taxable income) is—		And you are—			
At least	But less than	Single	Married filing jointly *	Married filing separately	Head of a household
		Your tax is—			
65,000					
65,000	65,050	15,161	12,851	15,986	13,911
65,050	65,100	15,176	12,865	16,001	13,925
65,100	65,150	15,192	12,879	16,017	13,939
65,150	65,200	15,207	12,893	16,032	13,953
65,200	65,250	15,223	12,907	16,048	13,967
65,250	65,300	15,238	12,921	16,063	13,981
65,300	65,350	15,254	12,935	16,079	13,995
65,350	65,400	15,269	12,949	16,094	14,009
65,400	65,450	15,285	12,963	16,110	14,023
65,450	65,500	15,300	12,977	16,125	14,037
65,500	65,550	15,316	12,991	16,141	14,051
65,550	65,600	15,331	13,005	16,156	14,065
65,600	65,650	15,347	13,019	16,172	14,079
65,650	65,700	15,362	13,033	16,187	14,093
65,700	65,750	15,378	13,047	16,203	14,107
65,750	65,800	15,393	13,061	16,218	14,121
65,800	65,850	15,409	13,075	16,234	14,135
65,850	65,900	15,424	13,089	16,249	14,149
65,900	65,950	15,440	13,103	16,265	14,163
65,950	66,000	15,455	13,117	16,280	14,177
66,000					
66,000	66,050	15,471	13,131	16,296	14,191
66,050	66,100	15,486	13,145	16,311	14,205
66,100	66,150	15,502	13,159	16,327	14,219
66,150	66,200	15,517	13,173	16,342	14,233
66,200	66,250	15,533	13,187	16,358	14,247
66,250	66,300	15,548	13,201	16,373	14,261
66,300	66,350	15,564	13,215	16,389	14,275
66,350	66,400	15,579	13,229	16,404	14,289
66,400	66,450	15,595	13,243	16,420	14,303
66,450	66,500	15,610	13,257	16,435	14,317
66,500	66,550	15,626	13,271	16,451	14,331
66,550	66,600	15,641	13,285	16,466	14,345
66,600	66,650	15,657	13,299	16,482	14,359
66,650	66,700	15,672	13,313	16,497	14,373
66,700	66,750	15,688	13,327	16,513	14,387
66,750	66,800	15,703	13,341	16,528	14,401
66,800	66,850	15,719	13,355	16,544	14,415
66,850	66,900	15,734	13,369	16,559	14,429
66,900	66,950	15,750	13,383	16,575	14,443
66,950	67,000	15,765	13,397	16,590	14,457
67,000					
67,000	67,050	15,781	13,411	16,606	14,471
67,050	67,100	15,796	13,425	16,621	14,485
67,100	67,150	15,812	13,439	16,637	14,499
67,150	67,200	15,827	13,453	16,652	14,513
67,200	67,250	15,843	13,467	16,668	14,527
67,250	67,300	15,858	13,481	16,683	14,541
67,300	67,350	15,874	13,495	16,699	14,555
67,350	67,400	15,889	13,509	16,714	14,569
67,400	67,450	15,905	13,523	16,730	14,583
67,450	67,500	15,920	13,537	16,745	14,597
67,500	67,550	15,936	13,551	16,761	14,611
67,550	67,600	15,951	13,565	16,776	14,625
67,600	67,650	15,967	13,579	16,792	14,639
67,650	67,700	15,982	13,593	16,807	14,653
67,700	67,750	15,998	13,607	16,823	14,667
67,750	67,800	16,013	13,621	16,838	14,681
67,800	67,850	16,029	13,635	16,854	14,695
67,850	67,900	16,044	13,649	16,869	14,709
67,900	67,950	16,060	13,663	16,885	14,723
67,950	68,000	16,075	13,677	16,900	14,737

* This column must also be used by a qualifying widow(er).

Continued on next page

If line 38 (taxable income) is—		And you are—			
At least	But less than	Single	Married filing jointly *	Married filing separately	Head of a household
		Your tax is—			

68,000

At least	But less than	Single	Married filing jointly	Married filing separately	Head of a household
68,000	68,050	16,091	13,691	16,916	14,751
68,050	68,100	16,106	13,705	16,931	14,765
68,100	68,150	16,122	13,719	16,947	14,779
68,150	68,200	16,137	13,733	16,962	14,793
68,200	68,250	16,153	13,747	16,978	14,807
68,250	68,300	16,168	13,761	16,993	14,821
68,300	68,350	16,184	13,775	17,009	14,835
68,350	68,400	16,199	13,789	17,024	14,849
68,400	68,450	16,215	13,803	17,040	14,863
68,450	68,500	16,230	13,817	17,055	14,877
68,500	68,550	16,246	13,831	17,071	14,891
68,550	68,600	16,261	13,845	17,086	14,905
68,600	68,650	16,277	13,859	17,102	14,919
68,650	68,700	16,292	13,873	17,117	14,933
68,700	68,750	16,308	13,887	17,133	14,947
68,750	68,800	16,323	13,901	17,148	14,961
68,800	68,850	16,339	13,915	17,164	14,975
68,850	68,900	16,354	13,929	17,179	14,989
68,900	68,950	16,370	13,943	17,195	15,003
68,950	69,000	16,385	13,957	17,210	15,017

69,000

At least	But less than	Single	Married filing jointly	Married filing separately	Head of a household
69,000	69,050	16,401	13,971	17,226	15,031
69,050	69,100	16,416	13,985	17,241	15,045
69,100	69,150	16,432	13,999	17,257	15,059
69,150	69,200	16,447	14,013	17,272	15,073
69,200	69,250	16,463	14,027	17,288	15,087
69,250	69,300	16,478	14,041	17,303	15,101
69,300	69,350	16,494	14,055	17,319	15,115
69,350	69,400	16,509	14,069	17,334	15,129
69,400	69,450	16,525	14,083	17,350	15,143
69,450	69,500	16,540	14,097	17,365	15,157
69,500	69,550	16,556	14,111	17,381	15,171
69,550	69,600	16,571	14,125	17,396	15,185
69,600	69,650	16,587	14,139	17,412	15,199
69,650	69,700	16,602	14,153	17,427	15,213
69,700	69,750	16,618	14,167	17,443	15,227
69,750	69,800	16,633	14,181	17,458	15,241
69,800	69,850	16,649	14,195	17,474	15,255
69,850	69,900	16,664	14,209	17,489	15,269
69,900	69,950	16,680	14,223	17,505	15,283
69,950	70,000	16,695	14,237	17,520	15,297

70,000

At least	But less than	Single	Married filing jointly	Married filing separately	Head of a household
70,000	70,050	16,711	14,251	17,536	15,311
70,050	70,100	16,726	14,265	17,551	15,325
70,100	70,150	16,742	14,279	17,567	15,339
70,150	70,200	16,757	14,293	17,582	15,353
70,200	70,250	16,773	14,307	17,598	15,367
70,250	70,300	16,788	14,321	17,613	15,381
70,300	70,350	16,804	14,335	17,629	15,395
70,350	70,400	16,819	14,349	17,644	15,409
70,400	70,450	16,835	14,363	17,660	15,423
70,450	70,500	16,850	14,377	17,675	15,437
70,500	70,550	16,866	14,391	17,691	15,451
70,550	70,600	16,881	14,405	17,706	15,465
70,600	70,650	16,897	14,419	17,722	15,479
70,650	70,700	16,912	14,433	17,737	15,493
70,700	70,750	16,928	14,447	17,753	15,507
70,750	70,800	16,943	14,461	17,768	15,521
70,800	70,850	16,959	14,475	17,784	15,535
70,850	70,900	16,974	14,489	17,799	15,549
70,900	70,950	16,990	14,503	17,815	15,563
70,950	71,000	17,005	14,517	17,830	15,577

71,000

At least	But less than	Single	Married filing jointly	Married filing separately	Head of a household
71,000	71,050	17,021	14,531	17,846	15,591
71,050	71,100	17,036	14,545	17,861	15,605
71,100	71,150	17,052	14,559	17,877	15,619
71,150	71,200	17,067	14,573	17,892	15,633
71,200	71,250	17,083	14,587	17,908	15,647
71,250	71,300	17,098	14,601	17,923	15,661
71,300	71,350	17,114	14,615	17,939	15,675
71,350	71,400	17,129	14,629	17,954	15,689
71,400	71,450	17,145	14,643	17,970	15,703
71,450	71,500	17,160	14,657	17,985	15,717
71,500	71,550	17,176	14,671	18,001	15,731
71,550	71,600	17,191	14,685	18,016	15,745
71,600	71,650	17,207	14,699	18,032	15,759
71,650	71,700	17,222	14,713	18,047	15,773
71,700	71,750	17,238	14,727	18,063	15,787
71,750	71,800	17,253	14,741	18,078	15,801
71,800	71,850	17,269	14,755	18,094	15,815
71,850	71,900	17,284	14,769	18,109	15,829
71,900	71,950	17,300	14,783	18,125	15,843
71,950	72,000	17,315	14,797	18,140	15,857

72,000

At least	But less than	Single	Married filing jointly	Married filing separately	Head of a household
72,000	72,050	17,331	14,811	18,156	15,871
72,050	72,100	17,346	14,825	18,171	15,885
72,100	72,150	17,362	14,839	18,187	15,899
72,150	72,200	17,377	14,853	18,202	15,913
72,200	72,250	17,393	14,867	18,218	15,927
72,250	72,300	17,408	14,881	18,233	15,941
72,300	72,350	17,424	14,895	18,249	15,955
72,350	72,400	17,439	14,909	18,264	15,969
72,400	72,450	17,455	14,923	18,280	15,983
72,450	72,500	17,470	14,937	18,295	15,997
72,500	72,550	17,486	14,951	18,311	16,011
72,550	72,600	17,501	14,965	18,326	16,025
72,600	72,650	17,517	14,979	18,342	16,039
72,650	72,700	17,532	14,993	18,357	16,053
72,700	72,750	17,548	15,007	18,373	16,067
72,750	72,800	17,563	15,021	18,388	16,081
72,800	72,850	17,579	15,035	18,404	16,095
72,850	72,900	17,594	15,049	18,419	16,109
72,900	72,950	17,610	15,063	18,435	16,123
72,950	73,000	17,625	15,077	18,450	16,137

73,000

At least	But less than	Single	Married filing jointly	Married filing separately	Head of a household
73,000	73,050	17,641	15,091	18,466	16,151
73,050	73,100	17,656	15,105	18,481	16,165
73,100	73,150	17,672	15,119	18,497	16,179
73,150	73,200	17,687	15,133	18,512	16,193
73,200	73,250	17,703	15,147	18,528	16,207
73,250	73,300	17,718	15,161	18,543	16,221
73,300	73,350	17,734	15,175	18,559	16,235
73,350	73,400	17,749	15,189	18,574	16,249
73,400	73,450	17,765	15,203	18,590	16,263
73,450	73,500	17,780	15,217	18,605	16,277
73,500	73,550	17,796	15,231	18,621	16,291
73,550	73,600	17,811	15,245	18,636	16,305
73,600	73,650	17,827	15,259	18,652	16,319
73,650	73,700	17,842	15,273	18,667	16,333
73,700	73,750	17,858	15,287	18,683	16,347
73,750	73,800	17,873	15,301	18,698	16,361
73,800	73,850	17,889	15,315	18,714	16,375
73,850	73,900	17,904	15,329	18,729	16,389
73,900	73,950	17,920	15,343	18,745	16,403
73,950	74,000	17,935	15,357	18,760	16,417

74,000

At least	But less than	Single	Married filing jointly	Married filing separately	Head of a household
74,000	74,050	17,951	15,371	18,776	16,431
74,050	74,100	17,966	15,385	18,791	16,445
74,100	74,150	17,982	15,399	18,807	16,459
74,150	74,200	17,997	15,413	18,822	16,473
74,200	74,250	18,013	15,427	18,838	16,487
74,250	74,300	18,028	15,441	18,853	16,501
74,300	74,350	18,044	15,455	18,869	16,515
74,350	74,400	18,059	15,469	18,884	16,529
74,400	74,450	18,075	15,483	18,900	16,543
74,450	74,500	18,090	15,497	18,915	16,557
74,500	74,550	18,106	15,511	18,931	16,571
74,550	74,600	18,121	15,525	18,946	16,585
74,600	74,650	18,137	15,539	18,962	16,599
74,650	74,700	18,152	15,553	18,977	16,613
74,700	74,750	18,168	15,567	18,993	16,627
74,750	74,800	18,183	15,581	19,008	16,641
74,800	74,850	18,199	15,595	19,024	16,655
74,850	74,900	18,214	15,609	19,039	16,669
74,900	74,950	18,230	15,623	19,055	16,683
74,950	75,000	18,245	15,637	19,070	16,697

75,000

At least	But less than	Single	Married filing jointly	Married filing separately	Head of a household
75,000	75,050	18,261	15,651	19,086	16,711
75,050	75,100	18,276	15,665	19,101	16,725
75,100	75,150	18,292	15,679	19,117	16,739
75,150	75,200	18,307	15,693	19,132	16,753
75,200	75,250	18,323	15,707	19,148	16,767
75,250	75,300	18,338	15,721	19,163	16,781
75,300	75,350	18,354	15,735	19,179	16,795
75,350	75,400	18,369	15,749	19,194	16,809
75,400	75,450	18,385	15,763	19,210	16,823
75,450	75,500	18,400	15,777	19,225	16,837
75,500	75,550	18,416	15,791	19,241	16,851
75,550	75,600	18,431	15,805	19,256	16,865
75,600	75,650	18,447	15,819	19,272	16,879
75,650	75,700	18,462	15,833	19,287	16,893
75,700	75,750	18,478	15,847	19,303	16,907
75,750	75,800	18,493	15,861	19,318	16,921
75,800	75,850	18,509	15,875	19,334	16,935
75,850	75,900	18,524	15,889	19,349	16,949
75,900	75,950	18,540	15,903	19,367	16,963
75,950	76,000	18,555	15,917	19,385	16,977

76,000

At least	But less than	Single	Married filing jointly	Married filing separately	Head of a household
76,000	76,050	18,571	15,931	19,403	16,991
76,050	76,100	18,586	15,945	19,421	17,005
76,100	76,150	18,602	15,959	19,439	17,019
76,150	76,200	18,617	15,973	19,457	17,033
76,200	76,250	18,633	15,987	19,475	17,047
76,250	76,300	18,648	16,001	19,493	17,061
76,300	76,350	18,664	16,015	19,511	17,075
76,350	76,400	18,679	16,029	19,529	17,089
76,400	76,450	18,695	16,043	19,547	17,103
76,450	76,500	18,710	16,057	19,565	17,117
76,500	76,550	18,726	16,071	19,583	17,131
76,550	76,600	18,741	16,085	19,601	17,145
76,600	76,650	18,757	16,099	19,619	17,159
76,650	76,700	18,772	16,113	19,637	17,173
76,700	76,750	18,788	16,127	19,655	17,187
76,750	76,800	18,803	16,141	19,673	17,201
76,800	76,850	18,819	16,155	19,691	17,215
76,850	76,900	18,834	16,169	19,709	17,229
76,900	76,950	18,850	16,183	19,727	17,243
76,950	77,000	18,865	16,197	19,745	17,257

* This column must also be used by a qualifying widow(er).

Continued on next page

If line 38 (taxable income) is— At least	But less than	Single	Married filing jointly*	Married filing separately	Head of a household

(This column must also be used by a qualifying widow(er). "Your tax is—")*

77,000

At least	But less than	Single	Married filing jointly	Married filing separately	Head of a household
77,000	77,050	18,881	16,211	19,763	17,271
77,050	77,100	18,896	16,225	19,781	17,285
77,100	77,150	18,912	16,239	19,799	17,299
77,150	77,200	18,927	16,253	19,817	17,313
77,200	77,250	18,943	16,267	19,835	17,327
77,250	77,300	18,958	16,281	19,853	17,341
77,300	77,350	18,974	16,295	19,871	17,355
77,350	77,400	18,989	16,309	19,889	17,369
77,400	77,450	19,005	16,323	19,907	17,383
77,450	77,500	19,020	16,337	19,925	17,397
77,500	77,550	19,036	16,351	19,943	17,411
77,550	77,600	19,051	16,365	19,961	17,425
77,600	77,650	19,067	16,379	19,979	17,439
77,650	77,700	19,082	16,393	19,997	17,453
77,700	77,750	19,098	16,407	20,015	17,467
77,750	77,800	19,113	16,421	20,033	17,481
77,800	77,850	19,129	16,435	20,051	17,495
77,850	77,900	19,144	16,449	20,069	17,509
77,900	77,950	19,160	16,463	20,087	17,523
77,950	78,000	19,175	16,477	20,105	17,537

78,000

At least	But less than	Single	Married filing jointly	Married filing separately	Head of a household
78,000	78,050	19,191	16,491	20,123	17,551
78,050	78,100	19,206	16,505	20,141	17,565
78,100	78,150	19,222	16,519	20,159	17,579
78,150	78,200	19,237	16,533	20,177	17,593
78,200	78,250	19,253	16,547	20,195	17,607
78,250	78,300	19,268	16,561	20,213	17,621
78,300	78,350	19,284	16,575	20,231	17,635
78,350	78,400	19,299	16,589	20,249	17,649
78,400	78,450	19,315	16,603	20,267	17,663
78,450	78,500	19,330	16,617	20,285	17,677
78,500	78,550	19,346	16,631	20,303	17,691
78,550	78,600	19,361	16,645	20,321	17,705
78,600	78,650	19,377	16,659	20,339	17,719
78,650	78,700	19,392	16,673	20,357	17,733
78,700	78,750	19,408	16,687	20,375	17,747
78,750	78,800	19,423	16,701	20,393	17,761
78,800	78,850	19,439	16,715	20,411	17,775
78,850	78,900	19,454	16,729	20,429	17,789
78,900	78,950	19,470	16,743	20,447	17,803
78,950	79,000	19,485	16,757	20,465	17,817

79,000

At least	But less than	Single	Married filing jointly	Married filing separately	Head of a household
79,000	79,050	19,501	16,771	20,483	17,831
79,050	79,100	19,516	16,785	20,501	17,845
79,100	79,150	19,532	16,799	20,519	17,859
79,150	79,200	19,547	16,813	20,537	17,873
79,200	79,250	19,563	16,827	20,555	17,887
79,250	79,300	19,578	16,841	20,573	17,901
79,300	79,350	19,594	16,855	20,591	17,915
79,350	79,400	19,609	16,869	20,609	17,929
79,400	79,450	19,625	16,883	20,627	17,943
79,450	79,500	19,640	16,897	20,645	17,957
79,500	79,550	19,656	16,911	20,663	17,971
79,550	79,600	19,671	16,925	20,681	17,985
79,600	79,650	19,687	16,939	20,699	17,999
79,650	79,700	19,702	16,953	20,717	18,013
79,700	79,750	19,718	16,967	20,735	18,027
79,750	79,800	19,733	16,981	20,753	18,041
79,800	79,850	19,749	16,995	20,771	18,055
79,850	79,900	19,764	17,009	20,789	18,069
79,900	79,950	19,780	17,023	20,807	18,083
79,950	80,000	19,795	17,037	20,825	18,097

80,000

At least	But less than	Single	Married filing jointly	Married filing separately	Head of a household
80,000	80,050	19,811	17,051	20,843	18,111
80,050	80,100	19,826	17,065	20,861	18,125
80,100	80,150	19,842	17,079	20,879	18,139
80,150	80,200	19,857	17,093	20,897	18,153
80,200	80,250	19,873	17,107	20,915	18,167
80,250	80,300	19,888	17,121	20,933	18,181
80,300	80,350	19,904	17,135	20,951	18,195
80,350	80,400	19,919	17,149	20,969	18,209
80,400	80,450	19,935	17,163	20,987	18,223
80,450	80,500	19,950	17,177	21,005	18,237
80,500	80,550	19,966	17,191	21,023	18,251
80,550	80,600	19,981	17,205	21,041	18,265
80,600	80,650	19,997	17,219	21,059	18,279
80,650	80,700	20,012	17,233	21,077	18,293
80,700	80,750	20,028	17,247	21,095	18,307
80,750	80,800	20,043	17,261	21,113	18,321
80,800	80,850	20,059	17,275	21,131	18,335
80,850	80,900	20,074	17,289	21,149	18,349
80,900	80,950	20,090	17,303	21,167	18,363
80,950	81,000	20,105	17,317	21,185	18,377

81,000

At least	But less than	Single	Married filing jointly	Married filing separately	Head of a household
81,000	81,050	20,121	17,331	21,203	18,391
81,050	81,100	20,136	17,345	21,221	18,405
81,100	81,150	20,152	17,359	21,239	18,419
81,150	81,200	20,167	17,373	21,257	18,433
81,200	81,250	20,183	17,387	21,275	18,447
81,250	81,300	20,198	17,401	21,293	18,461
81,300	81,350	20,214	17,415	21,311	18,475
81,350	81,400	20,229	17,429	21,329	18,489
81,400	81,450	20,245	17,443	21,347	18,503
81,450	81,500	20,260	17,457	21,365	18,517
81,500	81,550	20,276	17,471	21,383	18,531
81,550	81,600	20,291	17,485	21,401	18,545
81,600	81,650	20,307	17,499	21,419	18,559
81,650	81,700	20,322	17,513	21,437	18,573
81,700	81,750	20,338	17,527	21,455	18,587
81,750	81,800	20,353	17,541	21,473	18,601
81,800	81,850	20,369	17,555	21,491	18,615
81,850	81,900	20,384	17,569	21,509	18,629
81,900	81,950	20,400	17,583	21,527	18,643
81,950	82,000	20,415	17,597	21,545	18,657

82,000

At least	But less than	Single	Married filing jointly	Married filing separately	Head of a household
82,000	82,050	20,431	17,611	21,563	18,671
82,050	82,100	20,446	17,625	21,581	18,685
82,100	82,150	20,462	17,639	21,599	18,699
82,150	82,200	20,477	17,653	21,617	18,713
82,200	82,250	20,493	17,667	21,635	18,727
82,250	82,300	20,508	17,681	21,653	18,741
82,300	82,350	20,524	17,695	21,671	18,755
82,350	82,400	20,539	17,709	21,689	18,769
82,400	82,450	20,555	17,723	21,707	18,783
82,450	82,500	20,570	17,737	21,725	18,797
82,500	82,550	20,586	17,751	21,743	18,811
82,550	82,600	20,601	17,765	21,761	18,825
82,600	82,650	20,617	17,779	21,779	18,839
82,650	82,700	20,632	17,793	21,797	18,853
82,700	82,750	20,648	17,807	21,815	18,867
82,750	82,800	20,663	17,821	21,833	18,881
82,800	82,850	20,679	17,835	21,851	18,895
82,850	82,900	20,694	17,849	21,869	18,909
82,900	82,950	20,710	17,863	21,887	18,923
82,950	83,000	20,725	17,877	21,905	18,937

83,000

At least	But less than	Single	Married filing jointly	Married filing separately	Head of a household
83,000	83,050	20,741	17,891	21,923	18,951
83,050	83,100	20,756	17,905	21,941	18,965
83,100	83,150	20,772	17,919	21,959	18,979
83,150	83,200	20,787	17,933	21,977	18,993
83,200	83,250	20,803	17,947	21,995	19,007
83,250	83,300	20,818	17,961	22,013	19,021
83,300	83,350	20,834	17,975	22,031	19,035
83,350	83,400	20,849	17,989	22,049	19,049
83,400	83,450	20,865	18,003	22,067	19,063
83,450	83,500	20,880	18,017	22,085	19,077
83,500	83,550	20,896	18,031	22,103	19,091
83,550	83,600	20,911	18,045	22,121	19,105
83,600	83,650	20,927	18,059	22,139	19,119
83,650	83,700	20,942	18,073	22,157	19,133
83,700	83,750	20,958	18,087	22,175	19,147
83,750	83,800	20,973	18,101	22,193	19,161
83,800	83,850	20,989	18,115	22,211	19,175
83,850	83,900	21,004	18,129	22,229	19,189
83,900	83,950	21,020	18,143	22,247	19,203
83,950	84,000	21,035	18,157	22,265	19,217

84,000

At least	But less than	Single	Married filing jointly	Married filing separately	Head of a household
84,000	84,050	21,051	18,171	22,283	19,231
84,050	84,100	21,066	18,185	22,301	19,245
84,100	84,150	21,082	18,199	22,319	19,259
84,150	84,200	21,097	18,213	22,337	19,273
84,200	84,250	21,113	18,227	22,355	19,287
84,250	84,300	21,128	18,241	22,373	19,301
84,300	84,350	21,144	18,255	22,391	19,315
84,350	84,400	21,159	18,269	22,409	19,329
84,400	84,450	21,175	18,283	22,427	19,343
84,450	84,500	21,190	18,297	22,445	19,357
84,500	84,550	21,206	18,311	22,463	19,371
84,550	84,600	21,221	18,325	22,481	19,385
84,600	84,650	21,237	18,339	22,499	19,399
84,650	84,700	21,252	18,353	22,517	19,413
84,700	84,750	21,268	18,367	22,535	19,427
84,750	84,800	21,283	18,381	22,553	19,441
84,800	84,850	21,299	18,395	22,571	19,455
84,850	84,900	21,314	18,409	22,589	19,469
84,900	84,950	21,330	18,423	22,607	19,483
84,950	85,000	21,345	18,437	22,625	19,497

85,000

At least	But less than	Single	Married filing jointly	Married filing separately	Head of a household
85,000	85,050	21,361	18,451	22,643	19,511
85,050	85,100	21,376	18,465	22,661	19,525
85,100	85,150	21,392	18,479	22,679	19,539
85,150	85,200	21,407	18,493	22,697	19,553
85,200	85,250	21,423	18,507	22,715	19,567
85,250	85,300	21,438	18,521	22,733	19,581
85,300	85,350	21,454	18,535	22,751	19,595
85,350	85,400	21,469	18,549	22,769	19,609
85,400	85,450	21,485	18,563	22,787	19,625
85,450	85,500	21,500	18,577	22,805	19,640
85,500	85,550	21,516	18,591	22,823	19,656
85,550	85,600	21,531	18,605	22,841	19,671
85,600	85,650	21,547	18,619	22,859	19,687
85,650	85,700	21,562	18,633	22,877	19,702
85,700	85,750	21,578	18,647	22,895	19,718
85,750	85,800	21,593	18,661	22,913	19,733
85,800	85,850	21,609	18,675	22,931	19,749
85,850	85,900	21,624	18,689	22,949	19,764
85,900	85,950	21,640	18,703	22,967	19,780
85,950	86,000	21,655	18,717	22,985	19,795

* This column must also be used by a qualifying widow(er).

Continued on next page

86,000

At least	But less than	Single	Married filing jointly *	Married filing separately	Head of a household
86,000	86,050	21,671	18,731	23,003	19,811
86,050	86,100	21,686	18,745	23,021	19,826
86,100	86,150	21,702	18,759	23,039	19,842
86,150	86,200	21,717	18,773	23,057	19,857
86,200	86,250	21,733	18,787	23,075	19,873
86,250	86,300	21,748	18,801	23,093	19,888
86,300	86,350	21,764	18,815	23,111	19,904
86,350	86,400	21,779	18,829	23,129	19,919
86,400	86,450	21,795	18,843	23,147	19,935
86,450	86,500	21,810	18,857	23,165	19,950
86,500	86,550	21,826	18,871	23,183	19,966
86,550	86,600	21,841	18,885	23,201	19,981
86,600	86,650	21,857	18,899	23,219	19,997
86,650	86,700	21,872	18,913	23,237	20,012
86,700	86,750	21,888	18,927	23,255	20,028
86,750	86,800	21,903	18,941	23,273	20,043
86,800	86,850	21,919	18,955	23,291	20,059
86,850	86,900	21,934	18,969	23,309	20,074
86,900	86,950	21,950	18,983	23,327	20,090
86,950	87,000	21,965	18,997	23,345	20,105

87,000

At least	But less than	Single	Married filing jointly *	Married filing separately	Head of a household
87,000	87,050	21,981	19,011	23,363	20,121
87,050	87,100	21,996	19,025	23,381	20,136
87,100	87,150	22,012	19,039	23,399	20,152
87,150	87,200	22,027	19,053	23,417	20,167
87,200	87,250	22,043	19,067	23,435	20,183
87,250	87,300	22,058	19,081	23,453	20,198
87,300	87,350	22,074	19,095	23,471	20,214
87,350	87,400	22,089	19,109	23,489	20,229
87,400	87,450	22,105	19,123	23,507	20,245
87,450	87,500	22,120	19,137	23,525	20,260
87,500	87,550	22,136	19,151	23,543	20,276
87,550	87,600	22,151	19,165	23,561	20,291
87,600	87,650	22,167	19,179	23,579	20,307
87,650	87,700	22,182	19,193	23,597	20,322
87,700	87,750	22,198	19,207	23,615	20,338
87,750	87,800	22,213	19,221	23,633	20,353
87,800	87,850	22,229	19,235	23,651	20,369
87,850	87,900	22,244	19,249	23,669	20,384
87,900	87,950	22,260	19,263	23,687	20,400
87,950	88,000	22,275	19,277	23,705	20,415

88,000

At least	But less than	Single	Married filing jointly *	Married filing separately	Head of a household
88,000	88,050	22,291	19,291	23,723	20,431
88,050	88,100	22,306	19,305	23,741	20,446
88,100	88,150	22,322	19,319	23,759	20,462
88,150	88,200	22,337	19,333	23,777	20,477
88,200	88,250	22,353	19,347	23,795	20,493
88,250	88,300	22,368	19,361	23,813	20,508
88,300	88,350	22,384	19,375	23,831	20,524
88,350	88,400	22,399	19,389	23,849	20,539
88,400	88,450	22,415	19,403	23,867	20,555
88,450	88,500	22,430	19,417	23,885	20,570
88,500	88,550	22,446	19,431	23,903	20,586
88,550	88,600	22,461	19,445	23,921	20,601
88,600	88,650	22,477	19,459	23,939	20,617
88,650	88,700	22,492	19,473	23,957	20,632
88,700	88,750	22,508	19,487	23,975	20,648
88,750	88,800	22,523	19,501	23,993	20,663
88,800	88,850	22,539	19,515	24,011	20,679
88,850	88,900	22,554	19,529	24,029	20,694
88,900	88,950	22,570	19,543	24,047	20,710
88,950	89,000	22,585	19,557	24,065	20,725

89,000

At least	But less than	Single	Married filing jointly *	Married filing separately	Head of a household
89,000	89,050	22,601	19,571	24,083	20,741
89,050	89,100	22,616	19,585	24,101	20,756
89,100	89,150	22,632	19,599	24,119	20,772
89,150	89,200	22,647	19,613	24,137	20,787
89,200	89,250	22,663	19,627	24,155	20,803
89,250	89,300	22,678	19,641	24,173	20,818
89,300	89,350	22,694	19,655	24,191	20,834
89,350	89,400	22,709	19,669	24,209	20,849
89,400	89,450	22,725	19,683	24,227	20,865
89,450	89,500	22,740	19,697	24,245	20,880
89,500	89,550	22,756	19,711	24,263	20,896
89,550	89,600	22,771	19,725	24,281	20,911
89,600	89,650	22,787	19,739	24,299	20,927
89,650	89,700	22,802	19,753	24,317	20,942
89,700	89,750	22,818	19,767	24,335	20,958
89,750	89,800	22,833	19,781	24,353	20,973
89,800	89,850	22,849	19,795	24,371	20,989
89,850	89,900	22,864	19,809	24,389	21,004
89,900	89,950	22,880	19,823	24,407	21,020
89,950	90,000	22,895	19,837	24,425	21,035

90,000

At least	But less than	Single	Married filing jointly *	Married filing separately	Head of a household
90,000	90,050	22,911	19,851	24,443	21,051
90,050	90,100	22,926	19,865	24,461	21,066
90,100	90,150	22,942	19,879	24,479	21,082
90,150	90,200	22,957	19,893	24,497	21,097
90,200	90,250	22,973	19,907	24,515	21,113
90,250	90,300	22,988	19,921	24,533	21,128
90,300	90,350	23,004	19,935	24,551	21,144
90,350	90,400	23,019	19,949	24,569	21,159
90,400	90,450	23,035	19,963	24,587	21,175
90,450	90,500	23,050	19,977	24,605	21,190
90,500	90,550	23,066	19,991	24,623	21,206
90,550	90,600	23,081	20,005	24,641	21,221
90,600	90,650	23,097	20,019	24,659	21,237
90,650	90,700	23,112	20,033	24,677	21,252
90,700	90,750	23,128	20,047	24,695	21,268
90,750	90,800	23,143	20,061	24,713	21,283
90,800	90,850	23,159	20,075	24,731	21,299
90,850	90,900	23,174	20,089	24,749	21,314
90,900	90,950	23,190	20,103	24,767	21,330
90,950	91,000	23,205	20,117	24,785	21,345

91,000

At least	But less than	Single	Married filing jointly *	Married filing separately	Head of a household
91,000	91,050	23,221	20,131	24,803	21,361
91,050	91,100	23,236	20,145	24,821	21,376
91,100	91,150	23,252	20,159	24,839	21,392
91,150	91,200	23,267	20,173	24,857	21,407
91,200	91,250	23,283	20,187	24,875	21,423
91,250	91,300	23,298	20,201	24,893	21,438
91,300	91,350	23,314	20,215	24,911	21,454
91,350	91,400	23,329	20,229	24,929	21,469
91,400	91,450	23,345	20,243	24,947	21,485
91,450	91,500	23,360	20,257	24,965	21,500
91,500	91,550	23,376	20,271	24,983	21,516
91,550	91,600	23,391	20,285	25,001	21,531
91,600	91,650	23,407	20,299	25,019	21,547
91,650	91,700	23,422	20,313	25,037	21,562
91,700	91,750	23,438	20,327	25,055	21,578
91,750	91,800	23,453	20,341	25,073	21,593
91,800	91,850	23,469	20,355	25,091	21,609
91,850	91,900	23,484	20,369	25,109	21,624
91,900	91,950	23,500	20,383	25,127	21,640
91,950	92,000	23,515	20,397	25,145	21,655

92,000

At least	But less than	Single	Married filing jointly *	Married filing separately	Head of a household
92,000	92,050	23,531	20,411	25,163	21,671
92,050	92,100	23,546	20,425	25,181	21,686
92,100	92,150	23,562	20,439	25,199	21,702
92,150	92,200	23,577	20,453	25,217	21,717
92,200	92,250	23,593	20,467	25,235	21,733
92,250	92,300	23,608	20,481	25,253	21,748
92,300	92,350	23,624	20,495	25,271	21,764
92,350	92,400	23,639	20,509	25,289	21,779
92,400	92,450	23,655	20,523	25,307	21,795
92,450	92,500	23,670	20,537	25,325	21,810
92,500	92,550	23,686	20,551	25,343	21,826
92,550	92,600	23,701	20,565	25,361	21,841
92,600	92,650	23,717	20,579	25,379	21,857
92,650	92,700	23,732	20,593	25,397	21,872
92,700	92,750	23,748	20,607	25,415	21,888
92,750	92,800	23,763	20,621	25,433	21,903
92,800	92,850	23,779	20,635	25,451	21,919
92,850	92,900	23,794	20,649	25,469	21,934
92,900	92,950	23,810	20,663	25,487	21,950
92,950	93,000	23,825	20,677	25,505	21,965

93,000

At least	But less than	Single	Married filing jointly *	Married filing separately	Head of a household
93,000	93,050	23,841	20,691	25,523	21,981
93,050	93,100	23,856	20,705	25,541	21,996
93,100	93,150	23,872	20,719	25,559	22,012
93,150	93,200	23,887	20,733	25,577	22,027
93,200	93,250	23,903	20,747	25,595	22,043
93,250	93,300	23,918	20,761	25,613	22,058
93,300	93,350	23,934	20,775	25,631	22,074
93,350	93,400	23,949	20,789	25,649	22,089
93,400	93,450	23,965	20,803	25,667	22,105
93,450	93,500	23,980	20,817	25,685	22,120
93,500	93,550	23,996	20,831	25,703	22,136
93,550	93,600	24,011	20,845	25,721	22,151
93,600	93,650	24,027	20,859	25,739	22,167
93,650	93,700	24,042	20,873	25,757	22,182
93,700	93,750	24,058	20,887	25,775	22,198
93,750	93,800	24,073	20,901	25,793	22,213
93,800	93,850	24,089	20,915	25,811	22,229
93,850	93,900	24,104	20,929	25,829	22,244
93,900	93,950	24,120	20,943	25,847	22,260
93,950	94,000	24,135	20,957	25,865	22,275

94,000

At least	But less than	Single	Married filing jointly *	Married filing separately	Head of a household
94,000	94,050	24,151	20,971	25,883	22,291
94,050	94,100	24,166	20,985	25,901	22,306
94,100	94,150	24,182	20,999	25,919	22,322
94,150	94,200	24,197	21,013	25,937	22,337
94,200	94,250	24,213	21,027	25,955	22,353
94,250	94,300	24,228	21,041	25,973	22,368
94,300	94,350	24,244	21,055	25,991	22,384
94,350	94,400	24,259	21,069	26,009	22,399
94,400	94,450	24,275	21,083	26,027	22,415
94,450	94,500	24,290	21,097	26,045	22,430
94,500	94,550	24,306	21,111	26,063	22,446
94,550	94,600	24,321	21,125	26,081	22,461
94,600	94,650	24,337	21,139	26,099	22,477
94,650	94,700	24,352	21,153	26,117	22,492
94,700	94,750	24,368	21,167	26,135	22,508
94,750	94,800	24,383	21,181	26,153	22,523
94,800	94,850	24,399	21,195	26,171	22,539
94,850	94,900	24,414	21,209	26,189	22,554
94,900	94,950	24,430	21,223	26,207	22,570
94,950	95,000	24,445	21,237	26,225	22,585

* This column must also be used by a qualifying widow(er).

Continued on next page

95,000

At least	But less than	Single	Married filing jointly *	Married filing separately	Head of a household
95,000	95,050	24,461	21,251	26,243	22,601
95,050	95,100	24,476	21,265	26,261	22,616
95,100	95,150	24,492	21,279	26,279	22,632
95,150	95,200	24,507	21,293	26,297	22,647
95,200	95,250	24,523	21,307	26,315	22,663
95,250	95,300	24,538	21,321	26,333	22,678
95,300	95,350	24,554	21,335	26,351	22,694
95,350	95,400	24,569	21,349	26,369	22,709
95,400	95,450	24,585	21,363	26,387	22,725
95,450	95,500	24,600	21,377	26,405	22,740
95,500	95,550	24,616	21,391	26,423	22,756
95,550	95,600	24,631	21,405	26,441	22,771
95,600	95,650	24,647	21,419	26,459	22,787
95,650	95,700	24,662	21,433	26,477	22,802
95,700	95,750	24,678	21,447	26,495	22,818
95,750	95,800	24,693	21,461	26,513	22,833
95,800	95,850	24,709	21,475	26,531	22,849
95,850	95,900	24,724	21,489	26,549	22,864
95,900	95,950	24,740	21,503	26,567	22,880
95,950	96,000	24,755	21,517	26,585	22,895

96,000

At least	But less than	Single	Married filing jointly *	Married filing separately	Head of a household
96,000	96,050	24,771	21,531	26,603	22,911
96,050	96,100	24,786	21,545	26,621	22,926
96,100	96,150	24,802	21,559	26,639	22,942
96,150	96,200	24,817	21,573	26,657	22,957
96,200	96,250	24,833	21,587	26,675	22,973
96,250	96,300	24,848	21,601	26,693	22,988
96,300	96,350	24,864	21,615	26,711	23,004
96,350	96,400	24,879	21,629	26,729	23,019
96,400	96,450	24,895	21,643	26,747	23,035
96,450	96,500	24,910	21,657	26,765	23,050
96,500	96,550	24,926	21,671	26,783	23,066
96,550	96,600	24,941	21,685	26,801	23,081
96,600	96,650	24,957	21,699	26,819	23,097
96,650	96,700	24,972	21,713	26,837	23,112
96,700	96,750	24,988	21,727	26,855	23,128
96,750	96,800	25,003	21,741	26,873	23,143
96,800	96,850	25,019	21,755	26,891	23,159
96,850	96,900	25,034	21,769	26,909	23,174
96,900	96,950	25,050	21,783	26,927	23,190
96,950	97,000	25,065	21,797	26,945	23,205

97,000

At least	But less than	Single	Married filing jointly *	Married filing separately	Head of a household
97,000	97,050	25,081	21,811	26,963	23,221
97,050	97,100	25,096	21,825	26,981	23,236
97,100	97,150	25,112	21,839	26,999	23,252
97,150	97,200	25,127	21,853	27,017	23,267
97,200	97,250	25,143	21,867	27,035	23,283
97,250	97,300	25,158	21,881	27,053	23,298
97,300	97,350	25,174	21,895	27,071	23,314
97,350	97,400	25,189	21,909	27,089	23,329
97,400	97,450	25,205	21,923	27,107	23,345
97,450	97,500	25,220	21,937	27,125	23,360
97,500	97,550	25,236	21,951	27,143	23,376
97,550	97,600	25,251	21,965	27,161	23,391
97,600	97,650	25,267	21,979	27,179	23,407
97,650	97,700	25,282	21,993	27,197	23,422
97,700	97,750	25,298	22,007	27,215	23,438
97,750	97,800	25,313	22,021	27,233	23,453
97,800	97,850	25,329	22,035	27,251	23,469
97,850	97,900	25,344	22,049	27,269	23,484
97,900	97,950	25,360	22,063	27,287	23,500
97,950	98,000	25,375	22,077	27,305	23,515

98,000

At least	But less than	Single	Married filing jointly *	Married filing separately	Head of a household
98,000	98,050	25,391	22,091	27,323	23,531
98,050	98,100	25,406	22,105	27,341	23,546
98,100	98,150	25,422	22,119	27,359	23,562
98,150	98,200	25,437	22,133	27,377	23,577
98,200	98,250	25,453	22,147	27,395	23,593
98,250	98,300	25,468	22,161	27,413	23,608
98,300	98,350	25,484	22,175	27,431	23,624
98,350	98,400	25,499	22,189	27,449	23,639
98,400	98,450	25,515	22,203	27,467	23,655
98,450	98,500	25,530	22,217	27,485	23,670
98,500	98,550	25,546	22,231	27,503	23,686
98,550	98,600	25,561	22,245	27,521	23,701
98,600	98,650	25,577	22,259	27,539	23,717
98,650	98,700	25,592	22,273	27,557	23,732
98,700	98,750	25,608	22,287	27,575	23,748
98,750	98,800	25,623	22,301	27,593	23,763
98,800	98,850	25,639	22,315	27,611	23,779
98,850	98,900	25,654	22,329	27,629	23,794
98,900	98,950	25,670	22,343	27,647	23,810
98,950	99,000	25,685	22,357	27,665	23,825

99,000

At least	But less than	Single	Married filing jointly *	Married filing separately	Head of a household
99,000	99,050	25,701	22,371	27,683	23,841
99,050	99,100	25,716	22,385	27,701	23,856
99,100	99,150	25,732	22,399	27,719	23,872
99,150	99,200	25,747	22,413	27,737	23,887
99,200	99,250	25,763	22,427	27,755	23,903
99,250	99,300	25,778	22,441	27,773	23,918
99,300	99,350	25,794	22,455	27,791	23,934
99,350	99,400	25,809	22,469	27,809	23,949
99,400	99,450	25,825	22,483	27,827	23,965
99,450	99,500	25,840	22,497	27,845	23,980
99,500	99,550	25,856	22,511	27,863	23,996
99,550	99,600	25,871	22,525	27,881	24,011
99,600	99,650	25,887	22,540	27,899	24,027
99,650	99,700	25,902	22,555	27,917	24,042
99,700	99,750	25,918	22,571	27,935	24,058
99,750	99,800	25,933	22,586	27,953	24,073
99,800	99,850	25,949	22,602	27,971	24,089
99,850	99,900	25,964	22,617	27,989	24,104
99,900	99,950	25,980	22,633	28,007	24,120
99,950	100,000	25,995	22,648	28,025	24,135

$100,000 or over — use the Tax Rate Schedules on page 51

* This column must also be used by a qualifying widow(er).

1997 Tax Rate Schedules

Caution: *Use **only** if your taxable income (Form 1040, line 38) is $100,000 or more. If less, use the **Tax Table**. Even though you cannot use the Tax Rate Schedules below if your taxable income is less than $100,000, all levels of taxable income are shown so taxpayers can see the tax rate that applies to each level.*

Schedule X—Use if your filing status is **Single**

If the amount on Form 1040, line 38, is: Over—	But not over—	Enter on Form 1040, line 39	of the amount over—
$0	$24,650	.... 15%	$0
24,650	59,750	$3,697.50 + 28%	24,650
59,750	124,650	13,525.50 + 31%	59,750
124,650	271,050	33,644.50 + 36%	124,650
271,050	....	86,348.50 + 39.6%	271,050

Schedule Y-1—Use if your filing status is **Married filing jointly** or **Qualifying widow(er)**

If the amount on Form 1040, line 38, is: Over—	But not over—	Enter on Form 1040, line 39	of the amount over—
$0	$41,200	.... 15%	$0
41,200	99,600	$6,180.00 + 28%	41,200
99,600	151,750	22,532.00 + 31%	99,600
151,750	271,050	38,698.50 + 36%	151,750
271,050	....	81,646.50 + 39.6%	271,050

Schedule Y-2—Use if your filing status is **Married filing separately**

If the amount on Form 1040, line 38, is: Over—	But not over—	Enter on Form 1040, line 39	of the amount over—
$0	$20,600	.... 15%	$0
20,600	49,800	$3,090.00 + 28%	20,600
49,800	75,875	11,266.00 + 31%	49,800
75,875	135,525	19,349.25 + 36%	75,875
135,525	....	40,823.25 + 39.6%	135,525

Schedule Z—Use if your filing status is **Head of household**

If the amount on Form 1040, line 38, is: Over—	But not over—	Enter on Form 1040, line 39	of the amount over—
$0	$33,050	.... 15%	$0
33,050	85,350	$4,957.50 + 28%	33,050
85,350	138,200	19,601.50 + 31%	85,350
138,200	271,050	35,985.00 + 36%	138,200
271,050	....	83,811.00 + 39.6%	271,050

Part 9

Glossary & Index

The following glossary and index will help you quickly find answers to your specific tax questions.

Glossary: The useful glossary explains technical tax terms in plain easy-to-understand language.

Index: The index directs you to both the exact page and section where an item you are interested in is discussed

A

Accelerated Cost Recovery System (ACRS). A statutory method of depreciation allowing accelerated rates for most types of property used in business and income-producing activities during the years 1981 through 1986. It has been superseded by Modified Cost Recovery System (MACRS) for assets placed in service after 1986; *see 42.4.*

Accelerated depreciation. Depreciation methods that allow faster write-offs than straight-line rates in the earlier periods of the useful life of an asset. For example, in the first few years of recovery, MACRS allows a 200% double declining balance write-off, twice the straight-line rate; *see 42.5–42.8.*

Accountable reimbursement plan. An employer reimbursement or allowance arrangement that requires you to adequately substantiate business expenses to your employer, and to return any excess reimbursement; *see 20.31.*

Accrual method of accounting. A business method of accounting requiring income to be reported when earned and expenses to be deducted when incurred. However, deductions generally may not be claimed until economic performance has occurred; *see 40.3.*

Acquisition debt. Debt used to buy, build, or construct a principal residence or second home and which generally qualifies for a full interest expense deduction; *see 15.2.*

Active participation. Test for determining deductibility of IRA deductions. Active participants in employer retirement plans are subject to IRA deduction phase-out rules if adjusted gross income exceeds certain thresholds; *see 8.4.*

Adjusted basis. A statutory term describing the cost used to determine your profit or loss from a sale or exchange of property. It is generally your original cost, increased by capital improvements, and decreased by depreciation, depletion, and other capital write-offs; *see 5.24.*

Adjusted Gross Income (AGI). Important tax term representing gross income *less* allowable adjustments, such as for IRA, alimony, and Keogh deductions. AGI determines whether various tax benefits are phased out, such as personal exemptions, itemized deductions, and the rental loss allowance; *see 12.1.*

Alimony. Payments made to a separated or divorced spouse as required by a decree or agreement. Qualifying payments are deductible by the payor and taxable to the payee; *see 37.1–37.8.*

Alternative minimum tax (AMT). A tax triggered if certain tax benefits reduce your regular income tax below the tax computed on Form 6251 for AMT purposes; *see* Chapter 23.

Amended return. On Form 1040X, you may file an amended return within a three-year period to correct a mistake made on an original return; *see* Chapter 49.

Amortizable bond premium. The additional amount paid over the face amount of an obligation which may be deducted under the rules of *4.17.*

Amortization. Writing off an investment in intangible assets over the projected life of the assets; *see 42.18.*

Amount realized. A statutory term used to figure your profit or loss on a sale or exchange. Generally, it is sales proceeds plus mortgages assumed or taken subject to, less transaction expenses, such as commissions and legal costs; *see 5.18.*

Amount recognized. The amount of gain reportable and subject to tax. On certain tax-free exchanges of property, gain is not recognized in the year it is realized; *see 6.1.*

Annualized rate. A rate for a period of less than a year computed as though for a full year.

Annuity. An annual payment of money by a company or individual to a person called the annuitant. Payment is for a fixed period or the life of the annuitant. Tax consequences depend on the type of contract and funding; *see 7.22–7.31.*

Applicable federal rate. Interest rate fixed by the Treasury for determining imputed interest; *see 4.31* and *4.32.*

Appreciation in value. Increase in value of property due to market conditions. When you sell appreciated property, you pay tax on the appreciation since the date of purchase. When you donate appreciated property held long term, you may generally deduct the appreciated property; *see 14.7.*

Assessment. The IRS action of fixing tax liability that sets in motion collection procedures, such as charging interest, imposing penalties, and, if necessary, seizing property; *see 47.3.*

Asset. Anything owned that has cash or exchange value.

Assignment. The legal transfer of property, rights, or interest to another person called an assignee. You cannot avoid tax on income by assigning the income to another person.

At-risk rules. Limits loss deductions to cash investments and personal liability notes. An exception for real estate treats certain nonrecourse commercial loans as amounts "at risk"; *see 10.17.*

Attorneys' fee awards. Taxpayers who prevail in the Tax Court or other federal court may recover up to a certain amount for attorneys' fees, plus other litigation expenses, by showing that the IRS position was unreasonable; *see 48.7.*

Audit. An IRS examination of your tax return, generally limited to a three-year period after you file; *see 48.1.*

Averaging. Some retirees may use favorable averaging methods to compute tax on a lump-sum distribution if they participated in the plan for at least five years; *see 7.3* and *7.4.*

Away from home. A tax requirement for deducting travel expenses on a business trip. Sleeping arrangements are required for at least one night before returning home; *see 20.3* and *20.6.*

B

Balloon. A final payment on a loan in one lump sum.

Basis. Generally, the amount paid for property. You need to know your "basis" to figure gain or loss on a sale; *see 5.20.*

Boot. Generally the receipt of cash or its equivalent accompanying an exchange of property. In a tax-free exchange, boot is subject to immediate tax; *see 6.3.*

C

Calendar year. A year that ends on December 31.

Cancellation of debt. Release of a debt without consideration by a creditor. Cancellations of debt are generally taxable; *see 11.83.*

Glossary

Capital. The excess of assets over liabilities.

Capital asset. Property subject to capital gain or loss treatment. Almost all assets you own are considered capital assets except for certain business assets or works you created; *see 5.7*.

Capital expenses. Costs that are not currently deductible and that are added to the basis of property. A capital expense generally increases the value of property. When added to depreciable property, the cost is deductible over the life of the asset.

Capital gain or loss. The difference between amount realized and adjusted basis on the sale or exchange of capital assets. Capital gains are given tax benefits as explained in Chapter 5. Capital losses are deducted first against capital gains, and then against up to $3,000 of other income; *see 5.2* and *5.3*.

Capital gain distribution. A mutual-fund distribution allocated to gains realized on the sale of fund portfolio assets. You report the distribution as long-term capital gain even if you held the fund shares short term; *see 32.5*.

Capital loss carryover. A capital loss that is not deductible because it exceeds the annual $3,000 capital loss ceiling. A carryover loss may be deducted from capital gains of later years plus up to $3,000 of ordinary income; *see 5.3*.

Capitalization. Adding a cost or expense to the basis of the property.

Carryback. A tax technique for receiving a refund of back taxes by applying a deduction or credit from a current tax year to a prior tax year. For example, a business net operating loss incurred in 1997 may be carried back for three years.

Carryforward. A tax technique of applying a loss or credit from a current year to a later year. For example, a business net operating loss may be carried forward 15 years instead of being carried back for three years.

Cash method of accounting. Reporting income when actually or constructively received and deducting expenses when paid. Certain businesses may not use the cash method; *see 40.3*.

Casualty loss. Loss from an unforeseen and sudden event that is deductible, subject to a 10% income floor and $100 reduction for personal losses; *see 18.10*.

Charitable contributions. An itemized deduction is allowed for donations to qualifying charities. For property donations, the deductible amount depends on the type of property and donee organization, your holding period, and in some cases how the property is used; *see* Chapter 14.

Check the box. A term describing a classification rule that provides automatic partnership pass-through treatment for most businesses with two or more members when they elect on Form 8832 to be taxed as corporations.

Child and dependent credit. A credit of up to 30% based on certain care expenses incurred to allow you to work; *see 25.1*.

Child support. Payments to support a minor child generally to a custodial parent under a divorce or separation decree or agreement. The payments are not deductible; *see 37.5*.

Clifford trust. A short-term trust in which the principal is reserved by the grantor and current income is paid to the beneficiary. The tax-saving features of such trusts have been blocked by current tax rules; *see 33.3*.

Community income. Income earned in community property states and treated as belonging equally to husband and wife; *see 1.9*.

Condemnation. The seizure of property by a public authority for a public purpose. Tax on gain realized on many conversions may be deferred; *see 18.18* and *18.25*.

Constructive receipt. A tax rule that taxes income which is not received by you but which you may draw upon; *see 2.1*.

Consumer interest. Interest incurred on personal debt and consumer credit. Consumer interest is not deductible.

Convention. Rule for determining MACRS depreciation in the year property is placed in service. Either a half-year convention or mid-quarter convention applies; *see 42.5–42.7*.

Corporation. An entity organized under state law and generally treated as a separate taxpayer unless an S election is made.

Credit. A tax credit directly reduces tax liability, as opposed to a deduction that reduces income subject to tax.

D

Declining balance method. A rapid depreciation method determined by a constant percentage based on useful life and applied to the adjusted basis of the property. For example, a 40% declining balance rate applies to business automobiles, but it must be reduced by a half-year or mid-quarter convention; *see 42.5* and *42.8*.

Deductions. Items directly reducing income. Personal deductions such as for mortgage interest, state and local taxes, and charitable contributions are allowed only if deductions are itemized on Schedule A, but deductions such as for alimony, capital losses, moving expenses to a new job location, business losses, and IRA and Keogh deductions are deducted from gross income even if itemized deductions are not claimed; *see* Chapter 12.

Deferred compensation. A portion of earnings withheld by an employer or put into a retirement plan for distribution to the employee at a later date. If certain legal requirements are met, the deferred amount is not taxable until actually paid, for example, after retirement; *see 2.8*.

Deficiency. The difference between the tax assessed by the IRS and the amount reported on your return; *see 47.1*.

Defined benefit plan. A retirement plan that pays fixed benefits based on actuarial projections; *see 41.2*.

Defined contribution plan. A retirement plan that pays benefits based on contributions to individual accounts, plus accumulated earnings. Contributions are generally based on a percentage of salary or earned income; *see 41.2*.

Dependency exemption. A fixed deduction allowed to every taxpayer, except those who may be claimed as a dependent by another person. Extra exemption deductions are allowed for a spouse on a joint return and for each qualifying dependent. A deduction of $2,650 is allowed for each exemption claimed on 1997 returns, but the deduction is phased out for certain high income individuals; *see 21.15*.

Dependent. A person supported by another person. If certain tests are met, a dependency exemption may be claimed for the dependent; *see* Chapter 21.

Depletion. Deduction claimed for the use of mineral resources; *see 9.15*.

Depreciable property. A business or income-producing asset with a useful life exceeding one year; *see 42.1*.

Depreciation. Writing off the cost of depreciable property over a period of years, usually its class life or recovery period specified in the tax law; *see 42.4*.

Depreciation recapture. An amount of gain on the sale of certain depreciable property that is treated as ordinary income in case of personal property. Recapture is computed on Form 4797; *see 44.1*. For recapture on sale of realty, *see*

726

44.2.

Disaster losses. Casualty losses such as from a storm, in areas declared by the President to warrant federal assistance. An election may be made to deduct the loss in the year before the loss or the year of the loss; *see 18.2.*

Dividend. A distribution made by a corporation to its shareholders generally of company earnings or surplus. Most dividends are taxable but exceptions are explained in Chapter 4.

E

Earned income. Compensation for performing personal services. You must have earned income for a deductible IRA; *see 8.2,* or to claim the earned income credit; *see 25.10.*

Earned income credit. A credit allowed to taxpayers with earned income or adjusted gross income (AGI) below certain thresholds; *see 25.10.*

Estate tax. Imposed if the value of a decedent's taxable estate, after deductions and credits; *see 39.5.*

Estimated tax. Advance payment of current tax liability based either on wage withholdings or installment payments of your estimated tax liability. To avoid penalties, you generally must pay to the IRS either 90% of your final tax liability, or either 100% or 110% of the prior year's tax liability, depending on your adjusted gross income; *see 27.2* and *27.5.*

Exemption. *See* **Dependency exemption**.

F

Fair market value. What a willing buyer would pay to a willing seller when neither is under any compulsion to buy or sell.

Fiduciary. A person or corporation such as a trustee, executor, or guardian who manages property for another person.

First-year expensing. In 1997, a deduction of up to $18,000 (or $38,000 for qualifying businesses in an enterprise zone) of the cost of business equipment in the year placed in service. In 1998, the deduction is $18,500; *see 42.3.*

Fiscal year. A 12-month period ending on the last day of any month other than December. Partnerships, S corporations, and personal service corporations are limited in their choice of fiscal years and face special restrictions.

Flexible spending arrangements. A salary reduction plan which allows employees to pay for enhanced medical coverage or dependent care expenses on a tax-free

basis; *see 3.14.*

Foreign earned income exclusion. In 1997, up to $70,000 of foreign earned income is exempt from tax if a foreign residence or physical presence test is met; *see 36.2.* In 1998, the exclusion increases to $72,000.

Foreign tax credit. A credit for income taxes paid to a foreign country or U.S. possession; *see 36.14.*

401(k) plan. A deferred pay plan, authorized by Section 401(k) of the Internal Revenue Code, under which a percentage of an employee's salary is withheld and placed in a savings account or the company's profit-sharing plan. Income accumulates on the deferred amount until withdrawn by the employee at age 59 ½ or when the employee retires or leaves the company; *see 7.17.*

G

Gift tax. Gifts in excess of a $10,000 per donee annual exclusion are subject to gift tax, but the tax may be offset by a unified gift and estate tax credit; *see 33.1.*

Grantor trust rules. Tax rules that tax the grantor of a trust on the trust income; *see 33.3.*

Gross income. The total amount of income received from all sources before exclusions and deductions.

Gross receipts. Total business receipts reported on Schedule C or Schedule C-EZ before deducting adjustments for returns and allowances and cost of goods sold; *see 40.6.*

Group-term life insurance. Employees are not taxed on up to $50,000 of group-term coverage; *see 3.3.*

H

Head of household. Generally, an unmarried person who maintains a household for dependents and is allowed to compute his or her tax based on head of household rates, which are more favorable than single person rates; *see 1.10.*

Hobby loss. Hobby expenses are deductible only up to income from the activity; loss deductions are not allowed; *see 40.10.*

Holding period. The length of time which an asset is owned and which generally determines long-, middle-, or short-term capital gain treatment; *see 5.13–5.16.*

Home equity debt. Debt secured by a principal residence or second home to the extent of the excess of fair market value over acquisition debt. An interest

deduction is generally allowed for home equity debt up to $100,000 ($50,000 if married filing separately); *see 15.3.*

I

Imputed interest. Interest deemed earned on seller-financed sales or low-interest loans, where the parties' stated interest rate is below the applicable IRS federal rate; *see 4.31* and *4.32.*

Incentive stock option. Options meeting tax law tests that defer tax on the option transaction until the obtained stock is sold.

Income in respect of a decedent. Income earned by a person before death but taxable to an estate or heir who receives it; *see 1.12* and *11.4.*

Independent contractor. One who controls his or her own work and reports as a self-employed person; *see* Chapters 40 and 45.

Individual retirement account (IRA). A retirement account to which up to $2,000 may be contributed annually, but deductions for the contribution are restricted if you are covered by a company retirement plan. Earnings accumulate tax free on IRA contributions. Restrictions and limits are discussed in Chapter 8.

Innocent spouse. A spouse who claims that he or she should not be liable on a joint return because of ignorance of the other spouse's omission of income or claiming of excessive write-offs; *see 1.4.*

Installment sale. A sale of property that allows for tax deferment if at least one payment is received after the end of the tax year in which the sale occurs. The installment method does not apply to year-end sales of publicly traded securities. Dealers may not use the installment method. Investors with very large installment balances could face a special tax; *see 5.25.*

Intangible assets. Intangible assets that come within Section 197, such as goodwill, are amortizable over a 15-year period; *see 42.18.*

***Inter vivos* or lifetime trust.** A trust created during the lifetime of the person who created the trust. If irrevocable, income on the trust principal is shifted to the trust beneficiaries; *see 33.3.*

Investment in the contract. The total cost investment in an annuity. When annuity payments are made, the portion allocable to the cost investment is tax free; *see 7.22* and *7.27.*

Investment interest. Interest or debt used to carry investments, but not including interest expense from a passive activity.

Glossary

Deductions are limited to net investment income; *see 15.10.*

Involuntary conversion. Forced disposition of property due to condemnation, theft, or casualty. Tax on gain from involuntary conversions may be deferred if replacement property is purchased; *see 18.19.*

Itemized deductions. Items, such as interest, state and local taxes, charitable contributions, and medical deductions, claimed on Schedule A of Form 1040. Itemized deductions are subtracted from adjusted gross income to arrive at taxable income; *see* Chapter 13. The amount of itemized deductions is also subject to a 3% reduction when adjusted gross income exceeds certain limits; *see 13.7.*

J

Joint return. A return filed by a married couple reporting their combined income and deductions. Joint return status provides tax savings to many couples; *see 1.3.*

Joint tenants. Ownership of property by two persons. When one dies, the decedent's interest passes to the survivor; *see* Chapter 38.

K

Keogh plan. Retirement plan set up by a self-employed person, providing tax-deductible contributions, tax-free income accumulations until withdrawal, and favorable averaging for qualifying lump-sum distributions; *see* Chapter 41.

Kiddie tax. The tax on the investment income of a dependent child under age 14 in excess of $1,300, based on the parents' marginal tax rate and computed on Form 8615; *see 24.3.*

L

Legally separated. A husband and wife who are required to live apart from each other by the terms of a decree of separate maintenance. Payments under the decree are deductible by the payor and taxable to the payee as alimony; *see 37.2.*

Like-kind exchange. An exchange of similar assets used in a business or held for investment on which gain may be deferred; *see 6.1.*

Lump-sum distribution. Payments within one tax year of the entire amount due to a participant in a qualified retirement plan because of retirement, separation from service, reaching age 59 ½, death, or, in the case of a self-employed person, disability or reaching age 59 ½.

Qualifying lump sums may be directly rolled over tax free, or, in some cases, eligible for current tax under a favorable averaging method; *see 7.2.*

Luxury automobile limits. Ceiling placed on annual depreciation deductions for autos used for business; *see 43.3* and *43.4.*

M

Marital deduction. An estate tax and gift tax deduction for assets passing to a spouse. It allows estate and gift transfers completely free of tax; *see 39.6.*

Market discount. The difference between face value of bond and lower market price, attributable to rising interest rates. On a sale, gain on the bond is generally taxed as ordinary income to the extent of the discount; *see 4.20.*

Material participation tests. Rules for determining whether a person is active in a business activity for passive activity rule purposes. Unless the tests are met, passive loss limits apply; *see 10.6.*

Medical Savings Account (MSA). A type of medical plan combining high deductible medical insurance protection with an IRA-type savings account fund to pay unreimbursed medical expenses; *see 17.17.*

Miscellaneous itemized deductions. Generally, itemized deductions for job and investment expenses subject to a 2% adjusted gross income floor; *see* Chapter 19.

Modified ACRS (MACRS). Depreciation methods applied to assets placed in service after 1986.

Mortgage interest. Fully deductible interest on up to two residences if acquisition debt secured by home is $1 million or less, and home equity debt is $100,000 or less; *see 15.1.*

Moving Expenses. Certain expenses of moving to a new job location are deductible if distance and time tests are met; *see* Chapter 12.

N

Net operating loss. A business loss that exceeds current income may be carried back against income of prior years and carried forward as a deduction from future income until eliminated. The carryback and carryforward periods are discussed in *40.1.*

Nonperiodic distributions. A 20% withholding rule applies to nonperiodic distributions, such as lump-sum distributions, paid directly to employees from an employer plan; *see 7.8* and *26.11.*

Nonrecourse financing. Debt on which a person is not personally liable. In case of nonpayment, the creditor must foreclose on property securing the debt. At-risk rules generally bar losses where there is nonrecourse financing, but an exception applies to certain nonrecourse financing for real estate; *see 10.17.*

Nonresident alien. A person who is not a United States citizen or a permanent resident. Tax is generally limited to income from U.S. sources; *see 1.14.*

O

Ordinary and necessary. A statutory requirement for the deductibility of a business expense; *see 40.6.*

Ordinary income. Income other than capital gains.

Ordinary loss. A loss other than a capital loss.

Original issue discount (OID). The difference between the face value of a bond and its original issue price. OID is reported on an annual basis as interest income; *see 4.19.*

P

Partnership. An unincorporated business or income-producing entity organized by two or more persons. A partnership is not subject to tax but passes through to the partners all income, deductions, and credits, according to the terms of the partnership agreement; *see* Chapter 11.

Passive activity loss rules. Rules that limit the deduction of losses from passive activities to income from other passive activities. Passive activities include investment rental operations or businesses in which you do not materially participate; *see 10.1.*

Patronage dividend. A taxable distribution made by a cooperative to its members or patrons.

Pension. Payments to employees from an employer-funded retirement plan for past services; *see 7.25.*

Percentage depletion. A method that applies a fixed percentage to the gross income generated by mineral property; *see 9.15.*

Personal exemption. An automatic exemption given to a taxpayer unless he or she may be claimed as a dependent by another taxpayer. For 1997, the exemption amount is $2,650. Exemptions are phased out for certain high income taxpayers; *see 21.15.*

Personal interest. Tax term for interest on personal loans and consumer purchases.

Such interest is not deductible.

Placed in service. The time when a depreciable asset is ready to be used. The date fixes the beginning of the depreciation period; *see 42.5.*

Points. Charges to the homeowner at the time of the loan. A point is equal to 1 percent. Depending on the type of loan, points may be currently deductible or amortized over the life of the loan; *see 15.8.*

Premature distributions. Withdrawals before age 59 ½ from qualified retirement plans are subject to penalties unless specific exceptions are met; *see 7.14.*

Principal residence. On a sale of a principal residence, you may avoid or defer tax or gain under the rules explained in Chapter 29.

Probate estate. Property held in a decedent's name passing by will; *see 39.1.*

Profit-sharing plan. A defined contribution plan under which the amount contributed to the employees' accounts is based on a percentage of the employer's profits; *see 8.5 and 41.2.*

Provisional income. If your provisional income exceeds a base amount, part of your Social Security benefits may be subject to tax. To figure provisional income, *see 34.3.*

Q

Qualified charitable organization. A nonprofit philanthropic organization that is approved by the U.S. Treasury to receive charitable contribution deductions; *see 14.1.*

Qualified plan. A retirement plan that meets tax law tests and allows for tax deferment and tax-free accumulation of income until benefits are withdrawn. Pension, profit-sharing, stock bonus, employee stock ownership, and Keogh plans and IRAs may be qualified plans; *see Chapters 7, 8, and 41.*

Qualifying widow or widower. A filing status entitling the taxpayer with dependents to use joint tax rates for up to two tax years after the death of a spouse; *see 1.6.*

R

Real estate investment trust (REIT). An entity that invests primarily in real estate and mortgages and passes through income or loss to investors; *see 31.1.*

Real estate professional. An individual who, because of his or her real estate activity, qualifies to deduct rental losses from nonpassive income; *see 10.3.*

Real property. Land and the buildings on land. Buildings are depreciable; *see 42.13 and 42.16.*

Recognized gain or loss. The amount of gain or loss to be reported on a tax return. Gain may not be recognized on certain exchanges of property; *see 6.1.*

Recovery property. Tangible depreciable property placed in service after 1980 and before 1987 and depreciable under ACRS; *see 42.11 and 42.16.*

Refundable tax credit. A credit that entitles you to a refund even if you owe no tax for the year.

Residence interest. Term for deductible mortgage interest on a principal residence and a second home; *see 15.1.*

Residential rental property. Real property in which 80% or more of the gross income is from dwelling units. Under MACRS, depreciation is claimed over 27.5 years under the straight-line method; *see 42.13.*

Return of capital. A distribution of your investment that is not subject to tax unless the distribution exceeds your investment; *see 4.11.*

Revocable trust. A trust that may be changed or terminated by its creator or another person. Such trusts do not provide an income tax savings to the creator; *see 33.6.*

Rollover. A tax-free reinvestment of a distribution from a qualified retirement plan into an IRA or other qualified plan within 60 days; *see 7.3, 7.8, and 8.10.*

Roth IRA. A nondeductible contributory IRA that allows for tax-free accumulation of income, effective in 1998; *see 8.20.*

Royalty income. Amounts received for the use of property such as mineral property, a book, a movie, or a patent; *see 9.11.*

S

Salvage value. The estimated value of an asset at the end of its useful life. Salvage value is ignored by ACRS and MACRS rules.

S corporation. A corporation that elects S status in order to receive tax treatment similar to a partnership; *see Chapter 11.*

Scholarships. Grants to degree candidates receive tax-free treatment if awarded after August 16, 1986, and used for tuition and course-related expenses, but not room and board. More favorable exclusion rules apply to awards made before August 17, 1986; *see 38.1.*

Section 179 deduction. Year expensing deduction, in 1997 up to $18,000, al-

lowed for investments in depreciable business equipment in the year the property is placed in service. The deduction may be as high as $38,000 for qualifying businesses in an enterprise zone; *see 42.3.*

Section 457 plan. Deferred compensation plan set up by state or local government, or tax-exempt organization, that allows tax-free deferrals of salary, generally up to the lesser of $7,500 or one-third of pay; *see 7.21.*

Section 1231 property. Depreciable property used in a trade or business and held for more than a year. All Section 1231 gains and losses are netted; a net gain is treated as capital gain, a net loss as an ordinary loss; *see 44.8.*

Self-employed person. An individual who operates a business or profession as a proprietor or independent contractor and reports self-employment income on Schedule C; *see Chapters 40 and 45.*

Self-employment tax. Tax paid by self-employed persons to finance Social Security coverage. In 1997, there are two rates. A 12.4% rate applies to a taxable earnings base of $65,400 or less; and a 2.9% rate on all net earnings; *see Chapter 45.*

Separate return. Return filed by married person who does not file a joint return. Filing separately may save taxes where each spouse has separate deductions, but certain tax benefits require a joint return; *see 1.2.*

Short sale. Sale of borrowed securities made to freeze a paper profit or to gain from a declining market; *see 30.5.*

Short tax year. A tax year of less than 12 months. May occur with the startup of a business or change in accounting method.

Short-term capital gain or loss. Gain or loss on the sale or exchange of a capital asset held one year or less; *see 5.13.*

Simplified employee plan (SEP). IRA-type plan set up by an employer, rather than the employee. Salary-reduction contributions may be allowed to plans of small employers; *see 8.16.*

Single. The filing status of an individual who is not married on December 31 of the year for which the return is filed; *see 1.1.*

Standard deduction. A fixed deduction allowed to taxpayers who do not itemize deductions. The amount depends on filing status, age, and blindness; *see 13.1.*

Standard mileage rate. A fixed rate allowed by the IRS for business auto expenses in place of deducting actual expenses; *see 43.1*.

Statutory employees. Certain employees, such as full-time life insurance salespersons, may report income and deductions on Schedule C rather than on Schedule A, as a miscellaneous itemized deduction; *see 40.6*.

Stock dividend. A corporate distribution of additional shares of its stock to its shareholders; *see 4.6*.

Stock option. A right to buy stock at a fixed price.

Straddle. Taking an offsetting investment position to reduce the risk of loss in a similar investment.

Straight-line method. A method of depreciating the cost of a depreciable asset on a pro rata basis over its useful life; *see 42.9, 42.12*.

T

Tangible personal property. Movable property, such as desks, computers, machinery, and autos. Depreciable over a five-year or seven-year period; *see 42.4*.

Taxable income. Net income after claiming all deductions from gross income and adjusted gross income, such as IRA deductions, itemized deductions, or the standard deduction, and personal exemptions; *see 22.2*.

Tax deferral. Shifting income to a later year, such as where you defer taxable interest to the following year by purchasing a T-bill or savings certificate maturing after the end of the current year; *see* Chapter 4. Investments in qualified re-

tirement plans provide tax deferral (*see* Chapters 7, 8, and 41).

Tax home. The area of your principal place of business or employment. You must be away from your tax home on a business trip to deduct travel expenses; *see 20.6–20.9*.

Tax identification number. For an individual, his or her Social Security number; for businesses, fiduciaries, and other nonindividual taxpayers, employer identification number.

Tax preference items. Items that may subject a taxpayer to the alternative minimum tax (AMT); *see 23.3*.

Tax rate schedules. Used by taxpayers with taxable incomes of $100,000 or more; *see* Part 8.

Tax-sheltered annuity. A type of retirement annuity offered to employees of charitable organizations and educational systems, generally funded by employee salary-reduction contributions; *see 7.20*.

Tax tables. Used by taxpayers with taxable incomes of less than $100,000 to look up their tax; *see* Part 8.

Tax year. A period of 12 months for reporting income and expenses; *see 40.4*.

Tenancy by the entireties. A joint tenancy in real property in the name of both husband and wife. On the death of one tenant, the survivor receives entire interest.

Tenants in common. Two or more persons who have undivided ownership rights in property. Upon death of a tenant, his or

her share passes to his or her estate, rather than to the surviving tenants.

Testamentary trust. A trust established under a will.

Trust. An arrangement under which one person transfers legal ownership of assets to another person or corporation (the trustee) for the benefit of one or more third persons (beneficiaries).

U

Useful life. For property not depreciated under ACRS or MACRS, the estimate of time in which a depreciable asset will be used.

V

Vacation homes. The tax law limits deductions for vacation homes, broadly defined as any dwelling unit used by the owner or the owner's relatives for more than a specified period; *see 9.7*.

W

Wash sales. Sales on which losses are disallowed because you recover your market position within a 61-day period; *see 30.6*.

Withholding. An amount taken from income as a pre-payment of an individual's tax liability for the year. In the case of wages, the employer withholds part of every wage payment. Backup withholding from dividend or interest income is required if you do not provide the payer with a correct taxpayer identification number. Withholding on pensions and IRAs is automatic unless you elect to waive withholding; *see* Chapter 26.

Index

interest on loans to buy, 15.10:294–95
reporting income on, 4.20:74–76
original issue discount (OID), 4.18:73
reporting, 4.19:73–74
private activity, 4.24:78, 4.25:79
AMT and, 23.3:415–16
with put privileges, 30.11:475–77
sale or retirement of, 4.23:77–78
state and local (municipal bonds; tax-exempts)
investing in, 30.13:477–79
market discount, 4.26:79
original issue discount (OID), 4.26:79
stripped, 4.26:79
taxable interest, 4.25:78–79
tax-exempt interest on, 4.24:78
Treasury
interest on, 4.27:79–80
investing in, 30.12:477
unit investment trust, 30.14:479–80
U.S. Savings
charitable donation of, 14.6:273–75
interest on, 4.28:80–81, 4.29:82–83
tax-free exchange rules not applicable to, 6.6:127–29
U.S. savings
investing in, 30.16:481–82
wash-sale rules, 30.6:470–72
worthless, reporting on Schedule D, 5.7:94
zero coupon, 30.11:475–77
Treasury bonds, 30.12:477
Bonuses, employee, 20.25:384–85
Boot, tax-free exchanges and, 6.3:124, 6.8:129
Borrowing. *See* Debts; Loans
Bribes, 40.8:574
Building contractor, fraud by, 18.8:334–35
Bullion, tax-free exchanges of, 6.10:130
Business activities, classifying, 10.5:216–17
Business expenses. *See also* Itemized deductions
medical expenses deductible as, 17.14:322–23
taxes deductible as, 16.11:306
Business income. *See* Self-employed income (or loss) from business or profession
Business interruption insurance proceeds, 45.1:633
Business inventory, charitable donation of, 14.13:279
Business premises test, for employer-furnished meals or lodging, 3.11:54
Business property, sale of, Ch. 44
gifts and inheritances of depreciable property, 44.4:628
installment sale of depreciable property, 44.6:628

involuntary conversions, 44.5:628
property for business and personal uses, 44.9:630
recapture of depreciation on, 44.1:626
recapture of first-year expensing, 44.3:627
recapture on depreciable realty in service pre-1981, 44.2:626–27
sole proprietorships, 44.7:628
tax-free exchanges, 44.5:628
trading in business equipment, 44.10:630–31

C

Cab fare, as de minimis fringe benefit, 3.9:53
Cafeteria plans, 3.13:57
Calculators, 19.10:356
Call privileges, bonds with, 30.11:475–77
Canada, aliens who commute from 183-day test and, 1.16:21
Cancellation of debt, 11.8:240–42
Cancellation of leases, 31.6:488
Capital gains (or losses), Ch. 5
abandonments, 31.12:492–93
bad debt deductions
bank deposit losses as, 18.4:330–31
business, 5.9:97
guarantor or endorsement losses, 5.10:98
nonbusiness, 5.9:97
relatives, loans to, 5.12:99–100
rules to prove, 5.10:98
statute of limitations, 5.10:98
stockholders, loans by, 5.11:99
tax consequences, 5.9:97
bank deposit loss, 5.8:97
bonds and notes, 4.23:77–78
short-term obligations, 4.21:76–77
calculating, 5.17:102 (*See also* Basis)
amount realized as total selling price, 5.18:103
unadjusted basis of property sold, 5.19:103
cancellation of a lease, 31.6:488
carryovers of capital losses, 5.3:91–92
dates for reporting 1997 sales, 5.2:90–91
distributions, from mutual funds, 4.3:63
easement, granting of, 31.8:489
foreclosure sales and voluntary conveyances to creditors, 31.10:490–91
foreign tax credit and, 36.15:540–41
holding period, long-term or short-term
gifts, 5.16:101
inherited property, 5.16:101
involuntary conversions, 5.16:102
partnership property, 5.16:102
real estate transactions, 5.15:101
rules for counting, 5.13:100
securities transactions, 5.14:100–101

holding periods, 5.2:90–91
installment sales
contingent payment sales, 5.29:115–16
electing out of installment method, 5.27:114
escrow and other security arrangements, 5.30:116–17
figuring taxable part of payments, 5.26:111–13
interest tax on sales over $150,000 plus $5 million debt, 5.35:119–20
like-kind exchanges, 5.34:119
minimum interest, 5.31:117
relatives, restriction on sales to, 5.28:114–15
repossession of personal property sold on installment, 5.33:118–19
switching from full reporting to installment method, 5.27:114
tax advantage of, 5.25:110–11
transfer of installment notes, 5.32:117–18
losses disallowed on sales to related persons, 5.5:92–93
lump-sum distributions from retirement plans attributable to pre-1974 participation, 7.5:138–39
married couples, capital losses of, 5.4:92
mutual fund dividends, 4.3:63
not considered self-employment income, 45.1:633
options, sale of, 31.7:488–89
rates for net capital gains, 5.2:90–91
release of restrictive covenants, 31.9:490
S corporation stock, 5.8:97
Small Business Investment Company (SBIC) stock, 5.8:96–97
stock and bond sales
convertible securities, 30.7:472
corporate liquidations, 44.11:631
earmarking stock lots, 30.2:466–67
short sales, 30.5:469–70
SSBIC stock, 5.6:93–94
stock received as dividend or in a stock split, 30.3:467–68
stock rights, sale, exercise, or expiration of, 30.4:468–69
wash sales, losses from, 30.6:470–72
worthless securities, 5.7:94
on subdivided land sales, 31.3:485–86
from tax-exempt bond funds, 4.3:63
worthless securities, 5.8:96–97
Car service, as de minimis fringe benefit, 3.9:53
Carryovers
capital losses and, 5.3:91–92
of disallowed losses, 10.21:232
of excess foreign tax credit, 36.16:541
of loss from prior year, 40.18:583–84
Cash allowances for meals and lodging, 3.11:56

Index

F

Index

adoption credit, 25.15:435

Form 8844, 40.23:586–87

Form 8845, 40.23:586–87

Form 8847, 40.23:586–87

Form RRB-1099, 7.1:133–34

Form SS-5, 1.11:18

Form SSA-1099, 7.1:133–34, 34.2:516–17

Form TDF 90-22.1, 36.13:539

Form W-2, 2.1:28–30, 26.2:438
 categories in, 2.1:28–29
 sample form, 2.1:30

Form W-2G, 26.9:441

Form W-4, 26.4:439
 for children, 1.11:18
 when to file, 26.7:440

Fortune tellers, 18.8:334–35

Foster care payments, support test for dependents and, 21.7:397–99

Foster children
 expenses as charitable contributions, 14.4:271–72
 relationship test for claiming exemptions, 21.3:394–95

Foundations, private, grants to employees' children, 2.18:41

403(b) plans
 employees of tax-exempts and schools, 7.20:151–53

401(k) plans
 corrective distributions from, 7.14:147–48
 for executives, 2.14:38
 limit on salary reduction deferrals, 7.18:150–51
 nondiscrimination rules, 7.17:149–50
 partnership plans, 7.17:149–50
 restrictions on withdrawals, 7.19:151
 tax benefits of, 7.17:149–50

401(k) SIMPLE plans, 8.18:189

Fractional shares, 4.6:64

Franchises, Section 197, 42.18:609–11

Fraternal organizations, conventions held by, 20.12:379–80

Fraud, theft losses due to, 18.8:334–35

Freedom shares, 4.28:81

Friends, exemption for, 21.4:395–96

Fringe benefits, Ch. 3
 adoption benefits as, 3.5:49–50
 cafeteria plans, 3.13:57
 company cars, 3.7:51–52
 company services provided at no additional cost, 3.15:58–59
 day care as, 3.4:49
 de minimis, 3.9:53
 death benefits, 3.4:44–45
 dependent care assistance, 3.4:49
 discounts on company products or services, 3.16:59
 education assistance plans, 3.6:50
 employee achievement awards, 3.10:53–54

flexible spending arrangements (FSAs), 3.14:57–58

group-term life insurance premiums, 3.3:48–49

health and accident plans, 3.1:43–46, 3.2:46–48

meals or lodging, 3.11:54–56

minister's rental allowance, 3.12:56–57

for stockholders of S corporations, 45.10:587

working condition, 3.8:52

Frozen deposits, interest on, 4.13:68

Fuel-related credits, 40.24:587

Fulbright awards, 38.3:550

Furniture, used, charitable donation of, 14.7:275

FUTA (federal unemployment taxes), for household employees, 25.7:431, 25.9:432

Futures contracts, marked-to-market rules for gain or loss on, 30.9:430–31

G

Gambling winnings and losses, 11.3:235–36
 withholdings on, 26.9:441

Gasoline and fuels tax credit, 40.24:587

Gasoline taxes, deductibility of, 16.2:301

General business credit, 40.23:586–87

Generally related test, for dining and entertainment expenses, 20.17:381–82

G.I. Bill education assistance, support test for dependents and, 21.7:397–99

Gift tax
 basis of property received as gift and, 5.21:106
 custodian account, 33.2:506–7
 filing a gift tax return, 33.1:506
 on loans, 4.31:84
 overview of, 33.1:506

Gifts, 11.1:208. See also Charitable contributions
 basis of property received as, 5.21:105–7
 to business customers, 20.25:384–85
 of depreciable property, 44.4:628
 from employers
  tax free, 2.4:32
  as taxable income, 2.4:32
 holding period for, 5.16:101
 loans as, 4.31:84–85
  payable on demand, 4.31:84
 loss on sale of home acquired by, 29.14:462
 of mortgaged property, 31.16:496
 of passive activity interest, 10.13:224–26
 sale of stock received as, 5.7:94
 of Series E or EE bonds, 4.28:81
 strike and lockout benefits as, 2.7:34

Ginnie Maes, 30.12:477

Going-concern value, Section 197, 42.18:609–11

Golden parachute payments
 salary or wage income (compensation), 2.1:32

Goodwill
 amortizing, 42.18:609–11
 entertaining, 20.18:382
 exchanges of, 6.2:123

Government benefits. See also Social Security benefits
 as support, 21.7:397–99

Government employees. See also Elected and public officials
 deferred pay plans for, 7.21:153–54

Government services, assessments, 16.5:302–3

Grandfather election, penalty for excess distributions, 7.15:148

Grantor trusts, 33.3:507–9

Grants. See Scholarships, fellowships, and grants

Green cards, resident aliens, 1.16:21

Groceries, employer-furnished, 3.11:56

Gross income
 deductions from, 12.2:252–53

Gross income test for dependents, 21.5:396

Ground rents, redeemable, 15.6:290–91

Group life insurance
 for executives, 2.15:38

Group-term life insurance
 assigning, 33.6:510–12
 premiums
  for dependents, 3.3:48
  as fringe benefit, 3.3:48–49

Guam, 36.9:537–38

H

Half-year convention, MACRS, 42.6:601

Handicapped persons. See also Disabled,; Medical or dental expenses
 business expenses, expenses deductible as, 17.14:322–23
 home improvements as medical deductions for, 17.13:321–22
 job expenses, 19.4:351
 schooling for, 17.10:318–19

Hardship withdrawals from 401(k) plans, 7.19:151

Head of household
 child as, 1.10:17
 costs of maintaining household and, 1.10:16
 exemption phaseout, 21.15:404–5
 filing as, 1.3:10, 1.10:16–18
 qualifying tests, 1.10:16–18
 tax rates, 1.2:9
 temporary absences and, 1.10:18
 two-family house and, 1.10:17

Index

Index

Index

NOTES AND MEMOS

NOTES AND MEMOS

THE *J.K. LASSER YOUR INCOME TAX 1998* CONSUMER SURVEY AND REBATE

Your comments and suggestions on Your Income Tax 1998 will help us provide a better product line for you in the future. Thank you in advance for taking the time to complete the survey. We look forward to providing you more of the best tax guidance available.

1. Gender
___ Male   ___ Female

2. Age
___ Under 25   ___ 25-29   ___ 30-39
___ 40-49   ___ 50-59   ___ 60-69
___ 70+

3. Household Income:
___ Under $25,000   ___ $25,000-$34,999
___ $35,000-$49,999   ___ $50,000-$74,000
___ $75,000-$99,000   ___ $100,000 or more
___ Do not care to comment

4. How many people are in your immediate family?
_____

5. What is the highest level of education you have attained thus far?
_____

6. What is your occupation?
_____
_____

7. When did you purchase *J.K. Lasser's Your Income Tax 1998* (Month and date)?
_____

8. Where did you purchase *J.K. Lasser's Your Income Tax 1998* (Name of store and city)?
_____

9. Have you purchased *J.K. Lasser's Your Income Tax* in prior years?
_____ yes   _____ no

10. If yes, for how many years have you been using *Your Income Tax*?
_____

11. Which of the following tax guides have you purchased in the past (please check all that apply)?
___ *H&R Block Income Tax*
___ *Consumer Reports Guide to Income Tax*
___ *Ernst & Young Tax Guide*
___ *Taxes for Dummies*
___ *Idiot's Guide to Doing Your Income Tax*

12. What specifically led you to purchase *Your Income Tax 1998* over other available tax guides?
_____
_____
_____

13. Do you plan on purchasing *J.K. Lasser's Your Income Tax 1999* next year?
_____ yes   _____ no

Why or why not?
_____
_____

14. Were there any specific sections of the book that were of particular help to you?
_____ yes   _____ no

If yes, please elaborate:
_____
_____
_____

15. Are there any tax topics that you would like the book to treat in greater depth?
_____yes   ___no

If yes, please explain
_____
_____
_____

16. Do you now or have you ever had a professional tax preparer complete your tax forms?

_____ yes   _____ no

17. Do you have access to a computer?

_____ yes   _____ no

18. If yes, have you ever used tax preparation software to help you file your income taxes?

_____ yes   _____ no

19. Do you have access to the Internet?

_____ yes   _____ no

20. If yes, have you:
• Visited the J.K. Lasser Web Site at JKLasser.com?

_____ yes   _____ no

• Filed your taxes on-line?

_____ yes   _____ no

21. What features would you like to see added to the web site?

_____

_____

22. Do you now or have you ever subscribed to our Monthly Tax Letter?

_____ yes   _____ no

23. If you are not a subscriber, would you be interested in receiving a sample issue?

_____ yes   _____ no

24. Which of the following J.K. Lasser products would you consider purchasing?
___ *Taxes Made Easy for Home-Based Businesses*
___ *How to Pay Less on Retirement Savings*
___ *Tax Deductions for Small Businesses*
___ *Face to Face with the IRS*
___ *Year-Round Tax Strategies*
___ *Smart Finances for Your 20's and 30's*
___ *Gay & Lesbian Financial Planning Guide*

25. Did you take advantage of any of the offers in the book?
___ Bloomberg
___ Free Supplement
___ TurboTax

26. Is there an offer you would like to see? Please explain.

_____

_____

_____

Thank you for choosing the J.K. Lasser Institute!
Please send your completed survey and rebate coupon
to the address below.

GET A $2.00 RETURN FROM J. K. LASSER!

1. Mail your completed survey (no photocopies or facsimiles will be accepted) along with a dated cash register receipt or a UPC code from the back cover as proof of purchase to the following address.
2. Legibly fill out the information below.

J.K. LASSER'S REBATE
P. O. Box 9100
Bridgeport, NJ 08014-9100

Name_____

Address_____
(No P. O. Box #s Please)
City_____ State_____ Zip_____

Offer Valid Only in USA.
(Limit one rebate per name or address. This offer expires and all material must be received by 5/1/98.
Not responsible for lost, late, or misdirected mail. Please allow 4-8 weeks for processing and delivery.)

TurboTax Deluxe $15 Rebate

❏ **YES!** Send me $15 back on my purchase of TurboTax Deluxe® software for tax year 1997!

See reverse side for rebate details. Valid for retail purchases only. Not valid with any other offer. Offer ends May 15, 1998.

The easiest, fastest, most complete way to do your taxes

Tax experts are calling the 1997 tax laws the most complex in a decade. Now more than ever, using TurboTax software is the easiest, most complete way to do your taxes.

If you're really into REDUCING your taxes as much as possible — and if you want even more guidance on how to lower your tax bill — you'll want TurboTax Deluxe. There's no better way to get through the twists and turns of this year's convoluted tax laws.

How TurboTax Deluxe works

- Step 1: Answer easy-to-understand interview questions. TurboTax Deluxe then puts your answers in all the right places and performs all the calculations automatically.
- Step 2: TurboTax Deluxe reviews your return thoroughly to help you make certain that nothing has been left out or overlooked. It even alerts you to missed deductions and entries that could possibly trigger an IRS audit.
- Step 3: Print ready-to-file forms on plain white paper right from your printer. You just sign them and drop them in the mail or file electronically.

What's included

On screen Tax Library provides thousands of pages of money-saving tax guidance:

- IRS publications — tax information straight from the source
- On screen Books
  - Money® Magazine's Income Tax Handbook — excellent tax advice from former IRS Group Audit Manager, Mary Sprouse
  - How To Pay Zero Taxes — help on cutting your tax bill

Integrated VIDEO tax help from three of America's top financial advisors:

- Former managing editor of Fortune® and Money magazines, Marshall Loeb
- Tax attorney and former IRS Group Audit Manager, Mary Sprouse
- Former IRS executive, Bob Carver

New and improved TurboTax Deluxe features for 1997

Revised And Updated
- Incorporates ALL 1997 tax law changes to guide you through your taxes — and help you take advantage of more deductions

Improved Navigation
- Go anywhere in your tax return with a click
- Find what you're looking for faster with the improved search feature

Customized Interview
- Get through your return in less time
- Answer only questions geared to your specific tax situation

Tax Report
- Automatically create a customized action plan to save on next year's taxes
- Print and save a Tax Report to refer to throughout the coming year

Enhanced Electronic Filing
- File your return the fastest, safest way possible — it's easier than ever this year

One-Click Access To Technical Support Web Site
- Get the answers to the top 10 most frequently asked questions

Get Product Updates Fast If Tax Laws Change Again
- Download product updates from our web site — it's automatic, fast and FREE

Quick Reference Link
- Gives you easy one-click access to exactly the information you need from IRS publications and on screen books

Common Tax Questions
- Click to find the answers to over 200 of the most commonly asked tax questions, compiled from exhaustive interviews with CPAs

More And Even Better Videos
- Guides you through this year's tax law changes to help you reduce your taxes

32-Bit Performance
- Get through your return even faster

TurboTax Deluxe $15 Rebate

To receive your $15 rebate:

1. Complete the following information:

Name _____

Address_____

City_____ State _____ ZIP _____

Phone_____

E-mail _____

2. Attach both your original sales receipts from your J.K. Lasser™ book AND from your TurboTax Deluxe software to this original coupon. (Purchases from retail dealers only)

(If you do not have the receipt for your J.K. Lasser book, send the UPC code on the back cover as proof of purchase. Photocopied coupons, receipts and UPC codes will not be honored.)

3. Mail this coupon to:

JK Lasser Rebate
P.O. Box 4390
Department A
St. Cloud, MN 56398-4390

4. Limit one rebate per household. Offer ends on April 15. Must be postmarked no later than May 15, 1998.

5. We will forward your rebate check in approximately 6 to 8 weeks. If you do not receive your rebate within 8 weeks, please call 1-800-950-0017.

Rebate Coupon Rules: This rebate is for TurboTax Deluxe software for tax year 1997 purchased between October 1, 1997 and April 15, 1998. This coupon is not valid with and cannot be combined with any other offer. TurboTax Deluxe must be purchased from a participating retail dealer. All rebate coupon requests must be postmarked no later than May 15, 1998 and received by Intuit no later than May 31, 1998. Intuit assumes no responsibility for late, lost, incomplete, postage-due, or misdirected mail.

© 1997 Intuit. TurboTax is a registered trademark of Intuit Inc. All other trademarks are the property of their respective owners.

561212